Globalizing Automobilism

GLOBALIZING AUTOMOBILISM

*Exuberance and the Emergence of Layered Mobility,
1900–1980*

Gijs Mom

berghahn
NEW YORK • OXFORD
www.berghahnbooks.com

First published in 2020 by
Berghahn Books
www.berghahnbooks.com

© 2020, 2026 Gijs Mom
First paperback edition published in 2026

All rights reserved. Except for the quotation of short passages
for the purposes of criticism and review, no part of this book
may be reproduced in any form or by any means, electronic or
mechanical, including photocopying, recording, or any information
storage and retrieval system now known or to be invented,
without written permission of the publisher.

Library of Congress Cataloging-in-Publication Data
Names: Mom, Gijs, 1949- author.
Title: Globalizing automobilism : exuberance and the emergence of layered
  mobility, 1900-1980 / by Gijs Mom.
Description: New York : Berghahn Books, 2020. | Includes bibliographical
  references and index.
Identifiers: LCCN 2020012739 (print) | LCCN 2020012740 (ebook) | ISBN
  9781789204612 (hardback) | ISBN 9781789204629 (ebook)
Subjects: LCSH: Automobiles--Social aspects--History--20th century. |
  Transportation, Automotive--History--20th century. |
  Globalization--Social aspects--History--20th century.
Classification: LCC HE5611 .M55 2020 (print) | LCC HE5611 (ebook) | DDC
  303.48/320904--dc23
LC record available at https://lccn.loc.gov/2020012739
LC ebook record available at https://lccn.loc.gov/2020012740

British Library Cataloguing in Publication Data
A catalogue record for this book is available from the British Library

EU GPSR Authorized Representative
LOGOS EUROPE, 9 rue Nicolas Poussin, 17000, LA ROCHELLE, France
Email: Contact@logoseurope.eu

ISBN 978-1-78920-461-2 hardback
ISBN 978-1-83695-389-0 paperback
ISBN 978-1-80758-813-7 epub
ISBN 978-1-78920-462-9 web pdf

https://doi.org/10.3167/9781789204612

to Karel

Contents

List of Illustrations	x
Preface	xii

Introduction. Questioning the Car: Prolegomena for a Historical Analysis of Global Mobility	1
New Perspectives, New Questions	1
Looking Back: Emergence and Persistence of the Adventure Machine	5
Extending Adventure: The Car as Possession and Status Symbol	13
Producing Commodification: Status, Narcissism, and Self-Development	17
Diversifying Automotive Identities: The Non-hegemonic Self	21
New Mobility Studies: Bodily Senses, the Car as Medium, and the Challenge of Representation	28
The Trouble with Travel Writing: Meandering between Fictionality and Representation	38
This Study: Sources and Terminology	42

Part I. Emergence and Persistence (Again): The Shaping of Mobility Layeredness beyond the West

Chapter 1. Modernizing without Automobilization: Subverting and Subalternizing Mobility History (1890–1945/1950)	57
Imperialist Mobilities: Japan and the Modernization of Manchuria	57

Urban Mobilities: The Rickshaw and the Motorization
of Asian Cities   72

Between Long March and Long Haul: Rail and Road
Network Building in China   99

Dual Networks of Rails and Roads: The Modal
Configuration in Other Asian Countries   119

Migration, Colonialism, and the Struggle between Rail
and Road: The Case of Africa   133

More Than Modern: Constructing a Latin American
Adventure Machine   152

The Rest and the West: Subversive and Subaltern
Mobilities?   166

Part II. Exuberance, with a Twist: Spreading the Gospel of Automobilism

Chapter 2. Fragmenting Automotive Adventure: Western Exuberant Automobilism and Middle-Class Guilt (1945–1973)   205

"Why I Want to Fuck Ronald Reagan"   205

A Multimedia Feast: Folk, Beat, Rock, and Other
Mobilities   209

Motorizing the Worker: Fragmentation and
Convergence of Western Car Cultures   231

The Attack on Public Transport: Hegemonic Car
Cultures in a Cold War Setting   247

Experiencing the Car in a Fragmented Culture:
Shifts in Autopoetic Adventures   284

Songs and Movies: Rejuvenating the Adventure Machine
in Popular Culture   329

Flow Interrupted: *Crash* and the Systemic Aspects of
Automobilism   340

Chapter 3. Layered Development: The Transnational Construction of a World Mobility System (1940s–1970s)   384

What Is 'Layered Development'?   384

Alternative Developments: Soviet Mobility and the
Modernization of China and India   387

Conceiving 'Development': Mobilizing the 'Rest'	428
Mediating Modernization: Japan and Asian 'Development'	462
Constructing 'Circulation': The IRF and the "Development" of Africa	482
Developmentalism versus *Dependentismo*: Latin American Mobilities and the Frustrations of Middle-Class Modernity	504
Conclusions: Road, Rail, and Development	524
Layered, Fragmented, Subversive, Subaltern: Conclusions	562
Bibliography	575
Index	639

Illustrations

Figures

1.1.	Rickshaw pullers in Tokyo	74
1.2.	Licensed rickshaws in Singapore, 1887–1939	79
1.3.	Urban modal configuration in Hong Kong, 1896–1940	81
1.4.	Railway network length in China (without Taiwan)	99
1.5.	"Motor road" construction in China in km	114
1.6.	Cars and heavy motorized vehicles in some Indian provinces, 1915–1940	126
1.7.	Motor vehicle (car and truck) import in Gold Coast (Ghana), 1900–1939	146
1.8.	Spread of the car and Argentine Automobile Club membership in Argentina, 1901–1942	158
1.9.	Imported cars and trucks in Dahomey	171
2.1.	Modal split for journeys to work in the United Kingdom	211
2.2.	Share of different social groups in the purchase of new cars in Germany, 1958–1964	239
2.3.	Car densities in several Western countries	251
2.4.	Modal configuration during the main holiday trip in Germany, 1954–1988	254
3.1.	Roads in the Soviet Union by pavement type, 1936–1965	394
3.2.	Network lengths in China, 1949–1983	404
3.3.	Annual bicycle production in China, 1949–1978	407
3.4.	Relative registration figures of vehicles in India, 1951–2006	418

3.5. Map of the Asian Highway, avoiding the Soviet Union
and China   466
3.6. Cars, trucks, and motorized two-wheelers in Japan's
motorization explosion of the 1960s and 1970s   474
3.7. Analysis of the commodity flow on a market day in Ghana   487
3.8. Registered trucks in Mexico, 1924–1956   513
3.9. Gross investments in Brazil's transport sector   517

Table

0.1. Transfer processes and practices in new mobility studies   28

Preface

This book is not the work of a lifetime (as my previous one was announced to be), but it should have been. Half a year after *Atlantic Automobilism* appeared in the fall of 2014, it formed the core of my farewell party at the Eindhoven University of Technology. But I was already working on a sequel covering the second half of the twentieth century: letting untouched the piles of photocopies and the reams of notes about Western automobilism after 1945 I had produced during the production of the first volume seemed such a waste. I estimated I needed another year or two to get it done, which I reckoned I could easily do when we, my partner Charley and I, would live in Andalucía where we moved upon our retirements. After that, we could work on our orange and olive trees (harvesting, trimming). How short-sighted! For meanwhile, my views on transport history had changed drastically, and so did my views on this book project. It was all my own fault: it had started when, in 2010, I founded and became editor of *Transfers: The Interdisciplinary Journal of Mobility Studies* as an alternative to my editorship of the *Journal of Transport History* (*JTH*), where I had not been able to refocus editorial policy toward a broader and more activist approach of "transport" and bring the journal more in line of what I saw changing in the field of transport and mobility studies. With the editorial team of *Transfers* (Georgine Clarsen, Nanny Kim, Cotten Seiler, Charissa Terranova, Rudi Volti, Dorit Müller, and Kurt Möser, later joined by others: Deborah Breen, Fernanda Duarte, Anne-Katrin Ebert, Chia-ling Lai, Katariina Mauranen, Peter Merriman, Liz Montegary, Liz Millward, Stéphanie Ponsavady, Mimi Sheller, Sunny Stalter-Pace, and Heike Weber) I embarked on an adventurous bus tour through what we called new mobility studies, along the way decentering the car, the nation-state, the West, and even history. The impact of this move, disturbing as it might have seemed to several colleagues at the time, could be observed in the International Association for the History of Transport, Traffic and Mobility (T²M) where a *Yearbook* appeared in which not only a programmatic expansion took place of the geographic coverage beyond the West, but also the need of a more theoretical underpinning was lively debated. One of the results, brought about by many members of a new generation of young scholars, was a cooperation with social scientists, in the form of common annual conferences. The Cosmobilities network, with its journal *Mobilities*, proved a welcome partner who could help historians reequip their theoretical and methodological toolbox.

Then, luck struck (irony is one of the topics of this book). My application for a prestigious European ERC grant of 2.4 million euros was rejected. The project I proposed was fully geared to the world beyond the West, especially Asia. For this I was able to engage Nanny Kim (Heidelberg University) and Zhu Jianjun (Ocean University of China, Qingdao), who introduced me to China, and especially to literary-history professor Wang Guangdong and his PhD student Yang Weijian (meanwhile a professor himself) at Shanghai University. Together with a librarian from Tokyo, Toshihiko Saito, one of the few specialists in Japan's and Asia's rickshaw history, we designed, in the unheated rooms of Shanghai University in February 2010, a research program that in the end, as I already said, did not get funded. It goes without saying that I owe a lot to the people mentioned so far (as well as those that will be mentioned later), not only because their willingness to cooperate and to negotiate about topics and concepts questioned the very basics of my scholarship, but also because they formed the core of a new mobility studies network in the making. In hindsight, this first phase just seemed to add another vehicle, the rickshaw, to the existing assortment, although the combination of historical study and the confrontation with the conditions of the utterly poor was an eye-opener. It is my firm conviction that scholarship is a mix of study and action, reflection and organization, so the generous consolation grant from the Excellence Fund my university awarded me (the size of such awards are tuned to my colleagues at engineering departments who cannot reequip their laboratories with a couple thousand euros!) enabled me to expand the network through the funding of workshops and visits to research institutes and interested colleagues in a large variety of countries. Relieved from the burden to pull the rickshaw on my own, I could now indulge in discourses and debates with scholars from so many different disciplines and with so many interests that it became difficult to find a common denominator of what slowly seemed to become a journey toward a world mobility history.

I want to enumerate the workshops I was able to (co-)fund with my university grant, and the local organizers who made this all possible, and to whom I am most grateful. To begin with, in August 2009, I co-organized, with Director Pabrita Giri and with the help of Gaur Kapur (State Governor, Indian National Trust for Art and Cultural Heritage), an overview seminar at the University of Calcutta's Center for Urban Economic Studies about the state of the art of transport (history) research in West Bengal (title

"Mobility, Modernity and Transport"), where also street-corner workers were present who worked with the many thousands of rickshaw pullers in the city. Rajesh Agrawal, Executive Director (Heritage) of India's Ministry of Railways, also presented at that seminar. Later, when I stayed at his house in Kolkata, he would arrange a visit to one of the rickshaw repair shops as well as a bus body workplace, where the workers handled sheet aluminum with their bare hands. Two years later, in December 2011, at Jadavpur University in the same city, I co-organized with Joyashree Roy the workshop "Subversive Niches: Tracking Mobility Studies and Transitions in India and Bangladesh." Both workshops gathered historians, as well as social scientists, economists, and transport experts. Papers presented at these workshops flowed into *Transfers* and other outlets.

On to China, with a body invaded by sick-making bacteria. In Shanghai, at the Shanghai Academy of Social Sciences (SASS), specialist in Chinese bicycle history and friend Xu Tao set up a splendid overview workshop, under the presidency of his former PhD supervisor, Xiong Yuezhi of SASS and Fudan University, charting the state of mobility history research in China (title: "Mobility in Daily Life," January 2012), which expanded my knowledge of non-Western railways, bicycles, camel caravans, and riverboats considerably. Nanny Kim translated. One of the attendants, Chinese railway specialist Ding Xianyong, invited me to his Zhejiang university in Hangzhou. He not only organized lively discussions with his colleagues and students but also took me (his son Liu Ying as interpreter) to a Long Ying tea farm in the countryside where I ate my first (and my last) toad. His son also took me to James Ballard's Amherst Avenue (now Xinhua Road) home in Shanghai. At SASS, I spent two fellowships and other visits of several months to half a year each, in 2014, 2015, and 2016, to work on my manuscript. Shao Jian, a specialist in automotive history, allowed me to interview him. I used these months also to interview transport experts at Tongji Universiy in Shanghai (Pan Haixiao, Li Keping) and at several universities (Shao Chunfun, Beijing Jiaotong University; Yang Xinmiao, Tsinghua University, Deputy Director Institute of Transportation Engineering; Chen Yanyan, Peking University of Technology) and government bureaus of transportation in Beijing, as well as consultants (Robert Earley and Will Shaw). The organization of these interviews was done by PhD student and teacher Agnes Kneitz (Renmin University of China, Department of History, Center for Ecological History) and student Tu Zhouxin (Tsinghua University, Department of Automotive Engineering). The latter also taught me the skills of dealing with the statistics of the Ministry of Communication. From these interviews, I learned about the state of the art of current transport research in China, especially the efforts to introduce electric bikes and motorcycles, and the attempts of the Beijing government to introduce electric vehicles and abate pollution. Agnes also helped me find documentation about roadbuilding at the National Library in Beijing. I also wish to thank Bao Hui for her lessons Chinese and the help in getting me settled in Shanghai, and Carlos Galviz (now at Lancaster University) for the many happy hours we spent in his selection of bars and restaurants in Shanghai. I will never forget the support from Xu Tao, from purchasing of my first new bike to negotiating with my landlords of the several apartments I stayed in.

Back in New Delhi, in July 2012, my university and the Transportation Research and Injury Prevention Programme, led at the time by Dinesh Mohan (soon to be succeeded by Geetam Tiwari), part of the Indian Institute of Technology Delhi, co-organized a workshop "Cycle Rickshaws in India," where I also befriended a rickshaw puller activist, Rajendra Ravi (see the bibliography for his activist contribution in *Transfers*), who took me to one of the biggest slums in India, where I met a rickshaw fleet owner who had started a homeopathic pharmacy because his rickshaw fleet was being "regulated" away by the local government. There, I stepped, walking back when taking a photo of women and children squatting around a fire, with one leg in the open sewer, treating the passengers of my plane to Hyderabad that evening with an olfactory reminder of Delhi's poverty. At the University of Dhaka, in January 2013, I co-organized, with Maksudur Rahman (Department of Geography and Environment) and Director Shahnaz Huq-Hussain and her research assistant Umme Habiba of the Disaster Research Training and Management Centre, a workshop on "Informal Mobilities," particularly on the tens of thousands of hand-pulled rickshaws and many more poor in Bangladesh. This was followed by an excursion, with my friend Gopa Samanta from the University of Burdwan in West Bengal, to a hellish shipbreaking site at a beach of Chittagong, where the West dumps its obsolete ships to be dismantled by hand and torch. Gopa also arranged a meeting with Maps Steel Ltd. (ShipBreaking Ind.) Chairman Al-haj Nur Uddin Mohd. Jahangir Chy. Back in Dhaka, we visited the atelier of a rickshaw artist, Syed Ahmed Hossain (examples of his art can be seen in *Transfers*; see the bibliography under Samanta). The visits to India and Bangladesh opened my eyes to the importance of the informal sector and its subversive and subaltern mobilities. There, I was the farthest away from the Western automotive "adventure machine." It kept me thinking about the centrality of the passenger car in mainstream transport studies and its repercussions for solving transport problems beyond the West, both now and in the past. It also kept me thinking about my health: whenever I returned to India, the subversive and subaltern bacteria had their feast. They clearly didn't like my indulging in Indian mobilities. Had they been against China (the plumbing in Shanghai apartments and hotels made me learn to see urban China as a communist version of the United

States, something one cannot say of India), the following chapters would have been quite different.

On the other side of the Pacific, Rodrigo Booth of the School of Architecture and Urban Studies at the University of Chile in Santiago invited me to his workshop "Transport and Mobility Studies in Latin America." There, Tomás Errázuriz (now Universidad Andrés Bello), Dhan Zunino Singh (Universidad Nacional de Quilmes), Melina Piglia (Universidad Nacional de Mar del Plata) and several others introduced me to Latin modernism and the core-periphery question, a question that got a follow-up during the workshop organized by Simone Fari and Gregorio Nuñez at the Faculty for Economics and Business of the University of Granada. The attendants of that workshop formed their own network pursuing the core-periphery problematics in several consecutive workshops. In Leuven, Katrien Pype (KU Leuven), Jeroen Cuvelier (Ghent University), and Clapperton Mavhunga (Massachusetts Institute of Technology) introduced me to the anthropology and history of African mobility, in October 2013, at the workshop "Mobility and Technology in Africa: Exploring a New Analytical Field." In Munich, the Rachel Carson Center for Environment and Society (RCC), where I was one of the first fellows back in 2010–2011 to work on *Atlantic Automobilism*, again was very supportive, first with a workshop I could organize with RCC directors Helmut Trischler and Christoph Mauch on environmental mobility history (a topic and approach largely neglected within mobility studies) and then with one on bicycles and recycling, co-organized by Ruth Oldenziel and Heike Weber. Katie Ritson was very supportive in improving my English. At RCC, I started a discussion group on "risk" (as I was struggling with the paradox of car adventure and fatalities) with fellow fellows Lawrence Culver, Heike Egner, Agnes Kneitz, Cheryl Lousley, Uwe Lübken, and Diana Mincyte, culminating in a discussion with the risk master himself, Ulrich Beck (see the bibliography under Culver for an account of this discussion). Together, we undertook several excursions into the Bavarian Alps, Eva of TomTom navigation announcing the *afslags* to take. The discussions and lectures of the several dozens of historians and social scientists who took part in these workshops, whom I often met again at the annual T²M conferences and who were often willing to publish their articles in *Transfers* (or their dissertations and other manuscripts in the Explorations in Mobility book series of *Transfers*'s publisher, Berghahn Books, which I edited with Georgine Clarsen and Mimi Sheller), formed, as it were, my second scholarly, mobile education away from a narrow transport approach to the new subfield of politico-historical mobility studies.

The next phase started with Ruth Oldenziel becoming a full-time professor at Eindhoven's history department in 2016, which cemented mobility history at our university through the inclusion of the bicycle (and its activism) and made it possible to invite our new colleagues to Eindhoven for a lecture or a visiting professorship and receive invitations for lectures elsewhere, among them Martin Emanuel and Peter Norton. Ruth initiated the CP-SUM (CP Cultural Politics of Sustainable Urban Mobility) network grafted partially upon my own network and thus emerged a research network of scholars interconnected through *Transfers*, *JTH*, T^2M, *Mobilities*, and a series of funded workshops in several European countries (the final one in Eindhoven, in June 2018), dedicated to theorizing the city as a unit of mobility. The project resulted in an edited volume in Berghahn's Explorations in Mobility series. Another memorable visit to Eindhoven (with our PhD student Sun Qi translating) was by CASS's (China Academy of Social Sciences) Wu Li, Vice Director of the Institute of Contemporary China Studies; Zheng Yougui, Head of the institute's Department of Economic History; and Wang Lei (specialized in the economic history of China's Belt and Road initiative) in Beijing, as well as their colleagues from SASS's Institute of History Zhang Liuli and Lin Chaochao, whom I met at the workshop "Forty Years of Reforms in China's Long 20th Century of Modernization" in November 2018 at KU Leuven (organized by Valeria Zanier of its Sinology Research Unit) and who later visited our university just over the border in Eindhoven. We established an extensive cooperative research program on industrial and mobility history, to be continued by my lecture on China's modernization at a conference in Beijing in September 2019, organized by CASS, on the occasion of the seventieth anniversary of the People's Republic. A common research program, including China Science Publishing in Beijing, is in the making. For me, this was the culmination of a long sequence of invited lectures during the past decade or so, and I thank the colleagues who invited me, and who enabled me to sharpen my argumentation and learn about local conditions and research.

Thus, I was able to develop my thoughts further and to absorb unique expertise on local mobilities in India: University of Hyderabad (E. Haribabu, December 2010), Bangalore University (T. Sitharam, November 2010), the Jawaharlal Nehru University (Pranav Desai, December 2010), University of Burdwan (Gopa Samanta, December 2010); in China: Beijing (conference "Manufacturing Landscapes: Nature and Technology in Environmental History," co-organized by Renmin University China and the RCC, May 2015; conference "Sustainable Mobility," China Academy of Sciences, May 2015, organized by Zhao Hong, who took us to a new energy vehicle test and exhibition site outside Beijing), Tongji University (conference "The Historical Development of Sustainable Mobility," March 2018, invited by Pan Haixiao); in Japan: Sophia University in Tokyo (Asian Studies Conference, June 2014, invited by historian and Japanologist Bill Steele); in Singapore: National University of Singapore, (lecture,

Asia Research Institute, August 2016, invited by Asian migration specialist Brenda Yeoh and Asian mobility scholar Lin Weiqiang); in the United Kingdom: University of Birmingham (conference "[Auto-]Mobility in the Global Middle East: Defining the Field," organized by Simon Jackson, November 2015, opening my eyes for the Riyadh drifters); in France: Paris (lectures on the history of the electric vehicle [2012] and on the futures of mobility [2014], both invited by my friend Mathieu Flonneau), Bretagne (Cité des Télécommunications, a summer school "Mobility and Information Technology: A Long-Term Perspective," organized by Pascal Griset and Mathieu Flonneau, Paris-Sorbonne, September 2011), Mulhouse (Musée EDF Electropolis, organized by the Gesprächskreis Technikgeschichte; lecture on the conference "Mobilität durch Elektrizität in Deutschland und Frankreich – gestern – heute – morgen," June 2012); in Germany: the Christian Albrecht University of Kiel (conference "Travelling Goods, Travelling Moods," organized by Christian Huck, April 2011), University of Heidelberg (conference "Asia and Europe in a Global World," April 2013), Karlsruhe Institute of Technology (conference "The Contribution of the History of Technology for Understanding Technology Futures," organized by Marcus Popplow and Silke Zimmer-Merkle, September 2018), the VDI Arbeitskreis Technikgeschichte in Berlin (lecture "Automobilnutzung im Westen im Kontext einer Welt-Mobilitätsgeschichte," hosted by Stefan Poser and Hans-Liudger Dienel); in Canada: University of York (conference "Models of Mobility," organized by Matthias Kipping, together with the German Historical Institute in Washington, DC, March 2012); in the United States: German Historical Institute in Washington, DC (lecture, June 2012); in Switzerland: Geneva (colloquium "Histoire des transports et de la mobilité: Entre concurrence et coordination (1918 à nos jours)," organized by Olivier Perroux and Gérard Duc [Maison de l'histoire], Vincent Kaufmann [*École Polytechnique fédérale de Lausanne*], Hans-Ulrich Schiedt [ViaStoria, Zenrum für Verkehrsgeschichte], and Giuseppe Pini [Observatoire universitaire de la mobilité, Université de Genève], November 2013); in Australia: University of Wollongong, where Georgine Clarsen and Frances Steel organized a workshop on "Gendered Adventurism" (including ocean surfing) in 2010, with Jennifer Bonham, Carrol Purcell, Gordon Waitt, and others attending, resulting in lively debates about, among others, the gendered character of my concept of the car as an "adventure machine."

There are so many whom I owe so much that I certainly am going to forget some when I would even try to include them all in my thankfulness. But some *must* be mentioned. For instance, because they provided me with material, be it their own work, a crucial illustration, or suggestions for further study: Irene Anastasiadou, Georgine Clarsen, Colin Dival, Karl Gerth, Julia Hildebrand, Philip Holden, Thomas Kaiserfeld, Maxwell

Lay, Cheryl Lousley, Massimo Moraglio, Patricia L. Mokhtarian, Peter Norton, Lynne Pearce, Lü Pengyue, Stéphanie Ponsavady, Edward Rhoads, Dominic Sachsenmaier, Frank Schipper, Cotten Seiler, Victor Seow, Mimi Sheller, Dhan Zunino Singh, Stefan Tetzlaff, Lee Vinsel, and James Warren. Others must be mentioned because they were willing to read (often quite substantial) parts of my manuscript: Rodrigo Booth, Sina Fabian, Nanny Kim, Fabian Kröger, Gaële Lesteven, Chris Lezotte, Liu Wennan, Kudzai Matereke, the late Clay McShane, Federico Paolini, Gordon Pirie, Luísa Sousa, Steven Spalding, and Bill Steele. And, of course, the two anonymous reviewers of my final manuscript. At Berghahn Books, during the book production, I enjoyed the support from Marion and Vivian Berghahn, Chris Chappell, Mykelin Higham, Caroline Kuhtz and Kristyn Sanito. My former student assistant Texas van Leeuwenstein not only helped standardizing the graphs, he also assisted me in making the index.

In this excursion with a large carbon footprint, a special word of thanks goes to Dagmar Schäfer (Max Planck Institute for the History of Science, who succeeded me as editor of *Transfers*) for putting me in contact with Niu Weixing, Director of the School of History and Culture of Science at Shanghai Jiao Tong University, founded long ago as a transport research university. His invitation to give a summer school course on Modernization of China (with the emphasis on mobility history) in 2017 at his institute enabled me to present my new mobility studies ideas for the first time in a comprehensive form and to work with thirty-five students on issues of modern Chinese mobility culture. Hou Kun was my student assistant there. The students read recent Chinese novels, watch Chinese TV soap series, and analyze the Hollywood *Fast and Furious* and *Transformers* film series (and the online discussion forums in China) from a Chinese perspective. During a later visit to Shanghai, as a fellow of the Center for the History of Global Development at Shanghai University led by Iris Borowy, I was able to finalize my manuscript, including the bibliography, the latter with the crucial help of literary history students Wu Xiaoyan and Lou Shuyan. At Iris's center, I was able to initiate a new research project, together with the center's students, on the Chinese Belt and Road Initiative, the results of which will hopefully flow into the final volume of this trilogy on the world history of automobilism-in-the-making.

Closer to home, I must thank the members of the *ouwemannenclub* (old guys' club, meeting in Nijmegen), old (very old!) study friends Harry Mazeland, Michel van Nieuwstadt, Piet Rademakers, and Gerard Snels, whose discussions on irony, pop and rock, politics and novels, populism and Italian proletarian culture, as well as the lunches during our Sunday afternoon sessions, kept me on track. I thank Anneke Voeten for helping me select some Turkish novels. Qasim Barrio at the local café Barraka (no alcohol!) in

Órgiva (Granada province) deserves my thanks because he managed to keep the subscription of the *New York Times International Edition* active even when normal delivery stagnated and he had to switch to delivery by snail mail. At Eindhoven University, I must thank the library team, especially Peter Smits, who kept the stream of photocopies and books through the interlibrary loan system (ILS) going. Bert Toussaint of the Rijkswaterstaat agency deserves my gratitude because of the stream of assignments and projects that enabled me not only to use the Netherlands as a "silent model" of Western modernization-through-mobility but also to finance the increasingly expensive ILS flow. I thank Erik van der Vleuten, Hans Jeekel, and, again, Ruth Oldenziel for their support during the final years of my stay in Eindhoven. The same goes for Sonja Beekers and Sonia Parker, whereas Iris Houx was instrumental as a liaison once I settled in Spain. From then on, group chairman Rudi Deckers (later succeeded by Floor Alkemade) let me continue to use the university's ILS, as well as the university address for the dozens of books I ordered online, accurately managed by Iris. With Jan Korsten, Director of the Foundation for the History of Technology, I was able to negotiate a project with Rijkswaterstaat on the history of international road safety, to be executed with Ruud Filarski during the coming years. I also would like to thank two perhaps unusual subjects: the anonymous people behind the H-Soz-Kult website who perform an incredibly worthwhile and time-consuming job of keeping us informed about the field, and the Surface Pro tablet (despite Microsoft's questionable service), which stored literally thousands of scanned books, reports, papers, and articles, enabling me to read and make pen notes on-screen in planes, trains, and subways; hotel rooms, guest houses, and rented apartments; coffee shops and parks all over the world.

Having said this, the remaining errors in the following pages are of course fully my responsibility. Talking of errors, many readers with a local specialism may be inclined to read this book as an encyclopedic exercise of an international and transnational "world mobility history"—and no doubt will find many a hiatus. But this book is conceived, rather, as a kaleidoscope, a bricolage of snippets, fragments of history: such sections have been written as an invitation, a provocation perhaps, to expand, contradict, particularize. I really don't have the pretension to write a "definitive" form of historical analysis. Together, these "histories," as I would like to call them, are meant to show a certain pattern, such as the "layering" of mobilities beyond the West, the enormous and often neglected influence of the so-called informal economy (including the jeepneys, *matatus*, mosquito buses, and motorcycle taxis), the importance of the bus (and collective transport in general), and the overwhelming presence, often forgotten or neglected, of so-called slow mobilities, from walking, to head porterage, to rickshaw pulling and one-wheeled barrow pushing, to cycling. In such a setting, subversive and subaltern mobilities appear to be more important than the latest car model. Also, the Cold War, the Decade of Development, and the forced spread of the road network over the globe make this history deeply political. No wonder, then, that this mobility history is richly embedded in a societal story, contrasting the car "exuberance" of the West with the alleged "chaos" of the East and South. Wait for the next sequel to appear, and you will *really* know what I mean!

In a way, this book is at the same time a personal history, as I was a witness of many events described in chapters 2 and 3: the songs cited are mine, the university study indirectly enabled by the Marshall Plan enabled my later career in the first place, and the resistance against roadbuilding was part of my political education. This is also the place to thank my (now) wife Charley Werff (we had to marry, because Spain does not recognize cohabitants) for her support throughout this project. I dedicate this book to my deceased, younger brother Karel, whom I would have liked to know better.

Shanghai University, 29 September 2019

Introduction

QUESTIONING THE CAR
Prolegomena for a Historical Analysis of Global Mobility

> History … should be a left hand to us, as of a violinist.
> —William Carlos Williams

New Perspectives, New Questions

In a recent ethnography of China's fledgling culture of automobilism just after the turn of the new century, peri-urban outings are described that easily would engender a déjà vu experience among students of early Western road motorization. Caravans of automobiles driven by adventurous car owners roam the Chinese countryside, just like the automobile club excursions in Europe more than a century ago, or so it seems. The comparison seems all the more convincing when we realize the Chinese SUVs that take part in such adventures can be considered a revival of the large, heavy contraptions for the European aristocratic and bourgeois extended family, a wrong deviation, it soon turned out, on a path toward more affordable, miniaturized versions, then and now.[1]

So, history repeats itself? Perhaps with a twist? Didn't Karl Marx predict it would appear as a farce the second time? And didn't Gilles Deleuze expand on this by saying "repetition is comic when it falls short—that is, when instead of leading to metamorphosis and the production of something new, it forms a kind of involution, the opposite of authentic creation"?[2] Subtle differences with what I have described in a previous publication as an Atlantic culture around the car as "adventure machine" should warn us against premature conclusions as soon as we shift toward what we, in a similar sketchy (and catchy) style, could call Pacific automobilism. This book documents and analyzes the first phase of this shift: the explosion of Western automobilism and the ambitious and self-confident activities to spread this automobilism beyond the West in an effort to make the world into one giant 'car society.' But that is the story of the West, shared, perhaps, by the elite of 'the Rest.' From the perspective of the earth's majority, including many in the West, the story reads quite differently. For them, automobilism appeared as a way of life imposed upon an existing, rich fabric of mobilities. The result was very different from what we have seen emerge and persist in the prewar West, and explode there as exuberant automobilism in the immediate postwar years.

The crucial point here is that we can see this only if we try to look over the shoulder of the mobile Other—if we look, in the words of Michael Hardt and Antonio Negri, "from below."[3] That would mean we should zoom out of our stare at the car and its immediately surrounding culture (something the ethnography of the Chinese excursions failed to do) and refocus on the multiple mobilities of these societies. What we then see is what I will call a "layeredness" of these mobilities, a coexisting old and new, the old no less 'modern,' as we will see, than the new. The central question of this book, then, is what happens with the characteristics of the prewar 'car society' when it not only explodes into Western exuberance, reaching well beyond the prewar, relatively prosperous rural and urban middle class into societal pockets occupied by marginals and minorities still in the full process of emancipation, such as children, women, ethnic and sexual minorities, the physically impaired, but also, and at the same time, when it travels beyond the West in much larger amounts than only for the prewar colonials and their indigenous superelites. This central question, governing this book, has two answers: one historical, the other methodological.

From a *historical* perspective, the question arises whether the concept of the automotive adventure, as it emerged during the first half of the twentieth century as the very core of Western car culture, remains valid as a "master category" in a Deleuzian sense if we turn our attention to other countries not covered by our original North Atlantic focus. The second perspective is methodological: what could or should history bring to this issue? Is not social science quite competent in answering such questions, based on a thorough analysis of global car culture's predicaments? And if history *does* bring something to the analysis that social science cannot provide, can we use the same mix of conventional (archives, trade journals, secondary literature) and unconventional sources (artistic utterances written by and for an 'automotive middle class' such as novels and poems) as we did when dealing exclusively with the prewar West? Are the latter sources as generous in bringing out hidden motifs and motivations as they were in the case of the West? Shouldn't we revise our toolbox before we start to follow the car into the postwar period and beyond the West, if only to include sources from popular culture (such as films and songs, and so-called lowbrow literature) that seem to require a different approach than linear narrativity analysis? And do we need other tools when analyzing the collective mobility of the subaltern than the ones we used to analyze middle-class automobilism, such as the concept of the 'ironic car'?[4]

The answer is a clear and double 'yes.' In an effort to answer the questions formulated above, this book provides an extension and a shift of my previous perspective in two directions: it not only tries to decenter the West methodologically, by complexifying mobility culture from a global perspective, but it also covers the third quarter of the century, by the end of which the West seemed to be on the verge of being dethroned as the natural locus of automotive culture, as the first signs of the next period, that of Doom, became visible by the end of the 1960s. There is one small problem, however: we lack a prehistory of non-Western automobilization, which would only strengthen the prejudice that the car, well prepared during half a century, 'invaded' the South and East as an extraneous object. Therefore, first of all, I owe a correction to my previous analysis of the West by revisiting the pre–World War II period from a non-Western perspective (part I, chap. 1). In so doing, I will continue using the periodization developed on the basis of my 'Western' analysis (Emergence, until World War I; Persistence, until World War II, in this case taken together into one large period of Emergence and Persistence), but with a small, critical addition (also for the postwar periods: "again," "with a twist"), to indicate the periods themselves may fit but that their names may be up for revision once my analysis turns global. So, after the previous two periods of Emergence and Persistence, I will enter the postwar period announced in my previous study (Exuberance) but now described and analyzed from a global point of view (part II, chaps. 2–3), limiting my postwar excursion to the first period of the three, and reserving the other two (Doom, Confusion) for a later publication. World War II, not included in the previous study, appears in this one only in hindsight (from chap. 2, looking back); this is justified, in my opinion, because this war did not form such a breach as did World War I (to which an entire chapter was dedicated in my previous study, as it brought a 'systems approach' to automobilism).

Despite the Anglophone sources on which this study is largely based, the shift to the global perspective will be made visible in two respects: I will, whenever the sources allow, describe Western automobilism through non-Western (or better, formulated from the perspective of mobility studies:

non-canonized) eyes, taking the latter as "point of departure," following the suggestion by anthropologists Jean and John L. Comaroff that "it is the global south that affords privileged insight into the workings of the world at large, as old margins become new frontiers." The Comaroffs claim, quoting an American senator, the East and South are a "perfect petri dish of capitalism ... challenging the myth that there is only one authentic version of it." As I have argued in *Atlantic Automobilism*, this is certainly also the case for both American and European automobilisms before the war. The question, then, is, echoing the Comaroffs (including their assertion that "the line of demarcation" between North and South "is not actually drawn in a stable way" and that "the south" is "a *relation*, not a thing in or for itself"): does the "north appear ... to be 'evolving' southward" in automobilistic terms as well, and does the South thus "prefigure the future of the global north?" The Comaroffs gave as an example of the non-West figuring as the "laboratory" of global culture the "experiments ... in urban architecture and planning," as well as "in untried practices of governance and extraction, bureaucracy and warfare, property and pedagogy": modernity was from the outset a (highly asymmetrical) collaborative endeavor, in which the "peripheries" functioned as places of modernity production "at a discount," places where "the violence and the magic, the expropriation and alienation, the syncretism and archaism suppressed in Europe ... were often promiscuously visible." To give a more recent example: "Secure labor contracts have now evaporated such that the precarity that has long been the experience of workers in the subordinated countries and among subordinated populations in the dominant countries is now becoming universal." Can we find examples, in global automotive culture, of this *prefiguration* that go beyond Hartmut Böhme's observation that commodity fetishism was transferred from Africa right "into the very core of the European societies"?[5]

Second, heeding anthropologist Paul Rabinow's warning that one should not replace Orientalism by Occidentalism in an act of "reverse essentialism," the Western vision on global developments (such as its attempts to 'develop' the rest of the world through roadbuilding, a major revolution in the history of global mobility, described in chap. 3) will be explicitly described as a "gaze to the East." This does not make me immune, *hélas*, to the pitfalls of what David Spurr has called the "curious phenomenon," that "the West seeks its own identity in Third World attempts at imitating it; it finds its own image, idealized, in the imperfect copies fabricated by other cultures."[6] So be it. In the conclusion to this study, I will reach back to the following sections of the introduction, in which I first will provide a recapitulation of the previous study (emphasizing its main conclusions and concepts), concluding that we need to rethink the car as 'adventure machine,' especially in relation to its role as a status symbol. We also need to rethink automotive subjectivation, now that groups and classes other than the white male part of the middle class enter our narrative. Next, we will have to deal with some methodological issues additionally necessary to support the postwar analysis, such as some insights from media studies and travel writing, and the problem of representation: can we trust our popular-culture sources? At the end of this introduction, some paragraphs will be dedicated to the selection of the sources and the use of certain terms.

Looking Back: Emergence and Persistence of the Adventure Machine

I developed the concept of the adventure machine through my analysis of the electric vehicle: it formed the main explanation for this vehicle's 'failure' at the start of Western automobilism, which, from a technological-evolutionary point of view, was not a failure at all, as the vehicle's technology formed a grab bag of innovative solutions taken over by its main competitor, the gasoline car, a phenomenon without which the latter could not have become mainstream so easily.[7] Only if historians aim, as is often the case, at the entirety of the car as a commodity (only if they chose the history of the car as framework instead of the history of automobilism or of mobility in general) can the electric vehicle be said to have failed, as it could not get rid of its symbolic stereotype of being a woman's (or feminized) car. Instead, the 'adventurous' attractiveness of its internal-combustion rival in a male-dominated culture of sport and leisure was irresistible, in three realms of practices: temporal (racing and speedy touring), spatial (unlimited roaming in the countryside), and functional (tinkering, even if many pioneer motorists, especially in the United States, employed a chauffeur). All three practice-complexes were connected to uncertainty about their outcomes (hence the term adventure), engendering (bodily) thrill. This explanation, based on what I have called inter-artifactual technology transfer (resulting in the gasoline vehicle, once it became mainstream, to 'steal,' as it were, all benign functions of its electric rival, such as the closed body, the cord tire, and electric starting, to name only a few, to prevent potential users to opt in favor of the alternative) avoids the tautological dilemma of explaining the failure of one technology from the success of its rival, an explanation that fosters, misleadingly so, the belief in ubiquitous radical rather than incremental change.[8]

My subsequent analysis of the early gasoline car culture, mostly based on 'autopoetics' (novels, poems, songs, movies, paintings, not necessarily sources on cars, but also including sources in which the car figures directly or indirectly in selected passages, passages I described as 'autopoetic'), revealed two additional aspects of the automotive adventure. They were not found in my earlier study on the emergence of the electric car, because they were not so crucial in the struggle between the electric and the gasoline option, but also because I did not use autopoetics for that study. It confirms that conventional sources do not form a reliable entrance into the motifs and motivations of historical actors. The two new adventurous aspects were subsumed, in my *Atlantic Automobilism* study, under the term conquest, a "war metaphor" (in the analysis of George Lakoff and Mark Johnson) covering the masculine adventure of capturing the passenger (mostly a man 'conquering' a woman, although Proust, as a passenger, admired his masculine driver), as well as the touristic "surveying" (by men and some women alike) of the 'periphery,' either the noncore parts of the continents under investigation (the Southern United States, Eastern and Southern Europe), or those countries and continents, such as Africa, that were considered a 'periphery' in a colonial context. The study of postwar American women's literature in chapter 2, however, now suggests "control" captures the situation better than 'conquest.'[9]

This often violent (if not performative, then certainly structural) amalgam of aggressive attitudes and practices also applies to the colonial context, and one can wonder (as I will do in the following chapters) whether one can still call such experiences 'adventurous,' if the experience of the addressee of such "adventures" includes so much suffering and cruelty. This will be one of the main themes of my analysis. After all, 'adventure' was coined in a situation of leisurely, tongue-in-cheek play with near death, and the suffering of 'Others' was limited to what was deemed acceptable in a 'modern,' motorizing society, such as fear for life and limb, and the occasional traffic fatality, that is, if the 'victim' was a consideration at all in this largely narcissistic adventurous practice. However named, this fourth aspect, of conquest or control, is a secondary experience, as it presupposes the existence of one of the other three adventurous traits. All these adventurous traits of early car use were part and parcel of the emerging risk society, where danger was gradually being replaced by the calculable occurrence of an 'accident,' a shift in which the car played a supporting role, as the choice to take a ride increasingly involved the suppression of the fear for disaster. *Atlantic Automobilism* showed how motorists were supported in the statistical reproduction of automotive 'safety' by the fledgling expertise of traffic engineering, one of the systemic vanguards of the 'car society.'[10]

Methodologically, in an effort to explain the breakthrough of the gasoline car through the 'motifs, motives, and motivations' of early automobilism, the analysis of autopoetic sources took place on three 'levels': content, symbols, and affinity. I do not claim, as some recent social scientists using literature as a source do, "the novelist, poet, librettist or film director can often grasp the phenomenology of an event with a sharpness, clarity and resonance which makes the efforts of social and cultural analysts appear (as they indeed often are) clodhopping."[11] The choice of this type of sources was (and in this study again is) justified not only by the insight that they contain information not easily to be found in the traditional historical sources such as archives and trade journals (for instance, because they are taboo as a masculine conversation topic, or because they are part of subconscious, corporeal drives not easily expressed in words) but also by the realization that, historically, literary (or more generally, artistic) and automotive (or more generally, mobility) avant-gardes largely overlapped.

Indeed, we should "take ... advantage of what fiction can do better than polemic or history: put us in the room [with] other human beings," or, in our case, put us in their car.[12] For the first period of automotive pioneering (and to a certain extent, this applies to the bicycle pioneers a decade or so earlier), one can even claim not a few of the pioneers were writers, who helped shape the experience of driving as much as driving shaped their own literary experiments of a new sensorial 'grammar.' Written artistic utterances, I found, are especially attractive as a source because their authors are forced to "translate" their multisensorial experiences into 'text,' a skill in which writers are considered exceptionally trained: as such, they can function, the previous study showed, as the contemporary witnesses of the historian. But this is not a free ride: I will come back to the precarious issue of translation, but first let us investigate the three levels of analysis of this type of sources.

As to the first level of analysis, close reading the *textual content* resulted in the conclusion that the automotive adventure during the first Emergence phase was a white, heterosexual, male, urban, middle-class pastime imbued, if not saturated, by violence and aggression, from fantasies of intimidation of farmers and the rape or automotive penetration of villages, to 'hooliganism' (the elite counterpart of the Luddism of the movement's adversaries) and the actual killing of other road users. It is perhaps difficult to see this from a standpoint in history where the number of fatalities of global road traffic are in the order of one million, but for the contemporaries of the pioneers, this was nothing but obvious. The 'vandalism' of early automobilism is not a byproduct of an intrinsically benign technology; this insight should work as an antidote to those histories that depict the pioneers as a nostalgic fraternity of car lovers. They were not: they behaved like vandals loyal to their reputation of motorized narcissists. They were not a minority that soon got pushed out of the movement leaving the 'reasonable motorists' to spread their gospel of automobilism further, but they represented the very core of what automobilism was all about. This hegemonic minority was able to define automobilism as a seemingly innocent, but deeply violent and aggressive practice.

The crucial second Persistence period of early automobilism then established the systemic character of what after World War II would be called a 'car society,' a period in which highway network building channeled the 'swarms' of motorists into traffic flows and 'traffic engineering' helped make many violent aspects go underground, in a 'covert culture' of road safety statistics. Swarms are groups that act quasi-coordinated without any central command. Fear for disorder inspired this traffic engineering project, enabling the motorists to experience 'transcendence,' the reassuring feeling that one is not alone, despite the 'cocooning' of the driver and his (and increasingly, her) passengers in a capsule that distanced them from their environment. Hence, the coalescence of fear for chaos and desire for swarm-like transcendence enabled the systematization of automobilism into 'traffic.' By the end of this period, the closed 'affordable family car,' governed by a 'tamed adventure' of less aggressive (but, in terms of safety statistics, no less violent) weekend excursions and car holidays, and still mostly driven by the father of the 'nuclear family,' hurried over the highway network that became more or less completed in all industrialized Western countries well before World War II. Women and other marginalized would-be motorists (such as blacks or homosexuals) had a hard time to enter automobilism in the prewar period, and if they did, this took place under the hegemonic conditions of the dominant group (which often boiled down to a reduced and a seemingly more passive role of 'passengering,' a heavily under-researched automotive practice, I concluded at the end of my previous study), thus joining those that already deployed such practices, such as children and the physically impaired (who are virtually invisible as actors in prewar Western automobilism).

Indeed, automobilism in the first half of the twentieth century was far from inclusive, as some historians would have it: even the white worker refrained from joining the middle-class movement, also to a large extent in the United States, despite extensive credit facilities and despite the possibility of alternative, less individualized user practices such as shared car ownership. In the West, the passenger car had become firmly inscribed in a paradigm of individualism, testified, for instance, by the fate of the collective 'jitney' (often operated by Blacks), which was made illegal and then chased from the American urban roads.[13] And yet, public road transport, especially the bus, slowly emerging from its decade-long struggle against the railway alternative, was the vehicle of choice for all those waiting to become 'free' through car mobility. In other words, by the end of the interbellum, one did not have to own a car in order to feel part of a car society, or indulge in 'road experience,' which from then on decisively would shape the national and transnational discourses on mobility (including the urban crisis, which remained unresolved before the war), as the current study will abundantly show.

Told in this way, the first half of twentieth-century automobilism is a refutation of two powerful myths, still haunting mobility studies: the *functionalist* belief that the success of the car can be attributed to its evolution from a toy of the rich to a petty bourgeois utilitarian contraption,[14] and the *diffusionist* assumption that this transformation took place in the United States, which hence forms the universal model of 'motorization.' Instead, this analysis acknowledges the existence of 'multiple mobilities' (national and subnational) that—contrary to the diffusion thesis (this remnant of "historicism," which "assumes we are all heading in the same direction, but that some have got there first and must direct the travel for later arrivals")— developed in parallel to each other, coagulating in two large 'Atlantic' subcultures, a European and an American, a diversity that during the following half-century will increase spectacularly, as we will see in this study, and become one of the main characteristics of postwar, global automobilism.[15] The multiplicity of mobilities extends even into the mainstream, where we will distinguish, in the following chapters, between hegemonic mobilities in a certain culture, and alternative mobilities. The latter are often at the same time 'subversive mobilities,' because they go against the hegemonic grain, as anti-modernist modernities. As such, they must on their turn be distinguished from 'subaltern mobilities' that are (as we will see in this introduction) not only subversive but also not a part of the mainstream. We will also witness, in the first chapter, the importance of 'forced mobilities.'[16] Contrary to the functionalist belief, the use profile of the car has been dominated, over the entire two periods of Emergence and Persistence, by pleasure and hedonism, even, as often as not, in the fledgling flows of the first car commuters in the 1930s. Indeed, pleasure and violence, hedonism and aggression form mutually enhancing conceptual clusters of experiences in and around the car (albeit in a moderate, middle-class flavor), especially as narrated in novels and other artistic utterances.

This is especially apparent when the second, *symbolic* level of analysis is included. Based on my initial conviction that the dynamic, adventurous use was more important for an explanation than its static, symbolic use (quite adequate for the Western realms, it seemed), I limited my symbolic analysis to the metaphorical realm. During the first period, the car appeared to be compared to a monster or a woman (both to be tamed); it was described as a liberator (of men and especially women), as a unifier of humankind or a compressor of time and space, as vehicle of progress and restorer of the past, while the car trip functioned as the image of life itself or as a Quest of the Self. I identified the latter aspect as a distortion because of the type of sources, which privilege the car trip as a journey into the Self (a perspective uncritically followed by many students of travel writing and of literature), thus hiding the fundamental collective aspects of early automobilism, from the outings guided by car club officials and in general the multiple car and touring club events, to the hidden pleasure of being part of a flow and indulging in collective overspeeding, feeling strong against an often powerless police force, to the family as collective subject during the Persistence phase, or the 'situational group' of the taxi or bus trip. During the second, more systemic period, the car then also functioned, conversely, as a reservoir of metaphors to characterize nonautomotive phenomena in society, showing that automobilism had become a dominant cultural trait even if the movement itself was carried by a societal minority. Hegemony does not need to be "dominant in quantitative terms."[17]

But the most remarkable result of my symbolic analysis was the discovery of two metaphorical clusters (metaphor specialists Lakoff and Johnson would call it "lexical items ... coherently structured by a single metaphorical concept") to be found all over the sources: those related to the car as a 'shell' (a protective cocoon but also a grenade, now protective, then aggressive, or both at the same time) and the experience of 'flight' while driving, the elevated feeling that the motorist left the bumpy road and indulged in a womb-like poising. Flight, indeed, is the literal experience of transcendence, according to Zygmunt Bauman on the first page of his treatise on the individualized society. As such, 'flight' is in itself a form of mobility, a transformation from one state into another, into a field of mediated, "transcendental experience" according to Edmund Husserl, from a "field of direct experience."[18] However, as soon as we extend our analysis beyond the prewar phase and beyond the West, it becomes rapidly clear that the symbolic aspects of the car should be given more attention, a first recognition of the insight of the Comaroffs. After all, the car is not only an adventure machine but also a costly possession, even more so in societies with extreme inequalities. We will come back to this metaphorical level later in this introduction.

It is the third level of analysis, that of the *affinity* between the practice of driving and writing, between the production of a text and of a driving experience, that brought us nearest to an explanation of early Western automobilism. In *Atlantic Automobilism*, I have called the crucial driving experience an "ironic mobile sublime, enabling transcendence, but tongue-in-cheek, in a distanced way." I called it ironic because of its affinity with the literary technique of irony (defined in its verbal form as "the use of words to express something other than and especially the opposite of the literal meaning," a form of nonliteral language use, next to, for instance, the use of metaphors), which has helped the (middle-class) writer keep his distance to the world, just like the car cocoon brings the (middle-class) motorist close to the gazed-at other, but always in a distanced way, protected by the shell.[19] For the purpose of our postwar analysis, we should develop this concept of the 'ironic car' one step further. Borrowing from literary and linguistic studies of irony, we can now define the car as a vehicle of nonverbal irony, but in a sense other than the "Louvre's glass pyramids," proposed by Rebecca Clift as an "ironic play on our prototypical knowledge of pyramids as solid." Rather, the car's irony rests on the affinity between the production of the car trip and the production of texts, both resulting in a distancing effect toward the world. Tellingly, modern studies of linguistic irony distinguish between "wolves" (those who understand irony) and "sheep" (those who do not).[20] Others fine-tuned this distinction by adding another opposite pair (those who agree with the intended message and those who do not), resulting in a four-quadrant matrix of "wolf-confederates," "wolf-victims," "sheep-confederates," and "sheep-victims." Such studies also distinguish between ironic factors and ironic markers (the latter, contrary to the former, can be removed without the irony disappearing).[21]

Thus, automotive perception was shaped by, and on its turn shaped, automotive technology, which in this phase underwent one of the most costly operations in its history: the conversion from an open (like one half of a clam) to a closed body (a shell or cocoon), a process I described as encapsulation. The "ironist," Italian psychologists have observed in the case of prosodic (vocal nonverbal) irony, uses "his own voice for calibrating strategically his way of (un)masking himself to others." Just like the car had to undergo technical changes at the factory (ironic factors such as the closed body) and additional changes by the users (ironic markers such as tinted glass) to enable automotive irony, the human voice is inflected to produce ironic markers. Irony (and its somewhat more aggressive twin, sarcasm) thus are "considered as a cold way to wound the victim more harshly: unlike an open insult produced in a moment of rage, a sarcastic comment is more calculated, as it arises from rational and intentional planning." One can read this last form of linguistic violence as an ironic (if not sarcastic) statement about the car as well (as we have seen in our previous study when dealing with the "cold persona" as motorist, and his statistical inclination to wound and kill): "using irony you can say what you mean without meaning what you say …, because of the distinction between sentence meaning and intended meaning."[22] In the terms of automotive irony: one can kill (or be killed) on the road as long as one adheres to the rules and regulations of traffic.

In this study, we will witness the gradual loss of irony in the automotive adventure, a shift we will connect to a shift in the class base of automobilism. Indeed, in this study, there is a lot on class, especially middle class. We will use the class concept in a somewhat multilayered, eclectic way, now emphasizing its economic base, then its cultural aspects, then its Weberian (emphasizing status), sometimes its Marxist 'flavor,' and sometimes its "wedding" into Bourdieuian practices of the reproduction of hierarchical 'distinctions.'[23] "Distinction work" is often very mobile: it travels by car. In this study, following Bourdieu through Amy Hanser, class is "an activity or practice rather than … a category." For E. P. Thompson, class is a human relationship. Mobility, after all, is part of a possible definition of classes as "broad aggregates of individuals and families, … distinguished from each other by inequalities in wealth, income, power (or at least access to it), authority, prestige, freedom, life-styles and life chances, including mobility into a different aggregate of individuals."[24] Other forms of affinity—for instance, between the production and consumption of early movies and the vision through the windshield (or windscreen)—helped discover the very core of the automotive experience in this phase: the transcendental experience of going beyond the individual driver (just like literature allows "to draw us into a world beyond ourselves"), the godlike feeling of power, the entrance into the swarm of motorists, being part of a flow, yet only a monad.

For our current project, however, we need a subtler insight into the intricacies of the transcendental process. For instance, seen from the transcendental perspective, the experience of 'flight' (popping up time and again in early autopoetic novels counterintuitively: the bumpy roads and the harsh suspension systems really did not seem to allow it) appeared to be a crucial element of the automotive adventure, as it emphasizes the haptic basis of the car driving experience and as such forms a correction to those studies that see the car primarily as an instrument of vision. This is not to say vision is not important as a constitutive element in the automotive adventure, not so much as a gaze, as John Urry argued borrowing a-historically from an earlier phase of railway sensibilities (privileging the static train passenger, or the slow-moving walker), but as a furtive glance, produced at high speed, and constantly changing its direction. Differently put, the 'gaze' metaphor universalizes the driver's experience of the second half of the century along the straight freeways (and projects it back into history), but it neglects the prewar sweeping glances of the driver meandering over the national road system, as well as the car passenger whose vision is not (necessarily) a controlling one.[25] Vision may still be the predominant sensation while driving, but this is modulated and enhanced by a multisensorial experience, dominated by touch.[26]

The question, then, is whether this prewar ironic, moderately adventurous automobilism that draws its energy from a kind of collectively experienced, but covert culture of transcendence can stand the test of the postwar world: what happens to the automotive adventure if its carrier tries to migrate to other continents, and how is the original adventure affected by feedback from these places? To give only one example: if it is true that the colonial state's hegemony was the result of a shift in the balance between persuasion and coercion toward the latter, then Cotten Seiler's illuminating analysis of the role of the car in the United States as a historical stimulant of the 'persuasion side' of the state's hegemony might not be valid, as such, in a colonial society, and its successors.[27] Similarly, what happens on a more regional or local scale, when the white, heterosexual, middle-class man is joined by women, blacks and other people of color, homosexuals and other people with marginalized sexual proclivities, children in the passenger seat or even behind the steering wheel, as we will witness in the following chapters? Or when the car 'lands,' as an alien contraption, in a society where the appropriating upper or middle class is not white? And most of all: does our thesis, that car and middle class are historically intrinsically linked through the concept of 'adventure,' still hold when confronted with the majority-Rest, and its particular tradition of mobility, in a *multilayered world of increasing multimobility* (through the plane, motorized two-wheelers, but also in the non-West by the persistence of 'old' mobilities such as the rickshaw, the bullock cart, the trishaw, cycling, and walking)? It seems, indeed, we need to further fine-tune and extend our methodological and theoretical toolbox for this task, equip it with tools able to handle motorists other than the white, middle-class male, and other modes than the affordable family car. In the following four sections, we will do so by investigating two aspects of automobilism hitherto somewhat underexposed in our previous study: the commodity and the media character of the car.

Extending Adventure: The Car as Possession and Status Symbol

In our previous analysis, we emphasized (under the influence of the declared 'liquidity' of life, and the 'fluidity' of society and its 'mobility turn') the *dynamic character of car use,* experienced from the perspective of the human (predominantly white male) bodily sensorium. This was necessary to *corporeally,* haptically ground the concept of automotive adventure. Thus, the car adventure and the adventure car both fitted in the concept of the 'dual nature of technology': the technical *properties* (its physical qualities such as weight, color, and maximum engine speed) of the artifact car *afford* (in the terminology of ecological psychologist James Gibson) a set of relational, user *functions*.[28] In our previous analysis, these functions were mostly limited to the practice (or user function) of driving, from the internal handling of the car to taking part in road traffic or navigating along the highways on a holiday trip, to name only a few elements of the *use profile* as this emerged during the first decades of the last century. In my previous study, I drew up a matrix of car-related practices as a basis for a taxonomy. At the same time, however, most cars were and are owned by their user, and *ownership* does not fully overlap with *use,* at least not if we define the latter (perhaps somewhat) narrowly as a dynamic process of driving the car, or passengering in it. After all, the car is immobile (parked, stuck because of a defect, standing in traffic) during by far most of the time, time during which other car-related practices are deployed, such as maintenance and repair in the garage, do-it-yourself activities at home (including washing and polishing), vehicle modifying in the context of a youth culture, studying others stuck in the same jam, and showing off the results through 'cruising' and other forms of more static exhibitionist performances such as car shows, or museums.

Thus, 'consuming the car' involves not only the 'use profile' for which traffic engineering coined 'modal split,' a term I try to avoid in the following chapters because of its Western bias, opting for the alternative 'modal configuration' if we wish to refer to the competition of several *mobility modes*, such as the car, the bicycle, walking, and the train. Car consumption also involves the act of *purchase* as well as the *display of ownership*—also, and especially, if not moving. And although I dedicated, in my previous study, quite some space to the sociological aspects of the car as commodity (for instance, how it crept into the household budget of the Western nuclear family during the interwar years), there is also an important *corporeal* side to this which would allow us to distinguish between an aggressively masculine form on the one hand, and other forms of masculine and feminine behavior on the other, in the West and especially beyond. Instead of as an aggressive 'adventure machine,' the car then appears as a 'fashion machine,' a suit in metal and plastic; this would extend our conception of the automotive adventure considerably. In our earlier analysis, we briefly discussed the fetish character of the car as commodity, but for the period under scrutiny here, we need a broader take from the history and theory of consumption. We can do this along several paths, acknowledging that the quite repetitive and abstract treatise on "conspicuous consumption" by Thorstein Veblen from 1899 is no longer adequate.[29] One path is psychoanalytical as it is based on Sigmund Freud's later work, especially *Beyond the Pleasure Principle* (1920), in which he distinguished between pleasure and satisfaction and "turned his focus to the satisfaction that the subject derives from repeating experiences that don't provide pleasure." Todd McGowan called Freud's conclusion about the 'death drive' "misleading," and instead used his distinction between pleasure and satisfaction to emphasize that we "enjoy ... what we don't have," as the title of one of McGowan's books (2013) runs. "The fundamental gesture of capitalism is promise ... The promise ensures a sense of dissatisfaction with the present in relation to the future," a phenomenon I have called "expectation" and identified as the basis for innovation.[30]

On the consumption side, commodification functions through this "promise of a better future," an insight enabling us to reformulate 'adventure,' for the purpose of the present study that includes the car as commodity, as a risky chase after the future and its promises, "just like auto racing fans go to see cars crashing (or potentially crashing), though this desire remains unconscious." In this characterization, the commute is no adventure, despite efforts by the Western middle class to reshape it as such (remember, for instance, Sinclair Lewis's *Babbitt* [1923] and his efforts in this direction), but car *purchase* is, as an adventurous form of appropriation, a third element of the conquest or control aspect of the automotive adventure, accompanied by 'thrill,' if only because of the large amount of money involved. People who don't own a car *yet* may engage in a derived adventure of desiring the car and fantasizing about its future use. Societies or parts thereof with a large share of commuting in their 'modal split' may then have a less adventurous car culture, but an echo of the 'adventure machine' is kept alive by its commodification, the desire to acquire a confirmation of one's societal status, as we will investigate in the case of the American suburbanite in chapter 2. As we will see, car driving thus not only becomes a rite of passage into adulthood; its possession also cements one's social position as part of the car-owning class, and the ostentatious display of this possession gives an extra twist to car adventurousness. Adventure is the experience of playing out desires; it enjoys the road over the destination, celebrating the struggle over the fulfillment. "The *aim* is the way taken," in the words of Jacques Lacan. More even: this adventure is intrinsically ironic, as it needs distance: "Proximity has a deleterious effect on both the subject's desire and the objects desirability." Also, commodification transforms the sublime that every society needs: "the act of sublimation occurs when the subject creates an object that is out of reach." Under capitalist conditions, the sublime is tamed ("less terrifying"): commodification "transforms ordinary objects into commodities, which are mystical entities endowed with sublime properties." This "victory over utility" enables "the transcendence of the everyday ... One buys the SUV for its sublimity even if one insists on its usefulness for hauling things."[31]

And yet, McGowan's exclusive focus on the car as (static) object fully neglects the dynamics of the automobile's use: "Once we traverse the distance and acquire the commodity, we experience the profound disappointment" and

> the sublime becom[es] quotidian ... Before we purchase an object, it has transcendent quality, akin to a religious icon from the Middle Ages. After the purchase, the sublimity rushes out of it, and we are left with an ordinary object that falls far short of our expectations ... Immediately after buying the car, it ceases to be sublime, even if one is relatively content with one's choice ... The religious experience of seeking the commodity becomes immediately secular after one has it.

This may be true for a refrigerator, or a couch, but cannot be true for mobile objects such as dresses and especially automobiles. As we have shown repeatedly for the pre–World War II era (and will do again for the post–World War II era, even if it seems to erode in the West), it is the *dynamic use* of the car that rekindles the sublime, the transcendence, and the religious feeling of being part of the 'swarm.' Whereas the user aspect of "consumption" of a refrigerator consists in the opening and closing of its door (and, of course, if it is a prestigious brand, its conspicuous presence in the kitchen), a car or a dress is consumed through driving and wearing. Whereas the milk is kept cold as long as we don't touch the refrigerator, the car trip is produced by a complex cluster of practices, extensively described in the novels we will deal with (that is, as long as we do not have a refrigerator-prone 'driverless car'). Indeed, McGowan's conclusion seems the result of a universalization of the boring experiences of the Western commuter, as we will see in the following chapters. Likewise, mobility history has moved beyond generalizations about the "irrelevance" of "self-conscious 'display.'" Lynn Pearce, who put forward this claim of irrelevance in her recent analysis of autopoetic British novels, unfortunately does not qualify who those "many drivers" are, who, according to her, are insensitive to their status.[32] Let us not forget that a dilapidated Volvo station wagon in the outskirts of Berkeley is as much a status symbol as a red Ferrari stopping in front of the Ritz in Paris.

Another possible conceptual entrance (another 'path') into the commodification of the car is provided by social psychologist Helga Dittmar, whose analysis is attractive for our project not only because she emphasizes the social constructedness of personal and social identities (she herself uses the term constructionism) but also because her analytical overview of the discipline is historical. Dittmar focused not on (the promise of) purchase but on (the performative practice of) *ownership*. Tellingly, her first example of the psychological importance of "individual ownership" was the car, in a quote from Erich Fromm, who in 1978 emphasized its status-symbolic character and its ability to provide an "extension of power," its acquisition adding "a new piece of ego." Following a long tradition in the social sciences, Dittmar derived the "symbolic meanings of material goods" (which "extend far beyond their immediate physical qualities") from advertisements, the symbols' paradise. This strategy is attractive because of the simplicity and one-dimensionality of the message, but I am reluctant to follow her here, as it is conceived from the perspective of the manufacturers and exclusively aimed at inciting its consumers to buy, and buy again. Advertisements are "extremely limited in its expressive range," anthropologist Grant McCracken, specialized in the study of culture and commerce, opines.[33]

Advertisements, despite their "hypnotic spell, especially on sociologists" (*dixit* Marshall McLuhan), are not the best way to enter the world of motorists' motivations, even if we acknowledge their power derives from the fact that their content resonates with what is already there, as the objects they praise are "magically loaded."³⁴ Our autopoetic sources, on the other hand, are aimed at complexifying the imagined lifeworlds of motorists (just like historians tend to do), offering the reader or viewer a set of alternative options for the 'I,' as well as insights into their motives. Advertisements indeed "provide the meanings of material symbols," but, especially in a mass market, they have a controversial relation with humor, let alone irony, which makes the 'translation' of their messages toward the motives of the motorists much more complex than is the case for fictionally narrated driving experiences. Asking people about their relation with their possessions and their identity, as the surveys do that form the basis of much of advertising scholarship, is extra problematic if we realize that although the respondents "seem aware of the link between possessions and identity, [they] are less happy to admit it—particularly with respect to themselves." Furthermore, those ads that consciously mobilize "rhetorical irony ...[,] demand sophisticated language skills," and are seen by marketing students as "best aimed at an elite or 'class' audience, for downscale targets may miss the point" and "tend in some cases to take the messages literally." Apparently, like experience, meanings are layered: some people (the 'sheep' from literary irony studies) tend to stick to the "surface meaning" of this type of "traditionally postmodern" advertising, missing the nonliteral, "underlying meaning." They miss the ironic "markers" or "cues."³⁵ Irony splits the audience of autopoetic utterances in two, just like the capsule of the ironic car separates the motorists from the 'Other.' I will nevertheless, in this study, have to grant more attention to the contents and symbols of car advertisements (compared to my previous study), as they can provide evidence of the role of the car industry in enforcing masculinity upon a reluctant market, at a moment when women start attacking the masculinist bastion in massive numbers. Advertisements were (and are) a weapon in the masculinization of the car discourse. They are tools of power, powerful tools.

Producing Commodification: Status, Narcissism, and Self-Development

At the start of the post–World War II period, the breakthrough of the mass market of the automobile makes the selection of our sources into a crucial, strategic issue indeed. This is all the more true because translating advertisement messages into the lifeworld of consumers, an operation often neglected in analyses of the symbolisms of the car in advertisements, is a much more burdensome endeavor than in the case of autopoetic novels or movies, even if the makers of these novels or movies do not coincide anymore with the mainstream motorist, as will increasingly be the case during the phase under scrutiny in this study. Under these conditions, a less ironic car culture seems to emerge, better covered by media belonging to what has been called "popular culture," such as films, songs, and later (to be analyzed in a later study) the so-called new media. Dittmar's social constructivism of "symbolic consumption" implies that a symbol, as "an entity which represents and stands for another entity ...[,] can have meaning only to the extent that individuals share the belief that they possess that meaning."

The symbol as a mediator of meaning between individuals (alone or as part of a group) includes the aspect of *status*, the place an individual or a group is considered to occupy within a social hierarchy, but under one important condition: "driving a 'prestige' automobile," Dittmar quotes marketing scholar Elizabeth C. Hirschman, "will not serve as an effective symbol of one's social status unless others in the relevant social groups share the driver's belief that the automobile is, indeed, prestigious." The coming chapters will give several examples of autopoetic utterances that do not share anymore such a belief, and we have seen Pearce confirming this trend. If a particular market is saturated, then the absence of an object in a household may be a "sign of poverty," as in the case of television in the West and increasingly, so it seems, in the case of the car. But as long as (or wherever) this is not the case, the car's transcendental function is twofold: it allows owners to realize functions that go way beyond "instrumental and utilitarian" functions. Second, as a motorized possession on wheels, it enables them to feel part of a *swarm*, as we argued before: a somehow coordinated group of cars without a proper 'leader.'[36] The car is a *social machine*, despite marketeers' hammering on its individualism.

Often, automotive mobility is approached through the car as a unit of analysis, whereas the collective aspect is then limited to the group of passengers, be it the family, the situational group, or the fleeting group of bus passengers. The swarm concept, on the contrary, enables us to follow a middle road between the 'collective subject' and the anonymized flow of traffic. As we will see, the swarm is not necessarily "linked to the narrative of fighting back against the established system" (as Mikkel Thelle concluded in his analysis of the [pedestrian] multitude on a Copenhagen square around 1900) but can also be very system-enhancing. Whether people share the belief about the prestige of the car or not, their response is not instinctual, as psychology would have it (the "acquisitive instinct") until well after World War II, revived recently by sociobiology. Instead, theories about the social construction of the self, theories that view "material possessions as socially shared symbols for identity," see the function of (status) symbols as an extension of the self, as a prosthesis. Commodities are used as markers of difference, and, as English and American studies scholar Walter Hesford asserted, "difference—the threat or promise of 'the Other'—will continue to be the central organizing category for postmodernist culture."[37]

In the 1960s, anthropologist Claude Lévi-Strauss analyzed "goods" as "not only economic commodities but vehicles and instruments for realities of another order: influence, power, sympathy, status, emotion." Also, sociologist Georg Simmel's "trickle-down" effect (describing, in the paraphrase of Dittmar, how "social groups imitate and adopt the status symbols of those groups slightly more affluent than they are") has meanwhile been superseded by mechanisms of "advertisement-driven fashion." Theories of "symbolic self-completion" describing mechanisms of "identity-creating and identity-enhancing" have been followed by suggestions that the postmodern self is "empty." The latter approach (based on the identity-is-a-container metaphor), proposed by psychotherapist and historian Philip Cushman, emphasized the "loss" of previously highly appreciated values such as "shared meaning" or "family, community, and tradition," and although historically grounded like Dittmar's analysis, Cushman's seems to presuppose an 'absolute self' as a container that can be emptied and "'filled up' with food, consumer products, and celebrities." The "gap between society's expectations of high-sufficiency and the lessened ability of narcissistically wounded individuals to achieve it" creates a "'false self' that masks the frightened, hidden 'true self'" and can be healed only by "advertising and psychotherapy." From this perspective, the car functions not only as a physical but also as a psychological prosthesis, of the narcissistic automotive self.[38]

Criticizing Fromm's very broad definition (equating narcissism nearly with egotism), Christopher Lasch in his famous 1978 book on this topic used a neo- or post-Freudian definition ("narcissism as essentially a defense against aggressive impulses rather than self-love") that allowed him to draw parallels "between the narcissistic personality type and certain characteristic patterns of contemporary culture, such as the intense fear of old age and death, altered sense of time, fascination with celebrity, fear of competition, decline of play spirit, deteriorating relations between men and women." At first sight, the connection between narcissism and automobilism (as I posited in my previous study) is not immediately clear from Lasch's more psychoanalytic than cultural characterization, but this changes when we understand the very basis of psychoanalytical research: the "primary narcissist," the newborn male child, "does not perceive his mother as having an existence separate from his own and he therefore mistakes dependence on the mother, who satisfies his needs as soon as they arise, with his own omnipotence … If the child for some reason experiences (the subsequent) separation trauma [from the mother] with special intensity, he may attempt to reestablish earlier relationships by creating in his fantasies an omnipotent mother or father who merges with images of his own self."

Car driving, as argued in my previous study, provided this immediate, but surrogate, seemingly unmediated satisfaction by simulating the womb. This is a *historical* phenomenon: "patients who began to present themselves in the 1940s and 1950s 'very seldom resembled the classical neuroses Freud described so thoroughly,'" mostly related to what at the turn of the century was called neurasthenia, a condition typical for early motorists; instead, they complained about "vague, diffuse dissatisfactions of life ... subtly experienced yet pervasive feelings of emptiness and depression [and] violent oscillations of self-esteem." Such postwar patients, Lasch concluded, "'act[ed] out' their conflicts instead of repressing or sublimating them." From this perspective, early car pioneers can be seen as an *avant-garde* whose aggressive "acting out" prefigured the narcissist that offered himself for therapy after World War II. The evidence is paradoxical, however: although the narcissist is "chronically bored, restless in search of instantaneous intimacy—of emotional titillation without involvement and dependence," Lasch also emphasized the narcissist "has little capacity for sublimation," whereas we found the pre–World War II car to be an excellent platform for transcendence.[39]

In theories about the 'construction of the self,' we should be aware of the danger of Eurocentrism, as "the role of possessions in self-development may be a phenomenon which is particularly prominent in [the Western] part of the world," where individualism has been shaped and defined differently. Dittmar quoted research suggesting the "main distinctive feature (of the West) is the notion of an *independent self*, which contrasts with the *interdependent self* of many non-Western cultures ... and our [Western] very own history," the latter addition implying a questionable diffusionism, as if the non-West is a replica of the West's own past. However this may be, "the Western notion of identity combines a sharp distinction of self from others and environment with an emphasis on the autonomy and self-determination of the individual," a condition we are inclined to call, in light of the distancing effect of the car we analyzed previously, an ironic self. Dittmar even suggested this individual should be characterized as an "Anglo-American" self, concluding: "Our contemporary Western notion of the decontextualized, autonomous and unique person, which does not acknowledge material context, seems [viewed from a global perspective] to be the exception rather than the rule." Likewise, women and men "undergo very different identity construction processes," further complexifying the analysis of autopoetic utterances, as we will see later in this book.

Women, recent psychological studies argue, describe themselves in terms of a "relational mode of discourse"; against such "communal" qualities stand the "individualistic" qualities men ascribe to themselves. According to several psychological case studies reported by Dittmar, men emphasize the "instrumental" or "pragmatic" aspects of their possessions, while women emphasize "emotional" aspects, an essentialist dichotomy that can no longer be upheld, as the following chapters will show, once one goes beyond the self-declaration and -explanation of ethnographic interviews. Similarly, such surveys show how "working-class people seem more concerned with economic security, whereas middle-class people value self-actualization and self-development more highly." Anthropologist Mary Douglas and economist Baron Isherwood concluded already in the 1970s, "Whereas the middle-class use their possessions for long-term self-development, the working-class engage in repetitive short-term uses."[40] In the following chapters, we will encounter motorists (either in real daily life or as virtual personae) who exemplify many of the traits, biases, and dichotomies exposed in this section. However, before we deal with the second new element of postwar automotive culture, the media character of the car as possessive symbol, we will first dig somewhat deeper in the intricacies of the postwar 'automotive self.' For this we will borrow extensively from anthropological and ethnographic analyses of mobility phenomena, as it is ethnography that recently gave us a completely new thick narrative about the road, including its occasional breakdown.[41]

Diversifying Automotive Identities: The Non-hegemonic Self

Anthropology, including its ethnographic tradition, helped bring about a turn toward the reconstruction and deconstruction of a multiplicity of "non-hegemonic" selves, defined, among others, by their possessions. Such selves varied from women, feminine men, and queers to ethnic minorities in the West and even entire non-Western populations or large parts thereof, such as Chinese men, whether in China or in the diaspora. Parallel to the multiplicity of mobilities, we observe a multiplication of selves. Positioning itself in a sociological rather than psychological tradition, students of cultural studies and related disciplines could refer to early predecessors such as Max Weber and Thorstein Veblen who related "lifestyles, including material lifestyles, … to social stratification." With the car as one of the "important examples of visible consumer behavior" (a less morally loaded term, perhaps, than Veblen's "conspicuous consumption"), a historical comparison of American research from the 1970s with that of the 1920s suggested not only that "material lifestyles appear to have become more differentiated" but also that income "fails to predict several consumer behaviors effectively." In the specific case of research quoted here, however, nearly a quarter of the respondents (all white, young, and "native") from the 1970s in the United States (those who did not have cars?) failed to rate car makes and models in a hierarchical order. This, of course, is to say not that car ownership as a status symbol did not exist but only that no consensus existed among a rather limited group of Americans about which car does its job of 'fine distinction' best. Also, status may come from accessories such as excessive trimming or special wheel hubs, or the possession of a new or secondhand car, as we will see in the following chapters. Yet, it is worthwhile to realize, according to a recent semiotic analysis of Canadian car advertisements by sociologist Jim Conley, in only one-fifth of them is "a message of status or domination ... conveyed."[42]

Conley relativized David Riesman's thesis from the American 1950s of "the symbolic meanings of automobiles [that] overwhelmed instrumental meanings," as well as Roland Barthes's and Henri Lefebvre's assessment of the car as a "magical" object, worthy of worship. Instead, he argued for a balanced approach, stressing the "potent combination" of "the magical [and] the mundane." But it cannot be denied that "vehicles," in the generalization of the ethnographer, "possess totem-like qualities," providing "the agencies by which the moral boundaries of collective life may be traversed." Conley's semiotic analysis revealed connections between terms like "excitement," "luxury," and "status & dominance" ("luxury is not enough; it needs to be exciting too") but also confirmed our earlier thesis of the alibi character of the utilitarian argument among motorists.[43] No wonder, then, did contemporary transport researchers such as Linda Steg, together with Patricia Lyon Mokhtarian and their coauthors, revive the debate raging in the 1920s about the "necessity" of the passenger car, by emphasizing "motivational factors," as Steg calls them, in the purchase decision of a car. However, as Todd Litman stressed, "prestige value alone increases vehicle ownership only modestly, perhaps 5–15 percent in the short term ... These impacts probably increase over the long run as higher vehicle ownership further increases automobile dependency."[44]

Yet, surveys of this type, and research based on them, can have only a limited value for our historical study, not only because they are nonhistorical cross-sections undertaken quite late in the century but also, and mostly, because the multiple opposites of 'prestige value' are often grouped under terms like "functional" or "mundane" or "instrumental," the latter encompassing not only what we have called 'utilitarian' functions (such as bringing children to school, doing errands, commuting) but also all our adventurous traits. To give only one example: cultural sociologist Gerhard Schulze, who coined 'event society' (*Erlebnisgesellschaft*), claimed on the first page of the introduction to his seminal study:

> Since the post-war era the relationship of people to their goods and their services has changed continuously. The direction of this development can be

gauged very clearly from the changes in advertising. While initially the use value of the product formed the core of the presentation—longevity, purposefulness, technical perfection—meanwhile the user is ever more exposed to the event values (*Erlebniswerte*) of the goods on offer. Products are not any more presented as a means to a goal, but as a goal in itself (*Selbstzweck*). They should satisfy as such, independent from their usefulness for a certain purpose.

Schulze illustrated his thesis, for the development of which he "time and again makes a recourse to the artistic realm," by pointing at the "aesthetics" of products being "obfuscated (*verschleiert*) *ironically* as purposiveness. All-terrain cars, for instance, are first and foremost purposive (*zweckmässig*), only an all-terrain capacity in our asphalted and concreted environment has hardly a user value, and thus this attribute transforms (*entpuppt sich*) into an aesthetic attribute." Hence, Schulze claimed, the massive chromed bumper beams on current all-terrain vehicles.[45] In our reading of the emergence and persistence of the car society, the car challenges this split into two distinct phases of history, which seems to be the result of a lack of knowledge of prewar automobilism followed by a projection of the opposite of the dichotomous pair back into history. It may be true that accurate information regarding reliability and performance was more common in prewar advertising than it is now, but the *pleasurable* driving and passengering *experience* has always been predominant. Instead of the declared attraction of the car's 'freedom of mobility,' the slogan could better be the *pleasure* of mobility.

Similarly, Roland Barthes's famous assessment of the car as the equivalent of a Gothic cathedral not only emphasized the (quasi-)*static* totemism of the car (for instance, when it is parked in front of the house, or passed by a somewhat faster-cruising car on the freeway, in the latter case representing a totemism among motorists), but it also took the manufacturer's advertisement (in this case, the DS as *staged* by Citroën at the Paris Motor Show of 1955) at face value as it seemed to ignore a previous half-century of automotive transcendence. One can hardly maintain that the first gasoline cars manufactured by Benz and Daimler can be seen as cathedrals, so there must be a moment, or a phase, when the "mystification" started, and this was certainly not the case when Barthes made his famous discovery. When Barthes observed through the Citroën DS (the abbreviation for the French equivalent of "goddess") that the sacred had fallen from heaven, she was already driving millionfold over the earth providing transcendence. The result is the same: the Western motorist, as we have argued, experiences heaven on earth[46]

Literary sociologist Hartmut Böhme, who used Barthes's analysis as a point of departure for his own analysis of commodity fetishism, likewise characterized the car as "jewellery, ego equipment (*Ich-Ausstattung*), requisite, accessory, protective space, weapon, lover, companion, in short: a semantically variable sociocultural figuration." The current study tries to *historicize* this figuration, to trace how, when, and why (and at the cost of what) these single elements emerged before they accumulated (when?) into this metaphorical and fetishistic cocktail, and whether this is typical for the West or more a global phenomenon. This also means, however brilliantly such characterizations might be formulated and however they may guide us in historicizing automotive adventure (some of these with a morbid ending: Barthes died in an accident with a laundry truck), they will have to be treated in this study as part of the empirics, as historical actors. In other words: we need a much more sophisticated diversification and stratification of automotive functions (including symbolic functions) and automotive users, and their identities. After all, Schulze himself stressed the multilayeredness (*Mehrschichtigkeit*) of "personal styles," even if one of his critics rightly asserted this multilayeredness related to the "*fine* distinctions in a Bourdieuian sense …, distinctions within the broad middle class," and not to less fine distinctions such as those between core and periphery, North and South, middle class and working class, and so on.[47]

Against this background, and for the purpose of the current analysis, it is necessary to diversify and stratify mobility identities. This was first realized by the feminist discovery of "gendered mobilities." In an excellent overview, Chris Lezotte recently positioned Virginia Scharff and Georgine Clarsen, with their analyses of women's role in early Western automobilism, as founding scholars of this tradition, rightly so, even if Scharff's analysis can be said to ignore the social constructedness of the electric car and to follow the historical and, to a certain extent, current myth of this vehicle as inadequate, as I have argued elsewhere.[48] In *Atlantic Automobilism*, I dedicated many pages to the (supposed lack of) adventurousness in women drivers, but I measured their form of automobilism mostly along a scale of aggressiveness and violent musings in novels. The current study continues this thread but expands it toward other automotive functions, in a context of a much broader analysis of other marginalized (would-be) motorists. This is possible because of the explosion of women writers who formulate their own discourse of automobilism, emphasizing, as we will see, concepts such as 'escape' and the fear for physical threats.[49] In terms of scholarly attention, the next step in this diversification of automotive identities was a further nuancing of automotive masculinity itself and its "embodied symbiosis with [the] machine" (including the "noncognitive dimension of embodiment"), based initially on Australian sociologist Raewyn Connell's concept of "hegemonic masculinity" (and its somewhat dichotomous opposition to non-hegemonic variants such as complicit, subordinated, and marginalized masculinities). Soon, however, a more open investigation into the diversity and multiplicity of the "materially and symbolically powerful relationship between men and technology" took place, into their cars, and into their characteristic "car talks," saturated with "metaphors so full of human analogies indicat[ing] an intimate and embodied knowledge about the technology." Indeed, car talk is as metaphorically loaded ("the car talks to you, the car is stubborn, the car is friendly, and so on"), just like autopoetic texts, but often, it seems, more celebratory and 'caring' than critical. "Animating and anthropomorphizing machines," however, has a long tradition reaching back to the beginnings of automotive times (as I concluded in my previous study), which is often not acknowledged by social scientists unfamiliar with automotive history.[50]

Men and women construct "hybrid masculinities," a postmodern mixing of hegemonic and non-hegemonic elements. Whatever the type of masculinity, however, ethnographic research unearthed comparable transcendental experiences beyond the mere practice of car driving, such as when tinkering brings a "total absorption in a mechanical problem, when time stops and one gets fully *entranced* by the machine." Some ethnologists propose the term personification for this type of practice, but "tinkering" seems to be better at capturing its historical roots, going back to the very beginnings of automobilism's 'functional adventure.' In general, such masculinities are characterized by forms of "bodily intelligence, a kind of savoir faire," even if they are generated within a relation with the *static* machine (as object of tinkering and do-it-yourself culture), not during driving or passengering. Masculinity studies, however, still suffer from an unresolved contradiction within the practices of the gendering of the car itself, which is simultaneously called an "extension of the man" and a "feminine persona," a contradiction that may be resolved by approaching this relationship primarily as covertly homoerotic, masqueraded by an overt heteroerotic relationship, as I have argued elsewhere: it would explain the equally eroticized 'handling' of the gearshift lever better. Here, too, just like in women's mobility studies, young PhD researchers such as Swedish cultural studies scholar Dag Balkmar meanwhile have presented excellent overviews of the varieties of car-related masculinities, in both a static (tinkering, car shows) and a dynamic setting (street racing, low riding). Car tuning for them is "ego tuning" (*Ich-Tuning*, in Böhme's fetishistic vocabulary) at the same time. Unfortunately, however, such studies are mostly limited to special, car-related (if not car-friendly) subcultures (a term we will keep using throughout our study, despite recent criticism that it would "obscure … within-group differences").[51]

Balkmar and Lezotte analyzed car modifiers in Sweden and muscle car chicks (young women in souped-up production cars) in Michigan as (what I claim to be) the new, postwar counterparts of the prewar automotive avant-gardes. Such avant-gardes, I contend, were and are instrumental in shaping special "cultural icons," super-symbolic archetypes of car models that stand for a certain experiential complex, such as the Ford Falcon muscle car.[52] And although there are hardly any studies on the late twentieth-century versions of the Babbitts among the motorists (Babbitt being the 'common,' mainstream motorist, after American prewar writer Sinclair Lewis's iconic protagonist), the ethnographical character of these studies (describing these subcultures as tribes with their "rituals through which they construct [their] identities") provide us with a unique (albeit often poorly historicized) insight in the subversive "performative practices" of these groups, by "modify[ing] their cars into other designs than those originally given them" or by displaying a 'provocative' behavior as a female owner of a muscle car.[53] Next to subversive car-related practices, we distinguish in the following chapters between several *subaltern practices*, practices by groups that don't have their own voice, are generally outside mobility historiography, or (in our much more extended definition, well beyond the originators of this historical subfield intended)[54] stay largely below the radar of ethnographers. Lezotte said it loud and clear in her presentation of her chicks and muscle car drivers: she wanted to "giv[e] the woman driver a voice." As Chris Brickell in his study of "Men and Masculinities" has argued, "subversive performances and resistances may initially occasion the empowerment of subaltern groups before diffusing into wider social settings," and even become mainstream.[55]

What is most important for our subsequent analysis, however—next to the already well-established blurring of production and consumption (in the do-it-yourself world around the car)—is the gradual confusion of the borders of the male and female body, as well as the intertwining of the masculinities and femininities of these bodies, in the displayed practices of the masculinized women as muscle car chicks and the feminized men in their care for their modified cars. In the case of the muscle cars, queer theory can help "undermine the more or less taken-for-granted connection between masculinity and the male body." In his ethnography of "gendered bodies in motorsport," for instance, Ehren Helmut Pflugfelder met a woman racecar driver who "articulated a sexualized, feminine identity that she blends with her position as an aggressive racer." These subcultures are important from a historical point of view, because they attract and organize motorists that clearly belong to social strata well 'below' the traditional automotive middle-class constituency; such studies thus can help us analyze the process of social stratification within automobilism, but only if we will be able to historicize them: by acknowledging they provide a snapshot of a moment and place indicated by the date and location of the ethnographic research.[56] They thus form a welcome entrance into the presumed postwar shift in automotive adventure when groups other than the still dominant white, heterosexual, middle-class men appear on the scene in increasing numbers.[57] But this is still a shift within *Western* automobilism in a phase that the car as a mass-market article starts to appear in every inhabited spot on the globe. The next step, then, in this postwar fledgling tradition of the diversification of automotive subjectivities is undertaken in the vast world of non-Western automobilism, by Western and non-Western scholars alike. These scholars must struggle against a long Western tradition "to feminize the portrayal of Oriental men."[58]

Now that the postwar gendering of emerging consumption patterns in Asia is being analyzed extensively, for instance, by the Scandinavian Gendering Asia Network, which is busy developing "a 'new mobility paradigm' with a southern focus," Asian masculinities can be compared with Western patterns. Australian sinologist Kam Louie has been one of the pioneers studying Chinese masculinity as described in belletristic literature, coining the combination of *wen* (cultural attainment) and *wu* (martial valor) as its characteristic. Lamenting the "poverty of theory on the generic man" in the West, and referring to Edward Said's famous dictum that "the Orient is feminised to such an extent that it 'is penetrated, silenced and possessed,'" Louie's social-constructivist analysis (not only of images but also of the body) started by observing "images of Chinese men on billboards in the streets of Beijing or Hong Kong as well as in the American media do not conform to the 'macho' stereotype of masculinity currently circulating in the West." And although we have just seen how this Western image is now in the full process of being nuanced as well, Louie claims not only images of masculinity but also "many Western feminist paradigms" have been shown, by subaltern studies, to be "inapplicab[le] to women of Africa or Asia." Historically, Western men were stereotypically seen by their Chinese counterparts as "stripped of their civilisation—men of animal instincts and animal sexual drives."

In contrast, Louie coined a *wen-wu* image to conceptualize the "Chinese [post–Mao Zedong] masculinity matrix," against the "Western stereotype of the 'real man'" as someone adorned with "an adventurous spirit, a proclivity to violence, a tendency towards physical rather than oral expression of thoughts and a callous attitude to sexual relations," but also against the stereotype of the "*yin-yang* notion" of Chinese culture (*yin* being the female, *yang* the male component). Not denying "there is a macho tradition in China," Louie claimed this tradition is "counterbalanced by a softer, cerebral male tradition—the *caizi* (the talented scholar) and the *wenren* (the cultural man)," also among nonintellectuals, "not found to the same degree in contemporary Western conceptions of maleness." One wonders what happens with the automotive adventure in such circumstances of self-declared 'male weakness.'⁵⁹ What is more, such developments bounce back to the West (à la the Comaroffs) through the Chinese diaspora: American research revealed that "while white men considered masculinity to be a highly important component of who they were, this was not so for US-born Asian men and was less so for migrant Asian men." The result of this *mobility of identities* by immigrant men and women is that they "selectively mix and match 'traditional' norms and values with 'modern' options to improve their position in the contestant domains of gender and sexuality," and in a lot more domains, one is inclined to add, a layeredness of identities similar to the layeredness between old and new mobilities we will observe, in the following chapters, to emerge in the Global South.⁶⁰

New Mobility Studies: Bodily Senses, the Car as Medium, and the Challenge of Representation

For an increasing number of those feminized male and masculinized female would-be motorists, car ownership and car use have been constitutive when it comes to subjectivity formation. And whether this identity, as far as it is related to the car, develops in some way adventurous or not thus becomes increasingly more complex to determine, let alone explain, certainly not with the tools developed so far by mobility history, or, for that matter, transport history. This becomes extra complicated, because most research cited so far is nonhistorical, so it is not clear when the traits unearthed by the surveys and the cross-section analyses have emerged. Historian Kate McDonald adds an extra complication by reminding us "scholars of mobility history take movement as the trans-historical basis with which one might explore the constitution of societies past and present. Yet we also write from the vantage point of a modernity that is in part defined by movement."⁶¹ Because of this tautological conundrum, it is a welcome development to see mobility studies align with media studies in an effort to come to a transdisciplinary field called new mobility studies in which the "transfer" of signs, the translation between mobility realities, is considered at least as important as the "transport" of people, goods and ideas (table 0.1).

Table 0.1. Transfer processes and practices in new mobility studies

MOBILITY			
Transfer processes and practices			
Process	Change	Screen	Flow
Practice	Translation	Mediation/Medium	Transportation

Indeed, even if the second meaning of the term transport may be considered to refer to the transcendental effects of moving and being moved in a vehicle (perhaps more so in French than in English), we need a much more sophisticated toolbox to understand what happens in and through the use and the possession of an automobile, a motorcycle, or a motorbus. "The ultimate purpose of media," Jay David Bolter and Richard Grusin asserted on the first page of their study of new media, "is ... to *transfer* sense experiences from one person to another." If this 'other' also includes the mobility history scholar (and why not?), then this is exactly what we need: a technique enabling us to transfer *historical* driving and passengering experiences to the present. I consider 'transfers' a better term than "transition," proposed, for instance, by Glenn Hooper and Tim Youngs in their introduction to their study on travel writing, not only because of the former's material connotations (just like transport) but also because 'transition' has been colonized by the very successful field of transition studies, where it functions in a rather teleological context.[62] 'Transfer' is also a translation of 'metaphor' (like cars, metaphors are 'vehicles'), expressing intention as well as topographic movement. The concept of translation, as a form of transfer, an "articulation" of something stemming from another medium, is a welcome addition to our toolbox, especially what translation studies scholar Michael Cronin calls "intersemiotic translation or translation into or from something other than language," a procedure described as "the interpretation of verbal signs by means of signs belonging to non-verbal sign systems." In a way, the "transfer (of) the symbolic meanings of material goods to (individuals), by a number of social practices," is also a form of translation. Translation, its students propose since they undertook a "cultural turn" in the 1990s, "emerges as the central category for the negotiation of difference beyond representation."[63]

Some scholars, however, claim translation happens unmediated. Sociologist John Tomlinson, for instance, observed "a cluster of new cultural phenomena" in the history of speed increase in modern society, engendering a "new condition [that] is coming to influence cultural practices, experiences and values in contemporary, that is to say early-twenty-first-century modernity." He called this condition "immediacy," illustrating it, among many other things, by pointing at a "global youth culture in which mobile phones have become defining elements both in terms of style icons and as modalities of interpersonal relationship." Bolter and Grusin have criticized such observations as a "denial of mediation," an illusion provoked by the media themselves, a process that "dictates that the medium itself should disappear and leave us in the presence of the thing represented." In my previous study, this vanishing effect of media was already visible in some early autopoetic travelogues (Edith Wharton springs to mind, when she hardly mentioned the car as a conveyance through which she made her touring observations),[64] but the phenomenon seems to take on such a flight in the second half of the century that I will reserve in the chapters that follow a special phrase for it: the 'absent car,' present in the description of the movement and the navigating without being mentioned as such (as in "we turned right"; question: how? on foot? on the bike? in a car?).

If we agree translation is mediating, then we can follow Margrit Pernau and Imke Rajamani, who have, in the context of conceptual history (a field of study initiated by Reinhart Koselleck and Raymond Williams, among others), proposed a staged model, in which the corporeal sensorium plays a pivotal role. Emotions, they pointed out, "are developed not only in texts, but in pictures, in sounds, in the way space is organized, and in how people move." Koselleck's assertion that "it is the body and the senses that convey experiences to human beings" and that political iconography is "communicated through aesthetic experience, … those dimensions forming history, which were not and cannot be transmitted in written sources," also forms the incentive to bring media studies (preferably in its postcolonial form) into the investigation of postwar global automobilism. From the start, cars have been designed with (kin)esthetics in mind, not only within the domain of exterior design (the car as an aerodynamic 'sculpture,' worthy of exposition in art museums) but also in the domain of nonvisual aesthetics, such as the "orchestration of sound" when the car body became closed in the 1920s. As I argued in a previous study, the human bodily sensorium is much broader than the shortlist of five senses suggests, one of the other senses being proprioception, the perception of small movements by body parts, such as gestures, from waving to smiling.[65]

In an effort to challenge the "ocularcentric view" on the senses, a group of philosophers, psychologists, neuroscientists, and an artist, meeting in 2009, formulated a "Hand Manifesto," in which they analyzed the hands as "perceptual organs." One of them, Croatian philosopher Zdravko Radman, argued: "There is something like a vocabulary of movement that the body has internalized—a language of manual embodiment according to which the environment means something to the organism just as other forms of perception do in their own way." "Feeling the car," in Mimi Sheller's vision of "an emotional sociology of automobility," is indeed multisensorial and influences decisively the perception of the world 'outside' as well as 'inside,' but we should not forget that 'feeling' itself is multidimensional: it "refers to a situation or an activity, and these are usually linked. We feel something in order to have a feeling of it."[66] Applied to the car, this is true not only for the hands (when they steer and shift the transmission, or push a button at the dashboard) but also for the feet (when they push the pedals), and, in fact, for the entire skin (realizing, it is true, the hands are "the eyes of the skin"). The skin (especially of the face) is crucial in "producing the feel of affect." In my previous study, I showed how the car industry became aware of this from the 1920s when American manufacturers and university research teams started to investigate the elusive phenomenon of 'comfort,' including the body's sensitivity to vibrations and rhythms. The authors of the Hand Manifesto, however, also provided an additional conceptual basis for my 'adventure experience': whereas "vision reveals a world *seemingly* uncorrupted by any relationship with the viewer, a world that appears as 'out there,' 'independent of me,'" this is not the case for touch, as Merleau-Ponty already argued also, "I cannot forget [in the case of touch] that it is through my body that I go to the world."[67]

Recently, Ole B. Jensen and Phillip Vannini even observed vehicles (in their case, airplanes) "might not quite 'feel' as humans do but still 'feel' in consequential ways," as they are "highly sensitive to certain changing levels of stimuli." Cars, indeed, might not feel as humans do, but they *do* use anthropomorphic *sensors* that, for instance, lately can *detect* when a driver is falling asleep. And in general, the practice of 'handling the car' is a subtle mutual exchange between the two parts of the automotive cyborg: look what happens if you steer too much into a curve; the car will 'respond' to your 'steering error,' hopefully in a 'benign' way. In the following chapters, I will repeatedly point at practices, developed in mature car societies, of communication between motorists, or between those in the interior of a car cocoon and the exterior world, reminiscent of what Raymond Williams already observed when he wrote "private small family units" and "deliberately self-enclosed individuals" experience a "quite unprecedented mobility ... All the other shells are moving, in comparable ways but for their own different private ends. They are not so much other people, in any full sense, but other units which signal and are signalled to." This communication takes place not only through the human body but also through (literally and figuratively) the car body, for instance, when someone on the freeway suddenly brakes and an entire column of vehicles is forced to brake. For both bodily forms of communication, mostly performed without recourse to verbal language, I will use the term *body language*, as a special form of nonverbal, not very articulated, but nonetheless very important sign language developed within the motoring swarm. The body, according to Donna Haraway, indeed is a medium: she conceptualized the "posthuman" techno-organic "cyborg identity" as a "creation of social reality as well as a creature of fiction." This type of corporeal language is communicated, Guillemette Bolens assumed (perhaps leaning a bit too much on the cognitive characteristics of this process), by "kinesthetic empathy": "I cannot feel the kinesthetic sensations in another person's arm. Yet I may infer his kinesthetic sensations on the basis of the kinetic signals I perceive of his movements. [Thus], I may internally simulate what these inferred sensations feel like via my own kinesthetic memory and knowledge."[68]

In a less neuroscientific setting, body language (or "body idiom," in Erving Goffman's words) has from the 1970s been studied within the subfield of an "anthropology of human movement" in linguistic terminology (of a basically static interpretation of the "problem of embodiment"), often applied to "choreographed movement systems" such as rituals, ethnic dance, and martial art. Geographer and mobility scholar Peter Merriman even investigated the relation between dance and architecture, "exploring," in the words of Julia Hildebrand, "space and the possible choreographies that media and modes [of mobility] afford and that messages and moods follow." Such insights can help us get a grip on the repertoire of bodily movements and skills—their "grammar," so to speak—inside and around the car. One such movement, of the car-driver ensemble, is the meandering and slow movement of the flaneur that several students of mobility have tried to apply to the movements of the car, inspired by Walter Benjamin's analysis of Charles Baudelaire's peripatetics in the arcades of mid-nineteenth-century Paris.[69] It seems to me that the elasticity of this metaphor, just like Urry's tourist gaze, is stretched too much to describe a historical car involved in twentieth-century urban traffic. The metaphor of uninhibited flow seems to be more adequate here. By performing a multisensorial approach of automotive practices, I am heeding not only Cronin's warning (who was aiming at Urry, among others) against "'an overly visual reading of the travel phenomenon in cultural formation' at the expense of language," but also Merriman's assertion that trying to "separate the physical landscapes of roads [and by extension, the materiality of the car society in general] from the diverse representations that both aestheticize and present them in distinctive ways" is "futile." In this, indeed, I follow ethnographer David Lipset, who recently coedited a study on 'moral vehicle metaphors,' "adopting a position of methodological ambivalence with respect to the politics of representation, one that [is] not entirely given over to poststructural nihilism."[70]

How, then, does this theory of (metaphorical) translation fit in a media theory of the car? One possible answer goes through the concept of 'representation.' Since Roland Barthes's and Umberto Eco's "semiotic media theory" was attacked by poststructuralists such as Jacques Derrida (1966), Michel Foucault (1970), and Jean Baudrillard (1978), the value and existence of "representation" (especially historical representation) has been severely put to the test, so much so that some historians see this as the start of a "general epistemological uncertainty that characterizes large areas of academic-intellectual life in the humanities and social sciences in the late twentieth century." Derrida questioned the semiotic authority of symbol "decoding," whereas Foucault posited that historians can have a "discourse" only *about* history, a discourse shaped through power relations, including the power of the *dispositif* (a term developed by Jean-Louis Baudry). Baudrillard sharpened Foucault's critique by introducing the concept of simulacra, "in which the borders of fiction and reality are mutually transgressed." Jean-François Lyotard (1979) then announced "the end of metanarratives," but the result, the postmodern text, was criticized by Fredric Jameson as "pastiche," a de-historicized "failure of the new, [an] imprisonment in the past."[71] For literary theorists, more under the spell of postmodernism than many other disciplines, postmodernism "reveal[s] a general 'mistrust of the epistemological authority of the interpretive novel' largely because the complexities of contemporary society ma[kes] 'all interpretations of "reality" arbitrary and therefore at the same time both accurate and absurd.'" The postmodern novelist uses "a flat, expressionless narrative style to encompass reality as 'it is, quite simply' rather than to interpret reality by means of a strong narrative voice and a defined philosophical attitude (as seen in modernist fiction)." Collage rather than plot, one finds in postmodernist novels. Tellingly, and central to our thesis of the fundamental 'middle classness' of the twentieth-century automotive project, Mike Featherstone sees postmodernism as the "lifestyle" of the middle class constituted by "new cultural intermediaries" and the "helping professions."[72]

No wonder young scholars within the Association for the History of Transport, Traffic and Mobility (T²M) started to question whether they should "throw away more traditional methods and approaches such as interviews, surveys, and archive work" and instead use "ethnography and a focus on new media/communication technology [that promised to offer] a better view onto the phenomenon of mobility than previous methods." Colin Divall, a 'veteran' of the field of transport and mobility history they interviewed, called the idea that one could reach 'reality' without representations (what nineteenth-century German historians would call *Verstehen*) "epistemological nonsense," but he found that "we do have to 'move beyond' representations precisely to appreciate the *fuller reality* of which those traces were but a part," and that, perhaps, "the methodologies of mobility studies [as a set of social sciences] have something to teach us." Another interviewee, media scholar Sunny Stalter-Pace, suggested exactly the opposite: to work with the specificities of representations in order to gain more, as these representations could "give us insight into embodied experiences of movement that we should not get through studying the experiences themselves." We need, indeed (I would like to add), autopoetic translations to get access to these embodied experiences. Such representations, according to Tim Cresswell (another interviewee), should be seen as practices too: we move and at the same time we say, write, imagine to move. But we also just move, as a practice. And for this, we need "tools to think about that which doesn't make it into the text (to mistranslate Derrida's famous pronouncement)," Stalter-Pace responded. "This means a heightening attention to bodies, sensations, and prelinguistic processing of experience." In doing so, we should always notice representations are not "innocent windows on reality but active agents in the constitution of reality." Representations "fail to *translate* some portion of reality into another domain and ... they simultaneously succeed in constructing their own truth." Cresswell, who formulated these words, called representations "not very trustworthy."[73] On the other hand, they may be trusted if they resonate with other 'reading' experiences, and if so, then they may be very evocative, as the following chapters will show. But they are not so in every sense: for instance, their structure may privilege certain experiences (such as the Quest of the Self of prewar autopoetics), and as such, they may be very misleading, indeed. But their advantage remains, namely that their authors have had to perform an *intersensorial translation*, from whichever combination of senses into written text. To the benefit of the mobility historian.

It may come as no surprise, then, that travel writing students especially caution against "a postmodernist mire of co-extensive textuality, the loss of referential worlds and a weakened sense of reality." Indeed, the present study also benefits from travel writers' "traffic between 'real' (mediated) geopolitical worlds, representational worlds (including contexts and intertexts), imaginary worlds (including simulated and artificial) and alternative worlds (including transgressive and counter-hegemonic)." Autopoetic novels, like novels in general, share this intratextual 'mobility,' including the traveling back and forth between the 'real' and a 'parallel,' 'virtual' world, as we will see in the following chapters. However, as late as 2015, a handbook on travel writing studies, complaining about the "invisibility of infrastructures in travel writing [studies]," shows how "infrastructural readings of travel texts bring travel writing studies in line with recent developments in object-oriented ontology and new materialism," although the vehicles themselves are still largely excluded.[74] The "crisis of representation in ethnographic writing," brought about by, among others, the postwar critique of colonialism and anthropology's role therein (but also because of historians' skeptical attitude toward "narrative's abilities to represent historical objects" after the Holocaust), resulted in the "fus[ing]" of "literary theory and ethnography," as writing itself had become central to the scholarly practices of the anthropologist, whose use of "literary processes—metaphor, figuration, narrative—affect the way phenomena are registered." Anthropologists now produce "true fictions," characterized by, among others, "a rejection of 'visualism.'" This causes some intriguing epistemological problems, especially for a discipline that prides itself to become performative, for what are true fictions? How do we recognize them? To take an example from a fully different realm, when General Richard Shireff, NATO's second-in-command, wrote a novel about Russia's bellicose intentions and declared: "This is not fiction as such. This is fact-based prediction, very closely modelled on what I know, based on my position as a very senior military insider at the highest and best-informed level," one wonders whether one should act on such a clearly fictional account.[75]

"Rather than mirroring the world, the ethnographer interprets, represents and constructs social reality," a reality that exists beyond "the limits of our minds … It is deplorably anthropocentric to insist that reality be constrained by what the human mind can conceive," philosopher Colin McGinn argues. "We need to cultivate a vision of reality (a metaphysics) that makes it truly independent of our given cognitive powers, a conception that includes these powers as a proper part." A part of anthropology's move "into areas long occupied by sociology, the novel, or avant-garde cultural critique" is a special care for the mechanisms of "the translation of cultures," especially the "*tolerance* of [one's] own language for assuming unaccustomed forms." This leads to the following question: How tolerant is mobility history in its translation of the Chinese (Thai, Huasa, mestiza, etc.) automotive experience? And how does it deal with the problems of representation? The point is that when a novelist has her protagonist accelerate her car as an expression of anger, as we repeatedly will observe in all its gendered versions during our readings of contemporary autopoetic novels, she does not claim the real existence of her protagonist, or her car, or all other elements of her physical environment, but the connection between pushing the accelerator pedal and emotion is offered to the reader as something to reexperience, to reimagine (enabled by the Aristotelian process of "mimesis," which is another word for representation) in the hope that she will conclude, indeed, that is how it works (or not), more or less along the lines as explained by Bolens in the case of 'kinesthetic empathy.'[76] But it is well understood that this mimesis of social practices is loaded with several steps of translation, loaded with their risks of mistranslation and "loss of meaning" even when the translations can be considered technically successful. In my previous study, I gave as an example of such a loss of translation the privileging, by autopoetic authors as well as their students, of the Quest of the Self, ignoring all collective aspects of prewar automobilism (such as the traveling family).[77]

Translating bodily experiences, however, is complexified in another sense: the body is no longer a purely organic entity, nor are its borders well-defined and clear-cut. Instead, the human body is embedded in a nonhuman material base covered by the discipline of media studies, a field that unfortunately got uncoupled in the nineteenth century, when it was subsumed under the umbrella term communication (or *Verkehr*). This is not only true for scholarship, however: since the emergence of telegraphy, media as material artifacts have been "uncoupl[ed] from their previous reliance on physical movement," a practice quite usual in engineering when it comes to optimizing one technology (in this case, communication) by isolating it physically from the other technologies. Consequently, "traffic and communication were predominantly understood and analyzed as separate entities, often neglecting the simple fact that any news or press agency requires traveling journalists, that global television pictures since the 1960s were based on satellite technology and space flight, and that even telegraphy had heavily relied on physical transport, including the final door-to-door-delivery of telegrams." Whereas it often took less than a generation in the history of automotive technology before the split functions were integrated again (for instance, in the case of the automotive suspension's damping function, which was split from the leaf spring with its internal damping through friction, only to be conceived as an integrated coil spring / friction damper system soon thereafter), it took more than a century to reintegrate media and vehicles, only reluctantly followed by a similar process on their reflexive sides called mobility studies and media studies. Indeed, the split in scholarship did not coevolve with a split in technological development: "media were never that 'distinct' as many histories written so far let us assume." Whereas both technological complexes were considered in competition (the telephone competing with the car, for instance) before this reintegration, by the latter quarter of the past century, they were considered to influence, reinforce, and enhance each other, so much so that present researchers propose to simultaneously analyze "the 'mobilization' of media technologies (e.g., the mobile internet) and the 'mediatization' of transportation technologies (e.g., the media-saturated car)."[78]

The car, indeed, is a welcome terrain for such investigations, also in the period well before 'the latter quarter of the past century.' After all, Raymond Williams used a car metaphor when he characterized television culture as "mobile privatization" (he even used the "flow" metaphor in this context), whereas transport historians (including this one) started to analyze the view through the windscreen as a new type of furtive glance along the landscape. The French discipline of *médiologie* around Régis Debray made Catherine Bertho Lavenir, who wrote her dissertation on telephony, publish a seminal study about the relationship between car driving and writing. One step further and we call theory traveling, as literary theorist Janet Wolff proposed.[79] At the same time, and parallel to the simultaneous broadening of the concept of 'transport' to that of 'mobility,' the concept of 'media' broadened toward 'mediations,' addressing "questions on how ideas or mentalities are manifested via different kinds of transmissions and translations in both the symbolic and in the material world."[80] Media studies witnessed a "conceptual shift ... from a past focus on individual media to a present one on the history of media constellations and their 'interferences and resonances.'" From this perspective, it is important to notice that irony (and the ironic car) is (are) not the only distancing tool(s): symbols have a similar function, as they "sustain … the minimum of critical/reflective attitude," according to the Lacanian-inspired vision of Slavoj Žižek. Referring to Jean Baudrillard and Paul Virilio, Žižek claims "today, in the digitized universe of simulation, Imaginary overlaps with the Real, at the expense of the Symbolic … reality itself becomes indistinguishable from its simulated double." In this world, transcendence is impossible; the sublime (Žižek calls it appearance) is lost. Like McGowan's consumption analysis, Žižek observed, but along another route, the end of the transcendental experience, observations we will find reflected, as the following chapters will show, in many Western autopoetic utterances. Again: we need more sophisticated tools to deal with these changes, an insight that forms, in recent "culturalization of everyday life as being a defining feature of a new, postmodern age," part and parcel of the "cultural turn" in the social sciences and the humanities, a turn that may protect us from what Charles Taylor has called "the Enlightenment package error." This scholarly misunderstanding is the result, he claimed, from the use of "an acultural theory [which] unfits us for what is perhaps the most important task of social science in our day: understanding the full gamut of alternative modernities that are in the making in different parts of the world. It locks us into an ethnocentric prison, condemned to project our own forms onto everyone else, and blissfully unaware of what we are doing."[81]

The need of a more sophisticated toolbox than the one offered by transport history becomes all the more urgent if one realizes motorized vehicles, especially passenger cars, from World War II onward, have become more and more *automated*, first by mechanical means (for instance, in the automatic transmission's breakthrough in the United States after the war) and then slowly (even if it was continuously, and erroneously so, called a revolution) through electronic control systems that took over more and more functions that before the war had belonged to the proudly guarded domain of the masculine motorist. The 'dethronement' of the 'sovereign captain' of the car into a pilot performing tasks suggested by an ever 'smarter' car (against the price of a diminished 'immersion' in the intricacies of handling the moving car), enabled other, less knowledgeable motorists all over the planet to join the 'movement' of automobilism. This process started well before 'electronification' and can be seen as a power struggle between the engineer (as a representative of the manufacturer) and the knowledgeable user, who saw the car under her hands evolve into a foolproof contraption (*narrensicher*), a derogatory qualification still reminiscent of the eventual victory of the engineer in this struggle, a victory that was sealed by a gradual shift from the 'software' (of the human and the mechanical body) to the hardware (of the car). Electronification (also in the realm of production, allowing the development of sophisticated, fine-tuned suspension systems, engines, and dashboard consoles, to name only a few) supported the shift toward the car interior as an 'entertainment center,' for children during long holiday trips but also for navigating an unknown city or cruising on the freeway with one's feet from the pedals. This provisional end phase of the 'encapsulation' of the driver and her passengers (before the announced full 'smartification' of the car) does not only apply to the car: Jensen and Vannini observe a similar trend of "decreasing the potential for passengers to sense the unique characteristics of airplane travel."[82] In other words, the 'loss of the sublime' of car travel has a technical base: it enables the shift from a vertical to a horizontal transcendental experience, from feeling godlike to being transferred to a parallel 'reality.'

The Trouble with Travel Writing: Meandering between Fictionality and Representation

As I have already indicated, one adjacent academic discipline that came under the influence of media studies was travel writing, especially since its revival since the 1970s, when travel texts "began to be considered worthy of academic study." At the same time, the growing interest in 'popular culture' relativized former judgments of these texts as written by "second-rate talents," in the words of a snobbish literary historian, Paul Fussell. Suddenly, travel writing became "vital and generative" for postcolonial theory. Postcolonialism, together with postmodernism, became "the conceptual cornerstones of contemporary Western culture," which can be seen as "the result of the arrival of the Third-World intellectual in the First-World academy." It also became vital for the future of Western anthropology, "part of the necessary reimagining of the world first occasioned by the post–World War Two resistance movements and wars of liberation in the former European colonies, as well as by the wave of immigration that followed." After all, Edward Said's *Orientalism*, the seminal attack on the racist Western gaze on the 'East,' was partly based on this type of sources. Postwar iconic travel writers such as V. S. Naipaul (*The Middle Passage*, 1962, on the West Indian islands, and three travel books on India), Peter Mathiessen ("I am here to be here," but how did you get there?), Bruce Chatwin (*In Patagonia*, 1977) and, of course, Claude Lévi-Strauss (*Tristes Tropiques*, 1955: "Adventure has no place in the anthropological professions") belong to the preferred objects of study.[83] Despite the affinity between the practices of the travel writer and the anthropologist (Ivona Grgurinović calls it analogies), we preferred analyzing "autopoetic" fiction over the declared nonfictionality of the travelogue in our previous study, mainly because the latter's increasing emphasis (during the first part of the century) on the Quest of the Self and its neglect of the technological and infrastructural aspects of travel "block[ed] our view of the crucial bodily experience." We were not alone in this opinion: Tim Youngs, in his introduction to a special issue of *Studies in Travel Writing*, as late as 2013 lamented: "in discussions of travel writing a vital aspect often gets overlooked: namely, the traveller's mode of transport."[84]

In the second half of the century, when autopoetics became more and more an ironic, outsider's view on mass mobility (rather than being conceived and written by, on behalf of, and for the same societal group as the authors of such texts), the advantages of the one over the other type of sources have greatly diminished, all the more so as travel writing came out of its crisis by also including, to some extent, the material base of the journey, although many a scholar still seems hesitant to extend this materiality into the realm of mobility.[85] Also, "a remarkable number of novelists and poets were *travelling* writers" (just as was the case with our autopoetic pioneers at the beginning of the last century), even if they meanwhile represented mainly themselves, as a group of 'hypermobile' globetrotters. Critical travel writing scholars Patrick Holland and Graham Huggan now call the object of their study "a refuge for complacent, even nostalgically retrograde, middle-class values." What makes these sources even less attractive for our study is that travel writers are, within this critical tradition, seen as "retailers of mostly white, male, middle-class heterosexual myths and prejudices, and ... their readers as eager consumers of exotic—culturally 'othered'—goods." It seems as if our study of the non-West can expect to profit only negatively from texts that "provide ... an effective alibi for the perpetuation or reinstallment of ethnocentrically superior attitudes to 'other' cultures." Another reason for being skeptical about their usefulness for this study is that the "predominantly Anglophone" travel books "are unreliable to the extreme": the 'lie' of autopoetic fiction is a different one than the nonfictional 'lie' from a travel writer. Last, most travel writers, in their "poetics of the wandering subject" and their "*pseudo*ethnography" indulging in the "metaphysics of restlessness," consider speed "antithetical to (their) physical and verbal meandering ..., which relies on modes of transportation (walking, cycling, railtravel) that require the passage of time." Ironically, travel writing studies seems to have a truly problematic relationship with its object of study, even more so than historical mobility studies with the car!

On the other hand, Holland and Graham call travelogues "one of the most popular and widely read forms of literature today," and despite their middle classness, they have been compared to the popular culture of the "literary romance," navigating, as Fussell argues, "between the picaresque mode of comic misadventure and the pastoral mode of contemplation and elegiac reverie." And although the (ironic?) critique by travel writing scholars on the "cheerful superficiality" of these texts is reminiscent of Fussell's derogatory judgment, their inclination to adventurousness (even if travel writers are said to "hid[e] behind the mask of escapist explorer-adventurers") and their "cool detachment" remind us of the adventure novels of the beginning of the twentieth century analyzed in our previous study and the 'cool persona' of the autopoetic art of the 1920s and 1930s in Europe.[86] Again: travelogues and *some* (lowbrow, autopoetic) novels meanwhile intertwine. Also, like car use, travel (writing) requires a "back home," which makes it fundamentally different from migration and the flows of refugees, even if the travel writer (and the field's students in her wake) likes to compare herself with the nomad. Like the car journey, the adventures of the travel writers are circular and, generally, "related to pleasure … For many travellers the return home is (also) a source of considerable enjoyment." And like the car trip, travel writing is invasive and colonizing, because never "is the account written for the people or places experienced." Navigating between travel writing studies' "hypertheorization of travel-as-displacement" and "its opposite, the naively untheorized celebration of travel-as-freedom," Holland and Graham see a possibility for critical travel writing studies to benefit from the fact that travel is still "a crucial epistemological category for the displacement of normative values and homogenizing, essentialist views" (started with Said, as we saw), especially since women travel writers and postcolonial writers have discovered its "transgressive potential."[87] This is all the more true for the current project, as I am primarily interested in the 'motifs, motives and motivations' of the drivers and passengers depicted in the texts, and not in the factual information on mobility and its enveloping system (which I draw from more conventional sources).

As to its history, Helen Carr distinguishes between "three stages" of travel writing so far: a realist period until 1900, a more subjective one during the interbellum, and the period of the emergence of the literary travel book since World War II. Thus, the travelogue became an "alternative form of writing for novelists," written in a "more impressionistic style" and "focused as much on the travellers' responses or consciousness as their travels."[88] What, then, do both autopoetic texts and travelogues *represent*? Travelogue (*récit de voyage*; *Reisebericht*) is not a literary genre, a recent handbook asserts, but "a loosely defined body of literature." The representational aspect of a travelogue (that "makes use of fictional techniques") rests on a "*referential pact … between text and reader*" and can be defined as "*any narrative characterized by a non-fiction dominant that relates (almost always) in the first person a journey or journeys that the reader supposes to have taken place in reality while assuming or presupposing that author, narrator and principal character are but one or identical* ... the reader will presume that the author is *predominantly* concerned with the account of a journey he or she actually made" (emphasis in original). In another handbook of the subfield, similar struggles with the issue of fictionality can be observed: "the conventions of the genre with respect to embellishment and minor invention," argues Peter Hulme, "are well-understood by readers." Such arguments can be read as an effort to address some "issues that haunt discussion of travel writing in evolving forms, in particular the truth value or representations, inexpressibility and 'translation,' and the difficulty of imagining or representing the Other." The problem of "translating experience into text" haunts both the ethnographer and the travel writer (as well as the historian, I am inclined to add): they struggle with the "narration—description duality ... Unlike travel writing, in ethnographies description was superior to narration, which remained restricted to the 'arrival stories' which 'display [in the words of Mary Louise Pratt] clear continuities with travel writing.'" One of the literary techniques travel writers apply is *irony*, in the period under investigation here especially *self-irony*, for instance, when the 'I' assumes the role of the "nomad figure."[89]

From this perspective, the difference between autopoetics and travel writing is that the latter can turn into the former if (one of) the vehicle(s) used is the automobile, or even can be used to illustrate and analyze automobile use, whereas the former encompasses much more. Autopoetics is fictional, can be extraliterary (as film or a television series), but most of all, it is a set of texts (and autopoetic parts thereof) characterized by depicting the movements, the navigating, the internal and external practices while underway, as well as the immobilities (the flow interruptions, the borders as obstacles) of driver-car and passenger-car ensembles. Autopoetics also cover the commute, or the shopping trip, or the weekend spin, the illegal street race and the low-riding experience—practices that are generally not considered 'travel.' Perhaps because of the heterogeneity of this scholarly field, travel writing does not seem capable or willing to formulate its proper set of governing research questions, although its obsession by the representation, rather than the represented, seems undeniable. A revealing example is well-known travel writing scholar Mary Louise Pratt's remarkably morally charged (if not hostile) analysis of Joan Didion's *Salvador* (1983), a comment nearly fully devoid of information about the country itself, targeting instead Didion's way of traveling. Holland and Graham, who place themselves in Pratt's tradition, see the travel book, despite its often condescending attitude against 'the mass tourist,' as a constitutive part of the tourism industry, not only where "the spirit of adventure can hold off the threat of exhaustion," but also where the industry itself can use this literature "to lure the adventure-minded traveler onto an alternative beaten track," in order "to fuel [its] expansionist ambitions." They are, indeed "tourists with typewriters." Thus, the travel narrative is not a substitution for travel (just like the telephone was not an exclusive alternative to the car in the 1930s, as we saw), but it is "helping to sell holidays," or better: touristic events and experiences. Tourism agencies nowadays "don't sell travel anymore, but freedom and adventure ..., unique, emotional-intensive experiences," as part of what Marvin Zuckerman has called "sensation seeking."[90]

This Study: Sources and Terminology

I use belletristic utterances, but also genres from popular culture, to help identify the myriad forms of mobility, including (and especially) its subversive and subaltern forms. I selected these sources through several search strategies, the most important one being following, during the past two decades or so, the public literary, pop-musical, and filmic spaces as discussed in some major newspapers, from the two Dutch (internationally orientated) *De Volkskrant* and *NRC Handelsblad*, to the *New York Times International Edition*, as well as the *New York Review of Books*, *Times Literary Supplement*, and the *London Review of Books*. To identify older work, I used specialized secondary sources cited in the chapters to follow, but the first strategy differs from the second, because I selected the (literary) sources based on not whether they contained some clearly announced physical movement (either in the title or in the review) but rather whether they were considered to be(come) part of a literary canon and thus, in some way, expressed a certain kind of 'popularity' among the reading public (or expected or hoped-for popularity in the reviews). As to the sources for popular culture: apart from the handbooks and other overviews, I used Google searches to identify the most popular (in terms of size of audience, or simply by consulting 'best of' lists, well aware that the way these lists are made are opaque, to say the least, and in some cases the memory of friends old enough to remember pop songs from the 1960s and 1970s).

Now that Theodor Adorno's critique of the "culture industry" has cured us from the illusion that this culture arose "spontaneously from the masses themselves," and cultural and American studies convinced us popular culture is neither a false consciousness imprinted "from above" nor an "expression ... of a genuine people's culture, opposing and resisting the dominant culture," the complexity of the phenomenon urges us to define some of the concepts used in this study very clearly.[91] Thus, I call 'hegemonic' those (sub)cultures and their traits that dominate a certain society at a certain point in time, even if they are produced by a quantitative minority (for instance, as we will see in the following chapters, many traits of the Western 1960s youth culture became hegemonic in the following decades, challenging the up to then hegemonic middle-class culture). 'Hegemonic' should be clearly distinguished from 'mainstream,' which I use as another term for popular culture or media culture. I call cultural traits that challenge either hegemonic or mainstream culture 'subversive,' also if they are not characterized by a left-wing signature. I call 'subaltern' all those utterances and practices by people who normally leave no trace in the historical records, or who do not wish to be seen or heard. I included popular-cultural utterances not because they express the culture of the 'lower' societal echelons better but because they apparently appeal more to their taste, which is not the same! Lastly, if it is true that irony is rare in such utterances, then we have two different accounts on the mobility universe as it changes over time. Would we, consequently, also have two different car types, an ironic and a non-ironic? And two 'adventures'? Let's wait and see.

Let's wait for the chapters to be read and seeing their main thrust: after chapter 1, which returns to the first half century covered by *Atlantic Automobilism* (revisiting the Emergence and Persistence periods), but now told from a world-mobility point of view, we pick up the narrative where we left it in that study: in chapter 2, we analyze the Western car abundance, experienced in full ignorance of what happened beyond the West, observing for the first time a leveling off of the car adventure. Remarkably, this observation does not come from the conventional sources (and thus, one is inclined to say, it is not picked up by 'conventional' histories that celebrate this abundance as the very epitome of modernity) but is the result of a close, if not subtle, reading of the literary canon of this phase and especially of the Hollywood movies. At the same time, as already hinted at here, we see alternative mobilities emerge, of women, children, ethnic, and sexual minorities. While these automotive novices mobilize the car in their emancipatory practices, a popular mass culture of what we will call carnivalesque automobilism, as a flight forward, indulges in what seems to be a caricature of the prewar periods of the adventure machine. Once established as the more or less routine icon of Western mobility, the car becomes the central part of the Western mission to globalize the 'car society,' but indirectly so, as a promise, to be realized only once the Global Other is willing to build a road network. Chapter 3 analyzes this missionary ambition of the West, to plug the car as the very epithet of universal modernity, willing to make road (network) building into the very core of "development." It is the unashamed, naively arrogant conviction that the Other is like 'us,' the middle-class fantasy that the 'freedom of mobility' is 'our' gift to the world, 'our' civilizing mission repackaged in asphalt, steel, and plastic. The result looks like 'chaos,' a 'layered' amalgam of old and new, but it isn't. It's just different. In the conclusion, we will come back to the issues raised here, enriched by an overview of the results of the previous three chapters.

Notes

Epigraph: William Carlos Williams quoted in James Clifford, "Introduction: Partial Truths," in *Writing Culture; The Poetics and Politics of Ethnography*, ed. James Clifford and George E. Marcus (Berkeley/Los Angeles/London: University of California Press, 1986), 1–26, here: 3.

1. Jun Zhang, "Driving toward Modernity: An Ethnography of Automobiles in Contemporary China" (PhD diss., Yale University, 2009), 147; Gijs Mom, *Atlantic Automobilism: Emergence and Persistence of the Car, 1895–1940* (New York: Berghahn Books, 2015), 99.
2. Jedediah Purdy, *For Common Things: Irony, Trust, and Commitment in America Today* (New York: Alfred A. Knopf, 1999), 11; Marx ("The Eighteenth Brumaire of Louis Bonaparte," 1852) and Deleuze (*Difference and Repetition*, 2001) quoted in Keir Milburn, *Generation Left* (Cambridge: Polity, 2019), 67.
3. Michael Hardt and Antonio Negri, *Assembly* (Oxford: Oxford University Press, 2019), 78–83 ("What does 'from below' mean?").
4. Gyan Prakash, "Can the 'Subaltern' Ride? A Reply to O'Hanlon and Washbrook," *Comparative Studies in Society and History* 34, no. 1 (1992): 171 (Deleuzian); Mom, *Atlantic Automobilism*, 649 (ironic car).
5. Jean Comaroff and John L. Comaroff, "Writing Theory from the South: The Global Order from an African Perspective," *World Financial Review* (September–October 2013), 17 (departure, margins), 18 (petri dish, prefigure), 19 (demarcation); Jean Comaroff and John L. Comaroff, *Theory from the South or, How Euro-America Is Evolving toward Africa* (London: Boulder, 2012), 5 (laboratory), 6 (peripheries), 47 (*relation*); Hardt and Negri, *Assembly*, 103 (universal); Hartmut Böhme, "Das Strahlen fetischistischer Dinge des Konsums: Autos und Mode," in *In Gegenwart des Fetischs: Dingkonjunktur und Fetischbegriff in der Diskussion*, ed. Christine Blättler and Falko Schmieder (Vienna: Verlag Turia + Kant, 2014), 32.
6. Paul Rabinow, "Representations Are Social Facts: Modernity and Post-modernity in Anthropology," in *Writing Culture: The Poetics and Politics of Ethnography*, ed. James Clifford and George E. Marcus (Berkeley: University of California Press, 1986), 241; David Spurr, *The Rhetoric of Empire: Colonial Discourse in Journalism, Travel Writing, and Imperial Administration* (Durham, NC: Duke University Press, 1993), 36.
7. Gijs Mom, *The Electric Vehicle: Technology and Expectations in the Automobile Age* (Baltimore: Johns Hopkins University Press, 2004). In this book, I use "mainstream" as a quantitative qualifier, and I use the term interchangeably with popular culture; however, I use "hegemonic" as an indicator of a dominant cultural trait, which may be represented by a minority. See also the last section of this introduction.
8. For an elaboration of this evolutionary perspective, see Gijs Mom, "Translating Properties into Functions (and Vice Versa): Design, User Culture and the Creation of an American and a European Car (1930–1970)," *Journal of Design History* 20, no. 2 (2007).
9. George Lakoff and Mark Johnson, *Metaphors We Live By* (Chicago: University of Chicago Press, 2003), 48; Marie T. Farr speaks of "govern[ing] (the woman's) conduct" in "Freedom and Control: Automobiles in American Women's Fiction of the 70s and 80s," *Journal of Popular Culture* 29, no. 2 (1995): 164. On the cultural relationship between "core" and "periphery," see Ulf Hannerz, *Cultural Complexity: Studies in the Social Organization of Meaning* (New York: Columbia University Press, 1992), 239ff. The two terms seem to have been coined by the Latin American *dependentistas* who formulated a critique on the mainstream modernization theory called developmentalism (see chap. 3, "Developmentalism versus *Dependentismo*").

10. Mom, *Atlantic Automobilism*, 596–606.
11. John Tomlinson, *The Culture of Speed: The Coming of Immediacy* (Los Angeles: Sage Publications, 2007), 12.
12. Francine Prose, "The Passion and Rage of Arundhati Roy," *New York Review of Books* 64, no. 12 (13 July 2017): 17.
13. Mom, *Atlantic Automobilism*, 612–613.
14. Such as, quite recently, in Katherine J. Parkin, *Women at the Wheel: A Century of Buying, Driving, and Fixing Cars* (Philadelphia: University of Pennsylvania Press, 2017), 63: "The wealthy enjoyed cars as playthings, while the middle and working classes used their cars for both job opportunities and social excursions."
15. Sol Inés Peláez, "Beyond Post-dictatorship: Transnational Latin American Literature and the Violence of Writing" (PhD diss., State University of New York, 2010), xxiii (Peláez aims not at the car in her dissertation but on writing in general under and after dictatorships); Vasant Kaiwar, "Towards Orientalism and Nativism: The Impasse of Subaltern Studies," *Historical Materialism* 12, no. 2 (2004): 192 (historicism).
16. Tim Cresswell, "Black Moves: Moments in the History of African-American Masculine Mobilities," *Transfers* 6, no. 1 (2016): 14. Cresswell also mentions "furtive" mobility as a reason for New York police officers stopping black and Latino citizens. Ibid., 15.
17. Mom, *Atlantic Automobilism*, 200–201; Michael Hardt and Antonio Negri, *Multitude: War and Democracy in the Age of Empire* (New York: Penguin, 2005), 107 (dominant).
18. Lakoff and Johnson, *Metaphors We Live By*, 51; Zygmunt Bauman, *The Individualized Society* (Cambridge: Polity, 2004), 1; Toru Tani, "Transzendenz und Medium," in *Figuren der Transzendenz: Transformationen eines phänomenologischen Grundbegriffs*, ed. Michael Staudigl and Christian Sternad (Würzburg: Königshausen & Neumann, 2014), 143 (experience).
19. Mom, *Atlantic Automobilism*, 650; Salvatore Attardo, "Irony as Relevant Inappropriateness," *Journal of Pragmatics* 32, no. 6 (2000): 794 (definition). For a taxonomy of nonliteral language, see Richard M. Roberts and Roger J. Kreuz, "Why Do People Use Figurative Language?" *Psychological Science* 5, no. 3 (1994). For an effort to establish a phenomenological affinity between driving and "the way we think," see Lynn Pearce, *Drivetime: Literary Excursions in Automotive Consciousness* (Edinburgh: Edinburgh University Press, 2016), 1 (quote).
20. Rebecca Clift, "Irony in Conversation," *Language in Society* 28, no. 4 (1999): 535; Attardo, "Irony as Relevant Inappropriateness," 794; Christian Burgers and Margot van Mulken, "Het ironisch spectrum: Een overzicht van onderzoek naar het begrip en de retorische effecten van verbale ironie," *Tijdschrift voor Taalbeheersing* 35, no. 2 (2013): 184 (wolves, sheep). This is not to be confused with situational irony, as in Reinhold Niebuhr's *The Irony of American History* (1952), a Cold War pamphlet trying to invite sympathy for a country that desperately attempts to be the ideal of humankind. However, Niebuhr also acknowledges "the knowledge of irony is usually reserved for observers rather than participants." For an analysis of the ironic sensibility needed for television watching, see, e.g., John Caughie, "Playing at Being American: Games and Tactics," in *Logics of Television: Essays in Cultural Criticism*, ed. Patricia Mellencamp (Bloomington / London: Indiana University Press / BFI Publishing, 1990), 52–53.
21. Raymond W. Gibbs Jr., "Are Ironic Acts Deliberate?" *Journal of Pragmatics* 44, no. 1 (2012): 110 (matrix); Christian Burgers, Margot van Mulken, and Peter Jan Schellens, "Verbal Irony: Differences in Usage Across Written Genres," *Journal of Language and Social Psychology* 31, no. 3 (2012): 292; Christian Burgers, Margot van Mulken, and Peter Jan Schellens, "The Use of Co-textual Irony Markers in Written Discourse," *Humor*

26, no. 1 (2013). I thank Harrie Mazeland, formerly of the University of Groningen, for this suggestion.
22. Luigi Anolli, Rita Ciceri, and Maria Giaele Infantino, "From 'Blame to Praise' to 'Praise to Blame': Analysis of Vocal Patterns in Ironic Communication," *International Journal of Psychology* 37, no. 5 (2002): 266 (ironist), 267 (sarcastic; some researchers distinguish between sarcasm [as a violent form] and irony proper, while others do not), 268 (prosodic, last quote).
23. The same applies to the elusive concept of "middle class," as we will see in the following chapters. In this study, I use a hybrid approach of this concept, sometimes using econometric data, sometimes lifestyle characteristics to identify middle-class groups. See also Danièle Bélanger, Lisa B. Welch Drummond, and Van Nguyen-Marshall, "Introduction: Who Are the Urban Middle Class in Vietnam?" in *The Reinvention of Distinction: Modernity and the Middle Class in Urban Vietnam*, ed. Van Nguyen-Marshall, Lisa B. Welch Drummond, and Danièle Bélanger (Dordrecht: Springer, 2012).
24. Amy Hanser, *Service Encounters: Class, Gender, and the Market for Social Distinctions in Urban China* (Stanford, CA: Stanford University Press, 2008), 5 (wedding), 7 (category), 9 (distinction work), 187 (Thompson); A. Marwick quoted in Lutz Raphael, "Transformations of Industrial Labour in Western Europe: Intergenerational Change of Life Cycles, Occupation and Mobility 1970–2000," *German History* 30, no. 1 (2012): 103 (class definition). For a recent refutation of the idea that classes are vanishing (on the contrary, they are "very stable over time"), see Geoffrey Evans and James Tilly, *The New Politics of Class: The Political Exclusion of the British Working Class* (Oxford: Oxford University Press, 2017), 43 (quote).
25. Walter Hesford, "Overt Appropriation," *College English* 54, no. 4 (1992): 406 (beyond ourselves); John Urry, *The Tourist Gaze: Leisure and Travel in Contemporary Societies* (London: Sage, 1990); Jonas Larsen, "Tourism Mobilities and the Travel Glance: Experiences of Being on the Move," *Scandinavian Journal of Hospitality and Tourism* 1, no. 2 (2001). In all fairness, Urry acknowledged there exist "various ways of capturing sights in passing, from a railway carriage, through the car windscreen, the steamship porthole, the camcorder viewfinder, or the mobile phone." John Urry, *Mobilities* (Cambridge: Polity, 2007), 49. But the "gaze" metaphor has stuck in mobility (especially tourism) researchers' mind. The distinction between gaze and glance is also used in the media studies treatise by Jay David Bolter and Richard Grusin, *Remediation: Understanding New Media* (Cambridge. MA: MIT Press, 2000).
26. Gijs Mom, "Orchestrating Car Technology: Noise, Comfort, and the Construction of the American Closed Automobile, 1917–1940," *Technology and Culture* 55, no. 2 (2014).
27. Kaiwar, "Towards Orientalism and Nativism," 200 (persuasion, coercion); Cotten Seiler, *Republic of Drivers: A Cultural History of Automobility in America* (Chicago: University of Chicago Press, 2008).
28. Zygmunt Bauman, *Liquid Life* (Cambridge: Polity, 2006); John Urry, "Moving on the Mobility Turn," in *Tracing Mobilities: Towards a Cosmopolitan Perspective*, ed. Weert Canzler, Vincent Kaufmann and Sven Kesselring (Aldershot: Ashgate, 2008); Edward Reed and Rebecca Jones, eds., *Reasons for Realism: Selected Essays of James J. Gibson* (Hillsdale, NJ: Lawrence Erlbaum, 1982).
29. Mom, *Atlantic Automobilism*, 36 (properties), fig. 0.2 (matrix), 287–306 (budget), 654 (fetish); Thorstein Veblen, *The Theory of the Leisure Class* (New York: Dover Publications, 1994). Although Veblen seems to equate consumption with use, he emphasized the "pecuniar emulation" and focused on commodities for the home and the body. Ibid., 15. However, as a *historical* analysis, his book deals extensively with the violent and aggressive

(predatory, masculine) roots of consumption acts. In this book, I will refer to secondary sources in the past tense, whereas I retell fictional narratives in the present tense.

30. Todd McGowan, *Capitalism and Desire: The Psychic Cost of Free Markets* (New York: Columbia University Press, 2016), 12 (promise), 15 (repeating), 28 (misleading); Todd McGowan, *Enjoying What We Don't Have: The Political Project of Psychoanalysis* (Lincoln: University of Nebraska Press, 2013); Gijs Mom, "'The Future Is a Shifting Panorama': The Role of Expectations in the History of Mobility," in *Zukünfte des Automobils: Aussichten und Grenzen der autotechnischen Globalisierung*, ed. Weert Canzler and Gert Schmidt (Berlin: edition sigma, 2008); see also Harro van Lente, *Promising Technology: The Dynamics of Expectations in Technological Developments* (Delft: Eburon, 1993).

31. McGowan, *Capitalism and Desire*, 12 (better future), 29 (racing fans), 31 (Lacan quote), 37 (proximity), 215 (engine and out of reach), 216 (terrifying), 218 (mystical, everyday), 219 (utility), 221 (SUV); Mom, *Atlantic Automobilism*, 465 (*Babbitt*). All italics are found in the original sources unless otherwise noted (i.e., emphasis added).

32. McGowan, *Capitalism and Desire*, 226–227; L. Pearce, *Drivetime*, 38.

33. Helga Dittmar, *The Social Psychology of Material Possessions: To Have Is to Be* (Hemel Hempstead / New York: Harvester Wheatsheaf / St. Martin's Press, 1992), 1 (Fromm), 2 (advertisements), 42 (constructionism) ("culture and commerce" quoted in "Grant McCracken," https://en.wikipedia.org/wiki/Grant_McCracken [consulted 23 December 2016]). Two reviewers of my earlier monograph lamented the absence of advertisement analysis. Certainly, for the first period, and to a certain extent the second (until 1940), autopoetic novels and other artistic utterances were written by and for the same social group, so they provide a much better entrance into the intricacies of interbellum car culture than advertisements. See Mom, *Atlantic Automobilism*, 177; Peter Merriman, review of Mom, *Atlantic Automobilism*, *Journal of Transport History* 37, no. 1 (2016): 109–111; Donald Weber, Hubert Bonin, and Antonia Mackay, review of Mom, *Atlantic Automobilism*, *European Review of History* 24, no. 1 (2017): 158–166.

34. Marshall McLuhan, *Understanding Media: The Extensions of Man* (London: Routledge, 2005), 248; Aida Bosch, *Konsum und Exklusion: Eine Kultursociologie der Dinge* (Bielefeld: transcript, 2010), 145 (magical loading). For an example of a failed advertisement study in mobility history, see Dhan Zunino Singh and Mikkel Thelle, "Mobilities and Representations: A Conversation with Peter Merriman, Colin Divall, Sunny Stalter-Pace, and Tim Cresswell," *Mobility in History* 8 (2017): 15, where railway historian Colin Divall recounts his study of railway advertising: "But we never cracked the conundrum of what the intended recipients of all this marketing made of it, or indeed how railing was experienced, bodily and affectively, by these different groups. Interesting, despite the hugely greater resources thrown today at marketing mobility, colleagues who work in the field tell me that while they recognize the importance of people's emotional responses, they often have a poor understanding of this affective dimension."

35. Dittmar, *Social Psychology of Material Possessions*, 187 (meanings), 197 (aware); Barbara Stern, "Pleasure and Persuasion in Advertising: Rhetorical Irony as a Humor Technique," *Current Issues and Research in Advertising* 12, nos. 1–2 (1990): 26 (controversial), 28 (skills), 33 (elite), 36 (literally); Burgers et al., "Use of Co-textual Irony Markers" (sheep); Ekin Pehlivan, Pierre Berthon, and Leyland Pitt, "Ad Bites: Toward a Theory of Ironic Advertising," *Journal of Advertising Research* 51, no. 2 (2011): 418 (surface, underlying), 420 (cues), 425 (postmodern). For an exemplary analysis of car advertising, see Matthew Paterson, *Automobile Politics: Ecology and Cultural Political Economy* (Cambridge: Cambridge University Press, 2007), 154–162.

36. Dittmar, *Social Psychology of Material Possessions*, 5 (symbolic consumption), 6 (share the belief), 63 (instrumental and utilitarian), 96 (poverty).
37. Mikkel Thelle, "Subversive Mobilities: The Copenhagen Riots, 1900–1919," *Transfers* 3, no. 1 (2013): 15; Dittmar, *Social Psychology of Material Possessions*, 19–20 (instinctual, sociobiology), 41 (extended self), 66 (identity); Hesford, "Overt Appropriation," 415 (the quoted sentence ends with "and literary theory").
38. Claude Lévi-Strauss, *Structural Anthropology* (London, 1968) as quoted in Dittmar, *Social Psychology of Material Possessions*, 95, 97 (Simmel), 101 (self-completion), 200 (empty); Philip Cushman, "Why the Self Is Empty: Toward a Historically Situated Psychology," *American Psychologist* 45, no. 5 (1990): 599 (filled up, healed), 600 (loss, shared meaning, family), 605 (false self); Lakoff and Johnson, *Metaphors We Live By*, 51 (container). For an analysis of the car as prosthesis from an art-theoretical point of view, see Charissa Terranova, "Mobile Perception and the Automotive Prosthetic: Photoconceptualism, the Car, and the Posthuman Subject," *Transfers* 1, no. 1 (2011).
39. Christopher Lasch, *The Culture of Narcissism: American Life in an Age of Diminishing Expectations* (New York: Norton, 1991), 31 (Fromm), 33 (celebrity), 36 (separation), 37 (dissatisfaction) ("acted out" from psychiatrist Otto Kernberg, *Borderline Conditions and Pathological Narcissism* [1975]), 40 (sublimation); David D. Gilmore, *Manhood in the Making: Cultural Concepts of Masculinity* (New Haven, CT: Yale University Press, 1990), 29 (post-Freudian definition).
40. Dittmar, *Social Psychology of Material Possessions*, 57 (Western part: "our part of the world"), 127 (women), 128 (relational), 132 (instrumental, emotional), 133 (pragmatic), 137 (working-class), 188 (independent self), 191 (autonomy), 193 (Anglo-American, exception), 201 (Douglas and Isherwood).
41. See, e.g., Luca Ciabarri, "Biographies of Roads, Biographies of Nations: History, Territory and the Road Effect in Post-conflict Somaliland," in *The Making of the African Road*, ed. Kurt Beck, Gabriel Klaeger, and Michael Stasik (Leiden: Brill, 2017); Mark Lamont, "Ruin, or Repair? Infrastructural Sociality and an Economy of Disappearances along a Rural Road in Kenya," in Beck et al., *Making of the African Road*, 177 (breakdown).
42. Marcus Felson, "Invidious Distinctions among Cars, Clothes and Suburbs," *Public Opinion Quarterly* 42, no. 1 (1978): 49 (social stratification), 50 (visible, income), 52 (failed), 52, table 1 (a quarter); Marcus Felson, "The Differentiation of Material Life Styles: 1925 to 1966," *Social Indicators Research* 3, nos. 3–4 (1976): 398 (visible rather than conspicuous), 408 (native); Jim Conley, "Automobile Advertisements: The Magical and the Mundane," in *Car Troubles: Critical Studies of Automobility and Auto-mobility*, ed. Jim Conley and Arlene Tigar McLaren (Farnham: Ashgate, 2009), 51 (19.4 percent).
43. Conley, "Automobile Advertisements," 37 (Riesman, etc.), 40 (potent), 44 (alibi confirmation); David Lipset, "Introduction: Charon's Boat and Other Vehicles of Moral Imagination," in *Vehicles: Cars, Canoes, and Other Metaphors of Moral Imagination*, ed. David Lipset and Richard Handler (New York: Berghahn Books, 2014), 3 (qualities, agencies); Mom, *Atlantic Automobilism*, 325 (alibi thesis).
44. Linda Steg, "Car Use: Lust and Must—Instrumental, Symbolic and Affective Motives for Car Use," *Transportation Research Part A* 39, nos. 2–3 (2005); Linda Steg, Karst Geurs, and Michael Ras, "The Effects of Motivational Factors on Car Use: A Multidisciplinary Modelling Approach," *Transportation Research Part A* 35, no. 9 (2001); P. L. Mokhtarian, "Travel as a Desired End, Not Just a Means (Guest Editorial)," *Transportation Research Part A* 39, nos. 2–3 (2005); Sangho Choo and Patricia L. Mokhtarian, "What Type of Vehicle Do People Drive? The Role of Attitude and Lifestyle in Influencing Vehicle Type Choice," *Transportation Research Part A* 38, no. 3 (2004); Todd Litman, "Mobility

as a Positional Good: Implications for Transport Policy and Planning," in Conley and McLaren, *Car Troubles*, 204–205.
45. Litman, "Mobility as a Positional Good," 199 (functional); Conley, "Automobile Advertisements," 40 (mundane), 42 (instrumental); Gerhard Schulze, *Die Erlebnisgesellschaft: Kultursoziologie der Gegenwart* (Frankfurt: Campus Verlag, 2000), 13; Katharina Scherke, "Die These von der 'Ästhetisierung der Lebenswelt' als eine Form der Analyse des Modernisierungsprozesses," in *Analyse und Kritik der Modernisierung um 1900 und um 2000*, ed. Sabine A. Haring and Katharina Scherke (Vienna: Passagen-Verlag, 2000), 111 (recourse). For another, quite devastating critique of Schulze's study, which allegedly acknowledged only utilitarian and experience values and neglected social, ecological, medical, economic and other values, see Armin Günther, "20 Jahre Erlebnisgesellschaft-- und mehr Fragen als Antworten: Zwischenbilanz oder Abgesang auf die Erlebniswelten-Diskussion," in *Postmoderne Freizeitstile und Freizeiträume: Neue Angebote im Tourismus*, ed. Paul Reuber and Peter Schnell (with Birthe Linden) (Berlin: Erich Schmidt Verlag, 2006), 56.
46. Roland Barthes, "La nouvelle Citroën," in *Mythologies* (Paris: Éditions du Seuil, 1957); for an English translation, see, e.g., "The DS by Roland Barthes" Citroënët, accessed 19 October 2019, http://www.citroenet.org.uk/passenger-cars/michelin/ds/32.html; Böhme, "Das Strahlen fetischistischer Dinge des Konsums," 37.
47. Böhme, "Das Strahlen fetischistischer Dinge des Konsums," 41 (jewellery); Stephen Bayley, *Sex, Drink and Fast Cars: The Creation and Consumption of Images* (London: Faber & Faber, 1986), 7 (laundry truck); Schulze, *Die Erlebnisgesellschaft*, 114 (personal styles); Scherke, "Die These von der 'Ästhetisierung der Lebenswelt,'" 117.
48. Chris Lezotte, "The Evolution of the 'Chick Car' Or: What Came First, the Chick or the Car?" *Journal of Popular Culture* 45, no. 3 (2012): 531; Virginia Scharff, *Taking the Wheel: Women and the Coming of the Motor Age* (New York: Free Press, 1991); Georgine Clarsen, *Eat My Dust: Early Women Motorists* (Baltimore: Johns Hopkins University Press, 2008); Mom, *Atlantic Automobilism*, 277–278 (critique on Scharff). Lezotte wrote her dissertation at age sixty, after a career in car advertising. Christine L. Lezotte, "Have You Heard the One about the Woman Driver? Chicks, Muscle, Pickups, and the Reimagining of the Woman behind the Wheel" (PhD diss., Bowling Green State University, 2015), v.
49. Patrick Holland and Graham Huggan, *Tourists with Typewriters: Critical Reflections on Contemporary Travel Writing* (Ann Arbor: University of Michigan Press, 2000), 20 (explosion), 113 ("fear of rape"); Heidi Slettedahl Macpherson, *Women's Movement: Escape as Transgression in North American Feminist Fiction* (Amsterdam: Rodopi, 2000).
50. Ulf Mellström, "Machines and Masculine Subjectivity: Technology as an Integral Part of Men's Life Experiences," *Men and Masculinities* 6, no. 4 (2004): 368 (symbiosis), 369 (powerful), 371 (noncognitive), 377 (metaphors, stubborn), 378 (animating); Dag Balkmar, "On Men and Cars: An Ethnographic Study of Gendered, Risky and Dangerous Relations" (PhD diss., Linköping University, 2012), 45n20 (hegemonic and other masculinities).
51. Chris Lezotte, "Out on the Highway: Cars, Community, and the Gay Driver," *Culture, Society & Masculinities* 7, no. 2 (2015): 126 (hybrid); Kam Louie, *Theorising Chinese Masculinity: Society and Gender in China* (Cambridge: Cambridge University Press, 2002), 162 (postmodern); Balkmar, "On Men and Cars," 83 (personification); Mellström, "Machines and Masculine Subjectivity," 374 (intelligence), 377 (entranced; emphasis added), 379 (extension, feminine persona); Mom, *Atlantic Automobilism*, 97; Böhme, "Das Strahlen fetischistischer Dinge des Konsums," 37.

52. For the distinction between archetypes (really existing cars that stand for a certain period or geographic area), average types, and ideal types (the latter two virtual artifacts), see Gijs Mom, *The Evolution of Automotive Technology: A Handbook* (Warrendale, PA: SAE International, 2014), 10.
53. Balkmar, "On Men and Cars," 12 (modify), 27 (rituals), 36 (performative).
54. See, e.g., Gayatri Chakravorty Spivak, "Can the Subaltern Speak?" in *Marxism and the Interpretation of Culture*, ed. Cary Nelson and Lawrence Grossberg (London: Macmillan Education, 1988).
55. Lezotte, "Have You Heard the One about the Woman Driver?" vi; Chris Brickell, "Masculinities, Performativity, and Subversion," *Men and Masculinities* 8, no. 1 (2005): 39.
56. Balkmar, *"On Men and Cars,"* 47 (queer theory), 51 (subcultures); Pflugfelder, "Something Less Than a Driver," 423; Böhme, "Das Strahlen fetischistischer Dinge des Konsums," 39.
57. Robin Law, "Beyond 'Women and Transport': Towards New Geographies of Gender and Daily Mobility," *Progress in Human Geography* 23, no. 4 (1999).
58. Ragnhild Lund and Anna Karlsdottir, "Editorial: Gendered Mobilities in Asia," *Norsk Geografisk Tidsskrift / Norwegian Journal of Geography* 67, no. 4 (2013): 185; Henry Yu quoted in Kam Louie, "Chinese, Japanese and Global Masculine Identities," in *Asian Masculinities: The Meaning and Practice of Manhood in China and Japan*, ed. Kam Louie and Morris Low (London: Routledge, 2005), 2.
59. Louie, *Theorising Chinese Masculinity*, v (*wen* and *wu*), 2 (poverty), 3 (Said quote and macho image), 6 (body), 7 (feminist paradigms), 8 (adventurous; *caizi* quote), 9 (*yin-yang*), 12 (animal instincts), 161 (matrix); Xueping Zhong, *Masculinity Besieged? Issues of Modernity and Male Subjectivity in Chinese Literature of the Late Twentieth Century* (Durham, NC: Duke University Press, 2000), 11 ("in Chinese literature of the 1980s … Chinese men are seen as 'weak' and 'unmanly.'").
60. Roy Hibbins, "Male Gender Identities among Chinese Male Migrants," in Louie and Low, *Asian Masculinities*, 199, 200.
61. Kate McDonald, "Imperial Mobility: Circulation as History in East Asia under Empire," *Transfers* 4, no. 3 (2014): 68.
62. Bolter and Grusin, *Remediation*, 3 (emphasis added) (I thank James Miller for providing me with his (then not yet published) chapter on "Mediatization of the Automobile," in *Dynamics of Mediatization: Institutional Change and Everyday Transformations in a Digital Age*, ed. Oliver Driessens, Göran Bolin, Andreas Hepp, and Stig Hjarvard [London: Palgrave Macmillan]); Glenn Hooper and Tim Youngs, "Introduction," in *Perspectives on Travel Writing*, ed. Glenn Hooper and Tim Youngs (Aldershot: Ashgate, 2003), 1; for a recent example of transition studies as applied to the car, see Frank W. Geels, René Kemp, Geoff Dudley, and Glenn Lyons, eds., *Automobility in Transition? A Socio-technical Analysis of Sustainable Transport* (New York: Routledge, 2012); for an attempt to line up transition studies with the no less successful mobility turn, see Laur Kanger and Johan Schot, "User-Made Immobilities: A Transitions Perspective," Science Policy Research Unit Working Paper Series SWPS 2016–13 (University of Sussex, July 2016); for an example of a "historical" transition study fully neglecting mobility history, see, e.g., Benjamin D. Leibowicz, "Policy Recommendations for a Transition to Sustainable Mobility based on Historical Diffusion Dynamics of Transport Systems," *Energy Policy* 119 (2018).
63. Lipset, "Introduction," 2 (metaphor); Bauman, *Individualized Society*, 9 (articulation); Michael Cronin, *Across the Lines: Travel, Language, Translation* (Cork: Cork University

Press, 2013), 2; Zannagh Hatton, "The Tarmac Comboys: an Ethnographic Study of the Cultural World of Boy Racers" (PhD diss., University of Plymouth, 2007), 31 (transfer); Margrit Pernau and Imke Rajamani, "Emotional Translations: Conceptual History beyond Language," *History and Theory* 55, no. 1 (2016): 52.

64. Tomlinson, *Culture of Speed*, 72–73; Bolter and Grusin, *Remediation*, 6 (disappear), 229 (denial); Mom, *Atlantic Automobilism*, 158–159.
65. Pernau and Rajamani, "Emotional Translations," 47, 48 (Koselleck) (for an effort to design the concept of postcolonial media studies, see Kai Merten and Lucia Krämer, "Introduction," in *Postcolonial Studies Meets Media Studies: A Critical Encounter*, ed. Kai Merten and Lucia Krämer [Bielefeld: transcript Verlag, 2016]); Mom, "Orchestrating Automobile Technology."
66. Jesse J. Prinz, "Foreword: Hand Manifesto," in *The Hand, an Organ of the Mind: What the Manual Tells the Mental*, ed. Zdravko Radman (Cambridge, MA: MIT Press, 2013), ix (ocularcentric, organs), xi (linked); Zdravko Radman, "On Displacement of Agency: The Mind Handmade," in Radman, *Hand*, 379; Mimi Sheller, "Automotive Emotions: Feeling the Car," *Theory, Culture & Society* 21, nos. 4–5 (2004): 223.
67. J. Cole and A. Dawson quoted in Filip Mattens, "Perception and Representation: Mind the Hand!" in Radman, *Hand*, 159 (eyes); Nigel Thrift, "Intensities of Feeling: Towards a Spatial Politics of Affect," *Geografiska Annaler* 86B, no. 1 (2004): 61 (affect); Mom, "Orchestrating Automobile Technology"; Matthew Ratcliffe, "Touch and the Sense of Reality," in Radman, *Hand*, 131 (vision, Merleau-Ponty).
68. Ole B. Jensen and Phillip Vannini, "Blue Sky Matter: Toward an (In-Flight) Understanding of the Sensuousness of Mobilities Design," *Transfers* 6, no. 2 (2016): 38; Raymond Williams, *Television: Technology and Cultural Form* (London: Routledge, 1974) quoted in Nicola Green, "On the Move: Technology, Mobility, and the Mediation of Social Time and Space," *Information Society* 18, no. 4 (2002): 283; Bolter and Grusin, *Remediation*, 237 (body as medium); Haraway quoted in Pflugfelder, "Something Less Than a Driver," 418; Guillemette Bolens, *The Style of Gestures: Embodiment and Cognition in Literary Narratives, Foreword by Alain Berthoz* (Baltimore: Johns Hopkins University Press, 2012), 3.
69. Brenda Farnell, "Moving Bodies, Acting Selves," *Annual Review of Anthropology* 28 (1999): 346 (problem), 348 (static), 351 (Goffman), 354 (anthropology, ritual, linguistic), 355 (choreographed); Peter Merriman, "Roads: Lawrence Halprin, Modern Dance and the American Freeway Landscape," in *Geographies of Mobilities: Practices, Spaces, Subjects*, ed. Tim Cresswell and Peter Merriman (Farnham: Ashgate, 2011); Julia M. Hildebrand, "Media and Mobilities: Modes, Messages, Movements, and Moods" (unpublished manuscript, Drexel University, 2016), 15 (exploring), 16 (flaneur example). I thank Julia Hildebrand for providing me with this manuscript, which has since been published as "Modal Media: Connecting Media Ecology and Mobilities Research," *Media, Culture & Society*, 40, no. 3 (2018).
70. Bolter and Grusin, *Remediation*, 6; Cronin quoted and partly paraphrased in Tim Youngs, "Where Are We Going? Cross-Border Approaches to Travel Writing," in Hooper and Youngs, *Perspectives on Travel Writing*, 174; Peter Merriman, "Road Works: Some Observations on Representing Roads," *Transfers* 5, no. 1 (2015): 113; Lipset, "Introduction," 13. Urry later shifted toward "a broader sensory paradigm," according to Carolyn Birdsall in Carolyn Birdsall, Jan-Friedrich Missfelder, Daniel Morat, and Corine Schleif, "Forum: The Senses," *German History* 32, no. 2 (2014): 272.
71. Geoff Eley, "Is All the World a Text? From Social History to the History of Society Two Decades Later," in *The Historic Turn in the Human Sciences*, ed. Terrence J. McDonald

(Ann Arbor: University of Michigan Press, 1996), 194 (uncertainty); Rabinow, "Representations Are Social Facts," 249.
72. Christina Murphy, *Ann Beattie* (Boston: Twayne, 1986), 8 (all quotes), 9 (collage); Featherstone quoted in Hans Bertens, "The Sociology of Postmodernity," in *International Postmodernism: Theory and Literary Practice*, ed. Hans Bertens and Douwe Fokkema (Amsterdam: John Benjamins Publishing Co., 1997), 109.
73. Singh and Thelle, "Mobilities and Representations," 7 (traditional methods), 9 (Divall; emphasis added), 10 (Cresswell: "Representation is always also practice and doing stuff"; emphasis added), 13 (prelinguistic, active agents), 16 (trustworthy).
74. Julia Kuehn and Paul Smethurst, "Introduction," in *New Directions in Travel Writing Studies*, ed. Julia Kuehn and Paul Smethurst (London: Palgrave Macmillan, 2015), 2–3 (mire, traffic); Caitlin Vandertop, "Travel Literature and the Infrastructural Unconscious," in Kuehn and Smethurst, *New Directions in Travel Writing Studies*, 132 (invisibility), 141 (readings). On postmodernism and travel writing, see, e.g., Holland and Huggan, *Tourists with Typewriters*, chap. 4 ("Postmodern devices have not so consistently infiltrated the travel book as they have the contemporary novel").
75. Rabinow, "Representations Are Social Facts," 251 (crisis); James Clifford, "Introduction: Partial Truths," in Clifford and Marcus, *Writing Culture*, 2 (central), 3 (fuse), 4 (processes), 6 (fictions), 11 (visualism); Seamus O'Malley, *Making History New: Modernism and Historical Narrative* (Oxford: Oxford University Press, 2015), ix (Holocaust); for a recent example of an ethnography written "as if it were fiction—not as fiction," see Cecilia McCallum, "Racialized Bodies, Naturalized Classes: Moving through the City of Salvador da Bahia," *American Ethnologist* 32, no. 1 (2005): 102; for an example of mobilizing a novel as support of ethnographic scholarship (based on the *affinity* of both in terms of participant observation), see Akhil Gupta, "Narratives of Corruption: Anthropological and Fictional Accounts of the Indian State," *Ethnography* 6, no. 1 (2005); Richard Shirreff, *2017: War with Russia—An Urgent Warning from Senior Military Command* (2016) quoted in Robert Cottrell, "Russia, NATO, Trump: The Shadow World," *New York Review of Books* (22 December 2016), 97.
76. Balkmar, "On Men and Cars," 73 (mirroring); Colin McGinn, "Can We Solve the Mind-Body Problem?" *Mind* 98, no. 391 (1989): 366; Clifford, "Introduction," 23 (areas); Talal Asad, "The Concept of Cultural Translation in British Social Anthropology," in Clifford and Marcus, *Writing Culture,* 141 (translation of cultures), 157 (tolerance; emphasis added); Jan Borm, "Defining Travel: On the Travel Book, Travel Writing and Terminology," in Hooper and Youngs, *Perspectives on Travel Writing*, 21 (Aristotelian). Nonetheless, it is quite remarkable none of the reviewers of my earlier study remarked on the "truth value" of belletristic sources, used so prolifically in that study. See Weber et al., review of Mom, *Atlantic Automobilism*.
77. Pernau and Rajamani, "Emotional Translations," 55 (loss); Mom, *Atlantic Automobilism*, 425.
78. Pernau and Rajamani, "Emotional Translations," 53 (complexified); Gijs Mom, Georgine Clarsen, Peter Merriman, Cotton Seiler, Mimi Sheller, and Heike Weber, "Editorial," *Transfers* 3, no. 1 (2013): 1 (*Verkehr*); Dorit Müller and Heike Weber, "'Traffic': On the Historical Alignment of Media and Mobility," *Transfers* 3, no. 1 (2013): 65 (reliance, traffic), 67 (technologies); Mom, *Evolution of Automotive Technology*, chap. 7 (damping); Regine Buschauer, "The 'Ambulant in-Between': Media Histories of Mobile Communication," *Transfers* 3, no. 1 (2013): 97 (assume); Claude S. Fischer and Glenn R. Carroll, "Telephone and Automobile Diffusion in the United States, 1902–1937," *American Journal of Sociology* 93, no. 5 (1988) (telephone). For an effort to rewrite

media history as mobility history, see Christoph Neubert and Gabriele Schabacher, eds., *Verkehrsgeschichte und Kulturwissenschaft: Analysen an der Schnittstelle von Technik, Kultur und Medien* (Bielefeld: transcript verlag, 2013).
79. Raymond Williams, *Television: Technology and Cultural Form* (London: Routledge, 2003); Margaret Morse, "An Ontology of Everyday Distraction: The Freeway, the Mall, and Television," in Mellencamp, *Logics of Television*, 218n22 (flow metaphor); Catherine Bertho Lavenir, *La roue et le stylo: Comment nous sommes devenus touristes* (Paris: Editions Odile Jacob, 1999); Janet Wolff, "On the Road Again: Metaphors of Travel in Cultural Criticism," *Cultural Studies* 7, no. 2 (1993): 225.
80. See, e.g., Catherine Gudis, *Buyways: Billboards, Automobiles, and the American Landscape* (New York: Routledge, 2004); Müller and Weber, "Traffic," 66 (broadening).
81. Buschauer, "Ambulant in-Between," 97 (shift); Slavoj Zizek [sic], "What Can Psychoanalysis Tell Us about Cyberspace?" *Psychoanalytic Review* 91, no. 6 (2004): 809–810; Taylor quoted in Dominic Sachsenmaier, *Global Perspectives on Global History: Theories and Approaches in a Connected World* (Cambridge: Cambridge University Press, 2011), 144 (postmodern), 145 (blissfully).
82. Mom, *Evolution of Automotive Technology*, esp. chap. 9 ("Automation"); Jensen and Vannini, "Blue Sky Matter," 27.
83. Sara Mills, *Discourses of Difference: An Analysis of Women's Travel Writing and Colonialism* (London: Routledge, 2001), 2 (Fussell); Mary Baine Campbell, "Travel Writing and Its Theory," in *The Cambridge Companion to Travel Writing*, ed. Peter Hulme and Tim Youngs (Cambridge: Cambridge University Press, 2002), 261 (vital, result), 266 (Said); Holland and Huggan, *Tourists with Typewriters*, xii (cornerstones); Kaiwar, "Towards Orientalism and Nativism," 210 (First-World academy); iconic writers mentioned in Peter Hulme, "Travelling to Write (1940–2000)," in Hulme and Youngs, *Cambridge Companion to Travel Writing*, 89–92.
84. Ivona Grgurinović, "Anthropology and Travel: Practice and Text," *Studia ethnologica Croatica* 24 (2012): 46; Mom, *Atlantic Automobilim*, 141; Tim Youngs, "Introduction," *Studies in Travel Writing* 17, no. 4 (2013): 331.
85. E.g., S. Mills, *Discourses of Difference*, dedicated to nineteenth-century women travelers, discusses clothes and personal paraphernalia as part of the women's travel preparations, as well as "preparations for accidents." Ibid., 100–103, 100 (quote). Grgurinović, "Anthropology and Travel," 58 (travel writers "rarely take into account the material conditions," paraphrasing Caren Kaplan).
86. Holland and Huggan, *Tourists with Typewriters*, vii (travelogues), viii (remarkable, refuge), x (Anglophone), xiii (extreme), 6 (cheerful), 7 (mask, cool), 10 (reverie); 12 (*pseudo*ethnography), 14 (poetics, metaphysics), 23 (speed); Mom, *Atlantic Automobilism*, 142–143 (adventure novel), 499 (cool persona).
87. Holland and Huggan, *Tourists with Typewriters*, ix (crucial), 4 (transgressive), 5 (home, "round trips"), 11 (account); Charles Burdett, *Journeys through Fascism: Italian Travel Writing between the Wars* (New York: Berghahn Books, 2010), 7 (pleasure).
88. Helen Carr, "Modernism and Travel (1880–1940)," in Hulme and Youngs, *Cambridge Companion to Travel Writing*, 74 (impressionistic and focused), 75 (three stages).
89. Hooper and Youngs, "Introduction," 2 (loosely defined); Borm, "Defining Travel," 15 (techniques, *pact*), 17 (*narrative*); Hulme, "Travelling to Write (1940–2000)," 99; Campbell, "Travel Writing and Its Theory," 267 (haunt); Grgurinović, "Anthropology and Travel," 54 (duality); Patrick Holland and Graham Huggan, "Varieties of Nostalgia in Contemporary Travel Writing," in Hooper and Youngs, *Perspectives on Travel Writing*, 144 (nomad). "In historical scholarship … interest is increasingly turning toward approaches

drawn from anthropology—the portrayal of complex cultural forms, customary ways of life, etc.," Marcus and Clifford conclude in their report of the famous 1984 seminar on the making of ethnographic texts. George E. Marcus and James Clifford, "The Making of Ethnographic Texts: A Preliminary Report," *Current Anthropology* 26, no. 2 (1985): 267. On the role of narration in both fiction and history writing, see O'Malley, *Making History New*. For a German and French example of travel writing studies, respectively, see Gerrit Walther, "Auf der Suche nach der 'Gattung': Interdisziplinäre Reiseliteraturforschung," *Archiv für Sozialgeschichte* 32 (1992); Roland Le Huen, "Qu'est-ce qu'un récit de voyage?" *Littérales* 7 (1990).

90. Mary Louise Pratt, *Imperial Eyes: Travel Writing and Transculturation* (London: Routledge, 1992), 225–227 (the quoted section is—ironically—titled "The Lady in the Airport"); Holland and Huggan, *Tourists with Typewriters*, ix (expansionist), 2 (exhaustion), 3 (beaten track, holidays); Günther, "20 Jahre Erlebnisgesellschaft," 48 (freedom); Marvin Zuckerman, *Behavioral Expressions and Biosocial Bases of Sensation Seeking* (Cambridge: Cambridge University Press, 1994).

91. LeRoy Ashby, "The Rising of Popular Culture: A Historiographical Sketch," *OAH Magazine of History* 24, no. 2 (2010).

Part I

EMERGENCE AND PERSISTENCE (AGAIN)
The Shaping of Mobility Layeredness beyond the West

Chapter 1

MODERNIZING WITHOUT AUTOMOBILIZATION
Subverting and Subalternizing Mobility History
(1890–1945/1950)

The dragon-monsters continue to fight on the highways
at night
… another epoch is approaching.
—Zeng Pu, "A Flower in a Sinful Sea"

Imperialist Mobilities: Japan and the Modernization of Manchuria

At the very start of the new century, from 1900 to 1902, Natsume Sōseki (1867–1916), nowadays regarded as "one of Japan's greatest writers," spent "the most unpleasant years of [his] life" in London, living "like a poor dog that had strayed among a pack of wolves." In terms of mobility, Sōseki (Natsume being his family name, Sōseki his pen name) most of all practiced and experienced pedestrianism, observing how Londoners "were in no way ill at ease in a crowd." Prefiguring the 'swarm' I have used elsewhere to explain the emergence of the automobile, he described in one of his short stories how a "sea of humanity" followed "the watery movements of the ocean." "There could be no thought of escaping from it … I too progressed forward, adapting my step to that of the thousands of dark beings who appeared to have agreed among themselves to move at one uniform rate," in a city darkened by "soot-colored smoke."[1] Sōseki's early fictionalized experience of the movement of a pedestrian swarm (a group moving without a proper control center) in what he conceived as a fluid society, reads as an experience of transcendence, where the individual becomes larger than herself, part of a seemingly unstoppable and inevitable "progress" observed in a modernizing context.

This was only the beginning of his submergence in mobile modernity. Advised by a Japanese roommate to combat his upcoming depression through a therapeutic bicycle ride, he also experienced the cyborg condition that has been described as so typical for Western-style modernity. Because of his small stature opting for a lady's bicycle (thus confirming the stereotype that the non-West is not masculine), he incorporated his not-so-hilarious trip (with lots of falls and confrontations with the police) in the short story "The Diary of a Bicycle Rider" (1903). "Finding myself stuck to the bicycle and glued to its saddle, as it were—a perfect communion between the man and his machine!" he soon discovers the bicycle rather than himself is in charge. When he manages to avoid a collision with a tram car by diving, a gentleman in a horse-drawn cabriolet shouts: "'Everything's all right. You're not going to be killed, don't worry!' Stupefied, I murmured to myself, 'Is it possible that they get people to ride bicycles in order to kill them? England's certainly a fearful place!'"[2]

Little did Sōseki realize how this relationship between modern mobility and killing would become quite close pretty soon, in the annual production of traffic victims. What he could not avoid realizing, however, was the flip side of what he called "Westerners' logic," for instance, when another cyclist whom he caused to fall called him a "Chink." In London, while his homesickness heightened because his wife back in Japan delivered a son, he discovered the color of his skin: "Since I have been here," he wrote to his wife, "I have fretted at finding myself so yellow. Furthermore, I am small. I have not yet met anyone smaller than me. Nor am I broad shouldered. When I think to myself, 'Look, there's a funny person coming towards me!' it's my own reflection that I see in the mirror … I wish I were taller … I shut myself away in my boarding house as in a besieged castle, and my only resource is to study."[3] Sōseki's comparative attitude emphasizes the differences between a 'Western' and a 'Japanese' modernization path, in which the mobility mode and the intensity of its use will soon develop into crucial measuring tools, which allow characterization of Japan as an "Asian Prussia" that skipped the (European and American) shift from *Gemeinschaft* to *Gesellschaft* away from the family as all-pervasive basis.[4] Traffic (swarm) and transport (cyborg) were the metaphors he used to make his readers feel the ill fit of a Japanese modernist in London's modernity. If he became yellow, feminine, and small (also to himself) only through the gaze of a Westerner, one wonders what such Westerners did with non-Western mobility. We will find some clues for an answer in the reception of Sōseki's work.

As the iconic transitional writer of the Meiji Restoration, Sōseki had gone to the United Kingdom to study English literature. Combined with his previous studies of the Chinese classics, his celebrated modernism was constantly held back by the old society and its customs, as later literary students diagnosed. In this sense, he was a solid representative of Japan's 'partial modernization.' This is not surprising to a Western observer: Western literary modernity also struggled with reconciling the old and the new, as the work of Marcel Proust and his memories of things past testify. Japanese modernization initially followed the new railway lines: British firms had built the first Japanese railway line in the 1870s, but Japanese engineers soon took over, helping set in motion a process of labor-intensive industrialization and a growth ratio unique in the world. All rails and locomotives were imported until the turn of the century, and in 1890, 1,400 miles had been constructed, 40 percent "owned and operated by the government ... The state financed and ran a number of so-called model enterprises," from shipyards to beer factories, following "a German philosophy of state-led development." The "call for a constitution" prompted the emergence of anti-government institutions, led by "journalists and educators, often former samurai, who made up the urban intelligentsia of the Meiji era."

The constitution made the military "directly responsible to the emperor," not to parliament. Within three decades, Japan made itself into the Workshop of Asia, populated by forty-five million inhabitants, with more women than men being part of the labor force, mostly in the textile and the sex industries. When the Japanese government nationalized the railways in 1906, there was a network of five thousand miles of tracks in the country. The standard work on Japanese railways by Steven Ericson, however, argued "for the relative unimportance of railroads to the economy of Meiji Japan." Next to this modernization, which made Japan "the first non-Western industrial, capitalist economy," a "Japanese" tradition was invented, including Shinto worship and modernized forms of martial arts and Noh and Kabuki theater, whereas a military culture was shaped along Prussian lines, with "military drills at schools" and "a spirit of sacrifice for the state." In 1894, a war with China was fought in Korea, and Japan's victory gave it the control of Taiwan and "railroad building rights in southern Manchuria." The war with Russia in 1904 provided Japan with the control of the Russian railroads in Manchuria; in 1910, Japan annexed Korea "outright as a colony."[5]

However, there is also a global dimension to this story. The spread of the railway over the globe as the first modern land mobility system took place in the decades around the turn of the century. While virtually all railway mileage was laying in the West in the 1870s, by 1910 Asia and Latin America each were equipped with one-tenth of the drastically increased global railway network length (Africa's network size was half this). Transport infrastructure formed a central element in the struggle for hegemony between the industrializing West and the Rest: in 1750, the sum of the GDP of both amounted to $35 billion and $120 billion (of 1960), respectively, but in 1900, this had turned around to $290 billion and $188 billion (a difference that further increased to $3 trillion and $1 trillion in the 1970s). In this setting of explosive modernization with a twist, "an impossible hybrid of eastern and western civilization" in the eyes of one of Sōseki's translators, he became the center of a neo-idealist avant-garde, publishing his work in serial form in the newspaper *Asahi*, for which he managed the literary columns for a while. His work invites us to rethink both modernity and mobility, compared to the French and Belgian avant-garde I have analyzed elsewhere. While the latter discovered the car as the mobile equivalent of their literary adventures, Sōseki found his adventures in literary experiments, "casting aside all the reticence of convention," as he claimed in one of his short stories.[6]

This is not to say Sōseki did not include cars, especially streetcars, in his work. On the contrary, in *After the Spring Equinox* (*Higan sugi made*, 1912), for instance, the streetcar functions as an extension of the opportunity during walking to encounter strangers. "Civilization," Sōseki said in a lecture from 1911, "is something that moves." But civilization stands for "alienation and dehumanization," too. When the protagonist in *Sanshiro* (1908, set in 1907) boards a streetcar, he "mutters loudly enough for the other passengers to hear, 'Ah, it's moving. The world is moving,'" a nice example of nonautomotive inversion. "All of [Sōseki's] important characters," his translator said, "both long for and fear the movement." One protagonist observes, "Wherever you have motion, you must also have vulgarity." And another: "All the mundane world's vomit comes from movement." In her literary analysis of Japanese rail and road transport, Alisa Freedman observed the motion of the train (depicted in the novel in three types: "cross-country railroads, inner-city streetcars, and a commuter line") is a metaphor for "rapid national changes that have not been fully understood." *Sanshiro* is a novel not only about fear of trains, Freedman concluded, but also "of romantic relationships with women." In *The Three-Cornered World* (1906), the protagonist describes the train as affected with "contempt for individuality." The train, appearing "at either the beginning or the end of almost every of Sōseki's novels and reflect[ing] this author's fascination but ambivalence toward these machines," is portrayed as a machine of coercion.[7]

In a lecture on "The Civilization of Modern-Day Japan" ("Gendai Nihon no kaika," 1911), he explained Japan could not enjoy 'civilization,' because it had not freed its energies enough. The car, he claimed, is only used as a timesaving device and does not address its "desire for enjoyment, urging us to do exactly as we please." His observation of London's fledgling automobilism fully coincides with ours: Western car culture was hedonistic, nonutilitarian. Consequently, in a comparison with the rickshaw, Sōseki labels the car as an energy-saving device. Whereas "Western civilization (that is, civilization in general)" is intrinsically motivated, Japanese's development is "the result of pressure from outside." This leads Sōseki to pessimistically conclude "we have no choice but to develop in unnatural ways." Because Japan "has had to leap all at once from a barely attained complexity level to [a very high level] in both time saving and consumption, it runs the risk of a nervous breakdown." This clash of old and new, a phenomenon we will call 'layeredness' in this study, leads to internal turmoil. And perhaps to external turmoil as well, because here Sōseki may have referred, implicitly, to what historians have called "the era of popular riot" of two decades that started at the turn of the century: a list of nine riots between 1905 and 1918 in Andrew Gordon's monograph on Japan gives four in which streetcars are smashed and stoned.[8]

Where I emphasized in the French-Belgian case the dynamic 'affinity' between car driving and writing, Sōseki observes a comparable homology between mobility and the act of reading ("My mind was riveted to the pages, yet it glided over them as smoothly as a sleigh over the snow") and writing ("I am driving my fountain pen forward"), although in Sōseki's case, the vehicle that should function as an intermediary between these experiences was not very well defined. In another essay, Sōseki emphasizes the social implications of his modern "individualism": "It goes without saying that it is reassuring for twigs to be in a bundle." Although he does not lay a connection with traffic here, in yet another essay he nonetheless observes an affinity with the writing process, which, "if it succeeds in achieving 'correspondence' with readers achieves a form of community." In Japan, as in the West (as we saw in the introduction), transport modernity became closely connected with media modernity: the introduction, after 1872, of the movable type revolutionized book printing and consumption, as novels and other texts depended less on illustrations than on "descriptive prose," enabling the middle class to verbalize its observations (similar to what Catherine Bertho has analyzed for early French motorization) while at the same time individualizing the reading process by replacing "traditions of communal reading aloud with solitary and silent reading." Part of this revolution was the serialized publication of a novel, as Sōseki practiced, thus "blurring the distinctions between fact and fiction."[9]

Yet, Sōseki's work has been described by his many translators and other literary students as adorned with a "static quality" that "lack[s] the dynamic rhythm of action." This seems to be an echo of the stereotyping dichotomy between West as mobile and East as immobile, masculine versus feminine. At closer look, his short stories and his novels are full of mobility, traditional and modern. They are, indeed, the first indications of the importance of the *layeredness* of modernization in the world beyond the West. Whereas the literary-cum-automobile avant-garde in France dived head-on into the violent acceleration enabled by the bicycle and the car, Sōseki's transcendence is brought about by religion or, if that is impossible, "self-absorption," an "authentically Oriental" solution according to his translator. Sōseki, therefore, is an attractive case for whoever wishes to study the mobility side of Edward Said's Orientalism, the analysis of the West's patronizing, if not racist gaze to the 'East.' Racism is not a prerogative of the West, although it seems to be invented, and developed into seemingly perfect ideological constructs, in a colonial setting, remarkably often related to mobility, a setting where the "native races" were declared "unfit to operate motorized vehicles," unless they were trained by their superiors.[10]

***

Let us read in more detail, and in a contextualized way, one of Sōseki's major works, *The Wayfarer* (*Kōjin*, serially published in *Asahi*, 1912/1913), to find out more about this 'layeredness.' At first sight, nothing seems to happen and mobility seems to be pushed away as far as possible from a life described as extremely sedentary: "At home in Tokyo things seemed to be going as usual, with little change to speak of ... While things seemed to happen with me but nothing really did, the seemingly long but actually short winter—drizzling rains, thaws, dry winds—ran its own predestined course with monotonous regularity, and then it was gone." Mobility in Sōseki's literary universe seems to be confined to the gestures of the protagonist's body, such as the movement of his arm while shaving, an activity described in detail. "The house where I was born is four or five hundred meters from the one in which I live," he confesses in a serialized bundle of short stories published a year before his death in 1916. Yet, the novel's title already suggests otherwise: the tragic battle between the sexes, reenacted in the struggle between the protagonist's intellectual brother Ichiro and his brother's wife, who are forced by tradition to live together, leads to a distancing from and alienation in society comparable to what the French avant-garde described at about the same time. And just like in the latter's case, the pedestrian wayfarer advises his brother to undertake travel as a remedy against his depression. Visiting the mediator who arranged the trip for his brother, the protagonist, Jiro, an office clerk in Tokyo, finds near the entrance of this mediator's house "many rickshaws ... There were a couple of carriages but no automobiles."[11] This focus on the car as a measuring tool of modernity, mobilized by contemporary novelists and many mobility historians and social scientists in their wake, hides the fundamental synchronicity of 'West' and 'East.'

Indeed, the last quote is one of the very few occasions the car is mentioned in the novel: as an absence. But the rickshaw is everywhere. Born in Tokyo when there were neither trams nor rickshaws, Sōseki in *The Wayfarer* makes the latter abound as feeder to the tram, as a vehicle for emergencies ("I hurry by rickshaw" to a hospital) and as a means to fetch forgotten items, a form of mobility unheard of in the West at that time, based on a special role of the rickshaw puller: "I do not know of any supreme being as trustworthy as a ricksha man." Invented just a couple years after the start of the Meiji period (1868–1912), the *jinrikisha* (*jin* = man, *riki* = power, *sha* = vehicle) was an astounding success, not in the least after Emperor Meiji himself "made a series of peregrinations between 1872 (Meiji 5) and 1875 (Meiji 8) to promote its diffusion." It reminds us of the early proliferation of the bicycle in the West: by the latter year, there were more than one hundred thousand rickshaws plying on Tokyo's streets. But the rickshaw was first and foremost utilitarian: it was very useful in a walking city with narrow and winding streets, "with numerous T-junctions and dead ends to confuse and thwart would-be attackers." By the time Sōseki had portrayed it in his novel as a matter of course (he mentions it about twenty times), the total Japanese fleet of the new vehicle (like the period a hybrid of modern technology and traditional, cheap propulsion by the Other's muscle) amounted to more than two hundred thousand. Not only that: it also had already spread over the rest of Asia, standing for the urban conveyance par excellence during the first decade of the twentieth century.[12] For a global mobility history that takes its self-imposed task of decentering the West seriously, it is worthwhile to realize the car was just one of the world's vehicles of modernization at the turn of the last century

In the novel, the brother's existential problems are directly related to mobility. "Your brother is frustrated," an intermediary tells the protagonist,

> for he thinks whatever he does, no matter how, becomes neither his end nor his means. He is completely insecure; as a result he cannot stay still. He gets up because he cannot sleep in peace, so he contends. Once he gets up, he cannot stand being merely awake, so he walks. Once he walks he cannot just keep walking, so he runs. And once he starts running he cannot stop no matter where he may run. Not only must he not stop anywhere, but he cannot help accelerating his speed every moment. And he says it frightens him to imagine what it will ultimately lead to; he says it is so frightening that he breaks into a cold sweat. Yes, he says it is unbearably frightening.

The remedy, according to the brother, is a triple transcendence: "To die, to go mad, or to enter religion—these are the only three courses left open for me." The brother, longing for "everything that is at rest," then makes the connection to the general condition of modernity, complete with a linear picture of its development: "Man's insecurity stems from the advance of science. Never once has science, which never ceases to move forward, allowed us to pause. From walking to ricksha, from ricksha to carriage, from carriage to train, from train to automobile, from there on to the dirigible, further on to the airplane, and further on and on—no matter how far we may go, it won't let us take a breath. How far it will sweep us along, nobody knows for sure. It is really frightening."[13] Sōseki's novel, with its one-way ticket from pedestrianism to aerospace, shows that as a modern person one does not have to produce car-driving experiences oneself, or fly (in) an airplane, to experience mobility. The novel also shows how the layeredness of this mobility is experienced from the 'periphery': as a nerve-wracking predicament. Invoking the Comaroffs' thesis (see the introduction), Sōseki prefigures the neurasthenia of the West, which on its turn will be one of the drivers of Western automobilism, as we concluded in our earlier study. The solution to the modern predicament as experienced in transition Meiji Japan, Sōseki seems to claim, is self-absorption and unification with nature, transcendence preceded by distance (alienation), exactly the same result that in the West was reached by the 'distancing' effect of the ironic car trip and the subsequent transcendence and the 'sublime of violence' this offered. "Present-day Japanese society," the brother opines, "and perhaps the same might be said of western society, works in such a way that only superficial, clever fellows can live."[14] Modernity, one is inclined to conclude after comparing Sōseki with his European counterparts, does not need the car. But while the Franco-Belgian avant-garde engaged in a 'flight forward' (celebrating modernization), Sōseki's protagonists are engulfed in fear. In hindsight, they had all reasons to be anxious. Against the thrill of speed stands the anxiety of acceleration. Mobility stands in the middle.

***

Modernity was not only invading a fledgling metropole such as Tokyo, however. While Sōseki witnessed how his home town suburbanized, he was invited in 1909 to travel through Manchuria, the northwestern part of China near the Russian border, where Japan's military, supported by tens of thousands of Japanese settlers, undertook what Michael Mann has called social imperialism, a violent settler colonialism aimed to exploit the rich Manchurian metal ores and minerals and to create *lebensraum* for the home country.[15] When Japan struck Russian forces preemptively in 1905, its victory set in motion a wave of nationalist feelings among the peoples of South-East Asia, as Russia was considered a representative of the West. During World War I, Japan sided with the United Kingdom and took control of German railways in China's Shandong province. After the war, the United States recognized Japan's colonial possessions in Asia, a position joined by the League of Nations after its founding in 1920 (without acknowledging Japan's request for a "racial equality clause" in the league's statutes). When the victorious powers rejected China's claim on Shandong, the geopolitical dice were cast for decades to come, as we will see later in this chapter.[16] From 1859, when Han Chinese lifted the prohibition on settling in the area, about thirty million farmers and workers had migrated to Manchuria, most of them coming—in families—from southern coastal provinces like Guangdong, Fujian, and Zhejiang. They were joined by two million Koreans. The discipline from which this information has been drawn, migration studies, usually does not tell us much about the way people migrated and the means they used: on foot? By train? On bullock cart or one-wheeled barrow?

But the Japanese came by boat: when Chinese nationalism emerged, a faked sabotage of a railroad line in 1931 provoked the Japanese army to wage a full-scale attack on the armies of the Chinese warlords, and Manchuria was overrun by the Japanese. The number of settlers now amounted to more than a million, one-tenth of them farmers, the rest "bureaucrats in the occupation authority or white-collar workers in industries." The Japanese decided to conquer the Manchurian space by expanding the railway network, in classic colonial style: from the ports 'penetrating' into the land. Japan effectively tried to make its colony into a hub in a Pacific transport network, connecting its local network (taken from the Russians) to the Trans-Siberian Railway, but failed to build a network of steamer lines, thus creating what Kate McDonald called "railway imperialism," thus blurring the distinction with "railway internationalism" allegedly meant to unite a nation (as in the case of European unification). While Chinese laborers' wages were kept low and more than 114,000 Chinese were killed or injured at work until 1931, Sōseki wandered through the new colony, his meandering style straightened by the linearity of the railway, and condescendingly commenting on the "filth" of the "coolies" and their rickshaws, who were "swarming like angry wasps" on the shore when Sōseki's boat arrived. He called them a "mob," quite appropriate considering the etymology of the term, which goes back to the issue of (uncontrolled) mobility.[17]

Modernization may have been 'frightening' for Sōseki's protagonists, but this does not prevent the writer from using it as a yardstick to judge other peoples' 'civilization,' or lack thereof. The difference is not in the technology, however, but in its handling. "The rickshaw is a Japanese invention," his travelogue claims, "however, when it is drawn by Chinese or Koreans, one can no longer rest. They regard the rickshaw as a foreign invention and have a way of jerking it about that shows a lack of respect for this mode of transportation." The puller Sōseki hired had the "idea that his task was to gallop along without exercising any judgment [which] was also very characteristic of the Koreans. While being bumped about, I thought to myself that any rickshaw driver who does not give proper consideration to his passengers' nerves cannot be called a competent professional, even if he is a good runner." Although his judgment on the puller's skills coincided with the pullers themselves, as we will see later, Sōseki was soon blamed for his racism, but the editors of the translation, undertaken on the occasion of the centenary of Sōseki's stay in London, point at his 'unpolitical' aesthetic theory and suggest, in a typical tournure of literary theory, the travelogue is more fictional than hitherto recognized, and the protagonist 'Sōseki' does not coincide with the real one.[18]

So much for the distancing effect of irony (if not sarcasm, as Joshua Fogel calls it) in modern literature. Fogel, who wrote an overview of Japanese travel writing related to China, and calls Sōseki's text "the first important account of travel to the Asian mainland by a Japanese literary figure," also emphasized Sōseki's "objective style of reportage in opposition to the naturalism so prevalent in Japan at the time," soon to become "the roots of modern Japanese realism." He also said Sōseki's travelogue does not refer whatsoever to the Japanese hotels and railways he made use of. Sōseki was certainly not alone in his judgment on rickshaw pullers, however: Tsarist travelers in Japan also expressed their repulsion about "the mingling of feudal and early-capitalist ways to exploit human labour," but that was part of a left paradigm to condemn the rickshaw culture because of its inhumane traits, as we will witness on several occasions elsewhere later in the century.[19]

***

To sum up, apart from the difference in vehicles between East and West, there does not seem to be much difference in the experience of modernity, or mobility, even if the author of the serialized stories in *Asahi* confesses he is "completely ignorant" about how the "great war [that] broke out last year in Europe" started "and what turns it is to take." The 'mobility' of modernity over the globe is not necessarily a phenomenon of cognition: it travels through objects (such as bicycles, rickshaws, cars, the tram) that afford certain 'modern' practices. Vehicles, indeed, are messages. They have the remarkable property of 'inviting' similar behavior in quite far apart places, although Sōseki, nervous and fearful, emphasized utility rather than adventure. But Sōseki was certainly not the only one struggling with modernization. Fogel mentioned more than twenty other artists, journalists, and literati traveling through the colony during the interwar years. Shortly before the trips became less frequent in the beginning of the 1930s, according to Fogel because "the exercise may have seemed less *adventurous*," it was Yosano Akiko, a writer no less famous whose travel account through Manchuria informs us better about the imperialist sides of Japanese mobility. Yosano's journey was undertaken during the second half of the 1920s, the "high point of Sino-Japanese tensions," just when Japanese army officers had murdered Manchurian warlord Zhang Zuolin (she heard the "loud blast" of "the explosion that ended Zhang Zuolin's last train ride") and a "turn toward fascism" of a special type took place, "military fascism" without a working- or middle-class base, according to Mann.[20]

Like Sōseki invited by the South Manchurian Railway Company (SMRC), and like him having traveled to Europe before World War I, Yosano, traveling with her husband and like him using the protection of the train wagon to write poetry, now could also make use of automobiles (with a driver) for local trips at every stop. The cars were used in a manner similar to the way I have analyzed elsewhere in the case of Northwestern Europe, testifying to the proscriptive power of a vehicle's affordances: leisurely touring, the vehicle reinforcing their isolation from the Other, its high-speed potential celebrated now and then by "rac[ing] along the road at a fearful breakneck speed, an experience I never had had before. Sitting up front with my husband, [railway poet] Mr. Satō from time to time raised his hand and called out, 'What great fun!' The reverberations … were ghastly. We occasionally encountered Chinese walking along the road, and the men on the car would repeatedly scream warnings to them. Fortunately, we arrived at Jilin station without incident." During the car trips, the Japanese Other (as Sōseki had experienced in London) became the Self, glancing at the Chinese, secondary Other. This glance on the Other is enhanced, in Yosano's travelogue, by a telescope.

With the car at the ready, we now can extoll the disadvantages of traveling by train: "That afternoon, we grew tired of the monotony of the vista from the train window, which looked out onto sand and more sand. Everyone picked up a notebook and composed a poem." A well-known feminist and critical to her country's imperialism, Yosano and her company are nonetheless treated with respect. The railway company's high officials, often as literarily educated as their famous guests, even provide special trains, couple special wagons to trains, change departing schedules, and arrange "palenquins" and other vehicles (sedan chairs for her, horses for her husband), so much so that the practice of walking becomes worthy of mentioning: "We were now moving straight up a precipitous peak, so I got down from the sedan chair and walked. The men had earlier returned the horses at Shangshiqiaozi, so we were all now walking." When the couple enters Inner

Mongolia, Yosano does not see a single rickshaw, but she sees one-wheeled barrows used for transporting goods.[21]

Nowadays, we would say Yosano's trip was fully 'embedded': the journey to Beijing was canceled because of a "chaotic" situation around China's capital. Indeed, Manchuria and other parts of North China with its extractive and heavy industries were fiercely contested (and received disproportional investments in its infrastructure), with peasants self-organizing against ravaging warlords. Yosano travels well prepared, although she herself finds her reading of three books on Mongolia "poor." The anti-Japanese riots disturb her: "When I consider the Sino-Japanese issue from the perspective of a Japanese, or when I try to consider it from the perspective of our neighbor the Chinese, or from my position as a citizen of the world, I cannot remain indifferent as these despicable bloodcurdling facts press in before my eyes." But she allows herself the comfort of the doubt: "For my part, I privately was unable to make up my mind on the issue of how the Japanese economy in Manchuria and Mongolia could be beneficial to both Russia and China and come to resolution without contradiction." Traveling in "Western dress," she comes nearest to a "European flavor" when crossing the northeastern part of Mongolia where Russian girls wear bobbed hair and short skirts, an American "saccharine" movie is shown with Chinese subtitles, and a club is adorned with the same name as in Paris: *Folies Bergères*.[22]

***

The railway company's invitations to famous writers and journalists over a period of more than two decades was part of a conscious strategy to present Northeast China as an international tourist destination, offering "such charming mingling of the modern with the historic and romantic," as one of its brochures claimed. Such campaigns were aimed at the new middle class (*koshi-ben* [a *bentō* being a lunch box] or *sarariiman* [salaryman], accompanied by "modern girls" [*modan gaaru*]), which in Tokyo already in 1921 comprised one-fifth of the labor force. Fogel lamented "the general lack of adventuresomeness … in Japanese travelers as a group," a deficit he contrasted with "Westerners, who have often endeavored to travel to places long ignored or hitherto thought impossible to reach," a judgment that may have been influenced by his perception of the difference in adventurousness between the train and the car. From our point of view, Yosano's witnessing of the assassination of Zhang Zuolin may be enough to qualify her trip adventurous (even if she traveled mainly by train). In general, however, we need much more detailed research into the more frivolous *lüyóu* (Mandarin for touristic) sides of traveling, if only to investigate whether Fogel's own anecdotal mention of a wild nocturnal (car?) trip during Japanese writer Jun'ichirō Tanizaki's second visit to Shanghai in 1926, driven "in a speedy and altogether reckless manner" by his drunken host, is only incidental, or whether this was part of a wider automotive adventurous culture. We do not know.

With 250,000 employees in 1930, the SMRC transported forty million passengers and forty-nine million tons of freight per year. But it was much more than a railway company: as the infrastructural arm of Japanese 'social imperialism,' it "supervised schools, hospitals, sanatoria, libraries, agricultural stations, chemical facilities, dormitories and international hotels. The electricity and gas network, a steamship service, as well as postal, tram, and bus routes were also under the Company's responsibility." The company published *Official Guides to Eastern China* (suggesting "ways to avoid dealing with Chinese and Koreans," as one of its students concluded), had its own 'railway poet' as we saw, and boasted its hotels were "thoroughly modern ... managed on American lines." An analysis of the railroad publications from the period reveals, however, how "the idolatry of progress that the Japanese railroad administration professed" was combined with "a racial division between the 'capable' Japanese and the 'not yet civilized' Chinese and Koreans."[23]

What is much less known, however, is that Japan undertook similar initiatives in the realm of road transport. On the Japanese mainland, car registrations had increased from 8,000 in 1921 to a modest 56,000 by the end of 1930, a number that was not even very much compensated by a vast proliferation of motorcycles, although their fleet size increased faster (tenfold), from 2,500 to 24,000 in 1930. After the 1923 Great Kantō earthquake, the Japanese government imported Ford T trucks and adapted these to motorbuses to replace the electric trams; "bus girls" (*basu gāru*), as the female conductors were condescendingly called until they disappeared from the "one-man buses" in the 1960s, formed the iconic symbols of "the human effects of technological modernization," as a recent study of these women's representation in some Japanese novels concluded. In 1930, there were forty thousand buses and trucks in Japan, but like in its colony, there were many more bicycles and "a few private autos." The first subway line was opened in Tokyo in 1927. By then, a "new political order that bore great similarity to the fascist systems of Germany and Italy," had been put in place. Whereas an activist middle class opposed the "running dogs of big capital," the "economic miracle" of the 1930s ushered in the construction of twenty-six big cartels, as well as economic planning, through a Cabinet Planning Bureau that designed a first Five-Year Plan in 1937. More than the railways, it was the urban department store that now became the icon of daily consumerist life, and perhaps the car, too.[24]

The urge to 'modernize' Manchuria, however, remained very prominent, so much so that more roads were built there than in the mainland. "For

Manchukuo," a Japanese newspaper declared, using the Japanese name of the colonial puppet regime, "development begins with roads." During the 1930s, "several thousand idealist engineers flocked to Korea, Taiwan, Manchukuo, and China … to construct roads, canals, dams, cities, irrigation, sewage and water works, and electrical and communication networks." In 1933, Japan's aggression was condemned by the League of Nations, and the country withdrew from the league. In 1938, the Japanese government drew a plan to build a 5,490-mile highway joining Korea, China, Indo-China, and its colony, as part of a Great East Asian Highway, modeled after European freeway planning and aimed at "the construction of Greater East Asia," under Japanese leadership. Explicitly Japanese planners dreamt of a "bullet highway" (*dangan dōro*), similar to their parallel development of high-speed bullet trains (*dangan ressha*). Whereas on the Japanese islands themselves a thirty-year plan to develop a national road plan was formulated already in 1920, military spending soon prevented the network from being completed there: by 1940, less than 2 percent of the roads (and 18 percent of the nearly 9,000 km of national highways) were paved.

In Manchuria, however, 30,000 km of (largely unpaved) roads were built, "despite the scarcity of motor vehicles to use them." One can hardly think of a better example of a road network built way ahead of demand, as a simple, powerful token of 'development,' as we will observe on several occasions later in this book: by 1936, only three thousand motorcars were registered in the colony, part of a motorized vehicle fleet of only 5,300, against more than 100,000 bicycles and about 550,000 animal- and human-powered vehicles. Car density in the colony was about four times lower than in Japan. Nonetheless, construction of an expressway (*kosoku dōro*) one thousand kilometers long between Dalian and Harbin as part of the Great East Asian Highway started in 1942, to be paved with concrete for speeds up to 160 km/h. One of its leading civil engineers attended the Permanent International Association of Road Congresses (PIARC) conference in The Hague in 1938: the decision to make the Manchurian expressway as straight as possible was clearly inspired by the Italian autostradas (built since 1922 in the northern flat Po area) rather than Hitler's autobahns, which were curved to 'fit' into the German southern hilly landscape. The supervising engineer's report on the project (which was discontinued in 1944, only to be completed nearly half a century later, in 1990 during China's 'opening up') would function as "the Bible for Japan's postwar highway engineers."[25]

***

Summarizing, we conclude the diffusionist thesis, which would depict Sōseki's and Yosano's mobility as only partially modern (because it lacks a car), is misleading, and highly biased toward the West.[26] This is all the more true if one realizes that Sōseki's and Yosano's travelogues should be seen in a context of increasing Japanese interests in its neighbors' modernization. This became apparent not only in Manchuria, as we saw, but also in China proper. In 1923, as an offshoot of the Travel Department of the Shanghai Commercial and Savings Bank, the China Travel Service (Zhongguo Lüxing She—CTS) was founded, which was to become "the first and largest travel agency owned and run by Chinese in Republican China." This agency and its bank (which organized the financial support for military campaigns of Chiang Kai-shek, in China known as Chiang Chungcheng and romanized as Jiang Jieshi), was connected to Japan's East Asia Common Culture Academy (Tōa Dōbun Shoin), and together they sent out groups of senior students into the Chinese hinterland, publishing their travel accounts in an annual volume. It also published a touristic magazine, *China Traveler* (in which Zhang Henshui, the Chinese writer we will encounter later in this chapter, also published). Shoin was a hotbed of Japanese "Pan-Asianism" and had its origins in two institutions in Tokyo, one of them, the Research Institute of Sino-Japanese Trade (Nisshin Bōeki Kenkyūjo) founded by two military officers and evolved by 1890 in a true business school to train Japanese students in the Chinese language and Sino-Japanese trade, explicitly meant to "curb the advance of Western powers in Asia."

Important parts of the curriculum were field trips into China. This was the result of an idea from an intelligence officer of the Japanese army, who himself had in the 1880s opened a pharmacy as a cover in a town along the Changjiang (Long River, the lower part of which is known as Yangzi). When the first seven student groups set out to Northern (Beijing-Tianjin region) and Southern China (Guangdong and Fujian provinces) in 1907, the students were clad in a military-type of outfit inspired by European Africa explorers. Sometimes, they disguised themselves as Chinese, remodeling their samurai-style hairdo into a queue, and when they got caught by suspicious Chinese, they were instructed to declare they did not wear guns, and came in peace. The student reports, which we will revisit later in this chapter, did not celebrate the Pan-Asianism of the founders, however; instead of considering themselves part of a 'Yellow race' of Chinese and Japanese resisting Western influence together, they appeared appalled by the 'backwardness' of China, characterized the Chinese as "ignorant, indolent, violent, and extremely greedy," and often took the Nationalist side (and the side of its Western supporters) rather than the side of the 'revolutionaries.'[27] When Japan in 1937 started its undeclared "Pacific War," well ahead of the European Fascists, an orgy of aggressive mobility ensued. Westerners tend to see World War II as an Atlantic affair, but just as mobility history has to acknowledge the existence of 'Pacific automobilism,' so for most of the world's inhabitants the war was Pacific in the first place.

Urban Mobilities: The Rickshaw and the Motorization of Asian Cities

The self-appointed 'civilizing' role of Japan in Asia, directed partly against the West and partly mediating in the spread of modernity, allows for a different approach of modernization in this part of the world. If mobile modernity in the non-West should not and cannot be analyzed through the lens of automobility, then would that other nearly simultaneous invention, the bicycle, do as a substitute? Like the pedestrian, the bicyclist was another traffic participant the colonial authorities proved incapable to control. Therefore, as a privately owned and used vehicle, even if its collective, swarm-like behavior in traffic was more pronounced than that of the car, it became an "icon of the accessibly modern." In this section, we will investigate the bicycle, and especially its two- and three-wheeled derivative, the rickshaw, as a potential candidate for Asia's 'mobilization,' its modernization through mobility. In India shortly before World War I, around thirty-five thousand bicycles were imported annually, at a moment local and national governments started providing bicycles to its staff, from postal workers to vaccination squads.

The number of annually imported cycles reached a peak in 1928/1929 with 163,432; between 1910 and 1946, about 2.5 million bicycles had been shipped to India, mostly from Britain. The British brand Raleigh started a cycle factory in West Bengal. Whereas the bicycle came to India from the United Kingdom, fellow imperial power Japan threatened "to undermine the commercial dominance of colonial powers" in other Southeast Asian countries, for instance, by exporting bicycles to the Vietnamese market. There, a traffic census at the end of the 1920s on a bridge in Hanoi showed how about 15,000 pedestrians per day were joined by 141 animal-drawn carts, nearly 1,200 rickshaws (*pousse-pousses*, as they were called in Francophone colonies), 344 bicycles, 116 cars, and 79 buses. Shanghai, "more Western than Chinese" according to Japanese journalist Ryūnosuke Akutagawa who visited the city in 1921, by the end of the decade counted fifty thousand bicycles on its streets. In 1927, Ailing Soong (of the wealthy Soong family) "made a scandal-raising trip in the International Settlement," allegedly as the "first Chinese girl in the city to ride a bicycle." In Asian cities, a blossoming repair culture (including "the pavement repairman in India or Vietnam") emerged, the bottom line of what the World Bank would later call an "informal economy," fed also by a culture of bicycle theft.[28]

The Rickshaw as Urban Utilitarian Hybrid: Tokyo and Singapore

And yet, a much better candidate as iconic vehicle of modernity than the bicycle is the rickshaw, a two-wheeler with parallel wheels, based on a technological tradition (still rather poorly documented) similar to its Western counterpart with its wheels in line. The spread of the rickshaw from Japan through Southeast Asia during the latter quarter of the nineteenth century has been described, if at all, as a classic diffusion story: a package prepared in Japan and sent over sea to the British colonies and China. Often, we lack the local details about technology and its use necessary for a more balanced treatment of the local 'cultural appropriation' process, including the mysterious origins of the vehicle, which according to some was invented by an American Baptist missionary, according to others put on the market by two Japanese entrepreneurs (who incorporated Dutch and French horse-cart design influences), and according to yet others by an out-of-work samurai. The best overview of its early spread in English has been given by transport planner Peter Rimmer, who performed extensive fieldwork to compensate for the lack or inaccessibility of archives, and used London's transport system as a model to compare several urban transport cultures in Southeast Asia.[29]

Rimmer's analysis shows that at the moment Sōseki incorporated the ubiquitous rickshaws in his narratives, the success story of the rickshaw was in full flow, well before the breakthrough of the car. Contrary to Japan's Asian export markets for rickshaws, their number started declining on the domestic market around 1910, while exports peaked a decade or so later (fig. 1.1). One of the earlier, smaller export peaks was in 1907 with more than thirteen thousand, most of them to Singapore, but also, for instance, to Durban, South Africa (and two dozen to North America and forty to England). In Durban, ten rickshaws had been imported since 1892 by a "Natal sugar magnate," but by the start of the new century, there were more than two thousand in use directly ordered in Japan, and only in the 1930s, when the automobile spread among the local middle class, did the rickshaw become known as the 'poor man's taxi." There were also private rickshaws in use, in the early days both pulled and pushed, by African men. As we will see later in this chapter, rickshaws were also imported in Ghana.

In Japan, where, during the Tokugawa period (1615–1868), "all forms of wheeled transport" were "virtually banned" and only water and pedestrian transport (including the sedan chair or palanquin) existed, the coming of the rickshaw meant a true revolution. Originally used for long-range transport, the vehicle soon became the iconic urban contraption that reduced sedan chair transport drastically.[30] They were produced in a "fairly sophisticated manufacturing process" of a truly transnational character: materials came from India, Britain, Germany, China, Spain, and Japan. The vehicle received rubber tires in 1904, and pneumatics four years later. Its use in Japan was elitist (the rickshaw was "one of the most fashionable appointments for dashing young men"), but when large numbers of ex-palanquin bearers, made unemployed, turned to rickshaw pulling and especially when equally jobless ex-samurai joined them, the trade got the reputation of passenger overcharging and cheating. Pullers formed communities that easily went on strike, for instance, against the emergence of the horse-drawn omnibus: they could block or delay substitution.

Nonetheless, it was the tram, first the horse-drawn and then the electric version, together with the emergence of the bicycle, that triggered a substitution wave from 1904 onward, further enhanced by the motorized taxi and bus, which appeared in the Japanese urban transport fabric in 1912/1913. The rickshaw's fate appeared to be sealed by the emergence of the private car, even if it spread less spectacularly than in Western countries: a survey on a railway crossing in as late as 1921 in Kanazama (one of the second-tier cities with populations between 50,000 and 150,000, in contrast to the 3.3 million in Tokyo) showed nearly 6,000 pedestrians, 234 bicycles, about 750 horse-drawn vehicles, and only 5 cars. In Tokyo, too, the car for the first time outnumbered its rickshaw rival only in 1930 (of which there were still more than 5,000 in Tokyo and more than 42,500 in all of Japan). By then, the city had grown into the third largest in the world, after New York and London, yet its modest automobilism can function as another 'model' of mobility modernization. Ford (which opened an assembly plant in Yokohama in 1925) and General Motors (with an assembly plant in Osaka) dominated the market, and their products, remarkably, were advertised from a "nuts-and-bolts" perspective, emphasizing they were *keizai-teki jidōsha* (economical vehicles). Just

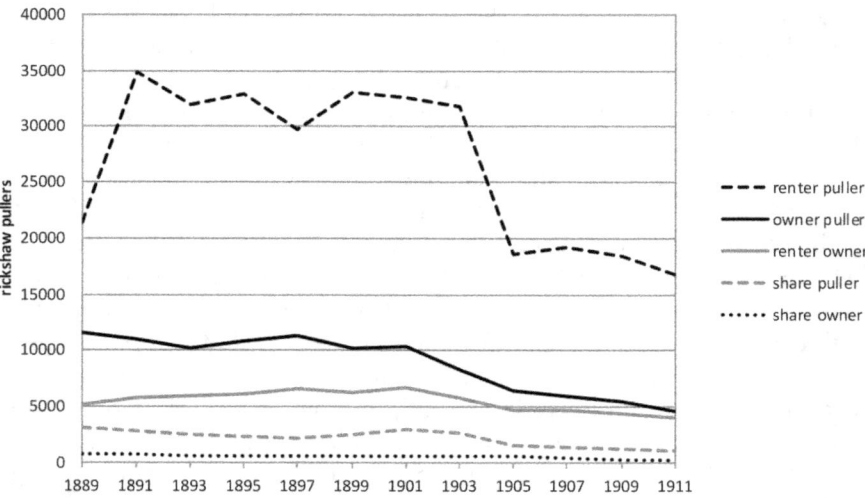

Figure 1.1. Rickshaw pullers in Tokyo. Source: Steele, "Mobility on the Move," based on Toshihiko Saito, *Jinrikisha* (Tokyo, 1979), 223. Figure created by the author.

as in the emergence phase of the rickshaw, the imperial family gave the example; hardly a hundred cars were driving around Tokyo in 1910, but the Imperial Household possessed a small fleet: two Daimlers, two Mercedes, and four Fiats, although Japanese efforts to develop a local version of a cheaper European model such as the Austin Seven (UK) and Benjamin (France) came to naught: the Datsun/Nissan brand, specially founded for this purpose, before World War II ended up making trucks.[31]

Indeed, we need much more detailed studies to verify this simple picture of substitution, especially to ascertain in which points of the user spectrum of the competing vehicles substitution really occurred, and in which points other forces were at work. There is no doubt, however, that rail-bound public transport came under attack from motorized buses (such as eleven-seat remodeled Ford trucks, acquired after the Great Kantō earthquake of 1923), both legal and illegal. This is nothing new for those familiar with the history of urban transport in the West, as we will be led to remark on several occasions in this chapter, but the man-powered, semipublic rickshaw, particularly fit to function in a capillary, fine-mazed street system (and thus not forcing a redesign of the urban fabric), made the 'modal split' in Tokyo fundamentally different from what mainstream urban transport history so far has unearthed.[32]

The term modal split seems to be conceived when Western urban planners started separating traffic streams to facilitate friction-free car flows. Therefore, in the present study, we prefer to use a more neutral term: modal configuration. This configuration was severely reshaped when the earthquake of 1923 destroyed the Japanese rickshaw factory in Tokyo, opening up new mobility options in a reconstructed Tokyo, one of the contenders being the cycle rickshaw, perhaps first developed in Singapore as a "hybrid" of the bicycle and the rickshaw, which indeed replaced the hand-pulled rickshaw by the end of World War II. In 1930, the national rickshaw fleet had shrunk to 43,000 (from 150,000 twenty years earlier), and the number of carriages had declined (from 8,600 to a bit more than 2,000), but the number of cars had exploded to 58,000 (still quite low compared to the West). The number of freight carriages exploded, too (it doubled to 309,000), while the number of bicycles had risen by far the most spectacularly: from 240,000 to 5.8 million. These vehicles could use about one million km of roads, including somewhat more than eight thousand km of national highways, most of them unpaved.[33]

***

The importance of the rickshaw in an urban setting is especially clear in the case of its best-covered application: Singapore. We owe the Singapore story to the excellent historical detective work of Australian historian James

Warren. Warren used the court archives of the colonial coroner (who was obliged to write a report on every 'mysterious' death) and oral history to reconstruct an entire *mobility community*'s culture based on an historical ethnography comprising two hundred individuals. He thus tried to answer what it means to be (and to control, as a passenger) a human vehicle motor, and what, in the parlance of the Colonial Office, drove poor migrant peasants from China to be regarded no better than "a beast of burden." The only information wanting is of a technical nature: apart from some paragraphs on the maintenance culture, and the insight that local owners tinkered with their vehicles, we only learn the vehicle's components were creatively deployed: "the wheel was used as a suicide device; its removable wicker seat as a weapon for self-defence; and its tarpaulin hood, as a shroud."[34]

Singapore was one of the destinations of a massive "coolie trade" from China, part of what migration historians nowadays see as a *longue durée* of Chinese migration history that started when Chinese traders (*huashang*) ventured abroad, well before the nineteenth century. Set up by Great Britain after the abolishment of the slave trade at the beginning of the nineteenth century, the "indentured labor" of millions of Indian and Chinese peasants (three to seven million from 1845 to 1871 alone) was organized based on five- and eight-year contracts for work in plantations and mines in British colonies and Latin America. Varying from voluntary engagement to sheer kidnapping, the recruitment was a highly modern undertaking in the sense that its logistics were well organized and its sheer explosion depended much on the emergence of a new mobility paradigm based on steam: shipping ("ocean railroads," according to Daniel Headrick) and railways, the true "tools of empire." The dependent relation often lasted much longer because of a monopoly by employers in the sale of food and shelter. Indian and Chinese coolies built the Transcontinental Railroad in the United States and the Canadian Pacific Railway in Canada and worked on the plantations in the Caribbean, and Chinese coolies formed one-third of the unskilled workers in South Africa's gold mines (organized in 1907 into "passive resistance" against the government by Gandhi). By the abolition of the system in 1917, Indian and Chinese coolies formed a worldwide part of the Indian and Chinese diasporas, which could not have been formed without modern forms of transport and communication, based on an informal recruiting system rooted in the family and the village of origin.[35]

***

In 1880, the rickshaw in Singapore, coming from Shanghai, joined (and partially substituted) the horse-drawn carriages imported from England since the 1820s. Within one year, more than a thousand plied on the streets, virtually all their pullers having migrated from the two South Chinese coastal provinces of Fujian and Guangdong. In general, it seems safe to conclude the spread of the rickshaw over the 'Pacific' world is related to the migration flows from China. Pullers were organized in secret societies, "quasi-kinship organizations with secret swearing-in ceremonies, oaths and rituals, [that] provided financial assistance to the ill and destitute, protected the monopoly of occupations of its members from all walks of life," including rickshaw pulling, and organized funerals. The secret society made rickshaw pulling a subaltern form of mobility in a very literal sense, and was one of the few elements of stability for coolies in a colonial society. Because of their competing governing power declared illegal in 1890, the "wealthy headmen of these societies were actually the central arm of the British government." When a strike, organized from above, failed, the societies, representing half of the Singapore population around the turn of the century and a stunning three-fourths by 1930, started to criminalize and be criminalized by the authorities. Like in big Western industrializing cities, where they were described as 'hooligans,' such workers at the 'underside' of the class spectrum belonged to the "dangerous classes," often criminalized. The four puller strikes of 1903, 1919, 1935, and 1938, analyzed in detail by Warren, reveal the dependence of city life on the Chinese and their rickshaws, although the strikes' disrupting effect diminished during the years. The first strike showed three-fourths of the Europeans relied on the rickshaw for their commute, "and for the rest of Singapore's population it was the only form of public transport." During one of the interwar strikes, pullers burned their own vehicles out of anger about Japanese aggression against China.[36]

Before the colonial government started restricting the number of rickshaws in 1928, about a thousand, mostly very wealthy fleet owners managed fleets of up to twenty vehicles each, on average. Some exceptional entrepreneurs kept fifty first-class rickshaws, adorned with rubber pneumatic tires, English wooden furniture, and a single seat. Second-class rickshaws were iron-tired, and together with the two-seaters, they were abolished under pressure of the Colonial Office, which used humanitarian arguments. A good rickshaw cost the equivalent of three trips to China in 1894, a third of the cost of a high-quality English bicycle in 1901, or the annual income of a rickshaw puller in 1917. In 1902, twenty thousand pullers (all men) were officially registered, most of them renting their vehicles in shifts of half a day, and only 1 percent of them owners. The rent was exceptionally high, about one-quarter of the puller's revenue, making rickshaw ownership a highly lucrative business. The pullers' nearly exclusively male culture was not the result of choice: "civil war, famine, epidemics and forced migration" formed the most important "push factors" setting in motion these men's highly mobile lives, connected reciprocally by bonds of kinship or affinity. Their clan structure divided by dialect groups was highly dynamic: by 1902, the cheap labor offered by men from Fuzhou (the capital of Fujian province in the far southeast of China) dominated Singapore rickshaw culture, after they had driven the men from the Fujian countryside and from Guangdong province out of the trade.[37]

The working conditions were grueling: pulling a rickshaw through a foot of water during floods brought triple fares in, against the danger of stepping in an open sewer. Warren dedicated a separate chapter to coroners' reports on pullers' suicides, mostly triggered by job loss. Europeans especially were appalled: "Rickshas ply day and night to the number of 20,000," a British reverend in a book on *Sunny Singapore* wrote, "drawn by an almost naked army of Chinese pullers. There is not a single man of any other nationality doing this really hard work." Several pullers had second jobs, and their involvement in traffic accidents was high: one-third of the inquests analyzed by Warren regarded traffic issues, a situation that became lethal from the moment the electric tram, car, and truck appeared on the streets:

> When motorists hit their horn they expected pullers to get out of the way quickly. In such frightening moments rickshaw coolies wondered if they were supposed to move to the right or left, and they knew what an enemy fear was if they did not react at all. If a puller froze on the spot in terror as a car bore down with its horn honking, he would be killed for not having been able to budge, before the driver would stop.[38]

The use(r) profile of the rickshaw was dominated by commuting, social visits, and going to the market (together representing 90 percent of rickshaw trips in 1900), mostly by Europeans and Asians going to their offices, children going to school (in the morning and afternoon), and sex workers and their clients at night. There were also ambulance rickshaws, and many trips were dedicated to the transport of goods. Calling rickshaw pulling unskilled labor, however, would deny the bodily versatility needed for the job. Learning to go uphill and downhill and the making of a smooth turn took weeks or months before the pain in the muscles and the chest (out of a lack of air) disappeared. Pullers were held in low regard, which "clearly had racist underpinnings."[39]

Whereas the electric tram wiped the last remnants of horse-carriage transport from the streets of Western cities (a process partially emulated in Tokyo, as we saw), the rickshaw in Singapore effectively was *stimulated* by the tram (electrified since 1905) and only started to decline in the early 1920s; the fleet size peaked in 1922, at around thirty thousand (fig. 1.2). This is not to say the local authorities did not try to regulate the business, if only to address the fear of the urban elite that the vehicles would be used for the "transport of pigs, goats, poultry, fish manure, buckets of indigo dye, hog's wash and many other abominations which need not here be detailed," as a report from the municipal Hackney Carriage and Jinrikisha Department in 1891 stated. Perhaps as a response to the motorization of the urban elite, cycle rickshaws instead of hand-pulled ones were tried as early as 1914, but they were soon sold to Jakarta; only in the mid-1930s did the cycle rickshaws reappear, and then they soon amounted to more than six thousand. Efforts to phase the rickshaws out were unsuccessful, however, even if strikes, set up by the headmen, were severely repressed, with deportation of those responsible. Only in 1947, when the hand-pulled rickshaw was forbidden, did the "trishaw" (three-wheeled bicycle rickshaw) "[experience] a phenomenal growth," most of its riders again coming from Fujian province in China. By the 1960s, when Singapore's rapid economic growth started, the cycle rickshaw remained on the streets as a touristic conveyance.[40]

***

On the other side of the urban transport spectrum, the bad electric tram service incited Chinese entrepreneurs to start seven-seater "mosquito" bus services based on remodeled Fords (there were 147 of these in 1921, and 171 plying twenty-two routes, managed by twelve registered companies in 1939), but even these did not reduce the amount of rickshaws, nor did the trolley, introduced in 1926. It was, again (like in Tokyo), the private motorcar that seriously started to challenge the reign of the rickshaw: while a traffic census on a central bridge in 1917 showed how both rivals held each other in check quantitatively, a count five years later revealed twice as many cars as rickshaws passed this bridge. The discontinuation of licensing in 1924 heralded the vehicle's decline, after nearly half a century of a

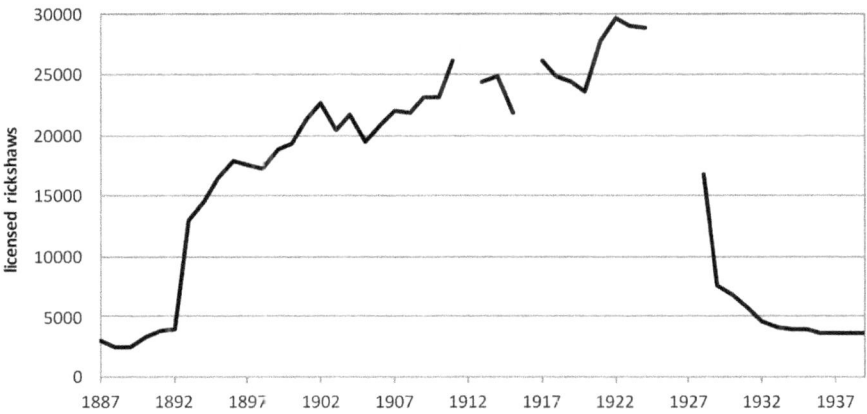

Figure 1.2 Licensed rickshaws in Singapore, 1887–1939. Source: Warren, *Rickshaw Coolie*, 61, table 6.2. Figure created by the author.

blossoming mobility culture. In other words, the decline was primarily the result not of market forces but of municipal policy. Buses pushed rickshaws out of outlying districts into the inner city, where they caused heavy congestion, the beginning of the construction of the "rickshaw problem," which got accompanied by a conflagration of narratives about the inhumane working conditions and the unmodernity of poor straining and sweating Chinese laborers on the public streets.

When such stories proliferate, we know the middle class is emerging. Unlike the very successful "coordination" of bus and rail transport in the British motherland, the Singapore authorities did not succeed in regulating the mosquito buses off the streets. And only after World War II were hand-pulled versions simply prohibited and replaced by cycle rickshaws. By then, at least four thousand motorized "pirate taxis" plied the streets of Singapore, adding to the exceptionally variegated modal configuration of this city, again proof of mobility 'layeredness,' an indication of a typical hybridization of urban traffic.[41] In sum, where the bicycle and the car functioned as the harbingers of modernization in the West, driven by urbanites who roamed the peri-urban countryside, in Asia it was a human-propelled bicycle-hybrid with its local origins and embedded in a collective, subaltern urban culture of utilitarian deployment that opened up the existing animal-drawn and pedestrian mobility culture. Next, we will investigate in how far this culture was pervaded by 'adventure,' as was the case in the Western cycle and car culture.

An Inhumane Profession? Rickshaw Pulling in Shanghai

In urban China, rickshaw cultures thrived in many places, one count from the late 1920s amounting to 150,000 pullers in fifteen ports and inland cities. In Beijing alone, their number reached a staggering 60,000, representing 20 percent of the urban population and taking half a million fares per day. In Hong Kong and Canton (current Guangzhou), 3,411 and 3,600 rickshaws, respectively, were counted in 1924 (fig. 1.3). In Shanghai, then already an important international port (producing 7 percent of China's GDP), a French businessman imported 300 as early as 1874, a number that grew precipitously to 2,500 five years later, when there were 260 carriages. At Shanghai's Willis Bridge (now Waibaidu Bridge) across Huangpu River, no less than 21,000 rickshaws were counted during a three-day traffic census in 1889, against 2,800 single-wheel carts and 1,600 carriages (and only 27 sedan chairs). A traffic survey in Shanghai's International Settlement counted 14,663 rickshaws in 1918, only 722 bicycles, no sedan chairs, but 1,863 cars. Sinologist Frank Dikötter estimated the number of Chinese rickshaws at four hundred thousand during the interwar years, one-quarter of them in Beijing. He also mentioned the adjustment to local needs and tastes, such as the lengthening of the handlebars, the lowering of the wheels, and the heightening of the passenger seat. Glass lanterns were added, and bells.[42]

Apart from the one-wheeled barrow, which was also used for passenger transport, urban Chinese traffic was also characterized by the bicycle, of which Guangzhou counted 8,000 in 1934, nearly as much as the number of handcarts and freight carts. Cycles were recycled, repainted, and equipped with new chains and tires. Like the wheelbarrows, they were especially useful because only a narrow path was necessary. Shanghai had 230,000 bicycles in 1948. The availability of this information reveals how historians are especially sensitive to a 'shock of the old,' as they appear fascinated by the traffic mix: Lu Hanchao, for instance, is amazed "how some 'outmoded' conveyances such as the sedan chair and wheelbarrow continued to ply the streets at a time when Shanghai had already become a motorized city," containing half of all the "motor vehicles" in China, with a population by the late 1920s of three million. Regarding the single-wheeled barrow: in the international concessions, this typical Chinese vehicle "became a popular form of public transportation," accommodating up to eight passengers.[43] This 'layeredness' indeed seems to be one of the characteristics of non-Western traffic, perhaps a result of the limited regulating power (or interest?) of local authorities, fed by the fact that much of this traffic represented the very livelihood of the urban poor.

The introduction of the rickshaw in China can best be studied in Shanghai, because its rickshaw culture is among the best documented, perhaps because of the attention it received from (politicized) middle-class members: the Chinese Communist movement started there, as a traditional Communist

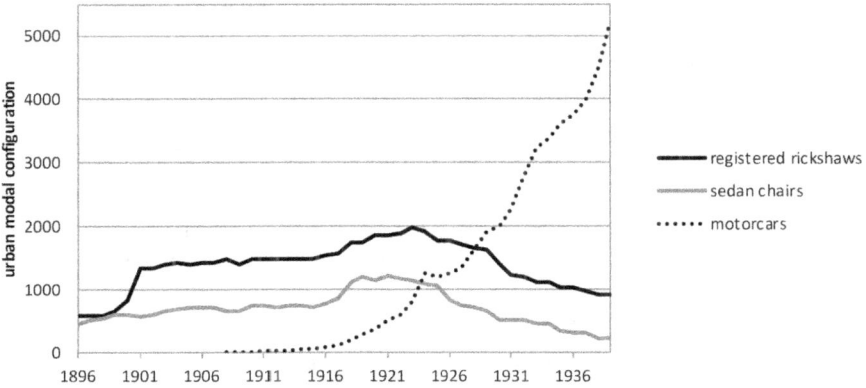

Figure 1.3. Urban modal configuration in Hong Kong, 1896–1940. Source: Ming, *Reluctant Heroes*, 119, table 7.2. Figure created by the author.

party, "with an intellectual leadership provided by students and teachers and a rank and file of urban workers—especially skilled workers." Shanghai is a special case, however, because its population consisted of a majority of rural migrants, and a wealthy minority of cosmopolitans, a "half-breed" culture, expressed in the *lilong* houses (a combination of traditional Chinese and Western architecture), the Zhongshang suit ("an amalgam of the Chinese long gown and the Western suit"), and, one is inclined to add, a similar hybrid layeredness of road traffic.[44]

Introduced in the early 1870s, the first ten rickshaw companies were all in foreign hands, the reason why the vehicle was called *dongyangche* (Eastern-overseas vehicle = Japanese vehicle). Public rickshaws were painted yellow, private ones black. By 1914, there were about 10,000 on the streets, a decade later double that amount (half of which were private), and during the 1930s, 23,000 public rickshaws were counted. More than 80,000 pullers competed to rent them, feeding 340,000 people, one-tenth of the city's population, which illustrates its importance within the urban culture. Most of the pullers came from the rural area of Subei to the north of Shanghai, "the source of Shanghai's poorest immigrants," and most of them were unmarried men, causing an uneven sex ratio in the city population. When Chinese adaptations to its originally Japanese technical structure appeared on the market after the 1880s, a gradual transfer of ownership was set in motion, until the entire fleet was in Chinese hands by the end of the 1920s, mostly belonging to the Green Gang. The sector was hierarchically structured: a cascade of middlemen owned licenses and rented rickshaws. In 1934, only one-third of the license holders owned rickshaws.

Pullers were poor, but this should be contextualized: there were also twenty thousand people picking up trash (more than five thousand of them children aged seven to fourteen). Several of the pullers had second jobs, and if they were living with a woman, income could be shared, as well as the sorrows, as the "Song of Women [Filature] Workers" ("Sichang nügong qu") expresses: "I lowered my head and thought of my husband, / Who ... must be pulling the rickshaw; / He must be dripping wet with sweat."[45] So much is clear: one can hardly talk of an adventurous (hedonistic, tongue-in-cheek) culture here, at least not for the *producers* of the rickshaw trip. For the *consumers*, this may have been different in a limited sense (for instance, through the enjoyment of high running speed), but the crucial adventurous trait of Western bicycle and car adventure is missing here: the uncertainty of the destination, and the thrill of self-propelled, self-directed roaming. About the rickshaw in private ownership (and its driving and passengering experiences), we know virtually nothing (but see Lao She's novel in the next subsection).

There is also a social argument why we cannot call rickshaw use (as driving and as passenger) adventurous: the middle class became partially opposed to it. In Shanghai, rickshaw pulling became a concern of the local middle class from the 1910s onward, but when the number of pullers suddenly rose to 100,000 in the 1930s, the rickshaw became the subject of a true cultural crisis of 'moral panic.' At that moment, there were 7,000 cars registered in Shanghai (1930, against only 19 in 1904, and 1,900 in 1919), whereas the number of tram passengers had increased tenfold over the same period (to 130 million at the end of the 1920s). Licensed rickshaws were limited (in the International Settlement to 8,000 between 1917 and 1924, 15,000 thereafter; for the entire Shanghai areas, the Ricsha Committee calculated a total of about 70,000 licenses), but the increase of the number of "tramp" rickshaws indicated private rickshaws were used to circumvent the city's regulations.

Why this crisis emerged is not fully clear, but Tim Wright's study of the "rickshaw reforms" of 1934 suggests this was because "the industry ... was widely perceived to have deteriorated into a 'racket.'" Communists and rickshaw owners both suggested the reform was inspired by local tramway and bus interests (in Nanjing, for instance, the introduction of the bus led to a halving of the pullers' income). Such reforms often were accompanied by proposals to improve the technical setup of the rickshaw. In the Shanghai "Rickshaw War" of the 1930s, Christian churches, reformist Chinese and foreigners (such as the Shanghai branch of the American Association of University Women, the Rotary Club, and the YMCA), and foreign-owned transport companies were opposed by a Rickshaw Association of owners with connections to the Shanghai underworld and the Nationalist Guomindang government; several hundreds of rickshaws were damaged during riots in this period. The report by the Ricsha Committee clearly indicated how the grip of the underworld on the industry kept rent fees high (three times higher than in Beijing and Chengdu). But Wright convincingly showed "pullers ... in Shanghai were unlikely to have been worse off than those in Beijing," their average income "on a par with the least-skilled and lowest-paid factory workers." The largest owner had a fleet of about two thousand rickshaws, the second and third largest about four hundred and three hundred, respectively, but most of the license holders had between ten and one hundred.[46]

According to Lu Hanchao, who studied the Shanghai rickshaw in detail, the subsequent surveys reflected the viewpoint of the social elite and may well have shaped the later 'humane' attitude against rickshaw pulling. The Ricsha Committee report spoke of "mostly destitute farmers" who "earn their living by toiling after the manner of draught-animals," but the reform initiative failed nonetheless; this was certainly also true for the minority report that held a plea for municipalization of the rickshaw trade.[47] Although Lu depicted a bleaker picture of the pullers' income than another study on Beijing's rickshaw culture suggested, he too rejected (based on interviews with pullers he conducted in 1989) "the idea that pulling a rickshaw was a death sentence," an idea that "sprang mainly from the everyday image of a ragged, sweat-soaked coolie pulling a corpulent, richly dressed customer," a picture that may also have been spread among students of the rickshaw because of Warren's early (and for some time only) analysis of Singapore. Lu concluded, "without a real solution for the livelihood of thousands of pullers, calls for abolishing rickshaws can only be regarded as cheap talk. In fact, … the rickshaw competed with motorized vehicles and served as one of the major means of public transportation in Shanghai for well over half a century."

With urban boulevards and streets in reasonable condition, pulling a rickshaw cost six or seven times the energy of a wheelbarrow pusher, and the former peasants often opined the 120-kilogram loads transported through a bamboo pole balancing on their shoulder when working the land was much more strenuous. What is more: a scientist working at the Sun Yat-sen University of Guangzhou had minutiously calculated that, if properly balanced, the puller's expenditure of energy was not so large: the center of gravity with an average person in the seat was exactly above the wheels, so once in motion, the only energy to be deployed was meant to overcome the rolling resistance of the pneumatic tires, on a level road. "In sum, the design of the rickshaw, the puller's limited working hours (which allowed rest and recreation), and the short-distance service in one way or another explain why many rickshaw men could work for decades without collapsing and why some aged men were still able to pull a rickshaw for a living." One of the skills pullers learned on the job was winding through dense traffic, so much so that they were often faster than cars, causing them to "laugh and joke and tease the uniformed conductors of official traffic." Indeed, the Chinese rickshaw-puller experience teaches us 'slow traffic' is a misnomer for nonmotorized flows.

Another skill the pullers had to learn was negotiating with customers, especially the many foreigners, who paid more (the basis for the stereotype of the dishonest puller), but they were heavier than Chinese "and usually asked the puller to run faster." Perhaps they were eager to experience 'adventure,' mimicking what they knew from the bicycle and car adventure back in Europe. One attribute for which rickshaw men were praised (as one Westerner wrote) was their willingness to carry customers from their front door into the rickshaw, during the typhoon season. Such foreigners related in their memoirs how after a short while they forgot about the 'inhumane' character of the rickshaw and considered it "'a grown-up's perambulator,' and almost cease[d] to think of the puller as a human being." "The most significant aspect of the story of the rickshaw," Lu concluded, "was that this simple vehicle had transformed peasants into 'petty traders' who, with their muscles as their only commodity for sale, daily involved themselves in endless marketing (soliciting customers in the streets) and bargaining (over fares with customers and over rent with owners)."⁴⁸ But adventurous, like the tripartite culture in the West? Let us investigate further, in Guangzhou, and in Beijing, where the pullers' life became the topic of a novel.

A Communist Avant-Garde? Rickshaw Culture in Beijing and Guangzhou

Contrary to Singapore, and perhaps to a certain extent to Shanghai, the capital's rickshaw culture was characterized by the presence of an outspoken Chinese middle class, whose intellectuals dominated the discourse on modernization during the republican period, the period between the ousting of the emperor in 1911 and the installation of Communism in 1949.⁴⁹ In David Strand's excellent study of its culture, the rickshaw arrived in Beijing in 1886, where its original technical structure was improved around the turn of the century into a modern vehicle adorned with ball bearings, a lighter frame, and rubber tires making a second 'pusher' at the back superfluous. This was supported by newly paved avenues. The new rickshaws were mostly used by "Beijing's middle classes, not the rich": shopkeepers, teachers, minor officials. The rickshaw culture in the capital was based on fleets of about thirty vehicles on average, managed by garages, without the middlemen, as was usual in Singapore and Shanghai, but at times as despotic as was the case in the British colony. The small scale gave the community of pullers around a garage the character of a (masculinized) family. One-quarter of the pullers were former peasants. Many others were also rural migrants (seasonally going back home to work in the fields), but much less than in cities like Shanghai, where nearly all came from the rural area north of the Yangzi river. In Beijing, most pullers were city people. They had a "relatively high standard of living" (they were "poor but not impoverished"), so much so that even some women seem to have disguised themselves as male pullers to earn their living. In the city, they came from the lower segments of the working classes, earning as much as a police officer, an unskilled artisan, a servant, or a shop clerk, but their mobile culture made them share the universe of "beggars, those who eat at soup kitchens, and all the rest of the poor who do not have enough to eat and wear." As Beijing did not have slums, the poor gradually came to live at the outskirts. They were "at least marginally literate," often spending their spare time reading a tabloid.⁵⁰

Only 3 percent of the pullers owned their vehicle. They were on the street for nine to twelve hours, pulling passengers about half that time, and if the competition was not too fierce, working every other day. A rickshaw ride cost twice as much as a streetcar's, and the average trip took about thirty to forty minutes, for two to three miles. Their mobility was considered high speed, not in the least because of the *feipao* (flying run), for which especially the Beijing rickshaw culture was well known. The run became even faster in the 1910s and 1920s, when fares got under pressure and were reduced to more than half. Some pullers were called "Yili Horse" (after Yili, a town in Xinjiang province, indicating a fast steed), or "Locomotive." An American in Beijing of the 1920s described in her memoir that pullers could hardly "resist the urge to race, to show off their strength and dexterity, and also their style of running," According to her, "they loved the sensation of control given them by turning the corners neatly and at as great a speed as they could."[51] At first sight, this 'speedy,' daredevilish behavior is similar to what we observed in the Western cycle and car culture, but the rickshaw puller also had to develop additional skills, mostly of a political nature.

The subaltern but nonetheless highly visible rickshaw culture made its participation immediately political, all the more so when middle-class reformers, influenced by the May Fourth Movement that started in 1919 against a background of expanding modern universities and colleges in the capital, began comparing them with automobiles: "We talk about democracy and humanism, about everyone being treated equally and having an equal opportunity," the journal *New China* opined. "How can we sit in a rickshaw with the puller working like an ox or a horse in the rain and the mud? Urging him to risk his life running … faster … faster … faster." The emergence of the car is important here, as we know from the West that criticism of an older technology (such as horse traction's stench) starts off in earnest once an alternative allows users to compare. In the more openly violent May Thirtieth Movement (triggered when Shanghai police killed twelve protesters in 1925), several "dirty-faced, raggedly dressed" rickshaw pullers participated under the banner of the Beijing Rickshaw Pullers Patriotic Group. When treated badly by a student, a rickshaw puller reportedly countered: "Mister, let's not have that sort of thing. We are both Chinese. How can you curse me like that? Even though I pull a rickshaw, I'm still a human being as you, a gentleman. In school, don't they teach you about equality? I haven't studied, but that is what I often hear you gentlemen discussing."[52]

However, not so much the reformers as the Communists seem to have enjoyed a welcome reception among pullers. It began with the intellectual May Fourth Movement during which the "laborers sacred" concept took hold and resulting in several writers dedicating texts to the fate of the pullers, whose constant deep inhaling of street dust caused many pullers to die of pulmonary diseases. Several poems dealt with rickshaw pulling, such as Liu Bannog's "Che Tan" and "Ni Ni song": even a young Zhou Enlai wrote a poem ("the deadening enjoy a happy life"). Rickshaw pullers were attractive for the Communist Party because of their "disorderly life," enabling them to "escape some of the customary controls that dictated life in the shops and factories," the very reason why they were considered "cunning and untrustworthy" by police and public alike. Wu Guang, sent by the Communist underground to infiltrate in the puller community in the early 1930s, describes in his memoirs how his metamorphosis took shape as he walked from his house to the puller garage: "First I took off my long, unlined blue gown and threw if over my shoulders. Then I twisted the gown and wrapped it around my waist, concealing it beneath my shirt. Then I took out cloth bands to tie up the bottoms of my trouser legs. Finally, I took a towel out and wrapped it around my head. The transformation of a student into a rickshaw man was complete!" It is Wu who recounts the "constant beatings and scoldings" the pullers received from the police.[53]

The Beijing pullers' reputation has been especially shaped by the "wild riot" against the emergence of the motorized bus and the tram, in October 1929.[54] Since the fall of the previous year, they had gathered in a pullers' union, which soon became the largest within the Federation of Trade Unions. The petition to the local authorities to restrict the deployment of buses and trams is worth mentioning, as it explicitly acknowledged the competition's higher efficiency but nonetheless rejected its service. Rickshaw pullers desired modernity without efficiency, that is, from a planner's perspective, as its speed in dense traffic was often higher than its rivals,' as we saw. The reason for this subversiveness was that their mobility was at the same time their very livelihood, which also motivated their subsequent behavior, starting with spontaneous Luddite activities, developing into controlling and policing their own ranks and in the end slipping fully out of union control. They wanted to do their "own singing," a reference to the usual "street songs that portrayed them in a pathetic light," as we can confirm referring to the song cited earlier. The streetcar company agreed to retreat from the nonutilitarian segments of the market (touristic trips were the most lucrative for the pullers), but by then it was too late, despite union officials' assurance that streetcars and buses were a "natural phenomenon" standing for "social advancement."

Now, violence, abduction of strikebreakers, and other "illegal acts" became the norm, and for a short while, the rioters controlled the city's street traffic. On 22 October, twenty-five thousand pullers, many other workers, and two thousand Buddhist monks and priests destroyed sixty of the ninety streetcars. Asked by a leftist member of the Nationalist Party after their motives, they responded, "overthrowing buses," "showing worker anger," and "not allowing workers to be bullied." No "proletarian consciousness," this observer concluded, they were "hooligans," driven by a "mad ambition to riot." The riot, the first since an army riot in 1912 and the Boxer Rebellion of 1900, ended with the execution of four union officials, the arrest of more than a thousand rioters, and the expulsion from the city of nine hundred of them.⁵⁵ It also resulted in a turn of the pullers' consciousness toward the Communist Party, although by then this party began increasingly being rooted in peasant society (while the Nationalists were more at home among the urban middle classes).⁵⁶ Rickshaw pullers, with their double urban-rural background, may have formed a crucial transitional mass basis for the Communist Party, which to my knowledge has not yet been given its full due (in English, at least).

*　*　*

In how far the Canton Uprising, carried out for the most part by Communist-led rickshaw pullers (most of them of rural origin), formed an inspiration for the Beijing riots is not recorded either (in English-language documents). In December 1927, a short-lived Guangzhou (Canton) Soviet was set up, another example of rickshaw pullers' variegated mobility, including their political mobilization. Next to Beijing, Guangzhou is the second element in our argumentation that it was not so much their poverty that triggered the pullers into revolution but rather an expectation of a better future, a desire (in Todd McGowan's words; see the introduction).⁵⁷ In Guangzhou, too, it was the May Fourth Movement that inspired intellectuals to rethink mobility. Anarchist student Liu Shifu, for instance, "argue[d] for abstention from riding rickshaws," and Hu Shi, a leader of the Chinese Literary Renaissance, drew a "line of demarcation between Eastern and Western civilizations" coinciding with "the line of demarcation between rickshaw and automobile civilizations." According to Liang Qichao, a "new citizen" (*xinmin*) was necessary, adorned with a "sense of adventure, … which Chinese subjects had not possessed in the past."⁵⁸ He may have referred to people like Meiling Soong (younger sister of the alleged first female bicycle rider in Shanghai, Ailing) who drove around dangerous Shanghai in a limousine "with only a maid for company," according to gangster Big-Eared Du, who captured the women and brought them back to Chiang Kai-shek's house. The protest against the 'inhumane' conditions of rickshaw pulling expanded to many Asian cities with large rickshaw cultures, including British Malaya and Indonesian Palembang, where Chinese inhabitants petitioned the Dutch colonial authorities to prevent pullers from emigrating from Singapore, "arguing that rickshaw pulling was degrading." Chinese students in France also protested in mid-1931 when the Paris Colonial Exhibition was scheduled to employ a hundred Chinese pullers to transport visitors. Here, as elsewhere, the classic two positions about 'human motoring' were produced, the other one being the concern that a prohibition would ruin the livelihood of the poor.⁵⁹

As elsewhere, new waves of rural migration during the Depression (in the case of Guangzhou aggravated by the Guangdong floods in 1934) coincided with the breakthrough of the car and other motorized vehicles. The Guangzhou Rickshaw Pullers' Union, with a membership of more than six thousand in 1926, demanded a limitation of the number of buses, a reduction in their route length, and a ruling to pick up passengers only at bus stops. Against a background of increasing confrontations between Communists and Chiang Kai-shek's Guomindang, the insurrection broke out in December 1927 when pullers stormed the headquarters of the Public Security Bureau, resulting in a victory of the revolutionaries. As a response, and perhaps triggered by the Ricsha Committee set up in Shanghai, Guangzhou local authorities started a reform program, driven by "high-ranking Chinese officials previously trained in the West and Japan" who wished "to turn Kwantung [Guangdong] into a model province for China's modernization" and who were led by Mayor Liu Jiwen, a graduate of London University. These reformers initiated a survey among more than five thousand pullers and proposed to found "pullers' hostels" (to be paid from a rickshaw tax), a law to enforce carrying hats while at work, the installation of tea stands for refreshments in summer, measures to regulate rickshaw rent, and a "rickshaw ownership scheme." At the same time, however, Communists were ousted from the unions, and a government-controlled union was set up in 1936, excluding from membership "opium smokers, men stripped of civic rights," and "counter-revolutionaries." By 1936, they had four thousand members, one-third of the Guangzhou puller constituency. In Guangzhou, even proposals to municipalize the rickshaw trade were heard, and 'coordination' (the regulating of street traffic to protect rail-bound public transport) was attempted under direct supervision of Chiang. The war prevented these plans from being implemented. Shortly after World War II, the Guomindang central government announced the abolition of the hand-pulled rickshaw in Chinese cities, a measure that was implemented to the full after the Communist takeover of the country in 1949.[60]

The Middle-Class Appropriation of the Rickshaw Puller: Lao She and Tâm Lang

China's rickshaw culture has been monumentalized by a realistic, "proletarian" novel written by May Fourth writer and schoolteacher Lao She (pen name of Shū Qìngchūn, 1899–1966), who had taught Chinese at the University of London from 1924 to 1929, and at his return dedicated a short story to the Beijing Streetcar Riot.[61] His *Rickshaw* (or "Camel Xiangzi," as the literal translation of the Chinese title *Luotuo Xiangzi* runs) was written in the for the May Fourth or (in a more restricted sense, without the politics) New Culture Movement typical vernacular (*baihua*) style. It was serialized in 1936 and 1937 and has since reached such an iconic status that it is indiscriminately used as a reliable representation of rickshaw culture tout court, even for the culture of as unlikely a place as Singapore. Indeed, one study of the author and his novel speaks of a "masterpiece and, perhaps the best work of its kind in modern Chinese literature." It was soon translated in English, French, German, Italian, Japanese, Czech, and Spanish.[62]

Yet, the depiction of protagonist Xiangzi's tragic life, which in an earlier American (best-selling) translation was given a happy ending, does not coincide at all with the relatively positive picture sketched in Strand's study. This happens, as we observed in our study about the Western car culture, when (middle-class) authors start depicting the culture of another class. However, started as an owner-puller, Xiangzi's experiences as a human motor as formulated by Lao She are remarkably parallel to what I elsewhere have identified as characteristic for the early car pioneers: apparently, the cyborg feeling ("There was simply no reason to separate man from rickshaw"), the anthropomorphizing of the vehicle ("It seemed to understand everything and have feelings after he had pulled if for six months"), and the feeling of 'flight' ("the rubber tires seemed to have left the ground ... blown along by a fierce wind"), connected so much to the dynamic experience of Western mobile modernity, does not need an engine to be produced, at least not in the fantasy of the middle-class Lao She, as it did in the related middle-class minds of his French and Belgian colleagues.[63]

In other words, the 'adventure machine' may be propelled by human muscle and does not necessarily have to be individually owned. It is the risky movement as such, in this case, experienced in a traffic 'swarm,' that triggers the experience of adventurousness. But the Belgian and French writers were expressing their own experiences, and those of their fellow middle-class car pioneers, whereas Lao She had to creep into the mind of his proletarian 'camel.' This makes one wonder, following up on what we said in the introduction about the problem of representing 'subaltern mobility,' certainly in a novel that uses the perspective of the 'omniscient narrator,' who at closer look conveys the perspective of the middle class. In Lao She's vision, there is also poetry in *cars*: during one of his rare taxi trips, Xiangzi marvels at "those little brushlike things hanging down in front of the driver outside [early windshield wipers pivoted around their axles mounted *above* the windshield] that move[s] back and forth by themselves to clean the glass." But the 'human motor' invites the most admiration. After more than seven hundred pages of Western autopoetic literature in my previous study, it would not bother the staunch reader too much, I hope, to read extensively how Lao She described the mobility of this human motor:

> He knew his way of running really looked good. The way a rickshaw man ran was proof of his ability and qualifications. That splayfooted fellow, flapping his feet down onto the ground like a pair of rush leaf fans, is undoubtedly a

beginner fresh from the village. That man with his head sunk way down and his feet scraping the ground, who puts on a show of running but isn't moving much faster than he walks, is one of the fellows over fifty ... [Xiangzi] certainly never chose to conduct himself in any of these ways. His legs were long, his stride was long, his torso was firm. There was scarcely a sound when he set out. His stride seemed to expand and contract. The rickshaw shafts did not wobble, which made the passenger feel secure and comfortable. Tell him to stop and no matter how fast he was going at the time, he'd be standing still in two more light steps. His strength seemed to permeate every part of the rickshaw. He ran with his back bent forward, his hands gripping the shafts lightly; he was energetic, smooth in his motions, precise.[64]

Although the novel does not try to reveal the protagonist's view of the world, the narrator, and Lao She by extension, was a careful observer indeed. But what makes Lao She's novel special, from our mobility point of view, is the tone of the despondency and tragedy, which is clearly not the protagonist's but rather a comment by the author. No irony here, as in Lu Xun's life of Ah-Q, but outright morality, of the author *against* his 'hero.' Despite Lao She's description of an athletic puller (he was not the first to praise the shape of the rickshawman's body),[65] Xiangzi's life went from bad to worse, until he lost his rickshaw, his wife, and his child, and ended a traitor in the revolutionary turmoils of his time. The novel describes how the protagonist's morality is undermined by his lust for money and his individualism. The novel is about the bankruptcy of this individualism, if ever that existed in interbellum Beijing. In fact, the novel is less about an individual who becomes dishonest (as some analysts want to have it) and more an utterly pessimistic narrative, situated in an endlessly senseless world of poverty, a narrative on a tragic hero who starts ambitiously and ends without any hope, losing from day to day, in utter loneliness and selfishness. In short, he is one of the 'mob,' the mobile collective often described as 'subaltern.' Rarely has a novelist discarded his hero so disdainfully as a "degenerate, selfish, unlucky, offspring of society's diseased womb, a ghost caught in Individualism's blind alley," even if one study (by Ranhir Vohra) vehemently tries to rescue the novel as basically solidary with the puller culture. But even Vohra cannot deny the narrator's sympathy is with the middle-class Mr. Ts'ao in the novel: "a scholar and yet reasonable in everything."[66]

This solidarity could only be constructed, because author and Communist commentators shared (and still share) the basic view of the rickshaw pullers' life as basically inhumane. Nor does the novel, despite Vohra's praise of Lao She's feminism, give a flattering picture of women, who cheat men into marriage (by simulating pregnancy) and generally are not trustworthy, if not simply monsters (and there is no irony here). Rarely, too, does a case study of a novel's content so blatantly show the cleft between fictional representation and reality as constructed on the basis of other sources, such as I just did through the use of secondary literature based on municipal reports and coroner's affidavits. It also shows there *is* a difference between fictional and nonfictional representation (see also the introduction). After the Communist Revolution, Lao She's novel was criticized and the author "possibly beaten up, definitely humiliated" by the Red Guards, his paintings, sculptures, and manuscripts destroyed in 1966. He drowned himself in a nearby canal, and his books were taken from the Chinese market. He was posthumously rehabilitated by the Communist Party in 1979, followed by a movie three years later.[67]

***

A similar middle-class perspective on the puller profession was published at about the same time by Vietnamese journalist Tâm Lang, whose "Tôi kéo xe" (I pulled a rickshaw) appeared in 1932 in a Hanoi newspaper as an early example of investigative journalism. "I no longer feel like a human being," Tâm Lang wrote after his first days as a puller amid the busy car traffic, "but like a steam engine." Construed as a frame tale containing the life story of puller Tu', Tâm Lang, like Lao She, admires the multiple skills needed to be a good puller: "When you pick up the shafts, you take a look at the way the passenger is sitting and work out the balance before you start running … Don't run on a full stomach, and make sure your belt is tight; if it's not, you'll have to support your midriff, and if you eat too well, you'll throw up." Another crucial skill is to get as much money as possible out of the customer. Like Lao She, Tâm Lang sees the Vietnamese rickshaw puller being corrupted by money, and like Lao She, he tells the rickshaw story as a story of poverty, ending in a plea to gradually abandon the profession and to introduce the cycle rickshaw, at a moment there were fifteen hundred (two-wheeled) rickshaws in the city.[68]

Yet, the Vietnamese culture of the *xe-kéo* (Vietnamese) or *pousse-pousse* (French), "a hybrid between a sedan chair and Western-style wheels," and "the most popular form of transportation in Hà Nôi and Sài Gòn from the 1910s through the mid-1930s," was unique because of its penetration by French colonial capital, which managed to acquire a monopoly, at least in Hanoi, so much so that it also could keep high the renting fees for the "coolies" (as the pullers were called by the colonizers). It seems the close collaboration between municipal authorities (who in Hanoi limited the fleet size, first to fifteen hundred, then to three thousand, then to less) and French capitalists made the rickshaw trade very lucrative in a mutual sense, as rickshaw taxes represented no less than 15 percent of some cities' municipal budgets. Although the Vietnamese case could need some further scrutiny beyond the current analysis, which is mainly fed by a municipal perspective (and the perspective of its reports and committee minutes), its uniqueness is further supported by some evidence of technical innovations to the rickshaw itself, most particularly a drastic weight reduction because of the application of aluminum by French manufacturers.

Vietnam also had two rickshaw qualities, one luxury (with rubber tires) and one common (with iron tires). While its popularity started through the use by a European colonial clientele, the constant efforts of French interests to acquire a monopoly against an increasing presence of Chinese rickshaw firms make the Vietnamese rickshaw history an interesting case of competition between two 'foreign' influences. Representing a staggering 10 percent of the population in Hanoi (despite the fact that the French colonial authorities were probably the only ones in Asia who managed to 'regulate' the trade in terms of numbers), the history of Vietnamese rickshaw pullers confirms the general picture that the rickshaw remained basically a hardly controllable contraption, their pullers largely migrants from rural areas (who in Vietnam often ran sixty km per day and were denied unionization), which may partly explain commentaries (by Hanoi's mayor) on the pullers as "an immoral criminal group that included recruiters for shade establishments of debauchery, brothels and gambling dens, as well as thieves and members of secret societies." Perhaps this combination of condescendence and exploitation explains the extremely short 'longevity' of the puller who "lasted three years at the most" and sometimes was so weak that customers were thrown to the ground from a rickshaw out of balance.

So much for history's irony: the true inhumane conditions of puller culture were to be found in a place dominated by Western capitalists. This is all the more remarkable as some Vietnamese pullers made extremely long trips, as they were integrated in a modal cocktail as a tourist attraction: "five hours by car, two hours by rickshaw, and five hours by buffalo-pulled cart." Called "man-horse" (*người ngựa*), the condition of the pullers "under the tropical climate of Cochinchina" was apparently so appalling that a chief editor of a Catholic newspaper started a campaign against this "new form of slavery." But only some French students vowed not to use the rickshaw, and a competing newspaper found "rickshaw pulling was no more problematic than many other types of work, including journalism." Patronage of the Vietnamese rickshaw remains unclear, however: when a municipal councillor in 1920 objected to limiting the number of rickshaws by pointing out it was "a proletariat's means of transportation," the mayor replied that "bicycles were used by even poorer people." The special conditions of the authoritarian, but meticulous colonial rule also managed to regulate the "incredible disorder" of urban traffic during the 1920s and beyond, through efforts to separate the traffic in three flows of different speed, a measure that was explicitly justified by a reference to the American "Eno system," which had meanwhile gained some popularity back in the Parisian metropole and was, according to the regulators, "used in all the modern cities."

But the municipality's control appeared elusive in the end: when it tried to decrease the fleet size, private persons started buying their own rickshaws. Indeed, the rickshaw remained, until the end of the interwar years, "the most convenient and affordable means of transport used by the great majority of the French and Annamite [Vietnamese] population," an observation that was confirmed when a pullers' strike in 1926 "affect[ed] everything in the city." By the end of the 1920s, more rickshaws were registered in Hanoi than cars and motorcycles combined (1,500 vs. 1,270), against 7,264 bicycles, a number that had more than doubled by 1935. In fact, the number of rickshaws was larger than the officially registered fleet, because when Hanoi's mayor in 1935 announced a plan to reduce the number of public rickshaws by 20 percent (to 1,355) in ten years, the number of privately owned rickshaws increased from 1,580 to 3,250 by 1939. The strict regulation of the Vietnamese rickshaw trade was not a capitalist privilege, however: when the Popular Front came to power in 1936, it "sought to reform the condition of the rickshaw pullers by applying rigorous regulations."[69]

***

Lao She's novel allows us a glance at Beijing's traffic, especially the rickshaw pullers' rivalry with the car and the obsession with unhampered flow as soon as the car appears: "All the cops cared about was keeping the road open for motor cars. Their sole fear was that the cars wouldn't go fast enough and wouldn't bring along enough dust. [Xiangzi] was no cop. Why should he let the cars race by?" Conversely, "chauffeurs felt it would diminish their prestige if they were to have anything to do with rickshaw pullers." Congestion lurks around the corner, in a traffic situation replete with variety and 'chaotic' meandering, including pigeons in the sky: "The rickshaws all had their tops down and their brasswork shone with a yellow gleam. Camels moved slowly and stolidly along the sides of the streets while automobiles and trolley cars hurried down the middle. Pigeons flew in the sky and pedestrians and horses passed by below." Even in 1944, when Lao She was looking back on his career as a writer, his metaphors were accordingly: "The twenty years have not been easy. They were just like twenty years of sedan-chair carrying or rickshaw pulling."[70]

Lao She depicts Xiangzi's mobility as part of the urban human fabric, especially when he is employed by a private citizen: the novel lists the task of a puller, which go way beyond the provision of transport and resembled the servant-like status of Western, pre-automobile carriage drivers: Xiangzi had to shop, take the children to school, bring his employer to his office, bring his junior wife to the market and to friends, collect the children for lunch and bring them back again, haul water (not the drinking water, which was delivered, but the washing water), sweep the courtyard and the rooms, fetch the master's guests, keeping "running in circles until midnight when he finally found a moment to breathe." This life should not be glorified, Lao She suggests. Poets may chant about rainbows, "but poor people suffer from hunger when the wage earners are sick … But the truth is that the rain is not evenhanded at all because it falls on an inequitable world." Xiangzi's conclusion is clear: "The rickshaw pulling was a dead end street! No matter how hard you work or how ambitious you are, you must not start a family, you must not get sick, and you must not make a single mistake … Being good wouldn't work and being bad wouldn't work either. There was only death ahead on this road … "[71]

To summarize, rickshaw pulling was much more than a profession; it was a way of life, an existential condition, of subalternity. Mobility in this condition was everywhere: in the movement of the puller's body; in the 'chaotic,' hardly controllable network of messages, freight, passengers, rickshaw stands, garages, lodgings, food stands, and brothels; in the trajectory of the rickshaw's diffusion through the Southeast Asian trade network; and in the dynamics of the rickshawmen's migratory movements. It was a collective, communal culture, even including the owners and bosses. The puller's labor was embedded in a culture of domestic servants. As such, it formed a bridge between the private and the public, the individual and the collective. It was also highly political, as it was a livelihood of last resort, and as such subversive, a countermobility against the grain of mainstream modernization and at the same time highly constitutive of the latter. It was modernity not based on individual property by the many: the special fleet structure based on daily rent made fleet owners rich and powerful, and made the pullers and their families hope for social mobility through physical mobility—hope to own your own rickshaw.

***

How, then, did the car emerge in this urban fabric of mobility? At first, rickshaw culture was hardly affected by the car, as the first cars were used by the very elite who did not frequent the rickshaw. This elite was aristocratic, not bourgeois, which may partially explain the very modest spread of the car in early twentieth-century Chinese society.[72] Other reasons were the instable political situation, also in the cities (which, in contrast, stimulated rickshaw culture as a lifesaving culture), as well as the problem most non-Western countries struggled with compared to the industrialized countries in the West: the lack of a middle class. Unsurprisingly, then, early cars had a high conspicuous consumption value, painted in bright colors rather than in black or gray and called by peasants "the foreign 'oceanic' house walking" (*yáng fángzi zǒulù*), the "oceanic" to be understood as a reversal of Western 'orientalism.' Perhaps this characteristic, emphasized in the introduction as possibly constitutive of the car culture beyond the West, explains the enigmatic photograph that pops up now and then in relation to the earliest car culture in urban China: the car is on fire, Chinese citizen with queues walking by.

Banker James Lee was the first Shanghainese who owned a car (a French De Dion Bouton) in 1909, the first of a string of other makes, including an electric one. But most of the earliest cars were official vehicles, or taxis, also used for pleasurable purposes: going for a ride was called "chasing the wind" (*doufeng*). The first cars in China (eight hundred by 2013 in Shanghai but only six in Beijing [where motorization started after World War I, with fifteen hundred cars in 1922] and a dozen in Tianjin in 1911), driven by the elite, "from warlords to government officials," were clearly dominated by Ford, imported as "completely knocked-down" cars from an assembly plant in Japan; a Ford plant in China was planned, but the Japanese invasion prevented its realization. Cars bought by the elite (such as the "Packard belonging to the Chiang family in Beijing") were "never large enough to hold the entire family." As late as 1929, Shanghai counted only a hundred motorized cabs. The *Bulletin de l'AIPCR* in 1926 gave for China 11,200 passenger cars, 480 buses, and 2,000 trucks; in 1931, it mentioned 35,489 "motor vehicles" (*véhicules automobiles*).[73]

In Vietnam, "the relatively lower costs of the colony permitted Europeans who might otherwise ride trains at home to own cars and drive them poorly at the expense of 'our brothers of Europe and Asia.' Likewise, those Europeans who could only afford small cars in Europe had large, chauffeur-driven cars in the colony." David Del Testa, who read "a hundred or so colonial-era novels, short stories, plays, and poems by Vietnamese authors," concluded trains are used "as a background on which to describe collective syndromes or tensions while [their authors] used automobiles as a site to discuss more individual struggles or problems." The train stands for a "microcosm" of colonialism, whereas the car separates people and shows their differences through commodity ownership. His analyses confirm my earlier work on European automobilism: "automobiles appear to serve as sites particularly of symbolic, physical, and sexual violence." In his novel *The Tempest* (*Giông Tô*, 1936), to give only one example, Vũ Trong Phung describes "the rape of a peasant woman on the backseat of a wealthy man's car while his driver and aide look on and snigger." When, as another expression of automotive violence (much less acknowledged by mobility historians), road accidents started increasing in the late 1920s, a recent analysis by Linh Vu of a hundred reports from three Vietnamese periodicals around

1930 reveals a systemic discourse of 'blaming the victim': "To be fair," one report read, "the injuries were not serious at all, but the old woman was old and feeble, and it must have been due to fright that she died in the hospital at the end of that day."[74]

Stéphanie Ponsavady's recent study of the early history of the car in Indochina (the protectorates of Cambodia, Laos, Annam, and Tonkin [now central and north Vietnam], Cochinchina [directly ruled southern Vietnam] and a leased Guangzhouwan on the southern coast of China) finds Cotten Seiler's thesis of the role of the American car as a self-governing device applicable to the Asian colonial setting: the car "helped to maintain beliefs in the colonial empire and the French republic" and at the same time helped "recapture a sense of lost superiority in the wake of the military defeat" against Germany in the 1870s. Although I recognize the importance of synchronicity with the West in the mobility realm, this Foucaultian effect must have been limited to the minority of colonists, despite their evocation of France's Roman imperial heritage. Nevertheless, colonial automobilism proliferated, because the French constructed (according to a colonial officer) a "magnificent road network of 35,000 kilometers and a fleet of 26,000 automobiles" in 1934, "the finest system of roads in the Far-East," built mostly by prisoners and designed by "the quintessential road-builder who succeed[ed] the explorer." The French colonists decided to improve the existing imperial road networks of the Lao and Khmer kingdoms, which did not have a central hub but "radiate[d] from different centers." Their first "systematized plan for road development" dates from 1897. Colonial Road 1 was "nicknamed the 'Mandarin Road' after the pre-colonial route that mandarins took between Hanoi and Saigon."

The first cars arrived in Saigon in 1902, a fleet of sixty-eight vehicles; three years later, Hanoi counted a dozen on its streets, all owned by Europeans. The cars were used for so-called *tours d'inspection*, pleasurable trips like the earlier ones undertaken in carriages, but now farther away; later, the car use profile was extended to sightseeing tours and picnics, indeed, all a part of what we have observed as the core of the car adventure in Europe: the 'adventure machine' was simply exported to the colonies, where French colonists and indigenous elites indulged in its thrills. Of the eight thousand cars in Indochina in 1931, 60 percent were owned by Europeans and one-quarter by indigenous inhabitants. Especially the French colonists were adventure-prone: in 1940, the car density in Indochina among Europeans was five times higher than in the metropole. Ponsavady described several adventurous long-distance journeys, from the commercial *Croisière Jaune* from Beirut to Saigon in 1932 sponsored by Citroën, through the Paris to Saigon trip by the Boy Scout Guy de Larigaudie in 1937. After 1914, and like in Manchuria, the French rulers invited artists to visit the colonies, offering them free transport, thus enabling the resulting travelogues being used as "colonial propaganda," in which the car played a crucial role, often driven by Vietnamese drivers. In the south, the 6,000 km of roads were called *l'écrasodrome*, because of its notorious unsafety.[75]

***

Adventure, so it seems, was a privilege of colonists and local elites. We may expect, if native-speaking scholars start reading the magazines of the local car and touring clubs, similar adventurous stories to emerge, as we saw in our previous study. Ponsavady's Vietnam study may serve as support for this suggestion: there does not seem to be much of a time lag here. In Singapore, the first car appeared in 1896, and, like in Europe, the government began regulating motor traffic quite early, in 1907, a reflection of the close relationship and personal overlap between the motoring and administrative elites. By 1920, there were around thirty-five hundred cars in the colony. Amid the Chinese-owned mosquito buses and commercial vans, and the fifty-six municipal motorbuses, the car expressed status and "racial divide": by 1939, a Japanese journalist observed how "all of the British managers and most of the younger assistants owned motor-cars driven by Malai chauffeurs," but already in 1912 a colonial guide of the Malay Peninsula noted "rich Chinamen outvie the heads of the European mercantile houses in ostentatious display … Everyone appears to own a car in Singapore—be they European, Eurasian, Chinese, Indian, Malay or Javanese." So, apart from adventure, we witness status appeal (as discussed in the introduction). An American manager in Singapore observed in 1939, that he "could live a simple life" in Akron, Ohio, but here "we must have six servants and a new motor-car every year." Rivalry between local elites made the wealthy Chinese "outshine the Europeans 'in ostentatious display.'"[76]

The spread of the car over the globe was remarkably fast, even if it was only a tiny trickle compared with the West: the first car in Java appeared in 1894, in Bangkok three years later, in North Sumatra in 1902, and in Rangoon in 1905. Forty years later, on the eve of World War II, Southeast Asia counted one hundred thousand passenger cars and half as many commercial vehicles.[77] Like in the West, cars were purchased not so much for intracity use but rather for peri-urban and intercity use, thus jeopardizing the monopoly of the railroads. It is this competition between rail and road, known in the West as 'coordination crisis,' that we will investigate in detail during the remainder of this chapter. We will do so in several case studies, starting with China, India and other Asian countries, Africa, and Latin America. The primary question is about timing: if these cases confirm the fundamental synchronicity of this crisis, as hypothesized in our previous study, then we have a powerful counterargument against the stagist, diffusionist thesis.

Between Long March and Long Haul: Rail and Road Network Building in China

Like in Japan, mobility modernization in China started, for everyone to see, with the railways. Businessmen in Shanghai took the initiative in 1876, before any permission from the national government had been granted, whereupon the governor of the region bought out the foreign capitalists and shipped the equipment to Taiwan.[78] But from shortly after the turn of the century, well before the revolution of 1911, national railroad network building started at high speed (fig. 1.4).

Nation Building and Development: Sun Yat-sen's Rails and Roads

The upbeat to this explosion was the "scramble" for railway concessions to France (1895), Germany (1896), and Russia (1898). A decade later, the Qing court's decision to nationalize the railways (and seek "loans from foreign banking consortiums") may well have been one of the triggers of the 1911 revolution, which broke out in Wuchang and spread within weeks through the provinces of Hunan, Hubei, and Sichuan. One player in the turmoils was the Railway Protection Movement, which opposed nationalization. When Sun Yat-sen (known in China as Sun Zhongshan) became president of the new republic, he set out to "make capitalism create socialism in China" by trying to attract foreign capital to realize what he saw as a "new law in Railway Economics which hitherto had not been discovered by railwaymen and financiers." His discovery of railway's promise of uniting the country through the massive construction of national (railway) infrastructure would more than half a century later be mimicked by Deng Xiaoping

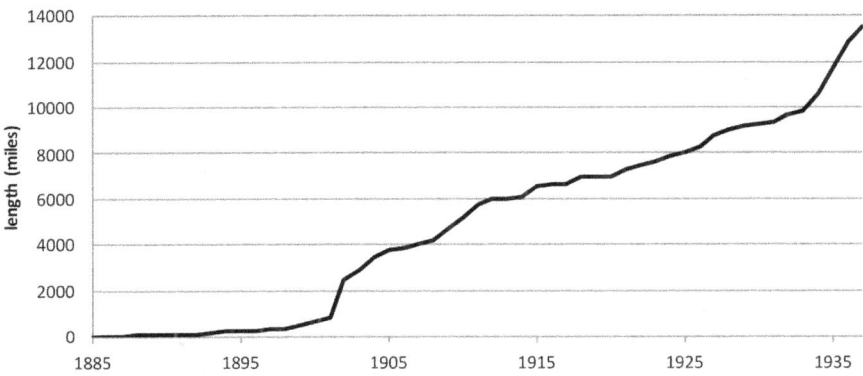

Figure 1.4. Railway network length in China (without Taiwan). Source: Huenemann, *Dragon and the Iron Horse*, 76–77, table 3. Figure created by the author.

and would become one of the pillars of 'state developmentalism.' It is indeed truly remarkable to observe how this medical doctor, nominated National Railway Supervisor of the new republican government before his rise to presidency, designed a national railway network of more than 200,000 km, inspired, among others, by a visit in 1913 to several Japanese large cities and, according to technical adviser to the Nationalist government (in 1930) Lieutenant Colonel Kenneth Cantlie, by "a concept of China developed to the population density of Europe," the three ports to be built "capable of equalling New York in the future."

Sun's house in Shanghai, meanwhile refurbished as a museum, still shows his impressive maps of China crisscrossed by trunk lines, to be realized in ten years. However, not more than 8,000 km appeared to be constructed by the time of his death in 1925, and according to a financial adviser to the Chinese government whom we will meet soon, the immediate prewar decade added another 47 percent (3,700 km). Although the network remained small in comparison to other modernizing nations in Asia (one source gives only 2 miles of railway track per 100,000 population, versus 11 for Japan, 28 for Russia, between 50 and 65 for France, Germany and the United Kingdom, 261 for the United States and 404 for Australia), the pace of its growth after Sun's death was nonetheless remarkable (undertaken by Sun's son, Sun Fo, Communication Minister of the Nationalist government), given the chaos the warlords created during the remainder of the interbellum period. Indeed, one of the arguments against railroad construction was the fear for rebellion, illustrated, for instance, by "displaced transport coolies [who] joined in the increasing banditry around Canton [current Guangzhou]." Ralph Huenemann, who did a Fogel type of calculation on Chinese railroads, concluded China did benefit economically from its "foreign-built railways," for instance, in the order of half a percent of GDP in 1933. By 1940, a direct railway link was completed between Beijing all the way to Guangzhou.[79]

What is less well known, however, is that Sun also envisioned constructing a network of "one million miles of road built in a very short time as if by a magic wand." He was fully aware of the 'layeredness' of his programs: "China has to begin," he wrote in his treatise on *The International Development of China*, "the two stages of industrial evolution at once." Sun's modernization projects (other promises included the taming of the Yangzi, the damming of the Three Gorges, and the manufacturing of cars so cheap that "everyone who wishes it, may have one") got massive support from the literary May Fourth Movement that exploded on the scene when the Versailles Peace Conference in 1919 proposed to give the German bases and rights in Shandong province to Japan. Dockers and rickshaw pullers were among the first to initiate anti-Japanese demonstrations and riots. In Hangzhou, rickshawmen refused to transport Japanese, and rickshaw pullers, seamen, and street porters started violent protests in Guangzhou.[80] Sun seems to have written to Henry Ford, who was known as an "amateur sinophile." In Ford's spirit, he formulated China's modernization path: the country, he wrote, "in order to catch up with modern civilization, must move." And for this, "the motor car … is a necessity." Roadbuilding was a political project: after Sun's death, much of it "was concentrated in areas where the army was fighting the Communists."

Such developments question the easy thesis that Chinese modernization equals industrialization.[81] The fascination among Chinese intellectuals for the Enlightenment values excluded in its radicalism traditional Confucian values: they were first mobilized through Japan (where at least 20,000 Chinese youths were studying in 1905) and then from the West, either directly (1,800 Chinese students in the United States in 1924; in 1931, 4,500 to 6,000 "American returned students in China" were estimated, technical students among them being the "most successful") or indirectly, through the many American missionaries and mission schools in China after the "European War" of 1914–1918. This is especially clear in the case of literature: Chinese intellectuals joined the protest movement and set up a blossoming "publishing infrastructure for a new literature," enabling the "avant-garde centers of Beijing and Shanghai" to reach their peers in smaller towns and the countryside. Most of them would soon form the core of the Communist Party, established in 1921. In their texts, these literati aimed at "exposing the evils of society or propagating the various isms that they exposed," pleading in favor of an unlimited Westernization, "based on the European model." This example was followed, amid alternative solutions proposed (such as one decentering Europe), by Guomindang and the Communist Party alike. China, in this vision, was a "nation of moderation," contrasted with Europe as a "nation of extremes."[82]

The Guomindang years in China, however, provide enough material to seriously question this self-definition of moderation. Hsieh Ping-Ying's *Autobiography of a Chinese Girl*, covering the years around what she calls "the great Revolution of 1926," shows how the May Fourth Movement had decisive impact on the Chinese youth, setting in motion fierce struggles within the family. Born into the family of a classical scholar in a southern small town she manages to "convince" (through the threat of suicide) her dictatorial mother (who forces her to bind her feet) to send her to school. Apart from the European classics (such as Goethe's *Das Leiden des jungen Werthers*), she confesses she "also liked to read stories of adventure and detective novels." By then, radical teachers tell their pupils that bound feet are part of the 'old system,' and she manages to have her feet unbound. She publishes her first short story when she visits a general who just had bought a thirteen-year-old "slave girl." She takes part in demonstrations ("Down with Imperialism") and joins the army to avoid an arranged marriage. At the military school, she joins a group of girl propagandists, who nearly all had fled "their families, by whom they were suppressed."

They take part in the Northern Expedition against the warlords, but when the tensions between the Communists and the followers of Chiang Kai-shek increase, the former decide to demobilize and Hsieh must go back home, where she continues her struggle against her family, from which she in the end escapes. "I wanted to be independent," she writes, and she starts a "wandering life. Like a fallen leaf in autumn wind, I would stay wherever I drifted to." Here is a remarkable element of synchronicity: whereas Hsieh's desires and mobile practices are (formulated) as adventurous as those of the European modernizing car pioneers, the technology (the car, the bicycle) is lacking. As much as she hates the "old system," she hates her mother. Mobility in Hsieh's life is mostly on foot, but for lengthy trip of ninety *li* (about thirty miles) a sedan chair is used. One such trip (a pilgrimage to a sacred mountain, five hundred *li* away) even takes five days; at the end of the trip, "all my bones ached." Her teacher uses a privately owned rickshaw to move from school to school within the city, and when Hsieh leaves for Shanghai, she uses river steamboats. Arriving in Shanghai, "on the bank of the Woo Sung River were motor-cars, tramcars, carriages and buses moving very busily before a background of high chimneys and factories and lofty buildings."[83]

Historians in East and West agree modernization, which accelerated during the "Nanjing decade" (1928–1937), when Chiang Kai-shek's government was located at the new capital of Nanking (current Nanjing), largely failed. Slowly, however, it began to dawn among the Chinese elite that "what some of the most brilliant minds in the modern West [such as Hegel] assumed to be self-evidently true had turned out to be parochial, a form of local knowledge" that within a couple decades would have "lost much of its universal appeal. In both the Western and the non-Western worlds, the projected transition from tradition to modernity never occurred. As a norm, traditions continue in modernity," the very basis of what we have called layeredness. Nonetheless, after the initial 'explosion' at the turn of the century, the curve of the railway network expansion becomes less steep until well into the 1930s. Nonetheless, this 'decade' saw a new national currency emerge, income tax collected, joint ventures formed with German firms for the production of trucks and aircraft, airlines established with the help of German and American companies, and the Academia Sinica University founded, as well as a "simplified textual language" designed, "restricted to 800 characters," meant as "an aid to literacy."[84]

The 'moderation' of the Chinese nation collapsed fully in 1934, when eighty-six thousand men (and thirty-five women) started their one-year

Long March of six thousand miles, the "migration of a nation" of which less than half survived, including Mao Zedong and Zhou Enlai. This (soon to become iconic) enterprise had its roots in the defeat of the urban workers movements in Shanghai, Guangzhou, and Wuhan in 1927, the shift to a peasant struggle emanating from the Soviets of Jiangxi province (1927–1934) and the "military encirclement based on coordinated road systems and blockhouses [micro-forts]" by Chiang in 1934. The withdrawal from Jiangxi managed by Zhou Enlai, the eighty thousand men followed "a round-the-clock policy of four hours' marching and four hours' rest [over] atrocious or nonexistent roads of the Guanxi–Hunan border region." They carried their supplies (including the parts of a printing press, machines for making arms and ammunition and "supplies of silver bullion") on their backs and on the backs of hundreds of horses confiscated from warlords and captured from Nationalist General Chiang's army, the latter attacking the Communists using Italian bomber planes. Meanwhile, as we saw, the Japanese had occupied Manchuria (1931) and had attacked Shanghai (1932), accompanied by "assassinations and betrayals, secret arrests, and executions; and the mass graves dug up on the information of defectors."[85]

***

Lately, the dichotomy of Chinese 'Fascism' versus "Communism" during the 1920s and 1930s has been questioned by historians, partly as a results of biographies of some warlords. One of them, on the "Model Governor" Yan Xishan of the conservative-agrarian province of Shanxi, west of Beijing, an anti-modern modernist who ran his geographically isolated and impoverished province as a "police state," may function as example. Without a classical Chinese education, Yan, just like Chiang Kai-shek drilled in Japan, where he learned to appreciate the dominant role of the army, and, like Chiang, considering his realm as his family and its citizens as his children, both of which needed to be 'developed' and 'uplifted,' he made his soldiers help the peasants and build roads. Impressed by the Soviets' 'development,' he constructed factories, bought aircraft, tried to eradicate banditry and abandon queue wearing and foot binding, initiated campaigns against female illiteracy and "homosexuality and prostitution," all this ideologically underpinned by an amazing, ideologically multilayered eclecticism of (in his own words) "militarism, nationalism, anarchism, democracy, capitalism, communism, individualism, imperialism, universalism, paternalism, and utopianism." In his booklets, distributed millionfold among the population, he fantasized about a classless society of a population that had to learn to "repress their desires," but, in constant fear of a mass uprising, he was as ruthless and cruel as his warlord colleagues, whose politics have been characterized as "Confucian authoritarianism" or, in Chiang's case, even

"Confucian Fascism." Yan considered representative democracy disorderly and anarchistic, and his regime was as corrupt and nepotistic as Chiang's: Yan's son was never punished for the accidents he caused with his cars.[86]

With assistance from the American Red Cross and missionary organizations, Yan Xishan built one thousand km of roads in the 1920s in a province that knew only mule trails, but lack of maintenance made these roads so dangerous that "generally merchants preferred to employ traditional forms of transportation like camels and rickshaws." Bus and truck services, monopolized by landlords and gentry, were asking "exorbitant rates" (in some provinces, warlords themselves monopolized transport, such as the "Christian general" Feng Yuxiang with his Northwest Automobile Transportation Company), but Shanxi's roads appeared to be crucial when it came to defend the province against neighboring warlords. Similarly, railroads were military-political instruments: Chiang used his grip on the northern rail network to frustrate Yan's efforts to export its rich coal resources to Japan, so Yan built his own (small-gauge) railroad, with German material, often using existing roadbeds, thus frustrating his rich gentry's road monopoly, whom he coerced in paying exorbitant taxes. He even contemplated building his own planes and cars but managed at least to develop a truck engine running on charcoal. Opposing Chiang in the latter's failure to resist the Japanese invasion in Manchuria, Yan formulated a Ten-Year Plan inspired by Soviet and American planning (which on its turn may have been the inspiration for Chiang's Five-Year Plan) but was supported by Chiang in his struggle against an invasion of the Red Army in 1936. His subsequent battle against the invasion by Japan (which on its turn dumped its surplus manufactures in an effort to destroy the fledgling Chinese industrialization) was inspired by the mobile warfare of his Communist adversaries, who enjoyed an "enormous popularity" among the devastated peasants, whereas the gentry collaborated with the Japanese. In the end, the Communists occupied those parts of the province not taken by Japan.[87]

After the war, until February 1947, Yan made his Japanese archenemy stay to resist the Communist revolution; when he at last fled to Taiwan, he became its premier until 1950. Mao Zedong would later ironically 'thank' the Japanese for making his revolution possible, but at least as important was the weakening of the Chinese ruling class by the revolution of 1911, when military rules displaced the mandarins. Some historians (such as Jonathan Fenby) add to this shortlist the gullibility and arrogance of the American government, who first saw the Communists as "what in our country we would call Socialists," as President Franklin D. Roosevelt declared. "We like their attitude towards the peasants, towards women and towards, Japan." And then they sent George Marshall as Chiang's chief of staff, who "spoke like a colonial governor 'and severely lectured us,'" as one Nationalist general remembered. All in all, the Nationalists received $3 billion in aid and $1 billion extra in "cut-price equipment." Fenby, who wrote a biography of Chiang, adds the ideological 'emptiness' of the Nationalist regime and its blatant cruelty and corruption to the factors supporting the Communist Revolution, a regime in which a "tiny upper crust prospered, making fortunes on the black market and driving around big cities in imported limousines."[88]

Indeed, if we are to trust Fenby's observations (who meticulously registered the cars and trains this upper crust used during Chiang's reign on China's mainland, in a typical way, that is, often characterizing them with make and model name, color, and some extra epithets such as 'large,' 'armoured,' or 'luxury'), there is no doubt the cars were owned exclusively by the very top of the ruling and the urban middle class, from the governor, ambassadors, Shanghai gangsters (a "bullet-proof limousine"), Shanghai's "most powerful union leader" in his "chauffeur-driven car," to a "former judge" in a "large car," American (a "new Cadillac") and Russian (an "old car") military advisers, and, of course, Chiang himself, who brought four of his cars to Taiwan as a sign of the Nationalists' impending retreat to that island. Cars clearly had a super-status symbolic function (confirmed by a visiting scholar, Robert Payne, who described in his diary "to ride in motorcars" as a typical trait of Chinese parvenus). This status also functioned in a negative sense, such as when a top official of Chiang's government followed the leader's campaign against corruption by "using a public rickshaw instead of his limousine," or when a Chinese delegation had to walk back to their train after a meeting with their Japanese victors, who humiliated them, as the *New York Times* wrote, because "no automobiles or carriages had been provided." For the enthronement of the "last emperor" of Manchukuo, a "bullet-proof Lincoln limousine [was] followed by nine new Cadillacs." One macho American military adviser refused his Cadillac and used a jeep instead; a no less macho Chinese warlord refused using his "white Buick" and preferred a truck instead.

By the end of the war, the new American ambassador "ordered a new Cadillac," whereas Mao came to meet him in Yan'an in a Chevrolet ambulance, a gift from the diaspora in the United States. Cars were a sign of corruption: when Americans entered the Nationalist capital Chongqing, they were "shocked by the extent of the trading with the enemy which saw Japanese-made cars running on the streets of [Chongqing] and medical aid sold by the Nationalists to Japan." The local fleets were modest at best: Xi'an counted four hundred "motor vehicles" in 1934, and five years later, the entire army possessed fifteen hundred "vehicles."[89] At the same time, the Chinese masses moved (fled, mostly) on foot; within cities, they also fled in rickshaws, carts, and sometimes buses and trucks. But, despite Ford being appointed Chiang's "adviser," the railroads remained the "key" in the warlord era (no Taxis de la Marne here!): as transport of troops but also as "personal trains"—in Chiang's case, often three armored ones in a row—as protection. Different from the West perhaps, the eight-year World War II in China and its generals' preference for motorized vehicles induced such a spectacular extension of the road vehicle fleet that other options (such as electric propulsion) lost their credibility, a role I attributed to World War I in the Western struggle between road and rail. Before China's Communist Revolution became part of the Cold War, Moscow remained the main source of supplies, sending, by the end of the 1930s, "900 planes, 82 tanks ... and 2,000 vehicles as well as 2,000 airmen and 3,000 advisers," among others. The United States shipped five hundred trucks to Burma for a campaign to reopen a supply road to China, and Japan supported its massive Ichigo campaign in 1944 with eight hundred tanks, twelve thousand to fifteen thousand "vehicles," and, not to be forgotten, seventy thousand to one hundred thousand horses, many of them captured by the Red Army.[90]

Shanghai Express: Modernity and Motorization in Chinese Literature

In a way, the May Fourth literati may be compared to the Belgian-French avant-garde (such as Octave Mirbeau, Maurice Leblanc, and Cyriel Buysse) we identified in the introduction as the initiators of a modernization wave in both transport and literature in Europe. One of their Chinese counterparts was Zhang Henshui (1895–1967, pen name of Zhang Xinyuan), a writer of popular (*tongsu*) novels in the style of the "Mandarin duck and butterflies school" (*yuanyang hudie pai*; the duck being a love bird), of which he wrote "between sixty and ninety-one" according to his English translator. Working on "at least half a dozen novels simultaneously," Zhang once apologized for his "superficial and pointless" style, which, like the large middlebrow movement of "colloquial fiction" he was a part of, was a hybrid of "the traditional Chinese novel, influenced by Western literary techniques" such as "methods of characterization and uses of nature to advance the narrative." He also applied the technique of linked chapters (*zhanghui xiaoshuo*), using cliffhangers, and he limited his main vocabulary to "only a few hundred characters." The son of rich noodle business parents, he was already popular among the "urban petty bourgeoisie" (to whose "vulgar tastes" he catered) when he published, in 1935, his *Shanghai Express* (*Ping Hu tong che*) in a serialized form in a travel magazine.

By then, indeed, Zhang was already famous because of his "perennial bestseller" *Fate in Tears and Laughter* (*Tixiao yinyuan*), "phenomenally successful, one of the best-selling Chinese novels of the twentieth century." Zhang was later praised by Zhou and Mao, probably because he included in his *Return of the Swallow*, written in travelogue-style, a journey to the famine-stricken northwest (based on a trip he undertook himself) by a patriotic hero-engineer on his way "to help in the development of the region." Zhang never experienced the harsh treatment during the post–World War II Cultural Revolution of some of his colleague-writers of the May Fourth Movement, unless one considers as such the invitation to provide the Lu Xun museum with a load of his Lu Xun novels as props. Analyzing "popular fiction" for our purpose of digging into the Chinese mobility history is attractive because it "yields the richest information on the domestic and social lives of Chinese people in the early 20th century." Even Zhang's dreamlike and fantastic passages "do … not contradict their informational value, serving as they do to help later readers appreciate the emotional and private worlds of their predecessors."[91]

***

Zhang's *Shanghai Express* is the story of a wealthy bank manager from Beijing who is seduced and robbed from his bonds and cash by a "modern and uninhibited" woman (reading foreign books) during his railway journey of two days and two nights to Shanghai. It is telling that the train functions as an intercity conveyance in this novel: in this microcosm of class differences, protagonist Ziyun, because of his financial mishaps fallen back to third-class status, observes how Shanghai railway station is so crowded with "silver and pale green automobiles" that pedestrians and the few rickshaws can hardly move through them. But he is not impressed: "'What's the big deal about the automobile?' he asked himself. 'Back then, yours truly had so many cars he got sick of riding in them!'" This is how status can be mobilized as a counterstrategy: without much irony (as would have occurred in a 'Western' novel), the declassed banker is portrayed as a parvenu. *Shanghai Express* illustrates that although the car may be ubiquitous in the big cities (in the 1930s, and especially in Shanghai), between these cities the train was the modern conveyance. In Zhang's novel, the story unfolds mostly without any irony and without much inversion (the Proustian technique to see the environment speed by the narcissistic individual in the vehicle). Here and there, we find glimpses of experiences as we know them from the West, such as the 'distancing' train window that separates the peasants outside from the elite inside, who then can romanticize about the 'pureness' of the farmer's mind, and we witness one rare example of inversion, when "the scenery roll[s] past outside."

This does not mean 'adventure' is absent, however. *Shanghai Express* is Zhang's first novel with a (female) "adventurer" (*chaibaidang*) as a protagonist and as such can be considered part of a long tradition of "adventure novels," including martial stories of chivalry, "hardly inferior to some

Western paperback best-sellers." But the 'adventure' is mainly erotic in a veiled way (the woman giggling and blushing, the man 'attacking' in the "war of aggression that man wages against woman" [perhaps some irony here?], but also ashamed if he breaches the rules of elite "social graces"), and not at all fast: the interior mobility is limited to visiting of the second and the overcrowded and smelly third class, where the heating is bad and "nobody is really interested in progress." In fact, the woman takes the initiative of seduction, deciding to get off the train to travel by road, thus circumventing a time-consuming river crossing by train ferry. The adventuress takes the car. Mobility is triple in this novel: the train in the landscape, hardly noticed, the movements inside the train, and the suggestion of social mobility between the classes, up the ladder (the woman-seductress) or down (the fallen protagonist). In two of his later novels (*Goblin Market* and *Chungking Gold Rush*, published as late as 1941 and 1946, respectively), a "station for out-of-town buses" and "a band of ... long-distance lorry drivers" appear, as well as a description of a protagonist's bus trip to his family home, all embedded in a dreamlike atmosphere. Other novels describe an "escape to a different, parallel world."[92]

***

But the real canonized May Fourth icon was Lu Xun (1881–1936, pen name of Zhou Shuren), son of an impoverished, landowning family and pupil of the Military Academy's School of Mines and Railways (which did not charge tuition fees), followed by medical studies in Japan, where he decided instead to "cure [his countrymen's] mind" by becoming a writer. Inspired by Eastern European writers, Lu can be compared to the Belgian-French group of literary and automotive pioneers because of the former's "ironic realism," and perhaps, therefore, among others, boxed in as a 'modernist.' The protagonist of his best-known book, *The Real Story of Ah-Q*, is the Chinese counterpart of the American *Babbitt*, not because the former is as wealthy as the latter (he is not) but because he is an "idiotic, able-bodied everyman," and "allegorically, China itself." Much more than Zhang's popular 'pointlessness,' Lu's "genius," as British cultural historian and translator Julia Lovell called it, is to grasp the "paradox" between the objectivist stance of literary realism and the need to talk on behalf of, or at least *on*, the poor Chinese masses. One tool to enhance this grasp is the literary technique of irony, the same style figure we observed the Western middle-class literati use to distance themselves from these same masses. This "unsettling implicat[ion] [of the] reader in the violence of literary voyeurism," as well as his later radicalization leading to his endorsement of "proletarian literature" (after a thorough study of Soviet literary theories, he became head of the League of Left-Wing Writers in Shanghai), may have been why Mao Zedong and his fellow

Communist leaders praised his work, although this "saint of modern China" later declined the party's invitation to write a grand novel on China's rural revolution, and he never became a party member.

Despite Mao's "glorification" of Lu, which made hundreds of millions of China's post–World War II schoolchildren familiar with his work (until he recently began to be replaced by "escapist kung fu texts"), more radical factions of the intelligentsia from as early as the end of the 1920s started criticizing his ironic approach. More than Zhang Henshui, Lu's application of what literary scholar Liu Ts'un-yan [Liu Cunren] called the "euphuistic [excessively literary] style" allows him to construct two parallel worlds of readers, the more educated ones understanding all kinds of hidden references to the Chinese classics.[93] For Mao, Lu Xun's "burning satire and freezing irony" were understandable, as he "liv[ed] under the rule of dark forces and deprived of freedom of speech," whereas under revolutionary conditions "we can shout at the top of our voices and have no need for veiled and roundabout expressions." If you're not a middle-class writer, Mao suggested, but a peasant or soldier amid revolutionary struggle, you don't need irony (translated into Chinese as *fan-hua*, back-speech or counter-speech). Mao's verdict was not unique: the "failure of modernism" in China, in literary scholar Wang Ning's words, was based on "the traditional Chinese literary conviction in 'art for life's sake' [which] was absolutely opposite to the modernist 'art for art's sake.'"[94]

***

From a mobility point of view, Ah-Q's fictional life story, written in 1921 but playing when the Republican Revolution of 1911 reaches Ah-Q's village, strikes particularly because of its lack of attention for mobility in general, whether 'modern' or not. Amid an avalanche of ironical twists (about "the global superiority of Chinese civilization" or "women [as] the root of all evil"), Ah-Q's *adventures* are multiple (a fistfight, stealing turnips from a monastery's garden), but the train and the car are totally absent. And when he suddenly leaves town for a while, the omniscient narrator tells us there is nothing to tell about his trip, as the trips to town only by the local elite are "public events." Travel, Lu Xun's narrator suggests, is only worth telling when its practitioner has status. The rest is unknown (made subaltern, I would say), including the mobility of the masses: in Lu's *The Real Story of Ah-Q* we find the Chinese equivalent of the absent car that will characterize the post–World War II Western (and especially American) novel (see chap. 2). Only at the end, when Ah-Q is paraded through town toward his execution by a firing squad, does this happen in an "open cart" surrounded by soldiers and militia.[95] So much is clear: whether we follow Mao or his saint, as soon as one left the few intercity corridors of the railways, mobility in rural

China was of an animal- and human-powered nature, apart from the occasional train moving over the modest network, and the exceptional car for Zhang Henshui's 'adventuress.' Next, we will investigate how easily or difficultly an 'adventuress' would be able to navigate on China's road network.

Road Mobility: Pedestrians, Horses, Buses, and an Occasional Car

After Sun Yat-sen's fantasy of the people's car, the Chinese roads seem to have been constructed primarily with public transport in mind. According to Dikötter, the importance of buses (or trucks simultaneously used for freight and passengers, called *huangyu*, yellow fish) in the countryside "has hitherto been underestimated by historians." In Shanxi province, buses and trucks did exist, as we saw, but their monopolistic position provided their owners (mostly the landowning gentry) with extraordinary profits. "However poor the roads and packed the buses, a national network which partly compensated for the inadequacy of railway transport and allowed merchants and farmers to make journeys unheard-of only a few years before was in place by the 1930s," testifying to our thesis that Western and non-Western synchronicity in the major characteristics of mobility modernization is more important than distinctions in 'civilization.' Dikötter said Beijing alone had ten factories specializing in body making and that a "national network" was in place by the 1930s, which is hard to reconcile with Mann's statement that at the end of World War II, "little Korea had half as many miles of modern roads as the whole of China."[96] It is clear: the definitive history of prewar Chinese motorization still has to be written. Let us make a first, modest start.

China's roads in this phase seem to have been mostly subsidized by its diaspora. Perhaps the proximity to Western funding also explains a remarkable proposal in the 1920s by the Italian Piero Puricelli, one of the imitators of the Italian autostradas, to build a freeway along the coast near Beijing. Whereas before 1920 "perhaps a hundred miles of improved roads suitable for motor traffic" had been built near Beijing and some port cities, during the famine of 1920–1921 it was the American Red Cross that used the Chinese eagerness for relief funds to make them build roads: in the provinces of Shandong, Shanxi, Hunan, and Zhili, more than a thousand km of motor roads were built in this way, but the number of motor roads built during the 1920s is unknown: estimates vary between nine thousand and thirty-five thousand miles. Gasoline imports increased by a factor of eight during this decade, indicating an increase of automobilism. American urban planner Thomas Campanella mentioned civil engineer Oliver J. Todd as the pivotal advisor to the Chinese government about "Red Cross roads" building: his assistant engineers "were trained in the United States." He showed the roads were financed out of the so-called Boxer Protocol funds, the $300 million the Qing court had been forced to pay Britain and the United States in 1901 "for having failed to quell the Boxer Rebellion," funds that also were used to found Tsinghua University in Beijing, "as a preparatory school for Chinese students planning to study in the United States."[97]

Puricelli's proposal to build freeways becomes understandable in light of the infrastructure planning by the Nationalist government once this was moved to the new capital of Nanjing in 1927. Although students of the Japanese Tōa Dōbun Shoin business school in Shanghai reported interruptions of train traffic in the mid-1920s because of civil unrest, during the Nanjing decade, the government started a series of infrastructure projects supported by the League of Nations. Founded on recommendation by US President Woodrow Wilson (who subsequently did not manage to make his country a member), the league, with thirty-two member states and thirteen additional candidates, propagated "a kind of world federalism" and had the International Labour Organization as one of its "most activist bodies." Following up on Sun Yat-sen's grand railway planning of a decade earlier, the Nanjing regime managed to "interlink … the north-south and east-west railway arteries" within a decade, "with minimum intervention from the imperialist powers." But they also planned the construction of a number of highways: within a decade, the road network length increased from eighteen thousand (1927) to sixty-nine thousand miles (1936), a "new (inter)urban network" beyond the lower Yangzi area consisting of a Three Provinces Road (*Sansheng gonglu*, in Jiangsu, Zhejiang, and Anhui provinces), a Southeast Five Provinces Road (*Dongnan wusheng gonglu* in Jiangsu, Zhejiang, Anhui, Jiangxi and Fujian provinces), and a Seven Provinces Road (*Qisheng gonglu* in Jiangsu, Zhejiang, Anhui, Jiangxi, Henan, Hubei, and Hunan provinces). The network was largely concentrated in central and northwest China (traditionally, the South and to a certain extent Central China were where water transport dominated).[98]

A very detailed report drawn up by the US Department of Commerce allows a unique view of the state of the art of China's roadbuilding around 1930. This report, based on information provided by local consuls, businessmen, and other sources, reveals quite clearly that there were no more than ten thousand miles of "roadways" (exclusive of what the Japanese were constructing at the same time in Manchuria), but it also shows a planning and building frenzy at the province and district level. China's road network seems to have been conceived for the first time in 1919 by an engineer called Luo Kou-shin, trained at Rensselaer Polytechnic Institute in the United States, who also proposed a road classification system. Virtually all roads were paved with broken stone, produced manually by thousands of workers, who also had to pull gigantic steel rollers, as China had only a few rollers propelled by steam, and some railroad dump trucks. Asphalt was used only in large treaty port concessions and some other cities. There were also asphalt roads in the British colony of Hong Kong, for a domestic fleet of 1,700 passenger cars, 460 motorcycles, 498 trucks, and 162 buses.

Apart from these local initiatives, other factors that stimulated this first wave of roadbuilding were the famine relief activities undertaken by the American Red Cross in 1920, from which a National Good Roads Construction Association (1921) was set up, backed by private bus interests. From 1922, they also published a magazine, *Good Roads Monthly*. A few provinces started their own road programs, coordinated by a National Highway Planning Commission, which made up a first national highway plan in 1929. The report claimed that China had fewer than 40,000 motor vehicles in 1930, one-third of which were in Shanghai (including 8,500 passenger cars that caused quite a busy traffic, according to a picture of a local crossroads), where 302 miles of roads were built, as well as four toll roads to nearby cities. This is consistent with a recent retrospective overview from the Chinese Ministry of Communications, which claims about fifty thousand motor vehicles were imported in China (most of them American makes) between 1901 and 1949 and that between 1913 and 1949, "over 130,000 km of highways were constructed successively throughout the country."

The report on 1930 provided a detailed overview of provincial road planning. To give only some examples: in Guangxi, 1,200 miles were built; in Guizhou, two hundred thousand laborers constructed 600 miles; and on 1 January 1930, Hainan Island counted 628 motor vehicles, 625 buses, 3 tractors, but not a single passenger car.[99] It is difficult to distinguish plans from implementation here. For instance, in mountainous Shanxi, roads were so badly maintained that they soon deteriorated into uselessness. The roads there were "terrible," as the participants of the Long March experienced. Perhaps the Chinese road conditions are best represented in the bulletins of the international road engineering association PIARC (China was a member; see later in this chapter); in a 1926 edition, 61,000 km of "improved roads" were given, but an estimate of 33,600 km was quoted from *Foreign Highway News* three years later. Again, a "total road length" of 56,000 km was given in 1931. Apparently, to impress on its readers the sheer size of the projects, the Southwestern Highways management office produced a map in 1940, on which its network was projected over a map of Europe, covering an area from Paris to Prague, and from Berlin to Rome.[100]

***

Nowadays, out of a "rising interest in historical continuity," some historians seem to be willing to reinterpret the role of the Guomindang (however "corrupt and dominated by the upper classes" it may have been, in the words of Mann) as a correction to earlier conclusions about the disruptive role of the Communist takeover in 1949 in the process of China's development. They thus side with the opinions of technical advisers such as Kenneth Cantlie or "financial adviser" Arthur N. Young, the latter a witness of the government's financial policy in nearly two decades (1929–1947). Young testified that "experts from the League of Nations played an important role in the work of the NEC [Nation Economic Council, founded in 1931 on the league's recommendation] [which] cooperated actively with a number of provinces, notably in highway construction, agricultural activities, and rural rehabilitation."[101]

In a bulletin of its Council of International Affairs, the Nationalist government in Nanjing explained how the "technical co-operation" with the league started in 1922, on recommendation of Japan (which in general played a driving role in the fledgling league), in the realm of epidemics management, provoking multiple visits from Geneva by high-placed officers such as Albert Thomas (of the ILO); by the beginning of the next decade, when the Nationalist government seemed to have brought a larger part of China under its control, plans for reconstruction were discussed with the league, bringing new visits to China, such as by Sir Arthur Salter (who later would chair an important coordination commission in the United Kingdom) and by later key figures in the founding of the European Community (such as the French Robert Haas, Director of the Transit and Communications Organization, who advised on China's waterways, and Jean Monnet).

They reported back on "the remarkable, not to say alarming, consequences of the excessive influence of the American model on Chinese education." Mussolini sent airplanes, against the "cut-throat competition and sharp practices among American aviation interests in China." Although the United States was not a member of the league, Young showed some surprise that it "sent no American experts to China." The first task formulated within an ambitious "Ten-Year Plan" of 1931 regarded the "building of harbours, canals, railways, and roads," among others, in order to open "the vast undeveloped area of the Northwest" (the ninth task mentioned in the plan was the "manufacture of vehicles of all types"). A Polish and a Dutch civil engineer were then sent to China as "permanent representative" to advise in roadbuilding. Roadbuilding on a national scale by the Nationalist government started with the already mentioned "three-province project" in 1932: six roads around the new capital, but a road conference in Hankou (now Wuhan) in the same year resulted in a "seven-province project" of 22,000 km, a length that was increased to more than 30,000 a year later, when more land surface was captured on the Communists. In 1936, nearly 24,000 km were completed, half as earthen roads, the other half paved with broken stone (fig. 1.5).[102]

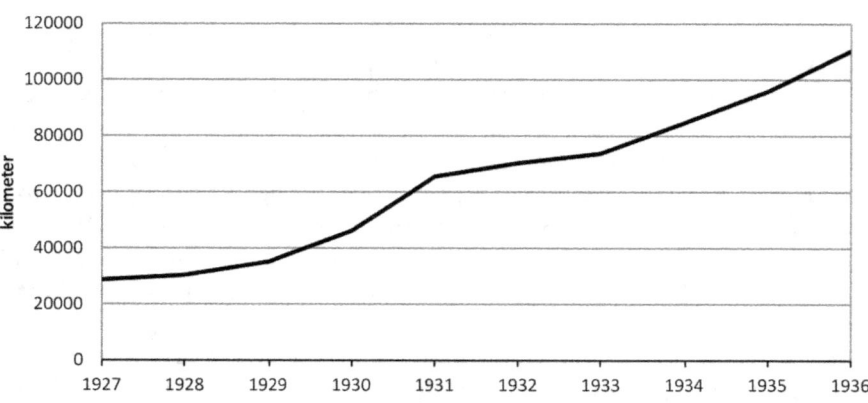

Figure 1.5. "Motor road" construction in China in km. Source: Young, *China's Nation-Building Effort*, 396–397, table 27. Figure created by the author.

Young, too, speaks of "great progress" made by the Guomindang government and bestows China the role of a pioneer in what he called "the field of economic development … , the promotion of progress of less developed countries." Indeed, this advisory work can be considered a prelude to the large-scale, Western, post–World War II development 'mission' (as analyzed in chap. 3) and as such is a nice example of the Comaroffs' thesis (see the introduction) of the non-West being the laboratory (and predecessor) for the West: 65 civil advisers, most of them from Europe, and 175 military advisers, mostly German (Chiang Kai-shek "broke with Russia," which thereupon withdrew its advisers invited by Sun Yat-sen, who then replaced them with Germans), were active in Nanjing, competing with members of the American (Kemmerer) Commission of Financial Experts (Young himself being one of them), arranged by a Chinese government official in an effort to counter the influence of the Europeans, which he "regarded as colonialists." Young also described the decentralization of Chinese roadbuilding to the provinces (the same trend as we observed earlier in the West), led by a Bureau of Roads set up in 1933, despite the extremely centralized governance structure endorsed by Chiang, inspired by European Fascism.

Involved in the NEC road program was the China International Famine Relief Commission and its missionaries, set up in the early 1920s on the occasion of the famine in the northwest; this commission made roadbuilding a precondition of its relief funding and "built or improved 3825 miles of road." But when the government in 1933 wanted to expand aid from the League of Nations, it failed, "largely because of Japanese hostility" within the league. Soon thereafter, the British Boxer Indemnity Scholarship funds (largely Chinese money) started investing heavily in railroad building: its network doubled between 1927 and 1930 to 2,300 miles. They were joined by Germans, after their trade with the Soviet Union was discontinued. A one billion Chinese dollars plan drawn in 1937 to develop "a mixed economic system of public and private enterprise, reserving to government the public utilities and the heavy industry closely related to defense but leaving light industry to private enterprise," was not executed but "became available to the Communists" after World War II. Nor was much of the railway network expansion realized, because of the Japanese invasion in 1937, the year in which the United States changed its China policy and allowed its Export-Import Bank to "finance half the cost of locomotives sold by American companies," and China's railway network had the same size as that of the state of Illinois.[103]

The eagerness to 'modernize' in the 1930s was so great that one of the Guomindang officials responsible for cultural policy proposed to close university courses on humanities and law for a decade in order to increase the number of road engineers. There are indeed accounts of at least one highway between Shanghai and Hangzhou, part of the Seven Provinces trunk line and finished in 1932, that showed "alignment and grades meeting international standards"; two hundred passenger cars drove the seven-hour trip during the opening day. During the "fifth and finally successful campaign" against the Communists in October 1933, Chiang Kai-shek mobilized a force of a million men, "mov[ing] slowly, building networks of roads to facilitate supply lines." A new road between Shanghai and Nanjing, also on the East Coast, was finished in 1935, "complete with service and aid stations equipped with telephones." A government bulletin speaks of one road in the province of Jiangxi, where seventy thousand workers finished a three-hundred-mile stretch in less than three months. China was also present at the 1934 PIARC conference, which convened in Nazi Germany.

William Kirby showed how the regime founded a state-owned China Automobile Manufacturing Company (Zhongguo Qiche Zhizao Gongsi) assembling "diesel trucks on a Daimler-Benz model," and it organized drivers and mechanics courses. Joint ventures with Pan American and Lufthansa intended to build up a domestic aviation network. The road network was considered a cheaper alternative to the railroads, but until 1932, a car licensed in one province could not drive in another without a local license. The use of these roads, and their interconnectedness, must have been wanting: one Shoin report questioned the wisdom of their construction, considering the resistance by representatives of old transport modes, as well as the very limited supplies of gasoline. This was mostly imported from India, with the United States as a second supplier, its volume increasing nearly twentyfold between 1919 and 1936, the annual amount being above ten million US gallons from 1928, reaching forty-six million US gallons in 1936.[104] Nevertheless, roadbuilding in this phase was quite remarkable given the "residual warlordism" still going on in the 1930s, the devastating influence of the Depression, and the general state of the Chinese road infrastructure at the beginning of the Republican period, and was certainly not a "drop-in-the-bucket accomplishment," as China historian R. Keith Schoppa concluded, although it is true that by the end of the 1930s, China "had the same mileage of modern highways as Spain."[105]

***

Considering the limited amount of information (especially the distinction between plans and execution), it is difficult to assess the extent of the road network in China, let alone its use. The best estimate is a table in a government bulletin from 1937 that gives a total network length of nearly 110,000 km (the longest portion of which was in the southeastern province of Guangdong), only one-fifth of this paved (with another 16,000 km under construction and 46,000 km projected). The same difficulty applies to urban renovation: it seems the Nationalist regime developed rudimentary urban planning "according to international standards" and supervised by "an American-trained engineer," in the capital city of Nanjing, where a "comprehensive system of parkways and main arteries" had to be realized, including a six-lane Zhongshan Road (or Sun Yat-sen Road), which was "bulldozered forty meters wide through the city center ... Residents in the way were given ten days to leave their homes." Proposed already as a "model capital" by Guomindang party founder Sun Yat-sen, "clean and efficient, offering the latest in technological conveniences" and attractive because of its centrality, Nanjing was conceptualized (by a planning commission chaired by an American) as "the new Washington, D.C." (and a bit modeled on Paris). Tellingly, the Ministry of Railways was the first building realized of the plan. The plan, however, was abandoned soon out of a lack of funding.[106]

The American report we cited earlier indicated walls were replaced by "city highways" in Guangzhou, Shanghai, Nantong, Hangzhou, Changsha, Zhengzhou, Huizhou, and Nanchang (all paved with "broken stone"), while dozens of cities were planning such renovations, but we need much more research into this period, at a national as well as regional and local level, to enable us to construct a picture of China's mobility modernization before the founding of the People's Republic in 1949. Only that would enable us to compare China's modernization with that in the Soviet Union, where the railroads (and its workers) played a crucial role in the revolution of 1917, a role that was taken over by the automobile during the first five-year plan of 1928–1932, when volunteers gave driver courses and organized rallies and races in order to spread socialist ideology in the countryside (and the first traffic jam appeared on the streets of Moscow in 1925, testifying to the "dreams of prosperity" hopefully soon to be realized).[107] But whatever comparisons will be made, and whatever in-depth studies will be performed, they will not be able to hide the scarcity of cars, which in my opinion can be connected to "the bankruptcy of the middle-class revolution" of the Chinese republican period.[108]

***

As to the *use* of the road and rail networks, even less information is readily available. What we know is that the Nationalist government dedicated some effort into promoting the railway network for tourism. Like the South Manchurian Railway Company did with Sōseki and Yosano, Chiang Kai-shek's government invited famous writers to produce travelogues while developing the new networks, and indeed, Zhang Henshui undertook a three-month journey (which may have inspired his novel we investigated earlier), also along highways. Shion students reported about excellent roads in the South, but they also observed its network was not complete, and as late as 1932, there was no road network in the Northwest. When the government moved to Chongqing after the Japanese invasion of 1937, a massive wave of migration to the Southwest took place. Shion students traveling in that area reported they used steamers and junks on the rivers but also an occasional bus, or they managed to rent an animal-drawn cart for their luggage, walking along. The Shanghai China Travel Service was allowed to sell bus tickets (the buses driven only by "middle school graduates" who mastered "basic vehicle repair skills"), thus assuming a role that in Europe was performed by the touring clubs.[109] It is difficult to determine whether these roads were built ahead of demand, but there cannot be much doubt that this was the case if their purpose was to enable passenger car traffic. It seems fair to say that outside the towns, mechanized road mobility was largely on "barrows, carts, mules, donkeys and camels," and human-powered water transport was predominant. The CTS published a brochure called "Romance of Transport" in which it printed pictures of a bus, a rickshaw, and a passenger car. Yet, the CTS signed contracts with Soviet and other travel agencies (such as Thomas Cook), offering its customers an Asian network for leisure travel. From 1926, it also published a pictorial periodical called *Liangyou*, in which photographs accompanied travel accounts.[110]

But when American missionary R. A. Boshardt and his wife (accompanied by "a Chinese girl, our own cook, and four coolies," two of the latter carrying his wife's "mountain chair") were captured by Mao's Communists, they traveled the entire six thousand miles on foot; the trip cost him a pair of shoes. Occasionally, they could use one of the mules. Once, he spotted one of Chiang Kai-shek's airplanes overhead. Boshardt generalized his experiences as to the condition of the roads: "The word 'road' in Chinese does not convey the same meaning as it does in English. A road in China is often just a narrow stony path which in times of rain is very slippery." Other anecdotal evidence confirms this general picture. From Lanzhou, the geographical center of China, to Xi'an, it took four to seven days by car in the late 1930s, whereas an airplane needed three hours. Despite the famines, floods, civil war, warlords, and long-marching Communists, China apparently offered enough space for the more traditional travel writers to wander around, such as the American Harry Franck, publishing his experiencing in *Wandering through Northern China* (1923) and *Roving through Southern China* (1925), who brought his family to China and set them down in several cities "while he struck off into the interior," by tram or car (in the case of the concessions of Tianjin, for instance). Like other Westerners, he was struck by the "honking automobiles that cluttered roads like 'the back streets of any second-class American city.'" In the 1930s, several Westerners pilgrimaged to the Communist headquarters in Yan'an, starting in "a ramshackle and overcrowded bus," and continuing on foot or horseback.[111] It took at least a quarter-century in the West to reconcile railway and road interests; in China, managing the railroad controversy was not that easy, if the report about farmers who had built a "stone wall" across one of the highways appears to be more than incidental.[112]

***

By the end of the war, in 1945, China's "death toll [had been] so immense that it will never be known for certain." Fenby calculated China's losses at thirteen million. Japan, which lost three million of its citizens, seemed to have alienated itself from the Chinese population forever, as it used poison gas, deployed a germ warfare program, gave Chinese children "buns laced with cholera and [had its] planes drop ... plague[-]carrying fleas and anthrax-laden feathers." By now, "the Americans got a global empire," and in China, the world war ushered in civil war. Manchuria again appeared crucial as "the acid test during the final stages of the Civil War. Whoever controlled its industrial resources would probably win." Whereas the Communists were supplied by arms captured in Manchuria from the Japanese by the Russians (who had supported the Nationalists during the war), the Guomindang "were armed and transported to Manchuria by the United States. The Communists got there first and occupied the cities. For the first time they had to defend cities, not attack them ... If the Communists had possessed any boats, they would have taken Taiwan ... most capitalists who had collaborated with the Japanese had fled to Hong Kong." Ji Xianlin, an Indologist at Peking University, remembered how the Nationalist regime had by then "dropped all pretense of good governance and was showing its true colors. Corrupt tax officials lined their own pockets, buying houses, cars, and mistresses." As late as 1949, according to Dikötter, the bicycle was "the only modern means of transportation" in the countryside, but this must be an observation of decline, after the somewhat more extended transport network condition of the 1930s. While the "antipathy toward the British" may have helped the popularity of American cars, it also may have eased the change to driving on the right, recommended by the American military in 1945.[113]

Dual Networks of Rails and Roads: The Modal Configuration in Other Asian Countries

Let us now visit a contrasting case, that of the full and longtime colony of India, where the 'coordination controversy' may be expected to end in a victory of the railways, considering the strict regulation of road transport in the United Kingdom. Remarkably, however, on the emergence of Indian urban transport, let alone the rickshaw (which nowadays, together with Bangladesh, forms the major contingent of this versatile vehicle in the world), much less is known, a regrettable omission of subaltern studies with its focus on the countryside rather than the urban poor (who often came from the countryside). Here, too, like in China and Singapore, its culture cannot be understood without considering the migration of tens of thousands of impoverished peasants from the surrounding countryside, in the Indian case especially from the state of Bihar. Indian migration amounted to 10 percent of the population during the eighty years since the mid-nineteenth century, more than 80 percent of them internal, as "circulating migratory workers."[114]

India and the Tools of Empire: The Emergence of the Layeredness of Modern Mobility

At first sight, on an abstract level of modal split (and only if one neglects the non-Western particularities such as one-wheeled barrows and rickshaws), early twentieth-century traffic in Indian cities showed no surprises: in 1908, Mumbai had 276 cars and 1,088 bicycles, and Chennai (Madras) 250 and 3,146, respectively. Kolkata (Calcutta) had more than 750 cars in 1914 (including 240 taxis, increasing to 2,000 in 1921), as well as 152 motorcycles and 21 trucks. The first motorcar (*hawah garhi*) seems to have been imported in 1898, one or two years—depending on the interpretation—after the Netherlands, and like in the Netherlands, the "stiff collared aristocrats" of Mumbai rejected them; they "found them too noisy and bizarre." A commercial publication from 1968 estimated the total number of "motor vehicles" in India in 1913–1914 at 4,419; this rose about sixfold by 1927–1928 to 25,950. But by then, the colonial powers had already started doing what they couldn't or wouldn't do to that extent in the United Kingdom: in 1921, the Indian government declared motor vehicles to be luxury goods and levied an import duty of 11 percent on trucks and buses, no doubt to protect the railways from competition. Like in several other Asian countries and the West, motor traffic grew exponentially in India after World War I (but its accident rates in 1935 were three times higher than in the United Kingdom). In 1928, General Motors started assembling cars and trucks in Mumbai, followed by Ford in Chennai (1930), and both a year later in Mumbai and Kolkata.[115]

In terms of density (per capita), Indian car statistics dwindled compared to Europe, let alone the United States, but comparing averages can be utterly misleading when it comes to assessing the car's local embeddedness. After all, the difference between the 'core' and the 'periphery' was at least as large within Europe itself (and even in the United States to a certain extent, between the Midwest and the South), as it was between the West and the Global South: the GDPs per capita of Bulgaria and Greece in 1929 were one-quarter of that of Switzerland, and one-third of Germany or the Netherlands. The rate of urbanization, the spread of mobility infrastructure, and the number of prosperous, middle-class members (all factors favoring the emergence of a motorized mobility culture) were equally much lower: the length of railway tracks per inhabitant, as well as the number of annual railway trips per capita, were a factor ten lower in what economic historian of transport Derek Aldcroft called "Europe's Third World" (a comparison he based on the same "degeneration of the state" as in "many latter day African countries") than in Northwestern Europe. And although the differences between Europe's North and South/East diminished during the interbellum, differences in GDP per capita in 1939 between the countries mentioned was still in the order of 1:2.[116]

But just like in Southern and Eastern Europe, as people in the street see not densities but concrete cars, there is no doubt, in terms of public visibility, that Indians, especially in the big towns, could consider themselves witness of the emergence of an automobile age, if only because the increasing motor traffic in the cities, just like in the West, started producing their first victims (a dozen in Kolkata in 1908). Earlier than in the Netherlands, for instance, the Punjab police made "motor accidents" a separate entry in their annual reports (in 1922). In other words, the debates on the car's role in modernizing societies happened at more or less the same time all over the world, but the form this debate took differed per local culture, of course.

In Kolkata, after World War II, "angry residents attacked truck-drivers and burned vehicles that had injured or killed pedestrians and cyclists," among them heavy US and British army lorries, again showing that Western patterns of resistance against the car were acted out, in non-Western countries, in a much harsher, and at the same time clearer, way, as if the 'irony of the car' was not taken at face value.

Mahatma Gandhi was no exception to the automobile craze, although he later openly confessed "constant motor-riding has evidently coarsened me." His car killed a villager in 1929, and he criticized motorists for being "as inflammable as the petrol with which they come into daily contact" (suggesting some *literal* intoxication?), although he blamed himself later for not getting out and attending to the young victim. Gandhi's attitude toward the car is remarkable, because in his "disavow[al of] modern civilization," he was one of the few who opposed the train as a colonial trap: they "propagate evil," as they, "along with doctors and lawyers had impoverished India; without railways … 'the English could not have such a hold on India as they have.'" Historians like to recount the story of Gandhi's expulsion from "a first-class railway carriage in South Africa" and his extreme mobility while back in India to contrast this with the fact that "more Indians must have seen Gandhi in a railway station than in any other physical forum—and yet he spoke of fixity as some sort of Indian idyll."[117] And although current mobility history does not have a problem with including the fixity of infrastructure in mobility (see the introduction), this does not diminish Gandhi's role as a symbol of a colony's ambiguous dealing with mobilities.

***

Indeed, by 1900, the motherland had already covered India with a vast railway network, creeping onto the subcontinent from the ports in the west, south, and east, along with a telegraph network, making "the British Indian Empire (covered by the world's) first global electronic communication network," and showing transport and communication were closely linked at this early date in global mobility culture. Although critiqued by later historians of technology as determinist, Daniel Headrick's study of the role of mobility in the British colonial era claimed the technologies of communications (e.g., the telegraph and mail) and transport (e.g., the steamship and train) were indispensable "tools of empire" and have been all too often neglected by historians. Both elements of mobility were fully intertwined: "Even more than goods, information was the lifeblood of European imperialism; business deals, administrative reports, news dispatches, and personal messages sustained the colonizers and assured them the support of their own people," needed badly in a situation where the colonizers were mostly a tiny minority compared to the people they came to 'civilize': "The 'new' imperialism of the nineteenth century was not new merely because it had been preceded by 'old' imperialisms. It was a qualitatively different phenomenon. For the first time in history, colonial metropoles acquired the means to communicate almost instantly with their remotest colonies and to engage in an extensive trade in bulky goods that could never have borne the freight costs in any previous empire."[118]

The technologies of mobility functioned as a "double-edged sword," however: the telephone network laid out in India, for instance, was effectively used by the Nationalist followers of Gandhi, who also traveled extensively by train, while the rapid proliferation of the news about the Japanese victory over Russia in 1905, which triggered a wave of enthusiasm through all sorts of fledgling independence movements, would not have been possible without the intercontinental telegraph cable between Britain and its colony. Nonetheless, the structure of the communications network was fully geared toward the control and exploitation of colonial space, just like the transport network. The technology thus worked mostly in favor of the colonizers, whose deployment of violence has meanwhile been qualified as genocide as defined by the United Nations after World War II. In India, for instance, most efforts to "construct hegemony through the legitimation of civilization" failed, so the presence of the British in India "rested ... in essence on the bayonet" until the very end. State terrorism, punishment, and other forms of disciplining and control were the stages of intrusion tested in the colonies as laboratories of violence, including the use of tattoos for identification of criminals and the constant observation of "criminal tribes" (through the Criminal Tribes Act of 1871), Indian nomadic, or semisedentary groups of people living in mountainous forest regions that had to be 'sedentarized' by force. Their mobility was punished with jail sentences, they were deported, and their children were taken away and sent to Christian mission schools.[119]

The fact that we can corroborate this general judgment through detailed research on some twentieth-century peasant uprisings is owed to subaltern studies scholars: historian Shahid Amin, founding editor of *Subaltern Studies*, investigated the killing of twenty-three policemen in Chauri Chaura (Uttar Pradesh) in 1922 by a peasant crowd, who were immediately condemned by Gandhi and subsequently erased from Nationalist history, only to be stylized as martyrs after Independence. Ironically, arrested peasants later declared they were inspired by Gandhi's "triumphant train tours of 1920" to spread the "*asahyog*, ... a boycott of the commodities and institutions through which England was able to rule India with the aid of Indians." Chauri Chaura was a creation by the Indian railways, who combined the names of the two villages of "agriculturalists" (up to one-half to two-thirds of both populations) when it built a station in between them in 1885. Amin, loyal to his postmodernist stance, in his study (in which he is very much present as an actor in a kind of historical detective story) writes less about the *kānd* (riot) itself than about how Gandhi and his fellow-Nationalists of the Congress organization have cleansed history of "the crime of Chauri Chaura," executed by "undisciplined 'hooligans,'" who created "disorder (*utpāt*)."

When Gandhi's train stopped at the Chauri Chaura railway station and other stations in the district in 1921, he wanted the "'insistent and assertive crowds' ... disciplined by trained volunteers." The Luddism of the estimated 6,000 'hooligans' (who displayed "crowd discipline, respond[ding] to pre-arranged signals"), 225 of whom were put on trial, of whom 172 received the death penalty (later limited to 19 "ringleaders"), also targeted telegraph and railway equipment, to prevent the quick dispatch of police reinforcements.[120] The history of Indian independence struggle since 1922 is colored by the Chauri Chaura metaphor, the fear for mob violence, and the *mobilization* of peasant anger: when student and peasant Nationalists targeted railway stations in 1942 again in a campaign to make Britain "Quit India," local authorities referred to the railway station's name to warn for undisciplined turmoil. From a mobility point of view, 'Chauri Chaura' and similar uprisings stand for the struggle between the order of the (colonial, postcolonial) railways and the disorder of the seminomadic volunteers and the mobs they were considered to discipline.[121]

Chauri Chaura also illustrates the fact that India, as an 'empty' country of thousands of isolated villages, became a 'railway society' (in contrast to the Western 'car societies-in-the-making'): the rail network functioned as a crucial alternative to India's dirt roads (which "in the rainy summer monsoons [became] impassible") and represented, in Headrick's words, "the most monumental project of the colonial era; it involved the largest international capital flow of the nineteenth century, and produced the fourth longest rail network on earth, behind only those of the United States, Canada and Russia." Whereas the railways before Independence stood for Britain's robber capitalism intent to protect the interests of the "cotton barons of Lancashire" through its resource-extractive (cotton) and military function (there was a "rash of railroad building" after the Indian Rebellion of 1857/1858), Headrick still called India in the beginning of the 1980s "the world's most railroad[-]dependent nation."

With one of the world's widest gauges (1.67 m), the network was built for one-third of what it would have cost in Britain, and its length in 1902 (26,000 miles) was three times that of Africa's, one-third of it government-owned, easily "the largest railway system in the colonial, Global South," but it was less beneficial to the Indian economy than often assumed: cliometricians calculated "social savings" of less than 10 percent of GDP.

Later extensions added one-meter gauge lines that had to be replaced after Independence. But Marx's and many others' expectation that constructing a railroad network would automatically lead to an industrial revolution turned out to be an illusion (it *did* affect village handicraft negatively, however, accelerating rural-urban migration). Until Independence, Britons held the best jobs in the enormous railroad company, while the tickets of first-class passengers were subsidized by the poor "pack[ed] [in] their third-class compartments," whose willingness to "put up with the hardships of railway travelling [was] a sign of our unmanliness," according to Gandhi.[122]

In 1919 (when Gandhi became the leader of the Indian National Congress), network length reached thirty-five thousand miles (its rails—not its engines!—mostly delivered by Tata Iron and Steel Company), and the railways employed sixty-nine thousand people. Just before Independence, the one-billion-passenger threshold was passed on a network that was already nationalized in 1924. It now became Indian Railways, with more than a million employees. At least as important was freight transport (nearly one hundred million tons in the mid-1920s). Together with passenger transport, it formed "a serious drain on the finances of the Government of India." No wonder, then, have Indian writers included the train's "symbolic presence of the British imperialism" into their work, up to the *Peshawar Express* by Krishan Chander, where the train becomes the narrator to account of the atrocities during the Partition of 1947 (see chap. 3). But already in 1929, Indian Bengali writer Budhhadev Bose asked his readers, "Our streets crowded with trams and motor cars, [our] trains—why would not they find places in our poetry?"[123] Yes, why not? Was it because road traffic generated more adventurous fantasies?

***

Because of the tight British grip on Indian colonial mobility development, it may not come as a surprise that Indian and British (and by extension, European) mobility histories show many striking parallels. In fact, the Indian mobile tabula rasa (in British eyes) was used to function as a laboratory for extreme experiments in what in the West has been called the 'coordination debate,' the struggle between a 'railway society' (for long-distance transport of bulk goods) and a 'car society' (for short-haul commodity transport), discussed in a report of the Mitchell-Kirkness Committee of 1933, followed by the Wedgwood Committee of 1936. Roadbuilding in India seemed aimed more at improving the existing network than expanding it, the paving of the famous precolonial 1,600-mile Great Trunk Road from current Kolkata to current Pakistan being a case in point. The Indian colonial government decided to protect its railway interests aggressively against competing trucks and buses but (advised by House of Lords member

Montagu of Beaulieu, doyen of British automobilism, and pressured by a growing international car lobby) accepted road transport (both buses and trucks) in a feeder function to the railways by granting transport companies, especially in India's densely populated central and western provinces, a monopoly on the use of the roads provided they maintained them. Like in Europe, many soldiers after World War I became truck and bus drivers, and like in Europe, it was the owner of a single truck or bus who competed head-on with the railways and formed, in the process, the basis of a new "rural bourgeoisie."

Later, the railways themselves introduced automobile feeder traffic (a maneuver never to be accepted in several European countries with a stronger car lobby), its self-made bodies mounted on American chassis. In many cases, this did not prevent bullock carts (e.g., for cotton transport) or ekkas and tongas (animal-drawn passenger vehicles) from increasing at the same time. Like in Europe, the engineer's dream of (expensive) concrete pavement for roads (but in India's case, expressly introduced to enable dominant animal traction on these roads) was gradually replaced by asphalt, and like in Europe, road planning was decentralized to provincial authorities (who immediately suspended the road monopolies granted by the central state) and local authorities. Indeed, there was a clear synchronicity between Indian and European road policy development. Initially, the Government of India Act 1919 delegated the entire responsibility of road-building to the provincial governments, who on their turn passed most of it to the local bodies. But the national trunk roads remained under central control, for which purpose a Central Road Fund was initiated in 1930, against the Nationalists, who had proposed plans inspired by Italian and German Fascist freeway planning.[124]

In 1909, an automobile club (the Western India Automobile Association) was founded in Mumbai as an active part in the road lobby (fig. 1.6). After Bengal, Mumbai had by far the most cars, more so than Delhi. Stefan Tetzlaff, who wrote the first comprehensive analysis of India's small-town road motorization, showed how landlords used "illegal exactions ... from peasants to purchase motorcars." He also gave an interesting (new in the current state of the art) explanation of the role of the Depression: it "promoted local transport," triggering the railways to send alarming messages to the Indian government. All in all, a very complex multiple-mobilities development took place, challenging easy notions of linear substitution. Against the increase in bullock-cart transport stood the demise of camel transport in hilly terrain (in favor of the truck), and the disappearance of many interurban ekkas and tongas because of the emerging bus.

And while the bus took away third-class passengers from the train, the car targeted the railway's first- and second-class clientele. Likewise, bullock carts were modernized by mounting pneumatic tires. Road censuses in the district of the city of Burdwan in West Bengal in 1936 and 1937 also produced a variegated picture, but many of the census points convey the pattern of pedestrianism outperforming all other modes by far, while rickshaw, passenger car, and motorbus were equally visible in road traffic, each mode often transporting about an equal daily amount of passengers. Carts clearly outnumbered trucks. Of the nearly three thousand vehicles per day, counted during a traffic census in northern India, only a thousand were motor vehicles. Nonetheless, a conference at Nagpur in 1943 not only formulated a road development program but also designed a classification of roads (see chap. 3).[125]

In Indian cities, the local modal configuration was mostly tainted by the rickshaw. Chennai had 2,090 rickshaws in 1913, and their numbers peaked in the mid-1930s with nearly 7,000. At that moment, about 6,000 rickshaws were registered in Kolkata, where the vehicle was introduced only around 1900 by the Chinese community for freight transport, and deployed for passenger transport from 1914 only. "Bengali chemist" Prafulla Râurrency observed in his memoirs of 1932, however, how "the custom for local people belonging to the so-called lower castes to supplement their agricultural income by serving as palanquin bearers" was becoming obsolete, as they "now ... would rather starve than undertake such a 'humiliating' task." In Burma (made into a province of India by the British in 1886), the first rickshaw appeared in the capital Rangoon in 1893 (the first car in around 1905). There were 426 cars and trucks ten years later,

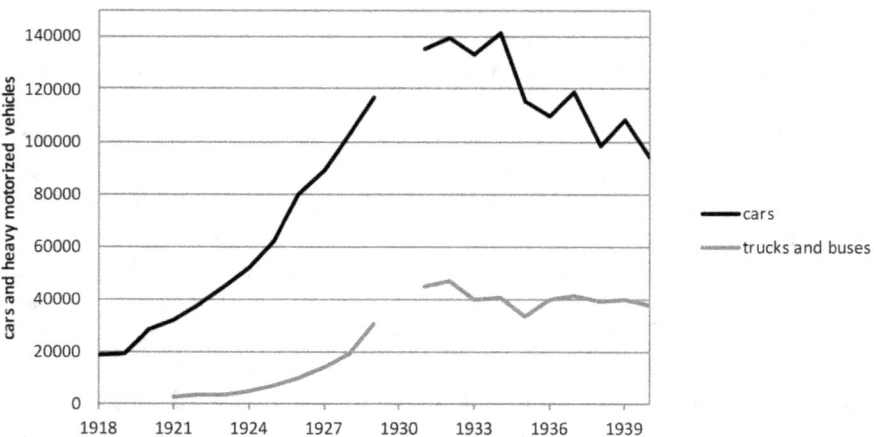

Figure 1.6. Cars and heavy motorized vehicles in some Indian provinces (Bombay, Bengal, Uttar Pradesh, Punjab, Madras, Central Provinces, Delhi), 1915–1940. Source: Tetzlaff, "Motorisation of the 'Mofussil,'" 288, table 2. Figure created by the author.

as well as 39 motorcycles. In 1923, W. Somerset Maugham was surprised Rangoon was as "modern" as Singapore or Shanghai (American cars were running "along trim, wide roads"). The number of rickshaws increased to 2,812 in 1920 (the first users were prostitutes), the year the local authorities tried to restrict their number. Three years later, these restrictions were lifted, and the rickshaw fleet increased to nearly 5,000 in 1924. It seems the introduction of the motorbus made their numbers decrease from 1926. Western observers commented on the "bizarre mixture of lorries, rickshaws, buses 'festooned with human beings,' bicycles, bullock carts, cows, copulating dogs, a stray horse, a five-seater car occupied by a family of ten, and handcarts with 'long bamboo poles hanging over the back.'"[126] This comment on the 'layeredness' of non-Western urban traffic from a British Army officer stems from 1950, so it misses the palanquin, but it is typical for the xenophobic and tendentially racist stance of the superior white, whose home situation is the norm and who observed deviating traffic conditions mostly as 'chaos.'

This chaos applied only to the large cities. In villages such as Karimpur, east of Agra near Delhi, the first (cycle) rickshaws appeared only around 1960, but bicycles for private use, although scarce, were around in 1930. This was observed by Charlotte and William Wiser, two American missionaries who, like Robert and Helen Lynd did on Muncie, Indiana, wrote an anthropological survey of the inhabitants' life in this village during a stay of several years, and who, like the Lynds, came back many years later to register its 'progress.' The Wisers arrived in Karimpur in a car, which, typically perhaps, was soon instrumentalized for errands and emergencies by the villagers. Different from the Lynds, however, was that they did not dedicate a large part of their report to car mobility: Karimpur's mobility was fully pedestrian. When Charlotte came back thirty years later (her husband had died), she reported how the children were disappointed about the new car design: "No mudguards, no running boards, not a thing to cling on." The Wisers were a part of a "transnational development regime" (including "the state, … bilateral and international development agencies, international foundations and NGOs, and institutions of expertise") of (mostly American) missionaries sent to Asian countries during the Progressive Era (1870–1920), supported by the Rockefeller foundation eager to promote "Christian ethics and civilisation on a global basis," a form of "professional philanthropy" pursuing "a program of robust capitalism, active democracy, private initiative, social service, and Christian virtue epitomizing the 'American way of life.'"[127]

However, the (mobility) historian may construct striking parallels between the West and the Rest at their own peril: it is through the inclusion of subaltern mobilities that the real differences become apparent. In a bundle of studies gathered by French Indologists undertaking their own 'mobility turn' (and coining the term circulation instead, to limit their analysis to circular mobility), the self-image of the colonizers bringing movement in an immobile agrarian society is fundamentally challenged: "Colonialism, far from being associated, as the wisdom of an earlier historiographical moment was prone to claim, with a greater freedom to circulate, and greater possibilities, linked to the advent of a new regime of surveillance which would have made circulation in fact more difficult and controlled." From this perspective, mobility per se was "potentially subversive." To illustrate this, subaltern studies unearthed "various types of peddlers," whose mobility was seen by the new rulers "as a social practice alien to processes of frontier building and administrative regulation. Therefore, circulation on the margins was understood to be a phenomenon which, by its very existence, represented a radical contestation of colonial rule," a contestation that on its turn prompted the colonizers to classify especially mobile groups as "criminal tribe."[128]

One such a mobile group were the Banjaras, an umbrella term for hundreds of tribes of "gypsies," buyers and sellers of draft animals and involved in transport for at least the last seven centuries. And although some of them started using trucks in the 1920s and 1930s, most kept walking with their oxen, the Banjara *qafila* (caravan) being a common sight at least until Independence. Historians also have described the "wandering castes of Bhojpuri singers" in Northern India (part of Uttar Pradesh and Bihar, before the provinces impoverished by the demise of the saltpeter trade in the 1920s) and their accompanying peddlers who sold "printed chapbooks" to a largely male public, consisting partly of sedentary urbanites but mostly of "rickshawalas, coolies, boatmen, wandering *baniyas*, cattle-sellers, slay-housebuilders, rope-makers, and *chaukidars*, i.e., people who leave their homes for long stretches to carry these travel-tales with them," tales replete with the themes of "wandering, violence, rebellion and renunciation." Such wandering castes were often martial, as they were used as spies and informants, just like the urban rickshaw pullers. Peddlers walked, and were often to be found on "cattle fairs," where "elephants, camels, sheep, buffaloes, horses and birds" were traded, and from where caravans departed to Nepal, and Bengal in the north and east. Caravans benefited not only from the itinerants' songs but also from their protection against bandits. Many of the bullock cart drivers and cattle drovers belonging to the Ahir, Teli, Noniya, and Banjara communities later became truck drivers. Singers who could "save enough money to buy a small truck ... place[d] a tape-recorder on a platform, and microphones, and drive slowly through cities to deliver their message."[129] It is amid this melee of mobility that the elite's motorization should be situated. This, indeed, is the most 'spectacular' difference with the 'coordination controversy' between road and rail in the West: in India, this controversy became embedded, if not overwhelmed and covered over, by the extreme layeredness of mobility.

***

The true token of Indian urban modernity, however, was not so much the car but rather apartment housing: the establishment of suburbs (in the case of Mumbai [Bombay] lying within the city limits) where "lower- and middle-class neighborhoods [were] always interspersed with slums," a response to "the emergence by the 1920s of a new upper-caste lower middle class" consisting of "clerks and typists" "working in the white-collar sector." In a study of these "walled compounds" of "multistory apartment buildings," Nikhil Rao described how such dwellings first got connected by "commuter trains" and then, in 1917, by an extension of the tramway. He uncovered a "questionnaire" from 1907 that asked stakeholders about their preferences regarding housing, roads, and rail connections in the future suburbs. The respondents rejected the possibility of the rich as potential inhabitants of the new suburbs, who "could build big bungalows, and they could afford the motor vehicles or carriages that would be necessary to move to and from the commercial districts." On the other hand, "the working classes … were simply working too many hours of the day to be able to spare the time to commute," let alone "afford even the modest sums that tram and train demanded. The middle classes, hence, were settled upon as those who would be 'forced' to [inhabit the suburbs], since they would be able to afford the rents and the costs of commuting."

To enable these people, who were mostly migrants from the South of India, to live there, the government should "have to take more of an initiative," for instance, through house purchasing via installment plans. However, Indian urban modernization was far from a copy of the West: the neighborhoods should reflect the "caste and community" characteristics of the social stratification and allow the middle class "to mix," as one stakeholder formulated it, "with his poor relations who are very often useful to him and to whom he is also a great help." Rao described a Gandhian revolt (*satyagraba*, a "form of nonviolent campaign through the force of truth") by angry commuters who stopped all traffic on the rail tracks out of protest against a lack of sufficient train capacity, the armed police arriving per truck, and the protest soon taking on "the aspect of a carnival … onlookers jeering and ridiculing the ranks of policemen." And although a bus service was opened in 1934, it is unlikely the suburbanites would be able to buy one of the 125,000 motor vehicles in the colony in 1936, a quarter more than in the Netherlands at about the same time.[130]

Natives as Subaltern Drivers of Mobility: The Cases of Malaysia and Indonesia

Other Asian countries show mobility configurations somewhere between the extremes of the two giants: India with its fully developed railway system, versus China with its dominant inland navigation, but both with an underdeveloped road network if placed in comparison with the West. As elsewhere, Malaya showed a half-century-long struggle between rail and road, as Thomas Leinbach revealed in his study of the peninsula's three-pronged "development." Whereas the tin ore was transported "through a complementary rail and road system," the latter functioning as "feeders" to the former, the rubber plantations farther away from the railroads benefitted from the newly built road network, followed by a phase that the system also supported the "rural level." This truly was 'development by road.' By 1921, Chinese and Indian migrants outnumbered the Malays, while Europeans and Eurasians represented not more than 3 percent of the population. As such, Malaysian mobility history is an example of the limits of the alleged universalism of Western concepts and methods. Such concepts and methods focus on the spread of the railway network over the country's surface similar to the Indian example, but they often forget to include a "people's history," in Malaysia's case, based on the labor of a "multi-ethnic community" of about thirteen thousand workers, where Indian were preferred by the British colonizers over Chinese, because the former were considered "passive and easily governed."[131]

The basis of such a people's history of Malaysian mobility has been written by Thomas Williamson, whose account of interbellum roadbuilding in the colony is exemplary in reflecting the tensions of colonial rule: the first road was cut through the jungle by the British invaders in the 1870s (when there were "virtually no roads" in the Malay-dominated states); the road aimed not only at reaching the mining centers from their base at Kuala Kangsar but also at confronting the Malay rebellion of 1875. By 1920, the British boasted that "no country situated in the tropical zone has a better road system," just like what the French said about their colonies in Indochina. Indeed, like in other colonies around the globe, roads were the tokens of modernity: "Everyone moves about; everyone reads newspapers," the colonial journal *British Malaya* wrote in 1926. Railways, especially the feeder roads to the tin mines and rubber cultivation sites, enabled at least twenty million migrants to "move ... through" the colony, most of them from China. The British consciously created this mobile modernity, for instance, by loaning money to officials "to buy a car or motor cycle," enabling them, according to a publication from the government, to drive "over 3,000 miles of excellent public roads, and an unknown mileage of roads through estates and up to mines," where they could indulge in the automotive adventure "no different from Europe." By then, the 1931 census revealed migrants had meanwhile outnumbered the indigenous population by 2.2 to 1.9 million inhabitants. In a serialized novel by Harun Aminurrashid (*The Rose of Kuala Lumpur*, 1930) the protagonist is "racing between rural and urban locations" in his car described as a cocoon, the only place where he "would feel calm." Soon, this quiet would be interrupted by the Japanese invasion, on the bicycle.[132]

***

In Indonesia, too, a dual network of roads and railroads was constructed by the Dutch colonizers, 44,000 and 6,500 km in length, respectively, connecting the coal fields with the big rivers and the coast. Some of the roads, such as the "Napoleonic" Great Daendels Mail Road on Java, were built as a defense against a possible British invasion already back in the early nineteenth century. On the "sugar road" on the same island, an amazing variety of draught animals were to be seen, from camels, donkeys, and buffaloes to llamas and elephants. Long before the coming of the motorbus, the *dokar* (pony cart) was used as a collective public transport vehicle. Here, too, the "earth-moving and stone-crushing" labor was provided by "the population ... free of charge or, at worst, it can be paid in rice and salt," as a local colonial newspaper formulated it. They were mostly Indies Chinese, or natives, part of the 60 million inhabitants (1900), of which the Europeans, mostly Dutch, formed less than 1 percent (60,000 in 1900, 208,000 in 1930). All technical equipment came from the West.

By the end of the interbellum, shortly before the Japanese would invade the colony in 1942, the number of cars in Indonesia was more than fifty thousand (mostly assembled locally by GM, since 1927), causing in its competition with the train the same coordination crisis that happened in the West in that phase. Like in the West, "wild buses and trucks" started to capture the lucrative routes from the train service. But apart from the equipment, the colonial elite also imported the automotive adventure, including the killing of chickens on the road, tongue in cheek, likewise provoking the violence from the original road users, who resisted the invasion through stone throwing. Indeed, it was not so much the machine that was exported but a fledgling elite 'car society,' with a twist: car accidents easily became racialized, as in the case of a European motorcyclist who killed a native cyclist, who, according to the journal *Magneet*, clearly was *bingoeng* (Malay for 'confused'), because "he zigzagged on the road in a most awkward way." When the Dutch governor-general made his inspection tour in 1915, he used a car for the first time, "sometimes at a racing speed."

When, by the end of the interbellum, the painter Soedjojono (who would become famous after the war as a painter of the revolution), like his Indian poet colleagues, asked himself how to represent the modern Indies, he favored the "sugar factories and starved peasants, automobiles of the rich, and pantaloons of the youth: shoes, trousers, and gabardine jackets of tourists on asphalt roads," instead of "the lush tropics, with the half-naked women." Rudolf Mrázek, who quotes the artist in his excellent analysis of "technology and nationalism in a colony," observed how, indeed, in the colony there was "an increasing eagerness to attain modernity by technologies that were unabashedly frivolous, and by machinery that served primarily to produce an appearance and an amusement … Much more than in the West, progress in the colony was identified with fashion." Indeed, it is in the colonies (especially in their fast-growing big cities) that the Western middle class felt the urge to emphasize the conspicuousness of its consumption, a flight forward in a condition of general uncertainty and insecurity.[133] Together with the indigenous elite, they forged a conspicuous, status-orientated car culture that would characterize much of the postwar, postcolonial societies. But what is instructive from a mobility point of view is the elite's monopoly on automotive adventure through an 'ironic car' that absolutely excluded the 'chaotic Other' from its adventurous bubble, including its violence.

Similar stories can be told about other urbanized parts of Indonesia, such as Surabaya, where the first motorbus appeared in 1924, when there were 800 taxis and 3,300 individually owned passenger cars. A close reading by Johny Khusyairi of two local newspapers revealed the racialized character of colonial mobilities: natives ran a six to ten times higher risk of being killed in traffic than Europeans and Chinese, a reflection of the quantitative composition of the population. Racism extends beyond the grave: in the Dutch *Soerabaiasch Handelsblad*, European victims were described with their initials, while Chinese victims were given full names. No name at all was given to the "natives." These natives, indeed, provided the (historically hidden) drivers of local mobility. Their relative vulnerability may also have been determined in part by the type of road Khusyairi saw represented on early Indonesian films of road traffic: the 'mixed road,' rejected in the European core by most traffic experts in favor of the automobile-only highway, may have persisted in the 'periphery' much longer, a phenomenon worthy of further study by historians of colonial mobility.[134]

***

As we have seen, rickshaws were to be found in the big cities such as Singapore, but they also appeared in Ceylon (current Sri Lanka) and as far away as South African Durban. Not only were the mobility configurations in all these places different, but also the ethnic configuration differed substantially. In Singapore, as we saw, "all transport workers were Asians," but in British Malaysia, horse carriage and motor vehicle drivers were mostly Malay, while the Chinese controlled the garage business and were bus and tram conductors, as well as rickshaw pullers. Indians (Sikhs) were tram drivers, and not a single European was involved in the transport business. In Philippine Manila, on the other hand, where some seven thousand carriages still plied the streets as late as 1941, transport-related occupations were characterized by "racially homogeneity," as they were dominated by Filipinos themselves. This is not to say Manila was free of racism; on the contrary, *cocheros* (carriage drivers) were often seen as "belonging to the same class as criminals," and especially the native Tagalogs among them were considered to have a "natural propensity to be reckless on the street," as Michael Pante's reading of Filipino newspapers revealed. A recent study of the "American-colonial masculinities" in the Philippines shows not only how a "masculinisation" of the transport sector in Manila was fueled by American entrepreneurs who dominated the sector but also how the subsequent motorization led to "the demise of the *paseo*, a late nineteenth-century urban ritual" of upper-class conspicuous mobility consumption in horse carriages.[135]

Migration, Colonialism, and the Struggle between Rail and Road: The Case of Africa

The rickshaw was the global expression of modernity, as it tainted the mobility of urbanization. Beyond city life, mobility was no less modern, as the massive migratory flows were an expression of industrialization, urbanization, and "second imperialism." Migration, therefore, should be part and parcel of a mobility history that takes itself seriously as a way to get a grip on the global 'mobility turn' of the nineteenth and twentieth centuries. Migration started well before the colonial period, but in early modern times, it took on a new character, stimulated less by disaster and war but more by emerging capitalism and long-distance mobility (both communication and transport), without which its unfolding would have been unthinkable. Between 1850 and 1940, on a global scale, about 150 million people migrated over transoceanic long distances, grossly one-third from Europe to the Americas, one-third from India and South China to countries around the Indian Ocean and the South Pacific, and one-third from Northeast Asia and Russia to Central Asia, Manchuria, and Japan. On average, and compared to a world population in the order of two billion, the annual flows of about one to two million people were tiny (maximum 1.5 percent) compared to a sessile majority, even if one takes the internal, many times larger migration flows into account. Most of these flows, "externally" per ship in third class or steerage, internally on foot, per train, per river boat, or otherwise, "took place beyond the direct influence of Europe," especially the 'migratory systems' in Asia; they showed two peaks of about 1.6 million migrants, one transatlantic in the decade before World War I, the other Asian in the decade before World War II.[136]

But real historical events do not work with averages: they come with surges and bounds; with this in mind, the number of ships and trains needed to transport the migrants over the entire globe was indeed massive. These flows were not spontaneous, to say the least: their logistics were highly organized, first through "facilitators" and then through professional agencies who provided the "credit tickets" taken over by the migrants' future employers, the beginning of their often lifelong dependency on their exploiters. Thus, from the point of view of the migrant, the dichotomy between a mobile West and an immobile Rest is an absurd construction, as are many of the other epithets Western colonizers reserved for themselves such as "rational, hard-working, productive, sacrificial and parsimonious, liberal-democratic, honest, patronal and mature, advanced, ingenious, proactive, independent, progressive and dynamic. The East was then cast as the West's opposite." The Rest was also depicted as alluring, exotic, and passive, inviting the colonizers' mobility, as it were.[137]

***

Colonial mobility infrastructures on the African continent were mostly ports, as well as telegraph and railway lines to the north and the south: the first railway line was part of the Red Sea Route to India, between Alexandria and Cairo, and the first two construction waves were inspired by the discovery of diamonds in the 1870s and gold a decade later. After 1914, the network did not change much until the end of the century, a network of "only scattered unconnected lines, serving mainly Europe's need for raw materials" and, of course, the ostentatious demonstration of occupation, after the 'scramble for Africa' at the Berlin Conference of 1885 by the colonial powers in Berlin. This scandalous "lack of inter-territorial rail links ... effectively dismembered the African market," the roads built as feeders to the railways. Everywhere, the colonial government "resorted to communal labour of a kind traditionally owed to chiefs, and to compulsory labour," triggering "the migration of large numbers of the male population," disintegrating social life and creating the first pockets of a wage-earning proletariat. They also created a "new kind of African city" on a continent that at the time was not very densely populated (about two hundred million as late as 1950), so much so that colonial governments started importing workers from India, Southeast Asia, and the West Indies.[138]

The new mobilities created a second layer upon an existing mobility culture, generating what we have called 'layeredness.' For instance, next to the traditional communication systems based on messengers, the telegraph and telephone emerged, from which black Africans were mostly excluded.

Similarly, next to the animal paths and the camels or human head porterage used along the trading routes, railways and concrete and asphalt roads were constructed, but here it was not possible to exclude the local population from using the new networks, although the type of mobility deployed was highly dependent on ethnic and racial dichotomies: motorized transport here, pedestrianism there. Nonetheless, road network building was surrounded with the same modernization mythology we have observed in Asia: in Zaïre, for instance, a report by a commission "for the Protection of the Indigenous" concluded: "There are roads but no vehicles," despite the decree from the provincial governors "to forbid long-distance porterage in regions where modern means of transport were more or less developed," a form of rigorous traffic regulation we will encounter quite often in a colonial setting, and, again, proof of the construction of colonial mobilities as 'laboratories.'[139]

From the Belgian Congo and its ruler, King Leopold (against whose atrocities Joseph Conrad's *Heart of Darkness* [1899] was directed), to the genocide on the Herero by the German colonizer in Southwest Africa (present-day Namibia), the cruelty was indescribable. In the case of the latter alone, between 1904 and 1908, "60,000 Herero, 10,000 Nama and up to 250,000 Ngoni, Ngindo, Matumbi, and members of other ethnic groups were either directly killed or starved to death." And although an 'efficient' and 'scientific' form of colonization emerged in the course of the early twentieth century, the open violence based on a not-less-open racism was never abandoned, whether one analyzes the history of settler colonies or other types of colonization. All in all, some scholars have tried to estimate the number of indigenous people who died as a direct cause of colonial rule, and they end up with numbers between fifty million and one hundred million.[140] Against this background, the emergence of the bicycle and the car should be analyzed. Africa, near the cradle of these vehicles (Europe), offered itself as a welcome terrain for experiments in this direction. Perhaps for the same reason, anthropologists flocked to the continent, more so, it seems, than to Asia, to study and in some cases even accommodate its modernization. The historian of mobility can benefit from this abundance.

The Construction of 'Layeredness': Colonial Mobility in Dahomey (Benin)

Indeed, several well-researched case studies, undertaken by economic historians as well as geographers (and later, anthropologists), make Africa an excellent starting point for an investigation into the relationship between colonialism, migration, and mobility.[141] Patrick Manning's very detailed history of Dahomey (current-day Benin), 1640–1960, for instance, clearly showed how African merchants continued the slave trade after the European powers (France, Portugal, England) discontinued it at the beginning of the nineteenth century. Triggered by the expansion of Brazilian plantations in the 1630s, Benin exported two million slaves, "one fifth of the total Atlantic slave trade." The princely class in Dahomey gained "European recognition and maintain[ed] dominion over a large precapitalist domestic economy." When Britain seriously started trying to stem the export of slaves, and after a slave revolt in Bahia in 1835, several slaves returned and became merchants themselves, increasing the local mix of religions, spoken languages, and ethnicities. With industrialized soap production in England emerging, slave trade changed into slave labor, on palm oil plantations run by Europeans as well as indigenous warlords, belonging to the Fon monarchy, which became dominant after a revolt of Yoruba slaves. During the remainder of the nineteenth century and far into the twentieth, two societies struggled for hegemony: a mercantile based on caravans and head porterage, canoe and sailing ship, and a capitalist, industrial technology driven by the steamship and the steam train. The main impulse to the struggle, and the eventual victory of capitalism, was coming from diminishing "costs of transport, marketing and finance." In the process, the Europeans favored capitalism under European rule, and in 1890–1893, France conquered the land, joined by Britain and Germany in neighboring areas, and the mercantilist system was by 1930 "absorbed into the capitalist mode of production."[142]

Indeed, the mercantile system first felt the onslaught of the new era in long-distance shipping, when British and German steamships began to dominate, and the Brazilians, unable financially to make the change, reoriented their commerce to Europe. On the coast of Dahomey, France built first a wooden and then a steel pier protruding into the ocean for several hundred meters, and equipped it with a railroad track allowing ships to be loaded much faster compared to the canoes that had to feed and unload the big ships one kilometer out of the shallow coast line. France also installed a postal system, set up telegraph lines, and built a narrow-gauge railroad that charged very high tariffs but nonetheless was much cheaper than head porterage, forcing the latter to develop into a feeder system around the railway stations. Although the palm oil economy was hardly affected by the new technologies, the maize plantations further into the hinterland would not have been possible without the railways. Meanwhile, the long-distance caravans had been pushed north, still carrying textiles, guns and gunpowder, alcoholic beverages, matches and tobacco.

In fact, apart from the long-distance sea transport, the actual conquering of the land was preceded by the installation of innovative communication systems, as the French based their first entries on indigenous transport technologies such as the horse, the palanquin, and the indigenous's own body. Precolonial Africa had been receptive to the import of guns but not to the wheel: long before, Saharan wheeled transport had been replaced by the camel. In sub-Saharan areas, carriages, if they were used at all (and mostly for ceremonial purposes by local sovereigns), were drawn by humans, because horses were extremely costly if they were around at all, because of the threat of trypanosomiasis, caused by the tsetse fly. But most of all, colonizers soon discovered (like the Dutch in Indonesia) it was not so much (or only) the vehicles they had to export, but an entire transport system: for the carriage presented to the king of Asante on the Gold Coast, a new road had to be constructed in order to get the vehicle to its destination.[143] Although we will deal later with how the railroads and roads were built under colonial circumstances, it is important to stress how the colonial state crept (or better, elbowed itself) in between the metropolis and the local elite. The local administrators concentrated their efforts on collecting taxes and organizing the construction of railroads and especially roads.

The classic (and traditionalist) tale of colonial transport development has been accompanied by an ongoing debate among students of African colonialism on the usefulness of roads; the economist Manning theorized their construction must be seen "as an effort in socialization rather than in investment. Administrators were trying to teach Dahomeans to be ready to work for the state on whatever they were asked to do, with enthusiasm, and regardless of compensation." The efforts undertaken by the colonizers to resettle villages close to the road were measures of control and dominance. This was for instance the case in Northern Angola, although the displaced natives often kept their houses in their fields in the bush, where they grew their own products. In other words, early twentieth-century infrastructure projects were exercises in hegemony. Meanwhile, "the French colonial state appropriated for itself a large and growing portion of the economic surplus of Dahomey, and then allocated it in a manner which, while tending to provide support for the capitalist sector at the expense of other sectors, was detrimental to the cause of economic growth," so much so that Manning claimed, using a counterfactual argumentation, the entire colonial project did not improve the economic condition of the area at all: "economic growth in the late nineteenth and early twentieth century would have been greater if the French had not conquered Dahomey."

For a student of Western mobility history, this does not come as a total surprise: roadbuilding in the West was also loaded with noneconomic values of modernity and a struggle between 'two societies.' In the colonies, however, such conditions came out much harsher and clearer: when the administrator of a certain district "conscripted virtually the entire [local] adult male population" to build a 150-kilometer road, "at the successful conclusion of which the Governor general was able to ride triumphantly from the coast to Parakou in a motorcar," villagers must have wondered about the disproportionate efforts to accomplish this feat, all the more so because all those men were taken from their work at the plantations. Indeed, on the fledgling road network, "the administrator or merchants could now ride to outlying areas on their bicycles."[144]

The Diversity of African National Mobility Developments: Uganda, Tanzania, Ghana, and Mozambique

Other case studies, undertaken in other countries, largely confirm the Dahomean pattern of mobility development. Uganda was special, however. Like in other colonies, modern transport started with a combined slave and ivory trade, the latter commodity carried by the former (in the parlance of the colonizers, they were called "joint products"). But John Speke, one of the first Europeans to visit the country, as early as 1862 commented on the roads as being "as broad as our coach-roads, ... a strange contrast to the wretched tracks in all the adjacent countries." Why this was so is unclear, but local peoples were required to maintain their roads (called *Luwalo*, imposed after the arrival of the British as a tax of one month's work per year), which also benefitted from the presence of good gravel material.[145] East African Tanzania, on the other hand, followed the usual pattern. Its history of mobility is adorned with two detailed studies and starts with caravan trade in ivory and slaves by Arabs to India and Arab countries, mobilizing an estimated five hundred thousand porters (many of them recruited among the people of Nyamwesi of central Tanzania) passing through Tabora in the middle of the country during the 1860s, a time when an annual seventy thousand slaves were sold at the market in Zanzibar. By the turn of the century, one hundred thousand to two hundred thousand people were involved in the caravan trade on the main route through the colony on an annual basis.

When Germany constructed East Africa, efforts to send German engineers to build roads were to no avail, mostly because the tsetse fly prevented the use of draught animals. As elsewhere, the railways during the two first decades of the twentieth century enabled the establishment of a capitalist plantation agriculture, aided by new efforts to build feeder roads, on which by 1914 fifteen motorcycles, six passenger cars, and five trucks were deployed. Indeed, initially, before the 'coordination crisis' of the interwar years, road and rail cultures coexisted peacefully, the former supporting the latter by expanding its area of influence. Here, as elsewhere, roadbuilding developed in two phases, first by widening existing paths (including caravan paths, providing them with rest houses, ferries, and bridges) and routes, and then, mostly during the interwar years, on a more scientifically inspired engineering basis. Planning of the network was strategic rather than economical: profitability was not envisaged, and "all transport investments of this period must generally appear over-sized in direct relation to the given level of economic development."[146]

When Great Britain received the mandate over Tanganyika from the League of Nations after Germany's defeat in World War I, the second half of the 1920s witnessed a rapid expansion of the road system, until the Depression led to stagnation from which the colony would emerge only after World War II. Whereas, in 1921, the colony had 2,650 miles of roads "passable for light motor vehicles during the dry season" and built by non-specialists, later road planning, if at all, was constrained by a rigorous 'coordination policy' that forbade the construction of roads parallel to railways. The proposal to construct a bridge in 1932 was rejected by authorities because it would have created a road competing with the railway. Nonetheless, in the 1930s the "Great North Road" was built, as part of "the famous dream concept of a road connection from the Cape to Cairo." Apart from the construction of local roads in areas of major economic activities, the length of classified main roads only increased from 2,159 to 2,956 miles between 1929 and 1946, and they did not form an integrated trunk road network. Nonetheless, the entire patchwork of networks comprised 16,400 miles of roads passable by automobiles, nearly all constructed during the interwar years. They allowed that "large parts of the country were for the very first time being drawn into the modern economy." In other words, the same phenomenon can be discerned in the colonies and the metropoles. Although major factions within government circles defended the railways, others built roads, laying the foundation for the demise of the former after World War II. In the colonies, however, government rule took on a harsher shape, as we saw, through a more aggressive 'coordination' policy aimed at outright prohibiting road competition against the railway interests. The state was held in check to a lesser extent than in the metropolises.

In Tanzania, by 1938, more than five thousand motor vehicles were registered, most of them trucks. Whereas some private trucking firms tried their luck, head porterage remained important until the early 1930s (even as late as the 1970s, some Tanzanians referred to a *barbara y Wapagazi* [porter's highway] when directing visitors to the main road; by 1938, this form of freight mobility had virtually disappeared). The endurance of porterage may also have been due to government policy, which in 1934, by special ordinance, prohibited transport of imported goods on roads parallel to the railways. And when, nearly a decade later, the advantages of trucking could no longer be denied by a government boasting on its rationality, it gave the monopoly of trucking to the railway company, exactly as European governments also tried to do, often to no avail.

Meanwhile, inland water transport had been handed over exclusively to the Kenya-Uganda Railway company, while British Imperial Airways started a regular civilian air service in 1931–1932, from England through Cairo all the way to Cape Town. River transport's role in both precolonial and colonial times should not be underestimated, but the railways remained the basic support structure of colonial exploitation: whereas the transport of high-valued goods such as ivory, kapok, and rubber may have been possible without it (undertaken through head porterage), the transport of bulk freight such as sisal, cotton, and coffee certainly would have not. Later products such as tea, tobacco, and cashews were not dependent on railway per se, although they too depended on a minimum form of infrastructure, be it railway or road. The post–World War II basic Tanzanian mobility structure of two East-West railway lines starting at port cities, and two trunk roads in the South, also starting at ports, is a direct heritage of the colonial logic of resource exploitation.[147]

***

An analysis of mobility history in Ghana from an economic-geography point of view and based mostly on colonial reports (1895–1946) confirms this picture, except that it emphasizes another freight mobility form: barrel rolling, "an innovation of the late nineteenth century" especially popular in the Golf Coast, mostly of palm oil, for which smooth roads were essential and draught animals were impossible to deploy because of the tsetse fly. But in Ghana, too, the watershed in transport history is situated in the 1920s, when the railways started to feel competition from the road system, the latter's function being changed from an independent role in the nineteenth century into a feeding role for the railways, "link[ing] formerly inaccessible areas of agricultural production to the railway and world markets." The study of Ghanese mobility history shows how the direction of the flow of the costly commodities (such as gold, ivory, and pepper) changed three times in two centuries, first to the coast in the south, then to the north, away from the sea, through porterage for the Portuguese, and then to the south again to the ports, when the Ashanti pushed the middlemen at the coast away and the railway was established. The latter, built in the first place for the European gold mining companies, also acquired a military function after the Ashanti revolt of 1901, for troop transport. Remarkably, the railway tracks also opened an extra possibility as a footpath for porterage.

In their road classification, the British rulers distinguished between "bush roads" and "main trade roads," the latter used for the intensive barrel rolling of cocoa and palm oil. With four hundred tons per month after the opening of a new road, barrel rolling seemed to be constrained only by the problem of recruiting labor. In this country too, a Great North Road was built, from Kumasi to Tamala, and here (like in Europe), heavy trucks with non-pneumatic tires ruined the roads, leading to regulation. Cocoa shipments per train diminished by the impact of trucking, a condition that was enhanced later during the interwar years by the Depression. These formed extra incentives to regulate 'wild' trucking, especially when the new roads "enabl[ed] the lorries to snatch not only the cocoa traffic to the port, but the high rated import traffic on the return journey" as well. Passenger transport by rail also decreased, both through the use of trucks (providing passenger transport at the same time as they transported freight) and through the Depression. In 1928, a Central Road Board was installed to sort out this situation, but the meetings ended in a quarrel between railway and road interests. In Ghana, as elsewhere in Africa, trucks were mostly Fords.[148]

***

A more recent analysis of the colonization of Moçambique (1900–1961), a district in Portuguese Mozambique, added to this general picture of 'colonial modal split' in a classic (economically dominated) transport context by giving a view on the mobility-related sufferings of the African population. Based, partially, on oral history and the interpretation of "songs and mockeries," this study, by Arlindo Chilundo, argued that porterage "antedated the colonial period." What the study especially showed, however, is the disrupting effect of the colonial tax system, as it forced peasants to carry their produce (millet, maize, rice, peanuts, rubber, wax, coffee, sesame, tobacco) to the coast to exchange for money. Porterage as forced labor was first introduced by the military, most particularly during the "pacification campaigns" starting shortly after the Berlin Conference of 1885, where European powers had divided Africa among themselves. The recruiting for porterage, and for the building of railroads and roads, led to a massive flight of sometimes entire villages deeper into the forests, which incited some factions within the colonial apparatus to hold a plea for the introduction of trucks and cars, which not only were more "humane" but also would prevent "a great number of natives [from ruining] themselves and put[ing] themselves out of action" and would "divert man-power, especially during the harvest when the number of porters reach the figure of 80,000."

In some areas such as Ghana, up to 60 percent of the women were also recruited for forced labor on the roads. The same applies to Mozambique, where female tax defaulters in the early 1930s were forced to work in the cotton fields. The usual efforts of colonizers, mimicking the practice in the mother country, to classify roads reveals its racism in these particularly harsh circumstances: distinguishing between three types of roads (A: arterial main roads, C: local roads, and B: all roads not being part of the first two categories) "enabled the colonial state to shift greater responsibilities to local communities." Class A was used by European firms and the state, and their maintenance was done by forced labor. The classification was slightly changed when the Forced Labor Convention (1930) in Geneva was signed, to which no colonial government adhered. "Overall, the paradox of the colonial situation enabled the colonial state to exploit forced labor while apparently championing free labor," one student of Ghana opines, but from a racist perspective, sadly, there is no paradox at all: freedom only counts for civilized people.[149]

An oral-historical and museological study of the palanquin/machilla (or *hamac* in French Senegal, hammock in English) gives a vivid picture of its use in Mozambique. It may have been the simplest "vehicle" ever, after walking: a two-by-one-meter rectangular cotton cloth, consisting of multi-colored bands ten to twenty centimeters wide, was suspended on a single pole of wood or bamboo (the pole itself sometimes wrapped in a colorful textile 'envelop'), resting on the heads of the two porters for and aft, and balanced on a shock-damping cloth on the porters' heads. Sometimes, a little tent against the sun and a pillow were added. Designed by Portuguese officers as a response to the total lack of roads in the colony in the nineteenth century, the hammock was used (by force of custom) exclusively for the transport of the African sovereign and for whites. The carrying of the vehicle required great skill, and at the court, porters exercised constantly in the art of balancing without their hands touching the pole. The first porter (in Fon, the local language, *kponhinto*) was the subject of legend formation, while the aft man went nameless, even if he had to steer. For a fifty-kilometer journey, about ten porters were necessary, and longer journeys might require fifty. Each group of porters consisted of three teams: the two main porters, up to six lateral porters (*dôkànto*) who had to help maneuver the hammock through difficult terrain, and a large reserve, from which new teams of porters were formed every fifteen to sixty minutes, depending on the condition of the path. The speed, realized as the team "jog-trotted along, chanting a song," varied from 3 to 10 km/h, with an average of 6.5 km/h, more than 50 percent faster than an average pedestrian (4 km/h). At the end of the trip, the hammock could be used as a bed or a seat. One European user preferred the hammock above all other forms of transport: "One smokes, one reads, one dreams or one sleeps and the variety of visions is a treat for the eye."[150]

When the machilla was officially prohibited in the early 1930s (but they were still used in the backcountry well into the 1940s), a nurse who had the right to use them, and who was later interviewed by Chilundo, said he was "barred from traveling in a rick-shaw. Because rick-shaws had to be imported, they remained a luxury reserved for only the high ranked European colonial officials," showing how again a vehicle, in this case used by the lower middle classes of China and India, does not come with a 'script' of its use. The script had to be formulated locally, as a part of the appropriating process. Here is how porters experienced this type of mobility:

Along with my colleagues, we carried the administrator (*chefe de posto*). He was a Portuguese. As the time passed, he started gaining weight and he was becoming heavier. So they brought in two more *mashilèros*. Sometimes we had to carry the *chefe de posto* and his wife from here (Muite) to Namialo. This always happened when his wife got sick. Under these circumstances, we had to carry the couple to Namialo in order to get to the hospital in Moçambique Island.

We would leave at dawn on Saturdays and hurry without stopping even if it rained, in order to reach the Monday train at 8.00 a.m., in Namialo. Then the train would take them to Moçambique Island.

Porters sang lyrics while portering to alleviate the pain of being away from home for so long (the porterage season could take six to twelve months). Peasants who saw the *mashilèros* coming ran away to avoid being recruited as porters themselves, or out of outright fear, remembering how during the 'pacification campaigns' their villages had been destroyed, "especially in areas whose chiefs had resisted militarily." Therefore, the porters, approaching a village, sang: "Wani Ho! / Nàruaka muhita wé / Ni-nluha Muretelle" (You there in the household, do not run away, because all we are bringing … is peace). The colony rested on other forms of forced labor as well. Roadwork, for instance, started during the campaigns of the late nineteenth century, when paths were widened and new roads were hastily built without much planning. "Those roads were designed," one interviewee remembered, "to ease the passage of the white people to my land." Indeed, like railways in an earlier phase, roads were constructed as tools of control. Interviewed peasants claimed they "were beaten more often than before the introduction of motor vehicles … When we were in the cotton fields, sometimes the settlers would appear in their cars and then violently beat us, maltreat us … we did not even have time to eat."[151]

The particular circumstances of the Portuguese regime also led to the installation of state-run trucking, as an extreme example of protecting the state's investments in the railroads. Until 1929, trucking was private, but when the railroads lost half their merchandise, truckers in the north were wiped from the roads by a state monopoly. Such measures, unheard of in the mother country, culminated in "a new law forbid[d]ing farmers who owned trucks to use them to haul their own produce if they happened to be along the railroad or the state trucking route." Such measures, also proposed by railroad companies in Europe, appeared impossible to implement there because of inviolable property rights. Not so in the colony: by the end of the 1930s, the state monopoly was extended to river boats, canoes, and rafts.[152]

This remarkable immobilizing of the natives was continued after World War II, when peasants needed travel permits from local authorities if they wished to leave their village. And yet, from the beginning of the 1940s, peasants managed to acquire bicycles: there were nearly 3,000 sold in 1942, growing to more than 15,500 in 1950 and double that amount ten years later. Such developments, as well as the impact of roadbuilding on women, brings most students of African colonialism to the conclusion that roads had an ambiguous effect: they enhanced the colonizers' exploitation, but at the same time "broadened the range of coping opportunities ... While it deepened the exploitation of rural women, the transportation revolution seems to have enhanced women's coping strategies by facilitating their direct access to commodity markets." Nonetheless, "road and rail transportation were the cornerstone of the colonial system."[153]

Roads Versus Rails: The Synchronous Emergence of the Automobile as a Frivolous Vehicle

It is quite revealing how, during the 1920s and 1930s, a small number of trucks could threaten the railway's monopoly. It shows how, although the scale of motorized mobility may have been different from the metropolis, its impact was at least as acute. Indeed, studying road traffic in the first half of the century in Africa shows how the amount of ownership and the character of driving experience should be clearly distinguished in analyzing motorization. If ownership triggers conspicuous consumption of trucks and especially passenger cars as it emphasizes their commodity character, then seeing and perhaps using them helps putting them squarely in a global mobility history as a tool of movement in all its varieties. In other words, the African colonial variety is clearly dominated by the 'serious mobility' of the transport economist (and as such resonates with what we found so far for Asia), but a recent study exclusively dedicated to the emergence of the car in Africa argues (although itself caught in the "impact" paradigm of early historians of automobilism such as John Rae and James Flink) that the vehicles' scarcity also granted an extra dimension to the car's iconic status. The "impact" of these vehicles therefore "stretches beyond [the state and the political and economic elite] into the everyday lives of people in the smallest villages." The car started in Africa as a colonial tool of "extension and enforcement of ... control at a symbolic and functional level," but later it also developed into an anti-colonial tool (just as we saw for the case of the Indian railways), for instance, when buses were boycotted during apartheid in South Africa or when Ghana's independence was partly realized by the use of propaganda vans touring the countryside. But between the one and the other practice, fifty years of motorization passed, hardly described and analyzed, in which the indigenous people had to deal with car and truck as a new phenomenon: "He made us work long hours on the roads," a colonial district official in Tanzania was remembered, "and he was the only one who had a motor car."[154]

Road motorization studies in Africa reveal, for instance, how in Zambia the truck competed with the *gareta*, a one-wheeled barrow reminiscent of what we encountered in China. Metal rods fore and aft permitted two men pulling and pushing "at a slow but steady jog trot," as a female colonizer explained in the late 1930s based on her own riding experience, while her husband used a bicycle. Ox wagons and sleds in sandy areas (including used canoes) were other vehicles deployed, dependent on the presence or absence of the tsetse fly. The first cars appeared in the first decade of the twentieth century and in Zambia, for instance, bought by a "settler [hero] of German colonialism": "Bwana Tucka Tucka" Paul Graetz. Whereas porterage and forced labor for roadbuilding already convincingly showed how mobility in Africa, also of the Europeans, would not have been possible without indigenous efforts, this is no less true for the early car trips along the very same roads, using petrol sent ahead through head porterage.[155]

Like in Europe, authorities predicted or pleaded in favor of the emergence of the car, such as the British governor of Ghana who in 1901 "advocated the building of roads good enough for motor cars and traction engines," followed, indeed, by the construction of several of such roads. Tarring, let alone the application of asphalt, was not common; in fact, the Ghanese Transport Department performed tests in 1908 "to tar the feet of the carriers it employed," a common reflex (to opt for the solution on the 'vehicle side') among road engineers when the infrastructural solution seemed too difficult. In this case, as in most others, a cheap version of the latter was eventually chosen: a combination of a tarred and a metal road, hence the name "tarmet." In the British Gold Coast (Ghana), the first car (a French Gardner Serpollet steamer, purchased in 1902 for the governor) was "dumped in the sea' after it could not be made to start, but after World War I, the country imported motor vehicles (cars and trucks) with two clear peaks in the mid-1920s and mid-1930s (fig. 1.7). And like in Europe, World War I precipitated the use of motorized transport, if only because for long journeys "a carrier would ... eat the full weight of his load in 24 days, that is on a 12-day journey outward (180 miles) and 12 days return." Hilarious is therefore the experience of a colonial official in Tanzania who in the 1920s "recruited unwilling Chagga porters to go on tour with him, only to find that they all chipped in to hire a lorry to transport his loads."[156]

Jan-Bart Gewald, one of the few Africanists who dedicated a study on early road motorization (in Zambia), confirms the pivotal role of the 1920s as a turning point in the history of African automobilism, putting this history in synchronicity with our earlier Asian history, and with Europe for that matter, including the car's pleasurable sides. However, much more than in Europe, Westerners and local elites practiced their automobilism, however adventurous, inside a bubble, given the modest size of a middle class in this period. A French consul in Bissao opined, "A drive in a motor car on a good road … is not an administrative tour, for it is not in the vicinity of the areas frequented by Europeans that the natives usually prepare their rebellion against the authorities." Like I have analyzed in detail elsewhere for early European and North American automobilism, the car distanced its passengers from the environment, at the same time protecting them from the Other. While whites, in their 'ironic cars,' distanced themselves technologically from blacks, the latter were forced to come closer and live near roads, as we saw. Wives of civil servants were driven in government cars to visit the cinema or a spin in the country with their children. And in case of repair, they could witness (but often did not notice!) a kind of reversed maintenance: during the job, usable parts were replaced by older ones, the harvest being sold. In Bissau, a certain stretch of road was used for "obligatory Sunday outing for the wealthy population of the town, both national and foreigners."[157]

When the Senegalese government in 1931 signaled that its indigenous people vehemently developed "a taste for displacement, in cars particularly," it could not observe any "economical motive." As I argued in my earlier study, this is typical for the state's response to fledgling mass motorization: compared to the 'seriousness' of the railroad, supervised by economists, the car appeared as frivolous. And yet, the number of cars in the two French colonies of Senegal and Dakar increased from 16 before World War I to 2,250 ten years later (equally distributed among both colonies), only to

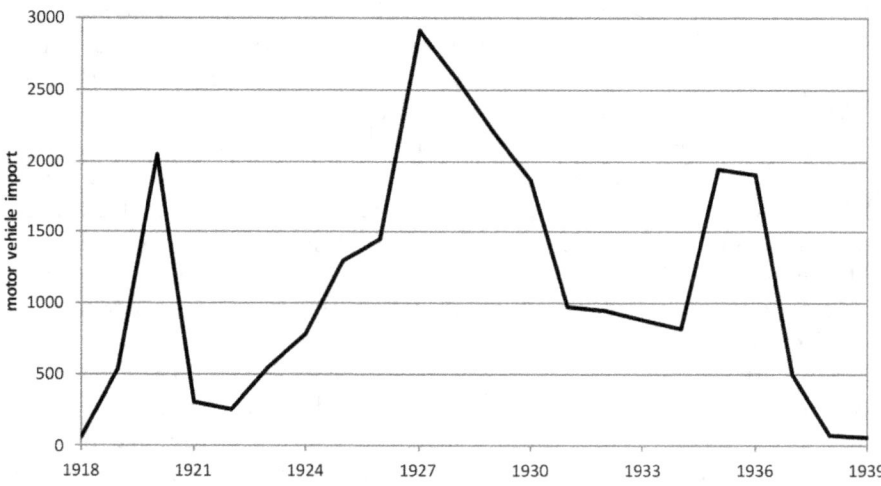

Figure 1.7. Motor vehicle (car and truck) import in Gold Coast (Ghana), 1900–1939. Source: Heap, "Development of Motor Transport in the Gold Coast," 24, table 3. Figure created by the author.

be more than doubled before World War II and then doubled again until 1950, after which year the numbers started to increase precipitously, near exponentially.

This rhythmic pattern of proliferation also resembles very much the spread of the car in Europe and the United States. American cars (Ford, GM after 1927) were preferred above British makes, because of their lighter weight and the availability of spare parts, the same arguments used by car buyers in the US countryside. One of the early dealers in Nigeria was W. Dawodu of Lagos (who also built rickshaws), one of several indigenous merchants who dominated the business until the 1920s, when Europeans started to join them. In Afrique Occidentale Française (French West Africa), an active policy was deployed to push these middlemen out of their businesses in favor of "les Européens et assimilés"; similarly, indigenous transporters did not have access to the "coordination committee" installed in 1936 to resolve the competition with railway freight transport. The latter part of the 1920s seems to have been the boom years (just like in Europe): in French Guinea, car advertising in the *Journal Officiel de la Guinéee française* blossomed in the short period between 1928 and 1931, mostly by Citroën and Michelin, who could boast on their *croisière noire* (Black Cruise) in 1924–1925 through the desert.[158]

***

In sum, except in South Africa, with its large 'white' cities, there were not many cars in Africa before World War I. After the pioneers, who receive much attention in the hobby books but did not play a role of much importance in the early African mobility culture, it was the 'official' cars, owned or driven by colonial civil servants and local chiefs, that for the first time offered a glimpse on a future, alternative society beyond the train. The governor of French Dahomey, for instance, made his first official car trip in 1915, and the colonial authorities in Paris immediately received dozens of letters of local commanders and indigenous chiefs applying for a similar treatment. Some chiefs wanted to use the money they had earned recruiting twelve hundred soldiers for the European Great War, to purchase a car, but the maintenance costs were too high for their budget, so the governor proposed to take over these costs in exchange for using the car as a representative vehicle. Early dignitaries in the colonies, whether European or African, were really car-horny, so much so that the indigenous contenders were eventually excluded from ownership: they had to wait another decade to be allowed access to this so eagerly sought-after contraption.[159] The status of ownership was clearly an important motive, more so perhaps than (the possibilities of) use.

Other early users with status appeal were anthropologists such as Max Gluckman, whose account of the inauguration of a bridge in Zululand in 1938, where all dignitaries arrived by car (some of them giving less lucky chiefs a lift) acquired some iconic status in post–World War II Africanist circles.[160] Missionaries, too, were among the early frequent car users, such as in Namibia, where their motorization started in the early 1930s and where car density figures were among the highest per (settler) population in Africa. The price they paid for their new status sounds familiar: the indigenous Herero did not let the missionaries camp in the village anymore; instead, they were "assigned a spot where the 'chicken and the dogs scratch around.'" For the missionaries, the car was a handy extension of their office; the Herero, however, deployed "various means to discover what it was the missionaries sought to hide in their cars." This gives us a rare glimpse of the 'underside of the ironic car,' as it enables us to gain a subaltern mobility perspective: for the indigenous 'hosts,' irony excludes, and fosters, inequality. It makes other, nonmotorized road users into potential victims. Remarkably, the isolation the car provided also impacts the historian, such as Gewald, for whom the higher speed and the lack of spare time to write during the journey led to a "dramatic decline ... in the content and quality of the missionary sources available."[161]

Trucks dominated, if only because of their economic advantage over head porterage, at least if there were roads. And yet, porterage was revived in Belgian Congo during the Depression. In this period, cycling, too, proved to be a serious competitor: in Nigeria, nearly all palm oil transport per truck was shifted to "native cyclists with the result that the lorries are being laid off the roads." Fitted with a carrier at the rear, cycle transporters loaded up to three four-gallon tins on their vehicle, using the rail lines as routes into the hinterland. During the 1930s, fifteen hundred cyclists were engaged in this trade in Calabar province alone. Whereas 'wild' trucks in Europe were a constant source of anxiety by national railroad companies and governments alike, the fully synchronous phenomenon of private trucking by indigenous entrepreneurs in Africa easily acquired a racist side, as they were called "pirates" by their European competitors. Constantly overloaded, 'African' trucks were simultaneously used for freight and passenger transport. In fact, the relatively low purchase and operating costs of the trucks were to the advantage of the small indigenous entrepreneur with one or two vehicles: buying a chassis and having a body mounted locally resulted in a very flexible solution, adjustable to the seasonal nature of the trade. Like elsewhere, pleasurable use in road motorization was never far away. The Herero, for instance, were renowned for their high mobility after World War II: football fans rented trucks bearing flags and banners in the colors of the Ethiopian freedom movement. Subversive forms of mobility were developed as truck drivers formed information networks just as rickshaw pullers did in Chinese cities. Again, trucks are not inherently subversive, as is shown by the South African settlers of German descent, who in majority joined the Nazi Party and used trucks to patrol the streets of Windhoek. One of the few students of road mobility in Africa concluded that the introduction of railways did not so much change the power structure within the colony fundamentally (it enhanced it by changing trade), but roadbuilding and the use of the truck did.[162]

***

Given the highly utilitarian character of African mobility during the first half of the twentieth century, how important was the automotive adventure (if it existed at all) in this setting? White automobile tourism to Africa did play a role as well, but at a much more modest scale than the exclusive focus on the 'conquest of Africa' by motorists from a Western perspective would suggest. Recently, Libbie Freed has argued the emphasis in the travel guides for Africa, during the "first phase" until 1930, was not so much on leisurely touring but on the serious task of conquest, where the behavior of the traveler had to be shaped in accordance with the 'civilizing' task of the European home countries (with the emphasis on 'European,' as a national perspective was not apparent): "the African, like all savages, ceases to respect the white who through an excess of benevolence, allows himself to be treated as an equal." Once the conquest was accomplished, rental cars became available, which enabled, supported by the start of commercial aviation, an expensive but exotic touristic experience of hunting and encounter with the Other, such as "pygmies," who, "once ferocious, come to eat out of the traveler's hand." In other words, European tourism was "part of the colonial project."[163] Despite Freed's assessment of the travel guides, however, these guides could not prevent early travelers from producing comparable landscape experiences as travelers did back in Europe, although the "colonial landscape experience" with its wide vistas 'empty' of people, had a special tone, as "a symptom of suppressed violence" governed by fear for the local population, and wild animals.[164]

There is no doubt that from an early date, tourism and imperialism were closely connected, such as in Libya, where three years after the Italian conquest of 1911, the Touring Club Italiano arrived with a group of 430 tourists, followed in 1920 by a second large excursion. Despite the atrocities of the "'pacification'—among them aerial bombardments, chemical warfare and 'settling' nomadic tribes in concentration camps—which resulted in a protracted genocide," Italian tourists visited desert oases "while ignoring rebel gunfire, or turning a blind eye to concentration camps while en route to archaeological ruins." They "became complicit in the violence of the colonial everyday," a form of 'thanatourism' that is usually connected to the world wars, but which, from a global mobility perspective, should be extended to the imperialist experience. In Libya, a picturesque *strada litoranea* was constructed, 1,811 km along the coast between the Tunisian and Egyptian borders. Some Italian travel writers conveyed the regime's "concerted attempt to foster interest in the colony as a place that showed the decisiveness of Fascist action in dealing with opposition to its rule." Angelo Picciolini's *La porta magica del Sahara* (*The Magic Gate of the Sahara*), praised, among others, by German writer Stefan Zweig, opined the inhabitants of the capital Tripoli "valued above all else a state of 'calm immobility,'" the same immobility he saw reflected in the repetitiveness of the ornaments in the mosques. Traveling by car, he had, like many other Western motorists in this period, his 'flight' experience, the feeling that "one's life had somehow left its ordinary plane, and that one entered a new state of consciousness ... a state of eternity." Touring in Libya was like entering "a hallucinogenic fantasy," an "encounter between Italy and Libya," in the words of Italian studies scholar Charles Burdett; it was a meeting "between a masculinist notion of vitality and a feminized idea of decadence."[165]

Often, the distinction between mimicking 'conquest' and indulging in 'adventure' was blurred, for instance, in the many efforts to cross the Sahara, to which recently a German amateur historian dedicated nearly nine hundred pages without much attention for indigenous people.[166] In this overview, ending in a description of the first family trip through the desert in 1929 and the establishment of bus and car tourism around the same time, extensive attention is given to Citroën's pioneering Black Cruise, which has its English counterpart in an expedition through the Kalahari with Morris six-wheeled trucks. Citroën had hoped to use its products "to establish permanent communications between Algeria and western Africa," but when they had reached the sultan of Tessaoua in the desert, he appeared to possess a brand-new Ford. This is ironic, too, but in quite another sense. Early cycling and motoring long-distance trips were serious business, their adventurousness on par with the seriousness of the civilizing task of the colony. Gordon Pirie records similar connections with the imperialist agenda in his overview of South African car tourism. Boasting a fleet of 138,000 cars in 1930, the local car and touring clubs (one of them becoming the African section of the Alliance Internationale de Tourisme in 1938), formed the backbone of a white middle-class endeavor to force the continent wide open for automotive 'penetration,' supported by similar clubs in Nairobi, Salisbury, Lourenço Marques and ... Brussels (for the *Touring Club du Congo Belge*). Founded as early as 1901, the Cape Town club was soon joined by others who amalgamated into a federation in 1919; they had to face the same resistance ("sticks and rocks being 'flung at passing cars'" as early as 1917), as has been reported for Europe and the United States. By 1947, a handbook called *Trans-Africa Highways* saw the light with all the long-distance trails that had been discussed during the Second International Congress of African Touring in Algiers that same year.[167]

The South African early motorization story is a story of settler colonial mobility. As Georgine Clarsen defines in her study of "overland" cycling journeys in Australia around the turn of the twentieth century, settler societies were "created in everyday movements across contested territory, as settlers' cumulative mobilities work[ed] to shape and reshape indigenous landscapes into settler places and incrementally produce[d] nativized settler subjectivities." Clarsen's work in 'settler mobility history' is an important addition to the mobility historian's toolbox, also for the African continent. In *Atlantic Automobilism*, I dedicated quite some pages to this 'colonial,' aggressive part of the European and American automotive adventure.

Pirie also wrote an overview of "non-urban motoring in colonial Africa in the 1920s and 1930s," in which he claimed a focus on the spectacular cross-continent journeys distorts a much richer and less adventurous or "quite ordinary" motoring. But of the impressive seventy-five or so travelogues he discovered, the "utility motoring" he evoked appears to boil down to similar use profiles as we have seen in, for instance, Indochina: inspection tours, road surveys, "off-rail travel" organized by Thomas Cook, safaris, motor races, and trips by missionaries, colonial administrators, and anthropologists, all apparently worthy of publication in books and booklets, and all full of elements of our tripartite adventure (high speed, roaming, tinkering, with conquest/control as additional trait; see the introduction), that is, if one does not take the declarations of the motoring subjects themselves at face value.[168]

***

On the other extreme of the African continent, and beyond (that 'black hole' in world mobility history, the Middle East), historians only very recently started digging into local automobilisms. Perhaps the first to do so for interwar Lebanon was Kristin Monroe, who revealed not only a typical car subculture of "summering" (*taṣīyf* or *iṣṭiyāf*) "in the mountain and rural regions" but also a heavy emphasis, in the "newspaper discourse," of the car as "a 'distinction-making' commodity. For instance, motor vehicle travel in the private car between the urban and the rural or mountain areas of Lebanon became a marker of bourgeois habitus, rather than a feature of democratization." Likewise, research into interwar roadbuilding in Morocco not only uncovered the very mobility of the country's borders but also certain peculiarities of local travel, such as the obligation, when using public roads (called "routes du Sultan," *triq as-sultan*), to hire "une escorte (*ztata*)."

In this French colony, a "touristic" road network of 2,700 km was realized by the beginning of the 1920s, supplemented by a secondary network of "strategic" and "colonization" roads, well before the construction of a railway network.[169] In other words, as soon as the car appeared on the continent, its adventurous characteristics were immediately mobilized to realize a frivolous deployment. The car was rare (except, perhaps, in the extreme South and North), but always immediately acknowledged as an adventure machine. How would this vehicle behave when it reached a continent that acquired colonial independence a century earlier?

More Than Modern: Constructing a Latin American Adventure Machine

Whereas Africa's motorization should be analyzed against a background of (settler) colonization, Latin American countries had their colonial experiences more than two centuries ago. Yet, several students of the continent see the influence of the United States (after it took over from the United Kingdom, a process of mutual rivalry coming to a close around 1930) as an "empire by invitation," an "informal empire laced with covert operations, proxies, and gunboats." Latin American countries function as an example of "authoritarian stability" supported by economic and military power of the United States to local elites "not ... weakened [as the countries in Asian had been] by war or anticolonialism."[170] At the same time, however, Latin Americanists struggle with the continent's "alterity": in the eyes of Walter Mignolo, for a long time the continent simply was invisible. "'America' only existed in 'Europe,'" and it suffered from "a second subalternization in de modern/colonial world imaginary, as a consequence of its colonial past in the hands of an empire in decay." Latin America was "the extreme West, not its alterity." Another student of Latin America's history, Ricardo Salvatore, said in a review of one of Mignolo's books: "Rather than establishing a separate intellectual path—as the US founding fathers did with regard to European ideas—, the elites of Spanish and Portuguese America placed the European civilizing project in a privileged place, while subordinating and erasing the traces of Indian and African cultures." Meanwhile, local governments were constantly concerned about the possibility of Indians revolting and taking over their position.[171]

Like the inhabitants themselves, Latin Americanists are still struggling with the continent's legacy: with independence from Spain and Portugal acquired at the beginning of the nineteenth century, concepts such as 'colonial' and 'postcolonial' are problematic, and modernity takes on a hybrid character as both a derivative of the same (European, American) and something distinct (Indian, Creole, the latter standing for "American-born European elite"). According to Néstor Canclini, Latin America may have had "an exuberant modernism with a deficient modernization, ... colonized by the most backward European nations, subjected to the Counter-Reformation and other antimodern movements," and "only with independence could we begin to bring our countries up-to-date."[172]

Contrary to Africanists, Latin Americanists have not dedicated much attention to the continent's mobility history. A welcome exception to this observation is Jaime Moreno Tejada's recent study of the 'hybridity' of Ecuadorian mobility around 1900 near the capital of Quito ("crisscrossed by tramways, telephone cables, and a handful of thunderous automobiles"), where efforts to "improve communications with the Amazon frontier" by an "expanding middle-class" were frustrated by "lazy labor" of the indigenous Napo Runa. Functioning as porters and pilots, the subaltern Napo Runa "moved in rhythms dictated by history and nature" with a work ethic defined by the local adaption of the Spanish *trabajo* (*tarabana*: "work undertaken for others, ... drunken work, alienating work, consciously lazy work," properties constructed by the Taylorist middle class), thus "undermin[ing] modernity's foundations" of the local hegemonic colonizers, for instance, in the case of the porters who suddenly decided "to abandon their cargo altogether" and disappear into the jungle. Such "submissive mobility" is of course highly subversive, yet it forms an inextricable part of Latin American modernity.

Such research prompts some questions: Is there a 'Criollo mobility'? And what does Indian mobility look like? Does the *indigenismo* movement (Mexico, Peru) have a mobile side, and if so, how does it differ from what we are used to?[173] We don't know. What we *do* know is a classical story of railway building, which started at the mid-nineteenth century and was more or less completed around 1930, two decades after North America. By then, the continental network measured one-fourth (nearly sixty thousand miles) of that of the North. Different from the 'scandal' of the African continent, the national networks also reached far-off and isolated regions (in Chile, Argentina, Brazil) and even connected some countries (such as the Ferrocarill Trasandino por Juncal, the Juncal Trans-Andean Railroad between Chile and Argentina). The peak in railroad building in Brazil took place in the decade after 1905.[174]

Equally synchronous with the West was the Latin American interest in roadbuilding, testified by the resolution on "Cooperation in the Improvement of Communications" approved during the Fifth International Conference of American States in Santiago de Chile in 1923, followed by the founding of a Pan-American Highway Confederation in Washington and by a Convention on the Regulation of Automobile Traffic, accepted and discussed during conferences in Rio de Janeiro (1929) and Washington (1930). Although the dream of a 'Pan-American road' played an important role in the self-image of American national elites (not in the least those of the imperialist North), the South American road network expanded considerably during the 1930s, most importantly in Argentina, and often "absorb[ing] unemployed labour in many rural areas" or, in some cases such as Guatemala, built through "coercion." Such developments intrigued the "relatively numerous" middle classes, numerous "compared not only to the urban elite but to the working classes." This was related to the large number of small businesses, as well as the white-collar workers in government or private employment, whereas the working classes were dominated by "domestic servants, street sellers and labourers. An industrial proletariat was only to be found in the textile and food industries and then mainly in a few cities—Buenos Aires, São Paulo, and, to some extent, Lima and Mexico City."[175] Therefore, the contrast with Africa in terms of road and car densities could not be larger, and confirms our central thesis that without a sizable middle class, automobilism does not have a chance.

Early Motorizations in the Southern Cone: Pan-Americanism and Automobilism in Argentina and Chile

During the interwar years in some Latin American countries, a veritable roadbuilding frenzy occurred, coupled to an eager expectation, reception, and appropriation of the automobile by the local elites. Especially the Southern Cone (Chile, Argentina, Uruguay, and Brazil) motorized faster than other parts of South America. Compared to the Asian and African continents, automobilism took a much higher flight, both quantitatively and qualitatively. No wonder, then, did one of the seminal monographs on the continent's mobility history start with an invocation of the same 'autopoetic' literature I used for my analysis of 'Atlantic automobilism,' more particularly of Northwest Europe and the United States. Guillermo Giucci's engagement with Latin American car-related novels and poems, published before my study, does not result in an alternative perspective, however: instead, viewed from a global point of view, it enhances the impression that car culture was universal. This seems to be the first stage in the construction of a (national) car history, given our similar conclusions regarding Africa.

The second stage, then, is the elaboration of typicalities and exceptionalisms. For South America, this is perhaps the phenomenon that Latin American elites showed themselves off as even more modern than their examples in Paris and New York. In Brazil, for instance, they criticized the modernization tempo in their "country of tortoises." For Monteiro Lobato, who in 1927 visited the United States and immediately "acquired a car, a radio, and a beautiful apartment," felt fully "Americanized," while his home country "continues to carve stones." Most of his Latin American colleagues, however, were much more critical toward North America: still oriented toward Italy and France, they often belonged to the very core of the French avant-garde, including its car pioneering faction. In Paris alone, Latin Americans numbered in the thousands, including many women. It would be worthwhile to find out, in more detail, whether and how far the Latin pioneers were somehow directly tributary to the French-Belgian group of writer-motorists analyzed in our earlier study.[176]

In a certain sense, Latin car pioneers even outperformed their European counterparts. Germán Arciniegras, a Colombian in London, for instance, having reminded his readers that "in no other country in the world there were proportionally so many cars of high quality as in one of our Southern republics," was convinced "the car transformed the customs" as "a new phenomenon not belonging to the category of sports, nor of work." Acknowledging "the motorist infantilizes himself through [the] sensation" of driving, an insight quite new within the plethora of metaphors invented to characterize the experiences of automobilism, he remarkably singled out three characteristics of the car driver, one of which (the middle one) has not been emphasized so much by Western literary car pioneers, although they practiced it nonetheless: "individualist, *rebellious*, libertarian." Arciniegras observed in awe how the car as an 'adventure machine' was celebrated in the United States by fifteen- or sixteen-year-old high school and college kids, who ignored traffic signs shouting "hands up" while lifting their hands from the steering wheel. Arciniegas's Spanish colleague José Ortega y Gasset, observing at the same time how 'peripheral' Spain motorized, was less thrilled. In "La moral del automóvil en España" (The morality of the car in Spain), this iconic critic of Western decadence castigated the *señorito* (the wealthy young man) with his big car, "not an article of essential need. The constant shine revealed the nation's underdevelopment." The machine was an expression of "Celtiberian backwardness" because Spain "bought more cars from abroad than any other nation."[177] Like so many car critics of the period, Ortega made the mistake of buying into the alibi of the car proponents and their lobby, as if the car was a utilitarian contraption and its deployment as a toy of the rich was, by then, a thing of the past. Nothing was further from the truth, at least not in the West.

***

Indeed, while the railroads seemed "emblematic of British imperialism," the car became associated with the United States and its manufacturers, especially Ford and General Motors. The manufacturers' interests were spread along two trajectories: an aggressive marketing of their products and the active spread of the gospel of good roads, embedded in the perspective of Pan-Americanism. The two were closely intertwined, through their active support of the Brazilian Good Roads Movement, for instance: the first national road conferences were held in 1916, 1917, and 1919, well before the Netherlands, where the first national conference was organized in 1920, again testifying to the 'laboratory' character of the 'periphery.' As a consumer market discovered after the Spanish-American War of 1898, Latin America's elite became enthralled by the myth of Pan-Americanism through mobility, especially through the car. The Panama Canal was mostly beneficial to the United States: a "military bastion," it processed "coffee and rubber from Brazil, sisal from Yucatan, nitrates from Chile, tin from Bolivia, sugar from Cuba, and oil from Peru." But the Pan-American Railway, and especially the Pan-American Highway, mesmerized elites in the North and the South as a "road utopia," a "10,000-mile dream," an "extension and culmination of the Bolivarian dream, creating a common history for all the Americas." Shortly after the Pan-American Conference in Santiago de Chile in 1923, Mexico and El Salvador started constructing parts of this continental highway, while Guatemala and Nicaragua intended to start surveying. In the 1930s, the original idea of a "single longitudinal route connecting Latin America to the United States" became redefined as "a Pan American Highway System connecting all the countries in the Americas."[178]

In his 1973 dissertation on Pan-Americanism, Robert Seidel showed how the leading Pan-American Highway Commission was fully run by North American interests (one official advocating the export of the Good Roads Movement as a remedy against "revolution, decentralization, and political incompetence"). The 'Pan-American' institutions were dominated by US experts, who had identified Latin America in 1930 (when they estimated the global roadbuilding programs outside the United States to amount to $1.3 billion) as the "one logical and obvious field for development," because Europe was already "well endowed" with highways, and the Orient did not offer any perspectives "during the coming decade." But this does not mean the project was one-sided: during the Pan-American Highway Congress in 1939 a Peruvian engineer claimed the uniqueness of Latin American countries to oppose the consumption imperialism of the United States; instead, he eloquently proposed a Latin American 'cultural appropriation': "ours is a country special and unique, because of the nature of our territory, its race, its population, etc., and we cannot adopt the solutions employed in other parts to resolve analogous problems without a previous adaptation to our environment, which requires special study, our own techniques, a Peruvian technique, as a result of our own observation." But the 'solutions employed' were not as geopolitically neutral as it seemed: according to Herbert Hoover, "the engineers have carried a dream in their minds that they might some day have a railway from Canada to Tierra del Fuego. That dream is more likely of realization ... through the development of the great new form of transportation by automobile."

And like in the case of the French colonies, the pretension to recall the "glory of ancient Rome" was never far away. Nonetheless, the project, set up along fully diffusionist lines, failed in the eyes of the experts, because "road construction was not rapid nor was it necessarily correlated with economic development," and the railroad remained dominant in the mobility configuration. As late as 1942, when two American motorists sponsored by the American Automobile Association drove through the southern continent for 13,600 miles, they "found the Pan-American Highway to be still an undeveloped project." That does not mean, however, parts of it did not play a role in national mobilization histories, as it did with the Cape to Cairo Road in Africa: in Venezuela, oil wealth allowed the country to build paved highways for its "relatively large number of cars," and in Peru, "roads connected sugar and cotton haciendas." But outside these areas, roads were mostly unpaved, slippery in the rainy season, and narrow and dangerously steep in mountainous areas. South American "backwardness" prevented the two pioneers from crossing the heart of the continent, leaving this, as they formulated it, to the "adventurous motorist." Latin America was a patchwork of "a few isles of 'automobile culture,'" as Salvatore, who studied their trip, concluded, adding a quote from a contemporary American in 1941 who expected the airplane to solve the continent's "transportation problems," a conclusion doubted by Salvatore: "The simultaneity of Andeans carrying their cargoes on the backs of llamas and middle-class Latin Americans flying in airplanes to their pleasure destination reminds us of the limitations of machines in overcoming uneven development and inequality."[179]

Yet, despite the 'failure' of the Pan-American Highway project (the United States spent not more than $3 million on the project until as late as 1941, arguing the funding should come from private sources), "American automotive sales to South America boomed," providing the northern car industry a very welcome outlet during the Depression and in a saturated domestic market, making Argentina the United States' "second largest customer for automotive products in the 1920s," after Canada. Indeed, hardly known among Western mobility historians (and a confirmation of Arciniegas's claim), Argentina's car density figures in the 1920s were above those of Germany, and comparable to those of France and Great Britain ("its per capita income was higher than both France and Germany" in 1913). The country started to motorize well before any road policy was developed, fully contrary to many countries we have already visited, where roadbuilding forestalled motorization. Likewise, the car density in 1920 in Chile (which saw the first car appear in 1902, and imported seventy-five by 1911, mostly French and British) was higher than those of Germany and Italy. By 1929, Argentina as a whole counted 205,000 automobiles, against 61,000 in Brazil, Mexico with 38,000, and Chile with more than 43,000 (1930). In terms of car density (per capita), Argentina's population was five times more surrounded by cars than Brazil, despite its smaller size (fig. 1.8). Brazil's density was in the same league as Venezuela's, and both were four times as dense in cars per capita as Bolivia.[180] Such quantitative comparisons were made regularly in the trade press, an obsessive habit aimed at measuring each other's modernity.

In other countries too (as far as this is known), local adventurous car cultures emerged, especially in the more prosperous countries of the Southern Cone, such as Chile, where motorists as early as 1913 shaped a culture of weekend outings by car around the capital Santiago. But the Chilean elite also used their cars as "playthings" (*bien de lujo*) in another sense: as fetishized objects during *corsos de flores* (flower parades). The first car-friendly road (a stretch of five km) was constructed between Valparaiso and Viña del Mar on the coast, well before the founding of the Automóvil Club de Chile in 1916. Chilean road network expansion started in earnest after a Road Law was accepted in 1920, a development extensively analyzed in a recent dissertation by Rodrigo Booth. When, by the end of the 1920s, there were more than four thousand cars in Santiago, "an aggressive campaign of road segregation [had] marginalize[d] animal-drawn vehicles from main roads and streets," while pedestrians had been "dictated the way in which [they] walked so that they would not disrupt motorized movement."[181]

Like the touristic trips to the south of Europe and the United States, as I have described elsewhere, Latin American early motorists organized their

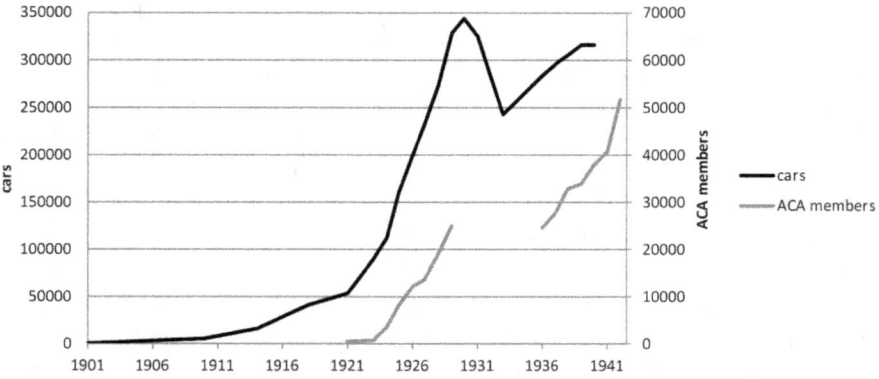

Figure 1.8. Spread of the car and Argentine Automobile Club membership in Argentina, 1901–1942. Source: Piglia, *Autos, rutas y turismo*, 31, table 1. Figure created by the author.

own 'conquests' of their 'periphery,' such as the Argentine José Piquero, who crossed the Andes in 1905 in an Oldsmobile, or the French Count Lesdain, who, having crossed Morocco, Algeria, and China, drove from Rio de Janeiro to São Paulo, or the Frenchman Roger Courtville and his wife and mechanic (both from Brazil), who crossed the entire continent from East to West in 1926. While they passed through towns where 'modern' traffic was already present (Salvatore's 'isles'), in order to get there they had to disassemble the entire car, load the parts on twenty mules, and cross the Andes (I did not know a car would fit on twenty mules!). Trying to "realize a Pan-American ideal," they were hosted by the Peruvian president.

Such experiences only heightened the hopes and expectations invested in an automotive future. Argentine's autopoetic culture expressed values similar to what we have unearthed in multiple variants and versions for European and American car culture, from Roberto Arl's many essays on the car, via Américo Netto, who in his poem "Automóvel" evokes the 'flight' sensation so ubiquitous in early car literature ("Mass flying forth / On invisible horses"), to Oswald de Andrade, who used the car metaphor in his poetry ("the meek, green Cadillac of illusion"). Argentina's literary avant-garde was certainly not alone in this respect: Uruguayan writer Alberto Lasplaces described in his short story "El automóvil" how his protagonist, while motoring, had similar transcendental experiences of an "oceanic fusion with the machine" as I analyzed for the early European automobilism scene: "he felt not like a man, but a God, and from that height, he envied absolutely no one."[182] As we have seen, it is a rare occasion to find such open adulation of the car as 'adventure machine' in Africa or Asia, but we, as a profession, did not yet look very thoroughly. And *if* we did (such as Ponsavady in Indochina), we found it.

Federalized Automobilism and Tropical Modernity:
The Adventure Machine in Brazil

The car was approached as a modernizer also in Brazil, most particularly as a national unifier in a giant country with an extreme form of federalism, after it had abandoned slavery as late as 1888 and "the declaration of the republic in 1889 signaled Brazil's final break with its colonial past." Even if it motorized more slowly than Argentina, most state capitals by the 1910s "had at least a few cars on their streets." Although this is no surprise after our earlier visits to Africa and Asia, what strikes the student of Brazil's automobilism first and foremost is its synchronicity with European culture. Celebrated in the new literary magazine with the ominous title *Fon-Fon!* (soon to be followed by another one, *Klaxon*), Rio de Janeiro's mobility culture was characterized by "cruising" and "rac[ing] up and down the Beira Mar an hour or two at a stretch," whereas the car figured in the city's Carnaval parade from 1907, the same year the Automóvel Clube do Brasil was founded. In the car club of São Paulo (Brazil's largest car market), more than 40 percent of the members called themselves farmer (*lavrador*) or rancher (*fazendeiro*). Brazil's road to "tropical modernity" went through two aborted efforts of military uprisings in 1922 and 1924 and was characterized by tensions between the agricultural interior (with coffee as main produce) and the urbanized coast. Car pioneers placed themselves in the adventurous tradition of the *bandeirantes*, who had formerly chased runaway slaves in the jungle and whose paths and roads were still often the only ways to give access to the hinterland.

The car (called a "tame and sublime mechanical *bandeirante*" by the automobile club) promised to be the tool of the new settler society in the making. Whereas three-quarters of imported cars came from Europe before World War I, the stagnation of European car production during the war gave US manufacturers the opportunity to conquer the new markets. Successfully so, as they dominated the postwar market by 83 percent, fed from the local assembly plants of Ford and GM set up during the 1920s. Ford also started his notorious Fordlândia rubber plantation project in this country, soon accompanied by a similar, less well-known project called Belterra. Especially the more prosperous countries of the Southern Cone were attractive targets: Argentina, Chile, and Uruguay had the highest average purchasing powers, while Brazil was the promising prospect, although it still lacked a middle class. As a "'consumer' South America," as North America's "hemispheric market," automotive Latin America "could be reduced to a few big cities (Buenos Aires, Rio de Janeiro, Santiago) and to certain emerging settler economies (Southern Brazil, the Argentine Pampas, and Uruguay). Second were smaller city markets such as those of Lima, Quito, Caracas, or Bogotá. The rest was barren land as far as consumer markets were concerned." Indeed, the car market showed large disparities between the states: São Paulo had by far the greatest concentration, representing about half the nation's motorized vehicles by the mid-1920s. In the second half of that decade, the fleet increased precipitously (to 160,000 road vehicles).[183]

***

But at closer look, differences with the European model start to pop up, phenomena called "differentiated commonalities" by historian Emily Rosenberg, referring to Arjun Appadurai—"commonalities that nevertheless manifested themselves differently depending on the unpredictable frictions arising from geographical, temporal, and sociocultural locations." One of these differentiated commonalities is the late start of the regular automobile shows (1923), which suggests the organizers' low expectations about the purchasing power of the middle class, because the purpose of such shows was the expansion of the market beyond the elite. Second, related to this was the disappointment, during one of the eager car density comparisons in the trade press, about Brazil's rate being in the same league as poor European countries like Serbia and Bulgaria. As the Brazilian middle class is under researched, an answer to the question of the country's specificities is difficult to give, although by the mid-1920s, "quite a few Brazilian commentators simply assumed that the middle class was defined by automobile ownership," and most members of Brazil's middle strata could not afford cars.[184]

A third characteristic, emphasized by contemporaries and historians alike, is the nation's eagerness for high power and speed. Joel Wolfe, who in terms of the empirics of automotive transport history provided the best analysis of a Latin American country so far (forming an excellent counterpart to the more cultural and literary history by Giucci on Argentina) started his study by quoting Alberto Santos Dumont, who at the end of the nineteenth century traveled to Paris "to explore the world of flying and ended up learning to drive." The real unification of the continent might have to come from the airplane (see Salvatore's earlier quote), but car driving was more fun (and perhaps more feasible under Latin American conditions). Foreign observers found Rio de Janeiro a city unequaled in the world when it comes to "expensive high-power cars," and the auto club's passion for racing was legendary, not the least feat of this being a Gran Premio Internacional del Norte race (1939) of no less than 7,300 km. Such feats, inspired by European races, are sometimes related to the special skills of the Creole pilots and mechanics and put in the context of a "national sporting style," especially manifest in the country's soccer culture. But in the end, the national government pursued the same goals as the European governments it wished to emulate: "Order and Progress," was the slogan, in that order.[185]

At the system level, the Brazilian automobile culture mostly spread along the coast: the state of São Paulo was quickly given a "comprehensive road network," which became connected to Rio de Janeiro by the "jewel" of Brazilian roadbuilding, the highway along which Washington Luís drove to get inaugurated as president of the republic in 1926. During Luís's reign, the centralization of road planning and building, set in motion by the military previously, acquired legal endorsement through the 1927 Federal Highway Act, complete with earmarking of a tax on imported cars for roadbuilding. Such roads also allowed the truck and bus to emerge. They were used by the army during the civil war of the early 1930s and the subsequent dictatorship of Getúlio Vargas and his Estado Novo of 1937, when roadbuilding was accelerated and the network doubled in less than a decade, to more than 200,000 kms. National tourism by car and bus, and car racing (the 1936 Grand Prix of São Paulo, watched by six hundred thousand Brazilians) were among the most visible feats of this period. Having "escaped" World War II,

Latin American countries continued to expand their highway networks, and in 1960, the largest was to be found in Mexico (26,000 km), followed by Argentina (23,000 km), which was nearly twice as large as Brazil's network. In density however, the Brazilian network was only one-fifth (per square kilometer) or even one-tenth (per capita), again confirming the 'emptiness' of Brazil. In my previous study, I used the 'emptiness' of certain countries and areas (United States, Southern Sweden, Southern France) to explain the eager proliferation of the car, more so than in 'full countries' (with a high population density).[186]

Revolutionary Mobility: Mexican Roadbuilding and Chicas Modernas

Perhaps the most extreme example of the hope of the national unification power of infrastructure network building is given by the case of revolutionary Mexico. Distinguishing between an armed phase (1910–1920, the decade of civil war in which estimates of up to a million deaths have been suggested) and a phase of revolutionary reconstruction (1920–1940), and recognizing that new communication media and means of transport formed a constitutive part of both, Mexicanists nowadays struggle whether the revolution can be called social (if so, it would be the first of the twentieth century), or political, benefitting only an elite, like the Chinese revolution of 1911. Although the relation between infrastructure formation and national identity, investigated by several scholars with a cultural studies background, has meanwhile become a cliché, in Mexico, during the postrevolutionary government of Elías Plutarco Calles, the dream of simultaneously constructing a transport channel for its agricultural and mineral products and creating a "new Mexican—a modern producer and consumer" came very close to realization, indeed.

What in Africa took place as coerced labor, the National Road Commission installed by Calles in 1925 tried to do by planning and executing a road network which "offered ordinary citizens the chance to do unskilled labor," paid for by gasoline and alcohol taxes and national treasury funds. Whereas the railroads, built during the long reign of Porfirio Díaz (1876–1911), asked for so much capital that its construction had to be given into foreign hands, the gradual expansion of the road network allowed the government to keep the planning under its control. Roads also were attractive over rails because of the steep grades in the country, as they allowed buses and trucks to be used as small units of transport. The capital investment was relatively low (and therefore realizable at both the national and the local and regional level), as long as one did not opt for the railway-like freeway systems Western engineers started discussing around this time (and rejecting, in most countries until well after World War II).

For the Mexican presidents of the interbellum, road network building had a double econo-political purpose: to stimulate domestic economic growth (and thus countering American imperialism) and to enable the transport of troops to "hotspots of resistance." For roadbuilding expertise, the government had to resort to an American engineering firm, but it stipulated in the contract that for unskilled work only Mexicans should be hired, while technical and administrative jobs also had to be filled by high quota of Mexicans. A law in 1934 (Ley Sobre Construcción de Caminos en Cooperación) enabled the founding of Local Roads Boards (Juntas Locales de Caminos), setting in motion a practice of decentralized planning (and "bipartite funding" by the local states and the federal state) that seems to have gone farther than European countries that around the same time also discovered the crucial role of the intermediary echelons of governances (such as provinces and regional institutions). Apart from the paving of roads and the construction of bridges longer than fifty meters (which remained a federal privilege), regional and local interest groups of "capitalists and entrepreneurs ... succeeded in their goal of keeping road building in Mexican hands." When one of the local military road builders (General Juan Almazán) was allowed to start his own business, "Mexicans constructed over ten thousand kilometers of roads" under his leadership until 1940. "Hundreds, perhaps thousands, of communities around the country answered the call [to "develop their own country"] and did their best to build roads or upgrade existing tracks to suit motor vehicles," a form of road network construction from below hardly paralleled during the global roadbuilding frenzy of the interbellum.[187]

Roadbuilding was also a clear federal project in Mexico. Before the revolution of 1910, the faena was the form of a voluntary labor system according to which Mexicans had to spend four to eight days per month on public works (those who could afford it paid a tax). It often degenerated into coerced labor, just like peasants were also obliged to work on plantations and haciendas. Although "obligatory unpaid labor" was outlawed in the constitution of 1917, the faena tradition was used by the government to advance the Nationalist project: "Communication is progress." Photographs show road openings using banners with "Paso al progresso" (Gateway to progress) and when the Nuevo Laredo (at the American border) to Mexico City part of the Pan-American Highway was opened, four days of festivities were needed to celebrate. Including the new road between the capital and Acapulco, the federal road network of nearly 10,000 km built between 1925 and 1940 stimulated North American car tourism. On the 4,000 km of local roads "built through the Roads in Cooperation program by 1940," buses made travel for women safer in a context of revolutionary violence, but when Luis Buñuel made his movie *Subida al cielo* (translated as *Mexican Bus Ride* when released in the United States in 1952), a tractor failed to pull a bus out of the mud, after which "a pair of hefty oxen led by a young girl" managed to pull *both* out.[188]

The federal government also set up a regulated trucking sector (by 1930, Mexico counted fewer than twenty thousand trucks, most of them converted passenger cars and all of them 'wild') after a European model, distinguishing between a public service (separate trucking companies) and private service (trucks and truck fleets owned by companies that were not specialized in transport). In 1932, these services were executed by twelve thousand and eight thousand trucks, respectively. Entrepreneurs that provided the same service were required by law to form cooperatives, a process that had its parallels in similar efforts in several European countries. Under President Lázaro Cárdenas (who came to power in 1935 and extensively traveled across the country to cement the support by workers and peasants), this was accompanied by "distributing unprecedented amounts of land to peasants," granting the local road boards more autonomy, and nationalizing the oil industry, generating more funds for the construction of "dams, railroads, port facilities, air travel, and telegraph and telephone installations." Indeed, the Mexican Revolution also was a communication revolution, as some recent cultural studies of the emergence of Mexican radio and film testify. In the case of the radio, consumers realized forms of subversive use not so easily observed in transport: they broke the seals of the radio sets tuned to an educational channel and listened to programs of their own choice, sometimes putting the set in a public space for every villager to enjoy.

In the case of the movie, the emergence of a Mexican film tradition also resulted in transport-related work, such as Enrique Rosas's *El automóvil gris* (*The Gray Car*, 1919), an "authentic" narrative of a gang of thieves active around Mexico City in 1915. Meanwhile, in the urban centers, *chicas modernas* were driving cars in the early 1920s (most often bought from the two assembly plants of Ford and GM, the latter opened in 1937), celebrating their "Mexican modernity," as an expression of "hybridity" combining "'two parallel and intersecting drives': the first, motivated by the growth of the middle class and the resulting expansion of European and U.S. ideals of capitalism, liberalism, democracy; the second, an effect of the 'interweaving' of local indigenous cultures and practices with modern, global social and economic institutions." In 1940, a road census revealed there were 145,000 automobiles in Mexico, 42,000 of them trucks.[189]

Latin American Layeredness: 'Coordination' of Roads versus Rails

Similar to Africa, automotive cultures in South and Central America were the result of a struggle between rail and road, of which we need much more thorough studies, if only to verify Salvatore's generalizing remark that the railroad "had not solved the transportation problem of sparsely populated areas." In any case, similar to the struggle between the car and horse-drawn carriages, there is no sign of a time gap with Western coordination struggles, if we may assume the statistics of investments in Colombian railroads and roads (where the share of the latter started dominating in 1931) are of any general value. But we need more local and regional empirical studies to investigate the claim the 'layeredness' of mobility is much more important than in the West, that, in other words, *coexistence* of the two systems is more normal than substitution, evolution more than revolution. In the case of Latin America, we have an excellent example of such a study in Fiona Wilson's analysis of Peruvian "transport and exchange relations" in the Andes as a struggle between indigenous and immigrant transport systems, showing "what the changing relationship (from complementarity to competition) [between road and rail in the central sierra from 1900 to 1940] meant for class formation and struggle." When the Carretera Central was completed in 1935 parallel to the British-owned railroad to Lima, which had for fifty years monopolized the transport of freight between the mines (owned by an American company) in the high Mantaro Valley and the coast, indigenous truckers started to compete. Facilitated by American truck manufacturers, truckers working for Italian and Chinese merchants first captured the transport of agricultural and livestock products and then took hold of the coffee flow and eventually even of the minerals.

Trucks also attacked animal transport undertaken by indigenous muleteers and llama drivers (employed by Italian immigrants), starting in 1916, shortly before a network of local roads emerged in the sierra province of Tarma, built by labor recruited under the new Ley de Conscripción Vial. By 1921, Tarma counted 83 cars and 28 trucks, ten years later increased (and turned around!) to 55 cars and 125 trucks (and 350 trucks by 1935), mostly General Motors, as Fords were considered unable to deal with the very steep gradients. "Truck driving became the preserve of very young men" from "comparatively wealthy immigrant and mestizo families," sons of the immigrant merchants. They "claimed a distinct social identity: they were the daredevils and adventurers." Truckers carried goods and passengers, also when many of them started working for themselves, and became "gipsy traders" in the eyes of the railroad and copper mine companies. A similar story can be told for Venezuela, where trucking appeared to be beneficial to small peasants who could now sell their produce directly along the roads, which by 1940 had a total length of 5,600 km, including the 500-km Carretera de los Andes, ready in 1925 and climbing up to 4,050 meters. There were 2,600 motor vehicles in 1922 in Venezuela, and 40,000 in 1940.[190] But how these vehicles were used, and whether similar *chicas modernas* were driving them as in Mexico, or whether the Brazilian and

Chilean adventurous car cultures were also to be found, say, in Paraguay, Colombia, or Surinam, we do not know.

The Rest and the West: Subversive and Subaltern Mobilities?

Latin America's mobility history raises questions about the extension of the 'West' when it comes to demarcating 'mainstream mobility history.' Has Latin American automotive mobility been 'invisible,' in the sense used by Mignolo, because it was not so different from what has been described for Northwest Europe and the United States? We have seen this can be true only if, at all, one mistakes 'Creole mobility' for the mobility of a continent, an obvious act of exclusion of entire populations of Indians, Africans, and many offspring of the *mestizaje* (miscegenation, culturally: the "mixing of European habits, beliefs, and forms of thought with those originating from American societies") taking place in the cities. So, does a 'mobility of the South' exist, parallel and in addition to Mignolo's "epistemology of the South"? Do we need an 'Other mobility' to cover the mobility of the Other?[191]

Even at the level of the relatively small middle class, it would be a methodological error to push Latin American mobility under the mainstream umbrella, as much as it would be a mistake to do the same with other 'peripheral' mobility cultures, such as Southern and Eastern Europe, whose histories have hardly been touched from a mobility perspective. What do we know, after all, of 'Soviet automobilism' (if such a thing exists as a separate category) in this phase, apart from the fact that during the revolutionary years avant-garde artists such as Futurist Vladimir Mayakovsky described experiences similar to his Western European vanguard counterparts, whereas Formalist and "dynamite thrower" Viktor Shklovsky saw the car as "a metaphor of revolutionary transformation," in which there was no place for electric propulsion? Do we need a third motorization model (next to that of Northwestern Europe and the United States) to characterize a country where, on the eve of World War II, only 78 tramway systems competed with 325 motorbus systems, statistics in which "numerous fleets maintained by individual enterprises or institutions for their employees, and the considerable use of buses for tourist, weekend or recreational trips" were not included?[192]

If so, we certainly need a fourth one for Latin America, where, as we have seen in the cases of Brazil and Mexico, subtle differences emerged, such as sport fetishism, road network building 'from below' as a Nationalist project, and the most important of all: a *small* but clearly visible (in terms of conspicuous consumption) middle class. And we need some space for a separate peripheral mobility, in which 'Westernization' is contested and discussed through the car. For instance, Turkish literary theorist Jale Parla unearthed an entire literary tradition of "car novels," in which modernization was discussed through the possession and use of the car (or vehicles in general) rather than other 'machines.' Such novels produced "enigmatic narratives of possession and dispossession, empowerment and loss of power, function and dysfunction, maturation and infantilism, narcissism and fetishism, fragmentation and self-destruction, not to mention a whole century of estrangement and a feeling of inferiority inspired by the contact with the West." In Recaizade Mahmut Ekrem's *Araba Sevdası* (*The Carriage Affair*, 1898, lit. "vehicle passion"), we see parts of the Western car-metaphorical cluster impinge on a 'peripheral' mobility, especially the 'flight' metaphor: the protagonist's carriage "speeds so fast down the slope … that the wheels do not touch the ground," and in the end, even the horse "frees itself [from the carriage] and flies into the air," a "masterpiece of satire and irony," according to Parla, in which "over-Westernization [is] producing the follies that reigned in the intellectual as well as the creative spheres," just like in the case of Sōseki.[193] If extended to the entire globe, interbellum mobility history becomes kaleidoscopic, indeed.

***

Indeed, all continents visited so far show characteristics that are not easily (or in some cases, not at all) to be found in the familiar (hi)stories. We have seen forgotten vehicles and draught animals (rickshaws, one-wheeled barrows, palanquins, hammocks and machillas, bullock carts, llamas, mules, and camels), and the most forgotten of all: human porterage, or, more generally, walking while carrying or pulling/pushing something, be it a palanquin or a rickshaw, or freight, on the head. There is, indeed, no doubt the non-West knows a much more variegated modal configuration, especially in the cities. We have called this phenomenon, which seems to be typical for the non-West, 'layeredness.' On top of this mobile richness, the coming of colonizers cemented another layer on an already existing, complex mix of old and new, a layer often functioning at quite a distance from the existing amalgam of vehicles, but very visible to everyone. The telephone or other devices of communicative modernity may be private, but the bicycle and the car are private only as 'public' vehicles.

Mobility layeredness resonates with claims by postcolonial scholars for whom "colonial capitalism and colonial modernity were not entirely a replica of their European counterparts but something *sui generis*, an 'original alloy' composed of the historic failure of capital to realise its universalising tendency under colonial conditions and a corresponding failure of the metropolitan bourgeois culture to dissolve or assimilate fully the indigenous culture of South Asia in the power relations of the colonial period." The main difference between the two cultures was that "while the metropolitan state was hegemonic in character 'with its claim to dominance ... based on a power relation in which *the moment of persuasion outweighed the moment of coercion*,' the colonial state was, by comparison, non-hegemonic with persuasion outweighed by coercion in its structure of dominance." Such a difference becomes apparent only if (in the case of India, to which this quote refers) the history of India is not reduced to "a history of the British in India." Writing a global mobility history as a history of car cultures would indeed neglect, as a violent act, the mobility of most of the planet's inhabitants. Including the history of the subaltern would make "colonial modernity more complex than European modernity, which undergoes a transition from feudalism to capitalism, shedding the ancien-régime values along the way."[194]

An example of this complexity is the Beijing rickshaw puller who, as we saw, struggled for 'modernity without efficiency.' Likewise, we also saw how Lao She's rickshaw puller produced modernist adventure machine experiences without the aid of an engine (no surprise if we realize the bicycle in the West generated similar experiences, to be enhanced and canonized only by the car). From this perspective, the car is only an 'enhancer' of experiences generated elsewhere, including adventure. Calling the car adventurous and all other vehicles not would thus result in a distortion of history by pronouncing, erroneously, the 'enhancers' as the true origin of adventurous feeling. This encourages us to look for broader 'vehicle experiences' in the chapters to follow, experiences that often emerge *outside* these vehicles, as resistance by pedestrians, porters, cyclists, rickshaw pullers, and muleteers. Other specific traits adding to colonial mobility's complexity are the supermacho qualification of car driving as childish and feminine by Latin American commentators, as well as this continent's obsession with speed and power, both phenomena an expression of a flight forward from, if not a caricature of Western modernity. From a sociohistorical mobility perspective, perhaps the most important difference is the role of the rickshaw, which was seen as a clear alternative to the car (a bad alternative, in the eyes of middle-class motorists); inextricably linked to this was the social and legal construction, by colonial authorities and local middle classes alike, of the 'mob,' the mobile collective Other, as a threat to the colonial 'order.' It is this mob that explains the 'mobility' of the rickshaw phenomenon throughout Asia, as the rickshaw is intimately linked to migration in the Pacific realm, especially of the Chinese diaspora.

Moreover, all cases discussed so far assume a basic sessility around which mobility modes spin their networks (the most conspicuous example being the apartment as iconic possession in India). But colonial mobility was special in that it actively tried, while mobilizing the colony's resources, to immobilize or at least control the mobility of the native population, especially its nomadic or pseudo-nomadic (circular-migratory) members. It seems, indeed, as if the nomads, especially the "pastoral nomads" (those who have specialized in animal husbandry, thus excluding "hunter-gatherers, Gypsies, migrant farm workers, or corporate executives who are nomadic but not pastoral") shape their mobility-as-life in animal rather than in any motorized form. From the south of the Sahara, through the Arabian deserts, the South American highlands, the Arctic North, and the Central Eurasian Steppe to the Tibetan Plateau, sheep, goats, cattle, horses, donkeys, camels, yaks, reindeer, and llamas have become, through selective breeding, the 'cultured' companions of nomadic families and tribes. Only Eurasia nomads seemed to have used wheeled vehicles drawn by oxen or horses. In many cases, it was the good-carrying capacity of the railroads that heralded the demise of nomadism, supported by enforced sedentarization and collectivization, such as in the case of the Kazaks, whose societies were destroyed by Joseph Stalin in the 1930s. Some nomads such as the Pashtun in Afghanistan adapted through the purchase of trucks. Northern Indian wandering singers did the same, as we saw. Even the American hoboes saw their nomadic culture disappear through the car.[195]

***

Despite these differences with a Western 'master narrative,' the global expansion of mobility history also reveals a remarkable *synchronicity* that severely questions the diffusionist stance: all major issues, from the shock about the lethality of automobilism, through the celebration of the car as 'adventure machine' in some Latin American countries, to the growth of the road network and the competition between rail and road, happened at more or less the same time as in Europe and the United States, irrespective of the *scale* of the phenomenon. Even in China, despite the internal 'disorder,' a network of rails and roads of a modest size was in place by the time of the Japanese invasion in 1937, wide enough for a 'national' bus culture (national without the Communists on their Long March, of course) to develop. Although the discourse (to which some scholars limit themselves, at a price) on these issues may have been limited to a middle class or an urban audience, or the literate community reading newspapers, the migrant descending from the Andes to the city could as easily (or even more easily, because of their lack of skills in negotiating motorized traffic) be killed by a speeding car as the skilled rickshaw puller. As a former car engineer specialized in combustion engines, I understand diffusion metaphorically as what combustion specialists call 'diffusionist combustion' (as occurs in a spark ignition engine). The spread over the globe of automotive mobility, however, seems to follow the diesel combustion process, called 'simultaneously explosive combustion': combustion kernels emerge simultaneously throughout the cylinder, wherever the conditions for ignition are present.

In social history, this phenomenon is sometimes called the "modern girl complex," which analyzes the nearly simultaneous emergence of "modern girls" (*chicas modernas*) in every part of the world in the early twentieth century, a phenomenon called 'modernity at large' by Appadurai. Automobilism, then, including its adventurous traits, is an accompanying phenomenon of 'modernity at large,' but not a precondition, as the 'modern rickshaw' testifies. Decentering Europe implies decentering the car. But we should be careful in the comparison West-Rest, as superficial similarities may hide deeper differences, as we already suggested at the start of the introduction. For instance, despite the undeniable parallel observation in Indonesia, as we saw, that 'progress' meanwhile comes in the guise of fashionable frivolity, and despite our observation of the same morbid 'thanatourism' in Libya as in Europe, we cannot ignore our overall impression that the non-West seems to be more impressed by the 'serious mobility' of buses, trucks, and, in general, the daily 'necessity' of transport, for instance, of the rickshaw for commuting.[196] If we exclude for the moment the tiny middle-class minorities who indulged in automotive adventurousness, and focus instead on the mobility of the majority, then motorized mobility seems to be less ironic (as we concluded in the case of Africa). This becomes understandable once one realizes mobility history of the 'Rest,' more conspicuously so than in the West, is racialized through and through, from the road-construction corvées in Africa to the inequalities in car ownership in Latin America. More so than in the West, roadbuilding in the non-West sometimes took place partially 'from below,' as it were, as we saw in the case of Mexico, or in the case of China.

***

About the other, more detailed aspects, we can only guess at the present scholarly state of the art. For instance, road construction in Africa seems to follow European and American patterns in that the length of local and regional roads during the interwar years grew faster than that of national roads, but some Latin American statistics seem to deviate from this pattern. Or was the local government less accurate in counting lower-order roads? One other possible difference worth investigating is the phenomenon that trucks sometimes seem to dominate the statistics of the country's motorized vehicle fleet (fig. 1.9). If this is not a local exceptionalism, it would provide room for speculation about the pleasurable sides of mobility, although we know from European and American early truck cultures (but also from the adventurous truck drivers in the Peruvian Andes) that they were at least as much 'driven' by adventure and pleasure than by business acumen and other traits of 'serious mobility.'

Nevertheless, the start of Japan's motorization as an exercise in economic utility (fed by transport companies rather than the adventures of individual motorists), as we have seen, seems to suggest we need some more nuance when it comes to the supposed universalism of the car as adventure machine. On a more general level, our excursions over the globe, as a first, albeit brief corrective to our earlier analysis of "Atlantic automobilism," also helps us rethink the debate on modernity, especially its relationship with tradition. It is quite clear that mobility forms, and should be seen as, a constitutive part of modernity, an insight that is far from general.[197] The mobility side of modernity is about control, and the decision of who is entitled to be mobile and who is not (as Tim Cresswell has eminently shown in the historical cases of his *On the Move*) is as much a part of colonial power deployment as the question of enforced labor or the grabbing of land by settlers. It is also highly gendered, from the exclusively male rickshaw culture (although we know from Lao She's novel about the role of women at home, and we know about some women masquerading as rickshaw pullers), to the high-power love of Argentine men, mimicking the European writer-motorist pioneers.

Mobile modernity is, from a global perspective, also about acknowledging the importance of subaltern and subversive forms of mobility, mobilities produced by those who have no voice in the historical record, or who move against the grain of hegemonic mobility. This conception of subalternity is deliberately kept very broad, parallel to Dipesh Chakrabarty's assertion in *Provincializing Europe* that the concept does not "refer … to any particular group or groups. We must assume that anyone who worlds the earth, experiences time, and so on, in ways to challenge the imperious code of

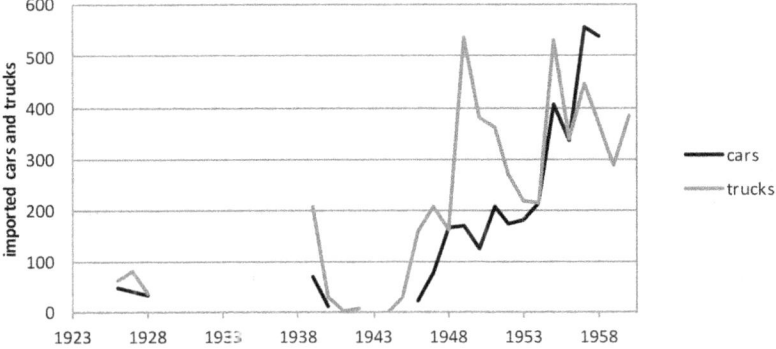

Figure 1.9. Imported cars and trucks in Dahomey. Source: Manning, *Slavery, Colonialism and Economic Growth in Dahomey*, 390, appendix 4. Figure created by the author.

historicism is a subaltern."[198] The problem of identifying and interpreting subaltern mobilities are legion, however. Should we make a much more radical move than we did in this chapter, and should the car be abandoned from a subaltern world mobility history? And should we instead unearth variants of walking, cycling, muleteering, smuggle with elephants, like the quoted French Indologists did, when they pointed at the circular mobility of singers and peddlers?[199] I think not.

Although 'slow mobility' indeed is heavily under researched (and not so slow after all, as we saw in the case of the rickshaw), snowed under the heaps of studies on speedy and motorized mobility that have fascinated Western and non-Western mobility scholars alike for the past thirty or so years, the constant and constantly increasing presence of the car in all local cultures visited so far crucially influenced mobility patterns and the way local people conceived them. Carlessness is as important a phenomenon as car ownership. As we will reiterate in the next chapter, the twentieth century has rightly been dubbed 'automobile age,' even in colonies (such as India), where the railway lobby was much stronger than the road lobby. As the previous pages make abundantly clear, the 'adventure machine' was not limited to the West. On the contrary, it was emphasized there, exaggerated, by colonists and indigenous elites alike, and spiced with a high sensitivity for status: wherever the car appears, we conclude, based on only limited evidence, frivolous images pop up. At first imported, then assembled, and only rarely produced locally from scratch in the period covered by this chapter, the car's spread over the globe, driven mostly by the two American giants Ford and GM, has been largely neglected here, but it is quite clear from the perspective of this 'production imperialism' that the globalization of motorized mobility easily takes the form of diffusion.

And yet, placed against a context of a walking majority, a world mobility history should perhaps abandon a *driver perspective*, certainly for the first half of the century. Walking and cycling may have been quantitatively dominant (and they still are), but the fact that we must constantly be reminded of this tells it all: in our discourse, in our thinking, we have developed a highspeed mind. Up to now, the Latin American Indians, with their llamas and mules and their rejection of wheeled mobility; the Africans, who drove camel caravans through the Sahara or were punished through their coerced building of colonial roads; the peasants in the fields of China, with their bullock carts and one-wheeled barrows, have been largely absent from our narratives so far, and I am afraid this will remain so for a while, except for the single peasant in Buñuel's film who, as a *deus ex animale*, pulled both the agricultural tractor and the urban bus out of the mud. Although the 'layering' effect of urban and rural mobilities over the non-Western world has kept those forms of 'primitive mobilities' alive, historians tend to be mesmerized by the 'shock of the new,' concentrated as they were (and often still are) on innovations in the history of technology and mobility much more than on the fuzzy mess of the traffic mix. In that mix, the old technology reigns, but the minds are full of a high-speed future. This is what Fernando Coronil called "subaltern modernities" and what I see as subaltern mobilities, understood as a crucial part of these modernities. In general, for mobility studies, the same applies as Darcy Ribeiro has formulated for subaltern knowledge:

> The colonial people, deprived of their riches and of the fruit of their labor under colonial regimes, suffered ... the degradation of assuming as their proper image that was no more than the reflection of the European vision of the world, which considered colonial people racially inferior because they were black, (Amer)Indians, or mestizos ... Even the brighter social strata of non-European people got used to seeing themselves and their communities as an infrahumanity whose destiny was to occupy a subaltern position because of the sheer fact that theirs was inferior to the European population.

From this follows, indeed, that "for purposes of world history, the margins sometimes demand more attention than the metropolis."[200] In the chapter 3, after our visit to Western automobility exuberance in chapter 2, we will wander through these 'margins' as much as our sources allow.

***

A second major consequence of penning toward the subversive and the subaltern is that it at the same time rebounds to the West: it urges mobility historians to rethink the mainstream narrative of an area that often is reduced to its Anglophone part. In this vein, the admonition of the Comaroffs that innovation starts in the 'Third World' also applied to our field: our global excursion invites us to revisit all those subaltern and subversive Western mobilities that have been mostly forgotten, such as the black jitney culture in the United States of the 1910s or the fact that early holiday excursions per bus in Europe were dominated by women.

One consequence of this is the relativization of vehicle *ownership*: the bicycle and car 'experience' also (and especially) was generated on the outside, by the onlookers, the victims, the pedestrians, the children and other excluded from riding and driving. It not only brings to the fore the importance of 'passengering,' for which sociologists and geographers of mobility have recently asked our attention (as we saw in the introduction) and which is fatally under researched in a historical sense, it also relativizes the perspective of the *production* of the driving experience (with all its connotations of speed, fetishism, transcendence) and brings Western 'slow traffic' back into the orbit of mobility history, as the mobile activity of by far the majority of inhabitants of this planet, despite the ubiquity of the 'automotive age.' Conversely, it would also bounce back to analyses of non-Western mobilities, where in ethnographic and anthropological studies, the 'possession' of a bicycle or a car often takes center stage (for instance, in studies of 'cultural appropriation'), enhancing a 'transport development' perspective or, more generally, neglecting the nonuser.[201]

A further impulse to rethink Western mobility comes from the insight, generated through the study of world mobility, that much of mobility, also in the West, is a collective experience, of the 'swarm' of pedestrians (despite the loneliness of the flaneur in the crowd, as during Sōseki's stay in London), of the situational group of bus passengers, of the community of rickshaw pullers, and the family of migrants. The individualist experience of bicycle and car driving, on which many Western mobility historians have placed so much emphasis to enable them to fit their analysis in the modernity discourse (and on which the Western literary tradition rests), has distorted our picture of Western mobility, where jitneys in the 1910s in the Southern United States were used by blacks in a collective way, or the passengers who in their nearly fully neglected bus travel formed their 'situational groups,' or the early bicycle and car pioneers who shaped their fledgling culture as a collective effort undertaken by groups of touring and car club members.

***

A third argument for why rethinking Western mobility on the basis of non-Western mobility studies is called for is the importance of the systemic aspect of mobility, which most clearly revealed itself in the African case, where the import of cars without roads did not make much sense. This argument especially plays a role in an important aspect of Western mobility: the long-distance journey as part of the imperialist project. Elsewhere, I have extensively dealt with this version of mobility, as it shares the adventurousness and the male aggression with mainstream mobility. In fact, the current preliminary sketch of non-Western mobility history in this chapter shows it is the other way around: the emergence of individual mechanized (bicycle) and motorized (car) mobility is unthinkable without the imperialist mind-set. Preceded by long-distance cycling (including trips across the world such as George Burston and Harry Stokes's ride from Melbourne to London [1890] or Annie Kopchovsky's ride around the world [1895]), automobile pioneers surveyed the route from Beijing to Paris (1907), traversed Africa from Cairo to the Cape, and tried to cross the Andes preparing for the Pan-American Highway. They were often sponsored by governments or companies, as in the case of the Black Cruise into Africa, or, even more spectacular, the Yellow Cruise (*croisière jaune*) into Central Asia during the 1930s, which produced 5,000 photographs and 230,000 feet of film. As a

British motoring pioneer said in 1908 (notice the past tense, as well as the sexual metaphor), "the joy of the motorist was as that of the conqueror," a joy that could be appreciated now that "the heart of Africa has been penetrated" by the car.[202]

Such stories illustrate the relationship between imperialism and modernity is controversial. Whereas Sanjay Joshi opted to "put slavery and terror at the very heart of any definition of modernity" and "much of what we know of modern bourgeois identities was formed in relation to colonial encounters in which ideas of racial distinctions were central," Mann warned against "exaggerat[ing] the significance of empire back home. Its profits were not enormous, providing just above 1 percent of British annual GDP, only a tenth of British trade with [the rest of] Europe." But imperialism is not only about profit making. It is also about prestige and status as an owner of colonies, as economic historian Walter Rostow reminded us. For Joshi, "a close examination of the discourse of modernity deployed reveals its illiberal and perhaps non-modern sub-strata," whereas Mann observed for the case of the largest empire ever, the United Kingdom, that "empire rarely dominated politics back home," that "imperialists—a diverse group of overseas business interests, adventurers, missionaries, and other ideologists—wanted more resources than the politicians would finance."[203] That does not mean, also according to Mann, imperialism wasn't through and through violent and aggressive. This is especially true for European imperialism, as "Europeans were probably more warlike than the inhabitants of any other continent." Europe's conquest of the colonies rested on "superior military power" in the first place: "From 1871 to 1914, the British fought about thirty colonial wars (not counting perennial violence along the northwest frontier of India). Between them, the British, French, and Dutch fought at least 100. In Kenya alone, the British fought one battle per year over a twenty-year period ... European losses in these colonial wars amounted to 280,000–300,000; the conquered people lost around 50–60 million, of whom 90 percent were civilians."

Especially the settler colonies were violent: at the census of 1900, more than 95 percent of North American natives appear to have died, and Australia lost 75 percent of its Aborigines by 1921. They died mostly by disease, although "settlers rejoyced at the death-toll and supplemented it with rolling waves of genocide. The more representative the settler politics, the greater the killing—democratic genocide." Hence, Alfred Crosby's distinction in four types of settlers: humans, as much as domestic animals, weeds and microbes, all of them deadly or devastating for indigenous species, were an integral part of "ecological imperialism." Imperialism was, to borrow a phrase Mann applied to World War I (showing he is as much driven by mobility metaphors as the objects of his study), a "high-octane masculine adventure." There is a comprehensive study to be undertaken of the meanderings of Europeans and other Westerners over the different continents, from the mass tourist to the elite literary visitor such as German globetrotter Clärenore Stinnes visiting Chile in 1927, Rudyard Kipling in Brazil in the same year, French dandy Raymond Roussel to Ceylon (Sri Lanka) and India, or Robert Byron, who in his *Road to Oxiana* "observed [the landscapes of Persia and Mesopotamia] from the windows of cars and gas-fuelled lorries, buses, and speedboats."[204]

***

Perhaps the most spectacular tale in this respect is American writer Frederic Prokosch's "rich sequence of adventures" as "a hitchhiker with little money" among the "Asiatics." Son of a professor at Yale, at twenty he purchased, according to his biographer, "a 'tumbledown' Ford roadster and enrolled at the University of Pennsylvania as a graduate student in English." When Klaus and Erika Mann (son and daughter of Thomas Mann, both in their early twenties) in 1927 made their tour along American universities, talking about their plan to make a world tour, Frederic was "breathless with envy," Klaus remembered.[205]

Less than a decade later, Prokosch would write an exemplary travelogue, in which about every conceivable vehicle (plane, steamer, lots of trucks, sleigh, camel and donkey caravans, horses, bullock carts, including his feet and an old Belgian expensive Minerva) was applied in an itinerary from Beirut to Hong Kong, carefully avoiding China. This is not a 'normal' travelogue, as much of the border crossing is undertaken illegally and stealthily, and the erotic adventures (the seduction of travel companions) are competing for the reader's attention with the adventures in physical mobility, including a plane crash, the pilot killed. His descriptions of cities in the Middle East resonate with what we know from other travelers from the 1930s (such as Harry Franck in Shanghai): Teheran disappoints because of "the new steam tramway and the new hotel and the new cinema theater and the new motorcars. Thoroughly Western."

On the road, he is living as much among the local elite and the Europeans, as among the marginals. Amid the usual racist remarks ("the dead rat, grinning terribly like a Chinaman") and the equally usual understanding, albeit put in the mouth of one of the protagonists, of the devastating impact of the West ("Bring in the Fords and the factories. What's a bit of faith compared to a fresh oil well or a new road? Civilization. Rot."), his descriptions of local traffic are very instructive for a study of non-Western mobility at the eve of World War II. In one scene along the "Teheran-to-Meshed road," the narrator spots "numerous post-carriages and motor-trucks" but also "single donkeys under terrific loads of grain and fagots, and twice we saw Junker airplanes flying high overhead." At a party of the local maharaja in India, a "stream of motor-cars, tongas, rickshas and victorias [a carriage] passed under the main portico." Sometimes, the perspective is from so high up that the traveling becomes a litany: "We rode and rode, and sometimes walked; past the abysses, along the sickling torrents, over the bridged ravines, between the brittle crags," until one starts to wonder why the landscape descriptions are so fleeting and at times quite superficial.

But then again, the response of the natives in India to his host's Minerva resonates with scenes familiar to those who studied the merging automobilism in Europe: "The villagers jumped up as we passed, assuming quite simply and amiably that we—Hamadullah, I, and the Minerva—were creatures superior to themselves. They peered, they whispered. Out of one door two naked little boys were watching us, out of another a cow." Enter the well-known ingredients of the automotive adventure, including the admiration for the driver's skill: "Hamadullah drove extremely well. He avoided many an unexpected creature, wild, domestic, human, or mechanical, for whom the road was a gathering-place rather than a thoroughfare." By the end of his trip, in Saigon, one of the protagonists discovers the essence of life: "Move, move, keep on moving, that's the whole thing. That's the way to survive." There, at last, walking down one of the main roads

> everywhere we saw brightly colored sport cars, American makes, most of them—Cadillacs and Chryslers and so on ... Now and then a fat sleek Chinese merchant would drive by in an expensive motor-car ... Ladies in the latest Paris gowns drove by in long motor-cars with iridescent hoods and chromium superchargers like great silver serpents ... Big open cars were being driven by sweating Frenchmen slowly along the avenue; straight-lipped nurses with gaily tinted parasols were taking their little girls for a walk; lovely dark concubines were riding by in freshly painted victorias and gaudy rickshas; down by the fountains two little children were playing nakedly in the stone basin.[206]

How amazing! What a detailed richness this account offers the student of non-Western mobility! Or not? Prokosch's novel appears to be part of the same "enormous hoax" as his memoirs from 1983: fascinated by maps, his sister recalls how he, "in a hammock" at his family's home, "surrounded by tomes of exotic photos and descriptions, munching on oranges, jott[ed] down ideas." His travelogue was an instant success, and famous reviewers could hardly believe it was all made up (in 1937, he would make an extensive motor tour of Europe, and his *Night of the Poor* [1939] is an adventurous road novel playing in the United States). Thomas Mann praised its "audacious, adventurous spirit," and although others called it the "Journey of a Narcissus," André Gide judged it an "authentic masterpiece," because of its "astonishing feat of the imagination." Others praised its lack of a plot, the adventures following each other "like beads on a string" (an affinity with the travel itinerary, moving from one location linearly to the next), and as late as 1964, a *Guide to American Literature* presented it as "among the best books to offer a picture of the world struggle up to the time of World War II."

Imaginative Italian filmmaker Federico Fellini in 1984 called Prokosch one of his favorite writers. Prokosch had produced the ultimate projection of his Western ideas, including his 'mobility cocktail,' on a continent reconstructed from books, maps, and hearsay: mobility history's Orientalism. "I went there and he didn't," Klaus Mann remembered, adding ironically: "Yet he saw more of it than I did." Tellingly, the narrative stops short of the Chinese border, to the north of Hanoi, where Communists had just arrested, tortured, and executed forty natives: in China, the closing message of Prokosch's novel seems to be there is no place for his protagonists' adventures, or for the author's irony: "hot coals had been ticked between their toes, long hot needles gently inserted in their ears, strange insects set nibbling away at their genitals. Not very pleasant."[207] In other words: shortly before World War II, virtual travel writing could be as convincing as the real stuff. But it was as 'untrue fiction,' as these histories that limited themselves to the West.

How did the subaltern (in the sense used by Chakrabarty) respond to these mobilities? We do not know, although one form of response sounds familiar to anyone who has studied Western folklore around the car: in East Africa, stories abounded about bloodsucking cars, especially those painted red, "drain[ing] the blood from lone pedestrians captured along the Kisumu to Busia highway" in Kenya. They seem to originate in the late 1910s and early 1920s, the moment of the first non-incidental appearance of the car.[208] In Mexican Tepoztlán, there were rumors that "the devil had made a pact with the engineers" of the nearby road that should pull the peasants out of the mud. In a cave, the devil hid "the souls of those who perished in motor vehicle crashes." In Chiapas, in the 1940s, there were fears that Indians were sold to the chiefs of the roadbuilding crews, "who turned them into grease to lubricate their road-building machinery." Where have we heard this before? During the Russian Revolution, about the cars driving in the night through Moscow abducting citizens? Or in Western folklore tales about hitchhikers in the night, leaving their severed hand behind the bumper after they failed to get onto the car? Folklore, in the West and in the East, has surrounded the car from its very beginnings, a reservoir of metaphors and anxieties from which higher-brow literati sometimes draw, such as the German Otto Julius Bierbaum and the British Marie Corelli, who—the former as a private indulgence in the 'thrill' of motoring, the latter as its rejection—mobilized vampiristic images of automotive violence and aggression at the very beginning of European automobilism.[209]

On the other hand, we should be wary of equating the subaltern's mobility to a response of Western automobilism: "the Third World contributes to modernity at the same time that modernity produces the Third World," Mignolo rightly claims, echoing the Comaroffs. The "moral economy of the peasant" in Southeast Asia is as much tainted by his mobility as it is by his "rebellion and subsistence," even if its students prioritize the latter over the former. But Mignolo also, rightly, argues that to analyze subalternity, we need new tools, as Western knowledge may be inadequate for the task. Mignolo gives the example of psychoanalysis, "created to deal with the problem of class society in Europe," which "may not work for a *caste* society in Calcutta." We will, in chapter 3, analyze the case of traffic engineering, and reach a similar conclusion. In addition, 'provincializing Europe,' also in the realm of mobility studies, at the same time means 'anthropologizing Europe,' studying its (auto)mobilists anew as a foreign tribe in order to "show how exotic its constitution of reality has been."[210] We will do so for the 'exuberant phase' of Western mobility in the next chapter.

Notes

Epigraph: Tseng P'u [Zeng Pu], "A Flower in a Sinful Sea," trans. Rafe de Crespigny and Liu Ts'un-yan [Liu Cunren], in *Chinese Middlebrow Fiction From the Ch'ing and Early Republican Eras*, ed. Liu Ts'un-yan [Liu Cunren] (Hong Kong: Chinese University Press, 1984), 137

1. Sammy I. Tsunematsu, "Introduction," in *Spring Miscellany and London Essays* by Natsume Sōseki (Boston: Tuttle Publishing, 2002), 7; Gijs Mom, *Atlantic Automobilism: Emergence and Persistence of the Car, 1895–1940* (New York: Berghahn Books, 2015), 138–139; Natsume Sōseki, "A Sweet Dream," in Sōseki, *Spring Miscellany*, 54–55; Natsume Sōseki, "Impressions," in Sōseki, *Spring Miscellany*, 57; Natsume Sōseki, "The Carlyle Museum," in Sōseki, *Spring Miscellany*, 126 (smoke).
2. Natsume Sōseki, "The Diary of a Bicycle Rider," in Sōseki, *Spring Miscellany*, 139, 147.
3. Natsume Sōseki, "To Kyō (22 January 1901)," in Sōseki, *Spring Miscellany*, 153.
4. See, e.g., Manfred Garhammer, *Wie Europäer ihre Zeit nutzen: Zeitstrukturen und Zeitkulturen im Zeichen der Globalisierung* (Berlin: edition sigma, 2001), 169, where the ownership of a car by most households is used as a measure of "modern time culture." Garhammer distinguished between three modernization "routes": a European, an American, and a Japanese. Ibid., 16 (shift).
5. Steven J. Ericson, *The Sound of the Whistle: Railroads and the State in Meiji Japan* (Cambridge, MA: Council on East Asian Studies, Harvard University, 1996), 32 (imported); Andrew Gordon, *A Modern History of Japan: From Tokugawa Times to the Present* (New York: Oxford University Press, 2003), 71–73 (model enterprises, German), 80 (constitution), 83 (samurai), 94 (workshop), 99 (1906), 100, table 7.1 (women), 101 (industries), 110 (Shinto), 111 (drills), 114 (first), 117–118 (1894), 121 (colony); Louise Young, *Beyond the Metropolis: Second Cities and Modern Life in Interwar Japan* (Berkeley: University of California Press, 2013), 92 (Ericson).
6. Steven C. Topik and Allen Wells, "Commodity Chains in a Global Economy," in *A World Connecting 1870–1945*, ed. Emily S. Rosenberg (Cambridge, MA: Belknap Press,

2012), 643, table 4.5; Armand Mattelart, *The Invention of Communication* (Minneapolis: University of Minnesota Press, 1996), 165; Beoncheon Yu, "Introduction," in Natsume Sōseki, *The Wayfarer: Kōjin* (New York: Perigree Books, 1982), 21–22 (hybrid), 16 (neo-idealists); Mom, *Atlantic Automobilism*, 161–170; Natsume Sōseki, *Inside My Glass Doors* (Boston: Tuttle Publishing, 2002), 33.

7. James A. Fujii, "Networks and Modernity: Rail Transport and Modern Japanese Literature," *Japan Railway & Transport Review* 13 (1997): 13 (extension); Ericson, *Sound of the Whistle*, 56 (alienation); Alisa Freedman, *Tokyo in Transit: Japanese Culture on the Rails and Road* (Stanford, CA: Stanford University Press, 2011), 23 (1907), 69 (women), 70 (metaphor), 90 (ambivalence), 113–114 (three types); Jay Rubin, "Sanshiro and Soseki: A Critical Essay," in *Sanshiro: A Novel* by Natsume Sōseki, trans. Jay Rubin (Seattle: University of Washington Press, 1977), 237 (characters).

8. Natsume Sōseki, "The Civilization of Modern-Day Japan (Gendai Nihon no Kaika)," in *The Columbia Anthology of Modern Japanese Literature: Abridged*, ed. J. Thomas Rimer and Van C. Gessel (New York: Columbia University Press, 2011), 155 (enjoyment), 157 (outside), 158 (unnatural), 159 (level) (I thank M. William (Bill) Steele for pointing me to this publication, as well as guiding me through Japan's early modernization); Gordon, *Modern History of Japan*, 132, table 8.1.

9. Sōseki, *Wayfarer*, 279, 281; Natsume Sōseki, "My Individualism," in Natsume Sōseki, *My Individualism and the Philosophical Foundations of Literature*, trans. Sammy I. Tsunematsu (Boston: Tuttle Publishing, 2004), 53 (twigs); Sōseki quoted from his essay "The Philosophical Foundations of Literature" in Inger Sigrun Brodey, "Introduction," in Sōseki, *My Individualism*, 19 (community); Christopher A. Reed and M. William Steele, "The Modern History of the Book in China, Japan and Korea" (manuscript draft, February 2016), 2 (movable type), 3 (revolutionized), 4 (serialized), 9 (blurring) (I thank Bill Steele for providing me with this manuscript); Catherine Bertho Lavenir, *La roue et le stylo: Comment nous sommes devenus touristes* (Paris: Editions Odile Jacob, 1999).

10. Yu, "Introduction," 18 (static), 25 (self-absorption); Michael D. Pante, "Racialized Capacities and Transgressive Mobility: 'Asian' Laborers and 'Western' Urban Transportation in Colonial Manila and Singapore," *Transfers* 4, no. 3 (2014): 50.

11. Sōseki, *Wayfarer*, 163 (home), 174 (shaving) 230 (things), 260 (rickshaws); Sōseki, *Inside My Glass Doors*, 54 (born).

12. Sōseki, *Inside My Glass Doors*, 5 (fetch), 60 (no trams or rickshaws), 63 (emergencies); Sōseki, *Wayfarer*, 300 (trustworthy); Peter J. Rimmer, *Rikisha to Rapid Transit: Urban Public Transport Systems and Policy in Southeast Asia* (Sydney: Pergamon Press, 1986), 40 (T-junctions), 42–43 (Emperor Meiji); James Francis Warren, *Rickshaw Coolie: A People's History of Singapore 1880–1940* (Singapore: Singapore University Press, 2003), 14 (hybrid); M. William Steele, "Mobility on the Move: Rickshaws in Asia," *Transfers* 4, no. 3 (2004): 90 (fleet).

13. Sōseki, *Wayfarer*, 284–285 (frustrated, automobile), 287 (at rest), 296 (remedy). From a feminist point of view, however, the brother's ailment may well lie elsewhere, in his violence toward his wife: "Women are far more cruel than men who resort to force. I wonder why the devil she didn't stand up to me when I hit her. No, she didn't need to resist, but why didn't she say so much as a single word back to me?" Ibid., 294.

14. Gijs Mom, "Civilized Adventure as a Remedy for Nervous Times: Early Automobilism and *fin de siècle* Culture," *History of Technology* 23 (2001); see also Joachim Radkau, "'Die Nervosität des Zeitalters': Die Erfindung von Technikbedürfnissen um die Jahrhundertwende," *Kultur & Technik* 3 (1994); Yu, "Introduction," 25 (nature); Sōseki, *Wayfarer*, 197.

15. Sōseki, *Inside My Glass Doors*, 66 (suburbanization); Michael Mann, *The Sources of Social Power, vol. 3: Global Empires and Revolution, 1890–1945* (Cambridge: Cambridge University Press, 2012), 111; Philippe Fôret, "Railroad Literature on Suitable Places: How the Japanese Government Railways Forged an 'Old China' Travel Culture," in *Die Internationalität der Eisenbahn 1850–1970*, ed. Monika Burri, Kilian T. Elsasser, and David Gurgerli (Zürich: Chronos Verlag, 2003), 311 (*lebensraum*). The inner-city "ward area" declined between 1891 and 1940 from 79 percent to 38 percent of Tokyo's population. Rimmer, *Rikisha*, 56. For a definition of settler colonialism (that erroneously assumes settlers are white), see Lorenzo Veracini, *Settler Colonialism: A Theoretical Overview* (London: Palgrave Macmillan, 2010), 4–5.
16. Mann, *Sources of Social Power, vol. 3*, 111, 117; Daniel R. Headrick, "A Double-Edged Sword: Communications and Imperial Control in British India," *Historical Social Research* 35, no. 1 (2010): 59; Gordon, *Modern History of Japan*, 173 (World War I), 174 (US, clause).
17. Jens Damm and Bettina Gransow, "Zwischen Kuli-Export und Business-Netzwerken: Muster interner, inter- und transnationaler chinesischer Migration seit dem 19. Jahrhundert," in *Migrationen: Globale Entwicklungen seit 1850*, ed. Albert Kraler, Karl Husa, Veronika Bilger and Irene Stacher (Vienna: Mandelbaum Verlag, 2007), 227 (migration); Mann, *Sources of Social Power, vol. 3*, 375 (sabotage), 377 (bureaucrats); for penetrating, see, e.g., Mattelart, *Invention of Communication*, esp. chap. 7 ("The Hierarchization of the World"); Kate McDonald, "Asymmetrical Integration: Lessons from a Railway Empire,' *Technology and Culture* 56, no. 1 (2015): 118 (Trans-Siberian), 121 (failing), 142 (imperialism, blurring); Natsume Sōseki, "Travels in Manchuria and Korea," in *Rediscovering Natsume Sōseki*, ed. and trans. Sigrun Brodey and Sammy I. Ysunematsu (Folkestone: Global Oriental, 2000), 39. The contradiction between Sōseki's wandering and the train's linearity is observed by Sigrun Brodey, "Introduction," in Brodey and Ysunematsu, *Rediscovering Natsume Sōseki*, 29 (19: swarming).
18. Sōseki, "Travels," 123; Brodey, "Introduction," 21, 28. Brodey goes even so far in this idiosyncratic distinction between "travelogue or … travel narrative" and "travel diary" that Sōseki finds himself converted from an imperialistic fellow traveler into a Japan critic: from that perspective, the racist remarks become subtle comments on Japan's imperialist ambitions. Ibid., 24. Whether Sōseki's or his protagonist's, the xenophobic diatribe reminds one of the attack on Belgians in Octave Mirbeau, *Sketches of a Journey: Travels in an Early Motorcar* (London: Philip Wilson Publishers, 1989). See Mom, *Atlantic Automobilism*, 179.
19. Joshua A. Fogel, *The Literature of Travel in the Japanese Rediscovery of China 1862–1945* (Stanford, CA: Stanford University Press, 1996), 252 (first, objective), 253 (sarcasm, hotels); Andreas Renner, "Watching Foreign Neighbours: Russian and Soviet Travel Writing about Japan in the First Half of the Twentieth Century," *Journal of Tourism History* 3, no. 1 (2011) 50.
20. Sōseki, *Inside My Glass Doors*, 5, 88; Joshua A. Fogel, "Yosano Akiko and Her China Travelogue of 1928," in Akiko Yosano, *Travels in Manchuria and Mongolia: A Feminist Poet from Japan Encounters Prewar China*, trans. Joshua A. Fogel (New York: Columbia University Press, 2001), 3; Fogel, *Literature of Travel*, 267 (blast), 273 (adventurous; emphasis added); Yosano, *Travels*, 119; Mann, *Sources of Social Power, vol. 3*, 371 (turn), 380–381 (military fascism). In this book, I follow the Chinese habit of giving the family name first, with one exception: I follow the name order on the title page of Anglophone books, also if they put (as they often do) the Chinese family name last.
21. Yosano, *Travels*, 22 (wagon), 24 (chairs, horses), 29 (walking), 39 (schedules), 64–65 (poem), 82 (special train), 105 (telescope), 107 (racing). On the early history of the one-

wheeled barrow in China, and for passenger transport, see Nanny Kim, "Single-Wheeled Mobility: The Housed-Wheel Barrow on the Plains of Pre-industrial China," *Journal of Transport History* 28, no. 2 (2007).

22. Yosano, *Travels*, 56 (perspective), 69 (poor), 74 (dress), 95 (contradiction), 96–97 (flavor), 99 (movie), 118 (canceled); Mann, *Sources of Social Power, vol. 3*, 115 (warlords).

23. Gordon, *Modern History of Japan*, 149–150 (new middle class), 150 (21 percent), 155 (*sarariiman*), 156 (girls); Fogel, *Literature of Travel*, 265 (Shanghai trip), 301 (adventuresomeness); Fôret, "Railroad Literature," 314 (250,000), 316 (schools), 320 (modern), 324 (idolatry); Yosano, *Travels*, 79 (railway poet).

24. Freedman, *Tokyo in Transit*, 173 (girls), 182 (Fascist), 183 (dogs), 192 (miracle), 193 (cartels), 194 (planning), 200 (autos, subway); Louise Young, "Marketing the Modern: Department Stores, Consumer Culture, and the New Middle Class in Interwar Japan," *International Labor and Working-Class History* 55 (1999): 52 (department store).

25. M. William Steele, "A Modern Infrastructure of Manchukuo: Where Did All the Cement Come From?" paper presented at the East Asian Environmental History Conference, Kagawa University, Japan (22–25 October 2015), 2 (newspaper), 4 (*kosoku*) (I thank Bill Steele for providing me with this paper); M. William Steele, "Roads, Bridges, Tunnels and Empire: Highway Construction and the Great East Asian Co-prosperity Sphere," 2 (road network), 9n4 (Manchukuo statistics), 12n33 (idealist engineers), 12n34 (vehicle statistics); Freedman, *Tokyo in Transit*, 190 (league); Koichi Shimokawa, "Japan: The Late Starter Who Outpaced All Her Rivals," in *The Economic and Social Effects of the Spread of Motor Vehicles: An International Centenary Tribute*, ed. Theo Barker (London: Macmillan, 1987), 215–216 (Japanese islands statistics). On European prewar freeway construction, see Gijs Mom, "Roads without Rails: European Highway-Network Building and the Desire for Long-Range Motorized Mobility," *Technology and Culture* 46, no. 4 (2005).

26. A similar conclusion (a "virtual temporal simultaneity of modernity in Europe, the USA and Japan") in Fujii, "Networks and Modernity," 15; and (regarding the emergence of an adventurous form of automobilism) Beirut in Kristin V. Monroe, "Driving Then and Now: The History and Anthropology of Automobility in Beirut" paper presented at the conference "(Auto)mobility in the Global Middle East: Defining the Field," University of Birmingham (6 November 2015), 11.

27. Yajun Mo, "Itineraries for a Republic: Tourism and Travel Culture in Modern China, 1866–1954" (PhD diss., University of California, Santa Cruz, 2011), 6 (CTS), 15 (academy), 190 (campaigns), 207 (Zhang), 336–337 (Pan-Asianism, business school, curb), 341 (intelligence), 344 (outfit), 348 (queue), 349 (guns), 359 (indolent), 380 (Yellow race).

28. David Arnold and Erich DeWald, "Cycles of Empowerment? The Bicycle and Everyday Technology in Colonial India and Vietnam," *Comparative Studies in Society and History* 53, no. 4 (2011): 973 (accessibly modern), statistics on 975, 980, 994; Fogel, *Literature of Travel*, 260 (more Western); Jonathan Fenby, *Chiang Kai-shek: China's Generalissimo and the Nation He Lost* (New York: Carroll & Graf Publishers, 2004), 163 (Soong). For China, see Xu Tao, "Making a Living: Bicycle-Related Professions in Shanghai, 1897–1949," *Transfers* 3, no. 3 (2013).

29. One of the most knowledgeable about the early rickshaw history is amateur historian and former university librarian Toshihiko Saito, who wrote several books on this topic in Japanese. Personal communication, Tokyo, 10 February 2010; Rimmer, *Rikisha*, 6–7; Warren, *Rickshaw Coolie*, 19n2. (samurai).

30. Peter J. Rimmer, "Structure, Conduct and Performance of the Rickshaw Industry in East and South East Asian Cities, 1869–1939," in *Transport Policy, Management and Technology towards 2001: Selected Conference Proceedings of the Fifth World Conference on*

Transport Research (Western Periodicals, 1989) (paper no. 3-19–3), 601 (long-range), table 2 (production peak in 1902), 604 (sedan chair); Ros Posel, "Amahashi: Durban's Ricksha Pullers," *Journal of Natan and Zulu History* 13, no. 1 (1990): 51 (two thousand); Ros Posel, "The Durban Ricksha Pullers' 'Strikes' of 1918 and 1930," *Journal of Natan and Zulu History* 8, no. 2 (1985): 87 (pull), 91 (African men).

31. Rimmer, *Rikisha*, 44–55; Freedman, *Tokyo in Transit*, 116; Young, *Beyond the Metropolis*, 7 (second-tier), 23 (survey); Stewart Lone, "Japan and the Age of Speed: Urban Life and the Automobile 1925–1930," in *The Automobile in Japan*, London School of Economics and Political Science Suntory and Toyota International Centres for Economic and Related Disciplines Discussion Paper no. IS/05/494 (July 2005), 3, 5 (Ford, GM, nuts-and-bolts); Christopher Madeley, "Kaishinsha, DAT, Nissan and the British Motor Vehicle Industry," in *Automobile in Japan*, 15 (a hundred), 16 (Imperial fleet), 21 (Austin Seven), 25 (Benjamin).
32. Rimmer, *Rikisha*, 267.
33. Steele, "Mobility on the Move," 14–15 (Tokyo, Singapore); Steele, "Roads, Bridges, Tunnels and Empire" (statistics).
34. Warren, *Rickshaw Coolie*, vii (200), 7 (suicide), 53 (beast), 54 (tinkering), 58 (workshops). From Japan, mostly third-class vehicles were imported, versions that were not used in that country. Ibid., 54.
35. Damm and Gransow, "Zwischen Kuli-Export und Business-Netzwerken," in Kraler et al., *Migrationen*, 225 (*longue durée*), 228–229; Karl Husa and Helmut Wohlschlägl, "Globale Märkte—lokale Konsequenzen: Arbeitsmigration in Südostasien seit der Mitte des 19. Jahrhunderts, " in Kraler et al., *Migrationen*, 176–177 (well organized); for a convincing plea to consider transport as the very backbone of nineteenth-century imperialism, see Daniel R. Headrick, *The Tools of Empire: Technology and European Imperialism in the Nineteenth Century* (New York: Oxford University Press, 1981), esp. 149 (ocean railways); Michael Mann, "Mobilität und Migration von Menschen in und aus Südasien 1840 bis 1990," in Kraler et al., *Migrationen*, 202–203; Susanne Weigelin-Schwiedrzik and Kim Rottenberger-Kwok, "Chinese Migration im Indischen Ozean," in *Der Indische Ozean: Das afro-asiatische Mittelmeer als Kultur- und Wirtschaftsraum*, ed. Dietmar Rothermund and Susanne Weigelin-Schwiedrzik (Vienna: Verein für Geschichte und Sozialkunde / Promedia Verlag, 2004), 153–154.
36. Warren, *Rickshaw Coolie*, 9 (1880), 14–15 (thousand), 17–18 (societies), chap. 8 (four strikes), 109 (commute), 116 (burned). On the criminalized class, see Mom, *Atlantic Automobilism*, 636–637; and Louis Chevalier, *Labouring Classes and Dangerous Classes in Paris during the First Half of the Nineteenth Century* (London: Routledge & Kegan Paul, 1973).
37. Warren, *Rickshaw Coolie*, 21–22, 24, 28–29, 33–36, 45, 58.
38. Ibid., 6, 47, 57, 62 (reverend quote), 71–72, 296, chap. 17 (suicide).
39. Ibid., 70 (profile), 138–139 (labor) (69: the user profile is contradicted by a remark in which "the coolie class" is identified as "the principal users of rickshaws precisely because of their 'low fares, brisk motion, and ready availability'"; in general, secondary sources are ambiguous when it comes to identifying rickshaw patrons); Michael D. Pante, "Mobility and Modernity in the Urban Transport Systems of Colonial Manila and Singapore," *Journal of Social History* 47, no. 4 (2014) (underpinnings).
40. Fu-Chia Chen, "Cab Cultures in Victorian London: Horse-Drawn Cabs, Users and the City, ca 1830–1914" (PhD dissertation, University of York, 2014) (tram in Western cities); Peter J. Rimmer, "Hackney Carriage Syces and Rikisha Pullers in Singapore: A Colonial Registrar's Perspective on Public Transport, 1892–1923," in *The Underside of Malaysian History: Pullers, Prostitutes, Plantation Workers …*, ed. Peter J. Rimmer and

Lisa M. Allen (Singapore: Singapore University Press, 1990), 137 (peaked); Rimmer, *Rikisha*, 112 (report); Warren, *Rickshaw Coolie*, 73, 77 (cycle rickshaw in 1936), 100; Jason Lim, *A Slow Ride Into the Past: The Chinese Trishaw Industry in Singapore, 1942– 1983* (Clayton, VA: Monash University Publishing, 2013), 124–125 (trishaw).

41. Rimmer, *Rikisha*, 107–120; Gijs Mom, "Clashes of Cultures: Road vs. Rail in the North-Atlantic World during the Inter-war Coordination Crisis," in *The Organization of Transport: A History of Users, Industry, and Public Policy*, ed. Christopher Kopper and Massimo Moraglio (London: Routledge, 2015) (coordination); Pante, "Mobility and Modernity" (1939); Warren, *Rickshaw Coolie*, 65 (congestion).

42. Fung Chi Ming, *Reluctant Heroes: Rickshaw Pullers in Hong Kong and Canton, 1874– 1954* (Hong Kong: Hong Kong University Press, 2005), 1, 92; David Strand, *Rickshaw Beijing: City People and Politics in the 1920s* (Berkeley: University of California Press, 1989), 20–21; Mann, *Sources of Social Power*, vol. 3, 115 (7 percent); Hanchao Lu, *Beyond the Neon Lights: Everyday Shanghai in the Early Twentieth Century* (Berkeley: University of California Press, 2004), 349n16 (1889 survey); Edward J. M. Rhoads, "Cycles of Cathay: A History of the Bicycle in China," *Transfers* 2, no. 2 (2012): 99 (1918 survey); Frank Dikötter, *Exotic Commodities: Modern Objects and Everyday Life in China* (New York: Columbia University Press, 2006), 82–89.

43. Dikötter, *Exotic Commodities*, 85 (230,000); Lu, *Beyond the Neon Lights*, 297 (outmoded), 305 (wheelbarrow); Fenby, *Chiang Kai-shek*, 133 (half, three million).

44. Mann, *Sources of Social Power*, vol. 3, 398 (leadership); Lu, *Beyond the Neon Lights*, 294 (migrants), 295 (*lilong* house, Zhongshan suit). The suit (later called the Mao suit) was designed by Sun Zhongshan (Sun Yat-sen). Fercility, "Zhongshan Suit," *China Highlights*, 17 June 2019, https://www.chinahighlights.com/travelguide/traditional-chinese-clothes-zhongshan-suit.htm.

45. Lu, *Beyond the Neon Lights*, 67–105, 75 (Subei), 80 (lyrics).

46. Tim Wright, "Shanghai Imperialists versus Rickshaw Racketeers: The Defeat of the 1934 Rickshaw Reforms," *Modern China* 17, no. 1 (1991): 77 (racket), 80 (new model), 81 (war), 84 (7,000 and 130 million), 85 (licenses), 86 (tramp), 90 (fees), 94 (on a par), 101 (Communists), 106 (Guomindang); Rhoads, "Cycles of Cathay," 8 (1,900 in 1919); Ricsha Committee, "Report of the Ricsha Committee," special issue *Municipal Gazette* (13 February 1934), 60 (70,000), 61 (largest fleet).

47. Ricsha Committee, "Report of the Ricsha Committee," 68 (destitute) 91, appendix B (initiative).

48. Lu, *Beyond the Neon Lights*, 92 (perambulator), 92–93 (idea, sprang, solution), 98 (design, laugh), 102 (faster), 105 (transformed peasants), 352n92 (1989).

49. Mann, *Sources of Social Power*, vol. 3, 113.

50. Strand, *Rickshaw Beijing*, xii (republican period), 25–26 (not rich); 28–31, 29 (standard, poor, beggars; the beggar quotation is from a Chinese source), 43 and 57 (city people), 45 (slums), 47–49 (garages).

51. Ibid., 41, 298–299n2; Warren, *Rickshaw Coolie*, 140 (American).

52. Strand, *Rickshaw Beijing*, 34 (*New China*), 177 (Mister), chap. 8 (May Fourth and the May Thirtieth Movements).

53. Ibid., 47, 50, 52, 54; on Zhou Enlai and Liu Bannog, and pulmonary disease, see Zhang Sheng, "Rickshaw and China's New Literature 1917–1927," paper presented at the conference "Mobility in Daily Life," Shanghai Academy of Social Sciences (4–7 January 2012), 3, 5, 9.

54. The following is based on Strand, *Rickshaw Beijing*, chap. 11 ("Machine-Breakers: The Streetcar Riot of October 22, 1929").

55. Ibid., 242 (songs), 250 (phenomenon, advancement), 251–255.

56. Mann, *Sources of Social Power, vol. 3*, 414–415.
57. Ming, *Reluctant Heroes*, 3 (Soviet); Mann, *Sources of Social Power, vol. 3*, 419, gives five reasons for a revolution to be triggered successfully, engaging himself in a debate with other students of this topic: "dependent economic development; an economic downturn; a repressive, exclusionary and personalist state; a strong political culture of opposition; and a 'world system opening,'" the latter referring to Wallerstein's world system history. See, e.g., Immanuel Wallerstein, *World-Systems Analysis: An Introduction* (Durham, NC: Duke University Press, 2004).
58. Luo Xu, *Searching for Life's Meaning: Changes and Tensions in the Worldviews of Chinese Youth in the 1980s* (Ann Arbor: University of Michigan Press, 2001), 8–9 (adventure). There is a personal note to Hu Shi's distinction: he was robbed by a puller when drunk. His distinction was also honed by his visit to the United States, to study. Lu, *Beyond the Neon Lights*, 347, 348n2.
59. Fenby, *Chiang Kai-shek*, 171 (women riders); Ming, *Reluctant Heroes*, 95, 116–118.
60. Ming, *Reluctant Heroes*, 87–92, 99–103, 165–169.
61. Strand, *Rickshaw Beijing*, 281; Lao She's "Black Li and White Li," 282, tells the story of two brothers involved in the riots, suggesting that "participating in modern politics kills one's sense of moral responsibility."
62. Warren, *Rickshaw Coolie*, uses Lao She's novel without any comment throughout his analysis as an illustration of local Singapore rickshaw culture, probably because of the dominance of the Chinese in this culture. Rey Chow, *Woman and Chinese Modernity: The Politics of Reading between East and West* (Minnesota: University of Minnesota Press, 1991), 34 (vernacular); for the New Culture Movement, see R. Keith Schoppa, *Revolution and Its Past: Identities and Change in Modern Chinese History* (Boston: Prentice Hall, 2011), 163; and Maurice Meisner, *Mao's China and After: A History of the People's Republic* (New York: Free Press, 1999), 14–16; Ranbir Vohra, *Lao She and the Chinese Revolution* (Cambridge, MA: Harvard University Press, 1974), 99 (serialized).
63. Lao She, *Rickshaw: The Novel Lo-t'o Hsiang Tzu* (Honolulu: University Press of Hawai'i, 1979), 10, 11, 62. The earlier publication, titled *Rickshaw Boy*, came out in 1945. The original Chinese version also made it into a movie, with the same title, in 1982. A Cantonese movie (*Humiliation of Rickshaw Pulling*) from 1940 was loosely based on Lao She's novel, which was also serialized in Hong Kong's leading magazine *Yuzhoufeng* (Universal winds). Ming, *Reluctant Heroes*, 123.
64. Lao She, *Rickshaw*, 7 (block quote), 102; as analyzed in Mom, *Atlantic Automobilism* (seven hundred pages).
65. But the "physique" of Singaporean pullers in the 1930s was "poor." Warren, *Rickshaw Coolie*, 148.
66. Vohra, *Lao She*, 113.
67. Lao She, *Rickshaw*, 249 (inhumane), 142–143; Vohra, *Lao She*, 4 (market), 165 (drowned). A Japanese movie—directed by Hiroshi Inagaki, called *The Rickshaw Man* (*Muhomatsu no issho*; lit. "the life of wild Matsu"), and based on a novel by Shunsaku Iwashita from 1943—was released in 1958. I thank Bill Steele for bringing this movie to my attention (emails, 12 August 2013, 9 May 2018).
68. Tâm Lang, "I Pulled a Rickshaw," in *The Light of the Capital: Three Modern Vietnamese Classics* (Kuala Lumpur: Oxford University Press, 1996), 52 (investigative), 60 (steam engine), 63 (cars), 74 (start frame tale), 82 (shaft quote), 102 (corrupts), 107 (customer), 114–115 (poverty), 118–119 (plea).
69. H. Hazel Hahn, "The Rickshaw Trade in Colonial Vietnam, 1883–1940," *Journal of Vietnamese Studies* 8, no. 4 (2014): 47 (hybrid, most popular, *xe-kéo*, clientele), 49 (manufacturers, 10 percent), 51 (aluminum), 52 (Chinese firms), 53 (15 percent; this

percentage is quoted for Hanoi; Hahn also mentions the occurrence of *auto-pousses* [auto rickshaws] as early as 1911), 54 (iron tires), 55 (immoral, proletariat; the latter quote is Hahn's rephrasing of the councillor's and mayor's words), 56 (rural), 57 (sixty kilometers, unionization), 57 (three days, out of balance, tourist attraction), 59 (disorder, Eno), 60 (three thousand), 61 (convenient, strike), 62, table 1 (rickshaw statistics), 63 (more than doubled, reduce, Popular Front), 64 (*người ngựa*), 65 (Cochinchina), 66 (slavery), 67 (problematic).

70. Lao She, *Rickshaw*, 76 (chauffeurs), 213 (cops), 224 (brasswork); Vohra, *Lao She*, 128.
71. Lao She, *Rickshaw*, 43–45 (45: quotes), 183, 185.
72. Mann, *Sources of Social Power, vol. 3*, 113.
73. Dikötter, *Exotic Commodities*, 89–97, 90 (oceanic; the quote stems from a farmer who saw a car for the first time in his life in 1940; I thank Nanny Kim for her explanation of oceanic), 92 (family) 93 (chasing); Thomas J. Campanella, "'The Civilising Road': American Influence on the Development of Highways and Motoring in China, 1900–1949," *Journal of Transport History* 26, no. 1 (2005): 80 (Shanghai), 82 (warlords), 83 (assembly plants), 84 (1911), 85 (1922); "Les Progrès de l'Industrie automobile et les Routes aux Etats-Unis," *Bulletin de l'Association Internationale Permanente des Congrès de la Route (AIPCR)* 15, no. 46 (July–August 1926): 202–207, here 203; "Les Véhicules automobiles et les Routes dans le monde au 1er Janvier 1931," *Bulletin de l'AIPCR* 20, no. 77 (September–October 1931): 335–342, here 341, table.
74. David Del Testa, "Automobiles and Anomie in French Colonial Indochina," in *France and "Indochina": Cultural Representations*, ed. Kathryn Robson and Jennifer Yee (Lanham, MD: Lexington Books, 2005), 63 (chauffeur), 70 (violence), 71 (rape), 72 (microcosm), 73 (syndromes); Linh D. Vu, "Careless and Carless Natives: Automobile Accidents and the Project of Modernity in French Indochina," *Sojourn: Journal of Social Issues in Southeast Asia* 27, no. 2 (2012): 332.
75. Stéphanie Ponsavady, *Cultural and Literary Representations of the Automobile in French Indochina: A Colonial Roadshow* (New York: Palgrave Macmillan, 2018), 2 (Seiler), 6 (1934), 8 (finest), 17 (1940), 23 (statistics 1921 and 1931); 42 (radiated), 44 (prisoners), 48 (Mandarin, artists, propaganda), 51 (explorer); 64 (fleet), 65 (dozen), 66 (*tours*), 80 (sightseeing), 81 (picnic), 89 (drivers). I thank Stéphanie Ponsavady for providing me with the first three chapters of her manuscript before it was published. One of the chapters was published as Stéphanie Ponsavady, "*Indigènes* into Signs: Incorporating Indigenous Pedestrians on Colonial Roads in 1920s and 1930s French Indochina," *Transfers* 4, no. 3 (2014): 6 (1897), 7 (*l'écrasodrome*).
76. Pante, "Mobility and Modernity," 5 (1896, 1907, 1920), 6 (mosquito), 9 (journalist, divide, outvie; the last sentence in this quote is from Pante's original manuscript, in my possession); Pante, "Racialized Capacities and Transgressive Mobility," 53 (American manager).
77. Howard Dick and Peter J. Rimmer, *Cities, Transport and Communications: The Integration of Southeast Asia since 1850* (London: Palgrave Macmillan, 2003), 66 (firsts), 68 (one hundred thousand).
78. Ralph William Huenemann, *The Dragon and the Iron Horse: The Economics of Railroads in China 1876–1937* (Cambridge, MA: Harvard University Press, 1984), 2–3, 5 (Shanghai businessmen).
79. McDonald, "Asymmetrical Integration," 117 (scramble); Wang Xudong and Li Junxiang, "Modernization and the Study of Modern Chinese History," *Chinese Studies in History* 43, no. 1 (2009): 55–56 (triggers); Mo, "Itineraries for a Republic," 350 (nationalization); Huenemann, *Dragon and the Iron Horse*, 4 (Sun Yat-sen), 38–39 (rebellion), 228 (GDP), 247 (benefit); Huang Yaping, *Rediscovering China: Sun-Yat-Sen*

in Shanghai, trans. Pan Qin (Shanghai: Shanghai Century Publishing Co., 2010), 10 (200,000 km), 65–68 (maps); Kenneth Cantlie, *The Railways of China* (London: China Society, 1981), 25; Arthur N. Young, *China's Nation-Building Effort, 1927–1937: The Financial and Economic Record* (Stanford, CA: Hoover Institution Press, 1971), 292 (New York), 392 (47 percent); John Earl Baker, "Transportation in China," *Annals of the American Academy* 152 (1930): 166, table 2 (railway track density figures; the China figure is from 1923, while all others are from 1924); Fenby, *Chiang Kai-shek*, 182 (Sun Fo); David Strand, "'A High Place Is No Better Than a Low Place': The City in the Making of Modern China," in *Becoming Chinese: Passages to Modernity and Beyond*, ed. When-hsin Yeh (Berkeley: University of California Press, 2000), 99 (Guangzhou).

80. Sun Yat-sen, *The International Development of China* (Shanghai: Commercial Press, 1920), ii (two stages), iii (one million), 152 (wand); Jean Chesneaux, *The Chinese Labor Movement 1919–1927*, trans. H. M. Wright (Stanford, CA: Stanford University Press, 1968), 151–152.

81. Campanella, "Civilising Road," 81 (sinophile); Sun, *International Development*, 151; Fenby, *Chiang Kai-shek*. 228 (Communists); Xudong and Junxiang, "Modernization," 47 (modernization). In all fairness, the authors rather seem to imply modernization is not an option *without* industrialization.

82. Chih Meng, "The American Returned Students of China," *Pacific Affairs* 4, no. 1 (1931): 3 (20,000), 5 (1,800; 6,000; European War), 12 (successful); Eva Shan Chou, *Memory, Violence, Queues: Lu Xun Interprets China* (Ann Arbor, MI: Association for Asian Studies, 2012), 19–20 (publishing); Julian Gewirtz, *Unlikely Partners: Chinese Reformers, Western Economists, and the Making of Global China* (Cambridge, MA: Harvard University Press, 2017), 126 (core); William A. Lyell, "Translator's Afterword," in *Shanghai Express* by Zhang Henshui (Honolulu: University of Hawai'i Press, 1997), 241 (isms); Julia Lovell, "Introduction," in *The Real Story of Ah-Q and Other Tales of China: The Complete Fiction of Lu Xun* by Lu Xun, trans. Julia Lovell (London: Penguin Books, 2009), xix (Westernization); Tze-ki Hon, "The Chinese Path to Modernisation; Discussions of 'Culture' and 'Morality' in Republican China," *International Journal for History, Culture and Modernity* 2, no. 3 (2014): 212 (European model), 215 (decentering Europe), 225 (Guomindang, Communist Party).

83. Hsieh Ping-Ying, *Autobiography of a Chinese Girl* (London: Pandora Press, 1986), 34 (ninety *li*), 40 (military school), 54 (suicide), 57 (teacher), 61 (detective), 67 (Imperialism), 74 (slave girl), 91 (great Revolution), 93 (suppressed), 116 (Northern Expedition), 131 (demobilize), 155 (five hundred *li*), 158 (bones), 193 (independent), 199 (wandering), 204 (steamer), 216 (motor-cars); Elisabeth Croll, "Introduction," in Hsieh, *Autobiography of a Chinese Girl*, 10 (scholar), 21 (1936).

84. Weiming Tu, "Implications of the Rise of 'Confucian' East Asia," *Daedalus* 129, no. 1 (2000): 198 (minds, traditions); Fenby, *Chiang Kai-shek*, 226–227.

85. Schoppa, *Revolution and Its Past*, 234 (Long March); Edgar Snow, *Red Star over China* (New York: Grove Press, 1968), 204 (horses), 205 (migration), 355 (bomber planes); Jean Chesneaux, *Le mouvement paysan chinois 1840–1949* (Paris: Éditions du Seuil, 1976), 156 (defeat), 157 (shift); Jonathan D. Spence, *The Search for Modern China* (London: Hutchinson, 1990), 397–400 (Soviet, atrocious, bullion); Chou, *Memory, Violence, Queues*, 43 (Manchuria, Shanghai).

86. Fenby, *Chiang Kai-shek*, 98 (Confucian authoritarianism), 104 (questioned), 226 (Fascism); Donald G. Gillin, *Warlord Yen Hsi-shan in Shansi Province 1911–1949* (Princeton, NJ: Princeton University Press, 1967), 3 (isolated), 11 (Japan), 22 (Model Governor), 25 (peasants, roads), 28 (factories), 29 (aircraft), 30 (banditry), 35 (queue,

illiteracy, homosexuality), 42 (anarchistic), 50 (son), 59 (fear), 63 (anarchism), 64 (millionfold), 66 (desires).

87. Gillin, *Warlord Yen Hsi-shan*, 37 (Red Cross), 55 (high taxes), 90–91 (one thousand), 92 (camels, exorbitant), 103 (crucial), 118 (failure), 122 (Manchuria), 127 (1936), 167 (New Deal), 193 (Five-Year Plan), 181 (Chiang), 182 (German), 187 (planes, cars), 189 (engine), 209 (export), 210 (surplus), 227 (supported), 246 (warfare), 262 (collaborated), 268 (popularity), 271 (occupied); Fenby, *Chiang Kai-shek*, 109 (Feng). For the "distant affinity" between Soviet and American planning during the 1930s, see Wolfgang Schivelbusch, *Entfernte Verwandtschaft: Faschismus, Nationalsozialismus, New Deal 1933–1939* (Munich: Carl Hanser Verlag, 2005).

88. Gillin, *Warlord Yen Hsi-shan*, 285 (1947), 291 (1950), 295 (1911), Fenby, *Chiang Kai-shek*, 366 (Roosevelt), 460 (Mao), 463 (limousines), 465 (Marshall), 471 (aid).

89. Fenby, *Chiang Kai-shek*, 122 ("the governor was caught [during the battle around Wuhan] fleeing in his car"), 125 (Soviet adviser Borodin "drove round the city in [warlord] Wu Peifu's old car"), 147 (union leader), 149 (judge), 186 (Buick), 223 (no automobiles), 243 (Packards), 259 (Xi'an), 298 (gangster), 326 (rickshaw), 349 (Payne), 358 (army), 371 (jeep), 413–414 (shocked), 438 (new Cadillac), 439 (Mao), 487 (four cars). I counted about forty mentions of cars, limousines, and trucks, and about fifteen mentions of armored and personal trains.

90. Fenby, *Chiang Kai-shek*, 112 (key), 171 (three trains), 181 (Ford), 221 (a warlord "aboard his personal train"), 322 (Moscow), 361 (Burma), 365 (main source), 416 (Ichigo); Mom, *Atlantic Automobilism*, chap. 3 (role of World War I for the breakthrough of the car), 243–245 (Taxis de La Marne).

91. Thomas Michael McClellan, *Zhang Henshui and Popular Chinese Fiction 1919–1949* (Lewiston, NY: Edwin Mellen Press, 2005), 1 (duck, vulgar), 11 (Xinyuan), 14 (successful), 127 (region); Lyell, "Translator's Afterword," 242 (props), 243 (*tongsu*, superficial), 244 (characters), 245 (parents), 246 (linked chapters), 247 (hybrid, bourgeoisie), 250 (magazine), 251 (famous), 253 (Zhou and Mao); Chow, *Woman and Chinese Modernity*, 36 (*yuanyang*, etc.); Liu Ts'un-yan [Liu Cunren], "Introduction: 'Middlebrow' in Perspective," in Ts'un-yan [Cunren], *Chinese Middlebrow Fiction*, 3 (colloquial); Stephen C. Soong and George Kao, "Preface," in Ts'un-yan [Cunren], *Chinese Middlebrow Fiction* (bestseller); Zhang, *Shanghai Express*, 218 (example of a cliffhanger); Bonnie S. McDougall, "Preface," in McClellan, *Zhang Henshui*, iv (yields, contradict).

92. Zhang, *Shanghai Express*, 13 (uninhibited), 17 (two days), 39 (giggling), 44 (ashamed), 70 (progress), 72 (graces), 86 (war), 156 (pureness), 158 (scenery), 203 (get off), 225 (silver), 226 (big deal), 264–265 (bus, truck drivers, dreamlike), 266 (escape); Ts'un-yan [Cunren], *Chinese Middlebrow Fiction*, 32 (adventure novels); McClellan, *Zhang Henshui*, 238 (*chaibaidang*).

93. Lovell, "Introduction," xiii (landowning), xxii (everyman), xxiv (voyeurism), xxiii (paradox, genius), xxix (proletarian), xxx (declined), xxxii (saint), xxxiv (ironic realism, glorification), xxxv (kung fu); Chou, *Memory, Violence, Queues*, 22 (Eastern European), 29–30 (brief biographical sketch of Lu Xun), 30 (School), 33 (cure); Fredric Jameson, "Third-World Literature in the Era of Multinational Capitalism," *Social Text*, no. 15 (1986), 74 (allegorically); Ts'un-yan [Cunren], *Chinese Middlebrow Fiction*, 26.

94. Mary Scoggin, "Wine in the Writing, Truth in the Rhetoric: Three Levels of Irony in a Chinese Essay Genre," in *Irony in Action: Anthropology, Practice, and the Moral Imagination*, ed. James W. Fernandez and Mary Taylor Huber (Chicago: University of Chicago Press, 2001), 158 (Mao), 160 (*fan-hua*); Wang Ning, "Confronting Western Influence: Rethinking Chinese Literature of the New Period," *New Literary History* 24, no. 4 (1993): 918.

95. Lu Xun, "The Real Story of Ah-Q," in Lu, *Real Story of Ah-Q and Other Tales*, 93 (superiority), 94 (evil), 102 (public events), 121 (open cart).
96. Dikötter, *Exotic Commodities*, 73 (underestimated), 94 (*huangyu*), 96 (unheard-of); Mann, *Sources of Social Power, vol. 3*, 118.
97. Juan Pablo Cardenal and Heriberto Araújo, *China's Silent Army: The Pioneers, Traders, Fixers and Workers Who Are Remaking the World in Beijing's Image*, trans. Catherine Mansfield (London: Allen Lane, 2013), 37 (diaspora); Massimo Moraglio, "Transferring Technology, Shaping Society: Traffic Engineering in PIARC Agenda, in the early 1930s," *Technikgeschichte* 80, no. 1 (2013): 32; Baker, "Transportation in China," 162 (estimates, eight); Campanella, "Civilising Road," 88 (trained), 92 (Boxer funds, Tsinghua University).
98. Mo, "Itineraries for a Republic," 187 (interruptions), 188 (intervention), 189 (sixty-nine thousand), 189n28 (province roads); Young, *China's Nation-Building Effort*, 393 (central and northwest); Emily S. Rosenberg, "Transnational Currents in a Shrinking World," in Rosenberg, *World Connecting*, 837 (federalism), 841 (members and candidates), 842 (ILO); Dikötter, *Exotic Commodities*, 74 (water transport). The length of the highway network is more or less confirmed by Ronald Hsia, "On Capital Formation through Highway Construction in Communist China," report for the Center for International Studies, Massachusetts Institute of Technology, April 1954, 31, who claimed: "Between 1927 and 1947, a total of 105,268 kilometers of highways was reportedly constructed … Of this total, however, only 44.5 per cent represented national highways built under the auspices of the Central Government." Hsia added the annual average (of 2,231 km) built under the Nationalist government was higher than under the Communists during the first half of the 1950s (1,610 km). This report was some months later republished as *The Role of Labor-Intensive Investment Projects in China's Capital Formation* (Cambridge, MA: Center for International Studies, MIT, 1954). Dikötter, *Exotic Commodities*, 80, claimed "roads passable for cars" increased from 75,000 km in 1935 to 176,000 km in 1937 (a very improbable increase of 100,000 km in two years), less than a quarter paved with macadam or gravel; "the results were generally judged impressive."
99. A. Viola Smith and Anselm Chuh, *Motor Roads in China* (Washington, DC: US Government Printing Office, 1931), 2 (ten thousand), 8 (Rensselaer, Good Roads; the name of the engineer is unclear, written in nonstandard transliteration as Luo Kou-shin; I thank Nanny Kim for pointing this out to me), 9 (national plan), 23 (asphalt, hand-pulled roller), 26 (provincial roads), 55 (Hainan), 58 (Hong Kong), 72 (Shanghai roads), 81 (Shanghai motor vehicles); *Highways in China 1949–1990* (Beijing: Ministry of Communications, [1990]), 15 (imported, constructed). T. K. Chao, "Highway Construction and Transport in China," *Information Bulletin: Council of International Affairs, Nanking, China* 4, no. 7 (4 August 1937): 163, gives a total of forty-five thousand cars, most of them in Shanghai and the "3 Eastern Provinces."
100. Mo, "Itineraries for a Republic," 283 (map), 347 (terrible); S. H. Pan, "Le développement des routes en Chine," *Bulletin de l'AIPCR* 16, no. 49 (January–February 1927): 11, table; "Chine: L'Amélioration des Routes," *Bulletin de l'AIPCR*, 18, no. 65 (September–October 1929): 316 (*Foreign Highway News*); "Les Véhicules automobiles," 341, table.
101. Dominic Sachsenmaier, *Global Perspectives on Global History: Theories and Approaches in a Connected World* (Cambridge: Cambridge University Press, 2011), 203 (continuity); Mann, *Sources of Social Power, vol. 3*, 382; Young, *China's Nation-Building Effort*, 298 (NEC).
102. Tze-hsiung Kuo, "Technical Co-operation between China and Geneva," *Information Bulletin Council of International Affairs* (1 July 1936), 1 (Japan), 2 (Thomas), 3 (Salter, Haas); Young, *China's Nation-Building Effort*, 345 (Monnet, American model, experts);

Kuo, "Technical co-operation between China and Geneva," 8 (Plan), 13 (engineers); Chao, "Highway Construction," 151 (three-province project), 152 (seven-province project), 153 (30,144 km), 155 (half).

103. Young, *China's Nation-Building Effort*, v (great progress), ix (less developed), 336–337 (advisers), 338 (Kemmerer Commission), 342 (Haas), 346 (Bureau), 350 (broke with Russia), 354 (Mussolini), 358 (CIFRC), 364 (hostility), 367 (Indemnity, realized), 372 (half), 388 (plans), 404 (Chinese money); Schoppa, *Revolution and Its Past*, 206–212 (extremely centralized), 213 (doubled, Illinois). For roadbuilding decentralization, see, e.g., Gijs Mom, "Decentering Highways: European National Road Network Planning from a Transnational Perspective," in *Die moderne Strasse: Planung, Bau und Verkehr vom 18. bis zum 20. Jahrhundert*, ed. Hans-Liudger Dienel and Hans-Ulrich Schiedt (Frankfurt: Campus Verlag, 2010), 77–100.

104. William C. Kirby, "Engineering China: Birth of the Developmental State, 1928–1937," in Yeh, *Becoming Chinese*, 145 (two hundred), 147 (humanities), 148 (Daimler, Lufthansa); Schoppa, *Revolution and Its Past*, 234 (campaign); Strand, "High Place," 99 (Shanghai to Nanjing); Mom, *Atlantic Automobilism*, 575 (PIARC); Chen, "Highways in China," 136 (seventy thousand), 146 (India, US); Chao, "Highway Construction," 165, table (gasoline), 166 (courses). From at least 1922, China is mentioned as a member of PIARC, for instance, in "Compte rendu de la reunion de la Commission Internationale Permanente tenue à Paris, le 10 Juin 1922," *Bulletin de l'AIPCR* 11, no. 24 (3e trimestre 1922): 451–479, here 452 (476–478: the country was represented first by a member of "the Chinese delegation in Paris," later by railway engineers from China's Ministry of Communications; in 1922, the delegate complained a car killed another member of his delegation walking on a Parisian sidewalk, and he asked for stricter punishment and better supervision when giving driver's licenses).

105. Schoppa, *Revolution and Its Past*, 213–214. In all fairness, Schoppa conceded, "probably the most successful areas of development were communications and transportation." Ibid., 215.

106. Chao, "Highway Construction," 160, table; Kirby, "Engineering China," 140 (Zhongshan); Charles D. Musgrove, "Building a Dream: Constructing a National Capital in Nanjing, 1927–1937," in *Remaking the Chinese City: Modernity and National Identity, 1900–1950*, ed. Joseph W. Esherik (Honolulu: University of Hawai'i Press, 1999), 139 (Sun Yat-sen), 140 (Washington), 142 (Paris), 149 (Ministry).

107. Smith and Anselm Chuh, *Motor Roads in China*, 7 (city highways); Tracy Nichols Busch, "'A Class on Wheels': Avtodor and the 'Automobilization' of the Soviet Union, 1927–1935" (PhD diss., Ferris State University, 2003); see also Tracy Nichols Busch, "From the Scythians to the Soviets: An Evaluation of Russian Mobility History," in *Mobility in History: The State of the Art in the History of Transport, Traffic and Mobility*, ed. Gijs Mom, Gordon Pirie, and Laurent Tissot (Neuchâtel: Alphil, 2009), 153–154; Lewis H. Siegelbaum, *Cars for Comrades: The Life of the Soviet Automobile* (Ithaca, NY: Cornell University Press, 2008), 185 (Moscow). I thank Nanny Kim for helping me with the transcription of older place names.

108. Jameson, "Third-World Literature," 75.

109. Ibid., 200 and 207 (Zhang), 209 (middle school), 231 (not complete), 234 (1932), 265 (Chongqing), 269 (junks), 282 (bus tickets), 347 (terrible), 297 and 395 (on foot). Kirby, "Engineering China," 145, gives one hundred miles of "improved roads" outside the concessions in 1920, twenty thousand miles in 1928, and seventy-five thousand extra roads built and planned during the Nanjing decade.

110. Mo, "Itineraries for a Republic," 192 (contracts), 199 (Romance), 213 (*Liangyou*); Dikötter, *Exotic Commodities*, 79 (donkeys).

111. R. A. Boshardt, *The Restraining Hand: Captivity for Christ in China* (London: Hodder & Stoughton, 1936), 11 (six thousand), 19 (mountain chair), 28 ("my shoes were nearly gone"), 32 (mule), 34 ("road"), 40 (spotted); Strand, "High Place," 98 (Lanzhou to Xi'an); Nicholas Clifford, "With Harry Franck in China," in *A Century of Travels in China: Critical Essays on Travel Writing from the 1840s to the 1940s*, ed. Douglas Kerr and Julia Kuehn (Hong Kong: Hong Kong University Press, 2007), 134–135 ("struck off" on 135), 138 (Shanghai); Nicholas Clifford, *"A Truthful Impression of the Country": British and American Travel Writing in China, 1880–1949* (Ann Arbor: University of Michigan Press, 2001), 168 (ramshackle). For a similar surprise about modernizing Middle Eastern towns in the 1930s, see Mom, *Atlantic Automobilism*, 655.
112. Kirby, "Engineering China," 146 (wall); Strand, "High Place," 127n7 (shortage).
113. Mann, *Sources of Social Power*, vol. 3, 386 (gas), 393 (empire), 413 (Manchuria); Fenby, *Chiang Kai-shek*, 291 (immense), 497 (deaths: "10 million or more" during the war with Japan, and "up to 3 million" during earlier campaigns of Chiang Kai-shek); Ji Xianlin, *The Cowshed: Memories of the Chinese Cultural Revolution* (New York: New York Review Books, 2015), 172; Dikötter, *Exotic Commodities*, 86; Campanella, "Civilising Road," 93 (antipathy), 94 (driving).
114. Mom, *Atlantic Automobilism*, 611 (UK); Mann, "Mobilität und Migration," 199–200.
115. David Arnold, "The Problem of Traffic: The Street-Life of Modernity in Late-Colonial India," *Modern Asian Studies* 46, no. 1 (2012): 124, 138; N. Das, *Road Transport in India: A Study* (Calcutta: Hindustan Motors Ltd., 1968), 10–11 (168,368 passenger cars in the last year of British rule, 1946/1947; ibid., 13); Sanjay Kathuria, "Commercial Vehicles Industry in India: A Case History, 1928–1987," *Economic and Political Weekly* (17–20 October 1987), 1809 (1898, GM, Ford), 1813 (11 percent); *Sixty Years of Motor Transport in India: A Dunlop Diamond Jubilee Publication 1898–1958* (Calcutta: Dunlop Rubber Co. Ltd., January 1959), 6 (first car appeared in India in 1897), 15 (*hawah garhi*), 17 (aristocrats), 36 (Kolkata taxis in 1921); David Arnold, *Everyday Technology: Machines and the Making of India's Modernity* (Chicago: University of Chicago Press, 2013), 163 (accident rates). On the explosion of motor traffic in the West, see Mom, *Atlantic Automobilism*, chap. 4.
116. Derek H. Aldcroft, ed. *Europe's Third World: The European Periphery in the Interwar Years* (Aldershot: Ashgate, 2006), 5, table 1.1 (GDP), 14 (middle class), 27, table 2.4 (railways), 173, table 9.1 (1:2).
117. Arnold, "Problem of Traffic," 132–133; Richard G. Fox, "East of Said," in *The Anthropology of Politics: A Reader in Ethnography, Theory, and Critique*, ed. Joan Vincent (Malden, MA: Blackwell, 2002), 146 (disavowal); Ian J. Kerr, "Representation and Representations of Railways of Colonial and Post-Colonial South Asia," *Modern Asian Studies* 37, no. 2 (2003) 313 (the second quote is Kerr's paraphrase); Claude Markovits, Jacques Pouchepadass, and Sanjay Subrahmanyam, "Introduction: Circulation and Society under Colonial Rule," in *Society and Circulation: Mobile People and Itinerant Cultures in South Asia 1750–1950*, ed. Claude Markovits, Jacques Pouchepadass, and Sanjay Subrahmanyam (Delhi: Permanent Black, 2003), 2 (idyll).
118. Deep Kanta Lahiri Choudhury, "Of Codes and Coda: Meaning in Telegraph Messages, circa 1850–1920," *Historical Social Research* 35, no. 1 (2010): 127 (first global); Lynne Hamill, "The Social Shaping of British Communications Networks Prior to the First World War," *Historical Social Research* 35, no. 1 (2010): 263 (closely linked); Hamill, "Social Shaping of British Communications Networks," 261 (determinist); Headrick, *Tools of Empire*, 129–130.
119. Headrick, "Double-Edged Sword," 54, 59, 62; Michael Mann, "Das Gewaltsdispositiv des modernen Kolonialismus," in *Kolonialismus: Kolonialdiskurs und Genozid*, ed.

Mihran Dabag, Horst Gründer, and Uwe-K. Ketelsen (Munich: Wilhelm Fink Verlag, 2004), 115 (laboratories), 131–133 (criminal tribes); Arnaud Sauli, "Circulation and Authority: Police, Public Space and Territorial Control in Punjab, 1861–1920," in Markovits et al., *Society and Circulation*, 233 (Act).

120. Shahid Amin, *Event, Metaphor, Memory: Chauri Chaura 1922–1992* (Berkeley: University of California Press, 1995), 10 (crowd), 12 (*asahyog*), 21 (1885), 22 (one-third nonagriculturalists in Chaura), 27 (one-half nonagriculturalists in Chauri), 47 (crime), 52 (hooligans, *utpāt*), 58 (ringleaders), 70 (equipment), 89 (signals), 95 (6,000), 138 (*kānd*), 163 (1921), 178 (peripatetic), 200 (martyrs), back cover (founding editor).

121. Ibid., 192–193, 197.

122. Headrick, *Tools of Empire*, 181 (impassible, monumental, railroad-dependent), 182 (barons), 183 (Rebellion), 186–187 (gauges, 26,000 miles), 188 (Marx), 189 (migration), 190 (jobs, class); Ian J. Kerr, "Colonial India, Its Railways, and the Cliometricians," *Journal of Transport History* 35, no. 1 (2014): 114 (largest), 116 (9.7 percent); Ian J. Kerr, *Engines of Change: The Railroads That Made India* (Westport, CT: Praeger, 2007), 118 (unmanliness). Robber capitalism: "All told, Britain stole $45 trillion from India—a conservative estimate that does not include debt placed on South Asia or the environmental cost of its aggressive deforestation of timber." Aditi Natasha Kini, "The British Stole Tipu's Magic Box: It Should Not Be for Sale," *New York Times International Edition* (29–30 June 2019).

123. Kerr, *Engines of Change*, 91 (billion), 114 (1919), 115 (Tata), 121 (nationalized), 163 (million); Daniel Thorner, "Great Britain and the Development of India's Railways," *Journal of Economic History* 11, no. 4 (1951): 392 (drain); Choudhury, "Of Codes and Coda," 137 (symbolic); Kerr, "Representation and Representations of Railways, 316 (*Peshawar Express*).

124. K. P. Bhatnagar, Satish Bahadur, D. N. Agrawal, and S. C. Gupta, *Transport in Modern India* (Kanpur: Kishore Publishing House), 515–519 (committees); Angelica Agredo Montealegre, "Roads and Road Transport in India during the Interwar Years" (MA, King's College London, 2015), 33 ("gradients were usually low and it was advised to break long gradients with flats to ease draft animals"), 51 (Great), 55 (improving); Stefan Tetzlaff, "The Motorisation of the 'Mofussil': Automobile Traffic and Social Change in Rural and Small-Town India, c. 1915–1940" (PhD diss., University of Göttingen, 2015), 17 (bullock cart), 18 (lobby), 23 (Fascist), 24 (Montagu), 25 (Lords), 28n58 (self-made), 37 (Fund), 93 (soldiers), 94 (single truck), 108 (ekkas, tongas), 124 (asphalt), 129 (monopolies), 150 (bourgeoisie), 165 (suspended). On the European coordination struggle, see, e.g., Gérard Duc, Olivier Perroux, Hans-Ulrich Schiedt, and François Walter, eds., *Transport and Mobility History: Between Modal Competition and Coordination (from 1918 to the Present)* (Neuchâtel: Alphil, 2014); for a history of animal-drawn vehicles in India, see, e.g., Jean Deloche, *Contribution à l'histoire de la voiture en Inde* (Paris: École Française d'Extrême-Orient, 1983); on the Indian views of Fascism during the interbellum, see Maria Framke, *Delhi—Rom—Berlin: Die indische Wahrnehmung von Faschismus und Nationalsozialismus 1922–1939* (Darmstadt: Wissenschaftliche Buchgesellschaft WBG, 2013).

125. Tetzlaff, "Motorisation of the 'Mofussil,'" 55 (association), 74 (landlords), 109 (camel), 140 (Depression), 142 (bus and car competition), 174 (emerging bus), 177 (pneumatic tires), 293, table 5 ("One-Weekly 4-Hour Traffic Censuses"); Montealegre, "Roads and Road Transport in India during the Interwar Years," 32 (thousand); Bhatnagar et al., *Transport in Modern India*, 272 (conference).

126. Warren, *Rickshaw Coolie*, 14 (Indian rickshaw numbers); Prafulla Chandra Rây, *Life and Experiences of a Bengali Chemist* (Calcutta / London: Chukervertty, Chatterjee & Co. /

Kegan Paul, Trench, Trübner & Co., 1932), 377 (man-power), 454 (humiliating); Beth E. Notar, Kyaw San Min, and Raju Gautam, "Echoes of Colonial Logic in Re-ordering 'Public' Streets: From Colonial Rangoon to Postcolonial Yangon," *Transfers* 8, no. 3 (2018): 57–60 (Burma vehicle numbers, Maugham, restrictions); Arnold, "Problem of Traffic," 127 (bizarre).

127. William H. Wiser and Charlotte Viall Wiser, *Behind Mud Walls 1930–1960, with a sequel: The Village in 1970* (Berkeley: University of California Press, 1971), 1, 137 (mudguards), 244–245; Subir Sinha, "Lineages of the Developmentalist State: Transnationality and Village India, 1900–1965," *Comparative Studies in Society and History* 50, no. 1 (2008): 60, 64.

128. Markovits et al., "Introduction," 3 (circulation), 4 (movement), 8 (surveillance, subversive), 16 (peddlers); Sauli, "Circulation and Authority," 216 (contestation).

129. Robert Gabriel Varady, "North Indian Banjaras: Their Evolution as Transporters," *South Asia: Journal of South Asian Studies* 2, no. 2 (1979): 1 (gypsies), 7 (seven centuries), 11 (trucks, *qafila*); Catherine Servan-Schreiber, "Tellers of Tales, Sellers of Tales: Bhojpuri Peddlers in Northern India," in Markovits et al., *Society and Circulation*, 277 (rickshawalas), 279 (spies), 287 (cattle fairs), 288 (protection), 304 (microphones).

130. Nikhil Rao, *House but No Garden: Apartment Living in Bombay's Suburbs, 1898–1964* (Minneapolis: University of Minnesota Press, 2013), 1 (slums), 2 (upper-caste), 4 (walled, white-collar, trains), 67 (questionnaire quotes), 68 (installment, mix), 71 (typists, tram extension), 79 (carnival), 77 (bus), 230 (multistory); Gijs Mom and Ruud Filarski, *Van transport naar mobiliteit: De mobiliteitsexplosie (1895–2005)* (Zutphen: Walburg Pers, 2008), 140 (about one hundred thousand motor vehicles in the Netherlands in 1940).

131. Thomas R. Leinbach, "Transportation and the Development of Malaya," *Annals of the Association of American Geographers* 65, no. 2 (1975): 270 (three-pronged); Peter J. Rimmer, Lenore Manderson, and Colin Barlow, "The Underside of Malaysian History," in Rimmer and Allen, *Underside of Malaysian History*, 21 (concepts), 22 (people's history); Amarjit Kaur, "Working on the Railway: Indian Workers in Malaya, 1880–1957," in Rimmer and Allen, *Underside of Malaysian History*, 102 (passive), 109, table 5.2 (thirteen thousand).

132. Thomas Williamson, "The Fluid State: Malaysia's National Expressway," *Space & Culture* 6, no. 2 (2003): 114 (rebellion, no country), 115 (1926), 116 (bicycle, novel, nineteen million from China and "millions more from India and the Netherlands East Indies"); Leinbach, "Transportation and the Development of Malaya," 271 (no roads in 1879 in the "Native States"); C. Mary Turnbull, *A Short History of Malaysia, Singapore and Brunei* (Singapore: Graham Brash, 1988), 199 (census).

133. Gerrit J. Knaap, *Changing Economy in Indonesia: A Selection of Statistical Sources Material from the Early 19th Century up to 1940, vol. 9—Transport 1819–1940* (The Hague: Royal Tropical Institute, 1989), 81, table 8 (roads), 99, table 12 (railroads); Rudolf Mrázek, *Engineers of Happy Land: Technology and Nationalism in a Colony* (Princeton, NJ: Princeton University Press, 2002), 4 (Mail and sugar roads), 5 (free of charge), 9 (60 million), 10 (equipment), 16 (GM), 17 (fifty thousand), 18 (wild buses), 20 (chicken), 21 (*bingoeng* stone throwing), 23 (racing), 37 (Soedjojono), 59 (fast-growing) 71 (1942), 132 (frivolous); Howard W. Dick, "Representations of Development in 19th and 20th Century Indonesia: A Transport History Perspective," *Bulletin of Indonesian Economic Studies* 36, no. 1 (2000): 190 (*dokar*).

134. Johny A. Khusyairi, "Modernity on the Road Traffic of Surabaya in 1920s," *Humaniora* 23, no. 3 (2011): [4] (periphery) [6] (taxis, cars), [9] (initials), [10] (six to ten times); for the 'mixed road,' see Gijs Mom, "Constructing Multifunctional Networks: Road

Building in the Netherlands, 1810–1980," in *Road History: Planning, Building and Use*, ed. Gijs Mom and Laurent Tissot (Lausanne: Alphil, 2007), 33–62.
135. Hahn, "Rickshaw Trade in Colonial Vietnam," 51 (Ceylon); Pante, "Racialized Capacities and Transgressive Mobility," 52; Michael D. Pante, "A Collision of Masculinities: Men, Modernity and Urban Transportation in American-Colonial Manila," *Asian Studies Review* 38, no. 2 (2014): 267 (seven thousand), 260 (*paseo*).
136. Benedict Anderson, "The New World Disorder," in Vincent, *Anthropology of Politics*, 265; S. Eben Kirksey and Kiki van Bilsen, "A Road to Freedom: Mee Articulations and the Trans-Papua Highway," *Bijdragen tot de Taal-, Land- en Volkenkunde* 158, no. 4 (2002): 838 (well before); Adam McKeown, "Global Migration, 1846–1940," *Journal of World History* 15, no. 2 (2004): 155–157, 165, fig. 1 (peaks); Betsy Hartmann, "Security and Survival: Why Do Poor People Have Many Children?" in *The Postcolonial Science and Technology Studies Reader*, ed. Sandra Harding (Durham, NC: Duke University Press, 2011), 310 (world population was about 1.7 billion in 1900 and 2.5 billion half a century later).
137. Husa and Wohlschlägl, "Globale Märkte—lokale Konsequenzen," 181, table 1 (surges, massive); Albert Kraler, "Zur Einführung: Migration und Globalgeschichte," in Kraler et al., *Migrationen*, 15 (facilitators); John M. Hobson, "Discovering the Oriental West," in Harding, *Postcolonial Science and Technology Studies Reader*, 44–45 (rational).
138. Headrick, *Tools of Empire*, 194–196 (quote on 196). I thank Kudzai Matereke for discussing these issues with me (email 20 June 2019); John Howe, "Transport for the Poor or Poor Transport? A General Review of Rural Transport Policy in Developing Countries with Emphasis on Low-Income Areas," International Institute for Infrastructural, Hydraulic and Environmental Engineering Working Paper IP-12 (October 1996), 23 (lack); Michael Brett, *Approaching African History* (Woolbridge: James Currey, 2013), 272–273 (resorted, etc.), 305 (population).
139. Alice L. Conklin, *A Mission to Civilize: The Republican Idea of Empire in France and West Africa, 1895–1930* (Stanford, CA: Stanford University Press, 1997), 215; Epanya Sh. Tshund'olela, "Motor Transport in a Developing Area (i): Zaïre, 1903–1959," in Barker, *Economic and Social Effects of the Spread of Motor Vehicles*, 239 (Zaïre), 241 (quote). For one of the few histories of mobility combining both transport and communication, applied to the case of Southern Africa, see Donal P. McCracken and Ruth E. Teer-Tomaselli, "Communication in Colonial and Post-Colonial Southern Africa," in *The Handbook of Communication History*, ed. Peter Simonson, Janice Peck, Robert T. Craig, and John P. Jackson Jr. (New York: Routledge, 2013), 425–426.
140. Dominik J. Schaller, "From Conquest to Genocide: Colonial Rule in German Southwest Africa and German East Africa," in *Empire, Colony, Genocide: Conquest, Occupation, and Subaltern Resistance in World History*, ed. A. Dirk Moses (New York: Berghahn Books, 2008), 296–297 (Herero); see also Mihran Dabag, Horst Gründer, and Uwe-K. Ketelsen, "Einleitung," in Dabag et al., *Kolonialismus*, 7; Alex Hinton, "Savages, Subjects, and Sovereigns: Conjunctions of Modernity, Genocide, and Colonialism," in Moses, *Empire, Colony, Genocide*, 442–443 (fifty million).
141. For an overview of very recent literature (from about 2000) on Africa, see Gordon Pirie, "African Mobility History: Recent Texts on Past Passages," in Mom et al. *Mobility in History*, 130, who calls "the 'field' of African mobility history … very small"; for a broader approach, see Clapperton Chakanetsa Mavhunga, "Which Mobility for (Which) Africa? Beyond Banal Mobilities," in *Mobility in History: Reviews and Reflections*, ed. Peter Norton, Gijs Mom, Liz Millward, and Mathieu Flonneau (Neuchâtel: Alphil, 2011).

142. Patrick Manning, *Slavery, Colonialism and Economic Growth in Dahomey, 1640–1960* (Cambridge: Cambridge University Press, 1982), 9 (one fifth), 15 (recognition), 15–16, 46–48, 50, 141 (absorbed).
143. Ibid., 143–145, 148, 152; Erdmute Alber, "Automobilismus und Kolonialherrschaft: Zur Bedeutung des Autoverkehrs für die Herrschaftsstrukturen in der westafrikanischen Kolonie Dahomey," *Paideuma* 46 (2000): 287 (systems, technologies); Robin Law, "Wheeled Transport in Pre-colonial West Africa," *Africa: Journal of the International Africa Institute* 50, no. 3 (1980): 253 (trypanosomiasis), 253–254 (Ansante), 257 (guns).
144. Manning, *Slavery*, 181–182, 182, 207, 229; Alber, "Automobilismus und Kolonialherrschaft," 290 (resettle); Inge Brinkman, "Refugees on Routes: Congo/Zaire and the War in Northern Angola (1961–1974)," in *Angola on the Move: Transport Routes, Communications and History*, ed. Beatrix Heintze and Achim von Oppen (Frankfurt: Verlag Otto Lembeck, 2008), 203–204 (Angola); on roadbuilding in the West, see Mom, *Atlantic Automobilism*, chap. 7 ("Swarms Into Flows: The Contested Emergence of the Automobile System").
145. E. K. Hawkins, *Roads and Road Transport in an Underdeveloped Country: A Case Study of Uganda* (London: Her Majesty's Stationery Office, 1962), 17 (joint products), 21 (*Luwalo*).
146. Rolf Hofmeier, *Transport and Economic Development in Tanzania, with Particular Reference to Roads and Road Transport* (Munich: Weltforum Verlag, 1973), 53–60 (quote on 60), 84–85 (for a periodization of transport history in Tanzania); Frank M. Chiteji, *The Development and Socio-economic Impact of Transportation in Tanzania 1884–Present* (Washington, DC: University Press of America, 1980), 21 (Nyamwesi), 31 (rest houses). The latter study, written as a dissertation, reads sometimes as a copy of the former (without referring to it), no doubt because both used the same sources.
147. Hofmeier, *Transport and Economic Development in Tanzania*, 63, 64, 67, 88–89, 101, 171, 172; Chiteji *Development and Socio-economic Impact of Transportation in Tanzania*, 21 (*Wapagazi*), 39 (disappeared); on the same phenomenon in colonies and metropoles, see Mom, *Atlantic Automobilism*, chap. 7; for river transport, see, e.g., Philippe David, "Iconographie de l'histoire des transports en Afrique noire: Les cartes postales," in *Les transports en Afrique (XIXe-XXe siècle): Actes du colloque organisé les 16 et 17 février 1990 à Paris*, ed. Hélène d'Almeida-Topor, Chantal Chanson-Jabeur and Monique Lakroum (Paris: L'Harmattan, 1992), 59; for the famous journey over the river Congo between Brazzaville and Kinshasa, see Ch.-Didier Gondola, "Typologie des sources pour la connaissance du transport interrive Brazzaville–Kinshasa," in d'Almeida-Topor et al., *Les transports en Afrique*, 200–209.
148. Peter R. Gould, *The Development of the Transportation Pattern in Ghana* (Evanston, Ill.: Department of Geography, Northwestern University, 1960), 1 (geography), 2 (link), 58 (snatch); Law, "Wheeled Transport in Pre-colonial West Africa," 255 (late nineteenth century).
149. Arlindo Gonçalo Chilundo, "The Economic and Social Impact of Rail and Road Transportation Systems in the Colonial District of Moçambique (1900–1961)" (PhD, University of Minnesota, 1995), 21 (colonial modal split), 28 (antedated, disrupting), 38 (military porterage), 45–46 (humane), 287 (Berlin), 181 (tax defaulters), 294–307 (for an analysis of the impact of infrastructure development on women's life); Kwabena Opare Akurang-Parry, "Colonial Forced Labor Policies for Road-Building in Southern Ghana and International Anti-forced Labor Pressures, 1900–1940," *African Economic History* 28 (2000): 8 (women), 18–20 (classification), 25 (paradox).

150. A. Félix Iroko, "Le transport en hamac dans le royaume du Danhome du XVIIe au XIXe siècle," in d'Almeida-Topor et al., *Les transports en Afrique (XIXe-XXe siècle)*, passim ("smokes" on 171); Jan Bart Gewald, "People, Mines and Cars: Towards a Revision of Zambian History, 1890–1930," in *The Speed of Change: Motor Vehicles and People in Africa, 1890–2000*, ed. Jan-Bart Gewald, Sabine Luning, and Klaas van Walraven (Leiden: Brill, 2009), 25 (jog-trotted).

151. Chilundo, "Economic and Social Impact," 52 (barred), 55 (block quote), 57 (lyrics), 156–157 (roadwork), 173 (designed), 227–229 (beaten); Chiteji, *Development and Socio-economic Impact of Transportation in Tanzania*, 22 (season).

152. Chilundo, "Economic and Social Impact," 245–246, 250 (forbid), 251 (rafts). That does not mean no harsh measures in the "metropole" were taken to force companies to be part of a state-controlled *grémio*. I thank Maria Luísa Sousa for this observation. See Maria Luísa Sousa, "A mobilidade automóvel em Portugal: A construção do Sistema sociotécnico, 1920–1950" (PhD diss., Universidade Nova de Lisboa, 2013).

153. Chilundo, "Economic and Social Impact," 261 (bicycles), 312–313.

154. Jan-Bart Gewald, Sabine Luning, and Klaas van Walraven, "Motor Vehicles and People in Africa: An Introduction," in Gewald et al., *Speed of Change*, 1–2, 4–6, 5 (district official); for a critique of the "impact" paradigm, see Mom, *Atlantic Automobilism*, 8.

155. Gewald, "People, Mines and Cars," 25 (*gareta*), 30 (sled), 38–39.

156. K. B. Dickson, "The Development of Road Transport in Southern Ghana and Ashanti since about 1850," *Transactions of the Historical Society of Ghana* 5, no. 1 (1961): 37–38, 40 (tarmet); Simon Heap, "The Development of Motor Transport in the Gold Coast, 1900–39," *Journal of Transport History* 11, no. 2 (1990): 21 (dumped); Gewald, "People, Mines and Cars," 42 (carrier), 43n73 (official).

157. Philip J. Havik, "Motor Cars and Modernity: Pining for Progress in Portuguese Guinea, 1915–1945," in Gewald et al., *Speed of Change*, 54 (good road), 55 (Sunday), 63–64; Mom, *Atlantic Automobilism*, 649.

158. Yves Hazemann, "Routes et routiers du Sénégal au XXe siècle: Les sources de l'histoire des transports," in d'Almeida-Topor et al., *Les transports en Afrique (XIXe-XXe siècle)*, 212–213, 213, 217, 219; Philip Drummond-Thompson, "The Development of Motor Transport in Nigeria: A Study in Indigenous Enterprise," in d'Almeida-Topor et al., *Les transports en Afrique*, 222–223 (European and US spread of car), 234 (Dawodu); Odile Goerg, "Publicité et transports routiers en Guinée dans l'entre-deux-guerres," in d'Almeida-Topor et al., *Les transports en Afrique*, 45–46 (advertising).

159. David, "Iconographie de l'histoire des transports en Afrique noire," 61 (not many cars); Alber, "Automobilismus und Kolonialherrschaft," 279–283, 291; for an English version of this brief but excellent overview, see Erdmute Alber, "Motorization and Colonial Rule: Two Scandals in Dahomey, 1916," *Journal of African Cultural Studies* 15, no. 1 (2002).

160. Max Gluckman, *Analysis of a Social Situation in Modern Zululand* (Manchester / New York: Manchester University Press / Rhodes-Livingstone Institute, 1958), 3–13; the bridge episode is reprinted in Vincent, *Anthropology of Politics*, 53–58, followed by Ronald Frankenberg, "'The Bridge' Revisited," in Vincent, *Anthropology of Politics*, 59–64; William Roseberry, "Social Fields and Cultural Encounters," in *Close Encounters of Empire: Writing the Cultural History of U.S.-Latin American Relations*, ed. Gilbert M. Joseph, Catherine C. LeGrand, and Ricardo D. Salvatore (Durham, NC: Duke University Press, 1998), 518 ("The Bridge" as "classic" among Latin Americanists).

161. Jan-Bart Gewald, "Missionaries, Hereros, and Motorcars: Mobility and the Impact of Motor Vehicles in Namibia before 1940," *International Journal of African Historical Studies* 35, nos. 2–3 (2002): 281, 283 (quotes).

162. Anthony I. Nwabughuogu, "The Role of Bicycle Transport in the Economic Development of Eastern Nigeria, 1930–45," *Journal of Transport History* 5, no. 1 (1984): 91–92 (cyclists); Heap, "Development of Motor Transport," 21 (wild), 35 (pirates); Philip Drummond-Thompson, "The Rise of Entrepreneurs in Nigerian Motor Transport," *Journal of Transport History* 14, no. 1 (1993): 48 (transport, costs, trade); Gewald, "Missionaries, Hereros, and Motorcars," 269–270 (football, networks, German); Alber, "Automobilismus und Kolonialherrschaft," 288.

163. Libbie Freed, "'Every European Becomes a Chief': Travel Guides to Colonial Equatorial Africa, 1900–1958," *Journal of Colonialism and Colonial History* 12, no. 2 (2011): 2, 4, 7.

164. Or their recorded experiences did not deal with landscapes at all, as in the "landscape writing" genre of Australian settlers. Alexander Honold, "Raum ohne Volk: Zur Imaginationsgeschichte der kolonialen Geographie," in Dabag et al., *Kolonialismus*, 108; Georgine Clarsen, "Cycling Settlers: Bicycles, Subjectivities, Landscapes," *Mobilities* 10, no. 5 (2015).

165. Stephanie Malia Hom, "Empires of Tourism: Travel and Rhetoric in Italian Colonial Libya and Albania, 1911–1943," *Journal of Tourism History* 4, no. 3 (2012): 284–285 (long quotes), 289 (*strada*); Charles Burdett, *Journeys through Fascism: Italian Travel Writing between the Wars* (New York: Berghahn Books, 2010), 37–43.

166. Werner Nöther, *Die Erschliessung der Sahara durch Motorfahrzeuge 1901–1936* (Munich: belleville Verlag Michael Farm, 2003). Yet, contrary to widespread belief, the Sahara was crisscrossed by indigenous people (see chap. 3).

167. Gewald, "Missionaries, Hereros, and Motorcars," 263 Guillermo Giucci, *The Cultural Life of the Automobile: Roads to Modernity* (Austin University of Texas Press, 2012), 63–65 (sultan); Gordon Pirie, "Automobile Organizations Driving Tourism in Pre-independence Africa," *Journal of Tourism History* 5, no. 1 (2013): 77 (138,000), 78 (sticks), 84 (1938), 85 (Algiers).

168. Clarsen, "Cycling Settlers," 11; Mom, *Atlantic Automobilism*, 154–161 ("Colonialism by Car: Gendered Travel Writing"), 426–439 ("An Avant-Garde in Autopoetic Travel Experience: The Conquest of the 'Periphery'"); Gordon Pirie, "Non-urban Motoring in Colonial Africa in the 1920s and 1930s," *South African Historical Journal*, 63, no. 1 (2011): 45 (off-rail), 56 (ordinary).

169. Kristin V. Monroe, "Automobility and Citizenship in Interwar Lebanon," *Comparative Studies of South Asia, Africa and the Middle East* 34, no 3 (2004): 523 (summering), 529 (marker); Frédéric Abécassis, "La mise en place du réseau routier marocain: Aperçu historique," paper presented at the conference "(Auto)mobility in the Global Middle East: Defining the Field," University of Birmingham (6 November 2015), [2] (routes, escorte), [4] (2,700), [5] (railway).

170. Mann, *Sources of Social Power, vol. 3*, 116–117. On the substitution of British interests by North American ones, see Robert Freeman Smith, "Latin America, the United States and the European Powers, 1830–1930," in *The Cambridge History of Latin America, vol. 4: c. 1870–1930*, ed. Leslie Bethell (London: Cambridge University Press, 1986), 119.

171. Walter D. Mignolo, *Local Histories / Global Designs: Coloniality, Subaltern Knowledges, and Border Thinking* (Princeton, NJ: Princeton University Press, 2000), 58 (extreme), 182–183; Ricardo Salvatore, "A Post-occidentalist Manifesto (review of Walter Mignolo, *The Idea of Latin America* [2005])," *A Contra corriente* 4, no. 1 (2006): 128; Ricardo Salvatore, "Re-discovering Spanish America: Uses of Travel Literature about South America in Britain," *Journal of Latin American Cultural Studies* 8, no. 2 (1999): 209 (concerned).

172. Mabel Moraña, Enrique Dussel, and Carlos A. Jáuregui, "Colonialism and Its Replicants," in *Coloniality at Large: Latin America and the Postcolonial Debate*, ed. Mabel

Moraña, Enrique Dussel, and Carlos A. Jáuregui (Durham, NC: Duke University Press, 2008), 6–7, 13–14; Mary Kay Vaughan and Stephen E. Lewis, "Introduction," in *The Eagle and the Virgin: Nation and Cultural Revolution in Mexico, 1920–1940*, ed. Mary Kay Vaughan and Stephen E. Lewis (Durham, NC: Duke University Press, 2006), 1 (Creole; Creolization originally "designates the language and culture created by variations from the base language and other languages in the context of slave trafficking," and has come to mean generally "cross-cultural mixes)"; Néstor García Canclini, *Hybrid Cultures: Strategies for Entering and Leaving Modernity* (Minneapolis: University of Minnesota Press, 1995), xxxiii, 41 (exuberant modernism) (I thank Rodrigo Booth for suggesting this source).
173. Jaime Moreno Tejada, "Lazy Labor, Modernization, and Coloniality: Mobile Cultures between the Andes and the Amazon around 1900," *Transfers* 6, no. 2 (2016): 4–5 (crisscrossed, improve), 5 (rhythms), 6 (*trabajo*), 9 (submissive), 12–13 (abandon); Stephen E. Lewis, "The Nation, Education, and the 'Indian Problem' in Mexico, 1920–1940," in Vaughan and Lewis, *Eagle and the Virgin*, 178. I thank Rodrigo Booth for enlightening me about *indigenismo*.
174. Robert T. Brown, *Transport and the Economic Integration of South America* (Washington, DC: Brookings Institution, 1966), 163 (two decades), 164, fig. 8.1 (sixty thousand), 165 (isolated regions), 167 (Trans-Andean); Álvaro Pachón and María Teresa Ramírez, *La infraestructura de transporte en Colombia durante el siglo XX: Una descripción desde el punta de vista económico* (Bogotá: Fondo de Cultura Económica, Banco de la República, 2006), 7, table 1.2A.
175. Pachón and Ramírez, *La infraestructura*, 194–195 (conferences); Victor Bulmer-Thomas, "The Latin American Economies, 1929–1939," in Leslie Bethell, ed., *The Cambridge History of Latin America, vol. 6: Latin America since 1930—Economy, Society and Politics* (London: Cambridge University Press, 1994), 108 (absorb); Orlandina de Oliveira, "Urban Growth and Urban Social Structure in Latin America, 1930–1990," in Bethell, *Cambridge History of Latin America, vol. 6*, 266–267.
176. Rodrigo Booth and Melina Piglia, "New Developments in a Neglected Field: Transport and Mobility in Latin American Recent Historiography," in Mom et al., *Mobility in History*, 163 (faster); Giucci, *Cultural Life of the Automobile*, 25; Ingrid E. Fey, "Frou-Frous or Feminists? Turn-of-the-Century Paris and the Latin American Woman," in *Strange Pilgrimages: Exile, Travel, and National Identity in Latin America, 1800–1990s*, ed. Ingrid E. Fey and Karen Racine (Wilmington, DE: Scholarly Resources Inc., 2000); Mom, *Atlantic Automobilism*, 161–170.
177. Germán Arciniegras, "El Automóvil," *Antorcha* (August 1931), 18, 19 (emphasis added); Giucci, *Cultural Life of the Automobile*, 147 (Ortega y Gasset quotes are Giucci's paraphrases).
178. Ricardo Salvatore, "Imperial Mechanics: South America's Hemispheric Integration in the Machine Age," *American Quarterly* 58, no. 3 (2006): 676 (utopia); J. Fred Rippy, "The Inter-American Highway," *Pacific Historical Review* 24, no. 3 (1955): 287 (10,000); Rosa Elena Ficek, "The Pan American Highway: Transformations of a Technology of Integration" paper presented at the T^{2}M conference "Spinoffs of Mobility: Technology, Risk and Innovation," Philadelphia (18–21 September 2014), 3 (Bolivarian dream), 8 (constructing parts), 10 (system); for a detailed treatment of the Pan-American Highway, see also Rodrigo Booth, "Automóviles y Carreteras: Movilidad, modernización y transformación territorial en Chile, 1913–1931" (PhD diss., Pontificia Universidad Católica de Chile, 2009), chap. 3; see also Ricardo Salvatore, "Panamericanismo práctico: Acerea de la mécanica de la penetración comercial norteamaericana," in *Culturas imperiales: Experiencia y representación en*

América, Asia y África. ed. Ricardo Salvatore (Rosario: Beatriz Viterbo, 2005), 269–300.
179. Robert Neal Seidel, "Progressive Pan Americanism: Development and United States Policy Toward South America, 1906–1931" (PhD diss. Cornell University, 1973), 273 (revolution), 283 (North American interests), 284 (pro-American), 299 ($1.3 billion), 306 (logical), 308 (diffusionist lines: "Assuming ... progress reasonably proportionate to that of the United States at a similar stage of its highway and automotive development"); Joel Wolfe, *Autos and Progress: The Brazilian Search for Modernity* (Oxford: Oxford University Press, 2010), 25 and 78 (Good Roads Movement); Ficek, "Pan American Highway," 6 (Peruvian engineer); Rippy, "Inter-American Highway," 290n9 (Hoover), 291 (Rome); Salvatore, 'Imperial Mechanics," 663 (contemporary quote), 680–682 (car trip, including backwardness, adventurousness, and isles), 686 (llamas).
180. Seidel, "Progressive Pan Americanism," 298 (boomed), 300 (second largest); Rippy, "Inter-American Highway," 293 ($3 million); Anahí Ballent, "Kilómetro cero: La construcción del universo simbólico del camino en la Argentina de los años treinta," *Boletín del Instituto de Historia Argentina y Americana "Dr. Emilio Ravignani,"* 27 (1er semestre 2005), 111 (Argentinian density); Mike Mason, *Turbulent Empires: A History of Global Capitalism since 1945* (Montreal: McGill-Queen's University Press, 2018), 217 (per capita income); Giucci, *Cultural Life of the Automobile*, 76–77, 101 (car numbers); Melina Piglia, *Autos, rutas y turismo: El automóvil club argentino y el estado* (Buenos Aires: Siglo Veintiuno Editores, 2014), 31, table 1, gives for 1929 a much higher number of cars in Argentina (330,000); Valeria Gruschetsky, "Argentina in Motion: Connections between Mobility, Politics, and Culture in Recent Historiography," in Norton et al. *Mobility in History*, 135 (road policy); Booth, "Automóviles y Carreteras," 46, table 1, 83, fig. 2 (Chile); Rodrigo Booth, "El automóvil: Un objeto técnico superior—Debates y experiencias en torno a la irrupción de la motorización privada en Chile (1902–1914)," in *À pied, à cheval, en voiture: l'Amérique indépendante et les moyens de transport*, ed. Isabelle Tauzin-Castellanos (Pessac: Maison des Sciences de l'Homme d'Aquitaine, 2011), 101 (1902).
181. Booth, "Automóviles y Carreteras," chap. 5 (adventurous car cultures), 57 (Road Law); see also Rodrigo Booth, "Turismo, Panamericanismo e ingeniera civil: La construcción del camino escénico entre Viña del Mar y Concón (1917–1931)," *Historia* 2, no. 47 (2014); Booth, "El automóvil," 101–102 (*bien de lujo, corsos de flores*), 109 (car-friendly, Club); Tomás Errázuriz, "When Walking Became Serious: Reshaping the Role of Pedestrians in Santiago, 1900–1931," *Journal of Transport History* 32, no. 1 (2011): 40 (campaign, dictated), 42 (four thousand).
182. Mom, *Atlantic Automobilism*, 328–344; Giucci, *Cultural Life of the Automobile*, 68, 75 (Piquero, Lesdain), 78. 84 (Andrade), 87 (flight), 162 (Lasplaces; "oceanic fusion" is Giucci's own paraphrase; Lasplaces's story appeared in his *El hombre que tuvo una idea* [The man who had an idea]); Roger Courteville, *La première traversée de l'Amérique du Sud en automobile: De Rio-de-Janeiro à Paz et Lima* (Paris: Barrères, [1954]), 75, 118. For a description of Argentina as "a special case of a settler nation" and for a shortlist of reasons why Argentina differs from "settler colonies" (lack of colonial rule, only a small British community, absence of legal discrimination), see Ricardo Salvatore, "The Unsettling Location of a Settler Nation: Argentina, from Settler Economy to Failed Developing Nation," *South Atlantic Quarterly* 107, no. 4 (2008): 779–780.
183. Wolfe, *Autos and Progress*, 16 (capitals), 18 (*Fon-Fon!, Klaxon*), 25 (slavery) 33 (tropical modernity), 39 (São Paulo), 52 (sublime), 82–84 (Fordlândia, Belterra); Richard Downes, "Autos over Rails: How US Business Supplanted the British in Brazil, 1910–28," *Journal of Latin American Studies* 24, no. 3 (1992): 557 (Clube); Downes,

"Autos over Rails," 569 (three-quarters); Ricardo Salvatore, "Early American Visions of a Hemispheric Market in South America," in *Transnational America: The Fading of Borders in the Western Hemisphere*, ed. Berndt Ostendorf (Heidelberg: Universitätsverlag C. Winter, 2002), 56–57 (consumer markets); Warren Dean, "The Brazilian Economy, 1879–1930," in *The Cambridge History of Latin America, vol. 5: c. 1870–1930*, ed. Leslie Bethell (London: Cambridge University Press, 1986), 712 (160,000). On Fordlândia, see also Greg Grandin, *Fordlandia: The Rise and Fall of Henry Ford's Forgotten Jungle City* (New York: Metropolitan Books / Henry Holt & Co., 2009).

184. Rosenberg, "Transnational Currents in a Shrinking World," 820; Wolfe, *Autos and Progress*, 44 (Serbia), 47 (car show), 75 and 221n66 (ownership).
185. Wolfe, *Autos and Progress*, 4 (slogan), 6 (Gran Premio), 9–10 (soccer, Creole), 14 (Santos Dumont), 16 (high-power); Melina Piglia, "Viaje deportivo, nación y territorio. El Automóvil Club Argentino y los orígines del Turismo Carretera'. Argentina, 1924–1938," *Nuevo Mundo Mundos Nuevos* (16 September 2008), 4 (European races).
186. Wolfe, *Autos and Progress*, 49–56 (jewel: 53), 91–99; Piglia, "Viaje deportivo, nación y territorio," 3; Salvatore, "Imperial Mechanics," 669, 680; Mann, *Sources of Social Power, vol. 3*, 423 (escaped); Pachón and Ramírez, *La infraestructura de transporte en Colombia durante el siglo XX*, 58, table 1.24 (statistics); Mom, *Atlantic Automobilism*, 69–70.
187. Claudio Lomnitz, "Final Reflections: What Was Mexico's Cultural Revolution?" in Vaughan and Lewis, *Eagle and the Virgin*, 221 (new Mexican, Road Commission), 224–225 (ten thousand), 335; Benjamin Fulwider, "Driving the Nation: Road Transportation and the Postrevolutionary Mexican State, 1925–1960" (PhD diss., Georgetown University, 2009), 5 (million deaths), 35 (hotspots), 47 (1934 law), 48 (bipartite), 49 (bridges), 50 (capitalists); Wendy Waters, "Remapping Identities: Road Construction and Nation Building in Postrevolutionary Mexico," in Vaughan and Lewis, *Eagle and the Virgin*, 221 (new Mexican, Road Commission), 224–225 (ten thousand).
188. Waters, "Remapping Identities," 226–229, 232–234, 237–238; Fulwider, "Driving the Nation," 66 (tourism), 79 (4,000).
189. Fulwider, "Driving the Nation," 51 (1930), 54 (1932), 57 (cooperatives), 61 (land to peasants), 64 (oil industry, autonomy), 76 (assembly plants), 80 (census); Joanne Hershfield, *Imagining la Chica Moderna: Women, Nation, and Visual Culture in Mexico, 1917–1936* (Durham, NC: Duke University Press, 2008), 12 (quote), 62–64 (*chicas modernas*); Joy Elizabeth Hayes, "National Imaginings on the Air: Radio in Mexico, 1920–1950," in Vaughan and Lewis, *Eagle and the Virgin*, 243–244; Hershfield, "Screening the Nation," in Vaughan and Lewis, *Eagle and the Virgin*, 262. On the European (especially Dutch) efforts to regulate the trucking industry, see, e.g., Gijs Mom, "Struggle of the Systems: Freight Mobility from a Transatlantic Perspective, 1920–2000," in Duc et al., *Transport and Mobility History*.
190. Salvatore, "Early American Visions of a Hemispheric Market in South America," 61; Pachón and Ramírez, *La infraestructura de transporte en Colombia durante el siglo XX*, 68, table 1.31 (statistics); Fiona Wilson, "The Conflict between Indigenous and Immigrant Commercial Systems in the Peruvian Central Sierra, 1900–1940," in *Region and Class in Modern Peruvian History*, ed. Rory Miller (Liverpool: University of Liverpool, Institute of Latin American Studies, 1987), 125 (relations), 127 (relationship), 142–143 (truck driving, identity), 151 (gipsy); Christoph Borcherdt, "Die neuere Verkehrserschliessung in Venezuela und ihre Auswirkungen in der Kulturlandschaft," *Die Erde* 1 (1968): 47 (Venezuelan vehicles).
191. I thank Rodrigo Booth ("we are in the extreme West and not in its alterity") for bringing the point about the extension of the West to my attention (email, 29 January 2015);

Salvatore, "Unsettling Location of a Settler Nation," 777; Salvatore, "Post-occidentalist Manifesto," 130; Canclini, *Hybrid Cultures*, xxxii (*mestizaje*).

192. Mom, *Atlantic Automobilism*, 507 (revolutionary, electric propulsion); Martin Crouch, "Problem of Soviet Urban Transport," *Soviet Studies* 31, no. 2 (1979): 237 (fleets).

193. Jale Parla, "Car Narratives: A Subgenre in Turkish Novel Writing," *South Atlantic Quarterly* 102, nos. 2–3 (2003): 536 (enigmatic), 537 (do not touch), 537–538 (into the air), 538 (masterpiece and follies). I thank Anne Voeten (Nijmegen, the Netherlands) for helping me read the Turkish *Wikipedia* article on *Araba Sevdası*.

194. Vasant Kaiwar, "Towards Orientalism and Nativism: The Impasse of Subaltern Studies," *Historical Materialism* 12, no. 2 (2004): 200 (persuasion), 202 (British), 212n81 (colonial modernity; the phrase in the original is formulated as a question). This is a review of Dipesh Chakrabarty, *Provincializing Europe: Postcolonial Thought and Historical Difference* (Princeton, NJ: Princeton University Press, 2000), and Ranajit Guha, *Dominance without Hegemony*.

195. Thomas J. Barfield, *The Nomadic Alternative* (Englewood Cliffs: Prentice Hall, 1993), 4 (husbandry), 5 (animals), 7–9 (overview of nomadic pastoral zones), 116 (Pashtun), 168 (railroads and Kazaks); on the fateful collectivization of the Kazaks, see Robert Kindler, *Stalins Nomaden: Herrschaft und Hunger in Kasachstan* (Hamburg: Hamburger Edition, 2014), on migration in general in twentieth-century Russia, see Lewis H. Siegelbaum and Leslie Page Moch, *Broad Is My Native Land: Repertoires and Regimes of Migration in Russia's Twentieth Century* (Ithaca, NY: Cornell University Press, 2014); Mom, *Atlantic Automobilism*, 443–444 (American hoboes).

196. Rosenberg, "Transnational Currents in a Shrinking World," 961 (modernity at large); for European motorists' thanatourism during World War I, see Mom, *Atlantic Automobilism*, 250–267.

197. A similar dominance of trucks and buses (*véhicules utilitaires*) has been observed for Morocco during the interwar years by Abécassis, "La mise en place du réseau routier marocain," [5]; for a recent definition of modernity in which mobility does not figure, see Hinton, "Savages, Subjects, and Sovereigns," 441.

198. Tim Cresswell, *On the Move: Mobility in the Modern Western World* (New York: Routledge, 2006); Kaiwar, "Towards Orientalism and Nativism," 207–208 (Chakrabarty).

199. See Markovits et al., *Society and Circulation*; Jacob Shell, *Transportation and Revolt: Pigeons, Mules, Canals, and the Vanishing Geographies of Subversive Mobility* (Cambridge, MA: MIT Press, 2015); see also Jacob Shell, "When Roads Cannot Be Used: The Use of Trained Elephants for Emergency Logistics, Off-Road Conveyance, and Political Revolt in South and Southeast Asia," *Transfers* 5, no. 2 (2015).

200. Mignolo, *Local Histories / Global Designs*, 13 (Coronil), 21 (Ribeiro); Arturo Escobar, "Development and the Anthropology of Modernity," in Harding, *Postcolonial Science and Technology Studies Reader*, 41.

201. Mignolo, *Local Histories / Global Designs*, 30; Mom, *Atlantic Automobilism*. 611 (women), 612–613 (jitney); on passengering, apart from the introduction, see, e.g., Peter Merriman, *Mobility, Space and Culture* (London: Routledge, 2012), 9, esp. 160n55, which contains more literature on the subject; see also Eric Laurier, Hayden Lorimer, Barry Brown, Owain Jones, Oskar Juhlin, Alyson Noble, Mark Perry, Daniele Pica et al., "Driving and 'Passengering': Notes on the Ordinary Organization of Car Travel," *Mobilities* 3, no. 1 (2008); possession, e.g., in Alber, "Automobilismus und Kolonialherrschaft," 294.

202. Clarsen, "Cycling Settlers," 9 (trips across the world); Giucci, *Cultural Life of the Automobile*, 68 (*croisière jaune*); Andrew Thacker, "E. M. Forster and the Motor Car," *Literature & History* 9, no. 2 (2000): 40 (joy).

203. Sanjay Joshi, "The Spectre of Comparisons: Studying the Middle Class of Colonial India," in *Elite and Everyman: The Cultural Politics of the Indian Middle Classes*, ed. Amita Baviskar and Raka Ray (London: Routledge, 2011), 104; Mann, *Sources of Social Power*, vol. 3, 32, 35; W. W. Rostow, *The Stages of Economic Growth: A Non-Communist Manifesto* (Cambridge: Cambridge University Press, 1971), 111.
204. Mann, *Sources of Social Power*, vol. 3, 22, 23, 30, 37, 148 (high-octane); Giucci, *Cultural Life of the Automobile*, 54–55 (Stinnes); Wolfe, *Autos and Progress*, 102–103, 232n47 (Kipling published *Brazilian Sketches* in 1940); Mark Ford, *Raymond Roussel and the Republic of Dreams* (Ithaca, NY: Cornell University Press, 2000), 117; Robert Byron, *The Road to Oxiana* (London: Penguin, 2007); Caitlin Vandertop, "Travel Literature and the Infrastructural Unconscious," in *New Directions in Travel Writing Studies*, ed. Julia Kuehn and Paul Smethurst (London: Palgrave Macmillan, 2015), 137 (Byron as an example of a travelogue in which infrastructure is not ignored).
205. Carl Van Doren, "Introduction," in *The Asiatics: A Novel* by Frederic Prokosch (New York: The Press of the Readers Club, 1941), vii ; Robert M. Greenfield, *Dreamer's Journey: The Life and Writings of Frederic Prokosch* (Newark: University of Delaware Press, 2010), 75 (Pennsylvania), 80 (envy), 92 (Yale); on Klaus and Erika Mann's world tour, see Mom, *Atlantic Automobilism*, 431–432.
206. Prokosch, *Asiatics*, 87 (sleigh, truck), 92 (Chinaman), 109 (bullock cart), 121 (Teheran), 133 (plane crash), 142 (Junker), 202 (rode and rode), 226 (Minerva), 236 (villagers), 248 (stream), 253 (extremely well), 273 (steamer), 313 (rot), 337 (keep on moving), 341 (brightly), 346 (Paris), 353 (concubines). "Frederic Prokosch," retrieved from http://en.wikipedia.org/wiki/Frederic-Prokosch on 21 February 2016 (hoax).
207. Greenfield, *Dreamer's Journey*, 80 (Klaus Mann), 108 (hammock), 124 (Thomas Mann), 126 (Narcissus), 129 (Gide), 130 (beads), 131 (struggle), 182 (Europe tour), 194–195 (road novel), 376–390 (hoax), 382 (memoirs), 398 (Fellini); Prokosch, *Asiatics*, 366–367.
208. Luise White, "Cars Out of Place: Vampires, Technology, and Labor in East and Central Africa," in *Tensions of Empire: Colonial Cultures in a Bourgeois World*, ed. Frederick Cooper and Ann Laura Stoler (Berkeley: University of California Press, 1997), 441–442; Chakrabarty, *Provincializing Europe*.
209. Waters, "Remapping Identities," 225–226 (grease); Stewart Sanderson, "The Folklore of the Motor-Car," *Folklore* 80, no. 4 (1969); Mom, *Atlantic Automobilism*, 148 (Bierbaum), 151 (Corelli).
210. Mignolo, *Local Histories / Global Designs*, 191 (psychoanalysis), 205 (Third World); James C. Scott, *The Moral Economy of the Peasant: Rebellion and Subsistence in Southeast Asia* (New Haven, CT: Yale University Press, 1976); Joshi, "Spectre of Comparisons," 105 (provincializing); Escobar, "Development and the Anthropology of Modernity," 278 (exotic).

Part II

EXUBERANCE, WITH A TWIST
Spreading the Gospel of Automobilism

Chapter 2

FRAGMENTING AUTOMOTIVE ADVENTURE
Western Exuberant Automobilism and Middle-Class Guilt
(1945–1973)

"Why I Want to Fuck Ronald Reagan"

At the end of the 1930s, "the bright but bloody kaleidoscope that was Shanghai" was bustling with pedestrians and rickshaws. Sitting in the back of a large American Packard, young James (Jim) Ballard was driven home by Chinese servant Yang. Honking at the "aggressive rickshaw coolies," Yang lashed "his leather riding crop at the thoughtless pedestrians, the sauntering bar girls with American handbags, the old amahs bent double under bamboo yokes strung with headless chickens." This is how Ballard remembered (and fictionalized) the mobilities in this "Western city," a place where he observed Britain's decline and America's rise, and where he shaped his fledgling imagination as an amalgam of East and West, the latter, as so often, reduced to the "Anglo-Saxon" West. Riding on his bicycle through the International Settlement in "his velvet trousers and silk shirt" during the Japanese invasion in 1937, the lonesome kid watched "the bloody heads of Communist soldiers mounted on pikes along the Bund," observed the thousands of Chinese refugees fleeing into the city and dying of cholera. Jim saw how Yang, driving out of their parental house at Amherst Avenue, crushed the foot of a beggar sitting just outside the gate. "Wooden carts and rickshaws crowded Amherst Avenue, each loaded with a peasant family's entire possessions," he remembered nearly half a century later, meanwhile tainted by his 'fleshy' style:

> Rickshaw coolies hauled at their shafts, chanting and spitting, veins as thick as fingers clenched into the meat of their swollen calves. Petty clerks pushed bicycles loaded with mattresses, charcoal stoves and sacks of rice. A legless beggar, his thorax strapped into a huge leather shoe, swung himself along the road through the maze of wheels, a wooden dumbbell in each hand. He spat and swiped at the Packard when Yang tried to force him out of the car's way, and then vanished among the wheels of the pedicabs [three-wheeled cycle rickshaws] and [hand-pulled] rickshaws, confident in his kingdom of saliva and dust.[1]

The year 1937 appeared to be only a rehearsal of the war exploding in full after Pearl Harbor. American journalist Edgar Mowrer witnessed in central China the fleeing flows of

> dainty Chinese girls in silken semi-modern dress and slippers, older women hobbling on surprisingly quickly on their bound feet with the aid of long poles on which they balanced; ... rich wives of merchants in rickshaws; ... whole families in heavy ox carts with solid wooden wheels, drawn by inconceivable combinations of domestic animals; ... babies in boxes on tiny wheels or strapped to the back of tottering older children, occasional sturdy farmers lifting the handles of gigantic loaded wheelbarrows, their remaining donkey or wife or children pulling in front ... [all of them] mixed with the retreating Chinese army. There were almost no motor vehicles, and the few were piled to the sky with women and goods and attempts to purchase transportation were sternly refused.

From early on, seeing war violence triggered a sequence of "desperate imagination" in the young Ballard, blurring reality and fantasy, as if his experiences were "part of a technicolor epic being staged at the Shanghai film studios." But the Japanese tank "crush[ing] a rickshaw against a telegraph pole" was very real, as were the Chinese "packed together on the quay" and "witnessing the complete humiliation of the Allied powers by the empire of Japan," a sight that made a deep impression on Jim. "A strange doubling of reality had taken place, as if everything that had happened to him since the war was occurring within a mirror. It was his mirror self who felt faint and hungry, and who thought about food all the time."

Like his father, owner of a cotton mill, Ballard admired the Americans because of their optimism and, later, during his three-year stay in the detention camp, their "good humour, verbal inventiveness and enormous laid-back style." In his fictional account of camp life, he survived on his own, shrewdly using the weakness of others, his parents detained in some other camp. As the seeming epitome of immobility, camp life in Jim's head was highly adventurous and mobile, from the secret escapes to the nearby airfield, where he witnessed the kamikaze pilots performing their last rituals, through the beating to death of a Chinese rickshaw puller by an dissatisfied Japanese officer returning from Shanghai (the adult British prisoners watching passively), to the raids by Japanese and American planes, even more beautiful than the large prewar Packards and Buicks But fictional or not, his reminiscences make us understand that whoever lived through the cruelties and the horrors of the camp wanted to shock the people in the petty-bourgeois world who had not gone through the pain and the sufferings. "The Communists had an intriguing ability to unsettle everyone, a talent [he] greatly respected," his biographer remarked.[2]

Arriving in England with his mother at the beginning of the "period of austerity," one of Jim's first observations regarded the "black perambulators, some kind of mobile coal shuttle, I assumed, used for bunkering ships. Later I learned that these were British cars (all made pre-war), a species I had never seen before." A foreigner in his own country, Ballard would remain, in his own words, a "lifelong outsider and maverick," especially toward the ever-expanding middle class, of which he could not deny being a part. He also would remain skeptical toward its "nuclear family, dominated by an overworked mother, ... in many ways deeply unnatural, as is marriage itself, part of the huge price we pay to control the male sex." Dropping out of his medical studies, he devoured American and continental European modernist writers, discovered Freud in his efforts to reconcile his inner struggles between technology fascination, death, and eroticism and found surrealism to be the channel of choice to express the blurring of his inner and external realities. With his ambition to become a pilot forgotten, Cold War technology offered a vista on a rebirth of the genre of science fiction, which he subverted by following J. B. Priestley's idea to tour "Inner Space." It was also attractive to Ballard because "SF [science fiction] writers weren't interested in the Self."

With the first thousand dollars earned after the publication of *The Drowned World*, the SF novel that made him part of the literary establishment overnight in 1962, he bought his first car, an Armstrong Siddeley Sapphire. His choice for the "New Wave" of a middlebrow genre was deliberate: "No one in a novel by Virginia Woolf ever fills up the petrol tank of their car," whereas "my entire fiction is the dissection of a deep pathology that I had witnessed in Shanghai and later in the post-war world." Ballard became interested in exposing "the violence that underpinned the entertainment culture," especially in so far as it touched the human body. So, whoever has read my previous study about prewar automotive adventurist culture will agree Ballard is the ideal candidate to start exploring the postwar continuation of this culture, in an era of fledgling globalization, a post–World War II counterpart of Natsume Sōseki of the previous chapter, as a bridge between East and West, a symbol of their mutual interdependencies.[3]

The New Wave SF scene "tried to give science fiction a more respectable character by steering it in the direction of normal literature" (by the fans most remembered because of American writer Philip K. Dick, known for movies like *Blade Runner, Total Recall,* and *Minority Report*). Ballard (in his own words) "sensed that a new kind of popular culture was emerging that played on the latent psychopathy of its audiences, and in fact needed to elicit that strain of psychopathy if it was to work. The modern movement had demonstrated this from its start, in the poetry of Baudelaire and Rimbaud, and the willing engagement of the audience's own psychopathy is almost a definition of modernism as a whole." This was not only fictional: SF, a Dutch philosopher maintained, is inspiring only as long as a "suggestion of realism" is present.

And so, this "misfit," this "casualty of war," started to provoke his audience, from his first novella "The Violent Noon" (1951, in which, according to his biographer, "in the smashed car and the helpless woman, Ballard for the first time links automobiles, violence and sex"), through "The Assassination of John Fitzgerald Kennedy Considered as a Downhill Motor Race" (1966, inspired by Alfred Jarry's 1907 "The Passion Considered as an Uphill Bicycle Race"), to the short piece "Why I Want to Fuck Ronald Reagan," published when the latter was still governor of California: "No," Ballard wrote, "John Wayne for President, Ronald Reagan for best friend."[4] By then, he had grown into a cult figure, especially in the emerging counterculture of the 1960s and 1970s, particularly known for his dystopian SF. How was this possible? How could a 'misfit' from Shanghai, an 'outsider' of a recovering England, a man fascinated by the mixture of violence, sex, and technology, and an author of dystopian science fiction, a reputed car lover, become an icon of a countercultural age known for its 'flower power'?

***

In this chapter, we will zoom, like Ballard, from the wider world mobility perspective we surveyed in the previous chapter, back to the West, where the post–World War II years were characterized by what since then has been called 'mass motorization,' its 'abundance' and 'extravagance' reducing the wider mobility spectrum to a monomodal phenomenon. We will try to answer the questions we have just formulated, first by investigating the relationship between the immediate postwar youth culture and mobility, resuming and continuing a narrative and analytic strand started elsewhere and going back to 1895, as recapitulated in the introduction. Where I previously dealt with the 'emergence' and 'persistence' periods before World War II, this chapter represents the zenith of the predominantly Western story, before the automotive story line dissolves into the multiple mobilities of the 1970s and beyond. We will study this culture through its music, focusing on the *affinity* between the mobility of the music itself (its rhythms) and of the musicians on the one hand, and (road) transport in general. Thus, in this chapter, we will practice for the first time the new mobility studies principle of merging transport and media under one and the same 'mobility' umbrella: the beat of the rock music informs us as prolifically about the youth's mobility as the rhythm of their car and motorcycle engines.

In the same vein, we will then zoom out to the postwar mass motorization in the West (sometimes looking back into the war and the interbellum) and analyze the relationship, assumed by James Ballard, between 'reality' and its underlying violence, again connecting to a thesis developed in a previous study about the car as 'adventure machine.' We will focus on a new group of car users: the Western working man. Then, we continue following the hegemonic middle class (the 'inventor' of automobilism before the war) and witness the erosion of the middle-class nuclear family. Finally, we will sketch a use and user profile within both the European and the American car cultures, continuing our earlier prewar story where we left the car as a tamed, affordable adventure machine in the hands of the white, middle-class nuclear family. We will first analyze hegemonic middle-class sources as an entrance in the Western middle-class car culture and then enter popular culture (especially film and, again, music, but now through a content analysis of its lyrics), tracing how it influenced hegemonic culture (in particular, the concept of the 'adventure machine'), becoming mainstream. We will wonder whether the car's 'affordances' (the practices it enabled) were changed under conditions of mass motorization, after which we will come back in the conclusions to Ballard, who will close the period under investigation here with *Crash*, a novel shocking many readers but nonetheless representing at least the violent part of the mobility history of this period.

A Multimedia Feast: Folk, Beat, Rock, and Other Mobilities

Young Ballard entered a motherland that was quickly leaving behind a condition of austerity, monitored and planned by the social democratic Attlee government, which kept consumption low in favor of export, its revenues needed to pay back the country's war debts. Some of the preferred export products were British-designed sport cars (especially the MG Midget, which sold more than 85 percent of its cars in the United States, and the larger Jaguar XK 120), a revival of the enthusiasm for British cars by American millionaires from the 1930s who wanted "to emulate the spectacles they saw on European racing circuits such as Le Mans, Silverstone and Nürburgring and in the Mille Miglia open road race," brought about by American military personnel enthralled by the handling of these cars on the winding European roads. While the Commonwealth started falling apart (initiated by India's independence in 1947), the government nationalized the rail and road transport business encompassing nearly nine hundred thousand employees, the biggest of the nationalized sectors.[5] The Conservatives, who won the elections of 1951, witnessed a first economic boom, expressed in an outburst of consumption, especially consumer durables, guided by the plans for a welfare society formulated in the famous Beveridge Report of 1942. The boom was interrupted by the Suez Crisis of 1956, but then the gates to British welfare society were pushed wide open, even if it was less spectacular than the large countries within the European Economic Community (EEC, founded in 1957, of which the United Kingdom was not a member). But the growth rate of even the British GDP per capita between 1951 and 1973 was a third higher than before the war, while unemployment was extremely low (2 percent), and the standard of living was climbing spectacularly: infant mortality halved in the same period, average income doubled, and by 1973, more than half the British owned their own home (against less than one-third in 1950).

The increasing affluence was measured in the acquisition and possession of the durables, even if already in the 1960s, it became clear "conspicuous consumption [and income were] relatively poorly correlated" and that "even automobile consumption is not so accurately predicted from income as one might think." Car ownership grew fivefold (already in 1966, "half of the nation's households owned one or more cars"), nearly every household had a television set, and the penetration rate of washing machines and refrigerators was in the order of two-thirds of all families by the end of the period covered in this chapter. For many, cars were "for leisure only," as one male interviewee of Colin Pooley's historical mobility reconstruction project explained, "It would not have occurred to you to use it for work."[6] In the trip to work, however, the car competed with walking, all other modes (but especially the rail-bound tramway and train) functioning as an intermediary solution (fig. 2.1). It is never too late to emphasize that the car started to dominate (with more than half of all trips) only in the 1990s. The welfare state, sketched in the Beveridge Report (and originally aimed at creating a "cradle-to-grave" welfare "as a universal right of citizenship for sickness, injury, unemployment, old age, maternity, orphans and widows"), took shape in the form of social insurance, a universal National Health Service, and measures to expand education and housing. Provided with leisure time (waiting between school and conscription at eighteen) and money ("without the burden of a family or home to support"), the war generation of the youth started indulging in rock 'n' roll, a transnational medium imported from the United States (as a fusion of "black gospel and blues ... with white country and western") but soon imitated in their own "skiffle bands," with makeshift percussion instruments, an acoustic guitar, and a banjo, the latter instrument originally coming from Africa.[7]

Some historians estimated the number of such bands in the United Kingdom at a staggering thirty thousand to fifty thousand around 1957. One of these was founded by Graham Nash, born in the slums of Manchester (in his neighborhood, "there were no cars in those days, just the horses and carts"), his father sacked as an employee of the car industry, "hungry a lot" with "dreams [as] the only way out." While perfecting their harmony singing, the first "gigs" of the band, which soon would be renamed into the Hollies, were in the blossoming local proletarian entertainment sector, just like other bands in the North did, such as Johnny and the Moondogs in Liverpool, soon to become the Beatles. Nash describes in his autobiography how this early rock culture, before the onslaught of the baby boom during the 1960s, was characterized by a continuous and delirious hunt for songs, how it was the rhythm (the beat) rather than the texts that initially attracted the hundreds of bands (thus prefiguring McLuhan's "the medium is the message"; see the introduction), how girls of the fledgling baby boom generation were the first ("total hysteria, wet panties") to attend their performances (undergone "like a religious experience") soon followed by the boys, and how these workers' kids started to write their songs, "combining personal feelings with poetry and music."

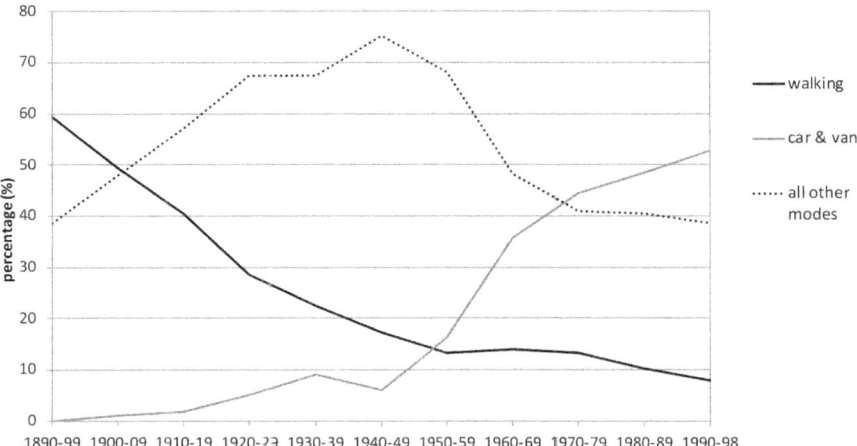

Figure 2.1. Modal split for journeys to work in the United Kingdom (percent of a sample of about twelve thousand). Source: Pooley and Turnbull, *Migration and Mobility in Britain since the Eighteenth Century*, 367. Figure created by the author.

The urge to develop their own 'language' (or, the obsolescence of the language of their parents) is one of the most remarkable phenomena of the fledgling youth and counterculture. Was mobility a part of this language, and will we encounter a new 'automotive adventure' here? Yes, we will: Nash also recounts the "murder" of playing the Northern provinces, touring in buses, continuing a prewar tradition of would-be motorists gaining their first 'road sense' in the collective bus. Time was experienced as flow: "Things were happening so fast; it was all so fluid." And then came the big jump over the ocean, in the slipstream of the Beatles, and followed by the Kinks, Gerry and the Pacemakers, the Dave Clark Five, and Herman's Hermits, also known as the "British invasion" of 1964/1965, "and the Hollies shifted gears, heading into the fast lane."[8]

The Beat of American Youth Mobility: Change as Normalcy, Mobility as Routine

The mobility of British rock, its becoming "mass media," had a devastating effect on a blossoming part of the American youth music culture, generally called the "folk revival." This revival got underway in 1958 when the Kingston Trio scored a hit with "Tom Dooley." It was a depoliticized version of an earlier folk revival, but this time driven by middle-class college students, less attractive to the record industry because they did not buy singles, as they preferred to wait for the LPs. The earlier, prewar revival had been a deliberate, romantic, and successful attempt of Northern bohemian and leftist urbanites to collect and record the voices of the 'people.' One of these voices of what sociologist Serge Denisoff termed the proletarian renaissance was the nasal and raspy voice of Aunt Molly Jackson, daughter of a miner in the Appalachian Mountains of Kentucky and Virginia. After her 'discovery' in 1931, she was brought to New York City by a group of radical writers led by Theodore Dreiser and John Dos Passos. Folk, as the "white man's blues" (Little Richard), was a direct expression of the sufferings of rural workers, including women, embedded in an activist context of musicians in the neighborhood of the Communist Party USA and radical unions (and even further back, the nomadic Wobblies of the first decades of the twentieth century), but also stimulated by Roosevelt's New Deal and the efforts to register and record the common American's voice, for instance, through the Federal Writers' Project.

The leaders of this project, B. Botkin and T. Couch, saw it also as a way to expose the public to the social conditions of Southern blacks and other poor, thus opposing opinions among Southern, white Federal Writers that industrialization and urbanization were the death of 'authentic' folk culture.[9] Woody Guthrie, "the dean of hard travelin'," with his *Dust Bowl*

Ballads, was the most famous urban expression of this rural-urban cultural mix (at the same time an expression of a hectic rural-urban mobility), but other subcultures were bluegrass ("a jazzed-up form of hillbilly music") and the (Mississippi) Delta blues of Chicago's migrated African Americans: "I'm goin' to get me a job, up there in Mr. Ford's place / Stop these eatless days from starin' me in the face," Blink Blake sang in his "Detroit Bound Blues." During the war, half a million people had migrated to Detroit.[10]

***

It is remarkable that the extensive literature on the folk phenomenon provides hardly any content analysis: folk appealed to something else, a feeling, of a community. "The response to the music is, to a large degree, physical. Interestingly, one of the effects of the music is the vicarious experience of producing it, as listeners mime the movement of the guitarist, the drummer, or the singer." This sensitivity toward the production of utterances and (the expression of) experiences is the very basis of what we have elsewhere characterized as the 'affinity' or "structural homology" between car driving (the production of the driving experience) and music (see the introduction). Music ("overtheorized and underresearched," in historian Tobias Becker's judgment) and mobility (likewise, in my judgment) go together: they 'move.' After the war, its content started to convey an (often commercialized) sentiment everybody could share. "We Shall Overcome," one of the iconic songs of the postwar revival, is a case in point: it became the anthem of the equal rights movement, but its lyrics were a far cry from the prewar agitprop.

But before the baby boomers incorporated this culture, it was the New York beatniks (the "ruffians [who] refused to work, hitchhiked across the country, and smoked a mind-altering drug called marijuana") who patronized the localities where the Almanacs and the Weavers performed their domesticated versions of folk, although still with "a definite left wing taint." The Almanacs, "four young men who roam around the country in a $150 Buick and fight the class war with ballads and guitars," did not break through to radio and TV, as they "refused to kowtow to the management's insistence that they wear hillbilly outfits," but were very popular among black and white migrants from the South to the Northern industrial cities during the war, for instance, when "they sang at a rally in Cadillac Square [in Detroit] for over thirty thousand auto workers" in 1942. Just as in other realms of mobility (such as the car culture), post–World War II folk revival was prepared during the interwar years.[11]

Indeed, focusing on the content of their songs, the mobility historian could easily be misled by the modest attention given to the car in folk music, and erroneously exclude it from our investigation. What we cannot overlook, however, is an entire mainstream popular culture of immediate postwar music emerging in the United States that can only be considered a giant bacchanal of eroticized car adventure constructed around the fledgling "hot rod" and "drag racing" cultures, suspiciously looked upon by a hegemonic culture still caught up in war austerity. From Kid Ory's Dixieland Jazz Band ("Saturday Night Drag Race") to Roy Brown's "Cadillac Baby" ("How that woman loves to ride / Yes, crazy 'bout that Hydramatic / Gives her such an easy ride"), from Howlin' Wolf ("I Asked for Water, She Gave Me Gasoline") to Bill Haley's gigs that led to the "first countrywide, bus-driven rock & roll tours ... of black and white musicians," popular music and car driving melted into a rebellious but eager-to-be-absorbed culture in which Ike Turner's "Rocket 88" performed by Jackie Brenston and His Delta Cats could celebrate Oldsmobile's 1949 Model 88 with its V8 engine using poisonous tetraethyl lead in the gasoline to master its enhanced compression ratio, only to be had with a Hydramatic automatic transmission, considered the fastest car at the time and "precursor of the muscle cars of the late 1960s." General Motors gave Brenston a Rocket 88, even if his idea was borrowed ("stolen," Paul Grushkin claimed in his nostalgic pop music history) from Jimmy Liggins's 1949 "Cadillac Boogie," which on its turn goes back to Robert Johnson's "Terraplane Blues" from 1936 that also celebrates a car, the Hudson Terraplane. The Cadillacs "turned to General Motors for permission to bask in their glory of the name, and other groups had to contend themselves with the names of particular models: the Fleetwoods, the Eldorados, the Sevilles." It was easy harvesting, playing mostly on the temporal (high speed and power) and the (erotic) conquest aspects of the car adventure, from Little Richard ("Got me a date and I won't be late / Picked her up in my 88") to Buddy Holly's "Not Fade Away ("My love is bigger than a Cadillac," which must be very big indeed).[12]

There was something new in the postwar mobility culture, however: an indulging in over-conspicuous consumption, represented by "white trash working-class male" former truck driver Elvis Presley's generosity, who spent $140,000 one day in 1975 to buy fourteen Cadillacs for his friends, family, and a total stranger (bank teller Minnie Person) who happened to be present. In this, rock and roll followed mainstream automotive culture, in which GM cleverly marketed Cadillac as the car a man (mostly an new middle-class small entrepreneur but also the parvenu gangster) had "earned" and as such was an expression of desire and hope, so GM's advertisements often placed in magazines of which the reader ("the man on his way up") could not yet afford the car. Whereas the prewar Cadillac had been four times as expensive as the average American car, it was only 70 percent more expensive in the 1950s. The car as "success symbol" was positioned in the status hierarchy without the help of motivation research, not too far above the potential customers' heads: "Tiptoe, we say, and you can reach us!"

Equipped with "juggernaut" V12 or V16 engines and weighing 2.5 ton, the customer was supposed to "relax. *You don't have to prove a thing*," but should questions be asked, the engine with its exuberant power "was put there for safety," of course. Cadillac's top management followed a conscious strategy of "trickle-down": every man just 'below' an owner should crave to get one. The trick worked: according to *Fortune*'s annual survey, 45 percent of its readers wished to buy one; in 1953, this was 61 percent. Rock 'n' roll fans were impressed by Hank Williams's death on the back seat of his "eggshell blue" Cadillac convertible during a three-day road trip on his way to a gig in Canton, Ohio, driven by a seventeen-year-old driver hired from his father's taxicab company.[13] Cadillac was not the only high-performance car. The first postwar "muscle car," the one that triggered the "horsepower race" between the Big Three, was the 1949 Oldsmobile Rocket 88, which figured in the eponymous rhythm and blues song by Jackie Brenston and his Delta Cats from 1951, based on "Cadillac Boogie" (1947) by Jimmy Liggins. We owe the "fuzz guitar" (with distorted sound from the amplifier) to the car as well: legend has it that an amplifier was damaged during a car trip from Mississippi to Memphis, Tennessee.[14]

***

There were also some mildly dissident sounds such as the Everly Brothers, who, perhaps unintentionally, suggested sex in a drive-in theater in "Wake Up Little Susie," or songs about car accidents, such as Mark Dinning's 1960 "too morbid" (in the judgment of UK radio officials) "Teen Angel." But most of the performers by far were as eager as their audience to get motorized, in a Cold War atmosphere. The Dictators said it for all to hear in "Cars and Girls": "The fastest car and a movie star are my only goals in life / It's the hippest scene, the American dream, and for that I'll always fight." Cartoons (including Ed Roth's T-shirts with pictures of monster mice in cars) and movies formed a part of this multimedia bacchanal: at the end of the movie *Rod Rumble* (1957), the hero and his conquest are, according to the film distributor's synopsis, "riding into the smog in his rod." So much for environmental consciousness in the early rock culture!

Several performers were hot-rodders themselves (just like the earliest autopoetic novel writers fifty years before were car pioneers), such as Dick Dale, "hot rodder, and guitar picker combined," with his "nitro" hit (its title referring to the fuel additive to enhance the car's performance), British Jeff Beck, Americans Brian Setzer (and his collection of vintage cars) and Billy Gibbons (who published a book on "his love of cars and guitars" in 2011), or Charlie Ryan, who described his album *Hot Rod* (1961) as follows: "This album has a 3/4 cam, two four-barrel carbs, a hot ignition, a 270 block, 456 rear end, and twin straight stacks. It's not music 'to relax to' [but] music that will have you hanging onto your chair [*sic*] at every screeching two wheel turn." One of the album's songs, "Hot Rod Race," tells us, "We were ripping along like white folks might," to whom he explains: "We had twin pipes and a Columbia butt, / You people may think that I'm in a rut / But to you folks who don't dig the jive / That's two carburettors and an overdrive." The album also contains sound effects: "engine knocking, horns squawking, fenders clicking against guardrail posts, and, most important, the culminating police siren." The Monkeys had their own Monkeemobile (1966), a Pontiac customized by a fledgling Californian car customizing industry. All in all, the number of "car songs" peaked at 1,500 in the first half of the 1960s. Songs by female performers were no less car-centered, such as Joni Mitchell's unreleased 1967 song "Born to Take the Highway" ("I was born to take the highway, I was born to chase a dream") and "All I Want" (1970), but like in the realm of literature, their emergence as text producers (using the car as a metaphor for "escape from male control") had to wait until the next period (and will thus be the subject of a later study).[15]

***

The West Coast's "schlock rock" (as it was condescendingly called by UK youth preparing their musical "invasion" into the United States, a paragon of what we called 'cultural appropriation') celebrated surf, hot-rodding, and car talk. In the East, an unlikely mix was in the making: while in New York, a "counterculture was developing by the mid-1950s, particularly in the Village, centered on modern jazz, abstract art, and the Beat writers," folk developed into folk-rock, which was perhaps a bit more acceptable to the middle-class hegemonic culture than the poetry of the urban nihilists. As local folk hero Dave Van Ronk observed: "The real Beats liked cool jazz, bebop, and hard drugs, and the folkniks would sit around on the floor and sing songs of the oppressed masses." The two subcultures were two different expressions of a countercultural sentiment, one rooted in leftist prewar party politics, the other expressing postwar disillusion and fear for the 'bomb,' and both, in Susan Sontag's analysis, a reaction against the "national psychosis" of "the unquenchable American moralism and the American faith in violence." In the eyes of the baby boomers' parents, folk functioned as a rescue of middle-class culture, but for the record companies (in the United States, losing an annual 10 percent of their business during the 1950s), rock and roll was much more attractive.

Technologically, the takeover of the youth culture by rock was supported by the "unbreakable vinyl 45-rpm record, the flood of transistor radios from Japan, the sudden appearance of many small, independent record companies, and the increase in local AM radio stations."[16] Soon, an unbelievable variety of styles and subcultures proliferated, accompanied by a no less fragmented mobility culture. Folk fueled the civil rights movement ("most often considered a southern and primarily rural struggle for desegregation and political enfranchisement"), which culminated in the "folk craze" of 1963–1964: the March on Washington, with Martin Luther King Jr.'s famous "I Have a Dream" speech, was supported by John Baez; Bob Dylan; Peter, Paul and Mary; Harry Belafonte; and Mahalia Jackson singing "We Shall Overcome" and "Blowin' in the Wind." In contrast, rock made inroads among the baby boomers. Toward the end of the period covered by this chapter, the global youth movement (someone once calculated there were student protests in fifty-six countries) became "split down the middle, … between people who became very hippy and people who became very political."[17]

The dichotomy between 'nihilists' and 'activists,' often used by historians to get a grip on the confusing variety of ideologies, lifestyles, and attitudes, is historically not very helpful, however. Dave Van Ronk, the Greenwich Village "Mayor of MacDougal Street" (whom the Coen brothers made into a protagonist in *Inside Llewyn Davis*, 2013), describes in his memoirs how he became a politically active anarchist with a disgust for the 'Stalinists' of the political folk movement but at the same time did not like to perform 'political' songs and instead opted for the blues of the Southern blacks, claiming this on itself was a political act, as the problems he experienced with 'normal' Americans when traveling through the country testified. Not in the possession of a driver's license, he describes how he hitchhiked the nine hundred miles from New York to Chicago only to follow up on a promise by a fellow folksinger to promote his demo. "Why didn't I just pick up the phone and call Grossman [the person in Chicago crucial in getting his songs on record]? And why hitchhike? I had enough money left for a bus or even a train. (It would never have occurred to me to fly out there; I had never been on a plane in my life)." He opted against the telephone because of his "firm conviction that all telephones were tapped." And he hitchhiked because

> hitchhiking was the way we traveled. We had all read Kerouac, after all. Money would be saved for food and drink … The main problem was sleep … There were some rest stops on the recently completed Ohio Turnpike, but if the cops caught you sleeping, they would roust you, and when they found that you had no car, they would run you in. You could get thirty days for vagrancy, so it was a good idea to stay awake.

Indeed, being in a car (and staying awake on the road), the hoboes before him had found out, was a guarantee against the accusation of vagrancy. Passengering as hitchhiker was the new mass-based form of youth mobility, preferably undertaken as a trip in more than one sense: when a trucker gives him a ride, "I gave him a couple of Dexies and took a couple myself, just to be sociable, and before we knew it we were pushing that semi 85 miles an hour down the Pennsy Turnpike, babbling at each other like happy lunatics," the same lunatics the FBI wanted American citizens to be protected against when it started its campaign against the danger of picking up hitchhikers (notice also that falling asleep in a rest stop was riskier than racing along the turnpike). Arrived in Chicago, Van Ronk "took a bus to the Loop and taxied from there to the [place where Grossman was to be found]." The entire trip took him twenty-four hours.[18]

Van Ronk and his fellow folksingers "wanted to distance themselves from the whole beatnik craze," which had turned the Village into a tourist attraction. Beat, a term from street slang, referred to a state one was in: "exhausted, poor and homeless," not the best base for car ownership. But beat icon Jack Kerouac gave the term an extra twist when he described his West Coast friend Neal Cassady as "beatific—short for beatific vision, you know, the highest vision you can get. A shortcut is via marijuana." A later commentator described this experience as "related to spiritual illumination, to an epiphany; to seeing the face of God." This beat student also characterized the subculture as a "reaction to the conservatism of '50s America ... through various radical actions: drug use, petty crime, sexual experimentation, religious exploration and travelling." This succession of 'radical actions' hides the reason we dwell on this for so long: apparently, they are all, in a way, 'adventurous experiences.'

It seems as if 'adventure,' shaped in the interior of the car half a century ago and still celebrated after the war in the hot rod and drag racing music, not only expanded and fragmented into all kinds of practices (such as hitchhiking) but also, in the process (and through it), got diluted, deemphasized. In this sense, the beats were an avant-garde *away* from the automotive adventure *as a driver experience* as we have known it before the war. Next to this transcendent desire, *emotionality* was part of the new urban adventurousness of the beatniks. "If a rational civilization could produce world war, the death camps, weapons of universal destruction," James Atlas wrote in his foreword to beat icon John Holmes's novel *Go*, "why not cultivate the irrational?" According to Norman Mailer in his controversial "The White Negro" (1959), "in such places as Greenwich Village, a ménage-à-trois was completed—the bohemian and the juvenile delinquent came face-to-face with the Negro, and the hipster was a fact of American life." These were "a new breed of adventurers, urban adventurers who drifted out at night looking for action with a black man's code to fit their facts."[19]

The hipster, in sociologist Mark Greif's analysis, is "the subcultural type generated by neoliberalism ... Hipster values exalt political reaction, masquerading as rebellion ... And hipster anti-authoritarianism bespeaks a ruse by which middle-class young can forgive themselves for abandoning the claims of counterculture ... while retaining the coolness of subculture." It is, in Jim McGuigan's terms, "cool capitalism," "the contemporary spirit of capitalist production and consumption that absorbs rebellion and neutralizes opposition, based no longer on Protestant ascetism, but rather on an ethics of narcissism, ironic detachment, and hedonism." The core of the New York beats (Allen Ginsberg, William S. Burroughs, Jack Kerouac) expressed their 'nihilism' in varied mobile ways: Ginsberg and Burroughs traveled abroad (South America, Mexico, India, Morocco, Japan, Europe), while Kerouac stayed within the country and chose emphatically for the car, as his patriotic and highly successful *On the Road* testifies. But comparing the beats' mobility to the nineteenth-century flaneur is a step too far: it reduces their movements to urban pedestrianism, despite the movie theorists who keep insisting on this metaphor.[20] Yet, English literature scholar John Lennon argues Kerouac's relation to the car was ambivalent (which is true) and that he in fact "more wistful[ly] long[ed] for the train" (which is true only if we reduce mobility history to transport history). As we will see, Kerouac's ambivalence was related to the fragmentation of the car culture, and his relation to the train was mostly nostalgic, fed by the same feelings he developed toward the hobo: the "romanticization of marginality." But the transcendental desire runs foul, in the end: "every trip that [Kerouac] takes in *On the Road* begins with excitement and enthusiasm filled with innumerable possibilities (a type of rebirth), all his trips end with intense sadness and a slinking back to a place he recognizes and knows—his home (a type of death)."[21]

***

Another characteristic of beats was their "sense of being outside of the vast bulk of American society," their "feeling of otherness" resulting in a rejection of its conventions, including the partitioning in artistic disciplines and styles. Beat artists practiced poetry as much as painting, music, and theater: they were "willing to experiment across media." John Holmes described the beats' world as "a world of dingy backstairs 'pads,' Times Square cafeterias, bebop joints, night-long wanderings, meetings on street corners, hitchhiking, a myriad of 'hip' bars all over the city, and the streets themselves." Adventure, diluted over so many urban practices, had to be reconstituted, as a personal piece of art. The beats deployed a similar 'bricolage' of mobile means and media. Their 'trips' were as much 'driven' by gasoline as they were by Benzedrine (amphetamine in the form of a bronchial inhaler) and science fiction magazines. The road network's anonymity also provided protection against the authorities, as in Kerouac's *On the Road* after the protagonists have stolen a police detective's car: "We ... stumbled off toward the protective road where nobody would know us."

Nor was beat an ideological or political monolith: while Kerouac soon would become the icon of the 'apolitical' counterculture, Burroughs opposed the "Beat/hip axis," who "want[s] to transform the world by love and non-violence." "This thinking is fostered by the establishment, they like nothing better than love and non-violence." Burroughs's opinions reveal the problem of calling the beatniks nihilists: "There should be more riots and more violence. Young people in the West have been lied to, sold out and betrayed. Best thing they can do is take the place apart before they are destroyed in a nuclear war." As Ginsberg formulated in one of his poems, "go fuck yourself with your atom bomb." In short, "the Beat's embrace of the marginal figure" encompassed, in the words of black beat poet LeRoi Jones, "Selby's hoodlums, Rechy's homosexuals, Burroughs's addicts, Kerouac's mobile young voyeurs, my own Negroes, [who] are literally not included in the mainstream of American life ... They are Americans no character in a John Updike novel would be happy to meet. [They] are ... the last romantics of our age."[22]

***

An explicit part of the beat style was travel, preferably in a car. As we will see, Kerouac's romantic rediscovery of an 'authentic' America was based on the figure of Dean Moriarty, representing Neal Cassady, whose "almost superhuman talent for long-distance driving" constituted the iconic, and idealized, mobility side of the beat generation. As we argued in the introduction, mobility encompasses all movements, material and virtual, bodily and technically, including its immobilities. Indeed, it encompasses all activities, but then seen from a transformative perspective. From this perspective, the beats were the epitome of change as normalcy, as routine. Most of this mobility was on foot, in an urban context, as always, but the 'vehicle' comes second. And yet, this subculture should not be described in terms of 'mobilities' (plural) because it is a state, a condition, like Bauman's 'fluidity,' in which moving and being are intertwined. Part of this fluidity was communication, which included the letters Neal wrote to Ginsberg and Kerouac, expressing his frustration about his inability to literary expression, but it also included the top speed with which Kerouac wrote the manuscript of *On the Road*, as well as the 'dynamics' of the jazz and folk music they were fascinated by. It is this transgression that from time to time ushered into transcendence, supported by the Benzedrine and the marijuana, which seems to be the very core of 'beat mobility.'

Cultural studies scholar Katie Mills, who wrote the best analysis of beat mobility so far, showed how Kerouac created a mobility universe quite different from what had been done before him, such as Henry Miller's *The Air-Conditioned Nightmare* (1945), John Steinbeck's *The Wayward Bus* (1947), or the "*noir film*" *The Hitch-Hiker* (1953) by Ida Lupino. Kerouac wanted to overcome the "sad imagery" of (pre)war road narratives, in which "their adventure ... was persecuting them," instead of they themselves creating the adventure in the first place. Beat poet Allen Ginsberg published a poetry bundle titled *The Gates of Wrath: 1947–1952*, which explicitly referred to Steinbeck's collective, Depression-style tale of the poor, white, and extended Joad family. He also wrote the poem "The Green Automobile" (1953–1954), dedicated to Cassady: "If I had a Green Automobile / I'd go find my old companion / in his house on the Western ocean. / Ha! Ha! Ha! Ha! Ha!" Mills analyzed what she called "'intermediary' possibilities created when one artistic medium ... bent in the direction of another medium," a phenomenon we called 'translation' in the introduction. Within these interstices, Mills saw the beats, especially Kerouac, finding "mysteries," which "reveal ... [his] yearning for transsubstantiation."[23]

There is a relation here with Roland Barthes's and Henri Lefebvre's characterizations of the car as "magic" (Barthes: "parfaitement magique"), which, again (just like Barthes's other remark about the car as a cathedral), makes these into *historical* qualifications rather than absolute ones, as we argued in the introduction. In my analysis, the magic is in and through the media themselves (not in between them): they apparently afford a route to God, transcendence. No dark uncertainty here, but bright divinity. Perhaps not even transcendence anymore, but the reverse: the automobile driver/rider becomes a "vessel of the divine" and "receives" an epiphany. One of the earliest post–World War II writers who grasped the media character of the car and its cyborgian traits while driving (instead of as a static cathedral, like Barthes would claim) was the German publicist in "philosophical-aesthetic theorizing" Max Bense, who in 1970 described driving as a practice "during which the car becomes me and I become the car," so much so that "I and the car are fusing ever more into a near-surreal automaton"; the car is a contraption, he added, that "processes information and generates communication."[24]

To give an example of this quasi-unhistorical 'mobility condition': Kerouac was fascinated by Cassady's unmediated, 'spontaneous' writing style, which the latter made into one of the very characteristics of avant-garde art: "Jan. 12—Bought a 1941 Packard club coupe," Cassady wrote to Kerouac in one of his famous letters,

> blue, spotlight, heater, radio, overdrive, seat covers, 6 cylinder. 80 top speed. Paid $1195 for it, $100 down, $75 a month. Raced 14,000 miles in 85 days—gave it back ... got so saturated with grief would tear across busy blvd.

intersections at 50, right thru the stop sign—hoping to get hit ... drove in a ditch & lay in back seat—tried to cry—couldn't—disgusting.

March 1st—Drove to Denver—2894 miles in 33 hrs no sleep—stuck on continental divide 7 hrs at 8' below zero—no anti-freeze in damn radiator—no [tire] chains-tried to freeze myself—got too cold & finally stopped a bus & got pushed.

March 5th—returned to Frisco, made it in 36 hrs thru Wyo. & Utah—picked up young girl—caught crabs from her."

Now, even someone who could not construct a proper sentence could become a 'writer.' According to Cassady students David Sandison and Graham Vickers, like in the folk music and the British rock, the "force" of Cassady's letters lay not in their content but in "the energy and imaginative dislocation of its style," but mentioning the distance and time needed for the car driver to cover it was of course nothing new but rather a cliché. It is less well known, however, that an earlier version of *On the Road* played with a similar grammatical fragmentation, but Mills argued convincingly that Kerouac's breakthrough was only possible when he, in his fifth version, compromised with the hegemonic narrative conventions, criticizing it at the same time through his development of 'spontaneous writing.' The same energy and imaginative dislocation governed Cassady's driving style, a nice example of 'affinity' (see the introduction).[25]

With a history of youthful car theft and juvenile penitentiary institutions, and his father an alcoholic bum, Cassady bought his first car in 1948, "a twenty-year-old Chevrolet with its original engine, paint job, and upholstery," in which he tried to sell encyclopedias. But as soon as he managed to 'organize' some money, he changed to a "shiny new Hudson saloon car" (unfit, as one of the book's commentators asserts, for planned obsolescence and unchallenged in stock car races during the early 1950s), using up "pretty well all of [his and his wife Cathy's] precious funds." From Cassady's and his friends' perspective, the 'trip' acquired a special meaning; it was a material as well as a virtual voyage, by car and by 'speed,' supported by sex and music, in that order. Overall, he used nineteen cars in two years, not much less than the number he had stolen and taken for joyrides in when he was an adolescent.[26] Cassady was a car addict, indeed, perhaps the first (known) personification of the carnivalesque car adventure, of the over-the-top adventure machine.

***

The same energy also governed the San Francisco Renaissance, the Western equivalent of the New York beat subculture. There, poet Lawrence Ferlinghetti opened a bookstore in 1953, where Ginsberg read his famous poem "Howl" in 1955 (subsequently seized by American authorities on an obscenity charge: "we went out whoring through Colorado in myriad stolen night-cars") and where Eastern and Californian beats (doing "poetry performance and, later, 'happenings'") met with folk and rock musicians. Groups like the Grateful Dead, Jefferson Airplane, Country Joe and the Fish, the Mamas and the Papas, the Lovin' Spoonful, and the Animals started writing songs "about personal experiences … just as the blues singers did for years" in their "'soundtrack' of the Great Migration" recorded since the 1910s, a "celebration of mobility." Anthropologist Ulf Hannerz described how the beats formed a "network" of "interlocking subcultures" characterized by "openness" ("which contributes so significantly to the vitality of urban cultures also in a way makes them more fragmented and vulnerable") and a desire for "diversity."[27] Indeed, like hitchhiking, the mobility of the beat subcultures has a clear network character: it behaves like spiders in a web, monads virtually connected by a common desire.

The movement was so pervasive that avant-garde classical music was influenced by it, and vice versa. In John Lennon and Yoko Ono's "Revolution 9," the final chords of Sibelius's Seventh Symphony are reproduced (according to reviewer Tim Page of *The Selected Letters of John Cage*, it is "pure Cage"), while members of the Grateful Dead and Jefferson Airplane attended classes of Karlheinz Stockhausen. Frank Zappa's love for Edgar Varèse is well documented, but it is less well known that the Velvet Underground took over La Monte Young's "drone aesthetics" and that David Bowie and Brian Eno (Roxy Music) visited concerts by minimalists like Steve Reich and Philip Glass who, like several of their colleagues, "evoke the experience of driving in a car across empty desert, the layered repetitions in the music mirroring the changes that the eye perceives—road signs flashing by, a mountain range shifting on the horizon, a pedal point of asphalt underneath," in short: 'affinity' between music production and the production of the trip, as we have defined this for an earlier phase of mobility history.

Glass and rock composer David Byrne of the Talking Heads cooperated in a theatrical production, while the Velvet Underground "closed the gap between rock and avant-garde" as they "specialized in art happenings and underground-film screenings," supported by Andy Warhol, who integrated them in his multimedia events, assisted by Nico, the singer recruited right from Warhol's Factory.[28] In other words, and again: the beat experience was an orgy of transmedial experimentation, including the automobile medium itself. By the end of the 1950s, the beat poets got pushed away by the singers on the New York countercultural stages and from bars and music cellars. Basically, the latter were "traveling folksingers" and as such formed a part of what one could call "folk mobility," which included the transfer of songs from one singer to the other, a process described by Van Ronk as evolutionary, with little personal (and often unconscious) changes made at every transfer. One of these folk singers was Bob Dylan, who, through his 'hobo' style of performing (listen to "From a Buick 6" on his 1971 album *Highway 61 Revisited*), represented folk mobility on stage. Like a true hobo, Dylan chose walking rather than car driving as a metaphor in "Blowin' in the Wind," asking the primary question, "How many roads must a man walk down?"

Female folksingers played a special role in this evolutionary transfer process: while "the boys were intentionally roughing up their voices," the girls tried "to sound prettier and prettier and more and more virginal," unconsciously mimicking an older folk style, which "gave them a kind of crossover appeal to the people who were listening to Belafonte and the old singers, and to the clean-cut college group."[29] It was in this culture that Graham Nash landed from the United Kingdom, after he had abandoned the Hollies. During the following years, he would become very successful as a member of Crosby, Stills, Nash and Young: "We were constantly writing ... After 'On a Carousel,' it felt like we were on an express train." The song brought them a check of $250,000, enabling Nash to buy his first car, a Rolls-Royce Silver Cloud, secondhand. Thus, he joined Sam Cooke and Miles Davis in their Ferraris, Aretha Franklin in her pink Cadillac (similar to the one Elvis Presley bought back in 1955), and later, Prince in his red Corvette.

Nash traveled to Morocco, to experience what he had read about in the works of Ginsberg and Burroughs, and wrote "Marrakesh Express ... It was an artistic breakthrough, more mature. Not about love, but about expanding our world. It was impressionistic, lots of black-and-white images. The characters were adult. It focused on travel to exotic, undiscovered places—and it was about dope," and it became an instant hit. They had transformed from a pop to a rock band, indulging in the well-known trio of sex, drugs, and rock and roll, spiced with large doses of esoterism and science fiction: "It was a hippie heaven," including traveling in former Canadian folksinger Dave Crosby's Volkswagen van. "We were as tight as our harmonies. And we were loose—man, were we loose." Despite the extravagance, they knew how to enjoy the simple things of life. Nash liked Canadian singer-songwriter Joni Mitchell: "She really liked men. She liked to repair cars, play guitar, and hang out with the guys."[30]

***

Mobility entered the 1960s youth culture in another form, that of the motor bus, such as in the Beatles film *Magical Mystery Tour* (1967), an "acid road film" (Mills) that in its "visionary chaos" (Wolfe) was conceived "like an abstract painting ... We did it," as Bob Neaverson in his analysis of the Beatles movies writes, "as a series of disconnected, unconnected events."

And it flopped on mainstream television. This film was inspired by a bus tour organized by Ken Kesey, author of *One Flew Over the Cuckoo's Nest* (1962), and his Merry Pranksters, located at his La Honda estate near Palo Alto. The idea was to make a road trip to the 1964 New York World's Fair. Neal Cassady (Sir Speed Limit) drove the 1939 International Harvester school bus, embellished by a "psychedelic paint job" and equipped with a movie camera and external microphones "to capture the sounds of the outraged citizenry." "There was going to be no goddamn sound on that whole trip," writer Tom Wolfe (with his "black shiny FBI shoes") claimed in his satire on the eleven-day bus trip in *The Electric Kool-Aid Acid Test*, "outside the bus, inside the bus, or inside your own freaking larynx, that you couldn't tune in on and rap off of."[31]

Wolfe's book, a "triumph of 'New Journalism'" managed to "write with an ethnographic intimacy" ("as if he is inside the Pranksters heads") and convey the experience of the "*now*, [being] in the moment," to "re-create the mental atmosphere or subjectivity reality," in Wolfe's own words. In Mills's analysis, Wolfe did what the Merry Pranksters did not manage to do: to record this trip on "the world's first acid film" in which "the U.S. nation [was captured] stream[ing] across the windshield like one of those goddamned Cinemascope landscape cameras that winds up your optic nerves like the rubber band in a toy plane." "The first psychedelic film to hit the mass market in 1967" was Roger Corman's *The Trip*, followed a year later by Bob Rafelson's *Head*. But the Pranksters movie, *Intrepid Traveler and His Merry Band of Pranksters Look for a Kool Place*, was placed only online in 1998, after Kesey had spent more than $100,000 to synchronize sound and image, recorded at different speeds. The film shows not only how the Pranksters were "unable or unwilling" to tell their own story (thus making Wolfe's book into a journalistic version of subaltern mobility studies) but also Cassady "rap[ping] out novels and tape record[ing] them [which] transformed the Pranksters' experiences into adventures," testifying to Sontag's observations that "a new non-literary culture exists today."[32]

"What we didn't know," one of the participants of Kesey's bus ride said later, "was that the thing we were just barely starting to explore … was the thing Cassady had been doing for years." Not totally, however: one of the bus passengers was Stewart Brand, an initiator of the environment-conscious *Whole Earth Catalogue*, who with his fellow "misfits" formed a countercultural group around the Grateful Dead and later would found the WELL, a computer-based communication network set up by "iconoclasts who had seen the LSD revolution fizzle, the political revolution fail." Network mobility had become mainstream. In the end, Cassady drove his human cargo along a serpentine road from the top of the Blue Ridge Mountains without functioning brakes. And while Kerouac had meanwhile developed into a counterculture icon, Cassady became the tragic clown of the West Coast counterculture. In the end, he died in 1968 (a year before his friend in the East died of liver cirrhosis), walking along a railway track, after spending his last years in Kesey's commune, living in a white Plymouth, "rant[ing] on about racing driver Juan-Manuel Fangio, Pliny the Elder, the Modern Jazz Quartet, and Elizabeth Barrett Browning while hitting riffs that prefigured modern rap: 'there we were coastin' through Houston, or roastin' in Austin if you will, but Proustian-wise, all the authorities agree.'"[33] The diverging life stories of the two beats are also symbolic in another sense: whereas Kerouac evolved into a middle-class icon, Cassady the worker's son was left along the railroad track after the latter had fed the former with his high-speed mobility culture. The alienation of the two beats symbolizes the political class division that would largely determine the development of American life during the coming decades.

***

For Graham Nash, and many others of his generation, the rock festival at the Altamont Speedway on 6 December 1969 marked the end of an era: meant to be the Western version of Woodstock and witnessed by three hundred thousand attendants, Altamont ended in the stabbing of a member of the public by the Hell's Angels, which Rolling Stones band leader Mick Jagger may or may not have seen happening during his performance (in any case, he saw it afterward on film footage), after the Grateful Dead had refused to play because of the atmosphere of mounting violence.[34] For many others, the end of the 1960s (also marked by the drug-induced deaths of Jimi Hendrix [or was it vomit?] and Janis Joplin) marked a watershed and a transfer into a new era characterized by violence and aggression, at the same time "mainstream conservatism began to fall apart." A study from 1975 of the American "modern family" contained a final chapter that drew a somber picture of the future: the "adolescent indifference to the family's identity," a shift "from parents to peer group" (a phenomenon "much more advanced in Europe than in the United States"), the "new instability in the life of the couple" with "skyrocketing divorce rates" created a "postmodern family" with children "escaping with increasing frequency into a subculture that is not so much in opposition to the dominant culture as independent of it." [35] According to Arthur Marwick, who dedicated a monumental (and controversial) study to the 'long 1960s' (1958–1974), "there was no 'collapse,' but the fine balance upon which the unique civilization of the sixties was based began to falter in the early seventies."

This lost "precarious balance between liberation and sensibility," according to Marwick, resulted in a wave of porn, a violent turn of both white and black activism such as the Weathermen (who "smashed up cars and business property") and the Black Panthers, most of this violence provoked by a violent police (killing protesting students at Kent State University) and the state, and its aggression deployed for the world to see in Vietnam. There is also reason to believe a more gendered history of the '60s (when there were ninety million Americans younger than twenty-five years, nearly half the population) would result in some important corrections on the myth of the "Summer of Love," proposed to be renamed into "Summer of Rape" by historian Gerard DeGroot, and described by a flabbergasted contemporary Joan Didion who lamented, "we had somehow neglected to tell these children the rules of the game we happened to be playing; maybe we had stopped believing in the rules themselves." "While hippies were dropping out, minority and lower-class youth struggled in," Russell Duncan concluded in his analysis of the Summer of Love, but sociologist Barbara Ehrenreich argued, and rightly so, "hippie women were far more dangerous to the prevailing culture than were those in [the radical student movement] SDS whose familiar kinds of protest were at least 'comprehensible.' Countercultural women exhibited a liberating cultural feminism in the rebellion of running away, refusal to conform to rules of protest, fashion, hair, sex, and more," the latter soon also including mobility, as we will see. The result, once again, was "an incredible diversity of lifestyles."[36]

***

Between 1955 and 1975, the United States lost fifty thousand military personnel in Vietnam (while the war severely disabled seventy-five thousand), but Vietnamese losses probably reached two million. Between 1964 and 1973, a spate of publications on American violence (such as *America the Violent* and *The Violent Women*) appeared, an extension of an interest from sociologists and others in "juvenile delinquency" in the 1950s. According to W. M. Frohock (*The Novel of Violence in America*, 1950), violence was "epidemic" in the American novel. Like transcendence, the violent aspects of the car adventure expanded to and diluted over other practices as well. For Marwick, "one of the most significant achievements of society in the sixties was the bringing of the basic amenities of civilized living to the vast majority of people. The next biggest change is in regard to 'personal transport': for good or for ill a major element in the growth of private freedom in the sixties was the private motor vehicle."[37] We will later on nuance Marwick's easy conclusions, which identify the 1960s with its material substrate (let alone equals the car to freedom), but it cannot be denied that the new generation of folk and rock singers did not express any reservation toward the car, and, indeed, that an element of 'youthful' emancipatory affordance was hidden in its 'script,' a power blossoming up when women and ethnic minorities discovered it, as we will see.

The Rock of European Youth Mobility: Recasting the Middle-Class Subject

When rock moved back to Europe, the images of a 'groovy' car culture moved with it, in the process reducing the vehicle to a two-wheeler. The Italian scooter Vespa, for instance, apart from borrowing from the animal kingdom's flexible but swarm-like mobility (*vespa* means 'wasp'), became the vehicle of choice of the British mod (a term derived from 'modern jazz'), the "lower-class dandy," the British white equivalent of the American zoot suiter. His spare time was partially dedicated to polishing his scooter, buying records (and Drinamyl pills), pressing his trousers, and washing his hair. The mods preferred customized scooters, with "foxtails, pennants, mascots, chromium, horns, extra lights and mirrors, whip aerials, fur trim and leopard-skin seats." They modified this "formerly ultra-respectable means of transport … into a weapon and a symbol of solidarity" (as became clear during their "scooter-charge" on Buckingham Palace in November 1966). In their conspicuous behavior, however, they "learned to make their criticism obliquely, having learned by experience (at school and work) to avoid direct confrontations where age, experience, economic and civil power would inevitably have told against them. The style they created, therefore, constituted a parody on the consumer society."

As "the first all-British White Negro of Mailer's essay," they differed very much from "the greasy Brylcreemed look of the Teddy Boy" and found the Beatles "too melodic and too respectable," despite the latter's change of name from the Beetles after a meeting between John Lennon and beat poet Royston Ellis. They were able to cross class boundaries "mix[ing] in middle- and upper-class circles where obvious Teds would be excluded." They were apparently also able to "masculinize" a vehicle that had been marketed in Italy as typically feminine, among others. This shows that artifacts do not have a 'script' but can function as empty containers that may be 'filled' with, afford, different practices. Teds, on the contrary, were "uncompromisingly proletarian and xenophobic." The mods on their turn triggered the emergence of "the rockers, in leather jackets, not smart suits, on powerful motorbikes, not scooters, and still dancing rock'n'roll and the twist." The Who, in their rock opera *Quadrophenia* (1973), which can be experienced as "Pete Townshend's artistic autobiography," portrays Jimmy (a clear mod) as a "man who drives a local bus / I take miners to work."[38]

In many industrialized European countries, similar developments can be observed. In the Netherlands, working-class youth in The Hague from Indonesian descent preferred driving an Austrian Puch moped. The Puch (1952) was the first moped conceived as a motorcycle "with its steel pressed frame, fan-boosted engine cooling, 2-speed handlebar-shifted gearbox and an elaborate electrical system." They introduced American rock culture in this city and stripped their Puchs of all luxury items. When college kids took over their culture (leading to a share of 10 percent around 1965 for the Puch in the Dutch moped market), these kids substituted the normal steer for an extravagant, high steer, and wore a knitted shawl as long as physically possible. But the best accessory was a Puch girl, preferably with a Françoise Hardy look (after the French singer with elongated bob hair). One of the Puch owners, interviewed much later, remembered: "One drove about 250 kilometres per week, only within the city, mostly during the weekend, but also at night. You just drove, that was the culture. Through the entire city, just for the heck of it, and to check whether there was something going on somewhere, looking at other Puchs, at chicks, of course ... and nearly exclusively in first gear, of course." One did not drive a white Puch; that was for girls. Another remembered: "The Puch brought us into the LPs we played." Many of the Puch youth took the little engine apart just for the heck of it, cleaning the piston, replacing the piston rings. "I don't remember why [we did this]. It was a feeling."[39] The ultimate l'art pour l'art of the functional adventure. Girls chose the French Solex, and when this went out of fashion because it acquired an image of an 'old ladies vehicle,' the equally French Mobylette and the many scooters. Girls and Mobylettes are not a fixed relationship, however: Bahar Emgin related, how Turkish "rowdy *mobilet* gangs" later in the century formed their lifestyle "around the image of a [tough] and strong commitment" to the moped, called mobilet after the French brand.[40]

***

As far as this is known, there was no youth car culture in the Netherlands in this phase, such as in Sweden, where a collective working-class youth culture around American gas guzzlers emerged (the cars adorned with the same foxtails and other proletarian paraphernalia as the mods' scooters), who displayed, especially during weekends, a provocative suggestion of free sex and an ostentatious, very loud indifference toward 'society.' In Finland, a similar subculture among young working-class men seems to have emerged around "old cars." Likewise, a nearly forgotten ostentatious and very loud subculture of Italian working-class *teppisti* (hooligans) practiced subversive activities such as "driving without a license, speeding, and road accidents without casualties," often in or on stolen cars, motorcycles, or scooters. All men, and all skilled workers, they refused to "defer satisfaction of a desire" (as the historian who rediscovered them concluded) and "stole for the fun of it," as one of them remarked. In the Netherlands, instead, there was a provocative urban culture, especially in Amsterdam (with connections to the beats through poets Robert Jasper Grootveld and Simon Vinkenoog) proposing a free and collective "white bicycle plan" as an alternative to the car.[41]

It was through such urban, anarchist groups that resistance against the car, until then accepted by beats and countercultural youngsters as a matter of course, emerged. By the end of the 1960s, the emergence of 'heavy metal' and hard rock music (started among the working-class youth as "a form of quiet deployment of violence" but later, in the 1990s, crossed over to a middle-class protest culture) heralded the transformation into another era. These developments already point us to one of the characteristics of this postwar youth movement, its seeming classlessness, the result of a unique phenomenon that "middle-class children were deliberately adopting lower-class values—'toughness, excitement, chance-taking, indulgence, "conning," autonomy and hardness'—and were thus making a conscious decision to oppose the values of their parents." If the 1960s resulted in anything new (as a consensus among students of the period seems to be), it was a "changed subjectivity," a recasting of the middle-class subject, a change that would have important repercussions for Western mobility culture in the years to come.[42]

What, then, happened here, exactly, in mobility terms? What happened here was a crucial crossover to another class, through the celebrated conviviality of youth cultures. Of course, there were large differences in musical preferences, but they all 'needed' music in some form or others, as a new way to breathe. Likewise, they used different vehicles, but they all practiced 'youth mobility' as part of an adventurous lifestyle. They were not against the car but wanted to drive another car, deviating from the hegemonic definition of what a car was all about.[43] Or they hitchhiked (as "prisoner[s] of the white lines on the freeway," in Joni Mitchell's words), in surprisingly large numbers, especially in Europe, the fifty million European border-crossing youth meanwhile representing "a significant social and cultural component to European integration" from below, a form of collective transnational adventurous culture of car passengering joined by one million Americans during the 1970s, practicing multimodality if they bought Eurail and Interrail passes. "We were young adventurers," one American remembered in the *New York Times* in 1989.[44] Every time this 'new subject' gets into her car (or "a car," as hitchhiker), they experience a feeling of independence, of public intimacy, of being part of 'modernity,' an experience that started to be exported beyond the West, together with the 'car system.' The question, then, is if and how this lifestyle made it into the mainstream culture, and whether this process influenced the very definition of the automotive adventure. Before we can answer this question, however, we will first have to turn to the hegemonic culture of the immediate post–World War II quarter century and its mobility.

Motorizing the Worker: Fragmentation and Convergence of Western Car Cultures

The immediate postwar years were years of industrial and infrastructural reconstruction for many European countries, although several countries in the European 'periphery' (Iceland, Ireland, Sweden, Spain, Portugal) and one in the middle, Switzerland, were less affected by the devastation of the war. The same applies, of course, to the United States. As James Ballard had witnessed in Shanghai, the United States came out of the war triumphant. In Michael Mann's words, it had "the only major functioning army, with more than half of all the usable productive capacity in the world, and [it emerged] as the banker and creditor to both former allies *and* former enemies." On top of that, the Bretton Woods Agreement of 1944 made the American dollar into the world's foremost currency, forcing, "as the price for international stability, foreign banks [to finance] the takeovers of their own countries' industry" by American multinationals. For instance, by the early 1970s, nearly one-third of US car manufacturers' investments took place abroad. The result was an "uninterrupted, unparalleled, and unprecedented economic expansion boom from the end of the 1961 (Eisenhower) recession to the 1969–70 (Nixon) crash": American families "saw their real incomes grow by a third." At the apex of this development, 1965, one-tenth of the value of all manufacturing shipments were cars and car parts, and by that year, about one-sixth of all Americans worked in the automobile industry or related branches. This America made Western European economies start to grow again, emulating the car exuberance of a country that by one of its leading economic historians, Walt Rostow, was described primarily as a car country.[45]

The 'European Model': Converging Car Ownership between Workers and Middle Class

European countries needed aid from the Marshall Plan (1948–1951) to get started, especially to repair or produce roads and railways, bridges and vehicles, as we will see in the next chapter, where we will deal with transnational road network building. What General George Marshall did not manage to accomplish in prewar, warlord China (see chapter 1) he now could try out in Europe. As a catalyst for the American export industry, this program (led, by the way, by Paul G. Hoffman, former CEO of Studebaker) increased the growth of the European gross industrial product by one-third. In the Netherlands, "the engine started running" in March 1951: between 1948 and 1954, the country received $1.127 billion, in 1949, for instance, representing more than 8 percent of its national income.[46] The

Dutch 'economic miracle' became visible most of all during the decade after 1963, during which real national income tripled and per capita income doubled. European consumption frenzy led some economists (and some historians in their wake) to conclude there were two "roads to prosperity," a Fordist (mass production, standardization, supermarkets, modern marketing) and a "European" consumption model. Consumption historians have described the latter model as "bourgeois" (*bürgerlich*), craft- and individuality-based and more skeptical toward the exuberance of the former, but perhaps it is better to call this model 'German,' as other countries such as the Netherlands, Sweden, France, and Italy tended more to the Fordist model. Indeed, the conclusion of these students is one of convergence called "Americanization," taking place from the 1980s, when Europeans started embracing the American concept of consumption (as an "Americanization from below," after the one from above had failed) as a celebration of the freedom of choice and as "a road to cultural equality." This shift has been described as "one of the most noteworthy phenomena in the recent history of ideas," ideas carried by "a new generation" of "citizen consumers."[47]

The alignment of the "structures" of European and American national industries (the ratio of industry to agriculture and service sector), income (GDP per capita), and consumption (share of durables in total expenses) has been called the "OECD profile," although the historian who observed this convergence also pointed at diverging trends between the United States and Europe in terms of the importance of industrial production (still growing in Europe, diminishing in the US); Japan followed Europe in this respect. It was Japan's increasing car production (with European production staying more or less at a constant level of one-quarter of the world's total) that pushed the American share in world car production back from nearly three-quarters in 1955 to a bit more than one-third by 1973, making 'Europe' into the largest car producer from the end of the 1960s, the decade in which also in Europe the trend toward larger cars began.[48] Ford produced a quarter of its world production in the EEC countries (GM only half that share, but its worldwide sales in absolute numbers exceeded those of Ford by more than 50 percent). America's share of car exports, however, was tiny (2.2 percent in 1960) compared to European countries (one-third in Italy and nearly half in Germany), but the latter exported largely to each other, while the upcoming market of Japan penetrated the United States and other parts of the world. According to behavioral economist George Katona and colleagues, the difference between America and Europe resided in "the perception of and the expectation about personal financial progress which makes for a greater frequency [in the United States] of purchases and plans to new durable goods," including *new* cars: Katona found there was not much difference in the acquisition of *used* cars.[49]

***

At the same time, 'Europe' was no monolith: never were the differences between what soon came to be called a (Northwestern) European 'core' and a 'periphery' as a ring of countries around it, so large as in the post–World War II years: a factor of three to four (Southern and Eastern Europe) to even six (Albania, Romania) in GDP per capita, while big differences between regions within the larger countries existed as well. The core-periphery tensions will become crucial, in the decades to come, to understand the development of Western car culture, even if the opposition between the two should not be seen as a fixed dichotomy. "As the world turns, today's periphery may be tomorrow's center," Hannerz suggested, but he was looking at geopolitics. Locally and regionally (nationally), whereas the core attracts capital flows as well as the flows of people and goods, the periphery is where the 'powerless' reside. And where in the core the "myth of the middle class" was taking shape in these years (so, not only the emergence of new middle-class culture but also the idée fixe that the white working class dissolved into the white middle class), the periphery's mobility culture should be the object of a 'subaltern study,' because it became the locus not only of "a disgruntled working class composed of ethnic minorities" (as the 'myth' suggested) but also of the white working class, made 'invisible' by postwar modernization. In the core, urbanization took place much faster (there, two-thirds of the population lived in cities by 1950, with large consequences for mobility, not yet fully investigated), and education and living standards were much more developed. In the periphery, 60 percent of the population worked in agriculture; analphabetism in Italy was 14 percent and in Portugal a staggering 44 percent. But whether in the East, the South, or the North, annual growth rates were unprecedentedly high (4 to 5 percent). What was new compared to earlier phases of strong growth was that also the periphery benefited, although the remaining differences were large enough to trigger large migratory flows of workers from the South to the North.

This enormous mobility on itself is a part of the explanation for the economic miracle that made Europe into an industrial society: by 1970, about eighty-three million people worked in industry (sixty-one million in 1950), against eighty million in the service sector (fifty-four million in 1950) and forty-one million in agriculture (sixty-six million in 1950). In other words, Europe immediately after the war was still a largely agrarian society, and the economic boom made it into an industrial society, much more than the United States and Japan, where the service sector had taken the lead. The enormous labor demand brought women into the workforce, leading to an unprecedented rise in income, both on a personal level and for the state. Tax revenues, indeed, grew twentyfold in Scandinavian countries and Austria; tenfold in France, Italy, and Germany; and fivefold in most other countries, which became the basis for building the infrastructures of a welfare state, education, health, the military, and transport and communication infrastructures. This resulted in a tighter cooperation between the countries, accelerated since the founding of the EEC in 1957. In 1974, the six founding nations (Belgium, France, Germany, Italy, Luxemburg, Netherlands) were expanded with three others (Denmark, Ireland, UK), and they decided to build a community based on four "basic freedoms of … mobility of goods, capital, people and services," in stages, at a moment when the United States was weakened by its Vietnam War. As a result of this, the differences between the core and the periphery started to diminish during the 1960s: the share of industrial production increased (to 41 percent in Southern Europe and 47 percent in Eastern Europe, although in Ireland and Portugal it remained below 10 percent), exports increased, as well as urbanization, real income, and consumption, including car ownership, especially in two 'peripheral' countries, Italy and Finland. In Eastern Europe, Czechoslovakia, leading in that area's car density in 1950, was overtaken by Poland, especially the German Democratic Republic (GDR), even if the middle classes were "marginalized and oppressed."

Most European countries lost their colonies in this period, even Portugal, as late as the early 1970s. Although the Cold War split the continent in two 'blocks,' they both witnessed similar growth rates, but their economic planning, their labor force (more women working in the East), and their health, education, and housing systems differed considerably. American tourists were lured to West Berlin, "the International City Behind the Iron Curtain," to gaze at East Berlin that "looks as if it lies in Asia." In the West, the Portuguese and Spanish dictatorships got company in 1967 from Greek colonels. Hartmut Kaelble, from whose overview of European history most of these trends are taken, concluded the postwar period until the early 1970s was "not a time of European convergence, but [resulted in] a divided and multifaceted continent."[50] To a certain extent, the "convergence in the sharing of progress" (*Angleichung im Fortschritt*), monitored in two famous surveys in 1956–1957 and 1963–1964 organized by the EEC and its predecessor (the European Coal and Steel Community), increased, but cars and TV sets lagged behind, especially in rural households, as the surveyors signaled in their final report, and they also pointed to Italy as the poorest country, compared to the richest, Luxemburg and the Netherlands. And although income differences diminished between the classes, a new cleft emerged vis-à-vis the immigrants, parts of which would later develop into a new 'underclass.' In Western Europe, the boom also had repercussions for the family in two opposing directions: on the one hand, the home with all its amenities (especially television) offered a private sphere away from public space, whereas other technologies (the car, the transistor radio) tended to help explode the family structure, even if the car offered a nice compromise as a 'family car,' a 'home away from home' especially during the holiday, as we will see in the next section. Indeed, the period from 1946 to 1965 has been dubbed the "golden age of the family," with 1965 as its absolute peak: right at that moment the audiences of the rock and pop groups started to be formed, as the first baby boomers came from school. Whatever the family's fate, however, sociological research showed a close relationship between this crucial social unit's two mobilities: geographical and social: "One leads to the other."[51]

Second (next to the convergence of inter-European development), the boom was characterized by a shift in consumption preferences from food and clothing toward furniture and mobility, although it took in Germany, for instance, about a decade or so before most "four-person salaried households" (*4-Personen-Arbeitnehmerhaushalte*) could afford a vacation. Indeed, against the idea that the economic miracle was an instant success for everybody, it is good to acknowledge the standard of living of worker families during the early years of the *Bundesrepublik* was lower than it had been during the boom in the early 1930s and even the years before World War I. Consciously constructed by the Western Allies as a "leveled middle-class society," its middle class "rema[d]e … in a republican mold," Germany counted 22 percent of its workers as car owners in 1962, which grew to 66 percent a decade later, a true internal convergence, as the corresponding percentages for white-collar families were 40 and 73, respectively. There is no doubt this growth was connected, in the minds of many Germans, with the spectacular rise of a middle class, to which social scientists considered nearly three-quarters of the German population to belong to at the start of the 1950s. Historians agree that during the 1950s and 1960s, "the new intelligentsia and the service class were recruited to a remarkable degree from lower-class families." Concerted propaganda efforts by both the German car industry and the largest touring and automobile club, the General German Automobile Club (ADAC), constructed a "close connection between car industry and reconstruction" and made Volkswagen into a symbol of the nation: for many Germans, the biography of this car resembled their own, with a "false start" during the Nazi period. Now, they could enjoy a true "family vehicle." Only during the 1970s had the income gap so much decreased and were car prices so much lowered that car consumption patterns could hardly be distinguished in a quantitative sense between social groups. During the two decades after 1950, relative expenses within the household budget for "transport" (*Verkehr*) nearly doubled, while expenses for food decreased, but Germans, like other Europeans, still spent a higher share of their income on food and clothing than US consumers did. The 'European consumption model' (as opposed to an American one) in this phase was characterized by a larger variety of products, including cars.[52]

***

Recently, the narrative that depicts Europe (and other parts of the world, for that matter) as passive recipients of "Americanization" has been challenged by a new generation of scholars, a welcome confirmation of my earlier conclusion about the untenability of the "diffusion myth." According to some scholars, the Marshall Plan, although "aimed to remake Europe in an American mode," even turned upside down, as conversely, "America was made the European way." Other scholars found "influence seemed to flow entirely in the other direction, from the New to the Old World."[53] Taken together, such studies reveal the major differences between European and American mass motorization. First, talking about "Westernization" rather than "Americanization," emphasizing mutual differences rather than convergence after a time gap, they show how a unique consumption culture emerged. This drift between a 'European' and an "American" consumption pattern can be illustrated through the case of Germany, where "pedestrian malls and numerous other examples from neighborhood shopping to the use of savings loans and public transportation [and less emphasis on suburban development, one is inclined to add] added up to a substantially different societal engagement with modern consumption goods," including cars. "Middle-class consumers, not just the poor, used public transportation."

Also, West Germans continued to spend more on food and "semiluxury food" (*Genussmittel*), "while expenses for housing, transportation, or household durable equipment never caught up to American levels." In addition, "household spending patterns continued to be more stratified by class differences," differences that further enable to nuance this analysis by suggesting the working-class Germans (especially the youth among them) were the ones practicing an "Americanization from below" ("blue jeans, bolo ties, and rock 'n' roll") or, in Rudi Koshar's characterization, "self-Americanization." But Americanization had its limits ("hegemonic Americanization has not occurred," historian Jan Logemann concluded): the "purchasing-power paradigm" (which also for Americans "broke down in the 1970s") made Americans "work much longer hours than their Western European counterparts," whereas Germany's housing conditions kept being characterized by a "division between a renting majority and a minority of homeowners reinforc[ing] this class stratification. The American credit-financed consumption pattern of home, car, and durables never gained quite the same importance in West Germany during the boom era [1945–1973]; nor did material consumption offer as viable a path to attaining middle-class respectability as it did in the United States." Germany's "social market economy" encapsulated "the preservation of inner-city retailing and the development of *Fussgängerzonen* [pedestrian zones]."

As far as transportation is concerned, this difference was expressed in the rapid emergences of the "two-car family," which "had become common by the end of the '60s." It was not so much the refrigerator but rather its contents that characterized German postwar mass consumption, economic historian Peter Kramper concluded. We will later see whether this also holds true for the car; for now, it suffices to observe that car technology differed greatly, so much so that it also in this realm seems justified to speak of a unique driving culture, which has up to now hardly been investigated. The European 'extravagance' manifested itself in Italy and France in the small car, in Germany in the lower-middle-class segments and in the United Kingdom in the middle-class segment. By the 1960s, the car as such in the UK had become "common place and [was] no longer a mark of social status although the *type* of car driven continued to be an indicator of distinction and social identity," a phenomenon that can be said to become universal in Western automobilism. "A part of these differences may be explained by differences in purchasing power, but another part is due to different preferences," preferences that formed the basis of much stereotyping such as the 'lazy' driving style in the United States versus the 'sporting,' agile cars in Europe; and cheap, mass-produced products versus quality manufacture ("In the US, cars are built not by engineers but by women and accountants [*Kaufleute*].") Stereotypes are very real, however: they are anchored in technology, for instance, in the struggle over the radial tire technology (the steel cord tire, invented by Michelin during World War II) that wreaked havoc among American tire manufacturers.[54]

The home away from home was produced by a growing domestic European car industry, which from the end of the 1950s was led by Germany (in terms of production numbers), closely followed by France, both overtaking Britain. PSA (Peugeot-Citroën) was the largest producer (with nearly one-fifth of total European output) and together with Volkswagen (which would soon overtake PSA in production figures), Renault, and Fiat, they captured nearly two-thirds of the European market. Several European car manufacturers were state or family owned. European countries were exporting a large part of their production, which helped finance their 'economic miracle.' The recession of 1967 briefly made Fiat the largest European car producer, overtaking Volkswagen, while Japan pushed Germany from second place among world car manufacturing countries. Like in the United States, the domestic car industry was increasingly challenged by foreign makes, the latter expanding its market share in Germany from one-tenth before the recession to more than one-quarter by 1972.[55]

This led to interesting stereotypes, such as in the following account of the Geneva International Motor Show of 1959 by the German magazine *Der Stern*: "We read about new constructive tendencies and shorter cars of pure rationality [*der reinen Vernunft*, an allusion to Kant]. In Geneva, however, we did not find American rationality, but united megalomania (*united Größenwahn*). It ruffles itself up (*plustert sich auf*) in sheet steel and chromium, it indulges in upholstered tastelessness and ugly folds and fake wings at the rear." Such stereotyping, however, took place on the basis of real differences, according to recent historical research into the modernization differences between Germany and the United States: "Despite West Germans' clear fascination with cars, their postwar standard of living had more to do with trams and trolleys than with chrome and tailfins," a revisionist history of mobility claimed.[56] We need more of this type of research to confirm whether this holds true for other European countries.

***

A second characteristic of the 'European model' (next to car technology as a token of Westernization rather than Americanization of European culture) was the preponderance of motorized two-wheelers immediately after the war, which makes the analysis of 'mass motorization' a delicate affair if one is inclined (as we are) to depart from a car fetishism induced by gazing at the American 'model.' The European motorcycle revival had a modest parallel in the United States, occurring in the late 1950s and the 1960s, but in the American case, the recreational aspects were more outspoken. The role of the motorcycle and especially the moped as a step up to the car or as a more autonomous development has not been properly investigated, but the differences between European countries were large. In Switzerland, motorcycles and scooters never outnumbered the car. Instead, the latter seems to have substituted the use of the bicycle, which diminished from the mid-1950s, only to explode alongside the car in equal absolute numbers from 1970. Most of the motorized two-wheelers were used by workers (80 percent in 1957). In Britain, "the moped and scooter came to symbolize the 1950s." Whereas a quarter of the population over sixteen used the bicycle in 1949, its use diminished quickly: from one-tenth of the passenger-miles in 1952 to less than 1 percent in 1970. Motorcycle use decreased, too.[57]

In Germany, workers bought more cars than motorized two-wheelers for the first time in 1957, just before the 'jump start' into mass motorization, the result of a conscious effort to "de-proletarianize" (*Entproletarisierung*) the working class against a Cold War background. It seems likely that business use of the car in the Netherlands (including a new group of traveling salesmen) ignited postwar motorization. Most Dutchmen (and ever more women) opted for the motorcycle and especially the moped, which soon, just like after World War I, outnumbered cars and were used for commuting. Especially at this level of mobility, that of the workers and lower middle classes, physical mobility increase cannot be understood without analyzing the social, 'vertical mobility': when, in 1958, German social scientist Morris Janowitz published a study titled "On the Size of Mobility in Our Society," he referred to the remarkable phenomenon of social mobility not only upward (toward the "lower middle class" and the "upper lower class") by farmers and agricultural workers (whose share in the working population decreased by half in one generation around 1955) but also downward, to the "lower lower class." The result was a social stratification in which the working class did not have a larger share than in the United States, but there were relatively more German independent entrepreneurs and fewer white collars. It seems that in these years especially the sons of schooled workers (*Facharbeiter*) and master artisans (*Meister*) transferred into the middle strata of *Angestellte* and civil servants.[58]

Similar developments were observed in the United Kingdom: "It was no longer a question of the old middle class absorbing new recruits from below in a manner which left their established position and form more or less intact," as had been the case before World War II. "Beginning in the 1940s and consolidating and accelerating after 1950, the general level of comfort, security and education of the formerly under-privileged and deprived masses was drastically uplifted. In the process many found themselves wanting to take up features of middle class lifestyle and were able to do so with relative ease." The Cold War background was called upon when German media compared West German motorization with East Germany: "For every thousand inhabitants of our country … there are 70 automobiles. In the so-called worker and farmer state of the Soviet zone, however,

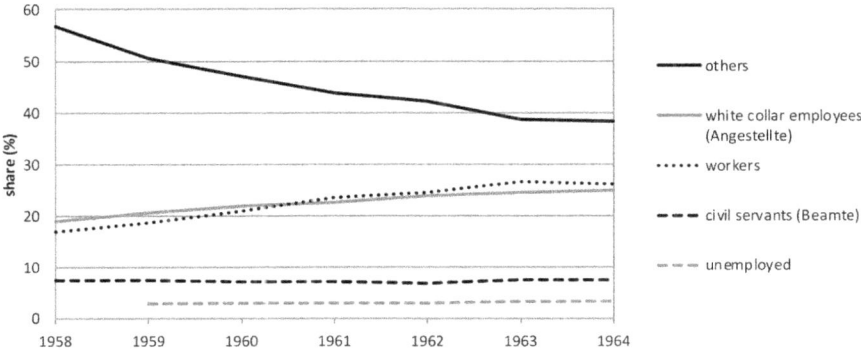

Figure 2.2. Share of different social groups in the purchase of new cars in Germany, 1958–1964. Source: Kopper, "Der Durchbruch des PKW zum Massenkonsumgut," 33, table 4. Figure created by the author.

there are only eight."⁵⁹ In the Cold War, the car became a measure of a country's modernization, as well as its 'democracy.'

The increase of relative worker car ownership paralleled the increase of car ownership by so-called *Angestellte*, the new, white-collar middle class employed in nonmanual jobs; against both trends stood a (relative) declining trend for other owner types, most particularly business men (fig. 2.2). No better proof can be found of the petit bourgeoisie and the skilled workers becoming (the graph is about purchasing) the carriers of post–World War II automobilism. In Germany, the motorized two-wheelers also compensated to a certain extent the inequalities in motorization between urban and rural areas, but never fully, although the share of motorized two-wheelers and bicycles was higher in the countryside than in the cities. Remarkably, the Ruhr area (the source of these observations) also shows rural car densities got equal to urban densities only in the 1970s, much later than in the United States (where rural densities already were higher way before World War II), but around the same time as in the highly urbanized Netherlands, where this took place around 1977. A similar development can be observed in Italy, where the South caught up in absolute number of cars with the Center, although the North still could boast to represent more than half the Italian car fleet. But in an 'empty country' like France, car densities were still highest in the Paris region and other highly urbanized regions (Bordeaux, Lyon, Marseille) as late as 1954.⁶⁰

***

A third possible characteristic, namely that the European car market initially was fragmented into national units, "despite the founding of the EEC in 1957," may hold true only if one limits one's analysis to the production side of the mobility equation (and thus to the larger European countries), and if one does not acknowledge the European car market consisted of a host of smaller countries as well, without much domestic production. For one of these countries, the Netherlands, the start of mass motorization can now exactly be pinpointed. And although there, again, a national debate took place about the 'necessity' of car use (just like in post–World War I days), after 1948 the combined effect of Marshall aid, followed by an explosion of the paid vacation as a result of an unprecedented economic boom and a very active field of private enterprises who quickly put a large fleet of modern motor buses on the road, resulted in a travel orgy (also to international destinations) that surprised even the specialists. The Netherlands until the early 1950s (when it was overtaken by France) had one of the largest fleets of motor buses per capita in the world, after the United Kingdom and the United States.⁶¹

Indeed, with the moped and the bus as appetizers, the Dutch motorization explosion by car can very precisely be located in time: the gradually increasing diffusion curve shows a first upward switch in 1953, upbeat for the real explosion in 1958 when the government lifted its consumption restrictions (*bestedingsbeperking*). It was first observed by a socialist journalist who saw car densities in Amsterdam quickly rising to a European average, and explained this by pointing at a paradigm shift within the household budget in favor of, first, durable consumption goods like radio and refrigerator, and then the car. In the Netherlands, by 1960, half the car park was owned by people earning less than 10,000 guilders per year, a level that even Royal Dutch Touring Club observers had seen up to then as an insurmountable threshold. Most of these cars were secondhand.[62]

Between 1936 and 1980, the share of 'transport' in the Dutch household income rose from 3 to 11 percent, a phenomenon also observable in other countries. In the United States, for instance, expenses for "automobile transportation" varied from 6 to 14 percent of the household budget, with an average of 11 percent.[53] These variations were indications of still existing class differences: in France (where the share of "transportation and holidays" in the household budget also doubled between 1950 and 1965), these costs' share in the budget varied between 6 percent for workers and farmers to 17 percent for the liberal professions. In 1967, more than half of French households owned a car. Unsurprisingly, given the close economic relationship with the Netherlands, Germany showed a similar "characteristic jump 1959/60" in consumption practices. There, too, in the same year (1953) as the Netherlands, the graph of monthly car sales shows a twist: the share of expenses for public and private transport tilted from 74–26 in 1952 to 47–53 in 1958. The turning point is also observable in the popularity of movie theaters, expenditure on electrical household appliances, and increasing expenses on vacations and outings.

In Germany, like in the Netherlands, the turning point toward mass motorization was accomplished mostly with secondhand cars, on the basis of bank credits that jumped from a growth rate of 6.5 percent to 23, 30 and 26 percent for 1958, 1959, and 1960, respectively. Remarkably, worker families profited the most from the credit system: their debt was larger than their white-collar counterparts' (this was also the case in the United States), while younger families borrowed more and easier than the elder. Between 1950 and 1973, the only two items in the worker families' household budget that grew relative to the other items were "household goods" and "transport and communication," benefitting from a decrease in relative expenses on food, rent, and clothing and, of course, a general increase in purchasing power. The year 1958 marked 'the end of modesty": Germany spent 5 percent of its GDP on cars, against 8 percent in the United States.[64]

***

Within the European car diffusion spectrum, mass motorization in the periphery started somewhat later. For instance, the peak of economic growth in Italy was 1964, the year in which the absolute number of registered cars overtook the 4.7 million registered motorcycles. The Italian consumption frenzy has been explained as a collective, "general rejection of poverty, of the 'ancient' world," initially symbolized by the Vespa scooter, the producer of which, Piaggio, was said to have "found a cure against communism." Production of the Vespa soared from 700,000 in 1956 to 4.3 million in 1964 (sharing the market with Innocenti's Lambretta). Advertised as "the small car with two wheels," the Vespa was especially popular in the Italian countryside (and later among London's mods, as we have seen) and was explicitly advertised as a "leisure-related tool." In 1958, Italians owned nearly three times as many motorized two-wheelers as cars (3.6 vs. 1.4 million). After the Vespa, Italy motorized in a Fiat, which represented 84 to 91 percent of the provincial markets in 1958, a monopoly that gradually was loosened toward larger domestic and foreign cars; in 1970, Fiat's market share had fallen to 63–76 percent, depending on the province. The Italian eagerness to motorize was exemplary, however: later analyses revealed national car diffusion curves followed the theory of the logistic curve so perfectly that one student of Italian motorization called the process "homeostatic," a quasi-autonomous process, like the 'contagious' behavior of multiplying bacteria in a petri dish. The growth of the fleet was very fast (around 20 percent per year) in the late 1950s and early 1960s. By 1973, Italian car densities were equal to those of Germany and Great Britain.[65]

In studies of Western mobility, mass motorization is often presented as a curve showing the relationship between car density and GDP per capita. In the case of Europe, quite surprisingly such curves show Romanic countries, as well as Greece and Austria, witnessed a higher car density per unit of income than other European countries, indicating an even greater eagerness to motorize, a phenomenon we also observed in the equally eager modernizing prewar middle classes in Latin America (chap. 1). But whatever the differences, motorization figures for all European countries are simply spectacular, following the German example where, between 1960 and 1970, the number of privately owned cars tripled, to fourteen million, while in Great Britain, France, and Sweden, it doubled over the same period.[66]

***

Several contemporary studies and surveys enable us to fine-tune our earlier observation of European automobilism being a combined worker/middle-class affair. In 1963, *Reader's Digest* organized for its advertisers a large survey into the buying habits in seven European countries (the six of the

European Community plus Great Britain) and observed their middle classes (comprising about 30 to 40 percent of the populations) and other "new Europeans" were busy buying cars, with France leading (where 40 percent of households meanwhile had acquired one). On average, in France, the car's penetration had reached nearly equal value as the penetration of TV sets (28 and 34 percent, respectively). The Netherlands (with 26 percent car penetration) could boast to have a bicycle density of 78 percent, nearly double the share of the other six countries. Its moped density was also double the 'European' average.

Diffusion had to be learned, however: German Minister for Economics (and later Chancellor) Ludwig Erhard in 1953 spoke out against the desires for equality (*Gleichmacherei*) in consumption among the population: "The first automobiles in America probably were not driven by retired citizens either, but ... by millionaires." Meanwhile, the diffusionist myth was fed by a continuous repetition of predictions about the further explosion of the car fleet size, started in Germany by Shell, which in 1958 published its first prognosis, thus making the car into a "political issue" (*Politikum*), so much so that there was hardly any difference between the governing coalition and the opposition, both giving in to a "severe public pressure." The still growing ADAC published a "Manifest of Automobilism" ("Manifest der Kraftfahrt") in 1965, in which it revived the prewar American insistence on the car being a utilitarian contraption (*Gebrauchsgegenstand*) "for everyone to satisfy daily needs, part of the progressive creation of a free world.[67]

In several studies by social scientists undertaken during the 1950s and 1960s, the emergence of European middle-class affluence can be followed in detail. In 1958, the Italian village of Bonagente had only two automobiles; eleven years later, most families had some form of motorized transport: scooters, motorcycles, and mopeds, while one-fifth to one-quarter of all families owned a car, most of them tiny Fiat Cinquecentos or Seicentos, as well as some small, three-wheeled Lurgoncino pickup trucks. Two interview rounds in 1971 revealed "the emphasis has shifted from community or collective toward individual and family goals." Most villagers opted for a house first (with a preference for a "kitchen *alla Americana*"), but for the young, "when they have the money, they buy a motorcycle or an automobile first. In general, the old walk or ride donkeys, the young motorcycles and automobiles. Only occasionally is the pattern reversed," but the entire community craved a smooth road. In the village of Plodémet in French Brittany, similar trends were observed, one interviewed citizen confessing he bought a Simca 500, which was "beyond our means, but it is our only luxury." The best-sold cars in France, rapidly becoming "an industrialized urban society," became the Renault 4CV (1946) and R4 (1961), as well as the Citroën 2CV and the Peugeot 203 (1949). These cars "symbolized the entrance of the workers into the consumption era": a quarter of them owned a car by the end of the 1950s, against only 8 percent in 1953. In Germany, it was the iconic Volkswagen Beetle that soon would push Ford's Model T from the throne as the world's best-sold car.[68]

***

And yet, the emergence of a new, quasi-proletarianized, middle-class youth subjectivity should not lure us into assuming working-class culture 'dissolved,' as it were, into a society-wide, middle-class culture (with a proletarian flavor). A 1969 ethnographic study of two distinct youth cultures of the 1960s in the United Kingdom by Paul Willis can clarify this. The first culture is produced by a working-class motorcycle youth, whose "values, attitudes and feelings were so deeply entrenched as to form part of an obvious commonsense reality." Contrary to what we will see emerging in middle-class car adventures (for instance, in Simone de Beauvoir's travelogue about the United States), "there was no abstract dimension to the world, no guilty reading, no burdened 'I'—just a straightforward physicality and confidence in things. The touchstone of this world were manliness, toughness and directness of interpersonal contact." Important values are "movement, noise, confidence," and constitutive elements of their bike culture are "music, bikes, excitement, disregard, speed and danger." Not a blurring of realities here but rather "the denial of other realities." Nor is there much room for irony left, no transcendence either, but the emphasis on "the importance of *control*[,] the capable handling of a bike." Hence, their adventure is near-deadly, quite different from the flirt with death in prewar middle-class car adventures: "Their frequently stated preference for an early death ... should not be taken as self-parody or mischievous posing." Willis gave an exemplary and brilliant analysis of both the technology of their bikes ("cattle-horn type" handlebars, forcing them in an "upright position, ... chromium-plated double exhaust pipes and high exuberant mudguards," the baffles removed from the silencer box, no helmets, goggles or gloves) and, most importantly, the affinity (he called it homology or "direct connection") "between rock music and fast bike-riding."

Their musical taste was "at least ten years out of date," directed at Elvis (and his lyrics "full of aggression"), Buddy Holly, Chuck Berry, Gene Vincent, and Edie Cochran. Biker Fred: "If I heard a record, a real good record, I just fucking wack it [the accelerator handle] open, you know, I just want to wack it open." Willis developed what I like to call an 'affinity chain' of music–dancing–violence–biking. Joe: "If you can't dance any more, or if the dance is over, you've just got to go for a burn-up," a fight. The beat, "rather than melody or harmony, is the basic organizing structure of the music. Its constancy and continuity mean that the music is, so to speak, a steady stream, rather than a varied structure." The beat often comes to a sudden stop, only to start again (as in Elvis's "Jailhouse Rock"), or fades "into nothing." Willis musicological analysis of rock's "repetition and 'timelessness'" allows us to discover a more general affinity with modernity, especially its early postmodern traits: "The whole motor-bike culture was an attempt to stop or subvert bourgeois, industrial, capitalist notions of time—the basic experiential discipline its members faced in the work they still took so seriously." How different this is from the hippie culture, and its preference for transcendence, expressed in the "post *Sergeant Pepper*" music of Frank Zappa, Cream, Jimmy Hendrix, Led Zeppelin, and the "acid rock" of the Grateful Dead, Jefferson Airplane, the Doors, Country Joe and the Fish, and Pink Floyd. Aided by LSD, 'hippies' did not need a car to get high. Their culture replete with "ironic detachment," producing a postmodern, anti-materialist lifestyle, their "progressive" pop music liked to play ironically with those conventions that rock 'n' roll tried to ignore.[69]

US Abundance: GIs and the Motorizing American Worker

The most spectacular developments were to be observed in the United States, not so much because of its car density growth rates (they were lower than the European ones, as they started from a much higher level) but because of its culture of abundance, expressed in staggering absolute numbers: twenty-one million cars bought in the 1950s alone (paid from indebtedness that rose three times faster than personal income, enabling Americans to travel "a billion miles a day on tyres"), nine million new homeowners, fifty million TV sets bought in the 1960s (compared to a total of seven thousand in 1946). With Europe's development of automobilism already spectacular, there is no other way to characterize American car culture of the 1960s and 1970s as exuberant.

This affluent culture was based on a consciousness of being the leader of the "free world" (as Henry Ford II declared in 1961) in car production. Rostow called World War II "a sort of deus ex machina which brought the United States back up to full employment." Also, "commitment to the cold war paid off domestically," as first the Korean War and then the rearmament race with the Soviet Union stimulated economic growth. Even in the United States, a welfare state was created consisting of the nine million veterans from World War II, for whom in 1944 the G.I. Bill of Rights passed Congress, a nearly $100 billion program that "created the most privileged generation in American history." US officials called the program to target GIs as consumption vanguards "Operation Abundance." The former GIs (Kerouac being one of them) benefitted from mortgage schemes (boosting suburban housing development) and other benefits, enabling "working class

GIs [to] become property owners and join the consumer suburban society." In 1946, nearly half of all college students were veterans. By 1984, nearly three-quarters of American whites owned their own homes (and only 25 percent blacks, who were mostly "excluded from suburban society").[70] There were two 'suburban societies,' however. The blue-collar version stood on wheels and was often labeled a slum, its two million inhabitants (in the immediate postwar years) derogatorily called "trailer trash." By 1965, 10 percent of newly constructed homes were mobile, in which about 3 percent of the American population lived, most of them just not being able to afford a permanent home and thus "fix[ing] the lower boundary of the middle majority market."

Trailer history started during the Depression as a home for the transient worker, and during the war used for those working in remote factories for the Army (60 percent of the two hundred thousand trailers during World War II were located in defense areas). After the war "the demand for residential trailers outstripped the demand for travel trailers," often used by GIs who could not find a permanent home in a seller's market. Trailers cost less than half of the mass-produced homes in new housing areas such as Levittown, Pennsylvania. By the early 1950s (when retired couples started replacing the GIs), the United States counted about twelve thousand trailer parks. Whether trailer or not, the suburb was the very basis of American automobile exuberance (historian Christopher Wells even claimed there is a "strong correlation between the spread of low-density landscapes during the postwar years and growing car ownership and use"), and its core was the white, middle-class nuclear family. With car ownership being "almost universal among wage-earner families by 1960," the American ideal of consumption became the second car, which would indeed revolutionize the family's internal functioning, especially the role of the wife.[71]

The famous kitchen debate of 1959 between Nixon and Khrushchev in Moscow, and many of its historians in its wake, not only ignored intimate culture under Communism and, as Ruth Oldenziel convincingly showed, the technology and culture of alternatives such as the Frankfurt kitchen, but also denied a role to the single mother or the extended family in the American 'home.' But most importantly, the event in Moscow formed the "apex" of a "conflation of mass consumption and middle-class gender ideology." This highly influential Cold War caricature of the East-West cleft was the focus of *My Son John* (1952), "one of the most important anti-Communist movies of the Cold War era." Indeed, we should not exaggerate the penetration of the car among American workers: according to a marketing study of the University of Michigan from 1968, half of all surveyed worker families in 1957 did not own a car, and if they did, it was mostly second-hand. Ten years later, still 32 percent did not own a car, and worker families owned more than half of all secondhand cars (more than half of all large cars were owned by white collars). Only in the 1960s did car ownership rates per American market segment start to converge.[72]

***

It was in this rapidly expanding (always almost) universal mass motorization that Marshall McLuhan in *Understanding Media* (as he had done before in his experimental *The Mechanical Bride*) called the car obsolete, referring to "observers" who had recently insisted the house as a status symbol had "of late, supplanted the car," an expression of a "growing uneasiness about the degree to which cars have become the real population of our cities." But the car "will go the way of the horse … 'Is the car here to stay?' The answer, of course, is 'No.' In the electric age, the wheel itself is obsolescent." Mobilizing the well-known substitution myth (see the introduction), McLuhan declared "it is TV that has dealt the heavy blow to the American car," quoting best-selling author John C. Keats to convince his readers the automotive adventure was over. It would die in ubiquitousness. The only thing to do now is to wait "for a decade more, by which time the electronic successors to the car will be manifest."

Perhaps the best remedy against this futuristic hubris is to place McLuhan in a long tradition of science fiction writers, some of whom exactly in this phase dreamed of another type of 'electric' future. Wilhelm Wolfgang Bröll, for instance, in his novel *Atomstadt UTO 2* (1952), depicted a world in which cars were propelled by small "atom batteries," whereas American film critic and University of California Press editor Ernest Callenbach in his "sustainability utopia" *Ecotopia* (1975) and subsequent Ecotopia books saw the private car disappear (echoing McLuhan) and replaced by electric taxicabs and buses. Videoconferencing made the car obsolete, whereas subterranean conveyor belts and electric trucks transported freight.[73]

The Attack on Public Transport: Hegemonic Car Cultures in a Cold War Setting

Now that we have described the material base of the postwar (mobility) boom in the West, we can zoom in on its motoring culture. It is better to talk of cultures, plural, as a focus on the 'cultural appropriation' of the car will illustrate. We will focus in this section on what transport planners have called the 'modal split' but what we will call 'modal configuration,' because we will also use it in traffic situations beyond the West, if only to rehabilitate the role of walking and other 'subaltern modes.' Postwar hegemonic car cultures cannot be understood without their Cold War context. This war (only in Europe was it really 'cold') knew its violent outbursts in Korea and Vietnam but had its 'cold' counterparts in US President Lyndon B. Johnson's other failed war, the War on Poverty, a $15 billion program (less than one-tenth of the costs of the hot war in Vietnam) to make America's poor participate in its consumer society including "mass-transit aid." A part of this war was the introduction of "busing," as "policy makers continued to believe that moving people [to and from school] was a better and easier solution than moving money and resources."

From a mobility perspective, the Korean War (starting in 1950) was "an old-fashioned conflict": the North was supplied through the Manchurian railway network, while the "US military had originally intended to target roads but then realized that the railways were far more important in the line of communication." This was reversed during the Vietnam War, when the "Ho Chi Minh trail, a jungle pathway that was gradually expanded into a road able to take the trucks supplied by the Russians and the Chinese. By the end of the war, the railway on both sides of the border was virtually derelict." In Europe, the blockade of West Berlin (1948); the insurgencies in the GDR and Czechia (both 1953), Hungary, and Poland (both 1956); and the erection of the Berlin Wall (1961) accompanied the consumer frenzy in the gloomy background. In the 1960s, the Cuban Missile Crisis (1962) and the oppression of the Prague Spring (1968) followed. The accompanying arms race and the expansion of military powers, as well as its spin-offs such as computers and electronic automation in general (also beneficial for automotive technology), formed one of the foundations of economic growth. "Until the 1970s [the] tacit agreement to treat the Cold War as a Cold Peace held good," Eric Hobsbawm concluded.[74]

Commute or Pleasure? The Breakthrough of the 'Ubiquitous Car'

In the mobility field, the Cold War extended into the realm of intermodal competition: a modern consumption society should be based on the car, as the always climbing curves of car use (expressed in passenger-miles) in the modal split graphs of the United States seemed to indicate.[75] And whoever did not believe the figures, there was always Rostow's *Non-Communist Manifesto* to make this crystal clear: America (clearly followed by 'the West') represented the end phase of humanity's history. The intermodal Cold War raged especially in the cities, most particularly the American cities, where motor buses succeeded street cars, giving rise to mythological conspiracies such as the 'Snell controversy,' presented at a congressional hearing, according to which General Motor had deliberately purchased many transit companies only to replace their tram cars with motor buses. As late as the 1950s, 70 percent of white families still used public transport for commuting and going to school (black families more), so GM's alleged move was fundamentally racist.[76]

Had Snell looked over the American border to Europe, and had he done some historical study, he would have found the 'coordination crisis' was a transnational phenomenon, 'solved' in the United States, as with so many issues, in an 'exuberant' way. In Germany, too, the car overtook public transport for commuting during the 1960s, but for holidays, the bus dominated the decade, suggesting a staged substitution of the bus by the car.[77] Not only the cities motorized: the motorization on farms (with trucks and tractors) showed similar ever-rising curves, even if the rural population decreased. In the case of the United States, such curves indicated the spread of the passenger car among farmers was a thing of the prewar period and thus did not contribute anymore to the national fleet growth, although the diminishing rural population implied rural car densities increased nonetheless.

In general, between the Cold War background and the foreground of hegemonic mobility, the contextual setting of a consumer society emerged, which one study (on Germany) tried to catch in five characteristics, most of them, tellingly, related to car culture. For a consumer culture to emerge, one needed, first, enough purchasing power, which, second, had to be spent to enhance the more nuanced distinctions between products as an expression, third, of a private lifestyle, which preferably had to be lived (fourth) in a suburb, where (fifth) a "work-and-spend culture" had spread. From these two interrelated perspectives (Cold War and consumer society), the devastation of the war in several European countries, but especially Germany, created a window of opportunity for the automobile system to make a jump start compared to its rival modalities. Large amounts of refugees migrated back to Germany in the immediate afterwar years (since the Nazis' seizure of power, fifty to sixty million people—one-tenth of the European population—had to leave their country of origin). Nine million of the Germans had to settle somewhere, for which the federal government selected three *länder* (agrarian regions of Lower Saxony, Bavaria, and Schleswig-Holstein). Soon, new refugees from the German Democratic Republic joined the migratory flows. No surprise, then, that European individual motorization started in Germany: public transport would never have been able to collect and distribute these dispersed people, although motor bus companies did their best, and buses boomed as a result, as did motorized bicycles. No surprise, too, that individual motorization in Germany took the form of commuting. Together with the trip to school, this mobility function soon formed about a quarter of German car fleet performance (in passenger-kilometers) for the remainder of the century.[78]

It comes as no surprise either that this early motorized migration to and from the cities formed the impetus to an early movement of suburbanization in a country where the ideal of the *Eigenheim* (owning your own home) formed the material base for what contemporary German observers called the emergence of "a new European man." This motorized "man" increasingly was a worker who during this phase was to enter the magic realm of middle-class consumption. In 1959, more than half the German passenger car fleet was owned by salaried persons, and by then, 80 percent of car purchase was done on credit. A year later, contemporaries observed a shift from commuting to leisure traffic being in full swing, without, of course, commuting stopping from being one of the constant drivers of motorization. In other words, a Germany prewar dominance of leisure use of the car was lost during the war, and regained dominance only after a short phase of a restart through commuting.

Whether commuting also formed the impulse for mass motorization in other European countries is not known, but there is no doubt that, in these years, the car became ubiquitous. Italian transport historian Federico Paolini claimed no less than 55 percent of the total car mileage was spent on commuting. But also, by the beginning of the 1960s, half of Italian motorists used their car for vacations. A recent study of interwar transport in London claimed commuting by car started there in 1939, but the evidence is rather thin.[79] The London Traffic Survey of 1964 showed half of the observed 11.3 million trips were commuter trips. What is more important, however, is the *nature* of the commutes: US work trips started taking place from suburb to suburb, a pattern that could have been impossibly performed by public transport. Also, another typical automotive phenomenon occurred: the linking of trips, especially by working mothers, who combined the commute with shopping or bringing children to school, a behavior that was hardly reflected in the surveys that increasingly were undertaken by social scientists and transport experts to monitor mobility landslides.[80]

In any case, the German 'economic miracle' was less miraculous than often thought, although the growth rate during the 1950s in Germany was rivaled only by the second loser of the war, Japan. Japan's automotive "extravagance," as Mary McShane and colleagues call it in their comparison of Japan's and Sweden's mass motorizations, is characterized by "actions [by Japan's government] which constrain private auto ownership and use," such as "parking requirements, fuel and automobile taxes, driver licensing requirements, and the auto inspection program," actions that partially were initiated in the period covered by this chapter. This resulted not only in a de facto limitation of household ownership of one car but also in the spread of very small cars and vans. This did not prevent motorists (especially the "kamikaze taxis") to indulge in the urban car adventure of "break-neck speeding." But like in Germany and other 'Atlantic' countries, the Japanese middle class, as Daniel Dhakidae argued, "absorbed the upper class, stripped of its power and economic privileges, and ceased to be middle in a strict sense."[81]

But Germany's rise (perhaps supported by a higher regional homogeneity than Italy, France, and the United Kingdom) formed part of a general European economic upswing into mass consumption. For instance, already during the first half of the 1950s, Germany's car density (in cars per capita) was overtaken by French motorists during their *Trente Glorieuses* ("glorious thirty" years after 1945), most other Western European countries following not far behind. This resulted in a veritable convergence of national average car densities in Europe in the subsequent 1970s, with the exception of Great Britain (fig. 2.3). Whereas French historians saw their 'propertied classes' diminish in size, Swedish researchers observed how "individual saving was to be viewed suspect … People in the new rich industrial society should not become *petit* [sic] *capitalists*; they should be happy *consumers*."[82]

It is unlikely this was caused by commuting: even in Germany by the early 1960s, nearly half the car fleet performance (in passenger-kilometers) was spent on the pleasurable sides of car mobility, a share that would remain stable for at least the next two decades, thus continuing a tradition started at the very beginning of Western automobilism and persisted during the interbellum. Pleasurable use (*activités extra-professionnelles*) also dominated the French car deployment profile in terms of expenses (50 percent). In fact, this was in accordance with the general shift in France toward pleasure in

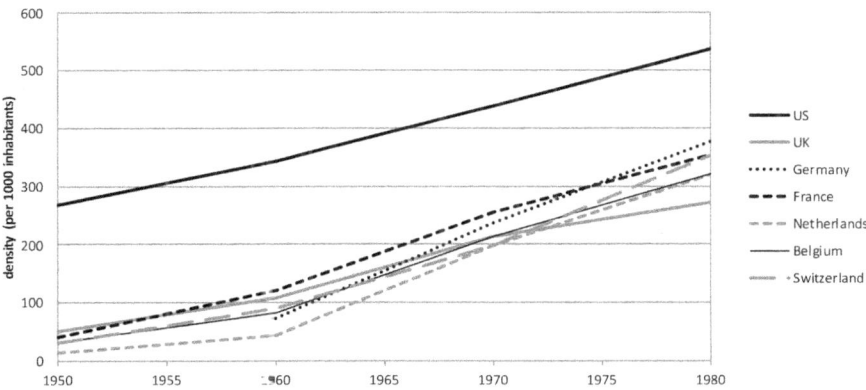

Figure 2.3. Car densities in several Western countries. Sources: Mitchell, *International Historical Statistics* (European vehicles and population); DOT, *Highway Statistics Series* (US vehicles); US Census Bureau, International Data Base (US population). I thank Luísa Sousa and Hanna Wolf for collecting and ordering the data.

consumption activities, but while consumption expenses between 1950 and 1962 doubled, expenses for leisure increased by a factor of 2.5, expenses on transport by a factor of 2.9 (and health by a factor of 3). American surveys indicated "leisure car use" (*automobilisme d'agrément* in the French report) was the most frequently performed leisure activity in the United States (with twenty-one days per year spent on this activity by Americans of twelve years and older, followed by hiking and walking with seventeen days). "Pleasure outings" dominated "weekend outdoor recreation" in the United States. Orvar Löfgren, student of Swedish tourism, even claimed (without giving evidence) "the great boom in Swedish car ownership during the 1950s and 1960s ... was not based so much on commuting to work as on a desire for leisure travel." Sweden was (and is) special not only because of its early enthusiastic embracement of the car in a social-democratic setting but also because the second position in its modal configuration, outside the city centers, was taken not by public transport but by cycling and walking.[83]

"I don't understand what we should do with a car," the narrator in Göran Rosenberg's *Ett kort uppehåll på vägen från Auschwitz* (translated into English as *A Brief Stop on the Road to Auschwitz*, published in Swedish in 2012 and looking back to the 1950s) observes:

> We walk or cycle to the beach. You guys cycle to work or take the bypass railway. To Stockholm and Borås we always go by train. Cars are unusual in the rowan berry lane ... Our car is a black Volkswagen ... The car as such doesn't interest me ... On a warm summer day he is simply there ... The car ... is not there to drive from one spot to another. It is there to drive if you don't need to go to a certain spot.

This is, of course, no evidence and may as easily be interpreted as a projection from a *current* indifference to the car, but for the Netherlands, qualitative evidence suggests pleasure *mobility* (which is not the same as pleasure car driving!) was at least as important, interpreted (and justified, against a skeptical government that emphasized a thrifty morale) by contemporaries as a reaction to restrictive war conditions. Slowly, all over the Western industrialized world, a more or less uniform division of car use over commuting, social visits, and vacations was established, but there were large differences, also *within* countries. As late as 1963, in Denver, Colorado, still one-quarter of commutes and one-third of shopping trips were done by public transport. In Germany, shopping (next to social visits) dominated the use profile of the car, before outings and commuting.[84]

But whatever the precise share of commuting or shopping, car use, in both absolute and relative terms, increased. For instance, in the United States, between 1969 (when 80 percent of all households owned at least one car) and 1983, households made nearly 40 percent more "family and personal business trips." The same increase was registered for the number of shopping trips, and their length increased by 20 percent at the same time. In general, during the 1970s alone, total fleet mileage increased by 40 percent, whereas population in the same period rose by only 8 percent.[85] From a longer-term perspective, the American car fleet increased 4.5 times from 1929 to 1979, but the mileage of the fleet 7 times. In other words, while car ownership grew, its use grew even more, testifying to the gradual transformation to a 'car society.' And although American historian Claude Fischer recently argued that evidence for the "unprecedented rate of geographical ... mobility in modern society" (as he quotes one of his targets of critique) is missing and that, on the contrary, Americans have become less mobile over the previous century, our and Fischer's findings are compatible if we realize the latter confines his remarks to *residential* mobility, the moving of the home. In other words, there is no doubt that once Americans (and Europeans for that matter) got hold of the car, their annual mileage and the frequency of their trips increased considerably. What is more, this mobility got enhanced by the increasing sessility of the Americans. But the increase was unequally divided among the population: "Salaried families [around 1950] who owned an auto spent one-fourth more on gas than wage-earner families, who spent one-seventh more than laborer families."[86]

Tourists to the South, Migrants to the North: Long-Range Car and Bus Travel

The most remarkable trend in the car use profile, however, was the growing share of long trips, mostly for pleasurable purposes and often in the context of family excursions or holidays. At the same time, "unstructured activities" (activities social scientists gathered under the term motoring) diminished, while "purposive traveling" increased. In her study of a Los Angeles workers' suburb, Becky Nicolaides quoted a local suburbanite: "I'd tell my wife, 'Let's get the hell out of here.' ... Sometimes we'd wind up having lunch in Oxnard ... We'd go to Big Bear for the day and I'd rent a cabin and we'd go to San Diego or we'd go to Mexico ... We were forever on the go," thus representing and shaping the hegemonic equivalent of Kerouac's and his friends' pseudo-nomadism. Tourism by car was accompanied by a new explosion in the 1960s and 1970s (after the ones in the 1910s for the US and the 1920s for the US and Europe) of enabling infrastructure, including facilities for motorized camping. A Gallup poll in 1954 revealed more than half the US interviewees had made a trip longer than six hundred miles during the previous year. In the United States, fifty million campers were counted by the 1980s.[87]

In Europe, too, long-distance touring and tourism by car exploded after the first consumption desires were satisfied: food, housing, clothing, and a "small margin of security." But in Europe, employees preferred "shorter hours to bigger paychecks" in order to expand the length of their annual holiday, resulting in the longest vacations in the world. During the first thirty postwar years, however, also the American working year diminished by one-tenth. In Germany, the modal configuration of holiday travel shifted from the train to the car between 1954 and 1972, with the motor bus acting as Trojan Horse, helping dethrone rail-bound transport. Germans were later than Britons in massively vacationing abroad, probably because they had to start from scratch. Only during the 1970s did aviation start to acquire important market shares, and after the 1970s, charter aviation took over the lead as the distance to vacation destinations continued to increase considerably, and the annual migration flows of pleasure from the North to Southern Europe shifted partially toward the airplane.[88] But the car remained dominant (fig. 2.4).

Italy was the second-largest destination for European tourists but a favorite of Germans in particular "because their common Fascist background largely guaranteed an avoidance of negative reactions from the population." Most managers in the early industry were former *Kraft durch Freude* employees, the prewar Nazi organization for national tourism. By the end of the 1970s, enabled by the cheap charter flights, many Germans, too, had shifted from Italy (where they had gone by car) to Spain, which received more than forty million tourists in 1981. Swedes (who enjoyed three weeks of paid vacation in 1951, four by 1963, and five by 1978) were the most eager participants in the annual flow (measured in package tours per capita):

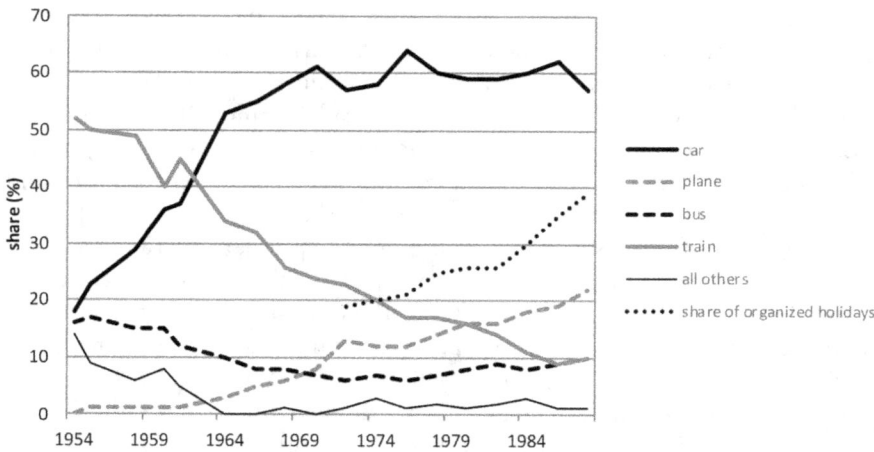

Figure 2.4. Modal configuration during the main holiday trip in Germany, 1954–1988. Source: Pagenstecher, *Der bundesdeutsche Tourismus*, 137, table 5. Figure created by the author.

they had started using the bus in the 1950s, but by 1965, nearly 90 percent of the 370,000 Swedish package tours were by airplane, most of them going to the Mediterranean. Postwar tourism showed that the car remained mainly a local, continental medium: its transnationalism consisted in its ubiquity (its gradual spread over the globe), not in any efforts to mimic the airplane's transcontinental reach.[89]

***

The development of international tourism was a crucial part of Marshall aid (called "travel development" by officials in Washington), if only to get Americans visiting Europe again and set in motion a flow of dollars (one-quarter of Western European dollars earned in 1949 came from this source), but also because of the Cold War, to show off the Western affluence to the 'others' in the East. The European tour was often treated by American travel writers as "a chance to escape modernity": a group of Midwestern farmers, after visiting Europe, wrote to their senator to "drastically cut" Marshall aid to Europe, because Europeans were "still worshipping their past history and old buildings. They do not understand the American idea of looking ahead." Aviation for touristic purposes really got started in 1958, when the "economy class" was offered at 20 percent lower fares than the previous "tourist class," introduced in 1952. Remarkably, these two years are exactly the two turning points mentioned when we discussed the breakthrough of mass motorization in Germany and the Netherlands. In 1958, for the first time, more passengers crossed the Atlantic Ocean by air than by ship. "Volume doubled between 1953 and 1959 and doubled again to 1.4 million by 1965," and Americans spent about double the government's foreign aid budget in Europe in 1955. But already in 1961, the new Kennedy administration tried to promote domestic travel and again in 1965 and 1968, President Johnson, facing "an acute balance-of-payments crisis," admonished his fellow Americans to refrain from "all nonessential travel" abroad.[90]

In Europe, UK tourists booked the largest absolute number of charter flights (37 percent), followed by Swedes (27 percent) and West Germans (23 percent), but related to population size, Scandinavians were the most eager of all European tourists to fly to the South, no doubt also because of the larger distance. By 1970, more than half of British tourists who went abroad used charter airlines offering "inclusive tours." By then, 5.8 million of the 34.5 million British (17 percent) vacationers went abroad. In Germany, "travel intensity" (the percentage of Germans going on vacations for at least five days) increased from 24 percent in 1954 to 49 percent in 1972 (when 12 percent went by air). Also in France, large flows were set in motion during the July holidays: half of the twenty million French tourists decided to take the road during that month, intent on reaching their nearly three million second homes in the countryside. Statistics revealed the French stayed more than twenty-five nights outside their homes on an annual basis. All in all, in 1970, about 156 million tourists roamed the planet (exploded from 25 million in 1950, and 75 million a decade later, so with the largest relative increase during the 1950s), dwindling the number of forced migrants. More than two-thirds of them had Europe as destination, most of them Italy (1970), later (in 1988) to be overtaken by France. Per capita, relatively few Americans traveled abroad: about 15 million in 1965, just 7 percent of the population. To Europe, only 1 percent of the tourists were black.[91]

***

Spain, as a 'peripheral' country isolating itself politically from the 'core,' may function as an exemplary case when it comes to the equalizing and differentiating effects of the European economic and mobility miracle. In 1955, one and a half million tourists visited the country, a number exploding to forty million during the years up to 1978, which was more than its thirty-seven million inhabitants. Spain earned about $400 million (1974) on tourism, but nonetheless experienced massive migratory flows: nine hundred thousand Spaniards to North and Latin America and four hundred thousand returning from there (1970), large migratory movements from the Spanish countryside to the cities, especially Madrid and Barcelona (one million agricultural workers traveled to the industrial cores between 1950 and 1960). The migration to Northern Europe took place mostly in buses. Meanwhile, in the country itself, the middle classes increased from 17 percent to 28 percent of the population, with an increase of nine million persons during the 1960s, forming the core of the motorization wave that would move through Spain as much as it moved elsewhere. But in terms of car density, the change in Spain was enormous: from 3 cars per thousand inhabitants in 1952 to 125, a more than fortyfold increase. Only Japan's change was more spectacular: in Japan, the *mai-ka* (my car) period started in 1966, when 10 million vehicles were registered, 3.8 million of them private cars.[92]

The equally seasonal counterflows of migrants from the Mediterranean countries to the Northwest from the late 1950s until well into the 1980s are heavily under researched from a mobility point of view, but a study by economic historian Paolo Guimarães shows that the motor bus (equally under researched) formed the backbone of these counterflows. The modest interest among mobility historians for these flows (which in the late 1950s started to change dramatically in "destination, character and scale" into "'managed' recruitment systems") is regrettable, because these flows are crucial for an understanding of the development of European integration "from below" (as opposed to and often prefiguring the unification efforts by the technocrats). From the 1970s these counterflows reversed direction during the summer months, as for more and more migrants "their country of origin now also became an aim for their holidays." Before Franco, Salazar, and the Greek and Turkish colonels and generals gave in to the mounting pressures from below and from their colleagues within the six countries of the EEC to liberalize international mobility, Italian immigrants formed the only available reservoir of manual labor on the European continent, a flow mainly directed to France and Switzerland. Half the workers and nearly all families were illegal before 1950. In 1970, Switzerland tried (but failed), by referendum, to restrict the influx of 'strangers' who meanwhile amounted to one-tenth of the population of six million.[93]

The migratory flows from Portugal can be 'read' as the paragon of transport coordination (the management of the struggle between road and rail) enforcing continental transnationalism and, in a certain way, even as one of the harbingers of Europe-wide parliamentary democracy. When the Portuguese government (as the last of the southern governments to make "the turn to Europe") in 1952 installed a coordination committee to monitor the effects of its demographic pressures on migration, it was surprised by the existence of a blossoming bus tourism organization called Europa-Bus, which served nearly nineteen thousand kilometers of lines throughout Europe, especially in a northwestern corridor to France and farther north, to Germany and the Benelux. During the second half of the 1960s, the flows of Portuguese migrants had increased to more than fifty thousand per year, at a moment when already half a million Spaniards were working in the North, mostly in France. Regulating these flows by the Portuguese government, however, was possible only through cooperation with the receiving countries, whose European Conference of Ministers of Transport had already addressed the issue of road-rail controversy, for instance, through the enforced regionalization of local bus companies. Portuguese smugglers, using local taxis, brought migrants to the Spanish border, from where illegal private bus companies transported them farther north.

'Coordination' implied, just as it had before the war, the protection of the national railways, who were given a monopoly through special national bus companies (in France and Spain) or through licensing regional private companies under strict coordination principles (as in Portugal), but international coordination also meant Portugal had to negotiated with Spain, France, Switzerland, Germany, and the Benelux countries about the partitioning of responsibilities and revenues. Thus, a "double tree structure" emerged, a corridor through Spain (that initially prohibited buses to pick up passengers) and a fine-meshed network to industrial sites in the North (avoiding France's autoroutes) and from tiny villages in Portugal. The 1,830-kilometer trip from Paris to Lisbon took thirty-one hours in 1984, tourists mingling with migrants. By the end of the period covered here, more than

1.4 million Portuguese had left the country (since 1957), 900,000 of them to France, a massive example of subversive mobility; by then, migrants started using the car and charter flights, but the bus lines never vanished: they merged into the Eurobus network, "the European Grey Hound [*sic*]." But in quantitative terms, the *internal* rural-to-urban migratory flows "by young men in search of work" were even more impressive, although it is difficult to find quantitative evidence for this.[94]

Television as Domesticated Adventure: The Family as the Subject of Car Mobility

The vacation frenzy of the third quarter of the twentieth century cannot be understood without considering two phenomena, always against a Cold War background: the middle class and the family, as several excellent studies within the field of tourism history have shown. For years, social scientists have argued against "the myth of the declining family," a paradox emerging during the "golden age of the family." But Theodore Caplow and colleagues, who coined this phrase in a study referring to the famous prewar *Middletown* study of the Lynd couple, do not dedicate much attention to the car, certainly not compared to the central role in *Middletown*.

Indeed, the golden age of the Euro-American nuclear family (heterosexual parents, as an "ethnocentric construct of the West") is mostly visible in the phenomenon that this functioned as the basic social unit, replacing social class. The nuclear family constituted the very basis of national welfare state policies, also in Germany, where the tradition of social security and the central image of the worker was particularly strong. Later, France, during "the years after electricity but before electronics" (the decade covering the late 1950s and early 1960s) transformed rapidly "from a rural, empire oriented, Catholic country into a fully industrialized, decolonized, and urban one." When the myth of the nuclear family could no longer be upheld, French marketeers started targeting the "young couple" (*jeunes* ménages, lit. young households) as a "new unit of middle-class consumption." The importance of French modernization, Kristin Ross concluded in her study of "fast cars and clean bodies," lies in "unifying the diverse middle classes," involving "leveling the difference between an older middle class and those two politically dangerous classes: the (potentially militant) working class and the traditional petite bourgeoisie."[95]

According to Ross, "neither Ford nor Lenin" was the preferred French "road to modernization." As so many social scientists and historians analyzing postwar Western modernization, she claimed, perhaps with the United States as a template, the worker got assimilated through the middle-class unit of the small family, basing her conclusions on novels, exactly the source we identified as becoming less and less reliable when it comes to depicting working-class life. Thus, her scholarship does in the cultural realm what capitalist elites did in physical reality: constructing the middle class as "presage[ing] a homogenous national class that is no longer, properly speaking, a class." In reality, nearly half a million people (19 percent of Paris's population but a staggering two-thirds of the inhabitants of the center) left the capital in the two decades after 1954, toward the suburbs, setting in motion a gentrification of the inner city, increasing the number of *cadres supérieurs* by 51 percent. In all fairness, Ross does document the reshaping of the big cities, but she explains this, from an American perspective, by using the concept of 'race' instead of class: her analysis thus results in the suburbs becoming populated by an "unskilled, large immigrant work force," whereas the original working class (most of the population!) has vanished from her narrative. No wonder, then, is the remainder of her book about "the *cadre* ... who defends both the interests of the factory and the interests of the work force," whose need for a "self-definition" on the basis of status rather than income is crucial to "[help] define [his] autonomy ... His leisure time is largely taken up ... with frenetic actual or imagined acquisition and accumulation, and with a kind of cult of comfort centered on the home," including the provision of a 'family car.'[96]

In the United States, the nuclear family competed with the car as "the most salient symbol ... of their newfound prosperity." The baby boom created a "'child-centered' society," with the birth rate for third children doubling between 1940 and 1960, and tripling for fourth children. Single-family home ownership between 1946 and 1956 grew more than during the entire previous 150 years. The family "also offered men a refuge from, as well as a justification for, increasingly bureaucratic and unsatisfying work lives," literary scholar Lyn Elliot observed. "No man who owns his own house and lot can be a Communist," builder William J. Levitt opined, "He has too much to do." One of these activities was transporting his kin around in a car, starting from a house in the suburbs, surrounded by a lawn as a "kind of verdant moat," in the words of urban historian Kenneth Jackson. Some families changed homes as often as their cars.[97]

A history of the United Kingdom lists the major transformations within the British family, illustrating the centrality of the family culture of mobility: the mean age for marriage plunged for both genders to values lowest since centuries (a process driven by worker families), while divorce rates kept increasing (since the 1960s, most divorce requests came from women), as did the remarriage rates. "The family was also resuming some of its earlier recreational self-sufficiency," which was possible because "affluence, birth control, car ownership, and the new media were domesticating recreation: the family that played together stayed together." Europe was the center of this transformation: nowhere else in the West was the "marriage boom" so large. The newly constituted social unit benefitted from parallel developments such as an acceleration in urbanization, an increase in state intervention, and the rolling out of the welfare state: in the mid-1970s, 16 percent of West European GDP was spent on 'welfare,' compared to 8–11 percent in the United States, Canada, Australia, and Japan (and 2–3 percent in Korea and Mexico). In the United States, the tax benefits for health insurance, social security, and private pension plans functioned as a "hidden welfare state," highly gendered and racialized once it became rooted in the suburbs. Of course, social scientists played the race card: "White workers now embraced more of a racial than a class identity"; they "battled to protect their neighborhoods from an invasion of blacks escaping the ghetto," resulting in a highly segregated housing space. But the results were no fantasy: from 1945 to 1960, "more than two hundred acts of violence were committed in Detroit against blacks moving into white neighborhoods. Militant blacks fought back … In 1964 … a fifth of families were living below the poverty level. Of them 78 percent were white, though they included an astonishing 80 percent of all nonwhites."[98]

Despite these conditions, the suburban nuclear family was seen as "a potent weapon against communism and a bastion of security in the atomic age." No surprise, then, did Marwick, in his extensive study of the 1960s, identify "the young and not-so-young married couple … with wives usually taking the initiative" as the real target of postwar marketing. In the United Kingdom, an American advertising agency called her the "mass market housewife." On the 'production side,' the peak of the baby boom was 1947, producing children who "achieved the magic age of 13 in 1960." The purchase power of these teenagers, marketing experts were quick to notice, was higher "than the total sales of General Motors." But their main target remained the young married couples, who were also the trendsetters, just as much as "America continued to set the standards," first in car ownership and then in the spread of television: "Affluence appeared merely to consolidate conventional, family-based America, America of the Rat Race." The "leisure-time family" (*Freizeitfamilie*) was also the aim of marketeers in Germany.[99]

***

"The television set is quite obviously keeping the family together," a British leisure study from the early 1970s opined. "It cuts down attendance at cinemas and even of public-houses," although "it does not much appeal to teenagers … By contrast with the television set, the motor-car might seem likely to break up the cohesion of the family," and that is why it was so important to conceive of the car as an "extension of the family living-room." This study subtly pointed at class differences in the use profile of the car: "Middle-class observers have remarked, with regret or amusement, that most working-class people do not know how to take advantage of a car. When they get to the countryside or the sea-front they do not always go for a good walk or swim. They are just as likely to sit in the crowded and fuggy machine, surrounded by food and newspapers, with the window steamed-up and a transistor blaring out the Light Programme." So much for the alleged fading of class in favor of race! Similar examples of working-class appropriation of the car and its culture can be observed for the Netherlands, where "roadside tourism" (*bermtoerisme*) incited road planners to reserve special parking lots along the new highways for these tourists to picnic and look at the passing (or congested) traffic.

We will, in the next sections, elaborate extensively on the split within national car cultures between a middle-class and a more proletarian flavor, but despite these differences, which were eagerly brought up by concerned middle-class observers, what is remarkable for this period is exactly the opposite: the enormous surge 'from below,' so to speak, toward a middle-class lifestyle. When British fashion guru Mary Quant, to give only one example, brought out her first set of 'hip' clothes, she had targeted "the spreading youth culture" and was fully surprised by her sudden success, realizing "we were interpreting the mood of the whole generation, not just smart art students."[100] Similar surprised reactions are known from the music world, where the 'invasion of the Beatles in America' pushed a subculture into the open, which seemed to cover an entire generation, irrespective of class.

Middle-class family outings and vacations, then, increasingly centered around the car, a fact that traffic experts had to get used to, as they were traditionally geared toward the more 'serious' forms of mobility. For instance, a British national leisure survey from 1967 does not include car touring in its listings of leisure "experiences," nor are cars included under the section of "sport equipment" (in all fairness, the report does mention the predominance of "going for a drive" in a separate section on "The Recreational Influence of Car-Ownership," where it is acknowledged that both the car and the TV set have "revolutionised our use of leisure time"). Not only that: with both media functioning as "representation of motherhood, marriage, and the family home," such durables not only were "an oasis for white women" but also helped cement "an ideology of familialism (and happy cleanliness)," forging this ideology into "a myth of the middle-class, happy family." There was also a homology in both media's respective societal roles, as Raymond Williams observed: they enabled "mobile privatisation," as people were "increasingly living as private small-family units, ... while at the same time there is a quite unprecedented mobility of such restricted privacies." Indeed, apart from a reality, the white, middle-class family was also a myth, an "ideological construct" as analyzed in their car dependence in recent studies by American studies scholar Cotten Seiler and media studies scholar Jeremy Packer. For this type of family, mobility and abundance became synonymous, a study of German consumption concluded: fledgling neoliberal convictions about the freedom of choice governing both consumption and democratic voting, created an atmosphere in which it was no longer the (German, prewar) "soldier man" (*soldatischer Mann*) who took center stage, but rather "daddy (*Vati*), who belongs to his family on Saturday."[101]

Television scholars have meanwhile developed theories that go far beyond Williams's simple analogy between car touring and television watching, especially for the United States, where, from 1948 to 1955, half of all homes had a television set installed. During the first years, high hopes were invested in the integrating influence on family coherence: an American survey from 1956 indeed found TV "had the effect of keeping the family at home more than formerly," quoting an interviewee who declared they "turn it on at 3 p.m. and watch until 10 p.m. We never go anywhere." But when the youth movement took on momentum, parents no longer believed "TV would keep their children off the streets," and the set was seen as "a family member" (not a seductive woman as in motorists toward their car), a "newborn baby," a "family friend," a "nurse," and a "family pet," listening to "his master's voice." Now, commentators started to worry about the "feminizing" effects of broadcasting ("momism") to a largely "passive" audience. Theorists (quite prolific in the discipline of TV studies, because "television overall seems to resist analysis" due to its "sheer extensiveness") have observed similar trends of the viewer becoming a "cyborg" to what we have seen in the history of automobilism, but here the cyborg has a "feminine body." To counter this trend, television developed strategies of the "construction of a violent hypermasculinity," through presenting "the discourse on sport as 'a place of "autonomous masculinity,"'" through the introduction of a plethora of "cop/detective shows" (*Miami Vice* being an example of "a show of male excess and display"), and through "mimicking cinematic conventions," making TV produce something more like the familiar movie experience. In this context, women "lack the distance required for 'proper' reasoning and viewing" (in our terminology: they are seen as less prone to irony). Irony, in this context, remained the privilege of the middle class, whose members wrote in *Harper's Magazine* of 1953 that the new domesticity of the suburbs enabled a "new form of social cohesion which allowed people to be alone and together at the same time."[102]

***

The affinities between television and the world of the car are striking, indeed, especially when, in the second half of the 1950s, the US Interstate Highway network was constructed, connecting the new suburbs with their shopping malls, of which the first was opened in 1956 (developed by Victor Gruen in Edina, Minnesota, after the Galleria Vittorio Emanuel in Milan). TV theorists were quick to discover deep analogies, as a postmodern version of what we found for car driving and writing at the start of the century. The "similar principles of construction and operation" of "freeways, malls, and television," such theorists claimed, produce a "*fiction effect* ... a partial loss of touch with the here and now, dubbed ... as *distraction*. This semi-fiction is akin to but not identical with split belief—knowing a representation is not real but nevertheless momentarily closing off the here and now and sinking into another world—promoted within the apparatus of the theater, the cinema, and the novel." If we limit this statement to *late* capitalism, it is indeed striking how often in the novels discussed in this and the next chapter the transfer into another, parallel world is described, as a prefiguration of the virtual extension of the automotive adventure. If TV afforded adventure, it was virtual and spatial, providing, in the words of early TV programmer Thomas Huntington, "a maximum extension of the perceived environment with a minimum of effort. Television is a form of 'going places' without even the expenditure of movement, to say nothing of money." The sense of "being there," provided by TV watching, produced "a kind of *hyper-realism*. Advertisers [of TV sets] repeatedly promised that their sets would deliver picture and sound quality so real that the illusion would come alive." The car also prefigured a new way of seeing, a "one-way view" from "every seat ... in the front row," allowing an "illusion of presence": "one could remain alone in the living room, but at the same time sustain an illusion of being in the company of others," the electronic-age equivalent of the 'ironic car.'

All these media, including the car, afford (or better, necessitate) "practices and skills that can be performed semiautomatically in a distracted state—such as driving, shopping, or television watching—[. . . They] are the barely acknowledged ground of everyday experience. This ground is without locus, a partially *derealized realm* from which a new quotidian fiction emanates." A mall, William Kowinski concluded in *The Malling of America* (1985), is a "TV you walk around in." Likewise, I would add, the freeway is a TV you drive around in: it "makes it possible to drive coast to coast and never see anything," as we will soon see when we analyze Kerouac's *On the Road*. Similarly, the mall is "the paradoxical promise of adventure on the road within an idyll of Main Street in a small town before the age of the automobile." Tellingly, this adventure of the experience of "an attenuated and controlled version of the crowded street" should be experienced on foot, *but one must drive to it*. The experience enhances the confusion of interior versus exterior, private versus public as analyzed by Walter Benjamin in his analysis of Baudelaire's Parisian nineteenth-century arcades. Just like "the sociality with the outside world ... has become physically impossible inside the automobile [and] is re-created via radio, disc and tape," so offers television a "similarly derealized communication." Mall, like television and cars, produce a "zombie effect" (Kowinski).[103]

In the introduction, we quoted Barthes's famous (and somewhat anachronistic, as we argued) dictum about the car as a cathedral. Much less known, however, is his use of car driving as a metaphor for the "operation of mythology itself": the glances through the windshield force one to "grasp the presence of the glass and the distance of the landscape," a "constant alternation [that] constitutes a spatial category of a continuous elsewhere which is [Barthes's] model for the alibi of myth." The windshield, TV analyst Margaret Morse concluded (somewhat biased toward vision, as we will see), "is not merely glass and image of the world into which one speeds, but also a mirror reflection of the driver and passengers; the rear-mirror displays the window of where one has been; the side-view mirror shows what to anticipate next. Meanwhile, the landscape unfolds right and left, distorted by speed," a multiple effect experienced "simultaneously." In short, the new media afforded "a celebration of the instantaneous," allowing "insistent 'present-ness.'" "The only excuse for writing a novel," former novelist Ken Kesey declared, "is if it can't be done as a movie." Barthes also grasped a phenomenon we will observe over and over again in Western postwar car culture as expressed in its autopoetic utterances: the phenomenon that the car's speed "expresses itself here [in the case of the Citroën] in less aggressive signs, less sporting, as if she [*sic*!] transferred (*passait*) from an heroic into a classic form." As such, the "Déesse" is "mediatized in less than a quarter of an hour, realizing, in this exorcism, the very movement of *petite-bourgeois* promotion."

Television sought to expose the plain underbelly of car culture, such as in the failed NBC sitcom *My Mother the Car* (1965) in which "a cheap family car" starts talking, the beginning of a whole series of movies of talking cars but, at this early date, not yet credible enough compared to the talking horse in *Mr. Ed* or the robots in the highly successful *Star Trek* series, enabling a frontier fantasy in outer space and offering the possibility to generate the hot rod experience in space or even in ancient Rome (*Ben Hur*, 1959). The analogy between TV watching and car driving is no fantasy of media theorists: Ford sponsored the *Ed Sullivan Show*, in which the Supremes, Martha and the Vandellas, and Marvin Gaye appeared, while GM supported the Western series *Bonanza*.[104]

Motivation Research: Bringing Class Back in Mobility History

Against this transmedial background, the nuclear family as collective-individual holiday subject needs to be analyzed here in quite some detail in order to assess the (dis)continuities of the automotive adventure developed in my previous study. French research, for instance, revealed the emergence of a two-pronged holiday, consisting of a part where parents were separated from their children as the latter went to holiday camp, followed by a commonly shared part. The holiday camp had a long tradition in France, based on prewar socialist and Catholic practices and expressed, for instance, in the Villages Vacances Familiales (Family Vacation Villages).

In the United States, where, by the 1970s (when the number of family trips started to decline), about an equal amount of tourists (sixty million) as in Europe (seventy million) took part in the annual 'pleasure migration' wave, it was the "dude ranch" (with a tradition going back to the prewar years) that attracted thousands of families to the West, creating an interesting fusion between car mobility and media, as by 1960, more than one-third of TV programming was covered by the Western. Experiences of car driving and TV watching both linked to the family ideal and to Cold War fears for the "bad guys." From 1953, California ranked first in American vacation destinations, and Colorado was second: "The children in the backseat were clad in cowboy gear, ready to shoot 'em up in a western vacation that blurred the boundaries between fantasy and reality." Dude ranches sold "an authentic western experience like the scenes vacationers saw in television western, with the comforts of home. Disneyland expanded this with other 'fantastic' experiences when the "western craze faded in the 1960s."[105]

By then, television had moved away from the beats and led its audience into outer space (*Star Trek*, aired from 1966). Thus, domesticity was part and parcel of Western mobility; more particularly, automobilism cannot be without sessility. It was this "California Culture" as a "symbol of relaxed, prosperous outdoor living, linked to a 'car culture,' that became the model of Western popular culture. Car design followed these trends (if it did not lead them): according to the Detroit "oligopoly," styling became "the most significant factor in creating the desire to buy." Avner Offer, who recently analyzed the American "challenge of affluence," argued car design aimed a "*sensual gratification*" rather than social distinction, or rather class distinction, because "non-class characteristics like age, gender and family status" (and ethnicity, one is inclined to add) remain important. Earlier, historian David Gartman had already shown how "by the end of the decade [of the 1950s], the qualitative differences in engineering, construction, and aesthetics between the automotive classes had virtually disappeared, replaced by small quantitative differences in size, horsepower, chrome, and price," but it is important to realize that these strenuous efforts to erase class are not the same as the disappearance of class. Yet, the classless myth of the 'middle-class society' was all pervasive: this became visible, for instance, in the marketing of the Cadillac as "everyman's luxury car," developed for "the man on his way up," a slogan deemed a bit too "ordinary" by several contemporary marketeers.[106]

Offering eighty-one models based on only three basic body types, GM had Harley Earl, in a blatant rejection of modernist principles, design its cars with "oversize curves, non-functional grilles, fake portholes[,] express[ing] a fantasy of affluence, luxury, sensual delight and power." Earl had started his career as a designer of customized car bodies for Hollywood stars, and now this "postmodernist before his time" gave his fellow Americans cars that "blend[ed] well with affluent suburbia" but proved "often incongruous in more workaday or countryside environments. Its natural habitat were the television commercial and the dealer's floor." And although the Big Three had tried, in 1957, to abandon stock car racing, the power and size of its engines soared precipitously, focused on the upper-middle class, who, during the 1950s, purchased half of all new American cars, spending much more than half the industry's revenue because they tended to buy the expensive models of what many Americans perceived as "The Classless Car." It is this segment of the middle class that personified the "American love affair with the automobile," which was, in fact, as historian Peter Norton convincingly showed, a social construction reaching back to the 1920s. Norton related how the television broadcast "Merrily We Roll Along," seen by millions, featured Groucho Marx, who told a history of American car love, in which "the hostility to the automobile typical of American cities in the 1910s and 1920s [was] never reckoned with." Marshall McLuhan surfed on this wave of love by calling his bundle of art and media critiques from 1951 *The Mechanical Bride*, but the essay with the same title in the bundle deals with women's legs, whereas the essay "Husband's Choice" (first sentence: "Love at first flight?") deals with the car.[107]

Designed for ultimate "comfort," the "softer" suspensions and very 'elastic' engines tended to "insulate its driver from the frictions of travel," much more so than European cars did, with a modest American market share in Europe as a result. This is perhaps the most astonishing of American car development in this period: American cars were consciously designed as impractical for everyday use, and their worldwide sales were consciously jeopardized in order to express affluence, hedonism, and exuberance. American car design of the 1950s was a flight forward (nearly) into the realm of the carnivalesque, a hysteria of greed. A junior designer at GM lamented the "superficial, fashion-oriented" design, culminating in the failure of the Ford Edsel, whose designer, Jack Reith, committed suicide. By the end of the decade, the American car as "a jukebox on wheels" (modernist designer Raymond Loewy; conversely, some jukeboxes looked like car fronts, by the way) drove into a crisis (as a result of this "great American auto war," in management and international affairs professors Lorraine Eden and Maureen Appel Molot's Cold War terminology), and the Volkswagen made its inroads. To the surprise of the industry, the Volkswagen was bought by "younger and wealthier [Americans] than the average Ford and Chevrolet buyer," inciting the American industry to develop its 'compacts' (such as the Ford Falcon). The Volkswagen minibus, which could be produced much cheaper than US equivalents because of lower labor costs, would appear to be the prototype of the sport utility vehicles (SUVs) of a later phase.[108]

***

And yet, Offer's analysis misses an important point, crucial for our argumentation, and brilliantly exposed by Shelley Nickles, who followed Victoria de Grazia and Lizabeth Cohen's plea to bring class back into consumption history: "A persisting working class in a supposedly classless middle-class society ... An increasing number of blue-collar workers now had middle-class pocketbooks that allowed them to live in suburban 'mass-produced domestic comfort' and participate in the white identity defined by that racially homogenous environment." Nickles's analysis of 'motivation research,' which we will introduce soon, can be substantiated by a much earlier, contemporary study of the "affluent worker" in the United Kingdom that effectively criticized the "*embourgeoisement* of the working class" thesis: "the life-styles that we recorded would seem better interpreted in terms of the adaptation of old norms to new exigencies and opportunities than in terms of any basic normative reorientation. What is clearer still is that affluence, and even residence in localities of a 'middle-class' character, do not lead on, in any automatic way, to the integration of manual workers and their families into middle-class society." Furthermore, in a British study on the "politics of class," sociologist Geoffrey Evans and political science scholar James Tilly convincingly showed "both [British] middle class and working class identities are very stable over time."[109] This conclusion would imply working-class automobilism may also differ from that of hegemonic middle-class culture, despite all those 'convergence' studies by contemporary observers and historians in their wake alike.

Indeed, marketing specialists in the United States observed such consumers "moved up economically but not culturally," and they developed new tools called "motivation research" to get a grip on the shifts in consumerism taking place under the surface of 'middle-class affluence,' and uncover "the persistence of working-class values, lifestyles, and taste within this middle-income mass market." Instead of asking simple questions (from people of the same class they themselves belonged to) and mold them into statistics, motivation researchers performed qualitative research through in-depth interviews and role playing to feel the pulse of their new potential clients, a difference in method that 'rhymes,' so to speak, with the difference between the analysis of highbrow autopoetic literature from the one-dimensional perspective of the Quest of the Self, versus scholarship on lowbrow utterances that must mobilize an array of transmedial methodologies to get a grip on popular (car) cultures. Contrary to widespread belief, the study of 'lowbrow culture' necessitates more sophisticated methods, no doubt also because now middle-class observers had to get acquainted with the habits and norms of people who were not in the same class (see also the introduction). The motivation researchers explained the necessity of this more elaborate method by referring to the "complex" character of consumer motivations, but we know, from our study of autopoetic novels, there is also an inability involved to verbalize one's motives—hence the need of a more elaborate 'apparatus' to dig into the 'popular mind.'

Against "professional middle-class values of hygiene, efficiency, and simplicity" (values expressed by hegemonic designers catering for an upper-middle class market), motivation researchers found three characteristic design features embraced by the new class: "bulk and size" (if "it looks bigger, it must be worth more"), "embellishment and visual flash" and "color." The magazine *True Story*, with a readership of twelve million (a "middle-class working class" consisting of 81 percent of "working class housewives," defined as "wives of blue-collar workers, including craftsmen, factory operatives, and service workers such as truck drivers"), published what postmodern anthropologists later would call "true fiction" (as we saw in the introduction) and what we could call "true romance" (after the eponymous title of *True Story*'s sister magazine): stories that denied, as most marketeers focused on the concept of the 'classless middle-class society' (but in fact "based on upper-middle class values and tastes") assumed, "that prosperity was eroding the class identity of the American worker." The magazine showed the emergence of "blue-collar aesthetics" of "a new social class of suburban workers." The "wage earner wife decides most family purchases," reflecting the gendered dichotomy of masculine "function and production" versus feminine "ornamentation and consumption." It was the car industry's Sloanism (after General Motors CEO Alfred Sloan) that led this shift toward "working-class purchasing power" through the introduction of a "ladder of consumption," in which it, by the end of the 1960s, introduced a new car type, the "intermediate," a 'middle-class car' in-between the "full-size" and the "compacts" (such as the 1969 models of the Ford Fairlane and the Mercury Comet), "appealing [not only] to budget-conscious family car consumers for being not too big and not too small" but also to their children, as they formed the base for the later "muscle cars."

In 1969 intermediates, led by Chevrolet (with nearly half a million sold) had a market share of one-quarter of total production of 8.8 million; virtually all were equipped with a V-8 engine. Motivation research confirmed this hierarchy through their introduction of a rank order of consumers: "upper-upper, old families; lower-upper, newly arrived wealthy;

upper-middle, professionals and successful businessmen; lower-middle, white-collar salaried; upper-lower, skilled, blue-collar wage earners; lower-lower, unskilled labor. The lower-middle and upper lower classes were the 'middle majority,' ... represent[ing] about 53 percent of all families in postwar America." From this perspective, the "application of ornament through chrome and color even to standardized refrigerators suggested the pervasiveness of working class taste." The preference for large cars with lots of power, adorned with flashy ornaments like tail fins and chrome strips were not an expression of "bad taste, fashion, or status-seeking," as Nickles argued against the manipulation thesis by contemporaries such as Vance Packard and his 1957 best seller *The Hidden Persuaders* (three million copies sold until 1975), "but ... social identity" of a "distinctive working-class culture created not by men but by women and united not by politics but in taste." The quoted British study from the 1960s confirms this: "Powerful motivations to gain higher material standards of living did not in the main appear to be accompanied by status striving [and] did not result in the acceptance of distinctively middle-class social perspectives."

Even the Museum of Modern Art (MoMA) with its 1950–1955 exhibition on *Good Design* could not influence this shift, nor could designer John Vassos, who removed the fins from his Cadillac and was praised by MoMA. Blue-collar consumers had the largest share in appliance purchases, and the largest share in purchasing the most expensive ones. They motivated marketeers to place the "V" emblem of Cadillac on RCA televisions and radios, testifying to the fact that even some functionalists started to give in to the new taste.[110] The 'brilliance' of Nickles's analysis resides here: she helps us 'defuse' those social scientists that did not manage to think beyond their own class base and hence could perceive of working-class culture only as 'not us,' 'manipulated,' 'ugly.' This does not only apply to publicists like Vance Packard: it was Theodor Adorno who interpreted this development as a "loss of luxury," comparing the 'fake' Cadillac (which emerged from the cheap Chevrolet through "only minor rearrangements") unfavorably with the "superior" Rolls-Royce. Instead, it was middle-class culture that got 'proletarianized,' for instance, in the spread of the "social kitchen," the kitchen in which the family gathered, testifying to "a working-class tradition influencing middle-class servantless homes." But marketing research kept being mesmerized by white, middle-class affluence: Marcus Felson's comparison of American lifestyle research in the 1920s and 1960s showed how middle-class blacks and women were excluded from much of this research.[111]

***

What often is neglected by mobility historians, however, is the importance of sedentarism in enabling the pseudo-nomadism of the car holiday. Even more than the car perhaps, the home defined the "middle-class revolution." According to a study on American suburbs from 1967 (remarkably enough not much dealing with the car), the home is clearly central: "If left to themselves, lower-middle-class people do what they have always done: put their energies into home and family, seeking to make life as comfortable as possible, and supporting, broadening, and varying it with friends, neighbors, church, and a voluntary association." And a car, one is inclined to add. Both, the home and the car, are, as cocoons of intimacy, a protection against the 'other,' part of "a construction of middle-class fears about an apathetic yet dangerous underclass," especially scary if they do not own a home. Soon, as we will see later in this chapter, the freeway network's anonymity would also provide a certain protection to the car driver and their passengers: the cocoon took on systemic traits. Mobility geographer Tim Cresswell explained in his excellent study *On the Move* how society and the state define who is allowed to move by forcing people to sedentarize. The home, then, allows the middle-class family to move, in a home away from home, on wheels. The classical form of this home on wheels is the station wagon, originally conceived to bring guests back to the station but in this period developed into an affordable family car designed with the family vacation in mind, offering seats for up to nine persons and, after the war, constructed as all-steel bodies, such as the 1946 Willys, the 1949 Plymouth and Chevrolet, and the 1952 Ford. By the end of the 1950s, 20 percent of all cars sold were station wagons, against only 3 percent of total production by the beginning of the decade.[112]

During the year, such cars could literally be used as living rooms and even dining rooms on wheels in drive-in movie theaters and drive-in restaurants: sitting in the car, "no one had to dress up." The movie *American Graffiti* (1973; director George Lucas used the near-hundredfold revenues [compared to the investment of only $1.25 million] to finance *Star Wars*) tries to give its audience the cruising experience of the car culture in and around such a drive-in, reminiscent of a high school culture in the 1940s where "boys talked in terms of pushing petting as far as their dates would allow, describing the experience as 'having fun' or 'taking them for a ride.'" It was, in Fredric Jameson's analysis, the "inaugural film of postmodern nostalgia." In Philadelphia, some drive-ins introduced live vaudeville shows, where audiences could honk their car horns as a sign of approval. Between 1941 and 1954, the number of drive-in theaters increased from 52 to 4,200, the largest growth occurring after the introduction of the decentralized sound system. The structural 'affinity' between car and cinema went even so far as the introduction of Cinerama, a three-camera system attempting "to imitate and exceed the automobile experience." Cinerama films were often shot from atop cars or planes, allowing a doubly enhanced experience of mobility. There can even be construed a mutual interplay between home and car when suburban houses came to be shaped into one-story ranch homes with "combined indoor and outdoor living" in which "domestic and nature experiences" could mix. "On vacations, sleeping in or beside the family car became an extended form of backyard living as millions of Americans discovered the sensory pleasures, intimacy, and economy of autocamping. The family sedan or station wagon became a ranch house on wheels."[113]

Soon, specialized camping vehicles came on the market based on pickup trucks, or vans and buses (such as the Merry Pranksters' bus we met earlier), or fully dedicated motor homes (including the headaches and respiratory problems caused by the formaldehyde in the plywood). The "motor home boom" took place between 1966 and 1973. For the youngsters, the vans—the most famous of them the Volkswagen bus—"combined the freedom of hippie buses with the hands-on appeal of hot rods and the versatility and privacy of the family station wagon." It was this culture that became the norm in the West, so much so that American surveys in 1950 revealed "spare-time habits and expenditure patterns of urban workers" differed only very slightly from this norm. The jury of social scientists is still out on whether we should call this a "leveled-off middle-class society" (*nivellierter Mittelstandsgesellschaft,* in the words of one of the leading researchers in this field in Germany, Helmut Schelsky), in which the distinction between consumers is to be found in "unequal consumption styles" (*ungleiche Konsumstile*), to quote another famous German sociologist, Ulrich Beck.[114]

Some observers hold a plea, instead, for "mass welfare" (*Massenwohlstand*) as a pluralized and individualized phenomenon, where classes have not disappeared but have "multiple-fragmented in its appearance" and are difficult to detect. Nonetheless, the debate on *Bürgerlichkeit,* which raged nowhere else so intensely as in Germany, seems to result in at least the consensus that lifestyle differences decreased and that "one cannot deny the continuity and the rise of the *bürgerliche* lifestyle after 1945." Neither noble, farmer, nor proletarian lifestyles have had a similar impact. This is all the more remarkable if one realizes the share of the German petty bourgeois (*Kleinbürger*) decreased (from 15 to 10 percent of the population, remarkably parallel to France, where the same group had diminished in size from 25 to 14 percent), whereas the number of dependent employees (*Arbeitnehmer*) increased faster than ever before. Even if one recognizes Germany is not a *bürgerliche* society, the concept of individual self-realization located within the family is part of a *bürgerliche* heritage, and the car seemed to contribute to this self-realization as no other consumption good. Students of German consumer society do not doubt consumption lured the Germans "in a soft manner" into modern individualism. Especially for this 'model' Western country, it is therefore all the more surprising how the higher echelons of the working class (*Facharbeiter*) assimilated so easily and eagerly in the new political order if one realizes surveys immediately after the war registered a widespread skepsis among young workers toward the new society and their lack of satisfaction in their jobs.[115]

***

However, all these suggestions of cultural convergence should not let us believe 'class' was no longer an adequate concept to describe postwar capitalist societies. Without this concept, it is hard to understand why the 1970s, first in the United States, became a "transitional moment between New Deal liberalism and Reaganesque conservatism." This was the period in which "votes from otherwise loyal, pro-New Deal working-class Democrats" brought Ronald Reagan, first, his Californian governorship in 1966 and then, in 1980, after two failed attempts, the presidency, intent on "undo[ing] [President Johnson's] Great Society." The American working class had, since 1896, more or less continuously supported the Republican Party, until President Franklin Roosevelt managed to gather them under the Democratic New Deal. His argument was that "the average American citizen ... had been so forgotten after the last war," exactly the phase in which American automobilism took on such a broad flight. After World War II, at a moment when the middle class, "our liberal friends" in the ironic words of Reagan during a televised endorsement of presidential candidate Barry Goldwater in 1964, not the least as a result of the New Deal, flourished as never before, these same workers started to agree with Reagan's condemnation of "a little intellectual elite in a far-distant capital [who think they] can plan our lives for us better than we can plan them ourselves."

While, as Reagan argued, the elite said they cared for their constituency, but in reality lured the country toward socialism and communism, he promised during his presidential campaign to "make America great again." The "Reagan coalition" would include "traditional business Republicans, southern whites, and blue-collar ethnic Midwestern and northeastern Democrats," an electoral basis the Democratic party was gradually replacing by "people of color (black, Hispanic, Asian, and multiracial individuals), college-educated whites working in information industries, and unmarried women," all of whom they reckoned would automatically endorse progressive policies through simple demographic growth. It was not Reagan alone who did this, an angry Thomas Frank (who dedicated a book to this shift) concluded, it was also due to "the capitulation of the Democrats."[116] It is one of the historical theses of this study that the class-denying surveys we cited in the previous pages formed the scholarly equivalent of this 'little intellectual elite'" against whom Reagan mobilized the blue-collar part of his electorate. Was that, perhaps, the deeper reason why Jim Ballard was so eager to 'fuck Ronald Reagan'?

Class to Group, Culture to Lifestyle? The Fragmentation of Car Culture in the United States

One of social science's strategies to erase class consciousness was 'lifestyle research.' Students of middle-class and consumption history observed increasing trends of fragmentation, into lifestyles of "peer groups," into alternative subcultures and countercultures, into hegemonic and non-hegemonic subcultures, including women and nonwhites. "Lifestyle" as a concept stems from the early 1960s, when it first appeared in *Webster's International Dictionary* (1961) as a successor of the more class-conscious concept of "way of life." These subcultures' different relations with mobility complicates the analysis of the post–World War II period further. In this subsection, we will prepare our cultural analysis of both mainstream and non-hegemonic subcultures of automobilism of the next sections by providing some basic material conditions for these cultures. Although women were increasingly seen as the center of the consumption module 'family,' knowledge production about their possible different car use profile is remarkably scarce, apart from some anecdotal (and easily stereotyping) information such as the redesign of gas stations, including the mounting of a "plastic covering to shield the driver's hand from the chill of the gasoline coming out of the underground tank," integrated in a lightweight nozzle "specifically designed for women." And although Marwick asserts "the American dream was in many ways a nightmare for American women," the gains in female-owned car density were large in quantitative terms: in 1964, 38.5 million American women (more than 40 percent of all licensed drivers) had a driver's license. Women were often driving second family cars, a phenomenon that had reached one-fifth of American families. By 1977, more than 42 percent of the American cars owned by men (three-fourth of all cars) were driven by woman as "principal drivers." In that year, nearly 64 million women had a driver's license (a share that had doubled since 1940), and they bought 25 percent (domestic cars) to 30 percent (imported ones) of cars.[117]

At a moment when, around 1963 in the United States, social scientists declared car driving "nearly universal among men" (and, famously, 40 percent of men proposing their girlfriends to marry did so in a car), they also observed "significant decreases in time spent on food preparation and ironing" among women, to be compensated only by "increases in time shopping and in travel, particularly travel associated with household errands and the chauffeuring of children." In general, such surveys revealed women's daily mobility was less (in length and number of trips) than men's, but the differences between the genders in this respect diminished, especially between 1963 and 1980. The gendering of the car culture followed the shift from a "neopatriarchal gender ordering" to a "difference-based ordering," taking place mid-century and extensively analyzed by women's studies, some of the latter arguing "the 1968 protest movement contributed largely to the emergence of women's liberation movements in Western industrial societies," movements that knew how to instrumentalize the car for their emancipatory ambitions.

According to Julie Candler, writing the "Woman at the Wheel" column in *Woman's Day* magazine, women who "hated housework and preferred interesting work in the business world" needed a car. She wrote for a readership (larger "than any of the automotive magazines," she boasted) consisting of (as the magazine's own surveys showed) "mothers with young children and full- or part-time jobs, who lived in suburbs and commuted thirty minutes or more to and from work. They took modest family vacations, often camping trips within ten miles of home, and they worried about their kids' safety and stretching the family budget." Such women were "more interested in safe driving and [their] car's operation than how it looked." Next to safety, Candler's columns were dedicated mostly to "car repairs and maintenance," followed by "buying a new or used car," "car related vacations," and "style features." "The hand that rocks the cradle," she wrote in 1964, "is the hand that most often turns the steering wheel of the family car."[118]

Chrysler, from 1955 to 1957, tried to address this female market segment through a stereotyped Dodge La Femme, with "pink trim[,] a matching rain hat, umbrella, and handbag." It soon became "the favorite car of pimps all over the country." Some attentive marketeers argued, against the "male chauvinist pigs" in their midst, that women wanted "functionality, passenger safety, and accident protection." Candler, as a 'business woman' struggling against the masculine image of the "great American consumer" (and probably addressing a "highly educated" audience) maintained as late as 1979 (citing a survey) that women were "more concerned than the average man" in power steering, automatic transmissions and other technologies that enhanced the car's ease of handling. Only when the car market threatened to crumble due to the energy crises of the 1970s did the car industry begin to target female consumers, in four segments: "staying-at-home housewives; plan-to-work housewives; just-a-job working women; and career women," suggesting that meanwhile the women's car market had expanded beyond Candler's 'business woman.' What is most astonishing, however, is that "local, male-oriented dealerships" kept pressuring the car manufacturers not to give in to these feminizing tendencies, until well into the 1990s. An aggressive male needs a domestic female, as Beth Kraig in her study of female violence argued: "Male adventuring and aggression are buffered by female domesticity and nurture."

There were changes in the air, however, to be seen, for instance, in the Hanna-Barbera cartoon *The Wacky Races*, with Penelope Pitstop as one of the protagonists, or the appearance of car care books such as Carmel Reingold's *A Woman's Guide to the Care and Feeding of an Automobile* (1973) ("if you can decipher a … recipe, … you can learn what makes a car run") and Patty De Roulf's *A Woman and Her Car* (1974), a rejuvenation of a long tradition, dating from the very beginnings of Western car culture. Fashion magazines such as *Vogue* (a column "Women & Cars") and women's lib magazine *Ms.* ("Populist Mechanics"), soon followed suit.[119]

***

In terms of a 'covert culture,' the automobility situation for nonwhites was not much different. The author of a prewar survey of an American city given the fictitious name of Southerntown reported on hardly any car culture, in sharp contrast to the prewar car ownership in (white) Middletown, after which the study was modeled. What he did was warn his audience that if the "Negro problem" would not be solved soon, the United States would fail to remain a worldwide example of peaceful affluence, and the problem "will be solved for us in ways not to our liking." Talking about black mobility in the twentieth-century West is talking about the American Southern Diaspora (1900–1980). A statistical overview of this remarkable phenomenon shows 3 to 4 percent of all Americans "undertook a long-distance move across state lines," involving in total 3.2 million whites, 1.1 million blacks, and 96,000 Hispanics in the 1950s alone, enabled by "the proliferation of cars and highways (not to mention moving vans)" and by a culture of "perpetual transportation," all in all totaling nearly 29 million migrants over the entire century.

Indeed, the African American emancipation struggle was crucially shaped by blacks' mobility cultures, from the earliest Jim Crow Supreme Court "separate but equal" decision in 1896 to way beyond the other Supreme Court decision in 1954 outlawing segregation. The latter decision had to be enforced by subversive mobility boycotts, starting in Baton Rouge, Louisiana, where blacks constituted two-thirds of all bus patrons. James Meredith intended to walk from Memphis to Jackson, Mississippi, to counter the "fear that dominates the day-to-day life of the Negro in the United States" but was attacked by a white man with a shotgun and declared white suburbanites a greater "threat to a just America than southern segregationists."[120]

When H. Rap Brown, in the middle of a series of more than five hundred uprisings during the five years since the Watt Rebellion of 1965, succeeded Stokely Carmichael as leader of the Black Power movement, he mimicked Hazel Motes in Flannery O'Connor's novel *Wise Blood* from 1952, when he "climbed atop a car in Cambridge, Maryland" and said, "violence is as American as cherry pie." When Rosa Parks made her historic bus trip in 1956, "igniting the modern civil rights movement," and Montgomery's black taxis were harassed by segregationist authorities, a pool of private motorists (including some whites) "supported the boycott by moving the elderly, infirm, and isolated into and out of the city with 'military precision,'" in the words of Martin Luther King Jr., a revival of the prewar jitney phenomenon run by blacks. The student of black culture who related this event concluded it was the car "as a kind of ur-commodity" that "tunes us in to the new conditions characteristic of consumer culture." Ironically, this black subversive mobility was at the same time in line with the general trend from collective to private mobility, from bus to car. With blacks spending nearly $40 billion on cars and related products and services, they formed one-third of the car-buying public, at the same time representing only a bit more than one-tenth of the American population. Although car ownership among blacks was still lower than among whites, "those who have a vehicle are more likely to have a luxury model and to have spent a higher percentage of their income on purchasing it."[121]

The reasons for this are not entirely clear, but one factor may have been the special configuration of the black middle class with its "three major segments—small capitalists, professionals, and clerical and sales workers … Clearly, the black middle class continued to differ substantially from the white middle class in that it was anchored by professionals and business people, whereas the white middle class had a sizeable contingent of (especially female) clerical and sales workers." Whereas the middle class in 1960 did not have a share larger than 10 percent in the black population, the white middle class occupied more than twice that share within the white population. Also, the black middle class grew slower than the white, and its growth was mainly to be found in its lower strata. The black middle class's mobility to the suburbs did not abolish segregation, however: "When African Americans moved to white suburbs, many whites moved out. In general, black suburbs [were] located near city limits … and are often the result of the 'spillover' of black urban enclaves into suburban municipalities." Up to now, no one has come up with a satisfactory explanation of the "uniquely intense association of cars and freedom in black American culture." The acceptance by Congress of President Johnson's Civil Rights Act of July 1964 was based on testimony during the hearings on the bill about statistics proving "the tremendous problem faced by Negro travelers along the highways in the South" (on highways elsewhere, it was not much better, as anecdotal evidence testifies).

However this may be, like the car, the racial issue also became a Cold War topic. Yet, some social scientists (the blacks' promise of consumption and its revenues in the back of their heads) did delve into the cultural differences between black and white car owners to probe the former's differences in appreciation of certain makes in the context of conspicuous consumption. One such study on "consumer motivations" among 1,106 blacks and 537 whites in some Southern cities revealed "Negroes want group identification; whites, feeling that they already have this, want group distinction." Confronted with several 1959 car models, blacks "labeled the [Ford] Mercury as 'sharp,' 'sophisticated,' and 'swinging.' Whites negated this judgment by calling the car 'horrible,' 'too bunglesome,' 'too chromy,' or 'too showy,'" thus showing how stereotypes of blacks' ostentatious consumption were formed in an early phase.[122] We will investigate in more detail some autopoetic novels dealing with this topic.

***

Even more elusive than black automobilism is the mobility culture of queer (LGBTQ) people. One of the rare studies is "Cars and Bars" by Tim Retzloff, who showed how changes in transportation, especially the postwar car, contributed to "the emergence of lesbian and gay communities." Retzloff tells the story of Melva Earhart, owner of the Poodle Bar in Flint, Michigan, who drove "'a pink Cadillac with two pink-dyed poodles in there, with blue ribbons in their hair[,]' [and] allowed Flint's gay and lesbian [often black] working class to dress up for a night out and to experience being of a higher class—the same effect many sought with their vehicles." Cars were used for courting, but also to escape the police. A study of automotive gay culture in southern Birmingham, Alabama, by John Howard, revealed the liberating function of the car in a white, upper-middle-class subaltern mobility culture as it "provided an escape from familial pressures and police prosecution." Howard described the 'body language' (see the introduction) developed by gay men while "cruising," initiated by "first establish[ing] prolonged eye contact with a passerby, then stop[ping] to strike up a conversation." But still more important were the "trick houses" ("trick" is slang for casual sex) that gay people rented, preferably on the city's outskirts reachable only by car.[123]

***

And how about the most elusive "minority" of all: youth? No doubt, the beat culture's mobility, described in the second section of this chapter, was constructed as deviant from mainstream youth culture, but the problem here is to decide what is mainstream and what is not. The jury is still out on whether the counterculture should be analyzed as a radical opposition to hegemonic culture, or if it was a part of it. One thing is certain, though: fragmentation, which started to characterize general culture, also governed the youth culture, enabling recent scholars to distinguish between radical and less radical movements. Gudrun Ensslin, shortly after her conviction in

1968 for firebombing a Frankfurt department store, gave a television interview in which she declared: "Wonderful, I too like the cars, I too like all the things one can buy in department stores. But when one is compelled to buy them, in order to remain unconscious, then the price is too high." That did not prevent Rote Armee Fraktion members from deploying used cars extensively to kidnap their capitalist victims.

Although Ensslin's stance against the car, certainly at this early point in time and even among the youth, was exceptionally radical, other youth subcultures' deviation from the norm worked, from hindsight, as an avant-garde within the general consumer culture, such as youth tourism in Germany: three-quarters of all twenty- to twenty-nine-year-olds in 1978 went on trips abroad, against one-third of all German citizens, their vacation culture described by concerned observers as a "subculture of a repressive society," consisting of swimming, suntanning, eating, and "late-night parties." This extraordinary German youth mobility (probably largest in Europe at that time with 76 percent of the German youth traveling abroad, followed by 67 percent of the French and 56 percent of the British youth), overtaken by mainstream tourism after the 1970s, on itself helped spread the youth culture and its music, against the grain, because the authoritarian regimes in Southern Europe wanted to ban the "hordes" and "swarm" of the "invasion of 'hippies,'" through a "war on hippies." Nonetheless, mobility had become part of a transnational 'community' of like-minded youngsters. Integration in the hegemonic culture went smoothly because, as German political science scholar Wolfgang Kraushaar claimed, the radical youth's worldview was nothing more than a libertarian, often anarchistic form of liberalism.[124]

***

Equally absorbed in hegemonic mobility culture became another product of the '1960s': the "Théorie de la Dérive" of the Bureau of Public Secrets, founded by the Situationists in Paris, artists becoming transport experts and traffic engineering theorists, the pinnacle of a converging process begun shortly after the turn of the century with the group of avant-garde Franco-Belgian writer-car pioneers. According to Guy Debord, "in a dérive one or more persons drop their relations, their work and leisure activities and all their usual motives for movement and action, and let themselves be drawn by the attractions of the terrain and the encounters they find there." Forming the majority in the Sorbonne Occupation Committee during the uprising of May 1968, the Situationists created the ultimate l'art pour l'art of mobility, a subversive pedestrian 'drifting': "slipping by night into houses undergoing demolition, hitchhiking nonstop and without destination through Paris during a transportation strike in the name of adding to the confusion, wandering in subterranean catacombs forbidden to the public, etc." "La beauté est dans la rue" (beauty is in the street), a 1968 poster read, depicting a protester throwing a brick, taken out of the pavement. Situationists were traffic experts: according to Raoul Vaneigem, "roads, lawns, natural flowers, and artificial forests lubricate the machinery of subjection and make it enjoyable," necessary because traffic circulation was "the organization of universal isolation," the "opposite of encounter."[125]

In an effort to revive the adventure ("urbanists of the twentieth century will have to construct adventures," *Internationale situationiste* declared), but now on foot (although sometimes taxis were used), as the true successors of the flaneur, Situationists practiced another technique, the *détournement* (reversal), to shift the meaning of an existing work of art into "one with revolutionary significance," and they aimed at "destructing idols, especially when they claim to represent freedom," for instance, by interrupting the press conference at the Paris Ritz by the "lugubrious and mercenary old man" Charlie Chaplin: "Go home, Mister Chaplin." Their strategy (a "permanent game" of "construction of situations") was systemic, however—aimed not against the car per se but against a society indulging in commodity fetishism. Their traffic theory, in a way, was way ahead of classic traffic engineering with its one-dimensional concept of 'flow,' because it emphasized "psycho-geographical" principles of movement, such as in the origin and destination study of sociologist Chombart de Lauwe, who followed "a student living in the 16th Arrondissement" and used only "a small triangle with no significant deviations, the three apexes of which are the School of Political Sciences, her residence and that of her piano teacher." Second, the *dérive* was an urban experience, because, as Debord posited, "Wandering in open country is naturally depressing." And third, the *dérive* was not an individual(ist) performance but had to be undertaken by "several small groups of two or three people," during "one day," an urban guerilla of subversive mobility. And as Debord had predicted ("the spectacle devours all opposition"), mass culture absorbed this subversiveness, for instance, through the Sex Pistols, who "wrote slogan on their clothes." It shows subversiveness and subalternity are not the same.[126]

***

But it is in their music ("based on emotional impulses" and hence excellently fit to absorb young people's values and interests) that the mechanism of absorption by late capitalist society of cultural counterproposals can best be studied. This absorptive mechanism is used to explain the remarkable explosion of the youth culture into the open in 1963, when the Beatles released their LP *Please, Please Me*, an explosion we touched upon at the beginning of this chapter to explain Graham Nash's rise to fame: "Pop [had] stopped being a spectacular but peripheral event, largely understood to be associated with teenage working-class taste, and became the central symbol of fashionable metropolitan, British culture ... Various European societies had reached a stage at which they started to project their own transformation onto their young generation and their offspring's culture." By the end of the period covered in this chapter, for instance, in Piaggio's advertising around the Vespa, "mobility and self-realization had ... been stripped of their connotations of opposition, and transformed into foundational elements of a new way of living in society, based on the use and possession of a scooter." This mechanism may have misled parts of the youth of the period to experience their radical practices as 'revolutionary.' Instead, youth culture became mainstream 'youthful culture,' acknowledging that teenagers had shifted toward a "self-directed socialization" (*Sozialisierung in eigener Regie*) which had "nothing to do with opposition or rebellion." It was "an attitude of rebellion within a framework of acceptance." And it was this self-directedness that fitted seamlessly in a culture of individual car (or motorcycle, or moped) driving, at a moment (the end of the 1970s) when "'youth' had seemingly transformed into a conglomerate of minorities."[127]

Such conclusions are the result of recent cultural studies scholarship that superseded the previous, neo-Marxist approach. At the same time, the scholarship that undertook this tournure should also be the subject of analysis, because it is indicative of a general shift inward of the middle class, away from the working class. In the United Kingdom, the neoliberal approach was led by the Birmingham Centre for Contemporary cultural studies of the mid-1970s, which had emphasized the heroic and violent sides of London's working-class youth, analyzed as a staged development toward an increased antagonism to society, starting with the mods, who had tried upward social mobility, and, when this had failed, ending in the "exaggerated lumpen style" of the Teddy Boys and the later skinheads and punks. This subculture (including its violent manifestations such as the Brighton riots of 1964 between mods and rockers, but also its typical musical style soon to be exported to the United States) was constructed as opposed to "the middle-class, to women, to the 'straights' or 'divis,' to the mass producers of fashion and music, to 'coobies' or 'hippies,' and to Asians." New research, for instance, into the "dance-based youth subculture" of British Northern soul, a male working-class subculture in the mod tradition, revealed this culture to be "a strong reflection of the parent culture, ... not a rebellion, [but] a culture of consolidation. Somewhere to escape the reality of work, home, family."[128] Thus, working-class youth culture (including its mobility) was deprived of its subversiveness and made into a 'culture of consolidation.' It opened the way toward research into (the mobility of) other minorities, the ones we have seen passing in the previous pages.

The results of this new research largely confirm Marwick's more aggressively formulated thesis (directed at both the neo-Marxists and the cultural studies scholars) of the 1960s being only a breach in mainstream culture rather than a revolution. This position is all the more cemented by a recent study of American marketing and fashion industry culture, undertaken by Thomas Frank as a dissertation in 1994, which argues adults were performing their own cultural revolution partly before the youth culture exploded into the open. Driven by a resistance against the planned Cold War society and the *Organization Man* (title of a famous book on American conformity by William White from 1956), whom historian Christopher Lasch, looking back from 1978, saw succeeded by "the narcissist" (defined by literary scholar Süha Oğuzertem as a person whose "normal tension between actual self on the one hand, and ideal self and ideal object on the other, is eliminated by the building up of an inflated self concept within which the actual self and the ideal self and ideal object are confused"), the "corporate revolution" criticized Cold War advertising that used the "idealized, white-family-at-play motif" to depict cars next to fighter planes and other paraphernalia "from the jet-age military," just like young James Ballard in the camp in Shanghai had learned to appreciate American cars.[129]

Frank, like Marwick, emphasized continuity and disjuncture at the same time: acknowledging the 'revolutionary' character of the cultural changes, he pointed at a process he called "co-optation" (and Marwick called "measured judgment") indicating the gradual absorption within mainstream culture, not by encapsulation but by similar, parallel revolutionary changes taking place within mainstream culture (this reference to encapsulation, by the way, brings Herbert Marcuse into the discourse, who coined "repressive tolerance"). Another historian of the 1960s, Detlef Siegfried, was less reluctant to apply Marcuse's thesis, when he pointed at the "principle of provocation" turned into a marketing tool and the phenomenon of "the young actors of the counterculture" being remodeled into "scouts of marketing development" and as "outsider-innovators." Marcuse's repressive tolerance is the social science application of a mechanism first occurring in the evolutionary realm of competing technologies, a phenomenon I called the Pluto effect, which describes the absorption of the advantageous functions of a competing technology by the mainstream technology, a phenomenon such as happened when the electric vehicle's seemingly 'unique' traits got 'encapsulated' by the hegemonic combustion-engined car. From this perspective, the counterculture appears as a new phase in middle-class culture, as a nonrevolutionary step toward "consumer subjectivity." Frank quoted Michael Harrington, who in 1972 saw the "massification of bohemia" occur, "an assumption of the values of Greenwich Village by the decidedly nonrevolutionary middle class." "Having professed their disdain for middle-class values," novelist Earl Shorris wrote in 1967, "the hippies indulge in them without guilt."[130]

Frank illustrated his thesis by studying car advertising, this practice of "transforming the language of objects to that of people," which changed overnight around 1965. "Anti-advertising" was a direct response to Vance Packard's consumer society critique and "appeal[ed] directly to the powerful but unmentionable public fears of conformity, of manipulation, of fraud, and of powerlessness," quasi-questioning consumerism itself, and meanwhile positioning Volkswagen in opposition to the Big Three's technocratic fantasies: "streamlined, finned like airplanes, … decorated with flashing chrome and abstract representations of rockets and airplanes." The Volkswagen was presented as an "honest" car: "if you simply want to get somewhere, get a bug," one of the lines in a VW ad ran. At the same time, a new 'adventure' was formulated. Advertising, *Fortune* magazine said in 1947, is about the "creation of new and daring, but fullfillable, consumer demands; demands that would not occur if advertising did not deliberately incite them." While deliberately ignoring those youngsters who did not take part in the counterculture, car advertising acquired a *youthful* image, propagating a new vitalism known from the "angry young [men]." The Ford Mustang, for instance, was advertised as the "Car of Young America"; 80 percent of its buyers requested a car radio to come with it (Martha and the Vandellas' clip for their hit song "Nowhere to Run" was made at the Mustang assembly line in Detroit's River Rouge factory).[131]

The Big Three learned quickly. Oldsmobile took on a youthful image, emphasizing "action, adventure, and daring" in its hip advertising. The 1970 Buick models were presented with the slogan "Light your fire" and the Dodge Rebellion (!) used slogans such as "Rise up" and criticized middle-class emptiness of "Dullsville." Frank concluded: "The sixties are more than merely the homeland of hip, they are a commercial template for our times, a historical prototype for the construction of cultural machines that transform alienation and despair into consent."[132] As we have seen, Piaggio in Italy, producer of the iconic Vespa scooter, was one of the first in Europe to apply the new marketing insights, pushing the scooter as an anti-car vehicle. The new values "served to legitimize a general transformation of the ways in which production and consumption are organized." The hippie, drug, and rock culture "supplied the ideological basis for [capitalism's] surprisingly persistent, post-Fordist phase of expansion." Even the family was not undermined by the increased permissiveness; it was strengthened by it. For the United Kingdom, for instance, one student of the middle classes claims, despite "the clash of two middle-class dogmas" (the free market and the idea that the middle class represented the nation), "the mass of the middle classes were content with the permissive society."[133]

Scholars such as Seiler and Packer suggested how this works: Seiler showed how "policing oneself" is the secret behind the apparent peacefulness of the "republic of drivers." The youth's "self-directed socialization" that upset the adults so much resonated with *Selbstführung* (self-guidance), as one analyst of the consumer society called it, which is much more than the ability, the skill to drive, although the self-policing begins through the bodily practice of handling the car (see the introduction). It is rather the willingness to self-control, to self-discipline, to make oneself governable, that is the core characteristic of modern car culture: "liberal-capitalist hegemony requires that its subjects submit by being *free* and *in motion*." This Foucaultian insight, applied to the Western car culture, boils down to the "internalization of hegemonic ways of being in the world, to such a degree that the threat of coercion recedes to the edge of perception."

Within this mainstream automobilistic universe, an exceptionalist stereotype of the "restless" and "moving American" was construed (despite studies showing, on the contrary, residential mobility *declined* in the course of the twentieth century, as we have seen). This stereotypical 'Moving American' was explained by one of its architects "because we attracted out of Europe the mobile temperaments, because these wanderers found themselves uprooted and unattached, because there were so many places to go, because there were so many means of going and rewards to be had for the venture, because the transformation of the old agrarian order now freed us for going, and because there were not and are not today the traditional social barriers to fence us in."[134]

***

In sum, the Western 'attack on public transport' took place through the youth and its 'rebellion.' Whereas its culture seemed to evaporate class differences and merge them into one, all-encompassing 'middle-class society,' the subsequent fragmentation into lifestyles seemed to cement this process into mainstream. At the same time, social science scholarship used this fragmentation to hide the working class and its cultures under the kaleidoscope of the lifestyle explosion. Car driving fitted seamlessly in this mainstreaming. But how effective was this? And how irreversible was this mainstreaming? The question, indeed, is how active the consumer-driver had to be before her self-discipline transcended the Foucaultian "panopticism"; where in this "neoliberal apparatus" did fragmentation turn into opposition, and when did the 'repressive tolerance' (Marcuse) implied in Frank's "co-optation" and even in Marwick's "measured judgment" (despite the latter's vehement rejection of Marcuse's thesis) lose its power?[135] Before we can answer such questions, we will have to characterize hegemonic car culture and its potential adventurous traits. We will do so, as usual, by studying the only sources able to dig deep into the motifs, motives, and motivations of Western motorists: novels, movies, and songs, both hegemonic and mainstream.

Experiencing the Car in a Fragmented Culture: Shifts in Autopoetic Adventures

The answer to the question of how the hegemonic nuclear family adopted the car should contain an emphasis on continuity with the pre–World War II mobility history, an insight we developed in the course of this chapter, and which is not really shared by many students of the 1950s and '60s (whether informed by transport history or literary history).[136] Often, post–World War II automotive culture is presented as if the nuclear family reinvented the wheel, whereas most of its 'discoveries' were already made way before the war. As we argued elsewhere (and repeated in abbreviated form in the introduction), the 'automobile system' was more or less established by the end of the interbellum, including car-friendly road networks but also a culture of automotive pleasure and (tamed) adventure dominated by the nuclear, white, middle-class family in an 'affordable family car.' We defined original automotive 'adventure' (as shaped during the early phase of 'emergence' of the car) as a highly gendered and racialized three-pronged temporal (speed), spatial (roaming), and functional (tinkering) practice, adding a desire to conquer (the woman, the colony) for the interwar phase of 'persistence.'[137] The question, then, is how the postwar car adventure (if it still existed at all) differed from its previous version. In an ever further fragmenting Western car culture, who were the drivers of change? The obvious candidate of this role is of course the beat generation, male and (beat and non-beat) female, whom we will investigate in the next two subsections. Then we will visit other American automotive subcultures, those of the hegemonic middle class, and those of their female counterparts, as well as blacks and other minorities, respectively. We will then delve somewhat deeper in the postwar Western adventure machine through the investigation of its aggressive and violent traits. The last subsection looks at the differences with European car cultures.

The Beat Adventure: A Breach in the Automotive Adventure's Historical Continuity

From the perspective of our continuity thesis, the mobility of the beats revived the prewar adventure but in a rather superficial way (as we will see later). The beats could look back on a prehistory of hoboing by car, hitchhiking, and "hop[ping] freights." Jack Kerouac himself pointed at this in a separate publication on "The Vanishing American Hobo," in which he emphasized the increasing threat of being hunted by the police. For modern hoboes "of sorts" (like himself, who knew he would in the end be "rewarded by social protection" after his impending literary success, as he self-confidently wrote) the experience of "absolute freedom" was worth the "few inconveniences like snakes and dust." The beats' main difference with the 'real' hobo (who "by the late 1940's [sic] ... was no longer a factor of any proportion in American political life") was the fact that their wandering around was a "quest," its "specific object ... spiritual."[138] Fodder for belletristic literature, one would guess, as literary students of mobility have often equated car driving with a "Quest of the Self." This misleading terminology, which reduces car driving experience to the 'individuality' of American society, even functions to suggest Kerouac's Quest for God makes him into "an everyman," and thus allows literary scholarship to remodel *On the Road* as a mainstream utterance, a practice that does not seem justified. Only now, when *On the Road* has been included into the literary canon, can the novel be analyzed (to quote one of the recent literary dissertations) as "pivotal ... in the transition from modernism to postmodernism," the latter characterized by "self-consciousness and reflexivity, fragmentation, discontinuity, indeterminacy, plurality, metafictionality, heterogeneity, intertextuality, decentering, dislocation, and ludism."[139]

Recently, the Quest-of-Self thesis has been challenged from a feminist cultural studies perspective by Alexandra Ganser, who distinguished in her excellent study of "American Women's Road Narratives" between three "tropes of movement": the quest, the para-nomadic, and the picaresque. Whereas the quest is "motivated by the desire to arrive," the nomadic protagonists are driven by "economic or political necessity," while the *picara*'s movements are "a pleasurable and empowering adventure." For Ganser, *On the Road* belongs to the first 'trope.' By contrast, our historical approach sees Kerouac's text as part of a *continuum* of automotive adventure, and not as the start of a movement whose roots go back at the most to the Depression era, as Ganser argued, although it cannot be denied that Kerouac's adventure differs substantially from prewar adventurous car experiences. This is all the more true from a mobility point of view, as Kerouac's car adventures took place in the late 1940s, a decade before the start of the construction of the Interstate Highway network (see chap. 3).[140] Perhaps this omission among literature students can be explained by pointing at the fact that the continuity before the war, especially in the strand of the female adventure, took place not in literary hegemonic culture but mostly in the middle- and lowbrow areas.

Four elements do set the beat mobility experience (as expressed in *On the Road* [1957] and related autopoetic utterances such as John Clellon Holmes's *Go* [1952]) apart from the prewar motoring experience, both mainstream and countercultural. The first element is the experience of *passengering*: Kerouac never in his life owned a car (nor did many other members of the beats' inner circle during the 1940s and 1950s), a circumstance that has not received much attention by Kerouac students. English literature student John Lennon argues, "Sal [Kerouac's alter ego in *On the Road*] hates to drive" (making his riding experiences into a special form of passengering), and Lennon even refers to the only occasion Sal is behind the wheel in *Visions of Cody* (another version of *On the Road* but published much later, in 1972) where he muses about the "whiteness" (in racial terms and in terms of boredom) of the suburban universe. The "greatest ride" in *On the Road* is "in the back of a flatbed truck" as a kind of "boxcar journey" with other 'hoboes,' "just as steady and straight" as "riding a railroad train." Kerouac's experiences were geared toward the home-away-from-home aspects of the modern, roomy car: the conversations, the sex, sleeping, making notes, against a background of a landscape that got its due attention as far as that was possible at the high speeds they mostly realized in their "recklessness without motivation." After all, "with [his fellow beat buddy] frantic Dean I was rushing through the world without a chance to see it."

Kerouac was not the only one indulging in this *automotive narcissism*: Andy Warhol made a car trip from New York to Los Angeles in 1963, "remaining studiously unmoved by the view from the car." Sometimes, not surprisingly so considering the prewar automotive culture, aggressive fantasies popped up, such as when Kerouac remembered how as a kid he had fantasized about holding "a big scythe in my hand and cut down all the trees and posts and even sliced every hill that zoomed past the windows," in the process producing an old trope of what we elsewhere called 'Proustian inversion,' the illusion that not the car but the environment moves, a literary technique we analyzed as being rooted in automotive narcissism. Yet, "adventure" or "adventuring" in Kerouac's travelogue-as-novel are used to connote the conquest of women, not the landscape, suggesting again that the car is seen as a tool to reach other goals, not as a goal in itself as in mainstream prewar car culture.[141]

Kerouac's "phobia" of car driving (according to one biographer triggered by an almost fatal accident before he met Cassady) prevented him from enjoying Dean's "violence of motion" and made him take sides with some of the women who refused to be a passenger because of Dean's scary driving style or obsessive endurance driving, without offering his passengers the possibility to pee. Nonetheless, Kerouac had worked for a while as a car mechanic, "wielding a tire iron, grease-gun, and monkey wrench." According to Kerouac himself, there was no violence in *On the Road*, but it is difficult to misinterpret his obsession to mention the car speed value (in 'mph') on many occasions of speedy endurance driving. Hollywood bosses who considered making *On the Road* into a movie agreed: one of them proposed to have Dean die in a car crash. Ellis Amburn, one of Kerouac's biographers, points at his misogyny as a counterargument against Kerouac's 'no violence' thesis, but his violence also is directed at objects: "We must admit," he wrote in 1943, "that there is a certain element of virility in ruining cars." Kerouac rejected the macho violence of fellow writer Ernest Hemingway (claiming as a student of Zen Buddhism that he did not need "'blood lust' [of the Spanish bullfight, the theme of Hemingway's *Death in the Afternoon*, 1939] to prove his virility"). Enthusiasts of drag racing and hot-rodding couldn't have agreed more. Kerouac's automotive machismo was often more symbolic, distancing himself from the "fag Plymouth" brought on the market by Chrysler. He found the Plymouth, in Amburn's words, "weak and girlish, without real acceleration or horsepower, a description that was as misogynous as it was homophobic." Later students of working-class car culture would not be surprised. In Kerouac's *Big Sur*, the protagonist "finds that automobiles are all family cars, presided over by women in 'sneering dark glasses.'" In other words, Kerouac and Cassady's automotive adventure was a ludic, if not a circus act, presented as mobility at a parking lot (where the admired Dean could park cars at high speed and with high precision) or as a pinball machine: the female characters as "bumpers" seemed to drive the men on, "propel[ling] the men ever faster."[142]

***

This brings us to the second element (next to the violent machismo of automotive narcissism) characterizing the adventurous beat car culture. *On the Road* does not describe touring in the classic sense, as one of the constitutive elements of the prewar automotive adventure, nor was it indulging in the vibrations of the driving (as was so characteristic of that adventure): it was a 'pure,' nearly abstract enjoyment of the 'freedom' and the detachment of the trip (in more than one sense) and its speed (in more than one sense as well: "chemical, musical and vehicular"), homological to "his playful use of language as pure sound." In that sense, the continuity with prewar adventure was only superficial. It is this *abstract character of the automotive adventure*, this general willingness to "take risks and journey into an emotional and intellectual wilderness," that attracted radical student leader Tom Hayden to Kerouac's book. This is quite different, for instance, from the hypocrisy of Henry Gregor Felsen's contemporary *Crash Club* (1958) and his related novels such as *Hot Rod* and *Road Rocket*, in which high school youth's drag races are a thrilling part of the mainstream, but which at the same time moralizes about "thoughtless, aggressive driving" that caused the death of one of the protagonists. The reference to "semi-Beatnik Southern California street racers" on the back cover is an illustration of the eager efforts of hegemonic culture to absorb what at that moment still resisted being absorbed. Nor can *On the Road* be rivaled by Theodore Weesner's novel *The Car Thief* (1972), even if sixteen-year-old protagonist Alex may have been inspired by Cassady/Moriarty; this novel describes the ennui of a school kid who steals cars as a protest against his social isolation, but whereas Weesner made Alex's adventures into "juvenile crime," Kerouac made Cassady into an avant-garde hero of counterculture. Weesner wrote about a rebel; Kerouac and Cassady were writing rebels themselves.[143]

The abstract, near-existentialist relationship with 'being on the move' (Norman Mailer called the hipster "the American existentialist") is also apparent in other literary utterances such as Bob Seger's song "Roll Me Away": "I could go east, I could go west / It was all up to me to decide." The same feeling was also expressed as early as 1946 in the song "(Get Your Kick on) Route 66" by Robert Troup, who got the idea for the title from his wife, Cynthia. The couple toured the entire route from Lancaster, Pennsylvania, to Los Angeles in their green Buick convertible. It was rerecorded (and its text rephrased) by Nat "King" Cole, Chuck Berry, Van Morrison's Them, and the Rolling Stones. Italian writer Luciano Bianciardi's best-selling novel *La Vita Agra* (1962)—translated into English in 1964 as *It's a Hard Life* and made into a movie in the same year—provided a European version: "In my opinion," one of the protagonists declares, "traveling serves no purpose nowadays, and you don't learn anything from it." In the novel, the narrator claims he could have written like "an angry beatnik" (*bitinicco*) at least ten years before "Mr. Jacques Querouaques." Kerouac's trips, however, always had a destination: they were not a 'roaming' in the countryside (just like their sex was always focused on the "big event," as one of their girlfriends later commented): *On the Road* was about "the purity of the entire trip" but clearly connected with (male) performance, just like he boasted of being "hard and fast" and reaching orgasm within sixty seconds. In that sense, it resembles this other form of bodily mobility that gained prominent importance during the 1960s. Dance was the most popular way to feel "alive again in the middle of this monstrous funeral parlor of western civilization" (it was Siegfried Kracauer, by the way, who already in the 1920s had compared car driving to dancing). The road cleanses, and allows one to start anew, but it is also a channel for a flight from "a feminized society."[144]

* * *

The third element characteristic for the beats is their 'nomadism,' despite the ultimate destination of most trips. After all, (pastoral) nomads, as we have seen, have a goal: the next pasture. Likewise, *On the Road* begins with a failure: a hitchhike based on studied maps, until Sal Paradise realizes he must "improvise" to get at his destination (which is Denver, where Dean lives).

The beats are the first to explicitly think about and practice the right method of getting somewhere in a car: despite the precise goal, the road toward it had to be navigated loosely, not like the straight line of the train. The beats could practice this because they often did not own a car: they could jump cars hitchhiking. They were, as we already concluded, *passengers*. Many beats did not own a house either, and even did not have a fixed residence: they 'hitchhiked' cars as they did rooms for the night. With his mother, Kerouac lived at least in twenty-six homes.

And if they got a home (like Kerouac, once his novel started to sell and he bought a house in Denver for he and his mother), the absence of a car led to quick failure (and they moved back to the East). This aspect made Cresswell claim the beats were engaged in an "exuberant resistance to hegemonic ideals of home and family," also in the novel's structure, which was as improvising and linguistically 'flowing' as jazz. Indeed, it is often the structural homology between the making of the autopoetic novel (or autopoetic elements in a non-autopoetic novel) and 'real life,' including car driving, that tells us more about the motifs and motives behind the car culture of a certain period (see the introduction). In this case, much of this 'affinity' was undoubtedly constituted through the speed of both: Sal's admiration for Neal's "kickwriting" (his "'virile' prose," as one student of the beats commented) was as large as his awe of his frantic driving. From that point of view, Kerouac's production (in his sweat-drenched T-shirt) of the 120-foot-long "scroll" of his manuscript (sheets glued together) is nothing more than his writing equivalent of Neal's unstoppable car driving (the trips glued together through a periodic intake of gasoline and other 'drugs'). Not only that: the "jazz way of knowledge, completing a chorus by improvising on it from every angle, with each version contributing to the whole," 'rhymed' with car driving to a well-defined destination, quite different from simply meandering around as was practiced in former days. But where he reached his geographical destinations (only to depart for the next one), Kerouac never realized the family and home ideal.[145] As Cresswell, however, in the same article related mobility to masculinity (and hence to femininity), he got a (belated) reply from feminist scholar Linda McDowell, who cited the memoirs *Off the Road* (1990) by Carolyn Cassady, Neal Cassady's wife, to show women's "immobility ... also offered possibilities of resistance." *On the Road*, in McDowell's feminist reading, is about failure and disappointment rather than a Quest for the Self, about home reappearing as a locus of "stability" in life. But although McDowell rightfully opened up the subversive character of mobility toward including the home (concluding Kerouac's 'resistance' is nothing more than "masculine selfishness"), Cresswell was not convinced: although "certain kinds of marginality" can be analyzed as resistance, he saw most of the beat women "only as marginalized and dominated."[146] Our excursion, in the next chapter, into non-Western mobilities will shed some more light on this issue. For the moment, we conclude with Simon Rycroft, in his response to Cresswell, that "the beat experience was a sedentary one" (because of the destination of their cross-country trips). However, it is quite clear the border between mobility and immobility started to get blurred, as the beats' sedentarism was highly mobile, and the car trips were like sitting in a room on wheels.

In this sense, Kerouac's tale was, indeed, very much (part of the) mainstream, as we will be able to witness in the next section. The first thing Kerouac did when he came "home" to his aunt's house, where he often stayed, was buy a refrigerator. For the patriot Kerouac, his real home was "America." Every time he earned money, he bought and sold his houses as if it were cars. Gilles Deleuze and Félix Guattari have coined the term rhizome for this type of mobility, literally meaning 'tuber' or 'root,' "a metaphor for modes of being that refuse the structured 'rootedness' of the 'arborescent,'" as Alex Young interpreted. "The rhizomatic ... exists on the same plane of immanence as the arborescent and it is in constant danger of transforming into it." Indeed, the beats were constantly in the process of becoming mainstream, a process celebrated by Kerouac in his later years and loathed by others, most eloquently by Ginsberg and Burroughs. Some students of the beats have misread this as mobile aimlessness (it is not: all trips in *On the Road* have a destination, as we already argued), although their emphasis on the homology between the writing of *On the Road* and the production of the car-driving experience, expressed in the concepts of "in-between-ness" and "repetition," is gratefully acknowledged.[147]

***

The fourth characteristic of the beats' mobility is their 'cross-mediality,' their easy transfer from one medium (the novel) to other media, especially film. Like the previous 'nomadic' trait, this characteristic blurs borders, mixes conditions. Parallel to this 'intertextuality' is a synesthetic practice, a "mixing of the senses." Katie Mills convincingly showed how Kerouac's rewriting of *On the Road*, published posthumously as *Visions of Cody*, breaks with the linearity of hegemonic mobility, at the same time prefiguring later experiments with cross-mediality: the rewritten texts mimic the restlessness of the camera eye, in the same way as Kerouac's introduction to photographer Robert Frank's famous photo book *The Americans* (1958), who also undertook a "year-long car trip around the country in 1955 and 1956," supported by a Guggenheim grant. In a way, this cross-mediality is already present in all previous versions of *On the Road*, where the car radio brings the 'bebop jazz' of fellow (ethnic) minorities into the car interior. Frank also operated the camera of Alfred Leslie's movie *Pull My Daisy*, originally intended to become "an art film version of *On the Road*," but eventually and remarkably filmed "on location," as utter sessility, in a room. The poem with the same name, written collectively by Ginsberg, Cassady, and Kerouac, and sung on the film's soundtrack by Anita Ellis, announced the end of the road novel ("woe my road is spoken"), suggesting that from now on, we should study other media to get a grip on the country's automobilism.[148]

In a certain sense, they had a point: as we will show later in this chapter, highbrow novels miss the fragmented 'bricolage' character of Western postwar (auto)mobilism. In another sense, they are wrong, as we will also show: discarding literature would rob us of the possibility to see the bifurcation of the car adventure into (at least) two quite different universes. Cross-mediality (to which the "road story" seems especially prone) was also practiced by Kerouac himself, who "appeared numerous times on television," lamented by several beats with their disdain for the mass character of this medium, among them the anarchist Kenneth Rexroth, who observed how "dissent has become a hot commodity." Rexroth criticized Kerouac for mentioning the brand name Cadillac in a positive way: "He *also* says the Studebaker is a car with a built-in engineering defect. Who is this guy working for? I mean values like this ... have nothing to do with a serious separation of the creative artist with society." Indeed, the big absorption of counterculture had started. Irony was dead. This became crystal clear when a television series called *Route 66* was broadcast from 1960 to 1964, which not only helped 'masculinize' TV's rather "feminized" content during its emergence in the late 1950s (as we have argued) but also helped "re-*familiarizing* the American wanderer," represented by a couple of bachelor buddies, vaguely resembling Kerouac and Cassady, who drove around in a brand-new Corvette sponsored by Chevrolet: absorption into mainstream apparently also needs a refashioning of the vehicle (its model name fitting nicely in the Cold War atmosphere: a corvette is a warship).

Television, Mills claimed, was a proper medium to convey "the tight space of a flashy sports car," when the protagonists were "filmed through the front window of the Corvette," and outside the car followed "new cinema vérité style of hand-held cinematography," thus enabling the television networks "to attract more men [through] such male-oriented gimmicks as fast cars, macho conflict, and big-busted actresses." Later television shows capitalized further on the beat phenomenon, such as *Then Came Bronson* (1969–1970; he came on a motorcycle) and *Three for the Road* (1975–1976), but by then *Star Trek* (1966) started to "replace ... both the Western and the road story as the new quest genre." It helped, of course, that the beats' rebellion was less antagonistic than contemporaries often assumed. For instance, despite Kerouac's sexual, gender-bending experiments, he and other beats "regard[ed] themselves and each other as very much in keeping with traditional formulations of American masculinity." However this may be, in 1960, television made the beats into "mainstream celebrities overnight," a development that showed American intelligentsia was "completely unprepared for the rise of pop art," which left the conquest of TV to "the *next* generation of the counterculture." Rexroth lamented that commercialization made people "read cheap sensationalism," where they perhaps expected "a trenchant and meaningful indictment of society." In short, what the beats did with automotive adventure was twofold. On the one hand, they abstractified it, made it into a vaguely (no longer 'subliminal') ironic attitude, and thus prepared it for absorption into mainstream mobility culture, at the same time giving it a multimedia twist.[149] On the other hand, they reformulated it toward proletarian, non-ironic violence. In the next subsection we will consider this process in more detail, enriched through the perspective of both beat and non-beat, romance-reading women.

***

But before we get there, how about the other elements deemed constitutive of the automotive-adventure experience? The cyborg experience, another part of the 'adventure machine,' and so often felt by motorists before the war because of defects in the mechanical side of the man-machine merger, had evidently become a matter of course in Kerouac's passengering experience. Indeed, *On the Road* is the first Western postwar passengering novel in which the perspective is not that of the driver. Perhaps as a consequence, the 'flight experience' aroused by the mechanical movements of the car and part of the driver's universe in nearly every prewar novel is hardly mentioned: the bodily insulation from the bumps and other irregularities in the environment, brought about by a combination of better springs and shock absorbers with smoother roads, became increasingly effective. At the moment car driving really started to resemble air flight, the 'flight' experience subsided and the bodily movements became comparable to the boring movements high in the air, in an airplane. Nor was there much feeling of 'multisensorial transcendence' during the car journey (as we have characterized the prewar car culture): Kerouac's "pursuit of excellence" was literary, not automotive, a pursuit he called "Self-Ultimacy." If he experienced some automotive transcendence, it was through Moriarty/Cassady, whom he once, in an appreciation of his being-as-driver, called "God." Hence, Kerouac's adventure (his urge to transgress limits and norms) was sexual rather than automotive, as he "somehow managed to convince himself he could dip deeply and regularly into homoeroticism and still be a part of society's heterosexual tyranny." [150]

There was, as Deborah Clarke observed, no "close personal sensation with the car," which—if true—would be a big difference with Karl Shapiro's poem "Buick" of only a couple years earlier (1940), which celebrates the "satisfaction of love" projected into the (anthropomorphized) car. It was also quite different from the "transcendental experiences" that, according to Timothy Leary, would soon pervade the psychedelic culture, but this was generated not so much by mobility as by a "Look within." "Girls, cars, and sex [made] for prosthetic masculinity," added Sidonie Smith in her analysis of *On the Road*, and the production of masculinity, we know from many studies, feminist or not, "always depends on a disavowal or flight from femininity." This is not to say that cyborg feeling (the unity with the machine) was absent in the beat automotive culture. For many male beats, *if* they owned a car, their relation to the car remained intense, if only because of the maintenance needed, just like in hegemonic car culture: "That guy spends more time with that old car than he ever does with me! ... It makes me feel like a who-er!" a woman complains at a party described in *Go*. No wonder, then, according to Kerouac's biographer Ellis Amburn, was *On the Road*, for many middle-class kids, a "tremendous trip ... the first word that we got ... about this gassy, groovy stuff going on." These kids loved the "footloose heroes, who've upset complacent America simply by driving through it," a practice that made Kerouac (and, although to a lesser extent, the kids who read him) "an outsider of modern Western culture."[151] No mainstream, in other words!

***

From that perspective (of the cyborg), there was not much difference with that other iconic novel, Robert Pirsig's *Zen and the Art of Motorcycle Maintenance*, published at the very end of our period (1974, translated into twenty-five languages), where, as a reflexive form of modernity (and an effort to convince his readers that Zen could be compatible with technology), even a whole plethora of theories on the relationship between man and machine is given and which has been interpreted as a multiplicity of journeys/plots (physical, mental, and between the father and his passenger, the son). Different from *On the Road*, however, the classic spatial adventure is revived: "Plans are deliberately indefinite, more to travel than to arrive anywhere."[152]

But the journey is an escape and a return at the same time: it is not a Quest of Self but an escape from his insane former self (figuring in the novel as a separate actor, Phaedrus) toward an ever more familiar landscape. If this is about adventure, it is an adventure of the mind, of the 'inside': it is the quintessential novel to study the domestication of the extreme within the middle-class mind and behavior. Quite distinct from Kerouac, Pirsig abhors the nihilistic "pure nothing" and comes out a pragmatist motorcycle "maintenance man." However different the outcome may be, Pirsig and

Kerouac both share the journey into the 'inner man.' What also sets Pirsig's novel apart from Kerouac's is the different vehicle used: the spatial part of the tripartite automotive adventure seems to be taken over by the culture around the motorcycle, a culture revived by the thousands of GIs and Vietnam veterans who founded the Bandidos Motorcycle Club in Texas, the Pagans Motorcycle Club in Pennsylvania, and the Pissed Off Bastards of Bloomington, who formed the Hells Angels Motorcycle Club.[153]

Their reputation was made when Marlon Brando featured in *The Wild One* (1953), which on its turn was based on the Hollister holiday run in 1947, when a frenzy of biker vandalism was picked up (and sensationalized) by the mass media and became one of the items of the 'delinquent youth' scare. From this perspective, the motorcycle movie *Easy Rider* (1969) was only a reminder that the violence also can come from the other side, the 'rednecks.' From the perspective of our general mobility history, however, the motorcycle culture can be seen as an open flirt with "danger, fear and antisocial behavior," enabling hegemonic automobile culture to hide its structural violence even further. But the "iconic images of motorcycling from movies are from slow rides," as Ted Bishop rightly claims in his analysis of "The Art of the Slow Ride" (referring to *The Wild One* and *Easy Rider*): Brando "may be wild, but his riding is almost meditative," and Peter O'Toole's *Lawrence of Arabia* moves "briskly but not blasting."

Zen and the Art of Motorcycle Maintenance seems to confirm this thesis, but even this "most widely read philosophy book, ever" claims the motorcycle at the beginning of the 1970s had taken over the car's adventurousness: "In a car you're always in a compartment, and because you're used to it you don't realize that through the car window everything you see is just more TV. You're the passive observer and it is all moving by boringly in a frame." Inversion as boredom! When the *Zen* protagonists cross a freeway jam of commuter cars they observe that the motorists "looked so sad … It's just they looked so *lost* … Like they were all dead. Like a funeral procession." The different, "meditating" mobility culture, in *Zen*, may also have been influenced by a conscious avoidance of freeways, of the hectic rat race. The main protagonist's celebration of the 'functional adventure' (the tinkering and the maintenance) becomes a tool to distinguish between those who are afraid of technology (such as the "beatniks" and "hippies") and those who are not. To prove this, the protagonist gives a list of tools he brings along, later followed by a treatise of the motorcycle's technical structure, both tropes well known from the car travelogues of the earliest period.[154]

***

But this is only the middle-class part of the story. From the mid-1960s, a working-class "biker culture" was revived, which received its own representational strands in the "exploitation 'biker' genre" of (lowbrow) movies such as Roger Corman's *The Wild Angels* (1966), Richard Rush's *The Savage Seven* (1968), and Anthony M. Lanza's *The Glory Stompers* (1967), with "rape of women ... a standard of the genre" and ethnic men figuring either as "drug dealers or incompetent Mexican policemen." Corman and others (including "gonzo" journalist Hunter S. Thompson, who wrote the famous ethnographic-style book *Hell's Angels*, 1966) "spent time with Hells Angels clubs as part of their research." Thompson became one of the iconic 'risk takers,' transferring the biker adventure to the car in his *Fear and Loathing in Las Vegas* (1973) with its "wild car trip ... while high on drugs between Los Angeles and Las Vegas." In the outlaw motorcycle movies, shown in suburban "drive-in movie theaters" for "teens with access to cars," bikers were turned "into unmitigated outlaws, whose machismo and misogyny offered a catharsis to working class youth who presumably felt alienated from both Kennedy's New Frontier and Lyndon Johnson's 'Great Society.'" *Easy Rider* borrowed from both cultures. For Mills, *Easy Rider* was the "artistic zenith" of both the exploitation movie (exploitation, if only because of the enormous difference between production costs and revenues, $360,000 versus $10 million in the case of *Wild Angels* alone, to which the Hells Angels served as "paid consultants," or $400,000 versus $50 million in the case of *Easy Rider*) and the psychedelic movie, such as *The Magical Mystery Tour*, a manifestation of the "mobilities of 'hip.'"

But whereas Kerouac and his buddies filled their trips with "manic talk," buddies Billy and Wyatt in *Easy Rider* produced "a knowing silence," or "emptiness of the rebellion," as Mills argued: "We want to be free," protagonist Blues (Jack Nicholson) explains, "we want to be free to do what we want to do. We want to be free to ride our machines without being hassled by the Man." Indeed, Mills concluded, "the critique must be vague so as to appeal to the largest possible audience." But it did not have to be vague in its sexual politics: although their inspiration partially came from underground movies such as Kenneth Anger's *Scorpio Rising* (1963) with their "homosexual and lesbian elements," in the biker exploitation movies the "characters yanked back the biker image from gay fantasy to straight society, presenting a virulent heterosexuality that titillated teen audiences at the dawn of the sexual revolution." However this may be, *Easy Rider* offers perhaps the best representation of the flight experience so central to the automotive adventure: Hopper and Fonda, on their "outlaw machine," are "flying down the road on their Harley choppers, leather fringe and long hair blowing in the breeze.[155] In sum, the automotive adventure is twisted, either toward an abstract experience (Kerouac) or toward a very concrete, unironic, violent one (working-class bikers). It is also split in two, along class lines, so it seems. In both versions, the tongue-in-cheek style is gone.

Mobility and/as Escape: Beat Girls and Romance-Reading Women

Kerouac considered his writing to be "teaching," and as *On the Road* was a narrative directed at a woman, one wonders how his lessons on mobility (sold three-million-fold until the end of the century) can be summarized. There is no doubt mobility was considered central to the beat life (see the book's title *On the Road*, or Holmes's *Go*), but the road was seen as a male playing field in which individuality is celebrated, in cars of which the interior was considered more important than the exterior: the outside of the characters was the inside of the car, the outside of the car reduced to a two-dimensional fantasy, flattened by a scythe.[156] Our main conclusion from close-reading *On the Road* is this: the mobile adventure was sexual rather than automotive. At the bottom line, *On the Road* deals with the question of whether the American 'good life' was possible without and outside the middle-class. The book's answer was no. Kerouac and his fellow beats were not "cool," as he emphasized time and again (he equated "cool" with "commercial" and with consumption), they were emphatically not hegemonic: they were "raw." Where Aldous Huxley before the war used the trance generated by a long car trip to fantasize about the effect of hashish, Kerouac and his fellow beats got high on the drug itself, renouncing Huxley's "passivity of the sleeper."[157]

Where Kerouac stands for the "relic of a working class that did not fit into the collegiate counterculture," Cassady (whose father *was* a hobo) managed to hop on the bus of the counterculture (even driving the Merry Pranksters' psychedelic bus) and died as a parody of the lonesome traveler. Perhaps Attilio Brilli, in his brilliant but, for historically inspired academic purposes, quite useless overview of a century of car-related mobility, touches on the core of *On the Road*, when he calls Kerouac's journey "ironic" in the sense that "it takes place at the same time as real journey and as journey in his imagination." This real and imagined trip is transformed into 'literature' while at the same time it is traveling through literary genres, forms and techniques: "confession, initiation journey, picaresque adventure novel." One cannot deny, however, "how invested" the beats, and in their wake the countercultural youth, "were in maintaining their reinterpretation of automobility as a means of connecting, not isolation," despite the Cold War paranoia about dangerous hitchhikers.[158]

***

But the "Beat and delinquent subcultures were predominantly male, and often working class, and were masculine in conventional and chauvinist ways," as Wini Breines concluded. The "bad girls" she studied, whose "'deviance' was more circumspect and less dramatic than was that of boys, especially working class boys," were as "excluded from and repelled by the prevailing youth culture" in the 1950s as the boys, "disgusted by the 'frivolity, antiintellectualism, and social indifference of the middle class peer culture.'" Beat girl Joyce Johnson describes in her memoirs *Minor Characters* how she longed for "Real Life. This was not the life my parents lived but one that was dramatic, unpredictable, possibly dangerous." Her beat boyfriend's dilapidated "1938 black Packard" (cars from this phase onward will often be referred to as make plus color, plus epithet [in this case, 1938]), "in which he spends more time roaming the country than he does studying," had to be scrapped after it broke down, and Johnson then experiences "the conundrum faced by restless young women in the 1950s—stay in New York and drive around in the broken down cars of male rebels who were dropping out of Columbia University, or go to Paris," or do both. Another beat girl, the British Sheila Rowbotham, described "how her image of the ultimate man was based on a mixture of James Dean, Marlon Brando, and the Beats, a man of few words but intense emotions, expressed through a grunt or a flick of the eye, always on the run." Like the boys, she was interested in "moments of intense subjectivity."

Breines argues the young women she interviewed showed themselves to be "interested in [the male beats] as models. They wanted to *be* them. Girls identified with the male adventures in *On the Road*, and there is evidence suggesting a profound rejection of gender mores, that many identified with male literary and movie heroes in order to achieve agency in the world." In other words, the male beats' 'abstractification' of the car adventure enabled its appropriation by women. And although this 'agency' included more and more the driving of a car (but most often experiencing the automotive adventure from the passenger or back seat, as we saw), their motives to do so have remained largely hidden. Male authors who created women often depicted them as "the quintessential hitchhiker," such as Sissy Hankshaw (nicknamed Thumbelina, because of her outsize thumb, which in the end becomes a persona in and of itself) in Tom Robbins's *Even Cowgirls Get the Blues* (1976, but playing in the early '70s), who, contrary to the destination-driven perspective of male protagonists, "prefers perpetual motion to the point of transforming it into stillness." And yet, she hitchhikes because of the "*greater freedom of movement*" it provides her.[159] Thus, the car adventure seemingly flattened into the 'car as freedom of mobility' myth but in the same vein was refashioned to suit the emancipation of women, first of all in the passenger seat.

***

Women who write while driving seem to take the stage only by the end of the period covered by this chapter. Even Janice Radway's ethnography of romance reading women (married, between twenty-five and fifty years of age, who mostly did not complete college) from the early 1980s does not present us with any clues as to a possible automotive adventurousness such as we know it as a celebration of masculinity. Reading "religiously every day," these women's declared reason for reading was escapist ("for simple relaxation," "because reading is just for me; it is my time"), and the way to reach that goal was not automotive but romantic-erotic, which, by the way (and not surprisingly so, considering our earlier study), produced a comparable transcendental effect ("I want to be entertained and feel lifted out of my daily routine," the flight metaphor again). By reading romance novels, these women showed they believed, according to Tania Modleski, "in the possibility of transcending the divided self." These women's desires were anti-adventurous (in our tripartite definition of the automotive adventure): analyzing the romances they disliked, Radway concluded they "dislike … 'about faces'; they prefer to see a hero and heroine *gradually* overcome distrust and suspicion and grow to love each other." Violence and all too explicit sex are taboo ("James Bond to the contrary," as one publisher commented), and a happy ending is necessary: the preferred romance does form the (inverted) literary equivalent of the 'tamed automotive adventures' offered by European touring clubs to their members, already before the war.

While the romance-reading women knew the outcome but not the (slightly accidental) way to get there, Dutch automobilists during their "trips with unknown destination" knew that if they followed their guides, they would be surprised, in the end, by a pleasant destination. Like car driving, romance reading was seen as therapeutic (short-lived, so inciting for more), and the thrill of the uncertainty resolved by the happy ending was another affinity with the car adventure. Reading, for these women, was indeed as performative an event as driving, and as immersive: instead of a Quest of the Self, it was the Loss of the Self that was sought. Reading these books, as a TV commercial promoting Harlequin Romance called it, was a "disappearing act." Since 1958, Harlequin by the end of the 1970s had produced 2,300 titles on 150 million books (50 million of them abroad, translated in 16 languages) and written by about 140 women, most of them British. By the beginning of the 1980s, the publisher occupied more than one-third of the paperback market in North America, producing 12 new books every month. Putting mystery or adventure in was allowed, "but these must be subordinate to the romance." The 'ironic function' of car driving (the distancing to the 'real world') apparently could also be reached through reading romances, and one did not need the violence of adventure: Radway quoted one of her interviewees' "belief that romances are a good substitute for the traveling she would like to do but cannot afford."[160]

Feminist critique of the "subliterary" genre of the popular romance since the 1990s has often used a psychoanalytical approach, trying to unearth the "encode[d] ideological information" of a genre that "nearly exclusively [has been] produced and read (*rezipiert*) by women," but published and marketed by men. Whereas some analysts see it as "a projection surface for the ideals of the hegemonic societal and intellectual class (*Schicht*)," others discern the possibility of women acquiring their "own voice ... with which they can express their unease (*Unzufriedenheit*) with the existing gender relations." And although Radway is considered part of the latter group, the patronizing tone of her analysis that tries to find out why these women did succumb to the seduction of patriarchy may resonate with Judith Williamson's accusation of "left-wing academics ... picking out strands of 'subversion' in every piece of pop culture from Street Style to Soap Opera." But in this case, there was no subversion to be found.

The critical treatment of such women's fantasies brings to mind Theodor Adorno's critique of popular culture of "the masses themselves," from which nothing of value "arises spontaneously," or American theologian Reinhold Niebuhr in 1952, for whom television was "our cultural analogous to the threat of atomic weapons to our civilization." Since then, as we argued in the introduction, cultural studies and American studies have developed more sophisticated tools, one of these being literary scholar Mikhail Bakhtin's "transgression of boundaries" thesis, thus, in the words of Peter Burke, "redefining the popular as the rebel in all of us (as Freud once wrote) rather than as the property of any social group."[161] This allows us to search hegemonic utterances (such as the ones discussed in the next subsection) for (at first sight, hidden) rebellious moments and actors, who resonate with the more tamed, ready-to-be-integrated, open rebellion of the beats and their followers. In other words, our search for adventure (tamed or not, abstractified or not) continues in (mostly American) highbrow literature.

The Absent Car: Hegemonic Car Adventure and the Middle-Class Motorist

It was John Updike who, as a conscious representative of American highbrow culture, conceived his novel *Rabbit, Run* (again showing in the title the centrality of mobility in his protagonist's life) as a counterargument against the beats' subversive mobility, without reading *On the Road*, as he later confesses in the introduction to his Rabbit tetralogy. While literary commentators could ventilate their doubts whether "the beats, and especially the work of Jack Kerouac, has any intrinsic value, either literary or human," nobody doubted the centrality of Updike's novel, written in 1959. His novel, Updike says in his introduction, "was meant to be a realistic demonstration of what happens when a young American family man goes on the road—the people left behind get hurt." Even his style (his novel is written in the present tense to create a movie-like directness) contrasted with *On the Road*'s affinity with music: vision (the dominant sense in automotive travel) versus improvised sound, outer-directedness versus inner trip.

Updike, who parodied Kerouac in the *New Yorker*, fled the country during the heydays of the 1960s countercultural turmoil, just like his "middle American" hero Harry Angstrom flees his house and wife, but Updike made his protagonist turn around in West Virginia, not without confessing he had "a good time." The trigger to his failed flight is his wife's aging body, and the reason he gets back is his "fear" of adventure ("It seemed safer to be in a place I know"). The entire novel (as well as its sequel, *Rabbit Redux*) is filled with fear, for women, the Bomb, the Russians, the dark (as a kid), blacks, the law, or sometimes just "a certain fear," the same residual fear that triggered the 1954 Seattle windshield pitting panic, when more than three thousand motorists reported their windshield suddenly becoming pitted and scratched. It was, of course, Cold War fear. "Fear. That's what makes us poor bastards run," Angstrom tells his new girlfriend in *Rabbit Redux*. He is, as one of the protagonists explains, "by nature a domestic figure," and as such, he invites comparison with this other iconic domestic figure, Sinclair Lewis's Babbitt from that other 'expansive' period, the 1920s.[162]

Indeed, there are many parallels between Babbitt's and Rabbit's mobilities, apart from their names' mutual rhyme: both take place in "semi-rural [America] where [in Rabbit's case] the telephone and the movies are the latest thing, and Jack Benny and Benny Goodman dominate the airwaves, and the spectres of Protestant morality still exercise a powerful pull," as Updike characterizes his hero's universe. But where Babbitt's car was crucial for him, and a source of pleasure and a commuting tool, Rabbit brings the *family car* back to his wife, Janice, once he has decided to leave her, and he uses the bus instead. Rabbit does not need a car, as "he has nowhere to go" in his "aimless middle-class suffering" and his "suburban homelessness" dominated by a vague "*fear* of falling." It seems as if Updike was quoting from John Keats's *The Insolent Chariot*, one of the many post–World War II critiques of the lost romance of prewar car driving, written under the impression of the 'invasion' of European compacts, and pointing at "terror or boredom" as the only emotions freeway travel could arouse, "depending on the individual phlegm quotient of the traveler, as influenced by speed."

Keats made clear that the answer to the question about the automotive adventure can be found no longer at the individual level but at the level of the family as subject in the 'lonely crowd.' "The automobile did not put the adventure of travel within reach of the common man," Updike could have read in *Insolent Chariot*, "instead, *it first gave him the opportunity to make himself more and more common*, so that when he reached the point in his development where he could leisure for travel, the lotus lands disappeared *because he was already there*." And yet, the novel's title, like those by Kerouac and Holmes, is resonating with mobility: in the case of Rabbit (modeled as an 'everyman' at least as emphatically as Kerouac's alter ego Sal Paradise and certainly as much as Babbitt), the title expresses an imperative, not often observed by later commentators (who seem to misread the title as conjugated in the present tense, as a description: 'Rabbit runs'): it makes the novel into a moralistic tract, as if the author himself incites his protagonist to move, but he won't, or can't.[163] Hegemonic literature's answer to the beats' vague adventurism was the family car, safely parked in the indoor garage.

Rabbit has often been placed in a world described in William Whyte's *The Organization Man* (1956), just as Babbitt was compared to the real live businessmen in the Lynds' sociological research in *Middletown*. Another comparison was provided by Sloan Wilson's novel *The Man in the Gray Flannel Suit* (1955), but there the house, not the car, is used to express the protagonist's sufferings. Just like for the 'organization man' and the 'man in the gray flannel suit,' the car enables Rabbit "to enter a dream world"; it functions "like a dip in a cool pool on a hot summer's day, or a small dose of aspirin," a medicine or drug rather than a full-blown therapy, as in prewar days. Like the beats' cars, Rabbit's car is an escape vehicle, but where the former keep trying, the latter realizes his escape is in vain. Yet, Rabbit is not more an 'organization man' than Dean Moriarty. This becomes apparent in Updike's sequel, *Rabbit Redux*, covering the 1960s, where his hero keeps his job in a printer's shop, whereas Janice has joined her father in his Toyota car dealership, the same dealership Rabbit will take over in the second sequel, *Rabbit Is Rich*, covering the 1970s. A Hollywood movie *Rabbit, Run* starring James Caan and Carrie Snodgrass and directed by Jack Smight premiered in Updike's hometown in 1970, but a wider release was aborted because of a poor reception.

"I like middles," Updike once said, and he liked "to give the mundane its beautiful due." His critics praise his ability "to make the ordinary seem strange," but "the American sublime will never touch his pages." From our mobility perspective, one is inclined to think this is because the car is so ostentatiously absent and that he, just like his literary rival Kerouac, "demonstrates a ... faith in the transcendent power of fiction and language" instead. Sublimity, the beats student Catharine Stimpson asserted, resulted from male friendship, "soar[ing] beyond any explanatory theory of sublimation, regression or repression."[164]

***

Remarkably, no less highbrow were Flannery O'Connor's Southern Gothic "grotesque" protagonists such as Hazel Motes in *Wise Blood* (1952), preacher of the Church without Christ, who buys a dilapidated car to use, in an utterly utilitarian way, as a tool, a pedestal for his sermons. The car is a second protagonist in the narrative, which works better "as a parable than as a representation of ordinary life, to which the author was largely a stranger." Nevertheless, the car took a prominent place in O'Connor's fictional universe: "There was only one thought in his mind," she describes Hazel, "he was going to buy a car. The thought was full grown in his head when he woke up, and he didn't think of anything else. He had never thought before of buying a car, he had never even wanted one before. He had driven one only a little in his life and he didn't have a license." But the car for Hazel is also a vehicle of escape, representing for him, as Clarke analyzed, "white, able-bodied American masculinity" and "a space away from the dominance of women."[165]

Mobility in O'Connor's universe primarily is depicted in the microphysics of bodily gestures (which also has the effect of blending out the environment). A close reading of the central chapters 6 and 7, however, also reveals how the car is used as a tool, a prosthesis, beyond the function of utilitarian driving: Hazel searches for someone while driving around (which implies the person he is looking for is expected to be found in public space, 'traffic space'), he follows others in his car, he stands on its hood to spread the word, he sleeps in it at night, he uses his car to ram someone else's car, and uses it to kill someone, running over him several times; he dreams of the car as a coffin, buried in it alive. The car is freaky, too: it sometimes "would go forward about six inches and then back about four; it did that now a succession of times rapidly," perhaps the weirdest phenomenon in the history of autopoetic literature. There were limits, however, to this 'automotive irrationality,' even in O'Connor's fictional universe: "Hazel tried to start the car by forcing his weight forward on the steering wheel, but that didn't work." When a police officer pushes his car off a cliff when he cannot show a license, Hazel blinds himself: without a car, there is no mobility, not even 'vision,' and he returns to his "mother," a motherly landlady. He dies like Neal Cassady, in a ditch along the road. For Kerouac, escape is futile; for Updike, it is impossible; and the same applies to O'Connor: escape is impossible, even from God. The centrality of the car in O'Connor's work ("The Essential Essex," in literary historian J. O. Tate's words, who sees O'Connor use the car metaphor "as a false God") reveals its *ubiquity*, now also in the American South.[166]

***

The same applies to that other Southern Gothic author, William Faulkner, although his *Reivers* (1962) and Snopes trilogy (1965) are set in a bygone prewar era. No less central (even if it is not mentioned so much) is the station wagon in Vladimir Nabokov's *Lolita* (1955), a "parody of American gentility and the standards of the middle class of the 1950s," in which the protagonist "plays make-believe adventurer, exotic lover, experienced traveller. In actual fact, he is always on the run" and fantasizes about being a "travelling family man." In fact, *Lolita* is one of the few early post–World War II autopoetic novels in which the automotive cocoon (owned originally by her mother) turns into a "cell," a "yearlong" prison for the twelve-year-old girl, the male protagonist's 'passenger.'

The beats' characteristic 'passengering' also has its Southern Gothic version, for instance, in O'Connor's short story "The Life You Save May Be Your Own," in which a tramp is allowed to sit in the back seat of the car, where he may sleep during the night. He accepts marrying the protagonist's daughter, only to abandon her as soon as he has taken hold of the daughter's price, which is the car. With O'Connor, herself far from an adventurer in the classical, corporeal sense (she did not take part in dance or sports during her student life, soon thereafter suffering from arthritis), we reenter a violent and aggressive car world (the world created before the war). In her short story "A Good Man Is Hard to Find," a bizarre family trip in the car ends in a near-fatal accident. "'We've had an ACCIDENT!' the children screamed in a frenzy of delight," as if a promise is fulfilled.[167] But like in *On the Road* and other autopoetic novels of the period, the attention from the inside of the automotive cocoon for the world out there is minimal: the road (network) itself, its traffic flow, instead of the automotive monadic capsule, starts to become a cocoon.

Even in John Steinbeck's traditional travelogue *Travels with Charley* (1962), the freeway experience in his camper on US 90 with its "centers for rest, food, and replenishment" prevents the author from seeing anything: "I must have crossed the river but I couldn't see it. I never did see it. I never saw St. Paul or Minneapolis. All I saw was a river of trucks; all I heard was a roar of motors." If this is the result of his being *In Search of America* (as the subtitle of his travelogue reads), then the result of his search is pretty meager. This, and similar utterances by other writers of autopoetics, form a counterargument against literary analyses that keep treating the fictional car trip as a 'Quest of the Self,' or, a more recent version of this trope, "the outer world as a reflection of the inner self." What then, does this postwar version of the prewar trope of 'the car as lens' (its windshield a moving movie theater screen) bring more than a sedentarist reflection of 'America'? Not much, or so it seems, as the car meanwhile enables a flight from 'the world' but also from the 'Self,' replacing manifold social interactions by a reduced form, a hypnosis, boredom, or some internal 'talks' (as in the case of *On the Road*) that helps go beyond the Self. Nor does the vehicle itself receive much attention. Although Steinbeck famously compared the new generation's limited knowledge of the clitoris with its prolific knowledge of the ignition coil, we don't hear much about "Rocinante," his truck-cum-mobile-home, but we are reminded of the ubiquitous autopoetic trope of the automation of the skills of car driving: "Nearly all the driving technique is deeply buried in a machine-like unconscious." Also, his trip is constructed as a lonely experience (except for Charley, his animal passenger): his wife flies in from the East for a brief visit to Chicago, which he subsequently and deliberately leaves out of his narrative. After all, the *illusion of the individualistic motorist* has to be kept up. Rocinante, called after Don Quixote's horse (and already used by Dos Passos as a metaphor), forms a part of what Steinbeck repeatedly calls his Operation Windmills. From his narrative, the pleasure of the journey slips away when he is confronted with "the racial conflict" in the South. Steinbeck's trip is at least as patriotic as Kerouac's, and he remarkably reaches the same conclusion as to trip planning: "I wonder why it is that when I plan a route too carefully it goes to pieces, whereas if I blunder along in blissful ignorance aimed in a fancied direction I get through with no trouble."[168]

The same freeway network also appears in Thomas Pynchon's postmodernist 1966 novel *The Crying of Lot 49*, in which the British music invasion of the United States is described through the experiences of the collective subject the Paranoids (the Beatles sometimes called themselves Los Paranoias) right at the moment Reaganism and the New Right started to appear, a fact often forgotten in the zeal to describe the countercultural impulses to the 1960s in Los Angeles: the most popular song in 1966 United States was Sergeant Barry Sadler's "Ballad of the Green Berets," Russel Duncan reminded us. Pynchon's novel is a celebration of postmodern mobility, dealing with "an underground organization whose main goal is to break the government's monopoly with an alternative, secret system for sending messages," the glue on the regular post stamps perhaps "saturated with LSD," a nice prefiguration of the later terrorism scare. The freeway system in such novels literally "panoramically lifted commuters above inner-city impoverishment," a city in which a year earlier the Watts riots had raged.

It is this universe, this freeway world isolated from urban America and at the same time the corridor through which urban culture is spread, that sets postwar mobility apart from the interbellum culture: it is the universe where serial killers such as Charles Starkweather (memorialized in Bruce Springsteen's "Nebraska," making Starkweather into an alternative Neal Cassady), "an angry young rebel against everything the nation held dear," killed eleven people in January 1958, driving around in a 1949 Ford. And although the 1950s does not seem to show "any measurable increase in juvenile crime," the FBI and the police helped create the idea that juvenile delinquency had spiked since the war.[169] Theodore Weesner, as we saw, capitalized on this fear through his novel *The Car Thief*. In sum, once the ubiquitous car is enabled to cruise on the new freeways (built from the end of the 1950s, as we will see in the next chapter), the abstractification is only enhanced into boredom and internalization. This, at least is the masculine experience. The question, then, is how the ubiquitous, utilitarian family car was able to include the woman—and whether she experienced a similar 'flattening' of the automotive adventure.

Women in the Hegemonic Autopoetic Universe: Very Young and Passengering

The utilitarian, tool-like character of the car is also apparent in the way women use the car, as we can gather from several recent dissertations. Such women are not necessarily depicted by women, however: with the exception of Flannery O'Connor, the female 'autopoetic' writers Deborah Clarke presented came to the fore only in the 1970s. Women, literature scholar Ronald Primeau concluded in an overview from 1999, "weren't allowed to, chose not to, or just didn't create their own unique version of America's road mythology until fairly recently." Literature scholar and Americanist Alexandra Ganser, too, saw women entering automobile culture as car drivers in the 1970s, at the moment second-wave feminism made women "taking back the streets." For Katie Mills, the real start of the female "road story" (celebrating "a self-consciously alienated subject position") took place somewhat (too?) late, "only after the rise of feminism, punk, and postmodern movements of the eighties," a hiatus she connected to the "repress[ion of] the production of road stories about girls" as a result of *Lolita*'s pedophilia. But because the beats themselves were specialists in 'passengering' as well, the difference with women is that the former "talked" (endlessly, as Sal and Dean in *On the Road*, the talking being the proof that one was being alive), whereas the latter struggled against their "speechlessness … and their status of decorative ornaments, 'anonymous passengers on the big Greyhound bus of experience.'"[170]

Although women writers may have been scarce in the 1950s and 1960s, this does not mean we cannot find autopoetic novels (or autopoetic parts in non-autopoetic novels) in which women protagonists (most of them belonging to the middle class) must deal with automobilism. Remarkably, women's dominant sphere of labor, the domestic sphere, was much less depicted than their behavior in traffic. Maybe movies give us a first clue: there, female traffic behavior is often represented by "bad" women, such as Ingrid Bergman's "reckless drunken driving" in *Notorious* (1946), or Marilee Hadley (played by Dorothy Malone) driving her own sports car and picking up men, as contrasted to the "demure domesticity" of Lauren Bacall, who lets men drive. "Women are variously struck down, blinded, or blown up by or in automobiles in *Suspicion* (1941), *Postman Always Rings Twice* (1946, 1981), *The Big Heat* (1953), *Magnificent Obsession* (1954), and *The Godfather* (1972), each narrative using the car to threaten or destroy romance, domesticity, or reproduction."[171] Novels offered a less risky universe for women, but before the 'explosion' of women writers in the 1970s (which will be a topic of a later study), the protagonists in hegemonic literature before that period are remarkably young, and most often passengers.

***

In her best-selling novel-as-memoir *Riding in Cars with Boys*, "bad girl" Beverly Donofrio describes her participation in a youth culture in an Italian American neighborhood that slowly slips into the (lower-middle-class part of the) counterculture. A car-related youth culture started before the war, as we showed in our earlier study, but now (belatedly, the memoir dates from 1990 and was made into a movie directed by Penny Marshall in 2001) former youth culture participants started writing about how the boys "rode real low in cars, elbows stuck out windows." It was a world where tinkering on cars was normal: "I figured he could probably fix cars because that's why hoods were called greasers." At fourteen, she was "speeding around Wallingford in crowded cars with guys who took corners on two wheels, flew over bumps, and skidded down the road to get me screaming. Whenever I saw a cop car, I lay down on the seat, out of sight."

Daughter of a policeman—sharing the family car now and then; enjoying the liberating music of the Four Tops, the Beatles, Led Zeppelin, and Jefferson Airplane; reading Hemingway, Steinbeck, and Faulkner; and watching *Easy Rider*—Donofrio's (or better: her alter ego's) struggle for independence is mediated by the car: "Why did [her husband Raymond] always get the car?" When she leaves, Raymond and starts living with her girlfriend Fay. Fay's husband "stole back the yellow Dodge, leaving us carless and furious—because it had been men who'd knocked us up, men who'd left us with kids, and men who got the cars." Not always, though: when Raymond's car gets repossessed by the credit union, the narrator lets him complain: "'I lost my car. I lost my son. I lost my wife,' in exactly that order." When she manages to get a scholarship for a community college, she at first cannot go, and only after acquiring a college loan can she buy "this beautiful fourteen-year-old with-a-rebuilt-engine emerald-green Volkswagen." Now, she "talked [herself] into feeling macho." In the car with her student friends, someone had put on Joni Mitchell: "'I am on a lonely road and I am traveling traveling traveling, looking for something what can it be,' and when I opened my eyes, I saw that my fellow women had taken their shirts off."

For women, the car seems to provide liberation, even if the scene is a memory from the 1990s, and no doubt colored by that period. But the car experience is adventurous, produced in an emancipatory mood. In a way, Donofrio's journey to a prestigious university (Wesleyan) can be read as the female counternarrative to and at the same time the successor of the beats' journey, all the more so as the 'necessity' of the car in Donofrio's case should not be exaggerated: at the end of her book, the narrator mentions there are students without a car. It seems her car dependence is a working-class fantasy: "There were plenty of students who went four years to college without ever having a car. I could walk to all my classes. I could shop at the little, though more expensive, corner market. I could hitch rides with neighbors. Eventually, I'd save the money to fix her [the car]. It would work out." Female adventure is different, the novel seems to suggest; the car dependence is less. Although hitchhiking creates dependence to men, dependence to cars appears as a station on the road upward, "preparing me for the upper middle class." Once graduated, she "totaled" her car. The car is like her friend Olivia's orthopedic shoes, which prevented her from traveling, or so she thought. At the end of the novel, the narrator "thought of Olivia and how her feet had hobbled her life. No. She had hobbled her life with her belief about her feet."[172]

***

Emily, Anne Roiphe's protagonist in *Long Division* (1972), drives with her ten-year-old daughter in her station wagon (the very icon of the American nuclear family) from New York to Mexico, to get her divorce papers, flying from her bohemian artist husband, and full of anticipation of "adventure." A part of her adventure as a "Wandering Jewess" is certainly not the tinkering, as she does not know how to change a tire: "Another generation of women might be able to change tires, having learned like their brothers at some early age, but I was born too late for that new liberty. I needed help." She hesitates whether she should not turn back, but unlike Rabbit Angstrom, she drives on ("the car keeps moving forward"), over the "screaming highways" into thrilling adventures (a kidnap of her daughter by gypsies, among others). She fantasizes about an accident ("What if a tire blew, what if I steered wrong, what if we crashed into the side of the train?") when she feels 'accelerated' by a parallel train, and produces a 'feminine' response: "I slowed the car to fifty, and then stopped entirely, letting the train go by till there was a distancing of noise and sudden silence." She gives an early description of what has since been called 'highway hypnosis': "the hypnotic effect of the constant motion on the smooth road," which makes her feel "like a monkey in a capsule a billion miles above the earth," giving us a rare post–World War II example of the ubiquitous flight metaphor of earlier days, the plane meanwhile morphed into a space capsule.

She takes on two hitchhikers (two youths with their "counterculture revolt against ... the Babbitlike mentality") to counter the "gray boredom" of freeway driving. During her trip, she is fooled by a black man who sells her pictures with "black men showing off their natural powers." When she later looks at the pictures, they appear to be magazine clippings, "each one of a different make of car, shiny chrome, big wheels and new paint job showing the body off to the best advantage. Cars! I had been had again. Five dollars' worth of Detroit's wet dreams. I felt fearful. Would I ever be able to ford the future?" For the female motorist, a man's genitalia are not equivalent to his car. Ironically, she calls her trip "seeing the country," but there are hardly any landscape descriptions, only her 'inner' adventures along the road and in the car's interior. Her adventures are limited: "Icarus was a male, not a female—a female would have waited for a boat " This limitation of the automotive adventure may be why Ganser analyzed Roiphe's text as part of the 'quest' trope: Emily's wanderings "are more a necessity, a consequence of her wish to quickly divorce her husband, than a choice based on wanderlust." Although Ganser conceded Emily's journey "transforms ... into a collective existential condition, with any potential destination continuously deferred," the individualistic bias of literature students (who tend to fall into the trap of literature's privileging of the individual's choice) prevents her from emphasizing the continuity with prewar female automotive 'adventurers,' a period in which the term necessity, especially in the United States, was used as an alibi to mask the fundamental adventurousness of automobilism.[173]

***

This cannot be said of Katherine Dunn's novel *Truck* (1971), fully written from the perspective of a drug-free, rebellious fifteen-year-old girl, Dutch, from Eugene, Oregon, who wants to become "invisible" amid a nuclear family she experiences as oppressive. The narrative can be seen as part of "a group of writings of the 1960s and 1970s which 'refine and enlarge antidomestic themes in grim road noir narratives that anticipate the final collapse of road romance.'" A novel about child passengering, *Truck* describes how Dutch spies on two of her friends petting in a drive-in theater, witnessed from the trunk of the car. The novel also portrays the microculture of bus passengering when Dutch muses:

> When it's good in a car I want never to stop. Just keep goin forever. The stopping makes me feel sick and tight like it's time to die. Just drive on, whoever was driving, not me. And I'd sit in the seat and we'd stop to piss and for gas and at drive-ins for hamburgers and get candy bars at gas stations and just go on fast down the road, not turning, just curving and I'd sleep sitting up or crawl in back and cover up and the driver would never sleep but just drive and the car would never break down or run out of gas.

Such is the experience of a child passenger on America's new highways: "not turning, just curving," enabling her to dream, and sleep. A child of baby boomers who does not want to "marry a service station attendant," Dutch personifies the beginning fragmentation of the nuclear family as she prepares her runaway very meticulously, driven by a lust for freedom denied her as a female, as her male friend Heydorf explains to her. The title refers to the jargon the girl uses to describe her mobile experiences ("We trucked down to the creek"; "I'm trucking along"; "He was trucking out with my money"), experiences that include her efforts to glance from the bus to the world outside at night: "I can see my eyes in the window. Somebody's reading light on. Yellow flat glass and my eyes huge and white all around the iris. Outside through the iris. There's no face. Just the outside and then the whites and in the middle of the whites little holes into the outside and the outside goes past very fast and dark." When in the end the police find her and she is recuperated, a "counselor" asks her at the police station (where another, twelve-year-old girl also appears to be arrested, who had stolen twelve cars and was caught joyriding the thirteenth into Mexico) why she ran away. "I just wanted the adventure," she replies, but the counselor does not believe her.[174]

***

When women appeared on the automotive scene as would-be owners in numbers (1 million annual car sales in the early 1960s, 1.5 million in 1977), they were not only identified (albeit reluctantly) by marketing specialists as the 'deciders' in family matters, including car purchase, but also were hailed as having a benign influence on car safety, as they admittedly caused more accidents than men, but these "were mostly fender-benders and resulted in little damage or injury." Psychologists observed women were no less aggressive than men, although they scored lower on the "sensation-seeking scale (SSS)" developed in the early 1960s, a measure of a "behavioral expression … found in various kinds of risk-taking behaviors such as driving habits, health, gambling, financial activities, alcohol and drug use, sexual behavior, and sports." That scale seemed to be developed to probe the violent inclinations of young, white, firstborn, Western, single or divorced men, inclinations that preferably could be observed in "driving behavior." Tellingly, one of the popular theories behind the human inclination toward thrill seeking was Freud's *Trieb* concept, which literally means "drive," although it is mostly translated into "instinct." Telling, too, was the special attention in the SSS questionnaire for the spatial adventure ("I would like to take off on a trip with no preplanned or definite routes or timetable," yes or no?), while the lust for high speed was measured through questions about water skiing, airplane piloting, parachute jumping, not car driving.[175]

Cadillac Flambé: Ethnic Minorities and Conspicuous Car Consumption

If there was, as we quoted Deborah Clarke, no "close personal sensation with the car" in this phase of car-cultural history anymore, one wonders which sensation the car exactly enabled to experience. Chicano "lowriding," for instance, was adventurous in quite a different way from the prewar mainstream, although Mexicanos in Los Angeles already started lowering their cars by putting cement bags in their trunks as far back as the 1930s. For them, hot-rodders must have been mainstream: a reader of *Low Rider* magazine in the 1970s characterized hot-rodders as "white people [who] *raise their cars*, making all kinds of noise and pollution, racing down the streets killing themselves, it not someone else." Their opinion did not differ very much from that of historian David Gartman, who saw hot-rodders emerge "in the late 1930s and early 1940s largely among working-class teenagers in Southern California," whose aesthetics, "however rebellious, ... was defined by the Fordist system it sought to reject." But Gartman presented "custom-car building," as a "spin-off movement of hot-rodding," undertaken by "working-class kids with sheet-metal and painting skills, popp[ing] up in Southern California in the late 1940s and early 1950s." For the car modifiers, however, the differences were big: instead of the "greasy coveralls" of the hot-rodders stood the clean, pressed, starched, and shiny clothes and shoes of the cholos. Cars were "status symbols" rather than adventure machines. After the war, sophisticated technical solutions were developed in a general climate of car tinkering, as hydraulic cylinders were mounted in the place of springs, such that the cars looked normal when the police was around. The do-it-yourself culture was certainly not limited to the poor, however: several contemporary observers were surprised to see how this 'functional' part of the automotive adventure predominantly spread among the middle and higher incomes, not much different from the fascination for small-scale technology expressed in the eagerness to build your own synthesizer and other forms of "playful use of technology." When Chicano youngsters started to die in the Vietnam War, lowrider clubs organized "lowrider funerals" for them.[176]

Here was a different and genuine car adventure in the making, resonating with the status-sensitive tradition we described in the previous chapter. In both the United Kingdom and the United States, surveys revealed about 20 to 25 percent of car owners tinkered on their cars themselves; in Germany, nine out of ten owners washed and maintained their cars regularly, often once a week. In the United States, the "Saturday mechanics" were often aiming at racing, or more generally, car sports. Whereas their sons were hitchhiking to Woodstock, the fathers (or their Southern brothers) drove to the stock car races in North Carolina, described in New Journalism style by Tom Wolfe in his *Esquire* article on "The Last American Hero" Junior Johnson, an eulogy on the racing David who challenged the Goliaths from Detroit in his Chevrolet: "You threw the car into second gear, cocked the wheel, stepped on the accelerator and made the car's rear end skid around in a complete 180-degree arc, a complete about-face, and tore on back up the road exactly the way you came from, God!" The power slides, Wolfe found out, had been practiced during "those goddamned *about-faces* running away from the Alcohol Tax agents."[177]

In the case of the Californian Chicanos, however, mobility was even less unproblematic: the ten days long Zoot Suit Riots in 1943 between second-generation Mexican Americans and gangs of GIs, who in a "carnival of drunkenness, violence, and sexual aggression" attacked all those who dared to walk around in suits (after "mid-thirties Negro fashions," but also practiced by "some ... Philipino youth"), all those who expressed "hostility to the established order," at the same time indulging in "the pleasures of shocking public opinion," was all about mobility. Adorned with "polka-dot shirts with outlandish trousers and jackets in yellow and purple, as well as string ties, pearl buttons as big as silver dollars, and trousers so tight they have to be zipped," zoot suiters became the target of racist hatred. "Marching through the streets of downtown Los Angeles," a journalist wrote, "a mob of several hundred soldiers, sailors and civilians proceeded to beat up every zoot suiter they could find."

The mobility background of the riot was a migration of Mexicans "on a scale unseen since the nineteenth century": the American industry after the Japanese attack on Pearl Harbor created 17 million new jobs (6.5 million of these acquired by women), in the Californian case meant to release American farmworkers. The aggression of the 'released' soldiers and sailors toward the zoot as "a badge of hoodlumism" (in the police's terms) was sanctioned by the local police ("if we can arrest people for being underdressed we can do so for being overdressed"). Some Mexican Americans drove past the police headquarters in their cars, showing banners reading, "We're good Americans," but other cars full of sailors cruised the barrios looking for victims (who subsequently were arrested by the police). "Seven truckloads of sailors came from Las Vegas, while taxis provided free transport to this 'mass lynching,'" fortunately without lethal casualties.[178]

***

Immediately after the war, it was the car's interior that attracted the young Chicanos' attention, but in the 1960s, Chicano muralists added paintings to the cars' exteriors, and when the Chicano civil rights movement erupted in the late 1960s, lowrider culture was fully developed and became one of its "lasting images." In fact, as we argued in the introduction, it was a revival of a very early 'feminized,' counter-adventurous part of automotive culture (one we have neglected somewhat in our earlier study), which started with flower contests (cars fully covered with flowers) before a jury but also took the form of gymkhanas, competitions in dexterity in handling the car in crammed spaces, a phase in a long tradition started in nineteenth-century horse riding and horse carriage culture. Moriarty's parking stunts can be seen in this light, but the Chicano lowrider culture surely was the most spectacular example of "overdecoration," which played with what Bakhtin called the "carnivalesque as a means of transgressing binary oppositions, particularly that [sic] between high and low." From this perspective, the mobility carnival is the popular-cultural equivalent of middle-class irony: it is the ostentatious flight forward, the creation of distance to the 'Other' through noise and exuberance rather than through doublespeak. The 'adventure' (if we can still call it that without losing sight that this Chicano culture was about 'conspicuous consumption' and 'rhymed' with fashion and styling) was an extension of an earlier Chicano urban culture of the pachucos, where youngsters dressed in "flamboyant zoot suits or 'drapes,' accessorizing with wide-brimmed hats and extremely long watch chains, speaking in a syncretic mixture of *caló* [a Spanish gypsy dialect] and hip, jazz-cat slang." This was, indeed, popular art rather than risky sports, quite different from its "exclusively phallic" counterpart of WASP hot-rodding.[179]

***

Packer has investigated similar connections between African Americans and cars, especially the stereotypical 'pimped' Cadillac, which was only advertised in the middle-class magazine *Ebony* (founded in the late 1940s and pointing the industry at an eager $15 billion market) as late as 1972. Packer's analysis of two decades of *Ebony* revealed that, again, vertical and horizontal mobility appeared to be closely intertwined (certainly in the case of 'minorities' and their emancipatory struggle) and that especially the Cadillac proved to be a "weapon in the war for racial equality." The industry, which even by 1963 did not have any African-American-owned dealerships, advertised their cars in *Ebony* surrounded by white families, and while it tried to accommodate women, it did the opposite toward blacks, avoiding at all costs that its products could be labeled "Negro cars," despite the five million African Americans who purchased a car annually. *Ebony* wondered why blacks worshipped the Cadillac, "an abnormal obsession, especially in Harlem," but as early as 1959, a small survey in Seattle in a neighborhood characterized as "conservative, middle-class, bourgeois, and anxious to preserve non-militant relations with the white group" had already established "the Negro and his Cadillac proved to be an unfounded stereotype," although it also found that in lower-class black areas, "there were more Negroes who drove Cadillacs than any other identifiable group."

Even black comedian Dick Gregory amused his audience in the Chicago Playboy Club in 1961 with jokes like: "Sometimes I think the only one who doesn't resent us owning a Cadillac is General Motors ... This car could be 6,000 skipped lunches standing out at the curb—but you can hear the teeth gritting a block away." What the survey especially revealed, however, was the collective use of these cars: "Three or four colored boys will go in together to buy a car and the one that makes the last payment will drive the car that month." In fact, the results of the survey were rather ambiguous, because at the same time, it reported on an observation on a "busy intersection" near a "lower-class area" about "more Negroes who drove Cadillacs than any other identifiable group," while "most Negroes who drive Cadillacs cannot afford them," a phenomenon a "Negro social worker" explained by referring to "the feeling [enabled by possessing a Cadillac] of more satisfaction than owning a home, because if it was a 'first class home,' it would have to be located in a white neighborhood."[180]

Mary Pattillo-McCoy, who analyzed the emergence of a black middle class, observed:

> African Americans have [bought things they often cannot afford in order to give others the impression that they can] for years, and with decidedly more vigor than whites ... African Americans use material goods as symbolic affronts to the power of whites. From the early 1950s through the 1960s, poor black men were more likely to buy expensive and prestigious cars (such as Cadillacs) and goods (like Scotch) than poor white men ... "Basically, a Cadillac is an instrument of aggression."

"The poor man's Cadillac," William Whyte wrote in *Fortune* commenting on "the Cadillac phenomenon," "sometimes *is* a Cadillac, and in some working class neighborhoods Cadillacs outnumber any other make." Packer concluded the car in general was never a simple tool of emancipation, not for women (stronger even, according to Packer, "there is ... no necessary correspondence between gender and driving") or for blacks or Hispanics: cars were used for lynchings and lowriding, rape and going to university. Indeed, the car as an 'umbrella' for a variety of functions fits very well in this black and subversive "social revolution," which "never has ... been so petit bourgeois; what blacks wanted more than anything was the very cliché of the American dream. As a member of the prototypically militant Deacons for Defense put it: 'I'm just a capitalist that don't have a damn thing.'" Ralph Ellison also plays with this "duality" in his 1973 short story "Cadillac Flambé," when the protagonist sets his Cadillac ablaze after a Southern governor called such cars "goon cages," suddenly realizing the car is "a means of trapping the black man into believing he was free." Ellison's story is one of the few postwar autopoetic revivals of the prewar trope of "that good old familiar feeling of *flying*" during his leisurely touring, but he also confirms the earlier quoted survey on the collective use of the car, speaking about "a power-drunk group" who forced him into a ditch.[181]

Even passengering is different in Ellison's car universe: in *Invisible Man* (1952), the protagonist may be "elated by the power he feels in commanding an automobile," as literary historian Roger Casey asserts, but he also senses an "impending doom because of his proximity to whiteness" (his passenger, Mr. Norton, whose chauffeur he is). Traveling "by bus from South to North—to Harlem, not Greenwich Village," Ellison's protagonist indeed produced a "very different road experience" than Kerouac. In contrast to this conspicuousness, when John A. Williams, upon invitation by the journal *Holiday*, as late as 1966 traveled through the United States to feel the pulse of its racism, he tried to be as inconspicuous as he could, especially when crossing the South. He suddenly regretted having ordered a brand-new station wagon, "a nine-passenger job with over four hundred horses hidden under the new white hood. Red upholstery, whitewalls, automatic. A gas-eater? Perhaps, but comfort and power."

Williams relates "how much nerve and courage it requires for a Negro to drive coast to coast in America. Nerve, courage, and a great deal of luck." He explains how blacks returning to the South from the North, where they had bought their Cadillacs and Lincolns earning their money in the car factories, hide their ownership by wearing chauffeur hats or "pretend they are just delivering the car." He is warned by friends to "stop for your gas in large cities … As soon as you see a speed zone, *slow up*; don't wait for another sign … Watch your step, keep your tongue inside your head, and *remember where you are*." Williams was also helped by his *Travelguide: Vacation and Recreation without Humiliation*, an essential tool for an African American to navigate the freeway system, as Seiler has shown in his seminal historical analysis of American automobilism. No black hitchhikers were to be found in the South, Williams pondered: that is too dangerous.

Indeed, by the end of his "non-fictional" account, after being followed, stopped, and harassed by state troopers and police officers during his fifteen thousand miles of wandering, he can't take it anymore and explodes in anger. In a "youthful dream," he often fantasized about the protective function of the car-as-capsule: "After every reported lynching I saw myself in a specially made car … heading South. Built into the front of the car were three machine guns, two .30 caliber and one .50. The two .30's could track 90 degrees to the side. The car, of course, was bulletproof, and being especially built, the engine was supercharged; nothing on the road could catch us."

Together with the adventure, black minorities revive its violence. Isolation and protection do not prohibit pleasure, however, but it is spatially (or better, geographically) distributed:

> I let the car out and it jumped ahead, moving cleanly and easily, and the joy of having so much power at toe tip filled me completely. Here it was, the ground-level height of Everyman's automated existence. Open the door, press a button and lower the window, turn the key, set the gear and mash down ... There had been times in the South when I hated to leave the car because it formed a vault of safety. But in New England and when I was emerging from the South, I did not want to get out of the car because of the sense of power it gave me.

Try to find such a text in postwar, highbrow, autopoetic literature! Williams's America trip showed that white, middle-class, hegemonic car culture, complete with the tropes of the power and pleasure of driving, started to become available for African Americans, ready to be appropriated within their own culture at the very moment the white adventure machine started to be domesticated beyond recognition. But it also shows how the narrative follows postwar hegemonic automobilism in the indifference the separate universe of the freeway system allowed toward other road users: "Some hours later we hit the Los Angeles freeway system ... Ahead of us, one car passing another hooked bumpers. Both cars flashed around in a blur of metal and glass ... and we went around, seeing the white startled faces still jerking and snapping. We left them, as other freeway riders left them, to their lawsuits and X rays, wrecking trucks and recriminations."[182] The car's irony, its ability to allow distance to the people outside, has a black side as well.

It is this Interstate freeway network that, according to Seiler, provided a first relatively free space for "driving while black." Seiler explained how from 1937 to well in the 1960s, the black, motoring middle class used the *Travelguide* and *The Negro Motorists Green Book* (a wordplay on the initiator, Victor Green) to "escape from Jim Crow." The early years of the 1950s saw the blacks in America become a weapon in Cold War rhetoric, for instance, in *Reader's Digest*, which declared that "the most 'exploited' Negroes in Mississippi are better off than the citizens of Russia or her satellites" (notice the refusal to call the Soviet Union by its proper name) or former President Herbert Hoover, who five years later in the same magazine opined that "our 14 million American Negroes own more automobiles than all the 200 million Russians and the 300 million Negroes in Africa put together." The guidebooks emphasized their readers' middle classness rather than their race: they were, according to Seiler, "mobile, affluent, benignant, and generally quiescent black travelers ... more identifiable by their status as consumers than by their race." The travel guides seemed to be less necessary when the civil rights movement in the late 1950s and early 1960s emerged, but the cocoon-like character of the interstate network, just being built, provided, in the words of Tom Lewis, "a measure of protection ... however thin a veneer as that protection might be."[183]

Chuck Berry's "Maybellene" (1955), adopted from a country song by Bob Wills, testifies to this discovery of the automotive adventure by black motorists: "As I was motivatin' over the hill / I saw Maybellene in a Coupe de Ville ... She's bumper to bumper rollin' side by side." The song, which introduced a neologism (motivatin') to suggest the sensation of car driving, ends with a race against Maybellene's Cadillac, a car that was especially popular as 'persona' in '50s and '60s songs, as we will see later. Berry's "No Particular Place to Go" (1964) celebrated not the temporal but rather the spatial aspects of the adventure machine. But this was the black youth fantasy. For their fathers and mothers, the protection the freeways provided can better be explained by referring to "the self-abstraction of the citizen" Michael Warner described as happening when this citizen "enters the public sphere, as a blank figure, divested of her particularities, and thereby empowered to speak, act, and move," a similar phenomenon of 'abstractification' as we observed happen with postwar, white middle-class automobilism.[184] Postwar hegemonic car culture made it easier for black automobilism to enter the fast lane, a phenomenon similar to what we observed when beat women joined their male friends in their 'abstractified' automobilism.

Prefiguring Road Rage: Aggression and Violence in Hegemonic Autopoetic Fiction

John Williams, in his travelogue, also refers to the "grim anarchy" he fears will erupt after the murder of John F. Kennedy, which happens during his journey, an anarchy expressed in "kids bombed to pieces, highway drivers and hitchhikers blasted by shotguns." Whether he was (or could have been) thinking of beat poet and Black Arts Movement (1967) founder LeRoy Jones (later Amiri Baraka)'s experimental novel *The System of Dante's Hell* from 1966 (with prepublications before that year) is not known; in this novel, Baraka describes "Falsifiers" in Dante's "Circle 8. Simply Fraudulent" (so, nearly at the bottom of hell), in which an especially cruel form of passengering is described:

> Sanchez threw the car in the wrong gear ... Donald was at the woman's left. I at her right. The other packed in the front ... The thunderous tires roared. And

roared ... I began to act ... The car moved at a steady rate. The dim lights on ... Big dogs barked at the car from the driveways ... "Bitch!" / What're you boys tryina do? No answer from us. The front riders sat tight in their seats ... we were deep in Montclair, and some car full of negroes up there wd be spotted by the police ... She screamed," [etcetera, ending in:] "Kick the bitch out!"

The precursors of "road rage," which erupted in the United States to its full variety in the late 1980s and became an object of study by psychologists by the end of the 1970s, consisted of "roadway assaults," including urban drive-by shooting, the latter a revival of a model developed by Italian mobsters in New York and Chicago during the 1920s.[185]

Connected by psychologists to the "territorial aggression thesis," automotive aggression and violence were also triggered by "frustration" caused by congestion, the interruption of the traffic flow, a phenomenon setting postwar car violence apart from its prewar precursors, which I have analyzed in much detail elsewhere. It took motorists a while to acquire new skills to enjoy the traffic jam as a locus of relaxation between work and family, motorists who systematically (and erroneously) were taken to be middle class. This was the case, for instance, in a publication edited by sociologist Murray Friedman (containing texts from Daniel Patrick Moynihan, Spiro Agnew, Edward S. Muskie, and many others, with a foreword by Hubert H. Humphrey) aimed at ways of *Overcoming Middle Class Rage*. The contributing politicians addressed the "silent majority" comprising "just under half the American population," and they referred to the sitcom *All in the Family* broadcast by CBS from 1971 to 1983, with tongue-in-cheek racist Archie Bunker as the iconic protagonist, living in Queens, New York City. Friedman blamed the positive discrimination allegedly enjoyed by African Americans to be partly at the root of the "decline in status of Middle Americans and attack on the heartland of their values and style of life." Such observations were made at a moment when, according to growth guru and economic historian Walt Rostow, "the automobile-durable consumers' goods-suburbia sectoral complex had lost in the 1950's [*sic*] the capacity to drive forward American growth."[186]

By the end of the period covered by this chapter, sociological studies started to appear questioning the biological grounding of traffic aggression, holding a plea for an "empirical sociology of the street." Such studies identified the young, male, middle-class motorist with a big car as the most aggressive "perpetrators" of "vehicular homicide" being "male, young, unmarried, and from lower status occupations" with "a high concentration of blacks."[187] By now, blacks were not only blamed for being dangerous drivers but also accused by part of the elite of ruining American 'middle-class society.'

***

We cannot leave this topic without mentioning the deplorable under-researched state of the black "migration narrative—musical, visual and literary [that] portray the movement of a major character or the text itself from a provincial (not necessarily rural) Southern or Midwestern site (home of the ancestor) to a more cosmopolitan, metropolitan area," or back again, as in the case of Toni Morrison's novel *Song of Solomon* (1977) analyzed by Farah Jasmine Griffin in her dissertation *"Who Set You Flowin'?"* In this novel, written by the first black American woman receiving the Nobel Prize in Literature in 1993, the protagonist makes the mistake of inquiring, in the town of Shalimar, Virginia, about buying a new car: "They looked with hatred at the city Negro who could buy a car as if it were a bottle of whiskey because the one he had was broken." True to its tributariness to migration studies, however, the flowin' in her otherwise excellent dissertation receives hardly any attention ("After leaving the South, the next pivotal moment in the migration narrative is the initial confrontation with the *urban* landscape"). Griffin identified six ways of responding to black repression: "the acquisition of religion, efforts at reform, the creation of new art forms, addiction to alcohol, formal education, and aimless rebellion." What is missing from this short list is mobility itself, as the examples she gave of "the Great Migration novel" suggest a prolific but still mostly barren field of study in black migratory autopoetic fiction, including "commercial deportation as rite of passage in black women's novels." Gladys Knight & the Pips' 1973 song "Midnight Train to Georgia" comments on the need to return ("I got to go, I got to go") to the South: "And he even sold his car / Bought a one way ticket back."[188]

Nor can we ignore the under-researched mobility experiences generated by poor whites, for instance, the "hill people" in the Appalachian Mountains who until well into the 1950s migrated to the car and steel factories in Ohio and Michigan along the "Hillbilly Highway" (such as US Route 23), so mostly by car. In his overview of *The Redneck Stereotype in Southern Fiction*, Duane Carr, as an American literary version of a subaltern studies scholar, debunked American writer Eudora Welty's claim that she could use her writing to overcome the distance to the rednecks' lives ("as I used to see from far off on a train") and to create a directness: "In writing the story I approached and went inside." Carr placed Welty's "stereotypical country bumpkins" (in her 1986 story "The Hitch-Hikers") against Harry Crews's "grits" (Crews's term for the derogatory 'rednecks') described "from *within the class*." Crews, too, sometimes succumbs to the stereotypes à la American 1960s TV sitcom *Beverly Hillbillies*, very loosely (through Erskine Caldwell's ironic, prewar *Tobacco Road*) referring to Steinbeck's equally prewar Joad family in *The Grapes of Wrath*. Clearly Caldwellian, for instance, is Crews's depiction of his protagonists in *The Gospel Singer* (1968), who "ruin the new truck their son has given them by putting water in the crankcase and oil in the radiator, after which they abandon it by leaving it in the front yard."[189]

Harry Crews as an autopoetic author is important because he is a specialist in the "southern grotesque" and can be seen as a latter-day convert to anti-automobilism, someone who "hate[s] [the car's] stifling presence and abhor[s] the sheer stupidity of the automobile industry," although "as a young man [he] loved cars with a deep, impossible, and idiotic lunacy," as he confessed in retrospect, in 1993. As few writers before him, he describes the lives (with their "constant threat of violence") of the Southern, white "dispossessed" "through the voices of a people left behind by prosperity." The mobility of the "grit émigrés," agrarian figures that migrate to the city whenever their crops have failed, living temporarily in the city "with no cultural antecedents as guides to behavior," is characterized by "their attempts to adapt to new environments often devolv[ing] into grotesque violence." The "nearly universal desire of [*The Gospel Singer*'s] characters to escape the rural poverty of Enigma, Georgia," represents an even broader universalism as soon as one ventures beyond the frontiers of Western automobility: "There are Enigmas all over this country, all over the world, and men everywhere are struggling to get out of them." In Crews's *The Hawk Is Dying* (1973), the protagonist, who has set up "a thriving automobile upholstery business," experiences his life in the city as "pervaded by abstraction, ... a pointless series of unessential motion," and decides to quit and start hawking: "*I'm at the end of my road ... Work hard, they say, and you'll be happy. Get a car, get a house, get a business, get money. Get get get get get get get. Well, I got. And now it's led me here where everything is a dead-end.*" In Crews's fictional migratory universe, "home" is everything, an "anchor in the world."[190]

But Crews's most devastating car criticism (prefiguring the coming ecological critique: "the roseburning, eyewashing emissions from hundreds of smoky tailpipes") is to be found in *Car* (1972, hardly mentioned in Carr's edited volume), on the Mack family in Jacksonville, Florida, and their "Auto-Town" junkyard. This gigantic slaughterhouse of cars is adorned with a "car-crusher" and a "red ten-wheeled tow truck" (called Big Mama), which is able to run at 115 mph by an especially built-in race gearing to get to leftovers of accidents quickly, surrounded by "abrupt cliffs of automobiles." Son Mister "dreams of one day owning a Cadillac. 'You show me a man who can trade in for a new Cadillac in October every year and I'll show you a man in the mainstream of America,'" he declares. *Car* is important as a harsh reckoning of middle-class guilt. Son Herman distinguished himself from his father Easy, sister Junell, and twin brother, Mister, by setting up a "history parade" of wrecks, representing "everything that's happened in this goddamn country in the last fifty years," because all that "has happened in, on, around, with or near a car." This "dreamer of mad dreams" decides to eat an entire car, a "brand-new Ford Maverick," according to some commentators "based on a real event": "I'm going to eat a car because it's there."

With this novel, Crews joined Barthes in his sacrality critique of the car: the ingesting of the car-as-god is like a sacrament, through which one hopes to become God oneself. But commentators hardly mentioned this hope is futile, according to *Car*: the countrywide media event runs foul after Herman has experienced a revelation. He does not manage to be transcended; instead, he falls down into the artifact itself, as it were: he becomes one: "He filled up with cars tighter and tighter ... He was a car ... it scared me, scared me bad." It is father Easy who formulates the core of the novel's car critique, a mixture of environmental concern and fear for addiction. "Every time he smelled an exhaust, he wanted to throw up." Easy also nearly throws up when he sees his son overwhelmed by 'car': "It was like finding out that your son liked to hang around public restrooms smelling the toilets, or that he was secretly eating shit." As for addiction: "America was a V-8 country, gas-driven and water-cooled, and ... it belonged to men who belonged to cars ... Either you master ... it," Easy tells his son, "or it master[s] you." Whereas his twin brother takes over and seems to end in a lot of blood (after the eating comes the "passing"), his father commits suicide, in the car crusher: it is eat or be eaten in Crews's gloomy automotive universe.[191]

One should realize, while reading this doom-filled novel, Crews, who himself meanwhile moved into the middle-class universe, uses working-class Americans to act out his guilt-ridden environmentalism. By the end of the decade, Crews added a biographical confession to his guilt, in the essay "The Car" (1979), emphasizing not so much the environmental argument from the novel than the addiction argument. "We have found God in cars, or if not the true God, one so satisfying, so powerful and awe-inspiring that the distinction is too fine to matter." What follows, typically, is an overview of his first cars, a "1938 Ford coupe" (that "turned over four times" in an accident), a "1940 Buick" (in "her," he practiced speeding), and a "1953 Mercury" (in which he practiced "power slide[s] ... a very *bored* expression on your face ... I remember them like people—like long-ago lovers," with whom he also experienced the functional adventure, "with my hands deep in crankcases"). But when he noticed "the car and I merged," his love for them "soured considerably." "The car owned me much more than I would ever own the car," and he does what smokers do when they decide to stop: "I drove to Jacksonville and left the Mercury on a used-car lot. It was an easy thing to do. / Since that day, I've never confused myself with a car, ... I use it like a beast, ... unlovely and unlikable but necessary."[192] Thus is revived the prewar 'necessity' argument, this time not outer motivated (as in the 1920s, when it was necessary as a political argument to silence the state's approach of the car as a luxury product), but inner motivated, loaded with guilt. We need the car, *hélas*.

Distant Exuberance: Fragmented Modernism in European Automotive Adventures

Compared to American autopoetics, the car in European literature seems to play a less prominent role, although the fascination is at least as powerful, if not more so, because the exuberant example is an ocean away. Whereas Baudrillard, as an intermediary between Europe and the United States, in *Le système des objets* (1968) found "mobility without effort constitutes a kind of unreal happiness," his compatriot Françoise Sagan enjoyed the traffic jam as "very peaceful. It's the only time you're alone." Recuperating in a hospital from a heavy car accident in 1957, Sagan kept being hooked to the car: "When would I have the strength to steer an Aston? To navigate the porte Maillot a bit fast? ... This black hood that leapt forward, this confident sound, friendly, Jaguar a bit long, Aston a bit heavy, I'm dying away without you, after almost dying because of you," typically granting agency to her car.

Like Crews's younger self, Sagan was an addict, a woman in the most densely motorized country in Europe, referring to prewar colleague Paul Morand, who like him wrote an eulogy on speed: "It lessens ... all of life's sorrows: you can be madly in love—in vain—but you are much less so at a hundred miles an hour." Five days after her eighteenth birthday, she got her driver's license, at a moment when she already drove in her father's Buick. She bought a Ferrari 250 GT in 1966, after the success of her novel *La Chamade*, and her friends avoided accompanying her in her "iron animal," especially when she drove at 200 km/h through the nightly Parisian streets, enjoying the proximity of "impending death." Eager to become an independent woman, she mobilized the entire gamut of prewar automotive adventure for her personal emancipation. No doubt she felt a bond with "the adventurers of the freeway," those "kamikazes" in their cocoons ("free at last, returned to the motherly womb"), who, like her, enjoyed this "precise pleasure" beyond the car's safety, "a joyous gamble with pure luck and oneself." Sagan was the living proof of the existence, or the postwar revival of the multisensorial car adventure: "To orchestrate everything oneself: these noises so subtly harmonious to the ear and body." Like Morand, she played with the opposition between speed and slowness (the latter observed at the timeless state at 200 km/h), and she even reported to experience 'inversion,' in a double, visual and acoustic, sense: "The road starts to oscillate and to murmur."[193]

***

Anthropomorphizing the car is part of a reawakened female automotive adventure, shared by several women writers. Such writers "measure [modernity] against American standards," and the result is not always positive, as in feminist Christiane Rochefort's novel *Les petits enfants du siècle* (translated as *Josyane and the Welfare*), which, according to Kristine Ross, "focused on the automobile as metonymy for the masculine embrace of the values and privileges of technocracy." And if the car is "man's friend," then it must be "woman's enemy." Dealing with the devastating emptiness of the Parisian suburban *grand ensemble*, the novel contains a hilarious conversation between "chaps" (*bonhomme*) on cars, where the merits and demerits of every make and model are discussed:

> The Aston and its fragile steering, the Jaguar and its fucking shock absorbers and the Alfa with its endless need for tuning (*réglages*), the [Mercedes] 220 SL now that is a true car but one needs to go to Germany every time one loses a nut, and as for the Americans we won't talk about them they are drags (*veaux*) and well, at last the best still is the small French Car, uniting the best quality in the smallest space, and thrifty, five litres to a hundred [kilometers] the [Renault] 4 CV is so practical with its engine in the back because you can put your luggage in the front.[194]

Not much adventure for young Josyane during her vacations, in a hotel more crammed than home, without a TV set.

***

Not so for Simone de Beauvoir either, who castigates the middle class for "inventing an epic style of expression in which routine takes on the cast of adventure, fidelity that of a sublime passion, ennui becomes wisdom, and family hatred is the deepest form of love." But she herself redirects her "love" from her American lover Nelson Alger to her new car, a Simca Aronde. De Beauvoir published *L'Amérique au jour le jour* (translated as *America Day by Day*) in 1947, in which she admired its highways "as spick-and-span as the tiled floor of a Dutch kitchen." De Beauvoir's four-month travelogue is a classic car adventure, indeed, although produced as a passenger: she experiences her travel across America (mostly in trains and buses, sometimes in a plane) as transformation ("I've already escaped myself. I am nowhere: I am *elsewhere*") and experiences "adventure on unknown routes" when passengering outside San Francisco in a car borrowed from a friend: "On the road in our car, these wild regions will offer us the risks and solitude of wandering in the mountains on foot." But the motor "gives out," and they are forced to visit a garage. Apart from her using the subways and walking ("I walk to Harlem, ... a kind of adventure"), the cars she uses to travel in and around cities are driven by her friends and acquaintances, whose parties convince her "superabundance ... is a curse."

Likewise, postwar American traffic adds new experiences to the classic adventurous tropes: urban traffic becomes a subliminal movement of a swarm: "The car drives so fluidly, the road beneath the wheels is so smooth ... Then, all at once, I see. I see broad, brightly lit streets were hundreds and hundreds of cars are driving, stopping, and starting again with such discipline you would think they were guided from above by some magnetic providence ... Paris has lost its hegemony," a judgment enhanced by the "tone of condescension that I've observed almost everywhere when France is mentioned," also among her American friends, who seem to be plagued by an "inferiority complex." Their "joking tone" irritates her ("you elude criticism by being ironic yourself"), and they lack transcendence: "The individual is too busy with telephones, refrigerators, and elevators, he is too invested in tools, to look above and beyond." At the same time, she is flabbergasted by what she sees: "The traffic [in Los Angeles] is terrifying; the broad roadways are divided into six lanes, three in each direction," and so on. In New York, she is "overwhelmed by [the] complexity" of the "multi-leveled highways, [their] spiraling intersections, [their] underground routes that avoid all crossroads." Reality and imagination become blurred: New York is "recognize[d]" from films she has seen. In Washington, she is "completely astonished to encounter a reality what looked to me like a studio set in the movies." Also in the countryside, the effect of automotive travel is alienating: "You could travel day after day in the same bus, across the same plain, and you'd arrive each evening in the same town, which would have a different name every time." The American landscape she finds "so ugly it won't distract me." America for her "is a country of mechanical wonders where, on an adult scale, the childish imaginings of travel literature are realized." And yet, the 'ironic car' does not work in this country:

> So often in Italy, in Greece, in Spain, I've felt such regret that my condition as a traveler separated me from the inhabitants, who hardly travel at all. In contrast, the average American devotes a great part of his leisure time to driving along the highways. The gas stations, roads, hotels, and solitary inns exist only for the tourist and because of the tourist, and these things are profoundly part of America. These landscapes in the Far West we're traveling through exist essentially for the sake of tourists. Almost no one lives here, and their only human significance is that they welcome people who pass through without stopping. By traveling in America, I'm not distanced from it.

Nonetheless, she is puzzled by the fact that "in this country, which seems so doggedly turned toward the concrete, the word 'abstraction' has come so often to my lips."[195]

***

Like in prewar days, Europeans visiting the United States drove through it as if visiting the future. Whereas de Beauvoir may not have met official approval with her critique of the "Red Scare," the experienced (Spain, 1955; Soviet Union, 1957) German travel writer Wolfgang Koeppen's trip to the United States in 1958 was partly sponsored by the US Department of State. Although he mostly traveled by train and walked the streets of big cities, he, too, observes the emptiness of the continent: "There was always as car to be seen on the horizon, struggling bravely and alone through the endlessness." But like de Beauvoir's, Koeppen's travelogue is "a book of cities." Conversely, Americans visiting Europe tended to describe their journeys as a trip into the past (as we already saw in Marshall Plan–induced tourism). Sybille Bedford is no exception. Her collection of travel essays *Pleasure and Landscapes* covers thirty years (1948–1978) of roaming through Europe, sometimes by train, but also by car, for instance, to Portugal at the end of the 1950s, in a further not identified car, or Yugoslavia in the 1960s, in a "rented Fiat." In 1948, she traveled to Italy to deliver Martha Gellhorn's Morris to the isle of Capri at a moment when "city streets were still crowded mainly with Vespas and pedestrians."[196]

Likewise, Stanley T. Williams's *Two in a Topolino* (1956) is a traditional, if not old-fashioned, travelogue of an 'I' and their female companion "M. L.," following the Marshall Plan's plea for more American tourists to Europe, a seven-thousand-kilometer trip from Rome first to Sicily and then to Venice, with all the classic ingredients: the tongue-in-cheek, ironic rendering of cultural differences, the "carnival of red tape" as preparation of the trips, the condescending way to address the natives ("the photographer, a sinister looking ruffian"), the save guidance of their "adventure" by the Touring Club Italiano, the small accident, and the projection of agency (including its anthropomorphisms) onto the car ("Topolino became restless"; he "was asleep in the hold" of the ferry from Palermo back to Naples; "We patted him affectionately. He had not failed us"). In their prewar Fiat Topolino, a "midget station wagon" bought secondhand, the two "college professors" must "unlearn [their] evil American habits" and "enjoy … the difference. We renewed our youth. We took the traffic as an adventure, and we mastered our little servant, so that he became marvelously docile."

In the 'Old World,' the adventure machine can still be enjoyed, but what is new compared to prewar 'European' travelogues (including those written by Americans such as Edith Wharton, with whom Williams can be compared in many respects, for instance, in his constant referring to famous literary predecessors like Italy travelers Henry James and Nathaniel Hawthorne), is the "madness of [Rome's] present traffic system" with zigzagging motorcycles and "breathless pedestrians" in one big "orgy of motion, a kinetic revulsion ... Motoring in Italy is so casual, so unrestrained, so exciting, that it is like a perpetual, gigantic sporting event in which the principle of 'devil take the hindmost' makes the participants uninhibited and gay. The point is that, after all, it is *fun* to drive a car in Italy." What is not new, but also reminiscent of Wharton, is the constant presence/absence of the car: it is a quotidian travel companion, who often disappears under unspecified verbs ("we now drove," "we descended," "we did a *giro* of country roads"). Nor is it new that the journey in the "Kidillac" is a trip into the past: "I rubbed my eye. Was I living in the Middle Ages?" But the car is masculine, and the narrator is reluctant to be engaged ("I regard a motor trip of more than twenty miles as torment") and is seemingly persuaded by M. L., who then hardly figures in the tale, making it into the type of pseudo-individual endeavor that has a long tradition.[197]

What a contrast with American James Salter's novel *A Sport and a Pastime*, written mostly between 1964 and 1966 based on his experiences as a US soldier in France in 1961, when "he met a young French girl ... and traveled the countryside with her." Published in 1967, the narrative is a true European road novel, a "hymn to 'green, bourgeois France,'" mixing "experiences of travel and sex, the exotic and the erotic," but told by an unreliable (and voyeuristic) narrator who may have made up most of the 'erotics.' Thus, we cannot know whether his intentions to "leav[e] Paris by train" and "walk these village roads" are 'true,' 'true fiction,' or simply 'fiction.' Sarah Hall, in her introduction to a reedition of Salter's "masterpiece" (according to Salter's biographer William Dowie) in 2007, nonetheless defended the 'truth' of the novel, written by a "writer's writer" (probably so because of his lyrical techniques). Salter's novel is one among many, from Nicolas Bouvier's *L'Usage du monde* (1963; translated as *The Way of the World*) about a "mid-1950s trip of two young Swiss men in a beat-up Fiat making their way across Turkey and Iran into Afghanistan," through Bernward Vesper's "German novel-essay" *Die Reise* (The trip; posthumously published in 1977), explicitly inspired by Kerouac's fiction, to René Barjavel's *Les chemins de Katmandou* (The road to Katmandu, 1969), James Michener's *The Drifters* (1971), or the Dutch "trans-European" Jan Cremer with his scabrous "autobiographical novel" *Ik, Jan Cremer* (1964).[198]

Salter wrote a true, classic road novel, but one in which (and that was new) the description of the car (and, in a way, the car itself: a Delage, "a splendid old car which yields nothing to popular taste") is as lyrical as the description of the many sex scenes between protagonist Dean (*nomen est omen*!) and the very young *française* Anne-Marie. "Is this your car?" she asks. "Yes, he insists I admire it, a convertible standing low and journey-dark in the dusk." They take a ride, and have the flight experience: "All the needles leap. / 'It's a dream to drive,' he says. 'It goes like the wind.' / 'I can imagine.' / 'No, really, it does.' / 'How fast?'" After the ride, Dean lifts the hood: "'Look at that,' he announces. / It's a distillery of ducts and hoses." This car is about status: "Through the doorway I can see people looking at the Delage. / 'Your car's creating a sensation.' / 'In Paris,' he says, 'they figured I was at least a duke.'" The novel is a concatenation of city walks, dinners, and sex scenes connected by intercity car trips ("we drive along empty streets"). The adventure is not in the car trips (despite the 'adventurous' jargon such as 'flight' and 'race' and the occasional inversion), but in the repeated conquest of the woman: "a long flight down the road to Paris, headlights cast ahead, the engine thrumming. Dean drives in cool excitement, in the electric hush of tires. He has a hard-on half the time … The real France, he is thinking. The real France." Europe excites the man.

The car, however, is used casually, its handling described in detail but without any sensationalist expression. The car is the fourth actor, as inconspicuous as the narrator: "They have come to the car. He opens the door for her and then walks around to the driver's side. He gets in himself, becomes busy with the keys … She undoes his clothing and brings forth his prick, erect, pale as a heron in the dusk, both of them looking ahead at the road like a couple." Even the experience of high speed is told as a matter of fact, for instance, when Anne-Marie tells him her mother needs a car, a Renault, and while she is telling this, the car becomes a cyborgian extension of Dean: "They come to a long, straight section of road, and he begins to accelerate. He seems absorbed in it. They go faster and faster. The gauge finally touches a hundred and sixty. Anne-Marie says nothing. She sits looking out the side." Salter's novel is early proof that the car, even a conspicuous Delage, becomes an inconspicuous driver of the narrative, including the car accident that kills him, back in the United States. And yet, the adventure between the two lovers was exceptional, the narrator tells us, closing his tale with the ironic observation that Anne-Marie is now immersed "deep in the life we all agree is so greatly to be desired."[199] The narrator may be ironic (he means petit-bourgeois life, of course), but the Delage is not.

***

German postwar literature offers a similarly fragmented picture of more adventure than in the American novels, but no less variegated, from enthusiastic embrace to near indifference. There is the usual violence: in Alfred Andersch's radio play *Fahrerflucht* (Hit and run), a woman cyclist is killed by a manager in a Borgward Coupe who flees from the scene. And the abstraction of the car trip à la Kerouac: in Martin Walser's "Kristlein trilogy," which includes his novel *Halbzeit* (Halftime, 1960): "I was pulled away by an engine that I didn't hear. In soundlessness I sat, in smell-lessness (*im Geruchlosen*), without resistance, in a vacuum, inside and outside not a whisper or sound, near happy, I thought: Thank God, you died with [the car]. Full synchronisation, steering gear with a circulating ball system, possibly even with a DB [Daimler-Benz] semi-independent rear axle (*Eingelenkpendelachse*) with hypoid gears and turbo-cooled brake shoes I drove, I drove for myself a heavy-blue dream cloud ... The king is dead, he li ... no, I can't do it. I am going on foot." The novel contains the same anthropomorphizing of cars, and the same tautological motivation of the car's necessity as in the United States: "and I need the car, because I need a car." Like in the United States, postwar German autopoetics also celebrates the car's status. In Friedrich Dürrenmatt's play *Der Besuch der alten Dame* (The visit of the old lady, 1956) we find the hierarchy of car ownership mapped: a Porsche for the "dynamic rich," a Mercedes for the "established physician," a sports-car-like Opel Olympia for the "ambitious youngster," a limousine for the "middle-class entrepreneur," an American Buick for the "extravagant *parvenue*," and a microcar Messerschmidt for the student.[200] The car is treated as a pure (but fragmented) status symbol, and the adventure is nowhere to be found.

Just like in Salter's *A Sport and a Pastime*, this is also the case in "angry young man" (the British counterpart of the beats) John Braine's *Room at the Top* (1957), in which protagonist Alice dies in a car crash while drunk driving (Alice played by Simone Signoret in the controversial film version of the book because of her "mature and illicit sexuality"). As in no other novel of the postwar decades, social and automotive mobility are closely intertwined in the ambitious aspirations of twenty-five-year-old accountant Joe Lampton, hypersensitive to class differences and eager to use the ownership of car makes and models as a ranking of wealth. Migrating, during the immediate postwar austerity years, from a mostly working-class town to a town called Warley with an outspoken middle-class flavor (and looking back from a point in time ten years later), here is how he meets the higher class for the first time: "Parked by a sollicitor's office opposite the café was a green Aston-Martin tourer, low-slung, with cycle-type mudguards. It had the tough, functional smartness of the good British sports car; it's a quality which is difficult to convey without using the terms of the advertising copywriter—made by craftsmen, thoroughbred, and so on—I can only say that it was a beautiful piece of engineering and leave it at that," and he remembers how in his town of origin his colleague just bought a "second-hand Austin Seven," the quintessential British equivalent to the Volkswagen Beetle and the Model T.

In his new surroundings, he observes how an acquaintance bought "a new Austin Eight; it was very difficult to get new cars—particularly small ones—at that time, and it occurred to me that whatever he did in textiles must be outstandingly profitable." A driver in a "grey Jaguar coupé ... sat bolt upright and disdainfully, as if giving the car its orders rather than driving it." And when his "working-class mentality" is exposed and he threatens to lose rich Susan: "I might as well face facts: good-bye Susan, good-bye a big car, good-bye a big house, good-bye power, good-bye the silly handsome dreams." Apart from class, car ownership is also gendered: Alice's car "a green Fiat 500, was parked outside. She unlocked the right-hand door then hesitated. 'Can you drive?'" Paranoid about his low status, he is immediately offended: "'Oddly enough, yes,' I said. / 'Don't be so bloody thin-skinned.' / 'I wasn't—' / 'You damn well were. I just thought you might like to drive. Most men hate being a woman's passenger. I'm an awful driver anyway.' / I didn't say anything but sat in the driver's seat and opened the other door for her," and he remembers how he learned to drive during the war, when he, as a soldier, shared the ownership of a seventeen-year-old "Austin Chummy" with three of his mates, a rare example of working-class shared car ownership.[201]

Many elements we identified previously as being part of the adventurous complex appear in the novel, such as the cyborg/body-language aspect: "'You were pretty good tonight [at amateur theater rehearsal],' Alice said in the Fiat afterward. / ... I turned the ignition key ... The engine started immediately, though I always had trouble with it normally ... the car rolling smoothly down the narrow street ... inside the car, the masculinity of steel and oil and warm leather and, best of all, Alice, her smell of lavender . . ." Car metaphors indicate he is living in a 'car society': ("I'm like a brand-new Cadillac in a poor industrial area, insulated by steel and glass and air-conditioning from the people outside"). There is even a premonition of Ballard's *Crash* when Joe describes his lovemaking with Alice as "melting into each other like amoebae but violently, like cars crashing head-on." The adventure machine pops up during a drunken drive in which "twice the car shimmied into a long skid the worst part of which was that though I knew I ought to care whether or not I came out of it alive, I didn't give a damn. I was, in a crazy way, enjoying it." The scene is a prefiguration of Alice's self-inflicted accident ("'She must have been going at the hell of a pace,' Teddy said. 'They say the car's bent like that'—he cupped his hand—'and there's blood all over the road.'") Handling the car appears to give pleasure: "I drove fast along the narrow switchback of Sparrow Hill Road, taking the corners as if on rails. I couldn't go wrong; the car felt as if it had two litres under its bonnet instead of just over a half." Or when Joe casually reveals to the reader he knows about cars: "I started the car with a jerk, but I soon got the hang of it. The steering was low-geared and more than a trifle soggy but the engine had plenty of power and I found that I was enjoying myself." But the status character overwhelms all, for instance, when a woman of modest means rejects "a common man with a motor-car" in favor of "something better than that." And then there is the scene with the 'absent vehicle': "When we reached Wool, Alica was asleep on my shoulder ... we'd had the window open all the way," and we discover they are traveling in a train.

Another woman (probably from Denmark) driving through France to Italy as "the Motherland of Sensation" is Lise in Muriel Spark's *The Driver's Seat* (1970), "the most successful *nouveau roman* in English" (made in 1974 into a film featuring Elizabeth Taylor and Andy Warhol) in which a woman in her "quest for autonomy" takes control of the car as well as the direction of her life, organizing her own death, a theme hardly fit to be the driver of an 'automotive adventure.' Spark's "female Gothic" novel follows not so much a Quest of the Self but rather a quest for the protagonist's oblivion, no random touring but a deliberate trail, "each move ... calculated."[202]

Songs and Movies: Rejuvenating the Adventure Machine in Popular Culture

Although the distinction between low- and highbrow culture in the gradually becoming postmodern West got more and more blurred, we will try, in this section, to get access to the automotive culture of motorists within but especially beyond the middle class through the analysis of mass media of film, pop songs, and lowbrow romance, although we should not forget that in capitalism, mass media are not necessarily consumed primarily by 'the masses': "It was those of high income, as ever, who consumed the bulk of popular culture products and services—whether sports event admissions, frozen foods, cars, or hi-fi components." In the United States, "those below the top 40 percent remained stationary in their proportion of national income during the 1950s, and all but the wealthiest lost in relative [purchasing] power," but one may question whether this constrained those below the top 40 percent from accessing the songs and movies we will be discussing here, and absorb the promises of new lifestyles conveyed by them.

It is indeed remarkable that the absence or at least the rapid erosion of adventurousness in the sense as we have defined it in its tripartite temporal, spatial, and functional aspects contrasts with the celebration of the 'adventure machine' in other parts of the popular culture spectrum. Given the hesitancy in hegemonic, middle-class, autopoetic utterances toward the automotive adventure, we may assume, indeed, the rejuvenation of this adventure was carried, or at least inspired, by those below the top 40 percent.

Roland Marchand, who investigated the 'classlessness' of the new lifestyles, gave Mickey Spillane's 1947 'invention' of detective Mike Hammer and his "self-righteous vigilantism" with his "escapes of vengeance" (including his "contempt for women, expressed in frequent violence and sadism") as an example of a new "popular culture hero," of whom we will soon meet several more. We could add other middle- and lowbrow novels such as Arthur Hailey's *Wheels* (1971) ("The World's #1 Storyteller," on the front cover), whose high-level car manufacturer executive "wheeled his cream sport coupé down the ramp," making "a fast 'S' turn, tyres squealing, ... then eased his lank figure out of the driver's seat. Leaving the keys inside."[203] But we will focus, in this section, on music and film.

Autopoetic Music: Celebrating Subversive and Conformist Mobility

Earlier in this chapter, we analyzed pop and rock in Europe and the United States in their *affinity* with automobilism's flows. Here we revisit this source, but now for a *content analysis* of its lyrics, to find out whether popular culture celebrated the automotive adventure when hegemonic, middle-class culture started to erode it, seemingly abandon it, and hide it in irony. In her excellent study of Motown music culture, Suzanne E. Smith not only convincingly showed how music was life for the black community in Detroit (instead of "a diversion from it"), she also unraveled how seemingly 'innocent' music like Martha and the Vandellas' "Dancing in the Street" (1964) became a martial song during the riots in Harlem (New York, 1964), Watts (Los Angeles, 1965, called "the *potlatch* of destruction" by *Internationale situationiste*), and especially Detroit (1967), as well as during the over five hundred other "major violent uprisings by African Americans." In the case of Detroit, this clearly "caused" "white institutional racism in the form of urban renewal, expressways, and white suburban resistance." Two hundred thousand Americans participated in these riots, while two million took part in political demonstrations mostly against the Vietnam War. As we have seen, the civil rights movement also was a struggle against hegemonic mobility: from the Montgomery bus boycott of 1954–1955 and the Freedom Rides of 1961 to the March on Washington in 1963, the movement showed that racial inequality literally (with the Jim Crow segregation legislation since the end of the nineteenth century) was at the heart of the conflict.

No wonder, then, was, like "Dancing in the Street," the "snotty escapism" of the Animals' "We Gotta Get Out of This Place," referring to a poor district, reinterpreted as a critique of America's Vietnam policy. Martha Reeves herself said "Dancing in the Street" was conceived simply as a "party song," but she was not heard. Nor was her band's name any secret reference to vandalism. "Masking" (hiding messages in seemingly innocent lyrics) was a well-known tradition going back to the slave trade period; this practice now produced songs that had different meanings for white and black audience, just like the car could function as an instrument of oppression and an emancipation tool, and just like irony divides a highbrow novel's readership into two camps of 'wolves' and 'sheep' (see the introduction). In the "crossover" from a black to a black-and-white audience, "a crossover song could change meanings." A related phenomenon was "signifyin'," coined by black literary scholar Henry Louis Gates Jr., linking "the double meanings to be found in homonyms whose one word-sound yields disparate meanings to black and white speakers." But during the riots, Marvin Gaye, a sympathizer of the black independence movement, did not need any masking or signifying to deplore the senselessness of the Vietnam War and to address themes like "ecology, racism, and urban violence" in his songs, for instance, on his album *What's Going On?* The radical Weathermen (who derived their name from a Bob Dylan song) were convinced "Dancing in the Street" "was coding for rioting."[204]

***

Apparently, not much masking was needed in the songs of the white youth culture. A rather random search resulted in a plethora of songs that express the special role of the car in daily life of the youth, especially regarding (male) eroticism and love, and speed, continuing a tradition started long before the war. The harvest is exceedingly rich. To start with, the lack of a car can be as painful as a broken heart, as the Beatles explained in "Drive My Car" (1965): "I got no car and it's breaking my heart / But I've found a driver and that's a start." The Rolling Stones didn't agree: in the same year, Mick Jagger announced he could not get any satisfaction from listening to the useless information coming from the car radio. The Who, on the other hand, indulged in "goin' mobile" ("Keep me movin'/ Over 50 / Keep me groovin' / Just a hippie gypsy"), the rhythm of the song reliving high-speed cruising. The pleasure of constantly being on the move, hobo-style, is absolute: "I don't care about pollution / I'm an air-conditioned gypsy / That's my solution." Steppenwolf's both popular and countercultural "Born to be Wild" (1968) prefigures the "heavy metal" of biker culture in its celebration of the pure adventure: "Get your motor runnin' / Head out on the highway / Lookin' for adventure," including the relationship between this adventure and violence, and including the flight metaphor ("Racin' with the wind"). A similar adventure machine is celebrated in the Beach Boys' 1964 "Little Honda" ("faster, faster"), its lyrics reading like a motorcycle advertisement.[205]

Many of these songs reproduced clichés (James Brown's "It's a Man's Man's Man's World" [1966]: "You see, man made the cars / To take us over the road / ... But it would be nothing, nothing / Without a woman or a girl"), another reason to believe it was the rhythm and other musicological traits that attracted Western youth to these songs rather than their content. Initially, when the boys start singing, it is love and/in cars that springs to their minds, but embedded in the indifference and routinized abstraction of middle class car culture, as we have come to know it in the previous section. Chuck Berry's "No Particular Place To Go" (1964) celebrated the aimless driving around (and the only aim to conquer fails, because he "couldn't unfasten her safety belt"). Dionne Warwick's "The Way to San Jose" promised that in the freeways of LA, if you "put a hundred down and buy a car / In a week, maybe two, they'll make you a star." Canned Heat, too, went "On the Road Again" in 1968, the cadence of the music mimicking the hammering of the car tires on the edges of the concrete slabs of the freeway. Joni Mitchell's "Blue" (1971) describes her being "on a lonely road ... / Traveling, traveling, traveling / Looking for something what can it be." Even at home, one is constantly reminded to live in 'car society,' according to Jim Morrison of the Doors: "The Cars Hiss By My Window" (1971). Also classic trucker songs were reinvented: the Flying Burrito Brothers, an offspring of the Byrds and fascinated by cars, planes, and boats ("Flying Again," "Airborne"), produced "Six Days on the Road," complete with an FBI check ahead, while the trucker is taking "little white pills." On the other side of the gender divide, it was a girl's adventurism that had to enable a hit, such as "Stick Shift" (1961) of the Duals, which came with a clip of a burning car chasing a boy running on the highway.[206]

***

When the song texts got more sophisticated, many old tropes from prewar 'Atlantic automobilism' were rediscovered, such as the use of the car and its components as metaphor, often for erotic purposes. Led Zeppelin's "Trampled Underfoot" (1975) says it thus: "Ooh, trouble-free transmission, helps your oils flow / Mama, let me pump your gas, mama, let me do it all." Creedence Clearwater Revival's 1971 hit "Sweet Hitchhiker" (band leader John Fogerty seemed to have written many songs in his car) alludes: "Won't you ride on my fast machine?" Meanwhile, Rod Stewart's "Let Me Be Your Car" (1974) describes his protagonist (the 'I') as "your automobile," and he explains: "I've got an engine / underneath my hood." Or, more ominously even, examine Bruce Springsteen's "Thunder Road," where the car takes on transcendental properties, with "redemption" on offer under its "dirty hood." Springsteen adds, "These two lanes will take us anywhere." For some, the systemic aspects of mobility formed the inspiration: the British psychedelic rock band Traffic (founded in 1967), its name conceived when they were standing at a crossroads in Dorchester, were a "jam band" (improvisational) and brought out the album *The Last Great Traffic Jam* when they briefly reunited in 1994. By the end of the period covered by this chapter, a Dutch group (successfully) tried to become popular by mobilizing the car trip experience in a way that fully resonated with the multimedia approach of new mobility studies: Golden Earring's "Radar Love" (1973) is sought through the car trip—"There's a voice in my head / That drives my heel / It's my baby callin'"—and they don't need "a phone" or "a letter" because "we've got a thing that's called radar love."[207]

As we claimed earlier, it is in this realm of popular culture that the exclusive focus on the content misses the point, more so perhaps than in highbrow culture. Like car culture, music was about rhythm, bodily experiences and emotions, feelings and illusions of freedom, escape, invitations to aggression. In this perspective, the analysis of car culture should be embedded in the study of the popular and the lowbrow, cultural studies, in film and media studies. This is not to say, of course, content is not important in analyzing rock 'n' roll, certainly not after the 'literary turn' of the mid-1960s (Bob Dylan, Paul Simon). To give only two examples: in the heyday of the black independence movement, it became increasingly difficult to see the song "We Shall Overcome" as the song of the movement: "Many fell silent at the stanza 'black and white together.'" Some even argued they should better sing "We Shall Overrun." But even then, the struggle was formulated in the terminology of mobility and its aggressive sides ("overrun"). Likewise, country-folk singer Michael Murphy wrote a song in 1972 called "Geronimo's Cadillac," referring to the famous 1904 photograph by Walter Ferguson of the Apache leader behind the steering wheel, a top hat on his head: "Ripped off his land, won't give it back; and they sent Geronimo a Cadillac."[208]

New Wave and the American Road Movie: Guilty Pleasures and Automotive 'Aimlessness'

European New Wave cinema appeared to be a bit more critical toward the car adventure, although it took some time to let the adventure machine erode into an ambiguous vehicle of fun and consumption critique simultaneously. In Italy, Michelangelo Antonioni's *L'avventura* (1960), starring Monica Vitti, experiences the adventure as sexual and automotive at the same time. Likewise, Federico Fellini's *La Dolce Vita* (The pleasant life, 1960) depicts Rome's postwar revival as an automotive celebration, showing mostly American (Cadillac Series 62, Chevrolet Corvette, Ford Thunderbird) and British (Triumph) cars, most of them convertibles, and all of recent design, whereas Dino Risi's *Il Sorpasso* (Overtaking, 1962; said to be the inspiration for Dennis Hopper's *Easy Rider*, 1969) appropriates the American road movie, experienced in a Lancia Aurelia. Somewhat later, Luigi Commencini would produce an even harsher Italian counterpart to Godard's *Weekend* called *Ingorgio* (Jam, 1978) in which a giant traffic jam leads to violence and rape. Similar developments can be observed in other European mass-motorizing countries, although German autopoetics added an atmosphere of class struggle combined with self-pity of the petty bourgeois, who feels his "right to motorize" was denied. This is, for instance, apparent in the "vacation movies" (*Urlaubsfilme*) *Italienreise—Liebe inbegriffen* (*Voyage to Italy, Complete with Love*, 1958) and *Schick deine Frau nicht nach Italien* (*Do Not Send Your Wife to Italy*, 1960), where, in the former, a physician and her married girlfriends travel to Italy in her car, while in the latter, the *Angestellte* protagonist travels by bus.[209]

More critical toward the car as icon of the ("Americanized") consumption society is Jean-Luc Godard, whose movie *Weekend* (1967) has long since gained an iconic status in its celebration of the car accident (prefiguring J. G. Ballard, who will soon add the sexual element to this, as we will see in the last section of this chapter) and the absurdity and violence of the traffic jam. Godard seems to have been inspired by Julio Cortázar's short story "La autopista del sur" (published in Cortázar's volume *Todos los fuegos el fuego* in 1966 and translated as "The Southern Highway") in which he, living in France, describes a traffic jam of at least five days (and possibly much more) on one of the French autoroutes, in which persons are called by their car's name, a community is formed in which fights break out, a suicide takes place and an old lady dies, nearby peasants become hostile, and a car is transformed in an ambulance. When breaking down, anonymous 'traffic' becomes a collective, if not a community, moving "as if an invisible gendarme at the end of the motorway were coordinating the advance." In the "frozen river of cars," motorists start to share each other's cars, self-organize into foraging groups, make coats and hats out of torn-off upholstery, and a coup against the group leaders is attempted.

In Godard's movie, a friend of protagonists Roland and Corinne asks: "Wouldn't it be great when Roland drives your father home if both of them died in an accident? ... Did he get his brakes fixed?" And Corinne answers: "No. I managed to make him forget." Roland and Corinne then begin their journey in their Facel convertible running into "a cinematically stunning traffic-jam scene that brings together many of [Godard's] most original and subversive ideas," showing "how the metaphorical meaning of cars has shifted in Godard's value system." In his earlier movies, the car "represented a Beat-style dream of liberation via speed, flexibility, elusiveness," but in *Weekend*, a "cynical" opinion prevailed, "paralyzing cars altogether by cramming them into a self-suffocating gridlock so devoid of action and energy that the movie itself almost stopped moving." Like in Crews's "The Car," middle-class guilt has overruled previous love of adventure. But there is enough energy left for "furious battles between motorists, complete with biting, hitting, hairpulling, and outrageous insults."[210] As soon as the flow stops, the violence hiding underneath comes in the open.

***

One of the peculiarities of the European movie seems to be the hesitance toward the exuberance of American car culture. We find a "compulsive hotrodder" in Risi's *Il Sorpasso* (1962), a race car driver (Jean-Louis Trintignant) in Claude Lelouch's *Un homme et une femme* (1966), and "two adolescents, seduced by automotive speed," in Louis Malle's *Ascenseur pour l'échafaud* (1957), but Robert Dhéry's *La belle américaine* (1961) and Jacques Rozier's *Adieu Philippine* (1962) both express an "ambivalence surrounding private ownership on the part of the first car owners in small, 'traditional' communities." Of course, there are also movies in which the car is simply celebrated as such, for instance, in Malle's *Zazie dans le métro* (1960) and Bertrand Blier's *Les Valseuses* (1974), in which the protagonists drive around in one of the 1.3 million iconic Citroën DS 19. But in most movies, the car seems to arrive from far away, as an alien, such as in the modernization parables of Jacques Tati in his *Mon Oncle* (1958) and *Playtime* (1967). While not many American cars were sold in France, a special agreement with the French government allowed Hollywood "a virtually total domination of the European movie market after the war … In production, cars had paved the way for film; now, film would help create the conditions for the motorization of Europe: the two technologies reinforced each other." In Marcel Carné's *Les tricheurs* (1958), the female protagonist says: "I wouldn't mind dying like Dean: young, and at great speed."[211]

Not only *within* films but also outside filmic imagination, there is a remarkably high number of casualties among the directors and cast of European and American movies: Godard suffered a grave moped accident (his mother was killed in an accident on a Vespa scooter), Tati was seriously injured behind the steering wheel of his Peugeot Frégate, and Sagan ended in a hospital writing her diary *Toxique*. In the United States, the most iconic victim was James Dean, who in his Porsche collided with "a milder-mannered Ford sedan, a vehicle symbolizing the timid velocity of the suburbs." Dean was one of the many real-life victims whose 'fate' was reenacted over and over again in filmic fiction, for instance, in Joseph Losey's *Accident* (1967). But despite the "watershed" of the late 1950s and early 1960s emanating in the "New Wave" cinema in Europe (fascinated by and at the same time increasingly critical of the United States) and the "unconventional adventures of perception" the young directors taught their audiences, movie theater visiting became "totally marginalized" as a cultural practice because of the emergence of television.[212]

***

How did the American movie industry respond to the double, and ambiguous, attack both from its own national television's shallowness and from European New Wave movie culture's consumption critique? Giant American production and distribution companies conquered the European market, but not without first having absorbed European stylistic traits ("jump cuts, split screens, slow-motion tableaus, freeze frames, and shots from a zoom lens—all the techniques of the European avant-garde") resulting in an "American New Wave," headed by young directors like Sam Peckinpah, Robert Altman, Martin Scorsese, Francis Ford Coppola, Steven Spielberg, and Woody Allen. We see here the same 'absorption' strategy of hegemonic culture toward alternatives we discussed earlier, referring to Marcuse's 'repressive tolerance.' Those who kept watching movies were individuals (as opposed to the family character of prewar moviegoing), "managerial and professional middle class and the clerks" and "secondary-school pupils and students," a development comparable to what happened in automotive culture: there, too, the family as automotive subject started to disintegrate, and individuals (Donofrio's Beverly, for instance) and 'dysfunctional' families (Updike's *Rabbit Redux*; Kerouac's *On the Road*) took over the wheel, if it was not simply stolen (Weesner's *The Car Thief*).²¹³

As we have seen, according to several literature students, the car in many postwar road novels was so ubiquitous that it was hardly mentioned. Again, such judgments missed the point, as they were apparently not including the prewar car culture, where this ubiquitousness made the car already invisible as far back as the travelogues of Edith Wharton, although, as I argued in my previous study, this may also have been the result of following a convention of avoiding the 'mundane.' Indeed, *invisibility of the vehicle* is an age-old trope, emerging in pre-car horse carriage days. Wolfgang Munzinger's qualification of the car as a 'stealthy protagonist' (*heimlicher Romanfigur*) is more to the point, also in its application to many road movies of the early postwar period, although the threat of the truck in Spielberg's debut *Duel* (1971) can hardly be called 'stealthy.' On the contrary, it seems the American road movie did the opposite of what happened in American novels: the car was very much present, loud, and clear. Especially in 'action movies,' the car competed with the protagonist for the audience's attention, reminiscent of the early slapstick era. In such movies, the car itself became an actor, such as in Nicholas Ray's *Rebel without a Cause* (1955) in which Jim Stark (James Dean) races "his customized 1949 Mercury coupe personif[lying] the struggle of disaffected middle-class youth."

Equally narcissistic are the motorcycles in Dennis Hopper and Peter Fonda's *Easy Rider* (1969), predecessor of the American road movie and considered by film students as "a loose film version of [*On the Road*]," where even the experience of 'flight' as the "sensual intensity of the gliding car movement" (which we identified as characteristic for prewar car driving experiences) was revived. In fact, the name was derived from the English title (*The Easy Life*) of the Italian movie *Il Sorpasso* (1962), but the term in American slang "refers to a man who lives off the earnings of his prostitute girlfriend." It was, as actor Peter Fonda explained in an interview, a movie in which "liberty's become a whore, and we're all taking an easy ride." Wyatt, played by Fonda, concludes at the end of the movie: "No man, we blew it," the road does not provide freedom. In other words, the illusion of the 'freedom of mobility' collapsed on its own, well before the ecologically inspired car criticism of the 1970s. *Easy Rider* is a film "completely bereft of personal revelation" and is characterized by Lyn Elliot as an act "not [of] self-discovery, but [of] self-assertion." The film is an "expression of the free self in public space." The road movie, Elliot concluded in a dissertation dedicated to "Liberating Domesticity," is "a genre obsessed with home," thus confirming current insights about the close connection between mobility and fixity (see the introduction). The genre "functions as a means of managing the anxieties and contradictions generated by … changes in family form or ideologies concerning the family." Indeed, as Elliot observed, "the birth of the road genre coincides with the emergence of a domestic ideology that posited the companionate nuclear family as the primary site for personal liberation." In this sense (by making home and family into one of America's "hegemonic norms," together with frontier and national identity), road movies, and the role of the car in them, are highly conservative.[214]

David Laderman, in his study of the American road movie, distinguished for this genre's first phase (1967–1975) between "quest road movies" and "outlaw road movies," the first starting to appear before the second. Elliot nuanced the latter category by distinguishing between "outlaw couple road films" and "male-buddy road films." But Laderman told his readers nothing about the relationship between the drivers (let alone the passengers) and their cars, thus placing himself in a long tradition of literary and media scholars mimicking the early bourgeois motorists like Wharton. Such motorists, and some scholars in their wake, were part of a pre-car tradition writing their travelogues as if traveling through thin air, dematerialized, as if prefiguring the virtual travel of the latter quarter of the century. The result is an emphasis on the individual quest, whereas we know it was the family or the small situational group that mostly traveled by car. Thus, *Bonnie and Clyde* (1967) and especially *Easy Rider* (1969), as precursors of the "road movie as a vital post-60s genre," are celebrated because "the quest [is established] as [*Easy Rider*'s] basic plot structure," and "driving" generally functions as "the foundational crux of the plot," in which a "subversion of conventional American institutions" is articulated and "transient mobility" is equated with "rebellious liberation." Bonnie and Clyde, director Arthur Penn observed, "literally spent their lives in the confines of the car," which is perhaps why the violent end of the movie includes an aggressive "assault on the car itself."[215]

Laderman observed a gradual depoliticization of the genre that assumes an "ironic attitude": "In this more existential focus, the genre's core conflict with conformist society has been internalized, 'rebellion' thus becoming an amorphous anxiety about self ... pushing the fusion of human and car more to the foreground," a similar conclusion we reached when dealing with *On the Road*. Indeed, in *Two-Lane Blacktop*, we are back in "a composition of pure movement," an "anti-action film" rhyming with Kerouac's *On the Road*: mobility has become abstract, if not virtual, the film "almost nihilistic in its sense of drift" depicting "driving as an enigmatic ritual." The outlaw road movies produced during the "classic stage" just before the 'lull' of the later 1970s (exactly when women started writing road novels, as we saw) and the subsequent "conservative turn" toward the blockbuster concept, convey a "general disillusionment pervading the aftermath of the counter-culture," depicting "unmotivated hero[es] on a journey" while "taking the road stands for the very quality of contingency." By then, the 'adventure' had solidified, was fossilized in a model "stuffed with explosions, car chases, and video-game annihilations, all designed predominantly for an adolescent audience." From a Quest of the Self, as literary students tend to analyze automotive adventure, it had evolved into the experience of "events."[216] This shift, in general, reflected the emergence of the 'event society' (see the introduction).

By the end of the period under investigation here, road movies presented rebellion for its own sake (a trait some observers see as a distinguishing characteristic of road *movies*, in contrast to road *novels*), just like automobility had become a mobile l'art pour l'art. This process can be followed through films like *Midnight Cowboy* (John Schlesinger, 1969), with its two bus trips "reveal[ing] the impossibility of autonomy and the futility of mobility for unheroic outlaws, hustlers, and rebels who, more often than not, are immobilized in their marginal lives"; or *The Rain People* (Francis Ford Coppola, 1969), in which a middle-class "road rebel" leaves her husband and drives off in a station wagon to get an abortion, picking up hitchhikers; or even independent filmmaker Barbara Loden's *Wanda* (1971), picturing a "working-class 'floater'" who "lacks passion and vision" and "whose aimlessness "undermines the American dream *and* the fantasy rebelling from it."

The same aimlessness haunts Madeleine in Alfred Hitchcock's *Vertigo* (1958) in her movement through San Francisco, or Marnie's drifting from city to city, in Hitchcock's eponymous 1964 movie. Although the 'aimlessness' of the road movie is observed by film students without any reference to the fact that this was nothing new (in fact, it was one of the three pillars [the spatial one] of the very car adventure), it cannot be denied this trait was celebrated time and again in postwar autopoetic movies (or movies with autopoetic scenes), such as Frank Perry's *Play It As It Lays* (1972). Other elements of the tripartite adventure could be watched in films like Guy Hamilton's *Goldfinger* (1964, conquest of the woman passenger), Peter Yates's *Bullitt* (1968, iconic car chase), Stanley Kubrick's *A Clockwork Orange* (1971, speeding and terrorizing pedestrians). "I'm not sure," Steve McQueen commented on his role in *Bullitt*, "whether I'm an actor who races or a racer who acts."[217] In other words, some road movies made the adventure machine invisible—made driving it an abstractified, aimless experience—whereas others exaggerated the adventure, making it no less 'unreal,' as a flight forward, a carnivalesque practice. In both cases, there was a relation with the new Interstate Highway network that would be spread over the United States in these years (see chap. 3).

***

The network inspired not only filmmakers. Photographers and painters "discovered a new world of aesthetic possibility from the windshields of their cars," such as Andy Warhol (who drove across the United States to California) and Roger Kurtz, whose painting *Arches* (1961) was the result of endless cruising over the LA freeways in his Aston Martin convertible, "using a 35mm camera and slide film." In many cities, "a full decade before the landmark national legislation," high-speed freeways were constructed or planned, by "pro-growth coalitions composed of business elites, mayors, and other city officials," keen on bringing 'development' to their cities. These freeways started enhancing suburbanization, which, given the lack of public transport, made the car into a real 'necessity.'

The lack of purpose, the abstractification, the aimlessness does not mean to imply mobility had lost its politics, of course. Seiler has shown how "to drive is to disappear," flowing "anonymously in the traffic stream" on the freeways, where driving is "inducing narcosis and invisibility" and a trance-like state, a first step toward a full "derealisation" of the subject. In the words of media scholar Margaret Morse, the car has become a "realm of passage" toward self-abstraction, "to divest of [the motorist's] particularity and enter on a par with the other individuals on the public road, all of whom are similarly veiled by their machines and following the uniform protocols of driving."[218] These "uniform protocols of driving" form the very foundation (often neglected by mobility students) for the emerging 'car society,' as well as the protests against it, to which we will turn in the next chapter. Before we do so, however, we will return to J. G. Ballard, whose novels started to emphasize the systemic aspects of automobilism, a vision rarely shared by immediate postwar autopoetics, and as such forming a bridge toward the global road building frenzy of the 1970s and beyond.

Flow Interrupted: *Crash* and the Systemic Aspects of Automobilism

We have, in the previous two sections, observed how belletristic literature after World War II perhaps is no longer the main locus to search for the motifs and motives of exuberant automobilism, and that middlebrow and popular-cultural utterances have become better indicators of automobility's pulse, at least if we wish to follow the historical fate of the car as 'adventure machine.' Otherwise put, we need both types of sources to document the split in Western automotive culture and to follow the divergences and convergences of middle-class and working-class subcultures (plural in both cases, to account for several additional subcultures around and within them). Indeed, we saw how avant-gardes such as the beats and their subversive successors eventually became integrated into a mainstream consumer culture, in which the car was one of the central and crucial icons. Whereas before the war, the automotive avant-gardes had won (and so put their adventure machine on the mobility map), now they "failed," according to Hobsbawm, as they "became a subdepartment of marketing," a double failure, as they also proved unable to "express the times." Differently put, the postwar years in the West saw a new automotive subculture emerge that expanded the up to then hegemonic automotive culture considerably, in the process slowly overshadowing the formerly hegemonic, middle-class experiences. Against the 'amorphous anxiety' of the middle class, base of an ironic attitude, now came to stand a carnivalesque adventurism, a flight forward into the extremes of the car adventure, up to a point that it could hardly be called 'tongue in cheek' anymore, as it became bloody serious. In Katie Mills's, words, "the road [and by extension, the automobile] has become one of the most powerful metaphors of transformation in American [and, again by extension, Western] pop culture."[219]

Our analysis resulted in the conclusion that the automotive adventure within hegemonic, middle-class culture became reformulated, fragmented, and diluted but did not disappear. It was *reformulated* into a more abstract phenomenon because of the new driving experiences offered by the highway-as-cocoon that seemed to annihilate the landscape, literally (as destruction) and figuratively (as loss of vision in a 'super-ironic' streak of isolation in the automotive capsule), infrastructure that really developed into countrywide systems in this period (see chap. 3). It became *fragmented* over several new subcultures (women, blacks, children, queers, the beats, the flower-power kids in their 2CVs and buses) and, within these subcultures, fragmented into specialized sub-subcultures, emphasizing either racing, roaming, tinkering or aggressive conquering, or combinations thereof. It became *diluted* because the middle class became embarrassed, so it seemed (at least according to its novels and its movies), by the emanations of automotive experiences beyond its own culture, from the Chicano lowriders, via the young white (street) racing enthusiasts, to the instrumentality of women drivers, and because the adventure now had to be shared much more with the (often female) passengers. The result was 'abstract,' ritualized driving, a rebellious automotive l'art pour l'art. It did not disappear, because it was rescued by the beats through their "transgression" experiences, and because it was revived by new adventurous contenders (including those on motorcycles, and including its dark sides in the form of its accidents, violence, and aggression), recruited most of all from the new suburban working class.

At the same time, we saw the instrumental deployment of the car increase (for instance, in the emergence of commuting as a mass phenomenon), which prompted contemporaries (and historians in their wake) to project this back into history, as if the success of the car could be explained by its 'serious' sides. Instead, the adventure became an object of "bricolage," a hybrid do-it-yourself experience that every novice was invited to produce during car driving. Whatever the exact flavor of this adventure, however, together, in their multifacetedness, they formed an exuberant expression of Western affluence marketed as 'freedom' and as such a powerful weapon in the "intermodal Cold War" between road and rail, West and East. The Western exuberance broke the prewar 'covert culture' (Leo Marx) of car pleasure wide open into a networked l'art pour l'art of mobility, for every earthling to see, especially those not living in the West, a spectacle that did not seem to stop increasing and intensifying. Unfortunately, we lack the resources to study the reception of this extravagance beyond the West. Such studies are very much needed, however, as the 'impact' of the 'American model' (as a pars pro toto of the 'Western model') on a 'Third World' local culture may have a high explanatory power.

***

By the end of this period, James Ballard, with whom we opened this chapter as he arrived from Shanghai in reconstruction England, published his novel *Crash* (1972). *Crash* is the story of a conversion: the narrator (Ballard) becomes "an eager disciple" of the "hoodlum scientist" Robert Vaughan, after the latter has killed himself in a car crash in an effort to kill Elizabeth Taylor, with whom he had hoped to be 'united' in steel and flesh, by a car collision. What Harry Crews describes as two separate spheres (the car erotics and the 'fleshy' cruelty of the car accident), Ballard merges into an explosive cocktail. But whereas Ballard's novel can be read as irony, Crews describes 'car erotics' in a much more down-to-earth style: Herman's brother, Mister, gets sentimental when he touches the "brand-new Maverick." He embraces the hood, "his pink lolling tongue lapp[ing] out of his mouth and touch[ing] metal," while his companion, "hotel whore" Margo, presses "her pussy … directly against the emblem on the front of the car," but Joe "didn't want to think about her ass. He wanted to think about car." Ballard tries to avoid this plebeian car porn. Driving in a Lincoln Continental, the same model in which President Kennedy was assassinated, Ballard and Vaughan have sex under the influence of LSD and despite his "horror and disgust at the sight of [Vaughan's] appalling injuries." In an introduction to the 1995 edition, Ballard gives the "marriage between reason and nightmare that has dominated the 20th century" in which "the balance between fiction and reality has changed significantly," as the background to his narrative: "We live inside an enormous novel … The writer's task is to invent reality."[220]

Within the novel, the narrator describes the acts of "a new sexuality born from a perverse technology" characterized by a "stylization of violence": "If one of [the firemen who rescues him from his car wreck] had unbuttoned his coarse serge trousers to reveal his genitalia, and pressed his penis into the bloody crotch of my armpit, even this bizarre act would have been acceptable." This fascination with the 'orifice' of the human body and of the car's streamlined body 'rhymes,' so to speak, with the nearly exclusive attention for the car's interior, where all sex acts take place. Car trips have no other purpose than to bring the passengers to places where these acts can be performed: the multimedia, multisensorial experience of 'automobilism' takes place now mostly at a standstill. The adventure as we know it from prewar novels is fully gone; it has dissolved in mutilation. As the interior (reminiscent of Ballard's main science fiction theme of 'inner space') acts as a stage, for fellow motorists as spectators ("three deep" around a crashed car), for the public to witness a staged car collision, the interior is at the same time an exterior (and vice versa), just like the wounds that generate so much excitement. Within the car's body, the sex acts are as violent as the world outside: "All those scenes of pain and violence that illuminated the margins of our lives—television newsreels of wars and student riots, natural disasters and police brutality which we [the narrator and his wife] vaguely watched on the colour TV set in our bedroom as we masturbated each other." The TV and photo camera are as much part of the protagonists' sexualized universe (and the narrator's own violent sexual fantasies: "ramming one of these massive steel plugs into a socket at the base of her spine") as are the cars. The crash with another 'collision partner' (as modern crash research would formulate it) represents the ultimate sexual act. At the same time, it is "the only way in which one can now legally take another person's life."[221]

This observation brings us to the 'systemic' aspects of the novel, as Ballard is one of the few modern writers who is not fooled by the smoothing road safety statistics: "After being bombarded endlessly by road-safety propaganda it was almost a relief to find myself in an actual accident." Instead, he dedicates an entire novel to these statistics' personal consequences, venting "premonitions of disaster" and observing "signs of [an] end of the world by automobile," of which the collisions are "rather like rehearsals. When we've all rehearsed our separate parts the real thing will begin." On the roadsides, the glass fragments form "a beach of sharp crystal" as a "new geological layer laid down by the age of the automobile accident." This collective, cumulative, systemic character of Ballard's novel has hardly been reflected on by reviewers: they have neglected the fact that Vaughan has worked as a "computer specialist" in "the application of computerized techniques to the control of all international traffic systems," including those of the airplanes that constantly roar above the heads of the protagonists when they drive around the London airport.

Sex in the car is controlled through the accelerator pedal, "stroking her rectum to the rhythm of the passing cars" and "inserting his penis in vagina, anus and mouth almost in response to the road along which we moved, the traffic density, the style of my driving." The sex scenes are described in the same medicalized and technical terminology as the staged crash test, which is set up in front of an audience that watches how a 'nuclear family' in the form of four dummies, "a husband, wife and two children," are used as props. One of the unique (compared to other crashes in novels of the period, but see Crews) features of Ballard's novel is a detailed description of what happens in the car interior during the pre-collision phase when the 'collision partners' (as in slow motion) approach each other head-on. The crash test results in what one reviewer has called a "grotesque" scene in which the head of a decapitated passenger flies through the interior at the same time as a "right cheekbone" is separated from another passenger's head by "the guillotine of the near-side windshield wiper."

It is remarkable that Crews's *Car* (published in the same year as *Crash*) also depicts human limbs flying through the car's interior after a collision. It is no coincidence that the year of publication coincides with the very top of the fatality curve in many Western countries. But Crews's novel can hardly be read as ironic when Easy's daughter, Junell, meets highway patrol Joe in a wreck, the only place where they are able to indulge in erotics, Joe tells her stories about cars, making her aroused by "telling her about a new fuel mixture," while in the background they hear "the scream [of] a six-year-old girl, ... the stick shift from the [Plymouth] Barracuda stuck through her pelvis ... One of her arms was torn off at the elbow. She was a lump of blood that screamed." In Ballard's novel, the "bored crowd" of a stock car race realizes the "real thing is available free of charge," in the public crash test.

It is this fetishization of the car and its 'orifices' (including its largest and crucial orifice, the interior) that sets this novel apart from many other published during this period: "It isn't sex that Vaughan is interested in, but technology," especially the technology of the "crippled" body. The fetish character of the car (which makes Ballard smear his semen on its "oily instrument panels and binnacles," as in a magic ritual) dominates the mobile aspects of car mobility: in the novel, the protagonists often end up in a traffic jam on the new freeway overpass. The "proximity" of the crashed cars is at the same time a metaphor of the *collapse of the distancing effect* of the automotive capsule, which was so important during the previous emergence and persistence phases of automobilism in the prewar years.[222] In Ballard's crashing universe, the irony of the car starts to collapse, and car culture becomes bloody serious.

***

When *Crash* appeared, car crashes were ubiquitous in belletristic literature, as well as in popular culture, as deus ex machina ("a cliché, a useful narrative device for introducing contingent events or unexpected encounters") or simply because of the thrill of its violence and (according to Ballard) hidden sexuality. Gregory Corso, a beat poet, versifies a night drive "not knowing how to drive," knocking down "people I loved / ... went 120 through one town." Gore Vidal's *Myra Breckinridge* is "struck by a hit-and-run automobile, I have been unconscious for ten days. I sustained twelve broken ribs, one cracked femur, one fractured shin, a dozen torn and bruised ligaments, as well as a concussion of the brain," her injuries enumerating as if they are trophies. Lolita's mother is lethally wounded in a car crash, enabling Nabokov's alter ego to spend most of the novel in the car with her daughter. Didion's characters "have nowhere to go" and "none of [them] knows what he or she wants"; her "fiction and essays show a preoccupation with accidents."[223] In short, the accident has become an inextricable part of autopoetics, for everyone to see.

From Ballard's perspective, Armenian American writer William Saroyan, in his short, traditionally (as a Quest of the Self) written travelogue *Short Drive, Sweet Chariot* (1966) from New York to Fresno in a 1941 Ford Lincoln, is still living in a modernist universe; for him, accidents are "shocking," "ugly," "dirty," and "obscene." The same even applies to Arthur Miller's play *Death of a Salesman*: Willy Loman kills himself in a car (off-stage, in this case, and represented by the sound of a crash). This is also true for the bus accident in the postmodern novel *Second Skin* by John Hawkes. Likewise, Madison Jones, in *A Buried Land* (1963), lets one of his protagonists use the car to murder someone by crashing into him, the actual impact only suggested by a very distanced description. Unlike Ballard, these authors do not connect the accident to a fetishist celebration of the car, although Saroyan sees "the healing of God in a variety of things, the most pleasant of which is probably automobile driving," the pleasure stemming from "this freedom in myself" generated by either writing or driving. Although car driving no longer has the connotation of "sex with Gods" (that seems to be reserved for flying), the transcendent experience of the car journey is still active among writing motorists: "We have found God in cars," Crews writes in his essay "The Car" (1979), having dedicated an entire novel to the world of cars and junkyards, "or if not the true God, one so satisfying, so powerful and aweinspiring that the distinction is too fine to matter." Like Ballard's middle-class copycats, Crews's 'redneck' protagonist "make love [no so much] *in* cars, but rather *to* cars": "With the gentleness of a lover he had stuck his hands into their dark greasy mysteries." [224]

James Agee's *Death in the Family* starts with an accident, and Karl Shapiro dedicates an entire, quite famous, poem to the "Auto Accident" as "an on-the-scene news report replete with sirens blowing, police lights turning and blood gushing—graphically painted." Of the nine autopoetic poems written during the period covered by this chapter and collected in Kurt Brown's anthology, seven are on accidents. Most of them are bloody and lethal, such as Robert Sward's "Scenes from a Text" (from *Kissing The Dancer and Other Poems*, 1964), where the car "lies on its side, windshield smashed / Doors off, bodies strewn, blood, brains" before it is towed away. The obsession for the car crash also was expressed in songs like "The Wreck on the Highway" (1949) by Roy Acuff ("I heard the groans of the dying / But, I didn't hear nobody pray") and Little Jimmy Dickens's "The Sign on the Highway" (1951) ("Their bodies were found near the sign board that read / Beer wine and whiskey for sale, just ahead"). Non-anglophone autopoetic texts also know how to include the car crash. Tankred Dorst's play *Die Kurve* (1960) shows a road crossing where a car mechanic is waiting for the crash victims and their wrecks to arrive, like Ballard playing with the (un)certainties of accident statistics. Claudia Lieb, who dedicated an entire dissertation to the "accident of the moderns," observed "aesthetic fatigue phenomena" around 1970, ushering in a new treatment of the car crash in a more grotesque and satirical way, such as in German-language authors Thomas Bernhard and Elfriede Jelinek.[225]

***

But no one generated so much controversy (this author "is beyond psychiatric help," one publisher's reader judged) or dedicated so much artistic energy to the car crash as Ballard, whose countercultural performance piece "Crash" already aroused some controversy when he saw "crash victims like Jayne Mansfield, James Dean, Aly Khan, Jim Clark and President Kennedy (the first man to be murdered in a motorcade)" as "act[ing] out the Crucifixion for us." Around celebrities who died in a car crash such as Dean, Mansfield, Sagan, Jackson Pollock, Grace Kelly, and Albert Camus, a "curious popular mythology" grew up. Indeed, Dean's wrecked Porsche Spyder was sold as a relic, reminding us of Barthes's qualification of the car as "the exact equivalent of the great Gothic cathedrals," a much too 'contemplative'" characterization compared to Ballard's bloody fetishistic magic. Whereas Ballard addressed mass culture, Barthes served the elite: blood and brains versus contemplation and worship. Ballard had his predecessors such as American artist Jim Dine, who set up a "happening" called *The Car Crash* in a gallery in New York in 1960, while French sculptor Arman dynamited a white MG and exhibited it as *White Orchid* in Paris in 1963. Warhol's famous *Death and Disaster* screenprints from the early 1960s and American sculptor Ed Kienholz's *Back Seat Dodge '38* ("a wrecked white car with the plastic dummies of a Third World War pilot and a girl with facial burns making love among the refuse of bubble gum war cards and oral contraceptive wallets") were both covered in Ballard's *The Atrocity Exhibition* (1969), in which also his "plan for the assassination of Jacqueline Kennedy" was included.

By now, Ballard also started to experiment with language, using "a cinematic technique of rapid cutting," including collages or applying a report-like style as in his short prose satire "Crash" (included in *The Atrocity Exhibition*). "If Christ Came Again," the tabloid *Sunday Mirror* headlined in May 1968 covering Ballard's "Crash" performance, "He Would Be Killed in a Car Crash." From this perspective, the exhibition in the New Arts Lab in 1970 called "Crashed Cars" could hardly stir more controversy. Ballard became a local celebrity, taking part in a movie made by the Automobile Association and participating in the launch of the Mercedes 320L, morbidly celebrated through a veteran car journey all the way to Stuttgart, Germany. Ballard's fetishism was supported by the car designers themselves, especially those of the American 'gas guzzlers' from the 1950s with their breast-like bumpers and "vaginal grilles." What could be more controversial than the sanctification of the crash, except perhaps the *eating* of an entire Ford Maverick, as described in all its bloody details in Crew's novel *Car*, as we saw. And like Crews's novel, Ballard's seem to be propelled by guilt, or, in the terminology of British author Joe Moran, his "passionate ambivalence toward roads," considering his publication of an article in the Automobile Association's magazine in 1971.²²⁶

***

The real explosion of controversy happened nearly two decades later, when David Cronenberg, the film director "relentlessly articulat[ing] a politics, a technology, and an aesthetics of the flesh," brought out his movie *Crash* in 1996. Influenced by beat authors like William S. Burroughs, whose *Naked Lunch* he made into a film in 1991, Cronenberg released *Crash* one year before Princess Diana's fatal crash in Paris. Cronenberg left out Ballard's celebrity obsession (after Ballard himself had self-censored his coprophiliac preoccupations from his original manuscript), but the "auto-sensation," the orgastic final and ultimate adventure for everyone to see, the violence (which around the same time was celebrated in Kubrick's *A Clockwork Orange* and Sam Peckinpah's *Straw Dogs*) shocked especially the American reviewers as "monstrous," but also let the British *Daily Mail* demand for a ban of this "sex film." On the other hand, the film premiered at the Cannes Film Festival (thanks to, according to Ballard, "the long tradition of subversive works in France"), and Helmut Newton photographed the cast. By the time of the film's release, the regular movie consumer already could have witnessed an orgy of car crashes, for France, for instance (where this has been excellently researched in a recent dissertation by Fabian Kröger) in Carné's *Les tricheurs* (1958) where a spectacular crash (a "female suicide") destroys the protagonist's Jaguar XK 140 convertible, whereas in Risi's Italian-French *Il Sorpasso* (1962) the protagonist is crushed under his Aurelia. All four of Godard's 1960s movies—*À bout de souffle* (1960), *Le Mépris* (1963), *Pierrot le Fou* (1965), and *Week-end* (1967)—contain car accidents.²²⁷

When Jean Baudrillard at the turn of the decade developed his famous "simulacrum" thesis through the analysis of Ballard's novel, Ballard's reputation as an icon of the 'motorway era' was also secured for many intellectuals who up to then had seen him as a middlebrow science fiction writer. Cronenberg's film was the crown on this development. Baudrillard emphasized the lack of "affectivity" ("no psychology, no ambivalence or desire, no libido or death-drive") and the "nonsensicalness" of Ballard's story. "The car is not the appendix of an immobile domestic universe: there are no more private and domestic universes, only figures of incessant circulation, and the Accident is everywhere as irreversible and fundamental trope, the banalizing of the anomaly of death.' Ballard's machines are "seductive" (not repressive, as in Kafka), and Baudrillard likened the scars they leave on the body ("itself ... only a medium") to the "ritual scarrings of aborigines." *Crash* is "the first great novel of the universe of simulation, the world that we will be dealing with from now on: a non-symbolic universe." And although Baudrillard emphasized "one must resist the *moral* temptation of reading *Crash* as perversion" (a point Ballard himself made in one of his autobiographical texts, expressing his regret that he had inadvertently emphasized the morality of his story), there is no doubt in my mind that *Crash* is a non-postmodern, moral tale: the protagonist time and again stresses the absurdity of his narrative and appears disgusted (and fascinated) by Vaughan's behavior, as Aidan Day convincingly argued. Baudrillard, however, saw in Ballard the beginning of a postmodern (automotive) era of simulation, of the hyperreal not to be distinguished from the unreal, of a blurring between the inside and outside, a world in which "form predominates over ... content," in which violence is tamed by artificiality, such as the crash test that is enacted instead of a 'real-world' crash. This "calming" is done by the new media (such as Vaughan's camera during the crash test), especially television.[228]

In my reading and viewing of *Crash*, the "internalized ... cameraman's perspective" is rehearsed and practiced in car driving: the 'glance' outside is no longer the touristic 'gaze' of prewar and immediate postwar days; it is the abstract, voyeuristic position the driver and his passengers put themselves in as soon as they enter the car. This voyeurism make the interior all-important, an interior that at the same time is also exterior, carefully prepared for everyone to see. *Crash* deals with this merger of mobility and media, as much as it deals with the merger of the organic body and the machine, the true, sexualized unification of man and technology. Ballard was certainly not the first science fiction writer investigating the consequences of Norbert Wiener's 1948 *Cybernetics* manifesto. Bernard Wolfe's "underground classic" novel *Limbo* (1952) also struggled with the "post-World War II cybernetic economy of information and simulacra," as Katherine Hayles calls the postmodern "technologies of control" developed by the US military that helped make a "shift from exo-colonization to endo-colonization," to conceptualize parts of the own population as the "enemy" within. Wolfe has his protagonist "perform ... lobotomies for the social good" in a situation where America's East Coast has been bombed back into a "virtually uninhabited wasteland." In this situation, the rulers formulate a policy called "Immob" aimed at ending wars by subjecting volunteers among the population to limb amputation according to the slogan "No Demobilization without Immobilization." Ironically, these volunteers are equipped with prostheses that enhance their human capacities, resulting in a "hybrid species that has the capacity to be humanity's evolutionary successors."[229]

Ballard's story is at the same time an abstract one, as the protagonists' fantasies reflect the *reality* of statistical predictability of the crash, not *their* crash, but *the* crash, abstract. This is what most reviewers (including Baudrillard) overlooked in Ballard's story: that it was written at what we now, from hindsight, know to be the zenith of road traffic lethality, at a moment when contemporaries could only think (if they had given it a thought, as we will investigate in the next chapter) the alarming increase of road casualties would only continue, into the apocalyptic afterworld described in Ballard's fiction, including his science fiction.

Feminist scholars have observed Ballard's car fetishism is "phallocentric" and that it "speaks male, not female, desire," in which the woman is "represented as the prosthetic other." For them, viewed from women's subjectivity, "the car can replace home and nation in shaping one's place in American culture," constructing "automotive citizenship," as Deborah Clarke argues in her analysis of women's autopoetic literature. This emancipatory, non-fetishized role of the car also applies to others "who may lack more solid standing within the community: 'white trash,' immigrants, nonwhites," the car forming "a bridge between dominant and nondominant cultures."

Except for these subjects living in "a kind of borderland but one grounded in material reality," the mainstream car in the hegemonic 1960s and early 1970s culture seems to be a part of a fetishized, male universe, in which the prewar tripartite adventure (speed, spatial roaming, tinkering) seems to have lost its attractiveness. In his study of modern space, Lefebvre calls the car "the epitome of 'objects,' the Leading-Object," which has "conceived (space) in terms of motoring needs." And he adds, "motorized traffic enables people and objects to congregate and mix without meeting, thus constituting a striking example of simultaneity without exchange, each element remaining enclosed in its own compartment, tucked away in its shell." Such conditions foster a "'psychology' or, better, a 'psychosis' that is peculiar to the motorist," which makes people prepared to take risks, "for the motor-car with its retinue of wounded and dead, its trail of blood, is all that remains of adventure in everyday life, its paltry ration of excitement and hazard."[230]

This car (use) loses its irony, because irony presupposes the wish to 'meet' the Other, even if it is only at a distance. In the new, 'systemic' car culture, the meeting is between cyborgs; the Other has become an invisible pilot of an adjacent vehicle in an anonymized and anonymizing flow. "With the car," a German motorist told his interviewer during a survey, "one can be so deliciously outlaw (*so herrlich gesetzwidrig*)," which reminds us of the American car tourists in the 1920s who defined their camping trips as "hoboing the luxe." Now, "one does not *depart* for adventure: risk is everywhere and nowhere": *Au coin de la rue, l'aventure*, the adventure is to be found on every street corner, as French philosophers Pascal Bruckner and Alain Finkielkraut claimed. An Australian study of 1950s tourism argued popular travel by then was marked by "a *retreat* from adventure" yet remained masculine. The car of the 1960s thus enabled people to "live in the middle," prefiguring Giorgio Agamben's assessment at the end of the century that "our current condition is characterized by the dominance of the planetary petty bourgeoisie." Living in the middle is possible, because, as we have seen in this chapter, "the petty bourgeoisie absorbed one cultural trend after another and meanwhile in all highly industrialized countries gained the cultural hegemony," but at the same time "does not possess any noticeable (*registrierbares*) self-consciousness[;] on the contrary, it has as always been characterized by self-hatred." Since the period under review here, the car functions as "a substitute for eroticism, for adventure." Car consumption has become "inconspicuous," and Bourdieu's 'distinction' has become commonplace (also, contra Bourdieu, for the workers, as Gartman argues, even if they were generally forced to "settle for second-hand autos from the middle class"), its "ordinariness" showing because the distinction, the slight 'subversion' of the Fordist paradigm, plays at the level of the model and the make, no longer at the level of the car itself.[231]

***

With Ballard's novel from 1973, the car has become like the horseshoe in physicist Niels Bohr's anecdote, in which a man is asked why he has put a horseshoe at his door. He answers that he is not superstitious but "they say that it also helps when one doesn't believe in it." Hartmut Böhme, who started his lengthy study of the role of the fetish in capitalist culture with this anecdote, asked about the agency in our dealing with fetishized objects, which are "overrated" in their importance, as they "belong to the periphery of a person—like a shoe, a garter, hair etc. [one is inclined to add the car to this short list]—whereas the person herself is not at all desired." Böhme distinguished between commodity fetishism and cultural fetishism and warned against reducing the latter to the former. The proliferation of fetishes and idols "de-enchants" (*Entzäuberung*) and enhances the playful character of a culture: "The integration within capitalist economy devaluates its sacrality; its performativity stimulates its non-conformist use; its circulation makes it public and prone to communication; its manifest visibility opens it to reflection. Fetishism has become an element of choice, multi-optional, carnivalesque, and as such also democratic."

From the 1970s onward, "cultural fetishism increasingly decoupled itself from its sexual and economic enclaves and became mainstream within popular culture." In *Crash*, the "enhanced body" (*erweiterter Körper*) becomes a fetish itself, so, during the crash, two body-cars (or car-bodies) meet: the people's body and the car's body. It is a fusion of cyborgs. Who drives? Böhme asked. "I drive, but the car drives too: some split and some fusion take place in ever-changing shares. Not only 'these two' drive, but other agents drive along: the street conditions, the traffic signs, the laws, the police, the courts, … but also my moods that just now make me feel aggressive or lenient."[232] Indeed, without the brand-new overpass near the

London airport, there would have been no *Crash*; without the fusion of wounds and metal, there would have been no start of Baudrillard's postmodern car society. We therefore will have to turn our attention to the system now, zooming out of the West again, and look over the freeway fence to the colonies and the motorizing 'Other.'

Notes

1. J. G. Ballard, *Miracles of Life: Shanghai to Shepperton—An Autobiography* (London: Fourth Estate, 2008), 5 (kaleidoscope); J. G. Ballard, *Empire of the Sun: A Novel* (New York: Simon & Schuster, 1984), 5 (chickens); 6 (Communist), 12 (Amherst Avenue), 18 (velvet); John Baxter, *The Inner Man: The Life of J. G. Ballard* (London: Weidenfeld & Nicolson, 2011), 265, 274; Arthur Marwick, *The Sixties: Cultural Revolution in Britain, France, Italy, and the United States, c. 1958–c. 1974* (Oxford: Oxford University Press, 1998), 319 (Anglo-Saxon).
2. Jonathan Fenby, *Chiang Kai-shek: China's Generalissimo and the Nation He Lost* (New York: Carroll & Graf Publishers, 2004), 313 (Mowrer); Baxter, *Inner Man*, 15 (Communists), 29 (telegraph), 36 (humiliation), 77 (mirror), 177 (desperate), 178–179 (puller); Ballard, *Miracles of Life*, 20 (optimism), 45 (father), 72 (humour).
3. Andrew Rosen, *The Transformation of British Life, 1950–2000: A Social History* (Manchester: Manchester University Press, 2003), xi (austerity); Ballard, *Miracles of Life*, 121 (perambulators), 127 (outsider), 134 (shifting roles), 145 (pathology, entertainment), 181 (Inner Space), 228 (nuclear family); Baxter, *Inner Man*, 65 (Cold War), 69 (Self), 97 (Woolf), 114 (establishment), 124 (first car).
4. Baxter, *Inner Man*, 49 (smashed), 90 (New Wave), 181–182 (Reagan); Fred Keijzer, *Filosofie van de toekomst: Over nut en noodzaak van sciencefiction* (Rotterdam: Lemniscaat, 2010), 44 (normal literature), 46 (realism); Ballard, *Miracles of Life*, 148 (Rimbaud), 177 (misfit, casualty; both used in their plural form in the quoted text).
5. Jeremy R. Kinney, "Racing on Runways: The Strategic Air Command and Sports Car Racing in the 1950s," *ICON* 19 (2013): 196 (Mille Miglia). See, also for the following Catherine R. Schenk, "Austerity and Boom," in *Twentieth-Century Britain: Economic, Social and Cultural Change*, ed. Paul Johnson (London: Longman, 1994), and Peter Howlett, "The 'Golden Age,' 1955–1973," in Johnson, *Twentieth-Century Britain*, 320–324.
6. Marcus Felson, "The Differentiation of Material Life Styles: 1925 to 1966," *Social Indicators Research* 3, nos. 3–4 (1976): 398 (predicted); Brian Harrison, *Seeking a Role: The United Kingdom, 1951–1970* (Oxford: Clarendon Press, 2009), 136 (1966); Colin Pooley, "Pedestrian Stories: The Changing Role of Walking in Urban Mobility," paper presented at the workshop "Large Metropolis Mobilities in Long-Term Perspective: For an Ecosystemic Approach of Sustainable Urban Mobilities," Paris (23–24 February 2017).
7. Howlett, "Golden Age," 337; Rodney Lowe, "Postwar Welfare," in Johnson, *Twentieth-Century Britain*, 357–358; Michael Mann, *The Sources of Social Power, vol. 3: Global Empires and Revolution, 1890–1945* (Cambridge: Cambridge University Press, 2012), 442 (cradle-to-grave); John Street, "Youth Culture," in Johnson, *Twentieth-Century Britain*, 462–463; Dick Hebdige, *Subculture: The Meaning of Style* (London: Routledge, 1994), 49 (fusion); on "skiffle" subculture, see, e.g., Ronald D. Cohen, *Rainbow Quest:*

The Folk Music Revival and American Society, 1940–1970 (Amherst: University of Massachusetts Press, 2002), 100–101, and Marwick, *Sixties*, 67–68; Fabian Brändle, "'Hard Travelin': Die Old Left und Folk Music im New Deal," *Moving the Social* 47 (2012): 45 (banjo).

8. Ronald D. Cohen, *Folk Music: The Basics* (New York: Routledge, 2006), 98 (thirty thousand); Graham Nash, *Wild Tales: A Rock & Roll Life* (New York: Crown Archetype, 2013), 13 (dreams, few cars), 25 (gig), 44 (songs), 47 (religious), 63 (married), 65 (hysteria), 65–66 (murder, fluid), 75 (fast lane), 77 (invasion); Peter Wicke, "Music, Dissidence, Revolution, and Commerce: Youth Culture between Mainstream and Subculture," in *Between Marx and Coca-Cola: Youth Cultures in Changing European Societies, 1960–1980*, ed. Axel Schildt and Detlef Siegfried (New York: Berghahn Books, 2006), 109–126 (language).

9. Simon Frith, *Sound Effects: Youth, Leisure, and the Politics of Rock 'n' Roll* (New York: Pantheon Books, 1981), 4 (mass media); Ronald D. Lankford Jr., *Folk Music USA: The Changing Voice of Protest* (New York: Schirmer Trade Books, 2005), xiii (Kingston Trio, college students); Shelly Romalis, *Pistol Packin' Mama: Aunt Molly Jackson and the Politics of Folksong* (Urbana: University of Illinois Press, 1999), 39 (Dreiser); for an analysis of the folklore studies within the New Deal's FWP, including the innovative use of cultural anthropology and ethnography and resulting in, among others, the publication *These Are Our Lives*, see Jerrold Hirsch, *Portrait of America: A Cultural History of the Federal Writers' Project* (Chapel Hill: University of North Carolina Press, 2003), chap. 8.

10. Lankford, *Folk Music USA*, 2–3; Brändle, "Hard Travelin,'" 44; Suzanne E. Smith, *Dancing in the Street: Motown and the Cultural Politics of Detroit* (Cambridge, MA: Harvard University Press, 2003), 12 (Blink Blake), 32 (migrated).

11. Frith, *Sound Effects*, 15 (physical) (14: "Sociologists of popular music have always fallen for the easy terms of lyrical analysis. Such a word-based approach is not helpful at getting at the meaning of rock"); Tobias Becker, "HT 2014: 'The Winner Takes It All'—Popgeschichtliche Narrative des 20. Jahrhunderts zwischen Ausbeutung und Emanzipation," conference review, H-Soz-Kult (14 November 2014), http://www.hsozkult.de/conferencereport/id/tagungsberichte-5669; Lankford, *Folk Music USA*, 24 ("We Shall Overcome"); Ronald D. Cohen, "Singing Subversion: Folk Music and the Counterculture in the 1950s," in *Beat Culture: The 1950s and Beyond*, ed. Cornelis A. van Minnen, Jaap van der Bent, and Mel van Elteren (Amsterdam: VU University Press, 1999), 119 (left wing); Cohen, *Rainbow Quest*, 29 (Buick), 33 (Detroit), 36 (migrants), 38 (prepared).

12. On hot-rodding, see, e.g., H. F. Moorhouse, *Driving Ambitions: An Analysis of the American Hot Rod Enthusiasm* (Manchester: Manchester University Press, 1991); and Peter Marsh and Peter Collett, *Driving Passion: The Psychology of the Car* (London: Jonathan Cape: 1986), 86–89; Paul Grushkin, *Rockin' Down the Highway: The Cars and People That Made Rock Roll* (St. Paul, MN: Voyageur Press, 2006), 18 (Ory), 20 ("Cadillac Baby"), 26 (muscle cars), 27 (stolen), 28 (Howlin' Wolf), 30 (bus-driven), 32 (Little Richard), 33 (Holly); Bernard Gendron, "Theodore Adorno Meets the Cadillacs," in *Studies in Entertainment: Critical Approaches to Mass Culture*, ed. Tania Modleski (Bloomington: Indiana University Press, 1986), 21 (Cadillacs).

13. Nancy Isenberg, *White Trash: The 400-Year Untold History of Class in America* (New York: Viking, 2016), 231 (white trash); Jefferson Cowie, *Stayin' Alive: The 1970s and the Last Days of the Working Class* (New York: New Press, 2010), 354 (truck driver); Grushkin, *Rockin' Down the Highway*, 76 (Presley); William H. Whyte Jr., "The Cadillac Phenomenon," *Fortune* (February 1955), 107 (1.7 times), 109 (way up, symbol,

motivation research), 174 (safety, relax), 175 (tiptoe, trickle-down), 184 (44.8 percent); Johnny Damm, "Editor's Corner: Stalking History on the Hank Williams Death Ride," *A Bad Penny Review*, accessed 23 October 2019, http://www.abadpennyreview.com/editors-corner-stalking-history-on-the-hank-williams-death-ride. I thank Piet Rademakers for suggesting Williams's fate to me, as well as the Rocket 88 story.

14. "Was the 1949 Oldsmobile 88 America's First Muscle Car?" *Pomona*, 11 April 2014, https://www.pomonaswapmeet.com/blog/2014/04/11/was-the-1949-oldmobile-88-americas-first-muscle-car; Aaron Severson, "Rocket Bomb: The Oldsmobile Rocket 88 and the Dawn of the American Horsepower Race," *Ate Up with Motor*, 20 August 2008, http://ateupwithmotor.com/model-histories/oldsmobile-rocket-88; "Rocket 88," s.v., *Wikipedia*, last edited 19 October 2019, https://en.wikipedia.org/wiki/Rocket_88.

15. Grushkin, *Rockin' Down the Highway*, 38 (Everly Brothers), 43 (Dictators), 45 (smog), 52 (Dale), 54 (Ryan), 55 (sound effects), 60 (Roth), 68 (morbid), 80 (Monkeemobile); Jeff Beck: https://www.grammy.com/grammys/news/multi-flavored-pop retrieved on 20 August 2017; "Billy Gibbons" (https://en.wikipedia.org/wiki/Billy_Gibbons, consulted 20 August 2017); "Brian Setzer Talks about His Classic Car Collection (1983)," video, 0:23, uploaded by cowsills2x2, 9 December 2013, https://www.youtube.com/watch?v=lfn8urU6AQk. "Car songs," s.v., *Wikipedia*, last updated 27 September 2019, https://en.wikipedia.org/wiki/Car_song (peaked); Chris Lezotte, "Born to Take the Highway: Women, the Automobile, and Rock 'n' Roll," *Journal of American Culture* 36, no. 3 (2013): 166 (Mitchell), 167 (control).

16. Andrea Carosso, "The Paradox of Re-colonization: The British Invasion of American Music and the Birth of Modern Rock," in *The Transatlantic Sixties: Europe and the United States in the Counterculture Decade*, ed. Grzegorz Kosc, Clara Juncker, Sharon Monteith, and Britta Waldschmidt-Nelson (Bielefeld: transcript, 2013), 130 (schlock rock); Cohen, *Rainbow Quest*, 96 (vinyl), 108 (Van Ronk), 133 (rescue); Russel Duncan, "The Summer of Love and Protest: Transatlantic Counterculture in the 1960s," in Kosc et al., *Transatlantic Sixties*, 153 (Sontag).

17. Cohen, *Rainbow Quest*, 204–205 (civil rights), 254 (hippy); Smith, *Dancing in the Street*, 23 (desegregation); Detlef Siegfried, "Understanding 1968: Youth Rebellion, Generational Change and Postindustrial Society," in Schildt and Siegfried, *Between Marx and Coca-Cola*, 61 (fifty-six).

18. Dave Van Ronk with Elijah Wald, *The Mayor of MacDougal Street: A Memoir* (Philadelphia: Da Capo Press, 2013), 56–57. On the campaigns against hitchhiking, see the excellent analysis by Jeremy Packer, *Mobility without Mayhem: Safety, Cars, and Citizenship* (Durham, NC: Duke University Press, 2008), chap. 2; see also Ginger Strand, *Killer on the Road: Violence and the American Interstate* (Austin: University of Texas Press, 2012), 66–69.

19. Van Ronk with Wald, *Mayor of MacDougal Street*, 127 (craze); David Sandison and Graham Vickers, *Neal Cassady: The Fast Life of a Beat Hero* (Chicago: Chicago Review Press, 2006), 260 (beatific); Jack Sargeant, *Naked Lens: Beat Cinema* (Berkeley, CA: Soft Skull Press, 2008), 10–11 (illumination, reaction); James Atlas, "Foreword," in *Go: A Novel* by John Clellon Holmes (New York: Thunder's Mouth Press, 1997), xv; Norman Mailer, "The White Negro: Superficial Reflections on the Hipster," in *Advertisements for Myself* (Cambridge, MA: Harvard University Press, 1992), 340–341. For an excellent sociological description of the beat culture, see Mel van Elteren, "The Culture of the Subterraneans: A Sociological View of the Beats," in Van Minnen et al., *Beat Culture*, 63–92.

20. Alexandra Ganser, "Reading Multiple Mobilities in Chuck Palahniuk's *Fugitives and Refugees*," in *Culture and Mobility*, ed. Klaus Benesch, 114–115 (Greif and McGuigan); Sargeant, *Naked Lens*, 12; metaphor insisted by, e.g., Steven Jacobs, "From *Flâneur* to Chauffeur: Driving Through Cinematic Cities," in *Imagining the City, vol. 1: The Art of Urban Living*, ed. Christian Emden, Catherine Keen, and David Midgley (Bern: Peter Lang, 2006), 215, who also mentions car chase movies as examples, hardly comparable with the pedestrian with a pet turtle on the leash (as mentioned in David Pinder, *Visions of the City: Utopianism, Power and Politics in Twentieth-Century Urbanism* [Edinburgh: Edinburgh University Press, 2005], 151). I thank Peter Merriman for suggesting this source to me (email, 11 November 2014).
21. John Lennon, *Boxcar Politics: The Hobo in U.S. Culture and Literature, 1869–1956* (Amherst: University of Massachusetts Press, 2014), 167 (possibilities), 169 (train); Katie Mills, *The Road Story and the Rebel: Moving through Film, Fiction, and Television* (Carbondale: Southern Illinois University Press, 2006), 38 (marginality).
22. Sargeant, *Naked Lens*, 12–13, 196 (nuclear war); Holmes, *Go*, 36 (wanderings), 47 (Benzedrine); Mike Jay, "Don't Fight Sober," *London Review of Books* 39, no. 1 (5 January 2017): 13 (inhaler); Jack Kerouac, *On the Road*, in *Road Novels 1957–1960: On the Road / The Dharma Bums / The Subterraneans / Tristessa / Lonesome Traveller / Journal Selections* (New York: Library of America, 2007), 201; Guy Norbury, "A Post-Generation X's View on Ginsberg," in Van Minnen et al., *Beat Culture*, 189 (atom bomb); Katherine Lawrie Mills, "Remapping the Road Story: Contemporary Narratives of Autonomy and Mobility in American Literature, Film, and Television" (PhD diss., University of Southern California, 2000), 37 (LeRoi Jones).
23. Sandison and Vickers, *Neal Cassady*, 169 (superhuman); Mills, *Road Story*, 35 (*noir*), 39 (transsubstantiation), 42 (adventure, Ginsberg), 58 (intermediary); Allen Ginsberg, "The Green Automobile," in *Selected Poems 1947–1995* (New York: HarperCollins, 1996), 23.
24. Roland Barthes, "La nouvelle Citroën," in *Mythologies* (Paris: Éditions du Seuil, 1957), 169. See also Mathieu Flonneau, *L'Automobile au temps des Trentes Glorieuses: Un rêve d'automobilisme* (Carbonne: Nouvelle Éditions Loubatières, 2016), 45–46; Mills, *Road Story*, 89 ("vessels of the divine" is a phrase written by Tom Wolfe in his description of the Merry Pranksters' "being on the bus"); Friederike Roth, "Einleitung: Max Benses poetische Texte," in Bense, *Ausgewählte Schriften, Bd. 4*, xi (philosophical); Max Bense, "Auto und Information: Das Ich, das Auto und die Technik," in *Ausgewählte Schriften, Bd. 4: Poetische Texte*, Max Bense, ed. Elisabeth Walther (Stuttgart: J. B. Metzler, 1998), 291 ("in dem das Auto zum Ich und das Ich zum Auto wird … Ich und Auto mehr und mehr zu einem beinah surrealen Automaten verschmelzen"), 292 ("Informationen verarbeitet und Kommunikation erzeugt").
25. Sandison and Vickers, *Neal Cassady*, 197 (dislocation), 154–155 (block quote); Mills, "Remapping the Road Story," 68; on affinity, see also Gijs Mom, *Atlantic Automobilism: Emergence and Persistence of the Car, 1895–1940* (New York: Berghahn Books, 2015), 137.
26. Sandison and Vickers, *Neal Cassady*, 135 (first car), 140 (nineteen), 165–166 (Hudson), 172 (the trip); Wolfgang Munzinger, *Das Automobil als heimliche Romanfigur: Das Bild des Autos und der Technik in der nordamerikanischen Literatur von der Jahrhundertwende bis nach dem 2. Weltkrieg* (Hamburg: LIT Verlag, 1997), 186 (unchallenged).
27. Sandison and Vickers, *Neal Cassady*, 233, 248; Sargeant, *Naked Lens*, 70 (happenings); Allen Ginsberg, *Howl and Other Poems* (San Francisco: City Light Books, 1996 [reprint of the 1956 edition]), 14; Cohen, *Rainbow Quest*, 254 (personal), 237 (Animals), 240 (Lovin' Spoonful), 253 (West Coast); Mills, "Remapping the Road Story," 16–17

(soundtrack, celebration); Ulf Hannerz, *Cultural Complexity: Studies in the Social Organization of Meaning* (New York: Columbia University Press, 1992), 197 (openness), 201 (diversity), 205 (network), 216 (fragmented).

28. Alex Ross, *The Rest Is Noise: Listening to the Twentieth Century* (New York: Farrar, Straus and Giroux, 2007), 515–518 (518: evoke), 554–555; Tim Page, "John Cage's Gift to Us," *New York Review of Books* 63, no. 16 (24 October 2016); Robert P. Morgan, *Twentieth-Century Music: A History of Musical Style in Modern Europe and America* (New York: Norton, 1991), 318 (Byrne).

29. Van Ronk with Wald, *Mayor of MacDougal Street*, 128 (pushed away), 138 (traveling folksingers), 167 (crossover); Sarah Hill, "'This Is My Country': American Popular Music and Political Engagement in '1968,'" in *Music and Protest in 1968*, ed. Beate Kutschke and Barley Norton (Cambridge: Cambridge University Press, 2013), 52 (Dylan); Lankford, *Folk Music USA*, x (Dylan lyrics).

30. Nash, *Wild Tales*, 95 (writing), 98 (train), 99 (Rolls-Royce), 106–107 (Marrakesh), 130 (heaven), 142 (Volkswagen), 145 (loose), 148 (Mitchell); Paul Gilroy, *Darker Than Blue: On the Moral Economies of Black Atlantic Culture* (Cambridge, MA: Belknap Press, 2010), 39 (singers' cars).

31. Mills, *Road Story*, 101 (FBI shoes), 103–104 (painting); Sandison and Vickers, *Neal Cassady*, 277 (Kesey), 282–284 (road trip), 288 (Speed Limit); Tom Wolfe, *The Electric Kool-Aid Acid Test* (New York: Bantam Books, 1999), 68. This was also the inspiration for a documentary including original footage of the Pranksters bus: Alex Gibney and Alison Ellwood, dir., *Magic Trip: Ken Kesey's Search for a Kool Place*, documentary (New York: Magnolia Pictures, 2011); see also Chris Knipp, "Alex Gibney: *Magic Trip* (2011)," *FilmLeaf*, 12 August 2011, http://www.filmleaf.net/showthread.php?3133-MAGIC-TRIP-(Alex-Gibney-2011).

32. Mills, *Road Story*, 88 (acid, triumph, *now*), 92 (rap, Sontag quote from 1965), 95 (re-create), 96 (intimacy), 97 (adventures), 100 (heads), 123 (mass market).

33. Sandison and Vickers, *Neal Cassady*, 291 (explore, brakes), 294 (Fangio), 296 (Plymouth); Wolfe, *Electric Kool-Aid*, 68 (coastin'); Stewart Brand and Howard Rheingold, *The Virtual Community: Homesteading on the Electronic Frontier* (Reading, MA: Addison-Wesley Publishing Co., 1993), 40 (passenger), 48 (LSD), 49 (Grateful Dead); Timothy D. Ray, "Merry Pranksters," in *Beat Culture: Icons, Lifestyles, and Impact*, ed. William T. Lawlor (Santa Barbara, CA: ABC Clio, 2005).

34. Nash, *Wild Tales*, 177–178; Jason Bezis, "Altamont Rock Festival: '60s Abruptly End (Part I of II)," *Livermore Heritage Guild* 42, no. 3 (2010): 3; "Death of Meredith Hunter: Under My Thumb," video, 9:28, uploaded by Car Chase Wonderland, 25 May 2016, https://www.youtube.com/watch?v=Jp_cSPztxOY (film footage: "We need an ambulance").

35. Thomas Ekman Jørgensen, "Utopia and Disillusion: Shattered Hopes of the Copenhagen Counterculture," in Schildt and Siegfried, *Between Marx and Coca-Cola*, 333 (Hendrix, Joplin); Jill Lynn Talbot, "This Is Not an Exit: The Road Narrative in Contemporary American Literature and Film" (PhD diss., Texas Tech University, 1999), 66 (conservatism); Edward Shorter, *The Making of the Modern Family* (New York: Basic Books, 1975), 269–273.

36. Marwick, *Sixties*, 733 (collapse), 749 (Weathermen); Duncan, "Summer of Love and Protest," 163 (DeGroot), 166 (dropping out), 168 (Ehrenreich); Paul van der Steen, "Luilekkerland van de liefde," *Historisch Nieuwsblad* 24, nos. 7–8 (2015): 24 (ninety million).

37. Nick Turse, *Kill Anything That Moves: The Real American War in Vietnam* (New York: Henry Holt & Co., 2013), 11 (Vietnam); Arthur Redding, *Raids on Human Consciousness: Writing, Anarchism, and Violence* (Columbia: University of South Carolina Press, 1998), 160–161 145 (Frohock); Marwick, *Sixties*, 761. For an analysis of the United States as a land of transcendence and the sublime (closely connected to its space program), see Daniel Sage, *How Outer Space Made America: Geography, Organization and the Cosmic Sublime* (Farnham: Ashgate, 2014).
38. Dick Hebdige, "Object as Image: The Italian Scooter Cycle," in *The Consumer Society Reader*, ed. Martyn J. Lee (Malden, MA: Blackwell, 2000), 153–155 (Drinamyl: 154); Hebdige, *Subculture*, 51 (Teds, xenophobic), 52 (mods); Stuart Hall and Tony Jefferson, eds., *Resistance through Rituals: Youth Subcultures in Post-war Britain* (London: Routledge, 2006), 76–77 (Buckingham, parody), 77 (White Negro); on the scooter charge, see, e,g., "Mod Style and Scooters," ModYourSpace.com, accessed 24 October 2019, http://modyourspace.com/description-mod-style.html; Marwick, *Sixties*, 77 (rockers, Teddy Boy); R. J. Ellis, "'They ... Took Their Time over the Coming': The Postwar British/Beat, 1957–1965," in *The Transnational Beat Generation*, ed. Nancy M. Grace and Jennie Skerl (New York: Palgrave Macmillan, 2012), 145 (Beetles); Bahar Emgin, "Rowdy Gangs on the Road: The Culture of Mobilet in Turkey," in *Nesneyi Okumak / Deciphering the Object*, ed. Tevfik Balcioğlu and Gülsüm Baydar (Izmir: Yaşar Üniversitesi, 2012), 38 (masculinized, feminine); Carosso, "Paradox of Re-colonization," 122–123 (Who).
39. Emgin, "Rowdy Gangs," 38 (pressed frame); Wim de Jong and Bas van Kleef, *De Puchstory en andere brommerverhalen* (Bussum: Thoth, 1994), 51, 38, 56, 119.
40. Mel van Elteren, "In het teken van vrijheid: Amerikaanse cultuur en jongeren in hun vrije tijd na 1945," in *Van ontspanning en inspanning: Aspecten van de geschiedenis van de vrije tijd*, ed. K. P. C. de Leeuw, M. F. A. Linders-Rooijendijk, and P. J. M. Martens (Tilburg, 1995), 65, 75–76; Emgin, "Rowdy Gangs," 37 (*mobilet*).
41. Henk Kleijer and Ger Tillekens, "The Lure of Anglo-American Popular Culture: Explaining the Rise of Dutch Youth Culture," in *American Culture in the Netherlands*, ed. Doeko Bosscher, Marja Roholl, and Mel van Elteren (Amsterdam: VU University Press 1996), 107; Tom O'Dell, "'Chevrolet ... That's a Real *Raggarbil*': The American Car and the Production of Swedish Identities," *Journal of Folklore Research* 30, no. 1 (1993); Tim Dant and Peter J. Martin, "By Car: Carrying Modern Society," in *Ordinary Consumption*, ed. Jukka Gronow and Alan Warde (London: Routledge, 2001), 157n2 (Finland); Simonetta Piccone Stella, "'Rebels without a Cause': Male Youth in Italy around 1960," *History Workshop* 38, no. 1 (1994): 160 (working-class), 164 (speeding), 173 (defer, fun); Detlef Siegfried, "Protest am Markt: Gegenkultur in der Konsumgesellschaft um 1968," in *Wo "1968" liegt: Reform und Revolte in der Geschichte der Bundesrepublik*, ed. Christina von Hodenberg and Detlef Siegfried (Göttingen: Vandenhoeck & Ruprecht, 2006), 57 (plan).
42. Bettina Roccor, "Heavy Metal: Gewaltdarstellung oder Gewaltverherrlichung?" in *Gewalt in der Kultur: Vorträge des 29. Deutschen Volkskundekongresses, Passau 1993, Teilband II*, ed. Rolf W. Brednich and Walter Hartinger (Passau: Lehrstuhl für Volkskunde Universität Passau, 1994), 645–646 (middle class), 657 (violence); for the "fantasies of violence" of hard rock, see also Wicke, "Music, Dissidence," 122; Wolfgang Kraushaar, "Die 'Revolutionierung des bürgerlichen Subjekts': 1968 als erneuerte bürgerliche Utopie?" in *Bürgertum nach 1945*, ed. Manfred Hettling and Bernd Ulrich (Hamburg: Hamburger Edition, 2005), 404 (*veränderte Subjektivität*); Frith, *Sound Effects*, 190 (toughness).

43. Detlef Siegfried, "Prosperität und Krisenangst: Die zögerliche Versöhnung der Bundesbürger mit dem neuen Wohlstand," in *Mit dem Wandel leben: Neuorientierung und Tradition in der Bundesrepublik der 1950er und 60er Jahre*, ed. Friedrich Kiessling and Bernhard Rieger (Köln: Böhlau Verlag, 2011), 74.
44. Richard Ivan Jobs, *Backpack Ambassadors: How Youth Travel Integrated Europe* (Chicago: University of Chicago Press, 2017), 1 (integration, fifty million), 3 (transnational), 4 (one million), 43 (Eurail), 137 (small groups of hitchhikers), 161 (adventurers); Mark Ford, "She Shampooed & Renewed Us," *New York Review of Books* (26 October 2017), 59 (Mitchell). For an introduction into European integration through mobility, see, e.g., Kiran Klaus Patel and Johan Schot, "Twisted Paths to European Integration: Comparing Agriculture and Transport Policies in a Transnational Perspective," *Contemporary European History* 20, no. 4 (2011).
45. Hartmut Kaelble, *Kalter Krieg und Wohlfahrtsstaat: Europa 1945–1989* (Munich: Verlag C. H. Beck, 2011), 14 (periphery); Barry Bluestone and Bennett Harrison, *The Deindustrialization of America: Plant Closings, Community Abandonment, and the Dismantling of Basic Industry* (New York: Basic Books, 1982), 112–115; W. W. Rostow, *The Stages of Economic Growth: A Non-Communist Manifesto* (Cambridge: Cambridge University Press, 1971), 84–85.
46. Kees Schuyt and Ed Taverne, *1950: Welvaart in zwart-wit* (Den Haag: sdu, 2000), 27–93; Jan Luiten van Zanden, *Een klein land in de 20° eeuw: Economische geschiedenis van Nederland 1914–1995* (Utrecht: Het Spectrum, 1997), 47; Piet de Rooy, *Republiek van rivaliteiten: Nederland sinds 1813* (Amsterdam: Mets & Schilt, 2005), 211; Kaelble, *Kalter Krieg und Wohlfahrtsstaat*, 15 (bridges, etc.); David W. Ellwood, "The Marshall Plan: A Strategy That Worked," *Foreign Policy Agenda* (April 2006) (downloaded from https://www.marshallfoundation.org on 5 August 2017), 19 (Hoffmann).
47. Siegfried, "Prosperität und Krisenangst," 63, 77 (the economists cited are George Katona, Burkhard Strümpel, and Ernest Kahn; the historian is Victoria de Grazia); Axel Schildt, "Amerikanische Einflüsse auf die westdeutsche Konsumentwicklung nach dem Zweiten Weltkrieg," in *Die Konsumgesellschaft in Deutschland 1890–1990: Ein Handbuch*, ed. Heinz-Gerhard Haupt and Claudius Torp (Frankfurt: Campus Verlag, 2009), 440–441 (from below); Andreas Wirsching, "From Work to Consumption: Transatlantic Visions of Individuality in Modern Mass Society," *Contemporary European History* 20, no. 1 (2011): 13–15 (equality).
48. Gerold Ambrosius, "Wirtschaftswachstum und Konvergenz der Industiestrukturen in Westeuropa," in *Der Boom 1948–1973: Gesellschaftliche und wirtschaftliche Folgen in der Bundesrepublik Deutschland und in Europa*, ed. Hartmut Kaelble (Opladen: Westdeutscher Verlag, 1992), 129, 134, 167; Peter J. Hugill, "Technology Diffusion in the World Automobile Industry, 1885–1985," in *The Transfer and Transformation of Ideas and Material Culture*, ed. Peter J. Hugill and D. Bruce Dickson (College Station: Texas A&M University Press, 1988), 126, table 6.2 (Japan); Lee Schipper, Ruth Steiner, and Stephen Meyers, "Trends in Transportation Energy Use, 1970–1988: An International Perspective," in *Transportation and Global Climate Change*, ed. David L. Greene and Danilo J. Santini (Washington, DC: American Council for an Energy-Efficient Economy, 1993), 63 (larger cars).
49. James J. Flink, *The Automobile Age* (Cambridge, MA: MIT Press, 1993), 294–297; George Katona, Burkhard Strümpel, and Ernest Zahn, *Aspirations and Affluence: Comparative Studies in the United States and Western Europe* (New York: McGraw-Hill Book Company, 1971), 69.
50. Kaelble, *Kalter Krieg und Wohlfahrtsstaat*, 119–147; Hannerz, *Cultural Complexity*, 266 (tomorrow's center); Christophe Guilluy, *Twilight of the Elites: Prosperity, the Periphery,*

and the Future of France (New Haven, CT: Yale University Press, 2019), 76 (myth); Hannes Siegrist, "From Divergence to Convergence: The Divided German Middle Class, 1945 to 2000," in *Social Contracts Under Stress: The Middle Classes of America, Europe, and Japan at the Turn of the Century*, ed. Olivier Zunz, Leonard Schoppa, and Nobuhiro Hiwatari (New York: Russell Sage Foundation, 2002), 28 (marginalized); Rudy Koshar, *German Travel Cultures* (Oxford: Berg, 2000), 170 (gaze).

51. Anne Lammers, "Daten für das 'Europa der Sechs': Sozialstatistiken in den Europäischen Gemeinschaften der 1950er- und 160er-Jahre," *Themenportal Europäische Geschichte* (2013), http://www.europa.clio-online.de/essay/id/fdae-1627; Anne Lammers, "Die Erfassung des Lebensniveaus in den Europäischen Gemeinschaften (1956/57 und 1963/64)," *Themenportal Europäische Geschichte* (2013), http://www.europa.clio-online.de/2013/Article=666; Kaelble, *Kalter Krieg und Wohlfahrtsstaat*, 46–49, 81–86, 90–95; Michel Hubert, "Démographie, femmes et famille entre spécificité et similitudes," in *Wandel und Integration: Deutsch-französische Annäherungen der fünfziger Jahre/Mutations et intégration—Les rapprochements franco-allemands dans les années cinquante*, ed. Hélène Miard-Delacroix and Rainer Hudemann (Munich: R. Oldenbourg Verlag, 2005), 370–371 (golden age); Colin Bell, *Middle Class Families: Social and Geographical Mobility* (London: Routledge & Kegan Paul, 1968), 23–24 (leads).

52. Sabine Haustein, *Vom Mangel zum Massenkonsum: Deutschland, Frankreich und Grossbritannien im Vergleich 1945–1970* (Frankfurt: Campus Verlag, 2007), 57, table 6; Hartmut Kaelble, "Auf dem Weg zur europäischen Konsumgesellschaft: Charakteristika in Frankreich und Deutschland im Vergleich," in Miard-Delacroix and Hudemann, *Wandel und Integration*, 197; Michael Wildt, "Konsumbürger: Das Politische als Optionsfreiheit und Distinktion," in Hettling and Ulrich, *Bürgertum nach 1945*, 288 (standard of living); Siegrist, "From Divergence to Convergence," 21 (leveled), 35 (intelligentsia); Siegfried, "Prosperität und Krisenangst," 67 (car ownership); Uta Gerhardt, *Denken der Demokratie: Die Soziologie im atlantischen Transfer des Besatzungsregimes* (Stuttgart: Franz Steiner Verlag, 2007), 289 (three-quarters); Gregor M. Rinn, "Das Automobil als nationales Identifikationssymbol: Zur politischen Bedeutungsprägung des Kraftfahrzeugs in Modernitätskonzeptionen des 'Dritten Reichs' und der Bundesrepublik" (PhD diss., Humboldt-Universität zum Berlin, 2008), 113–117 (false start); Bernhard Rieger, *The People's Car: A Global History of the Volkswagen Beetle* (Cambridge, MA: Harvard University Press, 2013), 163 (family vehicle); Karl Ditt, *Zweite Industrialisierung und Konsum: Energieversorgung, Haushaltstechnik und Massenkultur am Beispiel nordenglischer und westfälischer Städte 1880–1939* (Paderborn: Ferdinand Schöningh, 2011), 767 (1970s).

53. Geir Lundestad, *"Empire" by Integration: The United States and European Integration, 1945–1997* (Oxford: Oxford University Press, 1998), 157 (quoting Michael Hogan), 164 (Old World). For an earlier overview of the Americanization issue related to mobility, see Mom, *Atlantic Automobilism*, 12–13.

54. Jan L. Logemann, *Trams or Tailfins? Public and Private Prosperity in Postwar West Germany and the United States* (Chicago: University of Chicago Press, 2012), 2 (major differences), 3 (malls), 4 (Westernization), 7 (consumers, 1945–1973), 9 (*Genussmittel*, patterns), 76 (two-car), 80 (Kramper), 104 (working-class), 222 (purchasing-power, broke down), 224 (division, *Fussgängerzonen*), 226 (hegemonic); Dant and Martin, "By Car"; Rinn, "Das Automobil," 163 (engineers); Manuel Schramm, "Nationale Unterschiede im westeuropäischen Massenkonsum: Grossbritannien, Frankreich, Deutschland und Italien 1950–1970," in *Vergleich und Transfer in der Konsumgeschichte*, ed. Manuel Schramm (Leipzig: Leipziger Universitätsverlag, 2009), 73; Koshar, *German Travel Cultures*, 167;

for an effort to describe the evolution of a "European car," see Henry Lowe Brownback, "Comment la Voiture Européenne a évolué," *Journal de la S.I.A.* 32, no. 3 (1958); for a later English version, see Henry Lowe Brownback, "Why Is the American Car Built as It Is Built?" *FISITA Proceedings* (1960); on the differences between European and American car technology (including the radial tire controversy) in general, see Gijs Mom, *The Evolution of Automotive Technology: A Handbook* (Warrendale: SAE International, 2014); see also Paul Erker, "The Long Shadow of Americanization: The German Rubber Industry and the Radial Tyre Revolution," in *Americanization and Its Limits: Reworking US Technology and Management in Post-war Europe and Japan*, ed. Jonathan Zeitlin and Gary Herrigel (Oxford: Oxford University Press, 2000), esp. sec. 10.4 ("The Radial Revolution: The Decline of 'Americanized' Tyre Technology in the 1970s").

55. Hartmut Berg, "Motorcars: Between Growth and Protectionism," in *The Structure of European Industry*, ed. H. W. de Jong (Dordrecht: Kluwer, 1993); Flink, *Automobile Age*, 297 (PSA, etc.); Wildt, "Konsumbürger," 267 (economic miracle); Rinn, "Das Automobil," 181, 194.

56. Rinn, "Das Automobil," 157 (Geneva); Logemann, *Trams or Tailfins?* 2 (fascination).

57. Packer, *Mobility without Mayhem*, 124 (parallel); Benedikt Meyer, "Auf Schlingerkurs durch das 20. Jahrhundert," *Wege und Geschichte* 2 (2012): 29, fig. 1 (differences); Max Roland Jaisli, *Entwicklung, Stand und Auswirkungen der Motorisierung des individuellen Personenverkehrs in der Schweiz* (Aarau: Keller, 1958), 101 (Switzerland); Harrison, *Seeking a Role*, 137 (Britain).

58. Thomas Südbeck, *Motorisierung, Verkehrsentwicklung und Verkehrspolitik in der Bundesrepublik Deutschland der 1950er Jahre: Umrisse der allgemeinen Entwicklung und zwei Beispiele: Hamburg und das Emsland* (Stuttgart: Franz Steiner Verlag, 1994), 37, 40, 49; Elisabeth Tworek-Müller, *Kleinbürgertum und Literatur: Zum Bild des Kleinbürgers im bayerischen Roman der Weimarer Republik* (Munich: tuduv-Verlagsgesellschaft, 1985), 314 (de-proletarianize); Gijs Mom and Ruud Filarski, *Van transport naar mobiliteit: De mobiliteitsexplosie (1895–2005)* (Zutphen: Walburg Pers, 2008), 270–271 (Netherlands); Morris Janowitz, "Soziale Schichtung und Mobilität in Westdeutschland," Kölner Zeitschrift für Soziologie und Sozialpsychologie 10, no. 1 (1958); the title quote is from Karl Martin Bolte, "Vom Umfang der Mobilität in unserer Gesellschaft," following directly on Janowitz's article. Dagmar Hilpert, *Wohlfahrtsstaat der Mittelschichten? Sozialpolitik und gesellschaftlicher Wandel in der Bundesrepublik Deutschland (1949–1975)* (Göttingen: Vandenhoeck & Ruprecht, 2012), 320 (*Facharbeiter*). I thank Stefan Krebs (Luxemburg) for explaining the German terminology to me (email, 8 May 2018).

59. Alan A. Jackson, *The Middle Classes 1900–1950* (Nairn: David St. John Thomas Publisher, 1991), 332 (question, ease); Rinn, "Das Automobil," 143.

60. Joachim Scheiner, "80 Jahre Motorisierung in Stadt und Land: Fallstudie Nordrhein-Westfalen," *Internationales Verkehrswesen* 62, no. 12 (2010): 18; Gijs Mom, "Mobility for Pleasure: A Look at the Underside of Dutch Diffusion Curves (1920–1940)," *TST Revista de Historia* 12 (2007) (Netherlands and US); Federico Paolini, "A Country on Four Wheels: The Car and Society in Italy (1900–1974)," *TST Revista de Historia* 17 (2009): 120; Janine Morice, *La demande d'automobiles en France: Théorie—Histoire—Répartition géographique—Prévisions* (Paris: Librairie Armand Colin, 1957), 196.

61. Schramm, "Nationale Unterschiede," 72 (European market); Peter Rocholl, *Vergleichende Analyse der Entwicklung des Personenkraftverkehrs im westeuropäischen Wirtschaftsraum* (Düsseldorf: Droste Verlag, 1962), 129, graph 12 (Netherlands).

62. [A. Zewuster], *Een miljoen auto's in 1964* (Amsterdam: De Arbeiderspers, 1963), 23, 28; Pieter Schrijnen, "Autobezit en autogebruik" (Universiteit van Amsterdam, January

1986), 35. For Swiss evidence of this paradigmatic shift in household expenditures, see Jaisli, *Entwicklung, Stand und Auswirkungen der Motorisierung*, 86.
63. *How American Buying Habits Change* (Washington, DC: US Department of Labor, [1959?]), 31, 46–47, table 6, 50–51, table 8, 54–55, table 9; Theodore Caplow, Howard M. Bahr, John Modell, and Bruce A. Chadwick, eds., *Recent Social Trends in the United States 1960–1990* (Montreal: McGill-Queen's University Press, 1991), 399, table 2, gives 13–14 percent for the entire period 1950–1970. UK households spent 14 percent on transport in 2002. Department for Transport, *Focus on Personal Travel: 2005 Edition—Including the Report of the National Travel Survey 2002/2003* (Norwich: Her Majesty's Stationery Office, 2005), 89.
64. Joffre Dumazedier and Maurice Imbert (with Jean Duminy and Claire Guinchat), *Espace et loisir dans la société française d'hier et de demain* (Paris: Centre de recherche d'urbanisme, 1967), 25–27 (France), 54 (half); Michael Wildt, *Am Beginn der "Konsumgesellschaft": Mangelerfahrung, Lebenshaltung, Wohlstandshoffnung in Westdeutschland in den fünfziger Jahren* (Hamburg: 1995), 71–74 (jump: 74); Peter Engelhard, "Making Room for Beetle: Volkswagen's Impact on the German Motor Industry," *Automotive History Review* 54 (2012): 16, fig. 1 (twist in 1953); Wildt, "Konsumbürger," 272 (worker families); Christopher Kopper, "Der Durchbruch des PKW zum Massenkonsumgut 1950–1964," *Jahrbuch für Wirtschaftsgeschichte* 51, no. 1 (2010): 26–27 (credit); *How American Buying Habits Change*, 190 (US debt); Josef Mooser, *Arbeiterleben in Deutschland 1900–1970: Klassenlagen, Kultur und Politik* (Frankfurt: Suhrkamp Verlag, 1984), 81, table 11 (worker families' budget); Josef W. Schödermeier, *Die Entwicklung und Zusammensetzung des Personenkraftwagenbestandes in Westeuropa (Eine retrospektive Analyse)* (PhD diss., Universität Köln, 1961), 8–9 (5 and 8 percent).
65. Paolini, "Country on Four Wheels," 118, 122, table 7; Silvia Cassamagnaghi, "Vespa Piaggio: First Mass Motorization and Discovery of Leisure in Post-war Italy," paper presented at the conference "Inventing Europe," European Science Foundation workshop, Amsterdam (15–17 January 2009), 11–12 (communism); Adam Arvidsson, "From Counterculture to Consumer Culture: Vespa and the Italian Youth Market, 1958–78," *Journal of Consumer Culture* 1, no. 1 (2001): 49–50 (small car); Silvia Cassamagnaghi, "Dalla guerra alla Lambretta: L'Innocenti e l'invenzione di un prodotto di successo," *Contemporanea* 14, no. 4 (2011): 679 (three times); Gijs Mom, "Frozen History: Limitations and Possibilities of Quantitative Diffusion Studies," in *Manufacturing Technology, Manufacturing Consumers: The Making of Dutch Consumer Society*, ed. Ruth Oldenziel and Adri de la Bruhèze (Amsterdam: aksant, 2008) (petri dish); Federico Paolini, "'Torpedo blu' vs. 'Topolino amaranto': Appunti per una storia culturale dell' automobile in Italia," *Richerche Storiche*, nos. 2–3 (2004): 1 (20.7 percent).
66. Schödermeier, *Die Entwicklung und Zusammensetzung des Personenkraftwagenbestandes in Westeuropa*, 44 (the author explains this by pointing at the low car taxes in Greece and Austria and at "mentality; climate conditions" for the Romanic countries); Axel Schildt and Detlef Siegfried, "Introduction: Youth, Consumption, and Politics in the Age of Radical Change," in Schildt and Siegfried, *Between Marx and Coca-Cola*, 13 (motorization figures).
67. Reader's Digest Association, *Products and People: The Reader's Digest European Surveys* (London: Reader's Digest Association, 1963), tables 1 and 34; more details can be found in the German version: *Sieben-Länder-Untersuchung: Eine vergleichbare Marktuntersuchung in Belgien, Frankreich, Grossbritannien, Holland, Italien, Luxemburg und der Bundesrepublik Deutschland* (Düsseldorf: Verlag Das Beste, [1963]); see also U. W. Kitzinger, *The New Europeans: A Commentary on Products and People, a Marketing*

Survey of the European Common Market and Britain, 1963 (London: Reader's Digest, 1963); Wildt, "Konsumbürger," 271 (Erhard; I left the phrase *im Zweifelsfall* [in case of doubt] out of the quote, as it makes no sense in our context); Rinn, "Das Automobil," 119–120 (Shell), 120 (*Politikum*), 126 (pressure), 142 (free world).

68. Marwick, *Sixties*, 361 (Bonagente), 364 (luxury); Feliks Gross, *Il Paese: Values and Social Change in an Italian Village* (New York: New York University Press / University of Rome, Istituto di Statistica e Ricerca Sociale "C. Gini," 1973), 281 (emphasis), 284 (kitchen), 286 (young), 292 (road); David Inglis, "Auto Couture: Thinking the Car in Post-war France," in *Automobilities*, ed. Mike Featherstone, Nigel Thrift, and John Urry (London: Sage, 2005), 201 (best-sold cars in France); André Gauron, *Histoire économique et sociale de la Cinquième République, tome I : Le Temps des modernistes* (Paris: La Découverte / Maspéro, 1983), 19 (industrialized), 33 (symbolized); Rinn, "Das Automobil," 165–179 (Volkswagen).

69. Paul E. Willis, *Profane Culture* (London: Routledge & Kegan Paul, 1978), 11 (1969), 13 (toughness), 16 (*control*), 17 (no transcendence), 27 (posing), 32 (denial), 35 (Berry), 36 (values), 37 (danger), 55 (goggles), 56 (handlebars), 62 (out of date), 71 (aggression), 72 (connection, Fred), 73 (Joe), 76 (structure, "Jailhouse Rock"), 77 (timelessness), 86 (transcendence), 108 (Zeppelin, etc.; detachment), 154 (*Sergeant Pepper*), 167 (progressive, ignore). For prewar flirting with death, see, e.g., Mom, *Atlantic Automobilism*, 148.

70. Marwick, *Sixties*, 81; H. F. Moorhouse, "American Automobiles and Workers' Dreams," *Sociological Review* 31, no. 3 (1983): 419 (billion); Rostow, *Stages of Economic Growth*, 79; John Modell, *Into One's Own: From Youth to Adulthood in the United States 1920–1975* (Berkeley: University of California Press, 1989), 220 (commitment); Michael Mann, *The Sources of Social Power, vol. 4: Globalizations, 1945–2011* (Cambridge: Cambridge University Press, 2013), 57–58; Greg Castillo, *Cold War on the Home Front: The Soft Power of Midcentury Design* (Minneapolis: University of Minnesota Press, 2010), vii (Operation Abundance); Margaret Weir, "The American Middle Class and the Politics of Education," in Zunz et al., *Social Contracts Under Stress*, 182 (college students).

71. Andrew Hurley, *Diners, Bowling Alleys and Trailer Parks: Chasing the American Dream in the Postwar Consumer Culture* (New York: Basic Books, 2001), 196 (slum, trash), 197 (3 percent, majority), 202 (transient), 204 (defense), 206 (travel trailers), 211 (veterans), 216 (half), 221 (twelve thousand), 259 (couples); for a description of "1950s New Jersey trailer park life," see Allan Bérubé with Florence Bérubé, "Sunset Trailer Park," in *White Trash: Race and Class in America*, ed. Matt Wray and Annalee Newitz (New York: Routledge, 1997), 15–39; Clair Brown, *American Standards of Living 1918–1988* (Oxford: Blackwell, 1994): 14; Christopher W. Wells, *Car Country: An Environmental History* (Seattle: University of Washington Press, 2012), 280.

72. Isabel Heinemann, "Introduction: Inventing the 'Modern American Family': Family Values and Social Change in 20th Century United States," in *Inventing the Modern American Family: Family Values and Social Change in 20th Century United States*, ed. Isabel Heinemann (Frankfurt: Campus Verlag, 2012), 27; Ruth Oldenziel, "Exporting the American Cold War Kitchen: Challenging Americanization, Technological Transfer, and Domestication," in *Cold War Kitchen: Americanization, Technology, and European Users*, ed. Ruth Oldenziel and Karin Zachmann (Cambridge, MA: MIT Press, 2009), 321; Shelley Nickles, "More Is Better: Mass Consumption, Gender, and Class Identity in Postwar America," *American Quarterly* 54, no. 4 (2002): 614n20 (ideology); on the kitchen debate, see also Castillo, *Cold War on the Home Front*" ix–xi; William Henry Peters, "Variation in Consumer Buying Behavior: An Analytical Study of Automobile

Purchases" (PhD diss., University of Michigan, 1968), 36, table 4 (1957), 43, table 12 (1966/1967), 69, table 26 (converge).
73. Marshall McLuhan, *Understanding Media: The Extensions of Man* (London: Routledge, 2005), chap. 22 ("Motorcar: The Mechanical Bride"); Bernd Flessner, "'In jeder Hinsicht betriebssicherer': In der Science-Fiction stand der Umstieg auf den Elektromotor bereits vor 100 Jahren fest," in *Zeiten der Elektromobilität: Beiträge zur Geschichte des elektrischen Automobils—Beiträge der Tagung des VDE-Ausschusses "Geschichte der Elektrotechnik" in Kooperation mit dem VDE Rhein-Ruhr e.V. vom 7. und 8. Oktober 2010 in Dortmund*, ed. Theo Horstmann and Peter Döring (Berlin: VDE Verlag, 2018), 185–186.
74. Mann, *Sources of Social Power*, vol. 4, 63; Kaelble, *Kalter Krieg und Wohlfahrtsstaat*, 113–115; Cowie, *Stayin' Alive*, 245; Christian Wolmar, *Engines of War: How Wars Were Won and Lost on the Railways* (London: Atlantic Books, 2012), 266–272 (Korea and Vietnam); Blake McKelvey, *The Emergence of Metropolitan America, 1915–1966* (New Brunswick, NJ: Rutgers University Press, 1968), 227 (mass-transit aid); Eric Hobsbawm, *The Age of Extremes: The Short Twentieth Century 1914–1991* (London: abacus, 2013), 228.
75. The car *share* curve is flat, but the overall mobility curve increases steeply, indicating car performance (in passenger miles) increases as well.
76. Rostow, *Stages of Economic Growth*; Brown, *American Standards of Living*, 225; for the "Snell controversy," see, e.g., Robert C. Post, *Urban Mass Transit: The Life Story of a Technology* (Westport, CT: Greenwood Press, 2007).
77. Gert Schmidt, "Automobilkultur in der Bundesrepublik Deutschland: 50er und 60er Jahre" (unpublished manuscript, Munich, January 2010), 8–9. I thank Gert Schmidt for making his text available to me.
78. Schildt, "Amerikanische Einflüsse," 437–439 (five characteristics); Axel Schildt, "Konsum und Freizeit im 'Wirtschaftswunderland': Mit Streiflichtern auf den Alltag von Stadt und Landkreis Uelzen in den 50er Jahren," in *Von der Währungsreform zum Wirtschaftswunder: Wiederaufbau in Niedersachsen*, ed. Bernd Weisbrod (Hannover: Verlag Hahnsche Buchhandlung, 1998), 208–212; Thomas Mergel, "Transnationale Mobilität, Integration und Herkunftsbewusstsein: Migration und europäisches Selbstverständnis im 19. und 20. Jahrhundert," in *Selbstverständnis und Gesellschaft der Europäer: Aspekte der sozialen und kulturellen Europäisierung im späten 19. und 20. Jahrhundert*, ed. Hartmut Kaelble and Martin Kirsch (Frankfurt: Peter Lang, 2008), 275 (fifty to sixty million); Alexander Gall, "*Gute Strassen bis ins kleinste Dorf!' Verkehrspolitik in Bayern zwischen Wiederaufbau und Ölkrise* (Frankfurt: Campus Verlag, 2005), 229 (individual motorization), chap. 6 (for a unique analysis of postwar Bavarian commuting); for a study of commuting in Hamburg, see Südbeck, *Motorisierung*, 165ff.
79. Gall, *Gute Strassen*, 257 (new European); Südbeck, *Motorisierung*, 37 (magic), 40 (car fleet), 49 (leisure traffic); 68 (commuting as impulse); for an excellent overview of early postwar European car diffusion, see Rocholl, *Vergleichende*; Paolini, "Country on Four Wheels," 124–125; Michael John Law, *The Experience of Suburban Mobility: How Private Transport Changed Interwar London* (Manchester: Manchester University Press, 2014), 13 (1939). Law supported his claim by a reference to research by Colin Pooley (quoted earlier in this chapter) and his own analysis of some prewar road censuses of traffic to and from London. Ibid., 198–200.
80. Peter Hall, *Great Planning Disasters* (Berkeley: University of California Press, 1980), 65 (1964); Sandra Rosenbloom, "Why Working Families Need a Car," in *The Car and the City: The Automobile, the Built Environment, and Daily Urban Life*, ed. Martin Wachs and Margaret Crawford (Ann Arbor: University of Michigan Press, 1992), 45, 47.

81. Schildt, "Konsum und Freizeit," 207 (growth rate); Mary McShane, Masaki Koshi, and Olof Lundin, "Public Policy toward the Automobile: A Comparative Look at Japan and Sweden," *Transportation Research Part A* 18, no. 2 (1984): 97 (extravagance), 99 (parking), 100 (very small), 101 (break-neck); Daniel Dhakidae, "Lifestyles and Political Behavior of the Indonesian Middle Classes," in *Exploration of the Middle Classes in Southeast Asia*, ed. Hsin-Huang Michael Hsiao (Taipei: Southeast Asian Studies, Academia Sinica, 2001), 481.
82. Rocholl, *Vergleichende Analyse*, 128, graph 10 (overtaken); Kaelble, *Kalter Krieg und Wohlfahrtsstaat*, 81 (*Trente Glorieuses*); Gauron, *Histoire économique et sociale de la Cinquième République* chap. 1 ("Le déclin des classes possédantes" [The decline of the propertied classes]); Francis Sejersted, *The Age of Social Democracy: Norway and Sweden in the Twentieth Century* (Princeton, NJ: Princeton University Press, 2011), 317. I thank Luísa Sousa and Hanna Wolf for collecting and ordering the data in fig. 2.3.
83. Gall, *Gute Strassen*, 228 (Germany); Dumazedier and Imbert, *Espace et loisir*, 23 (health), 57 (50 percent), 177 (US); Philip L. Pearce, "Route Maps: A Study of Travellers' Perceptions of a Section of Countryside," *Journal of Environmental Psychology* 1, no. 2 (1981): 141 (outdoor); Orvar Löfgren, *On Holiday: A History of Vacationing* (Berkeley: University of California Press, 1999), 69; McShane et al., "Public Policy toward the Automobile," 104.
84. I used the Dutch translation: Göran Rosenberg, *Een kort openonthoud: Op de weg van Auschwitz*, trans. Jasper Popma (Amsterdam: Atlas Contact, 2014), 250–251; Mom and Filarski, *Van transport naar mobiliteit*, 270–271 (Netherlands); Owen D. Gutfreund, *Twentieth-Century Sprawl: Highways and the Reshaping of the American Landscape* (Oxford: Oxford University Press, 2004), 92 (Denver); Wolf Dieter Lützen, "Radfahren, Motorsport, Autobesitz: Motorisierung zwischen Gebrauchswerten und Statuserwerb," in *Die Arbeiter: Lebensformen, Alltag und Kultur von der Frühindustrialisierung bis zum "Wirtschaftswunder,"* ed Wolfgang Ruppert (Munich: Verlag C. H. Beck, 1986), 376.
85. Rosenbloom, "Why Working Families Need a Car," 40; Tim Retzloff, "Cars and Bars: Assembling Gay Men in Postwar Flint, Michigan," in *Creating a Place for Ourselves: Lesbian, Gay, and Bisexual Community Histories*, ed. Brett Beemyn (New York: Routledge, 1997), 230 (80 percent).
86. Caplow et al., *Recent Social Trends*, 457 (1929–1979); Claude S. Fischer, "Ever-More Rooted Americans," *City & Community* 1, no. 2 (2002): 177 (the quoted scholar is Peter Berger, *Invitation to Sociology*, 1963); Brown, *American Standards of Living*, 225.
87. John P. Robinson and Philip E. Converse, "Social Change Reflected in the Use of Time," in *The Human Meaning of Social Change*, ed. Angus Campbell and Philip E. Converse (New York: Russell Sage Foundation, 1972), 77 (79: whereas sleeping, eating, reading, moviegoing, sports playing, radio listening, "motoring," playing cards, and dancing now required less time, a trend connected to the emergence of television, Americans spent more time traveling, taking part in home- and family-related activities, and "perhaps working"); Becky M. Nicolaides, *My Blue Heaven: Life and Politics in the Working-Class Suburbs of Los Angeles, 1920–1965* (Chicago: University of Chicago Press, 2002), 242; George H. Gallup, *The Gallup Poll: Public Opinion 1935–1971, vol. 2—1949–1958* (New York: Random House, 1972), 1224; Löfgren, *On Holiday*, 64.
88. Françoise Monge, "Les vacances familiales," *après-demain* 137 (October 1971): 36 (margin); Löfgren, *On Holiday*, 172 (paychecks); Caplow et al., *Recent Social Trends*, 454 (one-tenth); Cord Pagenstecher, *Der bundesdeutsche Tourismus: Ansätze zu einer Visual History: Urlaubsprospekte, Reiseführer, Fotoalben 1950–1990* (Hamburg: Verlag Dr. Kovač, 2003), 136–139; Schmidt, "Automobilkultur," 9 (bus); Christopher M. Kopper,

"The Breakthrough of the Package Tour in Germany after 1945," *Journal of Tourism History* 1, no. 1 (2009): 77 (Germans later).

89. Herbert Jost, "Selbst-Verwirklichung und Seelensuche: Zur Bedeutung des Reiseberichts im Zeitalter des Massentourismus," in *Der Reisebericht: Die Entwicklung einer Gattung in der deutschen Literatur*, ed. Peter J. Brenner (Frankfurt: Suhrkamp Verlag, 1989), 499; Kopper, "Breakthrough of the Package Tour," 79 (Spain); Ray Hudson and Jim Lewis, "Introduction: Recent Economic, Social and Political Changes in Southern Europe," in *Uneven Development in Southern Europe: Studies of Accumulation, Class, Migration and the State*, ed. Ray Hudson and Jim Lewis (London: Methuen, 1985), 48, table 1.21 (forty million).

90. Marc Dierikx, "Sailing on a Cloud: The Development of Transatlantic Air Tourism" (unpublished manuscript); Marc Dierikx, "In Pursuit of the American Dream: The Spread of the Televised American Image and the Rise of European Tourism to the United States, 1945–1980," in Bosscher et al., *American Culture*, 119; Christopher Endy, *Cold War Holidays: American Tourism in France* (Chapel Hill: University of North Carolina Press, 2004), 33 (travel development), 105 (escape), 111 (worshipping), 125–131 (tourist class, volume, budget), 182 (nonessential), 186 (Kennedy).

91. Thomas Kaiserfeld, "From Sightseeing to Sunbathing: Changing Traditions in Swedish Package Tours: From Edification by Bus to Relaxation by Airplane in the 1950s and 1960s," *Journal of Tourism History* 2, no. 3 (2010): 150–153 (charter flights); Peter Lyth, "'Gimmy a Ticket on an Aeroplane … ' The Jet Engine and the Revolution in Leisure Air Travel, 1960–1975," in *Development of a Tourist Industry in the 19th and 20th Centuries: International Perspectives*, ed. Laurent Tissot (Neuchâtel: Editions Alphil, 2003), 115; Barrie Newman, "Holidays and Social Class," in *Leisure and Society in Britain*, ed. Michael Smith, Stanley Parker, and Cyril Smith (London: Allen Lane, 1973), 230; Cord Pagenstecher, "The Construction of the Tourist Gaze: How Industrial Was Post-war German Tourism?" in Tissot, *Development of a Tourist Industry*, 375, table 1 (Germany); Jean Fourastié (with Françoise Fourastié), *Des loisirs: pour quoi faire?* (Tournai: Casterman, 1970), 8 (France); Georges Cazes, "Les mobilités touristiques internationales," in *La planète "nomade": Les mobilités géographiques d'aujourd'hui*, ed. Rémy Knafou (Paris: Belin, 1998), 84–85, tables 1 and 2, 87 (156 million), table 3, 61 (dwindling); Erik Cohen, "The Sociology of Tourism: Approaches, Issues, and Findings," *Annual Review of Sociology* 10 (1984): 377 (25 and 75 million); for the statistical shakiness of France being the most-visited country (instead of the US and Italy as second and third), see Bertram M. Gordon, "The Evolving Popularity of Tourist Sites in France: What Can Be Learned from French Statistical Publications?" paper presented at the International Commission for the History of Travel and Tourism Congrès International des Sciences Historiques, Amsterdam (August 2010), 7; Americans abroad: Somerset R. Waters, "The American Tourist," *Annals of the American Academy of Political and Social Science* 368 (1966): 110, 114; Endy, *Cold War Holidays*, 131 (black).

92. Walther L. Bernecker, "Das spanische Wirtschaftswunder: Ökonomisches Wachstum und sozialer Wandel in der Franco-Ära," in Kaelble, *Der Boom 1948–1973*, 211, 213–214; Paolini, "Country on Four Wheels," 119, table 5 (car density); Joshua Hotaka Roth, "Is Female to Male as Lightweight Cars Are to Sports Cars? Gender Metaphors and Cognitive Schemas in Recessionary Japan," in *Vehicles: Cars, Canoes, and Other Metaphors of Moral Imagination*, ed. David Lipset and Richard Handler (New York: Berghahn Books, 2014), 91 (*mai-ka*).

93. Mergel, "Transnationale Mobilität," 283; Sandro Rinauro, "L'émigration illégale des Italiens en France et en Suisse après la Deuxième Guerre mondiale," *Journal of modern European history* 12, no. 1 (2014): 85 (Switzerland), 92 (illegal), 102 (referendum).
94. Paulo Guimarães, "Strassen des Friedens nach Europa: Migration und der Aufbau eines Freibusnetzes im Südwesten Europas (1960–2000)," *Zeitschrift für Weltgeschichte* 12, no. 2 (2011): 177 (democracy), 179 (Europa-Bus), 181 (Conference), 182 (turn to Europe), 183 (fifty thousand), 184 (taxi), 185 (illegal), 195 (prohibited, 1,830), 196 (avoiding), 198 (double tree), 208n45 (1.4 million); Victor Pereira, "Les réseaux de l'émigration clandestine portugaise vers la France entre 1957 et 1974," *Journal of Modern European History* 12 (2014): 108 (Grey Hound); Hudson and Lewis, "Introduction," 17 (young men).
95. Theodore Caplow, Howard M. Bahr, Bruce A. Chadwick, Reuben Hill, and Margaret Holmes Williamson, *Middletown Families: Fifty Years of Change and Continuity* (Minneapolis: University of Minnesota Press, 1982), chap. 13 ("The Myth of the Declining Family"); Hilpert, *Wohlfahrtsstaat der Mittelschichten?* 177; "CFP: Die Evidenz der Familie," H-SOZ-U-KULT@H-NET.MSU.EDU, 16 July 2012 (ethnocentric); Kristin Ross, *Fast Cars. Clean Bodies: Decolonization and the Reordering of French Culture* (Cambridge, MA: MIT Press, 1995), 2 (electronics), 4 (Catholic), 11 (unit), 135 (*ménages*), 138 (bourgeoisie).
96. Ross, *Fast Cars*, 127 (Lenin and modernization), 149 (homogenous), 150 (two-thirds), 151 (*cadres*), 152 (unskilled), 171 (*cadre*), 175 (leisure).
97. Stephanie Coontz, *The Way We Never Were: American Families and the Nostalgia Trap* (New York: Basic Books, 2000), 24–25; Lyn Elizabeth Elliot, "Liberating Domesticity: The American Road Narrative in Film and Fiction" (PhD diss., University of Iowa, 2000), 66 (refuge), 78 (Levitt), 79 (Jackson), 80 (changed homes). I thank Peter Norton (University of Virginia) for providing me with this dissertation, as well as the dissertations by Katherine Mills and Jill Talbot, also cited in this chapter.
98. Harrison, *Seeking a Role*, 293–299 (UK); Kaelble, *Kalter Krieg und Wohlfahrtsstaat*, 150–153 (marriage boom, parallel developments, welfare); Mann, *Sources of Social Power, vol. 4*, 59–61 (US).
99. Nicolaides, *My Blue Heaven*, 240 (weapon); Marwick, *Sixties*, 36 (not-so-young), 44 (wives), 45 (peak), 46 (GM), 80–81 (Rat Race); for a similar conclusion regarding the "young married couples with children" as the drivers of baby boom consumption, see Modell, *Into One's Own*, 221; Susan Nixon, "Mrs. Housewife and the Ad Men: Advertising, Market Research, and Mass Consumption in Postwar Britain, " in *The Rise of Marketing and Market Research*, ed. Hartmut Berghoff, Philip Scranton, and Uwe Spiekermann (New York: Palgrave Macmillan, 2012), 193–194 (housewife); Pagenstecher, *Der bundesdeutsche Tourismus*, 60.
100. Richard Hoggart, "Changes in Working-Class Life," in *Leisure and Society in Britain*, ed. Michael Smith, Stanley Parker, and Cyril Smith (London: Allen Lane, 1973), 32–34; Mom and Filarski, *Van transport naar mobiliteit*, 279 (Netherlands); Marwick, *Sixties*, 78.
101. *The Pilot National Recreation Survey: Report No. 1* (London / Keele: British Travel Association / University of Keele, July 1967), 69; motherhood and forging: Patricia Mellencamp, ed., *Logics of Television: Essays in Cultural Criticism* (Bloomington / Indianapolis: Indiana University Press / BFI Publishing, 1990), 4–5, 11; Eamonn Carrabine and Brian Longhurst, "Consuming the Car: Anticipation, Use and Meaning in Contemporary Youth Culture," *Sociological Review* 50, no. 2 (2002): 194 (the explanatory quote is a paraphrase of Williams); Cotten Seiler, "Anxiety and Automobility: Cold War Individualism and the Interstate Highway System" (PhD diss., University of

Kansas, 2002), 134; see also Cotten Seiler, *Republic of Drivers: A Cultural History of Automobility in America* (Chicago: University of Chicago Press, 2008); Packer, *Mobility without Mayhem*; Wildt, "Konsumbürger," 280–281.

102. Lynn Spigel, "Television in the Family Circle: The Popular Reception of a New Medium," in Mellencamp, *Logics of Television*, 74 (half), 79 (watch), 80 (streets), 82–83 (family friend), 87 (feminizing, momism); Mary Ann Doane, "Information, Crisis, Catastrophe," in Mellencamp, *Logics of Television*, 223–224 (resist analysis); Lynne Joyrich, "Critical and Textual Hypermasculinity," in Mellencamp, *Logics of Television*, 156 (cyborg), 161 (violent), 162 (distance), 166 (mimicking, *Miami Vice*); Lynn Spigel, "Installing the Television Set: Popular Discourses on Television and Domestic Space, 1948–1955," *Camera Obscura* 6, no. 1 (1988): 14 (cohesion).

103. Margaret Morse, "An Ontology of Everyday Distraction: The Freeway, the Mall, and Television," in Mellencamp, *Logics of Television*, 193 (*fiction, distraction*), 196 (*derealized*; emphasis added), 197 (Kowinski, coast to coast), 198 (idyll, crowded street), 200 (disc); David Brodsly, *L.A. Freeway: An Appreciative Essay* (Berkeley: University of California Press, 1983), 218n23 (Gruen); Spigel, "Installing the Television Set," 22–23 (*hyperrealism*), 32 (presence). For the affinity between car driving and writing, see Mom, *Atlantic Automobilism*, 648–650.

104. Morse, "Ontology of Everyday Distraction," 203 (the grasp quote is Barthes's, while the others are Morse's paraphrasings of Barthes's theory), 206 (mirror, simultaneously); Doane, "Information, Crisis, Catastrophe," 222 (present-ness); Mills, *Road Story*, 106 (Kesey); Barthes, "La nouvelle Citroën," 170 (classic), 171 (*petite-bourgeois*); Kenneth Hey, "Cars and Films in American Culture, 1929–1959," *Michigan Quarterly Review* 19, no. 4 (1980): 597 (*Bonanza*), 599 (hot rod).

105. Monge, "Les vacances familiales," 35 (French holiday); Ellen Furlough, "Making Mass Vacations: Tourism and Consumer Culture in France, 1930s to 1970s," *Comparative Studies in Society and History* 40, no. 2 (1998): 270 (Villages); Susan Sessions Rugh, *Are We There Yet? The Golden Age of American Family Vacations* (Lawrence: University Press of Kansas, 2008), 2 (decline), 31 (sixty million), 92 (Western), 93 (backseat), 98 (comforts). For a prewar description of the dude ranch, see John T. Faris, *Roaming American Playgrounds* (New York: Farrar & Rinehart, 1934), 273.

106. Mills, "Remapping the Road Story," 167–168 (*Star Trek*); Roland Marchand, "Visions of Classlessness, Quests for Dominion: American Popular Culture, 1945–1960," in *Reshaping America: Society and Institutions 1945–1960*, ed. Robert H. Bremner and Gary W. Reichard (Columbus: Ohio State University Press, 1982), 167 (California); Avner Offer, *The Challenge of Affluence: Self-Control and Well-Being in the United States and Britain since 1950* (Oxford: Oxford University Press, 2006), 193 (oligopoly), 194 (desire), 206 (*sensual*); David Gartman, "Three Ages of the Automobile: The Cultural Logics of the Car," *Theory, Culture & Society* 21, nos. 4–5 (2004): 185 (non-class); David Gartman, *Auto Opium: A Social History of American Automobile Design* (New York: Routledge, 1994), 156; Whyte, "Cadillac Phenomenon," 107 (ordinary).

107. See, e.g., Eric Larrabee, "Autos and Americans: The Great Love Affair—How Detroit Can Run a Heavy Industry on the Soft Winds of Whim and Romance," *Industrial Design* 2, no. 5 (1955); Peter Norton, "History as a Tool of Agenda Legitimation: US Urban Mobility Trajectories (Outline)," paper presented at the workshop "Large Metropolis Mobilities in Long-Term Perspective: For an Ecosystemic Approach of Sustainable Urban Mobilities," Paris (23–24 February 2017); see also Peter Norton, "Of Love Affairs and Other Stories," in *Incomplete Streets: Processes, Practices, and Possibilities*, ed. Stephen Zavestoski and Julian Agyeman (London: Routledge, 2015), 17–35; Marshall McLuhan,

The Mechanical Bride: Folklore of Industrial Man (Corte Madera, CA: Gingko Press, 2001), 82–84 ("Husband's Choice"), 98–101 ("The Mechanical Bride").
108. Offer, *Challenge of Affluence*, 197 (models, racing), 200–201 (Earl), 202 (upper-middle class), 207 (comfort), 208 (superficial), 209 (Reith), 211 (jukebox), 213 (younger), 214 (Falcon), 220 (minibus); Lorraine Eden and Maureen Appel Molot, "Made in America? The US Auto Industry, 1955–95," *International Executive* 38, no. 4 (1996): 503. I thank Piet Rademakers for bringing the car-like jukebox to my attention (email, 25 March 2016).
109. Nickles, "More Is Better," 582, 610n5, quoting Victoria de Grazia and Lizabeth Cohen, "Introduction: Class and Consumption," *International Labor and Working-Class History* 55 (1999); John H. Goldthorpe, David Lockwood, Frank Bechhofer, and Jennifer Platt, *The Affluent Worker in the Class Structure* (Cambridge: Cambridge University Press, 1969), 14 (*embourgeoisement*); Geoffrey Evans and James Tilly, *The New Politics of Class: The Political Exclusion of the British Working Class* (Oxford: Oxford University Press, 2017), 43. A similar conclusion on *die Kontinuität bürgerlicher Gruppen* (the continuity of the upper and lower middle classes) can be found in Regina Vogel, "Bürgertum nach 1945? Deutschland, Frankreich und Britannien im Vergleich," in Kaelble and Kirsch, *Selbstverständnis und Gesellschaft der Europäer*, 417.
110. Nickles, "More Is Better," 582 (social identity), 583 (moved up), 584 (eroding), 585 (upper-middle class), 586 (motivation research), 587 (uncovered, new social class, taste), 588 (color, wife decides), 589 (ladder), 591 (*Good Design*), 596 (role playing), 597 (majority), 598 (distinctive), 600 (largest share), 604 (middle-class working class), 609 (Packard), 610n3 (twelve million, 81 percent, *True Romance*), 618n54 (RCA); Kit Foster, "The Cars of 1969: A Rising Middle Class," *Collectible Automobile* 33, no. 4 (2016): 10 (intermediate), 11 (appealing, muscle cars), 13 (Fairlane, Comet), 15 (25.9 percent market share), 22t (8.8 million, V-8s); Goldthorpe et al., *Affluent Worker in the Class Structure*, 159 (powerful); Mark Crispin Miller, "Introduction," in *The Hidden Persuaders* by Vance Packard (Brocklyn, NY: IG Publishing, 2007), 15 (three million).
111. Theodor Adorno, *Minima Moralia* (1974) as quoted by Gartman, "Three Ages," 181 (superiority; "loss of luxury" is Gartman's paraphrase); for a defense of Adorno, see Gendron, "Theodore Adorno Meets the Cadillacs"; Nickles, "More Is Better," 584 (proletarianized); Felson, "Differentiation of Material Life Styles," 408–409: Felson observed an "omission of blacks, the aged, non-natives and their children" from the 1966 Detroit Area Study of household lifestyles.
112. Tim Cresswell, *On the Move; Mobility in the Modern Western World* (New York/London: Routledge, 2006); for a definition of middle class in terms of home ownership, see Clifford Edward Clark Jr., *The American Family Home, 1800–1960* (Chapel Hill: University of North Carolina Press, 1986), xiii; Arthur J. Vidich and Joseph Bensman, *Small Town in Mass Society: Class, Power and Religion in a Rural Community* (Princeton, NJ: Princeton University Press, 1968), 333 (revolution); Herbert J. Gans, *The Levittowners: Ways of Life and Politics in a New Suburban Community* (London: Allen Lane, 1967), 203 (association); Pamela Shurmer-Smith and Kevin Hannam, *Worlds of Desire, Realms of Power: A Cultural Geography* (London: Edward Arnold, 1994), 141 (construction, cocoon). Rugh, *Are We There Yet?* 20; Roger B. White, *Home on the Road: The Motor Home in America* (Washington: Smithsonian Institution Press, 2000), 95 (all-steel); Richard Ratay, *Don't Make Me Pull Over! An Informal History of the Family Road Trip* (New York: Scribner, 2018), 206 ("one in every five cars sold").
113. George Lucas, dir., *American Graffiti* (Universal City, CA: Universal Pictures, 1973); Peter N. Stearns, *American Cool: Constructing a Twentieth-Century Emotional Style* (New

York: New York University Press 1994), 241 (petting); http://nl.wikipedia.org/wiki/American_Graffiti, retrieved on 5 February 2014 (*Star Wars*); Cowie, *Stayin' Alive*, 353 (Jameson); Hey, "Cars and Films in American Culture," 594 (Cinerama), 595 (52), 596 (sound, honk); White, *Home on the Road*, 90, 98 (quote).

114. White, *Home on the Road*, 176, 185 (boom); Janet Ore, "Mobile Home Syndrome: Engineered Woods and the Making of a New Domestic Ecology in the Post–World War II Era," *Technology and Culture* 52, no. 2 (2011): 280 (formaldehyde); *How American Buying Habits Change*, 216 (spare-time); Dominik Schrage, "Der Konsum in der deutschen Soziologie," in Haupt and Torp, *Die Konsumgesellschaft in Deutschland 1890–1990*, 328–329.

115. Hans-Ulrich Wehler, "Deutsches Bürgertum nach 1945: Exitus oder Phönix aus der Asche?" *Geschichte und Gesellschaft* 27 (2001): 630 (*Massenwohlstand*), 633 (1945); a similar conclusion can be found in Vogel, "Bürgertum nach 1945?" 417; Hartmut Kaelble, "Boom und gesellschaftlicher Wandel 1948–1973: Frankreich und die Bundesrepublik Deutschland im Vergleich," in Kaelble, *Der Boom 1948–1973*, 234 (*Kleinbürger, Arbeitnehmer*); Manfred Hettling, "Bürgerlichkeit im Nachkriegsdeutschland," in Hettling and Ulrich, *Bürgertum nach 1945*, 25 (self-realization), 27 (soft), 28 (*Facharbeiter*).

116. Henry Olsen, *The Working-Class Republican: Ronald Reagan and the Return of Blue-Collar Conservatism* (New York: Broadside Books, 2017), xvii (pro-New Deal), 4 (1896), 8 (Roosevelt), 12 (forgotten), 24 (middle class, New Deal), 53 (1964), 56 (intellectual elite), 57 (liberal friends), 175 (great again), 246 (color); Thomas Frank, *Listen, Liberal or Whatever Happened to the Party of the People?* (Melbourne: Scribe, 2016), 106.

117. Marchand, "Visions of Classlessness," 169 (way of life); Greg Donofrio, "Gender Realignment: The Design and Marketing of Gas Stations for Women," in Berghoff et al., *Rise of Marketing and Market Research*, 258 (plastic, nozzle); Marwick, *Sixties*, 679; Charles Sanford, "'Woman's Place' in American Car Culture," *Michigan Quarterly Review* 19–20 (1980–1981): 542; Ellen J. Gerland and Craig L. Davis, "Selling Detroit on Women: *Woman's Day* and Auto Advertising, 1964–82," *Journalism History* 38, no. 4 (2013): 210.

118. Caplow et al., *Recent Social Trends*, 425–426 (universal); Sanford, "'Woman's Place' in American Car Culture," 532 (40 percent); Robinson and Converse, "Social Change Reflected in the Use of Time," 49; Ilse Lenz, "Feminismus und Fortschrittsdenken: Reflexive Brechungen und vielfältige Horizonte," *Vorgänge* 3 (September 2011): 113 (ordering); Kristina Schulz, "Feminist Echoes of 1968: Women's Movements in Europe and the United States," in *A Revolution of Perception? Consequences and Echoes of 1968*, ed. Ingrid Gilcher-Holtey (New York: Berghahn Books, 2014), 141; Gerland and Davis, "Selling Detroit on Women," 211 (children), 212 (boasted).

119. Gerland and Davis, "Selling Detroit on Women," 213 (pimps quote from Jane and Michael Stern in *Auto Ads* in 1978), 214 (protection), 215 (consumer), 216 (average man, highly educated, four segments), 217 (dealerships); Beth Kraig, "Are We There Yet, Driver? Searching for the Automotive Human," *Midwest Quarterly* 48, no. 2 (2007): 298; Penelope Pitstop quoted in Rachel A. Jennings, "Women Writers and the Internal Combustion Engine: Passing Penelope Pitstop," in *Gender, Genre, and Identity in Women's Travel Writing*, ed. Kristi Siegel (New York: Peter Lang, 2004), 97; Katherine J. Parkin, *Women at the Wheel: A Century of Buying, Driving, and Fixing Cars* (Philadelphia: University of Pennsylvania Press, 2017), 109 (Reingold and Roulf), 114 (*Vogue* and *Ms.*).

120. John Dollard, *Caste and Class in a Southern Town* (New York: Harpers & Brothers, 1949), xvi (Southerntown); James N. Gregory, *The Southern Diaspora: How the Great Migrations of Black and White Southerners Transformed America* (Chapel Hill: University

of North Carolina Press, 2005), 32, 330, table A.1 (whites, etc.); Gilroy, *Darker Than Blue*, 12–16; Robert D. Bullard, "Introduction," in *Highway Robbery: Transportation Racism & New Routes to Equity*, ed. Robert D. Bullard, Glenn S. Johnson and Angel O. Torres (Cambridge, MA: South End Press, 2004), 1 (Supreme Court); Robert D. Bullard, "The Anatomy of Transportation Racism," in Bullard et al., *Highway Robbery*, 16 (Baton Rouge); Stephen Tuck, *We Ain't What We Ought to Be: The Black Freedom Struggle from Emancipation to Obama* (Cambridge, MA: Belknap Press, 2010), 327–328 (Meredith).

121. Bullard, "Anatomy of Transportation Racism," 16 (igniting); Tuck, *We Ain't What We Ought to Be*, 330 (Carmichael).

122. Mary Pattillo-McCoy, *Black Picket Fences: Privilege and Peril among the Black Middle Class* (Chicago: University of Chicago Press, 1999), 17 (segments), 21 (slower), 24 (enclaves); Rugh, *Are We There Yet?* 90 (tremendous); Henry Allen Bullock, "Consumer Motivations in Black and White: I," *Harvard Business Review* 39, no. 3 (1961), 93, 104; on "black automobility as cold war imperative," see Seiler, *Republic of Drivers*, 111–128.

123. Retzloff, "Cars and Bars," 228 (emergence), 234–235 (police), 240 (the Cadillac quote is from *Hi-Spots* magazine from 1961); John Howard, "Place and Movement in Gay American History: A Case from the Post-World War II South," in Beemyn, *Creating a Place for Ourselves*, 212 (escape), 214 (cruising), 218 (trick house), 220 (outskirts), 224n13 (casual sex).

124. Uta G. Poiger, "Imperialism and Consumption: Two Tropes in West German Radicalism," in Schildt and Siegfried, *Between Marx and Coca-Cola*, 161 (Ensslin, kidnap); Axel Schildt, "Across the Border: West German Youth Travel to Western Europe," in Schildt and Siegfried, *Between Marx and Coca-Cola*, 150–151, 153 (repressive), 155–156 (spread); Schildt and Siegfried, "Introduction, " 26 (French and British youth); Michalis Nikolakakis, "Representations and Social Practices of Alternative Tourists in Postwar Greece to the End of the Greek Military Junta," *Journal of Tourism History* 7, nos. 1–2 (2015): 5 (invasion), 6 (war), 11 (hordes); Kraushaar, "Die 'Revolutionierung des bürgerlichen Subjekts,'" 392.

125. Guy Debord, "Theory of the Dérive," in *Situationist International Anthology*, ed. and trans. Ken Knabb (Berkeley, CA: Bureau of Public Secrets, 2006), http://www.bopsecrets.org/SI/2.derive.htm (demolition); Keith Miller, "Five Men in a Boat: Were William Hogarth and His Friends the First Situationists?" *Times Literary Supplement* (19 March 2010), 15 (Debord); "Situationist International" (http://en.wikipedia.org/wiki/Situationist_International, consulted on 6 April 2014), 1–19, here: 5 (majority); Pinder, *Visions of the City*, 137 (Vaneigem).

126. Quoted in Pinder, *Visions of the City*, 127 (*Internationale situationiste*, December 1959), 150 (taxis); "Situationist International," 3 (Chaplin and *détournement*), 5 (poster); Debord, "Theory of the Dérive"; Miller, "Five Men in a Boat," 15 (spectacle, Sex Pistols); Pinder, *Visions of the City*, 128 (game); "not the same": as argued by Dick Hebdige, "Towards a Cartography of Taste 1935–1962," *Block* 4 (1981): 41, who quotes Evelyn Waugh, who called Picasso "subversive high culture."

127. Wicke, "Music, Dissidence," 112–113 (pop), 114 (revolutionary, socialization; the attitude quote is from Ian Birchall), 116 (emotional impulses), 122 (conglomerate); Arvidsson, "From Counterculture to Consumer Culture," 65 (scooter).

128. Barry Doyle, "'More Than a Dance Hall, More a Way of Life': Northern Soul, Masculinity and Working-Class Culture in 1970s Britain," in Schildt and Siegfried, *Between Marx and Coca-Cola*, 314 (civis), 324–325; Carosso, "Paradox of Re-colonization," 123 (Brighton).

129. Thomas Frank, *The Conquest of Cool: Business Culture, Counterculture, and the Rise of Hip Consumerism* (Chicago: University of Chicago Press, 1997), 8 (revolution), 47 (resistance), 48 (fighter plane), 156 (motif); Christopher Lasch, *The Culture of Narcissism: American Life in an Age of Diminishing Expectations* (New York: Norton, 1991); Süha Oğuzertem, "Fictions of Narcissism: Metaphysical and Psychosexual Conflicts in the Stories of Ahmet Hamdi Tanpinar," *Turkish Studies Association Bulletin* 14, no. 2 (1990): 232.
130. Herbert Marcuse, "Repressive Tolerance," in *A Critique of Pure Tolerance*, ed. Robert Paul Wolff, Barrington Moore Jr., and Herbert Marcuse (New York, 1965), quoted by Marwick, *Sixties*, 808n15; Mom, *Evolution of Automotive Technology*, 28; Siegfried, "Protest am Markt," 54 (70: remarkably, when Siegfried described the electric guitar, amplifiers, LPs, transistor radios and cassette recorders, TV programs, the youth, and underground magazines as "transport vehicles" of countercultural values into mainstream culture, he did not mention the moped, the motorcycle, the bus, or the car); Frank, *Conquest of Cool*, 29–30 (Shorris).
131. Judith Williamson, *Decoding Advertisements: Ideology and Meaning in Advertising* (London: Marion Boyars, 1995), 12 (transforming); Frank, *Conquest of Cool* 49 (*Fortune*), 55–68 (Volkswagen), 111 (angry young); Smith, *Dancing in the Street*, 124–125 (Mustang), 127 (River Rouge).
132. Frank, *Conquest of Cool*, 136 (Buick), 157–159, 235 (consent). Frank also analyzed the failed Peacock Revolution in men's fashion as a second case to show how the "creative revolution" in several sectors of society preceded the counterculture's breakthrough. A similar effect is described for modern avant-garde music, for instance, by Robert Fink, who described how Philip Glass and other composers "used countercultural energy to break free from … the stifling technocratic conformity" of the American 1950s. He quoted Frank for this purpose. See Robert Fink, *Repeating Ourselves: American Minimal Music as Cultural Practice* (Berkeley: University of California Press, 2005), 68–69. For advertising of Renault as "feeling young behind the steering wheel of a young vehicle," see Frédéric Vieban, "L'Image de l'automobile auprès des Français 1930–1950" (unpublished Mémoire de maîtrise, Histoire Contemporaine, Université F. Rabelais, Tours, 1987), 136.
133. Arvidsson, "From Counterculture to Consumer Culture," 48 (legitimize); Marwick, *Sixties*, 383; Lawrence James, *The Middle Class: A History* (London: Little, Brown, 2006), 432 (clash), 443 (content).
134. Seiler, *Republic of Drivers*, 143; Peter-Paul Bänzinger, "Der betriebsame Mensch: Ein Bericht (nicht nur) aus der Werkstatt," *Österreichische Zeitschrift für Geschichtswissenschaften* 23, no. 2 (2012): 232 (*Selbstführung*); George W. Pierson, *The Moving American* (New York: Alfred A. Knopf, 1973), 35 (temperaments).
135. James Hay, "Unaided Viruses: The (Neo)liberalization of the Domestic Sphere and the New Architecture of Community," in *Foucault, Cultural Studies, and Governmentality*, ed. Jack Z. Bratich, Jeremy Packer, and Cameron McCarthy (New York: State University of New York Press, 2003), 167 (apparatus). For a critique of the repressive tolerance thesis, see Marwick, *Sixties*, 19.
136. The preparatory thesis about continuity between prewar and postwar history has been coined for the history of technology by Johan Schot and Dick van Lente, "Technology, Industrialization and the Contested Modernization of the Netherlands," in *Technology and the Making of the Netherlands*, ed. Johan Schot, Harry Lintsen, and Arie Rip (Cambridge, MA: MIT Press, 2010), 518–528.
137. Mom, *Atlantic Automobilism*, 643.

138. Kerouac, *On the Road*, 18 (hopping); Jack Kerouac, "The Vanishing American Hobo," *Hermitary*, accessed 12 December 2019, http://www.hermitary.com/lore/kerouac.html, 1 (the article was first published in *Holiday* in 1960 and in the same year reprinted in Kerouac's book *Lonesome Traveler*); Frederick Feied, *No Pie in the Sky: The Hobo as American Cultural Hero in the Works of Jack London, John Dos Passos, and Jack Kerouac* (San Jose, CA: Authors Choice Press, 2000), 57 (quest), 58 (1940s).
139. See, e.g., Nancy M. Grace, *Jack Kerouac and the Literary Imagination* (New York: Palgrave Macmillan, 2007), chap. 3; for a critique of the all-too-easy reduction of car mobility and inward journey, see Mom, *Atlantic Automobilism*, 425; for a succinct but good overview of the American critical reception of *On the Road*, see Elliot, "Liberating Domesticity," chap. 3; Talbot, "This Is Not an Exit," v (transition to postmodernism), 21 (ludism).
140. Alexandra Ganser, *Roads of Her Own: Gendered Space and Mobility in American Women's Road Narratives, 1970–2000* (Amsterdam: Rodopi, 2009), 33–34; the Interstate Highway System observation stems from Elliot, "Liberating Domesticity," 112n30 (quoting Kerouac student Robert Holton).
141. Atlas, "Foreword," xi; Mills, *Road Story*, 169 (hates, whiteness), 170 (greatest ride, straight), 171 (boxcar); Jack Kerouac, *Visions of Cody* (London: Penguin, 2012); Robert A. Hipkiss, "On the Road: Kerouac's Transport," *Kansas Quarterly* 21, no. 4 (1989): 19 (frantic Dean); Peter Conrad, *Modern Times, Modern Places* (New York: Alfred A. Knopf, 1999), 570 (Warhol); Kerouac, *On the Road*, 73 (adventure), 91 (adventuring), 186 (scythe; 104, another example of inversion: "the white line in the middle of the road that unwound, kissing our left front tire"); Mom, *Atlantic Automobilism*, 162–163 (inversion before the war).
142. Amburn, *Subterranean Kerouac*, 55 (phobia), 58 (grease-gun), 130 (pee), 144 (Plymouth); Lars Erik Larson, "Free Ways and Straight Roads: The Interstates of Sal Paradise and 1950s America," in *What's Your Road, Man? Critical Essays on Jack Kerouac's On the Road*, ed. Hilary Holladay and Robert Holton (Carbondale: Southern Illinois University Press, 2009), 51 (violence of motion); John Leland, *Why Kerouac Matters: The Lessons of On the Road (They're Not What You Think)* (London: Penguin, 2008), 17 (no violence), 55 (for a critique on Amburn's neglect of the "ambiguities" of Kerouac's sex life), 64 (ruining cars), 66 (precision), 94 (pinball), 136 (crash); Kerouac, *On the Road*, 8 (parking lot), 92 (example of mentioning speed), 183 (fag); for an analysis of the role of homosexuality in beat culture, see Oliver Harris, "Queer Shoulders, Queer Wheel: Homosexuality and Beat Textual Politics," in Van Minnen et al., *Beat Culture*; Ernest Hemingway, *Death in the Afternoon* (London: Arrow Books, 2004); on Hemingway's machismo and its influence on American masculinities, see David M. Earle, *All Man! Hemingway, 1950s Men's Magazines, and the Masculine Persona* (Kent, OH: Kent State University Press, 2009); Hipkiss, "On the Road," 20 (sneering).
143. Beth Kraig, "The Liberated Lady Driver," *Midwest Quarterly* 28 (1987): 395–396; Amburn, *Subterranean Kerouac*, 52 (pure), 364 (Hayden); Henry Gregor Felsen, *Crash Club* (Milton Keynes: Lightning Source, 2013), 193, back cover; Theodore Weesner, *The Car Thief* (New York: Grove Press, 2001).
144. Arthur Krim, *Route 66: Iconography of the American Highway*, ed. Denis Wood (Santa Fe, NM: Center for American Places, 2005), 116–117, 146 (Berry), 148 (Them), 149 (Stones); Mailer, "White Negro," 339; Luciano Bianciardi, *La Vita Agra, or It's a Hard Life* (London: Hodder & Stoughton, 1965), 185; the movie with the same name was directed by Carlo Lizzani: http://en.wikipedia.org/wiki/La_vita_agra_(film) (consulted 18 February 2014); Marwick, *Sixties*, 71 (dance), 171 (angry beatnik); Amburn, *Subterranean Kerouac*, 58 (sixty seconds), 149 (big event); Kerouac, *On the Road*, 32

(purity); the funeral parlor quote stems from political activist John Sinclair and is cited in Wilfried Mausbach, "'Burn, Ware-House, Burn!' Modernity, Counterculture, and the Vietnam War in West Germany," in Schildt and Siegfried, *Between Marx and Coca-Cola*, 194; Mom, *Atlantic Automobilism*, 447–448 (Kracauer); Larson, "Free Ways and Straight Roads," 48 (cleanses); Mary Parniccia Carden, "'Adventures in Auto-eroticism': Economies of Traveling Masculinity in *On the Road* and *The First Third*," in Holladay and Holton, *What's Your Road, Man?* 84 (feminized) (Carden's conclusion is based on two sources: Kerouac, *On the Road* and Neil Cassady, *The First Third and Other Writings* [San Francisco: City Lights, 1971]).

145. Amburn, *Subterranean Kerouac*, 148 (no house), 161 (kickwriting), 164 (scroll); Leland, *Why Kerouac Matters*, 11–12 (improvise), 24 (jazz), 107 (twenty-six homes), 113 (never realized); "virile" coined by William Plummer, quoted in Carden, "Adventures in Auto-eroticism," 96.

146. Tim Cresswell, "Mobility as Resistance: A Geographical Reading of Kerouac's 'On the Road,'" *Transactions of the Institute of British Geographers* 18 (1993): 254; Linda McDowell, "Off the Road: Alternative Views of Rebellion, Resistance and 'the Beats,'" *Transactions of the Institute of British Geographers* 21 (1996): 414, 417, 418; Tim Cresswell, "Writing, Reading and the Problem of Resistance: A Reply to McDowell," *Transactions of the Institute of British Geographers* 21 (1996): 422, 423; see also Jessica Lyn van Slooten, "Sexism and Misogyny," in Lawlor, *Beat Culture*.

147. Simon Rycroft, "Changing Lanes: Textuality off and on the Road," *Transactions of the Institute of British Geographers* 21, no. 2 (1996): 427; Carden, "Adventures in Auto-eroticism," 86; Kerouac, *On the Road*, 97; Amburn, *Subterranean Kerouac*, 348; Alex Trimble Young, "Settler Sovereignty and the Rhizomatic West, or, the Significance of the Frontier in Postwestern Studies," *Western American Literature* 48, nos. 1–2 (2013): 120; Marco Abel, "Speeding across the Rhizome: Deleuze Meets Kerouac *On the Road*," *Modern Fiction Studies* 48, no. 2 (2002): 233 (repetition), 243 (in-between-ness).

148. Jaap van der Bent, Mel van Elteren, and Cornelius van Minnen, "Introduction," in Van Minnen et al., *Beat Culture*, 8 (mixing); Mills, "Remapping the Road Story," 58–59 (car radio. road as "twin aspects of Beat automobility"), 68–69 (rewrite), 77 (art film), 78 (woe); Mills, *Road Story*, 58 (Guggenheim, car trip). Frank also filmed the 1972 Rolling Stones' American tour, but the recording called *Cocksucker Blues* was shelved, because of the footage on excessive drug taking and backstage parties. Ray Young, "Cocksucker Blues," *Flickhead* (2004), https://web.archive.org/web/20150930223332/http://home.comcast.net/~flickhead/Cocksucker-Blues.html.

149. Mills, "Remapping the Road Story," 83n1 ("cross-media quality of the road story"), 94 (dissent), 95 (numerous times, Studebaker), 103 (re-*familiarizing*), 116 (feminized); Mills, *Road Story*, 66 (cheap, next), 73 (vérité), 76 (macho), 83 (*Star Trek*); Stephen Bayley, *Sex, Drink and Fast Cars: The Creation and Consumption of Images* (London: Faber & Faber, 1986), 14 (warship); Elliot, "Liberating Domesticity," 72 (formulations); for the concept of the "ironic mobile sublime," see Mom, *Atlantic Automobilism*, 650.

150. Mom, *Atlantic Automobilism*, 516 (multisensorial); Amburn, *Subterranean Kerouac*, 82 (Self-Ultimacy), 102 (tyranny), 154 (God); on the "demystification" of the car in Kerouac's novel *Big Sur* (1962), see Hipkiss, "On the Road," 20.

151. Deborah Clarke, *Driving Women: Fiction and Automobile Culture in Twentieth-Century America* (Baltimore: Johns Hopkins University Press, 2007), 131; Jens Peter Becker, *Das Automobil und die amerikanische Kultur* (Trier: Wissenschaftliche Verlag Trier, 1989), 44–45 (Shapiro); Mills, *Road Story*, 89 (Leary); Sidonie Smith, *Moving Lives: Twentieth-Century Women's Travel Writing* (Minneapolis: University of Minnesota Press, 2001), 178;

Aaron Belkin, *Bring Me Men: Military Masculinity and the Benign Facade of American Empire, 1898–2001* (New York: Columbia University Press, 2012), 26 (disavowal); see also Melanie McCarry, "Masculinity Studies and Male Violence: Critique or Collusion?" *Women's Studies International Forum* 30, no. 5 (2007); Holmes, *Go*, 21–22; Amburn, *Subterranean Kerouac*, 276–277.

152. Robert M. Pirsig, *Zen and the Art of Motorcycle Maintenance: An Inquiry into Values* (London: Vintage, 2004), 26 (technology); Jeffrey Melton, "'Immediate Consciousness' and the American Open Road: Robert Pirsig's *Zen and the Art of Motorcycle Maintenance*," *Studies in Travel Writing* 17, no. 4 (2013): 398 (twenty-five languages); Michael Dick, *Die Situation des Fahrens: Phänomenologische und ökologische Perspektiven der Psychologie* (Hamburg: Technische Universität Hamburg Harburg, 2001), 142 (man-machine relation); Richard H. Rodino, "The Matrix of Journeys in *Zen and the Art of Motorcycle Maintenance*," *Journal of Narrative Technique* 11, no. 31 (1981): 54 (indefinite).

153. Beverly Gross, "'A Mind Divided Against Itself': Madness in *Zen and the Art of Motorcycle Maintenance*," *Journal of Narrative Technique* 14, no. 3 (1984): 201 (journey), 203 (maintenance man); William L. Dulaney, "A Brief History of 'Outlaw' Motorcycle Clubs," *International Journal of Motorcycle Studies* 1 (November 2005).

154. Packer, *Mobility without Mayhem*, 111–119 ("danger" on 112); Ted Bishop, "*Tempo Giusto*: The Art of the Slow Ride," in Benesch, *Culture and Mobility*, 83; Robert Pirsig, "Introduction to the Twenty-Fifth Anniversary Edition," in Pirsig, *Zen and the Art of Motorcycle Maintenance*, ix (philosophy book); Pirsig, *Zen and the Art of Motorcycle Maintenance*, 12 (TV), 15 (meditating), 17 (*lost*), 23 (afraid), 25 (beatniks), 48 (spare parts), 76–77 (structure).

155. Mills, "Remapping the Road Story," 132 (lowbrow movies), 133 (catharsis), 144 (zenith), 171n38 (*Magical Mystery Tour*); Hunter S. Thompson, *Hell's Angels* (New York: Ballantine, 1996); Mills, *Road Story*, 110 (Anger), 115 (outlaw machine), 116 (spent time), 117 (teens), 119 ($360,000, consultants), 120 (titillated), 122 (Nicholson quote, critique), 125 ($400,000), 129 (flying); Deborah Lupton, *Risk* (London: Routledge, 1999), 151 (wild car trip); Bishop, "*Tempo Giusto*," 112 (hip); Elliot, "Liberating Domesticity," 189 (manic, silence).

156. Leland, *Why Kerouac Matters*, 4 (teaching), 103 (directed); Amburn, *Subterranean Kerouac*, 380 (three-million) According to Deleuze, reading *On the Road*, "the inside is an operation of the outside … a fold of the outside, as if the ship were a folding of the sea." According to Abel, "Speeding across the Rhizome," 238, who quoted Deleuze, "there is too much 'outside' to describe for Kerouac to worry too much about the inside of his characters." The claim of this chapter is, however, that this outside is to be found inside the car.

157. Attilio Brilli, *Das rasende Leben: Die Anfänge des Reisens mit dem Automobil* (Berlin: Verlag Klaus Wagenbach, 1999), 144–145.

158. Leland, *Why Kerouac Matters*, 21 (hobo), 58 (relic), 87 (not cool), 121 (commercial), 130 (consumption); Brilli, *Das rasende Leben*, 180–181 (Brilli's analysis not only is poorly [thematically and temporally] structured but also has no source justification); Strand, *Killer on the Road*, 80 (invested).

159. Wini Breines, "The 'Other' Fifties: Beats and Bad Girls," in *Not June Cleaver: Women and Gender in Postwar America, 1945–1960*, ed. Joanne Meyerowitz (Philadelphia: Temple University Press, 1994), 384 (deviance), 385 (delinquent), 387 (repelled), 391 (Johnson), 392–393 (Rowbotham), 398 (agency); Mills, *Road Story*, 55–56 (Paris); Tom Robbins, *Even Cowgirls Get the Blues* (New York, 2003), 12 (Thumbelina), 13 (freedom), chap. 104 (thumb as persona); quoted in Ronald Primeau, "From Ma Joad to Elizabeth Berg: Women on the Road in America," *Midamerica* 26 (1999): 139 (perpetual motion).

160. Janice A. Radway, *Reading the Romance: Women, Patriarchy, and Popular Literature* (Chapel Hill: University of North Carolina Press, 1984), 4 (one-third), 55 (college), 59 (religiously), 61 (relaxation), 63 (lifted), 65 (gradually; emphasis added), 66 (happy ending), 69 (Bond), 85 (therapeutic), 94 (lose the self), 100 (real world), 110 (afford); for the prewar trips with unknown destination in the Netherlands (*tochtjes met onbekende bestemming*), see Mom and Filarski, *Van transport naar mobiliteit*, 242; Tania Modleski, "The Disappearing Act: A Study of Harlequin Romances," *Signs* 5, no. 3 (1980): 435 (disappearing), 436 (divided self), 437 (subordinate).
161. Vera Nünning and Ansgar Nünning, eds., *Erzähltextanalyse und Gender Studies* (Stuttgart: Verlag J. B. Metzler, 2004), 200–201; Meaghan Morris, "Banality in Cultural Studies," in Mellencamp, *Logics of Television*, 14 (Williamson); LeRoy Ashby, "The Rising of Popular Culture: A Historiographical Sketch," *OAH Magazine of History* 24, no. 2 (2010): 11 (Adorno, Niebuhr); Peter Burke, "Popular Culture Reconsidered," *Storia della Storiografia* 17 (1990): 42.
162. John Updike, "Introduction," in *Rabbit Angstrom: A Tetralogy* by John Updike (New York: Everyman's Library, 1995), viii (1959), x–xi (realistic demonstration), xiii (middle American); Melvin W. Askew, "Quests, Cars, and Kerouac," *University of Kansas City Review* 28, no. 3 (1962): 239 (style); Amburn, *Subterranean Kerouac*, 281 (*New Yorker*); John Updike, *Rabbit Run*, in Updike, *Rabbit Angstrom*, 24–25 (Angstrom's flight), 44 (good time), 48 (aging body), 92 (safer), 134 (domestic creature); John Updike, *Rabbit Redux*, in Updike, *Rabbit Angstrom*, 277 (certain fear), 412 (bastards), 583 (law); Marsh and Collett, *Driving Passion*, 74 (Seattle).
163. John Updike, *Higher Gossip: Essays and Criticism*, ed. Christopher Carduff (New York: Random House, 2011), 470 (airwaves); Catherine Jurca, *White Diaspora: The Suburb and the Twentieth-Century American Novel* (Princeton, NJ: Princeton University Press, 2001), 161–162 (*fear* of falling); John Keats, *The Insolent Chariots* (Philadelphia: J. B. Lippincott, 1958), 201 (terror), 207–208 (common man), 223 (compacts); Mary Gordon, "Good Boys and Dead Girls," in *Good Boys and Dead Girls and Other Essays* (London: Bloomsbury, 1991), 17, talks about Updike's title, suggesting "the innocent is urged to move."
164. Jurca, *White Diaspora*, 133–135 (Whyte, Wilson); Priscilla Lee Denby, "The Self Discovered: The Car in American Folklore and Literature" (PhD diss., Indiana University, 1981), 162–163; Updike, *Rabbit Redux*; John Updike, *Rabbit Is Rich*, in Updike, *Rabbit Angstrom*; Henry Ramont, "John Updike Completes a Sequel to 'Rabbit, Run,'" *New York Times*, 27 July 1970 (movie); Christopher Lehmann-Haupt, "John Updike, a Lyrical Writer of the Middle Class, Dies at 76," *New York Times*, 28 January 2009 (middles); John Updike, *The Early Stories: 1953–1975* (New York: Ballantine, 2004), xvii (mundane); Gavin Ewart, "Making It Strange," *New York Times*, 28 April 1985 (strange); Harold Bloom, ed. *Modern Critical Views of John Updike* (New York: Chelsea House, 1987), 7 (sublime); James Wood, "Gossip in Gilt," *London Review of Books* 23, no. 8 (2001) (faith); Elliot, "Liberating Domesticity," 136 (Stimpson).
165. Rosemary Magee, "Introduction," in *Conversations with Flannery O'Connor*, ed. Rosemary Magee (Jackson: University Press of Mississippi, 1987), xi (grotesque); Flannery O'Connor, "Wise Blood," in *Collected Works: Wise Blood / A Good Man Is Hard to Find / The Violent Bear It Away / Everything That Rises Must Converge / Essays and Letters* by Flannery O'Connor, ed. Sally Fitzgerald (New York: The Library of America, 1988), 37; Paul Binding, "Pure Terror" [review of Brad Gooch's biography of O'Connor], *Times Literary Supplement* (11 September 2009), 9 (stranger); Clarke, *Driving Women*, 90.

166. O'Connor, "Wise Blood," 7 (bodily gestures), 87 (six inches), 90 (tried to start), 110 (blending out), 113 (ram), 115 (kill), 118–119 (police officer), 131 (returns); Brian Abel Ragen, *A Wreck on the Road to Damascus: Innocence, Guilt, and Conversion in Flannery O'Connor* (Chicago: Loyola University Press, 1989), 181 (coffin); O'Connor, "Wise Blood," 118–119, 131; Clarke, *Driving Women*, 90 (mother); Jill P. Baumgaertner, "Foreword," in Ragen, *Wreck on the Road to Damascus*, xiii; J. O. Tate, "The Essential Essex," *The Flannery O'Connor Bulletin* 12 (1983): 54.

167. Richard A. Milum, "Continuity and Change: The Horse, the Automobile, and the Airplane in Faulkner's Fiction," in *Faulkner: The Unappeased Imagination—A Collection of Critical Essays*, ed. Glenn O'Carey (Troy, NY: Whitston Publishing, 1980); Mills, "Remapping the Road Story," 244 (station wagon, yearlong), 245 (prison); Mary F. Catanzaro, "The Car as Cell in *Lolita*," *Kansas Quarterly* 21, no. 4 (1989): 9 (cell); Ragen, *Wreck on the Road to Damascus*, 96–105 ("The Life You Save May Be Your Own"); Sally Fitzgerald, "Chronology," in O'Connor, *Collected Works*, 1239 (no dance or sport).; Flannery O'Connor, "A Good Man Is Hard to Find," in O'Connor, *Collected Works*, 145.

168. John Steinbeck, *Travels with Charley: In Search of America* (New York: Penguin, 1986), 91 (replenishment), 94 (machine-like), 123 (wife's visit), 128 (blunder along), 129 (St. Paul), 182 ("Rocinante has been neglected in this account"), 210 ("the American identity is an exact and provable thing"), 247 (racial conflict), 262 (pleasure); Talbot, "This Is Not an Exit," 28. (windmills), 30 (outer world); Brilli, *Das rasende Leben*, 64 (clitoris).

169. Casey Shoop, "Thomas Pynchon, Postmodernism, and the Rise of the New Right in California," *Contemporary Literature* 53, no. 1 (2012): 75; Carosso, "Paradox of Re-colonization," 138–139 (Paranoids); Duncan, "Summer of Love and Protest," 147 (Green Berets), 219 (underground); Strand, *Killer on the Road*, 34 (FBI).

170. Clarke, *Driving Women*, 88–95; Primeau, "From Ma Joad," 138; Ganser, *Roads of Her Own*, 48; Mills, "Remapping the Road Story," 10 (road story), 13 (punk), 28 (*Lolita*); on the beats' desire "to talk for years" (Dean Moriarty in *On the Road*), see Elliot, "Liberating Domesticity," 134 (190. Elliot, too, positions the emergence of the female protagonist in the "early 1970s").

171. Kathleen McHugh, "Women in Traffic: L.A. Autobiography," *South Atlantic Quarterly* 97, no. 2 (1998): 400.

172. Mom, *Atlantic Automobilism*, 405; Beverly Donofrio, *Riding in Cars with Boys: Confessions of a Bad Girl Who Makes Good* (New York: Penguin, 1990), 17 (cop car), 19 (real low), 27 (greasers), 34 (family car), 94 (credit union), 109 (Dodge), 144 (Volkswagen), 147 (macho), 153–154 (Mitchell), 170–171 (work out), 175 (totaled), 192 (Olivia).

173. G Anne Roiphe, *Long Division* (London: Secker & Warburg, 1973), 7 (screaming), 8 (station wagon), 10 (adventure), 29 (flight), 36 (Babbitt, boredom), 59 (no turn back), 85 (hypnotic), 101–103 (wet dreams), 133 (seeing the country), 170 (tire), 186 (Icarus); Ganser, *Roads of Her Own*, 159 (Wandering Jewess), 159–160; on the car as a necessity, see Mom, *Atlantic Automobilism*, 313–321.

174. Katherine Dunn, *Truck* (New York: Warner Books, 1990), 12 (fifteen), 14 (Eugene), 27–35 (drive-in), 75 (microculture), 82 (block quote), 117 (attendant), 120 (eyes), 136 (freedom), 147 (drug-free), 198 (invisible), 200 (joyriding), 203 (counselor), 204 (adventure); Lackey, *RoadFrames: The American Highway Narrative* (Lincoln: University of Nebraska Press, 1997) cited in Ganser, *Roads of Her Own*, 275 ("refine and enlarge").

175. Marvin Zuckerman, *Behavioral Expressions and Biosocial Bases of Sensation Seeking* (Cambridge: Cambridge University Press, 1994), unnumbered page on back of cover (SSS), 3 (*Trieb*), 44–45 (questionnaire), 122–123 (young men), 138–142 (driving behavior); Kraig, "Liberated Lady Driver," 380 (1 million), 385 (1.5 million), 389

(fender-benders); Rainer Schönhammer, "Was die an Frauen gerichtete Autowerbung lehrt," in *Frauen und Männer in der mobilen Gesellschaft*, ed. Antje Flade and Maria Limbourg (Opladen: Leske + Budrich, 1999), 52 (deciders). See also Emilie Sobel, "The Aggressive Female," in *Violence: Perspectives on Murder and Aggression*, ed. Irwin L. Kutash, Samuel B. Kutash, and Louis B. Schlesinger (San Francisco: Josey-Bass Publishers, 1978).

176. Michael Cutler Stone, "*Bajito y suavecito* [Low and slow]: Low Riding and the 'Class' of 'Class,'" *Studies in Latin American Popular Culture* 9 (1990): 102 (*raise*), 120n5 (clothes); Gartman, *Auto Opium*, 171–172; Denise Sandoval, "Bajito y Suavecito: The Lowriding Tradition," Smithsonian Latino Center (2003), accessed 5 June 2017, http://latino.si.edu/virtualgallery/lowrider/lr_sandovalessay.htm, 10 (status symbols), 11 (funerals); Mausbach, "Burn, Ware-House, Burn!" 194 (playful); for the American car maintenance culture, see, e.g., Kevin L. Borg, *Auto Mechanics: Technology and Expertise in Twentieth-Century America* (Baltimore: Johns Hopkins University Press, 2007).

177. *Pilot National Recreation Survey*, 23 (UK); Rinn, "Das Automobil," 140 (Germany); Mom and Filarski, *Van transport naar mobiliteit*, 293–294, show similar large percentages for the Netherlands; Borg, *Auto Mechanics*, 122–123 (racing), 126 (mechanics); Tom Wolfe, "The Last American Hero Is Junior Johnson. Yes!" *Esquire* (1 March 1965), 2 (second gear), 12 (*about-faces*).

178. Jon Savage, *Teenage: The Creation of Youth Culture* (London: Pimlico, 2007), 394–395 (background of the riot), 396–401; Sandoval, "Bajito y Suavecito," 38 (Philipino); Mauricio Mazón, *The Zoot-Suit Riots: The Psychology of Symbolic Annihilation* (Austin: University of Texas Press, 1984), xi (farmworkers), 1 (no casualties).

179. Ben Chappell, "'Take a Little Trip with Me': Lowriding and the Poetics of Scale," in *Technicolor: Race, Technology, and Everyday Life*, ed. Alondra Nelson and Thuy Linh N. Tu with Alica Headlam Hines (New York: New York University Press, 2001), 100–101 (muralists), 107 (overdecoration, carnivalesque), 108 (zoot suits); Mills, "Remapping the Road Story," 10 (lasting images); for carnivalesque, see also Lupton, *Risk*, 165; Denby, "Self Discovered," 336 (phallic).

180. Packer, *Mobility without Mayhem*, 200 ($15 billion, obsession), 205 (1972, five million); I. Roger Yoshino, "The Stereotype of the Negro and His High-Priced Car," *Sociology and Social Research* 44 (November–December 1959), 113 (conservative), 115 (stereotype), 116 (boys, social worker); on the symbolic role of the Cadillac, see also Marsh and Collett, *Driving Passion*, 64; the Cadillac as Black conveyance is also mentioned in Kerouac, *On the Road*, 180 ("a little taut Negro with a great big Cadillac"); and Updike, *Rabbit Redux*, 466 ("why do so few American Negroes want to give up their Cadillac"); Dick Gregory, *From the Back of the Bus*, ed. Bob Orben, photographs by Yerry Yulsman (New York: Avon, 1962), 14 (Playboy Club), 36 (joke; the book contains three jokes on blacks and Cadillacs).

181. Pattillo-McCoy, *Black Picket Fences*, 147 (concluding quote is from *Ebony*); Whyte, "Cadillac Phenomenon," 106; Packer, *Mobility without Mayhem*, 189–190, 259 (no correspondence), 315n22 (duality); Ralph Ellison, "Cadillac Flambé," *American Review* 16 (February 1973): 260 (*flying*), 267 (group).

182. Ralph Ellison, *Invisible Man* (London: Penguin, 2001); Roger N. Casey, *Textual Vehicles: The Automobile in American Literature* (New York: Garland Publishing, 1997), 134; Mills, *Road Story*, 49 (Harlem); John A. Williams, *This Is My Country Too* (New York: Signet, 1966), 29 (nine-passenger), 30 (courage), 36 (station wagon), 53 (returning South), 59 (speed zone), 60 (car fantasy), 63 (hitchhikers), 86–87 (block quote), 99 (15,000 miles), 109 (Los Angeles), 131–132 (state troopers); Talbot, "This Is Not an Exit," 26 (non-fictional), 44–53 (analysis of Williams's novel).

183. Cotten Seiler, "'So That We as a Race Might Have Something Authentic to Travel By': African American Automobility and Cold-War Liberalism," *American Quarterly* 58, no. 4 (2006): 1094 (Crow), 1096 (Mississippi), 1098 (Hoover), 1104 (benignant), 1110 (Lewis). This article reappeared in Seiler, *Republic of Drivers*, chap. 4.
184. Gilroy, *Darker Than Blue*, 28 (Willis); Marsh and Collett, *Driving Passion*, 17; Chuck Berry, "Maybellene" (1955), *SongLyrics*, accessed 27 October 2019, http://www.songlyrics.com/chuck-berry/maybellene-lyrics; Warner as paraphrased by Seiler, "So That We as a Race," 1092.
185. Williams, *This Is My Country Too*, 156; Amiri Baraka, *The System of Dante's Hell* (Brooklyn, NY: Akashi Books, 2016), 116–121; Mills, *Road Story*, 53 (Black Arts); Raymond W. Novaco, "Automobile Driving and Aggressive Behavior," in Wachs and Crawford, *Car and the City*, 234 (assaults), 243 (mobsters); Packer, *Mobility without Mayhem*, 233 (late 1980s).
186. Mom, *Atlantic Automobilism*, 177–183, 644; Murray Friedman, "Introduction: Middle America and the 'New Pluralism,'" in *Overcoming Middle Class Rage*, ed. Murray Friedman (Philadelphia: Westminster Press, 1971), 15 (majority, under half), 23 (*All in the Family*), 24 (decline); Murray Friedman, "Overcoming Middle Class Rage," in Friedman, *Overcoming Middle Class Rage*, 370 ("for Negroes only"); Rostow, *Stages of Economic Growth*, xv.
187. Joel Richman, "The Motor Car and the Territorial Aggression Thesis: Some Aspects of the Sociology of the Street," *Sociological Review* 20, no. 1 (1972): 24; see also Marsh and Collett, *Driving Passion*, 159–164 ("The Territorial Imperative"); Raymond J. Michalowski Jr., "Violence in the Road: The Crime of Vehicular Homicide," *Journal of Research in Crime and Delinquency* 12, no. 1 (1975): 42.
188. Farah Jasmine Griffin, *"Who Set You Flowin'?" The African-American Migration Narrative* (New York: Oxford University Press, 1995), 3 (narrative), 5 (*urban* landscape; emphasis added), 40 (*Song of Solomon*), 124 (six), 142 (Gladys), 174 (hatred); see also Gladys Knight & the Pips, "Midnight Train to Georgia," (1973), *Genius*, accessed 27 October 2019, https://genius.com/Gladys-knight-and-the-pips-midnight-train-to-georgia-lyrics; Joyce Hope Scott, "Commercial Deportation as Rite of Passage in Black Women's Novels," in *Matatu* 3, no. 6 (1989).
189. J. D. Vance, *Hillbilly Elegy: A Memoir of a Family and Culture in Crisis* (London: William Collins, 2017), 12 (hill people), 28 (highway), 30 (by car: "the trip in the 1950s [for Vance's grandparents] required about twenty hours of driving"), 36 (Route 23), 46 ("1950s, when the flood of migrants on the hillbilly highway slowed to a dribble"); Duane Carr, *A Question of Class: The Redneck Stereotype in Southern Fiction* (Bowling Green, OH: Bowling Green State University Popular Press, 1996), 115 (debunked), 117 (bumpkins), 135 (*within*; the quote is from the literary critic Frank W. Shelton), 136 (*Tobacco Road* and crankcase quote); Matthew Guinn, "The Grit Émigré in Harry Crews's Fiction," in *Perspectives on Harry Crews*, ed. Erik Bledsoe (Jackson: University Press of Mississippi, 2001), 106 (grits); on Caldwell's and Steinbeck's novels, see Mom, *Atlantic Automobilism*, 502 and 404–442, respectively.
190. Guinn, "Grit Émigré," 105 (violence, prosperity), 107 (émigré, behavior, Enigma), 108 (*dead-end*); Harry Crews, "Introduction," in *Classic Crews: A Harry Crews Reader* (New York: Touchstone, 1995), 16 (hates the car); Scott Romine, "Harry Crews's Away Games: Home and Sport in *A Feast of Snakes* and *Body*," in Bledsoe, *Perspectives on Harry Crews*, 117 (anchor).
191. Casey, *Textual Vehicles*, 164–165 (164: real event); Harry Crews, *Car: A Novel*, in Crews, *Classic Crews*, 331–334, 333 (Auto-Town), 338 (parade, goddamn), 341 (brand-new),

350 (shit), 352 (115 mph), 381 (was a car), 383 (scared me), 386 (V-8), 401 (passing), 402 (exhaust, mastered), 433 ("lump after bloody lump"); Nancy Corson Carter, "1970 Images of the Machine and the Garden: Kosinski, Crews, and Pirsig," *Soundings* 61, no. 1 (1978): 110 (Barthes).
192. Harry Crews, "The Car," in Crews, *Classic Crews*, 325 (God), 325–327 (overview)
193. Françoise Sagan, *Toxique*, illus. Bernard Buffet (Paris: Éditions Stock, 2009) (I thank Steven Spalding for helping me with the translation of Sagan's text and suggesting the car's agency to me); Ross, *Fast Cars*, 55 (traffic jam); Françoise Sagan, "La vitesse," in *Avec mon meilleur souvenir* by Françoise Sagan (Paris: Gallimard, 1984), 61 (love, death), 62 (animal, orchestrate), 63 (adventurers), 64 (kamikazes), 65 (womb, beach), 66 (oscillate), 67 (pleasure, bet); Marie-Dominique Lelièvre, *Sagan à toute allure* (Paris: Denoël, 2008), 121–122 (Ferrari, 200 km/h).
194. Ross, *Fast Cars*, 90–91 (standards, masculine), 59–60 (enemy); Matthew Taunton, *Fictions of the City: Class, Culture and Mass Housing in London and Paris* (London: Palgrave Macmillan, 2009), 107 (*grand ensemble*); Christiane Rochefort, *Les petits enfants du siècle* (Paris: Éditions Bernard Grasset, 1961), 48.
195. Christina Nehring, "No Exit" [review of Simone de Beauvoir and Jean-Paul Sartre's *Tête-à-tête*], *New York Times Book Review* (4 December 2005), 26 (inventing); Mills, "Remapping the Road Story," 270 (quote from *America Day by Day*); Douglas Brinkley, "Foreword," in *America Day by Day* by Simone de Beauvoir, trans. Carol Cosman (Berkeley: University of California Press, 1999), xi (1947); de Beauvoir, *America Day By Day*, 3 (*elsewhere*), 6 (smoothly), 12 (recognize), 13 (hegemony), 15 (superabundance), 34 (Harlem), 41 (condescension), 43 (inferiority), 78 (studio set), 83 ("I'm taken on a driving tour. This is the first time I'm immersed in the American countryside."), 92 (bus), 105 (ugly, childish), 108 (six lanes), 144 (adventure, risks), 157 (gives out), 164–165 (Far West), 171 (joking), 290 (plane), 312 (telephones), 343 (overwhelmed), 381 (four-month).
196. Michael Kimmage, "Introduction," in *Journey through America* by Wolfgang Koeppen, trans. Michael Kimmage (New York: Berghahn Books, 2012), 2 (DoS), 8 (cities); Koeppen, *Journey through America* (endlessness), 88; de Beauvoir, *America Day By Day*, 308 (Red Scare); Sybille Bedford, "Notes on a Journey in Portugal: 1958," in *Pleasures and Landscapes: A Traveller's Tales from Europe* by Sybille Bedford (London: Daunt Books, 2014), 107–108; Sybille Bedford, "A Journey in Yugoslavia: 1965," in Bedford, *Pleasures*, 115 (Fiat); Sybille Bedford, "A Homecoming: Capri 1948," in Bedford, *Pleasures*, 18.
197. Stanley T. Williams, *Two in a Topolino* (Rindge, NH: Richard R. Smith, 1956), 7 (seven thousand), 13 (torment, persuaded), 14 (Kidillac), 15 (carnival), 16 (individualistic: "my plan"), 17 (ruffian), 18 (Touring Club), 21 (unlearn), 22 (Rome), 23 (*fun*), 25 (differences), 34 (drove), 36 (descended), 43 (restless), 39 (*giro*), 57 (the car as "he"), 87 (asleep), 91 (affectionately), 93 (James and Hawthorne), 109 (Middle Ages), 146 (accident); on Edith Wharton, see Mom, *Atlantic Automobilism*, 157–160; for the Marshall Plan and tourism, see Frank Schipper, "Changing the Face of Europe: European Road Mobility during the Marshall Plan Years," *Journal of Transport History* 28, no. 2 (2007).
198. William Dowie, *James Salter* (London: Twayne Publishers, 1998), 47 (bourgeois, train, walk), 49 (exotic); Sarah Hall, "Introduction," in *A Sport and a Pastime* by James Salter (London: Picador Classic, 2017); novels mentioned in Jobs, *Backpack Ambassadors*, 140–142, 151, 231.
199. Salter, *Sport and a Pastime*, 30–32 (duke), 44 (empty streets), 56–58 (real France), 67 (conquest: "His hands … move to possess her"), 109 (heron), 125 (accelerate), 194

(killed), 198 (desired); Dowie, *James Salter*, 56 ("In his *Paris Review* interview [of 1993] Salter has admitted his intentions were ironic with these last words").
200. Jürgen Link and Siegfried Reinecke, "'Autofahren ist wie das Leben': Metamorphosen des Autosymbols in der deutschen Literatur," in *Technik in der Literatur: Ein Forschungsüberblick und zwölf Aufsätze*, ed. Harro Segeberg (Frankfurt: Suhrkamp Verlag, 1987), 474; Siegfried Reinecke, *Autosymbolik in Journalismus, Literatur und Film: Struktural-funktionale Analysen vom Beginn der Motorisierung bis zur Gegenwart* (Bochum: Universitätsverlag Dr. N. Brockmeyer, 1992), 236–238 (Dürrenmatt).
201. Marwick, *Sixties*, 121 (angry young men, illicit sexuality); John Braine, *Room at the Top* (London: Arrow Books, 2002), 28 (Aston-Martin), 29 (Austin), 33 (Eight), 50–51 (Fiat 500, Austin Chummy), 123 (ten years later), 127 (Jaguar), 151 (dreams), 219 (crash); Sean O'Connell, *The Car and British Society: Class, Gender and Motoring, 1896–1939* (Manchester: Manchester University Press, 1998) confirms this culture of shared car ownership through interviews (quoted in Mom, *Atlantic Automobilism*, 19).
202. Braine, *Room at the Top*, 79 (lavender), 84 (fast), 95 (common man), 124 (Cadillac), 179 (amoebae), 188 (jerk), 191 (shimmied), 217 (hell of a pace); Ian Rankin, "Surface and Structure: Reading Muriel Spark's *The Driver's Seat*," *Journal of Narrative Technique* 15, no. 2 (1985): 154–155; Martin Stannard, *Muriel Spark: The Biography* (London: Weidenfeld & Nicolson, 2009), 117 (Gothic), 366 (calculated).
203. Marchand, "Visions of Classlessness," 170 (below the top 40), 171 (Spillane); Arthur Hailey, *Wheels* (New Delhi: Rupa, 2006), 45.
204. *Visions of the City*, 142 (*potlatch*); Tuck, *We Ain't What We Ought to Be*, 330 (five hundred); Joe T. Darden and Richard W. Thomas, *Detroit: Race Riots, Racial Conflicts, and Efforts to Bridge the Racial Divide* (East Lansing: Michigan State University Press, 2013), 3 (caused); Caplow et al., *Recent Social Trends*, 201 (two hundred thousand); Mills, "Remapping the Road Story," 19 (signifying), 306 (civil rights movement); Pinder, Mausbach, "Burn, Ware-House, Burn!" 193 (snotty); Smith, *Dancing in the Street*, 170 (vandalism), 237 (Gaye); Mark Kurlansky, *Ready for a Brand New Beat: How "Dancing in the Street" Became an Anthem for a Changing America* (New York: Riverhead Books, 2013), 191 (masking), 186 (party song), 193 (Weathermen), 194 (crossover).
205. The search was aided by several friends and colleagues such as Piet Rademakers (Hengelo), Ed Simpson-Baikie (Amsterdam), and Drew Isenberg (Rachel Carson Center, Munich), and I thank them for their many tips about autopoetic songs; The Beatles, "Drive My Car" (1965), *LyricsMode*, accessed 27 October 2019, http://www.lyricsmode.com/lyrics/b/beatles/drive_my_car.html; The Rolling Stones, "(I Can't Get No) Satisfaction" (1965), *AZLyrics*, 27 October 2019, https://www.azlyrics.com/lyrics/rollingstones/icantgetnosatisfaction.html; The Who, "Going Mobile" (1971), *AZLyrics*, accessed 27 October 2019, https://www.azlyrics.com/lyrics/who/goinmobile.html; Steppenwolf, "Born to Be Wild" (1968), *Genius*, accessed 27 October 2019, https://genius.com/Steppenwolf-born-to-be-wild-lyrics; The Beach Boys, "Little Honda" (1964), *SongLyrics*, accessed 27 October 2019, https://songmeanings.com/songs/view/80401.
206. James Brown, "It's a Man's Man's Man's World" (1966), *AZLyrics*, accessed 27 October 2019, https://www.azlyrics.com/lyrics/jamesbrown/itsamansmansmansworld.html; Gilroy, *Darker Than Blue*, 29; Jaap Dekker, "Conamtune: No Particular Place to Go," *Conam Bulletin* 29, no. 1 (2019): 3; Dionne Warwick, "Do You Know the Way to San Jose," *Genius*, accessed 27 October 2019, https://genius.com/Dionne-warwick-do-you-know-the-way-to-san-jose-lyrics; Canned Heat, "On the Road Again" (1968), *Genius*, accessed 27 October 2019, https://genius.com/Canned-heat-on-the-road-again-lyrics; Ford, "She Shampooed & Renewed Us," 58 (Mitchell); The Doors, "The Cars Hiss by My Window" (1971), *Genius*, accessed 27 October 2019, https://

genius.com/The-doors-cars-hiss-by-my-window-lyrics; The Flying Burrito Brothers, "Six Days on the Road" (1972), *Genius*, accessed 27 October 2019, https://genius.com/Flying-burrito-brothers-six-days-on-the-road-lyrics; The Duals, "Stick Shift" (1961), video, 3:10, uploaded by doktorsung (10 July 2010) https://www.youtube.com/watch?v=Qp1FpvEA1H0.
207. Led Zeppelin, "Trampled Underfoot" (1975), *Genius*, accessed 17 November 2019, https://genius.com/Led-zeppelin-trampled-under-foot-lyrics; "Change in the Weather," *The Electric Bayou*, accessed 27 October 2019, http://sites.google.com/site/theelectricbayou/songs/change-in-the-weather ("Sweet Hitchhiker"); Rod Stewart, "Let Me Be Your Car" (1974), *AZLyrics*, accessed 27 October 2019, http://www.azlyrics.com/lyrics/rodstewart/letmebeyourcar.html.; Ragen, *Wreck on the Road to Damascus*, 65 (Springsteen); "Traffic (band)," s.v., *Wikipedia*, last edited 25 September 2019, https://en.wikipedia.org/wiki/Traffic_(band); Golden Earring, "Radar Love" (1973), *AZLyrics*, accessed 27 October 2019, http://www.azlyrics.com/lyrics/goldenearring/radarlove.html.
208. Smith, *Dancing in the Street*, 176; on the importance of "shared musical qualities" rather than "songs' individual lyrics" and the turn to 'literary' songs, see Frith, *Sound Effects*, 20–21; Philip J. Deloria, *Indians in Unexpected Places* (Lawrence: University Press of Kansas, 2004), 137 (photograph), 140 ("Geronimo's Cadillac").
209. Catherine Bertho Lavenir, "Flirting in a Car," paper presented at the T2M conference, "Energy and Innovation," Lucerne (5–8 November 2009); *L'avventura* quoted in Marwick, *Sixties*, 178–179; Fabian Kröger, "L'histoire des savoirs et des images de l'accident de voiture: L'interaction entre la recherche sur les accidents et les images des accidents aux États-Unis et en France (1945–1975)" (PhD diss., Université Paris 1 Panthéon-Sorbonne and Humboldt Universität, 2016), 113 (inspiration) (I thank Fabian Kröger for making his dissertation available to me); for an overview of Italian post–World War II autopoetic movies and novels, see Paolini, "'Torpedo blu' vs. 'Topolino amaranto'"; Siegfried Reinecke, *Mobile Zeiten: Eine Geschichte der Auto-Dichtung* (Bochum: Germinal Verlag, 1986), 123 (motorize); Maren Möhring, "Working Girl Not Working: Liebe, Freizeit und Konsum in Italienfilmen der frühen Bundesrepublik," in *Working Girls: Zur Ökonomie von Liebe und Arbeit*, ed. Sabine Biebl, Verena Mund, and Heide Volkening (Berlin: Kulturverlag Kadmos, 2007), 250–251 (vacation movies).
210. Julio Cortázar, "The Southern Highway," *Pegamequemegusta*, 3 February 2010, https://pegamequemegusta.wordpress.com/2010/03/02/the-southern-highway-julio-cortazar-trans-danny-fitzgerald, 5 (gendarme), 7 (frozen), 14 (suicide), 15 (hostile), 16 (coats), 18 (coup); David Sterritt, *The Films of Jean-Luc Goddard: Seeing the Invisible* (Cambridge: Cambridge University Press, 1999), 93 (accident, forget), 96–97, 101 (furious battles); see also Karen Beckman, *Crash: Cinema and the Politics of Speed and Stasis* (Durham, NC: Duke University Press, 2010), 205–213.
211. Ross, *Fast Cars*, 29 (hotrodder), 30 (ambivalence), 37 (domination), 38 (paved), 40 (adolescents), 46 (Dean).
212. Corinne François-Denève, "Moteur! La voiture comme dystopie dans le cinéma français des années soixante," *La voix du regard* 19 (October 2006): 10 (fascinated), 18 (vehicle deaths); Conrad, *Modern Times, Modern Places*, 560 (sedan); Marwick, *Sixties*, 476–477 (fate); Clarke, *Driving Women*, 73 (sitcoms); Pierre Sorlin, *European Cinemas, European Societies 1939–1990* (London: Routledge, 1991), 140 (perception), 142 (watershed), 149 (marginalized).
213. Richard Pells, *Modernist America: Art, Music, Movies, and the Globalization of American Culture* (New Haven, CT: Yale University Press, 2011), 295 (American New Wave), 301 (jump cuts); Sorlin, *European Cinemas*, 153 (middle class), 154 (students).

214. Becker, *Das Automobil und die amerikanische Kultur*, 101 (hardly mentioned), 173; Mom, *Atlantic Automobilism*, 157–160 (mundane), 192–194 (flight experience); Pells, *Modernist America*, 329 (*Easy Life*); David Laderman, *Driving Visions: Exploring the Road Movie* (Austin: University of Texas Press, 2002), 3 (hegemonic), 4 (obsessed), 66 (film version), 230 (companionate); Mills, "Remapping the Road Story," 148 (prostitute); Elliot, "Liberating Domesticity," 188 (bereft); Talbot, "This Is Not an Exit," 67 (interview), 68 (Wyatt).
215. Laderman, *Driving Visions*, 43 (post-60s), 44 (crux), 47 (subversion), 66 (plot structure), 71 (rebellious), 82–83 (quest road movies: *The Rain People* [Coppola, 1969], *Five Easy Pieces* [Rafelson, 1970], *Two-Lane Blacktop* [Hellman, 1971], *Duel* [Spielberg, 1971], *Vanishing Point* [Sarafian, 1971], *The Last Detail* [Ashby, 1973], *Paper Moon* [Bogdanovich, 1973], *Harry and Tonto* [Mazursky, 1974], *Bring Me the Head of Alfredo Garcia* [Peckinpah, 1974], *Road Movie* [Strick, 1975]; outlaw road movies: *Boxcar Bertha* [Scorsese, 1972], *The Getaway* [Peckinpah, 1972], *The Sugarland Express* [Spielberg, 1973], *Badlands* [Malick, 1973], *Slither* [Zieff, 1973], *Thieves LIKE Us* [Altman, 1974], *Thunderbolt and Lightfoot* [Cimino, 1974], *Dirty Mary, Crazy Larry* [Hough, 1974], *Crazy Mama* [Demme, 1974]); Elliot, "Liberating Domesticity," 74 (nuances), 157 (Penn), 174 (assault).
216. Laderman, *Driving Visions*, 82 (classic), 83 (existential), 85 (hero), 87 (blockbuster), 93 (drift), 93–105 (discussion of *Two-Lane Blacktop*); Becker, *Das Automobil und die amerikanische Kultur*, chap. 3, provides an analysis of fifty movies from a literary point of view, including *Duel* (147), action movies (161), *Easy Rider* (169), *Two-Lane Blacktop* (181); Pells, *Modernist America*, 375 (explosions); Bänzinger, "Der betriebsame Mensch," 230 (events).
217. Talbot, "This Is Not an Exit," 6 (distinguishing characteristic); Mills, "Remapping the Road Story," 152–153 (*Midnight Cowboy*), 192 (*Wanda*), 193 (passion); McHugh, "Women in Traffic," 393 (Hitchcock); Iain Borden, *Drive: Journeys through Film, Cities and Landscapes* (London: Reaktion Books, 2013), 26–27 (*Goldfinger*), 153 (*Play It*), 170 (*Clockwork Orange*), 191 (*Bullitt*), 195 (McQueen).
218. Eric Avila, *The Folklore of the Freeway: Race and Revolt in the Modernist City* (Minneapolis: University of Minnesota Press, 2014), 122; Roger Biles, "Expressways before the Interstates: The Case of Detroit, 1945–1956," *Journal of Urban History* 40, no. 5 (2014): 843 (coalitions), 844 (decade, suburbanization); Seiler, *Republic of Drivers*, 139–140.
219. Mom, *Atlantic Automobilism*, 176 (prewar avant-garde); Eric Hobsbawm, "The Avant-Garde Fails," in *Fractured Times: Culture and Society in the Twentieth Century* (London: Little, Brown, 2013), 241, 243; Mills, *Road Story*, 38.
220. J. G. Ballard, *Crash* (London: Vintage, 1973), 19 (hoodlum), 190 (disciple, horror), 194 (acid), 215 (Lincoln); Crews, *Car*, 364–366; J. G. Ballard, "Introduction," in Ballard, *Crash*, 4.
221. Ballard, *Crash*, 13 (perverse), 23 (stylization, acceptable), 37 (TV), 40 (ramming), 45 (only way), 147 (orifice), 154 (three deep).
222. Crews, *Car*, 358–360; Ballard, *Crash*, 19 (head-on), 39 (relief), 50 (premonitions, end of world, rehearsals), 56–57 (crystal), 63 (specialist), 81 (example of medicalized terminology: "Helen's perineum"), 84 (bored), 116 (technology), 122 (husband), 127 (cheekbone), 137 (example of traffic jam), 139 (Airport), 144 (rectum), 171–172 (penis), 224 (semen); Beckmann, *Crash*, 24 (proximity).
223. Ballard, *Crash*, 178 (device); Gregory Corso, "Last Night I Drove A Car," in *Gasoline and The Vestal Lady on Brattle* by Gregory Corso (San Francisco: City Light Books, 1981) (the poem is part of *Gasoline*); Gore Vidal, *Myra Breckinridge* (New York: Bantam Books,

1968), 261; Munzinger, *Das Automobil als heimliche Romanfigur*, 185 (Lolita); William Handley, *Marriage, Violence, and the Nation in the American Literary West* (Cambridge: Cambridge University Press, 2002), 196–197 (Didion).

224. William Saroyan, *Short Drive, Sweet Chariot* (New York: Pocket Books, 1967), 33 (ugly), 50 (God), 71 (Lincoln), 134 (freedom), 145 ("*total* freedom"); Arthur Miller, *Death of a Salesman: Certain Private Conversations in Two Acts and a Requiem* (New York: Viking, 1968), 136; John Hawkes, *Second Skin* (New York: New Directions, 1964), 34; Madison Jones, *A Buried Land* (Sag Harbor, NY: Second Chance Press, 1987), 224; Bayla Singer, *Like Sex with Gods: An Unorthodox History of Flying* (College Station: Texas A&M University Press, 2003); Jennifer L. Randisi, "The Scene of the Crime: The Automobile in the Fiction of Harry Crews," *Southern Studies* 25, no. 3 (1986): 213 (God), 219 (greasy).

225. Denby, "Self Discovered," 250 ("Auto Accident"), 179; Kurt Brown, ed., *Drive, They Said: Poems about Americans and Their Cars* (Minneapolis: Milkweed Editions, 1994), 179 (Sward), 214–215 (for Shapiro's poem "Auto Wreck," from his *Person, Place and Thing*, 1942); Roy Acuff, "Wreck on the Highway" (1949), *Genius*, accessed 27 October 2019, https://genius.com/Roy-acuff-the-wreck-on-the-highway-lyrics; Little Jimmy Dicks, "The Sign on the Highway" (1951), *Songs-Lyrics*, accessed 27 October 2019, https://www.songs-lyrics.net/so-%27LITTLE%27-JIMMY-DICKENS-lyrics-COUNTRY-BOY-01-lyrics-SIGN-BY-THE-HIGHWAY-lyrics-kgjhifvi.html; Claudia Lieb, *Crash: Der Unfall der Moderne* (Bielefeld: Aisthesis Verlag, 2009), 267 (Dorst), 273 (Jelinek).

226. Joe Moran, *On Roads: A Hidden History* (London: Profile Books, 2010), 43 (ambivalence), 191 (psychiatric); Baxter, *Inner Man*, 186, 188, 190, 193 (Christ), 202 (dummies), 211–212 (Association, Mercedes), 215 (vaginal); John Tomlinson, *The Culture of Speed: The Coming of Immediacy* (Los Angeles: Sage, 2007), 52 (mythology); J. G. Ballard, *The Atrocity Exhibition* (London: Fourth Estate, 2006); Lieb, *Crash*, 308–309 (tabloid, New Arts).

227. Steven Shaviro, "Bodies of Fear: The Films of David Cronenberg," in *The Politics of Everyday Fear*, ed. Brian Massumi (Minneapolis: University of Minnesota Press, 1993), 113–114; Sargeant, *Naked Lens*, 211 (Burroughs); Baxter, *Inner Man*, 217 (auto-sensation), 229 (monstrous), 317 (Diana, sex film); Ballard, *Miracles of Life*, 242–243 (subversive); Kröger, "L'histoire des savoirs," 100 ("suicide féminin"), 101 (*Les Tricheurs*), 117 (Aurelia), 119 (Godard).

228. Jean Baudrillard, "Two Essays," trans. Arthur B. Evans, *Science-Fiction Studies* 18, no. 3 (1991): 314–315, 319; the French original as "crash" published in Jean Baudrillard, *simulacres et simulation* (Paris: éditions galilée, 1981); Aidan Day, "Ballard and Baudrillard: Close Reading *Crash*," *English* 49, no. 195 (2000): 277 (content), 282 (television); Baudrillard, "Two Essays," 315 (temptation).

229. Day, "Ballard and Baudrillard," 284 (cameraman), 290 (regret); Bernard Wolfe, *Limbo* (New York: Carroll & Graf Publishers, 1987), 113–119.

230. Barbara Creed, "The *Crash* Debate: Anal Wounds, Metallic Kisses," *Screen* 39, no. 2 (1998): 178–179; for another feminist reading of *Crash*, see Beckman, *Crash*, chap. 5, esp. 161–163, who emphasizes the "traumatic movement between inside and outside, the movement *Crash* shares with pop art" and "remain[s] reluctant to dismiss the novel's feminist potential"; Clarke, *Driving Women*, 166; Henri Lefebvre, *Everyday Life in the Modern World*, trans. Sacha Ribinovitch (New Brunswick, NJ: Transaction Books, 1984), 100–101.

231. Mom, *Atlantic Automobilism*, 333 (hoboing); Pascal Bruckner and Alain Finkielkraut, *Au coin de la rue, l'aventure* (Paris: Seuil, 1979), back cover (quote); Richard White,

"The Retreat from Adventure: Popular Travel Writing in the 1950s," *Australian Historical Studies* 28, no. 109 (1997): 93 (*retreat*); Kai Arne Linnemann, "Die Sammlung der Mitte und die Wandlung des Bürgers," in Hettling and Ulrich, *Bürgertum nach 1945*, 203 (live in the middle); Heinz Bude, "Bürgertumsgenerationen in der Bundesrepublik," in Hettling and Ulrich, *Bürgertum nach 1945*, 111 (Agamben); Kraushaar, "Die 'Revolutionierung des bürgerlichen Subjekts,'" 402 (self-hatred); Jukka Gronow and Alan Warde, "Introduction," in Gronow and Warde, *Ordinary Consumption*, 4 (inconspicuous); Gartman, "Three Ages," 175 (Bourdieu), 176 (second-hand); Brian Longhurst, Gaynor Bagnall, and Mike Savage, "Ordinary Consumption and Personal Identity: Radio and the Middle Classes in the North West of England," in Gronow and Warde, *Ordinary Consumption*, 140 (ordinariness).

232. Hartmut Böhme, *Fetischismus und Kultur: Eine andere Theorie der Moderne* (Reinbeck: Rowohlt Verlag, 2006), 13 (Bohr), 77 (lenient), 344 (democratic), 347 (mainstream), 376 (periphery).

Chapter 3

LAYERED DEVELOPMENT
The Transnational Construction of a World Mobility System (1940s–1970s)

You tell all your friends about these lights.
Red is to stop, green is to go—
... All go on the same light.
—Flannery O'Connor

We have to go out from here as missionaries,
inspired by zeal and faith.
We have sold all this to ourselves.
But the world at large still needs to be persuaded.
—John Maynard Keynes

What Is 'Layered Development'?

In 1952, Ernesto "Che" Guevara made a tour on a Norton motorcycle through the Latin American continent. His voyage of personal awakening and radicalization is interesting, from a mobility point of view, for two reasons. First, and obviously, the youthful Che did not use a car, like Jack Kerouac would do during the same decade, a bit farther north. Instead, Che's vehicle stood for the postwar motorization in the 'periphery,' or, according to world-system historians, the semi-periphery.[1] Second, like Kerouac, Guevara's trip was continental, that is, from a 'world-system' point of view, local, or regional at most. Indeed, in physical mobility terms, the Western (American) empire was one of the sea, and soon would be one of the air. But as we will see in this chapter, in a nonphysical mobility sense, in terms of influence and knowledge diffusion (accompanied by very physical interests of construction assignments) the road network expansion was also 'developed' into a world mobility system.[2] Indeed, international travel on the road had (and still has) a clear continental (as opposed to *trans*continental) demarcation, despite efforts to create transcontinental highway systems as described in this chapter.

This chapter is especially interested in the emergence of a new layer of a heterogeneous motorized mobility system, superimposed on a resilient, no less heterogeneous layer of what Western observers keep calling 'traditional' mobilities. While motorization in the West has too easily been coupled to the emergence of the car, beyond the West this vehicle formed only a part of a much broader 'mobility network' on which people walked, cycled, drove trucks and buses, used animal- and human powered carts, barrows, and rickshaws. Studying the non-West, this chapter argues, teaches us the American and European 'exuberance,' as depicted in the previous chapter, was only one model of mobile modernization, spectacular and very influential, but enjoyed by a global *minority*. To illustrate this quantitatively: whereas in 1965, nearly 1.5 million Americans visited Europe, and nearly 600,000 Europeans visited the United States, the total "flow" of "foreign visitors" in the world amounted to 128 million.[3] This global *majority* was confronted and inspired by several models of motorization.

We study these phenomena under the terms of *development*, a highly value-laden and political practice, and defined by historian Mike Mason as "the theory and practice of turning the ex-colonies into subordinate economies [which] was simultaneously utopian and myopic."[4] We will use a somewhat broader definition, encompassing also the 'periphery' *within* the industrialized continents. We will focus on the infrastructural part of this development, especially road (network) building, which we consider as 'layered' as the flows it started to generate: after all, this too was imposed on a centuries-old system of roads, mostly geared to walking and animal transport. Through the lens of 'the road,' we will study the worldwide modernization discourse and the subsequent struggle between road and rail, the 'coordination crisis,' both highly dynamic processes with very variegated outcomes, but all of them geared toward the promises of the 'car society.' Contrary to the previous chapter (where we studied the motifs, motives, and motivations of stakeholders through the lens of artistic utterances), we will mainly (but not exclusively so) use reports from the World Bank and other transnational institutions, from think tanks (such as the Brooking Institution), as well as from anthropologists and other social scientists as basic sources, added with the results of a careful reading of road lobbyist IRF's magazine *Road International*. We can do so, because we are mainly interested in this chapter in (changes in) systemic properties of the car society and their effect on subaltern participants of the world mobility culture.

***

Although we do not pretend to write a history 'from below,' starting our analysis of postwar 'world mobility' beyond the West at least can give us a glimpse on alternative mobility options, as well as a fresh, critical look on the pretentions of the West. In the next section, we will therefore first sketch the partial emulation and appropriation of another, Soviet model of mobility configuration by the two largest motorizing countries in Asia: China and India. In the following section, we will have to zoom back to the West, where roadbuilding had evolved into such a frenzy that the 'car society,' more or less ready just before the outbreak of World War II, received an extra, spectacular layer of 'freeways,' rivers of high-speed car, truck, and bus traffic that could not stem the increasing unsafety, let alone the degradation of the environment, especially within the ever-growing cities. Whereas we will reserve the dark, ecological sides of this fast-growing network for a later study, here we will ask ourselves about the pervasive attraction of road construction (and the expectation that such roads would soon be filled by ever-increasing flows of car, truck, and bus fleets) as an icon of modernity. This section aims to deliver a transnational analysis of the global phenomenon of 'development' as core of the modernization process, especially the development of the road network, seen from the West, as the second (Western), and dominant, modernization practice. We then take a third model (next to the Euro-American and Soviet models) as point of departure: the Japanese mobility system as an 'intermediary' between the West and the Asian countries.

The two following sections then reconstruct the spread of the car system, infrastructure as well as fleet, to Africa and Latin America, the latter continent also where a counter-theory of development, *dependentismo*, was formulated. We will close this chapter with conclusions, where we will observe, among other things, the Soviet model and its initial followers did not develop their own development theory. Time-wise, the chapter has both a frayed beginning and a frayed ending, showing how difficult it is to develop a unified periodization on a global scale: while the abundance phase in the West *seemed* to end with the first energy crisis of 1973, when the modal configuration started to be fundamentally rethought, the struggle between road and rail was still in full flux for several Asian countries, necessitating us to follow this struggle until the end of the decade.

Alternative Developments: Soviet Mobility and the Modernization of China and India

From a cultural point of view, according to Petra Goedde, the immediate postwar years were phase 1 in the emergence of a world culture, when both the Soviet Union and the United States attempted to "achiev[e] global culture conformity," provoking on their turn all sorts of "dissident countercultures." The second phase (from the 1960s to the end of the Cold War) is then characterized by "cultural diversification," while the third saw "an increase in global migration and travel." Although the United States came out of World War II as the "unquestioned hegemonic power of the world-system," the so-called Third World (the term itself invented by French demographer Albert Sauvy, who meant to refer to the Third Estate in prerevolutionary France) became enough of "a locus of political turbulence" to capture both the West's and the East's anxious attention.[5] Indeed, the immediate postwar years saw a reformulation of East-West relations, which lately prompted development historians to reshape their approach from a Euro-Americo-centered to a more global approach, in an effort to counter the Western bias in the field, resulting, among others, in a reevaluation of the role of the United Nations' OECD, as well as of the explosion of NGOs (during "the NGO decade" of the 1980s) in the shaping of postwar development policy. In doing so, these historians constructed a counter-story to the largely technocratic mainstream history of Euro-American aid. OECD, they argued, not only was "instrumental in making development aid a normal function of a modern state" but also did so emphasizing the importance of "soft power mechanisms."[6] Walt Rostow, who soon would become one of the crucial Western policy makers in this domain, formulated it very clearly: "If American and Western output stagnates, we shall not be able to mount adequate programmes of military defence or of assistance to underdeveloped areas," in this order.[7]

On the one hand, the 'third decolonization' (after the first at the end of the eighteenth and beginning of the nineteenth centuries leading to independent states in North and South America, and the second at the turn of the twentieth century resulting in the independence of Australia, New Zealand, Canada, and South Africa) led to the definitive end of the European colonial period that had started in the sixteenth century. The wave of liberation began in Africa, through guerilla warfare, in Tunisia, Morocco and Sudan (1956) and the Gold Coast (Ghana, 1957), followed three years later by Nigeria and fourteen former French colonies, as well as the Belgian Congo.[8] Generally, this was a violent and especially cruel process; the Mau Mau Uprising in Kenya, for instance, was suppressed deploying "atrocities, occurring not in the 1850s but in the 1950s"; the British killed more than the French executed in Algeria. One of the tortured was the father of US President Barack Obama, who "had his testicles squeezed between metal rods." In 1962, the French fled from Algeria at the end of a war that raged from 1954, taking with them most of the settler colonists (soon, migrating Algerians formed France's largest ethnic group) in an era of "wild migration," before the French state started to regulate migration in 1974. In the 1960s, East Africa joined the independence movement, with Tanganyika (Tanzania, 1961), Uganda (1962), Kenya (1963), Zambia, and Malawi (1964). The Portuguese colonies Angola and Mozambique gained their independence in 1975, creating an African core of Communist countries. Another member of this group was Sudan, which between 1965 and 1967 had Lockheed Aircraft International draw up a detailed road construction scheme (which on its turn contracted Arizona University to do the actual designing) but, after the military coup in 1969, "aligned itself with the USSR—and that was the end of the scheme." This movement led to the dominance of non-Western countries in the UN, which during the period covered by this chapter saw 100 new countries be born such that by the mid-1970s, it counted 150 members, 25 of them European. "Strong supporters" of the United States decreased from a majority of 64 percent to 49 percent by 1966.[9]

Decolonization also led to a "global process of cultural heterogenization," brought about, among other factors, by increasing migration flows: the UN counted 73 million migrants in 1960 (as much, more or less, as there were international tourists) and 100 million in 1980 (versus 278 million tourists, on a total world population of 3 and 5.3 billion, respectively). Refugees represented nearly 3 percent of the migratory flows in 1960 (more than 2 million) and more than 9 percent (9 million) twenty years later. Immigrants in the United States (who in the prewar years had taken a share of more than 11 per thousand, which fell to 0.4 per thousand in 1940) reached its postwar peak of 4 per thousand in the 1990s, whereas in Europe their relative share became much higher: "Between 1965 and 2000, the foreign-born population in Western Europe rose from 2.2 percent to 10.3 percent." The rhythms of emigration from Southern European countries (including Turkey), mostly to Northern Europe, took place in two waves, and diminished from the mid-1970s, dominated by Italians. Migration, Goedde asserted, "became for a sizable proportion of the world's population a lifelong process." Some wealthy professionals, forming "a new social class of expatriates," now had "more than one household on more than one continent," whereas less wealthy migrants saw their "sense of belonging to a particular cultural community ... become deterritorialized." Against this background of a world 'on the move,' a new relationship between former colonies and the West was in the making, euphemistically called development, a term becoming prominent in the early 1960s as a combination of efforts to recast old dependency relations and counterefforts to 'provincialize Europe.' The UN Development Programme emerged in the early 1960s.[10]

***

But development as a concept has a much longer history: it was late nineteenth-century British anthropology with its evolutionary theory (making non-Western peoples into "living fossils" of a common human past, told as a converging "one-story") that coined the concept, and in its post-evolutionary, twentieth-century shapes "preserved the grand binary distinction between primitive and modern societies." After World War II, 'development' became a part of colonial empire planning, in which economists rather than anthropologists were called upon. Anthropologists, as "experts on 'backward people,'" especially the "applied" scholars with their "fieldwork," who "uncritically [embraced, in the early 1960s] such dubious modernization schemes as Rostow's *The Stages of Growth* (1960), offered a distinctive anthropological contribution: locating the cultural obstacles to economic 'take-off.'" From a colonial perspective, development can be seen as one of the versions (originally, especially an economical one) of the "civilization mission" or *mission civilisatrice*, a concept that at the same time made the performers of that mission into the civilized, of course.[11] Science played a special role in this scheme, as it enhanced the possibilities of control. One of the crucial elements of this scientification of 'development' was planning, the "*conditio sine qua non* of modernization." One of the instruments of this worldwide modernization endeavor was MIT's Center for International Studies (CIS), financed by the CIA in the context of the "soft power" psychological warfare against the Soviet Union, and set up for the "popularization of the modernization theory."

Rostow coauthored a CIS report in which regret was expressed that "we don't have the overt ideological philosophy that we can tell to the natives ... in the same sense that the Russians do." 'Development' as "evolutionary modernization" became the American, Western alternative to the Soviet paradigm. Sönke Kunkel, from whose analysis we derive these insights, concluded the scheme worked only if the new postcolonial nations "would accept their allocated status of underdevelopment ... Because of the Western socialization of colonial elites this willingness was remarkably high." Although Soviet aid to China was more than twice as large as the

Marshall Plan and lasted more than three times as long, the Western development paradigm reigned supreme during the golden years of the 1960s, until the Vietnam War (planned, among others, by Rostow) destroyed "the international credit of the modernization theory." But it would be a historical mistake to construe this pre- and postwar continuity as one of 'discourse' only. The continuity is also very concrete and personal: Corinna Unger showed how "numerous British officers who had been active in colonial development programs went to work for the World Bank, private development companies, and government agencies." Conversely, "the European Economic Community employed a significant share of former colonial administrators, several of whom engaged in 'developing' Europe's own 'backward' regions," such as Southern Italy and Turkey, the former a key player in the Cold War, the latter receiving "large amounts of West-German development aid in the late 1960s and early 1970s."[12] And we saw in chapter 1 how later EEC officials already during the 1930s studied and advised in China's 'development.'

***

To give the reader a first flavor of how 'development' worked out 'on the ground,' so to speak, let us briefly consider postwar Turkey and its continuity with prewar modernization. Jale Parla, the literary theorist we already encountered in chapter 1, saw the prewar tradition of "car novels" (or more general 'vehicle novels,' in which 'Westernization' was problematized and mobility symbolism merged with Turkish mobility 'layeredness') continue after the war, for instance with Ahmet Hamdi Tanpinar's *Saatleri Ayarlam Enstitüsü*, a short novel from 1949, in which a father wants to give his son a bicycle. As he likes the bicycle to protect from rain and sun, he develops the bicycle from a carriage but discovers that up-hill "somebody has to get off and push it," so he buys back the old horse that he sold, and "harnasse[s] [it] to the new vehicle," illustrating, according to Parla, "the absurd reappropriation of everything Western."

In 1975, Adalet Ağaoğlu wrote "a major Turkish novel" entitled *Fikrimin İnce Gülü* (The slender rose of my thought), in which Bayram, a Turkish "guest worker," drives a Mercedes (representing "status and power") back to his village. Like novelist Recaizade Mahmut Ekrem before the war (see chap. 1), Ağaoğlu has her protagonist "reenact the *clownish* infatuation with Westernization," because when the protagonist arrives, both car and man are a wreck. This Turkish road novel shows automobilism has no chance among the homeless: "At the end of the road, there, no one was waiting for Bayram."[13] In Turkey, automobilism was a Cold War phenomenon: the Turkish army received 7,551 American Jeeps between 1947 and 1952 under the Marshall Plan, as a substitution for mules in mountainous regions. An assembly plant in Tuzla (near Istanbul) started to produce the Jeeps, also meant for sales on the civilian market, but efforts to make the plant a part of an import substitution strategy failed because of a military coup in 1971. Prioritizing railways, the Turkish government initially considered roads dangerous for their sovereignty: they feared for a Soviet invasion. Highway network building was forced upon Turkey through US funds, backing "an ambitious program to build 23,000 km of new roads in nine years."[14]

Paradise of Utilitarianism: Rail and Road in Eastern Europe, Especially the Soviet Union

Western Europe and the United States were not the only contenders in the burgeoning development market, aimed at creating new interdependencies between 'core' and 'periphery' in a globalizing world. Corinna Unger argued "the Bolsheviks deserve the patent on modernization, for they were among the earliest and most ambitious advocates of modernization through technology, electrification, and state-run, big-push schemes in the 1920s and 1930s that aimed to produce a new kind of society constituted by the 'new Soviet man.'" And there were Fascist Germany and Italy with "their own models of a "new man" to be engineered by the state. "The creation of the American model of modernization [referring to David Ekbladh's *The Great American Mission*] was a reaction to European and Soviet modernization." Acknowledging "modernization was a global project in character and scope," a transnational analysis of 'development,' as one of the defining characteristics of this phenomenon would have to include the mobility of knowledge and attitudes across national and regional borders, as well as competition between blocs against a Cold War background, despite the near monopoly Western development acquired in the scholarly universe. Especially after the death of Stalin in 1953, a "Soviet economic offensive" (based on the principle of "peaceful coexistence" with the West) capitalized on the anti-Western feelings within large parts of the Third World, followed by several Eastern European countries, most of all the German Democratic Republic (GDR). Between 1954 and 1969, China (which joined—as aid provider—the USSR, which it considered "basically 'European'" and hence not receptive to the real needs of the Third World) provided only 9 percent of all 'Communist aid.' The bulk of Soviet aid (of $6.8 billion) went to India, followed by Egypt, Iran, and Indonesia (who together received about half).

China's aid was directed to Pakistan, Ceylon, Burma, Egypt, the Yemens, Guinea, West Africa, Tanzania, and the Palestinian guerilla (through Iraq). In total, about forty nations benefited from this aid (against about one hundred benefiting from Western aid), with Latin America heavily underrepresented, one of the main targets of American aid, as we will see.[15] According to Mark Lawrence, studying the postwar fate of Vietnam, "the East-West rivalry of the mid-twentieth century, while fragmenting the world into competing blocs, nevertheless powerfully advanced globalization by enmeshing the entire world in the struggle between two politico-economic systems that claimed universal applicability."[16] Seen from a mobility perspective, those Third World countries (divided by the Soviet leaders in 1964, after a phase of virtual ignorance about the Third World, in six types, from friendly to hostile) had a good reason to be inspired by the Soviet model: "traffic growth ... relative to output growth" tended to be higher in the USSR than in the United States, as a publication by the conservative Brookings Institution acknowledged in 1968. Even Rostow had to acknowledge "the current higher rate of increase in Soviet GNP." This places the Western ostentatious car exuberance, as described in the previous chapter, in a different light: it shows why in the West other arguments than purely economical had to be mobilized to make the car-based economy attractive for postcolonial governments. It also shows how the Western car society in its post–World War II shape, was largely a Cold War product. To quote Rostow's "Non-Communist Manifesto" again: "In the stages-of-growth sequence man is viewed as a more complex unit [than in the one-dimensional economic approach of Communism]. He seeks, not merely economic advantage, but also power, leisure, *adventure*, continuity of experience and security; he is concerned with his family, the familiar values of his regional and national culture, and a bit of fun down at the local."[17]

Remarkably, however, the Soviet economic growth was nearly fully brought about on the country's railway network, in accordance with the Soviet policy of industrialization and "the low priority accorded to the agricultural sector." During the fifteen years after 1950, freight transported over this network increased threefold, "with only a modest increase in the length of the network, very little rise in the operating labor force, and no increase at all in the number of locomotives," as Holland Hunter, the author of the Brookings publication, observed in admiration. Against the "chronic underutilization" of Western railroads, Hunter found the Soviets' "secret" in the electrification of their system. This was the result of a decision of the Central Committee of the Communist Party of the Soviet Union in 1955, which within a decade led to a slight reduction of the number of locomotives, as eight thousand of the steam locomotives (of a total steam fleet of twelve thousand) were replaced by three thousand electric and nearly four thousand diesel-electric versions. In 1956, the Ministry of Transport managed 121,000 km of railways, but the total length of the network was more than 200,000 km, the remainder owned by industry. This was about two-thirds of the length of the US network, employing four million workers, against only one million in the United States. To a Westerner at least, the Soviet Union's mobility configuration must have shown the world upside down: although the road-rail controversy played its role here as elsewhere, the solution the authorities tried to enforce were opposite to what a Western observer was used to. Short-haul freight was encouraged to be transferred to truck transport to alleviate threatening overcapacities, without any protest from the railroads, Hunter found. For him, Soviet mobility realized a Western railway management's dream: the deployment of truck transport as a pure feeder to and from the railroads. And although truck capacity more than doubled in the fifteen-year period mentioned, railroads by the end of that period still had a five times higher capacity than trucking. Remarkable, too, was that most of the road haulage was done by trucks owned by non-trucking organizations, the very sector that in the West had blocked a solution to the coordination crisis, because capitalist trucking regulations were mostly formulated such that production companies' possessions (such as their trucks) were exempted.[18]

For many knowledgeable observers such as transport experts in both the Third World and the West, Soviet mobility must have represented the paradise of superutilitarianism. In 1960, more than half the world's rail freight (55 percent, in ton-kilometer) was carried by Eastern European trains. As late as 1966, the minister of railroads complained at the 23rd Party Congress about trucks running empty "for hundreds and even thousands of kilometers," and in the same year, the head of the Party Central Committee's transport and communications section explained this further by pointing at the nearly tripling of long-haul road freight during the previous five years, freight that should have been transported by rail. The high costs of intercity trucking were also caused by the Soviet Union's notorious "roadlessness," a condition caused not so much by a lack of roads (the USSR counted about 1.5 million km in 1950) than by a lack of truck- and car-friendly asphalt pavement leading to the cutting off of thousands of villages during the spring and fall rain seasons. By the end of World War II, the USSR counted an astoundingly low amount of 4,400 miles of paved roads, mostly in and around cities. And although this length was increased twentyfold (to 82,000 miles) in 1965 (often carried out as a "people's project," as a modern form of the traditional corvée), the enormous size of the country gave the USSR a low road density (in length of roads per square kilometer). The Soviet road network further showed an internationally unique *reduction* of the overall road network during the 1950s, the result of an insufficient compensation by paved roads of the decrease of unpaved roads, very probably because of a lack of maintenance (fig. 3.1).[19]

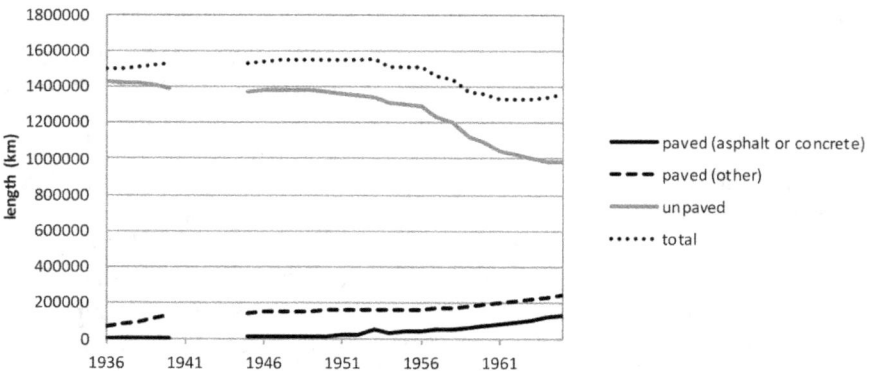

Figure 3.1. Roads in the Soviet Union by pavement type, 1936–1965. Source: Hunter, *Soviet Transport Experience*, 178, table C-12. Figure created by the author.

Only when, by the end of the period under investigation in this chapter, the country started to develop its agricultural sector did road network densities start to converge to Western values. But well before that moment, road investment shares within the overall annual investment in the transport sector overtook the railway share. And only then did the countryside become accessible by bus. By 1970, Soviet cities counted more than 2,000 bus systems (including 111 trolley bus systems and 5 metro systems). Five years earlier, the number of passenger trips by bus had for the first time surpassed that of "urban electric" forms of transport. But by then, the railroads share in public passenger transport in passenger-kilometer was still 66 percent. With its annual growth rates of 6 percent (compared to around 4 percent in the US) and its "lean pattern" of investments in transport (10 percent of total capital investment, versus double that share in the US), the Soviets showed modernization was possible without massive investment in roads and the automobile, but this 'lesson' did not come across the Cold War divide. And if it did (such as in the case of a comparison with Germany; see chap. 2), it functioned as proof of the USSR's backwardness. The insight that globalization came with 'multiple mobilities' was still hidden far ahead in the future: it had no place in a Cold War setting. For Rostow, the Soviet Union was thirty-five years behind the American 'model' (measured in "industrial output," and fifty years in "output per capita"). The country was simply "postponing or damping the advent of the age of high mass-consumption" and investing in military might instead.[20]

***

So, how about the passenger car, then, the very epitome of Western 'superior' modernity? Stalin's promise from 1929 that he would give his fellow compatriots "a country of automobilization" was apparently given without considering the passenger car. The passenger car's share was so "very modest" (*dixit* Hunter) that Soviet statisticians did not even bother estimating their number. Instead, the 'collective vehicle,' the bus, took on this road transport task. The lack of subways was another token of Communism's alleged backwardness: in Moscow, the forty-two prewar subway kilometers were extended to one hundred, while Leningrad and Kiev only started building their subway systems in 1955 and 1960, respectively. During a speech in Vladivostok after his visit to Beijing in October 1959, General Secretary Nikita Khrushchev declared, "It is not our aim to compete with the Americans in the production of large numbers of automobiles." Newly to be developed "public taxi pools" would be able to provide cars to his citizens "for necessary trips," a system of hiring from public garages that goes back to the beginnings of automotive history, when electric car fleets in particular were managed in such a way, and when it competed with the car as a private property, the latter especially popular among petrol car owners. Khrushchev's plan was based on a vision he unfolded during his secret talk at the famous 20th Party Congress in 1956, in which a part of his critique of the Stalin era was directed at the car as "the strongest status symbol of the elite."[21]

But most of Khrushchev's car-rental schemes failed, and after his removal from power in 1964 (not after he, at the 22th Party Congress, had predicted the Communist society would be reached in another two decades), "mass motorization" became the aim of his successors Leonid Brezhnev (who managed to raise the Soviet citizens' standard of living considerably) and Alexei Kosygin. But as Luminita Gatejel showed in her dissertation about the Soviet Union's motorization, Khrushchev's ideas appeared quite resilient and resonated among the population: by constructing a "large net of rental car garages ... we clearly need only one-tenth or one-fifteenth of the cars [compared to the West] ... After all, the people are no wanderers (*Herumtreiber*). They work. And while they work, the car is immobile." This was the closest Soviet socialism came to formulating its own 'car philosophy': like the electric fleet experiments of early automobilism, an engineer's dream (let's not forget that several Soviet leaders in this period were engineers).[22]

By 1965, about one million passenger cars were counted in the USSR, "mainly in the hands of state organizations." But then the Eastern Bloc started to motorize in earnest, the passenger cars produced, according to central planning in Moscow, in the USSR, Czechoslovakia, and the GDR.[23] And while a ninety-two-kilometer beltway was constructed in a vain hope to alleviate inner-city congestion around Moscow, in 1965 a six-lane road connection between the Kremlin and the Ministry of Foreign Affairs was pushed through an old neighborhood, "requiring demolition of more than a hundred stately homes." Remarkably, the American transport expert Hunter, who intended to draw "lessons for other countries" from the "Soviet transport experience," concluded "transport investment is a concomitant of, not a precondition for, economic development," the latter statement being the result of "a misreading of nineteenth century experience in the United States, that large-scale expensive transport facilities must be laid down before agriculture and industry can begin to grow," a lesson soon to be forgotten (if it were picked up at all) by subsequent transport experts under the 'development' ideology.[24] Hunter remained silent about the passenger car, however.

He also could have mentioned a phenomenon that would have disturbed his neat bipolar West-East picture: the 'development' of the vast eastern realm of the Soviet Union, where the low population density prevented the western railway network to be extended into. In rapidly industrializing Central Asia, for instance, truck transport increased precipitously during the 1950s in what three Soviet coauthors called "the opening up of virgin territory," a formulation reminding us of the American Western frontier. From a development perspective, the operation was very successful: after thirty-five years since 1950, freight transport in Tajikistan and Kirghizia (current Kyrgyzstan) had increased 70-fold (against a 55-fold increase of average USSR freight growth); in Turkmenia (current Turkmenistan) and Kazakhstan, it increased 80-fold, whereas in Uzbekistan the growth was a stunning 145-fold. But what is most revealing is how this freight was moved: by truck, in the case of Kazakhstan, fifteen times more so than by rail. In Kirghizia, nearly all freight and passenger transport took place by road, constructed through "people's projects." And although the purchase of private cars was modest (1,700 in 1965 in Uzbekistan), the Uzbeks motorized, like so many developing areas in the world, first and foremost through the motorcycle, of which they owned 167,200 by the end of the period covered by this chapter. They also used the bus, which in the case of Uzbekistan increased its patronage (in million passengers) nearly forty-fold between 1940 and 1960, and then again, until 1983, sixfold, half of this in rural areas. Bus use increase was similar in the Kazak, Kirghiz, Tajik, and Turkmen Soviet Republics. But as late as 1990, still half of all freight (in ton-kilometer) was hauled by the Russian railways (and 40 percent of passengers, in passenger-kilometer).[25]

***

Historians of Eastern European socialist states described how in these sates' "shortage economy" the "daily routines" of the people were dominated by "the state of the public transport systems," but next to their physical mobilities, "*imaginative mobilities*" were produced, especially fed by what Alexei

Yurchak has called the "Imagined West." Car maintenance in such economies "required subversive and resourceful behaviours," creating "new spaces of social bonding." The car market was coordinated through the Council for Mutual Economic Assistance (Comecon), established in 1949, but only in 1957 did this institution start to deal with transport issues: "By the 1960s and 1970s, the old Soviet Pobdas and Moskvitches gave way to a new generation of socialist cars such as the Wartburg and Trabant (produced in the GDR), the ... Czech Škoda, the Dacia (made in Romania), the Yugo (a Yugoslav version of the people's car), the Polski Fiat (a proud Polish achievement), and the Russian-made Lada and the Zhiguli, emerging from the conveyor belts of new car factories built in the Soviet Union."[26] Here (for instance, in former Yugoslavia, where the Brotherhood and Unity Highway was opened in 1963 between Ljubljana, Zagreb, and Belgrade), like elsewhere in Europe, freeway construction linked the capitals (in this case, of Slovenia, Croatia, and Serbia) but "peripheralized Bosnia and Herzegovina, Montenegro, Kosovo, and, partly, Macedonia. Thus, it additionally reinforced the already industrialized regions and neglected the less developed ones. Bogdan Mieczkowski's "empirical findings" of Eastern European transport (the first overview, he claimed, of Eastern European transport between 1945 and 1975 in English) did not find "direct evidence of a common transport plan," although he did observe a relative decline of railway transport after the construction of the Friendship oil pipeline (1964): "Road transport in the international trade within Comecon [was] small." The result was "autonomization of the republics, [heightening] tensions among them, which created conditions for future conflicts." In Yugoslavia, the road took over from rail (in both passenger and freight transport) in the second half of the 1960s.[27]

In Hungary, a recent study of five hundred cartoons by György Péteri from the satirical weekly *Ludas Matyi* during the era of explosive motorization between 1958 and 1970 (in the latter year, cars realized one-fifth of total passenger transport, its use growing faster than that of motorcycles and buses) gave a convincing impression of the *imaginative mobilities* of Eastern European citizens. His study revealed a remarkable critique of the "almost pathological concern with the good of the car, even at the expense of one's family's health and well-being." The critique was in fact directed at the elite, whose car *fetishism* sprang from their desire of acquisition. Although the average car density by the end of the period covered by this chapter was about one-tenth of Western European values (33 cars per 1,000 inhabitants in Hungary in 1972, 20 in Poland, 82 in the GDR, versus 269 in France and 262 in West Germany), experts hoped to overcome this "backwardness (*lemaradésunk*)" through a "system-neutral" mass motorization, thus producing "a conspicuous silence in the era about the questions of 'socialist car' or 'socialist automobilism,'" in which, as Péteri confirmed, Khrushchev "took a serious interest." Most car users were "spiritual workers" (managers, professionals, clerical workers who bought the Trabants, Wartburgs, Skodas and, from the 1970s, Zhigulis [Ladas]) and members of the *nomenklatura*, who used "general purpose personal vehicles" owned by the state, comprising one-fifth of the country's passenger car fleet, many of them Mercedes. *Ludas Matyi* documented a decade-long cultural shock among intellectuals and artists about the perversion of Hungary's socialist values by this "vulgar materialism." But central planners, aware of the social inequalities revealed by motorization, conceded that "to deny the satisfaction of the needs of this stratum would be incorrect and, indeed, it is impossible." Needless to say, Hungary's road fatality and injury rate was more than double of that of the Northwestern European countries (but in the same order of magnitude as Austria or Spain).[28] Chinese leaders, preparing for the 'opening up' of their economy, soon would send delegations to Hungary to study its reforms.

At that moment, "everyday life under [European] socialism" had seen, during the 'thaw' of the Cold War (the late 1950s and early 1960s; the building of the Berlin Wall happened in 1961) some first signs of "new mass leisure practices, such as tourism, hitchhiking, wild camping, listening to jazz, dancing to beat and rock and roll tunes, and the wearing of tight-fitting jackets and jeans, symboliz[ing] the youth's quest for everyday pleasures, adventure, and nonconformism, not just in the West, but in the Eastern Bloc as well." It is against this background that a Czech writer such as Václav Řezáč, in *Nástup* (Entrance, 1951; translated into German as *Die ersten Schritte* [1955], The first steps), a "for social realism typical work," could include a passus where the protagonist muses about the 'hypermodernity' of German cars ("Those Mercedes or BMWs, no match for any American car!"): "How is it possible to build miraculous [*fabelhafte*] cars and at the same time kill people. Either one is a motorist or one is a murderer."[29]

China's Mobility "On Two Legs": Making the Old New through Car and Bicycle

Much like Europe, Southeast Asia came out of World War II (which for China had taken three years more; Japanese called it the Fifteen Years War, starting in 1931) heavily marked by destruction. China (with a population of 450 million in 1949) counted 14 million deaths, Japan 2 million. Japan surrendered, according to Japanologist M. William Steele, not only because of the atom bombs dropped on Hiroshima and Nagasaki but also because of the invasion by the Soviet Union of its crucial economic asset, Manchuria. As witnessed by James Ballard, large migratory flows of returning forced laborers and Chinese and Japanese prisoners of war were set in motion, as well as Japanese refugees from Korea and China. While the

American occupying armies initiated political reform in Japan, China slid into a civil war of which it came out only in 1949 with the founding of the People's Republic. By then, the region represented one-tenth of the annual economic performance of the world, somewhat less in terms of exports. At the same time, the world population started to grow precipitously, mostly in this region. As a result, the countries of the Organisation for European Economic Co-operation and Development (founded 1961 as a successor to the Organisation for European Economic Co-operation [founded 1948] at a moment when Canada and the US joined, later followed by Japan) represented only 15 percent of the 5.2 billion people alive on the planet by the end of the 1980s.[30]

In China, mobility after the defeat of the Japanese army was dominated by the military: the Guomindang (GMD) equipped its troops with excellent American and Japanese trucks and other vehicles and engaged in a fierce civil war with the Communists, while "travel was controlled by a rigidly supervised passport system." Mobility was destructive and ravenous: between 1945 and 1947, the Communists destroyed more than 10,000 miles of railway track (of which the GMD rebuilt 3,700 miles), while they captured more than two thousand trucks and two hundred tanks. One of the enemies the Communists in the North were confronted with were flea-infested rats (a form of animal mobility hardly touched upon in the historiography of transport) released by the Japanese causing at least thirty thousand Chinese to die of bubonic plague in 1947. Shanghai, from where young James Ballard fled with his bourgeois family, seemed to offer the biggest chance of a GMD victory, although even Chiang Kai-shek's son, the Soviet-educated Chiang Ching-kuo, had to acknowledge the "parasitical" character of the local elite, whose "wealth and ... foreign style homes are built on the skeleton of the people. How is their conduct any different from that of armed robbers? Automobiles, refrigerators, perfumes, and nylon hosiery imported from abroad ... are like opium that destroy the national economy."[31] Cars as opium of the elite: Marx would have frowned.

But Shanghai was an exception. On the countryside, in 1948, Mao Zedong announced the shift from guerilla to open warfare, resulting in the seizure of the crucial railway junction at Zhengzhou by six hundred thousand troops backed by two million peasants in four provinces, whose logistics were organized by Deng Xiaoping. Remaining "stubbornly hostile to the idea of land reform," the GMD fled to the island of Taiwan with three hundred thousand troops, while intellectuals fled to Taiwan, Hong Kong, Macao, "and other parts of the world." When the People's Republic of China was inaugurated in 1949, "communist regimes ruled a third of the world." Article 5 of the Common Program for China guaranteed the right of freedom of speech, association, domicile, and "moving from one place to another" to all, except for "political reactionaries." Land reform set in motion an agricultural revolution and class war, which not only resulted in one to two million 'class enemies' killed, and another four to six million sent to "penal labor and reeducation camps," but also ushered in economic growth rates "exceeding [during the 1950s] what was seen in Eastern Europe." Not surprisingly, tourism came to a standstill. When the revolution hit the cities, similar amounts of casualties and forced laborers could be counted, this time accompanied by an anti-urban atmosphere, expressed, for instance, in campaigns against prostitution and opium use, and the abandonment of the hand-pulled and the cycle rickshaw, as we saw in chapter 1.[32] The pedicabs were from then on used only for urban freight traffic: when Marc Riboud published his collection of photographs on China from 1957 and 1965, only four showed a cycle rickshaw: "Rickshaws [hand-pulled] have disappeared all over China," he commented, "and most able-bodied people avoid even [cycle] pedicabs." When, at the beginning of the 1950s, a new classification system of social classes was introduced (identifying such people as "idler," "urban pauper," or "office employee"), "pedicab worker" was one of the sixty categories, but by 1956, the last pedicab in Shanghai was sent to the museum, except for those few vehicles that were kept for touristic purposes.[33]

***

The early 1950s generated much international sympathy for China, despite its invasions of Xinjiang (1949) and Tibet (1950). Also, domestically, hopes of a bright future were high: Indologist and university professor Ji Xianlin remembered how the revolution made him into a "changed person," expressed by his "wearing a modern Mao suit instead of traditional Chinese dress." The First Five-Year Plan (1953–1957), a "roaring success," increased industrial production considerably, backed by the Soviet Union. Among the twenty-four newly installed ministries, two were related to 'mobility': the Ministry of Communications and the Ministry of Railways, the latter soon to develop into a powerful player, with its own army section, including educational facilities. The investment in "transport and communications" represented 15 to 19 percent of capital investment in these years, the highest single item after "industry" (with 39 to 52 percent). Although the budget of the army (which encompassed an engineering corps, as well as a railway and signal corps) doubled between 1950 and 1960, its share in the total state budget decreased to one-fifth from a 1950 share of 42 percent. One of the army's feats was building the extensive road and rail system in the Northeastern Guanxi province to support Vietnamese Communist leader Ho Chi Minh with supplies in his struggle against the French colonizers.

By that time, the United States had become the number one enemy, mostly because of the Korean War (1950–1953) and their Seventh Fleet activities in the Taiwan Strait to protect Taiwan against mainland attacks. As a response, China sought cooperation with the 'nonaligned' countries who in their famous Bandung Conference in Indonesia in 1955 produced strong, anti-Western declarations (with a central role for Zhou Enlai: "the population of Asia will never forget that the first atom bomb exploded on Asian soil") and which China mainly used to strengthen its ties with the forty million or so of the Chinese diaspora, mostly coming from the two Southern provinces Guangdong and Fujian (who in Thailand represented one-tenth, in Malaysia one-fourth, and in Singapore even two-thirds of the population).[34] Whereas the United Kingdom tried to continue its imperialist relations with its former colonies through the Colombo Plan, formulated during the Commonwealth Foreign Affairs Ministers' meeting in Colombo, Ceylon, in 1950, "to counter communist expansion," Soviet leaders, "guided more by political considerations rather than profit and market concerns," soon granted India "the leading position as a recipient of Soviet aid," all the more reason for the United States to join the UK in its effort, in the words of US Undersecretary of State Dean Acheson, "to foster an environment in which our national life and individual freedom can survive and prosper." After all, the US regarded Germany and Japan as the "two great workshops of Europe and Asia, … necessary," according to Acheson, "for our national security." The young senator John F. Kennedy agreed: "If India collapses, so may all of Asia."[35]

One of the characteristics of the Chinese revolution, especially from a mobility point of view, is that it triggered enormous migratory waves: "In the early 1950s administrators in Shanghai and other major cities urged millions of refugees and unemployed urban workers and family members to go (or return) to the countryside." Although farmers' sedentary mobility was severely restricted (despite Article 5 of the Common Program for China) through the *hukou* regulation (1958), which compelled every citizen to obtain an official residence certificate from the local police (and which had to keep China free of a devastating mass urbanization as in other Third World countries), thirty million peasants had "drifted into the cities" by the end of the 1950s in an effort to escape the famine that, at the height of the Western abundance, cost at least twenty million lives, especially those of children. That was the result of the Great Leap Forward (1958–1961, connected to the Second Five-Year Plan), an effort, in the words of Mao, to "start a technological revolution so that we may overtake Britain in fifteen or more years."

This should be brought about through a radical decentralization of planning and can, from a mobility perspective, be interpreted as a (failed) effort to take the planning power out of the hands of the professional economic planners at the ministries. What did not fail, however, was the *hukou* system (perhaps inspired by the Soviet *propiska* [household registration] system), "a code of laws, regulations and programmes whose effect was formally to differentiate residential groups as a means to control population movement and mobility and to shape state development priorities," which according to Vivienne Shue brought down rural migration "close to zero." The Chinese government considered peasants "petty owners of productive property" and thus "carriers of bourgeois ideology," basing their production on "the family as a unit." Meanwhile, the railways appeared crucial in central planning, for instance, when the three hundred million peasants near railway lines were expected to store their grain, for later railway transport: "If we are in constant control of 100 billion *jīn* [half a kilogram, so fifty million ton] of grain," central economic planner and Party Central Committee member Chen Yun opined, "then [US President] Truman or [South Korean President] Syngman Rhee won't concern us."[36]

***

Indeed, "China's railway network … expanded enormously since 1949," as Jonathan Spence in his classic history of China asserts (without giving data). We know from a CIA analysis, however, that during the years 1952 to 1957 (covering the First Five-Year Plan of 1953–1957) the existing network of 22,000 km was increased by some 6,000. This work was undertaken by 1.5 million Chinese workers (counted at the end of 1956), whereas 15 percent of them were "permanent cadres of the Ministry of Railroads and the Railroad Engineering Corps of the PLA [People's Liberation Army] who did the design, planning, and semiskilled tasks associated with railroad construction." Workers were asked to bring their own tools, and their work was unpaid. A Central People's Government directive stipulated to the local authorities that such work should be done for a maximum of ten days per year (unless it was done by "volunteers"), and it was meant "to tap the [peasants'] seasonal underemployment."[37] After the founding of the People's Republic, China began reconstructing and reconfiguring its railway network "with some assistance from advisers from the U.S.S.R. and other Eastern European countries," starting with the return of a "large amount of Japanese-made machinery" (including the Japanese-built steelworks at Anshan) the Russians had taken from Manchuria during their brief occupation in the war. At that moment, most of China's railway lines (with different gauges) were located in the Northeast and along the coast, so much so that more than half the provincial capitals did not have a connection with Beijing. In Soviet style, roads were "planned not to compete with the railways but to supplement them." China spent nearly 70 percent of its investments in transport and communication during the First Five-Year Plan on railways.[38]

Work on roads was no less spectacular. The CIA analysis estimated the work done by the amount of "earthwork" moved. Although the earth moved for rail and road formed only a tiny fraction (6 percent) of the total (most of this total done "in support of water conservancy"), road expansion was nonetheless impressive, with the most spectacular increase in 1956, when more than 72,000 km of "simple roads" were added to the network (and another 15,000 km of "motor roads," "secondary roads," and "improved highways"). The CIA author was impressed, too, as he compared the total earth moved for railway building during the six-year period (461 million cubic meters) with the 425 million cubic meter moved during the twenty-five initial years of the English Industrial Revolution, for the building of 30,000 km of railroads.[39] In the case of the road, too, the period covered by the CIA report was preceded by the "rebuilding," during the first three years of the People's Republic, of 8,000 km of highways, while another 24,000 had been "repaired"; 1,640 km were newly built. Per km, highway building in China cost sixteen times less than in the United States. What the CIA report did not monitor was the *configuration* of the network: like in the Soviet Union, as we saw, "far more" highways were built "in the less developed regions than in the developed ones." And like in the Soviet Union (in Central Asia, as we saw), China undertook a form of 'socialist development' by constructing most of the new roads in the Northwest and Southwest, in an effort to unite the country through connections to the ethnic minorities, which meant in some cases (such as the roads from Qinghai, Xinjian, and Sichuan to Xizang [Tibet]) these roads were "major engineering achievements," as they were built up to four thousand meter above sea level.[40]

An official retrospective statistical overview of Chinese roadbuilding shows the steepest part of the curve occurring in the years just before and partially overlapping with the Great Leap (a period also called the Little Leap, just before the "second Great Leap"), and not during the 'reform and opening up' triggered by Deng Xiaoping in 1978, as many in the West and in China would have it.[41] If the figures for the Great Leap (when there were "appalling exaggerations in the statistical records of the country's economic performance") are correct (and we assume they are as they have been sanctioned—and perhaps corrected—by later statisticians who may have had an interest in emphasizing Deng's performance), it is indeed remarkable that the curve starts to flatten out in 1978 (fig. 3.2). According to these official statistics, the total length of roads at the start of the People's Republic was somewhat more than 80,000 km, which increased more than sixfold to 521,000 in 1960, only to increase further to 650,000 a decade later. During the first decade, half the roads were paved, while the share of paved roads increased clearly during the second decade, to about 75 percent of the total. "From early 1960s to mid-1970s," another Chinese retrospective publication said, "the focal point of highway construction was to upgrade the existing roads, rehabilitate dangerous bridges, improve ferries and build the 'Black Top' pavement"; in ten years, 100,000 km of "bituminous pavement" were laid.

Other spectacular statistics that easily dwindle the interstate rhetorics in the United States revealed that during the second half of the 1950s alone, 330,000 km of "county and township roads … of comparatively low standard and quality" were built, followed between 1965 and 1978 by another 360,000 km, most of the latter "in mountainous and remote areas." The statistics about the cumulative length of several types of bridges (including "dangerous bridges") from the same ministerial source shows a similar pattern as the start of the road curve of figure 3.2: the increase is largest during the first decade of the People's Republic, although in this case there is a clear steepening of the curve observable during the second half of the 1970s, at the end of which Deng Xiaoping started his 'opening up' campaign. And still, an MIT report from 1954 claimed this was less than the more than 100,000 km of new roads built by the Guomindang regime between 1927 and 1947. This study showed all these early roads were built by millions of farmers and PLA soldiers, without pay: five million peasants worked on the highway into Tibet, after its first section was laid by "inactive troops." In the planning, the remote areas were not forgotten. However, the building of *new* railway lines did not start before the mid-1950s. The completion of the Changjiang railway bridge at Nanjing was celebrated as a feat of Chinese engineering skills. Now, at last, the country possessed a

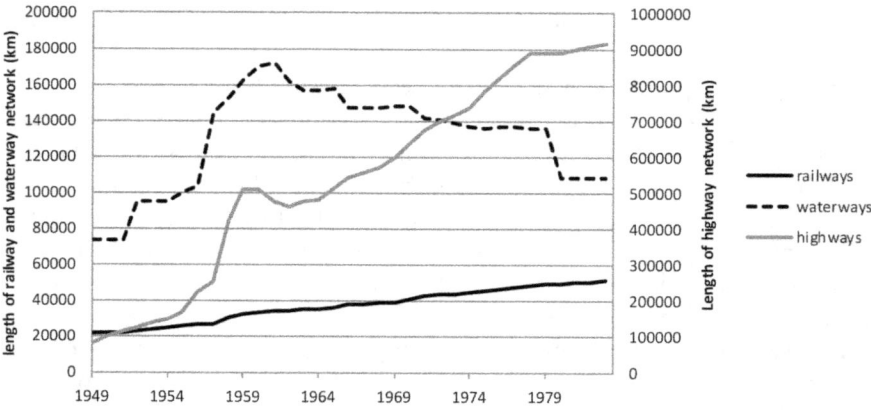

Figure 3.2. Network lengths in China, 1949–1983. Source: Comtois, "Transport and Territorial Development," 786–787, table 3.1. Figure created by the author.

fully integrated railway network supported by thousands of kilometers of short-distance feeder roads, like in the Soviet Union the dream of the utilitarian railway manager.⁴²

A politico-mobility history of the PRC from the mid-1950s would read like this. The Great Leap took place during the Second Five-Year Plan (1958–1962), when "everyone was called upon to maximize transport facilities, and to intensify transport construction" (without much attention spent on "the qualitative aspect"), emphasizing "short-distance transport." Chinese authorities called it "walking on two legs," using "both the resources of the central government and the resources of the local governments, the power of the state and the power of the masses, advanced means of transport and traditional means of transport." Meant to steer away from Soviet dependence, the Great Leap not only alienated intellectuals (many of them emanating from the prewar May Fourth Movement; see chap. 1), especially after Mao launched the Anti-Rightist Campaign, it also led to massive deforestation because the wood was needed to fuel the million tiny furnaces meant to produce steel decentrally. It also "clogged train yards and snarled train traffic throughout the country," because all these decentralized items had to be transported by railroads, and not, as in other less centrally controlled countries, by truck traffic. By mobilizing six million "units of female labor power," it further "undermined to a degree the closeness of the family unit" with its "daily coming together ... for shared meals," as American sinologist R. Keith Schoppa claimed.⁴³

After the Great Leap, road construction was "abruptly curtailed," and the emphasis shifted toward the maintenance of existing roads, such that road transport enterprises could be transferred to "rural and mountainous regions" in order to create a "Third Front" in a situation of increasing tensions with the Soviet Union, ending in the sudden withdrawal of thousands of Russian advisers in 1960. The Third Front period led not only to the construction of entire new cities in the Chinese countryside, especially in the West, but also to new railway lines, such as the one linking Chengdu with Kunming via Panzhihua and steel and truck plants, often at the price of "environmental disaster." Rural small-scale industry "owned by Chinese counties, communes and brigades" also made local roads necessary. This is also the period when special military roads were built near the borders with Southeast Asian countries (such as Vietnam). Both aims (the building of agricultural roads and of strategic roads) were continued in the Third Five-Year Plan (1966–1970). The break with the USSR also led to a reorientation of China's road construction knowledge procurement: whereas the Soviet Union and other Eastern European countries in the immediate postwar years were members of international roadbuilding association PIARC (Permanent International Association of Road Congresses), and China was not, the latter sent an "observer" to the 1964 PIARC conference in Rome and showed up with ten people three years later in Tokyo.[44]

Such visits would gradually open up China for the 'development' ideas of the West, a process that started during the second phase of the Cultural Revolution (1969–1976, after the three years of Red Guard class wars, 1966–1969), when China began rethinking its relation with the United States. In 1971, China replaced Taiwan as a permanent Security Council member, followed one year later by US President Richard Nixon's "historic visit," suggested for the first time in public by Edgar Snow's interview with Mao, published in *Life* magazine in April 1971. By then, the declarations to call itself a Third World country had been replaced by a realpolitik of diplomatic relations with the Fascist regimes in Spain, Greece, and Chile. At the same time, the Communist Party's membership had expanded to twenty-eight million. By the end of the Maoist period (Mao died in 1976), China's investment share of GDP in transport was 30 percent (double the share of 1952), "a very high figure for such a poor country."[45]

***

Russian assistance also had helped create the "cradle of the Chinese automobile industry" in the Northeastern provincial capital Changchun, after the model of a car factory near Moscow, a result of the signing of the Sino-Soviet Treaty of Friendship, Alliance and Mutual Assistance during Mao Zedong's visit to Moscow in 1950. Ironically, Changchun had been chosen by the Japanese invaders as the capital of their "puppet state" Manchukuo (see chap. 1) and for that occasion had been designed as a modern-style railway and car friendly city. The First Auto Works (FAW) was conceived to be the first of a future "China's Detroit" (*Zhongguo de Ditelü*), with the help of Soviet advisers. There, after three years of preparation, trucks of the Jiefang (Liberation) model were produced from 1956, its image reprinted in the billions on China's smallest bank note of 1 yuan. After 600 million yuan of investments, the four-ton, dark green truck, modeled after the Soviet ZIS-150, was produced by eighteen thousand workers, most of them from Shanghai. Five years later, not only a limousine (the Hongqi, Red Flag) for state leaders started production, also the "middle class car" Dongfeng (Eastern Wind) was developed. By then, sixteen automotive production plants had been founded, as part of the decentralization efforts at the start of the Great Leap in 1958, enabled by the dispatching from Changchun of 560 administrators and one thousand technicians. In 1969, the Second Auto Works in Wuhan (Hubei province) started producing trucks, but production was halted during the Cultural Revolution.[46]

In Shanghai, a sedan (Phoenix [Phenghuang], based on the Mercedes-Benz 220S) appeared, but until 1965, no more than a hundred passenger cars were produced annually. Only during a short break of two years, just before the outbreak of the Cultural Revolution, was the China National Automotive Industry Corporation (CNAIC) founded as an umbrella of some seventy-five plants, an initiative of the powerful First Ministry of Machine Building that soon was discontinued, but after Deng's opening and reform was revived in 1982, to play a catalyzing role in the relaunch of the Chinese car industry. As late as 1983, only sixty privately owned cars were registered in China. For the period under investigation here, however, more spectacular was the development of the production of bicycles, whose annual statistics showed a constantly rising line, with the steepest after the interruptions caused by the Great Leap and the Cultural Revolution (fig. 3.3). In his excellent description of Chinese village life, Huang Shu-min relates how by the early 1970s, when peasants were allowed to sell their surplus vegetables on the market, they started to "purchase things they wouldn't dare to think of before, such as a bicycle, a radio, or a wristwatch."[47]

China's average annual GDP growth of 9 percent during the First Five-Year Plan period was kept high by the growth of industrial GDP (16.1 percent per annum, agricultural GDP grew by only 5 percent). During the Great Leap, these figures were 9, 14, and 3 percent, in the *negative*. This was also caused, as sinologist Victor Seow showed, by the devastating role of the Jiefang truck: "In 1959 alone, there were purportedly over 50,000 professional and 70,000 non-professional transport groups established across more than 20,000 communes [of about 50,000 people each]. These groups, many of whom operated vehicles such as the 'Liberation' truck, were to carry grain and other products from farms to factories, mines and urban centres, coordinating with other road, rail and shipping services to complete these

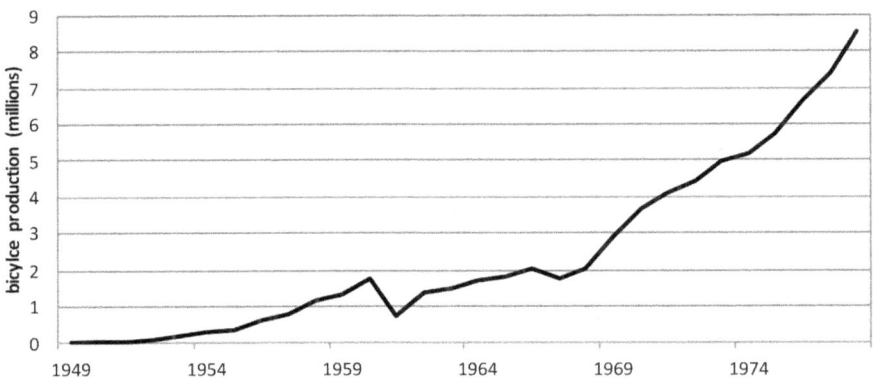

Figure 3.3. Annual bicycle production in China, 1949–1978. Source: Zhang, *Enterprise Reforms in a Centrally Planned Economy*, 9, table 2.1. Figure created by the author.

trips," meanwhile "leaving behind starving peasants." China also continued exporting grain to the Soviet Union, with a "death toll rang[ing] from about 28 to over 45 million" as a result.[48]

Xun-Hai Zhang, who worked in a Chinese bicycle factory between 1975 and 1978, distinguished in his subsequent dissertation between several phases of industrial planning, meandering between centralization and decentralization, each cycle preceded by a reform movement, thus realizing the Chinese proverb "crossing the river by touching stones," referring to the country's learning-by-doing style. The postwar cycle industry started in three factories in Shanghai, Tianjin, and Shenyang, confiscated from a Japanese businessman who had founded them in the latter half of the 1930s. During the First Five-Year Plan, another company in Qingdao was added, combining forty-nine small factories. In 1965, there were eleven bicycle factories in China, and forty-six fifteen years later. The largest was the Shanghai Bicycle Company. Because of the enormous demand, the Chinese government fixed bicycle prices and introduced a rationing system in 1973. Because of this, every province wanted to set up its own cycle factory: in 1976, only three provinces did not have such a factory.[49]

There exists an interesting anecdote, stemming from the biographer of Joseph Needham, the "railway mad" specialist of China's history of technology. Needham was summoned to Zhongnanhai, the party leaders' headquarters next to the Forbidden City in Beijing, for an "urgent matter of state business." There, Mao Zedong asked him about his love of cars, remembering even the make he was driving (an Armstrong Siddeley, which he, by the way, meanwhile had replaced by a more modest Ford Cortina) and then asked him "whether to allow my people to drive motor cars, or whether the bicycle is better for them." Needham, the guilty-feeling European, told Mao that back in Cambridge, the bicycle was "perfectly satisfactory for all of my needs," to which Mao replied: "Right, then. Bicycles it is."[50] *Se non è vero ...* What most students of Chinese mobility history so far have ignored, however, is its extreme duality: "traditional transport" in 1952 contributed 57 percent to the net domestic product, a share that was reduced to 38 percent five years later. Likewise, as much as 70 percent of all transport was done by boats before 1947, but this diminished to only 8 percent in 1979. China's policy of "walking on two legs" seemed to work: while bicycle production and roadbuilding formed the 'new modernity,' a conscious effort was undertaken to modernize the 'old,' by the production of ball bearings, axles, and pneumatic tires to improve the performance of wheelbarrows, hand carts, and animal-draft carts. In the 1960s, animal traction was deliberately introduced to replace human muscle power. Whereas nearly 150,000 motor vehicles were produced in 1978, the production figures for bicycles and handcarts were 8.8 and 10 million, respectively. If socialism did not produce a convincing alternative mobility theory, it at least produced another reality: the conscious construction of a two-pronged mobility system we called 'layeredness.'[51]

The 'Ten-Year Disaster': The Cultural Revolution and Revolutionary Mobility

Tellingly, all curves discussed so far flatten out somewhat during the Cultural Revolution (1966–1976), which began when Mao mobilized his three main supporters (the PLA; radical intellectuals, including his wife Jiang Qing and her "associates ... from the Chinese Academy of Sciences in Beijing and the Municipal Propaganda Department in Shanghai," as well as urban high school and college students; and urban workers) against the reformists within the party, represented, among others, by Vice Chairman Liu Shaoqi and General Secretary Deng Xiaoping. This revolution is nowadays taught in Chinese secondary-school classrooms as the "ten year disaster" and called, in official documents "the ten years of chaos," or, in the anti-Left jargon of mainstream reformers, "the grave left error of the Cultural Revolution, an error comprehensive in magnitude and protracted in duration, [for which the responsibility] does indeed lie with Comrade Mao Zedong."[52] The Cultural Revolution tried, along a different route (the mobilization of the youth organized into Red Guards, or *Hongweibing*, the baby boomers of China), to violently resolve the tension between rural and urban Chinese, between farmers and peasants on the one side and workers and middle class on the other. It was mainly a "city event," which partly explains the cruelty of the army when the time came to end the movement, as most soldiers came from the countryside. From a mobility point of view, the Cultural Revolution ("a caricature of the first" [New Culture Movement from the 1910s], according to Maurice Meisner) was probably the largest 'mobilization' ever in world history. Indeed, the rhetorics of the Cultural Revolution were replete with mobility metaphors: the initial enemies were identified as "capitalist roaders," and Mao's announcement of the "free mobilization of the masses" had been accompanied by the warning "not [to] be like women with bound feet." Mao borrowed the term itself (*wenhua geming*) from the New Culture Movement (1915–1919; see chap. 1), rejecting the 'stagism' of Soviet Marxism, because he intended to jump from an agricultural society directly into socialism.[53]

It was Mao who had brought the class element back into the political discourse in China, at the Tenth Plenum of the Eighth Central Committee in September 1962. In China, like in the West (where the emerging middle class started to make the working class 'invisible,' as we saw in chap. 2), the Communist Party bureaucrats had become blind to the consequences of their emergence as a class of "bourgeois without property." From 1965, clearly before the youth revolt in the West exploded in 'May 1968,' Mao decided to mobilize ("to rebel is justified") the "sent-down youth" or "educated youth," creating "unprecedented opportunities to travel about the country," thus enabling the development of "underground creativity forg[ing] the beginnings of distinctive youth popular culture in China," from wearing Sun Yat-sen jackets (called Mao jackets in the West), the "reinvention of opera and ballet forms" and street theater, to "mass singing" ("pioneered by Western missionaries and strengthened in secular schools by their inclusion in Japan-inspired school curricula," as a historian of China's youth culture analyzed). "Revolutionary tourism" generated massive waves of travelers: Shanghai counted nearly one million visitors on one day in 1966 alone. Likewise, thousands of Shanghai students visited the capital, waved through by "hapless railway ticket clerks [who] found it impossible to say no to hundreds of youth turning up together at stations an demanding passage north."[54] In fact, the wave was triggered by Shanghai workers who "commandeered a train bound for Beijing" to lay their complaints before the central party leaders. The "wanderlust" (Meisner) of around twelve million Red Guards who, between 18 August and 26 November, journeyed to Beijing to greet "Chairman Mao" in eight mass meetings at the Tiananmen Square, may well be considered the second empirical base (next to Khrushchev's plan for Soviet automobilism) of a potential 'socialist theory of mobility.' The vivid description of this "revolutionary tourism" (officially called *chuanlian*, "linking up" to experience and spread the revolutionary mood) was enabled by a declaration of the central authorities on 5 September 1966 that train travel to Beijing and accommodation along the journey would be free, provided one could show a signed certificate from the local Red Guard committee.

The flow was in two directions: at the start of the revolution, Beijing middle school students (middle schoolers formed the bulk of the Red Guards) appeared in the province on "chuanlian missions," while the flow in the other direction began shortly before the first of Mao's eight reviews of a million or so Red Guards on 18 August. The September declaration in fact implied 'taking the train' was considered a revolutionary act, as it mobilized the youth against the conservatives and other 'class enemies.' At the height of the 'movement,' Beijing's populations swelled from its regular 7.7 million to more than 10 million. At the largest rally, the crowd in front of the Forbidden City was so large that Mao was transported in an open jeep, greeting "2 million students in one fell swoop." Six thousand trucks were used for transport, but most Red Guards were marched to the square on foot, creating apocalyptic congestion and chaos. The crowd was so dense that some could simply lift their feet from the "puddle[s] of urine" on the ground, created because the boys were unable to visit the improvised toilets. Ken Ling, whose heavily redacted memoir provided most of the information given here, was a sixteen-year-old, middle-class Red Guard (his father a bank manager) who normally moved around the Southern city of Amoy (current Xiamen) on bicycle but now could confiscate and steal more than thirty jeeps and trucks (and later even a sedan) that he used for freight but also personal transport. In one house, they found two limousines in the garage. Status sensitive (wearing "white gloves of a leader"), he and his friends indulged in "wild" driving and driving "like mad," behaving as 'hooligans':

> We drove our jeep wildly around the city, putting the top down to let people see us, sprawling like the drunken American soldiers we had seen in propaganda pictures. We seldom ran across another car in the streets; after all, there were only 300 vehicles in Amoy City. My companions insisted that we drive to each of their homes, where we picked up passengers; before long there were more than half a dozen little brothers and sisters in the jeep, some sitting on our shoulders. Pedestrians were startled; people stuck their heads out of upper windows; I deliberately sideswiped a policeman's post. The police in Amoy learned a new traffic regulation—for the Red Guards there were no traffic regulations.

He went to Beijing twice, the train journey being a nightmare, with knife fights against a group of Mao-quoting beggars, demolishing baggage racks for weapons, and looting along the route. Shanghai was a "paradise of adventures," one of these being the sight of gigantic flows of girls on bicycles, when the workday in the factories ended. They went "sightseeing" in Qingdao, and when in Beijing, they had the chance to visit the Red Flag (Hongqi) sedan factory. Back home, he gave driving lessons to his girlfriend, but girls driving motorcycles (I am "so happy") Ling does not find appropriate. He tries to understand the motives for the desire to be a Red Guard, but in the end, he concludes that "in the monotonous life of this society people looked on participation in the Cultural Revolution as a kind of excitement." When, after a year, the factional struggles erupted, a "dangerous but exciting" "propaganda truck warfare" took place during the nights: more than fifty trucks with loudspeakers were "blaring denunciations … and colliding with one another until late into the night." Fully disillusioned, he flees to Taiwan.[55]

Dai Hsiao-ai [Dai Xiaoai], another participant, an elite, seventeen-year-old middle school student in Guangzhou (Canton), much more confused about the true motives of the belligerent factions than Ken Ling, also relates how the "struggle against the four olds" (for reactionary habits) was undertaken with "all sorts [of vehicles], even ambulances, to haul the stuff [found in the homes of 'class enemies']. It was very common to see a truck loaded with furniture, statues, clothing, and books with singing and chanting Red Guards hanging on in every corner." He also shows how some Red Guards managed to acquire "*chuanlian* prosperity" by shrewdly asking for money at the coordination centers, one of them collecting "enough to buy a bicycle after returning to Peking from his first trip. Wonder of wonders! While we were penniless and starving this clever Peking Red Guard was eating in restaurants every day!" He quickly learns the trick as well. Like Ling disillusioned, he flees to Hong Kong within less than two years.[56]

Liu Guokai, another participant, also relates about the class war between the "conservative" and the "rebel" factions in Guangzhou, how middle school students get bored and decide to take part, becoming highly mobile: "They ran around helping weak 'Rebel' organizations in other schools. They went to factories to organize 'Rebel' groups outside their units." For the victims it was, as Meisner formulated it, "a time of enormous human suffering," of which one gets only a glimpse when reading the memoir by Ruth Earnshaw, an American teacher in China married to Lo Chuanfang, together teaching at a university in Guangzhou. Typically, her memoir is full of irony, the well-known literary technique to create some distance between the narrator and (in this case, quite intimidating) reality, a reality of violence, a Communist version of social super-engineering, and micro-surveillance. After the ordeal, she realizes "we belonged to a doomed species in the new order." In the end, she returns "home," back into "freedom."[57] Curiously, a Chinese victim, Indology professor at Peking University Ji Xianlin, also uses irony (and a lot of sarcasm) to describe his sufferings as a "counterrevolutionary element" and a "capitalist academic authority" from the "psychopaths indulging their sadistic instincts under the cover of revolutionary instructions. Written sixteen years later and published thirty years later by an official publisher in Beijing, Ji's chronicle of a class struggle between workers and intellectuals provides the reader with a chilling account of violent 'struggle sessions' and a nine-month stay in the "cowshed," a makeshift prison on campus, constantly terrorized by "the mob."[58]

***

But for the Red Guards themselves, the orgy of mobility was adventurous: only later did they find out their youthful counterparts in the West had indulged in their own, automotive, versions of mobilities.[59] "We got hold of a letter of introduction and a jeep," a female member of a "gang of Red Guards" remembered, when interviewed by Zhang Xinxin and Sang

Ye in their excellent oral history project, "and went all the way to Yunnan province, seeing the world and 'promoting revolution.'" Another witness, a member of a girl group of Red Guards, recounts how they stopped a truck on the street, climbed aboard and "search[ed] people's homes and confiscat[ed] things ... I went on the great journeys to 'exchange revolutionary experience' as well. That was the first chance I'd ever had to go a long way from home—it didn't seem far then. Trains would be full of people in khaki wearing red armbands ... There was nothing to drink, and no way of going to the lavatory. Everyone would be playing the mouth-organ or singing." In general, it seems that "in aggregate, the female condition improved more than the male under Mao," according to an oral history by China's leading feminist, Li Xiaojiang.[60]

Frank Dikötter, who based his account of this phase mostly on Ling's diary, added that the "red tourists" sometimes "spent months crisscrossing the country" visiting Mao's birthplace, the site of the first peasant soviet in 1927, while they re'did' the Long March on foot, in such numbers that in some cases the army had to drop food and medicines from helicopters. Such students "without organization and without discipline" (as they were called) slipped through the checkpoints at the stations manned by Doctrine Guards who checked these students' *chengfen* (class background). Dikötter also mentioned the mobility of meningitis, due to the unhygienic circumstances, costing an extra 160,000 lives, upon the 400,000 mentioned by Meisner. Although the "free board and travel" were abolished on 21 December 1966, a new call to go home had to be broadcast in February of the next year.[61]

For our analysis, it is important to stress the absence, or so it seems, of any irony, at least among the Guardists: the memoirs and diaries give several examples of the bloody seriousness of the revolution. The second "anti-rightist campaign," for instance, was explicitly aimed against, among others, "grumbling and making of cynical remarks, etc." In fact, the Cultural Revolution itself started when literary critic Yao Wenyuan in November 1965 refused to accept the double entendre of the political satire of a play by Beijing's Vice Mayor Wu Han. And Dai Hsiao-ai [Dai Xiaoai] read in a big character poster in Shanghai during the "struggle against monsters and ghosts" (people in authority not following the Mao line) with which the Cultural Revolution started that a factory director had "portrayed workers as clowns," which resulted in hundreds of posters written against him, announcing that if he did not surrender, he would be "struggled against until he toppled and stank." By the end of the 1970s, the PLA intervened and a true factional struggle emerged (killing around half a million Chinese, purging from the party another three million, and paralyzing Deng Xiaoping's son, who fell from a building at Beijing University).[62]

***

PLA propaganda made army truck driver Lei Feng into a national hero. His posthumously discovered diary (he died in an accident) seems to have been largely "concocted by PLA propaganda writers." In his diary, Lei Feng compares Mao Zedong with the steering wheel of his truck. Lei Feng did not 'own' his truck: Chinese mobility was collective in both use and possession; this is even true for the seemingly 'individual' bicycle: relative very few Chinese, despite the high absolute production numbers, owned one, and certainly not in the countryside. There, the "barefoot doctors" (*chijiao yisheng*), "half-peasant half-doctors" (*bannong banyi*) who carried "one silver needle and a bunch of herbs" (well paid, but with no shoes, a mobility historian is inclined to add) and formed "mobile teams" during the height of the Cultural Revolution (1966–1976), were "mobilized" by the government to "walk the collective road" (instead of pursuing a practice in the city). By the mid-1970s, there were one million such "paramedics" in the countryside, a fourfold increase since 1965. In the village of Gao, to quote an example from American sinologist Edward Rhoads, who studied the postwar proliferation of the bicycle in China, the barefoot doctor was the only person in the "brigade" who owned a bicycle, thus continuing the traditional role of the Western medical doctor as the vanguard of individual 'mobilization.' Bicycles, Rhoads showed, together with wristwatches and sewing machines, belonged to the "three things that go round" (*san zhuan*), or, as Deng Xiaoping predicted in 1958, China would soon be "a nation of bicycles."[63]

By 1976 (from the spring of 1968), more than seventeen million youth had been sent to the countryside. Apart from "de-politicization" (factional power struggle replacing class struggle), the "failure of the Cultural Revolution" must be sought in the fact that workers and peasants disappeared from the leadership bodies, and the experts took over. It is, to conclude this account of the turbulent and violent beginnings of China's mass mobilization, hardly worth mentioning that road safety was no top priority of Chinese authorities, even if the first statistics for 1970 indicated a devastatingly high share of road casualties: the 400,000 "vehicles" in 1970 were involved in no fewer than 55,400 "road crashes" (meaning: every seventh vehicle had an accident that year). In a way, however, here too the automotive global world shows continuity rather than exceptionalism: also in the West, the pre-mass-motorization figures were extremely high, indicating the same learning-by-doing effects as must have been the case for China. But what stuck in the minds of observers in the West was that, in general, road casualties were an order of ten higher than in the Anglophone core, and pedestrians, not motorists, dominated the death statistics. The curves of mobility may have flattened out, but surprisingly this is not the case for rural industrialization. One of the lasting results of the Cultural

Revolution, in Meisner's analysis, was "the regeneration of the program to build industrial enterprises in the countryside," resulting in the creation of a twenty-million-strong class of industrial workers by the end of the 1970s. Private household plots existed before the Cultural Revolution, but their share had been limited from 15 to 5 percent of the cultivated land. During the previous decade, Zhou Enlai declared in 1974, China's industrial output had nearly doubled (it had grown by 10 percent per year, whereas tractor production had increased fivefold).[64]

"Developing India": Constructing a Cold War Modal Configuration

Like China, India started its postwar phase in turmoil. Famines had led to the death of at least one million, whereas a civil war between Muslims and Hindus from 1947 (the year in which India became independent) probably cost another million lives, while ten million fled, Muslims to newly founded Pakistan, Hindus back into India. It was one of "the most intense displacements, interethnic violence, and systematic sexual assaults of the twentieth century ... While well-to-do refugees traveled by airplane or car, and some of those heading to Bombay from Karachi took a ship, the vast majority walked or rode in bullock carts (a two-wheeled wooden vehicle pulled by oxen) in enormous caravans that stretched for miles." The dead, however, traveled by train, in the form of "a thousand charred corpses," as Khushwant Singh's famous novel *Train to Pakistan* (1956) dramatized. The dead were accompanied by 1.25 million Hindus and Sikhs who used the train to flee to India between August and November 1947. Within about two months, 673 trains transported 2.3 million refugees, 3,500 per train, one-third of them on the roofs. *Train to Pakistan* reveals, indeed, the centrality of the railways in postcolonial India, where the only other vehicles near the border with Pakistan are some bicycles, horse-drawn *tongas*, military trucks, and an 'official' motorcycle and "American car." Once, the railway junction at the remote border region where the novel is situated is visited by a military convoy of trucks and cars, preceded by a jeep with a loudspeaker.[65]

And yet, in a country ready to (be) modernize(d), where 80 percent of the population lived in 570,000 villages, *accessibility* through roads or tracks was essential. The emphasis in the government's transport policy initially was on intercity roads, however, meant to support industrialization. This is how 'development' works. The ambitious, twenty-year Nagpur Plan, from 1943, formulated at a Conference of Chief Engineers of the Provinces in the city of Nagpur, targeted a network of more than half a million kilometers, one-third of it paved. Like in China, the 1950s also saw a roadbuilding frenzy. Partition reduced the Indian planned road length by one-quarter, but in 1961, the revised plan was expanded to a total of one million km, with West Bengal as the "vanguard state" in terms of construction. The Nagpur project received loans from the World Bank of up to $700 million, which made India the largest user of World Bank funds until 1961. This had everything to do with India's strategic role in the Cold War. By the end of the 1960s, the Indian road network indeed had reached a total length of nearly one million km, one-third surfaced, on which a total Indian currency equivalent of $1.6 billion had been spent since 1943.[66]

But who was going to use this network? During the first three Five-Year Plans (1951–1966), truck traffic increased fivefold (against rail traffic 2.5 times). Within fifteen years, road freight's share had increased from 12 to 28 percent, and railway's share had likewise decreased. As a protectionist measure, the government increased the share of allocating public funds on railways according to the successive Five Year-Plans, from 55 percent in the first, to 68 and 67 percent in the second and third plans, respectively. In the fourth plan, covering the end of the 1960s and the beginning of the 1970s, half the funds spent on transport went to the railways, whereas the highway program received one-fourth. By the mid-1960s, still three-quarters of the freight transported (in ton-km) went by rail. These investment schemes were the result of a harsh struggle between rail and road proponents, the Indian equivalent of the (postwar part of the) Western coordination crisis. Following the Soviet model of industrialization, Indian national authorities intended to nationalize "road services," after they had already nationalized the railway system (in 1924). Private bus operators opposed these plans. When individual states nonetheless started to set up plans for nationalization through the founding of joint stock corporations (with the railways, state government institutions and bus operators as shareholders), and the bus companies suddenly withdrew from the schemes, the central government announced a moratorium until the end of the Third Five-Year Plan period, even if—after all states but one had introduced such schemes—almost all freight transport and more than half of passenger transport was still in private hands. By the end of the 1950s, bus routes had increased by 60 percent since 1954 (to 550 routes), and these routes' total distance by 95 percent (to 44,000 km); the number of buses deployed and of passengers carried had increased similarly, to 1,827 and 235,000, respectively. Also, the number of trucks had doubled during the same period.[67]

One of the most outspoken proponents of the road option was India's automobile industry. During World War II, Hindustan Motors (1942) and Premier Automobiles (1944) had been founded, while afterward Mahindra and Mahindra was set up (1945) and Tata Engineering and Locomotive Co started its automobile division (1954). The national government did not support this: at first, in 1949, it prohibited the import of complete vehicles (only "completely knocked down" vehicles were allowed, to be assembled in the country), and then it prioritized the domestic production of trucks (as recommended in the Tariff Commission Report of 1956). From 1953, it also "refused permission to Indian manufacturers to assemble imported vehicles without increasing local content," which made assemblers General Motors and Ford leave the country. According to Mike Mason, "in India [the] car manufacturing industry circumvented the expensive experimental stage by copying design of British Austins, Italian Fiats, and Japanese Suzukis." In the Indian planned economy, the Hindustan Motors' Ambassador (based on the Morris Oxford III and produced without much changes during four decades) became the "symbol of Indian independence and modernity," affordable only to "ministers, politicians and distinguished civil servants, and of a small segment of the upper middle class." By 1975, as many trucks were produced as passenger cars (about forty-three thousand).[68]

***

American transport expert Wilfred Owen, who wrote an extensive study of India's "transport and communications" for the Brookings Institution in 1968, signaled a total neglect of rural development in the Fourth Five-Year Plan, a phenomenon we also found in the postwar Soviet Union. In fact, already during the Second Five-Year Plan, "Indian planners ... driven by dreams of rapid industrialization, ... cut funding for agricultural projects [already] to a bare minimum." And although his book fits precisely in the American development ideology of the time (including his preference for roads over rails, as we will see), and thus should be analyzed in the context of the Cold War struggle around India, it cannot be denied that India's "transport problems [were] frustrating testimony to the impact of distance on development." Perhaps this was a blessing in disguise, as it meant that on the countryside, it was the short-distance vehicles like the bicycle and the bullock cart that were the main conveyances, next to walking and porterage (the latter still not to be neglected at the beginning of the 1960s), and not the bus, the truck, or the train, let alone the car. By the beginning of the 1960s, some 1.5 million horses and ponies, 60,000 mules, 1.2 million donkeys, 600,000 camels, and an unknown number of elephants were used for transport, but the "bullock remains the backbone of the agricultural economy," with no fewer than 9 million animals who carried 70 percent of the country's internal freight. One of the results of this was an Indian specialty: the 'mixed road,' where the seven-foot-wide lateral strips were meant for the heavy bullock carts.[69]

Like in China, India's bicycle usage was impressive: since the beginning of its import in 1912 until the year of independence in 1946, 2.5 million bicycles had been sold, but in the following six years alone, another 1.2

million were added, more than 200,000 annually, often adapted by local blacksmiths to the needs of Indian users. In 1946, Indians owned 1.5 million of the 70 million bicycles estimated to be in use all over the world, with 4 per 1,000 on a population of 400 million low compared to the 'bicycle nations' (e.g., in the Netherlands, 463 per 1,000), but by 1974, the Indian figure had increased to 30 million, while two- and three-wheeled motorized vehicles outnumbered four-wheeled ones by a factor of two. In this respect, India was a true two-wheeler country, but women were rarely seen on bicycles, even in towns. A recent study of India's mobility structure revealed a remarkable dance between motorized two- and four-wheelers around the totem of mobile hegemony, which, in relative terms, was convincingly won by the motorcycle. Figure 3.4 reveals a *retreat* of the car in relative terms during the entire period under investigation here: so much for an easy identification of modernization with the car. Clearly, the segment of Indian middle class wealthy enough to afford a car remained relatively modest in the first postwar decades. The passenger car lobby blamed this on the "heavy burden of taxation," which indeed was two times as high as in Germany, and four times as in the United States. A study by Hindustan Motors from 1968 (which, just like in Western countries, granted agency to the car-as-fetish [it "has brought revolutionary changes"], especially in the context of "the country's economic development") compared the "present morass" with the shining situation in the West, and although road transport performance increased more than rail traffic's, the latter still dominated in 1966. But it was, again, the size of the country and its population, just like in the previous case of China, that turned this 'modesty' into staggering figures: in 1971, there were 681,000 cars and jeeps registered in India, against 585,000 two-wheelers. The latter would then dominate the modal configuration for the remainder of the century.[70]

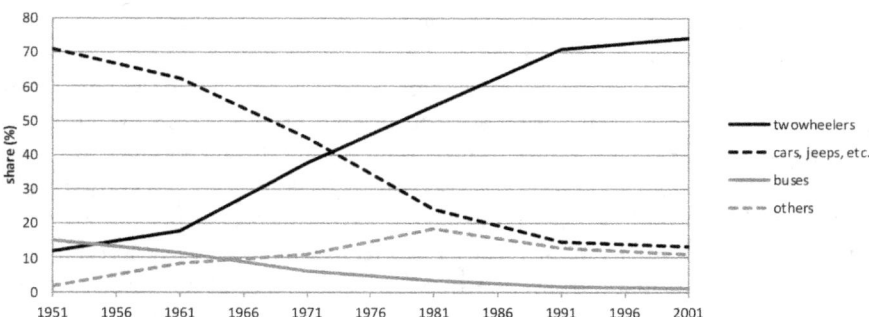

Figure 3.4. Relative registration figures of vehicles in India, 1951–2006. Source: Rahul and Verma, "Economic Impact of Non-motorized Transportation," 23, table 1. Figure created by the author.

By the mid-1970s, twelve million bullock carts were still in use, although the distance these carts produced were halved (from originally around fifty miles maximum per trip), because of the increasing availability of trucks. But Prime Minister Jawaharlal Nehru, seeking a "third way" between capitalism and socialism, was more interested in "big technology" and "big machines," including cars and planes. He accepted "a limited kind of national welfarism with the commanding heights of the economy, including banks and railways, controlled by the state but the rest of the economy in the hands of either local capitalists or multinationals." No wonder, then, did India become one of the most active members of the 'nonaligned' Bandung group of countries. Nonetheless, by the end of the 1970s, a detailed survey of the Indian Ministry of Transport left no doubt that 67 percent of land freight transport took place with animal traction (in ton-km; in tons, it was 72 percent), while about one-fifth was transported by truck and trailer (10 percent if the distance was not taken into account).[71]

India's mobility indeed, like several other Asian countries in this postwar phase, was dominated by what David Edgerton called "creole technologies," especially when the vehicles were improved with ball bearings, broader iron tires that ruined unpaved roads less, and other innovations (as with the bullock carts in India or the bicycles in China). Edgerton also mentioned Indian 'creole' motorized vehicles as examples, such as the Royal Enfield Bullet motorcycle (manufactured in India from the 1950s) and the aforementioned Ambassador produced by Hindustan Motors in West Bengal. Sushil Chandra and Sudhir Atreya also mentioned the specificity of Indian motorization in their brief history of the Indian motorcycle. They contrasted two movies, *Andaaz* (1970) and *Bobby* (1974), in which there is no bike-induced aggression (as in the American movies *The Wild One* and *Hell's Angels*; see chap. 2) but rather a romantic adventure: whereas the girl on the buddy seat in 1970 sits with both legs on one side, in 1974 she sits with legs parted, "nibbling the earlobes of the boy." India provides an interesting case of modernization in between the two rival capitalist and Soviet models.[72] Recently, David Engerman analyzed the Indian resistance to modernize Western-style as the result of a struggle between two personalities: economist Max E. Millikan, former CIA assistant director turned new director of MIT's Center for International Studies, and physics professor and self-made economic statistician Prasanta Chandra Mahalanobis.

Before Independence, in the late 1930s, the Indian National Congress had set up a National Planning Committee chaired by Nehru, who, as we saw, favored industrialization through heavy industry (contrary to Gandhi's emphasis on the cottage industry in the countryside). Immediately after independence, Nehru set up (and chaired) a Planning Commission as a "parallel Cabinet" in which Mahalanobis was invited, who started to cooperate with Soviet officials without following their advice of a nationalization of private enterprises. Mahalanobis's very extensive network—through, among others, the UN Statistical Commission and the UN Economic Commission for Asia and the Far East (ECAFE)—put him in contact with "Marxists without party affiliation" and related economists such as Harvard-based John Kenneth Galbraith. Galbraith would become the US ambassador to India in 1961, one year after "Indian nonalignment had metamorphosed from a policy of equidistance from the great powers to one that made partnership with Moscow the guiding lodestar of Indian foreign policy." These advisers started to visit India in such numbers that Chicago economist Milton Friedman (not invited but sent by "American officials") decided to visit the subcontinent if only to "counter the influence of the left-wing advice." Friedman also worried about the Rockefeller and Ford foundations, which were "highly sympathetic to the central planning propensities of Indian authorities." Rostow considered India "the big urgent test case for all these [developmentalist] principles." The American paranoia about Communism reached its zenith with the accusation, in congressional hearings, of the Ford Foundation being infected by the leftist virus.[73]

But American intelligence had its own way of countermeasures. When, in 1952, CIS was set up with CIA funds and started performing development surveys backed by private foundations, it initially focused on India (later expanding to Indonesia and Italy—countries, not by coincidence, with a strong left-wing tendency). Director Millikan (backed by his friend and former Yale classmate Walt Rostow) set up a Delhi office, but Mahalanobis's requests for a state-of-the-art Univac computer to perform his economic planning calculations were rebuffed, and India got a Soviet Ural computer, delivered "with great fanfare." CIS meanwhile performed its own analysis on its Univac, but its advice to focus more on agriculture caused such "an outcry in the Indian press" that CIS quietly withdrew from India in 1965. Its advice was fully in accordance with US foreign policy, which also opined that India should not follow the Soviet model by putting all its energy on industrialization, and deemphasize food production. In a military metaphor, Mahalanobis later explained he needed the American advice only as "airforce cover": "the very number of [hundreds of] visitors gave local officials room to maneuver. Paradoxically," Engerman concluded, "indigenous Indian economic policies took root only because of the volume and range of international traffic," a mobility of people and ideas that provided a protective shield in the Cold War for Indian planners to follow their own route.

This was all the more important because India, as an active participant to the Bandung conference of nonaligned countries in 1955, became involved in the expansion of the Cold War into a "tripolar" conflict, when it granted asylum to the Dalai Lama and seven thousand of his followers after a rebellion in Tibet in 1959. This was the culmination of an earlier sequence of conflicts over a road China had built between Xinjiang and Tibet, across the Aksai Chin plateau, claimed by India. When President Lyndon B. Johnson during the 1960s used its food aid as a weapon to force India to invest more in agricultural development, and on top of that India did not support the United States in its Vietnam War, the relation between the two countries deteriorated further. This was not improved, to say the least, when the war between US-backed Pakistan and India broke out in 1971, and more than ten million refugees crossed the border into Indian West Bengal from what soon would become Bangladesh. In 1971, President Richard Nixon canceled $87.6 million development aid to India, and his successor, Gerald Ford, did not allocate any further economic aid to this "test case." During the previous twenty years, the United States alone had spent $4 billion in "capital assistance" to India, but the Indian case clearly shows 'development' was a highly (geo)political practice. Much American aid, for instance, went into Pakistan and Afghanistan, as the many Western hippy and non-hippy travelers on their way to India could observe themselves, such as the British Dervla Murphy on her bicycle (a pistol in her pocket), all the way from Ireland: "This time it's 'God bless the Americans' who within four years expect to have completed the 320 miles from Kabul to Kandahar." At the same time, "nearly all the few Afghan-owned cars, jeeps and trucks seem to be Russian."[74]

***

Although there does not exist a separate study of India's road network building since Independence, it is quite clear that here, too, the Indian planners followed their own course, diligently using Western advice whenever they saw fit. With 9.6 million bullock carts and only 350,000 trucks, road freight transport was very 'layered' indeed. But whether looking west or east for support, mainstream 'development ideology' was never really questioned, thus revealing a continuity with colonial times. Indeed, back in 1929, a Central Road Fund had been set up, like in the West, fed by "a surcharge on fuel tax" and enabling the Nagpur Plan to be formulated during the war. Also, the Motor Vehicles Act of 1938 protected the railways against road competition, again just like in Western Europe, and again showing the 'coordination crisis' had spread to the colonies already well before the war. A comparison with Japan, the United States, and the United Kingdom revealed of course that India 'lagged behind' these examples of modernity considerably (despite the UK's reputation, among transport experts, of suffering from "public underinvestment in infrastructure"). And yet, India needed these roads, if only, as an overview by an Indian road engineer in

Road International argued, because of "an increasing need to develop the automotive industry which is most vital to the country for strategic as well as other reasons." He hoped "we should soon achieve self-sufficiency in this ideal."[75]

Emulating the West with limited financial resources proved impossible, though. Instead, together with other Western (former) colonies Indonesia, French Indo-China, Thailand, and Cambodia, India became an active member of the PIARC, where it contributed papers on a recurrent topic at every conference: the "low coast road" or the "roads in underdeveloped areas," or the "lightly trafficked road." The PIARC conference of 1963 was even scheduled to take place in India but was canceled (and shifted to Rome) at the last moment because of a "state emergency." In this situation, India had to find other sponsors, which it found in the UN's ECAFE. ECAFE indeed emphasized the importance of low-cost roads (it organized a special seminar in Delhi in 1958 on this topic), and initially its support was given within a context of postwar reconstruction. But the UN, too, succumbed to the lure of large-scale projects such as the Asian Highway. We will therefore continue this story later, where we will be able to embed it in the broader context of Western-inspired 'development.' Before we do so, however, we must first dedicate some thoughts to the still lingering 'urban crisis.'

'Layered' Asian Mobilities: Subversion in Urban Semipublic Transport

The mobility developments that regarded the people most took place locally, in the ever-expanding Asian cities. Here, urbanization was "proceeding at a scale and speed that [was] unprecedented in human history." Here, metropolises were in the making, often still around the traditional 'casbah' or 'medina' or 'old town,' the latter called such after the erection of the 'new town,' as in Delhi, where the government of British India had moved to in 1936 and which was designed as "a city built for the new technology of the motor car." This led to one of the typical phenomena of postwar mobility beyond the West: the 'layeredness' of urban mobility combining 'old-fashioned' bullock carts, rickshaws, and an increasing amount of 'modern' vehicles such as trucks, buses, motorcycles, and mopeds. Equally modern was the critique of rickshaw pulling being "injurious to the drivers," rejected by "medical authorities," as an authoritative overview of "transport in modern India" opined. This layeredness was enhanced precipitously when, from 1950 onward, millions of rural migrants per year entered these cities, and the share of the "informal sector" in total employment figures increased to 40 percent and in some cases even 70 percent. In the half-century after 1950, the world population grew from 2.5 to 6.1 billion people, a "population explosion" that took place in the Third World metropolises: whereas in 1950 of the six megacities with more than ten million inhabitants, only one (Shanghai) was to be found in developing countries, Shanghai had been joined by thirty of the forty-five megacities after the turn of the century.[76] In these cities, housing was the token of modernity, even more so than mobility, as we observed in the case of pre–World War II apartment building in Mumbai (chap. 1).

An excellent overview of the "integration" of Southeast Asian transport and communication over the past century and a half is given by geographers Howard Dick and Peter J. Rimmer specializing in urban mobility, who conceived their analysis as an antidote to the economists "who dominated the discourse of development after the 1960s." They charted the urbanization and motorization of the five original (1967) Association of East Asian Nations (ASEAN) members (Indonesia, Malaysia, the Philippines, Singapore, and Thailand), none of which (except Thailand) existed as such before the Pacific War. Consisting of 50 percent sea, the region's surface is half that of China's and is populated by half a billion inhabitants (as of 2000). Its core is the "Singapore-Bangkok-Hong Kong triangle," in which Bangkok (Thailand), Jakarta (Indonesia), and Manila (Philippines) belong to the world's twenty-five largest urban conglomerations, whereas Singapore and Hong Kong acquired the status of "world cities" through their banking and financing sectors. In 1950, Hong Kong, Jakarta, Manila, and Saigon each had more than one million inhabitants, followed a decade later by Singapore, Bangkok, and Surabaya, in which the hegemonic European elite had been replaced by "an indigenous middle-class elite."

Dick and Rimmer charted the modernization-through-motorization of this region, from the first railway opened in Java in 1867, through the first automobiles (1894 in Java, 1896 in Singapore, 1897 in Bangkok) and the spread of the Ford Model T among the wealthy Europeans and Chinese in the 1910s, so much so that the region counted about one hundred thousand passenger cars and half that amount of commercial vehicles on the eve of World War II. Apart from being a confirmation of our synchronization thesis (namely that quintessential developments in motorization time-wise did not differ fundamentally from those in the West), Dick and Rimmer's overview also emphasized the "uneven" developments across the region: "What demands explanation is … the slow diffusion of technology to the hinterlands," a development giving rise to a "fundamental dualism" in these societies, resulting in what one may characterize as 'two mobilities.' Against "the rapid diffusion of electric tramways" stood "the slow diffusion of railways," a phenomenon they explained by pointing at the role of the cities as "the point of contact between Southeast Asia and the world. Telegraphs, steamship mails and passengers, and later aircraft all touched there." Dick and Rimmer then provided extensive overviews of the infrastructural development and motorization of the main subregions (the islands of Java and Luzon, river systems such as the Mekong, peninsulas like Malaya and Annam) and their cities (Singapore, Manila, Jakarta, Bangkok, Rangoon, Saigon, and Kuala Lumpur). For instance, they explained how Java, despite its 140,000 automobiles in 1966, motorized on the motorcycle (216,000 in 1966, 8.4 million in 2000), after the island had experienced a "transport revolution" in the 1940s and 1950s on the basis of the bicycle: "The bicycle became to Indonesians what the car was to Europeans."[77]

In another publication, Rimmer gave three main differences with Western urban traffic: a much higher car density level (in cars per km of arterial road), a longer travel duration and a more pronounced urban structure in terms of social segregation. But to understand the full complexity of non-Western motorization and its interaction with Western and Soviet development models, we need more than this rather linear type of overviews. Tim Edensor and Mark Jayne, in their common effort to identify distinctive non-Western characteristics in both the structure of and the knowledge emanating "beyond the West," claimed (quoting Anthony King, and echoing the Comaroffs; see the introduction) "the first globally multi-racial, multi-cultural, multi-continental societies on any substantial scale were in the periphery not the core ... Only since the 1950s have such urban cultures existed in Europe." What we have called 'layeredness' they call "global mixing," and what several observers reject as 'chaos' they analyze as "modes and practices of urban ordering and disordering," partly a result of the colonial "dual city," with its white "cantonments" of "wide, tree-lined streets, parks and gardens, tennis courts and golf clubs, gothic style churches, domestic architecture that echoed suburban house and garden design, street names and statues of historic and colonial figures," and not to be forgotten in British colonies, the "club" with its indigenous servants, all this versus the "chaotic native quarter."[78]

***

How was this layeredness constructed? In India, the Mumbai government as early as 1963 assigned American consultants Wilbur Smith & Associates to conduct a first analysis of city traffic. Edensor and Jayne confirm the historical findings of the present study, that "accounts of flow, connections, and complexities that have constituted the recent 'mobility turn' in sociology and human geography have tended to focus on the mobility of elite groups," whereas "the retreat of the state" in a city like Mumbai "has produced a 'new, bazaar like urbanism,' created by those outside of the new elite, that 'slips under the laws of the city simply to survive'" and consists of "'processions, weddings, festivals, hawkers, street vendors and slum dwellers' who create an 'ever-transforming streetscape,' producing an urbanism that expresses the 'kinetic city,' the city in motion" that "exists alongside the 'static city,' the 'official, concrete and monumental,'" that in the course of the coming decades became equipped with "malls, gated communities, and architectures of commerce and powers and the new highways, flyovers, airports, corporate hotels, convention centres, galleries, and museums that declare the city's integration with the global." And although other scholars are left with the task of historicizing such shopping lists of findings, Edensor and Jayne discovered within this hybrid cityscape a new practice of "drifting ... that privileges 'ambivalence, contradiction, contingence and improvisation,'" including the meandering through traffic. This "weaving [of] a path" results in a "particular haptic geography" as well as "intense 'olfactory geographies,'" while "the combined noise of human activities, animals, forms of transport and music produces a changing soundscape."

In short, they described, in subaltern scholar Dipesh Chakrabarty's words, "the thrills of the bazaar" versus "the sterile supermarket," but others emphasize "not to over-romanticize" those "more sophisticated, resilient and adaptable form[s] of order," because the "central experience of ... urban life" is often "a story about terror" and "'abuse,' characterized by the symbolic violence of poverty and deprivation and the very real violence of political coercion, extortion, prostitution, crime and corruption." Delhi, for instance, became a "national icon" and a "national symbol of modernity" backed by a Master Plan of 1962 (co-funded by the Ford Foundation and conceived by the Delhi Development Authority, founded in 1957, which had to cope with two hundred thousand "unauthorized squatters"), in which decentralized growth in "ring-towns" (such as Loni and Ghaziabad, Faridabad, and Narela) was envisaged, connected to the inner city by a network of ring roads and radial roads, accompanied by several waves of slum clearance in and around the old city, which on their turn led to riots running "completely out of control." The police responded by using open fire, killing several protesters. Whereas the flyovers and road widening started in the 1960s (coinciding with a first slum clearance wave, followed by a second wave a decade later), the neglect of public transport made the plan "deficient": a metro system was not seriously considered before 1975 and became a priority project only in the 1980s (the first Indian metro system was constructed in Kolkata, from 1973).[79]

One cannot discuss Indian urban modernization without mentioning Chandigarh, the state capital of Punjab and Haryana. In the *development* context of this chapter, India's realization of French modernist architect Le Corbusier's *ville radieuse* (radiant city) in the foothills of the Himalayas went through several phases of adaption, one of them being a correction of the automobile-dependent fundamentals of its planning. To illustrate how Western arrogance worked, for example, an Indian planner had to change the Chandigarh plan because it was based on British planner Patrick Abercrombie's Greater London Plan of 1943: "The connection of the three satellite towns ["New Towns," one a garden city, another a university city, the third an administrative center] would have required a degree of motorization among the Indian population that was far from given in India in 1948." Also, the prediction of population growth was deemed much too low. Nonetheless, the road grid was set up according to seven standard road types (differentiated by speed of traffic) designed by Le Corbusier ("V7," for instance, was the standard for pedestrians and bicycles), such that "every citizen should be connected to the city's high-speed road network." In 1982 however, while Chandigarh's population had meanwhile exploded because of the migration flows as a result of Partition, most of the population moved on bicycles and rickshaws, while funds were lacking to develop a public transport system. And while the 1970s would herald the end of modernism and the beginning of postmodernism in the West, "in countries such as India," a recent analysis of Chandigarh asserts, "modernism has not lost all of its potential." This is also testified by subsequent development efforts in the Radiant City, despite amateur sculptor Nek Chand, celebrated by Edensor and Jayne in their search for differences with Western urbanism, who "secretly created a sculpture garden on informal scrubland[, built] out of the debris caused by demolition of the 42 villages that surrounded the new city."[80]

This is not to say differences between two urban 'mobility worlds' were not present in the West, as a result of modernization efforts there (see the "sleek business center" in London versus the "Cheapside"), but the changes in the East seem to have taken place much more suddenly, top down, on an often vibrant, extensive, very localized 'subaltern' network, often reminiscent of its agricultural origins. Modernization, in German historian Corinna Unger's view, "was an elite project." The sounds of this cityscape were different, too, as Edensor and Jayne already indicated and Salman Rushdie remembered in his novel *The Ground Beneath Her Feet*, whose protagonist is woken up by the "careless noise of shouts and engines and bicycle bells." In Delhi, these sounds were all the more coming from human voices rather than from motorized traffic, because of the "urban degeneration" that according to some observers had gripped urban development because of the Partition, which led to a "mammoth influx of refugees" into the city: between the censuses of 1941 and 1951, the capital's population nearly doubled to 1.7 million, causing the city to grow in a "totally chaotic manner," accompanied by a "big landgrab operation" and a racialized housing policy. One result of this development was the emergence of *nouveau riche puppies*, the latter term a derogatory mix of the terms Punjabi (Hindu and Sikh Punjabi fled to the city when the Partition migration started) and yuppies.[81]

It was in between these two layers that a special form of semipublic transport developed, carried by mopeds, motorcycles, and especially designed mini versions of trucks and buses, three-wheelers, and mopeds with sidecars, to negotiate the middle ground between the old city and the new, between the slums and the boulevards. By far the best overview of these developments has been given by Rimmer in his magisterial *Rikisha to Rapid Transit* (1986), who points at Hong Kong as the real archetypal Asian metropolis with a 'hybrid mobility,' "an amalgam of Western and Eastern technologies and organizations." Core of this hybridity was the "public light bus" (PLB, weighing, according to a regulation of 1982, not more than four thousand kilogram, with a maximum length of seven meter), a political term for a successful grassroots and subversive form of mobility leading "international agencies, notably the World Bank, to incorporate the minibus as part of their urban transport planning strategy for Southeast Asian cities," as we will see in the next section. Not every urban development took place as a top-down process, however. The history of Bangkok (which nearly doubled its surface between 1958 and 1971) gives a nice example of "uncontrolled" urban expansion lateral to the "ribbon-development" along some main arteries. These "sois," of which anthropologist Erik Cohen counted two thousand by 1971, and their branches ("sub-sois" and "sub-sub-sois") penetrated the "interstices" between the main arteries, enabling the construction of shop houses (primarily owned by Chinese), and slums. Originally emerging as "dirt roads and paths along irrigation canals (*klongs*)," the sois gradually became asphalted. They were served by urban bus systems, "*song-theo* (pick-up truck) collective services" or taxis and *samlors* (motorcycle taxis).[82]

***

There was more regulation in Hong Kong. Since World War II, this British colony had grown fivefold to five million inhabitants at the end of the 1970s, leading to serious "overcrowding" of the government-owned railways and the franchised bus companies. This prompted the emergence of small companies operating illegal minibuses called *pak pais*, hired either by groups who paid for the entire vehicle or by individuals who paid per seat. The government tried to legalize the *pak pais* by giving out licenses, but when a strike hit the official bus companies, the minibuses that operated as private cars were recognized in 1969 as "private light buses," while the others (used as taxis and "dual purpose vans") attained the status of PLBs. By then, nearly 90 percent of the minibus companies had only one vehicle, and another 8 percent had two, while the two largest companies owned fifty-two and fifteen units. They were patronaged mainly by blue-collar workers who previously had used the official buses. The deployment seems to have been derived from the rickshaw culture: drivers hired the buses per shift. By the beginning of the 1980s, there were 4,350 PLBs carrying 1.3 million passengers (300,000 fewer than during the peak year of 1976) and, in 1972 (with one million trips), performing one-third of all public transport trips.

Enter the experts: in their *Hong Kong Comprehensive Transport Study 1976*, American consultancy company Wilbur Smith & Associates supported the government's plan to build a Mass Transit Railway system, not only arguing that big buses and trams occupied less road space per passenger in high-density Hong Kong than the cheaper minibuses and thus were more efficient, but also accusing the "subversive elements" of "brinkmanship," a "selfish and aggressive attempt to pick-up passengers," a complaint that sounds familiar to the student of Western-style coordination struggle, where 'private' buses were accused of 'skimming' the best revenues off official public transport.[83] Although it was the local government that won this 'battle of the systems' in the case of Hong Kong, we will in the remainder of this chapter also look at cases such as Kuala Lumpur, where the 'subversives' won, or Singapore, where the government eventually rejected the World Bank's proposals. To understand both types of outcomes, however, it is important first to zoom back to the West, which meanwhile had become characterized by both the building of special road networks (freeway networks) and a specific outcome of the struggle between road and rail. There, the triumphant roadbuilding interests, not hindered by much knowledge about the local conditions in the Third World, as we just saw here and in the case of Chandigarh, sided with their governments to set up 'development' schemes that drove consultants such as Wilbur Smith & Associates to the East.

Conceiving 'Development': Mobilizing the 'Rest'

The aggressive, American form of road promotion is a post–World War II phenomenon.[84] It was first tested on Europe, where not only were Marshall Plan funds used to build up the local infrastructure (including traffic engineering knowledge) but also, remarkably enough (and against the intention of the Americans), colonial powers used part of this money to spend on infrastructures in their colonies.[85] Historically and theoretically, modernity was closely linked to mobility, according to German historian Hans-Ulrich Wehler's "dichotomy alphabet," which characterizes "social movement" as "stable" if it is "traditional," and "mobile" if it is "modern." Likewise, his overview of "most modernization theories" characterizes "traditional mobility" as "low" and "modern mobility" as "high." What is more, the "mobilization" within these theories (including Marxism, as a "special variation of modernization theories"), defined as the "generation of spatial and social mobility," is driven by a "revolution of rising expectations"—expectations, to be sure, that stayed within the consumerist paradigm, as the theories declared "revolutions in developing countries" to be "superfluous."

At the transnational level, roadbuilding expertise in Europe had traditionally, since 1908, been the domain of the PIARC. Dominated by engineers and planners officially representing their governments, the PIARC held transnational conferences where in a rather formal way members' reports on certain "questions" (topics) were gathered in one master report by the local organizer, the conclusions of which were often debated to the level of single words, as if it concerned a parliamentary debate. Although the conferences had no formal authority, they functioned for nearly half a century as a very effective consensus machine between national roadbuilding authorities, including those in the United States, who had until shortly before the war rejected the expensive and (according to the French delegations) 'undemocratic' freeway solution, only implemented on a massive scale in Fascist Italy and especially Fascist Germany. When former colonies joined the PIARC after the war, conference conclusions threatened to become so general as to lose their practical usefulness (at least for members from the West), which made the conferences of rival organization International Road Federation (IRF), set up after the war, all the more attractive as they dealt with concrete roadbuilding projects carried out all over the world, the more spectacular the better. The IRF's management was recruited from the car industry, and the glossy magazine *Road International* (in sharp contrast with the rather formal and dull PIARC periodicals) did not hide for a bit that its aim was to promote the diffusion of the road network over the world by Western construction companies.[86]

When the United Nations were founded, the close ties between IRF officials and the American government (a relic of the war) led to a consultancy status at the UN, whereas the US government refrained from reviving its PIARC membership. The PIARC on its turn refused to "expel all our members who are not Government representatives," and they were not prepared to ask non-UN members Switzerland and Spain to withdraw, concluding that this "makes our incorporation in U.N.O. impossible," creating a void eagerly occupied by the IRF. By 1955, there were seventy-five IRF branches in the world (one of the first was in Mexico, in 1949). Within a decade or so, however, the ideologies of both rivals converged considerably, probably under the pressure of Cold War solidarity, and they started organizing common activities while the PIARC acquired UN consultancy status as well. But by then, the hegemony in the transnational road engineering discourse had clearly shifted from Europe to the United States. The postwar domination by the IRF of the world roadbuilding community was an expression of this shift. It was cemented by a graduate course on traffic engineering organized by the Bureau of Highway Traffic at Yale University: the course, started in 1943, by the end of the 1960s had educated five hundred students from eighty-three countries.[87]

From Yale, the word from the road builders' bible (O. K. Norman's *Highway Capacity Manual*) was spread, first to the European 'periphery' and then to Europe's and the United States' common 'peripheries': the former colonies and other newly independent countries, most of them eager to start their modernization and motorization process through the building of national road networks. The magic word was 'freeways': roads exclusively used for high-speed road traffic, claimed to be much safer than ordinary roads (justifiably so), but most of all a token of a society's status as a modern nation. The iconic example of this modernization-through-motorization became the US Interstate Highway System, started in 1956 and soon encompassing 66,000 kilometer (41,000 miles), also crisscrossing the cities. By 1964, the road density (per capita) of the richest countries was at least a factor of ten higher than in all other countries: whereas New Zealand's record density in kilometer per capita reached 3,341 and France's 2,985, Spain's density (249 km/capita) was five times as high as India's (55 km/capita).[88]

Exuberant Infrastructures: Planning the Postwar Western Freeway System

The new US Interstate Highway System, built from the end of the 1950s to the mid-1970s, was a truly megalomaniacal project comparable to the parallel Cold War project of bringing an American to the moon. Although it would, when built, represent only 1 percent of the US road network, and the trucking lobby had to be convinced to accept raised taxes (on which they agreed, provided all the revenues would be spent on roadbuilding), the high-speed system paradoxically promised one-third fewer casualties because of the separated flows. Although Congress in 1944 had supported the plan if it would bypass the cities, the new postwar plans were quite clear about their main aim: the system had "to create new corridors of accessibility from city centers to potential suburbs," preferably by combining this with 'clearing the slums' near these centers, thus realizing its own domestic form of "development" and at the same time keeping the costs down because of the low land values of these slums. Many slums were inhabited by African Americans who had been "taking up residence in areas formerly occupied by European immigrants." The federal state successfully lured the local planners and authorities into its scheme by offering 90 percent subsidy if freeways ("a fundamentally rural design," using five hectares for every kilometer) were included in their urban plans.[89] Why did the federal government put so much effort in including the lower governmental echelons in its freeway planning? To answer this question, we must briefly switch back to the history of Western postwar roadbuilding and place the American initiative in an international context. This deeper investigation is also relevant for the core topic of the current chapter: understanding the roadbuilding schemes under the Western development ideology.

***

The planning and building of the postwar road system in the Western world could hardly cope with the mobility explosion. In the Netherlands (which in many respects may stand for several Western European countries), at the Ministry of Traffic, much of the prewar expertise had faded away, and the first postwar road plans of 1948 and 1958 were copies of the 1938 version (except for a road through the new Noordoostpolder). Funding of new plans was problematic, because the distribution of tax funds to the provinces and the cities first had to be sorted out. This was all the more problematic as the diffusion of the car all over the country suddenly made planners discover a quaternary, capillary road system that never had been part of any plan, a system that connected every farm and house to the other systems, and overnight made the entire administrative road network double in size. Like in Germany, the system had to be redesigned to car and especially truck use, to enable the explosion of farm mechanization. Moreover, under increasing pressure to address the road and traffic fatality problem (this was when representatives of the car and road lobby all over Western Europe accused national governments of 'murder' because they failed to address the 'road problem'), the central government decided to launch a plan for the construction of 1,200 kilometer of freeways, circumventing the traditional road planning procedures.

Only in 1965 and 1966 was the funding problem solved by law, resulting in the partial earmarking of automobile taxes for roadbuilding purposes (which were increased frequently and matched by a sum taken directly from the general tax revenues). From that moment, freeway building accelerated, and the subsequent decade can be called the golden era of freeway building in the Netherlands. The Road Plan of 1968 formed the ultimate expression of this 'building frenzy,' designed by a postwar 'system builder' at the ministry, civil engineer Bert Beukers. Beukers was a graduate of a new discipline at the Delft University of Technology called *Verkeerskunde* (traffic engineering, the equivalent of the German *Verkehrstechnik*). Initiated by leading officers of the ministry, J. Volmuller, a Dutch civil engineer with international experience in road planning at the World Bank, was made professor to develop this discipline next to existing courses on roadbuilding technology. The new expertise was largely imported from the United States: Volmuller and several other civil engineers after him (including Beukers) were sent to Yale to follow the famous course on traffic engineering and to get acquainted with the expertise behind Norman's *Highway Capacity Manual*. The Delft version of traffic engineering became a highly technicized form of traffic planning based on extrapolations of demographic phenomena, as well as traffic counts, resulting in large if not gigantomaniac road designs that followed assumed and projected 'desires' of future car use.

Compared to the other countries (including the US), there was nothing special here: all national networks were initially planned by uncritically following the demographers' inflated projections of future population growth; after the mid-1960s, however, national networks were based on systematic *under*estimations of future car ownership necessitating a continuous upgrading of network length and number of lanes per road. All this assumed, of course, that what was projected had to be built. British critics of this practice called it 'predict and provide.' What is different from these other countries, however, is the role of the Royal Dutch Touring Club (ANWB), which managed to become a part of the road community. Acknowledging it would soon be outperformed by academic road planning, it concentrated on the road safety issue and on the diffusion of roadbuilding expertise, organizing courses and workshops, toward the lower governmental echelons (where its particular strength resided, as the club was historically based on the local elite, called 'consuls'). In the 1950s and 1960s, it even managed to play an initiating role in the proliferation of this expertise among European road builders, by setting up an annual course in connection with a conference organized on behalf of the World Touring and Automobile Organisation (OTA).[90]

***

In Germany, road planning was literally based on the prewar autobahn system and started "surprisingly fast," even before a federal transport funding law (*Verkehrsfinanzgesetz*) was accepted by parliament in 1955, which earmarked the fuel tax above a threshold of 500 (later, 600) million DM for roadbuilding. The first road plan was never brought into parliament. It was based on preliminary prognoses of population, car ownership, and traffic, which were expected to saturate around 1990. This set free enormous sums questioned by nobody, resulting, just like in the Netherlands, in a "golden era" of roadbuilding between 1960 and 1973. In the course of the quarter century after the war, Germany developed "the most sophisticated" central road planning structure (compared to the US, UK, and France), based on four-year road plans (starting in 1959, five-year plans from 1971) and coordinated by a central planning division within the Ministry of Transport.

The "planning euphoria" also included the devastated German towns: as the municipalities and *länder* had to fund all other roads themselves if they were not part of the national road plan (*Bundesfernstrassenplan*), this may explain the ease with which these towns became crisscrossed by urban highways (*Stadtautobahnen*). First enabled by a share in the fuel tax revenues in 1960 (the *Gemeindepfennig*, municipal cent) the *Gemeindeverkehrsfinanzgesetz* (municipal traffic funding law) of 1971 made towns a part of national network planning.[91]

Equally remarkable, and different from the road planning and building practices in France and the Netherlands, the German transport ministry did not have branches at the intermediary level of the *länder*. The new federal constitution of the country had put all roadbuilding competence in the hands of the governments at the intermediary level, and although this had been criticized by contemporaries as critically undermining the planning authority of the federal state (which was also laid down in the constitution), this does not seem to have retarded in any way the same freeway building frenzy during the 1960s and 1970s as can be observed in other European countries. What is more, underneath this system, a fully independent system of state roads (*Bundesstrassen*) was constructed. It shows how every country mobilized its own institutional stakeholders to pursue a similar goal: covering the nation with a car-friendly road network. Critics lamented the weak position of the federal center: the *Bund* was reduced to a 'clearing house' of tax money in a planning process dominated largely by engineers and the *länder* could use their detailed knowledge of local building and planning practices as a de facto veto against proposals they did not like. A recent study of the state of Bavaria, however, convincingly showed regional representatives never violated each other's interests, in the process keeping overall costs at a high level. As long as tax revenues were increasing precipitously, road planning was evenly spread over the entire country, just like in the Netherlands, with perhaps a more powerful central planning authority. Only in France, with a weak and very young regional structure and a dominant orientation on catching up with 'Europe,' was an even distribution of the network over the entire national surface not realized until the 1990s.[92]

***

In Switzerland, a similar top-down approach of urban traffic problems was attempted. Conceptually justified by the central places theory of Walter Christaller only *after* the network had been planned, it was in reality a very 'practical' undertaking, geared at a double, seemingly contradictory aim: to connect Switzerland to the emerging European network and to alleviate the urban congestion problem. With "breathtaking speed," a national commission (without urban representatives) under the leadership of national system builder Robert Rucki in less than three years developed a road and freeway plan of unprecedented size and costs in which urban freeways formed an integral part. Indeed, against the wish of several local authorities, these freeways received the task to solve local traffic problems in seven larger Swiss cities. This has been explained by referring to leading national politicians and civil servants who shifted from Germany to the United States as a source of inspiration and who supported this shift by declaring their federal system of *Konkordanzdemokratie* (cooperative federal democracy) as more related to the American system (with an important role of localism) than to the centralized German federation. But such a formal comparison is rather limited, because planning rhetorics and actual building were two different worlds: German central planners were largely steered by the *länder*. In Switzerland, only when local democracy started to reject such ideas, the federal state withdrew from the cities, a move not unwelcome to national planners who saw the costs of the program rise precipitously. In the end, two towns rejected the *Expresstrassen* (Bern and Lausanne), two built a circumferential system (Basle and Geneva), while two others accepted urban highways only after some alignment changes. By 1980, a network of 1,464 km of freeways (80 percent of the entire network of *Nationalstrassen*) covered Switzerland, paid for by a frequently increased fuel tax that was partially earmarked for roadbuilding, resulting in a federal subsidy for the cantons of between 80 and 92 percent of their expenses.[93]

For the Swiss case, it has been described in detail how national parliament "disempowered" itself (*Selbstentmachtung*) by laying the planning competence at the executive level, when it accepted a National Road Law (*Nationalstrassengesetz*) in 1960, at the start of the network construction. Just like in the Netherlands, the Touring Club Suisse seems to have played an influential role, although many details have not been unearthed. In any case, close connections existed with the IRF. Indeed, as far as this has been researched, the IRF gained decisive influence in some countries, such as Sweden, and perhaps in the United Kingdom, one of the countries where it was founded. In the Netherlands, however, the local IRF branch—Stichting Weg (Road Foundation)—did not manage to get a grip on road planning, largely because its rival, the Dutch branch of the PIARC, absorbed several IRF ideas without taking over its confrontational style or its sophisticated PR techniques. The Dutch PIARC branch did gain access to the traffic engineering course at Yale, where it sent several of its members. As a result, civil servants remained in control in the Netherlands. In Germany, the Forschungsgesellschaft für Strassen- und Verkehrswesen (Research Society for Road and Traffic Issues) played a similar role, together with the powerful German Association of the Automotive Industry VDA and the touring club ADAC.[94]

When the European Economic Community was founded in 1957, transport became one of its raisons d'être, although several members were reluctant to give up the dominance of the railways in their national mobility policies. With Gunnar Myrdal as its first secretary-general, the UN Economic Commission for Europe (ECE) organized "Technical Assistance Mission 103" in 1952 within the framework of the Marshall Plan, to study the conditions in the United States. In a typical 'European' style, the subsequent proposal for a so-called E network was a clever plan to connect all existing national road networks by designating certain roads as "E routes" meant to be upgraded to freeway status in due course. From the M1 motorway between London and Birmingham (of which the first 125-km section was finished in 1959) to the Autostrada del Sole in Italy (ready in 1964), the European E-road network grew 'from below,' through the initiative of the individual countries, carefully guided by the coordination center in Brussels. Even Spain began construction of a freeway network in the mid-1960s, resulting, just like in other countries of the Southern European 'periphery,' in a widening of the gap between a more affluent core, and local, underdeveloped 'peripheries.' European freeway network length increased from 14,000 km in 1970 to 33,000 in 1986; especially France caught up with Germany, having 7,450 km in 1991, versus 9,000 in Germany.[95]

***

With every road planner gazing in awe at (or visiting) the United States, it may not come as a surprise that many European national networks showed such similar characteristics. After all, the US already had a highway planning tradition of several decades. This is not to say American planning was not perceived critically (it was), but this criticism mostly addressed the urban field, which, before the war in Europe, increasingly was taken out of the national planning discourse. In Switzerland, for instance, the connections on the planners' national road map accepted in 1960 stopped at the towns' borders, just as had been the case in the Netherlands in the 1920s and 1930s. America was perhaps the most extreme in its centralization of road planning power of all countries considered here, despite the admiration by Swiss politicians. This process has been studied in detail for the New York State Thruway Authority, which could collect fees from motorists independent of democratic control. This form of "supercentralization" (one critical historian even speaks of a "secret government") had a remarkable prewar tradition, the most famous example being the Tennessee Valley Authority (TVA) during the New Deal (1933). But there were more than a hundred of such "quasi-public corporations," managing from ports (New York, 1921) to vast areas of land in seven different states (such as the TVA).[96]

Although the importance (or not) of this type of "public enterprise" for a successful realization of such gigantic projects still waits for a thorough analysis, including its international diffusion, it is quite clear that in many countries similar strategies were tried: a "functional" task force (to use pre–World War I Dutch Minister of Transport Cornelis Lely's words) in some form had to be devised to enable the state to force the freeway concept through any bureaucratic and democratic resistance (which, admittedly, was hardly existent at the moment these schemes were first proposed). Supercentralization also had another important consequence worth mentioning in a mobility history: as we saw in chapter 2, Ronald Reagan's presidential campaigns were based on a rejection of the experts and other members of the 'elite' who made their decisions far away from the electorate, an accusation that resonated positively among those blue-collar voters who were becoming frustrated by the Democratic Party's turn toward the middle class and its slowly emerging preoccupation with 'identity politics.' The 'undemocratic' Interstate project proved to be a catalyst for a growing cleft between middle class and those 'left behind.' The NY Thruway Authority formed one of the models for the largest infrastructure project the world had ever seen: the sixty-six thousand kilometer Interstate Highway System, started in 1956. Cotten Seiler showed how President Dwight Eisenhower, a Republican, had to mobilize a new discourse around this project in order to distance it sufficiently from the New Deal public works tradition. Instead, the Interstate System was presented as a unique enabler of the freedom of mobility (and through this, the revival of the core values of the 'American way of life') in a world threatened by Soviet collectivism. Paradoxically, Americans accepted limited access to the system in order to indulge in this freedom.[97]

Eisenhower's "almost pathological fear of a depression" made him look for "a real public works program," in which "each federal dollar ... generated close to a half hour of employment" in one of the many industries related to road construction. He was helped in this by a strong road lobby, the American Road Builders Association, whose "key friends had found their way into influential posts in both houses of Congress." In the Cold War context, Eisenhower also needed a "dramatic" plan, although he seems to have been "furious" about the freeways crisscrossing the cities.[98] Indeed, according to some estimates, half of the sixty-six thousand planned kilometers (most of them newly built) were (sub)urban, their precise location "almost exclusively" determined by "traffic flow data and ... the near sovereignty in local affairs of the state and federal engineers who had prepared them." Seen from the perspective of the prewar rivalry between 'builders' and 'planners,' the Interstate project "propelled state engineers into the city planner's domain," where the former often bypassed the latter. The gigantic dollar stream ($100 billion were estimated to be spent until the network would be finished in 1971, later to be postponed to 1975) consisted of fully earmarked money, from a fuel tax, was collected by the federal state but sluiced to the states for further distribution according to centrally fixed formulas. In this tripartite system, the states were no doubt the crucial and most powerful players as long as they worked according to standards designed by the federal Bureau of Public Roads and cooperated with federal engineers stationed at the state public works departments.[99]

These standards included a fraud-free construction practice, hence the common (Democratic and Republican, right before the elections of 1960 that brought John Kennedy into the presidency) fight against a case of fraud in Massachusetts. Although half of the first allocated funds went into five thousand miles of bypasses around cities, a suburban "growth spurt" was set in motion, while around the interchanges, 'non-places' were created as they became "centers of service not only to passing motorists but also to local populations, offering commerce, manufacturing, distribution, and administration." The United States provides the classic example of what I would like to call 'forced demand' (as opposed to "latent demand"): the use of the system incited Americans to double their average annual mileage traveled by car. By 1962, about one-third (21,000 km) of the network had been built, and by the end of the decade, more than two-thirds (48,000 km) were ready.[100] Just like in European countries, the 'golden age' of US highway construction lasted about a decade, when a cluster of factors (analyzed by a plethora of researchers) including rising costs, diminishing tax revenues, and urban resistance caused a paradigm shift in the road planning discourse and practice, with a more 'comprehensive' approach, a reflection of the reappropriation of some influence by the 'planners' (as opposed to the engineers, the 'builders'). What has been less emphasized, however, is that by the mid-1970s, the job had been more or less done.

It must have been the inertia of road planning (in Germany, the interval between the starting dates of planning and building was at least eight years) that in all North Atlantic motorizing countries the "golden era of roadbuilding" took place at a time (the decade around 1970) when criticism of and resistance against roadbuilding already was in full swing, and no doubt it was this same inertia that then additionally fueled and deepened this criticism. However, incidental resistance can be observed as early as the mid-1950s in Switzerland, while the famous San Francisco revolt started in 1954 against the Western Freeway (which was lost) and was followed by a successful resistance against the Embarcadero Freeway. This sparked a chain of similar reactions, such as in Detroit, where already in 1953 seven hundred buildings were demolished, and two thousand black families displaced; this was repeated on a much larger scale during the "Negro Removal" of 1963, when forty-three thousand people had to move, 70 percent of them black. Freeway building in the United States peaked in 1966 and was from then on slowly brought to an end because of increasing costs (including the costs of displacement of people 'in the way') and resistance, which developed into a nationwide massive movement in the 1970s.[101] Because it can best be analyzed in the context of other resistance movements against the car, we will reserve the discussion of this 'freeway criticism' for a later study.

***

Whenever national governments contemplated scaling back their initial overambitious plans, the IRF was never far away to emphasize the necessity of these roads for an efficient and safe circulation of goods and people, and to mobilize counterforces. Therefore, the emergence of a globally dominant freeway paradigm should be analyzed against the background of three important trends: the immediate postwar decades as the heydays of the "planning euphoria," the struggle between road and rail, and the construction of a 'development ideology'—trends that became closely intertwined. As for the first trend, *economic planning* blossomed during the first postwar years of European reconstruction, but when planners tried to expand toward transport issues, they found the field already occupied by civil engineers from the roadbuilding community. This is not to say such engineers did not plan, but the concept of 'comprehensive planning,' which aimed at creating a balance between transport modes and in Europe was mostly furthered by social scientists with a social democratic or related background, often favored 'mass transport' modes such as the railways over roads. *Comprehensive planning* managed to gain a foothold within the planning paradigm only during and because of the disturbances and the crises of the 1970s. Nor is this to say such developments are universal: in the case of China, for instance, the 'planners' are often considered to represent the 'conservatives,' frustrating the modernizing efforts of the 'reformers.'[102]

Such conflicts between 'builders' and 'planners' (or perhaps better, between those who favored a 'technical fix' and those who included extra-technological arguments) became especially acute in a world increasingly characterized by an urban culture and infrastructure. Whatever the conditions, the planners' intention was nothing less than to fully reorganize society, according to what Marshall Berman has called a "Faustian model" of development, where Faust, "the public planner," was supported by "Mephistopheles, the private freebooter and predator who executes much of the dirty work," the latter's role often forgotten in histories of development, and only recently self-identified as 'economic hitmen.' As far as the second trend, the *struggle of the systems*, is concerned, the freeway movement sealed the fate of the European and North American railway networks for the coming three decades or so as a secondary, old-fashioned, but necessary mode (even in the United States, for freight), in the process, ironically, itself taking over railway-like characteristics.[103] When the IRF and its connected interests set out to conquer the rest of the world, this struggle acquired an extra dimension because of the 'layeredness' of non-Western mobility systems, and the indispensable character of most of the 'old' modes. This became especially acute in the growing metropolises, as we saw for the case of Hong Kong. It was, therefore, a very welcome circumstance that at about the same time, amid an emerging Cold War, and as a third trend accompanying the modernization-through-motorization history, *a new modernization theory* was developed by economists. It was this theory, "inspired by liberal anti-communism" and "soaked in Americans' self-confidence in the Cold War," that, together with "normative policy debates and political science[,] dominated the field of development studies" for "a long period," until the 1990s.[104]

Cementing Western Hegemony: Development and the Middle Class

According to this theory, often attributed to economic historian Walt Rostow, who programmatically coined his foundational book *A Non-Communist Manifesto* (1960), "modernization" was a "process by which historically evolved institutions are adapted to the rapidly changing functions that reflect the unprecedented increase in man's knowledge, permitting control over his environment." The theory, aggressive in its programmatic fantasy of 'conquering' the environment, construed a sharp dichotomy between "modern" and "traditional" societies, and was historical in that it assumed a modernizing nation goes through five "stages," in the course of which, in a telling rocket metaphor, modernization would "take off." In hindsight, however, it was unhistorical and deterministic in that this process was assumed to be linear and universal, and that traditional societies had to "catch up" with the more advanced one, most particularly, of course, the West, especially the United States. The theory was also chauvinist: it assumed modernization was "a genuinely American phenomenon, while the international and transnational dimensions of development and modernization discourse before and after World War II have been neglected." Rostow's manifesto (presented first as a series of lectures at Cambridge University) reads like an activist's pamphlet, fully focused on his own country's relationship with the world, especially the Soviet Union (and hardly anywhere mentioning Europe, except, of course, the UK). The United States, he declared, was now in the "post-maturity stage," and for this condition, "it has been a quite consistent feature of modern history for some groups to look out beyond their borders for new worlds to conquer."[105]

The "leading sectors in the American age of high consumption" were "the automobile, suburban home-building, road-building, and the progressive extension of the automobile and other durable consumers' goods to more and more families." Classic diffusion curves illustrated the "diffusion of the private automobile" in several industrialized and industrializing countries (including the Soviet Union). "All the post-war mature societies of the West and Japan," he concluded, "are behaving in a remarkably 'American' manner." This was also true for the Soviet Union (even if it did not have "a substantial and enterprising commercial middle class"): "Slowly, ever so slowly, the creep of washing machines, refrigerators, motor-cycles, bicycles, and even automobiles has begun—and the first Russian satellite town is under construction." The struggle is about the rest of the world: "We must demonstrate that the underdeveloped nations—now the main focus of Communist hopes—can move successfully through the preconditions [one of the earlier stages] into a well established take-off within the orbit of the democratic world, resisting the blandishments and temptations of Communism. This is, I believe, the most important single item on the Western agenda."[106] German historian Hans-Ulrich Wehler observed how most modernization theories assumed development equaled "linear rise" (*linearer Aufstieg*) and that "evident waves of reverse development, evoking mobility, de-differentiation, decay (de-development, de-mobilization … , dis-integration)" were ignored. Rostow's, in fact, was a "global theory of managed social change." Also, his motives were highly gendered: he worried about "what lies beyond the state of high mass-consumption," and concluded this was especially worrisome for men: "The problem of boredom is a man's problem, at least until the children have grown up."[107]

Bookshelves of publications have been dedicated to the central importance of the concept of the 'nation-state' within this theory, as well as "the pluralist legitimation of the American political system" it was intended to spread. Mobility was crucial in this legitimation. But the 'diffusionist' logic behind this was not the privilege of 'capitalist' economists: it was, and still is, a widespread myth of "modernization theory, whether in its Marxian or Weberian version," that sees a 'core' emulated by a 'periphery,' which makes this periphery per definition 'backward.' Starting with Karl Marx (for whom the "country that is more developed industrially only shows, to the less developed, the image of its own future"), via historicist scholars by the turn of the twentieth century who construed capitalism as the modern core within an imperialist framework, myriad historians and social scientists have helped cement the diffusionist tale, which proved so strong that even its critical historians are not immune to its influence. Michael Mann, for instance, in the fourth volume of his seminal series on *The Sources of Social Power*, saw the "American way of life … spread first to Europe, then to Japan and East Asia and to large parts of China and India," in between, one is tempted to say, touching on other 'peripheries' such as Southern and Eastern Europe, Latin America, and Africa. In this context, the "peasant" was and is the quintessential non-modern, "stand[ing] for all that is not bourgeois." Likewise, Eric Hobsbawm coined the immediate postwar decades as "the death of the peasantry" (excluding sub-Saharan Africa, China, and Southeast Asia, he conceded, which nonetheless represents half of the earth's population), an age in which "for 80 per cent of humanity the Middle Ages ended suddenly."[108] In contrast, and echoing the Comaroffs (see the introduction), recent students of the developing world's modernization (in this case, applied to Africa) have argued against the "popular and academic tendency to diminish, deny, or neglect the impact that African peoples, practices, and civilizations have had on the West's development, as well as to forget the extent to which these populations have sought paths that have veered away from Western modernities even while being interlocked with them," a phenomenon for which they coined the term Afro-modernity.[109]

From Adam Smith onward, transport had figured among economists as the 'engine' of economic growth, and Rostow was no exception: he equated "automobile-dependence" (the term seems to have been coined by him and was not meant to have any pejorative connotations when he did so) as "the highest stage of economic growth," a development that in all its societal consequences and mythologies can be called a "post-1950 phenomenon." Historical economist Charles Kindleberger was no less outspoken: "markets grow because of improvements in transportation and communication." And Wilfred Owen, who in 1964 wrote a programmatic monograph (quoted earlier) on *Strategy for Mobility* for the Brookings Institution's Transport Research Program—meant to investigate "the role of transport in development" and funded by the US Agency for International Development (USAID)—sketched a smoothly linear picture of transport mode succession and substitution:

> In Asia the ricksha and pedicycle are giving way to the truck, the bus, the motor scooter, and the taxi. The bullock cart is disappearing from Delhi and the camel from Karachi. On the Chao Phya in Thailand, ancient sampans are being pulled by diesel tows, and along the klongs of Bangkok fresh vegetables are propelled to market by outboard motor. Beef in Bolivia moves to consuming centers by air, pipelines distribute Sui gas over hundreds of miles of West Pakistan, and in Lagos a 1401 computer keeps track of railway freight cars. During the first election in Nigeria at least one tribal chief was campaigning by helicopter

We now know these innovations never fully annihilated 'tradition.' On the contrary, tradition fed innovation. 'Mobilizing' Rostow even further, Owen designed a "mobility index" on the basis of which he could divide the world in "immobile nations" and "mobile nations," Ethiopia and Nigeria being at the very bottom of the immobile nations scale (and Mexico and Israel at the top), whereas the United States was given the top position in the mobile nations scale, and Spain, Yugoslavia, and Argentina at the bottom, just below Chile and Japan. Some developing countries were more eager than others: Nigeria and Thailand spent more than 40 percent of their public spending on transport and communication, the average of the investigated countries being about one-quarter. Between 1960 and 1975, interrupted by its civil war from 1967 to 1970, Nigeria completed its road network of sixty-six thousand kilometer, about eight thousand of which were "National Trunk Roads." The Turkish military regime was even more extreme: they spent half their budget during the decade after 1948 on transport and communication, whereas Colombia, like Turkey, concentrated on transport "to the neglect of other needs." Owen recommended a balanced approach, but to prevent "transport problems … from frustrating economic growth," to avoid "critical congestion on the railway system," he emphasized the importance of investments in roads rather than rails, observing that the latter still dominated in Western development aid (half of all World Bank funds spent on transport was for rails, one-third for roads), even conceding the "highway truck" was 4.5 more expensive per ton-mile than the railway. No wonder he had to end his analysis by pointing at a "nearly universal trend … toward road transport."

Indeed, his argument in favor of roads was fully based on *expectations*, testifying to the validity of Björn Wittrock's conclusion that "modernity is a set of promissory notes, i.e., a set of hopes and expectations that entail some minimal conditions of adequacy that may be demanded of macrosocietal institutions no matter how much these institutions may differ in other respects." Such expectations on their turn were based on a trend toward "much more attention to road projects": "In balance … the changing composition for transport in underdeveloped areas *will* favor road carriers over rail for an increasing volume of traffic as economic development proceeds … Transport services have to be geared to a new mix of products as development creates new types of needs. Often the solution will be to substitute road services for rail." He claimed maintaining "uneconomical railway services" was a "common mistake," and the same was true, he concluded, for "restricting the use of motor vehicles on grounds of protecting the railways or conserving resources." The model to be emulated were the United States, which, for instance, in Iran supplemented local "oil revenues … to finance an extensive highway network … designed and supervised by foreign engineering firms" and using advice from the US Bureau of Public Roads. At the moment Owen wrote his monograph (which appeared in 1964), the US government, the World Bank, the International Development Association, the European Development Fund of the Common Market, the US Export-Import Bank (EXIM), and US-AID had spent, during the previous two decades, $7.2 billion, $700 million of which went toward (often Western-produced) equipment and $80 million toward (mostly Western) consultancy; five thousand persons had been trained in transport expertise in the United States.[110]

And although economic historians specialized in transport history such as the British Simon P. Ville (who quoted Rostow's framework approvingly) showed the advantage may lay not so much in backward linkages but rather in forward linkages (productivity growth), because of higher regularity and speed and reduced costs (and thus, one is inclined to add, only effective if the context is 'right'), the belief in the *magic* of transport investments remained unperturbed. To give only two examples of many: Brian V. Martin and Charles B. Warden, in their study of "Transportation Planning in Developing Countries" (with Colombia as case study) call "transportation investment ... the catalyst of economic development." And Wilbur Zelinsky declared, against all historical evidence to the contrary, circulation was "symptomatic of the problems of underdevelopment." John Galbraith was less orthodox: "With these ['a highly efficient transportation and an economic and reliable source of power'] available, something is bound to happen; without them, we can be less sure." The belief in the growth potential of highway building remained alive when one of the founders of the theory in the 1950s, Columbia University Professor Albert O. Hirschman himself (known for his two books on Latin American development), tried to nuance its influence by distinguishing between "development by shortage" and "development by excess," and opted for the former (investing in transport when congestion threatens to occur) rather than the latter (which emphasized the "catalytic" role of transport investments).[111] As such, his conclusion confirms our findings so far. Hirschman's admonition suggests many national road modernization projects were realized *ahead* of demand, as expectations cast into concrete.

Transport experts have also tried to distinguish between "unilineal 'phases' of mobility experience—premodern traditional, early transitional, late transitional, and advanced," constructing a "vigorous acceleration of circulation" during "the transformation from traditional-subsistence to an urban-industrial state." But they were much less successful than their colleague economists. Development through roadbuilding was also undertaken by private companies: Caltex, for instance, built a heavy-duty road to its oil fields in Indonesia. In short, most analysts do not doubt for a moment that mobility (transport and communication) is crucial for setting (and keeping) the 'development' dynamics in motion. To give only one European, non-Anglophone example: Erwin Gleissner, of the German Institut für Wirtschaftsforschung (Institute for Economic Research) cooperated with the German transport ministry for more than a decade when he published the results of a comparison of the relation between freight transport 'elasticity' and gross national product per capita for twenty-seven countries, Western and non-Western, and he found, predictably after our overview of the previous pages, that the richer the country, the less energy and freight transport it needed to produce one extra unit of GNP.[112]

***

Modernization theory as a "liberal theory of development" remained "ubiquitous in the late 1950s and early 1960s" and was then superseded by a version characterized by a "basic human needs approach," a process especially since the end of the 1960s taking place "under the influence of the Vietnam War and the attendant antiestablishment counterculture." But even its critics "were obliged to couch their critique in terms of the need for development, through concepts such as 'another development,' 'participatory development,' 'socialist development,' and the like … The fact that most people's conditions not only did not improve but deteriorated with the passing of time," one critic of the development paradigm concluded sarcastically, "did not seem to bother most experts." It seems the "grinding poverty that worsened, in many cases, through the 1960s and 1970s" hid from view the "real functions of modernization: to win the newly dependent nations for the 'free world' while at the same time securing unfettered access to their considerable natural resources and using the decolonized regions as a social scientific laboratory without having to bear responsibility for their experiments." Some of the results of these experiments were the "tight connections between scholars and policy. These connections were nowhere closer than in the world of development and modernization, where international fieldwork and government advising were common activities for scholars." Also, British officers active in colonial development later joined the World Bank and other private and government agencies.[113] And as we saw, Dutch World Bank employee Volmuller was sent back to the Netherlands to help 'develop' the country along car-friendly lines.

Development was big business: the World Bank and the Asian Development Bank (ADB) issued loan approvals for nearly $1 billion in 1979 alone, most of these flowing back into the coffers of American companies, as a frustrated and guilt-ridden Peace Corps volunteer observed. Initially, the World Bank focused nearly fully on "infrastructure" ("transportation, irrigation, and power"), whereas education and health were "completely neglected": excluding after-the-war reconstruction, two-thirds of all World Bank loans to developed countries were initially dedicated to electric power and transport (more than 80 percent even in "less developed countries," for the period from 1948 to 1961). Until 1956, nearly $900 million had been spent on electricity, immediately followed by transportation, with nearly $700 million. By mid-1963, the World Bank had spent $7 billion for eight hundred projects in sixty-four countries; one-third of this had been spent in Asia, and one-quarter each in Middle/South America and Europe, and only 13 percent in Africa. Overall, one-third had been spent on mobility infrastructures. More conservative than the American government, the World Bank was led by "businessmen, bankers, and lawyers [from] Wall Street [who] would not accept the New Deal and Keynesian policies, not to mention government planning, which to their eyes was like embracing socialism." Indeed, the US government's lending policy was more overtly political, aimed at preventing "another China."[114]

***

Development was not only big business but also a crucial element in geopolitical power play. Rostow, who left MIT's Center for International Studies to become a national security adviser, proposed to President Kennedy to make the 1960s an "economic development decade," suggesting in a memorandum in typical Cold War macho-cowboy language that the strategy of development was meant to "keep the 'underdeveloped' areas [of the world] 'off our neck as we try to clean up the spots of bad trouble.'" Initially, the United States prioritized Western Europe ($19 billion of Marshall aid until 1950), but when Fidel Castro's guerillas took hold of Havana in 1959 and Che Guevara had abandoned his motorcycle for a guerilla in the jungle, it was Brazil that convinced American policy makers to accept modernization programs as an antidote against Communism in Latin America, although the United States never gave up its reliance on "strategies based on force and coercion," such as launching a counterattack in Cuba's Bay of Pigs. The programs, New Deal veteran Adolf Berle asserted, had to take local needs and motives into account, but only to a certain extent: the plans were clearly aimed at strengthening national emerging middle classes, often neglected by the local Communists ("scavengers of the modernization process," in Rostow's words), who perhaps wanted to conceal their own descent from this class rather than make its basic preoccupations explicit. White House adviser and historian Arthur Schlesinger Jr. opined the Kennedy administration could bring about a "middle class revolution where the processes of economic modernization carry the new middle class into power and produce, along with it, such necessities of modern technical society as constitutional government, honest public administration, a responsible party system, a rational land system, an efficient system of taxation."

In the case of Latin America, the Kennedy administration included the development logic into an ambitious program called the Alliance for Progress, specifying growth rate targets and promoting reform of education, health care, housing, industrialization, land reform, and income redistribution. It was, indeed, and formulated with an eye on Communism, a "peaceful revolution," driven by (as well as fought on behalf of) the middle class. Schlesinger would later look back and muse: "Euphoria reigned; we thought for a moment that the world was plastic and the future unlimited." "One large surge of aid" would be needed, Rostow added, for "after 1970 these key nations would no longer be in need of assistance." The Development Decade confirms Americanist Ruth Oldenziel's thesis that "too often globalization is narrated like a process void of central control, government direction, or politics," often based on the argument, among others, of a rather weak American federal state. She quoted specialist on French Americanization Richard Kuisel, who said, "It is a mistake to discount American political, economic, and military dominance and to explain the success of American mass culture of consumer products simply by their inherent appeal," a warning that we, after the previous chapter in which the car was presented as a seductive commodity, may wish to heed particularly.[115] Development through road (network) building clearly shows this seduction theory is a myth, carefully fostered as it formed the very basis of Western middle-class self-confidence.

Recently, Francis Sutton gave an overview of the main characteristics of "the classical orthodox theory of development," at the same time, like Oldenziel, questioning the 'softness' of this power, as "nations that are underdeveloped have the responsibility to develop [according to the theory]. They are not free to make use of their freedom and self-determination in any way they please. Their governments are not to confine themselves to being guardians of law, order, and national defense. They must see themselves as organizers and agents of development," while developed countries have the responsibility "to help these countries develop successfully." Sutton saw the emphasis on economic growth as a post–World War II phenomenon, fed by fear for instability. Curiously, "former colonial powers were more generous toward their ex-dependencies after their independence than before when they were 'owned'": until 1960, most development aid (next to that from the United States) came from the former colonial powers, and only after Western prosperity started to grow were all non-Communist developing countries under the OECD umbrella included. Initially, the emphasis was on collective improvement (Sutton sees a connection with the prewar African Christian movement) and the central role of the state as subject of change, and "strong emphases on individual welfare did not emerge till later."

Indeed, initially, political leaders (such as in Japan) were interested primarily in "developing a powerful nation rather than a prosperous people," and the idea that "politically and culturally neutral" aid of a predominantly technical character would work in all circumstances haunted political leaders until the end of the last century. From this perspective, development ideology can be seen as the Western, liberal middle class's answer to "the doctrine of development that initially came out of Marxist thought." From a global point of view, Jean Franco's characterization seems adequate: "Under the hegemony of the United States, the goal of developmentalism was to remove opposition to the world system." And if the World Bank or related institutions were not willing or able to provide the funds, the American government did: Israel was "by far the largest recipient" ($81 billion since its creation), followed by Egypt ($53 billion during the last three decades of the century), South Vietnam ($24 billion during its existence), and sub-Saharan Africa ($32 billion since World War II until the end of the century). "While most US aid was tied to buying American products or was given as an accompaniment to military aid, some of the European aid—for instance from the Scandinavian countries—was given unconditionally." But the "often big and prestigious infrastructural plans" financed "in the worst tradition of colonial development schemes" were explicitly aimed, in Kennedy's words, to show "economic growth and political democracy can develop hand in hand."[116]

***

American economic development policies in Latin America largely failed, partly because of the misallocation of funds, partly because Latin American countries simply refused (or in any case, did not manage) to implement land and tax reforms. Plagued by "monetary instability that wracked Latin America from the 1950s," the continent often experienced a shift in the balance in US foreign policy to coercion (testified by the coups in Peru, Ecuador, the Dominican Republic, Honduras, Guatemala, and Argentina), but "modernization" as "ideology" stayed alive, especially when Kennedy agreed to found the Peace Corps. This organization, an expression of a new form of transnational mobility, used the idealism and adventurousness of American youth in the 1960s and 1970s to help diffuse the American model, supported by 'area studies' as new social science disciplines at the universities. Peace Corps volunteers, all of them "screened for leftist political activity and required to take loyalty oaths, and in some cases basic training included seminars in Marxist political thought," helped build roads as geologists, surveyors, and civil engineers, for instance, in Tanzania (one of the first Peace Corps projects, started in 1961), and by 1964, the Corps had trained seven thousand volunteers sent to forty-four countries, where they volunteered "building schools, introducing new methods of livestock breeding, demonstrating higher-yield crop varieties, providing medical care, and instructing farmers in the use of machine tools." Later, many volunteers taught English and helped in the realization of "community development" and other aspects of "social engineering." After one decade, the Peace Corps counted seventy thousand volunteers. When Guinea, as part of the group of African countries that leaned toward the Soviet Union, asked for "road builders and engineers," President Kennedy himself speculated, "If we can successfully crack Ghana and Guinea, Mali may even turn to the West. If so, [these] would be the first Communist-oriented countries to turn from Moscow to us." Amid the Cold War, a true volunteer 'arms race' started: Kennedy's brother-in-law Sargent Shriver, who designed the Peace Corps, reported on a Columbian "leading Commie" who on his return from Moscow accompanied 280 Columbian students, whereupon Shriver suggested to send 500 Peace Corps volunteers as countermeasure.[117]

The idealism of the Peace Corps volunteers did not prevent them from serving national interests. Local elites warned the Americans of the Communists' strange habits: "We like to eat good dinners and drive Cadillacs, but they don't care about anything like that ... They are working all the time." Peace Corps volunteers were popular among these elites, as well as among the population, because they (as "a new lay missionary army," in the words of British historian Arnold Toynbee) deployed similar attitudes: often they were attracted to this kind of work because it represented a "new frontier." After their duty abroad, many came back critical of American conformism. The volunteer "wants action; he wills himself to act ... Sophisticated, mature, toughened, confident and independent, the returned Volunteer [sic] refuses to be cast into a mold." The American civil rights movement and the Vietnam War had a deep impact on many of them (the latter showing that instead of planning to build, war offered the opportunity of planning to destroy: Vietnam called it the "War of Destruction" [*Chiến tranh Phá hoại*]). Many volunteers, once back home, would play a role in President Johnson's "War on Poverty." According to Shriver, the Peace Corps managed to combine a "sense of adventure" with "building a Great Society." One such adventurer was Peace Corps volunteer John Perkins, who later drafted reports to help governments of developing countries acquire World Bank and IMF loans, and, in the 1990s, consumed by guilt, wrote about his 'adventures' as an "economic hit man" employed by a consultancy with narrow ties to the CIA, who sometimes needed the brute force of the "jackals" to 'convince' government representatives. His is the type of cynical but guilt-ridden narrative that unmasked the World Bank reports as econometric humbug. Adventure, then, whether automotive or not, could be instrumentalized to enhance hegemonic culture, nothing new for who is familiar with Cotten Seiler's analysis of America's history of automobilism.[118]

Transport as Development: The World Bank and the Transnational Road Lobby

From this perspective, economic historians' doubts about the effectiveness of transport investment become increasingly futile. Indeed, as we saw, there is no consensus among transport experts about the relationship between road-building and economic growth. Most of them agree the influence of such investments is big when they lead to considerable time savings, so when the existing transport infrastructure is 'old' and the spatial density of population and economic activities is high.[119] A British report from 1999 answering the question, among others, "Do transport improvements lead to increased economic activity?" concluded only a "modest" effect could be observed: "We conclude that the theoretical effects [due to changes of 'costs of movement'] exist in reality, but that none of them is guaranteed," and they strongly depend on local conditions. The road lobby did not seem to be very much bothered by these doubts. Represented in a most outspoken way by the IRF but also fostered by its more 'official' PIARC counterpart, this lobby formed a crucial factor within the development paradigm, closely meshing with similar endeavors within the UN, and supported financially and ideologically by the World Bank and the Bank for International Settlements (the supercentral bank, interacting with the national central banks), and, through these, the US government. To give only one example of the latter: in the case of "The Failure of 'Liberal Developmentalism'" as a "United States's Anti-Communist Showcase in Guatemala, 1954–1960," the local US embassy counselor advised Washington to use the World Bank as "a reliable stand-in ... so that the Castillo Armas regime would not be 'accused of having their policy dictated by the Americans.'"[120]

The United Nations played a specific role in this process. First of all, as a true successor of the prewar League of Nations that had shaped two earlier 'conventions on road traffic' (from 1926 and 1931, on their turn replacing an earlier one from 1909, coinciding with the founding of the PIARC), the UN reformulated its Convention on Road Traffic in 1949. This was a clear (but largely failed) effort to universalize Western road traffic culture, as the convention was signed by only twenty European countries and the United States. The major result of this convention was perhaps that the UN installed a special body for traffic questions, the Organisation for Communications and Transit. In 1968, at the height of the worldwide roadbuilding frenzy, the UN Convention on Road Traffic in Vienna ended with the signature of two new International Conventions (again after consultation mainly with the ECE), one on "road traffic rules, drivers' permits, as well as documents and technical requirements for road vehicles" (which included "special rules applicable to motorways and similar roads"), the other on "road signs, signals and markings." About half of the seventy-one countries present in Vienna signed these conventions. Many developing countries, the reporting officer opined, showed an awareness "of the close relation between improvement in the standard of living and increases in national vehicle fleets and ... they desire to take at an early stage, adequate measures to ensure that pedestrians and other road users be duly prepared to cope with altered conditions resulting from an increased density of traffic, due either to an augmentation in national vehicle fleets or to an influx of growing numbers of 'motorized' foreign tourists." The "pedestrians and other road users" in this quote should be read as the transport expert's jargon for 'the poor.' Although the UN managed to convince the American participants to moderate their habit of using text on its signs (and instead to opt for graphic symbols of danger etc.), the conference could not agree to accept the proposal to use the European warning sign for danger (a triangle pointing upward, with a red border) or the American stop sign (a red octagonal with the word STOP) exclusively, or to the sign with a stag or deer as a warning for wild animals.[121]

***

Historical and social science research in freeway network building has revealed so far that at least two circumstances should be in place to launch a successful freeway building campaign: a strong central state, and funding. As to the former condition, a recent statistical overview of the correlation between types of regimes and freeway network size seems to indicate that the more authoritarian the national government is, the greater the chance of constructing an extensive road network. This is understandable, as the forces traditionally backing the exclusive 'national' transport mode, the railways, must be silenced or forced into compromise against a background of (often nationalistic) government campaigns about the modernistic promises of increasing road traffic. As to the latter condition (funding), by 1960, the International Bank for Reconstruction and Development (the World Bank's official name) and its "soft-loan wing," the International Development Association, as well as the Inter-American Development Bank, together had spent $175 million on highway construction loans. As of 1963, during the previous twenty years, "major United States and international donor agencies" had invested $7.2 billion in transport (39 percent on rails, 31 percent on roads, the latter percentage rapidly increasing), by far the most invested in Asia and the Middle East.[122] Such loans preferably were combined with loans for related purposes, such as electricity production, thus emphasizing that the provision of current for lighting, heating, and cooking was on par with the provision of car and truck driving experiences. Automobilism, we conclude again, thrives on the basis of sedentarism.

Venezuela, for example, invited a World Bank "general survey commission" to assess its 1963–1966 national economic plan, in which the highways of the country were considered to provide 95 percent of passenger and 90 percent of freight transport. Not doubting for a moment "the importance of transportation to economic growth," after nine years nearly $2 billion had been spent in Venezuela on "development loans," most of it dedicated to electric power development, more than half of the next item on the budget (transportation) to railways, and only one-fifth to highways. In some cases, however, such as the transport of copper and coal from the mines to the coast, the competition with road interests was so extreme that railroads had to be dismantled after World War II. At that moment, a large proportion of the World Bank loans had gone to Latin American countries, "explained by the fact that the countries involved are moving rapidly through the stages of basic development and urgently need new and improved highways to support their efforts," the "stages" an unmistakable reference to Rostow's modernization theory. By the beginning of the 1960s, Asia became the main recipient of the loans, representing 10 percent of the total capital of $20 billion, followed by $1 billion for Latin America, $1 billion for Africa and Australia together, and $1 billion for the European 'periphery' such as Norway, Finland, Austria, Turkey, and Yugoslavia. By 1964, the World Bank had given 480 loans worth $10 billion to eighty-five countries.[123]

***

As we have seen, the first decades of the World Bank were characterized by a Cold War form of "classical modernization theory" that assumed a connection between poverty and Communism, until the 1970s brought new forms of neoliberalism generally called the Washington Consensus to the fore and the notorious structural adjustment programs (SAPs) became the norm. The conditions under which the World Bank had to work and the requirements of its loans resulted in a "heavy concentration ... on power plants, railroad lines, highway networks, and similar physical facilities. The Bank became the leading proponent of the view that investment in transportation and communication facilities, port developments, power projects, and other public utilities was a precondition for the development of the rest of the economy," leaving no doubt that modernization was a highly technological affair, and mobility was part of this paradigm. Indeed, "for many developing countries, transport was the largest single sector for investment during the 1970s, with highway construction taking the lion's share ... By the late 1970s, transport accounted for almost a quarter of World Bank loans," the highest single issue on the bank's budget. By then, half that amount went into roads, a third into railways. Furthermore, 95 percent of the budget of research on transport was dedicated to roads. The layeredness-enhancing role of public investments in the transport sector becomes crystal clear in the case of Bangladesh, where, as late as the 1980s, nearly all "commercially operated vehicles" and two-thirds of their capacity were nonmotorized, whereas public investment in this sector was only 0.004 percent of the total investment in transport.[124]

When former General Motors CEO and "Cold War warrior" Robert McNamara became World Bank president (1968–1981), development was redefined through the inclusion of poverty relief through "projects focused on small farmers and provision of urban services." Before World War II, poverty had "largely [been] the province of religious and private philanthropic groups," but with the UN Universal Declaration of Human Rights in 1948, the issue "moved from what was essentially a domestic arena to an international one," but it is revealing that the period of Exuberance as described in the previous chapter was not accompanied by a debate on the world's poverty. Gunnar Myrdal's *Asian Drama: An Inquiry into the Poverty of Nations* (1968), on India and Pakistan, and the Institute for Development Studies at the University of Sussex (and its economist Dudley Seers), founded in the same year, started a movement to include poverty into the development paradigm, supported by President Johnson's War on Poverty. McNamara's predecessor, George Woods, had already allowed technical training programs to be funded and had included agriculture as a "directly productive" sector in the Bank's domain, but McNamara's Vietnam experiences as US Secretary of Defense probably made him aware of the security aspects of worldwide poverty at a moment that "between 500 and 700 million people were living in rural poverty," and "roads to markets" promised to alleviate this. Other analysts pointed at the "apparent failure of economically oriented approaches to development" as a cause of the World Bank's reorientation. However this may be, the decade before McNamara's famous Nairobi speech in 1973 on development and poverty saw the share of funded agricultural projects within the World Bank double to nearly a quarter, whereas infrastructure loans decreased from 55 to 30 percent over the same period. From then on, the Bank's policy reports increased considerably in quality, forming an important source for our overviews of the global mobility projects supported by the World Bank.[125]

Questioning Modernity: Development, Subalternity, and Alternative Mobilities

The question, then, is, what kind of modernity did the Peace Corps volunteers, as a vanguard of the 'soft side' of American foreign policy, foster? Some, within the ranks of high-echelon modernizers themselves, began to doubt development's effectiveness quite early. It was one of the founders of development economics, Albert Hirschman, who, through a historical reconstruction, showed the limited effectiveness of the World Bank's development policies. Partly based on an investigation of transport projects (roads in Ecuador, railways in Nigeria), he emphasized the large degree of uncertainty in the planning of many projects, as well as their highly technical approach, while also questioning the accuracy of the cost benefit analyses that formed the basis of the bank's assessments of the projects. Whereas, in the 'core,' time savings could be calculated and expressed in money, in the 'periphery,' with high unemployment rates, the benefits of time savings were controversial (although applied by many consultants without much reflection). In the periphery, economic growth and accessibility were proposed as better measures to estimate the benefits of infrastructure investments. By the end of the 1960s, the "flower[ing of the] old doctrines of development ... fell away with remarkable speed." They were replaced, as we will see later, by the emergence of the UN Conference on Trade and Development and Latin American *dependencia* theories. Thus, transnationally 'planning euphoria' came to an end, and a feeling of a "crisis of planning" set in.[126]

On the other hand, it would be naive to call this global project a "failure," as Amy Staples did in her seminal diplomatic history of the early development endeavor, a judgment inflated to an "ultimate failure" in the series editor's foreword. This would take the modernizers' pretensions at face value, and neglect the economic and other profits that Western construction companies and the consultant companies gained, and the propagandistic, anti-Communist role of their practices. We need the down-to-earth directness of a frustrated former Peace Corps volunteer-turned-"economic hit man" like John Perkins to remind us how "business schools, international organizations, and revered economists taught that building infrastructure projects was essential to development, the solution to poverty." He observed, without giving any proof, how governments in the developing world from the 1970s

> accepted outrageously large loans that were used to develop infrastructure projects that all too often served only the upper classes while leaving the country burdened with debt. / The results were disastrous ... Millions of people once hailed as members of the middle class lost their jobs and joined the ranks of the impoverished. As citizens [in Latin America] watched their pensions, health care, and educational institutions decline, they also noticed that their politicians were buying up Florida real estate rather than investing in local businesses.

Staples called the North-South debate on development a more "significant conflict ... than the ideological East-West armed standoff." She showed how the World Bank pushed the concept of the "denationalized expert" to the fore. Right after the start of the World Bank, John McCloy, one of its early presidents, had to convince Wall Street bankers he was "not controlled by New Deal idealists but by bankers, businessmen, and economists who were ready to work in partnership with private enterprise to manage the global economy." The World Bank "would aid private business by reinvigorating American and European faith in international investment and by making Third World economies more welcoming to multinational corporations and other foreign investors." This became clear when the loans were granted only if the requesting country was prepared to reform its tax system and deploy other "unpopular domestic measures," such that "the benefits of economic development were shared with the working classes," a condition especially important against the background of Cold War competition with the Soviet Union and China. The World Bank's first loans were to France ($250 million) and Chile ($40 million), but a loan request to rehabilitate mining in Eastern European Poland was rejected. McCloy's successor, Eugene Black, rejected an Argentinean loan request because of President Juan Perón's "extreme economic nationalism" and his striving toward "autarchy." But such countries could always try to get aid from the American government directly, such as the loans through EXIM to Mexico, Iran, and Brazil, whose requests had all been refused by the World Bank. And the World Bank's policy was not always consistent: the Netherlands received a loan that enabled the country to start a war against Indonesian nationalists. But by the end of the period under consideration here, Vice President Mohamed Shoaib conceded that alleviating the inequality between First and Third Worlds was not anymore "a realistic consideration."[127]

More recently, postmodern social scientists insisted we should distinguish between "modernity" (as a "metaphor for new or emerging 'here-and-now' materialities, meanings and cultural styles seen in relation to the notion of some past state of things") and "modernization" (as "a comprehensive package of technical and institutional measures aimed at widespread societal transformations and underpinned by neo-evolutionary theoretical narratives"), allowing for the existence of "multiple modernities," or "alternative or plural modernities." Others proposed the term "indigenous modernities." But when "modernization" is conceived as a practice "undertaken and implemented by cosmopolitan administrative and technological elites," one wonders why improvements made locally on rickshaws cannot be called "modernization" but should be labeled instead as "local modernities."[128] The answer to this question is probably that 'development' always is pervaded with a Western bias. However this may be, anthropologists and others have meanwhile acknowledged something like "modernization without the market" or even "modernization without capitalism" might exist, for instance, through research of the 'peripheral' Muslim areas in central Asia in the Soviet Union, brought about through "forced sedentarisation of nomadic populations" in the 1920s, and followed much later by "Soviet-style modernisation" such as "the emancipation of women, universal literacy, and the triumph of Soviet forms of expression over 'traditional' cultures." Other students of the modernization process coined terms like anti-capitalist modernity and postcolonial modernity. They followed, in a way, earlier subaltern studies scholars who, in their studies of the Indian peasantry, opened our eyes for the existence of "non-European modernity." These scholars also emphasized the intermediary role of local elites in the process of modernization, who in India, in the words of one of their contemporary critics, created "English rule without the Englishman." The modern, then, is something that has already happened elsewhere, only to be "reproduced, mechanically or otherwise, with a local content." This means, as Chakrabarty cleverly concluded in the case of India, the innovation often had to be found "in the sphere of the nonmodern." Instead of a not very fruitful dichotomy between modern and nonmodern, Chakrabarty proposed to deal with both as constituting the same process, which should be seen not so much as "British gifts to India [but] as fruits of struggles undertaken by the Indians themselves."[129]

***

Modernization theory was more than a euphemism taken from the "public transcript" (as opposed to the hidden transcripts of subaltern groups), however. As part of the hegemonic discourse, it has been analyzed lately as an ideology, providing guidelines for a practice that had more than a rocket metaphor in common with mobility studies. According to development economist Arthur Lewis, modernization implied the "mobilization" of capital and labor, and his colleague David Lerner identified in his study of the Middle East a "mobile personality" that should be encouraged to make "a personal choice to seek elsewhere his own version of a better life": "The mobile person is distinguished by a high capacity for identification with new aspects of his environment; he comes equipped with the mechanisms needed to incorporate new demands upon himself that arise outside of his habitual experience." Against such an individual with a "rationalist and positivist spirit," Islam would be "absolutely defenseless." Social psychologists further characterized this personality (based on interviews with nearly six thousand men) as having an "openness to new experience," a "readiness for social change," showing "effective use of time, a willingness to trust others, personal aspirations, and respect for the dignity of others. They then combined these qualities," concluded the anthropologist from whom these observations are quoted, "with a series of topical observations including kinship structure, attitudes towards women's rights, religion, commitment to work, and social stratification," which on their turn were combined with a third set of "behavioral measures based on voting, attendance at religious services, reading the paper, listening to the radio, and discussing political issues."[130]

Driving a car, one is inclined to add (had these scholars taken mobility into account), no doubt would have heightened the individual's score on the Overall Modernity Scale. It is quite clear that mobility formed a precondition of modernity, as it induced "modern men and women [to] learn to yearn for change." Such attitudes were certainly not limited to Peace Corps volunteers: when Charlotte Wiser, whom we met in chapter 1 as a missionary active in an Indian remote village in the 1930s, returned thirty years later, after the war (her husband, Bill, had died meanwhile), she came by "car and driver" borrowed from friends in Delhi. Oxcarts were still used for heavy loads, but the cycle rickshaw, coming to the village in 1960, had improved the connection to the bus depot and hence to the big town, leading to the prosperity of some (the local goldsmith who bought a cycle rickshaw) and the disaster of others (the cotton carder put out of work because of cheaper textile from the mills). Schoolchildren biked to town, communications (mail, telephone) improved, and sometimes "a group of men hired a whole bus to take them on the long journey" to a holy place in the Himalayas. This is what Wiser observed: "On every occasion when we are working together, we draw [the villagers'] attention to the existence of cause and effect, until they themselves are beginning to question some of their practices." Surveys won't help, she finds out, as the villagers confess: "We deliberately mislead the inquirer. We would be fools to give accurate figures, when there is a strong probability that they will be used to our disadvantage." The explanation is given alongside (complete with cause and effect): "Some may call our pretense of poverty, deception. Perhaps it is. But there are times when deception, as a means of self-protection, is justifiable. When a small mother bird knows that the hawk is overhead watching, does she fly straight to her nest?" Surveyors as predators attacking from above: so much for the successes of modernity in India. When Wiser returned ten years later, the village "had made more progress during those ten years than it had in the thirty years before."[131]

The close relationship between modernity and mobility led Marian Aguiar in her dissertation on railway modernity to propose a 'mobility definition' of modernity, as the latter "propels the present towards a possible future" at the same time as it "rejects the immediate past," a definition nicely encompassing the very important, and often neglected, *expectations* within the modernity discourse. Although, as Aguiar asserted, "modernity cannot be reduced to mobility," it was this willingness to constant change, this effort to mold the subjects and objects of modernization into a 'mobile individual,' that formed the very soft core of the modernization program, its hard, coercive flip side never far away. Indeed, students of modernization would be well advised to remember that "terror might lurk in the interstices of the modern," not so much because "the modernity's texture is violent; this claim, while true, does not interrupt the logic of modernity. The claim of the modern is to control violence legally and rationally," for instance, as a mobility history student might suggest, through the institutionalization of the 'hidden violence' of road accident statistics, as I have argued extensively elsewhere. History writing that wishes to be sensitive to these phenomena, needs to "deliberately make ... visible, within the very structure of its narrative forms, its own repressive strategies and practices. If "universalism" is the core of "the official gospel of modernity" of world capitalism, then the car, promoted by Henry Ford as a "universal car" and "a car for the multitudes," certainly forms an important part of it.[132]

***

But did these 'multitudes,' half of them poor peasants, agree? And if so, did they embrace its adventurous sides as well? We need the historical skills of an Eric Hobsbawm to remind us that "probably it was not until the 1960s or later that rural people outside parts of Latin America began systematically to see modernity as a promise rather than a threat." This happened in and through land reform, in which "almost half of the human race" got involved during the years immediately following World War II. Hobsbawm concluded that for many countries beyond the West, the "Second World" of the Soviet Union "appeared to provide a more suitable and encouraging model for progress than the West." We also need, however, the theoretical insights of subaltern and related scholars to show us how, next to the "public transcript," subaltern classes develop their own "hidden transcript," "a critique of power spoken behind the back of the dominant," as we already saw in the case of Wiser's Indian village. "The powerful, for their part, also develop a hidden transcript representing the practices and claims of their rule that cannot be openly avowed." From this perspective, James Scott, who coined these terms, conceded "even close reading of historical and archival evidence tend to favor a hegemonic account of power relations [Hamid Amin came to a similar conclusion in his study of the Chauri Chaura uprising; chap. 1]. Short of actual rebellion, powerless groups have ... a self-interest in conspiring to reinforce hegemonic appearances," the flip side of what we in the previous chapter encountered as 'repressive tolerance.' It results, instead, in the '*repressed* tolerance' by the subaltern masses of the hegemonic paradigm of modernity, including its mobility aspects.[133]

From this perspective, it is worthwhile to ask ourselves, do subaltern mobilities exist? If so, I would argue, they are to be found in unexpected places, in unexpected forms. "Subaltern politics," Chakrabarty asserted, "tended to be more violent than elite politics," but the "resistance to elite domination" would not have occurred without "subaltern mobilizations"—collective, deeply political actions that made the peasant, "instead of being an anachronism in a modernizing colonial world, ... a real contemporary of colonialism and a fundamental part of the modernity to which colonial rule gave rise in India." A historical investigation by one of the subaltern studies scholars of more than a hundred peasant rebellions during the nineteenth century showed "these always involved the deployment by the peasant of codes of dress, speech, and behavior that tended to invert the codes through which their social superiors dominated them in everyday life." In Scott's terminology, subaltern modernities (including mobilities) are to be found in the public transcript, but "in disguised forms."[134]

This book, which can sketch only a coarse framework for a world-historical analysis of alternative mobilities, cannot possibly begin to chart similar code inversions in the realm of mobility, but we will, in the course of this chapter, point at possible fissures where such inversions might be detected. Part of the 'subversive chaos' resulted from the refusal or inability to 'swarm' in what we called 'semipublic transport.' But this is urban stuff; we have no idea how subaltern mobilities looked like in a rural setting, although the central role of the bicycle in the "Telengana uprising of 1948–1951 [in Hyderabad state, when] women activists took to the bicycles that were otherwise the prerogative of men," suggests there is much to gain from a history of rural-urban subversiveness through a mobility lens. Likewise, later, during the Indochina wars, bicycles would become the "pack mules" of the revolutionary armies in the jungle. Therefore, despite the "assumed death of the peasant," these fissures will be found, as the following sections will show, at the interstices between rural and urban cultures. One characteristic of such fissures is the relationship between modernization and religion, mythology, superstition, witchcraft, and all other terms 'developers' have coined for the 'irrational' and "traditional" aspects of the modernization process, 'carnivalesque' aspects that also will taint our analysis of mobilities beyond the West.[135]

Exporting Megalomania: The IRF as Freeway Avant-Garde

In the global spread of 'mobile modernity,' the IRF, as vanguard of the transnational road lobby, used the specter of "congestion" as a crucial argument, a phenomenon that in the course of the previous decades had been redefined into a token of the nonmodern. As I have argued elsewhere, the success of the freeway lobby *before the war* in those Western countries that were hesitant to introduce this concept (such as in the Netherlands but also in France) used the *safety* argument to advocate their case: separating the traffic flow and then enabling its high-speed parts to increase their speed, paradoxically led to a decrease of fatalities. After the war, *congestion* became a second argument in favor of freeways. Both arguments (safety and congestion) were validated by the building of the American Interstate network, as we saw. For the IRF, Australian British Petroleum PR Manager Roth Jones confessed at a conference, "It is not difficult to 'sell' road construction because now there are few cities or countries in the world not facing the ever-growing problem of congestion." At a moment when there was "hardly a country in the world which is not undertaking some highway programme," Jones emphasized the road PR office, "like the engineer, is a specialist, and it cannot be left to the engineer to do the PR work on his own."[136]

Indeed, the IRF calculated that national road budgets of thirty-one countries nearly doubled between 1948 and 1954 (from $3.8 billion to $7.3 billion), the United States taking a diminishing share of 70 percent (1948) to 55 percent (1954), followed by Canada and Germany. American observers watched eagerly how the world motorized vehicle fleet increased to 76 million by 1953, an increase of 50 percent during the previous five years. In terms of growth rates, newcomers like Hong Kong and even Nigeria and Northern Rhodesia performed better than the US and the UK. By the end of the 1950s, the world motor vehicle fleet had increased to 122 million units, with the American (25 million) and Western European fleets (18 million) as the strongest (largest) growth cores, but, again, with the highest growth percentages in Asia. These vehicles drove on a global total of 5.7 million miles of high-grade highways (and an unknown number of many million miles more of lower-grade roads, one is inclined to add), Europe having the highest density (in miles per square mile), followed by North America (its density being less than half that of Europe, or even only a quarter when just the 'compact' EEC countries were taken into account), and Asia (with less than half the density of North America). A statistical overview by the World Bank showed the total road length in forty-three countries (from the US to Malawi) quite uniformly more than doubled during the 1960s (the average growth factor was 2.4, except for the rich countries, where it was 2.1).[137] This astounding result suggests a central command center, but there was none: it resulted from an aggressive and scientifically backed Western eagerness to build and advice, and a no less Eastern eagerness to modernize.

Although more research is needed, it seems IRF officials initially represented the hard-boiled modernization paradigm, but soon the propaganda for new roadbuilding got adjusted to include 'low-cost roads,' often constructed based on new knowledge collected on local soils and tropical climate conditions, and defined, at the PIARC conference in Istanbul in 1955, as a road "located and built to geometrical standards commensurate with future requirements, but ... constructed with bases and surface to meet the present traffic requirements." It is possible that Indian road engineers brought this perspective on the international agenda, through their active participation within the PIARC, after it had already occupied Western road engineers during the 1930s when it came to designing tertiary (agricultural) roads in remote areas in the West, but M. Luísa Sousa, Portuguese historian of technology specialized in mobility history, claimed "Portuguese road engineers working in Angola and Mozambique" put the issue on the agenda when the PIARC organized its conference in Lisbon in 1951. She showed how this road type received a specific definition within the transnational road engineering community of a non-Western road, "overseas/colonial."[138]

"Each country knows which are its own low cost roads," a British participant to the PIARC conference in Rio de Janeiro in 1959 opined. "In Germany, and in Poland, they are the minor rural roads serving small farms and villages away from the main centres. In Africa, on the other hand, almost all roads are still thought of as low cost roads." Low-cost roads offered a window of opportunity to indigenous expertise to seep into the roadbuilding paradigm, an example of "cultural appropriation" (Christian Huck) or "creative appropriation" (Frank Dikötter) that made the diffusion of technology into a two-sided process and led David Edgerton to speak of "creole technologies," as we saw. To give only one example of many: at the PIARC conference in Rio de Janeiro, a Malaysian engineer explained how his colleagues in a condition without a dry season used a very steep (nearly vertical) way of cutting the side banks of the road to prevent the very heavy rainfall from eroding the exposed earth surfaces. In many places, local engineers started to experiment with stabilizing tropical soils, while Western engineers proposed methods developed during the war for the rapid construction of airfields, for instance, in India. In Gambia, "in keeping with the client's wish, that indigenous material be used," the British contractor mixed the surface dressing with rolled cockleshells.[139]

***

Whereas the PIARC thus provided space to enhance appropriation from below, the IRF helped exporting the 'coordination debate' around the world, always emphasizing its "doctrine ... that roads must be given priority in the structural program of developing countries. They, together with the provision of water supplies, form the basis from which the economies of these countries must grow. Roads cause development: they should not be regarded as the result of it." And to underline where it got its wisdom from, the editorial in the IRF's *Road International* in mid-1969 continued:

"In the economic field roads make possible the change from a subsistence economy to a crash crop economy—a first stage in growth." From a social point of view, the journal stressed, roads bring "a sense of unity amongst the many tribes and the transformation of the warrior into a peaceful and useful worker." Transport experts delivered the scientific backing to this lobby, such as Wilfred Owen, who distinguished between three "transport patterns": those of the "advanced countries," of densely populated countries and some Communist countries, and of the "less populated undeveloped countries." The three groups of countries represented "different stages in an evolutionary process." Relative investment champions in roads were Colombia (74 percent of its public investment funds allocated to transport), Senegal (72 percent), and Iran (68 percent), whereas Argentina privileged the railways (with 55 percent). In Colombia (which published a transport plan in 1961, funded by the World Bank and executed by a US consultancy), railroad length started to decline from 1973 onward, after it had been stabilized during the 1960s and after $2.7 billion (10 billion pesos) had been spent, especially to construct the Atlantico Railroad, connecting the interior with the ports. The largest increase in rail freight performance (in ton-kilometer) between 1950 and 1960 took place in Asia (where it tripled) and Eastern Europe (where it doubled), but Owen predicted a "changing composition of the demand for transport in underdeveloped areas" in favor of road over rail.[140]

The IRF's preference was clearly for big if not megalomaniac projects, of which the usefulness only made sense from a prewar elite touristic perspective. Who needs a cross-continental road for automobiles, except for profit making by construction companies and consultancies, and except for ideological reasons, such as in the case of the Pan-American Highway, a project compared in several Senate and House reports with the "splendid road system" of the "Roman Empire"? Indeed, it is in *The Rhetoric of Empire* (the title of a book-length analysis of "colonial discourse" by David Spurr) that we can observe the emergence of the "curious phenomenon: the West seeks its own identity in Third World attempts at imitating it; it finds its own image, idealized, in the imperfect copies fabricated by other cultures." In Spurr's ironic comment, the point of view that goes with this phenomenon is that of "the conveniently middle-class shopowner, for whom Western-style consumption takes precedence over the realities of revolution," as the rhetoric within "journalism, travel writing, and imperial administration" (part of Spurr's subtitle) "seeks to minimize conflict and cultural difference by celebrating the unifying power of Western (or North American) commercial and cultural institutions."[141]

And yet, it is remarkable the United Nations ventilated similar grand visions as those of the IRF, mostly emanating from its regional economic commissions. The Economic Commission for Africa (ECA), for instance, initiated the Trans-African Highway network, from West to East, a suggestion made by a Japanese economic mission to Africa, with Mitsubishi Corporation being "prepared to build the road" and the Japanese government willing to give aid. By the time the PIARC reported about it in 1972, one-third of its length appeared to be paved (in Nigeria and East Africa), and for the remainder, the same strategy was used as in the case of the European E-road network: classifying some unpaved stretches as part of the network, later to be adjusted to the network's standard. This standard, a "pattern for African road development," as *Road International* called it, was South Africa. At the time of reporting, the British Transport and Road Research Laboratory had surveyed the "engineering properties of landscape" of the Kenyan and Nigerian parts, and "a firm of consulting engineers [had] been commissioned to prepare an economic assessment of the whole project." Four years later, the ECA held a meeting in Addis Ababa, where six countries agreed to build a "Trans-East African highway to link Cairo in Egypt with Gaborone in Botswana." After the failure of most of these projects, meant to "break [colonial] old patterns" of scandalous fragmentation of the continent in national networks, with hardly any interconnections between countries, the 1970s saw a shift toward the construction of rural roads. Africa's lack of continental intra-connectivity is not limited to roads but is a general mobility-wide phenomenon: it was easier to call or fly to European capitals from an African capital than to another African capital.[142]

Mediating Modernization: Japan and Asian 'Development'

After the excursion back to the West in the previous section, we can continue our analysis of Asian 'mobile modernization.' For China and India, although by far the largest, were not the only Asian countries engaging in an economic modernization process after the war. In this section, we will first describe the efforts by Asian countries and colonies to come to a common program of modernization, mostly through the UN. We will then focus on Japan's role as intermediary in the diffusion of Western expertise mixed with some 'Eastern' elements, within Asia.

'Developing Asia': The United Nations and the Comparison with the West

The United Nations founded, in March 1947, both the ECE and ECAFE (soon to be followed by similar commissions for Latin America and Africa), and although the latter covered an area containing more than half the earth's population (in 1960), the Western majority within ECAFE

(Australia, France, the Netherlands, Soviet Union, the UK, and the US, versus Taiwan, India, the Philippines, and Thailand) intended to organize the commission as "a purely research organization." In a context where the nation-state was "a fairly recent phenomenon" (except for Thailand), and where each young nation, after the period of decolonization finalized in 1960, had at least four of the "thirty-two ethnolinguistic groups" within its borders, the decision to found a "multisectoral" Regional Commission after the example of the ECE, led by Gunnar Myrdal (seeking "a middle way between the neoclassical approach and the Marxist alternative, which Continental Europe translated into the so-called social market economy") was inspired by the hope for an Asian version of the Marshall Plan. A year later, Latin American countries, which had crucially supported the founding of ECAFE within the UN, would set up the Economic Commission for Latin America (ECLA), under Raúl Prebisch, where the debate between developmentalists and *dependentistas* would rage, as we will see later in this chapter.

Initially, most of Western countries within ECAFE obstructed every proposal to strengthen Asia's economic integration, but the self-confidence of ever more independent Asian countries gradually increased, especially after it had become clear the Western countries were not willing to mimic the reconstruction efforts of the Marshall Plan. Thrown back on themselves, and fully aware they had long ago dominated worldwide GDP, Asian countries meanwhile represented a majority of votes within the commission, and gradually settled to improve their infrastructure through the founding, in 1949, of a Bureau of Flood Control and subcommissions on trade, industry, and iron and steel, whereas "ad hoc conferences on travel facilities and inland transport problems were also convened." Remarkably, and contrary to the ECE, Asian planners did not consider transport within ECAFE a priority, according to historian David Wightman, who was asked by the commission to write "a completely independent history" in 1958, "reflect[ing] to some extent the legacy of a colonial past when many Asians believed that transport existed primarily to serve the trading interests of the imperial power." This should have alerted transport planners, as several Asian former colonies had a transport network configuration similar to African countries: instead of a grid, linear connections between the coast and places of resource extraction.

But within ECAFE, transport was not considered "an international issue." Another reason was the fact that many countries produced the same raw materials (a heritage from colonialism), so experts initially did not see much chances for intra-regional trade. The first time Asian transport experts met was in 1949, in Singapore, at the first regional conference organized by ECAFE. In 1954, a Regional Training Centre for Railway Operating and

Signalling Officials was set up in Lahore, Pakistan, in an effort to improve the exploitation of the existing (mostly single-track) railway network, which indeed did not expand much, except in China and India. A study tour to Europe, Japan, and the United States was also organized. Within ECAFE, Japan (a full member since 1954) competed with the Western members in the export of transport expertise, for instance, through a "large-scale tour of Japan National Railways." India proposed its own diesel locomotives as a basis for standardization, but the differences between the member countries were too large to allow for any standardization. Although a proposed Organization for Asian Economic Cooperation did not materialize, Japan, in the context of ECAFE, set up its Asian Development Bank, which would be instrumental in the further dissemination of its planning practices and culture, as we will see later.[143]

In 1959, ECAFE's Inland Transport and Communications Committee (ITTC) held a meeting in Bangkok to discuss the construction of a transcontinental transport corridor, the so-called Asian Highway. At that moment, ECAFE had fourteen members (Australia, Burma, China, France, India, Indonesia, the Netherlands, New Zealand, Pakistan, the Philippines, Thailand, the USSR, the UK, and the US) and eight nonvoting members (they could vote in the commission's subcommittees): Cambodia, Ceylon (Sri Lanka), Hong Kong, the Republic of Korea, Laos, Malaya (Malaysia) and British Borneo (the northern part of this large island), Nepal, and Vietnam. ECAFE became "a truly regional organization" in 1960, and when it, in 1973, added not only 'Pacific' but also 'social' to its name (Economic and Social Commission for Asia and the Pacific—ESCAP), it counted twenty-nine members, including the three regional great powers India, China, and Japan. By then, ESCAP had been stripped from its political clout and remodeled to fit in the UN framework of 'technical assistance.' Ikuto Yamaguchi's historical study of the founding of ECAFE concluded that as late as 1962, its role "was still confined to the exchange of information, preparation of studies, and the academic exploration of projects," because of the "lack of funds," with two exceptions: the Lower Mekong River Basin project and the Asian Highway project. Road mobility appeared to be the loophole through which transnationalism could acquire momentum, but the local experts remained reluctant to follow the Western example of transport coordination (the road-rail competition): they felt they could not "afford the luxury of competition in the transport field, particularly between private and public enterprises" (meaning: between private trucks and buses and public railways).[144]

At the start of the highway project in 1958, the secretariat was relocated at the last moment from Shanghai to Bangkok. The planning of the network (according to official history tributary to ECAFE's Deputy Executive

Secretary Sithu U Nyun's "grand design" of 1958) shows many parallels with the European E-road network, especially in its strategy to take the "existing main national routes" as a basis, which made the International Chamber of Commerce complain that its shape showed "political and strategic considerations [instead of] economic considerations." A "uniform code of road signs, signals, and pavement markings" was taken over from the UN Convention of 1949. In 1961, the Indonesian network was added, connected through the ferry to the Malay peninsula. Between 1969 and 1972, ECAFE's ITTC organized a series of rallies for trucks, buses, and cars over finished stretches of the Asian Highway, between Vientiane (Laos) and Singapore, and between Tehran (Iran) and Dhaka (Bangladesh). The network (62,600 km) covered fourteen countries and included a smaller system of "priority roads: with a total length of 38,000 km, forming the Asian equivalent of the 28,000-km Pan-American Highway and the Trans-African Highway, avoiding, in true Cold War spirit, the territory of the Soviet Union and the People's Republic of China (fig. 3.5). There were also "missing links" in Burma, East Pakistan, and Thailand. Wightman saw the project as "a promotional one, … as a modern revival of the ancient caravan routes": such projects had to "create their own demand."[145]

By 1970, the end of the "UN Development Decade," $900 million had been spent on the construction of 12,750 km and the improvement of another 9,000 km, while another $1.8 billion were needed to complete the network. One through road was part of it, fully equipped with a bituminous surface between Turkey and Burma (except 400 km of gravel road in Iran). Another billion dollars would be necessary to convert the main artery into a two-lane road. What exactly the role of the IRF has been in this project is not clear, but the IRF, as an official UN adviser, was invited to the 1959 meeting in Bangkok. It is quite clear it was the IRF that advocated such international "uninterrupted through routes" as part of its PR efforts within the context of the road-rail struggle and, in a wider context, the Cold War. Later, this highway network was scheduled to be extended with a Central Treaty Organization (CENTO) network between Iran, Pakistan, and Turkey, thus providing a bridge between the Asian and the Western European networks. Supported by the United Kingdom, this intermediary network was introduced in *Road International* in a classic manner: first, the country was described as one where from ancient times onwards some animal (in this case the camel) reigned supreme; then, the arrival of 'modern times' was sketched, which made these solutions obsolete; and then the "enormous task" of modernization was depicted, the only way to propel the country into modernity. Nonetheless, in 1992, ESCAP developed a "new vision," a multimodal Asian Land Transport Infrastructure Development (ALTID), in which the Asian Highway and the Trans-Asian Railway were combined.[146]

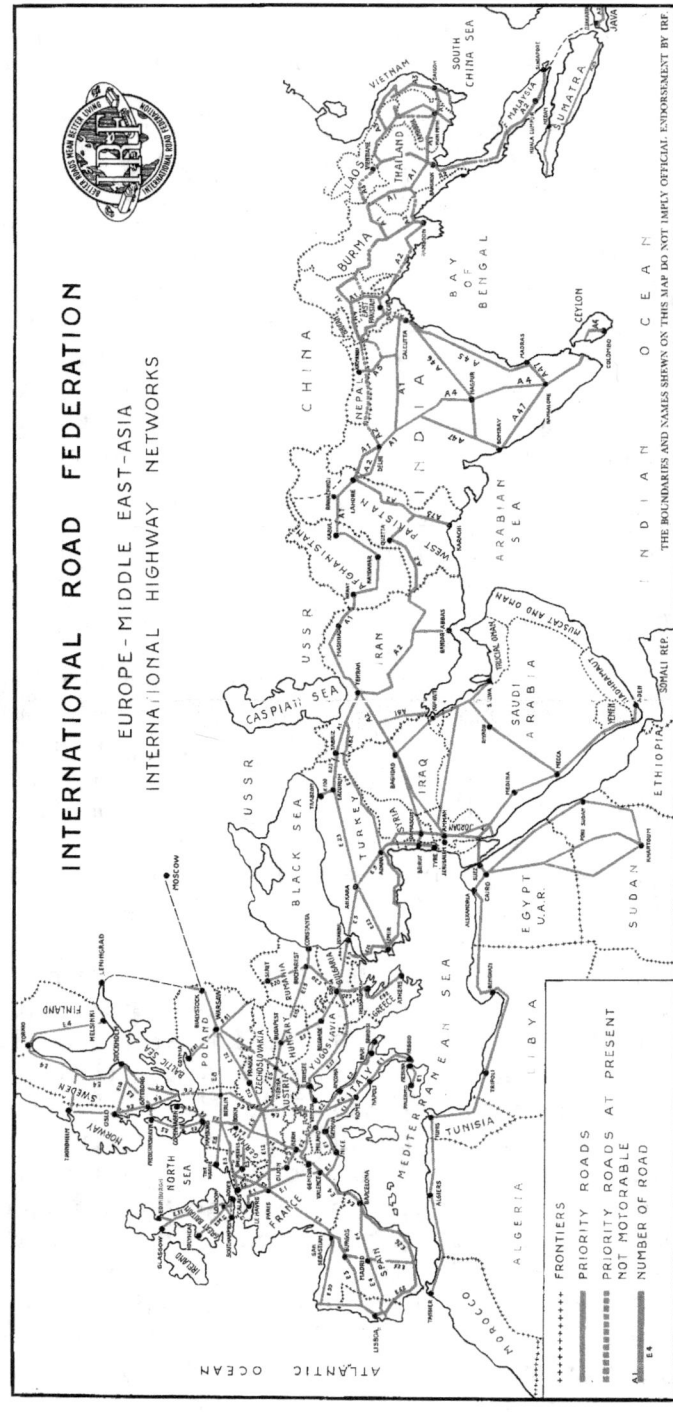

Figure 3.5. Map of the Asian Highway, avoiding the Soviet Union and China. Source: *Road International* (June 1970): 40–41. Published with permission.

***

The IRF, indeed, did not hide for a moment that the framework for development was defined not only through a comparison with the West but also with those growing factions within civil engineering circles and transport planners in favor of road over rail. An analysis of some pivotal articles in *Road International*, written by road engineers and planners, can illustrate this. In a discussion on the "bottleneck in Indian transport," civil engineer B. Vagh complained the Indian Five-Year Plans did not provide for a true road traffic planning. Although his comparison with the United Kingdom not only verged on the absurd (by converting the 9.6 million bullock carts on Indian roads to 195,000 trucks with an equivalent load), it did not at all support his complaint, instead clearly showing India needed railway wagons much more than it needed trucks. What is most revealing, though, is that we see here a mechanism emerging that certainly was not a prerogative of Eastern planners but that, in the case of the now very rapidly growing East, had an overarching converging effect on national fleets and networks: a comparison of the number of trucks per unit of national income for nine Western European countries clearly 'proved,' in the language of the development ideology, the 'backwardness' of Indian road transport. Although the differences between truck fleet sizes in Europe were large (France had about three times as many trucks per unit of income than did Switzerland or Sweden—the same, by the way, as Ceylon [Sri Lanka] and the Philippines), India, with about one-third of the latter countries' number of trucks, clearly 'lagged behind' and needed to 'catch-up.' The IRF point of view in Vagh's analysis became clear when he ended his comparison with a reference to the United States, where "some 26,000 miles of rail track were dismantled" between 1940 and 1945, which implied "India should proceed cautiously in extending its rail transport." Having thus coined the "transport problem" (others would soon follow specifying this into a "road problem"), Vagh advised the government to avoid "nationalization of goods transport for at least 15 years," to eliminate all "restrictions, regional or inter-State, on road transport," and to halve taxation on trucks.[147]

Likewise, the engineer who described the road system of Pakistan soon after the partition from India spoke of "roads, which are said to be a country's measure of civilization," a trait the fledgling country apparently lacked fully: a comparison with the "recognised standard (the United States of America)" resulted in the conclusion that Pakistan's road density (per square mile) did not even match the density of US "desert areas." "In the wake of good roads," he declared, "and through them alone, will follow the development of health services, the provision of educational facilities, the extension of technical information for improving agricultural production—in fact, the opening up of the village to the influence of progressive forces." Soon, Pakistan's road system would be expanded with US support. On the other side of the partition, in East Bengal (the later Bangladesh), a ten-year program of roadbuilding easily matched India's absurdity, when the government announced an area of 232 square miles, in which sixty-five rivers flowed, had to be crossed by roads, a task that, indeed, as the reporting engineer assured, "almost baffles description."[148] The eagerness with which colossal projects based on the road paradigm (and in this case, against the indigenous, hegemonic mobility mode) were proposed suggests the American Interstate project, as 'the largest public works project in the world,' not only reshaped domestic automotive culture, as we have seen, but also had a massive propagandistic function in the Cold War setting, although this cannot be supported by hard textual evidence from *Road International*. But the constant pounding on the urge to modernize suggested that investing enormous sums in high-grade roads and borrowing money to this end was nothing to be embarrassed about for the local elite; on the contrary, the additional use of comparative statistics set in motion a modernization and motorization race that determined the prestige of many a local government.

***

On the other hand, the 'low-cost road' paradigm generated local activities and knowledge production that have not yet been charted by mobility historians, for instance, through the founding, in 1959, of a South East Asia Treaty Organization (SEATO) Graduate School of Engineering in Bangkok. There, research on the "dominant tropical soil type" laterite ("a product of rock decay high in oxides of iron [hence the red color of dirt roads] and low in the proportion of silica") was initiated, and special "bituminous paving mixtures" were investigated, but also the lettering on road panels was tested, resulting in the conclusion that Latin letters were visible from a greater distance than Thai characters. Professor of Transport Engineering John Hugh Jones explained such research was important because, "in the developing countries, typically from 25 to 55 per cent of all public investment is devoted to the transport sector."[149]

Despite the technical adaptations, the intrusion on the landscape and the revolution of spatial arrangements was certainly not less than in the West. In Thailand, for instance, adorned with hardly any paved roads, the thousands of miles of *klongs* (canals connecting to the large rivers) had been the main traffic arteries for centuries, and the jungle was crossed either on foot or on elephants. Some railway lines had connected the main cities and had crossed the Cambodian and Malaysian borders, following North-South routes between the mountain ridges along the main rivers. Now, the Friendship Highway (financed by the US after it was rejected by the World Bank in the early 1950s) and the East-West Highway were forced on the landscape, ninety meandering miles necessitating "enormous [deforested] side cuts," with "a sub-base prepared from locally available materials," "carved out" by American construction contractor Raymond International with funding from USAID. As soon as the roads were ready, villages appeared along its trajectory, but as the road was constructed parallel to the railroads, a direct and major transfer of freight and passengers was the result, a policy turn hardly conceivable in the West at the time, again suggesting (*pace* the Comaroffs; see the introduction) the Global South functioned as a laboratory for the West. Meanwhile, the Ministry of Communications had realized another six thousand paved miles of highways, making Thailand, according to an anonymous article in *Road International*, "the leading exporter of food in Asia." USAID also was active in the Philippines, financing consultancy work by the US Bureau of Public Roads. America's extensive participation in many Southeast Asian highway construction projects was based on the conviction that such aid "would improve logistics capabilities against communist insurgency."[150]

'Accessibility,' catchword of transport planners to emphasize their concern for social equality, suddenly got an entirely different meaning: the whole earth had to be made 'accessible' to control the remotest areas. For Malaya, for instance, it is well established that the network of secondary roads built in central Kedah "had been constructed to combat the communist insurgency and to provide access to new rubber areas and irrigated padi land." In general, the Communist revolt of 1948 "ushered in decolonization via a fury of road making," a fury that also produced the construction of five hundred "fenced 'new villages'" for the Chinese population. "Before the Second World War the Malays had been content to leave the economy to foreigners [especially Chinese and Indians], provided they retained political supremacy. Now they awoke to the fact that they were not only outnumbered in their own country and had lost the lion's share of its wealth to outsiders [especially tin and rubber], but those outsiders now wanted equal political status too, and the colonial government backed these claims." A Federal Land Development Authority made "rural modernization" into an anti-Communist project. The roads connected cities but also led to a "further decline of 'empty areas,'" especially on the East Coast. Communist guerillas killed British High Commissioner Sir Henry Gurney in 1951. Independent since 1957 in a state of "Emergency," Malaysia forced Singapore (with a Chinese majority, and under the premiership of Lee Kuan Yew) out in 1965, because it feared a Chinese majority. After the first expansion phase of 1890–1930 (see chap. 1), a second phase started in the early 1950s. Thomas Leinbach claimed a "self-reinforcing system" had been put to work: "New or improved linkages stimulated additional growth which led to further elaboration of the network." Likewise, by 1975, Singapore, benefiting from the economic boom because of the Korean War, became "the third largest port in the world." Equipped with an "excellent communications system," Malaysia prospered too because of its rich resources of tin and rubber. By the beginning of the 1970s, it abandoned its anti-Communist stance and became the first ASEAN country "to seek out friendship with China." Singapore, meanwhile, had developed "its own branch of socialism" with "state participation in industry and commerce but with management in general in the hands of private enterprise," an example followed by Malaysia, which "moved from a free capitalist economy after 1969 to more state participation."[151]

'Development' through Motorization: Japan's Export of the 'Coordination War' and the 'Layering' of Urban Traffic

By the end of the 1960s, Taiwan, Hong Kong, South Korea, and Singapore, with their authoritarian governments, seemed to follow the development ideology by the book, neatly working through three consecutive phases, an example of the 'periphery' taking the lead of "the Sinic world ... proudly marching toward an Asian-Pacific century, the homeland [seemingly, at the time] remain[ing] mired in perpetual underdevelopment." In the case of Taiwan, its entire infrastructure, including its highways, were built "according to American standardization." South Korea went through a phase of import substitution (1954–1960), followed by export orientation (1961–1979), crowned by "stabilization" in the 1980s and beyond. During the Korean War (1950–1953), about four million people died (among them five hundred thousand to one million Chinese soldiers), not in the least through US carpet bombing, which destroyed the entire Korean infrastructure. The war split the country in a northern part supported by the Soviet Union who handed the government over to guerilla leader Kim Il-sung, whereas General Douglas MacArthur, relieved from his duties in Japan, installed a dictatorship "oiled by US military and Asian Development Bank," its new vertically integrated conglomerates (*chaebol*) modeled after Japanese *zaibatsu*. "No other country in the world received such large sums in per capita terms, with the exception of Israel and South Vietnam." Led by a military regime since 1961, and benefiting from the Vietnam War in which it also participated militarily (three hundred thousand soldiers), South Korea, like the other "East Asian Tigers," focused on the export of goods "for which the nation had a comparative advantage."[152]

In South Korea's case, these were automobiles and their parts, produced by Hyundai, a *chaebol* company in the hands of a "large, family-controlled, government-assisted corporate group." Quite appropriately, the modernization theorists considered the government in such a case a part of a "development state." A development state, according to Piotr Dutkiewicz and Robert Shenton, "was distinguished by the central and direct involvement of the state in the appropriation of surplus value from producers, and by the dependence of the 'ruling elite' upon this form of appropriation." In some of these countries, Japanese aid played an intermediary role. From the early 1960s, Japan "began to export capital to its neighbours, searching for cheap labour and lower manufacturing costs," first in Thailand and Malaysia, and then through the ASEAN. The countries that most benefited from this flow were South Korea (by far the most, with 17 percent), the Philippines (9 percent), Indonesia (7 percent), Taiwan (7 percent), and Thailand (6 percent). Japan was, according to some observers, in an ideal position to help shape a third model of motorization, next to the Euro-American and the Soviet model. During the 1970s, Japan's aid, through the Japan International Cooperation Agency (JICA), stressed technology transfer, funding surveys, planning, and construction of roads, railroads, and bridges in Burma, Indonesia, Korea, Philippines, Thailand, and Vietnam, but this could not prevent the eruption of anti-Japanese riots in several of these countries, the protesters accusing Japan of "economic penetration and domination of selected Third World countries to secure 'food bases' and 'natural resource bases.'"[153]

***

After the war, at a moment when Tokyo's local mobility depended partly on the cycle rickshaw again, economic reconstruction targeted both the railways and the road system, steered by the Supreme Commander for the Allied Powers and implemented by the Japanese government.[154] During their seven-year reign, the Americans allowed the continuation of Japan's "imperial democracy," established a form of "bank-centered capitalism," and had the Japanese government execute a "Red Purge" from 1949 to 1951, which made twenty-one thousand alleged Communists lose their job. The "indirect" occupation (as opposed to the "direct" of Germany) was led by General MacArthur, a conservative who undertook a "McCarthyist removal" of those members of his staff who were considered "active New Dealers." The American confiscated the island of Okinawa "to guard the gate to China" militarily. The railways, transporting one-third of domestic freight in 1946, received an enormous boost when the United States at the beginning of the Korean War (in 1950) decided to use Japan as a supply base: more wagons were deployed than during any similar period of the Pacific War. Also, the Korean War reversed American strictness vis-à-vis the *zaibatsu*, the monopolistic conglomerates considered so characteristic for Japanese capitalism before the war. Japan's economy now began to grow at an annual rate of more than 10 percent, a record "never … seen in world economic history," making the country's GNP the third largest in the world (after the US and the USSR, but above Germany). Cultural historian Shunsuke Tsurumi has the Japanese age of "prosperity" begin in 1960, although it took some time to convince the population "to strike a balance between consumption and saving," the former in its conspicuous form "widely represented as a threat to social stability." In relative terms, it was the road sector that benefited the most from the cold/hot wars of the postwar years, thus accelerating an encroachment of road on rail that had started in the 1930s and became known in the West as the 'coordination crisis.' For instance, and remarkably, two antitrust laws in 1947 broke open the monopoly of the largest road transporter in Japan, Nippon Tsuun, forcing small transporters onto a market that in the West had emerged spontaneously and gradually.[155]

Many of these small transporters started using small three-wheelers, resulting in a 'typical' Asian modal configuration, but as late as 1949, Japan still had more than 150,000 horse- and oxen-drawn carts on its streets. Others bought army surplus vehicles and from 1951 onward domestically produced trucks. The latter enabled medium- and long-distance trucking competing directly with the railways, predictably (if the West can be any measure of these developments) resulting in outcries about the road infrastructure limping behind the car and truck explosions. These cries increased after the cabinet of Prime Minister Ikeda Hayato had made "rapid growth" into one of Japan's top priorities, and Toyota, Nissan, Isuzu, and Hino acquired large loans from the government, the World Bank, and EXIM, enabling an "explosion in productivity" that jump-started motor vehicle production from 162,000 in 1955 to more than 11 million in 1980, more than half of the latter exported. This was the result of a second characteristic of Japanese capitalism (next to the monopolistic structure of its enterprises): the intimate cooperation between these enterprises and the "development state," represented by the Ministry of International Trade and Industry (MITI), which together with the Japan Development Bank (1951, set up by the ministry) created a form of "guided capitalism," a "strong-state model" (comparable to the system of France) in between liberal market systems and state-dominated "command economies." The "iron triangle" of conservative Liberal Democrats, the business monopolies, and elite bureaucrats received US aid from 1946 to 1952 of more than $15 billion, half of what the Americans spent on Germany.[156]

A Law on Motor-Vehicle Road Construction for National Development (1957) and a Law on Emergency Measures for Road Improvement (1958) already in their names (development, emergency) signaled how the Japanese government envisioned its trajectory toward supergrowth. These laws were extensions of the 1952 Road Law, which were formulated on order of the occupying forces (who commented in a memorandum that Japan's road system was not fit for a "civilized country") and led to a "complete-re-examination" of Japan's road legislation, resulting, for instance, in an extensive toll-road system. One of the consequences of this intervention was that the original freeway plans from the 1930s (inspired by Germany's autobahn system and never implemented; see chap. 1) were adapted to the American road (building) culture, upon advise by Ralph J. Watkins of the Brookings Institution in Washington, who wrote a feasibility study (1956) for the Nagoya-Kobe Expressway. Co-funded by the World Bank, the expressway was promoted as "a genuine extension of the modern production line." And like in the United States, military and strategic arguments were used to legitimate the enormous amounts of investments. The toll idea was suggested because at the time of the planning of these roads, the number of vehicles was not considered high enough to provide for funding through the 'spiraling' fuel and vehicle tax systems. This not only questions the earlier quoted outcries for a lack of adequate roads but also shows how these outcries were inspired by the well-known mythology of roadbuilding as the automatic trigger of modernization. The laboratory character of Japan's motorization shows—more clearly than the Western master narrative, where it has remained hidden under the car's 'ubiquity'—that road networks were created 'before demand,' and was not the result of some inherent 'human desire.' As late as 1952, bicycles accounted for 87 percent of the vehicles registered; horse-, ox-, and handcarts another 7 percent; and only then followed by motorized vehicles with 6 percent.[157]

This is not to deny the Japanese road system was in a modest technical state: of the more than 140,000 km of roads, only 5.4 percent was paved, and nearly half the bridges were wooden. Nor is this to deny investments in road construction and maintenance exploded only by the end of the period under investigation here, during the 1970s. With its extremely high population density (310 persons per square km, compared to 25 in the US and only 15 in Sweden), Japan started its freeway building as late as 1965. Whereas in Western countries (and in Thailand, for reasons unknown to me), road investment's share in GNP started to decline from around 1970 (by 1990 this had more than halved), Japanese investments in roadbuilding did not diminish, and remained higher, relatively speaking, than investments in the West had ever been (around 2.5 percent of GNP). Only in 1980 did the passenger car's performance (in passenger-km) overtake that of the train. From then on, however, Japan became a civil engineer's paradise, where the design rules of Norman and Yale's *Highway Capacity Manual* were adjusted to a higher lane capacity (from 2,000 to 2,500 vehicles per lane per hour), alignment and other geometric criteria were scaled down, and special toll collection "trumpet interchanges" were added. While a National Arterial Expressway Construction Law (1967) announced the construction of 7,600 km of freeways—of which the firsts were opened in 1963 (Meishin Expressway, between Amagasaki and Rittō) and 1969 (Tōmei Expressway), together linking Tokyo and Kobe—for Tokyo, a 71-km plan of ring and radial roads was designed (from 1958), scheduled to be ready for the 1964 Summer Olympics. The road signs became a hybrid of American and European lettering and symbol standards. By 1980, Japan had constructed 2,579 km of intercity freeways, and 253 of urban freeways.[158] Yet, the Japanese transport sector accounted for only 11 percent of GNP, against nearly double that share in the United States, at the other extreme end of the international scale.[159]

Another 'typical' Japanese innovation was an extreme adaptation of the American habit of extending the freeway system far into the city. In the eyes of the Japanese planners, urban freeways became a necessity once the government's development emphasis shifted from heavy industry (steel, chemicals, shipbuilding) to lighter industry, including motor vehicles and electronics, a shift enabled by the revision of the Security Treaty in 1960, which was expected to generate much more traffic in and around the big cities, especially Tokyo, where the light industry was located. Indeed, in its hybridization of European and American influences, Tokyo followed the American example in its uninhibited sprawl for which also the originally planned green belt was sacrificed, while the tramways were abandoned between 1965 and 1971 (as in most Japanese cities) and replaced by a subway system. During the quarter-century after the war, one million Japanese migrated to the cities annually, so much so that by 1975, three-quarters of the population lived in these cities.[160] The congestion resulting from these shifts could be solved, planners promised, by the construction of urban freeways.

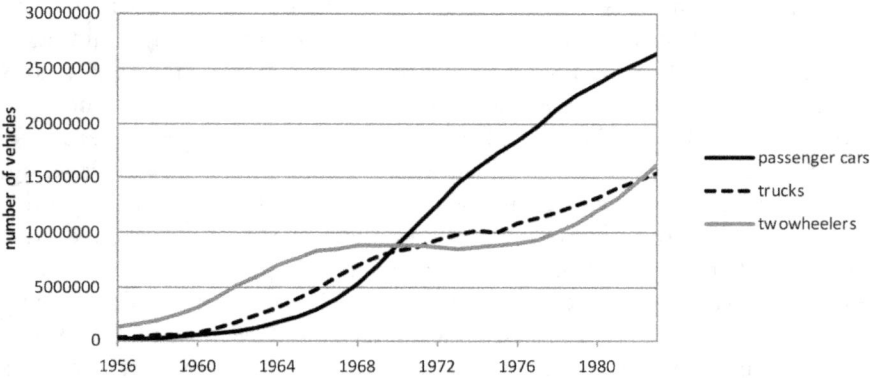

Figure 3.6. Cars, trucks, and motorized two-wheelers in Japan's motorization explosion of the 1960s and 1970s. Source: Shimokawa, "Japan," 224–225, table 11.6. Figure created by the author.

By then, Japan was quickly entering its own version of a 'car society,' aided, from 1963, by the financial benefits it harvested as no other Asian country did from the Vietnam War. Figure 3.6 shows how the car 'explosion' made the modal configuration pivot in 1970, the car curve forming a near-ideal representation of the logistic diffusion curve, although at closer scrutiny, two similar, hardly visible turning points (in 1962 and 1966) can be detected, just like the bumps occurring ten years earlier in the curves of the Netherlands and Germany (see chap. 2). By then, also the Japanese version of the coordination crisis seemed decided: whereas in 1965, still 52 percent of passengers were transported by rail, the balance was reversed five years later: rail had fallen to 41 percent, and road had taken over with 59 percent. In terms of performance (in passenger-km) too, this turnaround was measured: 65 percent by rail in 1965, exactly 50% five years later. In 1966, truck transport overtook railway transport (in volume). This all happened despite the development of another Japanese innovation, the high-speed Shinkansen ("new trunk line") train, the first of which (the Hikari on the Tōkaidō Main Line, inaugurated in 1964) at more than 160 kmh started to compete with motor traffic and subsonic jets with operational ranges of around 500 km, thus setting an example for France and other European countries.[161]

***

The first Social Stratification and Mobility Survey of 1955, undertaken by the Japan Sociological Society, discovered the emergence of a new middle class (*chūryū*, better to be translated, according to Japanologist William Kelly, as 'mainstream'), and when Ezra Vogel published his famous study of the rise of the *sararīman* and his family and working life governed by "group solidarity," the white-collar worker formed a quarter of the nonagricultural labor force in 1959, most of them commuting by rail (in Tokyo), because, as he concluded, "the salary man usually cannot afford such luxuries as a car or expensive entertainment." But many of their homes had one "Western style" room, "used for a sitting room or for entertaining guests." Their children were seeking "more challenge and excitement," although their responsibilities toward family and work "mollify [their] desires for new adventure," even if they started to buy cars on a massive scale, shaping a culture called *motarizeshon*. Tourism now started to grow precipitously, from 160,000 Japanese who traveled abroad in 1960 to 1 million a decade later, and four times as much another decade later. Coupled with a high participation rate in Japan's egalitarian education system and a high participation rate of women in the labor force (53 percent in 1970), an extremely high "middle-class consciousness" of 77 percent (1975) made Japanese first, during the 1950s and early 1960s, buy their "three sacred regalia" (black-and-white TV, washing machine, refrigerator [the regalia being a reference to the imperial regalia jewels, mirror and sword]; more than 90 percent had them by the mid-1960s), later followed by the "three new regalia," or the "three Cs": car, air-conditioner, color TV. According to Japanologist David Plath, 1966 was year 1 of the *maika gannen* (My-Car era), as the number of cars passed the ten million mark.[162]

Urban planning historians have criticized Japanese planners for missing a golden opportunity to become the region's very center of alternative mobility modernization, all the more so because of "the great similarity between small and medium-sized cities in Southeast Asia and the situation in their [Japan's] own country during the 1940s," where a mixture of slow and fast traffic formed what we have called a 'layeredness' of mobility. An elaborate planning protocol, constructed by the City Planning Bureau of the Ministry of Construction, allowed for the survey of different transport modes, including public transport options, as well as urban freight traffic networks complete with distribution hubs. For the export of planning knowledge, however, and despite the extensive studies undertaken into "the dynamics of slow and fast vehicles," Japanese planners focused on the metropolis, only "mildly refashioning American ideas and techniques." Nonetheless, the many "origin-destination surveys," transport "censuses," and surveys of "daily living activities," undertaken during the decade after 1958, revealed particularities that in hardly mediated form were transferred to the neighboring countries by JICA in a guilty mix of war damage repayment and competition with Australian, American, and European consultants, and which convincingly belies the easy diffusionist assumption that Japan's donorship was a copy of the American development practices.[163]

From 1974 to 1977, for instance, Indonesia received the bulk (43 percent) of the total Japanese aid of 572 billion yen. But it proved very difficult to plan and realize a road network in this country, although a Trans-Sumatran Highway was initiated in the 1970s with World Bank funding, a cross-insular corridor of 2,700 km finalized in 1985. This may also have been connected to the "staunchly anti-communist" affiliation of Indonesia, Malaysia, Philippines, Singapore, and Thailand in the ASEAN, rich in rubber and palm oil, representing in total more than two hundred million inhabitants who used the road for 86.5 percent of the passenger-kilometers they produced together in 1970. More than half the cars in these countries were to be found in the capitals. Japan's aid on the basis of its own experiences was all the more problematic, as not only did the urban freeway make Tokyo into a special case, but also the integration of the underground into the suburban railway systems was peculiar, as this necessitated tunnels with large bores (to allow for the pantographs instead of the third rail for power feeding), whereas some players (such as the Kobe high-speed railway) did not own rolling stock but operated trains provided by four private companies on its tracks. On the other hand, compared with the 'development' efforts of the West, Japan's lack of empathy for the particularities of its 'periphery' was not very special. In Japan's case, especially the urban component of its aid and development advises was "most controversial," as the experience of Manila (Philippines) will testify.[164]

***

Indeed, like several other large Asian towns, Manila was the scene of a veritable 'coordination war' between road and rail. With a population of nearly six million by the end of the period covered by this chapter, Manila was the scene of a struggle between the Philippine government, backed by the World Bank on the one side and the illegal services of minibuses, locally known as jeepneys, on the other. The jeepney's name derived from the wartime American Jeep and the prewar jitney. According to an analysis by Imes Chiu, the term emerged from an earlier handcrafted, horse-drawn version called *calesa*, in its first motorized version, the *auto-calesa*, allowing for ten passengers. The jeepney offered 'informal' but adequate and comfortable mobility to fourteen to eighteen passengers per vehicle. While the seventeen thousand mini taxis (as of 1982, in the form of motorized tricycles) served only very short trips of less than one kilometer on average, the fifty thousand to sixty thousand jeepneys (only one-third of them legal) dominated public urban road transport and directly competed with the 132 stage bus companies, but they also served the "tortuous and narrow streets inaccessible to buses." Of the 10 million daily passenger trips, 86 percent were realized by the jeepney. Like the prewar rickshaws, they were often rented from the owners on a daily basis, and more than half the jeepney enterprises were single-vehicle companies. Another 1.5 million trips were produced by the motorized tricycles that had replaced the cycle rickshaws in the 1950s.[165]

Chiu argued the *autocalesa* and the jeepney, contrary to the car in the West (which started its history as a horse*less* carriage, even though its initial use was clearly tributary to the culture of horse riding), openly celebrated its animal heritage, not only by using a chrome horse as an emblem on the hood but also by following the *calesa*'s "honor system . . ., by which passengers ride first and pay later." During the first postwar decades, the market was dominated by two carriage builders, and an "entire industry emerged devoted solely to the jeepney's decorative regalia, paintings, upholstery," as "customized folk art on wheels," so much so that "no two jeepneys were alike." This, too, was a direct reference to the *calesa* culture, when the horses "were embellished like kings, with little crowns on their heads." A picture book on *Painted Vehicles of the Americas* by Moira F. Harris showed vehicle painting has a long tradition, in Costa Rica, for instance, going back at least to the nineteenth century. In the Philippines, jeepneys were given a homelike feel, with curtains over the windows and religious paraphernalia on the dashboard, criticized by the middle class as *bakya* (literally, wooden clogs, "associated with the lower class particularly in the rural areas"), so after a while, these too started to vanish from the streets, being replaced by "surplus air-conditioned vans from Korea and Japan."[166]

In 1974, the government set up the Metro Manila Transit Corporation, a bus company placed directly under the responsibility of the Office of the President, inviting the private bus companies to form large consortia, and buying its own buses (financed by the Development Bank of the Philippines) to be leased by these companies. The government also tried to lure jeepney owners into cooperatives, but only when, in 1977, the rules were changed such that they could maintain their ownership as "symbols of their life savings," such measures met with some limited success. Meanwhile, the government gradually limited the number of corridors where jeepneys were allowed to compete with the buses, inviting the Japanese national aid agency to make a comprehensive survey, which resulted in the suggestion to improve the urban road network, build urban freeways, and upgrade the national railway system. Before these measures could be implemented, however, the World Bank financed a study to help plan a European-inspired Light Rail Transit System (1977), heightening fears among jeepney owners and drivers that the government thus wanted to "'zap' the jeepney completely." Indeed, plans were in the making to reroute the jeepney corridors accordingly. After the Manila failure, the Japanese decided to focus their aid on small- and medium-sized cities, with their 'layered' traffic patterns, but their tools often proved much too coarse for these applications.[167]

***

Similar coordination wars took place in other Asian cities, large and small. As a result, "pirate taxis" were made illegal in Singapore, whereas the *becak* (cycle rickshaw) and the "trishaw" (tricycle rickshaws) were chased from the central areas and important traffic corridors of Jakarta. Singapore as a city-state was created in 1965 through secession from Malaya (which had renamed itself Malaysia in 1963). Vogel called the new entity (accounting for 76 percent of Chinese, as of 1980) a "macho-meritocracy," run by leaders who "combine the articulate English-debating style with the confidence of the Chinese mandarin and the raw energy and wit of the street-smart, local Chinese trader." Deductions from paychecks (realizing "perhaps the highest savings ratings in the world") created funds to subsidize social housing projects and transport infrastructure. One of the Four Little Dragons (together with Taiwan, Hong Kong, and South Korea), Singapore implemented, according to Vogel, "strict and high-priced punishments for spitting, littering, jay-walking, and traffic violations," measures against "a perceived decline of civic morality in the West ... [The Four Little Dragons] are not so naive as to believe the nineteenth-century notion that they could combine Western technology with a supposedly moral Eastern spirit but they are, none the less intent on preserving the excess of individualism, egoism, and narcissism that they see destroying the fabric of Western society." Hence, these countries had a "basic effort in social engineering." The Singaporean government struggled with the colonial legacy of the monopolistic Singapore Traction Company, many Chinese-owned "mosquito" bus companies operating in the suburbs and the outskirts, and "pirate taxis."[168]

Also in other Asian countries, road motorization led to a multilayered traffic flow in which the rickshaw tended to disappear, substituted by a plethora of motorized micro and mini taxis and minivans. Take, for instance, Indonesian Jakarta: emerged during the war, 150,000 *becaks* were counted in 1970, only 20,000 of them officially registered. Most of their operators (115,000) had migrated to provincial centers by 1976, where they earned "the middle income among the poor" and where they lived "in relatively stable village communities, with a large number of communities making a city." The relationship with the riots of 1973, in which rickshaw drivers played a dominant role, is not known. In Malaysian Kuala Lumpur, too, the rickshaw virtually disappeared from the street in the 1950s, followed by the bullock carts during the next decade. Bangkok "eliminated pedicabs (*samlor*)" in 1962. In Jakarta, the "transport gap" was filled by the microbus (*opelet*), operating fixed routes along the former tramway routes, with rickshaws as feeders. There, the taxi fleet was legally expanded by mini taxis propelled by motorcycle engines, such as the *helicak* (a motorized *becak*), *superhelicak*, *bajaj*, and *mebea/bingo*. By the end of the 1970s, there were ten thousand such vehicles, most of them mini and micro vehicles, plying the Jakartan roads. By then a plan to replace the forty thousand *becak* with ten thousand motorized *bajaj* in five years after 1976 had only limited success.[169]

Peter Rimmer's conclusion after his thorough overview of Asian urban transport (which we enriched with information from Howard Dick) leaves no doubts: "From Istanbul to Ankara, through Amman to Hong Kong, the transport consultants united in their claim that the fixed route minibuses must be reduced to a feeder role." Against this background, Kuala Lumpur's urban transport development is of special interest, because it was here that the World Bank, which had changed course under President McNamara (who took office in 1968) to "improve the lot of the urban poor," issued a report in 1975 on "the urban transport problem" intended, with its emphasis on the informal transport sector, to have a moderating effect on the consultants' modernization frenzy, a World Bank "success story" held in check only by the government's reluctance to increase the number of minibuses.[170] In Singapore, however, the World Bank was less successful. In 1971, the Asian Development Bank published a transport survey, the result of a decision to build up a database on transport: Dutch consultants studied Jakarta, Japanese did Manila, Bangkok was done by US consultants, and Kuala Lumpur by the World Bank. In the same year, the UN finished its survey of Singapore, in which it advised to build 110 km of freeways, nearly 400 km of other roads, and a 36-km Mass Rapid Transit (MRT) system, at a cost of $10–15 billion.

The World Bank then undertook a second study in 1974, and it advised in the early 1980s, after a long struggle in which it mobilized an entire team of Harvard economists, against the government's intention to construct an MRT system. But Singapore insisted on its own course: it decided to implement the MRT plan in 1984, against a cost of $2.34 billion. It also started with a reorganization from 1970 of the public bus system consisting of family businesses "along typical Chinese traditions," which was accompanied by the elimination of "pirate taxis" through the imposition of a heavy diesel fuel tax, license withdrawals, and even vehicle seizures and arrests, many of the drivers becoming taxi or bus drivers. Two American consultancy bureaus (Crooks Mitchell Peacock Stewart and Wilbur Smith & Associates) produced reports, both based, according to Rimmer, on "methodologies and traffic models evolved in cities within developed countries and ... used in Singapore on the presumption that travel behaviour was the same in all countries of the world." The reports deviated from American practice, however, in that they both advised to use public transport extensively, whereas they also recommended "restraints on car ownership and use." Ironically, after the three major bus companies were amalgamated in 1973, Singapore became a possible model for other large cities in the world when it came to implementing policies to restrain car use, through the gradual increase of road taxes and license fees. Despite these harsh measures, however, the rickshaw survived until the second half of the 1980s, especially in villages.[171]

***

The history of the decline of these 'nonmodern' vehicles in *smaller* Asian cities has yet to be written, but Rimmer's analysis of some token cities (for instance, in the state of Penang in Malaysia), with their steep decline of the rickshaw fleet during the two decades after World War II, leaves no doubt that the general picture did not deviate considerably from the metropolises, albeit with some time lapse, although never too great. In Indonesian Surabaya, the cycle rickshaw had been introduced during Japanese occupation, replacing the horse-drawn two-wheeled *dokar* and four-wheeled *andong*. By the time manufacturing licenses were withdrawn by the government in 1974, there were twenty-five rickshaw producers. Surabaya's intermodal struggles reflected clearly what happened everywhere: state-owned stage buses tried to push the microbuses from the road, the latter shifting to other routes, where they "reduced [the rickshaws] to a feeder role (except at night and the early morning)." In the case of Surabaya, they had "eliminate[d] them completely by 1985 (except for those required for tourists)."[172]

In general, for Indonesia as a whole, the motorcycle (216,000 registered in 1966) seems to have pushed the cycle rickshaw from the road during the 1970s. It also threatened the bicycle. The rickshaws were owned mostly by "Hokkien [a former name of the current province of Fujian, here indicating a group of South Chinese dialects] Chinese who controlled the bicycle trade, but drivers were invariably indigenous Indonesians, often villagers who had migrated to the city in search of employment." And when, as a result of this intermodal struggle, the automobile started to penetrate in the urban household in Asia (one-third of the households owned a car in Bangkok, Kuala Lumpur, and Singapore by the early 1970s), their use seemed remarkably uniform, at least as far as the share of commuting within the car's use spectrum was concerned: whether in Sydney (with 88 percent of households owning a car in 1964) or in Bangkok, in Melbourne (with 101 percent!) or in Singapore, driving to work conquered one-third of the number of trips.[173]

***

By the end of the period described in this chapter, the 'layering' of 'new' upon 'old' had resulted in a surprisingly variegated (according to some observers, 'chaotic') spectrum of urban mobile media. Howard Dick, a leading specialist on Indonesian transport, gave a useful classification when he first distinguished between "two main groups, those which operate on fixed routes with set fares and those which offer door-to-door service as negotiated fares," the latter further divided in buses and jitneys. Jitneys come in various shapes—in Indonesia alone, in the form of the *bemo* (a fully or partially closed minibus), the *opelet* (named after the German Opel sedan), the *kolt* (probably named after the Mitsubishi Colt), and the *pikap* (a pick-up truck)—performing "frequent but unscheduled services, and stopping on demand." The technological variety corresponded with various functions in "price, speed, comfort, convenience and safety," but the hegemonic trend in all these setting has always been "to phase out jitneys … in favour of a four tier system modelled on western cities of electric trains, buses, taxis and *bajaj*," the latter being an autorickshaw imported from India, called after the mainstream brand name Bajaj and equipped with a Vespa (India) scooter engine.[174]

Constructing 'Circulation': The IRF and the 'Development' of Africa

In this section, we visit the highly variegated mobility landscape of Africa, so variegated, in fact, that it is difficult to paint an encompassing picture of the continent's 'development.' After a general introduction, depicting efforts of supranational network building including the role of road lobbyist IRF (and a small sidestep to the Middle East), we will first focus on the national road networks and its use in Ghana and Nigeria, and their diverging developments under the influence of the discovery of oil reserves. This is followed by a subsection dedicated to the breakthrough of car, bus, and truck (using several other African countries as case studies), showing it was in the collective truck and bus sector that indigenous entrepreneurs saw a chance to capture a sizable part of the mobility market. Then, we focus on what may be considered a particularity of non-Western mobility history: Africa's driver-induced automotive adventurism in a collective setting, produced in the motor bus. Nowhere else have anthropologists provided such a lively description as in Africa. This focus on drivers necessitates we spend some paragraphs to the issue of African labor studies. The last subsection deals with two typical road users in Africa: spirits and colonial soldiers. The description and analysis are rather eclectic, because of the scholarly state of the art, but we will focus on the logistic, statistical, and ethnic peculiarities of African mobilities, including its modal configurations. "Africa was the latest of the late developers, the least able to generate its own academic knowledge" on the issue of development. And yet, Africa knew a high level of personal mobility, because "the incomplete coverage of medical, educational, and other services (involved) long journeys for those who need[ed] them," while postal and telecommunication services were often lacking.[175] It was here that transnational road lobbyist IRF saw its chance, much less hindered (apart from a group of nonaligned countries) than in Asia (where China and India were inaccessible to the IRF).

The continent's colonial heritage did not bring a "panafrican traffic system or network, not even of one mode." The railway map of Africa in 1963 shows the mobility side of the continent's plunder: the 75,039 km of track (1962) on the vast continent not only produced a density (per square km) of less than half of those of Latin America, Australia (including New Zealand), and Asia (including the Soviet Union) (and ten times lower than North America's, and more than twenty times Europe [excluding the Soviet Union]), but also the tracks were of the 'penetrating' kind, starting in the harbors and reaching the farthest town or mine of the particular country. Of the 1.1 million km of roads (according to an estimate from 1958), 88 percent was unpaved, but a West-African Traffic Conference in

Monrovia in 1961 decided on the necessity of a road network between the West African nations (Dahomey, Ghana, Upper Volta, Niger, Nigeria, and Togo), which seems to have been realized by 1964, even if not all segments of the network were paved by then. No wonder did nearly all West African passenger traffic go by road. The German transport specialist who unearthed these data pointed at the "general lack of a policy of ordering intervention (*ordnungs-politischer Intervention*) by the state" as one of the major characteristics of the African transport sector. He quoted another German specialist who distinguished between three types of developing countries: those with large space with low population densities, equipped with railways in a phase that these were the only performative mode (Latin America); densely populated Asian countries (India, Pakistan, South Korea), equipped with railway networks; and African, as well as the less densely populated Asian, countries, which had to make the jump from "primitive transport" (such as bicycles) to high-performative road traffic.[176]

However, according to Africanist Michael Brett, Africa cannot be treated "as a single paradigm." For this, its culture has become "too eclectic an assemblage of equally valid elements." One of the consequences of not heeding this warning is the neglect of Saharan Africa and its history in the historiography of African mobility, as it does not seem to fit into this paradigm. Recent studies, however, have indicated the northern African desert was not a simple void for adventurous Europeans to conquer, as *Road International* suggested when it described the efforts by the Special Fund of the UN Development Programme to build the "Transsahara Road." Instead, it was a place of illicit trade between oases (themselves proof of "technical, logistic, and social achievement") and border-crossing trucking. The tremendous impact of 'development' on daily life can be illustrated through a case at the very edge (and well beyond) of the continent: the Middle East, where nomadic Bedouin tribes on the semiarid steppes of the northern Arabian plateau (covering Syria, Iraq, Saudi Arabia, and Jordan) had replaced their camels by Datsun and Toyota half-ton trucks and small tractors by the 1970s, their lives "no longer in balance with the seasonal pastoral cycle," having to drive to town to purchase "feed concentrates" for their sheep. In the case of "nomadic sheep husbandry," representing 35 percent of Syria's agricultural output, the trucks were used as camels: "to transport households and livestock from one camp to another and to carry water to the herds." Such trucks also allowed independence movements in Africa (often "led by men who viewed nomads as a socially backward element and as an obstacle to economic development") to try and "sedentarize pastoralists or at least restrict their movements."[177]

This anti-paradigmatic diversity does not mean, of course, that for a primer on world mobility, we should not look for common denominators between local cultures. We must make a clear distinction, however, between rural and urban mobilities, even if the postwar migration between both (thus forming a third form of migratory, rural-urban mobility) blurred the distinction between them. This third, hybrid form of mobility created a "semi-urban proletariat whose members retained close links with the rural areas, assuring a constant flow of goods and ideas between the city and the countryside." For African cities, where "a completely new culture of taxi and bus driving" emerged, often overlooked by anthropologists in "their bias towards the exotic," anthropologist Igor Kopytoff insisted

> the biography of a car ... would reveal a wealth of cultural data: the way it was acquired, how and from whom the money was assembled to pay for it, the relationship of the seller to the buyer, the uses to which the car is regularly put, the identity of its most frequent passengers, and of those who borrow it, the frequency of borrowing, the garages to which it is taken and the owner's relations to the mechanics, the movement of the car from hand to hand over the years, and in the end, when the car collapses, the final disposition of its remains.

"All of these details," he assured us (and he could have added the international dimension, as many cars in Africa would soon be bought secondhand, imported from Europe), "would reveal an entirely different biography from that of a middle-class American, or Navajo, or French peasant car."[178]

***

But road lobbyist IRF did not seem to be bothered by the warning that Africa should not be approached as a monolith. A color map in *Road International* showed large, red, "no road" areas that begged to be paved, in an atmosphere reminiscent of prewar enthusiasm about the Cape to Cairo road and other touristic megaprojects (and similar megafantasies). As we saw in chapter 1, it was South Africa (and the UK) and the North African rim (and France) that formed the cradle of these fantasies. In the north, the Arab League projected a road system connected to the European E-road network via Turkey. As for the south, what Japan was for South East and South Asia, South Africa was for the African continent: a self-declared "Pattern for African Road Development." To foster its spectacular projects, the IRF (helped) set up "regional road congresses" where such plans were discussed, as in Salisbury, Rhodesia, in 1957, where engineers and civil servants "convened to discuss a £10 million project whereby the road from Cape Town to Nairobi—along its whole length—would be brought up to international heavy duty standard." The attendants were told the road was "a modern version of Cecil Rhodes' Cape to Cairo railways" and would "open up for development vast tracks of what used to be known as darkest Africa."[179]

Initially, when IRF officials could surf on the activities of the British colonizer, it seemed as if the federation had carte blanche when it came to road planning. In Kenya, for instance, a former anti-guerilla brigadier of the Indian army chaired the Kenya Road Authority (in its name reminiscent of the extra-parliamentary planning initiatives of the New Deal era), which was backed by a local IRF branch (the East African Road Federation). He declared: "Kenya is underdeveloped and one of the reasons for its under development [*sic*] is its lack of communications. In this connection it should be borne in mind that so long as the road system is planned as an integral part of the development of the resources of a country, any reasonable expenditure upon it will always be justified." Ironically, similar to what happened in most African colonies shortly after the war (a phenomenon that begs for an explanation, but it is probably not too farfetched to assume a connection with the wave of declarations of independence), the modest "working capital" of 825,000 pounds was "no longer available" once it came to implementation of the plans. The brigadier thereupon suggested the inhabitants of Kenya themselves come up with proposals to raise their taxes.[180]

While World Bank and IMF money flowed into road projects in Ethiopia ("Opening Up Ethiopia") and Swaziland, among others, *Road International* showed pictures of gigantic earthmoving equipment next to women practicing head porterage on such roads. The contrast between 'modernity' and 'backwardness' (rural men and all women, respectively) always made for photogenic scenes. In Ethiopia's *limat* (development), after the visit of a World Bank mission, the World Bank's money was also (next to the dozers and graders) used to finance the "foreign experts." As a result, a "completely run-down network had been raised to the general standard of county roads in the United States." The costs of the coffee transport were diminished by 40 percent, which forced the railway monopoly to lower its tariffs.[181]

Historical Contingency: Oil and the Mobility Divergence of Ghana and Nigeria

The most advanced in the race toward modernity was Ghana (former Gold Coast). Ghana's immediate post–World War II mobility history has been analyzed as no other sub-Saharan African country. The country came out of the war with probably the densest road and rail network (per capita) of tropical Africa, which was, in a typical mobility metaphor coined by South African historian John Gunther, "on the march, and marching fast—towards western standards." Although the first part of this qualification was adequate (most Africans moved on foot), the second was less so, at least not in the metaphor's suggestion of linearity. Within less than half a century, Africa was changing from the least populated continent (after Australia) to the second most populated (after Asia).[182]

These populations moved continuously: more than half of Ghana's workforce in 1960 consisted of "mobile workers," half long-range, the other half intra-regional migrants. Many of them were part of what economists have come to call the "informal economy" or "petty capitalism," a form of value creation certainly not limited to the non-West, but there often "identified for heuristic purposes with the sub-proletariat of the slums," neglect of which can result in a skewed analysis of what others have called a "dualist" society. This concept was coined by colonial economist Jan Boeke in Anglophone literature and brought into mainstream by economists related to the ILO. We have characterized the mobility side of such dualist societies (with its "islands of modernism within a medieval economic system") as 'layeredness.' Transport researchers coined a new term for the subaltern layers of this type of "population mobility": circulation, the difference with 'migration' being "whether or not a return to place of origin is involved." Other students called it "return migration," "circular migration," "sojourner movements," "transhumance," or even "commuting." This form of migration involving "reciprocal flows" was presented as typical for non-Western countries, as a result of rural poverty and rapid urbanization, resulting in a hybrid form of activities, as these circular migrants "involved themselves in both capitalist and peasant modes of production." They were "'traditional men' with a strong stake in their villages of origin." Investigators tried to design taxonomies of these bi- or multi-local mobilities, pointing at the catalyzing role of roadbuilding, as in the case of China, where roads provoked the emergence of commuting by bicycle over distances up to 40 km. It was in 'backward' pockets that such circular forms of movements often found their origin, as in the case of the Moroccan Islamic Riff area from where, between 1960 and 1972 as a result of population pressure, many unskilled workers migrated to the Netherlands.[183]

***

Before Ghana's independence, the colonial army had educated drivers and mechanics for a fleet of nearly twenty-one thousand motor vehicles (eleven thousand of them commercial vehicles, and 70 percent of the latter "mammy wagons," two- to four-ton British Motor Corporation or Bedford trucks equipped with a covered wooden body for passenger transport, causing railway passenger numbers and freight volumes to drop. When the country declared independence from its British colonizers in 1957, Kwame Nkrumah became its first president. He had studied in the United States and had taken from the American black pride movement ideas that, back in Africa, resulted in Ghana becoming a founding member of the Non-Aligned Movement (see the Bandung Conference of 1955). At that moment, about thirty thousand kilometer of roads existed in the former colony, only 10 percent of which were bitumen-surfaced, and the majority by far were "feeder roads" from villages to the main roads. On the trunk roads, car and truck traffic had increased sixfold since the war (on the major roads, the increase was even tenfold), an annual growth of 11 to 12 percent, resulting in a fleet of nearly thirty-seven thousand motor vehicles by 1958. In *Road International*, an optimistic Ghanaian engineer reported an ambitious Second Development Plan had been formulated and that experiments were underway to investigate mixtures of bitumen with local soils, financed by a Road Fund that was largely fed by petrol taxes.[184]

On these roads, a unique (for Africa) survey of commodity mobility was undertaken in 1957 and 1958, extensively reported by anthropologist Peter Gould, allowing a detailed flow analysis of consumer goods. The survey saw the goods trickle into the feeder roads where head porterage, pack animals, and the bicycle took over, but where at the same time half of the heavier transports (such as the transport of zebus, on their own legs) had meanwhile been taken over by trucks. On market days, 80 percent of all goods (an impressive 65.5 tons in the case of one market) were brought there by "head loading." The flow charts describing these movement form a fascinating hybrid example of scientific scrutiny applied to one of the oldest forms of mobility in the world (fig. 3.7). While IRF engineers were dreaming about uniting the continent through infrastructure, Nkrumah promoted

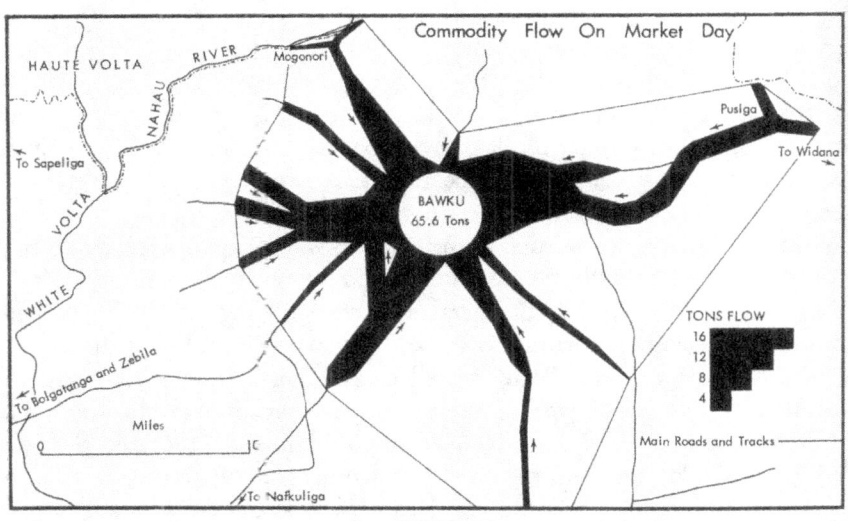

Figure 3.7 Analysis of the commodity flow on a market day in Ghana. Source: Gould, *Development of the Transportation Pattern in Ghana*, 139, fig. 96. Public domain.

Pan-Africanism, but during a visit to China, a military coup ended his presidency, bringing the hidden ethnic tensions to the open and resulting in a recession during the 1970s and a subsequent deterioration of the road network. First, the feeder roads from the villages worsened, and then, at the end of the 1970s, the major roads did as well. Such deterioration also resulted from modernization: it seems the development of the port of Tema (the place connected to the capital Accra) led to "stagnation" in other parts of the country because surf ports along the coast were abandoned.[185]

***

In an elegant comparative study of the postwar Nigerian and Ghanaian mobility histories, Africanist Gina Porter showed how historical contingency (the presence or absence of known oil reserves) made Ghana's subsequent development go down while catapulting Nigeria's development. In Nigeria, the hike in oil prices during the 1970s led to motorcycle and car purchases by "many ordinary working Nigerians," and entrepreneurs started taxi and "mammy-wagon" services (third class in the back, second class in front of the loading platform, first class inside the cabin), while farmers at the end of feeder roads were even able to buy a motorcycle. If they could not afford a motorcycle, farmers could use the mammy wagon, too, as these trucks also transported "loads [as] the property of the passengers," a practical form of collective freight transport. With the absence of regular buses, an overview from 1969 gives four possibilities for passenger transport: mammy wagons, intercity taxi services (based most often on the Peugeot 404, often the only intercity form of motorized transport), minibuses (Volkswagen, Ford [Germany], BMC J-class, Bedford, Fiat OM, Mercedes), and a transport form called "topping up," trucks in which "the passenger is secondary to freight," for which the law prescribed seating space on the wooden benches be at least fourteen by ten inches. A survey by the University of Ibadan in 1969 of Nigerians' travel motives found the "family motive" dominant, more so for women than for men, whereas men traveled to buy, women to sell. Generally, women dominated the flows.[186]

In Ghana, however, remote rural markets "collapsed, and others went into serious decline." Incomes of urban wageworkers declined during the 1960s. At the same time, Porter's study convincingly showed how modernization added another 'layer' upon the existing mobility pattern. Instead of replacing the 'old,' it either enhanced or sometimes deteriorated the conditions of the 'old,' as was the case with women in "off the road" villages, located only a couple of kilometers from the roads. Feeder road maintenance generally took place locally; all able-bodied villagers were mobilized (with fines for those who refused): "Women carry sand, gravel and stones to the potholes, men fill and level them, using their own shovels and pick axes." These women, forming the bulk of head porterage, which on its turn dominated freight transport, had more trouble establishing connections with the new layer of mobility, as the roads favored certain market places by abolishing other, smaller ones (nearer to these villages). It was only after the period described in this chapter that Africanists found increasingly convincing evidence of the "enormity of women's transport burdens in sub-Saharan Africa," on a road network of which the form was highly political in a special sense: Porter quoted a researcher who shortly after Ghanaian independence asked himself: "If an area is known as a stronghold of the Opposition, will it get funds for tarring its roads? And those roads that swing around the villages of Opposition chiefs, was it simply a matter of terrain and drainage?"[187]

***

Amid this modernization orgy, however, we should not forget that in a country like Ghana, as in many African countries, most of the people could only walk. In this "walking world" ("rural transport conditions in sub-Saharan Africa are remarkably poor by comparison with Asia and Latin America"), as late as the early 1990s, a bicycle in rural Tanzania cost "the equivalent of almost a year's minimum wage." Porter concluded her comparison twofold: "Roads in West Africa are not necessarily 'a good thing' for women who live by them because they are often not in a position to take advantage of the benefits that the road confers," and "for women (and other sectors of the rural poor) who live away from good roads [they] can actually make life harder."[188] In other words, even as critical an analyst as Porter acknowledged implicitly that roads are 'beneficial,' only that women cannot reap their benefits from them.

In most cases, however, local elites followed the transnational modernization call: in Zaire, entire villages were "resettled" to bring them near the main roads. This country is also a remarkable case because of its large contingent of "private roads" (18,000 km, half the length of national roads), giving rare evidence that private companies did their share in 'development.' In Zaire, road construction planning had to be scaled down in 1954 because of a lack of funding. Its road density (per square km) was half that of 'road champion Ghana' but double that of Guinea, Morocco, and Cameroon. Uganda showed another peculiarity: a split in the road system. Like in the West, the trunk road system was maintained by the central government. In Uganda, this was originally the colonial Protectorate Government, which decentralized the maintenance of the much larger subsidiary (gravel) road network to local governments, "but very little is known about the local government roads, even by those who build and maintain them." However, a survey unearthed a substantial growth of this secondary network since

1946, unnoticed so far because of a lack of statistics. The survey found that in the case of the largest province of Buganda, only one-fifth of the costs were provided by the colonial powers, while the rest was collected "from other sources." Construction and maintenance was often left in the hands of the local chiefs, the labor provided "by communal effort ... on a voluntary basis."[189]

Beyond Economics: 'Layeredness,' Subaltern Mobility, and the Precipitous Breakthrough of Car and Truck

But the benefits the roads offered may have been in unexpected places such as war scenes. Take Niger, the French colony to the north of Nigeria, where Djibo Bakary (a teacher and commis, a person "who had been to a colonial school or worked in the lower echelons of the colonial administration") founded the Union Démocratique Nigérienne in 1954 and won, with his progressive Sawaba movement, the first general elections in 1957 still under French tutelage, representing the urban semi-proletariat called *petit peuple*. Among these were the truck and bus drivers and other physically mobile Nigeriens such as traders, *marabouts* (Muslim preachers), and *karuwai* (sex workers). *Coxeurs* formed a part of the bus culture, "men who helped drivers to attract clients for a small commission [and] archetypical marginals, mobile and endowed with a horizon far beyond village life." This first wave of decolonization was brutally interrupted by the French, who toppled Bakary and manipulated his opponents of the Rassemblement Démocratique Africaine (RDA) (representing the commis and connected to similar movements in other French colonies) into power. It was under RDA governance that Niger declared independence "under French supervision" in 1960, immediately provoking a Sawaba guerilla resistance backed by Algeria, Ghana, and the Soviet Union and related countries.

The type of riots that broke out in 1958 between Sawaba and the RDA would have been inconceivable without the fledgling 'automobile system': while high party officials arrived on the spot by car such as the popular American-French Ford Versailles (testifying to the organized character of the riots), the "mob" was brought to the fighting scene in a new mobile phenomenon, trucks "of the open pick-up type." The mobility character of Niger's ethnic troubles even got a special dimension through the combined use of transport and communication devices, especially the telephone, resulting in a very 'fluid' conflict zone. An international dimension was added when it appeared truck drivers were instrumental in implementing "Opération Formation Cadres," the Sawaba clandestine network to send party officers to Eastern European countries for education. These "lorry driver[s] turned revolutionary" also took part in the armed Sawaba rebellion of 1963–1965, thus playing a role reminiscent of the rickshaw pullers of Beijing in the 1920s (see chap. 1), the commonality between them being that their mobility enabled them to function as the eyes and ears of a political movement. After the revolutionary tourism during the Cultural Revolution and Khrushchev's car-sharing plans, this may be considered the third empirical building block for a socialist theory of mobility. A coup in 1974 toppled the RDA regime.[190]

***

The cases dealt with in this section illustrate the reality of what anthropologists and other students of the development process after independence in the 1960s called "two economies, a small development sector generating exports and a large subsistence sector involving the rural masses. Eventually, it was assumed, the 'modern' economy would triumph, abolishing 'backwardness' as Africans joined the developed world." When this did not happen and poverty remained and even increased, social scientists forwarded other models and metaphors, such as the percolator model, consisting of a small passage between two economic spheres, along which a "small elite subsists by drawing wealth out of the villages." Such passages are replete with mobility, but the underlying, subaltern movements are hard to detect. In one of the few documented African histories 'from below,' Landeg White's *Magomero: Portrait of an African village* (advertised as "a kind of African Montaillou"), the author conceded "the fact that such movements occurred at all emerges only from biographies" and could best be investigated "not statistically but through its consequences. For the first time there was money in the village." But voicing the African subaltern should not take place, as Gayatri Chakravorty Spivak suggested, without leaving the 'voice-giver' out of the narrative: indeed, White recounts that he arrives in the village "to talk politics" with "three girl students as assistants, all English-speaking," by car.[191] The 'automobile system' not only enabled the changes in the relationship between rural and urban cultures; their description and analysis came to depend on this system as well.

In most countries, however, postwar motorization took place more or less as elsewhere in the world, although the differences with the Western model (either European or American) were substantial. In Uganda, for instance, a very detailed study undertaken just before independence (which occurred in 1962) showed how postwar motorization had started with a preponderance of commercial vehicles but that the passenger car took the lead in the course of the 1950s. Landlocked between Kenya, Tanganyika (Tanzania), Congo, and Rwanda, Uganda had a higher road density (per square kilometer) than its neighbors. On these roads, by 1958 more than half (about twenty thousand) of the registered vehicles were private cars (and one-quarter commercial vehicles), and they were accompanied by seven thousand motorcycles. Their growth as a fleet followed the usual logistic pattern, but at a rate much higher (18 percent per year) than its next neighbor in line (Nigeria with 14 percent), let alone the United Kingdom (with only 8 percent per year, a percentage we have called spectacular in the previous chapter). Received car diffusion wisdom tells us income and car diffusion are closely related, but the comparison with other African countries shows income per capita may function as a coarse indicator only and that the differences are so large as to beg for an explanation way beyond economics.

Up to now, transport studies have not come up with such explanations of a situation where Ghana, following (at a distance) directly after South Africa's income per capita, showed a much lower car density than Central Africa and Kenya (with much lower per capita incomes). What is important here, however, is not so much the quantitative differences but the fact that Uganda showed crucial differences with Western motorization models. This is testified not only by the passenger car fleet expansion stagnating around the mid-1950s (while it exploded in the West shortly thereafter) but most of all because of its racialized diffusion pattern, as one-third of the passenger cars were owned by "African" inhabitants (and one-quarter each by "European" and "Asian" owners), whereas most of the motorcycles (87 percent) were owned by "African" citizens. No wonder did Kenya's first president, Jomo Kenyatta, in an effort to deregulate the formal bus services in his country, consider the operators of the *matatu*, an illegal minivan bus used for informal transport, as embodying a spirit of indigenous "entrepreneurship." What was most remarkable, however, was that "Africans" were prepared "to acquire vehicles at a very much lower absolute level of income than is the case with Europeans or Asians," showing a converging mechanism that transport history so far has failed to explain, and which made the diffusion patterns in very differently structured countries resemble each other much more than one is inclined to assume on the basis of their average income or GNP. Indeed, the 'underside of the diffusion curve,' like the rest of the curve, is socially constructed. The Uganda transport survey even reported a series of traffic counts, showing that on a through road outside the capital of Kampala, the flow of vehicles was comparable to "the average traffic flow on some rural roads in the United Kingdom."[192]

A comparable detailed transport analysis was undertaken in 1971 by a German economist for Tanzania. His was a model of developmentalism, moderated by the warning that "there is no general agreement about the necessary size of the transport sector and about its causal relationships with other sectors of the economy, and in regard to the inducement of or influence on economic growth and development," but it did not leave the reader in doubt for a moment "that a certain minimum amount of transport facilities is absolutely essential to allow development of a modern economy and to encourage economic growth." The analysis constantly meandered between comparisons with other countries in terms of railway network densities in different dimensions (per square mile: comparable to its neighbors; per miles of track: much lower), and likewise for roads (only half of Kenya's density, per square mile). It showed how, if one would add the "unclassified roads and tracks" through the bush, total road network length increased by nearly 50 percent from twenty-one thousand to twenty-nine thousand miles.[193]

The railway network of Tanzania had been merged by the British in 1948 with the Kenyan and Ugandan networks into a system managed by the East African Railways and Harbours Administration, clearly in the expectation of the coming onslaught of road traffic competition, and a rare example of international network formation by the colonizers. But despite the ambitious postwar plans promised to be executed by the colonial powers, the explosion of construction costs moderated roadbuilding planning: a decade after independence, 1,500 miles of new roads were ready, while the amount of bituminous roads was doubled as well, also to about 1,500 miles. Only then, and in accordance with an international trend to improve rural accessibility and attack rural poverty, were "first attempts for the improvement of rural feeder roads" undertaken. Overall, the German analyst concluded in 1973, the development of the Tanzanian mobility infrastructure resembled "very closely" those of neighboring Ghana and Nigeria.

On these roads, traffic grew precipitously: the number of cars increased more than tenfold, from around eight thousand in 1947 to eighty-four thousand in 1970, with the highest growth rates during the decade immediately following the war, passenger cars taking a share of more than half, commercial vehicles around a quarter. Unlike in Europe and the United States, vehicle fleet growth briefly stagnated and even declined during the 1960s, but its obedience to the whims of the GDP remained undisturbed, even after recalculation of the latter. The German observer was surprised about the low share of long-distance traffic on these roads (traffic counts, undertaken regularly since the 1950s, showed only 150 vehicles per day on one of the national roads), even if road traffic's transport volume (in freight, and even more so in passengers) was significantly higher than all other modes combined. Characteristically, truck and bus fleets in Tanzania were owned mostly by small entrepreneurs (1,080 of the 1,600 buses were owned per one or per two by six hundred license holders), in which the share of Africans increased from just below half in 1963 to nearly three-quarters two years later.[194]

In Ghana, regular bus and truck transport between cities and the countryside came up in the 1960s, and their drivers "were much respected as they were associated with urban areas that were awe-inspiring places filled with promises of wealth and new goods," until, a decade later when road traffic and accidents increased, they inspired fear or awe, as in the case of the *khat* drivers, who raced toward the cities with their perishable stimulants. But this changed after the military coup by Jerry Rawlings in 1979 when professional car, bus, and truck drivers were consciously scapegoated as "scoundrels, cheats, liars, and thieves," a campaign that could harvest the results of a slow, thirty-year process, started under Nkrumah when such drivers went on strike (1957), against a regulation to introduce obligatory insurance.[195]

***

But it was in the truck and bus sector where Africans saw a chance to capture a part of the mobility market. In Uganda, for instance, where this has been studied in detail, road freight transport before independence was kept unregulated, while regulation of passenger transport on the road was "very strict," but soon after independence, most of the licensed vehicles (61 percent) were in the hands of the Asian part of the population. Again, we can observe the export of the Western coordination crisis (the struggle between rail and road), complete with the many efforts (a Traffic Amendment Bill of 1958, for instance) to combat the "pirate cars" (unlicensed vehicles) part of the 'informal economy.' These Asian entrepreneurs also employed African drivers for their private cars (as did some of the European and African car owners), thus creating another difference with the Western diffusion pattern.[196] Zaire may serve as an extreme example, where, different from Tanzania, the truck reigned supreme in a quantitative sense until the mid-1950s. Dahomey is another example, where, during the first postwar decade, more trucks were imported than passenger cars.

More is known about Nigeria, where Hausa migrants managed to protect their cattle and kola trade monopoly despite the surrounding Yoruba majority.[197] Living in a special enclave in 'Yoruba country' (an urban culture, itself in majority consisting of migrants), Hausa migrants coming hundreds of miles away from the savanna in the north for many generations had constructed an ethnic community in which class differences tended to loose their meaning. An institutionalized element of this Hausa diaspora is Sabo (an abbreviation of Hausa *sabor gari*), a "special settlement" within Yoruba-dominated Ibadan, capital of Ghana's Western Region (with 750,000 inhabitants) and a transport junction of roads and railway lines between northern Hausaland, southern Nigeria, and the rest of Ghana. Three-quarters of the nearly four thousand white-robed Hausa in Sabo were involved in long-range trading; most of them migrated after 1943, apart from a small group of Hausa, probably descendants of former slaves of Yoruba masters, "strangers" in the community because they could not anymore mention, upon being asked by other Hausa, their "home settlement" in the north.[198]

For generations, cattle was bought from the nomadic Fulani in the north and sold on cattle markets to Yoruba butchers. Like the delicate kola nuts transported to the north, cattle are highly perishable because of the tsetse fly that kills them as soon as they reach the forest areas, so high speed and, because of the large sums of money and the great risks involved, system reliability were very important; this was brought about not so much by a 'technical fix' but by a tribal monopoly that managed to control both the transport and the communication sides of the trading process. Thus, "mobility and stability" were two sides of the same coin. This insight is at the same time a confirmation, from a more general viewpoint, of our earlier thesis about the importance of sessility for automobilism. The thirty "landlords" who controlled the trade from the two Sabo truck parks (and the Ibadan Railway Station, but trucks were faster) had to maneuver socially and politically to keep the system working. They did so by following the tides of national politics, sometimes supporting one political party, sometimes the other (and sometimes both), and even influencing the shift to another form of Muslim cult, the Tijaniyya, at a moment when ethnic distinction with the Yoruba got blurred. The subsequent re-homogenizing of the local Hausa culture was undertaken through a process of "re-tribalization," thus reestablishing the distinction toward the Western-oriented Yoruba culture. It was highly effective, considering the failure of some Western businessmen to 'modernize' Ghanaian cattle trade with Nigeria.[199]

Reviving the 'Adventure Machine' in a Collective Setting: Driving, African Labor History, and Migration

Another ethnography of the Hausa transport community as part of an "urban service economy" in Nigeria showed the "urban informal sector" consisted of about a hundred bus owners (dominated by a core group of about twenty), drivers, and conductors amid a broader group of mechanics, petrol station owners, and spare part traders, all of them about 10 percent of the nearly two thousand Hausa men aged fifteen years and over. With bodies made locally and mounted on imported Leyland chassis, and rented out on a daily basis to the drivers and their conductor (sometimes two) in the style as we have seen in the rickshaw culture (see chap. 1), the buses plied the interurban roads "littered with the debris of vehicle parts and entire bodies." This, according to the analyst of the drivers' behavior in the early 1970s, was partly the result of bad roads but also of the "aggressive, belligerent character of bus driving in south-west Nigeria," requiring great driving skills. These buses were skimming the roads for lucrative passenger patronage in the style we have seen during the emergence of the West European bus in the 1920s and 1930s. Like the adventurers in those earlier days, Hausa bus drivers must be not

> faint-hearted [but instead] ambitious to succeed, physically and mentally prepared to withstand considerable buffeting and ready to be ruthless when the occasion demands … As drivers hurtle back and forth to arrive at heavily populated bus parks, they cut across in front of one another, engage in races two abreast along major highways and from time to time force one another off the road. Driving is hard work and the drivers are hard men, openly combative and full of bravado.

Once the urban culture became accepted as a field of study, anthropologists could not get enough of these special 'tribes' of truck and bus drivers. While on the road, these drivers maintained their "tough and combative form of urban entrepreneurship," their "micropolitics of mobility." Meanwhile, the bus owners (the elite that also owned passenger cars, together with "the town's leading traders, contractors, store owners and other successful entrepreneurs") sustained their relationships with local and national politicians and civil servants. Paying "regular and substantial bribes," they showed to practice another form of mobility as well, the "ability to move freely between two distant and disparate social worlds." At the same time, these "big men" functioned as 'godfathers' within their ethnic community, just like we encountered in chapter 1 in the case of the overseas Chinese rickshaw communities, testifying to the fundamental collective character of these forms of mobility, especially the blurring of the sharpest distinctions between bosses and drivers.[200]

A similar metamorphosis has been observed in 1971 for truck drivers in urban cultures in six West African countries (Ghana, Upper Volta [Benin], Ivory Coast, Togo, Dahomey, and Nigeria) in so much detail that students of Western mobility can only be envious of the anthropological and ethnographic energy invested in these non-Western mobilities. James Jordan traveled 3,462 miles as a participant-observer and related this behavioral change to the contrasting cultures of (what Ferdinand Tönnies in 1887 called) *Gemeinschaft* versus *Gesellschaft*, standing for a rural and an urban lifestyle, emphasizing ethnic kinship culture and a culture aimed at efficient, individualistic personal improvement, respectively. Jordan suggested part of the 'wild' road behavior might be explained by the corrugated shape of the laterite soils on the road, which necessitated either a very slow or a very fast (above sixty mph) driving style so as to negotiate these surfaces "in relative comfort." In Ghana, 13 percent of all nonagricultural wage earners were involved in transport (and only 7 percent in manufacturing), while state-owned transport companies only handled 5 percent of this business in Nigeria and Ghana. While Ivory Coast had by far the highest passenger car density of the countries mentioned (10 per 1,000 inhabitants, 2.5 times the densities of Ghana but five times as high as Upper Volta and Nigeria), a comparison with the United States (with 330 per 1,000 at that time) would miss the essence of West African mobility even if there, too, just like in the United States, "transport for the majority of persons and goods … mean[t] roads," and not railways.[201]

In the case of West Africa, however, this meant dirt roads, where thousands of trucks and buses created the local 'automobile systems' and where the layeredness of traffic, its mix with walking, porterage, cycling, motorcycling, made these systems near incomparable with the West. Jordan's research centered in and around Ghana's capital Accra's Central Lorry Park of about two hundred trucks, most of them heavy vehicles adapted for passenger transport, and some 'minibuses,' Land Rovers with extra seats inside. There were seventy-seven such parks in the eighty-three towns Jordan investigated, centers of a 'peripheral' feeder porterage system, all of them examples of the perfect symbiosis of 'old' and 'new.' In Koforidua, for example, Ghana's fifth-largest town, another anthropologist calculated a market day attracted a thousand headloads but that 85 percent of the total tonnage arrived by truck. The freight haulage and passenger transport system rested on a system of communication (*Gemeinschaft*, in Jordan's dichotomy), without which the drivers' person-oriented, *Gesellschaft* behavior would not have been possible. It is this switch from tribal to urban lifestyle that Jordan then researched in detail, observing that drivers were prepared to wait (1.5 hours on average) after boarding but that they often refused (in 86 percent of the observed cases) to stop along the roads, enmeshed in their *Gesellschaft* role (the 'necessity' to drive fast because of the 'washboard' road surface).

Also, extensive horn blowing formed a part of this role, as was the absence of humor and jokes, once the driver climbed behind his wheel. The "sullen look" that accompanied this change reminds us of the "cool persona" we have analyzed extensively for car drivers in the 1930s, especially in Germany. Jordan explained this behavioral flexibility by referring to J. Clyde Mitchell's "situational change." From this perspective, it would be a bit too easy to explain the "excessively rapid and careless" behavior out of a "lack of 'feeling' for machines," as some scholars did. Another projection of the 'lack of Western characteristics' on Africans reads like this: "The West African driver had not usually shown, in the past, the sense of awareness of slight changes in sound which indicate that mechanical trouble is impending." How could he, one is inclined to ask, if one reminds oneself of the washboard roads? Instead of stereotyping this behavior as "the result of a youth passed in a non-mechanical world," which reminds us of the 'chaos' Western observers saw (and still often see) in non-Western daily road traffic, it seems more to the truth to emphasize the extraordinary skills needed in negotiating both the roads and the passengers under conditions that still seem to make the 'automobile system' an ill-fitting entity in a largely rural world, resulting in extreme forms of 'layeredness.'[202]

***

If no special measures were taken (and they weren't) and if drivers also copied Western driving styles based on unhampered flows, accidents would predictably be more numerous than in the West. This not only resulted in higher road fatality numbers but also meant more work for mechanics and the repair sector. In Nigeria, for instance, "some of the earliest opportunities for Nigerians to engage in successful business expansion lay in road transport," especially when, after the mid-1970s, oil prices increased and the extra revenues were spent by an eager "state bourgeoisie and its clients" on cars, all the more so, as by that time Volkswagen had opened an assembly plant in the country. While the number of passenger cars did not increase much before the opening of the university in the late 1960s, the number of trucks started to rise in the 1950s because of new plantings of cacao by migrant farmers. The vehicles needed repairing, thus strengthening "the prevailing trend towards tertiary rather than industrial expansion in the Nigerian economy." The developmentalist American social scientist who investigated the mechanics trade in Nigeria confirmed the lack of managerial skills of the Yoruba as observed in earlier studies, but she found no indications that "their earlier socialization creates emotional inhibitions against mastering technical and organizational skills."[203] Nonetheless, contrary to the Hausa in their long-range trade, Yoruba mechanics were reluctant to organize along tribal lines, because kinship could interfere with managerial decisions.

African labor studies after independence could leave the previous, all-pervasive question among the colonizing powers aside how to attract laborers in the first place, and they did not spend much energy to the characteristics of a supposed African *civilisation du loisir* (leisurely civilization), but it did spend scholarly energy on the pressing question for the postcolonial social planners of the "militant and uncontrollable worker," who seemed to migrate in search for "adventure, and tests of manhood." What such labor studies emphasized was "stabilization," indicating an African form of (the Chinese "migration certificate") *hukou*, as "other countries [than South Africa, with its Apartheid system] are also anxious to block rural migrants from establishing themselves in town but hardly with the success, the ruthlessness, the political conviction, or the scale of the South African state." There, to give only one example of South Africa's racialized policy in the realm of mobilities, in 1953 "an Act of Parliament forbade whites from sharing any vehicle with a member of another racial group." Whoever is in doubt about the fundamental political character of mobility should study the South African black commuter culture, which can be followed back to the Alexandra bus boycotts of the 1940s and the Evaton and Alexandra boycotts in Johannesburg in the 1950s against the increase of bus fares by a monopolistic transport cartel formed in 1940. This culminated in the policy to relocate 3.5 million people between 1960 and 1980, including a plan to ban the entire South African proletariat toward the homelands and link them up "to the employment areas by a sophisticated high-speed transport system."[204]

In the 1960s, labor studies had departed from the *Gemeinschaft-Gesellschaft* dichotomy and began to focus on the question of "manpower" within the context of an upcoming "new hegemony of development as national ideology," all the more so after a successful general strike of Nigerian workers in 1964. This development perspective was abandoned by the end of the period covered by this chapter, when the ILO in Geneva broke with "modernization theory with its assumptions concerning the ability of Africa to replicate rapidly the economies of the industrialized nations." ILO's reorientation coincided with acknowledging that the "informal sector" often represented more than half of the urban economy and that it should be seen as "Africa pulling itself up with its own bootstraps," instead of as parasytical, and a source of crime, prostitution, and chaos. "The introduction of capitalist mining, farming, industry, and even administrative life everywhere in Africa evoked a host of service activities with a great impact on employment," so much so that the real problem in these countries appear to be not unemployment, the obsession of development bureaucrats, but rather underpayment and "often brutal exploitation." The urban life of the working class in the 'formal economy' also required services, including sexual ones. 'Informal,' therefore, is certainly not identical with 'marginal,' although the vast sector of domestic services, also provided by men, initially was fully neglected.[205]

***

Next to these typical issues of formal (and informal) labor, it is also only lately that "the magnitude of long-distance trade" in West Africa, covering distances of several hundred kilometers from savanna to the forest belt and back and often based on century-old trade routes started long before the European appeared, has been discovered, "without these being reflected in the official economic figures of the countries concerned … The West African long-distance trader is fully aware of the existence of the railway, the bank, the post office, the sollicitor, the police and the court, and he is no less rational in his economic activity than the European business man. Indeed, it is specifically because he is rational in the conduct of his business that he continues in the old traditional way," thus deploying what we have coined 'subversive mobilities,' and applying the practice of using tradition to shape modernity. Instead, it is more fruitful to learn from this à la the Comaroffs (see the introduction): lately, such regroupings of "political ethnicity" have also been observed in the West, leading to "new social forms," as members of such communities are "third or more generation immigrants," who "have lost their original language and many of their indigenous customs." But whether this re-ethnicization in the West causes similar problems as the 'layeredness' beyond the West is not known. In the latter case, mobility indeed took on a special character, as the moving not only was physical but also took place between two cultures and their lifestyles. In many areas of Africa where labor migrancy prevailed, it became ever more questionable to characterize a "town population" by an 'urban lifestyle,' as migrants "continue thinking of the hinterland, rather than the town, as their permanent 'home,' because of the greater security there."[206]

This 'mobility' between a rural and an urban identity can be experienced by reading Nigerian writer Cyprian Ekwensi's highly successful "brilliant evocation of modern Lagos," *Jagua Nana* (1961), in which the protagonist, called "after the famous British prestige car," manages to develop a city life, supported by one of the wealthy "Party People," Uncle Taiwo, who pays her rent and furnishes her house. Cars in this novel either are driven by the newly rich (or their chauffeurs, as in the case of Uncle Taiwo, owning "one of the long ones," a Pontiac), a "white face" (peering at her from a "gleaming black limousine"), or are dreamed about as tokens of future wealth. Jagua's lover, Freddie, a "poor teacher" who, like her, walks, rides the bus, and sometimes takes a taxi, intends to go to England, and when he returns, she fantasizes, he will drive "a big car." Surrounded by highlife music (an improvised and 'pidginized' blend of military, church, and local traditional music, sung by highly mobile performers), escaped from an arranged marriage, Jagua feels at home in "de fas' life" of the big city, of which "the air was thick with the smell of diesel oil from the buses; cycle bells were jangling, and the trains were shunting away at the railway yard; in the streets the hawkers were yelling their wares, weaving songs around simple commodities." When Jagua decides to visit Freddie's family in the countryside, she travels by "Mammy Wagon because it was much the quickest way."

She travels "'first class' which meant sitting beside the driver," but before she boards, she is deceived by the 'shadows' in the motor park where her mammy wagon departs: they are sitting on the truck bed, suggesting it is nearly full, and about to leave. The Nigerian countryside appears to be "the land of the bicycle-taxi where the people did not in the least depend on four wheels for their transport." Where the trucks stops, she must continue her journey through the Niger Delta by motorized canoe. There, she meets another type of limousine users: the "merchant princesses," independent women traders who sometimes also own several trucks. Back in Lagos, when she bumps into Freddie driving a car, she asks him how and when he got it. "'Is on loan,' Freddie told her. He turned a corner, away from the Main Road. 'Is party car for our people O.P. [Other Party] 1." During the subsequent dirty election campaigns between Freddie's O.P. 1 and Uncle Taiwo's O.P. 2, both of them protected by bodyguards but both, in the end, killed by their adversaries, one of the election promises relates to the construction of "wider roads." Devastated, her life in ruins (and unprotected) in Lagos, she returns home, buys a sewing machine and then a bicycle with the profits of her sewing business, intent on becoming, *deo voiente*, a "merchant princess" herself. Then, "I kin buy me own lorry and me own shop by the river" and "employ me own driver."[207]

Haunted Roads: Spirits and Soldiers Complexifying African Mobilities

Apart from the logistic, statistical, and ethnic peculiarities of the African mobilities investigated so far, these mobilities were also tainted by peculiar 'adventurous' experiences, as we saw. For many, the road's function was ambiguous. For the Hausaphone Mawri in southern Niger, for instance, the 905-km "Route Nationale 1" along the border with Nigeria, tarred in 1965, still provided the stuff for folktales, as its history was covered in blood and French colonial atrocities (see chap. 1). As a consequence, this *kwalta* (asphalt road) was fraught with cruel, bloodthirsty (and female) spirits, belonging to the bush, that either seduced male passengers and then killed them, or drove cars and trucks "that crash into oncoming vehicles or terrorize isolated villagers during the night."[208] The destruction of forest landscapes had robbed these spirits of their dwellings, and they now haunted the paved highways.

Wole Soyinka's satirical play *The Road* (1965) illustrates the close relationship between the African road network and death, represented in the play by the spider's web and its ability to provoke a sudden death. The first African to receive the Nobel Prize in Literature in 1986, Soyinka's Yoruba background and his education at the universities of Ibadan and Leeds enabled him to produce theater that critically discussed African modernization, without ignoring its mythologies. He was supported by a research grant from the University of Ibadan, which enabled him to buy a Land Rover to cross the country and investigate its modernization. In *The Road*, a *bolekaja* (mammy wagon) out of control wreaks havoc on a bridge near an "Aksident Store" where car parts can be purchased. Next to the usual tropes of autopoetic literature (the admiration for the skilled driver; the cyborg experience: "He is not complete without a motor lorry"), a recurring theme is the nearby "motor park" where one protagonist is a skilled mammy wagon driver, another a "tout," a "conductor" whose task is to lure passengers into the vehicle, in Yoruba. Driver and conductor are both very much aware of the hierarchy on the road and its related *status*:

> SALUBI: You say you get pride and still yet you are a conductor on bolekaja.
>
> SAMSON: Nonsense, we run a bus . . .
>
> SALUBI: . . . Me, I don't drive lorry. I drive only private owner—no more no less.

While they speculate what they would do if they were millionaires (one would buy ten wives, only because he can't count higher; another "all the transport lorries in the country"), the skilled driver wants to become a businessman, despite his reputation written on his lorry: "NO DANGER NO DELAY." Amid the Yoruba songs and dances, and the evocations of demons and spirits, what happens on the road is compared with a war. "It is peaceful to fight a war which one does not understand, to kill human beings who never seduced your wife or poisoned your water." At the same time, the road is a religion, as becomes clear when the shop owner (a former Sunday school teacher called Professor) asks: "May an ignorant man ask what god you pretend to worship?" And a police officer called Particulars Joe answers: "Same as the other sir, the road."[209]

But the haunting of the roads was done not only by spirits. Colonial soldiers also haunted them, for instance, in Angola, where Portugal resisted decolonization until 1975 by waging war. In such circumstances, the function of roads changes drastically, from arteries to barriers, 'ours' on this side, the enemy on the other, a situation coined by Kurt Lewin as "orientated landscape" (*gerichtete Landschaft*). "As soon as the war started in 1961, the Portuguese took to building roads, landing strips for aircraft, bridges, railways and other transport elements," Dutch Africanist Inge Brinkman concluded. The Portuguese colonial authorities thus implemented ultimately what they had failed to do during previous decades, as we saw in chapter 1. In one go, it created "the most comprehensive system of modern tarmac (asphalt) roads in the continent. This war the Portuguese committed themselves to winning on wheels." Commenting on the mobility characteristics of the guerillas, American Africanist Joseph Miller concluded that for them, "mobility was both their best offense and their readiest defense. The Portuguese, for all their modern vehicles, could not have men and guns fast enough to pursue the furtive fighters, who simply faded into the local population in a classic African strategy of mobility through multiple identities."

In a way, the peculiar frequent African switching between rural and urban identities provides a similar phenomenon. What did not change was the organization of forced labor for roadbuilding, this time of women and the elderly. But 'development under war conditions' had different aims: roadbuilding "hampered guerilla warfare," as it meant "victory over bandit and bush," the latter especially feared by Portuguese soldiers, as the "invisible enemy" was dwelling in there, the colonizers' counterpart of the indigenous spirits. Soldiers longed to return to their Portuguese urbanized world "of neon-lights, of cars that are not turned green, of large buildings, of asphalted roads, the World outside the green of grass and of the bush." Guerilas on their turn focused on blocking these roads: a missionary counted eight hundred felled trees and two hundred trenches dug on a thirty-kilometer stretch of road alone.[210]

The Portuguese classified the road network according to the question of whether their armored cars could pass, whereas knowledge of the footpaths through the bush (*mato* for the Portuguese), outward (abroad) for refugees, inward for guerillas, was a matter of life and death. During the first years of the war, an extensive secret footpath network existed, often parallel to the roads, a leftover from colonial times. Back then, farmers had been forced by the colonial powers to move from their farms in the direction of the roads. Now, they used these old farms, unknown to anybody, to hide. Skills of mobility now included knowledge of the terrain, as well as knowing how to survive in the bush. These skills were crucial, as, in the case of Angola, "hardly anybody, except in some of the largest settlements, stayed where s/he was before the war," despite the explicit Portuguese policy of "immobilizing" the local population. The guerilla strategy was exactly the opposite: using the aforementioned "classic African strategy of mobility through multiple identities," a special form of 'multiple mobilities' that, as we saw, was practiced during the migratory moves between the rural and the urban realm.[211]

Such strategies of developing multiple identities would also be needed by the poor Portuguese soldiers themselves, as back in Europe, a massive form of subversive mobility to Northern Europe was set in motion (nearly one million since 1957 until the revolution of 1974), most of them to France, and from the beginning of the 1960s often collected at the border by Spanish bus companies, after they had been brought to pensions near the border by taxis. In the previous chapter, we dealt with this bus migration in more detail. We can now add to this that after the Carnation Revolution of 1974, "between five and eight hundred thousand people migrated out of the colonies to Portugal."[212] Thus, Portugal evolved into a 'semiperiphery,' a type of country studied in detail by a new generation of development students we will focus on now, as they emerged in Latin America.

Developmentalism versus *Dependentismo*: Latin American Mobilities and the Frustrations of Middle Class Modernity

In the postwar history of African motorization discussed in the previous section, the national middle classes hardly appeared, so one is inclined to conclude (after the earlier discussion on Asia's motorization) automobilism's emergence was highly problematic. Those fragments of fledgling car subcultures that *did* appear, however, had a highly adventurous, if not carnivalesque, character, from maniacally racing khat transporters to near mortally competing bus drivers. Sometimes, the carnival turned sour, into motorized rioting and guerilla warfare, or it turned magic, into haunting spirits ready to kill. The mainstream forms of automobilism in Africa, however, had a strong collective character, from mammy wagons to buses. On the other side of the Atlantic, in Latin America, with a more pronounced middle class, we may thus expect a more developed automobilism. The leftist part of this middle class, especially the intelligentsia, became very articulate in rejecting developmentalism. By the end of the 1960s, hegemonic developmentalist thinking grew out of favor of academics as quickly as it had gained favor in the 1940s and 1950s, mostly because of frustration about its failure to deliver growth (which in theory was supposed to be easy), "even in rapidly industrializing states such as Brazil, South Africa, and Iran." Instead, "loss of theoretical direction" and "disillusionment" mounted about the coups d'état, increasing inequality and a lack of political democracy, not to speak of "debt, famine, environmental devastation, ethnocide, and civil war, to name but a few."

Critique increased on the "crises of planning," while Third World students started to question the wisdom of privileging industrialization over agriculture, all the more so as the usual strategy of "import substitution" did not seem to work ("an extremely inefficient method of saving foreign exchange," according to car industry investigator and economist Bernard E. Munk): instead of consumer goods, Latin American countries started to import capital goods in order to 'catch up' with a technologically more 'advanced' West, thus recreating a form of imperialism (through the generation of payment and trade deficits) that the theory had promised to avoid. Most frustrating, especially from a mobility development perspective, was what Third World students called "institutional weakness" in addition to a "profligate waste of resources," which made development champions such as David Lerner and Seymour Lipset cynically emphasize the need for "order and efficiency" instead of "Western-style democracy as the end point of development." Other critics of mobility-as-development observed the privileging of the urban culture led to serious deficiencies in "accessibility." In Indonesian Java, for instance, one-fifth of the villages had no access to a main highway; outside Java, the lack of connections was even one-third.[213]

Whereas a highway network in the West was superimposed on an already existing (but straightened and paved) older network of what later would be called 'secondary' roads, and the latter grew faster than the national networks during the interbellum because of decentralization, the highways in the Third World were often placed in an infrastructural vacuum, top down.

***

A nice example of this top-down development-through-roadbuilding is the Pan-American Highway system. Already introduced in chapter 1, this desire to mimic the railroads (or aviation, for that matter) to 'unify' an entire continent has a long tradition. The official theme of the ninth Pan-American Highway Congress held in Washington in 1963 as "Highways in the Alliance for Progress," placing the project clearly in the development schemes of the United States and "promis[ing] to reproduce in Latin America the prosperity observed in postwar U.S. through development aid." But during the motorcade of three GM buses carrying highway experts to celebrate the Inter-American Highway stretch between Mexico City and Panama City in the same year, one bus nearly fell off a precipice at the Cerro de la Muerte (what's in a name!) and another lost power causing the delegates to walk. Rosa Ficek, who revealed these events in her study of the Pan-American, suggested, however, the *regionalization* of the project, the addition of local and regional networks in an effort to create "common markets" by national governments, may have been the real driver of this project, initiatives supported by the ECLA, also known as CEPAL (Comisión Económica para América Latina [later extended by adding "y el Caribe").[214]

In the mid-1960s, CEPAL published a multivolume report on Latin America's transport condition, based on the plans designed by many of the continent's countries (information that flowed into the following pages when we deal with the individual countries). The commission lamented the primitive state of statistical reporting in many nations, reflecting that transport in Latin America had been "somewhat forgotten" in the past, but this was now changing. It concluded that transport investments were "a necessary but not sufficient condition" for economic growth. As usual in the '(semi-)periphery,' it compared these investments with those in Western countries (where their share was in the high seventies or eighties, but in the European periphery [Turkey, Greece], they were extremely high: more than 93 percent of all investments). There was one consolation: both the European and Latin American investment shares were higher than those in Asia.[215]

The international attention (also expressed through the organization of the fourth IRF World Congress in Mexico City held in 1958), concerned the spectacular parts of the highway project. After World War II, when Mexico, Nicaragua, and Argentina finalized their parts, Brazil constructed a stretch between its capital (Rio de Janeiro) and São Paolo; Colombia, Peru, and Chile also started their projects, some of them with direct US aid, both financial (through appropriation of funds in Congress) and technical (through the Bureau of Public Roads). But the mountains of Costa Rica and the Darién region in Panama still formed "barriers to even the most ambitious and intrepid adventurers." The Darién Gap between North and South America right through the jungle was never closed, despite coordinated efforts in 1955 by Panama, Colombia, the US Bureau of Public Roads, and an engineer specialized in tropical forests sent by Mexico. To acquire funding, the Darién Highway was presented in the US Congress as "an anti-revolutionary project that would promote economic development by opening access to undeveloped land in Eastern Panama and easing poverty." Construction started in 1973 by a firm specialized in military infrastructures in Afghanistan and Vietnam, but when the American Sierra Club sued the government because it did not investigate the project's ecological impact and Congress remained reluctant to grant funding, it was abandoned. Nicaragua's roads as part of the Pan-American were "unnecessarily winding in some places … and designed in such a way that they intersect with properties of the ex-President."[216]

In 1956, the IRF Washington office convened a regional conference in Guatemala to accelerate the finalization of the 1,573-mile Inter-American Highway between North and South America, a project the IRF estimated at $300 million and for which it proposed to set up an Inter-American Highway Maintenance Authority. Apart from President Carlos Castillo Armas, Guatemala's military dictator who had seized power in a CIA-sponsored coup in 1954 (and was assassinated three years later), who opened the conference, a delegation from the United Nations was present. In the American aid program for Guatemala, this highway's completion got "top priority," and the aid was given on the condition that the advice of the US Bureau of Public Roads be followed. The highway, at $266,000 per mile, became the most expensive in Central America and "absorbed more than half of all US grant aid to Guatemala." Historian Stephen M. Streeter, who analyzed this case, concluded the highways in Guatemala "did not improve the rural standard of living."[217]

Dependency Theory and Mobility: Modernizing through (Semi-)Peripheral Agency

With developmentalism failed, it was within CEPAL that dependency theory offered itself as an alternative. Gathered at universities in Santiago de Chile because of military coups in the region, leftist intellectuals invaded the commission, where they "criticized the Eurocentric assumptions of the [existing, developmentalist] *cepalistas*, including the orthodox Marxist and North American modernization theories." During the first two postwar decades, CEPAL's predecessor, the ECLA (as "an intergovernmental organization" with "its major training program of government bureaucrats") was "probably the most influential economic institution based in the Third World," fostering Argentinean economist Raúl Prebisch's "theoretical justification for import substituting industrialization (ISI) as a growth strategy," called *desarrollo hacia adentro* (inward-oriented development) formulated on the basis of the core-periphery dichotomy.

Dependentistas' critique within the ECLA (who, by the way, coined the terms center and periphery) was directed primarily against the diffusionist myth, which they called the "denial of coevalness," the latter term indicating synchronicity, similar to our 'layeredness' when applied to mobilities. They saw this denial as "central to Eurocentric constructions of 'otherness,'" and they attacked the fundamental liberalism of modernization theorists who had transplanted the Enlightenment concept of the free and sovereign individual onto the nation-state, thus assuming the "inevitable progress" of the nation-state could be achieved through a "rational organization of society." The *dependentistas* saw in the local elites not the bourgeoisie who in an orthodox Marxism (which in this sense appeared to be as 'stagist' as modernization theory) first had to be supported before socialism could be achieved, thus criticizing the Communist parties who had sided with this bourgeoisie. Instead, they saw them as intermediaries of new forms of imperialism, who had internalized the concept of Europe as the model to imitate and to catch up with.

The dependency theory never became as influential as its predecessor (nor were their main protagonists all Marxists, as many observers seem to think), but the Cuban revolution (which appeared to provide a vision to an alternative form of development "outside the world capitalist system") gave the fundamentally historical studies of Fernando Henrique Cardoso, Enzo Faletto, Andre Gunder Frank, Aníbal Quijano, and Theotonio dos Santos extra power. This happened, for instance, through its sloganesque formulation of the core of the theory as "development of underdevelopment" coined by economist Paul Baran, claiming both were intimately and dialectically related. The West created a "periphery" (and thus made itself into a "core") by "expropriat[ing] a significant part of the economic surplus produced in its satellites and appropriate it for its own economic development." In the process, it created "semiperipheries" (Taiwan next to China; Greece next to Eastern Europe; Nigeria next to Tanzania; Spain and Portugal next to Northwestern Europe) as icons of development in which large amounts of money were poured to contain the spread of Communism. Also, the dependentistas' historical approach (coinciding with the "historical turn" in the social sciences in general) attacked the unhistorical maxims of the developmentalists by claiming "the experience of the metropolitan societies cannot be repeated. Underdevelopment is a specific experience that needs to be analyzed as a historical and structural process." As an offshoot of these theories, "world-system analysis," coined by Immanuel Wallerstein, expanded the reach of the theory beyond Latin America. It also provoked a "revival of developmentalism among a new generation of social scientists" who started to work on a political economy of the Asian 'Tigers.'[218]

Dependentista theories were later criticized as being captured in the same modernist paradigm as the world it wished to overcome: the Latin American left "never radically problematized the racial/ethnic hierarchies built during the European colonial expansion." Perhaps because of this, the civil servants and civil engineers participating in the 1975 PIARC conference held in Mexico City were treated to a speech by civil engineer, member of the Institutional Revolutionary Party of President Luis Echeverria Alvarez, and Minister of Public Works Luis Enrique Bracamontes Gálvez, who explained why it was so difficult for his country to 'catch up': "The countries of the Third World must not indiscriminately copy the industrialised countries," he said in a nearly direct quote of the new *dependentista* theory, "for if we do so we will sink more and more into underdevelopment and will bring about the development of underdevelopment." Indeed, the minister showed what *dependentista* theory mostly accomplished: it brought 'agency' back into the 'core-periphery' equation, on the "periphery" side of this equation. A representative of Tunisia at the same conference, hesitating to take part in the discussion on low-cost roads in developing countries, as he "thought that this subject did not interest most of the representatives here," expressed as his "personal opinion" that the developed countries should provide the developing countries with "the whole of the existing armory which they have in their hands for the design of road projects," and not with only "the first generation of computers," a critique reminiscent of America's refusal to donate a high-performance computer to India.[219]

Dependentistas did not ignore mobility: in the early 1960s, CEPAL published an overview of the transport systems of seven Latin American countries, which showed, among other things, that apart from Argentina, all of them (Colombia, Chile, Bolivia, Peru, Brazil, and Venezuela) planned to invest more in roads than in rails. A study by the Brookings Institution from 1966 on the possibilities of continental "economic integration" teaches us that American analysts distinguished between an economic core in the eastern "coastal strip from Brazil to Argentina" surrounded by a "supporting hinterland" and the rest, the differences marked by per capita GNPs ranging from Venezuela to Bolivia, the former's being a factor of six higher than the latter's, which on its turn was one-quarter of that of the United States.

The Brookings study was road propaganda disguised as transport expertise, including a plea for "the completion of the Pan American Highway system [as] a prerequisite for producers to discover new markets in adjoining countries and for consumers to learn of new sources of supply." But to understand Latin American's motorization, we need extensive transport surveys of individual countries by studious anthropologists and transport experts such as in Africa. Ricardo Salvatore, one of the few who ventured a continental point of view on Latin America's 'modernization,' showed how many local elites in both regions (the Andean nations: "poor, populated by Indian majorities, technologically backward, and residual colonial in their social relations [servile labor, patrimonialism, and large landed estates]"; and the Southern Cone: Argentina, Brazil, and Chile) intended to emulate "the economic miracles of Japan in the postwar period and of the 'East Asian Tigers' in the 1960s and 1970s."[220]

Others have emphasized the role of the fledgling automobile industry in Latin American modernization: by the end of the 1960s, nine Latin American countries had their own automotive assembly industry, in Argentina, Brazil, and Mexico representing "the major source of supply for the home market." Whereas the ten most urbanized and industrialized countries counted half a million cars on its roads in 1945, twenty years later there were two million. It is in this phase that several countries, also outside Latin America (next to Argentina, Brazil, and Mexico, also Spain, India, South Africa, and Australia) planned "transition from assembly operations to automobile manufacturing." The Latin American car industry not only functioned as a model for industrialization through import substitution (autoworkers, in the words of Mexican Chrysler, representing "the aspirations for change of their societies at large"), which prompted Chile, for instance, to close its borders for "fully assembled automobiles for ordinary domestic use." At the same time, the industry also was a hotbed of violence and oppression. In Argentina, for instance, Ford executives collaborated with state authorities during the "dirty war" of the 1970s to denounce critical union members and even maintained a torture center in their Buenos Aires facility. In Mexico, in 1969, at Chrysler's Toluca plant, the secret security agency opened fire on six thousand protesters, while the company "blacklisted five hundred alleged subversives, dispatching guardias blancas (terror squads) to patrol the factory floor." The violence was most cruelly directed toward "the indigenous, who were deemed 'alien to modernity.'"[221]

In contrast, Cuba followed an alternative development path, of a scarcity economy, after Fulgencio Batista fled to Franco's Spain, and those who fled to the United States left their 167,000 cars behind. During the five years before the revolution of 1959, the Cuban car fleet had exploded (from 70,000 in 1950), with the highest per capita sales of Cadillacs in the world.

But when the revolutionaries had won, they did not reject the 'adventure machines.' While Fidel Castro took an Oldsmobile (in which he and his driver sped to the Playa Girón, the Cuban name for the Bay of Pigs), Che Guevara managed to acquire a brand-new "eight-cylinder Chevrolet Bel Air, Series 1600, … deep emerald green and (with) a white roof; with flat fins and a chrome strip on either side." Che's assistant Orlando Borrego "appropriated a virtually new Jaguar," but Che judged it a "pimp's car." However, and ironically, the American boycott changed the composition of the motorized vehicle fleet toward Skodas from Czechoslovakia, Ladas from the Soviet Union and Warsawas from Poland, minibuses all painted violet and driven by unemployed ex-prostitutes as *ruteros*, a revolutionary type of jitney, "running a standard fixed-rate route at five cents a passenger." The cars could be imported through the sale of Cuban sugar to the Soviet Union and the Eastern European socialist states, from where also came the automotive expertise to repair Soviet trucks.

And so, utilitarianism set in: "Those who got a car after 1960 hoped to get one that would keep running with a minimum of upkeep, burning as little gasoline as possible. How it looked was relatively unimportant; what mattered was getting from one place to another." But parallel to the official circuit a paradise of do-it-yourselfers emerged comparable to what cultural historian Kurt Möser has described for the GDR, showing an enormous creativity in adapting spare parts. Yet, despite the frustration about Latin America's "failing to keep pace with the growth of the world economy," it cannot be denied that by the 1960s, "most Latin American countries had in fact experienced a real improvement in general standards of living," changes that also expressed themselves in local waves of motorization, supported by national road construction programs.[222]

Mexico between Developmentalism and Dependentismo: *Acquiring Agency through Roadbuilding*

Mexico is an example of regained (or perhaps better, considering the interbellum history recounted in chap. 1, maintained) agency within a development context, certainly so in mobility terms. During the first three postwar decades, Mexico became a laboratory of 'development' for a complex set of actors, each with their particular interests. The United States, interested in stability at its southern border since its hectic Depression years, were eager to stimulate tourism and were even prepared to overrule the protests from Standard Oil of California and others against President Lázaro Cárdenas's nationalization of the Mexican oil industry. And indeed, already before the war, the Banco de México saw the percentage of foreign tourist cars on Mexican roads increase rapidly. With the tourists came millions of dollars of US aid to complete the Pan-American Highway, construct airports, and improve other infrastructures.[223]

World War II triggered radical changes in Mexico's mobility culture. The country "was a potential staging ground for Axis intelligence and even invasion. At the same time, Mexico became a crucial provider of the raw materials, products, and workers deemed critical to the U.S.'s capacity to wage an industrialized total war." We have already seen, from the other side of the border, the immigrants arriving to release American regular workers for military duties (see chap. 2). "In addition, U.S. automakers and road construction companies acquired a new interest in Mexico as a land of vast potential profits." On the Mexican side, President Manuel Ávila Camacho, who succeeded Cárdenas in 1940, considered building a road network as a way not only to boost economic growth, but also to "check… the power of railroad labor, keep the emerging industry in Mexican hands, and privilege large and politically connected groups over the needs of those with modest means." Camacho tempered Cárdenas's radicalism and his peasant-based policy, centralizing government power. Next to Cárdenas's prewar Confederación Nacional Campesina and the Confederación de Trabajadores de México, he founded the Confederación Nacional de Organizaciones Populares, gathering "shopkeepers, small businesses, and other non-worker urban groups" and thus opening the regime's basis toward the middle classes, who profited especially from Mexico's 34 percent growth of GDP during the war. This was the result of a shift of trade from Europe and Asia (blocked because of the war) to the United States and a growth of exports by 72 percent; imports grew 153 percent, setting in motion a process of inflation that increased inequality within Mexico.

The increasing American influence on the Mexican economy led to a more market-oriented agriculture, whereas adjustments in Mexico's legislation allowed plantations to grow, "away from [Mexico's prewar] collective forms of ownership." All these forces resulted in a fierce struggle, from 1943, between railroads (with their powerful unions, "counting thousands of Mexican communists among its ranks," and their reputation of struggle against the former American owners) and roads, all the more so when American consultants started to tour the Mexican countryside and advised Mexican authorities to follow the US example, where in 1941 Congress had passed the Defense Highway Act, the predecessor of the 1956 Interstate project legislation. These consultants vented a general concern in the United States about the availability of highways to transport troops in case of an Axis invasion (in the US itself) or to reach the Mexican oil fields. Within Mexico, opposition increased against the Alianza de Camioneros as a "state-sanctioned monopoly" of bus and truck concessions, a "monopoly of death," because of the alleged unsafety of its buses in Mexico City.[224]

Yet, like in the prewar phase, most of the annual average of 2,250 km of roads built between 1946 and 1952 (and most of the extra, annual 1,250 km during the war as well) were *caminos vecinales* (local roads), a result of a promise made in 1946 during the populist campaign of President Miguel Alemán, the "first postrevolutionary civilian president," who succeeded Camacho. What in the West was accomplished by decentralization (the expansion of the road network to the local level), necessitated a revolution in Mexico. And although Mexico's road network expanded to 25,000 km, including its 2,000-mile part of the Pan-American Highway, a fierce struggle between rail and road interests took place on these roads. Originally, before and partially during the war, the emphasis had been on freight mobility (the number of trucks more than doubled during the 1940s, to 106,321), and dozens of truck companies had captured this market, deploying, as one economist called it, a "destructive competition" with rail freight transport. By 1950, trucks hauled about the same amount of freight (in tons) as the train.

After President Camacho had started his aggressive industrialization policy based on import substitution (in which the domestic car industry would play a crucial role), and "the Revolution got down from its noble horse and settled into the pillowed seat of a Cadillac," the "politics of economic redistribution" was abandoned. Instead, a conscious strategy was now developed to increase the import tariffs on complete cars, to subsidize the national oil company PEMEX so that it could lower its gasoline price, and even to forbid the import of complete engines (in which 60 percent of the components should be produced within Mexico from then on). By 1960, seventeen enterprises produced forty-one passenger car models. Benefiting from the international economic boom after the war, Mexico was transformed into a car society, even if half of all cars were to be found within the capital. These middle-class-friendly policies coincided, at the start of the Cold War, with Alemán's campaign against the left in his party, renamed after the war into Partido Revolucionario Institutional. But *alemanismo* consisted, next to anti-Communism, of a focus on industrialization, like several of Latin American countries practiced after the war, one reason the continent did not become the subject of some sort of Marshall Plan.[225]

Yet, we should not forget that by 1970, only one-fifth of all trips within Mexico City were done by car, and the rest by "a diversity of public transport options from taxis, peseros, combis, micros, and electric trolleys to the newly built Metro." Also, a recent dissertation lamented "the countryside continued to suffer the consequences of infrastructural abandonment," quoting a report by a contemporary geographer that claimed only one-fourth of all *poblados* were connected by "roads suitable for vehicles of any type." One of the remarkable characteristics of the Mexican 'laboratory of road network building' was the emphasis on secondary and tertiary roads, especially in view of the fact that it was American consultants who supported this policy. During the 1940s, 4,000 km of roads had been constructed by private logging companies. Now, the American Road Builders Association convinced the Department of State to finance scholarships "to expose [Latin American] highway engineers to construction equipment built in the United States" (knowing that European equipment was 25 to 30 percent cheaper), thus prefiguring how 'development' would be shaped a decade or two later.

In his excellent dissertation (the only one that emphasized this transnational aspect of Mexico's road network building), Benjamin Fulwider concluded that "although national officials were careful never to admit it, it is hard to escape the conclusion that trucking was deliberately encouraged as a way to gain leverage against the railroad workers and their powerful union," confirming again that the coordination struggle is a highly political process. Indeed, when the truck and bus operators started to protest against Mexico's restricting regulations, Alemán suspended all restrictions during a brief period. By now, these vehicles could be maintained by a Mexican spare parts industry (emerged during the war). In 1950, the Mexican government lifted all restrictions to manufacture trucks, and in 1955, the semipublic Diesel Nacional factory started to build trucks and buses for the Mexican market. Whereas Alemán during the last three years of his presidency "spent unprecedented amounts of public money on dams, irrigation projects, roads and buildings," later presidents could deploy what one of them (Adolfo López Mateos, 1958–1964) called "stabilized development" in a further expansion of the Mexican 'laboratory.'

This type of development no doubt favored large-scale organizations, who (nothing new for those who know the history of the coordination crisis in Europe and the US) started to complain about *piratas* (illegal trucks and

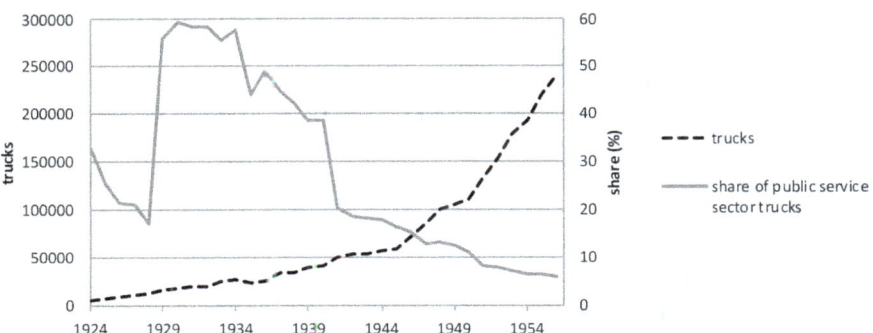

Figure 3.8. Registered trucks in Mexico, 1924–1956. Source: Fulwider, "Driving the Nation," 272, appendix A. Figure created by the author.

buses); at the same time, they were able to bypass regulations by purchasing their own truck fleets: between 1938 and 1952, public trucking decreased from 50 percent to only 10 percent of the Mexican truck fleet (fig. 3.8). And when student demonstrators in 1958 "hijacked city buses [in Mexico City] and burned them alongside effigies of José Valdovinos, the president of the [monopolist] Alianza [de Camioneros], [they] painted slogans on the walls of the National Palace calling for an end to national control over bus transportation in the city." By then, the Mexican middle class started to buy cars in large numbers, although the authorities' efforts to combat inflation through the imposition of production quotas, kept production lower than demand.[226]

One important aspect of the Mexican roadbuilding laboratory was the increasing financing by 'road bonds' (next to the already existing, and regularly increased, gasoline tax); such bonds were purchased predominantly by American investors. Another was the dominating influence of the IRF (a phenomenon missed by most students of the Mexican case), through its local chapter, the Asociación Mexicana de Caminos (and its monthly publication, *Más Caminos* [More roads]), founded 1949 and often the initiator of particular road stretches, through its connections within the Comité Nacional de Caminos Vecinales (founded by Alemán). Between them, they devised a "'tripartite' funding system," which gave local capitalists an important leverage of their investments in stretches of roads. Fulwider recounted the case of a road in the southern state of Oaxaca, where two earlier proposals (connecting many villages) were rejected in favor of a road that went right through a latifundia, and only passed through two communities. After what we have seen in Africa (where roads bypassed certain villages, and connected others), we already know road-building is a political process.

In 1960, Mexico counted 45,000 km of highways (about double the length of the network in 1940); ten years later, it had expanded to 71,000, covering the entire country. After 1960, road investments focused on maintenance and on adjusting the roads to the heavier vehicle loads. Whereas the Mexican motor vehicle fleet counted 200,000 units by the end of the war, ten years later there were more than half a million (of which 40 percent trucks); another decade later, there were 1.2 million. Nonetheless, about the question of whether the roads had caused economic growth, Fulwider was skeptical: "growth sometimes meant little more than the incorporation into the national economy of production that had previously been left out of national bookkeeping." Also, the public works projects contributed to large inequalities, mostly "boosting the value of real estate and other investments." Indeed, what the roads did was "incorporating more and more of Mexico's agricultural production into the sphere of a national market." It further "increased the wealth of those who were already well-off enough to own property."[227]

Venezuela and Colombia: Laboratories for Global Road Construction Projects

Other Latin American countries followed suit, such as Venezuela, which started the "greatest engineering project in South America since the Panama Canal," the "spectacular super-highway" connecting the capital Caracas with the airport and the harbor, and to the Pan-American Highway system, a nice example of the 'regionalization' of the Pan-American. Under President Marcos Pérez Jiménez (a developmentalist military dictator whose reign between 1952 and 1958 started and ended with a coup, in between supported by the US and Europe, especially Franco's Spain, where he fled after his presidency), "slices off the tops and sides of certain mountains" were made to fill the "giant gaps" between the peaks so that the highway could perform its climb up three thousand feet. Two thousand men and two hundred bulldozers did the job, figuring, as one student of expressway building in Caracas has hypothesized based on its synchronicity with developments in the United States, as a "territory of experimentation" for the rest of the world.[228] The project had to be ready for the sixth Pan-American Highway Congress held in July 1954 in Caracas, where again, the IRF hammered on the fact that the system was "not yet ready for pleasure travel, that a trip over the entire route … should be undertaken at present only as an expedition or adventure," just as it had been before the war. As usual, *Road International* played on the contrast of natural beauty and traffic quagmire:

> While depicting the natural beauty of Andean ranges and valleys, the wealth of archaeological relics, the Spanish colonial architecture, the colorful native life—all of which unfold along the highway route—the Pan American Union must present also the unromantic and often grim picture of travellers being bogged down in mud or sand, being stopped by landslides or unbridged rivers too deep to ford, or seeing the highway disappear into little more than a trail in certain sectors.

So much was clear: the automotive adventurer in the 1950s no longer was triggered by mud and physical effort, but instead followed, just like his counterpart in the United States, as we saw in the previous chapter, the Western pattern of unhampered flow. By 1958, the country had a fleet of 159,000 motor vehicles. That was two years before Ford joined General Motors with its own assembly factory, which would help grow the Venezuelan fleet further, causing 3,207 deaths and 24,510 injured in 1968 alone. By 1974, Venezuela produced more than a million vehicles in its assembly plants. Six years later, there were 1.8 million motor vehicles registered in the country,

1.4 million of these passenger cars. But the efforts to produce a *carro popular de bajo costo*, an ideal of any motorizing country in this phase, did not materialize.[229]

Likewise, with 17.5 million inhabitants in 1964, of which more than half lived in cities, Colombia started a railway and road modernization program backed by loans from the World Bank, while American and Dutch consultants advised for and against railway construction, respectively. Colombian modernization revealed the importance of institutionalizing design and maintenance through the foundation of a Department of Highways in the Ministry of Public Works. The ministry planned to hire foreign technical personnel for two years, after which period Colombians should be able to take over. By the mid-1960s, the railway network had been completed (in ten years, a thousand km had been added to the net), but in the 1970s, it started to be dismantled, as we have seen. During the 1950s, 1,800 km new roads were added to the network, and 2,800 km of existing roads were reconstructed, so by 1960, 17 percent of the 15,000 km of the Colombian road network was paved. During the previous decade, $2.7 billion had been spent on railway and road infrastructure, "each transport mode," as later critics would comment, "planned independently." The roads were (re)constructed by consortia consisting of American and Colombian construction companies. Meanwhile, the World Bank calculated how much the transportation costs had diminished through modernization. As a result, during the 1950s, road freight transport (in ton-km) surpassed rail freight transport, from a share of 43 percent to 77 percent.[230]

Tropical Mobility: The Creation of Brazil's Motorized Middle Class

Brazil, too, occupying half the South American land mass, started an ambitious highway building program in the densely populated "economic triangle" between Rio de Janeiro, São Paulo, and Belo Horizonte, set up along lines well tested in the west, such as the earmarking of fuel tax for roadbuilding (40 percent for federal, the remainder for the regional plans), whereas a selection of engineers was sent to the United States annually "to study and observe road building methods." According to urban planner Eduardo Vasconcellos, the federal state created a road fund in the 1950s, from which most of the 50,000 km of national highways were financed. Several of the twenty-one Brazilian states also started regional highway construction programs, the State of Rio de Janeiro purchasing its (foreign) earthmoving equipment with a World Bank loan. Only later would the connecting highways to the neighboring countries (Bolivia, Peru, Colombia, Venezuela, the Guianas) be built, as well as a network in the extreme South. This was possible because of a record economic growth of 6.5 percent annually between 1930 and 1980, "before the rise of China probably the fastest in the world."[231] Typically, the new prosperity was used to favor roadbuilding over railways (fig. 3.9).

More than in Africa, these networks were an obvious signal to the local middle classes that their wishes for the pleasurable sides of automobilism were taken care of. In the case of Brazil, as we saw in chapter 1, the interbellum was clearly a preparatory period for the postwar explosion, just like in the West. President Getúlio Vargas had taken a Fordist route to modernization, when he opened steels mills in Volta Redonda in 1946, a "government-sponsored version of Fordlândia" (see chap. 1), started an engine factory with support from the United States, which eventually began producing trucks under Italian Isotta-Fraschini license. He also started a campaign, "The Oil Is Ours," resulting in the founding of domestic oil company Petrobrás in 1953. It was, however, his successor, Juscelino Kubitschek, who made an ambitious roadbuilding program ("Fifty Years of Progress in Five," "More Energy, More Roads!") into a crucial element of his presidential campaign, during which he traveled more than 200,000 km. His views were inspired by UN's CEPAL in Santiago de Chile. During his presidency (1956–1961), he set up a domestic automobile industry, built highways, and constructed Brasília, "the car-dependent, modernist national capital in the interior" (and the Latin American counterpart of Indian Chandigarh), which opened in 1960. His developmentalist projects, after the top-down efforts of his predecessor (who ended his career by committing suicide) and inspired by

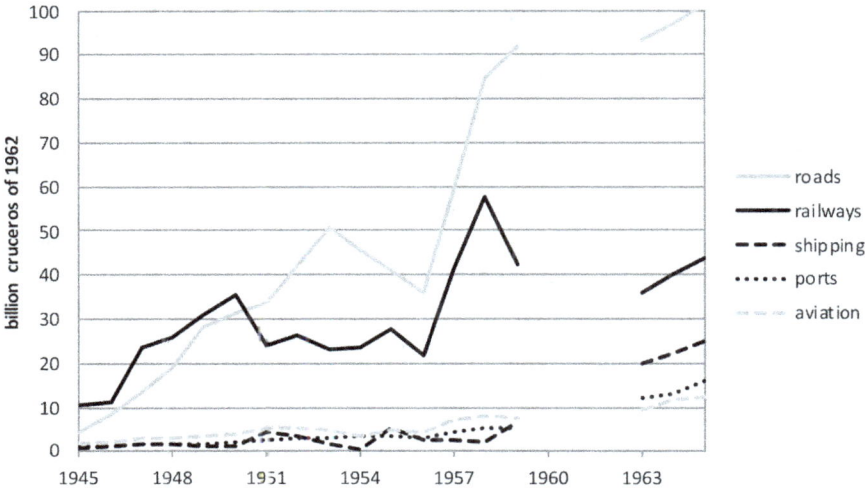

Figure 3.9. Gross investments in Brazil's transport sector (in billions of cruzeiros of 1962). Source: CEPAL, "El Transporte en America Latina," 716, table 196. Figure created by the author.

discussions in the Joint US-Brazil Economic Development Commission, were aimed at nothing less than "the creation of a middle class."

Around the mid-1950s, Brazil had only 2,000 km of high-quality highways, against double that amount in small countries like Puerto Rico and Cuba. According to a recent study of Brazilian automobilism, "Brazil had never had a powerful or effective central state," but Kubitschek seemed to be able to change this. As former mayor of Belo Horizonte, well versed in modern planning, he brought Volkswagen to Brazil and provided work for up seven hundred thousand Brazilians in the auto sector (using the steel mills in Volta Redonda), meanwhile trying to "integrat[e] through interiorization" the rest of the country along the newly built highways. In 1960, Brasília was connected to the state capitals by 5,611 km of newly built highways, on which, however, trucks soon began to dominate. On this system, also about 250,000 Brazilians migrated annually to the "interior frontier"; migration in this vast country was ubiquitous, indeed: "Between 1960 and 1990, more than eight million people left the northeast, the majority of whom went to the states of São Paulo and Rio de Janeiro." In the early 1960s, Brazil invested 8.3 percent of its GNP in transport; in absolute terms, it was the highest in Latin America and, according to a CEPAL report, "perhaps of the entire world."

After Kubitschek was succeeded by President Jânio Quadros, and then by João Goulart, and the latter gradually took the side of the workers in their conflict with their employers, women's groups and related middle-class members provoked a mass demonstration asking the military to intervene. In 1964, a coup started more than two decades of military dictatorship, during which the "Brazilian miracle of the late 1960s and early 1970s" took place. But the "experiment in 'rural urbanism,'" to be accomplished via the Trans-Amazonian Highway inaugurated in 1972, was a "dismal failure." By the mid-1960s (when 732,000 passenger cars were produced in the country), Brazil's car fleet may have been the largest on the continent, but in relative terms, motorization was low compared to Uruguay, Argentina, and Venezuela. In 1960, only half a percent of all Brazilians owned a car; twenty years later, this percentage had increased significantly (tenfold), but car density was still low. "Tropical modernity" had resulted in "a new working class," but the middle class must have been quite frustrated, judged by the frequent statistical comparisons with other countries' car densities in the press.[232]

***

Modernization theorists often emphasized the importance of the middle classes in stabilizing Latin American societies. In Brazilian Rio de Janeiro and São Paulo, for instance, the emergence of the middle class not only was heavily racialized (white-collar salarymen were mostly white- or light-skinned) and gendered (women played a dominating role only among elementary school teachers and retail clerks), but market surveys showed there was no gap with the West when it came to the acquisition of radios, or sewing machines, or the availability of credit. Yet, only 10–17 percent of middle-class members in 1946 owned a car (against 61–77 percent of the "rich," and 0–4 percent of the working class), despite the fact that many middle-class women joined their husbands in working outside the home. One reason for this was the low level of homeownership. As so often in similar situations, car and homeownership formed a powerful field of expectations as we saw: "Nearly half of [the middle-class interviewees] who said they intended to buy a house indicated that they would need a garage, though less than a fifth owned a car."

Novels of the period (such as Democrito de Castro e Silva's *Middle Class*) depicted the collective subject as "an unhappy class, because it cannot be rich and must not be poor." Such novels, as well as nonfictional commentaries, emphasized that this class "did not coalesce as a party, vote as a bloc, establish a clear direction, or push a unified agenda through its associations." Instead, Brian Owensby, who dedicated a separate study to this phenomenon, showed the middle class shared "the diffuse sense that the good life, or a least a life considerably better than most, is best protected and advanced through individual striving at work and at home," through personal "technical competence and domestic moralism.' As they could not, as a class, "make their will triumph in national politics," and hence felt "entirely abandoned" by mainstream politics, they had been "relegated to a secondary plane" in public life.[233]

Modernizing through 'Ordered Spending': Argentina and Peru

A comparable frustration must have captured the Argentinean middle class that saw the populist Peronist period (which ended in 1955 by a military coup) be dedicated to creating the *vida digna* of the working class. By then (in 1960), Argentina had by far the largest railway network in absolute numbers (nearly 44,000 km), as well as in network density (both per square km and per capita), followed by Brazil (38,000), Mexico (23,000) and Chile (8,400), but relatively speaking, Bolivia (with 10 km per 10,000 inhabitants) had a denser network than Brazil (with half that rate), testifying to the importance of population density and the size of the country, respectively.[234] The Argentinean middle class started buying radio sets and electric home appliances in the 1930s, often on consumer credit, but a 1937 survey revealed the average family spent 57 percent of its budget on food, 20 percent on housing, 10 percent on clothing, and only 8 percent on "general spending," which included "transportation."

Compared to the United States, a radio was seven times, a car five times, and a sewing machine three times more expensive than for a US worker. The period is remembered as "an age of abundance," but the Argentinean press complained about "the Perón government's neglect of the middle class—the 'Cinderella of Argentine society.'" The government published a transport plan in 1959, funded by the UN and the World Bank, and executed by American, Dutch, and Italian consultancies. In 1961, Argentina's enormous road network amounted to nearly 47,000 km of national roads (of which only 10 percent was paved by concrete, asphalt, or gravel), 142,000 km of provincial roads and 800,000 km of local roads.

But the Argentinean case illustrates that the automobile system not only (or even, not predominantly) consists of infrastructure. Building the system also implies creating a consumption attitude toward modernity. For (Western, middle-class) car consumption to become embedded in consumer society, we need a house, roads, and destinations such as recreation facilities, schools, shops, and work, as well as a nuclear family. And yes, we also need an average income enabling to transgress the threshold of car purchasing. And although Peronist consumption society was forced through the distribution ("through channels that bypassed markets") of "millions of consumer goods—clothing, toys, foodstuffs, and most famously, sewing machines," the car was not among them. New hotels, holiday complexes and swimming pools, parks, and beaches were made available for the nuclear working families, loudly advertised by a "virtual media monopoly by 1950." Eduardo Elena, who dedicated a study to Peronist consumerism, saw the absence of the car in the Peronist *vida digna* as a European (and Spanish) influence in a mostly American-inspired ideal of wellbeing (*bienestar*). In an atmosphere of "ordered spending," the hedonism of car consumption had no place.[235] My hypothesis, based on the available secondary literature, would be that the power of the working class (the sewing machines!) prevented the middle class from articulating its desires, which no doubt would have been mobility-related.

A dissertation, written in 1941 by one of the Peruvian founders of the Christian Democrat Party (in a country similarly haunted by an "almost castelike difference between the respectable *empleado* and the marginal, unwashed *obrero*"), formulated it unmistakably: there existed "essential" and "artificial" needs, and the "ostentatious and unnecessary use of the automobile and the telephone" belonged clearly to the latter. This anti-hedonistic attitude, fed by a populist stance, was widespread in Latin America: in 1954, amid the "Mexican miracle," the sixth Carrera Panamericana, the "world's most dangerous race," celebrating the recreational, hedonistic aspects of the use of the Pan-American Highway, was canceled by presidential decree, after the Mexican press had criticized the "danger, uselessness, and perceived idiocy" (in the words of the historian who analyzed the case) of this *carrera de la muerte*. Typically, the press found the explanation for the race's attractiveness in the threat to the pilots' lives, neglecting the possibility that it was the "idiocy" of the "uselessness" that indeed might have formed the major trigger for the sensation it created, as we would argue on the basis of the last eighty years of automotive adventure's history. And although Mexican President Miguel Alemán (1946–1952), predecessor of Adolfo Ruíz Cortines, who forbade the race, dreamed about (and ironized?) a future when every citizen would possess "a Cadillac, a cigar and a ticket to the bullfights," *cadillaquismo* was one of the token words to distance oneself from North American consumer hedonism, emulated by those members of the local Brazilian elite who had the means to buy one. Most of them in the early 1950s "relied on intercity bus travel much more than members of any other social class."[236]

Latin American populism heeded the dream of a car (and a cigar, and a bullfight), but it practiced an anti-hedonistic attitude. The Peronist moniker of 'dignity' for this attitude reflects a tradition going back to the early twentieth century of trying to play down the pleasure of consumption and instead emphasize the 'necessity' of relaxation within the family, after the seriousness of work: "Peronism was perceived, rightly or wrongly, as seeking to erode markers of class distinction, deference, and cultural hierarchy. Affluent sectors too may have seen their incomes rise during the postwar boom, but some felt their gains were matched, if not outstripped, by those of blue-collar workers and grew uneasy about being overtaken by their 'inferiors.'" Many in the "anti-Peronist middle class" saw the latter, especially the rural migrants among them, as *negros peronistas*. We should not forget, however, that even if the car may not have figured in the Peronist universe, this universe was nonetheless highly mobile: "Alpargatas [cord-soled shoes] sí, libros no," Peronist workers shouted during demonstrations. Like in Brazil, European (FIAT) and American car manufacturers (Kaiser) opened assembly plants in the 1950s, whereas Perón (who nationalized the British railway system, the American telephone system, and the French dock facilities) also started a Brazilian brand (Institec) of cars (a sedan named Justicialista, modeled after a 1951 Chevrolet), trucks, and motorcycles (the Puma) in 1952, in an effort to produce "affordable vehicles for the average household," but the coup of 1955 prevented these initiatives from really taking off.[237]

***

In Peru, too, a middle class that could have motorized on a massive scale had meanwhile been formed, especially after the 1930s and 1940s, when the number of *empleados* had "skyrocketed." By 1940, one-fifth of the empleados were women. Peru published its national transport plan in 1961, announcing it would invest three-quarters of its investments in transport during the coming decade in roads. Suburbanization and homeownership, access to consumer credit, and the possession of a radio, as well as visits to the movies and going on holidays, served as measures of distinction, perhaps—because of the enormous pressure from 'below' (see the Peronist populism)—even more so than in the West. Especially travel became a "virtual middle-class obsession," testified by the success of the organized tours of the *viajes para empleados*, but it was the mestizos rather than the Indians (who were "depicted as either enclosed in their communities and *haciendas*, or as rootless wanderers") who "were increasingly identified with mobility, being the archetypal muleteers, traders and brokers, moving with comparative ease between town and countryside," thus forming, one is inclined to conclude, the Latin American counterpart to the African Hausa. Despite the road propaganda, however, and just like in other 'developing' continents, rural areas were often without any road connection, for instance, "in Tarma province where the rural population (nonetheless) managed to lead mobile lives, and achieve relative autonomy, security and prosperity."

Colquemarca, in the Southern Andes, is another example of the 'delinking' that always accompanies 'linking' in mobility matters: this village had been prosperous in the 1930s, "transporting food surpluses by pack animal to the nearest railway. Once a road was built, the number of pack animals diminished and the village became accessible only in the dry season. People moved away, food production declined and the famous public lighting in the central square fell into disrepair." In other words, it became much clearer in Peru than in most Western countries (with the possible exception of the US) that middle-class formation was both a gendered and a racial phenomenon. This also seemed to make the "daily ordeal of riding the bus or streetcar" so crucial in the lives of the Peruvian urban middle class: "Streetcar ridership began to rise dramatically in 1940, peaked between 1947 and 1950, then fell off in subsequent years as the *transvias* were supplemented by buses and private cars." Protests (in which "*empleados* frequently joined with students and *obreros*") against rises in streetcar and bus fares testified of their importance. Like in most other countries, *empleados* spent about 6 percent of their "typical" household budget on transportation.[238]

In 1964, Latin America counted close to 4 million motor vehicles (excluding tractors), ranging from 1.7 million in Brazil, 1.4 million in Argentina, and 1.1 million in Mexico (the three countries with an extensive domestic car industry) to 2,200 in French Guiana. Small countries (Uruguay, French Guiana, Venezuela) had the highest car density; not all, however: Bolivia had a fifteen times lower density than champion Uruguay, whereas this country's vehicle density was also very low—10 per 1,000 inhabitants—while 67 percent of its motorized vehicles were commercial ones. Argentina had a road density similar to Venezuela. Especially in the Andean region, the length of paved roads was modest: Venezuela had the largest network, with 12,000 km, but Bolivia (which published a transport plan in 1961, aided by the UN and CEPAL experts) showed the other extreme, with less than 600 km of asphalt roads (and only 5,000 km of partially paved or unpaved roads). In between were Colombia (4,700 km), Peru (2,700 km) and Ecuador (1,100 km).

In short: like elsewhere, the enormous disparity in the spread of the car and the length of the road network were more characteristic than the proud values of one or two outliers. But it cannot be denied that, just like on other continents, several countries more or less doubled the length of their road networks in the period covered by this chapter: Argentina, Brazil, Chile, and Colombia. Overall, the continental passenger car and truck fleets increased even more: by a factor of four and five, respectively. As to the coordination struggle (between road and rail), the Latin American railway network by then had been expanded to nearly 66,000 km, about one-third of the American network, but in many Latin American countries, the motor bus played a crucial role: in Mexico, on about 1 million motor vehicles, there were 32,000 buses (more than in Canada, with 6.3 million motor vehicles); Brazil had 75,000 buses (on 1.6 million motor vehicles), 1.6 times more than France, with 8 million motor vehicles.[239]

"Cook Everything": Embellishing the Bus

It is around these buses that a typical, "Afro-Atlantic" culture arose of reappropriation through embellishment; for instance, in Haiti's capital of Port-au-Prince, the *tap-tap* (buses) "activate the streets … with a glittering mix of carnival, church, and crypto-Vodou," in bright colors. What we have analyzed for Western automobilism on the basis of the passenger car, Haitian citizens experienced by bus: transcendence on "altars on wheels." This tradition, to use painted signs and declarative sentences ("talking back," an aggressive stance related to one's vehicle is not a privilege of the West!) to protect drivers and passengers, seems to have been borrowed from Africa, where similar customs have been observed: invoking "sacrifice and purity of conduct as the cure for bad fortune," stemming from Yoruba philosophy. Sometimes the god of iron, Ogún, was called upon, as he "presides over violent death in accidents involving iron or metal." In Zaïre, for instance, during the early 1960s, a bus breaking down regularly was adorned with the nickname "Bring a Blanket" (*Nàta Vūnga*) as a satirical suggestion to passengers to be prepared for long waiting times. Another bus in the same period was called *Nléke Eto* ("There Goes Our Boy"), a declarative answer of the owner to his parents who did not want to lend him money to buy a bus.

Truck names, anthropologist Robert Thompson concluded, are "incantations," meant "to waft protection about the driver and all passengers. They prayerfully invoke an aura of humility and caring." They are all acts of aggression: *bolekaja*, which we translated to "mammy wagon," literally means "get out of that vehicle and let's fight." Anthropologist Ralph Bolton connected this culture with the culture of machismo (expressed, for instance, in another declarative sentence: "Super Male from Acomayo"), but he had to add an extra category, "religiosity," to be able to interpret all mottoes he had collected from Peruvian trucks at the end of the 1970s; he also found "aggression" to be "an integral part of machismo." In the 1970s, in the Muslim north of Nigeria, truck paintings (often violent) were inspired by foreign movies such as Italian "spaghetti westerns" (cowboy Django) and the "low-budget Chinese films made in Hong Kong," with cheap imitations of Bruce Lee. The anthropologist who reported this mentioned a Peugeot 504 station wagon, "widely used as a fast, long-distance taxi, [which] has been characterized by the nicknames *Shiga da alwalla* ('Enter with a prayer') and *Dafa Duka* ('Cook everything,' a reference to fiery crashes)." All these elements ("belief and bravado and affectionately named speed") were also to be found in Haiti. Although less well researched, slogans on buses have also been reported for Mexico during the 1940s through 1970s.[240]

Conclusions: Road, Rail, and Development

Statisticians have drawn up semilogarithmic graphs (the x-axis linear, the y-axis logarithmic) of car density versus per capita income that produced nice, straight lines of 'progress,' where the United States was always figuring on the far upper end of the line (its distance to the rest modestly tempered by the logarithmic scale), closely followed by a group of related countries (Canada, Australia, New Zealand). At a clear distance, the 'catch-up' was graphically depicted by some core European countries (UK, France, Belgium, Switzerland, Sweden), followed on their turn by some European 'latecomers' (the Netherlands, Germany, Norway), while at the lower left extreme, there were some 'peripheral' countries (Italy, Portugal, Argentina, Brazil). The countries not (yet) obeying to this law of development, like Thailand, Turkey, and India, were given dots at the bottom left of the quadrant. China, all African countries, and the Soviet Union were not even mentioned. Some students of world motorization even ventured somewhat further, presenting graphs that included such countries as Zaire and Cuba, confirming only how much car ownership depended on income.

Such insights also bounced back to the West, for instance, when analyzing the stratification of car ownership in the United States, where in 1974 less than half of the households earning less than $3,000 owned a car (and only 6.2 percent two cars), while nearly all households earning $10,000 or more (94 percent and higher) owned a car (and more than half two cars).[241]

In contrast to these easy pictures, the spread of the automobile system over the globe during the worldwide postwar boom has been analyzed in this chapter as a complex and messy process that defies the diffusion myth, the myth on which the dominance of the economists in the development discourse during the years covered by this chapter, was based. And yet, some dominant forces cannot be argued away: the previous pages do no leave much doubt that the all-pervasive development discourse was the result of a concerted effort of the West to refashion its imperialist drive. Under the guidance of world power America, a set of soft power tools were designed, varying from the Decade of Development and the Alliance of Progress to the Peace Corps, to enforce modernization if coercion was not needed. The enormous success of this formula, however, can be explained only through an eager reception, and adaptation to local circumstances, by national elites who struggled with the formidable task to overcome the inequalities and other harmful heterogeneities left behind by the colonizers and to lead their countries toward independence, and by a wealthy contingent of the middle classes in their wake. The wishes and expectations these elites represented remained largely in the dark in the present chapter (we know so little!), but the seeming generosity of the World Bank and related loan providers appeared to be crucial in the local decisions, remarkably uniform, to modernize. It was as if the *magic* of the car had been transferred to the road, to the car *system*. Now, transport investments formed the secret gateway to modernity.

The presence of such middle-class segments seems to have been crucial. Hence, we argued, the difference in motorization between Africa and Latin America, at least to a certain extent. We also gave several examples of national developments that relativized this conclusion: they do not explain why, for instance, Singapore, or Japan for that matter, followed a slightly different path of a restrained use of the car. But everywhere, roads had become a weapon in the Cold War, a weapon that became all the more effective because of, as a parallel process, the shaping of a "mobile personality," as we have seen. Roadbuilding, we concluded, was a deeply political process, just as much the spread of the car society over the global was equally deeply racialized. In other words, to modernize somewhere, people elsewhere had to suffer, and their sufferance was deemed 'inevitable,' a sacrifice for 'progress.' This was, to borrow the title of a recent analysis of the sufferings of Latin American people, the real face of "cruel modernity," and hence, one is inclined to say, of 'cruel mobility.'[242] We have seen in this chapter how the cruelest form of mobility, migration, and the proliferation of refugees colored the entire postwar phase, a form of mobility that represents the generally *carless* counterpart of Western Exuberance.

***

This chapter showed the 'export' of the car society took place primarily through infrastructure, the exact *opposite* of the spread of automobilism before World War II, when it was the car and its immediately surrounding cultural traits that got appropriated, often well before a national network was in place, by the early 1930s. Somehow, the idea had been formulated that roads incite automobilism to emerge and to grow, an idea that after the war would become one of the crucial 'soft weapons' in the cold war between road and rail, mobilized by an enormously powerful road lobby, consisting of construction companies and consultancies actively supported, if not ideologically steered, by lending agencies and the governments they represented. Whatever the motives of the local elites, it was clear from the onset that the 'export' of the car system also implied an export of a certain solution to the coordination crisis, the struggle between rail and road that had started in the 1920s in the West as well as in its colonies (see chap. 1), and which was finalized, in most cases, in a clear victory of the latter during the current phase. Indeed, the globalization of the 'car society' took place primarily through its systemic aspects, representing a mobility of ideas and concepts of managers, not primarily car users. From this perspective, the important role of the motor bus should not surprise us: modernization beyond the West had a clearly collective 'flavor' and, through this, a flavor of seriousness over hedonism as well. The automotive system was meant to be a counterforce against the 'collectivity' of public transport. There can be no doubt that this counterforce was applied aggressively, without much consideration for local circumstances.

***

We have seen an enormous variety of this struggle. Let us, to conclude, and in the light of the insights gained so far, analyze a typical "development and policy study" of the 1950s and 1960s, through which Uganda got its mobility history written for the British Colonial Office and the colonial Uganda government. An economist who consulted the traffic engineers of the (Tropical Section of the) Road Research Laboratory in the United Kingdom and stayed in Uganda for a year, the report's author (E. K. Hawkins) was explicitly asked by the government to advice on the future role of the railways and "the desirability of introducing road freight licensing in Uganda, both as a general measure, and also as a solution to the problem of road/

rail competition." As a landlocked country neighboring Kenya, Tanganyika, Belgian Congo, Ruanda Urundi, and Sudan, and one of the richest settler colonies with a dense transport network, Uganda cooperated with the first two neighbors (also English colonies) in a common railway company, as we have seen, mainly to transport cotton and coffee. On a population of 6.5 million, non-Africans formed only 1 percent, of which the largest group consisting of the Asian community had managed to capture trade and transport, including trucking.

By 1957, Uganda counted 8,369 miles of classified roads, and about 10,000 miles of local roads, resulting in a road density of 0.14 miles per square mile of land area (nearly double that of Tanganyika, 70 percent of South Africa, and one-tenth of the UK). By then, every other European owned a car, as did one in every ten Asians and one per thousand of African descent. Africans were driving motorcycles, which they used much less frequently and intensively than cars. Nonetheless, Hawkins's study revealed Africans were by then willing to buy a motorized vehicle at a much lower absolute level of income than Europeans and Asians were. Combined with its less frequent use, one wonders what different mobility culture is hiding behind these statistics, of which we know virtually nothing.[243]

What we *do* know is that expanding our analysis beyond the West, as we have done in this chapter, provided the counterexample of the Soviet Union that managed to modernize on the basis of its extremely intensely used railway system. This already suggests there were indeed many modernities, brought about by many modernization and motorization processes. In an earlier study, I already distinguished between two basic Western 'models,' one for 'full, urbanized countries' such as the UK and the Netherlands, another for 'empty countries' such as the United States, southern Sweden, and large parts of France, acknowledging the possibility (to be confirmed by further study) of a third subcategory, covering the European periphery, with its weakly developed middle class. Now, we are able to add a Russian model (modernization without the car), an Indian (meandering between a Western and a Soviet model), a Chinese (modernization 'on two legs,' consciously modernizing the 'old' at the same time), a Latin American (with a populist modernization, neglecting the middle class), and an African version (emphasizing road freight rather than the passenger car, and collectivity).

In-between subcategories can be distinguished, such as Japan (an extremely urban version of the Western model, with relatively few cars), or the South and South East Asian group of countries (Indonesia, Singapore, Vietnam) with a preponderance of two- and three-wheelers, rickshaws, and especially the minibus, and several African and Latin American countries that do not fit in their 'continental model,' such as Mexico, with its double emphasis on rural and intercontinental roads, or South Africa, or the Sahel countries, or the Bedouin nomads with their dominance of trucks replacing camels. Many of these 'multiple modernities' did not smoothly overlap but rather caused conflicts: "Modernity is a structure," Chinese thinker Wang Hui asserted, "that contains internal conflicts." The "contradictions of modernity" are "difficult to resolve." After the examples provided in the previous pages, this is perhaps a better acknowledgment of the fundamental contradictions within modernity itself than the often seen assertion that "the view that tradition and innovation are necessarily in conflict has begun to seem overly abstract and unreal." It is the conflict between municipal planners and minibus drivers, the struggle between rickshaw pullers and local politicians who wanted to get rid of them, that generated "counter-modernities."[244] From this perspective, the oxcart with new ball bearings in China and the jeepney adjusted to local needs in the Philippines were as 'modern' as the Shinkansen in Japan or the flyover in Delhi.

At the same time, we observed a converging trend, brought about by a very powerful roadbuilding lobby, led by the International Road Federation, and representing a driving force of this process that has hitherto been fully underexposed in the historiography: the lobby complex of construction companies, consultancies, intimately intertwined with government laboratories and related institutions such as the Bureau of Public Roads (US) and the Transport and Road Research Laboratory (UK), and, not to be forgotten, academia, from geographers to economists, traffic engineers to sociologists. The emphasis on high-tech solutions, and the costly earthmoving and other equipment necessary to bring this about, clearly favored Western businesses and advisers (which subsequently were financed from the World Bank loans), despite the many proposals at the conferences of both the IRF and the PIARC to emphasize the importance of low-cost solutions. At these conferences, the admiration for the very big schemes—the Pan-American, the Trans-Saharan, the Asian Highway—was always present. The convergent forces at this level were multiple, from the emphasis on roads and the car, via an urban bias in the planning, up to the all-pervasive force: the emergence of a middle class that in the car found an instrument of distinction that the concurrently rising working class could certainly not acquire, even not if it was backed by populist governments (such as in Argentina) who at least managed to distribute a flood of toys and sewing machines among the population.

***

The historian's stare at this modernist level, however, driven by a Western bias, has blocked our view on the extreme layeredness of the mobility system, as this level was superposed on an already existing level, thus creating two societies and two mobilities, in a way parallel with the rural-urban divide, partially coinciding with what economists later would call formal and informal economies, or dual structure, or coevalness, or, to quote Ernst Bloch, the *Gleichzeitigkeit des Ungleichzeitigen* (simultaneity of the nonsimultaneous). On top of that, regional disparities seem to have been much more crass than in the West, further adding to what Western observers often experienced as 'disorder,' but in any case necessitating a different type of analysis. How to deal, for instance, with the phenomenon of African urbanization without economic growth?[245] The underlying, 'subaltern' level consisted of head porterage and walking in general, along footpaths through the bush (in case of war even consisting of a secret network, as we saw in Angola), of wheelbarrows and bullock carts, of pirate taxis and mosquito buses, of hand-pulled rickshaws in Indian Kolkata, on the millions and millions of bicycles in the expanding cities and in the illegal jeepneys and other minibuses, that slipped through the mazes of the urban planners and the municipal authorities. The stare at the 'new' layer strengthens the diffusion myth, whereas the acknowledgment of the 'old' layer and its own processes of modernization (the ball bearings in China, for instance) help us to redefine mobility history, to relativize and critique the 'master narrative' of the fast lane.

This is not to say the "old layer" was indigenous while the "new layer" came from the West: "No one denies that Western invasion and expansion had a decisive influence upon the development of modern Chinese history," Wang Hui concedes, "but this is not equivalent to saying that Chinese history did not undergo its own particular evolutionary process. The seeds of modernity already existed." This is easier said than proven, however, as the studies that could unearth such 'countermodernities' are still to be undertaken. Such studies are thwarted by the cultural cleft that often keeps the two worlds apart: "The indigenous material [resulting from local research] frequently reveals ambiguities," researchers Murray Chapman and R. Mansell Prothero concluded, "which do not fit the discrete criteria of time and place associated with western concepts and terms." Commenting on the futility of organizing traffic surveys they add: "There is simply no point in selecting terms which are commonly used in western mobility studies, then attempting to translate them into indigenous language for a questionnaire survey in which they will not be understood by those to whom the questions are addressed." As to the new level: *if* there were origin and destination studies undertaken (further microstudies are necessary here, but it seems trendsetter World Bank contented itself with quite straightforward cost and benefit studies, limited mostly to calculations of transportation cost reduction), such deliberations did not play any role in the public debate, or in the specialized public sphere of *Road International* (or the *PIARC Bulletin*, for that matter). Road design and construction seemed to be a part of what Nebojša Nakicenovic in another context has called "homeostasis," the seemingly self-organizing process, which partly can explain the convergence trend.[246]

The constant statistical comparisons between countries regarding the relative length of their network, the size of their car and truck park (and the systematic neglect of all other mobility options), whether undertaken by a reformist military dictator or a Communist chairman, a Peronist president, or a civil servant in newly independent Ghana, accompanied a frenzy of road network building, largely independent from any demand (modernization theorists invented a nice term for this, as we saw: investment in excess) in the simple belief that the cars would automatically follow, whereas Western consultants meanwhile played on the fear for congestion and 'chaos.' As we saw earlier, a recent statistical analysis showed road networks were more extensive in countries reigned by authoritarian regimes, a phenomenon that already in 1952 had been given a historical basis by civil engineer "major" H. E. Aldington, who referred to Napoleon, Hitler, and Mussolini as "great road-builders—a sobering thought." Yet, there was not a modernizing country on earth that did not at least adorn itself with a basic network, even if this meant the destruction of parts of the underlying networks, especially the railroads.[247] This chapter showed that road (network) building formed the core of modernization in two respects: it enhanced transport efficiency (higher speed, ordered flow), and at the same time, it was a token of being at the very vanguard of modernization. We have seen, in this chapter, several examples of the latter taking the upper hand over the former. Mexico may serve as the most extreme example, with its new roads that hardly showed an increase of traffic. What was sold here was expectation rather than actual fact, ideology rather than rationality, despite the modernity claims.

When Indiana University's economist George W. Wilson was asked by the World Bank in the mid-1960s to assess the "impact of highway investment on development," his conclusion may have been disappointing for many developmentalists: those investments "may be a necessary but not sufficient condition to induce economic growth." Hence, "a "much more skeptical attitude toward transport appears essential," even if in all cases investigated, "there was a rise in traffic along the new facility." In general, he concluded, "where there is a *general* lack of dynamism, there is also a greater probability that a specific investment will not become much of a success." Apart from investments, this study seemed to suggest, modernization also requires a *willingness*, if not an *eagerness*, to be modern. In the "theory of transport and development" he tried to design based on these conclusions, he again warned against expecting "magical properties in transport investments that warrant the excessive attention frequently paid to them ... Transport investment is no more an initiator of growth than any other form of investment or deliberate policy. Under some conditions it may turn out to be strategic but the same can be said about any specific investment or policy." He then introduced the term accessibility to justify why investments in roads were preferable over all other alternatives.[248]

***

Whether the road filled up quickly or slowly (or not at all) with cars and motorcycles, the 'freedom of movement' indulged by a fledgling middle class was much more than a constrained pursuit of pleasure for the white nuclear family. If it is true, as some cultural studies scholars would have it, that 'classes' have become increasingly "products of the collective imagination," then the middle class is all the more convincingly defined by the car, as dream and expectation.[249] But like in the West, the expectation of automotive mobility proliferated beyond the middle class, into the lower middle class and the urban workers (as drivers of buses, taxis, and trucks), and even parts of the marginal and subaltern groups (as passengers of these buses, taxis, and trucks, or as pedestrians who had to cross or walk along these roads, when carrying their goods on their head). From this perspective, it is indeed astonishing that Communism did not come up with an alternative, apart from stubbornly (Soviet Union) sticking with an overburdened railway system or naively (Mao) opting in favor of the bicycle. It testifies to the poverty of Marxist theory when it comes to technology, let alone mobility, that, for instance, no efforts have been undertaken during the Western 'development decade,' to theorize the collectivity of public transport (or develop a critique of the individualism of the car) and the related phenomenon of 'passengering' as opposed to the driver experience. Or are we missing something here? Are Khrushchev's words about the lower need for the car in a Communist society an expression of alternative theorizing we, as Western mobility historians, know nothing about, yet?

Instead, we are stuck with the dichotomy of public versus private transport, a fully inadequate distinction between two systems emanating from two different centuries, which now, after a long period of gestation, start to form a comprehensive system, especially in the metropolises. Would such a theory have opened a vista on the existence of 'Communist mobilities,' or 'Muslim mobilities'? If we are to believe Tamim Ansary, who connected the problematic modernization of the Muslim world to the absence of "a collective 'self'" due to the only very recent emergence of many nation-states, and who defined Islam as "a framework" rather than a monolithic religion, the answer to such a question would clearly be positive. And such an answer, as far as motorization is concerned, would certainly be colored by the alleged absence of such a 'self,' although even the "countermodernity" of the Islamic world presupposes the emergence of a middle class. If the West was meanwhile fully discredited and could not provide the values, as Ansary asserted, it could and would nonetheless provide the cars.²⁵⁰

If it is true that Western automobilism has been decisively shaped by the desires of a middle-class nuclear family that needed to distinguish itself from a close-by working class through the acquisition of a very costly contraption, and if it is also true that it was this 'model' that was exported together with the spread of the road infrastructure (two conditions the present study supports), then the extreme layeredness of non-Western mobility cultures becomes understandable, not so much as a sequence of subcultures that should have its course, as diffusionists would have it, but as a persistent structure of inequality.

Notes

Epigraphs: Flannery O'Connor, "Wise Blood," in *Collected Works: Wise Blood / A Good Man Is Hard to Find / The Violent Bear It Away / Everything That Rises Must Converge / Essays and Letters* by Flannery O'Connor, ed. Sally Fitzgerald (New York: Library of America, 1988), 24; John Maynard Keynes quoted in Amy L. S. Staples, *The Birth of Development: How the World Bank, Food and Agriculture Organization, and World Health Organization Changed the World, 1945–1965* (Kent, OH: Kent State University Press, 2006), 40.

1. Ernesto Che Guevara, *Notas de viaje: Diario en motocicleta* (Buenos Aires: Distal, 2000); for a recent filmic rendering of Guevara's trip, see Walter Saller, dir., *The Motorcycle Diaries* (Universal City, CA: Focus Features, 2004). According to Manuela Boatcă, a semi-periphery belongs to "a middle stratum [of countries]—both agent of and subject to exploitation," giving the Eastern European socialist countries, Mexico, Brazil, and India as examples. Manuela Boatcă, "Semiperipheries in the World-System: Reflecting Eastern European and Latin American Experiences," *Journal of World-Systems Research* 12, no. 11 (2006): 322.
2. See Jennifer Van Vleck, *Empire of the Air: Aviation and the American Ascendency* (Cambridge, MA: Harvard University Press, 2013) as reviewed by Sabine Dworog, H-SOZ-U-KULT@H-NET.MSU.EDU (2 September 2014).
3. Richard N. Cooper, *The Economies of Interdependence: Economic Policy in the Atlantic Community* (New York: McGraw-Hill, 1968), 3 (128 million), 68, table 3-3 (Europeans and Americans).
4. Mike Mason, *Turbulent Empires: A History of Global Capitalism since 1945* (Montreal: McGill-Queen's University Press, 2018), 192.
5. Petra Goedde, "Global Cultures," in *Global Interdependence: The World after 1945*, ed. Akira Iriye (Cambridge, MA: Belknap Press, 2014), 540; Giuliano Garavini, *After Empires: European Integration, Decolonization, and the Challenge from the Global South 1957–1986*, trans. Richard R. Nybakken (Oxford: Oxford University Press, 2013), 11 (world-system).
6. As has been done convincingly, e.g., in Marc Frey, Sönke Kunkel, and Corinna R. Unger, eds., *International Organizations and Development, 1945–1990* (London: Palgrave Macmillan, 2014). On the OECD's and NGOs' role, see Marc Frey, Sönke Kunkel, and Corinna R. Unger, "Introduction: International Organizations, Global Development, and the Making of the Contemporary World," in Frey et al., *International*

Organizations, 8–11; and esp. Matthias Schmelzer, "A Club of the Rich to Help the Poor? The OECD, 'Development,' and the Hegemony of Donor Countries," in Frey et al., *International Organizations*, 172 (soft power); and Kevin O'Sullivan, "A 'Global Nervous System': The Rise and Rise of European Humanitarian NGOs, 1945–1985," in Frey et al., *International Organizations*, 196 (NGO decade).

7. Walt W. Rostow, *The Stages of Economic Growth: A Non-Communist Manifesto* (Cambridge: Cambridge University Press, 1971), 104.

8. Michael Brett, *Approaching African History* (Woolbridge: James Currey, 2013), 290–300; Hartmut Kaelble *Kalter Krieg und Wohlfahrtsstaat: Europa 1945–1989* (Munich: Verlag C. H. Beck, 2011), 154–167; Eric Hobsbawm, *The Age of Extremes: The Short Twentieth Century 1914–1991* (London: abacus, 2013), 246.

9. Michael Mann, *The Sources of Social Power, vol. 3: Global Empires and Revolution, 1890–1945* (Cambridge: Cambridge University Press, 2012), 38–39 (Mau Mau, Obama); Amelia H. Lyons, "French or Foreign? The Algerian Migrants' Status at the End of Empire (1962–1968)" *Journal of Modern European History* 12, no. 1 (2014): 126 (ethnic group, wild migration); Luca Ciabarri, "Biographies of Roads, Biographies of Nations: History, Territory and the Road Effect in Post-conflict Somaliland," in *The Making of the African Road*, ed. Kurt Beck, Gabriel Klaeger, and Michael Stasik (Leiden: Brill, 2017): 248 (Sudan); Tamim Ansary, *Destiny Disrupted: A History of the World through Islamic Eyes* (New York: PublicAffairs, 2009), 319 (new countries); Richard W. Mansbach, "The Soviet Union, the United Nations, and the Developing States," in *The Soviet Union and the Developing Nations*, ed. Roger E. Kanet (Baltimore: Johns Hopkins University Press, 1974), 261 (49 percent).

10. Migration and tourism statistics from Akira Iriye, "The Making of a Transnational World," in Iriye, *Global Interdependence*, 738, 740; Goedde, "Global Cultures," 560–561 (foreign-born), 563 (lifelong), 563–564 (wealthy and not wealthy migrants); Arturo Escobar, "Anthropology and the Development Encounter: The Making and Marketing of Development Anthropology," *American Ethnologist* 18, no. 4 (1991): 658 (prominent); Dipesh Chakrabarty, *Provincializing Europe: Postcolonial Thought and Historical Difference* (Princeton, NJ: Princeton University Press, 2000); Leelananda de Silva, "From ECAFE to ESCAP: Pioneering a Regional Perspective," in *Unity and Diversity in Development Ideas: Perspectives from the UN Regional Commissions*, ed. Yves Berthelet (Bloomington: Indiana University Press, 2004), 136 (UNDP). The program was the successor of its Expanded Program for Technical Assistance Board (TAB).

11. James Ferguson, "Anthropology and Its Evil Twin: 'Development' in the Constitution of a Discipline," in *International Development and the Social Sciences: Essays on the History and Politics of Knowledge*, ed. Frederick Cooper and Randall Packard (Berkeley: University of California Press, 1997), 153 (fossils), 154 (one-story), 155 (binary), 158 (imperial planning), 159 (economists, backward), 160 (dubious); Carey A. Watt and Michael Mann, eds., *Civilizing Missions in Colonial and Postcolonial South Asia: From Improvement to Development* (London: Anthem Press, 2011).

12. Sönke Kunkel, "Systeme des Wissens, Visionen von Fortschritt: Die Vereinigten Staaten, das Jahrzehnt der Modernisierungstheorie und die Planung Nigerias 1954–1965," *Archiv für Sozialgeschichte* 48 (2008): 162 (science), 163 (*conditio*), 164 (warfare), 165 (soft power, natives), 180 (evolutionary), 182 (credit, willingness); Jonathan Steele, "Who Started It?" [review of Odd Arne Westad, *The Cold War*, 2017], *London Review of Books* (25 January 2018), 25 (Soviet aid); Corinna R. Unger, "Histories of Development and Modernization: Findings, Reflections, Future Research," H-Soz-Kult (9 December 2010), 8–9.

13. Jale Parla, "Car Narratives: A Subgenre in Turkish Novel Writing," *South Atlantic Quarterly* 102, nos. 2–3 (2003): 540–541 (Tanpinar), 544 (Ağaoğlu; emphasis added). On Tanpinar's protagonists, whose narcissism seems to make them exceptionally prone to the modern craze of automobilism, see also Süha Oğuzertem, "Fictions of Narcissism: Metaphysical and Psychosexual Conflicts in the Stories of Ahmet Hamdi Tanpinar," *Turkish Studies Association Bulletin* 14, no. 2 (1990).
14. Serhat Güvenç, "The Cold War Origins of the Turkish Motor Industry: The Tuzla Jeep, 1954–1971," *Turkish Studies* 15, no. 3 (2014): 539 (Jeeps), 540 (invasion, 23,000), 541 (Marshall Plan, mules), 546 (Tuzla). For roadbuilding in Turkey and the Marshall Plan, see Frank Schipper, *Driving Europe: Building Europe on Roads in the Twentieth Century* (Amsterdam: aksant, 2008).
15. Unger, "Histories of Development," 10; David C. Engerman and Corinna R. Unger, "Introduction: Towards a Global History of Modernization," *Diplomatic History* 33, no. 3 (2009): 377 (scope), 379 (offensive); Roger E. Kanet, "Soviet Attitudes toward Developing Nations since Stalin," in Kanet, *Soviet Union and the Developing Nations*, 29 (coexistence); Jan S. Prybyla, "The Sino-Soviet Split and the Developing Nations," in Kanet, *Soviet Union and the Developing Nations*, 268 (European), 274 (1956), 289 ($6.8 billion, forty), 291, Appendix 10-A (9 percent), 292, Appendix 10-B (half).
16. Mark Atwood Lawrence, "Universal Claims, Local Uses: Reconceptualizing the Vietnam Conflict, 1945–60," in *Global History: Interactions Between the Universal and the Local*, ed. A. G. Hopkins (London: Palgrave Macmillan, 2006), 231. For a historical overview of USSR–Third World relations, see Andrzej Korbonski and Francis Fukuyama, eds., *The Soviet Union and the Third World: The Last Three Decades* (Ithaca, NY: Cornell University Press, 1987).
17. Kanet, "Soviet Attitudes," 32 (ignorance); Holland Hunter, *Soviet Transport Experience: Its Lessons for Other Countries* (Washington, DC: Brookings Institution, Transport Research Program, 1968), 41 (traffic growth); Rostow, *Stages of Economic Growth*, 102 (GNP), 149 (*adventure*; emphasis added).
18. Hunter, *Soviet Transport Experience*, 50 (low priority), 61 (modest, secret), 62, fig. 7 (reduction), 71 (underutilization), 80 (protest), 81 (capacity), 87 (non-trucking); J. N. Westwood, "Soviet Railway Development," *Soviet Studies* 11, no. 1 (2001): 24 (Soviet network length), 33 (US network length), 34 (workers); on prewar trucking regulation's exemption of non-trucking companies, see Gijs Mom and Ruud Filarski, *Van transport naar mobiliteit: De mobiliteitsexplosie (1895–2005)* (Zutphen: Walburg Pers, 2008), 297–309.
19. Wilfred Owen, *Strategy for Mobility* (Washington, DC: Brookings Institution, 1964), 11, table 1.2 (55 percent); Hunter, *Soviet Transport Experience*, 89 (minister and head quotes), 91 (roadlessness, cutting off), 92 (1.5 million [fig. 13], length of paved roads).
20. Martin Crouch, "Problem of Soviet Urban Transport," *Soviet Studies* 31, no. 2 (1979): 237, table 1 (bus systems, etc.), 238, table 2 (surpassed); Hunter, *Soviet Transport Experience*, 98 (66 percent); John Howe, "Transport for the Poor or Poor Transport? A General Review of Rural Transport Policy in Developing Countries with Emphasis on Low-Income Areas," International Institute for Infrastructural, Hydraulic and Environmental Engineering Working Paper IP-12 (October 1996), 27–28 (agricultural sector); Wilfred Owen, *Distance and Development: Transport and Communications in India* (Washington, DC: Brookings Institution, 1968), 160, table A-9; Rostow, *Stages of Economic Growth*, 93 (thirty-five), 133 (mass-consumption).
21. Hunter, *Soviet Transport Experience*, 96 (people's project), 100 (very modest), 102 (subway), 103n4 (Stalin), 105 (Khrushchev). According to György Péteri, quoted by Katalin Tóth, "The Invisible Cyclist and the History of Mobility in Budapest

(1930–2010)," paper presented at the CPSUM workshop in Munich (5–6 February 2016), 7n1, Khrushchev made a similar remark about rental car systems during a speech in Paris in 1960; Luminita Gatejel, *Warten, hoffen und endlich fahren: Auto und Sozialismus in der Sowjetunion, in Rumänien und der DDR (1956–1989/91)* (Frankfurt: Campus Verlag, 2014) 12 (20th Congress); on Khrushchev's plan, see also Jukka Gronow and Sergei Zhuravlev, "Soviet Luxuries from Champagne to Private Cars," in *Pleasures in Socialism. Leisure and Luxury in the Eastern Bloc*, ed David Crowley and Susan E. Reid (Evanston, IL: Northwestern University Press, 2010), 134–135; for the hiring of cars from public garages at the beginning of the twentieth century, see Gijs Mom, *Atlantic Automobilism: Emergence and Persistence of the Car, 1895–1940* (New York: Berghahn Books, 2015), 103–104.
22. Gatejel, *Warten*, 12 (Kosygin), 34 (one-tenth), 66 (standard), 104 (two decades), 109 (car-rental); Leonid Brezhnev, Alexei Kosygin, Andrei Gromyko, Yuri Andropov, and Mikhail Gorbachev had either an engineering or an agronomy degree. Joel Andreas, *Rise of the Red Engineers: The Cultural Revolution and the Origins of China's New Class* (Stanford, CA: Stanford University Press, 2009), 1.
23. Valentina Fava is the acknowledged expert on Eastern European car production. See, e.g., Valentina Fava, "In Search of a Czechoslovak People's Car: Skoda Auto and the 'Soviet Model of Management,'" *Actes du Gerpisa* 39 (December 2005).
24. Hunter, *Soviet Transport Experience*, 106 (one million), 112 (six-lane), 123 (misreading quote); Gatejel, *Warten*, 114 (GDR).
25. M. A. Akhunova, B. A. Tulepbaev and J. S. Borisov, "Motor Transport in a Developing Area (ii) Soviet Central Asia," in *The Economic and Social Effects of the Spread of Motor Vehicles: An International Centenary Tribute*, ed. Theo Barker (London: Macmillan, 1987), 258–259; Kazuyuki Fujita, Kiichiro Hatoyama, and Sergey V. Shaposhnikov, "A Historical Overview of Railway Construction and its Association with Economic Growth in Russia," *Journal of the East Asia Society for Transportation Studies* 12 (2017): 235, table 1 (1990).
26. Kathy Burrell and Kathrin Hörschelmann, "Introduction: Understanding Mobility in Soviet and East European Socialist and Post-Socialist States," in *Mobilities in Socialist and Post-Socialist States: Societies on the Move*, ed. Kathy Burrell and Kathrin Hörschelmann (London: Palgrave Macmillan, 2014), 9 (imaginative mobilities, Imagined West), 17 (bonding); Alexander Vari, "Introduction: Escaping the Monotony of Everyday Life under Socialism," in *Socialist Escapes: Breaking Away from Ideology and Everyday Routine in Eastern Europe, 1945–1989*, ed. Cathleen M. Giustino, Catherine J. Plum, and Alexander Vari (New York: Berghahn Books, 2013), 13 (Pobdas).
27. Lyubomir Pozharliev, "Collectivity vs Connectivity: The Techno-Historical Example of Motorway Peripherization in Former Yugoslavia," paper presented at the T²M conference "Spinoffs of Mobility: Technology, Risk and Innovation," Philadelphia (18–21 September 2014), 1 (peripheralized), 9 (two graphs: "share of railway and road transport," in percent [not explained as a share of what: trips or passenger- and ton-km?]). This graph is not reproduced in the eventual publication Lyubomir Pozharliev, "Collectivity vs Connectivity: Highway peripherization in former Yugoslavia (1940s–1980s)," *Journal of Transport History* 37, no. 2 (2016). Bogdan Mieczkowski, *Transportation in Eastern Europe: Empirical Findings* (Boulder, CO: East European Quarterly, 1978), 152 (no evidence), 158 (road transport within Comecon), 191 (first).
28. György Péteri, "Streetcars of Desire: Cars and Automobilism in Communist Hungary (1958–70)," *Social History* 34, no. 1 (2009): 3 (faster than buses), 4 (spiritual workers), 5, table 3 (densities), 6 (*lemaradásunk*), 7 (system-neutral), 8 (socialist car), 9 (*fetishism*),

10 (pathological), 12 (vulgar), 13 (impossible), 17, table 4 (fatality rates), 23 (general purpose), 24 (Mercedes).
29. Vari, "Introduction," 3 (leisure practices); Xavier Galmiche, "Die Kuh und der Mercedes: Die Umdeutung von Sinnbilder der Vergangenheit im tschechischen sozialistischen Aufbauroman," in *Zukunftsvorstellungen und Staatliche Planung im Sozialismus: Die Tschechoslowakei im ostmitteleuropäischen Kontext 1945–1989*, ed. Martin Schulze Wessel and Christiane Brenner (Munich: Oldenbourg Verlag, 2010), 242 (Řezáč).
30. Shunsuke Tsurumi, *A Cultural History of Postwar Japan 1945–1980* (London: KPI, 1987) 26 (Fifteen Years). Kaelble, *Kalter Krieg*, 62–68 (passim); R. Keith Schoppa, *Revolution and Its Past: Identities and Change in Modern Chinese History* (Boston: Prentice Hall, 20113), 305 (450 million); M. William Steele, "A Modern Infrastructure of Manchukuo: Where Did All the Cement Come From?" paper presented at the East Asian Environmental History Conference, Kagawa University, Japan (22–25 October 2015), 13; Hobsbawm, *Age of Extremes*, 243 (precipitously) (see esp. chap. 15, "Third World and Revolution"); Cooper, *Economies of Interdependence*, 195 (OECD).
31. Jonathan D. Spence, *The Search for Modern China* (London: Hutchinson, 1990) 471 (rats), 479 (Marx), 496 (rigidly); Jonathan Fenby, *Chiang Kai-shek: China's Generalissimo and the Nation He Lost* (New York: Carroll & Graf Publishers, 2004), 475 (railway destruction), 478 (tanks).
32. Spence, *Search for Modern China*, 487, 481–483 (Zhengzhou), 490 (reactionaries); Siu-tong Kwok, "Cultural Migration and Historiography in the Regions of China since the End of World War II," *Berliner China-Hefte* 26 (2004): 54 (intellectual flight); Mason, *Turbulent Empires*, 109 (land reform), 110 (a third); Michael Mann, *The Sources of Social Power, vol. 4: Globalizations, 1945–2011* (Cambridge: Cambridge University Press, 2013), 219 (casualties); Odd Arne Westad, "The Great Transformation: China in the Long 1970s," in *The Shock of the Global: The 1970s in Perspective*, ed. Niall Ferguson, Charles S. Maier, Erez Manela, and Daniel J. Sargent (Cambridge, MA: Belknap Press, 2010): 66 (growth rates); Yajun Mo, "Itineraries for a Republic: Tourism and Travel Culture in Modern China, 1866–1954" (PhD diss., University of California, Santa Cruz, 2011), 423 (tourism); Frank Dikötter, *The Tragedy of Liberation: A History of the Chinese Revolution, 1945–1957* (London: Bloomsbury, 2013), 257 (standstill); Spence, *Search for Modern China*, 493 (campaigns).
33. Edward J. M. Rhoads, "Cycles of Cathay: A History of the Bicycle in China," *Transfers* 2, no. 2 (2012): 106 (Riboud, museum); Spence, *Search for Modern China*, 513 (pedicab workers). The remark by one interviewee in Xinxin Zhang and Ye Sang, *Chinese Lives: An Oral History of Contemporary China*, ed. W. J. F. Jenner and Delia Davin (New York: Pantheon Books, 1987), 54, is somewhat enigmatic: as late as 1985, the interviewee tells about his wife's father, who "is a worker in a transport-cooperative. Or you can put it more bluntly and say he pedals a pedicab." The disappearance of the rickshaw in China is controversially discussed (interview, Shao Jian, 7 July 2014).
34. Mason, *Turbulent Empires*, 110 (Tibet), 112 (success), 139 (Xinjiang); Ji Xianlin, *The Cowshed: Memories of the Chinese Cultural Revolution*, trans. Chenxin Jiang (New York: New York Review Books, 2015), 173; Spence, *Search for Modern China*, 496 (1949), 515 (Five-Year Plan), 518–519 (1955 and 1956), 531–532 (army), 525 (Ho Chi Minh), 503–505 (enemy), 526–527 (Bandung); Hobsbawm, *Age of Extremes*, 358 (nonaligned); interview, Shao Jian (army in Railway Ministry); Jens Damm and Bettina Gransow, "Zwischen Kuli-Export und Business-Netzwerken: Muster interner, inter- und transnationaler chinesischer Migration seit dem 19. Jahrhundert," in *Migrationen: Globale Entwicklungen seit 1850*, ed. Albert Kraler, Karl Husa, Veronika Bilger, and Irene Stacher (Vienna: Mandelbaum Verlag, 2007), 223 (forty million); Tu

Wei-ming, "Cultural China: The Periphery as the Center," *Daedalus* 120, no. 2 (1991): 12, estimated the Chinese diaspora at twenty to thirty million (17: Guangdong and Fujian); Susanne Weigelin-Schwiedrzik and Kim Rottenberger-Kwok, "Chinese Migration im Indischen Ozean," in *Der Indische Ozean: Das afro-asiatische Mittelmeer als Kultur- und Wirtschaftsraum*, ed. Dietmar Rothermund and Susanne Weigelin-Schwiedrzik (Vienna: Verein für Geschichte und Sozialkunde / Promedia Verlag, 2004), 156, table (one-tenth, etc.).

35. Shiguru Akita, Gerold Krozewski, and Shoichi Watanabe, "Introduction: The Colombo Plan, Aid Relations, and the International Order of Asia, 1950–65," in *The Transformation of the International Order of Asia: Decolonization, the Cold War, and the Colombo Plan*, ed. Shiguru Akita, Gerold Krozewski, and Shoichi Watanabe (London: Routledge, 2015): 1 (1950), 21 (expansion); Ilya V. Gaiduk, "A Peace Offensive between the Two Wars: Khrushchev's Policy towards Asia, 1953–64," in Akita et al., *Transformation*, 207 (political considerations), 208 (recipient); Robert J. McMahon, "Development Assistance as a Cold War Tool: The United States, International Institutions, and the Political Economy of Asian Development, 1947–65," in Akita et al., *Transformation*, 216 (necessary; the workshop part of the quote is McMahon's conclusion), 217 (prosper), 224 (Kennedy).

36. Tiejun Cheng and Mark Selden, "The Origins and Social Consequences of China's Hukou System," *China Quarterly* 139 (September 1994): 647 (administrators); Spence, *Search for Modern China*, 547 (Mao), 553 (twenty million), 545 (planners), 469 (no mass urbanization); William Hinton, *Fanshen: A Documentary of Revolution in a Chinese Village* (1966), quoted in Bernard Galling, "Foreword " in *The Spiral Road: Change in a Chinese Village through the Eyes of a Communist Party Leader* by Shu-min Huang (Boulder, CO: Westview Press, 1989), x (bourgeois); Mason, *Turbulent Empires*, 114 (Second Five-Year Plan); Ming Ruan, *Deng Xiaoping: Chronicle of an Empire* (Boulder, CO: Westview Press, 1994), 67 (grain), 108–109 (Yun); Neil J. Diamant, *Revolutionizing the Family: Politics, Love, and Divorce in Urban and Rural China, 1949–1968* (Berkeley: University of California Press, 2000), 226 (*hukou*), 228 (Shue); Cheng and Selden, "Origins and Social Consequences," 644 (code of laws); Pál Nyíri, *Mobility and Cultural Authority in Contemporary China* (Seattle: University of Washington Press, 2010), 10 (*propiska*).

37. Spence, *Search for Modern China*, 690; "Value Added by Work Brigades in Railroad and Highway Construction in China, 1952–57; Research Aid," A (ER) 75–74 (Washington, DC: CIA, November 1975), 1–2 (CIA); these figures do not correspond with the data given by Comtois (see fig. 3.2). Regarding the 6,000, the report mentions 14,000 were renewed, 38 percent of this total being new lines and the rest repair of a heavily damaged network.

38. Kenneth Cantlie, *The Railways of China* (London: China Society, 1981), 37 (assistance); Claude Comtois, "Transport and Territorial Development in China (1949–1985)," *Modern Asian Studies* 24, no. 4 (1990): 784 (not compete), 785 (70 percent).

39. "Value Added by Work Brigades," 7, table 4. These statistics are somewhat inconclusive, as the report does not give any data for "simple roads" for the previous four years (cf. ibid., 9n16).

40. Ronald Hsia, "On Capital Formation through Highway Construction in Communist China" (report for the Center for International Studies, MIT, April 1954), 12 (8,000), 13 (repaired), 14, table 1 (newly built), 32 (sixteen times); Comtois, "Transport and Territorial Development," 788.

41. Schoppa, *Revolution and Its Past*, 336 (second Great Leap). In "History of Transportation in the People's Republic of China" (http://en.wikipedia.org/wiki/History_of_transportation_in_the_People%27s_Republic; retrieved on 9 March 2008) it is claimed

that "since 1949 … transportation occupied a relatively low priority in China's national development," while "(t)he drive to modernize the transport system … began in 1978."

42. Xin Liu, *The Mirage of China Anti-humanism, Narcissism, and Corporeality of the Contemporary World* (New York: Berghahn Books, 2009), 43 (appalling); *Highways in China 1949–1990* (Beijing: Ministry of Communications, [1990]), 39 (Black Top), 80 (spectacular); Hsia, "On Capital Formation," 4 (five million, inactive troops), 5 (first stretch), 25n1 (planning), 31–32 (Guomindang), 39 (new); Comtois, "Transport and Territorial Development," 795 (Changjiang).

43. Comtois, "Transport and Territorial Development," 791–792 (qualitative); Schoppa, *Revolution and Its Past*, 328–329 (intellectuals), 331 (deforestation, clogged rails), 332 (family).

44. Chris Bramall, *Chinese Economic Development* (London: Routledge, 2009), 266 (new railways), 269 (disaster, communes); Beverley Hooper, *Foreigners under Mao: Western Lives in China, 1949–1976* (Hong Kong: Hong Kong University Press, 2016), 164 (10,000 experts); Comtois, "Transport and Territorial Development," 793 (military roads); Xun-Hai Zhang, *Enterprise Reforms in a Centrally Planned Economy: The Case of the Chinese Bicycle Industry* (New York: St. Martin's Press, 1992), 12 (abrupt). In the list of members in *Bulletin de l'AIPCR* (2me trimestre 1956), 51–54, China is not mentioned as a member, but the Soviet Union is. (AIPCR is the French equivalent of PIARC.) Vietnam was also a PIARC/AIPCR member (*Bulletin de l'AIPCR* [1957], 3). Permanent International Association of Road Congresses (PIARC), *XIIth World Road Congress, Rome 1964: Proceedings of the Congress* (London, 1964), 320 (China as observer); PIARC, *XIIIth World Road Congress, Tokyo 1967: Proceedings of the Congress* (London, 1967), 6, table (397: China was not mentioned as a member).

45. Schoppa, *Revolution and Its Past*, 357; Maurice Meisner, *Mao's China and After: A History of the People's Republic* (New York: Free Press, 1999), 383 (Snow), 388 (diplomatic), 392 (twenty-eight million); Bramall, *Chinese Economic Development*, 157.

46. Susanne Stein, "'Wir haben nur etwas mehr als zwei Jahre gebraucht . . .': Die Umgestaltung Changchuns zur ersten 'Autostadt' des neuen China, 1953–1956," in *Autostädte im 20. Jahrhundert: Wachstums- und Schrumpfungsprozesse in globaler Perspektive*, ed. Martina Hessler and Günter Riederer (Stuttgart: Franz Steiner Verlag, 2014), 148–149 (Detroit), 153 (Manchukuo), 155 (modern-style), 156 (Moscow), 161 (bank note); G. E. Anderson, *Designated Drivers: How China Plans to Dominate the Global Auto Industry* (Singapore: John Wiley & Sons, 2012), 53 (Soviet advisers); Victor Seow, "Socialist Drive: The First Auto Works and the Contradictions of Connectivity in the Early People's Republic of China," *Journal of Transport History* 35, no. 2 (2014): 147 (Mao), 152 (eighteen thousand, dispatching), 153 (ZIS-150); Beth E. Notar, "Car Crazy: The Rise of Car Culture in China," in *Cars, Automobility and Development in Asia: Wheels of Change*, ed. Arve Hansen and Kenneth Bo Nielsen (London: Routledge, 2017), 154 (Second Auto Works).

47. Anderson, *Designated Drivers*, 53–54, 58; "Shanghai SH760" (http://en.wikipedia.org/wiki/Shanghai_SH760, consulted on 29 July 2019) (Mercedes); Howe, "Transport for the Poor," 29–31 (sixty); Zhang, *Enterprise Reforms*, 9 (bicycles); Huang, *Spiral Road*, 112.

48. Shenggen Fan and Connie Chan-Kang, "Road Development, Economic Growth, and Poverty Reduction in China," DSGD Discussion Paper no. 12 (Washington, DC: International Food Policy Research Institute, Development Strategy and Governance Division, August 2004), 12–13; Seow, "Socialist Drive," 155–156.

49. Zhang, *Enterprise Reforms*, 1 (phases), 8–9 (start of the industry), 9 (Chinese bicycle factory, proverb), 11 (Shanghai), 13 (fixed price), 17 (three provinces); Rhoads, "Cycles of Cathay," 106 (eleven, forty-six).

50. Simon Winchester, *Bomb, Book and Compass: Joseph Needham and the Great Secrets of China* (London: Penguin, 2009), 226 (railway mad), 245–246 (Mao).
51. Ezra Vogel, *Deng Xiaoping and the Transformation of China* (Cambridge, MA: Belknap Press, 2013), 702. For an overview of official modernization policies, see the many contributions to the journal *Chinese Studies in History*, e.g., Fangjun Cao, "Modernization Theory and China's Road to Modernization," *Chinese Studies in History* 43, no. 1 (2009). The layeredness of China's mobility system is also visible linguistically: the bicycle has been called (clearly before people became aware of the car, as *zixingche*, which literally means "vehicle moving on its own" or "autonomous vehicle"). The car's name is a reference to steam (*qi*) in *qi che*.
52. Oral communication with Xu Tao, 22 August 2014 (disaster); on the current leaders' "wholesome condemnations of the Cultural Revolution," see Meisner, *Mao's China and After*, 292–293; Central Committee of the Communist Party of China, "Circular Promulgating the 'Summary of the Guangdong, Fujian Provincial Conference' (Excerpts) (March 1, 1982)," in "China's Coastal Development Strategy, 1979–1984," ed. Lawrence C. Reardon, special issue, *Chinese Law and Government* 27, nos. 3–4 (1994): 84 (chaos); Schoppa, *Revolution and Its Past*, 364 (error). At a symposium in Hangzhou in 2002, Party Central Committee member Du Runsheng declared Mao's "shortcoming" was his too heavy emphasis on "egalitarianism . . ., representing only the demands of peasants." Quoted in Perry Anderson, "Imagining Alternative Modernities," in *The Chinese Model of Modern Development*, ed. Tan Yu Cao (London: Routledge, 2005), 19. At the same symposium, Yu Guangyuan regretted "the crimes committed during the Cultural Revolution cannot be exposed. Even books discussing the lessons of the Cultural Revolution can hardly get approval for publication." He mentioned one such lesson: the "high centralization of power" of "our economic management system." Yu Guangyuan, "Accomplishments and Problems: A Review of China's Reform in the Past Twenty-Three Years," in Cao, *Chinese Model of Modern Development*, 26, 29.
53. Paul Clark, *Youth Culture in China: From Red Guards to Netizens* (Cambridge: Cambridge University Press, 2012), 20 (*Hongweibing*); Huang, *Spiral Road*, 93 (city event); Meisner, *Mao's China and After*, 277 (bound feet), 295 (*wenhua*), 297 (rejecting), 319 (roaders, free mobilization), 367 (caricature). "If the Paris Commune of 1871 was a tragedy, was the Shanghai People's Commune merely a farce? Did Red Guards and 'revolutionary rebels' who imitated the Parisian Communards make history or merely act out a historical parody?" Meisner quoted in Lin Chun, *The Transformation of Chinese Socialism* (Durham, NC: Duke University Press, 2006), 166. On the Cultural Revolution as "an unprecedentedly violent, ignorant, farcical tragedy," see Ji, *Cowshed*, 182.
54. "The Course of Events and Critical Analysis," *Chinese Sociology & Anthropology* 19, no. 2 (1987): 15 (Plenum); Clark, *Youth Culture*, 11 (unprecedented), 12 (underground), 15 (jackets), 16 (reinvention), 17 (street theater), 19 (justified), 20 (*Hongweibing*), 21 (mass singing), 25 (one million), 26 (clerks); Dikötter, *Cultural Revolution*, 101 (5 September).
55. Meisner, *Mao's China and After*, 323 (wanderlust), 327 (Shanghai workers); Stanley Rosen, *Red Guard Factionalism and the Cultural Revolution in Guangzhou (Canton)* (Boulder, CO: Westview Press, 1982), 112 (missions), 116 (18 August); Frank Dikötter, *The Cultural Revolution: A People's History, 1962–1976* (London: Bloomsbury, 2016), 101 (linking up); Ken Ling, *The Revenge of Heaven: Journal of a Young Chinese* (New York: G. P. Putnam's Sons, 1972), 17 (middle-class), 23 (father), 64 (bicycle), 91 (more than thirty), 102 (block quote), 110 (knife fight), 113 (beggars), 116 (baggage rack), 117 (looting), 121 (paradise), 125 (girls on bicycles), 139 (limousines), 165 (Qingdao), 175 (urine), 184 (Red Flag), 238 (white gloves), 255 (sedan), 274 (like

mad), 295 (driving lesson), 318 (excitement), 328 (propaganda trucks), 365 (so happy), 388 (disillusioned); Dikötter, *Cultural Revolution*, 108 (jeep and trucks).
56. Gordon Bennett and Ronald N. Montaperto, *Red Guard: The Political Biography of Dai Hsiao-ai* (Garden City, NY: Doubleday, 1971) 29 (elite), 81 (vehicles), 123 (prosperity).
57. "Course of Events," 80 (ran around), 92 (class war); Meisner, *Mao's China and After*, 354 (suffering); Ruth Earnshaw Lo and Katharine S. Kinderman, *In the Eye of the Typhoon* (New York: Harcourt Brace Jovanovich, 1980), 124 (new species), 255 (freedom), 278 (home). Irony: when she, after a long period of uncertainty and loneliness, is called to report to a revolutionary committee at the university, she finds this "reassuring. It implied that somewhere in the rarefied upper regions of policy my existence was known." Ibid., 21. When her daughter needs a backpack, she refuses to use the new one, and her mother then patches up an old khaki one: "It looked satisfactorily proletarian when I had finished." Ibid., 65. When she is asked to watch a movie report on one of Mao's mass reviews in Beijing, she calls it a "treat." Ibid., 66.
58. Ji, *Cowshed*, 16 (mob), 41 (psychopaths), 43 (element), 50 (example of irony), 67 ("I realized that the Cultural Revolution was merely an elaborate excuse for workers to persecute intellectuals"), 139 (sixteen), 180 (capitalist); Zha Jianying, "Introduction," in Ji, *Cowshed*, vii (publisher).
59. When Earnshaw was able to read Western newspapers again in 1972, she learned about "the turmoil of the sixties in the United States ... Students in America, like those in China, were discontented, ... but they were not being used by politicians to kill each other." Lo and Kinderman, *In the Eye of the Typhoon*, 183–184.
60. Zhang and Sang, *Chinese Lives*, 76 (gang), 56 (girl group), 60 (chaos); Chaohua Wang, "Introduction: Minds of the Nineties," in *One China, Many Paths*, ed. Chaohua Wang (London: Verso, 2003): 34.
61. Rosen, *Red Guard Factionalism*, 116 (*chengfen*); Dikötter, *Cultural Revolution*, 101 (5 September), 107 (7.7 million), 108 (jeep and trucks), 111–114 (red tourists); Meisner, *Mao's China and After*, 354 (400,000). Dikötter gives 1.5 to 2 million dead.
62. "Course of Events," 22 (grumbling); Meisner, *Mao's China and After*, 312 (Wu Han); Bennett and Montaperto, *Red Guard*, 129 (clowns); Schoppa, *Revolution and Its Past*, 349–355.
63. Spence, *Search for Modern China*, 566–567 (Lei Feng); Pei-Kai Cheng and Michael Lestz (with Jonathan D. Spence), eds., *The Search for Modern China: A Documentary Collection* (New York: Norton, 1998), 421 (steering wheel); Xiaoping Fang, *Barefoot Doctors and Western Medicine in China* (Rochester, NY: University of Rochester Press, 2012), 1 (*chijiao yisheng*), 2 (needle), 23 (collective road), 30 (*bannong banyi*); Rhoads, "Cycles of Cathay," 106 (Deng Xiaoping), 109 (Gao); Meisner, *Mao's China and After*, 360 (one million).
64. Meisner, *Mao's China and After*, 357 (plots), 358 (enterprises), 359 (twenty million), 369 (seventeen million), 396 (Zhou Enlai), 409n41 (10 percent); Wang Hui, *The End of the Revolution: China and the Limits of Modernity* (London: Verso, 2009), 10–11 (de-politicization); Becky P. Y. Loo, W. S. Cheung, and Shenjun Yao, "The Rural-Urban Divide in Road Safety: The Case of China," *Open Transportation Journal* 5 (2011): 10, table 1; Mom, *Atlantic Automobilism*, 596 (road crashes); G. D. Jacobs and I. A. Sayer, *Study of Road Accidents in Selected Urban Areas in Developing Countries* (Crowthorne: Department of the Environment, Transport and Road Research Laboratory, Overseas Unit, 1977) (Western figures).

65. Marian Aguiar, *Tracking Modernity: India's Railways and the Culture of Mobility* (Minneapolis: University of Minnesota Press, 2011), 73–74 (intense), 87–91 (for a discussion of Singh's novel); Khushwant Singh, *Train to Pakistan* (New York: Grove Press, 1990), 18 and 78 (American car), 81 (trucks), 94 (corpses), 99 (bicycle), 110 (subinspector's bicycle), 121 and 164 (tonga), 133 (convoy); Ian J. Kerr, *Engines of Change: The Railroads that made India* (Westport, CT: Praeger, 2007), 136 (673 trains, but mentions 5,000 per train).

66. Owen, *Distance and Development*, 48 (570,000); Hindustan Motors, *Road Transport in India*, 15 (1958); "India," *Road International* 7 (Winter 1952/1953): 52 (West Bengal); J. Burke Knapp, "The International Bank for Reconstruction and Development," *Road International* 7 (Autumn 1961): 31–34, here 32 (World Bank); H. P. Sinha, "Road Development in India," *Road International* 51 (December 1963): 17–20; "India's Ambitious Highway Programme," *Road International* 7 (June 1970): 4–8 (one million); details about the Nagpur Plan can be found in K. P. Bhatnagar, Satish Bahadur, D. N. Agrawal, and S. C. Gupta, *Transport in Modern India* (Kanpur: Kishore Publishing House), 283–289.

67. Owen, *Distance and Development*, 7, table 1-2 (first three), 11 (fourth), 17 (three-quarters); Howe, "Transport for the Poor," 32 (freight shares; Howe does not clarify whether these shares related to tons or ton-km); Gijs Mom, "Clashes of Cultures: Road vs. Rail in the North-Atlantic World during the Inter-war Coordination Crisis," in *The Organization of Transport: A History of Users, Industry, and Public Policy*, ed. Christopher Kopper and Massimo Moraglio (London: Routledge, 2015) (struggle); Bhatnagar et al., *Transport in Modern India*, 374 (road services), 379 (operators), 380–381 (joint-stock corporations), 382 (all but one, more than half), 384, table (statistics), 389 (moratorium), 390 (trucks).

68. Sanjay Kathuria, "Commercial Vehicles Industry in India: A Case History, 1928–1987," *Economic and Political Weekly* (17–20 October 1987), 1809 (1956), 1810 (Hindustan Motors, etc.), 1813 (complete), 1816, table 2 (forty-three thousand); Kenneth Bo Nielsen and Harold Wilhite, "The Rise and Fall of the 'People's Car': Middle-Class Aspirations, Status and Mobile Symbolism in 'New India,'" in Hansen and Nielsen, *Cars, Automobility and Development in Asia*, 172 (refused, Morris), Mason, *Turbulent Empires*, 149.

69. Owen, *Distance and Development*, 13 (neglect: "entirely overlooked"), 146 (frustrating); Dennis Merrill, *Bread and the Ballot: The United States and India's Economic Development, 1947–1963* (Chapel Hill: University of North Carolina Press, 1990), 162 (minimum); Bhatnagar et al., *Transport in Modern India*, 318 (porterage), 321–322 (horses, etc.), 325 (bullocks).

70. David Arnold, *Everyday Technology: Machines and the Making of India's Modernity* (Chicago: University of Chicago Press, 2013), 53 (1946), 53–54 (bicycle imports), 85 (women); B. M. Birla, "Foreword," in Hindustan Motors, *Road Transport in India*, v (taxation); Hindustan Motors, *Road Transport in India*, 1 (revolutionary, development), 6 (comparison with the West), 22, table 5 (rail vs. road), 57, table 14 (motor vehicle revenue comparison); number of cars and two-wheelers calculated from T. M. Rahul and Ashish Verma, "Economic Impact of Non-motorized Transportation in Indian Cities," *Research in Transportation Economics* 38, no. 1 (2013): 23, table 1.

71. Owen, *Distance and Development*, 53 (twelve million, fifty miles); Arnold, *Everyday Technology*, 176 (Nehru); Mason, *Turbulent Empires*, 138 (third way); Howe, "Transport for the Poor," 35, table 3.3.

72. David Edgerton, "Creole Technologies and Global Histories: Rethinking How Things Travel in Space and Time," *HOST* 1 (Summer 2007): 10; Sushil Chandra and Sudhir

Atreya, "Lyricism in Design: A History of Motorcycles in India," *International Journal of Motorcycle Studies* 5, no. 2 (2009).

73. David C. Engerman, "The Political Power of Economic Ideas? Foreign Economic Advisors and Indian Planning in the 1950s and 1960s," in *India in the World since 1947: National and Transnational Perspectives*, ed. Andreas Hilger and Corinna R. Unger (Frankfurt: Peter Lang, 2012), 126 (Marxists), 128 (Friedman); Robert J. McMahon, "On the Periphery of a Global Conflict: India and the Cold War, 1947–1991," in Hilger and Unger, *India in the World*, 276 (lodestar); Merrill, *Bread and the Ballot*, 155 (test case); Mark Solovey, "The Politics of Intellectual Identity and American Social Science, 1945–1970" (PhD diss., University of Wisconsin-Madison, 1996), 131, 303.

74. Engerman, "Political Power of Economic Ideas?" 131 (fanfare), 133 (withdrew), 134–135 (air force); Merrill, *Bread and the Ballot*, 165 (foreign policy), 208 (ten million), 209 (Nixon, Ford), 210 ($4 billion); McMahon, "On the Periphery of a Global Conflict," 286 (rebellion), 288 (tripolar), 293 (weapon, Vietnam), 294 (Bangladesh); Schoppa, *Revolution and Its Past*, 342 (Aksai Chin); Dervla Murphy, *Full Tilt: Ireland to India with a Bicycle* (London: Eland 2010), 56–57.

75. E. A. Nadirshah, "A Review of Roads and Road Transport in India," *Road International* 22 (Autumn 1956): 28–30, here 30; Peter Scott, "Public-Sector Investment and Britain's Post-war Economic Performance: A Case Study of Roads Policy," *Journal of European Economic History* 34, no. 2 (2005): 393 (underinvestment).

76. Ansary, *Destiny Disrupted*, 339 (casbah); Heinz Schandl, Marina Fischer-Kowalski, Clemens Grunbuhel and Fridolin Krausmann, "Socio-metabolic transitions in developing Asia," *Technological Forecasting & Social Change* 76, no. 2 (2009): 273 (unprecedented); Diya Mehra, "Planning Delhi ca. 1936–1959," *South Asia: Journal of South Asian Studies* 36, no. 3 (2013): 356 (motor car); Bhatnagar et al., *Transport in Modern India*, 335 (injurious); Dirk Bronger, *Metropolen, Megastädte, Global Cities: Die Metropolisierung der Erde* (Darmstadt: Wissenschaftliche Buchgesellschaft, 2004), 76 (informal), 78 (6.1 billion, megacities).

77. Howard Dick and Peter J. Rimmer, *Cities, Transport and Communications: The Integration of Southeast Asia since 1850* (London: Palgrave Macmillan, 2003), xvii (specializing; Rimmer started his career in Thailand in the late 1960s, where he dealt with railroad competition, whereas Dick was active in Indonesia on interisland shipping in the early 1970s), 3 (ASEAN), 5 (dominated), 8 (sea), 21 (half a billion), 27 (triangle), 29 (twenty-five, world cities), 59 (1867), 66 (first cars), 68 (one hundred thousand), 71 (hinterlands, slow diffusion), 129, table 4.1 (140,000), 134 (bicycle), 222 (one million), 227 (middle-class).

78. Peter J. Rimmer, *Rikisha to Rapid Transit: Urban Public Transport Systems and Policy in Southeast Asia* (Sydney: Pergamon Press, 1986), 314–315; Tim Edensor and Mark Jayne, "Introduction: Urban Theory beyond the West," in *Urban Theory beyond the West: A World of Cities*, ed. Tim Edensor and Mark Jayne (London: Routledge, 2012), 12 (multi-racial), 19 (disordering).

79. Tarini Bedi, "Mimicry, Friction and Trans-urban Imaginaries: Mumbai Taxis/Singapore-Style," *Environment and Planning A* 48, no. 6 (2016): 1018 (1963); Edensor and Jayne, "Introduction," 18 (drifting), 21–22 (geographies), 22 (Chakrabarty, sophisticated), 23 (terror; this is a paraphrase of Edgar Pieterse's study about Africa); Mehra, "Planning Delhi ca. 1936–1959," 354 and 370 (squatters); Michael Mann, "Delhi-Metro-Polis: Public Transport, Public Opinion and National Politics," in Hilger and Unger, *India in the World*, 141 (ring-towns), 142 (ring roads, metro), 153 (slum); Michael Mann, "Town Planning and Urban Resistance in the Old City of Delhi, 1937–1977," in *Urbanization and Governance in India*, ed. Evelin Hust and Michael Mann (New Delhi:

Manohar, 2005), 259 (deficient), 260 (slum), 266 (riots); Kerr, *Engines of Change*, 148 (Kolkata).

80. Boris Niclas-Tölle, "India's Ville Radieuse: Modernist Town Planning in Chandigarh," in Hilger and Unger, *India in the World*, 168 (Abercrombie), 173–174 (standard roads), 176 (1982), 181 (postmodernism); Edensor and Jayne, "Introduction," 10–11.

81. Ansary, *Destiny Disrupted*, 339 (Cheapside); Corinna R. Unger, "Industrialization vs. Agrarian Reform: West German Modernization Policies in India in the 1950s and 1960s," *Journal of Modern European History* 8, no. 1 (2010): 63; Salman Rushdie, *The Ground Beneath Her Feet: A Novel* (New York: Picador, 1999), 195; Ravinder Kaur, "Planning Urban Chaos: State and Refugees in Post-Partition Delhi," in Hust and Mann, *Urbanization and Governance in India*, 229–234.

82. Rimmer, *Rikisha*, 73 (amalgam, World Bank), 88 (four thousand); Erik Cohen, "A Soi in Bangkok: the Dynamics of Lateral Urban Expansion," *Journal of the Siam Society* 73, nos. 1–2 (1985): 2 (ribbon, interstices), 2n6 (surface), 3 (dirt roads, *song-theo*, etc.), 8 (uncontrolled), 11 (shop houses).

83. Rimmer, *Rikisha*, 77 (fivefold), 78 (overcrowding, *pak pais*), 80 (1969, 90 percent), 81 (blue-collar), 82 (shift), 54 (1972), 88 (4,350), 84–90 (90: subversive; the "selfish" quote on 87 is Rimmer's paraphrase); Mom, *Atlantic Automobilism*, 606–617 (skimming).

84. The following paragraphs are based on Gijs Mom, "Planning the Car System in the Netherlands: Mass Motorization in a North-Atlantic Context" (Casus No. 6 of the project "Dutch Mobility in a European Context: A Comparison of Two Centuries of Mobility Policy in Seven Countries"), paper presented at the Second International Workshop on Transport History and Policy, Utrecht (5–7 February 2009). Parts of this paper were published as Gijs Mom, "International Road Federation (IRF)," in *The Palgrave Dictionary of Transnational History*, ed. Akira Iriye and Pierre-Yves Saunier (London: Palgrave Macmillan, 2009), and Gijs Mom, "Decentering Highways: European National Road Network Planning from a Transnational Perspective," in *Die moderne Strasse: Planung, Bau und Verkehr vom 18. bis zum 20. Jahrhundert*, ed. Hans-Liudger Dienel and Hans-Ulrich Schiedt (Frankfurt: Campus Verlag, 2010). I thank the participants of the Utrecht workshop and the referees of the two publications for their constructive comments on earlier versions.

85. F. J. Erroll, "Transport in Africa: A Comprehensive Survey of Means of Communication throughout the Continent," *Road International* 3 (Winter 1951): 45–50, here 50. This is remarkable indeed, as the Netherlands felt threatened by an "alarming suspension of Marshall aid intended for the Dutch East Indies." Francis X. Sutton, Tom G. Kessenger, James P. Grant, and George Zeidenstein, "Development Ideology: Its Emergence and Decline [with Comments]," *Daedalus* 118, no. 1 (1989): 47. In the ten years since the Colonial Development and Welfare Act of 1945, Great Britain had spent 118 million pounds under this act, 16 percent of which went to roads. "Britain's Contributions to Colonial Road Programmes," *Road International* 23 (Winter 1956/1957): 56.

86. Hans-Ulrich Wehler, *Modernisierungstheorie und Geschichte* (Göttingen: Vandenhoeck & Ruprecht, 1975), 14–15 (high, etc.), 17 (expectations), 18 (superfluous), 23 (decay), 51 (variation); "Messages of Welcome to *Road International* from the Chairmen of the International Road Federation," *Road International* 1 (Autumn 1950): 10–11, here 11.

87. Daniel Boutet, "Permanent International Association of Road Congresses: Its Origine [sic] and Its Activity," *Bulletin de l'AIPCR* 40, no. 128 (1951): 1–8, here 5; Benjamin Fulwider, "Driving the Nation: Road Transportation and the Postrevolutionary Mexican State, 1925–1960" (PhD diss., Georgetown University, 2009), 168 (1955); Mom, "International Road Federation (IRF)," 583 (Yale).

88. Theodore M. Matson, "The Traffic Engineering Profession," *Road International* 7 (Winter 1952/1953): 8–12, here 8 (peripheries); Hindustan Motors, *Road Transport in India*, 33, table 8.
89. Peter Hall, *Cities of Tomorrow: An Intellectual History of Urban Planning and Design in the Twentieth Century* (Malden, MA: Wiley-Blackwell, 2002), 317; John A. Jakle and Keith A. Sculle, *Motoring: The Highway Experience in America* (Athens: University of Georgia Press, 2008), 155 (trucking lobby); Paul Barrett and Mark H. Rose, "Street Smarts: The Politics of Transportation Statistics in the American City, 1900–1990," *Journal of Urban History* 25, no. 3 (1999): 416 (development, immigrants); Brian Ladd, *Autophobia: Love and Hate in the Automotive Age* (Chicago: University of Chicago Press, 2008), 103 (rural design; my calculation; the source gives twenty acres for every mile).
90. This section is based on Mom, "Planning the Car System in the Netherlands"; see also Mom and Filarski, *Van transport naar mobiliteit*, 311–325. On Yale, see Bruce Seely, "'Push' and 'Pull' Factors in Technology Transfer: Moving American-Style Highway Engineering to Europe, 1945–1965," *Comparative Technology Transfer and Society* 2, no. 3 (2004): 238–239.
91. Hans-Liudger Dienel, "Das Bundesverkehrsministerium," in *Handbuch Verkehrspolitk*, ed. Oliver Schöller, Weert Canzler, and Andreas Knie (Wiesbaden: VS Verlag für Sozialwissenschaften, 2007), 115; Dietrich Garlichs, *Grenzen staatlicher Infrastrukturpolitik: Bund/Länder-Kooperation in der Fernstrassenplanung* (Königstein im Taunus: Verlag Anton Hain, 1980), 117, 41 (surprisingly fast, federal comparison), 35 (most sophisticated); Ueli Haefeli, *Verkehrspolitik und urbane Mobilität: Deutsche und Schweizer Städte im Vergleich 1950–1990* (Stuttgart: Franz Steiner Verlag, 2008), 59 (*Gemeindepfennig*).
92. For a unique account from within the ministry, see Horst Heldmann, *50 Jahre Verkehrspolitik in Bonn: Ein Mann und zehn Minister* (Bonn: Kirschbaum Verlag, 2002); Garlichs, *Grenzen staatlicher Infrastrukturpolitk*, 125 (clearing house); see also Dietrich Garlichs and Edda Müller, "Eine neue Organisation für das Bundesverkehrsministerium," *Die Verwaltung* 3 (1977); Alexander Gall, *"Gute Strassen bis ins kleinste Dorf!" Verkehrspolitik in Bayern zwischen Wiederaufbau und Ölkrise* (Frankfurt: Campus Verlag, 2005) (Bavaria). For a comparison of French and American earmarking policies of motor tax and infrastructure building, see James A. Dunn Jr., "The Politics of Motor Fuel Taxes and Infrastructure Funds in France and the United States," *Policy Studies Journal* 21, no. 2 (1993).
93. Ueli Haefeli, "Stadt und Autobahn: Eine Neuinterpretation," *Schweizerische Zeitschrift für Geschichte* 51 (2001): 41, 183; George Kammann, *Mit Autobahnen die Städte retten? Städtebauliche Ideen der Expressstrassen-Planung in der Schweiz 1954–1964* (Zürich: Chronos Verlag, 1990), chap. 8; Michael Ackermann, *Konzepte und Entscheidungen in der Planung der schweizerischen Nationalstrassen von 1927 bis 1961* (Bern Peter Lang, 1991), 123, 210, 232, 251–253, 266; Robert Ruckli, "Der Ausbau des amerikanischen Hauptstrassennetzes: Vergleich mit dem schweizerischen Hauptstrassenprogramm," *Strasse und Verkehr* 32, nos. 14–15 / nos. 16–17 (1946); Jean-Daniel Blanc, *Die Stadt: Ein Verkehrshindernis? Leitbilder städtischer Verkehrsplanung und Verkehrspolitik in Zürich 1945–1975* (Zürich: Chronos Verlag, 1993), 95–96.
94. Kammann, *Mit Autobahnen die Städte retten?* 89, 105; Haefeli, *Verkehrspolitik und urbane Mobilität*, 72, 98; Mom and Filarski, *Van transport naar mobiliteit*.
95. Gijs Mom, "Roads without Rails: European Highway-Network Building and the Desire for Long-Range Motorized Mobility," *Technology and Culture* 46, no. 4 (2005); Schipper, *Driving Europe*, 168 (Myrdal), 177 (103); Peter Merriman, *Driving Spaces: A Cultural-Historical Geography of England's M1 Motorway* (Malden, MA: Blackwell,

2007); Tom Rallis and Uno Helk, "Story of the Motorways II," *European Asphalt Magazine* 1 (1993): 8 (Italy); Tom Rallis and Uno Helk, "Story of the Motorways III," *European Asphalt Magazine* 2 (1993): 20 (Spain); Antonio Vasquez Barquero and Michael Hebbert, "Spain: Economy and State in Transition," in *Uneven Development in Southern Europe: Studies of Accumulation, Class, Migration and the State*, ed. Ray Hudson and Jim Lewis (London: Methuen, 1985), 284 (peripheries); Winfried Wolf, *Eisenbahn und Autowahn: Personen- und Gütertransport auf Schiene und Strasse: Geschichte, Bilanz, Perspektiven* (Hamburg: Rasch & Röhring Verlag, 1992), 511; for a detailed analysis of the emergence of British freeway policy (and the road lobby's influence), see Geoffrey Dudley and Jeremy Richardson, *Why Does Policy Change? Lessons from British Transport Policy 1945–99* (London: Routledge, 2000).

96. Mom and Filarski, *Van transport naar mobiliteit*, 199 (Switzerland, Netherlands); Michael R. Fein, *Paving the Way: New York Road Building and the American State, 1880–1956* (Lawrence: University Press of Kansas, 2008), 202–218; Stephen V. Ward, *Planning the Twentieth-Century City: The Advanced Capitalist World* (Chichester: John Wiley & Sons, 2002), 122.

97. Robert G. Smith, *Ad Hoc Governments: Special Purpose Transportation Authorities in Britain and the United States* (Beverly Hills: Sage, 1974); Cotten Seiler, "Anxiety and Automobility: Cold War Individualism and the Interstate Highway System" (PhD diss., University of Kansas, 2002); Jakle and Sculle, *Motoring*, 160 (paradoxically).

98. Tom Lewis, *Divided Highways: Building the Interstate Highways, Transforming American Life* (New York: Penguin, 1999), 86 (depression), 99 (dramatic); Stephen B. Goddard, *Getting There: The Epic Struggle between Road and Rail in the American Century* (New York: HarperCollins, 1994), 197 (key friends).

99. For half of the Interstates being urban as "grossly misleading" (because most of these were suburban), see Owen D. Gutfreund, *Twentieth-Century Sprawl: Highways and the Reshaping of the American Landscape* (Oxford: Oxford University Press, 2004), 56; Barrett and Rose, "Street Smarts," 414 (sovereignty); Louis Ward Kemp, "Aesthetes and Engineers: The Occupational Ideology of Highway Design," *Technology and Culture* 27, no. 4 (1986): 762 (domain). For the history of the Interstate Highway project, see Mark H. Rose and Bruce E. Seely, "Getting the Interstate System Built: Road Engineers and the Implementation of Public Policy, 1955–1985," *Journal of Policy History* 2, no. 1 (1990); and Bruce Seely, *Building the American Highway System: Engineers as Policy Makers* (Philadelphia: Temple University Press, 1987).

100. Lewis, *Divided Highways*, 164–165 (fraud), 168 (one-third), 211 (two-thirds); Jakle and Sculle, *Motoring*, 157 (growth spurt), 158 (interchanges), 159 (1,100 miles); Marc Augé, *Non-lieux: Introduction à une anthropologie de la surmodernité* (Paris: Éditions du Seuil, 1992) (non-places).

101. Garlichs, *Grenzen staatlicher Infrastrukturpolitk*, 39 (Germany); Bernard Gutknecht, "Proteste gegen den Nationalstrassenbau 1957–1990: Von punktueller Opposition zu grundsätzlichem Widerstand," in *Rechte und linke Fundamentalopposition: Studien zur Schweizer Politik 1965–1990*, ed. Urs Altermatt (Basel: Helbing & Lichtenhahn), 62–94; James A. Dunn Jr., *Miles to Go: European and American Transportation Policies* (Cambridge, MA: MIT Press, 1981), 123 (Switzerland, San Francisco); Suzanne E. Smith, *Dancing in the Street: Motown and the Cultural Politics of Detroit* (Cambridge, MA: Harvard University Press, 2003), 35 (Detroit); Jeffrey Brown, Eric A. Morris, and Brian D. Taylor, "Planning for Cars in Cities: Planners, Engineers, and Freeways in the 20th Century," *Journal of the American Planning Association* 75, no. 2 (2009): 172–173.

102. Kaelble, *Kalter Krieg*, 111 (euphoria); Westad, "Great Transformation," 73; on the modest application of "comprehensive planning" in developing countries, see Brian V. Martin and Charles B. Warden, "Transportation Planning in Developing Countries," *Traffic Quarterly* 19, no. 1 (1965). More research is needed here.
103. For the struggle between "builders" and "planners" in the Netherlands, see Gijs Mom, "The West and the Rest: The Green Heart and the Breakthrough of Spatial Planning," in *Builders and Planners: A History of Land-Use and Infrastructure Planning in the Netherlands*, ed. Jos Arts, Ruud Filarski, Hans Jeekel, and Bert Toussaint (Delft: Eburon, 2016); Marshall Berman, *All That Is Solid Melts Into Air: The Experience of Modernity* (New York: Penguin, 1988), 74; John Perkins, *The Secret History of the American Empire: The Truth about Economic Hit Men, Jackals, and How to Change the World* (New York: Plume, 2008); Mom, "Roads without Rails."
104. Unger, "Industrialization vs. Agrarian Reform," 49 (anti-communism); Jiafeng Wang, "Some Reflections on Modernization Theory and Globalization Theory," *Chinese Studies in History* 43, no. 1 (2009): 75 (soaked); Alberto Arce and Normal Long, "Reconfiguring Modernity and Development from an Anthropological Perspective," in *Anthropology, Development and Modernities: Exploring Discourses, Counter-Tendencies and Violence*, ed. Alberto Arce and Normal Long (London: Routledge, 2006), 1 (normative).
105. Rostow, *Stages of Economic Growth*, 1 (historian), 73 (post-maturity); Michael E. Latham, *Modernization as Ideology: American Social Science and "Nation Building" in the Kennedy Era* (Chapel Hill: University of North Carolina Press, 2000), 3–4 (institutions); Arce and Long, "Reconfiguring Modernity," 5 (stages); Unger, "Histories of Development," 12 (phenomenon).
106. Rostow, *Stages of Economic Growth*, 78 (leading), 84–85, figs. 1–2 (curves), 87 (manner), 103 (slowly), 134 (agenda), 164 (middle class). In all fairness, Rostow conceded that developing nations now had two differences compared to those that had developed earlier: they had "an enormous back-log of technology," and they developed amid the Cold War. Ibid., 140–141.
107. Wehler, *Modernisierungstheorie und Geschichte*, 23 (linear); Catherine V. Scott, "Tradition and Gender in Modernization Theory," in *The Postcolonial Science and Technology Studies Reader*, ed. Sandra Harding (Durham, NC: Duke University Press, 2011), 292; Nathan Citino, "Suburbia and Modernization: Community Building and America's Post–World War II Encounter with the Arab Middle East," *Arab Studies Journal* 14, no. 1 (2005/2006): 41 (managed).
108. On the crucial importance of the concept of the nation-state among non-Western elites, see, e.g., Pankaj Mishra, *From the Ruins of Empire: The Revolt Against the West and the Remaking of Asia* (London: Allen Lane, 2012), 303; Leonard Binder, "The Natural History of Development Theory," *Comparative Studies in Society and History* 28, no. 1 (1986): 3 (pluralist); Partha Chatterjee, *The Politics of the Governed: Reflections on Popular Politics in Most of the World* (New York: Columbia University Press, 2004), 33 (Weberian, etc.); Chakrabarty, *Provincializing Europe*, 7 (Marx, historicists), 11 (peasant); Mann, *Sources of Social Power*, vol. 4, 45–46; Hobsbawm, *Age of Extremes*, 288 (Middle Ages), 289 (death), 291 (half).
109. Michael Hanchard, "Afro-Modernity: Temporality, Politics, and the African Diaspora," in *Alternative Modernities*, ed. Dilip Parameshwar Gaonkar (Durham, NC: Duke University Press, 2001), 273. Also, the critical historians cited at the beginning of this chapter, who emphasized the role of the OECD and the NGO explosion, pointed at the influence of the 1951 report *Measures for the Economic Development of Under-developed Countries*, written by Manchester economist W. Arthur Lewis (without mentioning Rostow). Frey et al. "Introduction," 36.

110. Schandl et al., "Socio-metabolic Transitions in Developing Asia," 273 (post-1950); Martin and Warden, 'Transportation Planning," 59 (Kindleberger); Owen, *Strategy for Mobility*, vii (role), 7 (block quote), 14, table 1.4 (index), 39 (other needs), 48 (Turkey), 44 (frustrating), 45, table 3.1 (average, Nigeria and Thailand), 58 (congestion), 98 (4.5), 99 (trend), 102 (*will*; emphasis added), 117 (model), 153 (one-third), 156 (attention, Iran), 170 ($7.2 billion), 173 ($80 million), 175 (five thousand: calculated as 8 percent of the total sixty thousand trainees), 198 (mistake); Björn Wittrock, "Modernity: One, None, or Many? European Origins and Modernity as a Global Condition," *Daedalus* 129, no. 1 (2000): 55; on the political epitetha of the Brookings Institution (from "conservative" to "centrist-left") see https://en.wikipedia.org/wiki/Brookings_Institution (retrieved 22 April 2016); Oladipo O. Olubomehin, "Development of the National Trunk Roads in Nigeria and the Socio-economic Impact, 1960–2013," *Lagos Historical Review* (2015): 3 (Trunk Roads).

111. Howe, "Transport for the Poor," 11–13 (Ville, Hirschman), 23 (Rostow); Rainer Fremdling, "Book Review: *Transport and the Development of the European Economy, 1750–1918*," *Journal of Transport History* 12, no. 2 (1991): 197 (approvingly); Martin and Warden, "Transportation Planning," 59 (catalyst); Murray Chapman and R. Mansell Prothero, "Themes on Circulation in the Third World," in *Circulation in Third World Countries*, ed. R. Mansell Prothero and Murray Chapman (London: Routledge & Kegan Paul, 1985), 15–16 (Zelinsky); Seah Chee Meow, *Infrastructural Growth and Development Planning: A Comparative Study of Road Infrastructure in the National Development of Asean Countries* (Singapore: Chopmen Enterprises, 1978), 5 (Galbraith); Michele Alacevich, *Visualizing Uncertainties, or How Albert Hirschman and the World Bank Disagreed on Project Appraisal and Development Approaches* (Washington, DC: World Bank, Information Management and Technology Network, Knowledge and Information Service Unit, November 2012), 8 (two books). I thank Colin Divall for drawing Ville's argument to my attention. For a schoolbook example of a Rostowian analysis of Venezuela, see John Friedmann, *Regional Development Policy: A Case Study of Venezuela* (Cambridge, MA: MIT Press, 1970).

112. Nathan Porath, "A River, a Road, an Indigenous People and an Entangled Landscape in Riau, Indonesia," *Bijdragen tot de Taal-, Land- en Volkenkunde* 158, no. 4 (2002): 275; Erwin Gleissner, *Transportelastizität und wirtschaftliche Entwicklung: Ein internationaler Vergleich* (Berlin: Juncker & Humblot, 1967), 22 (twenty-seven), 23 (richer).

113. Binder, "Natural History of Development Theory," 11 (ubiquitous); Arturo Escobar, "Development and the Anthropology of Modernity," in Harding, *Postcolonial Science and Technology Studies Reader*, 271 (human needs); Unger, "Histories of Development," 2 (counterculture), 8 (officers); Engerman and Unger, "Introduction," 375–276 (laboratory), 381–382 (tight connections).

114. John A. Black and Peter J. Rimmer, "Japanese Highway Planning: A Western Interpretation," *Transportation* 11, no. 1 (1982): 45 ($1 billion); Perkins, *Secret History*, 106 (coffers); Michele Alacevich, "The World Bank and the Politics of Productivity: The Debate on Economic Growth, Poverty, and Living Standards in the 1950s," *Journal of Global History* 6, no. 1 (2011): 61 (neglected), 62, table 2 ($900 million, $700 million), 69 (Wall Street), 71 (another China; quoting Devesh Kapur, John P. Lewis, and Richard Webb, *The World Bank: Its First Half Century, vol. 1—History* [Washington, DC: Brookings Institution Press, 1997], 112); Gunther Lübbeke, "Verkehrsprobleme der Entwicklungsländer und der Beitrag der Weltbank zu ihrer Lösung," *Archiv für Verkehrswesen* 16, nos. 1–2 (1964): 6 ($7 billion), 8 (one-third).

115. Latham, *Modernization* 68–81, 69 (neck, Alliance), 70 (revolution) 74 ($19 billion) 77 (coercion), 78–79 (Berle), 81 (Schlesinger), 86 (scavengers); Merrill, *Bread and the*

Ballot, 171 (plastic), 172 (key nations: Argentina, Brazil, Colombia, Venezuela, India, Philippines, Taiwan, Turkey, Greece, and "possibly" Egypt, Pakistan, Iran, and Iraq); Ruth Oldenziel, "Is Globalization a Code Word for Americanization?" *Tijdschrift voor Sociale en Economische Geschiedenis* 4, no. 3 (2007): 89 (appeal), 105 (too often).

116. Sutton et al., "Development Ideology," 37–39 (orthodox), 45 (powerful), 49 (OECD), 50 (growth, fear), 60 (Marxist); Jean Franco, *Cruel Modernity* (Durham, NC: Duke University Press, 2013), 6; Odd Arne Westad, *The Global Cold War: Third World Interventions and the Making of Our Times* (Cambridge: Cambridge University Press, 2014), 156.

117. Stefan Eich and Adam Tooze, "The Great Inflation," in *Vorgeschichte der Gegenwart: Dimensionen des Strukturbruchs nach dem Boom*, ed. Anselm Doering-Manteuffel, Lutz Raphael, and Thomas Schlemmer (Göttingen: Vandenhoeck & Ruprecht, 2016), 174 (instability); Latham, *Modernization*, 99–106, 112 (community development), 119 (area studies), 121 (geologists), 124 (social engineering), 133 (Guinea, Shriver); Merrill, *Bread and the Ballot*, 174 (screened); Goedde, "Global Cultures," 572 (seventy thousand); for an overview of transport-related Peace Corps activities, see Owen, *Strategy for Mobility*, 175–176.

118. Latham, *Modernization*, 149 (Cadillacs), 143 (missionary), 145 (frontier), 146 (mature), 149 (Shriver); Christina Schwenkel, "Traveling Architecture: East German Urban Designs in Vietnam," *International Journal for History, Culture and Modernity* 2, no. 2 (2014): 161 (destroy); Perkins, *Secret History*, 226 (guilt: "I was repeating the sins of those slavers"), 231 (adventurer: "a guy like me could make real money—and have some fun"), 238 (jackals); Cotten Seiler, *Republic of Drivers: A Cultural History of Automobility in America* (Chicago: University of Chicago Press, 2008).

119. I thank Carl Koopmans (Vrije Universiteit Amsterdam) and Colin Divall (University of York) for providing an overview of the state of the art in this field. See, e.g., Carl Koopmans and Rogier Lieshout, "Spoorwegen en groei," *Economisch Statistische Berichten* 93, no. 4535 (16 May 2008): 301–302. See also Jean-Marc Offner, "Les 'effets structurants' du transport: Mythe politique, mystification scientifique," *L'espace géographique* 3 (1993).

120. Standing Advisory Committee on Trunk Road Assessment, *Transport and the Economy: Full Report* (London: Her Majesty's Stationery Office, 1999), 2 (question, costs of movement), 3 (modest, guaranteed). I thank Vincent Lagendijk (Maastricht University) for suggesting literature in this domain: Patrick M. Wood, "The BIS: Bank for International Settlements," *August Review* 5, no. 11 (14 October 2005), http://www.bibliotecapleyades.net/sociopolitica/sociopol_globalbanking04.htm (supercentral); Stephen M. Streeter, "The Failure of 'Liberal Developmentalism': The United States's Anti-Communist Showcase in Guatemala, 1954–1960," *International History Review* 21, no. 2 (1999): 390 (stand-in).

121. F. D. Masson, "United Nations Conference on Road Traffic, Vienna, 1968," *Road International* 73 (June 1969): 22–27; M. H. Perlowski, "International Road Traffic: Its Problems and their Solution," *Road International* 2 (1951): 28–29, 32–33. On earlier road traffic conventions by the League of Nations, see also Schipper, *Driving Europe*.

122. Albert Saiz, "Dictatorships and Highways," *Regional Science and Urban Economics* 36, no. 2 (2006): 2: "in autocratic countries the share of paved roads in poor condition tends to be smaller"; "Loans by International Agencies for Highway Projects," *Road International* 40 (Spring 1961): 43–47; Jonathan Dawson and Ian Barwell, *Roads Are Not Enough: New Perspectives on Rural Transport Planning in Developing Countries* (London: Intermediate Technology Publications, 1993), 2 (soft-loan); Owen, *Strategy for Mobility*, 170–171, incl. table 6.5.

123. "World Bank Loans to Venezuela," *Road International* (December 1964): 21 (economic plan); "The Work of the World Bank in Financing Highway Projects," *Road International* 17 (Summer 1955): 37–41, here 38 ($2 billion); Christoph Borcherdt, "Die neuere Verkehrserschliessung in Venezuela und ihre Auswirkungen in der Kulturlandschaft," *Die Erde* 1 (1968) (extreme); Knapp, "International Bank for Reconstruction and Development," 31 (Asia, etc.); Alacevich, *Visualizing Uncertainties,* 2 (480).
124. Toby James Carroll, "The Politics of the World Bank's Socio-institutional Neoliberalism" (PhD diss., Murdoch University, 2007), 2 (new form); Sutton et al., "Development Ideology," 54–55 (concentration); Dawson and Barwell, *Roads*, 2 (single sector), 4 (0.004 percent).
125. Carroll, "Politics," 39 (warrior); Martha Finnemore, "Redefining Development at the World Bank," in Cooper and Packard, *International Development*, 204 (farmers), 206 (philanthropic, domestic), 208 (movement), 209 (Johnson), 210 (Woods), 211 (Vietnam), 216 (rural poverty, roads), 217 (double), 218 (reports); Escobar, "Anthropology and the Development Encounter," 659 (failure).
126. J. D. G. F. Howe, "Valuing Time Savings in Developing Countries," *Journal of Transport Economics and Policy* 10, no. 2 (1976): (benefits); Alacevich, *Visualizing Uncertainties*, 51 (doctrines), 52 (UN, *dependencia*), 54 (crisis).
127. Staples, *Birth of Development*, ix (ultimate), 1 (significant), 23 (denationalized), 28 (idealists), 29 (France, Chile), 31 (working classes, Perón), 32 (EXIM, American protectionism), 41 (Netherlands), 44 (failure, Shoaib); Perkins, *Secret History*, 106 (block quote), 282 (business schools).
128. Jyoti Hosagrahar, *Indigenous Modernities: Negotiating Architecture and Urbanism* (London: Routledge, 2005); Dipesh Chakrabarty, *Habitations of Modernity: Essays in the Wake of Subaltern Studies* (Chicago: University of Chicago Press, 2002), xx (plural); Arce and Long, "Reconfiguring Modernity," 2 (cosmopolitan).
129. Deniz Kandiyoti, "Modernization without the Market? The Case of the 'Soviet East,'" in Arce and Long, *Anthropology*, 52–53; Wang, *End of the Revolution*, viii (anti-capitalist); Chakrabarty, *Provincializing Europe*, 19 (non-European), 34 (English rule), 39 (local content, nonmodern); Chakrabarty, *Habitations*, 4–5 (British gifts).
130. On hegemonic public and hidden transcripts, see James C. Scott, *Domination and the Arts of Resistance: Hidden Transcripts* (New Haven, CT: Yale University Press, 1990); Latham, *Modernization* (ideology), 36 (Lewis), 52 (interviews); Arce and Long, "Reconfiguring Modernity," 6; Daniel Lerner, *The Passing of Traditional Society: Modernizing the Middle East* (New York: Free Press, 1965), 49 (mobile person).
131. Berman, *All That Is Solid Melts Into Air*, 95 (yearn); William H. Wiser and Charlotte Viall Wiser, *Behind Mud Walls 1930–1960, with a Sequel: The Village in 1970* (Berkeley: University of California Press, 1971), 35 (cause and effect), 121 (hawk), 140 (car and driver), 156 (bus hire), 183–184 (bicycles, telephone, mail), 189 (cotton carder), 236 (progress), 244–245 (rickshaws).
132. Aguiar, *Tracking Modernity*, 1–2; Pradeep Jeganathan, "On the Anticipation of Violence: Modernity and Identity in Southern Sri Lanka," in Arce and Long, *Anthropology*, 112 (terror); Mom, *Atlantic Automobilism*, 594–606; Chakrabarty, *Provincializing Europe*, 45 (practices); Immanuel Wallerstein, *World-Systems Analysis: An Introduction* (Durham, NC: Duke University Press, 2004), 38–39.
133. Hobsbawm, *Age of Extremes*, 354–355 (land reform), 371 (Soviet model); Scott, *Domination*, xii. This does not mean the hidden transcript cannot be studied: it can be read, against the grain, in "rumors, gossip, folktales, songs, gestures, jokes, and theater of the powerless as vehicles by which, among other things, they insinuate a critique of

power while hiding behind anonymity or behind innocuous understandings of their conduct." Ibid., xiii.
134. Chakrabarty, *Habitations*, 8–9 (the study has been done by Ranajit Guha); Scott, *Domination*, 136.
135. David Arnold and Erich DeWald, "Cycles of Empowerment? The Bicycle and Everyday Technology in Colonial India and Vietnam," *Comparative Studies in Society and History* 53, no. 4 (2011): 994; Chakrabarty, *Habitations*, 19 (assumed death); on religion and modernity, see, e.g., Chakrabarty, *Habitations*, chap. 2 ("Subaltern Histories and Post-Enlightenment Rationalism").
136. Roth Jones, "The Vital Role of Public Relations in the Development of National and International Highway Programmes," *Road International* 54 (December 1964): 44–47, here 44, 46; Mom and Filarski, *Van transport naar mobiliteit*, 194–195 (elsewhere).
137. "Uitgaven voor wegen in verschillende landen," *Wegen* 29, no. 10: 311; "Meer dan 76 millioen automobielen in de wereld op 1 Januari 1953," *Wegen* (November 1953): 311; "How the Number of Motor Vehicles Has Increased during Four Years," *Road International* 6 (Autumn 1952): 61–62 (25 million); Owen, *Strategy for Mobility*, 10, table 1.1 (122 million), 13, table 1.3 (density); World Bank, *World Development Report 1994: Infrastructure for Development* (Oxford: Oxford University Press, 1994), 140–142, table A.1 (Appendix: Infrastructure Data).
138. Rolf Hofmeier, *Transport and Economic Development in Tanzania, with Particular Reference to Roads and Road Transport* (Munich: Weltforum Verlag, 1973), 79 (requirements); M. Luísa Sousa, "Colonial Centres and Peripheries: Low-Cost Roads and Portuguese Engineers in the 1950s," in *Peripheral Flows: A Historical Perspective on Mobilities between Cores and Fringes*, ed. Simone Fari and Massimo Moraglio (Newcastle upon Tyne: Cambridge Scholars Publishing, 2016), 171 (Portuguese), 175 (overseas).
139. PIARC, *XIth World Road Congress, Rio de Janeiro 1959: Proceedings of the Congress* (London, 1959), 194 (British participant), 195–197 (Malaysian engineer); Christian Huck and Stefan Bauernschmidt, eds., *Travelling Goods, Travelling Moods: Varieties of Cultural Appropriation (1850–1950)* (Frankfurt: Campus Verlag, 2012); Arnold, *Everyday Technology*, 7 (Dikötter); Edgerton, "Creole Technologies." R. S. Colquhoun, "Low-Cost Roads in Undeveloped Countries: Road Expenditures in Proportion to National Revenues," *Road International* 1 (Autumn 1950): 54–57, here 56 (India); "New Roads for the Gambia," *Road International* 61 (June 1969): 28–29. See also L. Odier and Louis Loder, "What Is the Position Regarding Low-Cost Roads in 1970? An Example: Australia," in *AIPCR–PIARC 1909–1969* (Paris: Association Internationale Permanente des Congrès de la Route / Permanent International Association of Road Congresses, 1970).
140. [Editorial], *Road International* 73 (June 1969): 9; Owen, *Strategy for Mobility*, 87–89 (investment percentages; the figures were part of local plans), 94, table 4.3 (rail freight), 102 (composition); Comisión Económica para América Latina (CEPAL), "El Transporte en America Latina, Volumen III" (Naciones Unidas, Consejo Económico y Social, 11 February 1965), 718 (consultancy); Martin and Warden, "Transportation Planning," 62 ($2.7 billion); Álvaro Pachón and María Teresa Ramírez, *La infraestructura de transporte en Colombia durante el siglo XX: Una descripción desde el punta de vista éconómico* (Bogotá: Fondo de Cultura Económica, Banco de la República, 2006), 29, graph 2.6 (decline).
141. J. Fred Rippy, "The Inter-American Highway," *Pacific Historical Review* 24, no. 3 (1955) 291n10; David Spurr, *The Rhetoric of Empire: Colonial Discourse in Journalism, Travel Writing, and Imperial Administration* (Durham, NC: Duke University Press, 1993), 35–36.

142. Guy Arnold and Ruth Weiss, *Strategic Highways of Africa* (London: Julian Friedmann Publishers, 1977), 11 (Gaborone), 140 (call), 146 (fly), 151 (Japanese mission); P. J. Beavan and C. J. Lawrence, "The Application of Terrain Evaluation tho [*sic*] the Trans-African Project," *Bulletin de l'AIPCR* 61, no. 206 (1972): 55–73, here 55 (one-third), 65 (Laboratory), 67 (firm); Emil Millin, "The Union Is the Pattern for African Road Development," *Road International* 4 (Spring 1952): 28–30, 32 (patterns).

143. David Wightman, *Towards Economic Cooperation in Asia: The United Nations Economic Commission for Asia and the Far East* (New Haven, CT: Yale University Press, 1963), v (independent), vi (Latin America and Africa), 4 (more than half), 16–17 (March 1947), 18 (research), 20 (Western majority), 47 (reconstruction), 49 (Flood Control), 204 (colonial past), 205 (international, regional conference), 209 (not expand, study tour); Yao Souchou, "Introduction," in *House of Glass: Culture, Modernity, and the State in Southeast Asia*, ed. Yao Souchou (Singapore: Institute of Southeast Asian Studies, 2001), 4 (nation-state), 12 (ethnolinguistic); Yves Bertholet, "Unity and Diversity of Development: The Regional Commissions' Experience," in Bertholet, *Unity and Diversity in Development Ideas*, 1 (multisectoral) 5 (Myrdal, middle way); Ikuto Yamaguchi, "The Development and Activities of the Economic Commission for Asia and the Far East (ECAFE), 1947–65," in Akita et al. *Transformation*, 92 (Marshall Plan), 95 (inland, Lahore), 96 (large-scale), 103 (ADB); [Peter Stalker], *The First Parliament of Asia: Sixty Years of the Economic and Social Commission for Asia and the Pacific (1947–2007)* (Bangkok: United Nations, 2007), 21 (crucially supported), 39 (65 percent of worldwide GDP in 1500), 47 (extraction), 59 (intra-regional); Oba Mie, "Japan's Entry into ECAFE," in *Japanese Diplomacy in the 1950s: From Isolation to Integration*, ed. Iokibe Makoto, Caroline Rose, Tomaru Junko, and John Weste (London: Routledge, 2008), 99 (full member).

144. Yamaguchi, "Development and Activities," 96 (Bangkok, funds), 104 (Mekong); De Silva, "From ECAFE to ESCAP," 139 (truly), 163 (technical assistance); Wightman, *Towards Economic Cooperation*, 232 (afford; the quote stems from an expert interviewed by Wightman).

145. J. H. T. Clarke, "The Work of the Economic Commission for Asia and the Far East in the Field of Inland Transport," *Road International* 3 (Winter 1951): 51–53, here 51 (Bangkok); [Stalker], *First Parliament of Asia*, 51 (grand design), 53 (rallies); W. G. Kennedy, "The Asian Highway System," *Road International* (March 1964): 34–35; "The Asian Highway in the United Nations Development Decade," *Road International* 77 (June 1970): 35–41; Wightman, *Towards Economic Cooperation*, 218 (existing), 219 (Indonesian), 219 (missing links), 221 (signs, promotional); L. Odier, "Some Information on the International Road System in Asia (1)," *Bulletin de l'AIPCR* 61, no. 206 (1972): 41–48, here 43 (total length), 47 (rallies).

146. "Asian Highway," 36, 39; W. G. Kennedy, "The Role of E.C.A.F.E. in the Development of the Asian Highway," *Road International* 36 (Spring 1960): 37–39, 42 (42: uninterrupted); "Linking the CENTO Region," *Road International* 53 (June 1964): 26–28 (26: enormous); De Silva, "From ECAFE to ESCAP," 163.

147. B. V. Vagh, "The Bottleneck in Indian Transport: Increased Road Transport Facilities Urgently Needed," *Road International* 14 (Autumn 1954): 29–31 (quotes on 30–31).

148. Tajammal H. Hashmi, "Road Development in Pakistan," *Road International* 8 (Spring 1953): 20; Owen, *Strategy for Mobility*, 73 (expanded); Khun Sahib M. A. Jabber, "Road in East Bengal Pakistan," *Road International* 2 (Spring 1951): 70–71; for an incredibly detailed overview of the types and quality of roads (constantly compared with the West) in West Bengal, see Sukla Bhaduri, *Transport and Regional Development: A Case Study of Road Transport of West Bengal* (New Delhi: Concept Publishing Co. 1992).

149. John Hugh Jones, "Transportation Engineering Research at the SEATO Graduate School of Engineering," *Road International* 60 (March 1966): 20–27, here 21 (55 percent), 22 (lettering), 26 (laterite), 27 (bituminous); James William Jordan, "Role Segregation for Fun and Profit: The Daily Behavior of the West African Lorry Driver," *Africa: Journal of the International African Institute* 48, no. 1 (1978): 31 (silica).

150. "Modern Highways Open Thailand's Interior," *Road International* 60 (March 1966): 45–49, here 45 (*klongs*), 46 (carved), 47 (sub-based); Meow, *Infrastructural Growth*, 20 (rejected, insurgency); Thomas R. Leinbach, "Road and Rail Transport Systems," in *South-East Asian Transport: Issues in Development*, ed. Thomas R. Leinbach and Chia Lin Sien (with Christopher C. Kissling, Ross Robinson, and Andrew H. Spencer) (Singapore: Oxford University Press, 1989), 80 (transfer); Joe L. Campbell, "Report on U.S. Aid Programme for Highways in the Philippines," *Road International* 18 (Autumn 1955): 44–50, here 46.

151. Thomas R. Leinbach, "Transportation and the Development of Malaya," *Annals of the Association of American Geographers* 65, no. 2 (1975): 279 (Kedah), 280, fig. 5 (second phase), 282 (self-reinforcing); C. Mary Turnbull, *A Short History of Malaysia, Singapore and Brunei* (Singapore: Graham Brash, 1988), 229 (outsiders), 237 (1948), 240 (new villages, Gurney), 245 (Emergency), 248 (majority), 249 (premiership), 256 (port), 260 (resources), 269 (China), 281 (socialism and 1969); Thomas Williamson, "The Fluid State: Malaysia's National Expressway," *Space & Culture* 6, no. 2 (2003): 117 (fury); Thomas R. Leinbach, "The Spread of Modernization in Malaya: 1895–1969," *Tijdschrift voor Economische en Sociale Geografie* 63, no. 4 (1972): 274 (empty areas).

152. Tu, "Cultural China," 12 (Sinic world); Kuan-Hsing Chen, "The Formation and Consumption of KTV in Taiwan," in *Consumption in Asia: Lifestyles and Identities*, ed. Chua Beng-Huat (London: Routledge, 2000), 172 (Taiwan); Mason, *Turbulent Empires*, 95 (MacArthur), 96 (one million, carpet bombing), 97 (*zaibatsu*, Israel), 98 (three hundred thousand); Zhiqun Zhu, *Understanding East Asia's Economic "Miracles"* (Ann Arbor, MI: Association for Asian Studies, 2012), 24–25; Matthew Hilton and Rana Mitter, "Introduction," *Past and Present* 218, no. S8 (2013).

153. James Ferguson, *The Anti-politics Machine: "Development," Depoliticization, and Bureaucratic Power in Lesotho* (Cambridge: Cambridge University Press, 1990), 267 (Dutkiewicz and Shenton); Black and Rimmer, "Japanese Highway Planning," 39–41 (39: resource); Mason, *Turbulent Empires*, 83 (capital flow).

154. Rimmer, *Rikisha*, 58 (cycle rickshaw). The following paragraphs are based mostly on several contributions to Hirofumi Yamamoto, ed., *Technological Innovation and the Development of Transportation in Japan* (Tokyo: United Nations University Press, 1993).

155. Tsurumi, *Cultural History*, 1 (conservative), 2 (removal), 8 (20,997 lost their job), 22 (prosperity; this is confirmed by Shunya Yoshimi, "Consuming America, Producing Japan," trans. David Buist, in *The Ambivalent Consumer: Questioning Consumption in East Asia and the West*, ed. Sheldon Garon and Patricia L. Maclachlan [Ithaca, NY: Cornell University Press, 2006], 72: "Japan entered the era of economic growth in the late 1950s"); Mason, *Turbulent Empires*, 33 (Okinawa); Andrew Gordon, *A Modern History of Japan: From Tokugawa Times to the Present* (New York: Oxford University Press, 2003), 229 (seven), 234 (imperial), 236 (bank-centered), 239 (Red Purge), 246 (record); Sheldon Garon, "The Transnational Promotion of Saving in Asia: 'Asian Values' of the 'Japanese Model'?" in Garon and Maclaclan, *Ambivalent Consumer*, 164 (balance).

156. Koichi Shimokawa, "Japan: The Late Starter Who Outpaced All Her Rivals," in Barker, *Economic and Social Effects*, 218, table 11.2 (horse-drawn); Katsumasa Harada, "Policy," in Yamamoto, *Technological Innovation*, 222 (rapid); Hirofumi Yamamoto, "Roads," in

Yamamoto, *Technological Innovation*, 244 (explosion); Zhu, *Understanding*, 10 (development state), 12 (guided), 15 (aid).
157. Harada, "Policy," 224 (laws), 226; Michizo Kishi, "Road Financing in Japan: Report Presented at the I.R.F. Pacific Regional Conference, Sydney," *Road International* (Autumn 1961): 29–30 (reasons for toll roads); [editorial], *Road International* 51 (December 1963) 15 (extension); Black and Rimmer, "Japanese Highway Planning," 29 (7 percent, 6 percent) 31 (strategic).
158. Walter Hock and Michael Replogle, "Motorization and Non-motorized Transport in Asia: Transport System Evolution in China, Japan and Indonesia," *Land Use Policy* 13, no. 1 (1996): 75; Shimokawa, "Japan," 229 (1970s); Yoshitsugu Hayashi, Rithika Suparat, Roger Mackett, Kenji Doi, Yasuo Tomita, Nahoko Nakazawa, Hirokazu Kato, and Krit Anurak, "Urbanization, Motorization and the Environment Nexus: An International Comparative Study of London, Tokyo, Nagoya and Bangkok," *Memoirs of the School of Engineering, Nagoya University* 46, no. 1 (1994): 84 (share in GNP); Black and Rimmer, "Japanese Highway Planning," 31–32; Yamamoto, "Roads," 253. See also Akira Kikuchi, "Urban Motorways," in *AIPCR–PIARC 1909–1969* (Paris: Association Internationale Permanente des Congrès de la Route, 1970), 71–92.
159. Howe, "Transport for the Poor," 10n2; Black and Rimmer, "Japanese Highway Planning," 32, 35.
160. Gordon, *Modern History*, 251.
161. Mason, *Turbulent Empires*, 83 (Vietnam War); Shimokawa, "Japan," 226, table 11.7; Gordon, *Modern History*, 254 (trunk line).
162. William W. Kelly, "At the Limits of New Middle-Class Japan: Beyond 'Mainstream Consciousness,'" in *Social Contracts Under Stress: The Middle Classes of America, Europe, and Japan at the Turn of the Century*, ed. Olivier Zunz, Leonard Schoppa, and Nobuhiro Hiwatari (New York: Russell Sage Foundation, 2002), 233 (Survey), 234 (mainstream); Ezra F. Vogel, *Japan's New Middle Class: The Salary Man and His Family in a Tokyo Suburb* (Berkeley: University of California Press, 1971), 5 (*sarariman*), 6n3 (quarter), 11 (guests), 14 (commuting), 35 (afford), 265 (solidarity), 274 (excitement), 275 (adventure), 277 (cars); David W. Plath, "My-Car-isma: Motorizing the Showa Self," in *Showa: The Japan of Hirohito*, ed. Carol Gluck and Stephen R. Graubard (New York: Norton, 1992), 229 (*motarizeshon*), 230 (year); Gordon, *Modern History*, 255 (tourism, egalitarian), 256 (53 percent), 267 (regalia), 268, fig. 14.2 (77 percent of survey respondents self-defined as middle class).
163. Rimmer, *Rikisha*, 70 (similarity); Black and Rimmer, "Japanese Highway Planning," 30 (surveys), 37 (dynamics, refashioning).
164. Leinbach, "Road and Rail," 41 (aid), 42 (controversial), 79 (Trans-Sumatran); Meow, *Infrastructural Growth*, 7–8 (200 million), 11 (86.5 percent), 22 (capitals); Eiichi Aoki, "Railroads," in Yamamoto, *Technological Innovation*, 239 (pantographs).
165. Rimmer, *Rikisha*, 169–191 (174: tortuous); Imes Chiu, *The Evolution from Horse to Automobile: A Comparative International Study* (Amherst, NY: Cambria Press, 2008), 224–225.
166. Chiu, *Evolution*, 225 (literally), 227 (honor system), 232 (alike), 234 (crowns), 235 (upholstery), 240 (*barja*), 241 (Korea); Moira F. Harris, *Art on the Road: Painted Vehicles of the Americas*, photographs by Leo J. Harris (St. Paul, MN: Pogo Press, 1988), chap. 1 ("The Ox Carts of Costa Rica").
167. Rimmer, *Rikisha*, 188; Black and Rimmer, "Japanese Highway Planning," 43 (coarse).
168. Williamson, "Fluid State," 117; Ezra F. Vogel, "A Little Dragon Tamed," in *Management of Success: The Moulding of Modern Singapore*, ed. Kernial Singh Sandhu and Paul Wheatley (Singapore: Institute of Southeast Asian Studies, 1989), 1053 (macho, street-

smart), 1055 (narcissism, social engineering), 1056 (76 percent), 1061 (paychecks, savings); N. Varaprasad, "Providing Mobility and Accessibility," in Singh Sandhu and Wheatley, *Management of Success*, 421 (Company); Rimmer, *Rikisha*, 153 (pirate).

169. Rimmer, *Rikisha*, 155, fig. 5.1 (Kuala Lumpur), 159 (Bangkok), 180 (*opelet*), 160 (Jakarta, 150,000), 165 (115,000), 166 (riots); Gustav F. Papanek, "The Poor of Jakarta," *Economic Development and Cultural Change* 24, no. 1 (1975): 22 (city), 25 (middle income); Howard W. Dick, "Urban Public Transport, Part II," *Bulletin of Indonesian Economic Studies* 17, no. 2 (1981): 76–77 (*helicak*, 10,000), 78 (replace).

170. Rimmer, *Rikisha*, 168 (feeder), 204 (McNamara), 221 (problem), 224 (informal), 227 (success).

171. V. Setty Pendakur, "Elaboration of the Transport System," in Singh Sandhu and Wheatley, *Management of Success*, 400 (ADB, freeways); Rimmer, *Rikisha*, 123 (typical Chinese, pirate), 125 (bureaus), 126 (amalgamated), 134 (policies), 143 (Harvard), 148 ($2.34 billion), 150 (rickshaw); for an official report from the Singapore Institute of Planners, see Chua Peng Chye, ed., *Planning in Singapore: Selected Aspects and Issues* (Singapore: Chopmen Enterprises, 1973).

172. Rimmer, *Rikisha*, 232, fig. 7.1 (Penang), 247, fig. 7.4 (Surabaya), 247–248 (eliminated).

173. Howard W. Dick, "Representations of Development in 19th and 20th Century Indonesia: A Transport History Perspective," *Bulletin of Indonesian Economic Studies* 36, no. 1 (2000): 193–194; Q. Edward Wang, "Globalization, Global History and Local Identity in 'Greater China,'" *History Compass* 8, no. 4 (2010): 323 (Hokkien); Rimmer, *Rikisha*, 317, table AI.2.

174. Howard W. Dick, "Urban Public Transport: Jakarta, Surabaya and Malang, Part I," *Bulletin of Indonesian Economic Studies* 17, no. 1 (1981): 66 (taxonomy), 67 (*bemo, bajaj, kolt*); according to Yann-Philippe Tastevin, "Autorickshaw (1948– 2 . . .): A Success Story," *Techniques & Culture* 58, no. 1 (2012): 264, 266. The autorickshaw was a "scooter-based taxi" derived from the three-wheeled model "l'Ape" by the Italian scooter manufacturer Piaggio, made famous through its Vespa; the three-wheeler and its engine were produced since 1948; see "Auto Rickshaw," https://en.wikipedia.org/wiki/Auto_rickshaw (consulted 6 May 2016).

175. Frederick Cooper and Randall Packard, "Introduction," in Cooper and Packard, *International Development*, 12 (developers); Alan Hay, "The Importance of Passenger Transport in Nigeria," *Nigerian Journal of Economic and Social Studies* 11, no. 1 (1969): 21.

176. G. Wolfgang Heinze, *Der Verkehrssektor in der Entwicklungspolitik: Unter besonderer Berücksichtigung des afrikanischen Raumes* (Munich: Weltforum Verlag, 1967), 123 (panafrican), 127 (primitive transport, including porterage, canoes and rafts, animal traction, and bicycles), 128–129 (densities), 154, table 30 (nearly all), 157 (Monrovia), 183 (ordering), 184 (the taxonomy of countries stems from Günther Lübbeke). For a succinct overview of the railroad struggle in Africa, see Irene S. van Dongen, "Road versus Rail in Africa," *Geographical Review* 52, no. 2 (1962).

177. Brett, *Approaching African History*, 321; B. Bazabas, "The Transsahara Road," *Road International* 74 (September 1969): 10–13; Judith Scheele, *Smugglers and Saints of the Sahara: Regional Connectivity in the Twentieth Century* (New York, 2012), quoted in Joshua Grace, "Saharan Garages, Paper Economies, and Migrant Laborers: New Perspectives on Mobility in African History," in *Mobility in History: The Yearbook of the International Association for the History of Transport, Traffic and Mobility, Volume 5*, ed. Peter Norton, Gijs Mom, Tomás Errázuriz, and Kyle Shelton (New York: Berghahn Journals, 2014), 145 (achievement); Dawn Chatty, *From Camel to Truck: The Bedouin in the Modern World* (Cambridge: White Horse Press, 2013), 118 (1970s),

120 (concentrates), 141 (Toyota, households), 143 (semiarid, husbandry); Thomas J. Barfield, *The Nomadic Alternative* (Englewood Cliffs, NJ: Prentice Hall, 1993) 49 (nomads, pastoralists).
178. Jan-Bart Gewald, Sabine Luning, and Klaas van Walraven, "Motor Vehicles and People in Africa: An Introduction," in *The Speed of Change: Motor Vehicles and People in Africa, 1890–2000*, ed. Jan-Bart Gewald, Sabine Luning, and Klaas van Walraven (Leiden: Brill, 2009), 9 (new), 10 (exotic); Sjaak van der Geest, "'Anyway!' Lorry Inscriptions in Ghana," in Gewald et al., *Speed of Change*, 259 (Kopytoff).
179. Millin, "Union"; Anis Chebat, "International Routes and the Arab States," *Road International* 42 (Autumn 1961): 40–42; "The African Regional Road Congress: Report from Salisbury," *Road International* 25 (Summer 1957): 26–27, 29, here 26 (£10 million), 27 (Rhodes).
180. A. Felix-Williams, "The Kenya Road Authority: Kenya Colony and Protectorate—Its Formation and the Problems It Has to Face," *Road International* 4 (Spring 1952): 20–21.
181. "Opening Up Ethiopia: Progress under the International Bank's Loan," *Road International* 25 (Summer 1957): 44–48, here 46; "Economic Development in Swaziland: World Bank Finances Highway and Hydroelectric Projects," *Road International* 53 (June 1964) 58; on women as "the most 'backward' group in society," see Scott, "Tradition and Gender in Modernization Theory," 293; Daniel Mains, "Blackouts and Progress: Privatization, Infrastructure, and a Developmentalist State in Jimma, Ethiopia," *Cultural Anthropology* 27, no. 1 (2012): 8 (*limat*).
182. Peter R. Gould, *The Development of the Transportation Pattern in Ghana* (Evanston, IL: Department of Geography, Northwestern University, April 1960), 77 (densest); Brett, *Approaching African History*, 290 (Gunther), 297 (Brett's subsequent analysis points out the march's end was "inconclusive" at best), 305 (populated).
183. Keith Hart, "Informal Income Opportunities and Urban Employment in Ghana," *Journal of Modern African Studies* 11, no. 1 (1973): 61 (mobile), 86 (slum), 89 (neglect); Dick, "Representations," 205n1 (dualist); Heinze, *Der Verkehrssektor*, 115 (islands); Chapman and Prothero, "Themes on Circulation," xvii (origin), 1 (transhumance), 6 (traditional), 7 (example of such a taxonomy, where "shopping" is missing as one of the micro-circular movements), 20 (forty), 24 (Netherlands).
184. Gould, *Development*, 73 (mammy wagons), 83 (photograph of a mammy wagon); Hay, "Importance," 16–17 (mammy wagon definition); Awuleh Mensah, "Ghana Roads: A Second Five-Year Development Plan Now Starting," *Road International* 35 (Winter 1959/1960): 31–33.
185. Gould, *Development*, 135 (porterage), 137 (half), 138 (head loading); Gina Porter, "Reflections on a Century of Road Transport Developments in West Africa and Their (Gendered) Impacts on the Rural Poor," *EchoGéo* 20 (April–June 2012), 4.
186. Hay, "Importance," 15–18 (four forms), 23 (motives), 24 (women dominant).
187. Porter, "Reflections," 5 (collapsed); Hart, "Informal Income Opportunities," 64 (1960s); Gina Porter, "Living in a Walking World: Rural Mobility and Social Equity Issues in Sub-Saharan Africa," *World Development* 30, no. 2 (2002): 287 (fines), 292.
188. Porter, "Living," 286 (poor), 294 (Tanzania); Porter, "Reflections," 1.
189. Epanya Sh. Tshund'olela, "Motor Transport in a Developing Area (i): Zaïre, 1903–1959," in Barker, *Economic and Social Effects*, 177 (split), 191 (other sources), 192 (communal), 240, table 12.1 (roads), 245 (resettled), 248 (scaled down), 251, table 12.4 (density).
190. Gewald et al., "Motor Vehicles and People," 75 (*commis*), 76 (*petit peuple*), 81 (supervision) 83–84 (*coxeur*), 86 (pick-up), 91 (telephone), 96 (*Cadres*).

191. Landeg White, *Magomero: Portrait of an African Village* (Cambridge: Cambridge University Press, 2000), 252 (economies, subsists), 227 (fact), 245.
192. E. K. Hawkins, *Roads and Road Transport in an Underdeveloped Country: A Case Study of Uganda* (London: Her Majesty's Stationery Office, 1962), 23 (landlocked, density), 28, table 3 (vehicle statistics), 31 (growth rate and income), 35 (stagnating), 39, table 9 (racialized), 40 (level), 46 (United Kingdom); Amiel Bize, "Jam-Space and Jam-Time: Traffic in Nairobi," in Beck et al., *Making of the African Road*, 58 (minivan), 65 (Kenyatta); Gijs Mom, "Mobility for Pleasure: A Look at the Underside of Dutch Diffusion Curves (1920–1940)," *TST Revista de Historia: Transportes, Servicios y Telecomunicaciones* 12 (June 2007): 30–68 (curve).
193. Hofmeier, *Transport*, 19 (agreement), 37–38 (railway density), 39 (tracks), 40 (road density). For an attempt to quantify the modernization process in Tanzania and explain this through maps, see Peter R. Gould, "Tanzania 1920–63: The Spatial Impress of the Modernization Process," *World Politics* 22, no. 2 (1970).
194. Hofmeier, *Transport*, 68 (East African Railways), 83 (new roads), 85 (feeder roads), 86 (closely), 101 (growth of traffic), 102 (stagnation), 103, table 1 (quarter), 131 (150), 153 (all modes), 155, table 14 (buses), 156 (half).
195. Klaas van Walraven, "Vehicles of Sedition: The Role of Transport Workers in Sawaba's Rebellion in Niger, 1954–1966," in Gewald et al., *Speed of Change*, 76–77 (semi-urban); Gewald et al., "Motor Vehicles and People," 11 (drivers); Jennifer Hart, "'One Man, No Chop': Licit Wealth, Good Citizens, and the Criminalization of Drivers in Postcolonial Ghana," *International Journal of African Historical Studies* 46, no. 3 (2013): 375 (scoundrels), 377 (thirty), 381 (1957).
196. Hawkins, *Roads*, 101 (strict), 102, table 48 (61 percent), 131 (pirate), 168 (drivers).
197. For the following paragraphs, see Adrian Peace, "The Politics of Transporting," *Africa: Journal of the International African Institute* 58, no. 1 (1988); and esp. Abner Cohen, *Customs and Politics in Urban Africa: A Study of Hausa Migrants in Yoruba Towns* (Berkeley: University of California Press, 1969).
198. Cohen, *Customs and Politics*, 30 (home settlement), 32 (stranger), 103 (special settlement).
199. Ibid., 27 (cattle, etc.), 189 (landlords, etc.).
200. Peace, "Politics of Transporting," 14 (micropolitics), 15 (economy, debris), 16 (skills), 20–21 (block quote), 22 (bribes), 24 (contractors), 25 (big men), 26 (move freely, informal sector, 10 percent); Mom, *Atlantic Automobilism*, 614–617 (Western European).
201. Jordan, "Role Segregation," 32 (mile, wild, comfort, densities), 33 (13 percent); Bill Freund, "Labor and Labor History in Africa: A Review of the Literature," *African Studies Review* 27, no. 2 (1984): 3 (the *Gemeinschaft-Gesellschaft* dichotomy was introduced into African studies by Godfrey Wilson in 1941).
202. Jordan, "Role Segregation," (dirt roads), 39 (sullen), 42 (Mitchell); Mom, *Atlantic Automobilism*, 499 (cool); W. B. Morgan and J. C. Pugh, *West Africa* (New York: Methuen, 1969), 41 (non-mechanical).
203. Sara S. Berry, "From Peasant to Artisan: Motor Mechanics in a Nigerian Town," African Studies Center Working Paper no. 76 (Boston, 1983): 4 (opportunities), 12 (skills), 14 (tertiary).
204. Freund, "Labor," 2 (*loisir*), 4 (manhood), 20 (South Africa); Cheng and Selden, "Origins and Social Consequences," 656 (certificate); Bradley Rink, "Race and the Micropolitics of Mobility: Mobile Autoethnography on a South African Bus Service," *Transfers* 6, no. 1 (2016): 66 (1953); J. J. McCarthy, "South Africa's Emerging Politics of Bus Transportation," *Political Geography Quarterly* 4, no. 3 (1985): 236 and 238 (boycotts).

205. Freund, "Labor," 6 (*Gemeinschaft*), 30 (theory), 31 (mining, sexual), 32 (exploitation).
206. Cohen, *Customs and Politics*, 6–7 (fully aware), 191–192 (political ethnicity); Philip Mayer, "Migrancy and the Study of Africans in Towns," *American Anthropologist* 64, no. 3 (1962): 576.
207. Ekwensi, *Jagua Nana*, Cyprian Ekwensi, *Jagua Nana* (Melbourne: Heinemann, [1997?]), front cover (brilliant), 5 (prestige), 8 (big car), 13 (High-life), 28 (bus), 30 (poor teacher), 34 (long), 49 (white face, limousine), 55 (diesel), 57 (Pontiac), 58 (Party People), 68 (Mammy Wagon, first class), 72 (bicycle-taxi), 73 (deceived), 74 (canoe), 105 (princesses), 125 ("de fas' life"), 126 (rent), 135 (O.P. 1), 138 (wider roads), 139 (bodyguards), 155 (Freddie's death), 168 (marriage), 179 (sewing), 180 (bicycle), 186 (Taiwo's death), 187 ("God will help me for become real Merchant Princess"), 192 (lorry); Van der Geest, "Anyway!" 275 (pidginized).
208. Adeline Masquelier, "Road Mythographies: Space, Mobility, and the Historical Imagination in Postcolonial Niger," *American Ethnologist* 29, no. 4 (2002): 831.
209. "*The Road* by Wole Soyinka: Themes and Meanings," eNotes.com, accessed 29 October 2019, https://www.enotes.com/topics/road-wole-soyinka/themes (spider's web); "Wole Soyinka," https://en.wikipedia.org/wiki/Wole_Soyinka (retrieved on 11 May 2016) (Nobel Prize and Landrover); "The Road Themes; Wole Soyinka," http://www.enotes.com/topics/road-wole-soyinka (consulted 11 May 2016) (spider's web); Wole Soyinka, *The Road* [a play] (Oxford: Oxford University Press, 1965), 1 (*bolekaja*), 3 (motor park), 4 (block quote), 5 (ten wives), 35 (admiration), 37 (cyborg), 38 (business man), 51 (bridge), 55 (delay), 81–82 (war), 85 (worship), 89 (Sunday School).
210. Brinkman, "Refugees on Routes," 200 (aircraft, hampered, bandit), 201 (forced labor, trees), 202 (invisible enemy, neon-lights) (I thank Luísa Sousa [Lisbon] for bringing this source to my attention); Joseph C. Miller, "From Group Mobility to Individual Movement: The Colonial Effort to Turn Back History," in Heintze and Oppen, *Angola on the Move*, 258–259 (winning).
211. Brinkman, "Refugees on Routes," 209; Miller, "From Group Mobility," 258 (immobilizing), 259 (multiple).
212. Victor Pereira, "Les réseaux de l'émigration clandestine portugaise vers la France entre 1957 et 1974," *Journal of Modern European History* 12 (2014): 107–116; Christian Hadorn, "Tagber: Violence, Migration, Cooperation, Gender: Late Portuguese and Spanish Colonialism in Africa Reconsidered," H-Soz-Kult (29 January 2017), 2 (migrated).
213. Sutton et al., "Development Ideology," 54; Kate Manzo, "Modernist Discourse and the Crisis of Development Theory," *Studies in Comparative International Development* 26, no. 2 (1991): 4 (Brazil, famine), 15 (easy); Ramón Grosfoguel, "Developmentalism, Modernity, and Dependency Theory in Latin America," in *Coloniality at Large: Latin America and the Postcolonial Debate*, ed. Mabel Moraña, Enrique Dussel, and Carlos A. Jáuregui (Durham, NC: Duke University Press, 2008), 316 (substitution); Bernard E. Munk, "The Colombian Automotive Industry: The Welfare Consequences of Import Substitution," *Economies and Business Bulletin* (Fall 1970), 6; Leinbach, "Road and Rail," 71 (Java).
214. Rosa E. Ficek, "Imperial Routes, National Networks and Regional Projects in the Pan-American Highway, 1884–1977," *Journal of Transport History* 37, no. 2 (2016): 141, 142 (walk), 143 (common markets).
215. CEPAL, "El Transporte," 862 (sufficient), 885, table 242 (shares), 889 (Asia), 894 (somewhat forgotten: *un poco olvidado*).
216. Eduardo Dibos, "The Road Link Between North, Central and South America Still Has Some Gaps," *Road International* 4 (Spring 1952): 10–19, here 10 (adventurers) (Dibos

had been mayor of Lima in Peru and was now vice president of the Peruvian branch of Goodyear and president of the Touring and Automobile Club of Peru); Ficek, "Imperial Routes," 145–148 (147: poverty); Fulwider, "Driving the Nation," 252 (ex-President). On the stretch of the Pan-American Highway through Central America, see Rippy, "Inter-American Highway."

217. "The Inter-American Highway in Central America: Progress along the 1,573-Mile Link between the Americas," *Road International* 38 (Autumn 1960): 29–32; "Carlos Castillo Armas," *Wikipedia*, last edited 29 October 2019, http://en.wikipedia.org/wiki/Carlos_Castillo_Armas (Carlos Castillo Armas); Streeter, "Failure," 399–401 (expensive).

218. Grosfoguel, "Developmentalism," 307 (*cepalistas*), 319; Kathryn Sikkink, "Development Ideas in Latin America: Paradigm Shift and the Economic Commission for Latin America," in Cooper and Packard, *International Development*, 228 (influential, Prebisch), 229 (ISI, training), 231 (*desarrollo*); Arturo Escobar, *Encountering Development: The Making and Unmaking of the Third World* (Princeton, NJ: Princeton University Press, 2012), 80 (center and periphery); Ann Laura Stoler and Frederick Cooper, "Between Metropole and Colony: Rethinking a Research Agenda," in *Tensions of Empire: Colonial Cultures in a Bourgeois World*, ed. Frederick Cooper and Ann Laura Stoler (Berkeley: University of California Press, 1997), 17 (historical turn); Manzo, "Modernist Discourse," 4 (world-system), 5 (revival), 10 (Marxists), 11 (internalized), 16 (Baran), 17 (expropriating).

219. Grosfoguel, "Developmentalism," 327 (hierarchies); Manzo, "Modernist Discourse," 11 (agency) claims such critique misreads the truly "countermodernist" elements in *dependentista* theory; "Speech delivered by Mr. Luis Bracamontes," in *XVth World Road Congress, Mexico 1975: Proceedings of the Congress* by PIARC (London, 1975), 50–54 (53: Gálvez), 91–92 (Tunisia).

220. CEPAL, "El Transporte," 603, table 164; Robert T. Brown, *Transport and the Economic Integration of South America* (Washington, DC: Brookings Institution, 1966) 11 (strip), 14 (hinterland), 78, table 5-3 (GNP per capita), 228 (prerequisite); Ricardo Salvatore, "The Unsettling Location of a Settler Nation: Argentina, from Settler Economy to Failed Developing Nation," *South Atlantic Quarterly* 107, no. 4 (2008): 757 (regions), 776 (Tigers).

221. Bernard Munk, "The Welfare Costs of Content Protection: The Automotive Industry in Latin America," *Journal of Political Economy* 77, no. 1 (1969): 85 (market); Brown, *Transport*, 175, table 8-3 (cars); Güvenç, "Cold War Origins," 537 (transition); Steven J. Bachelor, "Miracle on Ice: Industrial Workers and the Promise of Americanization in Cold War Mexico," in *In from the Cold: Latin America's New Encounter with the Cold War*, ed. Gilbert M. Joseph and Daniela Spenser (Durham, NC: Duke University Press, 2008), 43–44 (Chrysler, autoworkers, Ford); Leland J. Johnson, "Problems of Import Substitution: The Chilean Automobile Industry," *Economic Development and Cultural Change* 15, no. 2 (1967): 202 (Chile); Franco, *Cruel Modernity*, 7 (alien).

222. Richard Schweid, *Che's Chevrolet, Fidel's Oldsmobile: On the Road in Cuba* (Chapel Hill: University of North Carolina Press, 2004), 176 (Cadillacs), 178 (Battista), 180–181 (Castro, Che, Borrego), 187 (boycott), 193 (sugar), 195 (Playa Girón), 199 (Oldsmobile), 200 (Skodas, etc.; upkeep); Kurt Möser, "Autobasteln: Modifying, Maintaining, and Repairing Private Cars in the GDR, 1970–1990," in *The Socialist Car: Automobility in the Eastern Bloc*, ed. Lewis H. Siegelbaum (Ithaca, NY: Cornell University Press, 2011); Tulio Halperín Donghi, *The Contemporary History of Latin America*, ed. and trans. John Charles Chasteen (Durham, NC: Duke University Press, 1993) 293, 299.

223. John Brian Freeman, "Transnational Mechanics: Automobility in Mexico, 1895–1950" (PhD diss., City University of New York, 2012), 180 (Cárdenas, 86 percent), 201

(dollars); Michael K. Bess, 'Routes of Conflict: Building Roads and Shaping the Nation in Mexico, 1941–1952," *Journal of Transport History*, 35, no. 1 (2014): 80 (overrule).
224. Fulwider, "Driving the Nation," 88 (profits), 89 (railroad labor), 92 (shopkeepers), 94 (GDP), 95 (trade), 97 (market), 98 (collective), 102 (consultants), 103 (oil fields), 110 (monopoly), 114 (state-sanctioned), 124 (Communists).
225. Freeman, "Transnational Mechanics," 174 (trucks), 205 (25,000), 175 (competition), 176 (same), 206 (Cadillac), 207 (strategy), 208 (half); Bess, "Routes of Conflict," 78–79 (2,250); Fulwider, "Driving the Nation," 129 (civilian), 130 (Partido), 131 (campaign), 135 (Marshall Plan), 136 (*alemanismo*).
226. Freeman, "Transnational Mechanics," 209 (one-fifth); Fulwider, "Driving the Nation," 138 (scholarships), 141 (union), 146 (brief), 149 (spare parts), 158 (Mateos), 181 (10 percent), 187 (1950), 189 (demand), 190 (Diesel), 208 (logging), 230 (*piratas*).
227. Fulwider, "Driving the Nation," 166 (bonds), 167–170 (Asociación), 172–174 (Oaxaca), 192 (km), 195 (units), 197 (growth), 200 (incorporating), 202 (property), 268 (maintenance).
228. "Marcos Perez Jimenez," s.v., *Wikipedia*, last edited 28 October 2019, http://en.wikipedia.org/wiki/Marcos_Perez_Jimenez (Marcos Perez Jimenez); José Ignacio Vielma-Cabruja, "Transfers, Influences and Experiences: Notes on the Development of Expressways in Caracas (1947–1973) and Its Actual Expression," paper presented at the workshop "Transport and Mobility Studies in Latin America," School of Architecture and Urban Studies of the University of Chile, Santiago de Chile (8–9 July 2013).
229. Eugene Wright, "Venezuela's 'Road to the Sea': The Autopista from Caracas to La Guaira," *Road International* 13 (Summer 1954): 11–17, 60 (block quote); Francisco J. Hernández, "A Continental Avenue of the Americas," *Road International* 13 (Summer 1954): 34–35, here 35 (pleasure); Alfredo Schael, ed., *Venezuela: 100 años en AUTOMOVÍL* (Caracas: Fundación Museo del Transporte, 2004), 185 (1958, Ford), 203 (*carro popular*), 205 (deaths), 207 (a million).
230. Robert O. Swain, "A Maintenance Programme for a National Highway System: Colombia Inaugurates Plan Proposed by World Bank as Second Phase of Road Construction Is Started," *Road International* 14 (Autumn 1954): 14–19; Pachón and Ramírez, *La infraestructura*, 235 (inhabitants), 265 (consultants), 291, graph 2.6 (railway network), 324–325 (American firms), 326 (road network), 362–363 (costs), 366, table 2.22 (road freight); Martin and Warden, "Transportation Planning," 62 (independently).
231. Benjamin B. Fraenkel, "Highways in Brazil's Future," *Road International* 18 (Autumn 1955): 12–17, here 14; Eduardo Alcântara Vasconcellos, "The Making of the Middle-Class City: Transportation Policy in São Paulo," *Environment and Planning A* 29, no. 2 (1997): 303n7; Mason, *Turbulent Empires*, 218 (fastest).
232. Joel Wolfe, *Autos and Progress: The Brazilian Search for Modernity* (Oxford: Oxford University Press, 2010), 105–110 (Vargas), 113 (Fifty Years), 114 (middle class), 115 (More Energy), 136 (central state), 150 (frontier), 153 (miracle), 155 (failure), 166 (statistics), 179 (modernity), 246n97 (CEPAL); CEPAL, "El Transporte," 713 (8.3), 717 (highest); Brian P. Owensby, *Intimate Ironies: Modernity and the Making of Middle-Class Lives in Brazil* (Stanford, CA: Stanford University Press, 1999), 246 (coup); Terry-Ann Jones, "Migration as a Response to Internal Colonialism in Brazil," *Transfers* 7, no. 2 (2017) (eight million); Eduardo Alcântara Vasconcellos, "Urban Development and Traffic Accidents in Brazil," *Accident Analysis and Prevention* 31, no. 4 (1999) 323 (732,000).
233. Owensby, *Intimate Ironies*, 5 (stabilizing influence), 45 (light-skinned), 103 (women), 112 (radios, sewing), 114 (credit), 115 (survey), 116 (survey quote), 127 (unhappy), 191 (abandoned), 202 (coalesce), 240 (triumph), 241 (relegated, diffuse), 242 (competence).

234. Pachón and Ramírez, *La infraestructura*, 7 (table 1.2A), 51 (table 1.21).
235. CEPAL, "El Transporte," 618 (Dutch), 637 (47,000); Eduardo Elena, *Dignifying Argentina: Peronism, Citizenship, and Mass Consumption* (Pittsburgh, PA: University of Pittsburgh Press, 2011), 31 (US worker), 39 (survey), 86 (abundance), 93 (Cinderella), 120 (sewing), 126 (monopoly), 185 (ordered).
236. The dissertation, written by Héctor Cornejo Chávez, is quoted in D. S. Parker, *The Idea of the Middle Class: White-Collar Workers and Peruvian Society, 1900–1950* (University Park: Pennsylvania State University Press, 1998), 214–216; John Brian Freeman, "'La carrera de la muerte': Death, Driving, and Rituals of Modernization in 1950s Mexico," *Studies in Latin American Popular Culture* 29 (2011): 3 (cigar), 13 (idiocy), 15 (pilots'), 18 (dangerous); Wolfe, *Autos and Progress*, 116 (*cadillaquismo*, bus travel), 236n8 (of Brazilian upper-class members, 90 percent had made such an intercity bus trip, compared to 77 percent of middle-class respondents and 57 percent of the poor and the working class; 79 percent of all men and 57 percent of all women had been among intercity bus traveler in the early 1950s).
237. See Mom, *Atlantic Automobilism*, 313–328 (tradition); Elena, *Dignifying Argentina*, 152 (the car), 156 (anti-Peronist), 157 (inferiors), 158 (*negros*), 160 (*alpargatas*), 243; Mason, *Turbulent Empires*, 221 (nationalized).
238. Parker, *Idea*, 117 (skyrocketed), 85–186 (suburbanization), 193 (women), 204–205 (streetcar), 213 (six percent); CEPAL, "El Transporte," 801 (three-quarters); Fiona Wilson, "Towards a Political Economy of Roads: Experiences from Peru," *Development and Change* 35, no. 3 (2004): 532 (Indians), 534 (Colquemarca), 536 (Tarma). The couple of terms "linking and delinking" emerged within the Tensions of Europe research program. See Thomas J. Misa and Johan Schot, "Introduction," *History and Technology* 21, no. 1 (2005).
239. Michael Marvin Self, "A Survey of Automobile Manufacturing in Latin America" (PhD diss., University of Texas, 1967), 114 (4 million), 115, table 13 (densities), 118 (buses); Brown, *Transport*, 172, table 8-1 (road length), 175, table 8-3 (fleets; the increases are measured between 1945 and 1962/1963); CEPAL, "El Transporte," 653 (experts), 683 (less than), 699 (Bolivian vehicle density); Jaime Salazar Montoya, *De la mula al camión: Apuntes para une historia del transporte en Colombia* (Bogotá: Tercer Mundo Editores, 2000), 149 (Andean road lengths).
240. Robert Farris Thompson, "*Tap-Tap, Fula-Fula, Kiá-Kiá*: The Haitian Bus in Atlantic Perspective," *African Arts* 29, no. 2 (1996): 36 (glittering), 37 (Afro-Atlantic), 38 (protection), 39 (Zaire), 40 (fortune, Ogún), 41 (prayerfully, altars, *bolekaja*), 43 (bravado); Ralph Bolton, "Machismo in Motion: The Ethos of Peruvian Truckers," *Ethos* 7, no. 4 (1979): 318 (*machismo*), 321 (religiosity), 322 (Super Male), 328 (aggression); Jack Pritchett, "Nigerian Truck Art," *African Arts* 12, no. 2 (1979): 27 and 30 (Nigeria); Fulwider, "Driving the Nation," 243 (slogans).
241. Krish Bhaskar, *The Future of the World Motor Industry* (London: Kogan Page, 1980), 43, table 3.5.
242. Franco, *Cruel Modernity*.
243. Hawkins, *Roads*, 3 (study), 10 (desirability), 23 (density), 40 (cars), 49 (less frequently). The preface suggests the Uganda government was not altogether happy with his results, perhaps because of the role given to road traffic.
244. Wang, *End of the Revolution*, 78–79; Joseph R. Gusfield, "Tradition and Modernity: Misplaced Polarities in the Study of Social Change," *American Journal of Sociology* 72, no. 4 (1967): 352; for the concept of "Counter-Moderns in the Islamic World," see, e.g., Mishra, *From the Ruins*, 257, where Turkey serves as an example of "indigenous

modernity that not only does not depend on the original Western [model] but seems also to rival it." Ibid., 284.
245. Chapman and Prothero, "Themes on Circulation," 16; Oliver Schöller-Schwedes and Stephan Rammler, *Mobile Cities: Dynamiken weltweiter Stadt- und Verkehrsentwicklung* (Berlin: LIT Verlag, 2008) 134 (German traffic analysts use the term parallel development to indicate layeredness); Anatol Lieven, "What Chance for Afghanistan?" *New York Review of Books* 63, no. 7 (21 April 2016): 47 (Bloch); Schöller-Schwedes and Rammler, *Mobile Cities*, 63 (disparities), 91 (growth).
246. Wang, *End of the Revolution*, 129; Murray Chapman and R. Mansell Prothero, "Conclusion," in Prothero and Chapman, *Circulation*, 439; Nebojša Nakicenovic, "The Automobile Road to Technological Change: Diffusion of the Automobile as a Process of Technological Substitution," *Technological Forecasting and Social Change* 29, no. 4 (1986).
247. Saiz, "Dictatorships and Highways"; H. E. Aldington, "The Civil Engineer and Road Transportation," *Road International* 1 (Autumn 1950) 29–23, here 33.
248. George W. Wilson, "What the Cases Show," in *The Impact of Highway Investment on Development* by George W. Wilson, Barbara R. Bergmann, Leon V. Hirsch, and Martin S. Klein (Washington, DC: Brookings Institution, 1966), 174 (sufficient), 177 (skeptical, rise), 189 (lack); George W. Wilson, "Toward a Theory of Transport and Development," in Wilson et al., *Impact*, 201 (accessibility), 218 (magical).
249. Parker, *Idea*, 234.
250. Ansary, *Destiny Disrupted*, 356; Mishra, *From the Ruins*, 264.

Layered, Fragmented, Subversive, Subaltern
Conclusions

> the only way to appear in public
> is to be mobile
> —Sarah Sharma and Armond R. Towns, "Ceasing Fire
> and Seizing Time"

The decentering of Europe, undertaken in chapter 1, forced us to decenter the car. Although the appearance of the latter beyond its cradle formed a first refutation of the diffusionist thesis (that its spread emanated from and proliferated the 'American model'), an excursion over 'the Rest' of our planet resulted in a long list of 'forgotten' or 'invisible' mobilities. One-wheeled barrows, palanquins, hammocks and machillas, bullock carts in the millions, idem rickshaws and bicycles, but also llamas, mules, camels, human porterage, and, the most widespread of all, walking—they all mingled with this alien contraption to create what Westerners experienced as 'chaos' but what, on closer look, could be defined as 'layeredness.' This entire amalgam of mobilities engaged in modernization and on its turn helped make the non-Western fledgling 'car society' modern, from the new ball bearings in the bullock carts, through the pneumatics on the rickshaws to the elite adventure machine, the car. The Comaroffs' thesis of the non-West as a laboratory of the West (see the introduction) helped us see beyond the myth of the monolithic car culture, how also in the West mobility was layered and that there, too, the majority walked. Likewise, David Edgerton's *Shock of the*

Old helped us defuse a second myth, that the car was 'modern' and the rest 'backward'—a myth all too often mobilized to ban 'the old' and please the local elite in their modernistic, but illusionary self-esteem.[1]

This kaleidoscopic variety (its fragmentation a better metaphor of road traffic than the concept of 'multiple mobilities') made us wonder whether something like an 'Other mobility,' a 'mobility of the Global South,' exists or existed. Can we point to a form of 'peripheral mobility'? Does (did) a Socialist or Communist mobility emerge? Considering the state of research, we can only say at this stage that in every *locale*, another mix, another setting of the kaleidoscope, was possible. Our first panoramic sketch of a world mobility history hopefully allows others to dig deeper in local specificities or regional commonalities, find continental typicalities or transnational trends only hinted at on these pages. Future research should confirm whether Khrushchev's car-sharing plans of the 1960s found a following in other places; perhaps the rickshaw culture with its collectivism and its emphasis on labor rather than consumption, or the explosion of 'informal transport' would be cases in point? Future research could confirm whether 'peripheral mobilities' exist with a higher share of 'serious mobility' (trucks, freight transport in general, commuting) than in the 'core.'

But what we know now is that after our analysis of the previous pages, only if we 'decenter Europe' (decenter the car) can we investigate a non-Western mobility history that could be as 'adventurous' (remember Lao She's rickshaw puller) but perhaps was less 'ironic.' The adventure beyond the West seemed less tongue in cheek, more utilitarian, closer to poverty, at times subaltern, and often somewhat grim. In other words, it had less trouble acknowledging it was class-based and collective, rather than celebrating individualism, and being vaguely middle class. But I have to be careful here: we might find adventure if we search for it more thoroughly, endorsed with knowledge of local languages, enabled to travel beyond the 'prison of English.'[2] After all, the decision to translate a 'foreign' novel into English (and only thus making it accessible to most of us) might be more inspired by a desire for exoticism (or at least 'difference') than commonalities with the West. In other words, does the corpus of Anglophone novels, songs, and movies play a similar trick on us as the prewar novels did that filtered out the collective basis of Western automobilism? Let us assume, for now (with no evidence to the contrary), this is not the case. But there is no doubt that the gaze to the East and vice versa are fraught with translation problems.

For instance, now that we, during the third quarter of world automobile culture, have observed so many parallel traits and developments of automobilism between Western and non-Western cultures, one wonders whether we should not rehabilitate the diffusionist thesis we have so apodictically rejected at the end of our study of the first half of the previous century (see the introduction). After all, the predominance of the American 'model,' constructed before the war, and after the war solidly cemented within a Western Cold War paradigm of freedom and mobility, based on (if not reduced to) the all-pervasive trope of the freedom *of* mobility, would warrant a reevaluation in the face of fledgling national car cultures characterized by poverty, Communism, or both. Did the car bring freedom and prosperity to the 'Rest,' *after* it had reached maturity in the 'West'? Does our earlier conclusion that Socialism and Communism did not formulate a convincing alternative to capitalist car culture (they did so in the realm of the arts, as Socialist realism, for instance) confirm the diffusionist thesis?

I believe the answer to this question should still be no.[3] The new evidence, spread out in the previous chapters, rather reinforces the alternative thesis of multiple mobilities, even more so: of fragmented, kaleidoscopic mobility cultures. Every country (and within each country: the different classes and minority groups) had its (their) own mobility 'flavor,' even if it is true that the most exorbitant one, the United States, functioned as an example to the up-and-coming cultures. If it is allowed to use a metaphor from the technical field I am coming from: while the Otto engine (with a spark plug) is characterized by diffusive combustion, the flame front around the plug traveling concentrically toward the cylinder walls, the Diesel engine has a so-called simultaneous-explosive combustion, small kernels of combustion emerging all over the cylinder simultaneously when and if the conditions locally are conducive to self-ignition. We need a mixture of the 'right' configuration, and self-ignition occurs. The spread of mobility cultures around the globe takes place simultaneous-explosively, although sometimes there is some 'delay,' because the circumstances are not conducive for a car culture to emerge. This is all the more true during the phase of transition we investigated here, a transition "from an auto-centered economy, with a continual increase in workers' wages and social redistribution organized by the state and the trade unions, to a liberal economy integrated into global trade and therefore export-orientated, specializing, privatizing profits, socializing risks and assuming a planetary increase in inequalities."[4]

The United States, in the words of Cotten Seiler, may have seen a "republic of drivers" emerge, after World War II, this became an 'empire of drivers,' unrolled over the planet through 'development,' most particularly roadbuilding and its systemic companions, including the adventure machine. Within the Empire, and borrowing from the Comaroffs, will the South prefigure the North, the Pacific the Atlantic? One indication that this is indeed the case is the questionable universality of Western concepts of mobility and its theorizing, expressed through urban planning turning into disaster when applied to the non-West, through the privileging of roadbuilding by Western consultants, through the very concept of 'modal split' (applied to a world of 'layered' mobilities) and even the seemingly universal 'fluidity' of society (see the introduction). First revealed in the non-West, they have all meanwhile bounced back to the West and help us reinterpret the West's mobility culture, too.

***

What, then, are these 'circumstances conducive for a car culture to emerge'? After all, it would be a fallback into national chauvinism if we were to accept the multiple-mobilities thesis as an end point of our argumentation. For, despite this multiplicity, we are now also able to distinguish a certain *pattern of 'automobilization'* with the following characteristics. First of all, people, initially, all over the planet and all over the previous century, seem to behave pretty uniformly when confronted with the car. Elites embrace it, subalterns (the eternal pedestrians) resist. After their home (which appears to be a precondition for an adventurous use of the car), the local elite, followed by the local middle class, wish to acquire it as a token of their societal *status*, and subsequently start to use it in a pretty much uniform way (which we have called 'adventure machine'), thus confirming, over and over again, the intimate connection between sessility and automobility. This phenomenon has often been called a 'script,' but our concept of the 'dual nature of technology' enables a better understanding of a variety of behaviors around a basic one. The technical properties of the car 'afford' a spectrum of functions (the relationship between these properties and functions being fuzzy, as we argued earlier), but one type of behavior dominates, and dominated over the previous century: its pleasurable use.

This is not a simple parti pris against the utilitarian thesis (in fact, already before World War II we have seen arise doubts, in our earlier study, about the hedonistic paradigm),[5] or even against the toy-to-tool thesis, explained in the introduction; it is much more: it says its so-called utilitarian uses are also governed by a certain pleasurable disposition, at least in men (and as we have seen: in quite a bit of women). Even the driver of a truck, the utilitarian vehicle par excellence, experiences (and experienced) constitutive elements of the automotive adventure, and even the seemingly ultimately utilitarian passenger car practice, the commute, is often strewn with pleasurable traits, as we have seen on several occasions in the previous chapters. The basis for this is what we in an earlier study called the *transcendental experience* the car allows: the bodily grounded, haptically induced experience of being more than the 'I,' to be a seemingly autonomous element (a monad) as an element in a pack or a swarm-in-flow, even if some motorists, as the previous pages testify, experience the freeway drive as utterly boring but at the same time remain receptive to the transcendental 'highway hypnosis.' It is this transcendental experience that forms the foundation for the 'adventure machine': the car as a provider of a temporal (speeding), spatial (roaming), functional (tinkering) and aggressive (conquering, controlling) adventure, the mechanical part of the driver-car cyborg.

Second, it seems the *middle class* has been crucial to this motorization project of nearly a century, even if, after World War II, the car has started to become embraced by other groups and classes. And even if the latter is not the case, such as in some African countries, the car has meanwhile acquired such a ubiquitous presence that also the carless are subject to its reign, and often under its spell. If they aren't, they will suffer, because they better first look to the left, to the right, and to the left again (or the other way around, in the UK, or Singapore), before they cross the street. From the 1970s at least, we are a true automotive world in which more often than not the car is dangerously invisible: in the previous chapters, we have deliberately included novels and other utterances that did not explicitly address automobilism in any form, in order to investigate this enigmatic phenomenon of the 'absent car.' The car is there, everywhere, so much so that it is not. Conversely, beyond the West: even if it is not, it is there, as an image, a fantasy, a ghost, a desire (or an impending nightmare).

Third, if we would stop at the 'absent car' as the ultimate postwar outcome of a near-century of automotive adventure, we would make the same mistake as all those social scientists who declared 'class' to be something of the past, and who embarked on devising research strategies aimed a investigating 'lifestyles.' However prolific their research appeared (and still appears) to be, unearthing 'subcultures' of car modifiers, of hot-rodders, muscle-car-driving women from which new mobility studies has benefited enormously, such results should not be mobilized to hide the fundamental cleft between a Western middle class that increasingly 'abstractified' and routinized the car adventure, and an emerging working-class culture of 'carnivalizing' this adventure, a flight forward into an exaggerated version of the 'adventure machine.'[6] It is this cleft, most visible in the United States, that would drive the mobility history of the coming decades, and would generate both postmodernism and neoliberalism.

***

Indeed, mass motorization and globalization of the car culture are not simple confirmations and extensions of what we found analyzing the pivotal interbellum gestation period of the Western car culture. Car Exuberance, the third global phase of world mobility culture, is not simply more Emergence and more Persistence (the two first phases). 'Exuberance with a Twist' (that is: seen against the background of the emergence of a global car culture) brought new elements to the car culture and its automotive adventure, so much so that one may wonder whether this qualification of adventurousness is still valid. First, mass motorization brought an explosion of problems that were already lingering during the prewar years, but that led to a massive countermovement against the car's unsafe, unhealthy, and degrading effects on the 'environment,' both rural and urban, as well as planetary. We will go into these problems more in depth in a later study (as they exploded in the latter quarter of the century), but for now, it is quite clear that the paving of the globe with millions of kilometers of asphalt and concrete did not benefit everyone equally, to say the least. We have seen *dependentismo* emerge in Latin America (and spread over the scholarly globe as 'world systems theory'). We have also seen expressed the first doubts about the viability of the car system because of its seemingly ever-increasing fatality statistics, especially in those novels that depicted the car as a dangerous machine.

Second, globalization brought to the fore other responses to the car than a previous exclusively Western 'master narrative' showed. One of the most obvious examples is the *ostentatious use of the car*: the slow, noisy parading of the car-as-sign, the car *as* medium rather than means of transport. But we must be careful here: the Western master narrative of car culture has always emphasized its masculine, risky use and has hardly investigated the flower parades and the gymkhanas organized by the automobile clubs from the very beginning as well, next to the races and tours through the countryside. Even at this level, the Comaroffs' thesis is active: if I had known this result when writing the previous study, I might have included a chapter on this 'forgotten,' 'feminine,' or 'feminized' part of pioneering car culture. The status-sensitive 'carnival' of the 'Rest' reminds us of the hidden, status-related traits of the Western early 'adventure machine.' Whereas the automotive middle class was busy 'civilizing' its ranks without jeopardizing the car's fundamental adventurousness (by distancing itself from the rowdy-adventurers and by redefining the car as 'necessity'), other more marginal motorizing groups (women, blacks, Latinos), kept other, less 'adventurous,' more seemingly 'feminine' elements of the earliest car culture alive, such as a more 'defensive' style of driving, a style of car consumption less driven by guilt in the form of the purchase of very 'fancy' cars, or a more sophisticated form of do-it-yourself culture in the form of low-riders and street racers. In the terms of our concept of the 'ironic car,' whereas the car isolated the mainstream elite from the 'common folk,' for the marginals of the mainstream, this same distancing effect afforded a certain relative autonomy enabling 'escape' from an oppressing condition.

The third new element that our study of the third quarter of the last century revealed is the proliferation of the study of *passengering* (stereotyped as a more feminized, non-male role), not only of those adults that are not allowed to drive although they have a driver's license, but also, and especially, of those who are not able or willing to drive, the bodily impaired, children, the poor, and those urbanites for whom the car represents only a nightmare of finding parking space, congestion and other unpredictabilities. Like the 'feminized' elements of the car culture, passengering and, in general, the ethnography of road and car (including the phenomenon of the professional 'chauffeur'), needs a lot more research before we can give it its proper place in the history of automobilism, but it is quite clear that both phenomena question the dominance of the car as adventure machine. Not only that: it also connects the car more easily with other, more collective forms of automobilism, such as the taxicab, the bus, and even rail-bound forms like the tramway and the train, as well as the airplane. Aren't we all passengers, sometime, somewhere, even if we never were drivers?

Fourth, the enormous expansion of the world's road infrastructure during the second half of the last century, a phenomenon that strikes the observer as so eagerly executed as if coordinated from a central command center (with the World Bank as the most likely candidate) deserves more scholarly scrutiny, from historians of technology to anthropologists. This study, confirming my earlier history of prewar automobilism, found again the crucial importance of the intermediary level of governance (the states in the US, the provinces elsewhere) in the spread of the network. What strikes me the most in the rollout of this icon of modernity (often well before the explosion of national car fleets) is the enormous amount of red tape (including the expert rhetoric) that also should be analyzed as a giant smoke screen around the naked interests of the West. Taking this rhetoric seriously, dedicating endless chapters to its rebuttal, is one of the weaknesses of the social sciences, and prevents us from calling what it was: a shameless, arrogant orgy of greed, of profit making by Western multinational corporations and their 'consultants.' In that sense, the export of the 'car society' through infrastructures (rather than directly through the car), starting with the Decade of Development of the 1960s and 1970s, was a blatant success, despite all the 'evidence' from social scientists of the roads' failed promises.

The confusion, of course, was caused by the fact that the road's promise seemed so universal, promoted by the capitalist as much as by the Communist Bloc within a Cold War setting, eagerly accepted by many in the developing world, most of all the local elite and the modernizing middle class. Perhaps this is also why neither Socialism nor Communism developed its own 'theory of mobility': there seemed to be no need to do so; modernizing through road and car seemed universal. Even *dependentismo*, as a Latin American alternative to *developmentalism*, was not able to formulate an alternative. The distinction between public and private transport does not help us much further: the enormous expansion of what transport planners came to call *informal transport* explains why. This often subversive, often subaltern mobility shows how the 'old,' the 'backward,' can be as 'modern' as the 'new.' Such an alternative theory, we argued, could be constructed on the basis of at least three empirical building blocks identified in this study: Khrushchev's car-sharing plans, the revolutionary traveling during the Cultural Revolution, and the revolutionary lorry drivers in Niger.

Fifth, wherever we have studied the roadbuilding lobby of the International Road Federation, the World Bank, and the International Monetary Fund, we found the road networks were built far 'ahead of demand'— hence the importance of the *motorbus*. The global roadbuilding frenzy tipped the balance between road and rail definitively toward the former: the collective bus paved the way for the individual car, the bus passengers for the car drivers, the carless for the middle class. Even in the West's very center, the United States, roadbuilding benefited the middle classes: "the success of the visible freeway revolt has left us with some of the nation's most exclusive enclaves of wealth and privilege," a gentrification on a national scale.[7] There, in the West, on its road network, the car, as an intrinsically modern machine (a contraption to experience constant change, change "becoming the only constant of modern society"),[8] managed to support the transition to postmodernity, because its 'ironic' features prefigured the postmodern mood. The conclusion seems inevitable: the car has been pushed and pushed through, against the train, against the bus (or perhaps alongside it), against the rickshaw, against walking, against animal traction. Aggressively and violently so.

***

Let us, to conclude, come back a bit more in depth to the cleft between two different class-based car cultures. Even without considering the five new phenomena just enumerated, the Western, white, middle-class man, and especially his urban, youthful counterpart, has witnessed the automotive adventure being tamed beyond recognition. For them, too, the postwar decades brought a new complacent, guilt-ridden car culture. It is as if the postmodern era promises to provide enough 'adventure' (risk, uncertainty) to make automotive adventure redundant.

But we have also seen on multiple occasions how this taming was accompanied by a *delegation* of adventurous behavior to other societal groups, within and outside the car culture proper: the hot-rodders, the rally drivers, the street racers, and their celebration in Hollywood movies. The adventure was also delegated to other modes, most particularly the motorcycle and, in general, the (motorized) two-wheeler. We need much more scholarly attention to the history of racing and other 'sporting' activities in an around the car, and the symbiotic relationship with other media, in order to trace the evolution of the adventure machine among the loud, the vulgar, the nonwhite, and the trash: in short, the subalterns and subversives of mobility, the 'barbarians' in Alessandro Baricco's ironic terminology, as the true heirs of automotive adventure. After all, NASCAR racing is "the second most popular sport in the United States (after the National Football League) as measured by TV ratings."[9]

We thus can distinguish between three main Western, transnational car cultures, against which our previous distinction between a European and a US car culture appears rather futile:

- a tamed, hegemonic, middle-class culture, obsessed with 'the crash' in all meanings of the term;
- an emancipatory culture celebrating the car as liberator, an escape vehicle, driven by minorities and the 'marginals' of the mainstream;
- a vulgar, carnivalesque flight forward into extreme adventure or extreme ostentatiousness, as a working-class, popular culture.

We deal here with a deep cleft between two cultures, two cultures in both of which the car plays a crucial but quite different role, cultures developing on both sides of a cleft that not only runs within single countries but also starts to spread over the globe, especially the third one. The split is between a 'civil' middle-class society and the 'mobile Other' in all kinds of guises, from the white young daredevil to the rickshaw passenger with her two kids.

***

So (coming back to the question asked in the introduction), apart from most of the insights formulated above, what did we gain more about the fate of the 'adventure machine' through our study of the high- and lowbrow autopoetic culture? For our mobility purpose, I conclude the most important result of this investigation is the observed *loss of the transcendent character* of the automotive ride. The novels, songs, and movies analyzed in the previous pages showed how the automotive adventure became not only fragmented (women, blacks, queers, beats, flower-power children) but also, in the process of fragmentation, *reformulated*. It became *abstracted* and *routinized* on the one hand, carnival on the other. Highbrow literature allowed us to reconstruct only one half of the equation: this trumpet of middle-class experience is not the right entrance into the popular culture of the car. We needed middle- and lowbrow utterances, popular culture in general, to discover the other half (however distorted by middle-class authors, to be read now against the grain), to identify other subjectivations in and around the car.[10]

Secondly, our study also showed that (contrary to some literary critics) there is an overwhelming amount, a veritable *mer à boire*, of autopoetic sources, of which this study only analyzed a small part. My latest additions to my collection however show me that my conclusions would not have been altered, had I taken on more of these sources.

Furthermore, this type of sources provided us with the insight, after our earlier study of the Western prewar car cultures, that the transcendental experience of the motorist, as the very foundation of the 'sticky' attractiveness of the automotive adventure, was in fact a secularization of the nineteenth-century sublime. At the moment when the automobilist reappropriated this experience, it was already mixed with the collective (the 'swarm,' as we called it, the flow of traffic), instead of a Supreme Being. It was an ironizing experience, creating a supreme state of euphoria by creating distance, in the automotive cocoon.[11]

There is a tension, if not a paradox, between this transcendence and automotive narcissism. The latter is centripetal, aimed at the 'I,' the former is centrifugal, but not so much aimed at the world, the environment, but beyond the 'I,' into another, higher-order 'I,' the transcendental subject that has left behind the 'I,' denies the 'I.' It is the 'I' in the crowd, the swarm-as-moving crowd. From this perspective, the regular reference to Roland Barthes's characterization of the car as a twentieth-century cathedral among social scientists is not adequate: the car's transcendence is produced while driving, not in contemplation in a cathedral (the metaphor stems from seeing the Citroën ID being positioned upright during the Paris Motor Show), but on the road.[12]

Indeed, the truth of automobilism is to be found on the road, but not necessarily while driving. Ask the families of the victims.

***

In 1949, during a college football game in Northern Californian Berkeley, the air was so bad that the historian who mentioned it compared it with the smog in Los Angeles that had appeared for the first time about a decade before.[13] Three years later, an estimated extra three thousand to four thousand people died in London, because of a similar phenomenon. Soon it was discovered, however, that well-known 'London smog' (linguistically a combination of 'smoke' and 'fog,' and the result of the burning in homes of 'fat,' highly sulfuric coal) was not the same as the new 'Los Angeles smog,' which did not contain much smoke from coal. The latter was the result of photochemical reactions in a climatic situation of 'inversion,' where air was trapped by a warmer layer in a bowl-shaped valley. This shift in content and material base of the smog phenomenon was a reflection of a shift toward the car, from coal to oil: after a fierce debate among specialists in which biochemistry professor Arie J. Haagen-Smit's opinion prevailed, photochemical smog appeared to be predominantly caused by exhaust gases from automobiles.[14] It is, therefore, all the more enigmatic why the developments within transport history did not reflect these changes: up to now, the field, even in its new 'mobility' appearance, has been remarkably silent on the car's energetic and environmental role.[15]

Pollution from road traffic was not the only issue of environmental concern for postwar Westerners. In 1956, strontium 90, an isotope released during hydrogen bomb test explosions in the atmosphere, was discovered in milk, leading to Women Strike for Peace organizing monthly marches in front of New York's United Nations building and resulting in the Limited Test Ban Treaty of 1963.[16] Whether from the perspective of the mobility of vehicles or the mobility of radioactive material, nobody could doubt anymore that the 'risk society' had arrived (Ulrich Beck seminal book appeared in 1986): next to the poisoning of children because they lived too close to the roads (where lead was emitted in the car exhaust), road accident statistics soared to unprecedented heights, even compared to the prewar situation.

These and similar events are often (or not so often, as with road safety) presented in environmental histories, to relativize the 'oil shock' of October 1973, when the oil-producing countries of OPEC implemented a fourfold price increase per barrel, and the Western world of abundance seemed to have come to an end.[17] The effects of this oil shock were so widespread that the entire world seemed to know a new historical phase had emerged, a phase that we, from a mobility perspective, have called Doom.

Notes

Epigraph: Sarah Sharma and Armond R. Towns, "Ceasing Fire and Seizing Time: LA Gang Tours and the White Control of Mobility," *Transfers* 6, no. 1 (2016): 40.

1. David Edgerton, *The Shock of the Old: Technology and Global History since 1990* (Oxford: Oxford University Press, 2007).
2. Anna Wierzbicka, *Imprisoned in English: The Hazards of English as a Default Language* (Oxford: Oxford University Press, 2014).
3. For a similar anti-diffusionist position in consumption studies, see Sheldon Garon and Patricia L. Maclachlan, eds., *The Ambivalent Consumer: Questioning Consumption in East Asia and the West* (Ithaca, NY: Cornell University Press, 2006), e.g., in "Introduction," 3.
4. Alain Badiou *The Rebirth of History*, trans. Gregory Elliott (London: Verso, 2012), 9.
5. See Gijs Mom, *Atlantic Automobilism: Emergence and Persistence of the Car, 1895–1940* (New York: Berghahn Books, 2015), 346.
6. It was Mikhail Bakhtin who, during the Interbellum in the Soviet Union, coined the term "carnivalization" when analyzing written narrative forms. See Graham Pechey, *Mikhail Bakhtin: The Word in the World* (London: Routledge, 2007), 96.
7. Eric Avila, *The Folklore of the Freeway: Race and Revolt in the Modernist City* (Minneapolis: University of Minnesota Press, 2014), 193.
8. Derek Sayer in his summary of Marx's *Communist Manifesto*, as quoted in Alberto Gomes, *Modernity and Identity: Asian Illustrations* (Bundoora: La Trobe University Press, 1994), 2.
9. Catherine Lutz and Anne Lutz Fernandez, *Carjacked: The Culture of the Automobile and Its Effects on Our Lives* (New York: St. Martin's Press, 2010), 6 (NASCAR); also see Evelyn Vingilis and Reginald G. Smart, "Street Racing: A Neglected Research Area?" *Traffic Injury Protection* 10, no. 2 (2009); Alessandro Baricco, *De barbaren*, trans. Manon Smiths (Amsterdam: De Bezige Bij, 2010).
10. Kai Merten and Lucia Krämer, "Introduction," in *Postcolonial Studies Meets Media Studies: A Critical Encounter*, ed. Kai Merten and Lucia Krämer (Bielefeld: transcript Verlag, 2016), 7: "literature is still over-represented as the [postcolonial studies] discipline's subject of textual criticism."
11. See Christian Burgers and Margot van Mulken, "Het ironisch spectrum; Een overzicht van onderzoek naar het begrip en de retorische effecten van verbale ironie," *Tijdschrift voor Taalbeheersing* 35, no. 2 (2013).
12. Hartmut Böhme, "Das Strahlen fetischistischer Dinge des Konsums: Autos und Mode," in *In Gegenwart des Fetischs: Dingkonjunktur und Fetischbegriff in der Diskussion*, ed. Christine Blättler and Falko Schmieder (Vienna: Verlag Turia + Kant, 2014), 37.
13. James E. Krier and Edmund Ursin, *Pollution and Policy: A Case Essay on California and Federal Experience with Motor Vehicle Air Pollution 1940–1975* (Berkeley: University of California Press, 1977), 6.
14. Frederick Buell, *From Apocalypse to Way of Life: Environmental Crisis in the American Century* (New York: Routledge, 2004), 70 (London smog); Krier and Ursin, *Pollution and Policy*, 42 (inversion). On the discovery of Los Angeles smog, see Scott Hamilton Dewey, "'Don't Breathe the Air': Air Pollution and the Evolution of Environmental Policy and Politics in the United States, 1945–1970" (PhD. diss., Rice University, 1997).
15. One of the few books that can function as an exception to this statement is Tom McCarthy, *Auto Mania: Cars, Consumers, and the Environment* (New Haven, CT: Yale University Press, 2007).

16. David Stradling, *The Nature of New York: An Environmental History of the Empire State* (Ithaca, NY: Cornell University Press, 2010), 184–185.
17. Fiona Venn, *The Oil Crisis* (London: Pearson Education, 2002), 1 (fourfold); on gasoline price development, see esp. Lee Schipper and Stephen Meyers (with Richard B. Howarth and Ruth Steiner), *Energy Efficiency and Human Activity: Past Trends, Future Prospects* (Cambridge: Cambridge University Press, 1992), 128.

Bibliography

(Not included are articles from periodicals that have been used as primary source, such as *Road International*, *IAPCR Bulletin*, and PIARC Road Congresses: an exception has been made for programmatic articles from these sources. Nor have most websites mentioned in the notes been included here if they have only been quoted for casual information. Novels and related artistic primary sources are marked by an asterisk [*].)

Abécassis, Frédéric. "La mise en place du réseau routier marocain: Aperçu historique." Paper presented at the conference "(Auto)mobility in the Global Middle East: Defining the Field." University of Birmingham, 6 November 2015.

Abel, Marco. "Speeding across the Rhizome: Deleuze Meets Kerouac *On the Road*." *Modern Fiction Studies* 48, no. 2 (2002): 227–256.

Ackermann, Michael. *Konzepte und Entscheidungen in der Planung der schweizerischen Nationalstrassen von 1927 bis 1961*. Bern: Peter Lang, 1991.

Aguiar, Marian. *Tracking Modernity: India's Railways and the Culture of Mobility*. Minneapolis: University of Minnesota Press, 2011.

Akhunova, M. A., B. A. Tulepbaev, and J. S. Borisov. "Motor Transport in a Developing Area (ii) Soviet Central Asia." In Barker, *Economic and Social Effects of the Spread of Motor Vehicles*, 256–263.

Akita, Shiguru, Gerold Krozewski, and Shoichi Watanabe. "Introduction: The Colombo Plan, Aid Relations, and the International Order of Asia, 1950–65." In Akita et al., *Transformation of the International Order*, 1–12.

———, eds. *The Transformation of the International Order of Asia: Decolonization, the Cold War, and the Colombo Plan*. London: Routledge, 2015.

Akurang-Parry, Kwabena Opare. "Colonial Forced Labor Policies for Road-Building in Southern Ghana and International Anti-forced Labor Pressures, 1900–1940." *African Economic History* 28 (2000): 1–25.

Alacevich, Michele. *Visualizing Uncertainties, or How Albert Hirschman and the World Bank Disagreed on Project Appraisal and Development Approaches*. Washington, DC: World Bank, Information Management and Technology Network, Knowledge and Information Service Unit, November 2012.

———. "The World Bank and the Politics of Productivity: The Debate on Economic Growth, Poverty, and Living Standards in the 1950s." *Journal of Global History* 6, no. 1 (2011): 53–74.

Alber, Erdmute. "Automobilismus und Kolonialherrschaft: Zur Bedeutung des Autoverkehrs für die Herrschaftsstrukturen in der westafrikanischen Kolonie Dahomey." *Paideuma* 46 (2000): 279–299.

———. "Motorization and Colonial Rule: Two Scandals in Dahomey, 1916." *Journal of African Cultural Studies* 15, no. 1 (2002): 79–92.
Aldcroft, Derek H., ed. *Europe's Third World: The European Periphery in the Interwar Years.* Aldershot: Ashgate, 2006.
Ambrosius, Gerold. "Wirtschaftswachstum und Konvergenz der Industiestrukturen in Westeuropa." In Kaelble, *Der Boom*, 129–168.
Amburn, Ellis. *Subterranean Kerouac: The Hidden Life of Jack Kerouac.* New York: St. Martin's Press, 1998.
Amin, Shahid. *Event, Metaphor, Memory: Chauri Chaura 1922–1992.* Berkeley: University of California Press, 1995.
Anderson, Benedict. "The New World Disorder." In Vincent, *Anthropology of Politics*, 261–270.
Anderson, G. E. *Designated Drivers: How China Plans to Dominate the Global Auto Industry.* Singapore: John Wiley & Sons, 2012.
Anderson, Perry. "Imagining Alternative Modernities." In *The Chinese Model of Modern Development*, edited by Tian Yu Cao. London: Routledge, 2005), 16–20.
Andreas, Joel. *Rise of the Red Engineers: The Cultural Revolution and the Origins of China's New Class.* Stanford, CA: Stanford University Press, 2009.
Anolli, Luigi, Rita Ciceri, and Maria Giaele Infantino. "From 'Blame to Praise' to 'Praise to Blame': Analysis of Vocal Patterns in Ironic Communication." *International Journal of Psychology* 37, no. 5 (2002): 266–276.
Ansary, Tamim. *Destiny Disrupted: A History of the World through Islamic Eyes.* New York: PublicAffairs, 2009.
Aoki, Eiichi. "Railroads." In Yamamoto, *Technological Innovation*, 229–243.
Arce, Alberto, and Norma Long, eds. *Anthropology, Development and Modernities: Exploring Discourses, Counter-Tendencies and Violence.* London: Routledge, 2006.
———. "Reconfiguring Modernity and Development from an Anthropological Perspective." In Arce and Long, *Anthropology, Development and Modernities*, 1–31.
*Arciniegras, Germán. "El Automóvil." *Antorcha* (August 1931), 18–21.
Arnold, David. *Everyday Technology: Machines and the Making of India's Modernity.* Chicago: University of Chicago Press, 2013.
———. "The Problem of Traffic: The Street-Life of Modernity in Late-Colonial India." *Modern Asian Studies* 46, no. 1 (2012): 119–141.
Arnold, David, and Erich DeWald. "Cycles of Empowerment? The Bicycle and Everyday Technology in Colonial India and Vietnam." *Comparative Studies in Society and History* 53, no. 4 (2011): 971–996.
Arnold, Guy, and Ruth Weiss. *Strategic Highways of Africa.* London: Julian Friedmann Publishers, 1977.
Arvidsson, Adam. "From Counterculture to Consumer Culture: Vespa and the Italian youth Market, 1958–78." *Journal of Consumer Culture* 1, no. 1 (2001): 47–71.
Asad, Talal. "The Concept of Cultural Translation in British Social Anthropology." In Clifford and Marcus, *Writing Culture*, 141–164.
Ashby, LeRoy. "The Rising of Popular Culture: A Historiographical Sketch." *OAH Magazine of History* 24, no. 2 (2010): 11–14.
Askew, Melvin W. "Quests, Cars, and Kerouac." *University of Kansas City Review* 28, no. 3 (1962): 231–240.
Atlas, James. "Foreword." In Holmes, *Go*, xi–xvi.
Attardo, Salvatore. "Irony as Relevant Inappropriateness." *Journal of Pragmatics* 32, no. 6 (2000): 793–826.
Augé, Marc. *Non-Lieux: Introduction à une anthropologie de la surmodernité.* Paris: Éditions du Seuil, 1992.

Avila, Eric. *The Folklore of the Freeway: Race and Revolt in the Modernist City.* Minneapolis: University of Minnesota Press, 2014.
Bachelor, Steven J. "Miracle on Ice: Industrial Workers and the Promise of Americanization in Cold War Mexico." In *In from the Cold: Latin America's New Encounter with the Cold War*, edited by Gilbert M. Joseph and Daniela Spenser (Durham, NC: Duke University Press, 2008), 253–272.
Badiou, Alain. *The Rebirth of History.* Translated by Gregory Elliott. London: Verso, 2012.
Baker, John Earl. "Transportation in China." *Annals of the American Academy* 152 (1930): 160–172.
Balkmar, Dag. "On Men and Cars: An Ethnographic Study of Gendered, Risky and Dangerous Relations." PhD diss., Linköping University, 2012.
Ballard, J. G. *The Atrocity Exhibition.* London: Fourth Estate, 2006.
*———. *Crash.* London: Vintage, 1973.
*———. *Empire of the Sun: A Novel.* New York: Simon & Schuster, 1984.
———. "Introduction." in Ballard, *Crash*, 4–6.
———. *Miracles of Life: Shanghai to Shepperton—An Autobiography.* London: Fourth Estate, 2008.
Ballent, Anahí. "Kilómetro cero: La construcción del universo simbólico del camino en la Argentina de los años treinta." *Boletín del Instituto de Historia Argentina y Americana "Dr. Emilio Ravignani."* 27 (1er semestre 2005), 107–137.
Bänzinger, Peter-Paul. "Der betriebsame Mensch: Ein Bericht (nicht nur) aus der Werkstatt." *Österreichische Zeitschrift für Geschichtswissenschaften* 23, no. 2 (2012): 222–236.
*Baraka, Amiri. *The System of Dante's Hell.* Brooklyn, NY: Akashi Books, 2016.
Barfield, Thomas J. *The Nomadic Alternative.* Englewood Cliffs, NJ: Prentice Hall, 1993.
Baricco, Alessandro. *De barbaren.* Translated by Manon Smiths. Amsterdam: De Bezige Bij, 2010.
Barker, Theo, ed. *The Economic and Social Effects of the Spread of Motor Vehicles: An International Centenary Tribute.* London: Macmillan, 1987.
Barrett, Paul, and Mark H. Rose. "Street Smarts: The Politics of Transportation Statistics in the American City, 1900–1990." *Journal of Urban History* 25, no. 3 (1999): 405–433.
Barthes, Roland. "La nouvelle Citroën." In *Mythologies* (Paris: Éditions du Seuil, 1957), 169–171.
Basiuk, Tomasz. "Fiction in the 1960s and the Notion of Change: American and European Concepts of Postmodernism." In Kosc et al., *Transatlantic Sixties*, 202–225.
Baudrillard, Jean. "Crash." In *Simulacra and Simulation* by Jean Baudrillard, translated by Sheila Faria Glaser (Ann Arbor: University of Michigan Press, 1994), 111–119. First published as "Crash," in *Simulacres et simulation* by Jean Baudrillard. Paris: Éditions Galilée, 1981).
———. "Two Essays." Translated by Arthur B. Evans. *Science-Fiction Studies* 18, no. 3 (1991): 309–320.
Bauman, Zygmunt. *The Individualized Society.* Cambridge: Polity, 2004.
———. *Liquid Life.* Cambridge: Polity, 2006.
Baumgaertner, Jill P. "Foreword." In Ragen, *Wreck on the Road to Damascus*, xi–xiii.
Baxter, John. *The Inner Man: The Life of J. G. Ballard.* London: Weidenfeld & Nicolson, 2011.
Bayley, Stephen. *Sex, Drink and Fast Cars: The Creation and Consumption of Images.* London: Faber & Faber, 1986.
Beck, Kurt, Gabriel Klaeger, and Michael Stasik, eds. *The Making of the African Road.* Leiden: Brill, 2017.
Becker, Jens Peter. *Das Automobil und die amerikanische Kultur.* Trier: Wissenschaftliche Verlag Trier, 1989.

Becker, Tobias. "HT 2014: 'The Winner Takes It All'—Popgeschichtliche Narrative des 20. Jahrhunderts zwischen Ausbeutung und Emanzipation." Conference review. H-Soz-Kult, 14 November 2014. http://www.hsozkult.de/conferencereport/id/tagungsberichte-5669.

Beckman, Karen. *Crash: Cinema and the Politics of Speed and Stasis.* Durham, NC: Duke University Press, 2010.

*Bedford, Sybille. "A Homecoming: Capri 1948." In Bedford, *Pleasures and Landscapes*, 15–22.

*———. "A Journey in Yugoslavia: 1965." In Bedford, *Pleasures and Landscapes*, 115–145.

*———. "Notes on a Journey in Portugal: 1958." In Bedford, *Pleasures and Landscapes*, 105–113.

*———. *Pleasures and Landscapes: A Traveller's Tales from Europe.* London: Daunt Books, 2014.

Bedi, Tarini. "Mimicry, Friction and Trans-urban Imaginaries: Mumbai Taxis/Singapore-Style." *Environment and Planning A* 48, no. 1 (2016): 1012–1029.

Bélanger, Danièle, Lisa B. Welch Drummond, and Van Nguyen-Marshall. "Introduction: Who Are the Urban Middle Class in Vietnam?" In *The Reinvention of Distinction: Modernity and the Middle Class in Urban Vietnam*, edited by Van Nguyen-Marshall, Lisa B. Welch Drummond, and Danièle Bélanger (Dordrecht: Springer, 2012), 1–17.

Belkin, Aaron. *Bring Me Men: Military Masculinity and the Benign Facade of American Empire, 1898–2001.* New York: Columbia University Press, 2012.

Bell, Colin. *Middle Class Families: Social and Geographical Mobility.* London: Routledge & Kegan Paul / Humanities Press, 1968.

Bennett, Gordon, and Ronald N. Montaperto. *Red Guard: The Political Biography of Dai Hsiao-ai* (Garden City, NY: Doubleday, 1971.

*Bense, Max. "Auto und Information: Das Ich, das Auto und die Technik" [Car and information: The I, the car and technology]. In *Ausgewählte Schriften, Bd. 4: Poetische Texte* by Max Bense, edited by Elisabeth Walther (Stuttgart: J. B. Metzler, 1998), 291–293.

Berg, Hartmut. "Motorcars: Between Growth and Protectionism." In *The Structure of European Industry*, edited by H. W. de Jong (Dordrecht: Kluwer, 1993), 121–146.

Berman, Marshall. *All That Is Solid Melts Into Air: The Experience of Modernity.* New York: Penguin, 1988.

Berna, Serge, Jean-Louis Brau, Guy Debord, and Gil J. Wolman. "No More Flat Feet!" Translated by Sophie Rosenberg. *Internationale Lettriste* 1 (November 1952).

Bernecker, Walther L. "Das spanische Wirtschaftswunder. Ökonomisches Wachstum und sozialer Wandel in der Franco-Ära." In Kaelble, *Der Boom*, 190–218.

Berry, Sara S. "From Peasant to Artisan: Motor Mechanics in a Nigerian Town." African Studies Center Working Paper no. 76. Boston, 1983.

Bertens, Hans. "The Sociology of Postmodernity." In *International Postmodernism: Theory and Literary Practice*, edited by Hans Bertens and Douwe Fokkema (Amsterdam: John Benjamins Publishing Co., 1997), 103–118.

Bertho Lavenir, Catherine. "Flirting in a Car." Paper presented at the T²M conference "Energy and Innovation," Lucerne, 5–8 November 2009.

———. *La roue et le stylo: Comment nous sommes devenus touristes.* Paris: Editions Odile Jacob, 1999.

Bertholet, Yves. "Unity and Diversity of Development: The Regional Commissions' Experience." In *Unity and Diversity in Development Ideas: Perspectives from the UN Regional Commissions*, edited by Yves Bertholet (Bloomington: Indiana University Press, 2004), 1–50.

Bérubé, Allan, with Florence Bérubé. "Sunset Trailer Park." In *White Trash: Race and Class in America*, edited by Matt Wray and Annalee Newitz (New York: Routledge, 1997), 15–39.

Bess, Michael K. "Routes of Conflict: Building Roads and Shaping the Nation in Mexico, 1941–1952." *Journal of Transport History* 35 no. 1 (2014): 78–96.
Bezis, Jason. "Altamont Rock Festival: '60s Abruptly End (Part I of II)." *Livermore Heritage Guild* 42, no. 3 (2010): 1, 3–5.
Bhaduri, Sukla. *Transport and Regional Development: A Case Study of Road Transport of West Bengal.* New Delhi: Concept Publishing Co., 1992.
Bhaskar, Krish. *The Future of the World Motor Industry.* London: Kogan Page, 1980.
Bhatnagar, K. P., Satish Bahadur, D. N. Agrawal, and S. C. Gupta. *Transport in Modern India.* Revised and enlarged edition. Kanpur: Kishore Publishing House, 1961.
Bianciardi, Luciano. *La Vita Agra, or It's a Hard Life.* Translated by Eric Mosbacher. London: Hodder & Stoughton, 1965.
Biles, Roger. "Expressways before the Interstates: The Case of Detroit, 1945–1956." *Journal of Urban History* 40, no. 5 (2014): 843–854.
Binder, Leonard. "The Natural History of Development Theory." *Comparative Studies in Society and History* 28, no. 1 (1986): 3–33.
Binding, Paul. "Pure Terror." *Times Literary Supplement*, 11 September 2009, 9.
Birdsall, Carolyn, Jan-Friedrich Missfelder, Daniel Morat, and Corine Schleif. "Forum: The Senses." *German History* 32, no. 2 (2014): 256–273.
Bishop, Ted. "*Tempo Giusto*: The Art of the Slow Ride." In *Culture and Mobility*, edited by Klaus Benesch (Heidelberg: Universitätsverlag Winter, 2013), 81–88.
Bize, Amiel. "Jam-Space and Jam-Time: Traffic in Nairobi." In Beck et al., *Making of the African Road*, 58–85.
Black, John A., and Peter J. Rimmer. "Japanese Highway Planning: A Western Interpretation." *Transportation* 11, no. 1 (1982): 29–49.
Blanc, Jean-Daniel. *Die Stadt: Ein Verkehrshindernis? Leitbilder städtischer Verkehrsplanung und Verkehrspolitik in Zürich 1945–1975.* Zürich: Chronos Verlag, 1993.
Bloom, Harold, ed. *Modern Critical Views of John Updike.* New York: Chelsea House, 1987.
Bluestone, Barry, and Bennett Harrison. *The Deindustrialization of America: Plant Closings, Community Abandonment, and the Dismantling of Basic Industry.* New York: Basic Books, 1982.
Boatcă, Manuela. "Semiperipheries in the World-System: Reflecting Eastern European and Latin American Experiences." *Journal of World-Systems Research* 12, no. 11 (2006): 321–346.
Böhme, Hartmut. "Das Strahlen fetischistischer Dinge des Konsums: Autos und Mode." In *In Gegenwart des Fetischs: Dingkonjunktur und Fetischbegriff in der Diskussion*, edited by Christine Blättler and Falko Schmieder (Vienna: Verlag Turia + Kant, 2014), 31–52.
———. *Fetischismus und Kultur: Eine andere Theorie der Moderne.* Reinbek: Rowohlt Verlag, 2006.
Bo Nielsen, Kenneth, and Harold Wilhite. "The Rise and Fall of the 'People's Car': Middle-Class Aspirations, Status and Mobile Symbolism in 'New India.'" In *Cars, Automobility and Development in Asia: Wheels of Change*, edited by Arve Hansen and Kenneth Bo Nielsen (London: Routledge, 2017), 171–190.
Bolens, Guillemette. *The Style of Gestures: Embodiment and Cognition in Literary Narratives.* Foreword by Alain Berthoz. Baltimore: Johns Hopkins University Press, 2012.
Bolter, Jay David, and Richard Grusin. *Remediation: Understanding New Media.* Cambridge. MA: MIT Press, 2000.
Bolton, Ralph. "Machismo in Motion: The Ethos of Peruvian Truckers." *Ethos* 7, no. 4 (1979): 312–342.

Booth, Rodrigo. "Automóviles y Carreteras: Movilidad, modernización y transformación territorial en Chile, 1913–1931." PhD diss., Pontificia Universidad Católica de Chile, 2009.

———. "El automóvil: Un objeto técnico superior—Debates y experiencias en torno a la irrupción de la motorización privada en Chile (1902–1914)." In *À pied, à cheval, en voiture: l'Amérique indépendente et les moyens de transport*, edited by Isabelle Tauzin-Castellanos (Pessac: Maison des Sciences de l'Homme d'Aquitaine, 2011), 99–110.

———. "Turismo, Panamericanismo e ingeneria civil: La construcción del camino escénico entre Viña del Mar y Concón (1917–1931)." *Historia* 2, no. 47 (2014): 277–311.

Booth, Rodrigo, and Melina Piglia. "New Developments in a Neglected Field: Transport and Mobility in Latin American Recent Historiography." In Mom et al., *Mobility in History*, 159–165.

Borcherdt, Christoph. "Die neuere Verkehrserschliessung in Venezuela und ihre Auswirkungen in der Kulturlandschaft." *Die Erde* 1 (1968): 42–76.

Borden, Iain. *Drive: Journeys through Film, Cities and Landscapes*. London: Reaktion Books, 2013.

Borg, Kevin L. *Auto Mechanics: Technology and Expertise in Twentieth-Century America*. Baltimore: Johns Hopkins University Press, 2007.

Borm, Jan. "Defining Travel: On the Travel Book, Travel Writing and Terminology." In Hooper and Young, *Perspectives on Travel Writing*, 13–26.

Bosch, Aida. *Konsum und Exklusion: Eine Kultursociologie der Dinge*. Bielefeld: transcript, 2010.

Boshardt, R. A., *The Restraining Hand: Captivity for Christ in China*. London: Hodder & Stoughton, 1936.

*Braine, John. *Room at the Top*. London: Arrow Books, 2002.

Bramall, Chris. *Chinese Economic Development*. London: Routledge, 2009.

Brand, Stewart, and Howard Rheingold. *The Virtual Community: Homesteading on the Electronic Frontier*. Reading, MA: Addison-Wesley Publishing Co., 1993.

Brändle, Fabian. "'Hard Travelin': Die Old Left und Folk Music im New Deal." *Moving the Social: Journal of Social History and the History of Social Movements* 47 (2012): 41–62.

Breines, Wini. "The 'Other' Fifties: Beats and Bad Girls." In *Not June Cleaver: Women and Gender in Postwar America, 1945–1960*, edited by Joanne Meyerowitz (Philadelphia: Temple University Press, 1994), 382–408.

Brett, Michael. *Approaching African History*. Woolbridge: James Currey, 2013.

Brickell, Chris. "Masculinities, Performativity, and Subversion." *Men and Masculinities* 8, no. 1 (2005): 24–43.

Brilli, Attilio. *Das rasende Leben: Die Anfänge des Reisens mit dem Automobil*. Translated by Annette Kopetzki. Berlin Verlag Klaus Wagenbach, 1999.

Brinkley, Douglas. "Foreword." In de Beauvoir, *America Day by Day*, xi–xvi.

Brinkman, Inge. "Refugees on Routes: Congo/Zaire and the War in Northern Angola (1961–1974)." In *Angola on the Move: Transport Routes, Communications and History*, edited by Beatrix Heintze and Achim von Oppen (Frankfurt: Verlag Otto Lembeck, 2008), 198–220.

Brodey, Inger Sigrun. "Introduction." In Natsume Sōseki, *My Individualism and the Philosophical Foundations of Literature*, translated by Sammy I. Tsunematsu (Boston: Tuttle Publishing, 2004), 9–23.

Brodey, Inger Sigrun. "Introduction." In *Rediscovering Natsume Sōseki*, edited and translated by Sigrun Brodey and Sammy I. Ysunematsu (Folkestone: Global Oriental, 2000), 1–32.

Brodsly, David. *L.A. Freeway: An Appreciative Essay*. Berkeley: University of California Press, 1983.

Bronger, Dirk. *Metropolen, Megastädte, Global Cities: Die Metropolisierung der Erde* (Darmstadt: Wissenschaftliche Buchgesellschaft, 2004.
Brown, Clair. *American Standards of Living 1918–1988*. Oxford: Blackwell, 1994.
Brown, Jeffrey, Eric A. Morris, and Brian D. Taylor. "Planning for Cars in Cities: Planners, Engineers, and Freeways in the 20th Century." *Journal of the American Planning Association* 75, no. 2 (2009): 161–177.
*Brown, Kurt, ed. *Drive, They Said: Poems about Americans and Their Cars*. Preface by Edward Hirsch. Minneapolis: Milkweed Editions, 1994.
Brown, Robert T. *Transport and the Economic Integration of South America*. Washington, DC: Brookings Institution, 1966.
Brownback, Henry Lowe. "Comment la Voiture Européenne a évolué." *Journal de la S.I.A.* 32, no. 3 (1958): 133–140.
———. "Why Is the American Car Built as It Is Built?" *FISITA Proceedings* (1960): 564–583.
Bruckner, Pascal, and Alain Finkielkraut. *Au coin de la rue, l'aventure*. Paris: Seuil, 1979.
Bude, Heinz. "Bürgertumsgenerationen in der Bundesrepublik." In Hettling and Ulrich, *Bürgertum nach 1945*, 111–132.
Buell, Frederick. *From Apocalypse to Way of Life: Environmental Crisis in the American Century*. New York: Routledge, 2004.
Bullard, Robert D. "The Anatomy of Transportation Racism." In *Highway Robbery: Transportation Racism & New Routes to Equityi*, edited by Robert D. Bullard, Glenn S. Johnson, and Angel O. Torres (Cambridge, MA: South End Press, 2004), 15–31.
———. "Introduction." In *Highway Robbery: Transportation Racism & New Routes to Equityi*, edited by Robert D. Bullard, Glenn S. Johnson, and Angel O. Torres (Cambridge, MA: South End Press, 2004), 1–12.
Bullock, Henry Allen. "Consumer Motivations in Black and White: I." *Harvard Business Review* 39, no. 3 (1961): 89–104.
Bulmer-Thomas, Victor. "The Latin American Economies, 1929–1939." In *The Cambridge History of Latin America, vol. 6: Latin America since 1930—Economy, Society and Politics*, edited by Leslie Bethell (Cambridge: Cambridge University Press, 1994), 65–116.
Burdett, Charles. *Journeys through Fascism: Italian Travel Writing between the Wars*. New York: Berghahn Books, 2010.
Burgers, Christian. "Verbale ironie: Een literatuurstudie." *Tijdschrft voor Taalbeheersing* 29, no. 2 (2007): 135–158.
Burgers, Christian, and Margot van Mulken. "Het ironisch spectrum: Een overzicht van onderzoek naar het begrip en de retorische effecten van verbale ironie." *Tijdschrift voor Taalbeheersing* 35, no. 2 (2013): 183–202.
Burgers, Christian, Margot van Mulken, and Peter Jan Schellens. "The Use of Co-textual Irony Markers in Written Discourse." *Humor* 26, no. 1 (2013): 45–68.
———. "Verbal Irony: Differences in Usage Across Written Genres." *Journal of Language and Social Psychology* 31, no. 3 (2012): 290–310.
Burke, Peter. "Popular Culture Reconsidered." *Storia della Storiografia* 17 (1990): 41–50.
Burrell, Kathy, and Kathrin Hörschelmann. "Introduction: Understanding Mobility in Soviet and East European Socialist and Post-Socialist States." In *Mobilities in Socialist and Post-Socialist States: Societies on the Move*, edited by Kathy Burrell and Kathrin Hörschelmann (London: Palgrave Macmillan, 2014), 1–22.
Busch, Tracy Nichols. "'A Class on Wheels': Avtodor and the 'Automobilization' of the Soviet Union, 1927–1935." PhD diss., Ferris State University, 2003.
———. "From the Scythians to the Soviets: An Evaluation of Russian Mobility History." In Mom et al., *Mobility in History*, 149–157.

Buschauer, Regine. "The 'Ambulant in-Between': Media Histories of Mobile Communication." *Transfers* 3, no. 1 (2013): 96–118.
Byron, Robert. *The Road to Oxiana*. Introduction by Colin Thubron. London: Penguin, 2007.
Campanella, Thomas J. "'The Civilising Road': American Influence on the Development of Highways and Motoring in China, 1900–1949." *Journal of Transport History* 26, no. 1 (2005): 78–98.
Campbell, Mary Baine. "Travel Writing and Its Theory." In Hulme and Youngs, *Cambridge Companion to Travel Writing*, 261–278.
Canclini, Néstor García. *Hybrid Cultures: Strategies for Entering and Leaving Modernity*. Translated by Christopher L. Chiappari and Silvia L. López. New introduction and foreword by Renato Rosaldo. Minneapolis: University of Minnesota Press, 1995.
Cantlie, Kenneth. *The Railways of China*. London: China Society, 1981.
Cao, Fangjun. "Modernization Theory and China's Road to Modernization." *Chinese Studies in History* 43, no. 1 (2009): 7–16.
Caplow, Theodore, Howard M. Bahr, Bruce A. Chadwick, Reuben Hill, and Margaret Holmes Williamson. *Middletown Families: Fifty Years of Change and Continuity*. Minneapolis: University of Minnesota Press, 1982.
Caplow, Theodore, Howard M. Bahr, John Modell, and Bruce A. Chadwick, eds. *Recent Social Trends in the United States 1960–1990*. Montreal: McGill-Queen's University Press, 1991.
Carden, Mary Parniccia. "'Adventures in Auto-eroticism': Economies of Traveling Masculinity in On the Road and The First Third." In *Your Road, Man? Critical Essays on Jack Kerouac's On the Road*, edited by Hilary Holladay and Robert Holton (Carbondale: Southern Illinois University Press, 2009), 77–98.
Cardenal, Juan Pablo, and Heriberto Araújo. *China's Silent Army: The Pioneers, Traders, Fixers and Workers Who Are Remaking the World in Beijing's Image*. Translated by Catherine Mansfield. London: Allen Lane, 2013.
Carosso, Andrea. "The Paradox of Re-colonization: The British Invasion of American Music and the Birth of Modern Rock." In Kosc et al., *Transatlantic Sixties*, 122–143.
Carr, Duane. *A Question of Class: The Redneck Stereotype in Southern Fiction*. Bowling Green, OH: Bowling Green State University Popular Press, 1996.
Carr, Helen. "Modernism and travel (1880–1940)." In Hulme and Youngs, *Cambridge Companion to Travel Writing*, 70–86.
Carrabine, Eamonn, and Brian Longhurst. "Consuming the Car: Anticipation, Use and Meaning in Contemporary Youth Culture." *Sociological Review* 50, no. 2 (2002): 181–196.
Carroll, Toby James. "The Politics of the World Bank's Socio-institutional Neoliberalism." PhD diss., Murdoch University, 2007.
Carter, Nancy Corson. "1970 Images of the Machine and the Garden: Kosinski, Crews, and Pirsig." *Soundings* 61, no. 1 (1978): 105–122.
Casey, Roger N. *Textual Vehicles: The Automobile in American Literature*. New York: Garland Publishing, 1997.
*Cassady, Neal. *The First Third and Other Writings*. San Francisco: City Lights, 1971.
Cassamagnaghi, Silvia. "Dalla guerra alla Lambretta: L'Innocenti e l'invenzione di un prodotto di successo." *Contemporanea* 14, no. 4 (2011): 645–679.
———. "Vespa Piaggio: First Mass Motorization and Discovery of Leisure in Post-war Italy." Paper presented at the conference "Inventing Europe," European Science Foundation workshop, Amsterdam, 15–17 January 2009.
Castillo, Greg. *Cold War on the Home Front: The Soft Power of Midcentury Design*. Minneapolis: University of Minnesota Press, 2010.
Catanzaro, Mary F. "The Car as Cell in *Lolita*." *Kansas Quarterly* 21, no. 4 (1989): 91–96.

Caughie, John. "Playing at Being American: Games and Tactics." In Mellencamp, *Logics of Television*, 44–58.

Cazes, Georges. "Les mobilités touristiques internationales." In *La planète "nomade": Les mobilités géographiques d'aujourd'hui*, edited by Rémy Knafou (Paris: Belin, 1998), 77–91.

Central Committee of the Communist Party of China. "Circular Promulgating the 'Summary of the Guangdong, Fujian Provincial Conference' (Excerpts) (March 1, 1982)." In "China's Coastal Development Strategy, 1979–1984." edited by Lawrence C. Reardon. Special issue, *Chinese Law and Government* 27, no. 3 (1994): 81–95.

———. "Circular Promulgating the 'Summary of the Work Conference on Guangdong and Fujian Provinces and the Special Economic Zones' (Excerpts) (July 19, 1981)." In "China's Coastal Development Strategy, 1979–1984." edited by Lawrence C. Reardon. Special issue, *Chinese Law and Government* 27, no. 3 (1994): 59–79.

"CFP: Die Evidenz der Familie." H-SOZ-U-KULT@H-NET.MSU.EDU, 16 July 2012.

Chakrabarty, Dipesh. *Habitations of Modernity: Essays in the Wake of Subaltern Studies*. Chicago: University of Chicago Press, 2002.

———. *Provincializing Europe: Postcolonial Thought and Historical Difference*. Princeton, NJ: Princeton University Press, 2000.

Chandra, Sushil, and Sudhir Atreya. "Lyricism in Design: A History of Motorcycles in India." *International Journal of Motorcycle Studies* 5, no. 2 (2009).

Chao, T. K. "Highway Construction and Transport in China." *Information Bulletin: Council of International Affairs, Nanking, China* 4, no. 7 (4 August 1937): 151–168.

Chapman, Murray, and R. Mansell Prothero. "Themes on Circulation in the Third World." In *Circulation in Third World Countries*, edited by R. Mansell Prothero and Murray Chapman (London: Routledge & Kegan Paul, 1985), 1–26.

———. "Conclusion." In *Circulation in Third World Countries*, edited by R. Mansell Prothero and Murray Chapman (London: Routledge & Kegan Paul, 1985), 437–440.

Chappell, Ben. "'Take a Little Trip with Me': Lowriding and the Poetics of Scale." In *Technicolor: Race, Technology, and Everyday Life*, edited by Alondra Nelson and Thuy Linh N. Tu with Alica Headlam Hines (New York: New York University Press, 2001), 100–120.

Chatterjee, Partha. *The Politics of the Governed: Reflections on Popular Politics in Most of the World*. New York: Columbia University Press, 2004.

Chatty, Dawn, *From Camel to Truck: The Bedouin in the Modern World*. Cambridge: White Horse Press, 2013.

Chen, Fu-Chia. "Cab Cultures in Victorian London: Horse-Drawn Cabs, Users and the City, ca 1830–1914." PhD diss., University of York, 2014.

Chen, Kuan-Hsing. "The Formation and Consumption of KTV in Taiwan." In *Consumption in Asia: Lifestyles and Identities*, edited by Chua Beng-Huat (London: Routledge, 2000), 159–182.

Chen, Lawrence M. "Highways in China." *Information Bulletin, Council of International Affairs, Nanking, China* 2, no. 8 (21 November 1936): 134–157.

Cheng, Pei-Kai and Michael Lestz (with Jonathan D. Spence), eds. *The Search for Modern China: A Documentary Collection*. New York: Norton, 1998.

Cheng, Tiejun, and Mark Selden. "The Origins and Social Consequences of China's *Hukou* System." *China Quarterly* 139 (September 1994): 644–668.

Chesneaux, Jean. *The Chinese Labor Movement 1919–1927*. Translated by H. M. Wright. Stanford, CA: Stanford University Press, 1968.

———. *Le mouvement paysan chinois 1840–1949*. Paris: Éditions du Seuil, 1976.

Chevalier, Louis. *Labouring Classes and Dangerous Classes in Paris during the First Half of the Nineteenth Century*. London: Routledge & Kegan Paul, 1973.

Chilundo, Arlindo Gonçalo. "The Economic and Social Impact of Rail and Road Transportation Systems in the Colonial District of Moçambique (1900–1961)." PhD diss., University of Minnesota, 1995.
Chiteji, Frank M. *The Development and Socio-economic Impact of Transportation in Tanzania 1884–Present*. Washington, DC: University Press of America, 1980.
Chiu, Imes. *The Evolution from Horse to Automobile: A Comparative International Study*. Amherst, NY: Cambria Press, 2008.
Choo, Sangho, and Patricia L. Mokhtarian. "What Type of Vehicle Do People Drive? The Role of Attitude and Lifestyle in Influencing Vehicle Type Choice." *Transportation Research Part A* 38, no. 3 (2004): 201–222.
Chou, Eva Shan. *Memory, Violence, Queues: Lu Xun Interprets China*. Ann Arbor, MI: Association for Asian Studies, 2012.
Choudhury, Deep Kanta Lahiri. "Of Codes and Coda: Meaning in Telegraph Messages, circa 1850–1920." *Historical Social Research* 35, no. 1 (2010): 127–139.
Chow, Rey. *Woman and Chinese Modernity: The Politics of Reading between East and West*. Minnesota: University of Minnesota Press, 1991.
Chun, Lin. *The Transformation of Chinese Socialism*. Durham, NC: Duke University Press, 2006.
Chye, Chua Peng, ed. *Planning in Singapore: Selected Aspects and Issues*. Singapore: Chopmen Enterprises, May 1973.
Ciabarri, Luca. "Biographies of Roads, Biographies of Nations: History, Territory and the Road Effect in Post-conflict Somaliland." In Beck et al., *Making of the African Road*, 116–140.
Citino, Nathan. "Suburbia and Modernization: Community Building and America's Post–World War II Encounter with the Arab Middle East." *Arab Studies Journal* 14, no. 1 (2005/2006): 39–64.
Clark, Clifford Edward, Jr. *The American Family Home, 1800–1960*. Chapel Hill: University of North Carolina Press, 1986.
Clark, Paul. *Youth Culture in China: From Red Guards to Netizens*. Cambridge: Cambridge University Press, 2012.
Clark, T. J. and Donald Nicholson-Smith. "Why Art Can't Kill the Situationist International," *October* 79 (Winter 1997): 15–31.
Clarke, Deborah. *Driving Women: Fiction and Automobile Culture in Twentieth-Century America*. Baltimore: Johns Hopkins University Press, 2007.
Clarsen, Georgine. *Eat My Dust: Early Women Motorists*. Baltimore: Johns Hopkins University Press, 2008.
———. "Pedaling Power: Bicycles, Subjectivities and Landscapes in a Settler Colonial Society." *Mobilities* 10, no. 5 (2015): 706–725.
Clifford, James. "Introduction: Partial Truths." In Clifford and Marcus, *Writing Culture*, 1–26.
Clifford, James, and George E. Marcus, eds. *Writing Culture: The Poetics and Politics of Ethnography*. Berkeley: University of California Press, 1986.
Clifford, Nicholas. *"A Truthful Impression of the Country": British and American Travel Writing in China, 1880–1949*. Ann Arbor: University of Michigan Press, 2001.
———. "With Harry Franck in China." In *A Century of Travels in China: Critical Essays on Travel Writing from the 1840s to the 1940s*, edited by Douglas Kerr and Julia Kuehn (Hong Kong: Hong Kong University Press, 2007), 133–145.
Clift, Rebecca. "Irony in Conversation." *Language in Society* 28, no. 4 (1999): 523–553.
Cohen, Abner. *Customs and Politics in Urban Africa: A Study of Hausa Migrants in Yoruba Towns*. Berkeley: University of California Press, 1969.

Cohen, Erik. "The Sociology of Tourism: Approaches, Issues and Findings." *Annual Review of Sociology* 10 (1984): 373–392.

———. "A Soi in Bangkok: The Dynamics of Lateral Urban Expansion." *Journal of the Siam Society* 73, nos. 1–2 (1985): 1–22.

Cohen, Ronald D. *Folk Music: The Basics*. New York: Routledge, 2006.

———. *Rainbow Quest: The Folk Music Revival and American Society, 1940–1970* (Amherst: University of Massachusetts Press, 2002.

———. "Singing Subversion: Folk Music and the Counterculture in the 1950s." In Van Minnen et al., *Beat Culture*, 117–127.

Comisión Económica para América Latina (CEPAL). "El Transporte en America Latina, Volumen III" (Naciones Unidas, Consejo Económico y Social, 11 February 1965).

Conklin, Alice L. *A Mission to Civilize: The Republican Idea of Empire in France and West Africa, 1895–1930*. Stanford, CA: Stanford University Press, 1997.

Conley, Jim. "Automobile Advertisements: The Magical and the Mundane." In *Car Troubles: Critical Studies of Automobility and Auto-mobility*, edited by Jim Conley and Arlene Tigar McLaren (Farnham: Ashgate, 2009), 37–57.

*Cortázar, Julio. "The Southern Highway." *Pegamequemegusta*, 3 February 2010. https://pegamequemegusta.wordpress.com/2010/03/02/the-southern-highway-julio-cortazar-trans-danny-fitzgerald.

Courteville, Roger. *La première traversée de l'Amérique du Sud en automobile: De Rio-de-Janeiro à Paz et Lima*. Paris: Barrères et Cie., [1954].

Comaroff, Jean, and John L. Comaroff. *Theory from the South or, How Euro-America Is Evolving toward Africa*. London: Boulder, 2012.

———. "Writing Theory from the South: The Global Order from an African Perspective." *The World Financial Review* (September–October 2013): 17–20.

Comtois, Claude. "Transport and Territorial Development in China (1949–1985)." *Modern Asian Studies* 24, no. 4 (1990): 777–818.

Conrad, Peter. *Modern Times, Modern Places*. New York: Knopf, 1999.

Coontz, Stephanie. *The Way We Never Were: American Families and the Nostalgia Trap*. New York: Basic Books, 2000.

Cooper, Frederick, and Randall Packard, eds. *International Development and the Social Sciences: Essays on the History and Politics of Knowledge*. Berkeley: University of California Press, 1997.

———. "Introduction." In Cooper and Packard, *International Development and the Social Sciences*, 1–41.

Cooper, Richard N. *The Economies of Interdependence: Economic Policy in the Atlantic Community*. New York: McGraw-Hill, 1968.

*Corso, Gregory. *Gasoline and The Vestal Lady on Brattle*. San Francisco: City Light Books, 1981.

*———. "Last Night I Drove a Car." In Corso, *Gasoline and The Vestal Lady on Brattle*, 52.

Cottrell, Robert. "Russia, NATO, Trump: The Shadow World." *New York Review of Books* (22 December 2016): 97–100

"The Course of Events and Critical Analysis." *Chinese Sociology & Anthropology* 19, no. 2 (1987): 15–129.

Cowie, Jefferson. *Stayin' Alive: The 1970s and the Last Days of the Working Class*. New York: New Press, 2010.

Creed, Barbara. "The *Crash* Debate: Anal Wounds, Metallic Kisses." *Screen* 39, no. 2 (1998): 175–179.

Cresswell, Tim. "Black Moves: Moments in the History of African-American Masculine Mobilities." *Transfers* 6, no. 1 (2016): 12–25.
———. "Mobility as Resistance: A Geographical Reading of Kerouac's 'On the Road.'" *Transactions of the Institute of British Geographers* 18 (1993): 249–263.
———. *On the Move: Mobility in the Modern Western World.* New York: Routledge, 2006.
———. "Writing, Reading and the Problem of Resistance: A Reply to McDowell." *Transactions of the Institute of British Geographers* 21 (1996): 420–424.
*Crews, Harry. *Car: A Novel.* In Crew, *Classic Crews*, 329–436.
*———. "The Car." In Crews, *Classic Crews*, 323–328.
*———. *Classic Crews: A Harry Crews Reader.* New York: Touchstone, 1995.
———. "Introduction." In Crews, *Classic Crews*, 9–16.
Croll, Elisabeth. "Introduction." In Hsieh, *Autobiography of a Chinese Girl*, 9–22.
Cronin, Michael. *Across the Lines: Travel, Language, Translation.* Cork: Cork University Press, 2013.
Crouch, Martin. "Problem of Soviet Urban Transport." *Soviet Studies* 31, no. 2 (1979): 231–256.
Culver, Lawrence, Heike Egner, Stefania Gallini, Agnes Kneitz, Cheryl Lousley, Uwe Lübken, Diana Mincyte, Gijs Mom, and Gordon Winder. "Revisiting Risk Society: A Conversation with Ulrich Beck." Special issue, *RCC Perspectives* 6 (2011).`
Cushman, Philip. "Why the Self Is Empty: Toward a Historically Situated Psychology." *American Psychologist* 45, no. 5 (1990): 599–611.
Dabag, Mihran, Horst Gründer, and Uwe-K. Ketelsen. "Einleitung." In Dabag et al., *Kolonialismus*, 7–18.
———, eds., *Kolonialismus: Kolonialdiskurs und Genozid.* Munich: Wilhelm Fink Verlag, 2004.
d'Almeida-Topor, Hélène, Chantal Chanson-Jabeur, and Monique Lakroum, eds. *Les transports en Afrique (XIXe-XXe siècle): Actes du colloque organisé les 16 et 17 février 1990 à Paris.* Paris: L'Harmattan, 1992.
Damm, Jens, and Bettina Gransow. "Zwischen Kuli-Export und Business-Netzwerken: Muster interner, inter- und transnationaler chinesischer Migration seit dem 19. Jahrhundert." In Kraler et al., *Migrationen*, 222–244.
Damm, Johnny. "Editor's Corner: Stalking History on the Hank Williams Death Ride." *A Bad Penny Review*, accessed 23 October 2019. http://www.abadpennyreview.com/editors-corner-stalking-history-on-the-hank-williams-death-ride.
Dant, Tim, and Peter J. Martin. "By Car: Carrying Modern Society." In Gronow and Warde, *Ordinary Consumption*, 143–157.
Darden, Joe T., and Richard W. Thomas. *Detroit: Race Riots, Racial Conflicts, and Efforts to Bridge the Racial Divide.* East Lansing: Michigan State University Press, 2013.
David, Philippe. "Iconographie de l'histoire des transports en Afrique noire: Les cartes postales." In d'Almeida-Topor et al., *Les transports en Afrique (XIXe-XXe siècle)*, 56–66.
Dawson, Jonathan, and Ian Barwell. *Roads Are Not Enough: New Perspectives on Rural Transport Planning in Developing Countries.* London: Intermediate Technology Publications, 1993.
Day, Aidan. "Ballard and Baudrillard: Close Reading *Crash*." *English* 49, no. 195 (2000): 277–293.
*de Beauvoir, Simone. *America Day by Day.* Translated by Carol Cosman. Berkeley: University of California Press, 1999.
de Jong, Wim, and Bas van Kleef. *De Puch-story en andere brommerverhalen.* Bussum: Thoth, 1994.

de Oliveira, Orlandina. "Urban Growth and Urban Social Structure in Latin America, 1930–1990." In *The Cambridge History of Latin America, vol. 6: Latin America since 1930—Economy, Society and Politics*, edited by Leslie Bethell (Cambridge: Cambridge University Press, 1994), 253–324.
de Rooy, Piet. *Republiek van rivaliteiten: Nederland sinds 1813*. Amsterdam: Mets & Schilt, 2005.
de Silva, Leelananda. "From ECAFE to ESCAP: Pioneering a Regional Perspective." In *Unity and Diversity in Development Ideas: Perspectives from the UN Regional Commissions*, edited by Yves Bertholet (Bloomington: Indiana University Press, 2004), 132–167.
de Grazia, Victoria, and Lizabeth Cohen. "Introduction: Class and Consumption." *International Labor and Working-Class History* 55 (1999): 1–5.
Dean, Warren. "The Brazilian Economy, 1879–1930." In *The Cambridge History of Latin America, vol. 5: c. 1870–1930*, edited by Leslie Bethell (Cambridge: Cambridge University Press, 1986), 685–724.
Debord, Guy. "Theory of the Dérive." In *Situationist International Anthology*, revised and expanded edition, edited and translated by Ken Knabb. Berkeley, CA: Bureau of Public Secrets, 2006. http://www.bopsecrets.org/SI/2.derive.htm.
Dekker, Jaap. "Conamtune: No Particular Place to Go." *Conam Bulletin* 29, no. 1 (2019): 28–30.
Del Testa, David. "Automobiles and Anomie in French Colonial Indochina." In *France and "Indochina": Cultural Representations*, edited by Kathryn Robson and Jennifer Yee (Lanham, MD: Lexington Books, 2005), 63–77.
Deloche, Jean. *Contribution a l'histoire de la voiture en Inde*. Paris: École Française d'Extrême-Orient, 1983.
Deloria, Philip J. *Indians in Unexpected Places*. Lawrence: University Press of Kansas, 2004.
Denby, Priscilla Lee. "The Self Discovered: The Car in American Folklore and Literature." PhD diss., Indiana University, 1981.
Department for Transport. *Focus on Personal Travel: 2005 Edition—Including the Report of the National Travel Survey 2002/2003*. Norwich: Her Majesty's Stationery Office, 2005.
Dewey, Scott Hamilton. "'Don't Breathe the Air': Air Pollution and the Evolution of Environmental Policy and Politics in the United States, 1945–1970." PhD diss., Rice University, 1997.
Dhakidae, Daniel. "Lifestyles and Political Behavior of the Indonesian Middle Classes." In *Exploration of the Middle Classes in Southeast Asia*, edited by Hsin-Huang Michael Hsiao (Taipei: Southeast Asian Studies, Academia Sinica, 2001), 475–513.
Diamant, Neil J. *Revolutionizing the Family: Politics, Love, and Divorce in Urban and Rural China, 1949–1968*. Berkeley: University of California Press, 2000.
Dick, Howard W. "Representations of Development in 19th and 20th Century Indonesia: A Transport History Perspective." *Bulletin of Indonesian Economic Studies* 36, no. 1 (2000): 185–207.
———. "Urban Public Transport, Part II." *Bulletin of Indonesian Economic Studies* 17, no. 2 (1981): 72–88.
———. "Urban Public Transport: Jakarta, Surabaya and Malang, Part I." *Bulletin of Indonesian Economic Studies* 17, no. 1 (1981): 66–82.
Dick, Howard, and Peter J. Zimmer. *Cities, Transport and Communications: The Integration of Southeast Asia since 1850*. London: Palgrave Macmillan, 2003.
Dick, Michael. *Die Situation des Fahrens: Phänomenologische und ökologische Perspektiven der Psychologie*. Hamburg: Technische Universität Hamburg - Harburg, 2001.

Dickson, K. B. "The Development of Road Transport in Southern Ghana and Ashanti since about 1850." *Transactions of the Historical Society of Ghana* 5, no. 1 (1961): 33–42.
Dienel, Hans-Liudger. "Das Bundesverkehrsministerium." In *Handbuch Verkehrspolitk*, edited by Oliver Schöller, Weert Canzler, and Andreas Knie. Wiesbaden: VS Verlag für Sozialwissenschaften, 2007.
Dierikx, Marc. "In Pursuit of the American Dream: The Spread of the Televised American Image and the Rise of European Tourism to the United States, 1945–1980." In *American Culture in the Netherlands*, edited by Doeko Bosscher, Marja Roholl, and Mel van Elteren (Amsterdam: VU University Press, 1996), 114–132.
———. "Sailing on a Cloud: The Development of Transatlantic Air Tourism." Unpublished manuscript.
Dikötter, Frank. *The Cultural Revolution: A People's History, 1962–1976*. London: Bloomsbury, 2016.
———. *Exotic Commodities: Modern Objects and Everyday Life in China*. New York: Columbia University Press, 2006.
———. *The Tragedy of Liberation: A History of the Chinese Revolution, 1945–1957*. London: Bloomsbury, 2013.
Ditt, Karl. *Zweite Industrialisierung und Konsum: Energieversorgung, Haushaltstechnik und Massenkultur am Beispiel nordenglischer und westfälischer Städte 1880–1939*. Paderborn: Ferdinand Schöningh, 2011.
Dittmar, Helga. *The Social Psychology of Material Possessions: To Have Is to Be*. Hemel Hempstead / New York: Harvester Wheatsheaf / St. Martin's Press, 1992.
Divall, Colin. "Railway imperialisms, railway nationalisms." In Monika Burri, Kilian T. Elsasser and David Gurgerli, eds., *Die Internationalität der Eisenbahn 1850–1970* (Zürich: Chronos Verlag, 2003), 195–209.
Doane, Mary Ann. "Information, Crisis, Catastrophe." In Mellencamp, *Logics of Television*, 222–239.
Dollard, John. *Caste and Class in a Southern Town*. New York: Harpers & Brothers, 1949.
Donghi, Tulio Halperín. *The Contemporary History of Latin America*. Edited and translated by John Charles Chasteen. Durham, NC: Duke University Press, 1993.
*Donofrio, Beverly. *Riding in Cars with Boys: Confessions of a Bad Girl Who Makes Good*. New York: Penguin, 1990.
Donofrio, Greg. "Gender Realignment: The Design and Marketing of Gas Stations for Women." In *The Rise of Marketing and Market Research*, edited by Hartmut Berghoff, Philip Scranton, and Uwe Spiekermann (New York: Palgrave Macmillan, 2012), 237–267.
Dowie, William. *James Salter*. London: Twayne Publishers, 1998.
Downes, Richard. "Autos over Rails: How US Business Supplanted the British in Brazil, 1910–28." *Journal of Latin American Studies* 24, no. 3 (1992): 551–583.
Doyle, Barry. "'More Than a Dance Hall, More a Way of Life': Northern Soul, Masculinity and Working-Class Culture in 1970s Britain." In Schildt and Siegfried, *Between Marx and Coca-Cola*, 313–330.
Drummond-Thompson, Philip. "The Development of Motor Transport in Nigeria: A Study in Indigenous Enterprise." In d'Almeida-Topor et al., *Les transports en Afrique (XIXe-XXe siècle)*, 222–246.
———. "The Rise of Entrepreneurs in Nigerian Motor Transport." *Journal of Transport History* 14, no. 1 (1993): 46–63.
Duc, Gérard, Olivier Perroux, Hans-Ulrich Schiedt, and François Walter, eds. *Transport and Mobility History: Between Modal Competition and Coordination (from 1918 to the Present)*. Neuchâtel: Alphil, 2014.

Dudley, Geoffrey, and Jeremy Richardson. *Why Does Policy Change? Lessons from British Transport Policy 1945–99.* London: Routledge, 2000.
Dulaney, William L. "A Brief History of 'Outlaw' Motorcycle Clubs." *International Journal of Motorcycle Studies* 1 (November 2005).
Dumazedier, Joffre, and Maurice Imbert (with Jean Duminy and Claire Guinchat). *Espace et loisir dans la société française d'hier et de demain.* Paris: Centre de recherche d'urbanisme, 1967.
Duncan, Russel. "The Summer of Love and Protest: Transatlantic Counterculture in the 1960s." In Kosc et al., *Transatlantic Sixties,* 144–173.
Dunn, James A., Jr. *Miles to Go: European and American Transportation Policies.* Cambridge, MA: MIT Press, 1981.
——— "The Politics of Motor Fuel Taxes and Infrastructure Funds in France and the United States." *Policy Studies Journal* 21, no. 2 (1993): 271–284.
Dunn, Katherine. *Truck.* New York: Warner Books, 1990.
Earle, David M. *All Man! Hemingway, 1950s Men's Magazines, and the Masculine Persona.* Kent, OH: Kent State University Press, 2009.
Eden, Lorraine and Maureen Appel Molot. "Made in America? The US Auto Industry, 1955–95." *International Executive* 38, no. 4 (1996): 501–541.
Edensor, Tim, and Mark Jayne. "Introduction: Urban Theory beyond the West." In *Urban Theory beyond the West: A World of Cities,* edited by Tim Edensor and Mark Jayne (London: Routledge, 2012), 1–27.
Edgerton, David. "Creole Technologies and Global Histories: Rethinking How Things Travel in Space and Time." *HOST: Journal of History of Science and Technology* 1 (Summer 2007): 75–112.
———. *The Shock of the Old: Technology and Global History since 1990.* Oxford: Oxford University Press, 2008.
Eich, Stefan, and Adam Tooze. "The Great Inflation." In *Vorgeschichte der Gegenwart: Dimensionen des Strukturbruchs nach dem Boom,* edited by Anselm Doering-Manteuffel, Lutz Raphael, and Thomas Schlemmer (Göttingen: Vandenhoeck & Ruprecht, 2016), 173–196.
*Ekwensi, Cyprian. *Jagua Nana.* Melbourne: Heinemann, [1997?].
Elena, Eduardo. *Dignifying Argentina: Peronism, Citizenship, and Mass Consumption.* Pittsburgh, PA: University of Pittsburgh Press, 2011.
Eley, Geoff. "Is All the World a Text? From Social History to the History of Society Two Decades Later." In *The Historic Turn in the Human Sciences,* edited by Terrence J. McDonald (Ann Arbor: University of Michigan Press, 1996), 193–243.
Elliot, Lyn Elizabeth. "Liberating Domesticity: The American Road Narrative in Film and Fiction." PhD diss., University of Iowa, 2000.
Ellis, R. J. "'They … Took Their Time over the Coming': The Postwar British/Beat, 1957–1965." In *The Transnational Beat Generation,* edited by Nancy M. Grace and Jennie Skerl (New York: Palgrave Macmillan, 2012), 145–163.
*Ellison, Ralph. "Cadillac Flambé." *American Review* 16 (February 1973): 249–269.
*———. *Invisible Man.* Introduction by John Callahan. London: Penguin, 2001.
Ellwood, David W. "The Marshall Plan: A Strategy That Worked." *Foreign Policy Agenda* (April 2006): 17–25. http://www.marshallfoundation.org/library/wp-content/uploads/sites/16/2014/05/The_Marshall_Plan_A_Strategy_that_Worked_000.pdf.
Emgin, Bahar. "Rowdy Gangs on the Road: The Culture of Mobilet in Turkey." In *Nesneyi Okumak / Deciphering the Object,* edited by Tevfik Balcioğlu and Gülsüm Baydar (Izmir: Yaşar Üniversitesi, 2012), 36–46.

Endy, Christopher. *Cold War Holidays: American Tourism in France*. Chapel Hill: University of North Carolina Press, 2004.
Engelhard, Peter. "Making Room for Beetle: Volkswagen's Impact on the German Motor Industry." *Automotive History Review* 54 (2012): 14–21.
Engerman, David C. "The Political Power of Economic Ideas? Foreign Economic Advisors and Indian Planning in the 1950s and 1960s." In Hilger and Unger, *India in the World*, 120–135.
Engerman, David C., and Corinna R. Unger. "Introduction: Towards a Global History of Modernization." *Diplomatic History* 33 no. 3 (2009): 375–385.
Ericson, Steven J. *The Sound of the Whistle: Railroads and the State in Meiji Japan*. Cambridge, MA: Council on East Asian Studies, Harvard University, 1996.
Erker, Paul. "The Long Shadow of Americanization: The German Rubber Industry and the Radial Tyre Revolution." In *Americanization and Its Limits; Reworking US Technology and Management in Post-war Europe and Japan*, edited by Jonathan Zeitlin and Gary Herrigel (Oxford: Oxford University Press, 2000), 298–315
Errázuriz, Tomás. "When Walking Became Serious: Reshaping the role of Pedestrians in Santiago, 1900–1931." *Journal of Transport History* 32, no. 1 (2011): 39–65.
Escobar, Arturo. "Anthropology and the Development Encounter: The Making and Marketing of Development Anthropology." *American Ethnologist* 18, no. 4 (1991): 658–682.
———. "Development and the Anthropology of Modernity." In Harding, *Postcolonial Science*, 269–289.
———. *Encountering Development: The Making and Unmaking of the Third World: With a new preface by the author*. Princeton, NJ: Princeton University Press, 2012.
Evans, Geoffrey, and James Tilly. *The New Politics of Class: The Political Exclusion of the British Working Class*. Oxford: Oxford University Press, 2017.
Fan, Shenggen, and Connie Chan-Kang. "Road Development, Economic Growth, and Poverty Reduction in China." DSGD Discussion Paper no. 12. Washington, DC: International Food Policy Research Institute, Development Strategy and Governance Division, August 2004.
Fang, Xiaoping. *Barefoot Doctors and Western Medicine in China*. Rochester, NY: University of Rochester Press, 2012.
Faris, John T. *Roaming American Playgrounds*. New York: Farrar & Rinehart, 1934.
Farnell, Brenda. "Moving Bodies, Acting Selves." *Annual Review of Anthropology* 28 (1999): 341–373.
Farr, Marie T. "Freedom and Control: Automobiles in American Women's Fiction of the 70s and 80s." *Journal of Popular Culture* 29, no. 2 (1995): 157–169.
Fava, Valentina. "In Search of a Czechoslovak People's Car: Skoda Auto and the 'Soviet Model of Management.'" *Actes du Gerpisa* 39 (December 2005): 147–170.
Feied, Frederick. *No Pie in the Sky: The Hobo as American Cultural Hero in the Works of Jack London, John Dos Passos, and Jack Kerouac*. San Jose, CA: Authors Choice Press, 2000.
Fein, Michael R. *Paving the Way: New York Road Building and the American State, 1880–1956*. Lawrence: University Press of Kansas, 2008.
Felsen, Henry Gregor. *Crash Club*. Milton Keynes: Lightning Source, 2013.
Felson, Marcus. "The Differentiation of Material Life Styles: 1925 to 1966." *Social Indicators Research* 3, nos. 3–4 (1976): 397–421.
———. "Invidious Distinctions among Cars, Clothes and Suburbs." *Public Opinion Quarterly* 42, no. 1 (1978): 49–58.
Fenby, Jonathan. *Chiang Kai-shek: China's Generalissimo and the Nation He Lost*. New York: Carroll & Graf Publishers, 2004.

Fercility. "Zhongshan Suit." *China Highlights*, 17 June 2019. https://www.chinahighlights.com/travelguide/traditional-chinese-clothes-zhongshan-suit.htm.
Ferguson, James. "Anthropology and Its Evil Twin: 'Development' in the Constitution of a Discipline." In Cooper and Packard, *International Development and the Social Sciences*, 150–175.
———. *The Anti-politics Machine: "Development." Depoliticization, and Bureaucratic Power in Lesotho*. Cambridge: Cambridge University Press, 1990.
Fey, Ingrid E. "Frou-Frous or Feminists? Turn-of-the-Century Paris and the Latin American Woman." In *Strange Pilgrimages: Exile, Travel, and National Identity in Latin America, 1800–1990s*, edited by Ingrid E. Fey and Karen Racine (Wilmington, DE: Scholarly Resources Inc., 2000), 81–94.
Ficek, Rosa Elena. "Imperial Routes, National Networks and Regional Projects in the Pan-American Highway, 1884–1977." *Journal of Transport History* 37, no. 2 (2016): 129–154.
———. "The Pan American Highway: Transformations of a Technology of Integration." Paper presented at the T²M conference "Spinoffs of Mobility: Technology, Risk and Innovation." Philadelphia, 18–21 September 2014.
Fink, Robert. *Repeating Ourselves: American Minimal Music as Cultural Practice*. Berkeley: University of California Press, 2005.
Finnemore, Martha. "Redefining Development at the World Bank." In Cooper and Packard, *International Development and the Social Sciences*, 203–227.
Fischer, Claude S. "Ever-More Rooted Americans." *City & Community* 1, no. 2 (2002): 177–198.
Fischer, Claude S., and Glenn R. Carroll. "Telephone and Automobile Diffusion in the United States, 1902–1937." *American Journal of Sociology* 93, no. 5 (1988): 1153–1178.
Fitzgerald, Sally. "Chronology." In O'Connor, *Collected Works*, 1237–1256.
Flessner, Bernd. "'In jeder Hinsicht betriebssicherer': In der Science-Fiction stand der Umstieg auf den Elektromotor bereits vor 100 Jahren fest." In *Zeiten der Elektromobilität: Beiträge zur Geschichte des elektrischen Automobils—Beiträge der Tagung des VDE-Ausschusses "Geschichte der Elektrotechnik" in Kooperation mit dem VDE Rhein-Ruhr e.V. vom 7. und 8. Oktober 2010 in Dortmund*, edited by Theo Horstmann and Peter Döring (Berlin: VDE Verlag, 2018), 181–192.
Flink, James J. *The Automobile Age*. Cambridge, MA: MIT Press, 1993.
Flonneau, Mathieu. *L'Automobile au temps des Trentes Glorieuses: Un rêve d'automobilisme*. Carbonne: Nouvelle Éditions Loubatières, 2016.
Fogel, Joshua A. *The Literature of Travel in the Japanese Rediscovery of China 1862–1945*. Stanford, CA: Stanford University Press, 1996.
———. "Yosano Akiko and Her China Travelogue of 1928." In Yosano, *Travels in Manchuria and Mongolia*, 1–8.
Ford, Mark. *Raymond Rousset and the Republic of Dreams*. Ithaca, NY: Cornell University Press, 2000.
———. "She Shampooed & Renewed Us." *New York Review of Books* (26 October 2017): 57–44.
Fôret, Philippe. "Railroad Literature on Suitable Places: How the Japanese Government Railways Forged an 'Old China' Travel Culture." In *Die Internationalität der Eisenbahn 1850–1970*, edited by Monika Burri, Kilian T. Elsasser and David Gurgerli (Zürich: Chronos Verlag, 2003), 309–326.
Foster, Kit. "The Cars of 1959: A Rising Middle Class." *Collectible Automobile* 33, no. 4 (2016): 8–25.

Fourastié, Jean (with Françoise Fourastié). *Des loisirs: pour quoi faire?* Tournai: Casterman, 1970.
Fox, Richard G. "East of Said." In Vincent, *Anthropology of Politics*, 143–152.
Framke, Maria. *Delhi—Rom—Berlin: Die indische Wahrnehmung von Faschismus und Nationalsozialismus 1922–1939.* Darmstadt: Wissenschaftliche Buchgesellschaft WBG, 2013.
Franco, Jean. *Cruel Modernity*. Durham, NC: Duke University Press, 2013.
François-Denève, Corinne. "Moteur! La voiture comme dystopie dans le cinéma français des années soixante." *La voix du regard* 19 (October 2006): 19–30.
Frank, Thomas. *The Conquest of Cool: Business Culture, Counterculture, and the Rise of Hip Consumerism.* Chicago: University of Chicago Press, 1997.
———. *Listen, Liberal or Whatever Happened to the Party of the People?* Melbourne: Scribe, 2016.
Frankenberg, Ronald. "'The Bridge' Revisited." In Vincent, *Anthropology of Politics*, 59–64.
Freed, Libbie. "'Every European Becomes a Chief': Travel Guides to Colonial Equatorial Africa, 1900–1958." *Journal of Colonialism and Colonial History* 12, no. 2 (2011).
Freedman, Alisa. *Tokyo in Transit: Japanese Culture on the Rails and Road.* Stanford, CA: Stanford University Press, 2011.
Freeman, John Brian. "'La carrera de la muerte': Death, Driving, and Rituals of Modernization in 1950s Mexico." *Studies in Latin American Popular Culture* 29 (2011): 2–23.
———. "Transnational Mechanics: Automobility in Mexico, 1895–1950." PhD diss., City University of New York, 2012.
Fremdling, Rainer. "Book Review: *Transport and the Development of the European Economy, 1750–1918.*" *Journal of Transport History* 12, no. 2 (1991): 197–198.
Freund, Bill. "Labor and Labor History in Africa: A Review of the Literature." *African Studies Review* 27 no. 2 (1984): 1–55.
Frey, Marc, Sönke Kunkel, and Corinna R. Unger, eds. *International Organizations and Development, 1945–1990.* London: Palgrave Macmillan, 2014.
———. "Introduction: International Organizations, Global Development, and the Making of the Contemporary World." In Frey et al., *International Organizations and Development*, 1–22.
Friedman, Murray. "Introduction: Middle America and the 'New Pluralism.'" In *Overcoming Middle Class Rage*, edited by Murray Friedman (Philadelphia: Westminster Press, 1971), 15–53.
———. "Overcoming Middle Class Rage." In *Overcoming Middle Class Rage*, edited by Murray Friedman, 367–383.
Friedmann, John. *Regional Development Policy: A Case Study of Venezuela.* Cambridge, MA: MIT Press, 1970.
Frith, Simon. *Sound Effects: Youth, Leisure, and the Politics of Rock 'n' Roll.* New York: Pantheon Books, 1981.
Fujii, James A. "Networks and Modernity: Rail Transport and Modern Japanese Literature." *Japan Railway & Transport Review* 13 (1997): 12–16.
Fujita, Kazuyuki, Kiichiro Hatoyama, and Sergey V. Shaposhnikov. "A Historical Overview of Railway Construction and its Association with Economic Growth in Russia." *Journal of the East Asia Society for Transportation Studies* 12 (2017): 234–250.
Fulwider, Benjamin. "Driving the Nation: Road Transportation and the Postrevolutionary Mexican State, 1925–1960." PhD diss., Georgetown University, 2009.
Furlough, Ellen. "Making Mass Vacations: Tourism and Consumer Culture in France, 1930s to 1970s." *Comparative Studies in Society and History* 40, no. 2 (1998): 247–286.

Gaiduk, Ilya V. "A Peace Offensive between the Two Wars: Khrushchev's Policy towards Asia, 1953–64." In Akita et al., *Transformation of the International Order*, 199–214.
Gall, Alexander. "*Gute Strassen bis ins kleinste Dorf!*" *Verkehrspolitik in Bayern zwischen Wiederaufbau und Ölkrise*. Frankfurt: Campus Verlag, 2005.
Galling, Bernard. "Foreword." In Huang, *Spiral Road*, ix–xii.
Gallup, George H. *The Gallup Poll: Public Opinion 1935–1971, vol. 2—1949–1958*. New York: Random House, 1972.
Galmiche, Xavier. "Die Kuh und der Mercedes: Die Umdeutung von Sinnbilder der Vergangenheit im tschechischen sozialistischen Aufbauroman." In *Zukunftsvorstellungen und Staatliche Planung im Sozialismus: Die Tschechoslowakei im ostmitteleuropäischen Kontext 1945–1989: Vorträge der Tagung des Collegium Carolinum in Bad Wiessee vom 22. bis 25. November 2007*, edited by Martin Schulze Wessel and Christiane Brenner (Munich: Oldenbourg Verlag, 2010), 235–252.
Gans, Herbert J. *The Levittowners: Ways of Life and Politics in a New Suburban Community*. London: Allen Lane, 1967.
Ganser, Alexandra. "Reading Multiple Mobilities in Chuck Palahniuk's *Fugitives and Refugees*." In *Culture and Mobility*, edited by Klaus Benesch (Heidelberg: Universitätsverlag Winter, 2013), 103–119.
———. *Roads of Her Own: Gendered Space and Mobility in American Women's Road Narratives, 1970–2000*. Amsterdam: Rodopi, 2009.
Garavini, Giuliano. *After Empires: European Integration, Decolonization, & the Challenge from the Global South 1957–1986*. Translated by Richard R. Nybakken. Oxford: Oxford University Press, 2013.
Garhammer, Manfred. *Wie Europäer ihre Zeit nutzen: Zeitstrukturen und Zeitkulturen im Zeichen der Globalisierung*. Berlin: edition sigma, 2001.
Garlichs, Dietrich. *Grenzen staatlicher Infrastrukturpolitik: Bund/Länder-Kooperation in der Fernstrassenplanung*. Königstein im Taunus: Verlag Anton Hain, 1980.
Garlichs, Dietrich, and Edda Müller. "Eine neue Organisation für das Bundesverkehrsministerium." *Die Verwaltung* 3 (1977): 343–362.
Garon, Sheldon. "The Transnational Promotion of Saving in Asia: 'Asian Values' of the 'Japanese model'?" In Garon and Maclachlan, *Ambivalent Consumer*, 163–187.
Garon, Sheldon, and Patricia L. Maclachlan, eds. *The Ambivalent Consumer: Questioning Consumption in East Asia and the West*. Ithaca, NY: Cornell University Press, 2006.
———. "Introduction." In Garon and Maclachlan, *Ambivalent Consumer*, 1–19.
Gartman, David. *Auto Opium: A Social History of American Automobile Design*. New York: Routledge, 1994.
———. "Three Ages of the Automobile: The Cultural Logics of the Car." *Theory, Culture & Society* 21, nos. 4–5 (2004): 169–195.
Gatejel, Luminita. *Warten, hoffen und endlich fahren: Auto und Sozialismus in der Sowjetunion, in Rumänien und der DDR (1956–1989/91)*. Frankfurt: Campus Verlag, 2014.
Gauron, André. *Histoire économique et sociale de la Cinquième République, tome I: Le Temps des modernistes*. Paris: La Découverte / Maspéro, 1983.
Geels, Frank W., René Kemp, Geoff Dudley, and Glenn Lyons, eds. *Automobility in Transition? A Socio-technical Analysis of Sustainable Transport*. New York: Routledge, 2012.
Gendron, Bernard. "Theodore Adorno Meets the Cadillacs." In *Studies in Entertainment: Critical Approaches to Mass Culture*, edited by Tania Modleski (Bloomington: Indiana University Press, 1986), 13–36.
Gerhardt, Uta. *Denken der Demokratie: Die Soziologie im atlantischen Transfer des Besatzungsregimes*. Stuttgart: Franz Steiner Verlag, 2007.

Gerland, Ellen J., and Craig L. Davis. "Selling Detroit on Women: *Woman's Day* and Auto Advertising, 1964–82." *Journalism History* 38, no. 4 (2013): 209–220.

Gewald, Jan-Bart. "Missionaries, Hereros, and Motorcars: Mobility and the Impact of Motor Vehicles in Namibia before 1940." *International Journal of African Historical Studies* 35, nos. 2–3 (2002): 257–285.

———. "People, Mines and Cars: Towards a Revision of Zambian History, 1890–1930." In Gewald et al., *Speed of Change*, 21–47.

Gewald, Jan-Bart, Sabine Luning, and Klaas van Walraven. "Motor Vehicles and People in Africa: An Introduction." In Gewald et al. *Speed of Change*, 1–18.

———, eds. *The Speed of Change: Motor Vehicles and People in Africa, 1890–2000*. Leiden: Brill, 2009.

Gewart, Gavin. "Making It Strange." *New York Times* (28 April 1985): 18.

Gewirtz, Julian. *Unlikely Partners: Chinese Reformers, Western Economists, and the Making of Global China*. Cambridge, MA: Harvard University Press, 2017.

Gibbons, Billy. *Billy F. Gibbons: Rock + Roll Gearhead*. Minneapolis, MN: MBI Publishing, 2011.

Gibbs, Raymond W., Jr. "Are Ironic Acts Deliberate?" *Journal of Pragmatics* 44, no. 1 (2012): 104–115.

Gillin, Donald G. *Warlord Yen Hsi-shan in Shansi Province 1911–1949*. Princeton, NJ: Princeton University Press, 1967.

Gilmore, David D. *Manhood in the Making: Cultural Concepts of Masculinity*. New Haven, CT: Yale University Press, 1990.

Gilroy, Paul. *Darker than Blue: On the Moral Economies of Black Atlantic Culture*. Cambridge, MA: Belknap Press, 2010.

*Ginsberg, Allen. "The Green Automobile." In *Selected Poems 1947–1995* (New York: HarperCollins, 1996), 23–27.

*———. *Howl and Other Poems*. San Francisco: City Light Books, 1996.

Giucci, Guillermo. *The Cultural Life of the Automobile: Roads to Modernity*. Translated by Anne Mayagoitia and Debra Nagao. Austin: University of Texas Press / Teresa Lozano Long Institute of Latin American Studies, 2012.

Gleissner, Erwin. *Transportelastizität und wirtschaftliche Entwicklung: Ein internationaler Vergleich*. Berlin: Juncker & Humblot, 1967.

Gluckman, Max. *Analysis of a Social Situation in Modern Zululand*. Manchester: Manchester University Press / Rhodes-Livingstone Institute, 1958.

Goddard, Stephen B. *Getting There: The Epic Struggle between Road and Rail in the American Century*. New York: HarperCollins, 1994.

Goedde, Petra. "Global Cultures." In *Global Interdependence: The World after 1945*, edited by Akira Iriye (Cambridge, MA: Belknap Press, 2014), 535–678.

Goerg, Odile. "Publicité et transports routiers en Guinée dans l'entre-deux-guerres." In d'Almeida-Topor et al., *Les transports en Afrique (XIXe–XXe siècle)*, 44–55.

Goldthorpe, John H., David Lockwood, Frank Bechhofer, and Jennifer Platt. *The Affluent Worker in the Class Structure*. Cambridge: Cambridge University Press, 1969.

Gomes, Alberto. *Modernity and Identity: Asian Illustrations*. Bundoora: La Trobe University Press, 1994.

Gondola, Ch.-Didier. "Typologie des sources pour la connaissance du transport interrive Brazzaville–Kinshasa." In d'Almeida-Topor et al., *Les transports en Afrique (XIXe–XXe siècle)*, 200–209.

Gordon, Andrew. *A Modern History of Japan: From Tokugawa Times to the Present*. New York: Oxford University Press, 2003.

Gordon, Bertram M. "The Evolving Popularity of Tourist Sites in France: What Can Be Learned from French Statistical Publications?" Paper presented at the International Commission for the History of Travel and Tourism / Congrès International des Sciences Historiques, Amsterdam, August 2010.

*Gordon, Mary. "Good Boys and Dead Girls." In *Good Boys and Dead Girls and Other Essays*. London: Bloomsbury, 1991), 3–23.

Gould, Peter R. *The Development of the Transportation Pattern in Ghana*. Evanston, IL: Department of Geography, Northwestern University, 1960.

———. "Tanzania 1920–63: The Spatial Impress of the Modernization Process." *World Politics* 22, no. 2 (1970): 149–170.

Grace, Joshua. "Saharan Garages, Paper Economies, and Migrant Laborers: New Perspectives on Mobility in African History." In *Mobility in History: The Yearbook of the International Association for the History of Transport, Traffic and Mobility, Volume 5*, edited by Peter Norton, Gijs Mom, Tomás Errázuriz, and Kyle Shelton (New York: Berghahn Journals, 2014), 143–149.

Grace, Nancy M. *Jack Kerouac and the Literary Imagination*. New York: Palgrave Macmillan, 2007.

Grandin, Greg. *Fordlandia: The Rise and Fall of Henry Ford's Forgotten Jungle City*. New York: Metropolitan Books / Henry Holt & Co., 2009.

Green, Nicola. "On the Move: Technology, Mobility, and the Mediation of Social Time and Space." *Information Society* 18, no. 4 (2002): 281–292.

Greenfield, Robert M. *Dreamer's Journey: The Life and Writings of Frederic Prokosch*. Newark: University of Delaware Press, 2010.

*Gregory, Dick. *From the Back of the Bus*. Edited by Bob Orben. Photographs by Yerry Yulsman. Introduction by Hugh Hefner. New York: Avon, 1962.

Gregory, James N. *The Southern Diaspora: How the Great Migrations of Black and White Southerners Transformed America*. Chapel Hill: University of North Carolina Press, 2005.

Grgurinović, Ivona. "Anthropology and Travel: Practice and Text." *Studia ethnologica Croatica* 24 (2012): 45–60.

Griffin, Farah Jasmine. *"Who Set You Flowin'?" The African-American Migration Narrative*. New York: Oxford University Press, 1995.

Gronow, Jukka, and Alan Warde. "Introduction." In Gronow and Warde, *Ordinary Consumption*, 1–8.

———, eds. *Ordinary Consumption*. London: Routledge, 2001.

Gronow, Jukka, and Sergei Zhuravlev. "Soviet Luxuries from Champagne to Private Cars." In *Pleasures in Socialism: Leisure and Luxury in the Eastern Bloc*, edited by David Crowley and Susan E. Reid Evanston, IL: Northwestern University Press, 2010), 121–146.

Grosfoguel, Ramón. "Developmentalism, Modernity, and Dependency Theory in Latin America." In *Coloniality at Large: Latin America and the Postcolonial Debate*, edited by Mabel Moraña, Enrique Dussel, and Carlos A. Jáuregui (Durham, NC: Duke University Press, 2008), 307–331. First published in *Nepantla: Views from South* 1, no. 2 (2000): 347–374.

Gross, Beverly. "'A Mind Divided Against Itself': Madness in Zen and the Art of Motorcycle Maintenance." *Journal of Narrative Technique* 14, no. 3 (1984): 201–213.

Gross, Feliks. *Il Paese: Values and Social Change in an Italian Village*. Preface by Vittorio Castellano. New York: New York University Press / University of Rome, Istituto di Statistica e Ricerca Sociale "C. Gini," 1973.

Großbölting, Thomas, Massimo Livi, and Carlo Spagnolo. "Einleitung." In *Jenseits der Moderne? Die Siebziger Jahre als Gegenstand der deutschen und der italienischen Geschichtsschreibung*, edited by Thomas Großbölting, Massimo Livi, and Carlo Spagnolo (Berlin: Duncker & Humblot, 2014), 7–14.

Gruschetsky, Valeria. "Argentina in Motion: Connections between Mobility, Politics, and Culture in Recent Historiography." In *Mobility in History: Reviews and Reflections*, edited by Peter Norton, Gijs Mom, Liz Millward, Mathieu Flonneau, and Tomás Errázuriz (Neuchâtel: Alphil, 2011), 136–141.

Grushkin, Paul. *Rockin' Down the Highway: The Cars and People That Made Rock Roll*. St. Paul, MN: Voyageur Press, 2006.

Gudis, Catherine. *Buyways: Billboards, Automobiles, and the American Landscape*. New York: Routledge, 2004.

Guevara, Ernesto Che. *Notas de viaje: Diario en motocicleta*. Buenos Aires: Distal, 2000.

Guilluy, Christophe. *Twilight of the Elites: Prosperity, the Periphery, and the Future of France*: Translated by Malcolm Debevoise. New Haven, CT: Yale University Press, 2019.

Guimarães, Paulo. "Strassen des Friedens nach Europa: Migration und der Aufbau eines Freibusnetzes im Südwesten Europas (1960–2000)." *Zeitschrift für Weltgeschichte* 12, no. 2 (2011): 175–212.

Guinn, Matthew. "The Grit Émigré in Harry Crews's Fiction." In *Perspectives on Harry Crews*, edited by Erik Bledsoe (Jackson: University Press of Mississippi, 2001), 105–115.

Günther, Armin. "20 Jahre Erlebnisgesellschaft—und mehr Fragen als Antworten: Zwischenbilanz oder Abgesang auf die Erlebniswelten-Diskussion." In *Postmoderne Freizeitstile und Freizeiträume: Neue Angebote im Tourismus*, edited by Paul Reuber and Peter Schnell (with Birthe Linden) (Berlin: Erich Schmidt Verlag, 2006), 47–62.

Gupta, Akhil. "Narratives of Corruption: Anthropological and Fictional Accounts of the Indian State." *Ethnography* 6, no. 1 (2005): 5–34.

Gusfield, Joseph R. "Tradition and Modernity: Misplaced Polarities in the Study of Social Change." *American Journal of Sociology* 72, no. 4 (1967): 351–362.

Gutfreund, Owen D. *Twentieth-Century Sprawl: Highways and the Reshaping of the American Landscape*. Oxford: Oxford University Press, 2004.

Gutknecht, Bernard. "Proteste gegen den Nationalstrassenbau 1957–1990: Von punktueller Opposition zu grundsätzlichem Widerstand." In *Rechte und linke Fundamentalopposition: Studien zur Schweizer Politik 1965–1990*, edited by Urs Altermatt (Basel: Helbing & Lichtenhahn), 62–94.

Güvenç, Serhat. "The Cold War Origins of the Turkish Motor Industry: The Tuzla Jeep, 1954–1971." *Turkish Studies* 15, no. 3 (2014): 536–555.

Hadorn, Christian. "Tagber: Violence, Migration, Cooperation, Gender—Late Portuguese and Spanish Colonialism in Africa Reconsidered." H-Soz-Kult, 29 January 2017. http://www.hsozkult.de/conferencereport/id/tagungsberichte-6956.

Haefeli, Ueli. "Stadt und Autobahn: eine Neuinterpretation." *Schweizerische Zeitschrift für Geschichte* 51 (2001): 181–202.

———. *Verkehrspolitik und urbane Mobilität: Deutsche und Schweizer Städte im Vergleich 1950–1990*. Stuttgart: Franz Steiner Verlag, 2008.

Hahn, H. Hazel. "The Rickshaw Trade in Colonial Vietnam, 1883–1940." *Journal of Vietnamese Studies* 8, no. 4 (2014): 47–85.

*Hailey, Arthur. *Wheels*. New Delhi: Rupa, 2006.

Hall, Peter. *Cities of Tomorrow: An Intellectual History of Urban Planning and Design in the Twentieth Century*. Malden, MA: Wiley-Blackwell, 2002.

———. *Great Planning Disasters*. Berkeley: University of California Press, 1980.

Hall, Sarah. "Introduction." In Salter, *Sport and a Pastime*, ix–xiv.

Hall, Stuart, and Tony Jefferson, eds. *Resistance through Rituals: Youth subcultures in Post-war Britain*. London: Routledge, 2006.
Hamill, Lynne. "The Social Shaping of British Communications Networks prior to the First World War." *Historical Social Research* 35, no. 1 (2010): 260–286.
Hanchard, Michael. "Afro-Modernity: Temporality, Politics, and the African Diaspora." In *Alternative Modernities*, edited by Dilip Parameshwar Gaonkar (Durham, NC: Duke University Press, 2001), 272–298.
Handley, William R. *Marriage, Violence, and the Nation in the American Literary West*. Cambridge: Cambridge University Press, 2002.
Hannerz, Ulf. *Cultural Complexity: Studies in the Social Organization of Meaning*. New York: Columbia University Press, 1992.
Hanser, Amy. *Service Encounters; Class, Gender, and the Market for Social Distinctions in Urban China*. Stanford, CA: Stanford University Press, 2008.
Harada, Katsumasa. "Policy." In Yamamoto, *Technological Innovation*, 222–229.
Harding, Sandra ed. *The Postcolonial Science and Technology Studies Reader*. Durham, NC: Duke University Press, 2011.
Hardt, Michael, and Antonio Negri. *Assembly*. Oxford: Oxford University Press, 2019.
———. *Multitude: War and Democracy in the Age of Empire*. New York: Penguin, 2005.
Haring, Sabine A., and Katharina Scherke. "Einleitung." In *Analyse und Kritik der Modernisierung um 1900 und um 2000*, edited by Sabine A. Haring and Katharina Scherke (Vienna: Passagen-Verlag, 2000), 11–32.
*Harris, Moira F. *Art on the Road: Painted Vehicles of the Americas*. Photographs by Leo. J. Harris. St. Paul, MN: Pogo Press, 1988.
Harris, Oliver. "Queer Shoulders, Queer Wheel: Homosexuality and Beat Textual Politics." In Van Minnen, *Beat Culture*, 221–240.
Harrison, Brian. *Seeking a Role: The United Kingdom, 1951–1970*. Oxford: Clarendon Press, 2009.
Hart, Jennifer. "'One Man, No Chop': Licit Wealth, Good Citizens, and the Criminalization of Drivers in Postcolonial Ghana." *International Journal of African Historical Studies* 46, no. 3 (2013): 373–396.
Hart, Keith. "Informal Income Opportunities and Urban Employment in Ghana." *Journal of Modern African Studies* 11, no. 1 (1973): 61–89.
Hartmann, Betsy. "Security and Survival: Why Do Poor People Have Many Children?" in Harding, *Postcolonial Science*, 310–317.
Hatton, Zannagh. "The Tarmac Cowboys: An Ethnographic Study of the Cultural World of Boy Racers." PhD diss., University of Plymouth, 2007.
Haustein, Sabine. *Vom Mangel zum Massenkonsum: Deutschland, Frankreich und Grossbritannien im Vergleich 1945–1970*. Frankfurt: Campus Verlag, 2007.
Havik, Philip J. "Motor Cars and Modernity: Pining for Progress in Portuguese Guinea, 1915–1945." In Gewald et al., *Speed of Change*, 48–74.
*Hawkes, John. *Second Skin*. New York: New Directions, 1964.
Hawkins, E. K. *Roads and Road Transport in an Underdeveloped Country: A Case Study of Uganda*. London: Her Majesty's Stationery Office, 1962.
Hay, Alan. "The Importance of Passenger Transport in Nigeria." *Nigerian Journal of Economic and Social Studies* 11, no. 1 (1969): 15–26.
Hay, James. "Unaided Viruses: The (Neo)liberalization of the Domestic Sphere and the New Architecture of Community." In *Foucault, Cultural Studies, and Governmentality*, edited by Jack Z. Bratich, Jeremy Packer, and Cameron McCarthy (New York: State University of New York Press, 2003), 165–206.

Hayashi, Yoshitsugu, Rithika Suparat, Roger Mackett, Kenji Doi, Yasuo Tomita, Nahoko Nakazawa, Hirokazu Kato, and Krit Anurak. "Urbanization, Motorization and the Environment Nexus: An International Comparative Study of London, Tokyo, Nagoya and Bangkok." *Memoirs of the School of Engineering, Nagoya University* 46, no. 1 (1994): 55–98.

Hayes, Joy Elizabeth. "National Imaginings on the Air: Radio in Mexico, 1920–1950." In Vaughan and Lewis, *Eagle and the Virgin*, 259–278.

Hazemann, Yves. "Routes et routiers du Sénégal au XXe siècle: Les sources de l'histoire des transports." In d'Almeida-Topor et al., *Les transports en Afrique (XIXe-XXe siècle)*, 210–221.

Headrick, Daniel R. "A Double-Edged Sword: Communications and Imperial Control in British India." *Historical Social Research* 35, no. 1 (2010): 51–65.

———. *The Tools of Empire: Technology and European Imperialism in the Nineteenth Century*. New York: Oxford University Press, 1981.

Heap, Simon. "The Development of Motor Transport in the Gold Coast, 1900–39." *Journal of Transport History* 11, no. 2 (1990): 19–37.

Hearn, Marcus. *The Cinema of George Lucas*. New York: Abrams Books.

Hebdige, Dick. "Object as Image: The Italian Scooter Cycle." In *The Consumer Society Reader*, edited by Martyn J. Lee (Malden, MA: Blackwell, 2000), 125–161.

———. *Subculture: The Meaning of Style*. London: Routledge, 1994.

———. "Towards a Cartography of Taste 1935–1962." *Block* 4 (1981): 39–56.

Heinemann, Isabel. "Introduction: Inventing the 'Modern American Family': Family Values and Social Change in 20th Century United States." In *Inventing the Modern American Family: Family Values and Social Change in 20th Century United States*, edited by Isabel Heinemann (Frankfurt: Campus Verlag, 2012), 7–28.

Heinze, G. Wolfgang. *Der Verkehrssektor in der Entwicklungspolitik: Unter besonderer Berücksichtigung des afrikanischen Raumes*. Munich: Weltforum Verlag, 1967.

Heldmann, Horst. *50 Jahre Verkehrspolitik in Bonn: Ein Mann und zehn Minister*. Bonn: Kirschbaum Verlag, 2002.

*Hemingway, Ernest. *Death in the Afternoon*. London: Arrow Books, 2004.

Hershfield, Joanne. *Imagining la Chica Moderna: Women, Nation, and Visual Culture in Mexico, 1917–1936*. Durham, NC: Duke University Press, 2008.

———. "Screening the Nation." In Vaughan and Lewis, *Eagle and the Virgin*, 259–278.

Hesford, Walter. "Overt Appropriation." *College English* 54, no. 4 (1992): 406–417.

Hettling, Manfred. "Bürgerlichkeit im Nachkriegsdeutschland." In Hettling and Ulrich, *Bürgertum nach 1945*, 7–37.

Hettling, Manfred, and Bernd Ulruch, eds. *Bürgertum nach 1945*. Hamburg: Hamburger Edition, 2005.

Hey, Kenneth. "Cars and Films in American Culture, 1929–1959." *Michigan Quarterly Review* 19, no. 4 (1980): 588–600.

Hibbins, Roy. "Male Gender Identities among Chinese Male Migrants." In *Asian Masculinities: The Meaning and Practice of Manhood in China and Japan*, edited by Kam Louie and Morris Low (London: Routledge, 2005), 197–219.

Highways in China 1949–1990. Beijing: Ministry of Communications, [1990].

Hildebrand, Julia M. "Media and Mobilities: Modes, Messages, Movements, and Moods." Drexel University paper, [2016]. Also published as "Modal Media: Connecting Media Ecology and Mobilities Research." *Media, Culture & Society* 40, no. 3 (2018): 348–364.

Hilger, Andreas, and Corinna R. Unger, eds. *India in the World since 1947: National and Transnational Perspectives*. Frankfurt: Peter Lang, 2012.

Hill, Sarah. "'This Is My Country': American Popular Music and Political Engagement in '1968.'" In *Music and Protest in 1968*, edited by Beate Kutschke and Barley Norton (Cambridge: Cambridge University Press, 2013), 46–63.

Hilpert, Dagmar. *Wohlfahrtsstaat der Mittelschichten? Sozialpolitik und gesellschaftlicher Wandel in der Bundesrepublik Deutschland (1949–1975)*. Göttingen: Vandenhoeck & Ruprecht, 2012.

Hilton, Matthew, and Rana Mitter. "Introduction." *Past and Present* 218, no. S8 (2013): 7–28.

Hindustan Motors. *Road Transport in India: A Study*. Calcutta: Hindustan Motors, 1968.

Hinton, Alex. "Savages, Subjects, and Sovereigns: Conjunctions of Modernity, Genocide, and Colonialism." In *Empire, Colony, Genocide: Conquest, Occupation, and Subaltern Resistance in World History*, edited by A. Dirk Moses (New York: Berghahn Books, 2008), 440–459.

Hipkiss, Robert A. "*On the Road*: Kerouac's Transport." *Kansas Quarterly* 21, no. 4 (1989): 17–21.

Hirsch, Jerrold. *Portrait of America: A Cultural History of the Federal Writers' Project*. Chapel Hill: University of North Carolina Press, 2003.

Hobsbawm, Eric. *The Age of Extremes: The Short Twentieth Century 1914–1991*. London: abacus, 2013.

———. "The Avant-Garde Fails." In *Fractured Times: Culture and Society in the Twentieth Century* (London: Little, Brown, 2013), 241–257.

Hobson, John M. "Discovering the Oriental West." In Harding, *Postcolonial Science*, 39–60.

Hofmeier, Rolf. *Transport and Economic Development in Tanzania, with Particular Reference to Roads and Road Transport*. Munich: Weltforum Verlag, 1973.

Hoggart, Richard. "Changes in Working-Class Life." In *Leisure and Society in Britain*, edited by Michael Smith, Stanley Parker, and Cyril Smith (London: Allen Lane, 1973), 28–39.

Holland, Patrick, and Graham Huggan. *Tourists with Typewriters: Critical Reflections on Contemporary Travel Writing*. Ann Arbor: University of Michigan Press, 2000.

———. "Varieties of Nostalgia in Contemporary Travel Writing." In Hooper and Youngs, *Perspectives on Travel Writing*, 139–151.

*Holmes, John Clellon. *Go: A Novel*. New York: Thunder's Mouth Press, 1997.

Hom, Stephanie Malia. "Empires of Tourism: Travel and Rhetoric in Italian Colonial Libya and Albania, 1911–1943." *Journal of Tourism History* 4, no. 3 (2012): 281–300.

Hon, Tze-ki. "The Chinese Path to Modernisation: Discussions of 'Culture' and 'Morality' in Republican China." *International Journal for History, Culture and Modernity* 2, no. 3 (2014): 211–228.

Honold, Alexander. "Raum ohne Volk: Zur Imaginationsgeschichte der kolonialen Geographie." In Dabag et al., *Kolonialismus*, 95–110.

Hook, Walter, and Michael Replogle. "Motorization and Non-motorized Transport in Asia: Transport System Evolution in China, Japan and Indonesia." *Land Use Policy* 13, no. 1 (1996): 69–84.

Hooper, Beverley. *Foreigners under Mao: Western Lives in China, 1949–1976*. Hong Kong: Hong Kong University Press, 2016.

Hooper, Glenn, and Tim Youngs. "Introduction." In Hooper and Youngs, *Perspectives on Travel Writing*, 1–11.

———, eds. *Perspectives on Travel Writing*. Aldershot: Ashgate, 2003.

Hosagrahar, Jyoti. *Indigenous Modernities: Negotiating Architecture and Urbanism*. London: Routledge, 2005.

How American Buying Habits Change. Washington, DC: US Department of Labor, [1959?].

Howard, John. "Place and Movement in Gay American History: A Case from the Post-World War II South." In *Creating a Place for Ourselves: Lesbian, Gay, and Bisexual Community Histories*, edited by Brett Beemyn (New York: Routledge, 1997), 211–225.

Howe, J. D. G. F. "Valuing Time Savings in Developing Countries." *Journal of Transport Economics and Policy* 10, no. 2 (1976): 113–125.

Howe, John. "Transport for the Poor or Poor Transport? A General Review of Rural Transport Policy in Developing Countries with Emphasis on Low-Income Areas." International Institute for Infrastructural, Hydraulic and Environmental Engineering Working Paper IP-12, October 1996.

Howlett, Peter. "The 'Golden Age,' 1955–1973." In Johnson, *Twentieth-Century Britain*, 320–339.

Hsia, Ronald. "On Capital Formation through Highway Construction in Communist China." Report for the Center for International Studies, MIT, April 1954. Later published as *The Role of Labor-Intensive Investment Projects in China's Capital Formation*. Cambridge, MA: Center for International Studies, MIT, 1954.

*Hsieh, Ping-Ying. *Autobiography of a Chinese Girl*. Translated by Tsui Chi. New introduction by Elisabeth Croll. London: Pandora Press, 1986.

Huang, Shu-min. *The Spiral Road: Change in a Chinese Village through the Eyes of a Communist Party Leader*. Boulder, CO: Westview Press, 1989.

Huang, Yaping. *Rediscovering China: Sun-Yat-Sen in Shanghai*. Translated by Pan Qin. Shanghai: Shanghai Century Publishing, 2010.

Hubert, Michel. "Démographie, femmes et famille entre spécificité et similitudes." In *Wandel und Integration: Deutsch-französische Annäherungen der fünfziger Jahre / Mutations et intégration—Les rapprochements franco-allemands dans les années cinquante*, edited by Hélène Miard-Delacroix and Rainer Hudemann (Munich: R. Oldenbourg Verlag, 2005), 361–378.

Huck, Christian, and Stefan Bauernschmidt, eds. *Travelling Goods, Travelling Moods: Varieties of Cultural Appropriation (1850–1950)*. Frankfurt: Campus Verlag, 2012.

Hudson, Ray, and Jim Lewis. "Introduction: Recent Economic, Social and Political Changes in Southern Europe." In *Uneven Development in Southern Europe: Studies of Accumulation, Class, Migration and the State*, edited by Ray Hudson and Jim Lewis (London: Methuen, 1985), 1–53.

Huenemann, Ralph William. *The Dragon and the Iron Horse: The Economics of Railroads in China 1876–1937*. Cambridge, MA: Harvard University Press, 1984.

Hugill, Peter J. "Technology Diffusion in the World Automobile Industry, 1885–1985." In *The Transfer and Transformation of Ideas and Material Culture*, edited by Peter J. Hugill and D. Bruce Dickson (College Station: Texas A&M University Press, 1988), 110–142.

Hulme, Peter. "Travelling to Write (1940–2000)." In Hulme and Youngs, *Cambridge Companion to Travel Writing*, 87–101.

Hulme, Peter, and Tim Youngs, eds. *The Cambridge Companion to Travel Writing*. Cambridge: Cambridge University Press, 2002.

Hunter, Holland. *Soviet Transport Experience: Its Lessons for Other Countries*. Washington, DC: Brookings Institution, Transport Research Program, 1968.

Hurley, Andrew. *Diners, Bowling Alleys and Trailer Parks: Chasing the American Dream in the Postwar Consumer Culture*. New York: Basic Books, 2001.

Husa, Karl, and Helmut Wohlschlägl. "Globale Märkte—lokale Konsequenzen: Arbeitsmigration in Südostasien seit der Mitte des 19. Jahrhunderts." In Kraler et al., *Migrationen*, 171–198.

Inglis, David. "Auto Couture: Thinking the Car in Post-war France." In *Automobilities*, edited by Mike Featherstone, Nigel Thrift, and John Urry (London: Sage, 2005), 197–219.

Iriye, Akira. "The Making of a Transnational World." In *Global Interdependence: The World after 1945*, edited by Akira Iriye (Cambridge, MA: Belknap Press, 2014), 679–847.

Iroko, A. Félix. "Le transport en hamac dans le royaume du Danhomè du XVIIe au XIXe siècle." In d'Almeida-Topor et al., *Les transports en Afrique (XIXe-XXe siècle)*, 159–177.

Isenberg, Nancy. *White Trash: The 400-Year Untold History of Class in America*. New York: Viking, 2016.

Jackson, Alan A. *The Middle Classes 1900–1950*. Nairn: David St. John Thomas Publisher, 1991.

Jacobs, G. D., and I. A. Sayer. *Study of Road Accidents in Selected Urban Areas in Developing Countries*. Crowthorne: Department of the Environment, Transport and Road Research Laboratory, Overseas Unit, 1977.

Jacobs, Steven. "From *Flâneur* to Chauffeur: Driving through Cinematic Cities." In *Imagining the City, vol. 1: The Art of Urban Living*, edited by Christian Emden, Catherine Keen, and David Midgley (Bern: Peter Lang, 2006), 213–228.

Jaisli, Max Roland. *Entwicklung, Stand und Auswirkungen der Motorisierung des individuellen Personenverkehrs in der Schweiz*. Aarau: Keller, 1958.

Jakle, John A., and Keith A. Sculle. *Motoring: The Highway Experience in America*. Athens: University of Georgia Press, 2008.

James, Lawrence. *The Middle Class: A History*. London: Little, Brown, 2006.

Jameson, Fredric. "Third-World Literature in the Era of Multinational Capitalism." *Social Text* no. 15 (1986): 65–88.

Janowitz, Morris. "Soziale Schichtung und Mobilität in Westdeutschland." *Kölner Zeitschrift für Soziologie und Sozialpsychologie* 10, no. 1 (1958): 1–38.

Jay, Mike. "Don't Fight Sober." *London Review of Books* 39, no. 1 (5 January 2017): 11–14.

Jeganathan, Pradeep. "On the Anticipation of Violence: Modernity and Identity in Southern Sri Lanka." In Arce and Long, *Anthropology, Development and Modernities*, 112–126.

Jennings, Rachel A. "Women Writers and the Internal Combustion Engine: Passing Penelope Pitstop." In *Gender, Genre, and Identity in Women's Travel Writing*, edited by Kristi Siegel (New York: Peter Lang, 2004), 97–119.

Jensen, Ole B., and Phillip Vannini. "Blue Sky Matter: Toward an (In-Flight) Understanding of the Sensuousness of Mobilities Design." *Transfers* 6, no. 2 (2016): 23–42.

*Ji, Xianlin. *The Cowshed: Memories of the Chinese Cultural Revolution*. Translated by Chenxin Jiang. New York: New York Review Books, 2015.

Jobs, Richard Ivan. *Backpack Ambassadors: How Youth Travel Integrated Europe*. Chicago: University of Chicago Press, 2017.

Johnson, Leland J. "Problems of Import Substitution: The Chilean Automobile Industry." *Economic Development and Cultural Change* 15, no. 2 (1967): 202–216.

Johnson, Paul, ed. *Twentieth-Century Britain: Economic, Social and Cultural Change*. London: Longman, 1994.

*Jones, Madison. *A Buried Land*. Sag Harbor, NY: Second Chance Press, 1987.

Jones, Terry-Ann. "Migration as a Response to Internal Colonialism in Brazil." *Transfers* 7, no. 2 (2017): 65–82.

Jordan, James William. "Role Segregation for Fun and Profit: The Daily Behavior of the West African Lorry Driver." *Africa: Journal of the International African Institute* 48, no. 1 (1978): 30–46.

Jørgensen, Thomas Ekman. "Utopia and Disillusion: Shattered Hopes of the Copenhagen Counterculture." In Schildt and Siegfried *Between Marx and Coca-Cola*, 333–352.

Joshi, Sanjay. "The Spectre of Comparisons: Studying the Middle Class of Colonial India." In *Elite and Everyman: The Cultural Politics of the Indian Middle Classes*, edited by Amita Baviskar and Raka Ray (London: Routledge, 2011), 83–107.

Jost, Herbert. "Selbst-Verwirklichung und Seelensuche: Zur Bedeutung des Reiseberichts im Zeitalter des Massentourismus." In *Der Reisebericht: Die Entwicklung einer Gattung in der deutschen Literatur*, edited by Peter J. Brenner (Frankfurt: Suhrkamp Verlag, 1989), 490–507.

Joyrich, Lynne. "Critical and Textual Hypermasculinity." In Mellencamp, *Logics of Television*, 156–172.

Jurca, Catherine. *White Diaspora: The Suburb and the Twentieth-Century American Novel*. Princeton, NJ: Princeton University Press, 2001.

Kaelble, Hartmut. "Auf dem Weg zur europäischen Konsumgesellschaft: Charakteristika in Frankreich und Deutschland im Vergleich." In *Wandel und Integration: Deutsch-französische Annäherungen der fünfziger Jahre/Mutations et intégration—Les rapprochements franco-allemands dans les années cinquante*, edited by Hélène Miard-Delacroix and Rainer Hudemann (Munich: R. Oldenbourg Verlag, 2005), 193–200.

———. "Boom und gesellschaftlicher Wandel 1948–1973: Frankreich und die Bundesrepublik Deutschland im Vergleich." In Kaelble, *Der Boom*, 219–247.

———, ed. *Der Boom 1948–1973: Gesellschaftliche und wirtschaftliche Folgen in der Bundesrepublik Deutschland und in Europa*. Opladen: Westdeutscher Verlag, 1992.

———. *Kalter Krieg und Wohlfahrtsstaat: Europa 1945–1989*. Munich: Verlag C. H. Beck, 2011.

Kaiserfeld, Thomas. "From Sightseeing to Sunbathing: Changing Traditions in Swedish Package Tours: From Edification by Bus to Relaxation by Airplane in the 1950s and 1960s." *Journal of Tourism History* 2, no. 3 (2010): 149–163.

Kaiwar, Vasant. "Towards Orientalism and Nativism: The Impasse of Subaltern Studies." *Historical Materialism* 12, no. 2 (2004): 189–247.

Kammann, George. *Mit Autobahnen die Städte retten? Städtebauliche Ideen der Expressstrassen-Planung in der Schweiz 1954–1964*. Zürich: Chronos Verlag, 1990.

Kandiyoti, Deniz. "Modernization without the Market? The Case of the 'Soviet East.'" In Arce and Long, *Anthropology, Development and Modernities*, 52–63.

Kanet, Roger E. "Soviet Attitudes toward Developing Nations since Stalin." In Kanet, *Soviet Union and the Developing Nations*, 237–264.

———, ed. *The Soviet Union and the Developing Nations*. Baltimore: Johns Hopkins University Press, 1974.

Kanger, Laur, and Johan Schot. "User-Made Immobilities: A Transitions Perspective." Science Policy Research Unit Working Paper Series SWPS 2016–13, University of Sussex, July 2016.

Kapur, Devesh, John P. Lewis, and Richard Webb. *The World Bank: Its First Half Century*, vol. 1—*History*. Washington, DC: Brookings Institution Press, 1997.

Kathuria, Sanjay. "Commercial Vehicles Industry in India: A Case History, 1928–1987." *Economic and Political Weekly* (17–20 October 1987), 1809–1823.

Katona, George, Burkhard Strümpel, and Ernest Zahn. *Aspirations and Affluence: Comparative Studies in the United States and Western Europe*. New York: McGraw-Hill, 1971.

Kaur, Amarjit. "Working on the Railway: Indian Workers in Malaya, 1880–1957." In Rimmer and Allen, *Underside of Malaysian History*, 99–128.

Kaur, Ravinder. "Planning Urban Chaos: State and Refugees in Post-Partition Delhi." In *Urbanization and Governance in India* edited by Evelin Hust and Michael Mann (New Delhi: Manohar, 2005), 229–249.

Keats, John. *The Insolent Chariots: Illustrated by Robert Osborn*. Philadelphia: J. B. Lippincott Co., 1958.
Keijzer, Fred. *Filosofie van de toekomst: Over nut en noodzaak van sciencefiction* [Philosophy of the future: On the usefulness and necessity of science fiction]. Rotterdam: Lemniscaat, 2010.
Kelly, William W. "At the Limits of New Middle-class Japan: Beyond 'Mainstream Consciousness.'" In Zunz et al., *Social Contracts Under Stress*, 232–254.
Kemp, Louis Ward. "Aesthetes and Engineers: The Occupational Ideology of Highway Design." *Technology and Culture* 27, no. 4 (1986): 759–797.
*Kerouac, Jack. *On the Road* in *Road Novels 1957–1960: On the Road / The Dharma Bums / The Subterraneans / Tristessa / Lonesome Traveller / Journal Selections*. Edited by Douglas Brinkley (New York: Library of America, 2007), 3–278.
*⸻. "The Vanishing American Hobo." *Hermitary*, accessed 12 December 2019. http://www.hermitary.com/lore/kerouac.html.
*⸻. *Visions of Cody*. Introduction by Allen Ginsberg. London: Penguin, 2012.
Kerr, Ian J. "Colonial India, Its Railways, and the Cliometricians." *Journal of Transport History* 35, no. 1 (2014): 114–120.
⸻. *Engines of Change: The Railroads that made India*. Westport, CT: Praeger, 2007.
⸻. "Representation and Representations of Railways of Colonial and Post-colonial South Asia." *Modern Asian Studies* 37, no. 2 (2003): 287–326.
Khusyairi, Johny A. "Modernity on the Road Traffic of Surabaya in 1920s." *Humaniora* 23, no. 3 (2011).
Kikuchi, Akira. "Urban Motorways." In *AIPCR—PIARC 1909–1969* (Paris: Association Internationale Permanente des Congrès de la Route / Permanent International Association of Road Congresses, 1970), 71–92.
Kim, Nanny. "Single-Wheeled Mobility: The Housed-Wheel Barrow on the Plains of Pre-industrial China." *Journal of Transport History* 28, no. 2 (2007): 229–251.
Kimmage, Michael. "Introduction." In Koeppen, *Journey through America*, 1–26.
Kindler, Robert. *Stalins Nomaden: Herrschaft und Hunger in Kasachstan*. Hamburg: Hamburger Edition, 2014.
Kini, Aditi Natasha. "The British Stole Tipu's Magic Box: It Should Not Be for Sale." *New York Times International Edition* (29–30 June 2019): 8.
Kinney, Jeremy R. "Racing on Runways: The Strategic Air Command and Sports Car Racing in the 1950s." In *ICON: Journal of the International Committee for the History of Technology* 19 (2013): 193–215.
Kirby, William C. "Engineering China: Birth of the Developmental State, 1928–1937." In Yeh, *Becoming Chinese*, 137–160.
Kirksey, S. Eben, and Kiki van Bilsen. "A Road to Freedom: Mee Articulations and the Trans-Papua Highway." *Bijdragen tot de Taal-, Land- en Volkenkunde (On the Road: The Social Impact of new roads in Southeast Asia)*, 158, no. 4 (2002): 837–854.
Kitzinger, U. W. *The New Europeans: A Commentary on Products and People, a Marketing Survey of the European Common Market and Britain, 1963*. London: Reader's Digest, 1963.
Kleijer, Henk, and Ger Tillekens. "The Lure of Anglo-American Popular Culture: Explaining the Rise of Dutch Youth Culture." In *American Culture in the Netherlands*, edited by Doeko Bosscher, Marja Roholl, and Mel van Elteren (Amsterdam: VU University Press 1996), 97–113.
Knaap, Gerrit J. *Changing Economy in Indonesia: A Selection of Statistical Sources Material from the Early 19th Century up to 1940, vol. 9—Transport 1819–1940*. The Hague: Royal Tropical Institute, 1989.

Koepnick, Lutz. *On Slowness: Toward an Aesthetic of the Contemporary.* New York: Columbia University Press, 2014.
*Koeppen, Wolfgang. *Journey through America.* Translated by Michael Kimmage. New York: Berghahn Books, 2012.
Koopmans, Carl, and Rogier Lieshout. "Spoorwegen en groei." *Economisch Statistische Berichten* 93, no. 4535 (16 May 2008): 301–302.
Kopper, Christopher M. "Der Durchbruch des PKW zum Massenkonsumgut 1950–1964." *Jahrbuch für Wirtschaftsgeschichte* 51, no. 1 (2010): 19–36.
———. "The Breakthrough of the Package Tour in Germany after 1945." *Journal of Tourism History* 1, no. 1 (2009): 67–92.
Korbonski, Andrzej, and Francis Fukuyama, eds. *The Soviet Union and the Third World: The Last Three Decades.* Ithaca, NY: Cornell University Press, 1987.
Kosc, Grzegorz, Clara Juncker, Sharon Monteith, and Britta Waldschmidt-Nelson, eds. *The Transatlantic Sixties: Europe and the United States in the Counterculture Decade.* Bielefeld: transcript, 2013.
Koshar, Rudy. *German Travel Cultures.* Oxford: Berg, 2000.
Kraig, Beth. "Are We There Yet, Driver? Searching for the Automotive Human." *Midwest Quarterly* 48, no. 2 (2007): 297–313.
———. "The Liberated Lady Driver." *Midwest Quarterly* 28 (1987): 378–401.
Kraler, Albert. "Zur Einführung: Migration und Globalgeschichte." In Kraler et al. *Migrationen*, 10–31.
Kraler, Albert, Karl Husa, Veronika Bilger, and Irene Stacher, eds. *Migrationen: Globale Entwicklungen seit 1850.* Vienna: Mandelbaum Verlag, 2007.
Kraushaar, Wolfgang. "Die 'Revolutionierung des bürgerlichen Subjekts': 1968 als erneuerte bürgerliche Utopie?" In Hettling and Ulrich, *Bürgertum nach 1945*, 374–406.
Krier, James E., and Edmund Ursin. *Pollution and Policy: A Case Essay on California and Federal Experience with Motor Vehicle Air Pollution 1940–1975.* Berkeley: University of California Press, 1977.
Krim, Arthur. *Route 66: Iconography of the American Highway.* Edited by Denis Wood. Santa Fe, NM: Center for American Places, 2005.
Kröger, Fabian. "L'histoire des savoirs et des images de l'accident de voiture: L'interaction entre la recherche sur les accidents et les images des accidents aux États-Unis et en France (1945–1975)." PhD diss., Université Paris 1 Panthéon-Sorbonne and Humboldt Universität, 2016.
Kuehn, Julia, and Paul Smethurst. "Introduction." In *New Directions in Travel Writing Studies*, edited by Julia Kuehn and Paul Smethurst (London: Palgrave Macmillan, 2015), 1–13.
Kunkel, Sönke. "Contesting Globalization: The United Nations Conference on Trade and Development and the Transnationalization of Sovereignty." In Frey et al., *International Organizations and Development*, 240–258.
———. "Systeme des Wissens, Visionen von Fortschritt: Die Vereinigten Staaten, das Jahrzehnt der Modernisierungstheorie und die Planung Nigerias 1954–1965." *Archiv für Sozialgeschichte* 48 (2008): 155–182.
Kuo, Tze-hsiung. "Technical Co-operation between China and Geneva." *Information Bulletin Council of International Affairs* (1 July 1936).
Kurlansky, Mark. *Ready for a Brand New Beat: How "Dancing in the Street" Became an Anthem for a Changing America.* New York: Riverhead Books, 2013.
Kwok, Siu-tong. "Cultural Migration and Historiography in the Regions of China since the End of World War II." *Berliner China-Hefte* 26 (2004): 53–62.

Lackey, Kris. *RoadFrames: The American Highway Narrative*. Lincoln: University of Nebraska Press, 1997.
Ladd, Brian. *Autophobia: Love and Hate in the Automotive Age*. Chicago: University of Chicago Press, 2008.
Laderman, David. *Driving Visions: Exploring the Road Movie*. Austin: University of Texas Press, 2002.
Lakoff, George, and Mark Johnson. *Metaphors We Live By*. Chicago: University of Chicago Press, 2003.
Lammers, Anne. "Daten für das 'Europa der Sechs': Sozialstatistiken in den Europäischen Gemeinschaften der 1950er- und 160er-Jahre." *Themenportal Europäische Geschichte* (2013), http://www.europa.clio-online.de/essay/id/fdae-1627.
———. "Die Erfassung des Lebensniveaus in den Europäischen Gemeinschaften (1956/57 und 1963/64)." *Themenportal Europäische Geschichte* (2013), http://www.europa.clio-online.de/2013/Article=666.
Lamont, Mark. "Ruin, or Repair? Infrastructural Sociality and an Economy of Disappearances along a Rural Road in Kenya." In Beck et al., *Making of the African Road*, 171–196.
*Lang, Tâm. "I Pulled a Rickshaw." In *The Light of the Capital: Three Modern Vietnamese Classics*. Translated by Greg Lockhart and Monique Lockhart. Kuala Lumpur: Oxford University Press, 1996.
Lankford, Ronald D., Jr. *Folk Music USA: The Changing Voice of Protest*. New York: Schirmer Trade Books, 2005.
Larrabee, Eric. "Autos and Americans: The Great Love Affair—How Detroit Can Run a Heavy Industry on the Soft Winds of Whim and Romance." *Industrial Design* 2, no. 5 (1955): 95–98.
Larsen, Jonas. "Tourism Mobilities and the Travel Glance: Experiences of Being on the Move." *Scandinavian Journal of Hospitality and Tourism* 1, no. 2 (2001): 80–98.
Larson, Lars Erik. "Free Ways and Straight Roads: The Interstates of Sal Paradise and 1950s America." In *What's Your Road, Man? Critical Essays on Jack Kerouac's On the Road*, edited by Hilary Holladay and Robert Holton (Carbondale: Southern Illinois University Press, 2009), 35–59.
Lasch, Christopher. *The Culture of Narcissism: American Life in an Age of Diminishing Expectations*. New York: Norton, 1991.
Latham, Michael E. *Modernization as Ideology: American Social Science and "Nation Building" in the Kennedy Era*. Chapel Hill: University of North Carolina Press, 2000.
Laurier, Eric, Hayden Lorimer, Barry Brown, Owain Jones, Oskar Juhlin, Alyson Noble, Mark Perry, Daniele Pica et al. "Driving and 'Passengering': Notes on the Ordinary Organization of Car Travel." *Mobilities* 3, no. 1 (2008): 1–23.
Law, Michael John. *The Experience of Suburban Mobility: How Private Transport Changed Interwar London*. Manchester: Manchester University Press, 2014.
Law, Robin. "Beyond 'Women and Transport': Towards New Geographies of Gender and Daily Mobility." *Progress in Human Geography* 23, no. 4 (1999): 567–588.
———. "Wheeled Transport in Pre-colonial West Africa." *Africa: Journal of the International Africa Institute* 50, no. 3 (1980): 249–262.
Lawrence, Mark Atwood. "Universal Claims, Local Uses: Reconceptualizing the Vietnam Conflict, 1945–60." In *Global History: Interactions Between the Universal and the Local*, edited by A. G. Hopkins (London: Palgrave Macmillan, 2006), 229–256.
Lefebvre, Henri. *Everyday Life in the Modern World*. Translated by Sacha Ribinovitch. New Brunswick, NJ: Transaction Books, 1984.
Le Huen, Roland. "Qu'est-ce qu'un récit de voyage?" *Littérales* 7 (1990): 11–27.

Leibowicz, Benjamin D. "Policy Recommendations for a Transition to Sustainable Mobility Based on Historical Diffusion Dynamics of Transport Systems." *Energy Policy* 119 (2018): 357–366.
Leinbach, Thomas R. "Road and Rail Transport Systems." In *South-East Asian Transport: Issues in Development*, edited by Thomas R. Leinbach and Chia Lin Sien (with Christopher C. Kissling, Ross Robinson, and Andrew H. Spencer) (Singapore: Oxford University Press, 1989), 60–96.
———. "The Spread of Modernization in Malaya: 1895–1969." *Tijdschrift voor Economische en Sociale Geografie* 63, no. 4 (1972): 262–277.
———. "Transportation and the Development of Malaya." *Annals of the Association of American Geographers* 65, no. 2 (1975): 270–282.
Leland, John. *Why Kerouac Matters: The Lessons of On the Road (They're Not What You Think)*. London: Penguin, 2008.
Lelièvre, Marie-Dominique. *Sagan à toute allure*. Paris: Denoël, 2008.
Lennon, John. *Boxcar Politics: The Hobo in U.S. Culture and Literature, 1869–1956*. Amherst: University of Massachusetts Press, 2014.
Lente, Harro van. *Promising Technology: The Dynamics of Expectations in Technological Developments*. Delft: Eburon, 1993.
Lenz, Ilse. "Feminismus und Fortschrittsdenken: Reflexive Brechungen und vielfältige Horizonte." *Vorgänge* 3 (September 2011): 111–119.
Lerner, Daniel. *The Passing of Traditional Society: Modernizing the Middle East*. Introduction by David Riesman. New York: Free Press, 1965.
Lewis, Stephen E. "The Nation, Education, and the 'Indian Problem' in Mexico, 1920–1940." In Vaughan and Lewis, *Eagle and the Virgin*, 176–195.
Lewis, Tom. *Divided Highways: Building the Interstate Highways, Transforming American Life*. New York: Penguin, 1999.
Lezotte, Chris. "Born to Take the Highway: Women, the Automobile, and Rock 'n' Roll." *Journal of American Culture* 36, no. 3 (2013): 161–176.
———. "The Evolution of the 'Chick Car' Or: What Came First, the Chick or the Car?" *Journal of Popular Culture* 45, no. 3 (2012): 516–531.
———. "Out on the Highway: Cars, Community, and the Gay Driver." *Culture, Society & Masculinities* 7, no. 2 (2015): 121–139.
Lezotte, Christine L. "Have You Heard The One about the Woman Driver? Chicks, Muscle, Pickups, and the Reimagining of the Woman behind the Wheel." PhD diss., Bowling Green State University, 2015.
Lieb, Claudia. *Crash: Der Unfall der Moderne*. Bielefeld: Aisthesis Verlag, 2009.
Lieven, Anatol. "What Chance for Afghanistan?" *New York Review of Books* 63, no. 7 (21 April 2016): 47–49.
Lim, Jason. *A Slow Ride Into the Past: The Chinese Trishaw Industry in Singapore, 1942–1983*. Clayton, VA: Monash University Publishing, 2013.
*Ling, Ken. *The Revenge of Heaven: Journal of a Young Chinese*. English text prepared by Miriam London and Ta-ling Lee. New York: G. P. Putnam's Sons, 1972.
Link, Jürgen, and Siegfried Reinecke. "'Autofahren ist wie das Leben': Metamorphosen des Autosymbols in der deutschen Literatur." In *Technik in der Literatur: Ein Forschungsüberblick und zwölf Aufsätze*, edited by Harro Segeberg (Frankfurt: Suhrkamp Verlag, 1987), 436–482.
Linnemann, Kai Arne. "Die Sammlung der Mitte und die Wandlung des Bürgers." In Hettling and Ulrich, *Bürgertum nach 1945*, 185–220.

Lipset, David. "Introduction: Charon's Boat and Other Vehicles of Moral Imagination." In *Vehicles: Cars, Canoes, and Other Metaphors of Moral Imagination*, edited by David Lipset and Richard Handler (New York: Berghahn Books, 2014), 1–17.
Litman, Todd. "Mobility as a Positional Good: Implications for Transport Policy and Planning." In *Car Troubles: Critical Studies of Automobility and Auto-Mobility*, edited by Jim Conley and Arlene Tigar McLaren (Farnham: Ashgate, 2009), 199–217.
Liu, Ts'un-yan [Liu, Cunren]. "Introduction: 'Middlebrow' in Perspective." In Ts'un-yan [Cunren], *Chinese Middlebrow Fiction*, 1–40.
Liu, Ts'un-yan [Liu, Cunren], with John Minford, ed. *Chinese Middlebrow Fiction: From the Ch'ing and Early Republican Eras*. Hong Kong: Chinese University Press, 1984.
Liu, Xin. *The Mirage of China: Anti-humanism, Narcissism, and Corporeality of the Contemporary World*. New York: Berghahn Books, 2009.
*Lo, Ruth Earnshaw, and Katharine S. Kinderman. *In the Eye of the Typhoon*. Introduction by John K. Fairbank. New York: Harcourt Brace Jovanovich, 1980.
Löfgren, Orvar. *On Holiday: A History of Vacationing*. Berkeley: University of California Press, 1999.
Logemann, Jan L. *Trams or Tailfins? Public and Private Prosperity in Postwar West Germany and the United States*. Chicago: University of Chicago Press, 2012.
Lomnitz, Claudio. "Final Reflections: What Was Mexico's Cultural Revolution?" In Vaughan and Lewis, *Eagle and the Virgin*, 335–349.
Lone, Stewart. "Japan and the Age of Speed: Urban Life and the Automobile 1925–1930." In *The Automobile in Japan*, London School of Economics and Political Science Suntory and Toyota International Centres for Economic and Related Disciplines Discussion Paper no. IS/05/494, July 2005, 1–13.
Longhurst, Brian, Gaynor Bagnall, and Mike Savage. "Ordinary Consumption and Personal Identity: Radio and the Middle Classes in the North West of England." In Gronow and Warde, *Ordinary Consumption*, 125–141.
Loo, Becky P. Y., W. S. Cheng, and Shenjun Yao. "The Rural-Urban Divide in Road Safety: The Case of China." *Open Transportation Journal* 5 (2011): 9–20.
Louie, Kam. "Chinese, Japanese and Global Masculine Identities." In *Asian Masculinities: The Meaning and Practice of Manhood in China and Japan*, edited by Kam Louie and Morris Low (London: Routledge, 2005), 1–15.
———. *Theorising Chinese Masculinity: Society and Gender in China*. Cambridge: Cambridge University Press, 2002.
Lovell, Julia. "Introduction." In *The Real Story of Ah-Q and Other Tales of China: The Complete Fiction of Lu Xun* by Lu Xun, translated by Julia Lovell (London: Penguin, 2009), xiii–xxxix.
Lowe, Rodney. "Postwar Welfare." In Johnson, *Twentieth-Century Britain*, 356–373.
Lu, Hanchao. *Beyond the Neon Lights: Everyday Shanghai in the Early Twentieth Century*. Berkeley: University of California Press, 2004.
*Lu, Xun. "The Real Story of Ah-Q." In Lu Xun, *The Real Story of Ah-Q and Other Tales of China: The Complete Fiction of Lu Xun*, translated by Julia Lovell (London: Penguin, 2009), 79–133.
Lübbeke, Gunther. "Verkehrsprobleme der Entwicklungsländer und der Beitrag der Weltbank zu ihrer Lösung." *Archiv für Verkehrswesen* 16, nos. 1–2 (1964): 5–12.
Lund, Ragnhild, and Anna Karlsdóttir. "Editorial: Gendered Mobilities in Asia." *Norsk Geografisk Tidsskrift / Norwegian Journal of Geography* 67, no. 4 (2013): 185–186
Lundestad, Geir. "*Empire*" *by Integration: The United States and European Integration, 1945–1997*. Oxford: Oxford University Press, 1998.
Lupton, Deborah. *Risk*. London: Routledge, 1999.

Lutz, Catherine, and Anne Lutz Fernandez. *Carjacked: The Culture of the Automobile and Its Effects on Our Lives*. New York: St. Martin's Press, 2010.

Lützen, Wolf Dieter. "Radfahren, Motorsport, Autobesitz: Motorisierung zwischen Gebrauchswerten und Statuserwerb." In *Die Arbeiter: Lebensformen, Alltag und Kultur von der Frühindustrialisierung bis zum "Wirtschaftswunder,"* edited by Wolfgang Ruppert (Munich: Verlag C. H. Beck, 1986), 369–377.

Lyell, William A. "Translator's Afterword." In Zhang, *Shanghai Express*, 239–258.

Lyons, Amelia H. "French or Foreign? The Algerian Migrants' Status at the End of Empire (1962–1968)." *Journal of Modern European History* 12, no. 1 (2014): 126–145.

Lyth, Peter. "'Gimmy a Ticket on an Aeroplane . . .': The Jet Engine and the Revolution in Leisure Air Travel, 1960–1975." In *Development of a Tourist Industry in the 19th and 20th Centuries: International Perspectives*, edited by Laurent Tissot (Neuchâtel: Editions Alphil, 2003), 111–122.

Madeley, Christopher. "Kaishinsha, DAT, Nissan and the British Motor Vehicle Industry." In *The Automobile in Japan* (London School of Economics and Political Science Suntory and Toyota International Centres for Economic and Related Disciplines discussion paper no. IS/05/494, July 2005), 14–38.

Magee, Rosemary. "Introduction." In *Conversations with Flannery O'Connor*, edited by Rosemary Magee (Jackson: University Press of Mississippi, 1987), vii–xxiii.

*Mailer, Norman. "The White Negro: Superficial Reflections on the Hipster." In *Advertisements for Myself* (Cambridge, MA: Harvard University Press, 1992), 337–358.

Mains, Daniel. "Blackouts and Progress: Privatization, Infrastructure, and a Developmentalist State in Jimma, Ethiopia." *Cultural Anthropology* 27, no. 1 (2012): 3–27.

Mann, Michael. "Das Gewaltsdispositiv des modernen Kolonialismus." In Dabag et al., *Kolonialismus*, 111–135.

———. "Delhi-Metro-Polis: Public Transport, Public Opinion and National Politics." In Hilger and Unger, *India in the World*, 136–160.

———. "Mobilität und Migration von Menschen in und aus Südasien 1840 bis 1990." In Kraler et al., *Migrationen*, 199–221.

———. *The Sources of Social Power, vol. 3: Global Empires and Revolution, 1890–1945*. Cambridge: Cambridge University Press, 2012.

———. *The Sources of Social Power, vol. 4: Globalizations, 1945–2011*. Cambridge: Cambridge University Press, 2013.

———. "Town Planning and Urban Resistance in the Old City of Delhi, 1937–1977." In *Urbanization and Governance in India*, edited by Evelin Hust and Michael Mann (New Delhi: Manohar, 2005), 251–278.

Manning, Patrick. *Slavery, Colonialism and Economic Growth in Dahomey, 1640–1960*. Cambridge: Cambridge University Press, 1982.

Mansbach, Richard W. "The Soviet Union, the United Nations, and the Developing States." In Kanet, *Soviet Union and the Developing Nations*, 237–264.

Manzo, Kate. "Modernist Discourse and the Crisis of Development Theory." *Studies in Comparative International Development* 26, no. 2 (1991): 3–36.

Marchand, Roland. "Visions of Classlessness, Quests for Dominion: American Popular Culture, 1945–1960." In *Reshaping America: Society and Institutions 1945–1960*, edited by Robert H. Bremner and Gary W. Reichard (Columbus: Ohio State University Press, 1982), 163–190.

Marcus, George E., and James Clifford. "The Making of Ethnographic Texts: A Preliminary Report." *Current Anthropology* 26, no. 2 (1985): 267–271.

Markovits, Claude, Jacques Pouchepadass, and Sanjay Subrahmanyam, eds. *Society and Circulation: Mobile People and Itinerant Cultures in South Asia 1750–1950.* Delhi: Permanent Black, 2003.

Markovits, Claude, Jacques Pouchepadass, and Sanjay Subrahmanyam. "Introduction: Circulation and Society under Colonial Rule." In Markovits et al., *Society and Circulation*, 1–22.

Marsh, Peter, and Peter Collett. *Driving Passion: The Psychology of the Car.* London: Jonathan Cape: 1986.

Martin, Brian V., and Charles B. Warden. "Transportation Planning in Developing Countries." *Traffic Quarterly* 19, no. 1 (1965): 59–75.

Marwick, Arthur. *The Sixties: Cultural Revolution in Britain, France, Italy, and the United States, c. 1958–c. 1974.* Oxford: Oxford University Press, 1998.

Mason, Mike. *Turbulent Empires: A History of Global Capitalism since 1945.* Montreal: McGill-Queen's University Press, 2018.

Masquelier, Adeline. "Road Mythographies: Space, Mobility, and the Historical Imagination in Postcolonial Niger." *American Ethnologist* 29, no. 4 (2002): 829–856.

Mattelart, Armand. *The Invention of Communication.* Translated by Susan Emanuel. Minneapolis: University of Minnesota Press, 1996.

Mattens, Filip. "Perception and Representation: Mind the Hand!" In Radman, *The Hand, an Organ of the Mind*, 159–184.

Mausbach, Wilfried. "'Burn, Ware-House, Burn!' Modernity, Counterculture, and the Vietnam War in West Germany." In Schildt and Siegfried, *Between Marx and Coca-Cola*, 175–202.

Mavhunga, Clapperton Chakanetsa. "Which Mobility for (Which) Africa? Beyond Banal Mobilities." In *Mobility in History: Reviews and Reflections*, edited by Peter Norton, Gijs Mom, Liz Millward, and Mathieu Flonneau (Neuchâtel: Alphil, 2011), 73–84.

Mayer, Philip. "Migrancy and the Study of Africans in Towns." *American Anthropologist* 64, no. 3 (1962): 576–592.

Mazón, Mauricio. *The Zoot-Suit Riots: The Psychology of Symbolic Annihilation.* Austin: University of Texas Press, 1984.

McCallum, Cecilia. "Racialized Bodies, Naturalized Classes: Moving through the City of Salvador da Bahia." *American Ethnologist* 32, no. 1 (2005): 100–117.

McCarry, Melanie. "Masculinity Studies and Male Violence: Critique or Collusion?" *Women's Studies International Forum* 30, no. 5 (2007): 404–415.

McCarthy, J. J. "South Africa's Emerging Politics of Bus Transportation." *Political Geography Quarterly* 4, no. 3 (1985): 235–249.

McCarthy, Tom. *Auto Mania: Cars, Consumers, and the Environment.* New Haven, CT: Yale University Press, 2007.

McClellan, Thomas Michael. *Zhang Henshui and Popular Chinese Fiction, 1919–1949.* Lewiston, NY: Edwin Mellen Press, 2005.

McCracken, Donal P., and Ruth E. Teer-Tomaselli. "Communication in Colonial and Post-Colonial Southern Africa." In *The Handbook of Communication History*, edited by Peter Simonson, Janice Peck, Robert T. Craig, and John P. Jackson Jr. (New York: Routledge, 2013), 424–439.

McDonald, Kate. "Asymmetrical Integration: Lessons from a Railway Empire." *Technology and Culture* 56, no. 1 (2015): 115–149.

———. "Imperial Mobility: Circulation as History in East Asia under Empire." *Transfers* 4, no. 3 (2014): 68–87.

McDougall, Bonnie S. "Preface." In McClellan, *Zhang Henshui and Popular Chinese Fiction*, iii–iv.
McDowell, Linda. "Off the Road: Alternative Views of Rebellion, Resistance and 'the Beats.'" *Transactions of the Institute of British Geographers* 21 (1996): 412–419.
McGinn, Colin. "Can We Solve the Mind–Body Problem?" *Mind* 98, no. 391 (1989): 349–366.
McGowan, Todd. *Capitalism and Desire: The Psychic Cost of Free Markets*. New York: Columbia University Press, 2016.
———. *Enjoying What We Don't Have: The Political Project of Psychoanalysis*. Lincoln: University of Nebraska Press, 2013.
McHugh, Kathleen. "Women in Traffic: L.A. Autobiography." *South Atlantic Quarterly* 97, no. 2 (1998): 391–412.
McKelvey, Blake. *The Emergence of Metropolitan America, 1915–1966*. New Brunswick, NJ: Rutgers University Press, 1968.
McKeown, Adam. "Global Migration, 1846–1940." *Journal of World History* 15, no. 2 (2004): 155–189.
McLuhan, Marshall. *The Mechanical Bride: Folklore of Industrial Man*. Corte Madera, CA: Gingko Press, 2001.
———. *Understanding Media: The Extensions of Man*. London: Routledge, 2005.
McMahon, Robert J. "Development Assistance as a Cold War tool: The United States, International Institutions, and the Political Economy of Asian Development, 1947–65." In Akita et al., *Transformation of the International Order*, 199–214.
———. "On the Periphery of a Global Conflict: India and the Cold War, 1947–1991." In Hilger and Unger, *India in the World*, 276–299.
McShane, Mary, Masaki Koshi, and Olof Lundin. "Public Policy toward the Automobile: A Comparative Look at Japan and Sweden." *Transportation Research Part A* 18, no. 2 (1984): 97–109.
Mehra, Diya. "Planning Delhi ca. 1936–1959." *South Asia: Journal of South Asian Studies* 36, no. 3 (2013): 354–374.
Meisner, Maurice. *Mao's China and After: A History of the People's Republic*. New York: Free Press, 1999.
Mellencamp, Patricia, ed. *Logics of Television: Essays in Cultural Criticism*. Bloomington / London: Indiana University Press / BFI Publishing, 1990.
Mellström, Ulf. "Machines and Masculine Subjectivity: Technology as an Integral Part of Men's Life Experiences." *Men and Masculinities* 6, no. 4 (2004): 368–382.
Melton, Jeffrey. "'Immediate Consciousness' and the American Open Road: Robert Pirsig's *Zen and the Art of Motorcycle Maintenance*." *Studies in Travel Writing* 17, no. 4 (2013): 398–410.
Meng, Chih. "The American Returned Students of China." *Pacific Affairs* 4, no. 1 (1931): 1–16.
Meow, Seah Chee. *Infrastructural Growth and Development Planning: A Comparative Study of Road Infrastructure in the National Development of Asean Countries*. Singapore: Chopmen Enterprises, 1978.
Mergel, Thomas. "Transnationale Mobilität, Integration und Herkunftsbewusstsein: Migration und europäisches Selbstverständnis im 19. und 20. Jahrhundert." In *Selbstverständnis und Gesellschaft der Europäer: Aspekte der sozialen und kulturellen Europäisierung im späten 19. und 20. Jahrhundert*, edited by Hartmut Kaelble and Martin Kirsch (Frankfurt: Peter Lang, 2008), 251–297.

Merrill, Dennis. *Bread and the Ballot: The United States and India's Economic Development, 1947–1963*. Chapel Hill: University of North Carolina Press, 1990.
Merriman, Peter. *Driving Spaces: A Cultural-Historical Geography of England's M1 Motorway*. Malden, MA: Blackwell, 2007.
———. *Mobility, Space and Culture*. London: Routledge, 2012.
———. "Roads: Lawrence Halprin, Modern Dance and the American Freeway Landscape." In *Geographies of Mobilities: Practices, Spaces, Subjects*, edited by Tim Cresswell and Peter Merriman (Farnham: Ashgate, 2011), 99–117.
———. "Road Works: Some Observations on Representing Roads." *Transfers* 5, no. 1 (2015): 108–113.
Merten, Kai, and Lucia Krämer. "Introduction." In *Postcolonial Studies Meets Media Studies: A Critical Encounter*, edited by Kai Merten and Lucia Krämer (Bielefeld: transcript Verlag, 2016), 7–22.
Meyer, Benedikt "Auf Schlingerkurs durch das 20. Jahrhundert." *Wege und Geschichte* 2 (2012): 29–33.
Michalowski, Raymond J., Jr. "Violence in the Road: The Crime of Vehicular Homicide." *Journal of Research in Crime and Delinquence* 12, no. 1 (1975): 30–43.
Mie, Oba. "Japan's entry into ECAFE." In *Japanese Diplomacy in the 1950s: From Isolation to Integration*, edited by Iokibe Makoto, Caroline Rose, Tomaru Junko, and John Weste (London: Routledge, 2008), 98–113.
Mieczkowski, Bogdan. *Transportation in Eastern Europe: Empirical Findings*. Boulder, CO: East European Quarterly, 1978.
Mignolo, Walter D. *Local Histories / Global Designs: Coloniality, Subaltern Knowledges, and Border Thinking*. Princeton, NJ: Princeton University Press, 2000.
Milburn, Keir. *Generation Left*. Cambridge: Polity, 2019.
*Miller, Arthur. *Death of a Salesman: Certain Private Conversations in Two Acts and a Requiem*. New York: Viking Press, 1968.
Miller, James. "Mediatization of the Automobile." In *Dynamics of Mediatization: Institutional Change and Everyday Transformations in a Digital Age*, edited by Oliver Driessens, Göran Bolin, Andreas Hepp, and Stig Hjarvard. London: Palgrave Macmillan.
Miller, Joseph C. "From Group Mobility to Individual Movement: The Colonial Effort to Turn Back History." In *Angola on the Move: Transport Routes, Communications and History*, edited by Beatrix Heintze and Achim von Oppen (Frankfurt: Verlag Otto Lembeck, 2008), 243–262.
Miller, Keith. "Five Men in a Boat: Were William Hogarth and His Friends the First Situationists?" *Times Literary Supplement* (19 March 2010), 14–15.
Miller, Mark Crispin. "Introduction." In *The Hidden Persuaders* by Vance Packard (Brooklyn, NY: Ig Publishing, 2007) 9–27.
Mills, Katherine Lawrie. "Remapping the Road Story: Contemporary Narratives of Autonomy and Mobility in American Literature, Film, and Television." PhD diss., University of Southern California, 2000.
Mills, Katie. *The Road Story and the Rebel: Moving through Film, Fiction, and Television*. Carbondale: Southern Illinois University Press, 2006.
Mills, Sara. *Discourses of Difference: An Analysis of Women's Travel Writing and Colonialism*. London: Routledge, 2001.
Milum, Richard A. "Continuity and Change: The Horse, the Automobile, and the Airplane in Faulkner's Fiction." In *Faulkner: The Unappeased Imagination—A Collection of Critical Essays*, edited by Glenn O'Carey (Troy, NY: Whitston Publishing Co., 1980), 157–174.

Ming, Fung Chi, *Reluctant Heroes: Rickshaw Pullers in Hong Kong and Canton, 1874–1954*. Hong Kong: Hong Kong University Press, 2005.
*Mirbeau, Octave. *Sketches of a Journey: Travels in an Early Motorcar*. London: Philip Wilson Publishers, 1989.
Misa, Thomas J., and Johan Schot. "Introduction." *History and Technology* 21, no. 1 (2005): 1–19.
Mishra, Pankaj. *From the Ruins of Empire: The Revolt Against the West and the Remaking of Asia*. London: Allen Lane, 2012.
Mitchell, B. R. *International Historical Statistics: Europe 1750–1993*, 4th ed. London: Stockton Press, 1998.
Mo, Yajun. "Itineraries for a Republic: Tourism and Travel Culture in Modern China, 1866–1954." PhD diss., University of California, Santa Cruz, 2011.
Modell, John. *Into One's Own: From Youth to Adulthood in the United States 1920–1975*. Berkeley: University of California Press, 1989.
Modleski, Tania. "The Disappearing Act: A Study of Harlequin Romances." *Signs: Journal of Women in Culture and Society* 5, no. 3 (1980): 435–448.
Möhring, Maren. "Working Girl Not Working: Liebe, Freizeit und Konsum in Italienfilmen der frühen Bundesrepublik." In *Working Girls: Zur Ökonomie von Liebe und Arbeit*, edited by Sabine Biebl, Verena Mund, and Heide Volkening (Berlin: Kulturverlag Kadmos, 2007), 249–274.
Mokhtarian, P. L. "Travel as a Desired End, Not Just a Means (Guest Editorial)." *Transportation Research Part A* 39, nos. 2–3 (2005): 93–96.
Mom, Gijs. *Atlantic Automobilism: Emergence and Persistence of the Car, 1895–1940*. New York: Berghahn Books, 2015.
———. "Civilized Adventure as a Remedy for Nervous Times: Early Automobilism and *fin de siècle* Culture." *History of Technology* 23 (2001): 157–190.
———. "Clashes of Cultures: Road vs. Rail in the North-Atlantic World during the Inter-war Coordination Crisis." In *The Organization of Transport: A History of Users, Industry, and Public Policy*, edited by Christopher Kopper and Massimo Moraglio (London: Routledge, 2015), 8–31.
———. "Constructing Multifunctional Networks: Road Building in the Netherlands, 1810–1980." In *Road History: Planning, Building and Use*, edited by Gijs Mom and Laurent Tissot (Lausanne: Alphil, 2007), 33–62.
———. "Decentering Highways: European National Road Network Planning from a Transnational Perspective." In *Die moderne Strasse: Planung, Bau und Verkehr vom 18. bis zum 20. Jahrhundert*, edited by Hans-Liudger Dienel and Hans-Ulrich Schiedt (Frankfurt: Campus Verlag, 2010), 77–100.
———. *The Electric Vehicle: Technology and Expectations in the Automobile Age*. Baltimore: Johns Hopkins University Press, 2004.
———. *The Evolution of Automotive Technology: A Handbook*. Warrendale, PA: SAE International, 2014.
———. "Frozen History: Limitations and Possibilities of Quantitative Diffusion Studies." In *Manufacturing Technology, Manufacturing Consumers: The Making of Dutch Consumer Society*, edited by Ruth Oldenziel and Adri de la Bruhèze (Amsterdam: aksant, 2008), 73–94.
———. "'The Future Is a Shifting Panorama': The Role of Expectations in the History of Mobility." In *Zukünfte des Automobils: Aussichten und Grenzen der autotechnischen Globalisierung*, edited by Weert Canzler and Gert Schmidt (Berlin: edition sigma, 2008), 31–58.

———. "International Road Federation (IRF)." In *The Palgrave Dictionary of Transnational History*, edited by Akira Iriye and Pierre-Yves Saunier (London: Palgrave Macmillan, 2009), 582–583.

———. "Mobility for Pleasure: A Look at the Underside of Dutch Diffusion Curves (1920–1940)." *TST Revista de Historia: Transportes, Servicios y Telecomunicaciones* 12 (June 2007): 30–68.

———. "Orchestrating Automobile Technology: Comfort, Mobility Culture, and the Construction of the 'Family Touring Car,' 1917–1940." *Technology and Culture* 55, no. 2 (2014): 299–325.

———. "Planning the Car System in the Netherlands: Mass Motorization in a North-Atlantic Context" (Casus no. 6 of the project "Dutch Mobility in a European Context: A Comparison of Two Centuries of Mobility Policy in Seven Countries"). Paper presented at the Second International Workshop on Transport History and Policy, 5–7 February 2009, Utrecht.

———. "Roads without Rails: European Highway-Network Building and the Desire for Long-Range Motorized Mobility." *Technology and Culture* 46, no. 4 (2005): 745–77.

———. "Struggle of the Systems: Freight Mobility from a Transatlantic Perspective, 1920–2000." In Duc et al., *Transport and Mobility History*, 177–195.

———. "Translating Properties into Functions (and Vice Versa): Design, User Culture and the Creation of an American and a European Car (1930–1970)." *Journal of Design History* 20, no. 2 (2007): 171–181.

———. "The West and the Rest: The Green Heart and the Breakthrough of Spatial Planning." In *Builders and Planners: A History of Land-Use and Infrastructure Planning in the Netherlands*, edited by Jos Arts, Ruud Filarski, Hans Jeekel, and Bert Toussaint (Delft: Eburon, 2016), 155–211.

Mom, Gijs, and Ruud Filarski. *Van transport naar mobiliteit: De mobiliteitsexplosie (1895–2005)*. Zutphen: Walburg Pers, 2008.

Mom, Gijs, Georgine Clarsen, Peter Merriman, Cotten Seiler, Mimi Sheller, and Heike Weber. "Editorial." *Transfers* 3, no. 1 (2013): 1–5.

Mom, Gijs, Gordon Pirie, and Laurent Tissot, eds. *Mobility in History: The State of the Art in the History of Transport, Traffic and Mobility*. Neuchâtel: Alphil, 2009.

Monge, Françoise. "Les vacances familiales." *après-demain* 137 (October 1971): 35–37.

Monroe, Kristin V. "Automobility and Citizenship in Interwar Lebanon.' *Comparative Studies of South Asia, Africa and the Middle East* 34, no. 3 (2004): 518–531.

———. "Driving Then and Now: The History and Anthropology of Automobility in Beirut." Paper presented at the conference "(Auto)mobility in the Global Middle East: Defining the Field," University of Birmingham, 6 November 2015.

Montealegre, Angelica Agredo. "Roads and Road Transport in India during the Interwar Years." MA thesis, King's College London, 2015.

Montoya, Jaime Salazar. *De la mula al camión: Apuntes para une historia del transporte en Colombia*. Bogotá: Tercer Mundo Editores, 2000.

Moorhouse, H. F. "American Automobiles and Workers' Dreams." *Sociological Review* 31, no. 3 (1983): 403–426.

———. *Driving Ambitions: An Analysis of the American Hot Rod Enthusiasm*. Manchester: Manchester University Press, 1991.

Mooser, Josef. *Arbeiterleben in Deutschland 1900–1970: Klassenlagen, Kultur und Politik*. Frankfurt: Suhrkamp Verlag, 1984.

Moraglio, Massimo. "Transferring Technology, Shaping Society: Traffic Engineering in PIARC Agenda, in the early 1930s." *Technikgeschichte* 80, no. 2 (2013): 13–32.

Moran, Joe. *On Roads: A Hidden History*. London: Profile Books, 2010.
Moraña, Mabel, Enrique Dussel, and Carlos A. Jáuregui. "Colonialism and Its Replicants." In *Coloniality at Large: Latin America and the Postcolonial Debate*, edited by Mabel Moraña, Enrique Dussel, and Carlos A. Jáuregui (Durham, NC: Duke University Press, 2008), 1–20.
Moreno Tejada, Jaime. "Lazy Labor, Modernization, and Coloniality: Mobile Cultures between the Andes and the Amazon around 1900." *Transfers* 6, no. 2 (2016): 4–22.
Morgan, Robert P. *Twentieth-Century Music: A History of Musical Style in Modern Europe and America*. New York: Norton, 1991.
Morgan, W. B., and J. C. Pugh. *West Africa*. London: Methuen, 1969.
Morice, Janine. *La demande d'automobiles en France: Théorie—Histoire—Répartition géographique—Prévisions*. Paris: Librairie Armand Colin, 1957.
Morris, Meaghan. "Banality in Cultural Studies." In Mellencamp, *Logics of Television*, 14–43.
Morse, Margaret. "An Ontology of Everyday Distraction: The Freeway, the Mall, and Television." In Mellencamp, *Logics of Television*, 193–221.
Möser, Kurt. "Autobasteln: Modifying, Maintaining, and Repairing Private Cars in the GDR, 1970–1990." In *The Socialist Car: Automobility in the Eastern Bloc*, edited by Lewis H. Siegelbaum (Ithaca, NY: Cornell University Press, 2011), 157–169.
Mrázek, Rudolf. *Engineers of Happy Land: Technology and Nationalism in a Colony*. Princeton, NJ: Princeton University Press, 2002.
Müller, Dorit, and Heike Weber. "'Traffic': On the Historical Alignment of Media and Mobility." *Transfers* 3, no. 1 (2013): 65–74.
Munk, Bernard E. "The Colombian Automotive Industry: The Welfare Consequences of Import Substitution." *Economics and Business Bulletin* (Fall 1970), 6–22.
———. "The Welfare Costs of Content Protection: The Automotive Industry in Latin America." *Journal of Political Economy* 77, no. 1 (1969): 85–98.
Munzinger, Wolfgang. *Das Automobil als heimliche Romanfigur: Das Bild des Autos und der Technik in der nordamerikanischen Literatur von der Jahrhundertwende bis nach dem 2. Weltkrieg*. Hamburg: LIT Verlag, 1997.
Murphy, Christina. *Ann Beattie*. Boston: Twayne, 1986.
*Murphy, Dervla. *Full Tilt: Ireland to India with a Bicycle*. London: Eland 2010.
Musgrove, Charles D. "Building a Dream: Constructing a National Capital in Nanjing, 1927–1937." In *Remaking the Chinese City: Modernity and National Identity, 1900–1950*, edited by Joseph W. Esherik (Honolulu: University of Hawai'i Press, 1999), 139–157.
Nakicenovic, Nebojša. "The Automobile Road to Technological Change: Diffusion of the Automobile as a Process of Technological Substitution." *Technological Forecasting and Social Change* 29, no. 4 (1986): 309–340.
Nash, Graham. *Wild Tales: A Rock & Roll Life*. New York: Crown Archetype, 2013.
*Natsume, Sōseki. "The Carlyle Museum." In Sōseki, *Spring Miscellany and London Essays*, 119–132.
*———. "The Civilization of Modern-Day Japan (Gendai Nihon no Kaika)." In *The Columbia Anthology of Modern Japanese Literature: Abridged*, edited by J. Thomas Rimer and Van C. Gessel (New York: Columbia University Press, 2011), 154–161.
*———. "The Diary of a Bicycle Rider." In Sōseki, *Spring Miscellany and London Essays*, 133–148.
*———. "Impressions." In Sōseki, *Spring Miscellany and London Essays*, 56–58.
*———. *Inside My Glass Doors*. Translated by Sammy I. Tsunematsu. Introduction and afterword by Marvin Marcus. Boston: Tuttle Publishing, 2002.

*———. "My Individualism." In Natsume Sōseki, *My Individualism and the Philosophical Foundations of Literature*, translated by Sammy I. Tsunematsu (Boston: Tuttle Publishing, 2004), 25–57.
*———. *Spring Miscellany and London Essays*. Translated and introduced by Sammy I. Tsunematsu. Boston: Tuttle Publishing, 2002.
*———. "A Sweet Dream." In Sōseki, *Spring Miscellany and London Essays*, 52–55.
*———. "To Kyō (22 January 1901)." In Sōseki, *Spring Miscellany and London Essays*, 149–155.
*———. "Travels in Manchuria and Korea." In *Rediscovering Natsume Sōseki*, edited and translated by Brodey and Sammy I. Tsunematsu (Folkestone: Global Oriental, 2000), 33–146.
*———. *The Wayfarer: Kōjin*. Translated and introduced by Beongcheon Yu. New York: Perigree Books, 1982.
Nehring, Christina. "No Exit." [Review of Simone de Beauvoir and Jean-Paul Sartre's *Tête-à-tête*.] *New York Times Book Review* (4 December 2005): 26–27.
Neubert, Christoph, and Gabriele Schabacher, eds. *Verkehrsgeschichte und Kulturwissenschaft: Analysen an der Schnittstelle von Technik, Kultur und Medien*. Bielefeld: transcript verlag, 2013.
Newman, Barrie. "Holidays and Social Class." In *Leisure and Society in Britain*, edited by Michael Smith, Stanley Parker, and Cyril Smith (London: Allen Lane, 1973), 230–240.
Nickles, Shelley. "More Is Better: Mass Consumption, Gender, and Class Identity in Postwar America." *American Quarterly* 54 no. 4 (2002): 581–622.
Niclas-Tölle, Boris. "India's Ville Radieuse: Modernist Town Planning in Chandigarh." In Hilger and Unger, *India in the World*, 161–181.
Nicolaides, Becky M. *My Blue Heaven: Life and Politics in the Working-Class Suburbs of Los Angeles, 1920–1965*. Chicago: University of Chicago Press, 2002.
Nikolakakis, Michalis. "Representations and Social Practices of Alternative Tourists in Postwar Greece to the End of the Greek Military Junta." *Journal of Tourism History* 7, nos. 1–2 (2015): 5–17.
Ning, Wang. "Confronting Western Influence: Rethinking Chinese Literature of the New Period." *New Literary History* 24, no. 4 (1993): 905–926.
Nixon, Susan. "Mrs. Housewife and the Ad Men: Advertising, Market Research, and Mass Consumption in Postwar Britain." In *The Rise of Marketing and Market Research*, edited by Hartmut Berghoff, Philip Scranton, and Uwe Spiekermann (New York: Palgrave Macmillan, 2012), 193–213.
Norbury, Guy. "A Post-generation X's View on Ginsberg." In Van Minnen et al., *Beat Culture*, 189–193.
Norton, Peter. "History as a Tool of Agenda Legitimation: U.S. Urban Mobility Trajectories (Outline)." Paper presented at the workshop "Large Metropolis Mobilities in Long-Term Perspective: For an Ecosystemic Approach of Sustainable Urban Mobilities," Paris, 23–24 February 2017.
———. "Of Love Affairs and Other Stories." In *Incomplete Streets: Processes, practices, and possibilities*, edited by Stephen Zavestoski and Julian Agyeman (London: Routledge, 2015), 17–35.
Notar, Beth E. "Car Crazy: The Rise of Car Culture in China." In *Cars, Automobility and Development in Asia: Wheels of Change*, edited by Arve Hansen and Kenneth Bo Nielsen (London: Routledge, 2017), 152–170.

Notar, Beth E., Kyaw San Min, and Raju Gautam. "Echoes of Colonial Logic in Re-ordering 'Public' Streets: From Colonial Rangoon to Postcolonial Yangon." *Transfers* 8, no. 3 (2018): 55–73.

Nöther, Werner, *Die Erschliessung der Sahara durch Motorfahrzeuge 1901–1936*. Munich: belleville Verlag Michael Farm, 2003.

Novaco, Raymond W. "Automobile Driving and Aggressive Behavior." In *The Car and the City: The Automobile, the Built Environment, and Daily Urban Life*, edited by Martin Wachs and Margaret Crawford (with Susan Marie Wirka and Taina Marjatta Rikala) (Ann Arbor: University of Michigan Press, 1992), 234–247.

Nünning, Vera, and Ansgar Nünning, eds. (with Nadyne Stritzke). *Erzähltextanalyse und Gender Studies*. Stuttgart: Verlag J. B. Metzler, 2004.

Nwabughuogu, Anthony I. "The Role of Bicycle Transport in the Economic Development of Eastern Nigeria, 1930–45." *Journal of Transport History* 5 no. 1 (1984): 91–98.

Nyíri, Pál. *Mobility and Cultural Authority in Contemporary China*. Seattle: University of Washington Press, 2010.

O'Connell, Sean. *The Car and British Society: Class, Gender and Motoring, 1896–1939*. Manchester: Manchester University Press, 1998.

*O'Connor, Flannery. "A Good Man Is Hard to Find." In O'Connor, *Collected Works*, 137–153.

*———. *Collected Works: Wise Blood / A Good Man Is Hard to Find / The Violent Bear It Away / Everything That Rises Must Converge / Essays and Letters*. Edited by Sally Fitzgerald. New York: Library of America, 1988.

*———. "Wise Blood." In O'Connor, *Collected Works*, 1–131.

O'Dell, Tom. "'Chevrolet ... That's a Real *Raggarbil*': The American Car and the Production of Swedish Identities." *Journal of Folklore Research* 30, no. 1 (1993): 61–73.

Odier, L., and Louis Loder. "What Is the Position Regarding Low-Cost Roads in 1970? An Example: Australia." In *AIPCR–PIARC 1909–1969* (Paris: Association Internationale Permanente des Congrès de la Route / Permanent International Association of Road Congresses, 1970), 71–92.

Offer, Avner. *The Challenge of Affluence: Self-Control and Well-Being in the United States and Britain since 1950*. Oxford: Oxford University Press, 2006.

Offner, Jean-Marc. "Les 'effets structurants' du transport: Mythe politique, mystification scientifique." *L'espace géographique* 3 (1993): 233–242.

Oğuzertem, Süha. "Fictions of Narcissism: Metaphysical and Psychosexual Conflicts in the Stories of Ahmet Hamdi Tanpinar." *Turkish Studies Association Bulletin* 14, no. 2 (1990): 223–233.

Oldenziel, Ruth. "Exporting the American Cold War Kitchen: Challenging Americanization, Technological Transfer, and Domestication." In *Cold War Kitchen: Americanization, Technology, and European Users*, edited by Ruth Oldenziel and Karin Zachmann (Cambridge, MA: MIT Press, 2009), 315–339.

———. "Is Globalization a Code Word for Americanization?" *Tijdschrift voor Sociale en Economische Geschiedenis* 4, no. 3 (2007): 84–10.

Olsen, Henry. *The Working-Class Republican: Ronald Reagan and the Return of Blue-Collar Conservatism*. New York: Broadside Books, 2017.

Olubomehin, Oladipo O. "Development of the National Trunk Roads in Nigeria and the Socio-economic Impact, 1960–2013." *Lagos Historical Review* (2015). https://www.t2m.org/wp-content/uploads/2014/09/Oladipo%20O%20Olubomehin_Development%20of%20the%20National%20Trunk%20Roads.pdf.

O'Malley, Seamus. *Making History New: Modernism and Historical Narrative*. Oxford: Oxford University Press, 2015.
Ore, Janet. "Mobile Home Syndrome: Engineered Woods and the Making of a New Domestic Ecology in the Post–World War II Era." *Technology and Culture* 52, no. 2 (2011): 260–286.
O'Sullivan, Kevin. "A 'Global Nervous System': The Rise and Rise of European Humanitarian NGOs, 1945–1985." In Frey et al., *International Organizations and Development*, 196–219.
Owen, Wilfred. *Distance and Development: Transport and Communications in India*. Washington, DC: Brookings Institution, 1968.
———. *Strategy for Mobility*. Washington, DC: Brookings Institution, 1964.
Owensby, Brian P. *Intimate Ironies: Modernity and the Making of Middle-Class Lives in Brazil*. Stanford, CA: Stanford University Press, 1999.
Pachón, Álvaro, and María Teresa Ramírez. *La infraestructura de transporte en Colombia durante el siglo XX: Una descripción desde el punta de vista éconómico*. Bogotá: Fondo de Cultura Económica, Banco de la República, 2006.
Packer, Jeremy. *Mobility without Mayhem: Safety, Cars, and Citizenship*. Durham, NC: Duke University Press, 2008.
Page, Tim. "John Cage's Gift to Us." *New York Review of Books* 63, no. 16 (24 October 2016).
Pagenstecher, Cord. *Der bundesdeutsche Tourismus: Ansätze zu einer Visual History: Urlaubsprospekte, Reiseführer, Fotoalben 1950–1990*. Hamburg: Verlag Dr. Kovač, 2003.
———. "The Construction of the Tourist Gaze: How Industrial Was Post-war German Tourism?" In *Development of a Tourist Industry in the 19th and 20th Centuries: International Perspectives*, edited by Laurent Tissot (Neuchâtel: Editions Alphil, 2003), 373–389.
Pan, S. H. "Le développement des routes en Chine," *Bulletin de L'Association Internationale Permanente des Congrès de la Route* 16, no. 49 (January–February 1927): 7–12.
Pante, Michael D. "A Collision of Masculinities: Men, Modernity and Urban Transportation in American-Colonial Manila " *Asian Studies Review* 38, no. 2 (2014): 253–273.
———. "Mobility and Modernity in the Urban Transport Systems of Colonial Manila and Singapore." *Journal of Social History* 47, no. 4 (2014): 855–877.
———. "Racialized Capacities and Transgressive Mobility: 'Asian' Laborers and 'Western' Urban Transportation in Colonial Manila and Singapore." *Transfers* 4, no. 3 (2014): 49–67.
Paolini, Federico. "A Country on Four Wheels: The Car and Society in Italy (1900–1974)." *TST Revista de Historia: Transportes, Servicios y Telecomunicaciones* 17 (2009): 108–130.
———. "'Torpedo blu' vs. 'Topolino amaranto': Appunti per una storia culturale dell' automobile in Italia." *Ricerche Storiche* 34, nos. 2–3 (2004): 427–444.
Papanek, Gustav F. "The Poor of Jakarta." *Economic Development and Cultural Change* 24, no. 1 (1975): 1–27.
Parker, D. S. *The Idea of the Middle Class: White-Collar Workers and Peruvian Society, 1900–1950*. University Park: Pennsylvania State University Press, 1998.
Parkin, Katherine J. *Women at the Wheel: A Century of Buying, Driving, and Fixing Cars*. Philadelphia: University of Pennsylvania Press, 2017.
Parla, Jale. "Car Narratives: A Subgenre in Turkish Novel Writing." *South Atlantic Quarterly* 102, nos. 2–3 (2003): 535–550.
Patel, Kiran Klaus, and Johan Schot. "Twisted Paths to European Integration: Comparing Agriculture and Transport Policies in a Transnational Perspective." *Contemporary European History* 20, no. 4 (2011): 383–403.
Paterson, Matthew. *Automobile Politics: Ecology and Cultural Political Economy*. Cambridge: Cambridge University Press, 2007.
Pattillo-McCoy, Mary. *Black Picket Fences: Privilege and Peril among the Black Middle Class*. Chicago: University of Chicago Press, 1999.

Peace, Adrian. "The Politics of Transporting." *Africa: Journal of the International African Institute* 58, no. 1 (1988): 14–28.
Pearce, Lynne. *Drivetime: Literary Excursions in Automotive Consciousness*. Edinburgh: Edinburgh University Press, 2016.
Pearce, Philip L. "Route Maps: A Study of Travellers' Perceptions of a Section of Countryside." *Journal of Environmental Psychology* 1, no. 2 (1981): 141–155.
Pechey, Graham. *Mikhail Bakhtin: The Word in the World*. London: Routledge, 2007.
Pehlivan, Ekin, Pierre Berthon, and Leyland Pitt. "Ad Bites: Toward a Theory of Ironic Advertising." *Journal of Advertising Research* 51, no. 2 (2011): 417–426.
Peláez, Sol Inés. "Beyond Post-dictatorship: Transnational Latin American Literature and the Violence of Writing." PhD diss., State University of New York, 2010.
Pells, Richard. *Modernist America: Art, Music, Movies, and the Globalization of American Culture*. New Haven, CT: Yale University Press, 2011.
Pendakur, V. Setty. "Elaboration of the Transport System." In Singh Sandhu and Wheatley, *Management of Success*, 399–419.
Pereira, Victor. "Les réseaux de l'émigration clandestine portugaise vers la France entre 1957 et 1974." *Journal of Modern European History* 12, no. 1 (2014): 107–125.
Perkins, John. *The Secret History of the American Empire: The Truth about Economic Hit Men, Jackals, and How to Change the World*. New York: Plume, 2008.
Permanent International Association of Road Congresses. *XIth World Road Congress, Rio de Janeiro 1959: Proceedings of the Congress*. London: PIARC, 1959.
———. *XIIth World Road Congress, Rome 1964: Proceedings of the Congress*. London: PIARC, 1964.
———. *XIIIth World Road Congress, Tokyo 1967: Proceedings of the Congress*. London: PIARC, 1967.
———. *XVth World Road Congress, Mexico 1975: Proceedings of the Congress*. London: PIARC, 1975.
Pernau, Margrit, and Imke Rajamani. "Emotional Translations: Conceptual History beyond Language." *History and Theory* 55, no. 1 (2016): 46–65.
Péteri, György. "Streetcars of Desire: Cars and Automobilism in Communist Hungary (1958–70)." *Social History* 34, no. 1 (2009): 1–28.
Peters, William Henry. "Variation in Consumer Buying Behavior: An Analytical Study of Automobile Purchases." PhD diss., University of Michigan, 1968.
Pflugfelder, Ehren Helmut. "Something Less Than a Driver: Toward an Understanding of Gendered Bodies in Motorsport." *Journal of Sport and Social Issues* 33, no. 4 (2009): 411–426.
Pierson, George W. *The Moving American*. New York: Knopf, 1973.
Piglia, Melina. *Autos, rutas y turismo: El automóvil club argentino y el estado*. Buenos Aires: Siglo Veintiuno Editores, 2014.
———. "Viaje deportivo, nación y territorio. El Automóvil Club Argentino y los orígines del Turismo Carretera. Argentina, 1924–1938." *Nuevo Mundo Mundos Nuevos* (16 September 2008) (downloaded from http://nuevomunod.revues.org/40923 on 15 September 2013).
The Pilot National Recreation Survey: Report No. 1. London / Keele: British Travel Association / University of Keele, July 1967.
Pinder, David. *Visions of the City: Utopianism, Power and Politics in Twentieth-Century Urbanism*. Edinburgh: Edinburgh University Press, 2005.
Pirie, Gordon. "African Mobility History: Recent Texts on Past Passages." In Mom et al. *Mobility in History*, 129–135.

———. "Automobile Organizations Driving Tourism in Pre-independence Africa." *Journal of Tourism History* 5, no. 1 (2013): 73–91.

———. "Non-urban Motoring in Colonial Africa in the 1920s and 1930s." *South African Historical Journal*, 63, no. 1 (2011): 38–60.

Pirsig, Robert M. "Introduction to the Twenty-Fifth Anniversary Edition." In Pirsig, *Zen and the Art of Motorcycle Maintenance*, ix–xii.

*———. *Zen and the Art of Motorcycle Maintenance: An Inquiry into Values*. London: Vintage, 2004.

Plath, David W. "My-Car-isma: Motorizing the Showa Self." In *Showa: The Japan of Hirohito*, edited by Carol Gluck and Stephen R. Graubard. New York: Norton, 1992.

Poiger, Uta G. "Imperialism and Consumption: Two Tropes in West German Radicalism." In Schildt and Siegfried, *Between Marx and Coca-Cola*, 161–172.

Ponsavady, Stéphanie. *Cultural and Literary Representations of the Automobile in French Indochina: A Colonial Roadshow*. New York: Palgrave Macmillan, 2018.

———. "*Indigènes* into Signs: Incorporating Indigenous Pedestrians on Colonial Roads in 1920s and 1930s French Indochina." *Transfers* 4, no. 3 (2014): 4–23.

Pooley, Colin. "Pedestrian Stories: The Changing Role of Walking in Urban Mobility." Paper presented at the workshop "Large Metropolis Mobilities in Long-Term Perspective: For an Ecosystemic Approach of Sustainable Urban Mobilities," Paris, 23–24 February 2017.

Pooley, Colin, and Jean Turnbull. *Migration and Mobility in Britain since the 18th Century*. London: Routledge, 1998.

Porath, Nathan. "A River, a Road, an Indigenous People and an Entangled Landscape in Riau, Indonesia." *Bijdragen tot de Taal-, Land- en Volkenkunde* 158, no. 4 (2002): 769–797.

Porter, Gina. "Living in a Walking World: Rural Mobility and Social Equity Issues in Sub-Saharan Africa." *World Development* 30, no. 2 (2002): 285–300.

———. "Reflections on a Century of Road Transport Developments in West Africa and Their (Gendered) Impacts on the Rural Poor." *EchoGéo* 20 (April–June 2012): 1–14.

Posel, Ros. "Amahashi: Durban's Ricksha Pullers." *Journal of Natan and Zulu History* 13, no. 1 (1990): 51–70.

———. "The Durban Ricksha Pullers' 'Strikes' of 1918 and 1930." *Journal of Natal and Zulu History* 8, no. 1 (1985): 35–106.

Post, Robert C. *Urban Mass Transit: The Life Story of a Technology*. Westport, CT: Greenwood Press, 2007.

Pozharliev, Lyubomir. "Collectivity vs Connectivity: Highway Peripherization in Former Yugoslavia (1940s–1980s)." *Journal of Transport History* 37, no. 2 (2016): 194–213.

———. "Collectivity vs Connectivity: The Techno-historical Example of Motorway Peripherization in Former Yugoslavia." Paper presented at the T²M conference "Spinoffs of Mobility: Technology, Risk and Innovation," Philadelphia, 18–21 September 2014.

Prakash, Gyan. "Can the 'Subaltern' Ride? A Reply to O'Hanlon and Washbrook." *Comparative Studies in Society and History* 34, no. 1 (1992): 168–184.

Pratt, Mary Louise. *Imperial Eyes: Travel Writing and Transculturation*. London: Routledge, 1992.

Primeau, Ronald. "From Ma Joad to Elizabeth Berg: Women on the Road in America." *Midamerica: The Yearbook of the Society for the Study of Midwestern Literature* 26 (1999): 138–146.

Prinz, Jesse J. "Foreword: Hand Manifesto." In Radman, *The Hand, an Organ of the Mind*, ix–xvii.

*Pritchett, Jack. "Nigerian Truck Art." *African Arts* 12, no. 2 (1979): 27–31.

*Prokosch, Frederic. *The Asiatics: A Novel*. Introduction by Carl van Doren. New York: The Press of the Readers Club, 1941.
Prose, Francine. "The Passion and Rage of Arundhati Roy." *New York Review of Books* 64, no. 12 (13 July 2017): 16–17.
Prybyla, Jan S. "The Sino-Soviet Split and the Developing Nations." In Kanet, *Soviet Union and the Developing Nations*, 265–293.
Purdy, Jedediah. *For Common Things: Irony, Trust, and Commitment in America Today*. New York: Knopf, 1999.
Rabinow, Paul. "Representations Are Social Facts: Modernity and Post-modernity in Anthropology." In Clifford and Marcus, *Writing Culture*, 234–261.
Radkau, Joachim. "'Die Nervosität des Zeitalters': Die Erfindung von Technikbedürfnissen um die Jahrhundertwende." *Kultur & Technik* 3 (1994): 51–57.
Radman, Zdravko. "On Displacement of Agency: The Mind Handmade." In Radman, *The Hand, an Organ of the Mind*, 369–397.
Radway, Janice A. *Reading the Romance: Women, Patriarchy, and Popular Literature*. Chapel Hill: University of North Carolina Press, 1984.
Ragen, Brian Abel. *A Wreck on the Road to Damascus: Innocence, Guilt, and Conversion in Flannery O'Connor*. Chicago: Loyola University Press, 1989.
Rahul, T. M., and Ashish Verma. "Economic Impact of Non-motorized Transportation in Indian Cities." *Research in Transportation Economics* 38, no. 1 (2013): 22–34.
Rallis, Tom and Uno Helk. "Story of the Motorways II." *European Asphalt Magazine* 1 (1993): 8–13.
———. "Story of the Motorways III." *European Asphalt Magazine* 2 (1993): 14–22.
Ramont, Henry. "John Updike Completes a Sequel to 'Rabbit, Run.'" *New York Times* (27 July 1970).
Randisi, Jennifer L. "The Scene of the Crime: The Automobile in the Fiction of Harry Crews." *Southern Studies* 25, no. 3 (1986): 213–219.
Rankin, Ian. "Surface and Structure: Reading Muriel Spark's *The Driver's Seat*," *Journal of Narrative Technique* 15, no. 2 (1985): 146–155.
Rao, Nikhil. *House but No Garden: Apartment Living in Bombay's Suburbs, 1898–1964*. Minneapolis: University of Minnesota Press, 2013.
Raphael, Lutz. "Transformations of Industrial Labour in Western Europe: Intergenerational Change of Life Cycles, Occupation and Mobility 1970–2000." *German History* 30, no. 1 (2012): 100–119.
Ratay, Richard. *Don't Make Me Pull Over! An Informal History of the Family Road Trip*. New York: Scribner, 2018.
Ratcliffe, Matthew. "Touch and the Sense of Reality." In Radman, *The Hand, an Organ of the Mind*, 131–157.
Ravi, Rajendra. "A Journey with Cycle Rickshaws: Identity, Respect, Equality, Space, and Sustainable Futures." *Transfers* 3, no. 3 (2013): 124–130.
Râycheu, Prafulla Chandra. *Life and Experiences of a Bengali Chemist*. Calcutta: Chukervertty, Chatterjee & Co. / Kegan Paul, Trench, Trübner & Co., 1932.
Ray, Timothy D. "Merry Pranksters." In *Beat Culture: Icons, Lifestyles, and Impact*, edited by William T. Lawlor (Santa Barbara, CA: ABC Clio, 2005), 230–231.
Reader's Digest Association. *Products and People: The Reader's Digest European Surveys*. London: Reader's Digest Association, 1963. Published in German as *Sieben-Länder-Untersuchung: Eine vergleichbare Marktuntersuchung in Belgien, Frankreich, Grossbritannien, Holland, Italien, Luxemburg und der Bundesrepublik Deutschland* (Düsseldorf: Verlag Das Beste, [1963]).

Redding, Arthur. *Raids on Human Consciousness: Writing, Anarchism, and Violence.* Columbia: University of South Carolina Press, 1998.
Reed, Christopher A., and M. William Steele. "The Modern History of the Book in China, Japan and Korea." Manuscript draft, February 2016.
Reed, Edward, and Rebecca Jones, eds. *Reasons for Realism: Selected Essays of James J. Gibson.* Hillsdale, NJ: Lawrence Erlbaum, 1982.
Renner, Andreas. "Watching Foreign Neighbours: Russian and Soviet Travel Writing about Japan in the First Half of the Twentieth Century." *Journal of Tourism History* 3, no. 1 (2011): 39–56.
Reinecke, Siegfried. *Autosymbolik in Journalismus, Literatur und Film: Struktural-funktionale Analysen vom Beginn der Motorisierung bis zur Gegenwart.* Bochum: Universitätsverlag Dr. N. Brockmeyer, 1992.
———. *Mobile Zeiten: Eine Geschichte der Auto-Dichtung.* Bochum: Germinal Verlag, 1986.
Retzloff, Tim. "Cars and Bars: Assembling Gay Men in Postwar Flint, Michigan." In *Creating a Place for Ourselves: Lesbian, Gay, and Bisexual Community Histories*, edited by Brett Beemyn (New York: Routledge, 1997), 226–252.
Rhoads, Edward J. M. "Cycles of Cathay: A History of the Bicycle in China." *Transfers* 2, no. 2 (2012): 95–120.
Richman, Joel. "The Motor Car and the Territorial Aggression Thesis: Some Aspects of the Sociology of the Street." *Sociological Review* 20, no. 1 (1972): 6–27.
Ricsha Committee. "Report of the Ricsha Committee." Special issue, *Municipal Gazette*, 13 February 1934.
Rieger, Bernhard. *The People's Car: A Global History of the Volkswagen Beetle.* Cambridge, MA: Harvard University Press, 2013.
Rimmer, Peter J. "Hackney Carriage Syces and Rikisha Pullers in Singapore: A Colonial Registrar's Perspective on Public Transport, 1892–1923." In Rimmer and Allen, *Underside of Malaysian History*, 129–160.
———. *Rikisha to Rapid Transit: Urban Public Transport Systems and Policy in Southeast Asia.* Sydney: Pergamon Press, 1986.
———. "Structure, Conduct and Performance of the Rickshaw Industry in East and South East Asian Cities, 1869–1939." In *Transport Policy, Management and Technology towards 2001: Selected Conference Proceedings of the Fifth World Conference on Transport Research* (Western Periodicals, 1989), 597–611 (paper no. 3-19-3).
Rimmer, Peter J., and Lisa M. Allen, eds. *The Underside of Malaysian History: Pullers, Prostitutes, Plantation Workers ...* Singapore: Singapore University Press, 1990.
Rimmer, Peter J., Lenore Manderson, and Colin Barlow. "The Underside of Malaysian History." In Rimmer and Allen, *Underside of Malaysian History*, 3–22.
Rinauro, Sandro. "L'émigration illégale des Italiens en France et en Suisse après la Deuxième Guerre mondiale." *Journal of Modern European History* 12, no. 1 (2014): 84–106.
Rink, Bradley. "Race and the Micropolitics of Mobility: Mobile Autoethnography on a South African Bus Service." *Transfers* 6, no. 1 (2016): 62–79.
Rinn, Gregor M. "Das Automobil als nationales Identifikationssymbol: Zur politischen Bedeutungsprägung des Kraftfahrzeugs in Modernitätskonzeptionen des 'Dritten Reichs' und der Bundesrepublik.'" PhD diss., Humboldt-Universität zu Berlin, 2008.
Rippy, J. Fred. "The Inter-American Highway." *Pacific Historical Review* 24, no. 3 (1955): 287–298.
"*The Road* by Wole Soyinka: Themes and Meanings." eNotes.com, accessed 29 October 2019. https://www.enotes.com/topics/road-wole-soyinka/themes.
*Robbins, Tom. *Even Cowgirls Get the Blues.* New York: Bantam Books, 2003.

Roberts, Richard M. and Roger J. Kreuz. "Why Do People Use Figurative Language?" *Psychological Science* 5, no. 3 (1994): 159–163.
Robinson, John P., and Philip E. Converse. "Social Change Reflected in the Use of Time." In Angus Campbell and Philip E. Converse, eds., *The Human Meaning of Social Change* (New York: Russell Sage Foundation, 1972), 17–86.
Roccor, Bettina. "Heavy Metal: Gewaltsdarstellung oder Gewaltsverherrlichung?" In *Gewalt in der Kultur: Vorträge des 29. Deutschen Volkskundekongresses, Passau 1993, Teilband II*, edited by Rolf W. Brednich and Walter Hartinger (Passau: Lehrstuhl für Volkskunde Universität Passau, 1994), 645–658.
*Rochefort, Christiane. *Les Petits Enfants du siècle*. Paris: Éditions Bernard Grasset, 1961.
Rocholl, Peter. *Vergleichende Analyse der Entwicklung des Personenkraftverkehrs im westeuropäischen Wirtschaftsraum*. Düsseldorf: Droste Verlag, 1962.
Rodino, Richard H. "The Matrix of Journeys in *Zen and the Art of Motorcycle Maintenance*." *Journal of Narrative Technique* 11, no. 31 (1981): 53–63.
*Roiphe, Anne. *Long Division*. London: Secker & Warburg, 1973.
Romalis, Shelly. *Pistol Packin' Mama: Aunt Molly Jackson and the Politics of Folksong*. Urbana: University of Illinois Press, 1999.
Romine, Scott. "Harry Crews's Away Games: Home and Sport in *A Feast of Snakes* and *Body*." In *Perspectives on Harry Crews*, edited by Erik Bledsoe (Jackson: University Press of Mississippi, 2001), 117–132.
Rose, Mark H., and Bruce E. Seely. "Getting the Interstate System Built: Road Engineers and the Implementation of Public Policy, 1955–1985." *Journal of Policy History* 2, no. 1 (1990): 23–55.
Roseberry, William. "Social Fields and Cultural Encounters." In *Close Encounters of Empire: Writing the Cultural History of U.S.-Latin American Relations*, edited by Gilbert M. Joseph, Catherine C. LeGrand, and Ricardo D. Salvatore (Durham, NC: Duke University Press, 1998), 515–524.
Rosen, Andrew. *The Transformation of British Life, 1950–2000: A Social History*. Manchester: Manchester University Press, 2003.
Rosen, Stanley. *Red Guard Factionalism and the Cultural Revolution in Guangzhou (Canton)* Boulder, CO: Westview Press, 1982.
Rosenberg, Emily S. "Transnational Currents in a Shrinking World." In *A World Connecting 1870–1945*, edited by Emily S. Rosenberg (Cambridge, MA: Belknap Press, 2012), 813–996.
*Rosenberg, Göran. *Een kort oponthoud: Op de weg van Auschwitz*. Translated by Jasper Popma. Amsterdam: Atlas Contact, 2014.
Rosenbloom, Sandra. "Why Working Families Need a Car." In *The Car and the City: The Automobile, the Built Environment, and Daily Urban Life*, edited by Martin Wachs and Margaret Crawford (with Susan Marie Wirka and Taina Marjatta Rikala) (Ann Arbor: University of Michigan Press, 1992), 39–56.
Ross, Alex. *The Rest Is Noise: Listening to the Twentieth Century*. New York: Farrar, Straus and Giroux, 2007.
Ross, Kristin. *Fast Cars, Clean Bodies: Decolonization and the Reordering of French Culture*. Cambridge, MA: MIT Press, 1995.
Rostow, W. W. *The Stages of Economic Growth: A Non-Communist Manifesto*. Cambridge: Cambridge University Press, 1971.
Roth, Friederike. "Einleitung: Max Benses poetische Texte." In *Ausgewählte Schriften, Bd. 4: Poetische Texte* by Max Bense, edited by Elisabeth Walther (Stuttgart: J. B. Metzler, 1998), vii–xiii.

Roth, Joshua Hotaka. "Is Female to Male as Lightweight Cars Are to Sports Cars? Gender Metaphors and Cognitive Schemas in Recessionary Japan." In *Vehicles: Cars, Canoes, and Other Metaphors of Moral Imagination*, edited by David Lipset and Richard Handler (New York: Berghahn Books, 2014), 88–108.

Routledge, Paul. "A Spatiality of Resistance: Theory and Practice in Nepal's Revolution of 1990." In *Geographies of Resistance*, edited by Steve Pile and Michael Keith (London: Routledge, 1997), 68–85.

Ruan, Ming. *Deng Xiaoping: Chronicle of an Empire*. Translated and edited by Nancy Liu, Peter Rand, and Lawrence R. Sullivan. Foreword by Andrew J. Nathan. Boulder, CO: Westview Press, 1994.

Rubin, Jay. "Sanshiro and Soseki: A Critical Essay." In *Sanshiro: A Novel* by Natsume Sōseki, translated by Jay Rubin (Seattle: University of Washington Press, 1977), 213–248.

Ruckli, Robert. "Der Ausbau des amerikanischen Hauptstrassennetzes: Vergleich mit dem schweizerischen Hauptstrassenprogramm." *Strasse und Verkehr* 32, nos. 14–15 / nos. 16–17 (1946): 200–210 / 217–231.

Rugh, Susan Sessions. *Are We There Yet? The Golden Age of American Family Vacations*. Lawrence: University Press of Kansas, 2008.

*Rushdie, Salman. *The Ground Beneath Her Feet: A Novel*. New York: Picador, 1999.

Rycroft, Simon. "Changing Lanes: Textuality off and on the Road." *Transactions of the Institute of British Geographers* 21, no. 2 (1996): 425–428.

Sachsenmaier, Dominic. *Global Perspectives on Global History: Theories and Approaches in a Connected World*. Cambridge: Cambridge University Press, 2011.

*Sagan, Françoise. *Avec mon meilleur souvenir*. Paris: Gallimard, 1984.

*———. "La vitesse." In Sagan, *Avec mon meilleur souvenir*, 59–67.

*———. *Toxique*. Illustrated by Bernard Buffet. Paris: Éditions Stock, 2009.

Sage, Daniel. *How Outer Space Made America: Geography, Organization and the Cosmic Sublime*. Farnham: Ashgate, 2014.

Saiz, Albert. "Dictatorships and highways." *Regional Science and Urban Economics* 36, no. 2 (2006): 187–206.

*Salter, James. *A Sport and a Pastime*. London: Picador Classic, 2017.

Salvatore, Ricardo. "Early American Visions of a Hemispheric Market in South America." In *Transnational America: The Fading of Borders in the Western Hemisphere*, edited by Berndt Ostendorf (Heidelberg: Universitätsverlag C. Winter, 2002), 45–64.

———. "Imperial Mechanics: South America's Hemispheric Integration in the Machine Age." *American Quarterly* 58, no. 3 (2006): 662–691.

———. "Panamericanismo práctico: Acerca de la mecánica de la penetración comercial norteamaericana." In *Culturas imperiales: Experiencia y representación en América, Asia y Africa*, edited by Ricardo Salvatore (Rosario: Beatriz Viterbo, 2005), 269–300.

———. "A Post-occidentalist Manifesto (review of Walter Mignolo, *The Idea of Latin America* [2005])." *A Contra corriente* 4, no. 1 (2006): 126–138.

———. "Re-discovering Spanish America: Uses of Travel Literature about South America in Britain." *Journal of Latin American Cultural Studies* 8, no. 2 (1999): 199–217.

———. "The Unsettling Location of a Settler Nation: Argentina, from Settler Economy to Failed Developing Nation." *South Atlantic Quarterly* 107, no. 4 (2008): 755–789.

Samanta, Gopa. "Art on the Move: Rickshaw Painters in Bangladesh" *Transfers* 3, no. 3 (2013): 131–134.

Sanderson, Stewart. "The Folklore of the Motor-Car." *Folklore* 80, no. 4 (1969): 241–252.

Sandison, David, and Graham Vickers. *Neal Cassady: The Fast Life of a Beat Hero*. Chicago: Chicago Review Press, 2006.

Sandoval, Denise. "Bajito y Suavecito: The Lowriding Tradition." Smithsonian Latino Center (2003), accessed 5 June 2017. http://latino.si.edu/virtualgallery/lowrider/lr_sandovalessay.htm.
Sanford, Charles. "'Woman's Place' in American Car Culture." *Michigan Quarterly Review* 19–20 (1980–1981): 532–547.
Sargeant, Jack. *Naked Lens: Beat Cinema.* Berkeley, CA: Soft Skull Press, 2008.
*Saroyan, William. *Short Drive, Sweet Chariot.* New York: Pocket Books, 1967.
Sauli, Arnaud. "Circulation and Authority: Police, Public Space and Territorial Control in Punjab, 1861–1920." In Markovits et al., *Society and Circulation*, 215–239.
Savage, Jon. *Teenage: The Creation of Youth Culture.* London: Pimlico, 2007.
Schael, Alfredo, ed. *Venezuela: 100 años en AUTOMOVÍL.* Caracas: Fundación Museo del Transporte, 2004.
Schaller, Dominik J. "From Conquest to Genocide: Colonial Rule in German Southwest Africa and German East Africa." In *Empire, Colony, Genocide: Conquest, Occupation, and Subaltern Resistance in World History*, edited by A. Dirk Moses (New York: Berghahn Books, 2008), 296–324.
Schandl, Heinz, Marina Fischer-Kowalski, Clemens Grunbuhel, and Fridolin Krausmann. "Socio-metabolic Transitions in Developing Asia." *Technological Forecasting & Social Change* 76, no. 2 (2009): 267–281.
Scharff, Virginia. *Taking the Wheel: Women and the Coming of the Motor Age.* New York: Free Press, 1991.
Scheiner, Joachim. "80 Jahre Motorisierung in Stadt und Land: Fallstudie Nordrhein-Westfalen." *Internationales Verkehrswesen* 62, no. 12 (2010): 17–21.
Schenk, Catherine R. "Austerity and Boom." In Johnson, *Twentieth-Century Britain*, 300–319.
Scherke, Katharina. "Die These von der 'Ästhetisierung der Lebenswelt' als eine Form der Analyse des Modernisierungsprozesses." In *Analyse und Kritik der Modernisierung um 1900 und um 2000*, edited by Sabine A. Haring and Katharina Scherke (Vienna: Passagen-Verlag, 2000), 109–131.
Schildt, Axel. "Across the Border: West German Youth Travel to Western Europe." In Schildt and Siegfried, *Between Marx and Coca-Cola*, 149–157.
———. "Amerikanische Einflüsse auf die westdeutsche Konsumentwicklung nach dem Zweiten Weltkrieg." In *Die Konsumgesellschaft in Deutschland 1890–1990: Ein Handbuch*, edited by Heinz-Gerhard Haupt and Claudius Torp (Frankfurt: Campus Verlag, 2009), 434–447.
———. "Konsum und Freizeit im 'Wirtschaftswunderland': Mit Streiflichtern auf den Alltag von Stadt und Landkreis Uelzen in den 50er Jahren." In *Von der Währungsreform zum Wirtschaftswunder: Wiederaufbau in Niedersachsen*, edited by Bernd Weisbrod (Hannover: Verlag Hahnsche Buchhandlung, 1998), 207–230.
Schildt, Axel, and Detlef Siegfried, eds. *Between Marx and Coca-Cola: Youth Cultures in Changing European Societies, 1960–1980.* New York: Berghahn Books, 2006.
———. "Introduction: Youth, Consumption, and Politics in the Age of Radical Change." In Schildt and Siegfried, *Between Marx and Coca-Cola*, 1–35.
Schipper, Frank. "Changing the Face of Europe: European Road Mobility during the Marshall Plan Years." *Journal of Transport History* 28, no. 2 (2007): 211–228.
———. *Driving Europe: Building Europe on Roads in the Twentieth Century.* Amsterdam: aksant, 2008.
Schipper, Lee, and Stephen Meyers (with Richard B. Howarth and Ruther Steiner). *Energy Efficiency and Human Activity: Past Trends, Future Prospects.* Cambridge: Cambridge University Press, 1992.

Schipper, Lee, Ruth Steiner, and Stephen Meyers. "Trends in Transportation Energy Use, 1970–1988: An International Perspective." In *Transportation and Global Climate Change*, edited by David L. Greene and Danilo J. Santini (Washington, DC: American Council for an Energy-Efficient Economy, 1993), 51–89.

Schivelbusch, Wolfgang. *Entfernte Verwandtschaft: Faschismus, Nationalsozialismus, New Deal 1933–1939*. Munich: Carl Hanser Verlag, 2005.

Schmelzer, Matthias. "A Club of the Rich to Help the Poor? The OECD, 'Development,' and the Hegemony of Donor Countries." In Frey et al., *International Organizations and Development*, 171–195.

Schmidt, Gert. "Automobilkultur in der Bundesrepublik Deutschland: 50er und 60er Jahre." Unpublished manuscript, Munich, January 2010.

Schödermeier, Josef W. *Die Entwicklung und Zusammensetzung des Personenkraftwagenbestandes in Westeuropa (Eine retrospektive Analyse)*. PhD diss., Universität Köln, 1961.

Schöller-Schwedes, Oliver, and Stephan Rammler. *Mobile Cities: Dynamiken weltweiter Stadt- und Verkehrsentwicklung*. Berlin: LIT Verlag, 2008.

Schönhammer, Rainer. "Was die an Frauen gerichtete Autowerbung lehrt." In *Frauen und Männer in der mobilen Gesellschaft*, edited by Antje Flade and Maria Limbourg (Opladen: Leske + Budrich, 1999), 49–62.

Schoppa, R. Keith. *Revolution and Its Past: Identities and Change in Modern Chinese History*. Boston: Prentice Hall, 2011.

Schot, Johan, and Dick van Lente. "Technology, Industrialization and the Contested Modernization of the Netherlands." In *Technology and the Making of the Netherlands*, edited by Johan Schot, Harry Lintsen, and Arie Rip (Cambridge, MA: MIT Press, 2010), 485–542.

Schrage, Dominik. "Der Konsum in der deutschen Soziologie." In *Die Konsumgesellschaft in Deutschland 1890–1990: Ein Handbuch*, edited by Heinz-Gerhard Haupt and Claudius Torp (Frankfurt: Campus Verlag, 2009), 319–334.

Schramm, Manuel. "Nationale Unterschiede im westeuropäischen Massenkonsum. Grossbritannien, Frankreich, Deutschland und Italien 1950–1970." In *Vergleich und Transfer in der Konsumgeschichte*, edited by Manuel Schramm (Leipzig: Leipziger Universitätsverlag, 2009), 69–85.

Schrijnen, Pieter. "Autobezit en autogebruik in Nederland." Universiteit van Amsterdam (report Instituut voor Verkeers- en Vervoerseconomie, Projectcentrum Milieubewegingsvraagstukken/ Wetenschapswinkel), January 1986.

Schulz, Kristina. "Feminist Echoes of 1968: Women's Movements in Europe and the United States." In *A Revolution of Perception? Consequences and Echoes of 1968*, edited by Ingrid Gilcher-Holtey (New York: Berghahn Books, 2014), 124–147.

Schulze, Gerhard. *Die Erlebnisgesellschaft: Kultursoziologie der Gegenwart*. Student edition. Frankfurt: Campus Verlag, 2000.

Schuyt, Kees, and Ed Taverne. *1950: Welvaart in zwart-wit*. Den Haag: sdu, 2000.

Schweid, Richard. *Che's Chevrolet, Fidel's Oldsmobile: On the Road in Cuba*. Chapel Hill: University of North Carolina Press, 2004.

Schwenkel, Christina. "Traveling Architecture: East German Urban Designs in Vietnam." *International Journal for History, Culture and Modernity* 2, no. 2 (2014): 155–174.

Scoggin, Mary. "Wine in the Writing, Truth in the Rhetoric: Three Levels of Irony in a Chinese Essay Genre." In *Irony in Action: Anthropology, Practice, and the Moral Imagination*, edited by James W. Fernandez and Mary Taylor Huber (Chicago: University of Chicago Press, 2001), 145–171.

Scott, Catherine V. "Tradition and Gender in Modernization Theory." In Harding, *Postcolonial Science*, 290–309.
Scott, James C. *Domination and the Arts of Resistance: Hidden Transcripts*. New Haven, CT: Yale University Press, 1990.
———. *The Moral Economy of the Peasant: Rebellion and Subsistence in Southeast Asia*. New Haven, CT: Yale University Press, 1976.
Scott, Joyce Hope. "Commercial Deportation as Rite of Passage in Black Women's Novels." In *Matatu* 3, no. 6 (1989): 127–154.
Scott, Peter. "Public-Sector Investment and Britain's Post-war Economic Performance: a Case Study of Roads Policy." *Journal of European Economic History* 34, no. 2 (2005): 391–418.
Seely, Bruce. *Building the American Highway System: Engineers as Policy Makers*. Philadelphia: Temple University Press, 1987.
———. "'Push' and 'Pull' Factors in Technology Transfer: Moving American-Style Highway Engineering to Europe, 1945–1965." *Comparative Technology Transfer and Society* 2, no. 3 (2004): 229–246.
Seidel, Robert Neal. "Progressive Pan Americanism: Development and United States Policy toward South America, 1906–1931." PhD diss., Cornell University, 1973.
Seiler, Cotten. "Anxiety and Automobility: Cold War Individualism and the Interstate Highway System." PhD diss., University of Kansas, 2002.
———. *Republic of Drivers: A Cultural History of Automobility in America*. Chicago: University of Chicago Press, 2008.
———. "'So That We as a Race Might Have Something Authentic to Travel By': African American Automobility and Cold-War Liberalism." *American Quarterly* 58, no. 4 (2006): 1091–1117.
Sejersted, Francis. *The Age of Social Democracy: Norway and Sweden in the Twentieth Century*. Translated by Richard Daly. Edited by Madeleine B. Adams. Princeton, NJ: Princeton University Press, 2011.
Self, Michael Marvin. "A Survey of Automobile Manufacturing in Latin America." PhD diss., University of Texas, 1967.
Seow, Victor. "Socialist Drive: The First Auto Works and the Contradictions of Connectivity in the Early People's Republic of China." *Journal of Transport History* 35, no. 2 (2014): 145–161.
Servan-Schreiber, Catherine. "Tellers of Tales, Sellers of Tales: Bhojpuri Peddlers in Northern India." In Markovits et al., *Society and Circulation*, 275–305.
Severson, Aaron. "Rocket Bomb: The Oldsmobile Rocket 88 and the Dawn of the American Horsepower Race." *Ate Up with Motor*, 20 August 2008. https://ateupwithmotor.com/model-histories/oldsmobile-rocket-88.
Sharma, Sarah, and Armond R. Towns. "Ceasing Fire and Seizing Time: LA Gang Tours and the White Control of Mobility." *Transfers* 6, no. 1 (2016): 26–44.
Shaviro, Steven. "Bodies of Fear: The Films of David Cronenberg." In *The Politics of Everyday Fear*, edited by Brian Massumi (Minneapolis: University of Minnesota Press, 1993), 113–135.
*She, Lao. *Rickshaw: The Novel Lo-t'o Hsiang Tzu*. Translated by Jean M. James. Honolulu: University Press of Hawai'i, 1979.
Shell, Jacob. *Transportation and Revolt: Pigeons, Mules, Canals, and the Vanishing Geographies of Subversive Mobility*. Cambridge, MA: MIT Press, 2015.
———. "When Roads Cannot Be Used: The Use of Trained Elephants for Emergency Logistics, Off-Road Conveyance, and Political Revolt in South and Southeast Asia." *Transfers* 5, no. 2 (2015): 62–80.

Sheller, Mimi. "Automotive Emotions: Feeling the Car." *Theory, Culture & Society* 21, nos. 4–5 (2004): 221–242.

Shimokawa, Koichi. "Japan: The Late Starter Who Outpaced All Her Rivals." In Barker, *Economic and Social Effects of the Spread of Motor Vehicles*, 214–235.

Shoop, Casey. "Thomas Pynchon, Postmodernism, and the Rise of the New Right in California." *Contemporary Literature* 53, no. 1 (2012): 51–86.

Shorter, Edward. *The Making of the Modern Family*. New York: Basic Books, 1975.

Shurmer-Smith, Pamela, and Kevin Hannam. *Worlds of Desire, Realms of Power: A Cultural Geography*. London: Edward Arnold, 1994.

Sieben-Länder-Untersuchung: Eine vergleichbare Marktuntersuchung in Belgien, Frankreich, Grossbritannien, Holland, Italien, Luxemburg und der Bundesrepublik Deutschland. Düsseldorf: Verlag Das Beste, [1963].

Siegelbaum, Lewis H. *Cars for Comrades: The Life of the Soviet Automobile*. Ithaca, NY: Cornell University Press, 2008.

Siegelbaum, Lewis H., and Leslie Page Moch. *Broad Is My Native Land: Repertoires and Regimes of Migration in Russia's Twentieth Century*. Ithaca, NY: Cornell University Press, 2014.

Siegfried, Detlef. "Prosperität und Krisenangst: Die zögerliche Versöhnung der Bundesbürger mit dem neuen Wohlstand." In *Mit dem Wandel leben: Neuorientierung und Tradition in der Bundesrepublik der 1950er und 60er Jahre*, edited by Friedrich Kiessling and Bernhard Rieger (Köln: Böhlau Verlag, 2011), 63–78.

———. "Protest am Markt: Gegenkultur in der Konsumgesellschaft um 1968." In *Wo "1968" liegt: Reform und Revolte in der Geschichte der Bundesrepublik*, edited by Christina von Hodenberg and Detlef Siegfried (Göttingen: Vandenhoeck & Ruprecht, 2006), 48–78.

———. "Understanding 1968: Youth Rebellion, Generational Change and Postindustrial Society." In Schildt and Siegfried, *Between Marx and Coca-Cola*, 59–81.

Siegrist, Hannes. "From Divergence to Convergence: The Divided German Middle Class, 1945 to 2000." In Zunz et al., *Social Contracts Under Stress*, 21–46.

Sikkink, Kathryn. "Development Ideas in Latin America: Paradigm Shift and the Economic Commission for Latin America." In Cooper and Packard, *International Development and the Social Sciences*, 228–256.

Singer, Bayla. *Like Sex with Gods: An Unorthodox History of Flying*. College Station: Texas A&M University Press, 2003.

Singh, Dhan Zunino, and Mikkel Thelle. "Mobilities and Representations: A Conversation with Peter Merriman, Colin Divall, Sunny Stalter-Pace, and Tim Cresswell." *Mobility in History* 8 (2017): 7–18.

Singh, Khushwant. *Train to Pakistan*. Introduction by Arthur Lall. New York: Grove Press, 1990.

Singh Sandhu, Kernial, and Paul Wheatley, eds. *Management of Success: The Moulding of Modern Singapore*. Singapore: Institute of Southeast Asian Studies, 1989.

Sinha, Subir. "Lineages of the Developmentalist State: Transnationality and Village India, 1900–1965." *Comparative Studies in Society and History* 50, no. 1 (2008): 57–90.

Sixty Years of Motor Transport in India: A Dunlop Diamond Jubilee Publication 1898–1958. [Calcutta]: Dunlop Rubber Co. Ltd., January 1959.

Slettedahl Macpherson, Heidi. *Women's Movement: Escape as Transgression in North American Feminist Fiction*. Amsterdam: Rodopi, 2000.

Smith, A. Viola, and Anselm Chuh. *Motor Roads in China*. Washington, DC: US Government Printing Office, 1931.

Smith, Robert Freeman. "Latin America, the United States and the European Powers, 1830–1930." In *The Cambridge History of Latin America, vol. 4: c. 1870–1930*, edited by Leslie Bethell (Cambridge: Cambridge University Press, 1986), 83–119.

———. *Ad Hoc Governments: Special Purpose Transportation Authorities in Britain and the United States*. Beverly Hills: Sage, 1974.

Smith, Sidonie. *Moving Lives: Twentieth-Century Women's Travel Writing*. Minneapolis: University of Minnesota Press, 2001.

Smith, Suzanne E. *Dancing in the Street: Motown and the Cultural Politics of Detroit*. Cambridge, MA: Harvard University Press, 2003.

*Snow, Edgar. *Red Star over China*. First revised and enlarged edition. New York: Grove Press, 1968.

Sobel, Emilie. "The Aggressive Female." In *Violence: Perspectives on Murder and Aggression*, edited by Irwin L. Kutash, Samuel B. Kutash, and Louis B. Schlesinger (San Francisco: Josey-Bass Publishers, 1978), 267–284.

Society for Anglo-Chinese Understanding. "The Chinese Car Industry." *China in Focus* 13 (2003).

Solovey, Mark. "The Politics of Intellectual Identity and American Social Science, 1945–1970." PhD diss., University of Wisconsin-Madison, 1996.

Soong, Stephen C., and George Kao. "Preface." In Ts'un-yan [Cunren], *Chinese Middlebrow Fiction*.

Sorlin, Pierre. *European Cinemas, European Societies 1939–1990*. London: Routledge, 1991.

Sousa, Maria Luísa. "Colonial Centres and Peripheries: Low-Cost Roads and Portuguese Engineers in the 1950s." In *Peripheral Flows: A Historical Perspective on Mobilities between Cores and Fringes*, edited by Simone Fari and Massimo Moraglio (Newcastle upon Tyne: Cambridge Scholars Publishing, 2016), 169–188.

Sousa, Maria Luísa de Castro Coelho de Oliveira e. "A mobilidade automóvel em Portugal. A construção do Sistema socio-técnico, 1920–1950." PhD diss., Universidade Nova de Lisboa, 2013.

*Soyinka, Wole. *The Road*. [A play]. Oxford: Oxford University Press, 1965.

Spence, Jonathan D. *The Search for Modern China*. London: Hutchinson, 1990.

Spigel, Lynn. "Installing the Television Set: Popular Discourses on Television and Domestic Space, 1948–1955." *Camera Obscura: A Journal of Feminism and Film Theory* 6, no. 1 (1988): 11–46.

———. "Television in the Family Circle: The Popular Reception of a New Medium." In Mellencamp, *Logics of Television*, 73–97.

Spivak, Gayatri Chakravorty. "Can the Subaltern Speak?" In *Marxism and the Interpretation of Culture*, edited by Cary Nelson and Lawrence Grossberg (London: Macmillan Education, 1988), 271–313.

Spurr, David. *The Rhetoric of Empire: Colonial Discourse in Journalism, Travel Writing, and Imperial Administration*. Durham, NC: Duke University Press, 1993.

[Stalker, Peter]. *The First Parliament of Asia: Sixty Years of the Economic and Social Commission for Asia and the Pacific (1947–2007)*. Bangkok: United Nations, March 2007.

Standing Advisory Committee on Trunk Road Assessment. *Transport and the Economy: Full Report*. London: Her Majesty's Stationery Office, 1999.

Stannard, Martin. *Muriel Spark: The Biography*. London: Weidenfeld & Nicolson, 2009.

Staples, Amy L. S. *The Birth of Development: How the World Bank, Food and Agriculture Organization, and World Health Organization Changed the World, 1945–1965*. Kent, OH: Kent State University Press, 2006.

Stearns, Peter N. *American Cool: Constructing a Twentieth-Century Emotional Style*. New York: New York University Press, 1994.

Steele, Jonathan. "Who Started It?" [Review of Odd Arne Westad, *The Cold War*, 2017.] *London Review of Books* (25 January 2018), 23–25.

Steele, M. William. "Mobility on the Move: Rickshaws in Asia." *Transfers* 4, no. 3 (2004): 88–107.

———. "A Modern Infrastructure of Manchukuo: Where Did All the Cement Come From?" Paper presented at the East Asian Environmental History Conference, Kagawa University, Japan, 22–25 October 2015.

———. "Roads, Bridges, Tunnels and Empire: Highway Construction and the Great East Asian Co-prosperity Sphere." Unpublished manuscript since published in *Asian Cultural Studies* 42 (2016): 87–101.

Steg, Linda. "Car Use: Lust and Must—Instrumental, Symbolic and Affective Motives for Car Use." *Transportation Research Part A* 39, nos. 2–3 (2005): 147–162.

Steg, Linda, Karst Geurs, and Michael Ras. "The Effects of Motivational Factors on Car Use: A Multidisciplinary Modelling Approach." *Transportation Research Part A* 35, no. 9 (2001): 789–806.

Stein, Susanne. "'Wir haben nur etwas mehr als zwei Jahre gebraucht . . .': Die Umgestaltung Changchuns zur ersten 'Autostadt' des neuen China, 1953–1956." In *Autostädte im 20. Jahrhundert: Wachstums- und Schrumpfungsprozesse in globaler Perspektive*, edited by Martina Hessler and Günter Riederer (Stuttgart: Franz Steiner Verlag, 2014), 147–165.

*Steinbeck, John. *Travels with Charley: In Search of America*. New York: Penguin, 1986.

Stella, Simonetta Piccone. "'Rebels without a Cause': Male Youth in Italy around 1960." *History Workshop* 38, no. 1 (1994): 157–178.

Stern, Barbara. "Pleasure and Persuasion in Advertising: Rhetorical Irony as a Humor Technique." *Current Issues and Research in Advertising* 12, nos. 1–2 (1990): 25–42.

Sterritt, David. *The Films of Jean-Luc Goddard: Seeing the Invisible*. Cambridge: Cambridge University Press, 1999.

Stoler, Ann Laura, and Frederick Cooper. "Between Metropole and Colony: Rethinking a Research Agenda." In *Tensions of Empire: Colonial Cultures in a Bourgeois World*, edited by Frederick Cooper and Ann Laura Stoler (Berkeley: University of California Press, 1997), 1–56.

Stone, Michael Cutler. "*Bajito y suavectio* [Low and Slow]: Low Riding and the 'Class' of 'Class.'" *Studies in Latin American Popular Culture* 9 (1990): 85–126.

Stradling, David. *The Nature of New York: An Environmental History of the Empire State*. Ithaca, NY: Cornell University Press, 2010.

Strand, David. "'A High Place Is No Better Than a Low Place': The City in the Making of Modern China." In Yeh, *Becoming Chinese*, 98–136.

———. *Rickshaw Beijing: City People and Politics in the 1920s*. Berkeley: University of California Press, 1989.

Strand, Ginger. *Killer on the Road: Violence and the American Interstate*. Austin: University of Texas Press, 2012.

Street, John. "Youth Culture." In Johnson, *Twentieth-Century Britain*, 460–475.

Streeter, Stephen M. "The Failure of 'Liberal Developmentalism': The United States's Anti-Communist Showcase in Guatemala, 1954–1960." *International History Review* 21, no. 2 (1999): 285–413.

Südbeck, Thomas. *Motorisierung. Verkehrsentwicklung und Verkehrspolitik in der Bundesrepublik Deutschland der 1950er Jahre: Umrisse der allgemeinen Entwicklung und zwei Beispiele: Hamburg und das Emsland*. Stuttgart: Franz Steiner Verlag, 1994.

Sun, Yat-sen. *The International Development of China*. Shanghai: Commercial Press, 1920.

Sutton, Francis X., Tom G. Kessenger, James P. Grant, and George Zeidenstein. "Development Ideology: Its Emergence and Decline [with Comments]." *Daedalus* 118, no. 1 (1989): 35–60.
Sweeney, Gael. "The King of White Trash Culture: Elvis Presley and the Aesthetics of Excess." In *White Trash: Race and Class in America*, ed. Matt Wray and Annalee Newitz (New York: Routledge, 1997), 249–266.
Talbot, Jill Lynn. "This Is Not An Exit: The Road Narrative in Contemporary American Literature and Film." PhD diss., Texas Tech University, 1999.
Tani, Toru. "Transzendenz und Medium." In *Figuren der Transzendenz: Transformationen eines phänomenologischen Grundbegriffs*, edited by Michael Staudigl and Christian Sternad (Würzburg: Königshausen & Neumann, 2014), 143–161.
Tao, Xu. "Making a Living: Bicycle-related Professions in Shanghai, 1897–1949." *Transfers* 3, no. 3 (2013): 6–26.
Tastevin, Yann-Philippe. "Autorickshaw (1948– 2 . . .): A Success Story." *Techniques & Culture* 58, no. 1 (2012): 264–277.
Tate, J. O. "The Essential Essex." *The Flannery O'Connor Bulletin* 12 (1983): 47–59.
Taunton, Matthew. *Fictions of the City: Class, Culture and Mass Housing in London and Paris*. London: Palgrave Macmillan, 2009.
Terranova, Charissa. "Mobile Perception and the Automotive Prosthetic: Photoconceptualism, the Car, and the Posthuman Subject." *Transfers* 1, no. 1 (2011): 73–96.
Tetzlaff, Stefan. "The Motorisation of the 'Mofussil': Automobile Traffic and Social Change in Rural and Small-Town India, c. 1915–1940." PhD diss., University of Göttingen, 2015.
Thacker, Andrew. "E. M. Forster and the Motor Car." *Literature & History* 9, no. 2 (2000): 37–52.
Thelle, Mikkel. "Subversive Mobilities: The Copenhagen Riots, 1900–1919." *Transfers* 3, no. 1 (2013): 7–25.
Thompson, Hunter S. *Hell's Angels*. New York: Ballantine, 1996.
Thompson, Robert Farris. "*Tap-Tap, Fula-Fula, Kiá-Kiá*: The Haitian Bus in Atlantic Perspective." *African Arts* 29, no. 2 (1996): 36–45, 101–102.
Thorner, Daniel. "Great Britain and the Development of India's Railways." *Journal of Economic History* 11, no. 4 (1951): 389–402.
Thrift, Nigel. "Intensities of Feeling: Towards a Spatial Politics of Affect." *Geografiska Annaler* 86B, no. 1 (2004): 57–78.
Tomlinson, John. *The Culture of Speed: The Coming of Immediacy*. Los Angeles: Sage, 2007.
Topik, Steven C., and Allen Wells. "Commodity Chains in a Global Economy." In *A World Connecting 1870–1945*, edited by Emily S. Rosenberg (Cambridge, MA: Belknap Press, 2012), 591–812.
Tóth, Katalin. "The Invisible Cyclist and the History of Mobility in Budapest (1930–2010)." Paper presented at the CPSUM workshop in Munich, 5–6 February 2016.
*Tseng, P'u [Zeng, Pu]. "A Flower in a Sinful Sea." Translated by Rafe de Crespigny and Liu Ts'un-yan [Liu Cunren]. In Ts'un-yan [Cunren], *Chinese Middlebrow Fiction*, 137–192.
Tshund'olela, Epanya Sh. "Motor Transport in a Developing Area (i): Zaïre, 1903–1959." In Barker, *Economic and Social Effects of the Spread of Motor Vehicles*, 236–255.
Tsunematsu, Sammy I. "Introduction." In Sōseki, *Spring Miscellany and London Essays*, 7–12.
Tsurumi, Shunsuke. *A Cultural History of Postwar Japan 1945–1980*. London: KPI, 1987.
Tu, Wei-ming. "Cultural China: The Periphery as the Center." *Daedalus* 120, no. 2 (1991): 1–32.
———. "Implications of the Rise of 'Confucian' East Asia." *Daedalus* 129, no. 1 (2000): 195–218.

Tuck, Stephen. *We Ain't What We Ought to Be: The Black Freedom Struggle from Emancipation to Obama*. Cambridge, MA: Belknap Press, 2010.
Turnbull, C. Mary. *A Short History of Malaysia, Singapore and Brunei*. Singapore: Graham Brash, 1988.
Turse, Nick. *Kill Anything That Moves: The Real American War in Vietnam*. New York: Henry Holt & Co., 2013.
Tworek-Müller, Elisabeth. *Kleinbürgertum und Literatur: Zum Bild des Kleinbürgers im bayerischen Roman der Weimarer Republik*. Munich: tuduv-Verlagsgesellschaft, 1985.
Unger, Corinna R. "Histories of Development and Modernization: Findings, Reflections, Future Research." H-Soz-Kult, 9 December 2010. http://www.hsozkult.de/hfn/literaturereview/id/forschungsberichte-1130
———. "Industrialization vs. Agrarian Reform: West German Modernization Policies in India in the 1950s and 1960s." *Journal of Modern European History*, 8, no. 1 (2010): 47–65.
*Updike, John. *The Early Stories: 1953–1975*. New York: Ballantine, 2004.
———. *Higher Gossip: Essays and Criticism*. Edited by Christopher Carduff. New York: Random House, 2011.
———. "Introduction." In Updike, *Rabbit Angstrom*, vii–xxii.
*———. *Rabbit Angstrom: A Tetralogy*. New York: Everyman's Library, 1995.
*———. *Rabbit Is Rich*. In Updike, *Rabbit Angstrom*, 621–1045.
*———. *Rabbit Redux*. In Updike, *Rabbit Angstrom*, 265–619.
*———. *Rabbit Run*. In Updike, *Rabbit Angstrom*, 3–264.
Urry, John. *Mobilities*. Cambridge: Polity, 2007.
———. "Moving on the Mobility Turn." In *Tracing Mobilities: Towards a Cosmopolitan Perspective*, edited by Weert Canzler, Vincent Kaufmann, and Sven Kesselring (Aldershot: Ashgate, 2008), 13–23.
———. *The Tourist Gaze: Leisure and Travel in Contemporary Societies*. London: Sage, 1990.
US Department of Transportation. *Highway Statistics Series 2017*. Washington, DC: DOT, 2018.
Vaaranen, Heli. "The Emotional Experience of Class: Interpreting Working-Class Kids' Street Racing in Helsinki." *Annals of the American Academy of Political and Social Science* 595 (September 2004) ("Being Here and Being There: Fieldwork Encounters and Ethnographic Discoveries"), 91–107.
Vaaranen, Heli, and Neil Wieloch. "Car Crashes and Dead End Careers: Leisure Pursuits of the Finnish Subculture of the *Kortteliralli* Street Racing." *Young* 10, no. 1 (2002): 42–58.
Van der Bent, Jaap, Mel van Elteren, and Cornelis A. van Minnen. "Introduction." In Van Minnen et al., *Beat Culture*, 1–11.
*Van der Geest, Sjaak. "'Anyway!' Lorry Inscriptions in Ghana." In Gewald et al., *Speed of Change*, 253–293.
Van der Steen, Paul. "Luilekkerland van de liefde," *Historisch Nieuwsblad* 24, nos. 7–8 (2015): 20–29.
Van Dongen, Irene S. "Road versus Rail in Africa." *Geographical Review* 52, no. 2 (1962): 296–298.
Van Doren, Carl. "Introduction." In Frederic Prokosch, *Asiatics*, v–vii.
Van Elteren, Mel. "The Culture of the Subterraneans: A Sociological View of the Beats," in Van Minnen et al., *Beat Culture*, 63–92.
———. "In het teken van vrijheid: Amerikaanse cultuur en jongeren in hun vrije tijd na 1945." In *Van ontspanning en inspanning: Aspecten van de geschiedenis van de vrije tijd*,

edited by K. P. C. de Leeuw, M. F. A. Linders-Rooijendijk, and P. J. M. Martens (Tilburg: Gianotten, 1995), 63–86.

Van Minne, Cornelis A., Jaap van der Bent, and Mel van Elteren eds. *Beat Culture: The 1950s and Beyond*. Amsterdam: VU University Press, 1999.

*Van Ronk, Dave, with Elijah Wald. *The Mayor of MacDougal Street: A Memoir*. Foreword by Lawrence Block. Philadelphia: Da Capo Press, 2013.

Van Slooten, Jessica Lyn. "Sexism and Misogyny." In *Beat Culture: Icons, Lifestyles, and Impact*, edited by William T. Lawlor (Santa Barbara, CA: ABC Clio, 2005), 324–325.

Van Walraven, Klaas. "Vehicles of Sedition: The Role of Transport Workers in Sawaba's Rebellion in Niger, 1954–1966." In Gewald et al., *Speed of Change*, 75–103.

Van Zanden, Jan Luiten. *Een klein land in de 20ᵉ eeuw: Economische geschiedenis van Nederland 1914–1995*. Utrecht: Het Spectrum, 1997.

Vance, J. D. *Hillbilly Elegy: A Memoir of a Family and Culture in Crisis*. London: William Collins, 2017.

Vandertop, Caitlin. "Travel Literature and the Infrastructural Unconscious." In *New Directions in Travel Writing Studies*, edited by Julia Kuehn and Paul Smethurst (London: Palgrave Macmillan, 2015), 129–144.

Varady, Robert Gabriel. "North Indian Banjaras: Their Evolution as Transporters." *South Asia: Journal of South Asian Studies* 2, no. 2 (1979): 1–18.

Varaprasad, N. "Providing Mobility and Accessibility." In Singh Sandhu and Wheatley, eds., *Management of Success*, 420–435.

Vari, Alexander. "Introduction: Escaping the Monotony of Everyday Life under Socialism." In *Socialist Escapes: Breaking Away from Ideology and Everyday Routine in Eastern Europe, 1945–1989*, edited by Cathleen M. Giustino, Catherine J. Plum and Alexander Vari (New York: Berghahn Books, 2013), 1–23.

Vasconcellos, Eduardo Alcântara. "The Making of the Middle-Class City: Transportation Policy in São Paulo." *Environment and Planning A* 29, no. 2 (1997): 293–310.

———. "Urban Development and Traffic Accidents in Brazil." *Accident Analysis and Prevention* 31, no. 4 (1999): 319–328.

Vasquez Barquero, Antonio, and Michael Hebbert. "Spain: Economy and State in Transition." In *Uneven Development in Southern Europe: Studies of Accumulation, Class, Migration and the State*, edited by Ray Hudson and Jim Lewis (London: Methuen, 1985), 284–308.

Vaughan, Mary Kay, and Stephen E. Lewis, eds. *The Eagle and the Virgin: Nation and Cultural Revolution in Mexico, 1920–1940*, edited by Mary Kay Vaughan and Stephen E. Lewis (Durham, NC: Duke University Press, 2006), 1–20.

Vaughan, Mary Kay, and Stephen E. Lewis. "Introduction." In Vaughan and Lewis, *Eagle and the Virgin*, 1–20.

Veblen, Thorstein. *The Theory of the Leisure Class*. New York: Dover Publications, 1994.

Venn, Fiona. *The Oil Crisis*. London: Pearson Education, 2002.

Veracini, Lorenzo. *Settler Colonialism: A Theoretical Overview*. London: Palgrave Macmillan, 2010.

*Vidal, Gore. *Myra Breckinridge*. New York: Bantam Books, 1968.

Vidich, Arthur J., and Joseph Bensman. *Small Town in Mass Society: Class, Power and Religion in a Rural Community*. Princeton, NJ: Princeton University Press, 1968.

Vieban, Frédéric. "L'Image de l'automobile auprès des Français 1930–1950." Unpublished Mémoire de maîtrise, Histoire Contemporaine, Université F. Rabelais, Tours, 1987.

Vielma-Cabruja, José Ignacio. "Transfers, Influences and Experiences: Notes on the Development of Expressways in Caracas (1947–1973) and Its Actual Expression." Paper presented at the workshop "Transport and Mobility Studies in Latin America," School of

Architecture and Urban Studies of the University of Chile, Santiago de Chile, 8–9 July 2013.
Vincent, Joan, ed. *The Anthropology of Politics: A Reader in Ethnography, Theory, and Critique.* Malden, MA: Blackwell, 2002.
Vingilis, Evelyn, and Reginald G. Smart. "Street Racing: A Neglected Research Area?" *Traffic Injury Protection* 10, no. 2 (2009): 148–156.
"Vision and Actions on Jointly Building Silk Road Economic Belt and 21st-Century Maritime Silk Road: Issued by the National Development and Reform Commission, Ministry of Foreign Affairs, and Ministry of Commerce of the People's Republic of China, with State Council Authorization." News release, 28 March 2015. https://reconasia-production.s3.amazonaws.com/media/filer_public/e0/22/e0228017-7463-46fc-9094-0465a6f1ca23/vision_and_actions_on_jointly_building_silk_road_economic_belt_and_21st-century_maritime_silk_road.pdf.
Vogel, Ezra F. *Deng Xiaoping and the Transformation of China.* Cambridge, MA: Belknap Press, 2013.
———. *Japan's New Middle Class: The Salary Man and His Family in a Tokyo Suburb.* Berkeley: University of California Press, 1971.
———. "A Little Dragon Tamed." In Singh Sandhu and Wheatley, *Management of Success*, 1049–1066.
Vogel, Regina. "Bürgertum nach 1945? Deutschland, Frankreich und Britannien im Vergleich." In *Selbstverständnis und Gesellschaft der Europäer: Aspekte der sozialen und kulturellen Europäisierung im späten 19. und 20. Jahrhundert*, ed. Hartmut Kaelble and Martin Kirsch (Frankfurt: Peter Lang, 2008), 381–417.
Vohra, Ranbir. *Lao She and the Chinese Revolution.* Cambridge, MA: Harvard University Press, 1974.
Vu, Linh D. "Careless and Carless Natives: Automobile Accidents and the Project of Modernity in French Indochina." *Sojourn: Journal of Social Issues in Southeast Asia* 27, no. 2 (2012): 329–341.
Wallerstein, Immanuel. *World-Systems Analysis: An Introduction.* Durham, NC: Duke University Press, 2004.
Walther, Gerrit. "Auf der Suche nach der 'Gattung': Interdisziplinäre Reiseliteraturforschung." [Book review essay.] *Archiv für Sozialgeschichte* 32 (1992): 523–533.
Wang, Chaohua. "Introduction: Minds of the Nineties." In *One China, Many Paths*, edited by Chaohua Wang (London: Verso, 2003), 9–45.
Wang, Hui. *The End of the Revolution: China and the Limits of Modernity.* London: Verso, 2009.
Wang, Jiafeng. "Some Reflections on Modernization Theory and Globalization Theory." *Chinese Studies in History* 43, no. 1 (2009): 72–98.
Wang, Q. Edward. "Globalization, Global History and Local Identity in 'Greater China.'" *History Compass* 8, no. 4 (2010): 320–329.
Wang, Xudong, and Junxiang Li. "Modernization and the Study of Modern Chinese History: A Brief Thesis." *Chinese Studies in History* 43, no. 1 (2009): 46–60.
Ward, Stephen V. *Planning the Twentieth-Century City: The Advanced Capitalist World.* Chichester: John Wiley and Sons, 2002.
Warren, James Francis. *Rickshaw Coolie: A People's History of Singapore 1880–1940.* Singapore: Singapore University Press, 2003.
Waters, Somerset R. "The American Tourist." *Annals of the American Academy of Political and Social Science* 368 (1966) 109–118.

Waters, Wendy. "Remapping Identities: Road Construction and Nation Building in Postrevolutionary Mexico." In Vaughan and Lewis, *Eagle and the Virgin*, 221–242.
Watt, Carey A. "Introduction: The Relevance and Complexity of Civilizing Missions c. 1800–2010." In Watt and Mann, *Civilizing Missions in Colonial and Postcolonial South Asia*, 1–34.
Watt, Carey A., and Michael Mann, eds. *Civilizing Missions in Colonial and Postcolonial South Asia: From Improvement to Development*. London: Anthem Press, 2011.
*Weesner, Theodore. *The Car Thief*. New York: Grove Press, 2001.
Wehler, Hans-Ulrich. "Deutsches Bürgertum nach 1945: Exitus oder Phönix aus der Asche? " *Geschichte und Gesellschaft* 27 (2001): 617–634.
———. *Modernisierungstheorie und Geschichte*. Göttingen: Vandenhoeck & Ruprecht, 1975.
Weigelin-Schwiedrzik, Susanne, and Kim Rottenberger-Kwok. "Chinese Migration im Indischen Ozean." In *Der Indische Ozean: Das afro-asiatische Mittelmeer als Kultur- und Wirtschaftsraum*, edited by Dietmar Rothermund and Susanne Weigelin-Schwiedrzik (Vienna: Verein für Geschichte und Sozialkunde / Promedia Verlag, 2004), 145–164.
Weir, Margaret. "The American Middle Class and the Politics of Education." In Zunz et al., *Social Contracts Under Stress*, 178–203.
Wells, Christopher W. *Car Country: An Environmental History*. Foreword by William Cronon. Seattle: University of Washington Press, 2012.
Westad, Odd Arne. *The Global Cold War: Third World Interventions and the Making of Our Times*. Cambridge: Cambridge University Press, 2014.
———. "The Great Transformation: China in the Long 1970s." In *The Shock of the Global: The 1970s in Perspective*, edited by Niall Ferguson, Charles S. Maier, Erez Manela, and Daniel J. Sargent (Cambridge, MA: Belknap Press, 2010), 65–79.
Westwood, J. N. "Soviet Railway Development." *Soviet Studies* 11, no. 1 (2001): 22–48.
White, Landeg. *Magomero: Portrait of an African Village*. Cambridge: Cambridge University Press, 2000.
White, Luise. "Cars Out of Place: Vampires, Technology, and Labor in East and Central Africa." In *Tensions of Empire: Colonial Cultures in a Bourgeois World*, edited by Frederick Cooper and Ann Laura Stoler (Berkeley: University of California Press, 1997), 436–460.
White, Richard. "The Retreat from Adventure: Popular Travel Writing in the 1950s." *Australian Historical Studies* 28, no. 109 (1997): 90–105.
White, Roger B. *Home on the Road: The Motor Home in America*. Washington: Smithsonian Institution Press, 2000.
Whyte, William H., Jr. "The Cadillac Phenomenon." *Fortune* (February 1955): 106–109, 174–184.
Wicke, Peter. "Music, Dissidence, Revolution, and Commerce: Youth Culture between Mainstream and Subculture." In Schildt and Siegfried, *Between Marx and Coca-Cola*, 109–126.
Wierzbicka, Anna. *Imprisoned in English: The Hazards of English as a Default Language*. Oxford: Oxford University Press, 2014.
Wightman, David. *Towards Economic Cooperation in Asia: The United Nations Economic Commission for Asia and the Far East*. New Haven, CT: Yale University Press, 1963.
Wildt, Michael. *Am Beginn der "Konsumgesellschaft": Mangelerfahrung, Lebenshaltung, Wohlstandshoffnung in Westdeutschland in den fünfziger Jahren*. Hamburg: Ergebnisse Verlag, 1995.
———. "Konsumbürger: Das Politische als Optionsfreiheit und Distinktion." In Hettling and Ulrich, *Bürgertum nach 1945*, 255–283.
*Williams, John A. *This Is My Country Too*. New York: Signet, 1966.

Williams, Raymond. *Television: Technology and Cultural Form*. London: Routledge, 2003.
*Williams, Stanley T. *Two in a Topolino*. Rindge, NH: Richard R. Smith, 1956.
Williams, William Carlos. "The Virtue of History." *In the American Grain* (New York: Albert & Charles Boni, 1925) 188–207.
Williamson, Judith. *Decoding Advertisements: Ideology and Meaning in Advertising*. London: Marion Boyars, 1995.
Williamson, Thomas. "The Fluid State: Malaysia's National Expressway." *Space & Culture* 6, no. 2 (2003): 110–131.
Willis, Paul E. *Profane Culture*. London: Routledge & Kegan Paul, 1978.
Wilson, Fiona. "The Conflict between Indigenous and Immigrant Commercial Systems in the Peruvian Central Sierra, 1900–1940." In *Region and Class in Modern Peruvian History*, edited by Rory Miller (Liverpool: University of Liverpool, Institute of Latin American Studies, 1987), 125–161.
———. "Towards a Political Economy of Roads: Experiences from Peru." *Development and Change* 35, no. 3 (2004): 525–546.
Wilson, George W. "Toward a Theory of Transport and Development." In *The Impact of Highway Investment on Development* by George W. Wilson, Barbara R. Bergmann, Leon V. Hirsch, and Martin S. Klein (Washington, DC: Brookings Institution, 1966), 190–218.
———. "What the Cases Show." In *The Impact of Highway Investment on Development* by George W. Wilson, Barbara R. Bergmann, Leon V. Hirsch, and Martin S. Klein (Washington, DC: Brookings Institution, 1966), 174–189.
Winchester, Simon. *Bomb, Book and Compass: Joseph Needham and the Great Secrets of China*. London: Penguin, 2009.
Wirsching, Andreas. "From Work to Consumption. Transatlantic Visions of Individuality in Modern Mass Society." *Contemporary European History* 20, no. 1 (2011): 1–26.
Wiser, William H., and Charlotte Viall Wiser. *Behind Mud Walls 1930–1960, with a Sequel: The Village in 1970*. Foreword by David G. Mandelbaum. Berkeley: University of California Press, 1971.
Wittrock, Björn. "Modernity: One, None, or Many? European Origins and Modernity as a Global Condition." *Daedalus* 129, no. 1 (2000): 31–60.
Wolf, Winfried. *Eisenbahn und Autowahn: Personen- und Gütertransport auf Schiene und Strasse—Geschichte, Bilanz, Perspektiven*. Hamburg: Rasch & Röhring Verlag, 1992.
*Wolfe, Bernard. *Limbo*. New York: Carroll & Graf Publishers, 1987.
Wolfe, Joel. *Autos and Progress: The Brazilian Search for Modernity*. Oxford: Oxford University Press, 2010.
Wolfe, Tom. *The Electric Kool-Aid Acid Test*. New York: Bantam Books, 1999.
———. "The Last American Hero Is Junior Johnson. Yes!" *Esquire*, 1 March 1965, 1–22. https://classic.esquire.com/article/1965/3/1/junior-johnson.
Wolff, Janet. "On the Road Again: Metaphors of Travel in Cultural Criticism." *Cultural Studies* 7, no. 2 (1993): 224–239.
Wolmar, Christian. *Engines of War: How Wars Were Won and Lost on the Railways*. London: Atlantic Books, 2012.
Wood, James. "Gossip in Git." *London Review of Books* 23, no. 8 (2001): 31–32.
Wood, Patrick M. "The BIS: Bank for International Settlements." *August Review* 5, no. 11 (14 October 2005). http://www.bibliotecapleyades.net/sociopolitica/sociopol_globalbanking04.htm.
World Bank. *World Development Report 1994: Infrastructure for Development*. Oxford: Oxford University Press, 1994.

Wright, Tim. "Shanghai Imperialists versus Rickshaw Racketeers: The Defeat of the 1934 Rickshaw Reforms." *Modern China* 17, no. 1 (1991): 76–111.
Xu, Luo. *Searching for Life's Meaning: Changes and Tensions in the Worldviews of Chinese Youth in the 1980s*. Ann Arbor: University of Michigan Press, 2001.
Yamaguchi, Ikuto. "The Development and Activities of the Economic Commission for Asia and the Far East (ECAFE), 1947–65." In Akita et al., *Transformation of the International Order*, 91–108.
Yamamoto, Hirofumi. "Roads." In Yamamoto, *Technological Innovation*, 244–253.
———, ed., *Technological Innovation and the Development of Transportation in Japan*. Tokyo: United Nations University Press, 1993.
Yao, Souchou. "Introduction." In *House of Glass: Culture, Modernity, and the State in Southeast Asia*, edited by Yao Souchou (Singapore: Institute of Southeast Asian Studies, 2001), 1–23.
Yeh, When-hsin. *Becoming Chinese: Passages to Modernity and Beyond*. Berkeley: University of California Press, 2000.
*Yosano, Akiko. *Travels in Manchuria and Mongolia: A Feminist Poet from Japan Encounters Prewar China*. Translated by Joshua A. Fogel. New York: Columbia University Press, 2001.
Yoshino, I. Roger. "The Stereotype of the Negro and His High-Priced Car." *Sociology and Social Research* 44 (November–December 1959): 112–118.
Young, Alex Trimble. "Settler Sovereignty and the Rhizomatic West, or, the Significance of the Frontier in Postwestern Studies." *Western American Literature* 48, nos. 1–2 (2013): 115–140.
Young, Arthur N. *China's Nation-Building Effort, 1927–1937: The Financial and Economic Record*. Stanford, CA: Hoover Institution Press, 1971.
Young, Louise. *Beyond the Metropolis: Second Cities and Modern Life in Interwar Japan*. Berkeley: University of California Press, 2013.
———. "Marketing the Modern: Department Stores, Consumer Culture, and the New Middle Class in Interwar Japan." *International Labor and Working-Class History* 55 (1999): 52–70.
Young, Ray. "Cocksucker Blues." *Flickhead* (2004). https://web.archive.org/web/20150930223332/http://home.comcast.net/~flickhead/Cocksucker-Blues.html.
Youngs, Tim. "Introduction." *Studies in Travel Writing* 17, no. 4 (2013): 331–334.
———. "Where Are We Going? Cross-Border Approaches to Travel Writing." In Hooper and Youngs, *Perspectives on Travel Writing*, 167–180.
Yoshimi, Shunya. "Consuming America, Producing Japan." Translated by David Buist. In Garon and Maclachlan, *Ambivalent Consumer*, 63–84.
Yu, Beoncheon. "Introduction." In Sōseki, *Wayfarer*, 9–26.
Yu, Guangyuan. "Accomplishments and Problems: A Review of China's Reform in the Past Twenty-Three Years." In *The Chinese Model of Modern Development*, edited by Tian Yu Cao (London: Routledge, 2005), 23–53.
Zeitlin, Jonathan. "Introduction: Americanization and Its Limits: Reworking US Technology and Management in Post-war Europe and Japan." In Jonathan Zeitlin and Gary Herrigel, eds. *Americanization and Its Limits: Reworking US Technology and Management in Post-war Europe and Japan* (Oxford: Oxford University Press, 2000), 1–50.
[Zewuster, A.] *Een miljoen auto's in 1964*. Amsterdam: De Arbeiderspers, January 1963.
Zha, Jianying. "Introduction." In Ji, *Cowshed*, vii–xvii.
Zhang, Jun. "Driving toward Modernity: An Ethnography of Automobiles in Contemporary China." Diss., Yale University, 2009.
*Zhang, Henshui. *Shanghai Express: A Thirties Novel*. Translated William A. Lyell. Honolulu: University of Hawai'i Press, 1997.

Zhang, Sheng. "Rickshaw and China's New Literature 1917–1927." Paper presented at the conference "Mobility in Daily Life." Shanghai Academy of Social Sciences, 4–7 January 2012.
Zhang, Xinxin, and Ye Sang. *Chinese Lives: An Oral History of Contemporary China*. Edited by W. J. F. Jenner and Delia Davin. New York: Pantheon Books, 1987.
Zhang, Xun-Hai. *Enterprise Reforms in a Centrally Planned Economy: The Case of the Chinese Bicycle Industry*. New York: St. Martin's Press, 1992.
Zhong, Xueping. *Masculinity Besieged? Issues of Modernity and Male Subjectivity in Chinese Literature of the Late Twentieth Century*. Durham, NC: Duke University Press, 2000.
Zhu, Zhiqun. *Understanding East Asia's Economic "Miracles."* Ann Arbor, MI: Association for Asian Studies, 2012.
Zizek [sic], Slavoj. "What Can Psychoanalysis Tell Us about Cyberspace?" *Psychoanalytic Review* 91, no. 6 (2004): 801–830.
Zuckerman, Marvin. *Behavioral Expressions and Biosocial Bases of Sensation Seeking*. Cambridge: Cambridge University Press, 1994.
Zunz, Olivier, Leonard Schoppa, and Nobuhiro Hiwatari, eds. *Social Contracts Under Stress: The Middle Classes of America, Europe, and Japan at the Turn of the Century*. New York: Russell Sage Foundation 2002.

Songs

Acruff, Roy. "The Wreck on the Highway." *Genius*, 27 October 2019. https://genius.com/Roy-acuff-the-wreck-on-the-highway-lyrics.
The Beatles. "Drive My Car" (1965). *LyricsMode*, accessed 27 October 2019. http://www.lyricsmode.com/lyrics/b/beatles/drive_my_car.html.
The Beach Boys. "Little Honda" (1964). *SongMeanings*, accessed 27 October 2019. https://songmeanings.com/songs/view/80401.
Berry, Chuck. "Maybellene" (1955). *SongLyrics*, accessed 27 October 2019, http://www.songlyrics.com/chuck-berry/maybellene-lyrics.
Brown, James. "It's a Man's Man's Man's World" (1966). *AZLyrics*, accessed 27 October 2019. https://www.azlyrics.com/lyrics/jamesbrown/itsamansmansmansworld.html.
Canned Heat. "On the Road Again" (1968). *Genius*, accessed 27 October 2019. https://genius.com/Canned-heat-on-the-road-again-lyrics.
Dickens, Little Jimmy. "The Sign on the Highway" (1951). *Songs-Lyrics*, accessed 27 October 2019. https://www.songs-lyrics.net/so-%27LITTLE%27-JIMMY-DICKENS-lyrics-COUNTRY-BOY-01-lyrics-SIGN-BY-THE-HIGHWAY-lyrics-kgjhifvi.html.
The Doors. "The Cars Hiss by My Window" (1971). *Genius*, accessed 27 October 2019. https://genius.com/The-doors-cars-hiss-by-my-window-lyrics.
The Duals. "Stick Shift" (1961). Video, 3:10. Uploaded by doktorsung, 10 July 2010. https://www.youtube.com/watch?v=Qp1FpvEA1H0.
The Flying Burrito Brothers. "Six Days on the Road" (1972). *Genius*, accessed 27 October 2019. https://genius.com/Flying-burrito-brothers-six-days-on-the-road-lyrics.
Gladys Knight & the Pips. "Midnight Train to Georgia," (1973). *Genius*, accessed 27 October 2019. https://genius.com/Gladys-knight-and-the-pips-midnight-train-to-georgia-lyrics
Golden Earring. "Radar Love" (1973). *AZLyrics*, accessed 27 October 2019. http://www.azlyrics.com/lyrics/goldenearring/radarlove.html.
Led Zeppelin. "Trampled Underfoot" (1975). *Genius*, accessed 17 November 2019. https://genius.com/Led-zeppelin-trampled-under-foot-lyrics.

Rolling Stones. "(I Can't Get No) Satisfaction" (1965). *AZLyrics*, accessed 27 October 2019. https://www.azlyrics.com/lyrics/rollingstones/icantgetnosatisfaction.html.

Steppenwolf. "Born to Be Wild" (1968). *Genius*, accessed 27 October 2019. https://genius.com/Steppenwolf-born-to-be-wild-lyrics.

Stewart, Rod. "Let Me Be Your Car" (1974). *AZLyrics*, accessed 27 October 2019. http://www.azlyrics.com/lyrics/rodstewart/letmebeyourcar.html.

Warwick, Dionne. "Do You Know the Way to San José" *Genius*, accessed 27 October 2019. https://genius.com/Dionne-warwick-do-you-know-the-way-to-san-jose-lyrics.

The Who. "Going Mobile" (1971). *AZLyrics*, accessed 27 October 2019. https://www.azlyrics.com/lyrics/who/goinmobile.html.

INDEX

Page numbers in italics indicate a definition or central treatment of the term. Only those contemporary scholars have been included whose names appear in the text more than in passing.

A

Abercrombie, Patrick, 426
absent car, 30, 109, *299–305*, 336, 566. *See also* abstractification
absent train, 329
abstractification (of the car), 292, 297, 305, 337, 570
    of middle class culture, 332
    See also absent car
accessibility, 415, *469*, 493, 504, 512, 531
action movies, 336
Acuff, Roy, 345
Allgemeine Deutsche Automobilclub ADAC, 434
Adorno, Theodor, 269, 299
adventure/adventurous, 1, 2, *13–17*, 24, 27, 40–42, 43, 60, 66, 68, 80, 82, 84, 88, 97–98, 107–10, 130–32, 145, 149–152, 157–158, 168, 171, 176–178, 214, 218–219, 221, 222, 227, 230, 244, 247, 250, 258, 263, 264, 279, 282, 284–301, 305–310, 312, 315, 316, 321–35, 338–342, 347, 349–50, 392, 398, 411–412, 419, 448, 475, 498, 501, 515, 521, 563, 569–571
    bus driving in Nigeria, 495

    conquest, 6, *15*, 145, 149–151, 159, 175, 214–215, 284, 286, 326, 332, 339, 341, 379n199, 483, 566
    demystification of the car, 372n150
    domestication, 293
    as elite privilege, 98
    fear of, 300
    flight experience, 10, 12, 90, 150, 159, 167, 292, 295, 298, 307, 314, 326, 331, 337
    fragmented, 340–341
    functional (tinkering), 5, 25, 229, 284, 294, 306, 310, 320, 329, 510, 566
    multisensorial, 321
    as near-death experience, 321, 328, 335
    rickshaw culture, 80, 82
    romantic motorcycle culture (Indian movies), 419
    spatial (roaming), 5, 263, 284, 293, 294, 309, 316, 329, 339, 349, 566
    tamed, 8–9, 15, 209, 282, 284, 298–299, 569–570
    temporal (speed), 5, 214, 284, 316, 320–321, 329, 339, 566
    touring, 287
    urban car, 250
    See also beat car culture, driving skills, female (automotive) adventure, flower parade, gymkhana
adventure beyond the West, 563
adventure machine, xv, 4, *5–13*, 90, 97, 152, 155, 159–60, 168, 169, 172, 209, 315, 324, 329, 495, 510, 562, 564–67

adventure novels, 107
adventurers, 165
   khat drivers (Africa), 494
advertisements, *16–17*, 22–23, 47nn33–35, 147, 214, 242, *280–282*, 312.
   See also consumption
affinity, *10*, 12, 38, 45n19, 52n75, 213, 222–23, 244, 270, 298
   between car driving and writing, 11, 61, 222, 289–290
   between mobility and music, 209, 213, 243–244, 289, 299–300, 330
   between television and the world of the car, 262
Agamben, Giorgio, 349–350
Ağaoğlu, Adalet, 390
Agee, James, 345
agency (and the car), 321, 324, 350, 378n193, 418
aggression, 7, 9, 70, 108, 174, 178, 226–227, 244, 274, 311, 313, *316–317*, 333, 341, 419, 524. See also violence
Agnew, Spiro, 317
Aguiar, Marian, 456–457
AIPCR. See PIARC
Aldcroft, Derek, 120
Alemán, President Miguel, 512–513, 521
Allen, Woody, 336
Alliance for Progress, 446, 505, 525
Alliance Internationale de Tourisme (AIT), 150
Almanacs, The, 213
Altman, Robert, 336
Alvarez, President Luis Echeverria, 508
Ambassador (Indian car model), 417, 419
Amburn, Ellis, 293
Americanization, 232, 236, 238, 446
Amin, Shahid, 122
Aminurrashid, Harun, 131
Andersch, Alfred, 326
Angola, 137, 338, 460, 502–503
angry young men, 327
animal traction
   four-wheel *andong*, 480
   two-wheel *dokar*, 480
   See also camel transport, caravan, carriage, cart, donkey, horse statistics, llama, mule, pack animals, elephants

Animals, The, 223, 330
Ansary, Tamim, 531
anthropomorphizing the car, 322, 327
Anti-Rightist Campaign (China), 405
Antonioni, Michelangelo, 333
ANWB (Algemene Nederlandse Wielrijdersbond; Royal Dutch Touring Club), 241, 432
Appadurai, Arjun, 170
appropriation, 142, 247, 460
   cultural, 80–81, 156
   See also reappropriation, rickshaw
Arciniegras, Germán, 155, 157
Argentina, *153–154*, *157–158*, 160–162, 199n182, 442, 447, 461, 505, 508–509, *518–519*, 522–524, 528
Arl, Roberto, 159
Arman, 346
Armas, President Carlos Castillo, 506
Asian Development Bank (ADB), 444, 464, 470, 480
Asian Highway, 70, 422, *464–466*, 469, 528
Asian Land Transport Infrastructure Development (ALTID), 465
Asian Tigers, 470, 508–509
Association of East Asian Nations (ASEAN), 423, 470–471, 476
Association for the History of Transport, Traffic and Mobility T2M, 33
Atreya, Sudhir, 419
autocamping, 271
automation of the car, 37, 304
Automobile Club India, 125
automobilism
   anti-, 319
   colonial, 6, 96–98, 120, 131, 147, 151
      (*see also* mobility, colonial)
   exuberant, 2, 153, *205*, *245*, 321, 340, 342, 430
   importance of sessility for, 495
   inclusive, 8
   systemic aspects of, 340
   working-class, 261, 267
   See also adventure, flower parade, gymkhana
automotive adventure. See adventure
automotive industry, 422, 509, 521
   Brazil, 517–518

China, 406
Europe, 237
France, 240
India, 416–417
Latin America, 509
automotive narcissism, 6, *17*, *19*, 107, 167, 219, 281, 286–297, 335, 479, 534n13, 571
autopoetics, 5–6, 12, 16, 17, 18, 20, 25, 33–35, 37, 39–41, 90, 154, 159, 167, 215, 264, 267, 268, *277*, *284*, 289, 302–05, 314, 316, 318, 319, 321, 327, 329, 330, 334, 339–40, 344–45, 349, 502, 570
autorickshaw, 481, *554n174*
autoroute. See freeway
avant-garde, 218, 223, 278, 336, 340, 571
  Belgian and French, 60, 62, 64, 90, 106, 108, 155, 278
  Japanese, 60
  Soviet Union, 166, *340*
aviation, 254. *See also under* tourism

B

Baez, John, 217
bajaj. See mini-taxi
Bakary, Djibo, 490
Bakhtin, Mikhail, 299, 312
Balkmar, Dag, 25
Ballard, James (Jim) G., *205–209*, 272, 281, 328, 334, 339, 341–349, 398–99
Bandung Conference, 401, 419, 420, 486
Bangkok, 427, 479–480
Bangladesh, 452, 468
Banjaras (India), 128
Bank of International Settlements, 449
Baran, Paul, 507
barefoot doctors (China), 414
Barjavel, René, 325
barrel rolling, 140
Barthes, Roland, 22, *23*, 24, 32, *221*, 264, 320, 346, 571
Baudrillard, Jean, 32–33, 321, *347–348*
Beach Boys, The, 331
Beat (culture), *209*, *212*, 216 *218–223*, 228, 277, *284–287*, 287–293, *296–297*, 316, 334, 344, 347, 353n19, 398

Beatles, The, 212, 331
beatniks, *213*, 218, 287, 288
becak (cycle rickshaw), 478–479
Beck, Jeff, 215
Beck, Ulrich, 271, 572
Bedford, Sybille, 325
Beijing Streetcar Riot (1929), 87, 89
Belafonte, Harry, 217
bemo (mini-bus), 481
Benin (Upper-Volta), 135, 138, 494
Bense, Max, 221
Bergman, Ingrid, 305
Berlin Conference of 1885, 134, 141
Berman, Marshall, 438
Bernhard, Thomas, 345
Berry, Chuck, 244, 288, 316, 332
Bertho Lavenir, Catherine, 36, 61
Beukers, Bert, 431–432
Bianciardi, Luciano, 288
bicycle, 72, 75, 81, 138, 144–145, 148, 414, 417, 458, 473, 481, 487, 489, 501, 529
  China, 72, 81, 88, 119, *398*, *407–408*, 411–412, *414*, 486, 531, 539n51
  density in India (1974), 418
  density in the Netherlands, 243
  in India, 417, 458
  fleet in India, 72
  fleet in Manchuria, 70
  fleet in Shanghai, 72
  fleet in Vietnam, 72
  Indonesia, 424
  industry/production, 407–408
  in Manila, 477
  statistics, 81, 94, 119, 144, 417
  taxi, 500
  white bicycle plan, 229
  and women, 72
bicycle rickshaw. *See* cycle rickshaw
Bierbaum, Otto Julius, 178
Bishop, Ted, 294
Black Cruise. *See Croisière Noire*
Black Panthers, 227
Blake, Blink, 213
Blier, Bertrand, 335
Bloch, Ernst, 529
body language, *31–32*, 277, 328

Boeke, Jan, 486
Böhme, Hartmut, 23, 350
bolekaja. *See* mammy wagon
Booth, Rodrigo, 158
Bose, Budhhadev, 124
Boshardt, missionary R. A., 117
Bourdieu, Pierre, 12, 350
Bouvier, Nicolas, 325
Bowie, David, 223
Boxer Rebellion (China), 87, 111
Boxer Protocol Funds (China), 110, 114
Braine, John, 327
Brand, Stewart, 225
Brando, Marlon, 294
Brasília, 517
Brazil, 159–161, 516, 518
Breines, Wini, 296
Brenston, Jackie, 214
Brett, Michael, 483
Brezhnev, Leonid, 395
Brinkman, Inge, 502
Bröll, Wilhelm Wolfgang, 247
Brookings Institution, 392, 417, 441, 473, 508–509
Brown, H. Rap, 275
Brown, James, 331
Brown, Roy, 214
Bruckner, Pascal, 349
Bunker, Archie, 317
Buñuel, Luis, 163
Bureau of Public Roads (US), 506, 528
Burma, 471
Burroughs, William S., 219–220, 224, 290, 347
bus, 80, 87, 110, 112, 117–118, 125, 129, 163, 249, 256, 275–276, 314, 323, 334, 338, 394–395, 514
   accident, 345
   company, 478
   culture, 490
   girls (Japan), 69
   park Nigera, 495–496
   passengering, 308
   riots Peru, 522
   riots South Africa, 499
   statistics India (1950s), 416
   statistics Tanzania, 493
   tourism, 150, 161, 257

   See also busing, motor bus, *coxeurs*, minibus
bush roads, 140
busing (US), 248
Byrne, David, 223
Byron, Robert, 176

C
Cadillac, *105*, 159, *214–215*, 224, 265, 269, 277, 291, *310–313*, 316, 319, 328, 333, 448, 509, 512, 521
Caldwell, Erskine, 318
Callenbach, Ernest, 247
Camacho, President Manuel Ávila, 511–512
camel transport, 125, 137, 417
Cameroon, 489
Canclini, Néstor, 153
Candler, Julie, 274
Canned Heat, 332
canoe, 501
Canton Uprising, 88
Cape to Cairo, 139
car accident in novels, 303. *See also* road safety
car and cinema, 270
car and driver, 456, 494, 568
car as a cell/prison, 303
car as cocoon, 131
car as a coffin, 302
car emergence. *See* motorization
car as lens, 303
car as medium, 567
car as necessity, 243, 307–308, 321, 327
car as a weapon, 302
car chase, 339
car commuting (quantitative) Germany, 250
car crash, 327–328, 345
   as grotesque, 345
   See also Princess Diana's fatal car crash, obsession for the car crash, road safety
car critique, 319–321
car culture
   African Americans, 312–316
   Chicano, 310–312
   non-whites USA, 275–277
   poor whites, 318
   queer, 277
   See also youth (car) culture

car density, 120, 524
  Argentina (1920s), 157
  Bolivia, 158
  Brazil, 158, 518
  Central Africa, 492
  Chile, 158
  Europe (1970s), 251
  Federal Republic of Germany (West Germany), 251, 397, 492
  France, 251, 397
  German Democratic Republic (GDR), 397
  and GDP, 242
  Ghana, 497
  Hungary (1972), 397
  Indochina, 97
  Italy, 242
  Ivory Coast, 497
  Japan, 70
  Kenya, 492
  Manchuria, 70
  Mexico, 512
  Nigeria, 497
  Poland, 397
  Spain, 256
  as typical for non-West, 424
  Upper Volta (Benin), 497
  Venezuela, 158
car dependence, 441
car fetishism. *See* commodity (car) fetishism
car holiday, 269
car industry. *See* automotive industry
car interior, 31, 38, 218, 263, 290, 296, 308, 311, 342–344, 348
car/mobility metaphors, 10, 12, 20, 29, 32, 36, 46n25, 159, 166–167, 175, 216, 219, 224, 264, 290, 298, 302, 304, 307, 328, 331–332, 344, 455, 485, 563, 571
car modifiers. *See* lowriders
car novels. *See* autopoetics
car ownership, 13–14, 16, 22, 28, 96, 114, 147, 161, 170, 172–173, 179n4, 210, 218, *231*, 234, 240, 242, 245–247, 250, 252–253, 259–261, 275, 327–328, 335, 432, 478, 480, 519, 524–525
  Blacks USA, 276, 314

  Bonagente (Italy), 243
  gendered, 328
  Plodémet (France), 243–244
  restrained, 480
  second-hand, 246–247
  shared, 8, 328, 379n201
  working class, *231*, 240, 242, 244–247, 250
  See also under rickshaw
car ownership (quantitative)
  France, 240–243
  Germany, 240, 242
  Manchuria, 69–70
  middle class, 240
  rural areas, 240
  Singapore, 75
  Sweden, 242
  United Kingdom, 242
  USA, 252–253
  women USA (1960s/1970s), 309
  working class, 240
car ownership statistics. *See* car statistics
car painting, 311
car production
  American (USA), 232
  Europe, 232
  Ford, 232
  General Motors, 232
  Japan, 232
  world, 232
  See also automotive industry
car purchase
  on credit, 8, 236, 241, 250, 306
  household Uganda, 527
  low financial threshold, 492, 520
car sales, 241, 309
car society, 131, 253
  as Cold War product, 392
car songs. *See* songs
car statistics, 94, 96, 132, 191n115
  Argentina (1929), 158, 199n180
  ASEAN (1940), 423
  Bangkok (1970s), 481
  Brazil, 158, 160, 518
  Chile (1930), 158
  China, 105, 112
  Cuba, 509
  Ghana, 145

Hongkong, 112
India, 119–120, 418
Indonesia (1942), 131
Java (1966), 424
Kuala Lumpur (1970s), 481
Latin America, 509, 523
Melbourne, 481
Mexico, 158, 164
middle class, 519
Santiago de Chile (1920s), 158
Shanghai, 83, 112
Singapore, 98, 481
South East Asia (1940), 98
Soviet Union (1965), 395
Spain, 256
Sydney (1964), 481
Tanzania, 139, 493
Uganda (1958), 491–92
Vietnam, 97
car technology, 237–238, 350n54
car tourism, 149–150, 161, 163, 253, 255, 261
car use profile, 9, 13, 97, 151, 209–210, 251, 252, 253, 260, 273, 481
caravan (animals), 136, 138, 465
Cardasso, Fernando Henrique, 507
Cárdenas, President Lázaro, 510
carlessness, 172
Carmichael, Stokely, 275
Carné, Marcel, 335, 347
carnival, 129, 311, 523, 567
carnivalesque, 266, 312, 339, 350, 390, 458, 504, 566, 570, 573n6
  adventurism, 340
  caricature, 409
  Luddism, 287
  parody, 228
  southern grotesque, 319
  youth, 539n53
Carr, Duane, 318
Carrera Panamericana, 520–521
carriage, 75, 80, 133, 137
cart
  animal-drawn, 72, 117, 192n124
  bullock 125, 128, 145, 415, 417, 419, 421, 456, 529
  horse- and oxen-drawn, 472
  pony, 131

Casey, Roger, 314
Cassady, Carolyn, 289
Cassady, Neal, 218, *220–222, 225–226, 286–288*, 291–292, 296, 302, 304
Castro, Fidel, 445, 510
Center for International Studies (CIS), 389, 419, 445
Central Treaty Organization (CENTO), 465
CEPAL. See Comisión Económica para América Latína y el Caribe
chaebol (South Korea), 470
Chakrabarty, Dipesh, 171, 178, 425, 455, 458
Chander, Krishan, 124
Chandigarh (India), 425–26
Chandra, Sushil, 419
chaos (of traffic), 8, 43, 123, 127, 424, 497, 529–530, 562. *Also see* layeredness
Chatwin, Bruce, 38
Chauri Chaura (India), 122–123
Chevrolet, 105, 222, 267–270, 291, 311, 333, 510, 521. See also Corvette
Chiang, Ching-kuo, 399
Chiang, Kai-shek, 71, 88–89, 102–105, 114–115, 117–118, 399
Chilundo, Arlindo, 141
China Automobile Manufacturing Company, 115
China National Automotive Industry Corporation (CNAIC), 407
Chrysler, 274, 287
CIA, 389, 402–403, 419–420, 448, 509
circulation, *128*, 443, *482*, 486
civil rights movement, 216, 275–276, 311, 330, 448. See also Freedom Rides, March on Washington, Montgomery bus boycott
Clarke, Deborah, 292, 349
Clarsen, Georgine, 24, 151
class, *11–13*, 21, 77, 165, 179, 213, 228, 230, *239*, 258, 261, *264–270*, 273, 274, *276–277*, 296, 328, 400, 406, 409–410, 412–413, 519–522, 563, *566*, 569
  as (analytical) concept, *11–13, 258–260*, 267, *272–273*
  differences, 236, 241, 283, 327
  division/stratification, 107, 226, 236, 494

identity and race, 260
See also middle class, working class
Cochran, Edie, 244
cocoon. *See* car as cocoon, road network as cocoon, freeway cocoon experience
coevalness, 507, 509. *See also* layeredness
Cohen, Lizabeth, 267
Cold War and the racial issue in the United States of America, 276
Cole, Nat "King," 288
collapse of the distancing effect, 344
collectivism/collectivity, 3, 8–10, 12, 18, 22, 35, 72, 80, 91, 95–96, 131, 168, 174, 212, 221, 229–230, 242–243, 264, 276, 304, 308, 313–314, 334, 343, 395, 414, 427, 436, 446, 458, 482, 488, *495–496*, 504, 512, 519, 526–527, 531, 563, 568–571
Colombia, 516
Colombo Plan, 401
colonial automobilism/automobilism in the colonies. *See* automobilism
colonial landscape experience, 149
colonial mobility. *See* mobility, colonial
colonial modal split, 141
colonial transport development, 137
Comaroff, Jean and John L., 4, 10, 28, 64, 114, 135, 156, 173, 179, 424, 441, 469, 500, 562, 564, 567
Comisión Económica para América Latina y el Caribe (CEPAL), 505–509, 517, 523
Commencini, Luigi, 333
commodification, 4–5, 13–19, 23, 47n29, 85, 96, 144, 151, 276, 279, 350, 446
commodity (car) fetishism, 4, 14, 23–25, 158, 166–167, 173, 238, 279, 344–346, 349–350, 397, 418
commuting, *15*, 22, 78, 129, 170, 239, 248–253, 300, 341, 362n78, 475, 481, 486, 499, 563, 565. *See also* circulation
compact (car USA), 267
conflicts between builders and planners, 438
congestion. *See* traffic jam
Congo, 148
conquest. *See under* adventure

conspicuous consumption, 14, 16, 18, 21, 95, 132–133, 144, 166, 168, 210, 214, 277, 310, 312, 567
consumerism, 69, 282, 429, 520
consumption/consumption society (middle class), 27, 37, 46n29, 156, 160, 210, 219, 228, 232, *237*, 241–246, 248–252, 262, 267, 271, 273, 276, 278, 281, 283, 296, 316, 333, 336, 340, 440, 461, 472, 487, 504, 509, 520, 563
anti-hedonist, 520
Argentina as, 520
black, 276–277
of the car/ as commodity, 14, 16, 210, 234–235, 237, 251–252, 283, *310*, 317, 350, 520, 567
on credit, 519, 522
European and American/ Fordist model of, 232, 236, 246, 253, 258, 267, 274, 334, 336, 521
female, 274 (*see also* female motorist)
mass, 237, 251, 329, 394, 440, 446
Peronist, 520
restriction of, 209, 241
working class, 269, 271
See also motivation research
Convention on Road Traffic. *See* UN Convention on Road Traffic (1949)
cool persona, 497
coordination, 106, 129, 139, 147, 164n166, 192n124, 385, 422, 438–439
crisis, 87, 98, 131, 249, 416, 421, 472, 475, 494, 526
debate/struggle/war, 124–125, 428, 460, 470, 477
Ghana, 140
Mozambique, 143
See also road-rail competition
Coppola, Francis Ford, 336, 338
core and periphery, 233, 391, 440, *507*, 508. *See also* periphery, semi-periphery
Corelli, Marie, 178
Coronil, Fernando, 173
Corso, Gregory, 344
Cortines, Adolfo Ruíz, 521
Corvette, 291

counterculture, 208, 212, 216, 219–220, 226, 277, 281, 282, 288, 291, 292, 296, 306, 307, 338, 444
Country Joe and the Fish, 223, 245
Courtville, Roger, 159
covert culture, 8, 12, 275, 341
coxeurs, 490
Crash (novel and movie), 209, 328, 340–351, 570
Creedence Clearwater Revival, 332
Cremer, Jan, 325
Creole, 153, 198n172
  mobility, 161, 166
  technologies, 419, 460
Cresswell, Tim, 33–34, 171, 270, 289–290
Crews, Harry, 318–321
criminal tribe (India), 128
Croisière Jaune, 97, 174
Croisière Noire, 147, 150
Cronenberg, David, 347. *See also Crash*
Crooks Mitchell Peacock Stewart (consultants), 480
Crosby, Dave, 224
Crosby, Stills, Nash and Young, 224. *See also* Graham Nash
cross-mediality/intermediality, 223, 264, 268, 290–292
cruising, 14, 23, 38, 159, 270, 277, 331, 339. *See also under* subaltern
Cuba, 507, 509–510
Cultural Revolution (China), 406–07, 409–414, 539n52
Cultural Studies, 280
custom-car building, 310
cyborg, 221, 262, 326, 349–350
  car experience, 31, 90, 159, 292, 293, 328, 502, 566
  experience on the bicycle, 58
cycle rickshaw, 75, 79, 471, 477–478, 480n81, 481. *See also becak*

D

Dahomey. *See* Benin
Dai, Hsiao-ai [Dai Xiaoai], 411–412
Dale, Dick, 215
Darién Gap, 506
David Clark Five, 212
Davis, Miles, 224
de Andrade, Oswald, 159

de Beauvoir, Simone, 244, 322
de Grazia, Victoria, 267
Debord, Guy, 278–79
Decade of Development, 525, 568
de Castro e Silva, Democrito, 519
decentering the car, 562–63
decentralization, 114, 125, 163, 406
decolonization, 258, *387–388*, 444, 463, 469, 490, 502
deforestation, 405
delegation of adventurous behavior, 569
Deleuze, Gilles, 290
Delhi/New Delhi, 125–127, 420, 425–426, 441, 456, 529
Deng, Xiaoping, 399, 403, 409, 413–414
denial of coevalness. *See dependentismo*
Denisoff, Serge, 212
Dependency Theory, *453*, 506–07
dependentismo, 507–508, 510–15, 567–68
development, 103, 113–114, 127, 156, 235, 339, 384–390, 385, 421, 428–430, 438, 525, 564
  of Africa, *482–501*
  alternative, 509
  as big business, 444
  as (national) ideology, 438, 499
  basic human needs approach, 444
  as geopolitical instrument, 445–447
  investment in excess, 530
  as middle class ideology, 446–447
  mobility as, 438, 441, 504–505
  and private companies, 489
  redefinition towards poverty relief, 452
  socialist, 403
  state, 100, *470–472*
  structural adjustment program (SAP), 451
  theory of, 446 (*see also* Dependency Theory, developmentalism)
  and transport investment, 443–444
  of travel, 255
  in Turkey, 390–391
  of underdevelopment, 507
development aid, 446
  by Scandinavian countries, 447
  by US government, 447
developmentalism, 492–493, 504, 506–507, 510–515, 568
  revival of, 508

See also development as (national) ideology
Dhéry, Robert, 335
diaspora, 105, 110
   Africa, 494
   Chinese, 21, 28, 76, 105, 110, 168, 401, 536n34
   Indian, 76
   Southern (USA), 275
Dick, Howard, 423–424, 479, 481, 542n77
Dickens, Little Jimmy, 345
Dictators, The, 215
Dinning, Mark, 215
Didion, Joan, 41, 227, 344
diffusion, 98, 120, 169, 440, 563–564. *See also under* myth
diffusionism/Marxism as, 429, 440, 507
Dikötter, Frank, 80, 413
Dine, Jim, 346
Dinning, Mark, 215
disorder. *See* chaos
Divall, Colin, 33, 47n34
do-it-yourself (DIY). *See under* adventure
dokar. See pony cart
donkey, 417
Donofrio, Beverly, 306
Doors, The, 245, 332
Dorst, Tankred, 345
dos Santos, Theotonio, 507
drag racing, 214, 218, 287
Dreiser, Theodore, 212
drifting, 425
driving skills, 498, 502
   admiration for the driver's, 177
driving while black, 315
dual nature of technology, 565
Duals, The, 332
dude ranch, 265
Dumont, Alberto Santos, 161
Dunn, Katherine, 308
Dürrenmatt, Friedrich, 327
Dylan, Bob, 217, 224, 333

E

Earl, Harley, 266
Earnshaw, Ruth, 412
East as feminine, the, 62
ECAFE. *See* ESCAP
ECE. *See* UN Economic Commission for Europe (ECE)
Economic and Social Commission for Asia and the Pacific. *See* ESCAP
Economic Commission for Europe ECE. *See* UN Economic Commission for Europe (ECE)
Economic Commission for Latin America (ECLA), 464, 505, 507
Economic Commission of Africa (ECA), 462
economic development decade, 445
economic growth and democracy, 447
economic growth and transport, 492–493, 505, 530
Ecuador, 153, 453
Edensor, Tim, 424
Edgerton, David, 419, 460
Ehrenreich, Barbara, 227
Eisenhower, President Dwight, 436
ekka. See cart
Ekrem, Recaizade Mahmut, 167
Ekwensi, Cyprian, 500
Elena, Eduardo, 520
elephants, 468
Elliot, Lyn, 337
Ellison, Ralph, 313
emancipatory role of the car/mobility, 2, 43, 227, 274–275, 297, 306, 312–313, 321, 331, 349, 455, *570*
Engerman, David, 419–20
Eno, Brian, 223
Eno system, 94
epiphany, 218, 221
E-road network, 435, 462, 465
ESCAP (Economic and Social Commission for Asia and the Pacific), 422, 462–65
escape/escape vehicle, 24, 86, 102, 108, 216, 277, 280, 293, *296*, 301–302, 315, 319, 323, 330, 500, 567, *570*
Ethiopia, 485
Eurobus network, 258
Eurocentrism, 20
European Development Fund, 443
European Economic Community EEC, 234, 435
event society, 338
Everly Brothers, 215
EXIM (Export Import Bank), 454, 472

expectation (as driver of change), *14*, 15, 19, 159, 429, *442–443*, *456–457*, 519, 525, 530–531

F
faena (Mexico), 163
Faletto, Enzo, 507
family, 234–235
  car, 259, 300–301
  postmodern, 226
  as subject, 300
  two-car, 237
  See also nuclear family
Faulkner, William, 302
Faustian model, 438
Fava, Valentina, 535n23
feeder to the railways, road traffic as, 63, 125, 136, 393, 479, 481
feeder road, 130, 138, 405, *487–488*, 493
Fellini, Federico, 178, 333
female (automotive) adventure, 107, 285, 307, 309, 322. *See also* escape, gender, women
female bicyclist, 88
female bus driver, 69
female motorists/car owners, 26, 28, *273–274*
female road story, 305. *See also* escape
female singer/writer, 216, 224, 303, 307, 329
Feng, Yuxiang, 104
Ferlinghetti, Lawrence, 222
fetishization of the car. *See* commodity (car) fetishism
Ficek, Rosa, 505
Finkielkraut, Alain, 349
First Auto Works (FAW) (China), 406
Fischer, Claude, 253
Five-Year Plans (China)
  First (1953–1957), 400, 402, 407–408
  Second, 401, 405
  Third (1966–1970), 405
Five-Year Plans (India), 416
  Fourth, 417
  Second, 417
flaneur, 32, 174, 219, 279
flight (experience). *See* adventure
Flink, James, 144

flower parade, 567. *See also* gymkhana
Flying Burrito Brothers, 332
flyover, 425
folklore around the car, 178
Fonda, Peter, 336–337
footpath network, 503
Ford, 74, 96, 120, 147, 155–156, 160, 164–165, 172, 264, 515
  collaborating with oppressive regime, 509
  Falcon, 267
  Foundation, 425
  Mustang, 282
Ford, Gerald, 421
Ford, Henry, 101, 105
Foucault, Michel, 32–33
Four Little Dragons (Asia), 478
fragmentation, 273, 283, 563
  of the car culture, 219
  of the nuclear family, 309
Franck, Harry, 118
Frank, Andre Gunder, 507
Frank, Robert, 290, 372n148
Frank, Thomas, 272, 281–282
Franklin, Aretha, 224
free railway travel (China), 410
Freed, Libbie, 149
Freedom Rides of 1961 (civil rights movement USA), 330
freeway, 339, 429, 430, 437–438
freeway building
  and authoritarianism, 450
  Eastern Europe, 397
  Japan, 473–474
freeway density, 459
freeway driving, 330, 308
  cocoon experience, 316, 340
freeway network length
  Europe (1970–1986), 435
  France (1991), 435
  Germany (1991), 435
  Switzerland (1980), 434
  USA (1960s), 437
  world, 459
freeway resistance, 437–438
Friedman, Milton, 420
Friedman, Murray, 317
Friendship Highway, 468
Fulwider, Benjamin, 513–514

Fusell, Paul, 38

G
Galbraith, John Kenneth, 420
Gálves, Luis Enrique Bracamontes, 508
Gambia, 460
Gandhi, Mahatma, 76, 121, 419
Ganser, Alexandra, 285
gareta, 145
Gartman, David, 265, 310, 350
Gatejel, Luminita, 395
Gates Jr., Henry Louis, 331
Gaye, Marvin, 264, 331
Gemeinschaft versus *Gesellschaft*, 496–497, 556n201
gender(ing), 28, 246, 265–273, 297, 299
 -bending, 291
 of the car culture, 273–275, 314, 332
 See also female, masculinity, women; *see also under* car
General Motors, 74, 120, 131, 147, 155–156, 160, 164–165, 172, 214, 264, 515
German Association of the Automotive Industry (VDA), 434
Gerry and the Pacemakers, 212
Gewald, Jan-Bart, 145, 148
Ghana, 140–141, 448, 485, 493–494, 496
Gibbons, Billy, 215
Gibson, James, 13
Gide, André, 177
Ginsberg, Allen, 219–222, 224, 290–291
Giucci, Guillermo, 154, 161
Gladys Knight & the Pips, 318
Glass, Philip, 223
Gluckman, Max, 148
Godard, Jean-Luc, 334, 347
Goedde, Petra, 387–388
Gold Coast. *See* Ghana
golden age
 of Dutch freeway construction, 431
 of US highway construction, 437
 See also nuclear family
Golden Earring, 333
Goulart, João, 518
Gould, Peter, 487
Grateful Dead, 223, 245

Great Leap Forward (China), 401, 403, 405–407
Gregory, Dick, 313
Griffin, Farah Jasmine, 318
Grootveld, Robert Jasper, 229
Gross National Product (GNP), 392, 444, 471, 473–474, 492, 518
 transport share of, 474
Guatemala, 154, 156, 447, 449, *506*
Guattari, Félix, 290
Guevara, Ernesto "Che," 384, 445, 510
Guimarães, Paolo, 256
Guinea, 448, 489
Guomindang, 101, 105
Guthrie, Woody, 212
gymkhana, 312, 567. *See also* flower parade

H
Haagen-Smit, Arie J., 572
Haas, Robert, 113
Hailey, Arthur, 330
Haiti, 524
Haley, Bill, 214
hamac. *See machilla*
Hamilton, Guy, 339
Hannerz, Ulf, 223
haptic basis of car driving, 12
Haraway, Donna, 31
haunted car, 302
haunted roads, 501–503
Hawkes, John, 345
Hawkins, E. K., 526
Hayato, Ikeda, 472
Hayden, Tom, 287
head porterage. *See* porterage
Headrick, Daniel, 121
hegemonic (car/mobility) cultures, 7–9, *42–43*, 44n7, 154, 168, 172, 209, 214, 216, 222, 230, 236, *247*, 249, 253, 267–268, *273*, 277–278, 281, 283–285, 287–290, 293–294, *299*, 301, *305–306*, *315–316*, 329–330, 336–337, 340, 349, 387, 423, 448, 455, 457, 468, 481, 504, *570*. *See also* masculinity, mobility, self
helicak. *See* mini-taxi
Hells Angels, 294–295

Hendrix, Jimi, 226, 245
Herman's Hermits, 212
hidden transcript, *457*, 549n133
hidden violence of road accident statistics, 457
highlife music, *500*
Highway Capacity Manual, 430, 432, 473
highway hypnosis, 307
Hillbilly Highway, 318
hipster, 218–219, 288
Hirschman, Albert O., 443, 453
Hitchcock, Alfred, 338
hitchhiking, 217–218, 289, 297, 307, 332, 338, 398
   by Blacks, 314
   'hoboing by car,' 284
Hobsbawm, Eric, 441, 457
Hoffman, Paul G., 231
holiday travel, 254
Hollies, The, 211–212
Holly, Buddy, 214, 244
Hollywood movies, 569
Holmes, John Clellon, 218–219, 285
home ownership, 270, 519
Hong Kong, 427, 459, 470, 478
Hongweibing (Red Guards, China), 409
hooligans, 77, 87, 123, 229, 410–411. See also *teppisti*
Hopper, Dennis, 336
horse statistics, 417
hot-rodding, 214, 215, 218, 264, 271, 287, 310, 312, 335, 352n12, 566, 569
household budget (share of car in), 14, 235, 241, 268, 274, 519, 522
housing, 129, 423
Howlin' Wolf, 214
Hsieh, Ping-Ying, 101–102
Huang, Shu-min, 407
hukou, 401–402, 498. See also *propiska*
Humphrey, Hubert H., 317
Hunter, Holland, 392, 396
Hyundai, 470

I
immobility, 150, 207, 289–290
impact paradigm, 144, 196n154
import substitution, 509, 512
indentured labour, 76

independence (movements), 122, 331, 333, *387–388*, 446, 525
   in Africa, 144, 483, 485–486, 489–491, 493–494, 498
   in India, 123–124, 128, 210, 417, 419, 421
   in Latin America, 152–153
   See also *dependentismo*
independence (personal), 230, 306. See also car dependence
India, 452, 467
Indian mobility, 153
indigenismo movement, 153
indigenous modernities, 454
Indonesia, 130–131, 471, 476, 481
informal economy/sector, 72, 422, 486, 494–495, 499, 529, 570
informal transport, 427, 477, 479, 492, 563, 568
   regulation and bans, 478
   share in modal configuration, 477
   statistics, 428
Inland Transport and Communications Committee (ITTC), 464
Inter-American Development Bank, 450
intercity bus travel, 521
interior. See car interior
intermediality, 290–292, 348
intermediary level of governance, 437, 568
International Development Association, 443, 450
International Labour Officie/Organization (ILO), 111, 113, 486, 499
International Monetary Fund (IMF), 448, 485, 569
International Road Federation (IRF), *429–430*, 434, 438–439, 449, *458–461*, 465, 467, *482–485*, 487, 505–506, 515, 528
Interstate Highway System, 262, 285, 315–316, 339, 404, *430*, *436*, 459, 468, 511
inversion, 60, 286, 294, 321, 326
invisibility of the vehicle. See absent car
ironic car, 10, 12, 15, 18, 37, 64, 121, 132, 146, 148, 263 296, 298, 315, 323, 344, 349, 521, 567
ironizing experience, 39, 571

irony/ironic, 10–11, 17, 37, 41, 43, 66, 91, 107, 108–109, 167, 170, 178, 219, 244, 245, 262, 272, 291–292, 295–296, 298, 312, 315, 318, 323, 324, 326, 330–331, 338, 340, 342–344, 349, 412, 413, 497, 540n57, 563, 569, 570, 571.
  as literary technique, 10
  in Lu Xun, 108–109
  non-, un-, 43, 292, 295
  See also ironic car, ironizing experience
Israel, 470

J
Jackson, Aunt Molly, 212
Jackson, Kenneth, 259
Jackson, Mahalia, 217
Jagger, Mick, 331
Jakarta, 79, 423–424, 478–480
Jameson, Fredric, 33
Japan, 232, 462, 470–477
  supergrowth of, 471–472
Japan Development Bank, 472
Japan International Cooperation Agency (JICA), 471, 476
Java, 98, 131, 423–424, 504
Jayne, Mark, 424
jeepney, *477–478*, 528, 570
Jefferson Airplane, 223, 245
Jelinek, Elfriede, 345
Ji, Xianlin, 412
Jiménez, President Marcos Pérez, 515
jitney, 8, *173–174*, 276, 477, 481, 510.
  See also bemo, kolt, opelet, pikap, bajaj
Johnson, Junior, 311
Johnson, President Lyndon B., 248, 255, 421, 448, 452
Johnson, Robert, 214
Jones, LeRoy, 220, 316
Jones, Madison, 345
Joplin, Janis, 226
Jordan, James, 496–497

K
Kaelble, Hartmut, 234
Katona, George, 232
Keats, John C., 247, 300

Kennedy, President John F., 255, 316, 401, 437, 445
Kenya, 485, 492
Kenyatta, Jomo, 492
Kerouac, Jack, 217–221, 225–226, 245, 284–296, 299–302, 314, 327, 373n156, 384–385
Kesey, Ken, 225
Khrushchev, Nikita, 246, 395, 398, 531, 535n21, 563. *See also* kitchen debate
Khusyairi, Johny, 132
Kienholz, Ed, 346
Kindleberger, Charles, 441
King, Martin Luther, 217
Kingston Trio, 212
Kinks, The, 212
Kipling, Rudyard, 176
kitchen debate, 246
Koeppen, Wolfgang, 324
kolt, 481
Kopytoff, Igor, 484
Korean War, 248, 401, 470–471
Koselleck, Reinhart, 30
Koshar, Rudi, 236
Kosygin, Alexei, 395
Kraig, Beth, 274
Kröger, Fabian, 347
Kuala Lumpur, 479–480
Kubitschek, Juscelino, 517–518
Kubrick, Stanley, 339, 347
Kuntz, Roger, 339

L
laboratory (periphery/Global South as), 4, 114, 124, 156, 444, 469, 562
  Japanese motorization as, 473
  Mexican roadbuilding as, 510–513
  See also Comaroff
Labour History/labour studies, 495, 498
Laderman, David, 337
landscape writing, 197n164
Lang, Tâm, 92
Lao She, 89–92
Lasch, Christopher, 19, 20, 281
Lasplaces, Alberto, 159
laterite, 468
Lawrence, Mark, 392

layeredness, xx, 2, 17, *24*, 28, 43, 61–62, 64, 80, 81, 82, 102, 119, 127, 129, 134–135, 164, 165, 167, 172, 384, 386, 390, 409, 421–422, 424, 439, 442, 452, 470, 476, 478–479, 481, 486, 488, 490, 497–498, 500, 507, 528, 529, 532, 539, 551, 561n245, 562
Le Corbusier, 425–26
League of Nations, 65, 70, 111, 113, 114, 139, 449
Leary, Timothy, 293
Lebanon, 151
Led Zeppelin, 245, 332
Lee, Bruce, 524
Lefebvre, Henri, 22, 221, 349
Lei, Feng, 414
Leinbach, Thomas, 130, 469
leisure use of the car, 250
Lelouch, Claude, 335
Lennon, John, 223
Lerner, David, 504
Lesdain, Count, 159
Lévi-Strauss, Claude, 19, 38
Lewin, Kurt, 502
Lewis, W. Arthur, 546n109
Lezotte, Chris, 24–26
LGBTQ. *See* car culture, queer; *see also under* subaltern
Li, Xiaojiang, 413
Libya, 149
Lieb, Claudia, 345
lifestyle (research), 273, 283
Ling, Ken, 410–411
Liggins, Jimmy, 214
Lipset, Seymour, 504
Little Richard, 214
Liu, Guokai, 412
Liu, Shaoqi, 409
llama, 157, 165
Lo, Chuanfang, 412
loans (to countries), 416, 444, 450, 454, 516, 525. *See also* Asian Development Bank, International Monetary Fund IMF, US Export-Import Bank (EXIM), World Bank
 personal, 306, 501
Lobato, Monteiro, 154

Loden, Barbara, 338
Loewy, Raymond, 266
Löfgren, Orvar, 252
logistic diffusion curve, 475
London Traffic Survey of 1964, 250
Long March (China), 103, 116–117
long-distance touring, 253, 261, 262, 287, 314. *See also* Cape to Cairo
long-distance trade in West Africa, 499
Losey, Joseph, 335
loss of the Self, 298
Louie, Kam, 27
Lovin' Spoonful, 223
low cost road, 422, 454–460, 468, 508, 513
lower class. *See* working class
lowrider/lowriding, *310–313*, 341
Lu, Hanchao, 83
Lu, Xun. *See* Zhou, Shuren
Lucas, George, 270
Luo, Kou-shin, 111, 189n99
Lyotard, Jean-François, 33

M
MacArthur, General Douglas, 470–471
machilla, 142–144
Mahalanobis, Prasanta Chandra, 419
Mailer, Norman, 218
mainstream, 5, 9, 18, 26, 43, 44n7, 44n9, 75, 95, 166, 173, 174, 209, 214, 220, 225, 230, 273, 277–284, 285–287, 290–293, 310, 319, 340, 349, 350, 409, 421, 475, 481, 486, 504, 519, 567, 570
 culture, 281
 development ideology, 421 (*see also* developmentalism)
Malaysia, 130, 469–471, 476
Mali, 448
mall, 263
Malle, Louis, 335
Mamas and the Papas, The, 223
mammy wagon, *486*, 500–501, *524*
Manchukuo. *See* Manchuria
Manchuria, 398, 402
Manila, 477–478, 480
Mann, Klaus, 178
Mann, Klaus and Erika, 176
Mann, Michael, 440

Mann, Thomas, 177
Manning, Patrick, 135, 137
Mao Zedong, 103, 106, 399, 405–406, 408–409, 414
March on Washington (1963), 330
Marchand, Roland, 330
Marshall, George, 104, 231
Marshall, Penny, 306
Marshall Plan, 231, 236, 240, 255, 324, 390–391, 428, 435, 445, 463, 512, 543n85
Martha and the Vandellas, 264, 482, 330
Marwick, Arthur, 226
Marx, Karl, 440
Marxism, 11, 280–281, 409, 420, 429, 440, 447, 463, 507. *See also* diffusionism
masculinity, 17, 25, 26, 27–28, 262, 289, 292–293, 298, 302, 328
   Chinese, 27
   hegemonic, 24–25
   hybrid, 25
   See also gender
masculinization, 133
masking, 330–331
mass motorization, 395
   Japan, 250
   jump start in Europe, 238
   start in European periphery, 242
   start in the Netherlands, 240
Mass Rapid Transit (MRT), 480
matatu, 492, 570
Mateos, Adolfo López, 513
Mathiessen, Peter, 38
Mau Mau uprising, 388
Maugham, W. Somerset, 127
May Fourth Movement (China), 86, 88, 405
May Thirtieth Movement (China), 86
Mayakovsky, Vladimir, 166
McDowell, Linda, 289
McLuhan, Marshall, 247, 266
McNamara, Robert, 452. *See also under* World Bank Presidents
mebeal bingo. See mini-taxi
media studies, 5, 28, 30, 35–36, 333
media theory of the car, 32
mediation, 28–29
merger of mobility and media, 348
Merriman, Peter, 32
mestizaje, 166
metaphor. *See* car metaphor
metro. *See* subway
Mexico, 153–154, 156, 158, *162–164*, 166, 170, 178, 219, 253, 260, 295, 307, 309, 442, 454, 505–506, 508–509, *510–515*, 520–524, 527, 530. *See also faena*, motorization; *see also under* car density, car statistics, modal configuration, motor bus statistics, motor vehicle statistics, railway network length, road labour, road network length, road safety, roadbuilding, truck statistics
Mexicanos / Mexican Americans, 310–311
Michener, James, 325
middle class (culture), 5, 21, 83, 85, 91, 117, 129, 145–147, 153–154, 160–161, 164, 166, 207, 212, 214, 216, 226, *228*, *230–231*, *239–240*, 243, 250, 256, *267–270*, 272, *276*, 281, 302, 306, 312, 322, 327, 367n112, 418, 436, *439*, 446, *504*, 511–512, 514, 516–521, 525, 528, 531–532, *566*, *570*
   and advertisements, 17 (*see also* advertisements)
   in Africa, 145–146
   African American, 312–313, 315
   automobilism/car culture, 3, 7–9, 11, 13, 21, 24, 27, 43, *46n23*, 67, 150, 168, 170, 209, 237, 242, 244, 258, 284, *399*, 315–317, *330*, 338, 340, 531, 567, 569
   Chinese, *82–86, 89–90*, 117
   consciousness, 475
   creation of/rise of, 80, 165, 235, 445, 518–519, 522, 531
   elite, 423
   emptiness, 282
   family, 261
   fantasy, 43, 307
   guilt, *205*, 244, 282, 319–321, 333–334, 341, 346, 408, 444, 448, 568–569
   in India, 129, 418
   Japanese, 68–69, 73, 251, 475

lack of, 95, 160
  in Latin America, 153, 157, 160–161,
    165–166, *504*, 514, 516, 519–522,
    525, 527–528
lifestyle, 33, 239
members, 81, 120, 219, 235, 305, 336,
  518
myth, 39, 233, 261
neglect of the, 520
proletarianization of, 269
revolution, 445
and rickshaws, 83
rural, 2
self-defined, 553n162
society, 179, 235, 265, 271, 283
  in Spain, 256
urban, 2, 105, 169–170
values/tastes, 39, *82–83*, 90, 92, 268–269,
  282, 293
writers/writing, 10, 61, 90, 108–109, 329
See also petty bourgeois, *sarariiman*
Middle East, *151*, 176, 450, *455*, 482–483
Mieczkowski, Bogdan, 397
Mignolo, Walter, 152, 166, 179
migration, 40, 88, 119, 129, 133–134, 169,
  387, 401–402, 426, 474, 486, 494–
  495, 498, 503, 518, 526
  in Africa, 134–35
  in American South, 223, 319
  Black, 318
  Europe, 38, 233, 250, 254, 256, 257, 388,
    503
  Indian, 119, 426–27
  in Latin America, 518
  peasants from China, 76–77, 117, 168,
    498
  in Portugal, 257–258
  rural-urban, 88, 124, 402, 422, 484, 500,
    522
  United States of America, 56, 311
  See also circulation, diaspora, refugees
migration studies, 65, 318
Miller, Arthur, 344
Miller, Joseph, 502
Millikan, Max E., 419–420
Mills, Katie, 220–222, 290–291, 295, 305,
  340

mini-bus, 427–428, 477, 479–481, 488,
  497, 510, 527–529
Ministry of International Trade and
  Industry MITI (Japan), 472
mini-taxi, 477, 479, *481*
missionaries, 73, 104, 114, 117, 127, 148,
  456
Mitchell, J. Clyde, 497
Mitchell, Joni, 216, 306, 332
mixed road, 132, 417
mob, 91, 123, 168, 412
mobile Other, 166, 570
mobile personality, 455
mobility/mobilities
  alternative, 9, 43, 168, 229, 386, 409,
    452, 458, 476, 564, 571
  colonial, 65, 72, 77, 88, 92–93, 121–
    124, 128, 131–135, 137, 140–142,
    144–145, 151, *168*, 172, 490 (*see also
    under* automobilism)
  Communist, 531
  folk, 223
  hegemonic, 9, 42–43, 171, 230, 247,
    249, 273, 278, 283, 290, 293–294,
    299, 315, 316, 329, 330, 340, 468
  imaginative, 396–397
  kaleidoscopic, 564
  multiple, 2, 9, 125, 209, 394, 454, 503,
    563–565
  Muslim, 531
  peripheral, 166–167, 563
  postmodern, 304
  serious, 144, 170–171, 563
  slow, 84, 172–173
  of the South, 166
  and stability, 495
  subaltern, 9, 43, 77, 86, 90, 91, 127,
    148, 152, 166, 171–173, 178–179,
    247, 277, 386, 452, 458, 486, 490,
    529, 565, 568
  submissive, 153
  See also network mobility
'mobility turn,' 128
Mobylette (moped), 229
Mods (UK), *228*, 280
modal configuration, 75, 126, 247, 408,
  475
  ASEAN, 476

Index • 655

India, 126–127, 416, 419
Japan, 473
Mexico, 512
typical Asian, 472
See also modal split
modal split, 75, 211, 238, 564
Germany, 251–252
Sweden, 252
USA, 248–249, 252
Western world, 252
See also modal configuration
modernity
Afro-, 441
anti-capitalist, 455
counter-, 528, 529
mobility definition of, 456–57
non-European, 455
postcolonial, 455
roadbuilding as token of, 130
modernization, 85, 115–116, 153–154, 233, 385–386, 389–390, 391, 394, 426, 439, 441, 443, 444, 451, 454–455, 457–459, 488, 501, 507, 516–517, 525–27, 529, 530, 539n51
in Africa, 135, 488–489, 501
American, 179n4
as anti-communist strategy, 445
in Asia, 72, 85, 129, 418–419, 425, 462
in China, 71, 85, 89, 101
Cold War background of, 239–240
through housing, 129
Japanese, 58–66, 69, 74, 462
in Latin America, 153–154, 509, 516, 517
through motorization, 74 110, 116, 385, 423, 430, 439, 462, 562
rural, 469, 473, 477
Soviet-style, 455
in Soviet Union, 391, 394
Western, 58, 80, 106, 167, 233, 238, 240, 258, 335, 426, 445, 465, 467, 479
See also development, Faustian model
modernization mythology, 135
modernization theory, 389, 428–429, 438, 439, 440, 444, 447, 451, 455, 499, 507, 518, 530
modernization without capitalism, 455

Mokhtarian, Patricia Lyon, 22
Monkeys, The, 216
Monnet, Jean, 113
Monroe, Kristin, 151
Montgomery bus boycott, 330
moped, 238
density (the Netherlands), 243
See also Mobylette, motorcycle, Puch, Solex
Moran, Joe, 346
Morand, Paul, 321
Moreno Tejada, Jaime, 153
Morrison, Jim, 332
Morrison, Toni, 318
Morrison, Van, 288
Morocco, 151, 159, 201n197, 219, 224, 387, 486, 489
Morse, Margaret, 339
Möser, Kurt, 510
mosquito bus, 79, 98, 479, 529
motivation research, 264–265, 267–268, 277
motor bus, 74–75, 127, 132, 254, 523, 526, 569
in Beatles film, 224
density, 240
in Japan, 69
Ken Kesey, 225–226
wild or pirate, 131
See also bus, busing, Eurobus, female bus driver, intercity bus travel, mini-bus, Montgomery bus Boycott, mosquito bus, passengering, public bus system, Public Light Bus, trolley bus; *see also under* adventure, truck
motor bus statistics
Brazil, 523
Canada, 523
France, 523
Mexico, 523
Singapore, 98
motor vehicle statistics
Argentina, 522–523
Bolivia, 522–523
French Guiana, 522–523
Ghana, 486–87
Latin America, 522–523
Mexico, 514, 522–523

Uruguay, 522–523
Venezuela, 515–516, 522–23
motorcycle, 29, 127, 138, 228, *238*, 243–244, 280, 291, 293–295, 331, 336, 384, 396, 415, 418–419, 424, 481, 488, 492, 527, 569
   European revival of, 238
   ownership (Germany), 240
   taxi, 427, 479 (*see also* mini-taxi)
motorcycle statistics, 94, 242, 424, 481
motorization
   Africa, 147
   Asia, 423
   Bangkok, 98
   Burma, 126
   Chile, 157–158
   China, 95–98
   European model of, 238
   India, 119–120
   Java, 98
   Latin America, 154
   Malaysia, 130
   models of, 527–528
   Rangoon, 98
   Senegal and Dakar, 146–147
   Singapore, 98
   South Africa, 150–151
   Sumatra, 98
   Vietnam, 96
   Tanzania, 138
   See also mass motorization
motorization through commercial vehicles
   Nigeria, 498
   Dahomey, 494
   Mexico, 512, 518
   Uganda, 491
   Uruguay, 523
   Zaire, 494
   movie, 68, 92, 163–164, 185n63, 185n67, 215, 225, 241, 262, 264, 270, 287–288, 290–291, 294–295, 297, 301, 306, 347, 371n144, 540n57.
   See also action movies, adventure, *Crash* (movie), Hollywood movies, road movie, talking cars (in movies), vacation movies
movie theorists, 219
Moynihan, Daniel Patrick, 317

Mozambique, 141–144
Mrázek, Rudolf, 132
mule, 417
muleteers, 165
Munk, Bernard E., 504
Munzinger, Wolfgang, 336
Murphy, Dervla, 421
Murphy, Michael, 333
muscle car, 25–26, 214, 215, 268, 566
Muskie, Edward S., 317
Mussolini, Benito, 113
Myrdal, Gunnar, 435, 452, 463
myths
   diffusionist, *9*, 70, 98, 157, *169*, 243, 440, 476, 507, 525, 529, 532, 562–564
   functionalist, *9*

N
Nabokov, Vladimir, 302, 344
Nagoya-Kobe Expressway, 473
Nagpur Plan. *See under* roadbuilding
Naipaul, V. S., 38
Nakicenovic, Nebojša, 529–530
Nanjing decade (China), 102
narcissism. *See* automotive narcissism
NASCAR racing, 570
Nash, Graham, 211, 224, 226, 279
Natsume Sōseki. *See* Sōseki, Natsume
Needham, Joseph, 408
Nehru, Jawaharlal, 419
neoliberalism, 218, 262, 280, 283, 451, 566
Netto, Américo, 159
network mobility, 225
New Culture Movement (China), 89, 409
New Mobility Studies, xii, xiii, 28, 209, 333, 566
Newton, Helmut, 347
Nickles, Shelley, 267–269
Nicolaides, Becky, 253
Niebuhr, Reinhold, 299
Niger, 489–491
Nigeria, 148, 453, 459, 462, 488, 494–495, 498, 524
Nixon, Richard, 246, 406, 421. *See also* kitchen debate
Nkrumah, Kwame, 486–488, 494

nomadism/nomads, 128, 169 288. *See also* pseudo-nomadism
non-Aligned Movement. *See* Bandung Conference
non-Western mobility history, 563
Norton, Peter, 266
nuclear family, 9, 14, 207, 209, 246, *258–260*, 264, 307–309, 338, 343, 520, 531–532
  golden age of, 235
  See also fragmentation
Nyun, Sithu U, 465

O
obsession for the car crash, 345
O'Connor, Flannery, 301–302
Oldenziel, Ruth, 246, 446
one-wheeled barrow, 68, 81, 145
Ono, Yoko, 223
OPEC. *See* Organization of the Petrol Exporting Countries
opelet, 481
ordered spending, 519–520
Organisation for European Economic Co-operation and Development (OECD), 399
Organization of the Petrol Exporting Countries OPEC, 572
orientated landscape, 502
Ortega y Gassset, José, 155
Ory, Kid, 214
ostentatious consumption. *See* conspicuous consumption
other mobility, 563. *See also* mobile Other
Owen, Wilfred, 417, 441–443, 461
Owensby, Brian, 519
oxcart. *See* cart

P
Pacific automobilism, 2, 71
pack animals, 487 522
Packard, Vance, 269
Packer, Jeremy, 262
pak pais. *See* mini-bus
Pakistan, 452, 467–468
palenquin/palanquin, 67, 73, 102, 126, 142

Pan-American Highway, 154, 156–157, 163, 198n178, 461, 465, 505, 509, 511–512, 515, 520, 528
Pan-American Highway Confederation, 153
Pan-American Railway, 156
Pante, Michael, 133
Paolini, Federico, 250
Parks, Rosa, 276
Parla, Jale, 167, 390
passengering, 173, 201n201, 217, 230, 286, 292, 303, 305, 308, 314, 316, 322, 531, 567, 568.
  child, 308
  See also bus
Passos, John Dos, 212
Peace Corps, 444, 447–449, 453, 525
Peckinpah, Sam, 336, 347
pedestrian zones, 237
pedestrians/pedestrianism. *See* walking
pedicab. *See* cycle rickshaw
periodization
  confusion, 3
  doom, 3, 572
  emergence, 3, 5–13, 23, 43, 57, 208, 566
  persistence, 3, 5–13, 43, 208, 284, 344, 566
periphery, 156, 233, 453. *See also* core and periphery, semi-periphery; *see also under* mass motorization
Perkins, John, 448, 453
Permanent International Association of Road Congresses. *See* PIARC
Perry, Frank, 339
Peru, 153, 156–157, 447, 506, 508, 516, *519, 521–523*, 558n216
pesero, 513
Peter, Paul and Mary, 217
Péteri, György, 397
petty bourgeois, 9, 106, 207, 271, 334, 350
Philippines, 133, 423, 463–464, 467, 469, 471, *476–478*, 528
PIARC, 70, 96, 190n104, 405–406, 422, 429, 434, 449, 460, 462, 508, 528, 538n44
Picciolini, Angelo, 150
pickup truck, 243, 271, 490
pikap, 481
Pink Floyd, 245

Piquero, José, 159
pirate cars, 494
pirate taxis, 478–480, 529
pirate trucks, 148
Pirie, Gordon, 150–151
Pirsig, Robert, 293–294
planning, 389, 402
   centralization of road, 161
   comprehensive, 437–38
   crisis of, 453, 504
   economic/general, 11, 69, 104, 234, 389, 395, 401–402, 408, 419–420, 445, 448, *453*, 464, 471, *504*, 518
   euphoria, 433, 438, 453
   freeway/road/railway/infrastructure, 70, 111–112, 125, 138–139, 143, 161–163, 404, *430–435*, 438, 443, 453, 467, 473, 485, 489, 493
   radical decentralization of, 401–402
   urban, 4, 116, 426–427, *476*, 528, 564
Plath, David, 476
plebeian car porn, 342
Pluto effect, 281
Ponsavady, Stéphanie, 97
Pooley, Colin, 210
popular culture, 3, 5, 18, 38–39, 42–43, *44n9*, 208–209, 214, 265, 299, 329–330, 333, 344, 350, 410, 570
Porter, Gina, 488
porterage, 135–136, 138–141, 145, 148, 153, 167, 417, 485, 489, 497, 529. *See also* barrel rolling
Portugal, *140–143*, 157, 231, 233–234, *257–258*, 324, 388, 460, *502–503*, 507, 524
postmodern advertising, 17. *See also* advertisements
postmodern car society, 348, 351
postmodern lifestyle, 245
postmodern novel, 345
postmodern self, 19
postmodernism, 25, *33*, 37, 263, 268, 270, *285*, 305, 329, 426, 454, 566, 569. *See also* family, mobility
Pratt, Mary Louise, 41
Prebisch, Raúl, 463, 507
'predict and provide,' 432
Presley, Elvis, 214, 224, 244–245

Primeau, Ronald, 305
Prince, 224
Princess Diana's fatal crash, 347
private road, 489
professional chauffeur, 568
Prokosch, Frederic, 176, 178
propiska (Soviet Union), 402
prosthesis, car as, *18–19*, 48n38, 302, 349
pseudo-nomadism, 253
public bus system, 480
public light bus (PLB), 427
public trucking, 513–514
Puch (moped), 228–229
punks, 280
Puricelli, Piero, 110–111
Pynchon, Thomas, 304

Q
Quadros, President Jânio, 518
Quest of the Self, 10, 34–35, 39, 267, 285, 289, 293, 298, 303, 329, 338, 344
Quijano, Aníbal, 507

R
racing, 161, 569. *See also* drag racing, NASCAR racing, sport cars, stock car racing, street racers
Radway, Janice, 297–299
Rae, John, 144
railway, 67, 96, 107, 140–141, 254, 393, 402, 404–405, 410, 415, 464, 475, 468, 471, 482
   in Africa, 134
   in China, 99–100
   emergence of Asian, 423
   in Japan, 59
   in Manchuria, 59, 69
   in Latin America in the 19th century, 153
   in literature, 60
   in the Soviet Union, 392
   in the world, 59–60
railway network (building), 115, 121–124, 153, 392, 402
railway network density, 482
   Bolivia, 519
   Brazil, 519
   Ghana, 485
   Tanzania, 493

railway network length, 153
  Africa, 482
  Argentina, 519
  Asia, 60
  Brazil, 519
  Chile, 519
  China, 99, 402–403
  Colombia, 516
  India (1919), 124
  Latin America, 60, 523
  Mexico, 519
  Soviet Union, 92–93
railway riot, 129
rally/rally drivers, 465, 569
Rao, Nikhil, 129
Ray, Nicholas, 336
Rây, Prafulla, 126
Reader's Digest, 242
Reagan, Ronald, 272, 436
reappropriation, 390, 523
Red Cross roads, 104, 110
red tourists, 413
Reeves, Martha, 330
refugees, 249, 388, 415, 421, 426, 503
Reich, Steve, 223
rental car (system), 149, 535n21
representation, 5, *28–29*, *32*, 34–35, *38*, 41, 52n73, 69, 89, *92*, 261, 263, 295, 302
repressed tolerance, 457
repressive tolerance, 281, 372n135
resettled villages, 137. *See also* settler (society)
restrained car use, 480
revolutionary tourism (China), 410
Rexroth, Kenneth, 291–92
Řezáč, Václav, 398
rhizome, 290
Rhoads, Edward, 414
Rhodesia, 459
Ribeiro, Darcy, 173
Riboud, Marc, 400
rickshaw, 72–98, 126–127, 132, 142, 400, 479–480, 528–529, 562
  appropriation, 85, 93
  ban, 77, 79–80
  criticism of inhumane rickshaw culture, 66, 78, *80*, 83–84, 91, 93, 422
  in Durban, South Africa, 73
  Japanese Emperor as first user, 78
  in Natsume Sōseki, 63
  outnumbered by car, 73–74
  ownership, 77, 82, 89
  patrons, 78, 93, 183n39
  pousse-pousse, *72*, 92
  private, 83, 102
  reform of, 83, 89 (*see also* rickshaw regulation)
  in Shanghai, 80–85
  in Singapore, 75–80
  in Tokyo, 63, 72–75
  use profile, 63, 78, 183n39
  and underworld, 83
  xe-kéo (Vietnam), 92
  See also autorickshaw, cycle rickshaw
rickshaw puller, 66, 74, 82, 85, 89, 93–94, 100, 168
  Camel Xiangzi (Lao She), 89
  skills, 84, 86, 90–92
  strike, 77, 94
  woman as, 85
rickshaw regulation, 78, 89, 92–93
rickshaw riot of 1929. *See* Beijing Streetcar Riot (1929)
rickshaw statistics, 82
  Bangkok, 479
  Hanoi, 94
  Jakarta, 479
  Kuala Lumpur, 479
Riesman, David, 22
Rimmer, Peter J., 73, 423–424, 427, 479–80, 542n77
riots
  Africa, 490
  Brighton (1964), 280
  China, 100, 471
  Harlem (1964), 330–31
  India, 425, 479
  student, 343
  in the US, 304
  Zoot Suit (1943), 311
  See also Beijing Streetcar Riot (1929)
Risi, Dino, 333, 335, 347
risk(-taking)/risk society, xvi, 6, 86, 132, 295, 309, 349, 569, 572

road census. *See* London Traffic Survey, traffic census/survey
road construction. *See* roadbuilding
road density, 430, 489
 Argentina, 523
 Brazil, 162
 Ghana, 485
 South Africa, 527
 Tanganyika/Tanzania, 493, 527
 Uganda, 491, 527
 United Kingdom, 527
 Venezuela, 523
road labour, 163
 forced, 141–143, 154, 163, 503 (*see also* Forced Labour Convention)
 in Mexico, 162
 by women, 141
 See also faena
road lobby, 449–450, 458, 526, 528. *See also* International Road Federation IRF
road movie, 333–339
road network, 421–422, 473
 as cocoon, 303
 in Manchuria, 69–70
 in interbellum China, 110–118
 in Vietnam, 97
road network density. *See* road density
road network length, 403–406, 415–416
 Argentina, 162, 520
 Brazil, 161, 162, 516, 518, 523
 China, 111, 116
 Colombia, 516, 523
 Cuba, 518
 Ecuador, 523
 Europe, 435
 Ghana, 487–487
 India, 124
 Japan, 75, 473
 Kenya, 493
 Mexico, 162, 512, 514
 Morocco, 152
 Nigeria (1970), 442
 Peru, 523
 Puerto Rico, 518
 Tanzania, 139, 493
 Uganda, 527
 Venezuela, 165, 523
road novel, 178, 291, 325, 336, 338, 390–391
road rage, 316–317
Road Research Laboratory (UK), 462, 518, 526, 528
road safety, 98, 121, 131–132, 309, 328, 335, 341–349, 414, 459, 498, 502, 567, 572
 Hungary, 398
 India, 120
 Mexico City, 511–512
 Venezuela, 515
 Vietnam, 96
roadbuilding, 113, 124, 138–139, 153, 386, 516, 564
 anti-revolutionary, 506
 China (Soviet advisers), 405
 against communist insurgency, 469
 decentralization of, 114
 and economic growth, 449
 expertise, 429
 frenzy, 154
 in Ghana, 145
 in Indonesia, 131
 investments in, 461, 473
 in Latin America, 508
 in Libya, 150
 in Malaysia, 130
 in Mexico, 162–164, 512–514
 in Morocco, 151
 Nagpur Plan (India), 126, 415–416, 421, 541n66
 national highway plan in China (1929), 112
 provincial, 112
 See also freeway building, low cost road
roadlessness (Soviet Union), 393
road-rail competition/controversy, 118, 130, 464–465, 469, 473, 493, 511–514, 526–527
 Colombia (1973), 461
 Ethiopia, 485–489
 India, 119–120, 467
 See also coordination
roadside tourism (*bermtoerisme*, The Netherlands), 261
Rochefort, Christiane, 322

Index • 661

rock 'n' roll, *209–230*, 235, 236, 244–45, 282, 332, 333, 398
Roiphe, Anne, 307
Rolling Stones, The, 288, 331, 372n148
romance novels, 39, 268, 292, *296–298*
Rosas, Enrique, 164
Ross, Kristin, 258, 322
Rostow, Walt, 231, 317, 387, 389–390, 392, 394, 420, 438, 441, 445–446
Roussel, Raymond, 176
Roxy Music, 223
Royal Dutch Touring Club. *See* ANWB
Rozier, Jaques, 335
Rucki, Robert, 434
rural road. *See* low cost road
Ryan, Charlie, 215
Rycroft, Simon, 290

S

Sagan, Françoise, 321
Sahara crossing, 150
Said, Edward, 27, 38, 62
Salter, Arthur, 113
Salter, James, 325
Salvatore, Ricardo, 509
Sang, Ye, 412–413
Santiago de Chile, 158
sarariiman (Japan), 475. *See also* middle class
Saroyan, William, 344
scarcity (economy), 117, 509
Scharff, Virginia, 24
Schelsky, Helmut, 271
Schlesinger, John, 338
Schlesinger Jr., Arthur, 445–446
Schoppa, R. Keith, 405
Schulze, Gerhard, 22–24
science fiction, 207–208, 219, 224, 247, 342, 347–349
scooter, 228, 238, 242, 280, 282, 335, 441, 481, 554n174
Scorsese, Martin, 336
Scott, James, 457
script, 142, 227, 228, 565
Seattle windshield pitting panic, 300
Second Auto Works (China), 406
second subalternization, 152
secondhand cars, 22, 224, 241, 246–247, 324, 484

sedan chair. *See* palanquin
sedentarism, 269, 290, 451, 565
sedentarization (forced), 503
Seger, Bob, 288
Seidel, Robert, 156
Seiler, Cotten, 97, 262, 314–316, 339, 436, 449, 564
Self, the, 18, 20, 207, 298, 303
   independent/interdependent, 20
   non-hegemonic, 21
   See also loss of the Self, postmodern self
semi-periphery, *385*, 503, 505, 507, 532n1
semi-public transport. *See* informal transport
Senegal, 142
sensation-seeking-scale (SSS), 309
Seow, Victor, 407
sessility. *See* sedentarism
settler (society), 64, 135, 145, 148, 151, 152, 160, 175, 181n15, 199n182, 388, 527
Setzer, Brian, 215
Shanghai Express (novel), 107–108
Shapiro, Karl, 292–293, 345
shell, *10–11*, 349. *See also* car as cocoon
Sheller, Mimi, 30
Shinkansen, 475
Shklovsky, Viktor, 166
Shriver, Sargent, 448
Siegfried, Detlef, 281
Simmel, Georg, 19
Simon, Paul, 333
Singapore, 469–470, 476, 478, 480
Singh, Khushwant, 415
Situationists, 278–279, 330
skinheads, 280
sled, 145
slum clearance, 425
smartification of the car. *See* automation of the car
Smith, Sidonie, 293
Smith, Suzanne E., 330
smog, 571–572
Snell controversy, 248
Snow, Edgar, 406
social engineering, 448, 479
social mobility, 239
Social Stratification and Mobility Survey (Japan), 475

socialist mobility theory, 397–398, 410, 491, 531, 563
soft power, *387*, 389, 446, 457, 525–526
Solex (moped), 229
songs, 3, 6, 18, 42, 87, 128, 141, 211, *213*, 215–217, 223–224, 282, 284, 288, 304, 316, 318, *329–333*, 345, 500, 502, 549n133, 563, 570, *637–638*
song-theo (Thailand), 427
Sontag, Susan, 216
Soong, Meiling, 88
Sōseki, Natsume, 57–68
Sousa, M. Luísa, 460
South Africa, 462, 498
South Korea, 470–471, 478
South Vietnam, 470
Southern Cone (Latin America), 509
Soviet Union, 394, 527
Soyinka, Wole, 501
Spark, Muriel, 329
Speke, John, 138
Spielberg, Steven, 336
spirits. *See* haunted car, haunted roads
Spivak, Gayatri Chakravorty, 491
sport cars, 209–210
sport utility vehicle (SUV), 267
Springsteen, Bruce, 304, 332
Spurr, David, 461
squatters, 425
Stalter-Pace, Sunny, 33
Staples, Amy, 453–454
station wagon, 16, 270–271, 302, 307, 314, 324, 338, 524
status, 18, 19, 22, 107, 109, 172, 214, 259, 265, 316, 328–329, 390, 565. 567
  of the car better than of the home, 313
  hierarchy, 214, 327
  See also conspicuous consumption
status symbol, 18, 19, 22, 310, 327, 395
  car as, 13, 15, 16, 98, 105, 132, 144, 147–148, 237, 269, 310, 326–327, 390, 395, 411, 502
  home as, 247, 313
Steele, M. William, 398
Steg, Linda, 22
Steinbeck, John, 303, 318
Steppenwolf, 331
Stewart, Rod, 332

Stinnes, Clärenore, 176
stock car racing, 266, 310
Stockhausen, Karlheinz, 223
Strand, David, 85, 90
street racers, 569
streetcar, 60, 63, 74, 79, 87, 522, 474
  statistics Shanghai, 83
Streeter, Stephen M., 506
Structural Adjustment Program (SAP). *See under* development
struggle between road and rail. *See* road-rail competition
Studebaker, 231, 291
subaltern, 91, 95, 109, 153, 171–173, 233, 529
  form of mobility, 77
  gay mobility culture USA, 277
  mobility, 90, 127, 148, 458
  mobility studies, 225
  modernities, 458
  network, 426
  studies, 119, 122–124
  See also second subalternization
substitution, 75, 125
  myth, 247
suburb, 253, 259–260
  as basis of American car culture, 246
  Black, 276
suburbanization, 250, 339, 522
subversive, 26, 43, 164, 173, 229, 278, 313, 334, 340, 347, 397, 428, 458, 562, 568
subversive mobility, 9, 42, 87, 95, 128, 148–149, 153, 166, 171, 258, 275, 276, 279, 289, 299, 330, 427, 500, 503
subway (system), 394–395, 425, 474
Sumatran Highway, 476
summering (Lebanon), 151
Sun, Fo, 100
Sun, Yat-sen, 99
  and cars, 100
  road network designed by, 100
Sun, Zhongshan. *See* Sun Yat-sen
superhelicak. *See* mini-taxi
Supremes, The, 264
Surabaya, 480–481
Sutton, Francis, 446
SUV. *See* sport utility vehicle

Sward, Robert, 345
swarm, 8, 12, 16, 18, 31, 57–58, 72, 90, 174, 228, 278, 323, 458, 565, 570–571
Swaziland, 485
synchronicity, 63, 97–98, 102, 110, 125, 145, 159, 169, 518
synchronization thesis, 423
systemic character of mobility, 174, 270, 279, 332, 340, 343, 349, 386, 526. *See also* automobilism

T

T²M. *See* Association for the History of Transport, Traffic and Mobility
Taiwan, 470–471, 478
talking cars (in movies), 264
Talking Heads, 223
tonga. See cart
Tanganyika. *See* Tanzania
Tanpinar, Ahmet Hamdi, 390
Tanzania, 138–140, 447, 492–493
tarmet, 145
Tata, 124, 416
Tati, Jacques, 335
taxi, 10, 74, 90, 96, 119, 132, 218, 250, 256, 279, 311, 427, 441, 481, 488, 500, 503, 512, 531, 568
  Black, 276
  company, 215
  drivers, 480, 484
  electric, 287
  intercity/long-distance, 483, 525
  'kamikaze,' 250
  poor man's, 73
  public pool of, 395
  scooter-based, 554n174
  See also mini-taxi, pirate taxis; *see also under* bicycle, motorcycle
taxi statistics, 119, 132
Taxis de la Marne, 106
Taylor, Elizabeth, 329, 341
Teddy Boys, 228, 280
telegraph (network), 121, 134, 136
Telengana uprising of 1948–1951 (India), 458
telephone (network), 122, 134
television, 260–264

teppisti (hooligans), 229
Terranova, Charissa, 48n38
Tetzlaff, Stefan, 125
Thailand, 401, 422–423, 441–442, 463–465, 468–469, 471, 473, 476, 524
thanatourism, 150, 170
Third Front (China), 405
Third World, 4, 38, 120, 173, 179, 341, 346, 387, 391–393, 401, 406, 423, 428, 454, 461, 471, 504–505, 507–508, 534n16
Thomas, Albert, 113
Thompson, Hunter S., 295
three-wheelers, 472
Tokyo, 63, 474, 476
toll-roads, 112, 473
Touring Club Italiano, 149
touring club of the Netherlands. *See* ANWB
Touring Club Suisse, 434
tourism, 41–42, 117, 149, 258, 349, 398, 510
  by bus. *See under* bus
  by car (*see* car tourism)
  by (charter) aviation, 254–255
  destination Spain, 256
  destinations, 254
  Europe, 252, 254–257, 278, 398, 400
  by Japanese, 475
  and Marshall aid, 255, 324
  revolutionary (China), 410, 491
  statistics, 256
  USA, 510
  See also car tourism, revolutionary tourism, roadside tourism, thanatourism; *see also under* bus
toy-to-tool thesis, 565
traffic census/survey, 64, 74, 79–80, 126, 313, 419, 476, 478, 480, 487–490, 492, 529. *See also* London Traffic Survey, Social Stratification and Mobility Survey
traffic engineering, 428, 430–432
  course at Yale, 430, 432, 434
traffic jam, 317, 321, 332, 334, 458–459, 530
trailer parks, 246
train tours by Ghandi, 122
tram/tramways. *See* streetcar

Trans-African Highway, 462, 465
Trans-African Railway, 465
Trans-Amazonian Highway, 518
transcendence/transcendental experience, 8, 10, 12, 15–16, 18, 20, 23, 25, 29, 37, 38, 58, 62, 64, 159, 173, 218–221, 227, 244, 245, 292–293, 298, 301, 323, 332, 345, 355n37, 523, 565, 570–571. *See also* epiphany
transhumance. *See* circulation
translation, 28–30, 32, 34, 35, 41, 221, 563
transmediality. *See* cross-mediality
Transport and Road Research Laboratory. *See* Road Research Laboratory
transport investments, 442, 450–451
    and economic growth, 451
    Asia, 505
    Brazil, 518
    Greece, 505
    Latin America, 505
    magic of, 443
    Peru, 522
    Turkey, 505
Trans-Saharan Road/Highway, 483, 528
travel. *See* holiday travel, intercity bus travel, free railway travel, train travel; *see also under* development
travel permits, 143
travel writing, 5, 9, 29, 34, 38–42, 178, 461
trishaw. *See* cycle rickshaw
trolley (streetcar), 79
trolley bus, 394
Troup, Robert, 288
truck/trucking/truck transport, 24, 104–105, 125, 139, 148–149, 161, 170, 286, 303, 319, 336, 386, 393, 396, 405–407, 411–414, 416–417, 419, 431, 441–442, 467, 472, 475, 482–483, 487, *490*, 493–495, 497, 500, 511–514, 523
    culture West Africa, 496
    drivers, 121, 125, 128–129, 144–146, 149, 165, 170, 214, 268, 414, 450–451, 490, 494, 496, 565
    embellishment, 524 (*see also* vehicle embellishment)
    Ghana, 497
    Japan, 69

    as laboratory (Venezuela), 515
    parks, 494–495, 502, 530
    regulation, 140
    Soviet Union, 396
    state-run, 143
    used as bus, 500 (*see also* mammy wagon, pickup truck)
    wild, 141
    See also pickup truck, pirate truck, public trucking
truck statistics, 421
    Ghana, 145
    India, 119
    Latin America, 523
    Mexico, 512
    Tanzania, 493
tsetse fly, 137–138, 140, 145, 495
    trypanosomiasis caused by, 137
Tsurumi, Shunsuke, 472
Turner, Ike, 214

U
ubiquitous car, 248, 250, 302, 304. *See also* absent car, abstractification
Uganda, 138–139, 489–492, 494, 526–527
UN. *See* United Nations (UN)
UN Conference on Trade and Development (UNCTAD), 453
UN Convention on Road Traffic (1949), 449–450, 465
UN Development Decade/Programme, 389, 465, 483
UN Economic Commission for Asia and the Far East (ECAFE), 420
UN Economic Commission for Europe (ECE), 435, 449, 462
UN Universal Declaration of Human Rights, 452
underclass, 234. *See also* working class
Unger, Corinna R., 390–391, 426
United Nations (UN), 122, 387, *429*, 449–450, 461–465, 480, 506, 520, 523, 572
Updike, John, 220, *299–301*
urban crisis, 8, 422
urban freeway, 116, 474
urbanism, 424

urbanization/urbanized condition, 120, 132–133, 160, 212, 233–234, 240, 250, 260, 401, 422–426, 486, 503, 509, 518, 527, 529
US Agency for International Development (USAID), 441, 443, 469
US Bureau of Public Roads, 442, 469
US Export-Import Bank (EXIM), 443

V
vacation movies, 334
Van Ronk, Dave, 216
Vargas, Getúlio, 517
Vasconcellos, Eduardo, 516
Veblen, Thorstein, 14, 21
vehicle embellishment
  Costa Rica, 477–478
  Manila, 477
  See also under truck
Velvet Underground, 223
Venezuela, 165, 451, 515
Vespa, 228, 242, 324, 481, 554n174. *See also* scooter
Vesper, Bernward, 325
Vidal, Gore, 344
Vietnam, 227, 405
Vietnam War, 248, 310, 330–331, 390, 421, 444, 448, 475
Ville, Simon P., 443
Vincent, Gene, 244
Vinkenoog, Simon, 229
violence, 7, 9, 11, 27, 64, 87, 96, 108, 122, 128, 131, 132, 135, 149, 163, 175, 178, 180n13, 206–209, 216, 220, 226–227, 230, 244, 260, 274–275, 286–287, 292, 294, 298, 303, 311, 315, 316, 317, 319, 20, 330, 331, 334, 335, 341, 342, 344, 347, 348, 412, 415, 425, 457, 509
  in the American novel, 227
  as aspect of car adventure, 227
  See also aggression, hidden violence of road statistics
vision (eye), 12, 31, 300, 302, 340
  gaze (Urry), 12, 32, 46n25, 348
  glance, 12, 46n25, 67, 305, 348
Vogel, Ezra, 475, 478
Volkswagen, 235, 266–267, 498, 518

Volmuller, J., 431–432
voyeurism, 348

W
walking, 13, 14, 39, 60, 63, 67, 72, 96, 117, 127, 128, 172, 177, 210, 224, 226, 247, 252, 279, 385, 417, 450, 479, 489, 529, 562, 569. *See also* palenquin, porterage, *machilla*
Wallerstein, Immanuel, 508
Walser, Martin, 327
Wang, Hui, 527
War on Poverty, 448, 452
Warhol, Andy, 223, 286, 329, 339, 346
warlords, 65, 67–68, 96, 100, 102–104, 116, 136
Warren, James, 75
Washington Consensus, 451
Weathermen, 226, 331
Weavers, 213
Wehler, Hans-Ulrich, 428, 440
welfare state, 234, 245, 258, 260
Wells, Christopher, 246
Westernization, 390. *See also* Americanization
wheelbarrow, 529. *See also* one-wheeled barrow
white trash, 214. *See also* trailer parks
white working class, 233
White, Landeg, 491
Who, The, 228, 331
Wiener, Norbert, 348
Wightman, David, 463, 465
Wilbur Smith & Associates (consultants), 424, 428, 480
Williams, Hank, 215
Williams, John A., 314
Williams, Raymond, 30, 31, 36, 261
Williams, Stanley T., 324
Williamson, Thomas, 130
Willis, Paul, 244
Wilson, Fiona, 165
Wiser, Charlotte, 456
Wiser, Charlotte and William, 127
Wittrock, Björn, 442
Wobblies, 212
Wolf, Joel, 161
Wolfe, Bernard, 348

Wolfe, Tom, 225
women
  and head porterage, 489
  and new roads in Africa, 489
  as passengers, 287, 324, 341
  as protagonists in novels, 305
  See also female, gender
  working class/underclass, 21, 24, 26, 67, 77, 214, 227–228, 233, 235, 238, *258–259*, *267–269*, 271–272, 277, 296, 327–328, 338, 341, 499, 519–520, 528, 566
    African-American, 277 (*see also* Cadillac)
    car ownership (*see under* car ownership)
    car culture, 242, 261, 287, 340, *566*, 570 (*see also* Cadillac)
    creation of, 518–519
    embourgeoisement of, 267
    motorcycle culture of, 228, 244, *294–295*
    protagonists in novels, 328
    in USA, 245–246, 272, 320, 436
    upward mobility of, 271
    values/tastes, 280, 328
    vanishing, 280
    youth (car) culture, *229–230*, 280, 310 (*see also teppisti*)
  See also white working class
World Bank, 416, 427, 442–444, 447–449, 461, 468, 472–473, 476–480, 485, 516, 520, 525, 528–530, 568–569
  funding (statistics), 444–445, 451–452, 454
  See also loans
World Bank Presidents
  Black, Eugene, 454
  McCloy, John, 453
  McNamara, Robert 452, 479

Shoaib, Mohamed (Vice President), 454
Woods, George, 452
world mobility system, 384–385
world motor vehicle fleet statistics, 459
world system theory/analysis, 508, 567

Y

Yamaguchi, Ikuto, 464
Yan, Xishan, 103–104
Yates, Peter, 339
Yosano Akiko, 67–68
Young, La Monte, 223
youth (car) culture, 14, 29, 42, 208, *211–212*, 216–217, 224, 227–230, *244*, 261–262, *277–281*, 284, 294, 296–297, 306, 331–332, 336, 410, 447
  Chinese, 101, *409–410*
  Dutch, 228–229
  See also under carnivalesque, working class
youth tourism, 278
Yurchak, Alexei, 396–97

Z

zaibatsu, 470–471
Zaire, 489, 523
Zambia, 145
Zappa, Frank, 223, 245
Zhang, Henshui, 71, 106, 117
Zhang, Xinxin, 412–13
Zhang, Xinyuan. *See* Zhang Henshui
Zhang, Xun-Hai, 408
Zhou, Enlai, 103, 106, 401, 415
Zhou, Shuren, 108–109
Žižek, Slavoj, 37
Zoot Suit Riot, 311
zoot suiter, 228

www.ingramcontent.com/pod-product-compliance
Lightning Source LLC
Chambersburg PA
CBHW071143070526
44584CB00019B/2644